THE CAMBRIDGE ANCIENT HISTORY

EDITORS

Volumes I–VI	*Volume* VII
J. B. BURY, M.A., F.B.A.	S. A. COOK, LITT.D.
S. A. COOK, LITT.D.	F. E. ADCOCK, M.A.
F. E. ADCOCK, M.A.	M. P. CHARLESWORTH, M.A.

VOLUME VII

THE
CAMBRIDGE
ANCIENT HISTORY

VOLUME VII
THE HELLENISTIC MONARCHIES
AND THE RISE OF ROME

EDITED BY

S. A. COOK, Litt.D.
F. E. ADCOCK, M.A.
M. P. CHARLESWORTH, M.A.

THIRD IMPRESSION

CAMBRIDGE
AT THE UNIVERSITY PRESS
1964

PUBLISHED BY
THE SYNDICS OF THE CAMBRIDGE UNIVERSITY PRESS

Bentley House, 200 Euston Road, London, N.W. 1
American Branch: 32 East 57th Street, New York 22, N.Y.
West African Office: P.O. Box 33, Ibadan, Nigeria

First Edition	1928
Reprinted with corrections	1954
Reprinted	1964

First printed in Great Britain at the University Press, Cambridge
Reprinted at the Whitefriars Press, Tonbridge

PREFACE

IN volumes v and vi Greece was the centre of the Mediterranean world; but the conquests of Alexander shifted the
centre of gravity eastwards and left room for the emergence of a
new great power, the Republic of Rome. Greece, in fact, was
destined to lose her primacy in the West without gaining complete political or intellectual domination in the East. But in the
early decades of the third century Rome was still occupied in
making good her hold upon the Italian peninsula, and no observer
of the time would have compared her progress with the brilliant
expansion of the Greeks eastwards. Out of the confusion which
followed the death of Alexander emerged the three great Hellenistic monarchies, Macedon, Egypt and the Seleucid Empire
of the East, whose making and organization are the main theme
of the first part of this volume. These three predominant powers
overshadowed the countries which bordered on the eastern
Mediterranean. The great days of Pergamum and Rhodes belong
to the next period, and the systematic account of their economy is
reserved for volume VIII.

The third century was an age of political experiment, and we
witness the birth of the Great State, instinct with Greek and
Macedonian ideas, learning from the ancient bureaucracies of
the East, and transcending the bounds of race. But in Egypt and
in Seleucid Syria the fusion of races was not complete: the military
needs of these monarchies compelled them to accord a special
position to Graeco-Macedonian settlers and to use the forms of
the Greek city-state to make homes for the governing class. This
fact doubtless did much to limit the efficacy of the new city-
settlements as centres of Hellenic culture; and imposing as was
the Seleucid Empire it had to face an Oriental reaction even
before the tide of Greek expansion had reached its full. In Greece
proper a marked advance was made in the federalism of the Aetolian
and Achaean Leagues, which acquired a cohesion and a strength
denied to the city-states, whose failure as political units had been
proved by the history of the preceding century. Yet the *polis*
meant much to the Greeks as the setting of their social life, and
the Hellenistic world was covered with cities, even where these
communities had no power to control their own fortunes.

Side by side with these political experiments we find in literature
and in philosophy new movements, which, if less splendid than
the achievements of the fifth and fourth centuries, were to

exercise a more widespread influence. The age which witnessed the rise of the Stoic and Epicurean philosophies made Athens not only the school of Greece but also the school of the Mediterranean world. In Alexandria, for this purpose a part of Greece rather than a part of Egypt, there arose the first academic community which, though it had its pedants, yet pursued the Greek way of wisdom, the way of the seeker rather than of the sage. Most striking of all the intellectual achievements of this period were those of the great mathematicians and astronomers. Even at a time when Greece was beginning to lose the political primacy which had been hers, the Greeks of the home-land and of the *Diaspora* remained the most effective fraction of the human race.

The final achievement of the Hellenistic movement was the conception of the world, that is the world of ancient civilization, as in a sense a single community—the *oecumene*, with the Greek *koine* as almost a universal language. But the conception was 'a leap of the imagination alone,' and was not translated into political or economic fact. The farther East remained in essentials unchanged. There was in externals a fusion of religions within the borders of the Hellenistic kingdoms, but Judaism, Zoroastrianism and the local cults of Egypt bided their time, and the way was being prepared for a religious reaction of the East upon the West which was to have the most momentous consequences. In the East there was a species of passive resistance to be followed by reaction; in the West the unity of the *oecumene* was broken by the intrusion of the Celts, who in the fourth century crossed the Alps and in the third century the Balkans. Their first coming, transient as were its political effects, yet had its historical significance, and it is not only because of chronological necessities that the account of the Celts is placed where it is in this volume but also in order to give a strong contrast to the Hellenistic order which conceived of the world of men in terms of Hellenistic thought. And further, even when Celtic raiders had been repelled or absorbed, the Celts remained to bar the north-western expansion of the older Mediterranean states and turn them upon themselves. But these invasions had slight effects compared with the making of a united state at Rome and the attainment of a Roman hegemony in a united Italy.

This state so built up was to dominate the remaining history of the ancient world, to create not a monarchy but an empire, and to rival Greece in the deep imprint which it made upon the mind of the modern world.

In this volume we witness only the rise of Rome, but the political achievements of that rise rank with the creations of the Hellenistic

monarchies and the Greek Leagues in their immediate importance
and in their permanent effect as models for later institutions.
The story is in itself less adventurous, because Rome's problems
were near at hand and did not call for the subtleties of Hellenistic statecraft. It was the good fortune of the Republic to keep
clear of far-flung entanglements until its strength was able to
break through them where its wisdom failed to solve them.
Thus the influence of Rome on the general course of the Mediterranean world-history was delayed, and it is this fact as well as
the need to treat continuously of what was so essentially continuous, that justifies the first appearance of Rome in this rather
than in an earlier volume.

The oecumenical importance of Rome itself, which for longer
than any other city was in reality or in sentiment the capital of
the European world, lends a peculiar interest to the problems of
its first foundation and its early monarchy; and the examination
of these problems is particularly instructive in showing how the
sciences of archaeology and historical research may correct, confirm, supplement or supplant tradition. The vigorous increase of
archaeological research in Italy will lay students of the beginnings
of Rome under ever deeper obligations.

Of yet greater importance is the study of Roman institutions,
which presents to the historian a peculiarly difficult problem
owing to the character of the ancient evidence. For the historical
tradition of the Romans about the growth of their constitution was
in the main the work of annalists who had little sense of historical
criticism and of jurists who had little sense of historical development. In the chapters on the growth of the Roman constitution
will be found a critical reconstruction intended to show how far
logic and a highly practical grasp of fact combined to build up
the strongest political structure which the world has yet seen.
Side by side with this we can trace, despite the accretions of fiction
which lie heavy on the Roman tradition, the shrewd tenacity which
guided the young Republic both in diplomacy and in war. It is
true that the advance of historical criticism has stripped the old
glamour from the story, and we have no means of re-capturing a
sense of close contact with the Rome of the fifth and fourth
centuries such as that which invests the history of Athens with
its peculiarly dramatic character. The Romans contrived to make
it seem inevitable that they should dominate Italy, and it is hard
to realize how unremitting were the efforts that gained them their
reward. Yet *tantae molis erat*.

Gradually the advance of Rome's power brought her into contact and conflict with the Greeks of Southern Italy; and in the

period which forms the main theme of the volume she measured her strength against Pyrrhus, a soldier of the new Greek school of war, and against the fleets and armies of Carthage, the oldest great power of the Western Mediterranean. Rome survived both these tests of her capacity and brought Sicily within the bounds of Roman Italy. Two centuries of wars in which the Republic had claimed as the reward of each war greater resources for the winning of the next had placed at her disposal a man-power stronger than that which any ancient state had yet controlled. This power rested not only on the military superiority of Rome but on ties of common interest and sentiment throughout Italy which the wise policy of the Roman federation had known how to evoke. Meanwhile the Greeks of the West had witnessed the career of Agathocles which both in its successes and its failures attested the political weaknesses which were to surrender the future to Rome. In the eastern half of the Mediterranean we see the struggle of Egypt with Syria and Macedonia and the rise in Greece of the two leagues, the Aetolian and the Achaean, whose fate it was to prevent the union of Greece under Macedon, while themselves achieving a form of union which transcended the limits of the Greek city-state. Finally, the pirate state of Illyria compelled the Republic to realize that the Adriatic has two coasts, and the Carthaginian Empire in Spain gave to Hannibal the means of accepting a conflict with Rome which was to end in the extension of Roman power along the northern coast of the Mediterranean to the Pillars of Hercules.

This conflict will be the first topic of volume VIII, which will proceed to treat of the period in which Rome thrust aside the Hellenistic monarchies and came to be acknowledged as the single great power in the Mediterranean world. It will also complete the picture of Hellenistic civilization and economic life and describe the rise of literature and the advent of philosophy in Rome herself, taken prisoner by the Hellenism which she dethroned.

In the present volume Professor Ferguson writes on the leading ideas of the new period (chapter I) and Mr de Navarro describes the Celts and their advent in the Mediterranean world (chapter II). Mr Tarn continues the political history of the Hellenistic states (chapters III, VI, XXII and XXIII), while Professor Rostovtzeff describes the organization, political and economic, of the Ptolemaic and Seleucid Empires (chapters IV and V). Mr C. F. Angus writes the account of Athens as the home of the New Comedy and the new philosophies (chapter VII), Mr Barber that of Alexandrine literature (chapter VIII), Dr W. H. S. Jones treats of Greek medicine and botany, and Sir Thomas Heath describes the achievements of the Greek in the field of mathematics and astronomy (chapter ix). A survey of Hellenistic art is reserved for a chapter in vol. VIII which will cover both the third and second centuries. In chapter x the account of the rise of Rome begins with a review of the sources and the making of the Roman tradition about the early Republic. This chapter is by Dr Stuart Jones, who in the following section of the volume treats of the primitive institutions of Rome and the constitutional development of the Republic. Mr Last writes on the foundation of the city, the Kings of Rome and the external history of the Early Republic together with its economic progress and problems. M. Homo describes the Gallic wars of Rome, and Professor Adcock the wars which enabled Rome to dominate central Italy. The account of the career of Agathocles is written by Dr Cary. The war of Rome against Pyrrhus and the first conflict with Carthage are recounted by Professor Tenney Frank, who also describes the Roman federation in Italy and the beginnings of its provincial system (chapters xx, xxi and xxv). Professor Schulten writes on early Spain and the Spanish empire of Carthage (chapter xxiv); the final chapter, that on the Romans in Illyria, is from the pen of M. Holleaux. The chronological note on the first treaty between Rome and Carthage is by Mr Last, the notes on the battles of Cos and Sellasia are by Mr Tarn.

The editors desire to thank all the contributors for their very ready co-operation. Apart from specific obligations mentioned below, they wish, in particular, to express their gratitude to Mr Tarn for constant and most generous help. Mr de Navarro thanks Professor A. A. Bevan and Professor Housman for assistance on particular points, Dr W. H. S. Jones wishes to acknowledge the help of Dr E. T. Withington, who read the proofs of his contribution and made valuable suggestions. Mr Tarn expresses his indebtedness to Mr Sidney Smith, Mr E. S. G. Robinson and Mr S. R. K. Glanville. Mr Last would like to record his thanks to Mr Cyril Bailey and Dr Ashby—to the former for some suggestions and to the latter for the privilege of seeing in proof the late Dr Platner's *Topographical Dictionary of Rome*, completed and shortly to be published by Dr Ashby.

The volume owes a debt to contributors in the preparation of maps to illustrate their chapters: to Mr de Navarro for Map 1; to Mr Tarn for Maps 2, 3, 4, 9 and 10; to Mr Last for Maps 5 and 6; to Dr Schulten for Map 11; to M. Holleaux for Map 14, and for co-operation with Mr Tarn in Map 10. Professor Adcock is responsible for Map 7, and for Map 8 in consultation with Dr Cary and Professor Tenney Frank, Mr Charlesworth for

Maps 12 and 13 in consultation with Mr Last and Professor Tenney Frank. In particular, students of the Hellenistic period will observe the value of Maps 3 and 4, which illustrate the spread of Hellenistic settlements in Egypt and the nearer East. The Genealogical and Chronological Tables of the Hellenistic Dynasties are constructed by Mr Tarn, who also supplied the material for the two centre columns of the General Chronological Table.

For the translation from the Russian of Professor Rostovtzeff's chapters we are indebted to the friendly help of Dr Minns. Mr D. H. Beves has translated chapter xvii, Mr B. L. Hallward chapter xxiv, and Mr W. Montgomery chapter xxvi.

The General Index and Index of passages referred to have been made by Mr B. Benham. In a volume of this complexity these tasks have been exceptionally difficult and we would thank him for the great pains which he has devoted to them. Finally we have again to express our gratitude to the Staff of the University Press for their unfailing skill and helpfulness.

We have chosen as the design on the cover the she-wolf from the famous group in the Museo dei Conservatori in Rome. (See Volume of Plates, i, 336, and below, p. 366.)

With this volume a change appears on the title-page. The death of Professor Bury in 1927 removed the great scholar who had made the general plan for the *Ancient History* and who for seven years had guided its progress as editor-in-chief. Despite failing health towards the end, his erudition and experience made him throughout these years a tower of strength to his two colleagues, who never turned to him in vain for help and counsel. He was ever ready to suggest or to welcome modifications of his general plan for the whole work, and, while the scheme of this volume follows the main lines which he had originally laid down, changes have been made of which those proposed before his death had his full assent. The responsibility for the final shape of the remaining volumes will rest with the editors, but they wish to make it clear how great is and will be their debt to Professor Bury's wide and deep understanding of the whole field of Ancient History.

In the summer of this year Mr M. P. Charlesworth of St John's College, who, after Professor Bury's death, had co-operated in the preparation of this volume, was appointed an editor by the Syndics of the Press.

S.A.C.
F.E.A.
M.P.C.

October, 1928

TABLE OF CONTENTS

CHAPTER I

THE LEADING IDEAS OF THE NEW PERIOD

By W. S. Ferguson, Ph.D., LL.D., Hon. Litt.D. (Louvain),
Professor of Ancient History, Harvard University

	PAGE
I. Salient features	1
An age of experiment	3
Religious syncretism	5
Science *versus* Revelation	6
II. Monarchy	7
Macedonian monarchy	8
Hellenistic kingship	11
III. Deification	13
Ruler-cult	14
The cities and the monarch	15
The imperial cult of the Ptolemies	17
The Egyptian rite of deification	18
Complex character of deification	20
IV. The large state and the polis	22
Decay of urban nationalism	23
The dependent *polis* and its protector	25
The absence of natural frontiers	26
Fiscality and prodigality of kings	28
The new capitals as centres of culture	30
The *malaise* of the Greek world	32
V. Cosmopolitanism, individualism, stoicism	33
Substitutes for the *polis*	33
Private clubs	34
The *oecumene*	37
The self-sufficiency of sages	38

CHAPTER II

THE COMING OF THE CELTS

By J. M. de Navarro, M.A.
Fellow of Trinity College, Cambridge, and University Lecturer
in Archaeology and Anthropology

I. The material civilization of the Celts during the La Tène period	41
Chronological subdivisions	42
Phase A or the earliest La Tène period	43
Phase B	44
Phase C	45
Coins	46

PAGE

II. The art of the La Tène period 47

III. Early traders and contacts with the Greek world . . . 49
    Early references in classical authors 49
    Avienus: Atlantic trade 51
    Pytheas of Massilia 53

IV. The early home of the Celtic peoples 54
    The origin of the Celts 55
    Celts and Galatae 56

V. Celtic migrations 59
    Movements to the south-west 59
    Movements southward 60
    The Alpine passes 61
    South-eastward expansion 64

VI. Causes of Celtic migrations 66
    Nordic pressure on the Rhenish area 67
    Nordic pressure in Central Germany 69
    Climatic change 71

VII. The life and character of the Celts 71
    The Druids: religion 71
    War and peace 73

CHAPTER III

THE NEW HELLENISTIC KINGDOMS

By W. W. Tarn, M.A., F.B.A.
Sometime Scholar of Trinity College, Cambridge

I. The years after Ipsus 75
    Demetrius after Ipsus 76
    Athens, Cassander, Lachares 78

II. Demetrius, king of Macedonia 79
    Demetrius and Greece 80
    Lysimachus and the Getae 82

III. Pyrrhus and Demetrius 82
    Demetrius at the height of his power 84

IV. The fall of Demetrius 85
    The freedom of Athens 86
    Demetrius in Asia 87
    The surrender of Demetrius 88

V. Lysimachus 89
    Lysimachus' realm: the cities 90
    Ptolemy, Seleucus 92

VI. Antigonus Gonatas 94
    Menedemus, Zeno 94

PAGE

VII. THE PASSING OF THE SUCCESSORS 96
    The fall of Lysimachus 97
    Seleucus and Keraunos 98
    The treaty of 279 B.C. 100

VIII. THE INVASION OF THE GAULS 101
    The Gauls and Greece 102
    Delphi 103
    The Gauls and Asia Minor 104

IX. ANTIGONUS, KING OF MACEDONIA 106
    Consolidation of the kingdom 107

CHAPTER IV

PTOLEMAIC EGYPT

BY M. ROSTOVTZEFF, Hon. D.Litt. (Oxon), Hon. Litt.D. (Wisconsin),
Professor of Ancient History, Yale University

I. THE CONDITIONS CONFRONTING THE PTOLEMIES 109
    The problems of the Ptolemies 110
    The new communities 111

II. THE FOUNDATION OF THE PTOLEMIES' POWER IN RIGHT AND PRACTICE 113
    The king and the Egyptians 114

III. ADMINISTRATION: EGYPT 116
    The court and the army 116
    The fleet 118
    The civil service 119
    Justice and finance 120
    Alexandria 121
    Polis: politeumata: the country 122
    Tax-officers 124

IV. ADMINISTRATION: PROVINCES 126
    Cyprus 126
    Cyrenaica 127
    The burden of taxation 129
    Tax-farmers 129

V. ECONOMIC CONDITIONS. THE RESOURCES OF EGYPT AND THEIR APPLICATION 130
    Cultivation 131
    Development of resources 133
    Growth of trade and industry 134

VI. TAXATION 136
    Economic policy: taxation of Egypt 137
    Soldier-settlers 138
    Land dues 139
    Monopolies: the corvée 140
    Coinage and coin-standards 141

PAGE

VII. Social, religious and intellectual life. The Hellenization of Egypt 142
    Life in Alexandria 143
    Egyptians and Greeks 144
    Sarapis 145
    Art and literature 146
    Culture 148
    The Egyptian priesthood: guilds 149
    Native risings 151
    Failure to make a nation 152
    The work of the Ptolemies 153

CHAPTER V

SYRIA AND THE EAST

By M. Rostovtzeff

I. The empire of the Seleucids, its character and development . 155
    Varied elements in the empire 155
    The task of the Seleucids 157
    Graeco-Macedonian settlements 158
    The Iranian reaction 160

II. The organization of the Seleucid empire 161
    A. The king's power 161
        The sanction of royalty 162
        Non-Greek peoples 163
    B. The court and central administration 164
        Government of the provinces 164
        The great officials 165
        The satrapies 166
        Taxation: law 168
    C. The army and fleet 169
        The *katoikoi* 171
        The fleet 172
    D. The economic policy of the Seleucids . . . 173
        The Far East 174
        Currency 176

III. The empire: Asia Minor 176
    The old Greek cities 178
    Colonization: the new cities 180
    King's lands and fiefs 182
    The temples 183

IV. The empire: Syria, Mesopotamia, and Babylonia . . . 184
    The heart of the empire 185
    Doura-Europos 186
    Seleuceia 187
    Babylon 188

CONTENTS

PAGE

V. The empire: Phoenicia and Palestine 190
   Phoenician cities 190
   Judaea 192
VI. The results of the Seleucids' work 194
   Seleucid Hellenism 195

CHAPTER VI

MACEDONIA AND GREECE

By W. W. Tarn

I. Antigonus Gonatas and Macedonia 197
   Race and religion 197
   People and land 198
   The cities and the army 200
   Basis of kingship 202
II. Antigonus and his circle 203
   Philosophy 204
III. Macedonia and her neighbours 205
   Athens 206
   Greece: Rhodes 207
IV. The Aetolian League 208
   The constitution 208
   Council and *Apokletoi* 209
   Aetolian policy 210
V. Social changes in Greece 211
   Humanity and war 211
   Wealth and population 212
VI. Pyrrhus 213
   Defeat and death of Pyrrhus 215
VII. Greece after Pyrrhus' death 216
   The position in Greece: Aetolia 217
VIII. Greece after the Chremonidean war 218
   Central Greece: the Peloponnese 219
   Antigonus and Athens 221
IX. Aratus of Sicyon 222
   The recovery of Corinth 222

CHAPTER VII

ATHENS

By C. F. Angus, M.A.
Fellow of Trinity Hall, Cambridge, and University Lecturer in Classics

I. The spirit of the new age 224
II. The new comedy 226
   Menander 227
   Fortune omnipotent 229

	PAGE
III. The new philosophies	230
Philosophies of resignation	230
IV. Epicurus	231
His life and work	232
Epicurus *Soter*	233
V. Zeno	235
Stoic idealism	235
A gospel of detachment	236
VI. The older schools	237
Academy and Lyceum	237
VII. Stoicism	238
Stoic physics	239
Stoic ethics	241
VIII. Epicureanism	243
Peace at any price	243
Epicurean atomism	245
The Hedonistic calculus	247
Friendship	248

CHAPTER VIII

ALEXANDRIAN LITERATURE

By E. A. Barber, M.A.
Fellow and Tutor of Exeter College, Oxford, and University Lecturer
in Greek and Latin Literature

I. Alexandria and Alexandrian scholarship	249
Patronage of letters	250
The library at Alexandria	252
Alexandrian scholars	253
II. Prose	255
Oratory and rhetoric	255
History	256
Theopompus	257
Local history	259
Biography	261
Geography	261
Eratosthenes	262
Popular prose-works: romances	264
III. Poetry: general features	266
Conditions of poetry	267
Themes not handled	269
Pedantry	270
IV. The Fore-Runners	273
Philetas and others	273

PAGE

V. The Golden Age 274
   Genus irritabile vatum: Callimachus 275
   Apollonius: the first romantic epic 276
   Theocritus 277
   Variety in the pastoral 278
   Herodas 280
   The aftermath 281
   A scholar's friendships 282

CHAPTER IX

HELLENISTIC SCIENCE AND MATHEMATICS

By W. H. S. Jones, Litt.D., Fellow of St Catharine's College, Cambridge, and University Lecturer in Classics, and Sir Thomas L. Heath, K.C.B., K.C.V.O., F.R.S., Sc.D., Hon. D.Sc. (Oxon), Hon. Fellow of Trinity College, Cambridge[1]

I. Medicine and surgery 284
   Surgery and pathology 285
   Medicine 286
II. Biology and botany 288
   Theophrastus 289
III. Mathematics created a science: Thales and the Pythagoreans . 290
   Pythagorean mathematics 291
   Astronomy 292
IV. Second stage: higher problems. The irrational and infinitesimals 293
   Higher Geometry 293
   Zeno and Eudoxus 294
   Plato and Aristotle 296
V. Alexandria: Euclid, Aristarchus, Archimedes, Apollonius of Perga 297
   Strato 297
   Euclid and his fore-runners 298
   The works of Euclid 300
   Aristarchus 301
   Conon: Archimedes 302
   The works of Archimedes 304
   Eratosthenes: mechanicians 306
   Apollonius of Perga 307
VI. Hipparchus 310

CHAPTER X

THE SOURCES FOR THE TRADITION OF EARLY ROMAN HISTORY

By H. Stuart Jones, M.A., D.Litt. (Oxon.), Hon. D.Litt. (Wales), F.B.A., Principal of the University College of Wales, Aberystwyth; formerly Camden Professor of Ancient History in the University of Oxford

I. Early monuments 312
   Fasti and list of triumphs 313
II. Extant historians 313
   Ancient historians and their sources 314

[1] Sections I–II are by Dr Jones, sections III–VI are by Sir Thomas Heath.

PAGE

III. THE EARLIER ANNALISTS 316
The Roman annalists 317
Diodorus 318
IV. SOURCES USED BY THE ANNALISTS 319
V. SYSTEMS OF CHRONOLOGY 321
Insertions and expedients 322
VI. LISTS OF MAGISTRATES 323
Roman family traditions 323
Typical legends of the early republic 324
VII. JURISTS AND ANTIQUARIANS 326
The work of the jurists 327
Varro and the antiquarians 329
Legal and constitutional history 331
The task of reconstruction 332

CHAPTER XI

THE FOUNDING OF ROME

BY HUGH LAST, M.A.
Fellow of St John's College, Oxford, and University Lecturer in Roman History

I. THE ORIGIN OF THE LATINS 333
The ancestors of the Latins 334
Cremators and inhumers 336
II. THE GEOGRAPHY OF LATIUM 337
The structure of Latium 338
The frontiers of Latium 340
III. EARLY LATIUM 341
The products of Latium 342
Life in Latium 344
The Latin communities 346
IV. THE BEGINNINGS OF LATIN UNITY 348
Latin unity 349
The early leagues 350
V. THE SITE OF ROME AND THE GROWTH OF THE CITY 351
The hills of Rome 352
The settlements of Rome 354
Roma Quadrata 356
The Septimontium 357
The four regions 358
The walls of Rome 360
The Servian city 362
VI. THE FOUNDATION LEGENDS 363
The coming of Aeneas 364
Romulus and Rhomos 365
Romulus and Remus 366
The Sabine women 368

CHAPTER XII

THE KINGS OF ROME

By Hugh Last

		PAGE
I. The early kings	.	370
The value of tradition	.	371
Titus Tatius	.	373
Numa	.	374
The institutions ascribed to Numa	.	375
Tullus and Ancus	.	377
II. Etruscan Rome	.	378
Etruscan origins	.	379
The meaning of Etruria	.	381
Etruscan influence on Rome	.	382
The Etruscans and Roman religion	.	383
The measure of Rome's debt	.	385
Rome not an Etruscan city	.	386
III. The later kings	.	387
The Tarquins	.	388
Servius Tullius and Mastarna	.	390
Historical character of Servius	.	391
The second Tarquin	.	393
The fall of the monarchy	.	394
Lars Porsenna	.	397
The achievements of the later kings	.	398
IV. The spread of Roman authority during the regal period	.	399
The extent of Roman territory	.	399
The wars of the kings	.	401
The beginnings of conquest	.	403
Rome and the Latins	.	404

CHAPTER XIII

THE PRIMITIVE INSTITUTIONS OF ROME

By H. Stuart Jones

I. Primitive monarchy	.	407
The king	.	408
II. Primitive divisions of the people	.	409
The three tribes: the *curiae*	.	410
The *comitia curiata*	.	412
III. The structure of society: patres and gentes: clients: plebeians	.	413
Patres and *paterfamilias*	.	414
Gens and *gentiles*	.	415
The family and the *gens*	.	417
Plebeian *gentes*	.	418
Clients	.	420
The *plebs*	.	421

PAGE

IV. Civic rights of plebeians 422
 Public rights 423
 The patriciate 424

V. Religious institutions 425
 The *flamines* 426
 Ius and *fas* 427
 Pontifices, Fetiales and Augurs 428
 Augury and divination 430

VI. Military institutions 431
 The earliest army 431

VII. Reform of Servius Tullius: the comitia centuriata and the census 432
 The *comitia centuriata* : the centuries 432
 The tribes 434

CHAPTER XIV

THE EARLY REPUBLIC

By H. Stuart Jones and Hugh Last[1]

I. The successors of the kings 436
 The supreme magistracy 437
 Italic institutions 439
 The dictatorship 440

II. The powers of the magistrates 441
 Imperium 441
 Limitations of the *imperium* 442
 The custom of the ancestors 444

III. Criminal jurisdiction: the right of appeal 445
 Duoviri perduellionis 445
 The right of appeal 447

IV. The early Republican Senate 448
 The formation of the Senate 449
 Mos maiorum 450

V. Plebeian institutions: tribunes: concilium plebis . . . 450
 The assemblies of *plebs* and *populus* 451
 Secessio 452
 The appointment of tribunes 452
 Assemblies of tribes 455

VI. The demands of the plebs: auxilium 456
 Popular jurisdiction 457

VII. The Decemvirate and the Twelve Tables 458
 Appointment of the Decemvirate 459
 Criticism of the tradition 461

[1] Sections I–VII and XIII are by Dr Stuart Jones, sections VIII–XII by Mr Last.

PAGE

VIII. THE ROME OF THE TWELVE TABLES 462
   The evidence of the Twelve Tables 463
   The sources of Roman wealth 464
   Archaeological evidence 465
   The life of fifth-century Rome 466

IX. LAND-TENURE AND THE DEMAND FOR LAND AT ROME 468
   Land-tenure 468
   The *heredium* 469
   The agitation for land 471
   The failure of demands for land 472

X. EARLY ROMAN COLONIZATION 473
   The purpose of colonies 473
   The evidence 474

XI. THE FOOD-SUPPLY 474
   Famine 475

XII. THE LAW OF DEBT 476
   Debt 476
   The *nexum* 478
   The plight of the debtor 479

XIII. THE VALERIO-HORATIAN LAWS 480
   The tradition of the Valerio-Horatian legislation . . . 481
   Plebiscita and *leges* 482

CHAPTER XV

ROME AND HER NEIGHBOURS IN THE FIFTH CENTURY

BY HUGH LAST

I. ROME, LATIUM, AND THE HERNICI AT THE BEGINNING OF THE FIFTH CENTURY 485
   The leagues of Latium 487
   Lake Regillus and the *foedus Cassianum* 488
   The date of the treaty 490
   Rome and the Hernici 492

II. THE SABINES AT ROME 493
   Theory of a Sabine conquest of Rome 494
   The gradual penetration of Sabines into Rome 496

III. THE VOLSCIAN ADVANCE 497
   The Volscian threat 497
   Coriolanus 498

IV. THE WARS WITH THE AEQUI 500
   Cincinnatus 501
   The battle of the Algidus 502
   The connection of Volscians and Aequi 503

V. THE ROMAN DEFENCE OF THE TIBER 504
   The Fabii on the Cremera 504
   Aulus Cornelius Cossus 507
   The clearing of Latium 509

	PAGE
VI. THE EASTERN OFFENSIVE	509
Aequi and Volsci	510
VII. THE CONQUEST OF SOUTHERN ETRURIA	511
Rome across the Tiber	511
The siege of Veii	512
The weakness of Etruria	515
The political situation	517
Rome's hegemony in Latium	518

CHAPTER XVI

THE MAKING OF A UNITED STATE

By H. STUART JONES and HUGH LAST[1]

	PAGE
I. CONSULAR TRIBUNES	519
The tradition of the consular tribunes	520
II. THE CREATION OF THE CENSORSHIP	521
Powers and functions of the censors	522
The roll of the Senate: state contracts	523
III. THE CLIMAX OF THE CONSTITUTIONAL STRUGGLE	524
M. Manlius Capitolinus	524
The Licinio-Sextian laws	525
The dictatorships of Camillus	526
The first plebeian consul	527
Patrician evasions	528
Leges Genuciae	529
Leges Publiliae	530
IV. APPIUS CLAUDIUS	531
The city tribes	532
The career of Cn. Flavius	533
Priesthoods thrown open to the Plebs	535
V. FOOD-SUPPLY, PUBLIC LANDS AND COLONIES	535
Sp. Maelius and L. Minucius	536
Public land	538
The Licinian rogation	539
Colonies	541
VI. DEBT AND THE NEXUM	542
Debt	543
Measures for the relief of debt	544
The lex Poetelia	545
VII. THE NEW NOBILITY	546
Latin rights	549
VIII. THE MACHINERY OF GOVERNMENT	550
Functions of the aediles	551
Minor offices: duoviri	552
The last secession: the Lex Hortensia	553

[1] Sections I–IV and VII–VIII are by Dr Stuart Jones, sections V and VI by Mr Last.

CHAPTER XVII

THE GALLIC WARS OF ROME

By L. Homo
Professor of Ancient History in the University of Lyons

PAGE

I. The evidence for the period 554
The literary and archaeological evidence 554

II. The Gallic conquest of northern Italy 555
Gauls and Etruscans in north Italy 556
Etruscan and Celtic culture 559

III. The Gallic catastrophe 561
Rome on the eve of the Allia 561
The Gauls before Clusium 562
The Allia 564
The Gauls in Rome 565

IV. The rebuilding of Roman power 566
The recovery 567
Military and political measures 568

V. Gallic incursions 570
Gallic raids 571
Roman successes 573

VI. The wars of Rome with her neighbours 574
Securing of the northern frontier 574
Wars with the Volsci and Latins 576
Prelude to Rome's mastery of Italy 579

CHAPTER XVIII

THE CONQUEST OF CENTRAL ITALY

By F. E. Adcock, M.A.
Fellow of King's College and Professor of Ancient History
in the University of Cambridge

I. The Roman tradition 581
The criticism of the tradition 582

II. The grouping of powers 583
The Sabellian movement 583
The Samnite league 585

III. Rome and the Latins 586
Latin disaffection 587
The Latin War 589

IV. The new Roman power 591
The settlement with the Latins 591
Campania and Rome 592

V. Roman policy and the Samnites 594
The breach with the Samnites 595
The Samnite power 596

		PAGE
VI. The great Samnite war: the first phase		597
The Caudine peace		599
VII. The great Samnite war: the second phase		600
The Samnite offensive		601
The Roman recovery		603
VIII. The Roman advance in central Italy		603
Rome and the Etruscans		604
The revolt of the Hernici		606
The Roman currency		607
IX. The last crisis		608
Umbria and the north		609
The invasion of Samnium		610
The crisis of Sentinum		612
X. The final victory		613
The last campaigns		614
Sabines and Samnites		615

CHAPTER XIX

AGATHOCLES

By M. Cary, D.Litt.
Reader in Ancient History in the University of London

I. The Rise of Agathocles		617
The Siceliote Greeks		617
Early Rises and Falls		619
Usurpation of Tyranny		620
II. The Sicilian Wars 316–310 b.c.		621
Conquests in Sicily		623
III. The African Campaign 310–309 b.c.		624
Invasion of Africa		625
Ophellas of Cyrene		626
IV. The African Campaign 308–307 b.c.		628
The Carthaginian Rally		629
Evacuation of Africa		630
V. Sicilian Affairs 310–304 b.c.		631
Sicilian Warfare		632
Agathocles king of Sicily		633
VI. Agathocles and South Italy		634
Descents upon Italy		635
VII. Conclusion		636
Results of his Rule		637

CHAPTER XX

PYRRHUS

By Tenney Frank, Ph.D.

Professor of Latin in the Johns Hopkins University

		PAGE
I. Rome and Magna Graecia		638
The Senones and Etruscans		638
The battle of Vadimo		639
The cities of Magna Graecia		640
II. Tarentum: the coming of Pyrrhus		641
Pyrrhus at Tarentum		642
III. The War and Peace-proposals		644
The tradition about Pyrrhus		644
Pyrrhic victory at Heraclea		645
Cineas negotiates for peace		646
Failure of peace-negotiations		647
The battle of Asculum		648
IV. Carthaginian Policy: Pyrrhus in Sicily		649
Rome's treaty with Carthage		649
Pyrrhus in Sicily		651
V. The End of the War		652
Pyrrhus defeated at Beneventum		653
Rome's activity in Magna Graecia		654
The siege of Tarentum		655
Rome's federation extended		657
Serf-rising at Volsinii		658
VI. The Roman Federation		658
Nature of Rome's federation		659
Differing status of allies		660
The federation		661
A new currency		662
The government		664

CHAPTER XXI

ROME AND CARTHAGE: THE FIRST PUNIC WAR

By Tenney Frank

I. Carthage		665
Constitution and government		666
II. The Alliance with the Mamertines		667
Affairs in Sicily		667
Rome's intervention in Messana		668
Causes of the War		670
Messana occupied		672

PAGE

III. The Crossing to Sicily: Alliance with Hiero 673
Warfare in Sicily 674
Hiero accepts terms of peace 675

IV. Siege of Agrigentum: the new Roman fleet 676
Agrigentum captured 677
Creation of a fleet 678
The first naval battle: Mylae 679
Battle of Tyndaris 680

V. Regulus in Africa 681
The invasion of Africa: battle of Ecnomus 681
The landing 682
Campaign of Regulus in Africa 683
Regulus defeated: the fleet wrecked 684
The disaster off Palinurus 686

VI. Stalemate by land and sea 686
War in Sicily: Lilybaeum; Drepana 687
Peace negotiations fail 689
Treaty with Hiero renewed: Hamilcar in Sicily . . . 690

VII. The Final Effort 691
The new fleet 691
The Aegates islands: terms of peace 692
The difficulties of Carthage 693
Reasons for Rome's victory 694

VIII. The effect of the War on Rome 695
The effect on the Roman constitution 695
Cultural influences from Sicily 696
Influence on Roman drama 697

CHAPTER XXII

THE STRUGGLE OF EGYPT AGAINST SYRIA AND MACEDONIA

By W. W. Tarn

I. Introduction: the First Syrian War 699
The Issues between Egypt and Syria 701
Success of Antiochus I 702
Arsinoe's triumph and honours 704

II. The Chremonidean War 705
Coalition against Antigonus 706
Antigonus takes Athens 708

III. The War of Eumenes 709
Eumenes I 709

IV. The Second Syrian War 710
Antiochus II 710
Antigonus' fleet 711
Asia Minor and Cyrene 712
The battle of Cos 713
Antigonus' monuments 714

PAGE

V. The Third Syrian or Laodicean War 715
    Berenice II 715
    Campaign of Ptolemy III 717
    The battle of Andros 718
    Asia Minor, Thrace 719

VI. The War of the Brothers: Attalus I 720
    Seleucus II and Hierax 720
    Attalus I: the Gauls 721
    The dedications of Attalus 722
    The success of Attalus 722

VII. Antiochus III 723
    Revolt and defeat of Molon 724
    Revolt of Achaeus 725

VIII. The Fourth Syrian War 726
    Ptolemy III 726
    Ptolemy IV 727
    Antiochus' invasion of Syria 728
    Antiochus advances to Raphia 729
    The battle of Raphia 730
    Its results 731

CHAPTER XXIII

THE GREEK LEAGUES AND MACEDONIA

By W. W. Tarn

I. Aratus and the Achaean League 732
    The expansion of Aetolia 733
    Aratus 733
    Aratus takes Corinth 734
    Attempts on Athens and Argos 735

II. The Constitution of the Achaean League 735
    The League officials 736
    Assembly and meetings 737
    Council and Assembly 738

III. Agis IV of Sparta and Reform 739
    The position at Sparta 739
    The problems 740
    Agis' reforms 742
    His death 743

IV. The War of Demetrius II with the Leagues . . . 744
    Demetrius II and Aratus 744
    Lydiades 746
    Dardania 747

V. The Triumph of Federalism 747
    Aetolia 747
    Athens 748
    The triumph of Aratus 750

VI. Antigonus Doson 751
    'The League of the Macedonians' 751

		PAGE
VII.	CLEOMENES III OF SPARTA AND THE REVOLUTION	752
	Cleomenes III	752
	The revolution at Sparta	754
	Cercidas	755
VIII.	CLEOMENES AND ARATUS	755
	Failure of the Achaean League	756
	Doson offers help to the Achaeans	757
IX.	CLEOMENES AND ANTIGONUS	758
	Doson in Greece	758
	His new League	759
	Megalopolis	760
	The battle of Sellasia	761
	Defeat of Cleomenes	762
X.	THE WAR OF THE ALLIES	763
	Philip V	763
	Aetolia and Philip	764
	Philip in the Peloponnese	766
	Successes of Philip	767
	The conference of Naupactus: Agelaus	768

CHAPTER XXIV

THE CARTHAGINIANS IN SPAIN

By A. SCHULTEN, Ph.D.
Professor of Ancient History in the University of Erlangen

I.	EARLY SETTLEMENTS IN SPAIN	769
II.	SPAIN IN THE GREAT AGE OF TARTESSUS	770
	The Massiliote *Periplus*	770
	The Empire of Tartessus	772
III.	THE CARTHAGINIAN CONQUEST	773
	Carthage and Tartessus	774
	Carthage and the Straits	776
IV.	THE FIRST CARTHAGINIAN EMPIRE IN SPAIN	777
	The Phoenician towns	778
	The natural wealth of Spain	778
	Archaeological finds and literary evidence	779
	Pytheas of Massilia	780
V.	THE IBERIANS	782
	Iberian Institutions	783
	Iberian civilisation	784
VI.	THE RE-CONQUEST OF SPAIN	786
	Hamilcar in Spain	786
	Hasdrubal: the Ebro treaty	788
VII.	HANNIBAL: THE CHALLENGE TO ROME	789
	The early campaigns	789
	Saguntum	790
	Hannibal in Spain	791

CHAPTER XXV

ROME AFTER THE CONQUEST OF SICILY

BY TENNEY FRANK

	PAGE
I. SICILY: TAXATION	793
The cities	793
The tithe imposed on Sicily	795
The *Lex Hieronica*	796
Status of subjects	797
II. SICILY: ADMINISTRATION	798
The rights of the cities	799
III. ITALY AND ROME	800
Falerii	800
Colonies: reforms	801
IV. CARTHAGE AFTER THE WAR	802
Rome's policy towards Carthage	803
Rome takes Sardinia	804
V. NORTH ITALY: FLAMINIUS	805
Pisa	805
The democrats	806
The *ager Gallicus* and Flaminius	807
The Claudian plebiscite	808
VI. THE GALLIC PERIL	808
Massilia and Carthage	809
The Ebro treaty	810
Levies throughout Italy: the Census	811
Victory at Telamon: Flaminius	813
Marcellus at Clastidium	814
VII. ROMAN POLICY	815
Border wars	815
VIII. THE ROMAN CONSTITUTION	817
The magistrates	818
The power of the Senate	819
The leading men	820

CHAPTER XXVI

THE ROMANS IN ILLYRIA

BY M. HOLLEAUX
Membre de l'Institut, Professor of Hellenistic History in the University of Paris

	PAGE
I. THE EARLY RELATIONS OF ROME WITH THE GREEK WORLD	822
Roman indifference to Greece	823
II. ILLYRIAN PIRACY	824
The Illyrian pirate fleets	825
Rise of an Illyrian state	826

PAGE

III. ILLYRIA UNDER AGRON AND TEUTA 827
        The Illyrian kingdom 827
        The Illyrian and Italian commerce 829
        Illyrian raid on Epirus 830

IV. THE FIRST ROMAN WAR WITH ILLYRIA 831
        Queen Teuta 831
        The battle of Paxos 833
        The first Roman expedition 834
        The Roman protectorate 836

V. THE ROMANS AND ANTIGONUS DOSON 837
        The motives of the Romans 837
        Antigonus Doson 839
        The first Roman envoys in Greece 841
        Recovery of Macedonia 842
        The embarrassments of Rome 843

VI. THE REBELLION OF DEMETRIUS OF PHAROS 844
        Character of Demetrius 844
        Antigonus and Demetrius 845
        The revolt of Demetrius 846

VII. THE SECOND ROMAN WAR WITH ILLYRIA 848
        The second Roman expedition 849

VIII. PHILIP V AND ROME AFTER THE SECOND ILLYRIAN WAR . 851
        Philip V and Rome 851
        Philip's successes 852
        The hopes of Philip 853

IX. SCERDILAIDAS' ATTACK ON PHILIP 854
        The defeat of Scerdilaidas 855

X. CONCLUSION 856

CHRONOLOGICAL NOTES:
        1. The date of the first treaty between Rome and Carthage . . 859
        2. The date of the battle of Cos 862
        3. The date of the battle of Sellasia 863

LIST OF ABBREVIATIONS 865

BIBLIOGRAPHIES

GENERAL BIBLIOGRAPHY 867
CHAPTER I 869
CHAPTER II 871
CHAPTERS III, VI, XXII, XXIII 874
CHAPTER IV 889
CHAPTER V 898
CHAPTER VII 902
CHAPTER VIII 904

CONTENTS

PAGE

CHAPTER IX 907
CHAPTERS X–XVI 909
CHAPTER XVII 918
CHAPTER XVIII 921
CHAPTER XIX 924
CHAPTERS XX AND XXI 925
CHAPTER XXIV 927
CHAPTER XXV 929
CHAPTER XXVI 931

GENERAL INDEX 935

INDEX TO MAPS 975

INDEX OF PASSAGES REFERRED TO 982

LIST OF MAPS, TABLES, PLANS, ETC.:

1. Map to illustrate the coming of the Celts . . . FACING PAGE 41
2. The Hellenistic Kingdoms c. 275 B.C. . . . . ,, 75
3. Hellenistic Egypt . . . . ,, 109
4. Hellenistic Asia . . . . ,, 155
5. Rome and her Neighbours in the Fifth Century . . ,, 333
6. Site of Rome . . . . ,, 351
7. The Roman conquest of central Italy . . . . ,, 581
8. S. Italy and Sicily . . . . ,, 617
9. The struggle of Egypt against Macedonia and Syria . ,, 699
10. Greece, Macedonia and S. Illyria in 228 B.C. . . . ,, 768
11. Carthaginian possessions in Spain c. 220 B.C. . . ,, 769
12. Map to illustrate Roman colonization . . . . ,, 820
13. Map to illustrate extension of Roman citizenship . . ,, 820
14. Illyria . . . . ,, 825
Comparative Chronological Table for Early Roman History . ,, 321
Hellenistic Dynasties . . . . AT END
Genealogical Tables . . . . ,,
Chronological Tables . . . . ,,

CHAPTER I

THE LEADING IDEAS OF THE
NEW PERIOD

I. SALIENT FEATURES

DURING the period of history covered in this volume the Greeks continued for a long time to occupy the centre of the stage[1]. The rôle they had to play was graver and more complicated than ever before. In the West they soon lost the initiative to Rome. All the time they were spreading themselves thinly over the East the Italians were being concentrated more and more completely and compactly under a single head. It would have been better for the political fortunes of the Greeks if the forces led by Alexander of Macedon into the East had supported Alexander of Epirus in Italy, and Hellas was destined to pay dearly for misdirecting thus its energy. So favourable a conjuncture for saving their western kinsmen was never to recur; and that not simply because of the marvellous growth of Roman power. For once the way into Persia was opened, thither for several generations streamed the surplus population of the Aegean Archipelago and its environs. The East became the land of opportunity for the Greeks. It was 'manifest destiny' that they should seek to possess it. And once they were committed to movement in that direction they could not draw back. No matter what happened in the West they had to hellenize the world in which the Macedonians had made them masters, or themselves go under.

They set about this task with energy and intelligence. It was twofold in character: the forging of instruments—institutions, ideas, devices—by which to make their culture more readily communicable to non-Greeks; and the transmutation of 'natives.' They ran great risks of losing their own soul in the process. Probably we should say, from our rich experience of imperialism, that success was excluded from the start. Hellenism failed to master the intractable soul of the Orient; but it acquired a capacity for world-culture in the attempt. What led the proud Roman conqueror captive was not the aristocratic civilization of Attic Greece but the more seductive, accommodating, catholic

[1] For contrasts with the civilization of this Hellenistic world see chap. II on the Celts and the chapters on Early Rome.

modification of it that we call Hellenistic. And, after all, the East *was* moved. It is hard to overrate an effort which, precisely by its partial failure, created the milieu in which heretical Judaism was fused with cosmopolitanized Hellenism to form Christianity.

The leaders of the Hellenes in their eastward expansion were Macedonians, the most forceful, if not the most cultivated, representatives of their race, but the prompters and agents of these leaders were for the most part Greeks of the old stock. The work had to be prosecuted in the midst of political disunion and intestine wars—hence without centralized direction—in Egypt in one way, in Syria and elsewhere in Asia in another; and not by states alone, but by scores of communes, hundreds of private associations, and thousands of individuals, acting ordinarily without set purpose, aggressive propagandists of Hellenism by their mere existence if by nothing else. The problems were so novel, the centres of irradiation, cities new and old, so numerous, the area of statecraft so circumscribed that, in the sense of drift and of the omnipotence of Tyche—Chance—then generally prevalent, conscious effort could seldom be long sustained.

Macedon exerted no such transforming influence on Greece as Rome did on Italy. There was no Hellenic analogue for Latinization. The *synedrion* of the various Hellenic Leagues, whether a reflex of Macedon or autonomous, proved an ineffective instrument of national consolidation. And, disunited at home, Greece lacked an organ, such as the governing society of Italy possessed, first in the Senate and later in the Princeps, for keeping its influence steadily applied in given directions abroad. Macedonian imperialism differed from Roman imperialism in its works as well as in its methods. Rome gave to the world order, law, roads, administrative centralization. The Greeks had only themselves to give—themselves and their views and ways of life. The only external authority they had recognized hitherto had come to each individual from his city-state, and in the new world this was diminished by the artificiality of the new cities, by monarchical interferences with their conduct of affairs, and, perhaps even more than by either of these sources of weakness, by the contacts in the routine of life between townsman and townsman throughout the length and breadth of a kingdom. The authority of city-states could not control situations and problems adequately when these ceased to be predominantly urban. The Greeks in the East were thus thrown even more than at home upon their own resources. In one sense their pronounced individualism was an asset: it multiplied indefinitely their propensity for contrivance. But the ordinary

Greek was not a masterful person like the ordinary Roman. He was too curious, too interested, too sociable to stand aloof among the 'barbarians' with whom his lot was cast. He could not forget that he was a Greek, but neither could he leave unsampled the goods of others. In their colonial environment the Hellenes had perforce to deviate from their traditions however much value they set on maintaining them. They were of course the imperial people; and in the *gymnasium*, which they took with them everywhere, they had an institution for the education of their youth that served to keep them socially apart from 'the lesser breeds without the Law.' Theirs was not the rôle to yield, least of all to subjects. But, this granted, they could not display their superiority in any way more clearly than by adapting themselves flexibly to changed circumstances.

It thus happened that the early Hellenistic age was an age of vast experiment in the most varied spheres of human endeavour. The capabilities of monarchical and federal states were tested simultaneously in many political laboratories. The manifold possibilities of municipal organization were explored more and more thoroughly. The old lines separating nations, classes, families, races, and sexes having faded, a new social cosmos had to be created. Social life, indeed, divorced from political life after two centuries of fusion, had to be re-cast in institutions of its own. Religion, too, had now to face a new problem, that of creating organs peculiar to itself and distinct from states. The whole economic order had to be remodelled. The office of governing natives was inseparable from that of exploiting them, and on this unhappy business much ingenuity was expended—so, too, on the management of state monopolies and of crown-lands. Protective tariffs were invented (p. 139). Transport, assuming added significance with the increased size of states, perplexed statesmen even more than it did merchants and manufacturers; and with good reason. For without effective communications big states were bound to be weak states. The time was rich in novelties in art and architecture, engineering and town-planning, education and scientific research. As was natural in an age when literature had to be re-shaped to meet the needs of a Hellenic *diaspora*, of a reading instead of a listening public, of a patronage which, while given mainly by courts and courtiers, was extended also by mobs and masses, often cosmopolitan, old literary types had to be discarded, replaced, re-combined, and new ones added (chap. VIII). With the widening of the world the public, with which in the olden time writers and artists had been in marvellously direct and mutually profitable contact, receded farther and farther in the distance or went completely out of sight. Athens did not cease at once to be the cynosure of Greece, but its leadership was contested by new royal capitals; and everywhere the effect was felt of the waning of its dominion in matters of taste. Like the sculptor and the painter, the man of letters, for whom his own city no longer sufficed, was allowed to feel that he had only his own taste to consult, his own moods to chronicle, his own personality to embody in his work.

Individualism thus became a dominant feature of the age. But, once the great Macedonian generals, whose pulses had been quickened by service with Alexander, had passed from the scene, it was not a magnificent individualism, arising, as it did, not so much from the greatness of individuals as from the weakness of society. Craftsmanship was free from control rather than inspired. Asceticism waxed; and it waxed from fear of the entanglements of ambition rather than from satiety. Introspection flourished, numbing the will and killing zest for action, and scepticism, with its arrest of judgment. The world had become too suddenly big, and too formless even for great social criticism. But there was one sphere in which this individualism was indeed magnificent— characterized by splendid achievements—that of pure science (chap. IX). *Nihil mathematicis inlustrius*, says Cicero[1]. The men of science alone rose to the height of the occasion and were the chief glory of their time; but they failed to make their knowledge a common possession because the mass of mankind was too remote and ill-organized to advance abreast of them.

Among the populations released from the old authority of city-state law and opinion but uncontrolled by the authority of their scientific leaders, religions grew and spread, especially those which promised to individuals knowledge of their future (astrology), cure of their diseases (Asclepius), salvation and immortality (Mystery cults). To this resurgence of superstition the new monarchies, while doing much for science, were either indifferent or sympathetic. Like other polytheistic peoples the Macedonians had no thought of extending their imperialism to religion. They did not view the gods of subjected peoples as subject to their gods or themselves as having a mission to proselytize. The Hellenes generally took their home gods with them to the East, as they had taken them to their colonies in times past. These, now as then, were the gods primarily recognized by both monarchical and city-state law—those, for example, for which public cults and festi-

[1] *Tusculan Disputations*, I, 2, 5.

vals were commonly instituted; but Greeks abroad readily identified them with local gods that looked like them, and, like their
ancestors, they had little or no religious repugnance to adopting
new gods found on the spot or new modes of worshipping old gods.
'In such an environment, as the history of emigration and colonization in modern times teaches us, fidelity to the religion of their
ancestors was a matter of individual determination.'[1] Cosmopolitanism in heaven was matched by religious individualism on earth.

To bring some semblance of system into the welter of worships
that ensued was a challenge to the official no less than to the
philosophic and the popular mind. By making the ruler-gods of
each dynasty share temples with one another and with other
deities, and by grouping under a single priesthood deities like
Sarapis, Isis, Harpocrates, and Anubis, governments did something to promote simplification. Rationalizing theology also
helped somewhat by substituting for the gods of common thinking
abstractions which could be symbolized adequately not by one
god-name alone but by two or more combined, as, for example,
Apollo-Helios-Hermes. But the general tendency, now as in all
periods of polytheistic expansion, was towards a cruder syncretism
—putting the name of a Greek god on a cognate deity, addressing
him as 'Thou of many names' or by all the names strung together
by which each worshipper happened to know him, accepting as
valid every local mode of divine approach when it was not too
repellent. From the fusion of deities—new and old—of a place
or region it was a short step, at least for the theologically-minded,
to their complete fusion into universal powers. The idea that was
their common character was subtracted. Zeus-Ammon-Yahweh-
Ahuramazda-Jupiter, for example, became the Highest God or
(since the Greek language was the *lingua franca*) Zeus simply.
Once this tendency was established, the differences in religion felt
to be important were peculiarities of ritual; and the local cults that
had the most potent ritual—the best accredited means of winning
the attention of the gods—had an almost infinite capacity of
migration. An ebb and flow of cults followed which brought alien
elements into both West and East—Dionysiac rites into Egypt
and Jerusalem and rites of Isis and Atargatis into Athens—but
which did not necessitate much change anywhere of fundamental
religious conceptions. Of these the most active transforming agent
remained the philosophic (scientific and mystic) speculation of the
Greeks; but now, even more than before, this was fed by Oriental
materials, by concepts native in Iran, Chaldaea, Egypt; and it was

[1] G. F. Moore, *Judaism*, I, p. 224.

menaced in its basic assumption—the efficacy of reason—by inner disintegration into dogmatism and scepticism, and, though more remotely, by an attitude of mind prevalent in the Orient and manifested in its most pure form in the fundamental tenet of Judaism, 'that religion must be revealed.'[1] *For the Jews require a sign and the Greeks seek after wisdom.*

Hellenism, like a corrosive fluid, spread round and ate into the foundations of the eastern cultures, rock-ribbed with religion though they were. It dissolved isolated particles, disintegrated detached masses, penetrated all crevices and softened the granite surfaces perceptibly wherever, as in and near the cities, its action was especially direct. The elements thus hellenized conformed to the amenities of cosmopolitan life, obtained access to offices and better openings for international business, entered through inter-marriage into the penumbra of 'society,' and thus formed a medium through which the acid of the West advanced yet farther, though doubtless with less transforming efficacy. But the great massifs remained impervious. The most resistant Oriental cultures, established, as they were believed to be, by the very presence of God, stood fast amidst the tide. Judaism threw the fence of the Law around its divine inheritance, and was strong enough, when the overt attack came, to assert its right to its own independent life (see further, vol. VIII). In Egypt the many local cults, through whose stiff and antiquated rites the ideal life of the people strove helplessly for expression, retained a strong hold on the mass of the peasants, while those cults whose appeal was wider had even greater success in preserving their ancient character through being indissolubly bound up with the crown not only by syndicated priesthoods but also by theology, ritual, festivals, and sacred ceremonies and representations of which the Pharaoh-Ptolemy was the interested object (pp. 113 *sqq.*). In Iran, where, too, national life was wrapped up in religion, and in eastern Asia Minor, whither Zoroastrianism had been carried by Persian colonization, Hellenism encountered successful opposition. The Magi had in their arsenal not merely sorcery, with which to combat malevolent demons, but also a creed which did justice to the reality of Evil yet taught men to hope that, with their help and for their salvation, its god of Goodness and Light, Ahuramazda, would, in the fullness of time, prevail over his great adversary, Ahriman, and the hosts of Darkness. In fact, so strong was the religion of Iran that orthodox Judaism at this time moulded its thinking more in conformance with Zoroastrianism than in conformance with

[1] G. F. Moore, *op. cit.* I, p. 112.

Hellenism. Here, then, and elsewhere in what had been Persia, notably in Babylonia, national streams of thought and feeling kept flowing steadily on through the sea of Hellenism, now broad now narrow, now mingling with one another and with their common medium or losing themselves in it altogether, now holding resolutely apart each in its own channel.

With the religions of the nations which they could neither ignore nor assimilate the Greeks came to terms, with some of them in our period—for example, the Egyptian cult of Sarapis, Isis, Harpocrates and Anubis and the Syrian cult of Hadad and Atargatis; with others, like that of the Jewish sect of the Nazarenes, not till five hundred years later. But they got terms as well as gave them, and the end of the matter was that these religions ceased to be Oriental and became Hellenistic. The rites may have remained essentially eastern; the plastic representations were mainly Greek. The religious services were quickened by Hellenic speculation into mysteries—Graeco-Oriental 'fake' mysteries, as they have been called (vol. VI, p. 166). Greek thinkers fitted into their own systems ideas for which they were ripe, from Zoroastrianism the concept of Eternity (Zervan-Aion), from Babylon the lore, so seemingly scientific, of the heavenly bodies as *Cosmocratores*—predeterminers of the fate of men and empires. It was ominous for Greek assimilation of this mass of alien matter that, after a long period of mutually profitable union, Greek philosophy and science parted company in the third century B.C.—the one to become more ethical, popular, sentimental, the other more mathematical, difficult, remote.

II. MONARCHY

Of the two expedients with which this age experimented for combining small states into large units—League[1] and Monarchy —the former has approved itself in our time as the most apt instrument of republican consolidation. Until the Great War (Switzerland apart) it achieved its real triumphs where, as in America, Canada, Brazil, South Africa, and Australia, it was applied to political entities in which state-distinctiveness and national individuality were blurred by prior membership in a larger political association. This, too, was the condition of its most

[1] Following popular usage this term is used to designate (a) coalitions (symmachies) possessing permanent organs of their own, even though their basis was the alliance of autonomous states; and (b) federations (sympolities) where the central organs were based on a common citizenship (see p. 751 n. 1).

striking, if not its only, success in Hellas. Behind the Greek
Leagues that achieved inner solidarity was almost invariably a
Greek tribe (*ethnos*), of which the federated states were in each
instance parts. As an agency of republican consolidation of
altogether separate nations the League laboured under the double
disadvantage (from which we to-day are spared) that self-government had come to be applied consistently to foreign relations and
that democracy could not be maintained when the population
concerned was widely dispersed. Wherever government was
organized without a primary assembly, it ceased to be self-
government even in city-states. Only where there was a common
Assembly could there be a common citizenship that meant anything politically important for the masses. And the greatest
significance of a primary Assembly, even in Leagues of moderate
compass like the Achaean, was to preserve the form rather than
the reality of democracy. Whether primary assemblies existed or
not, states in which the chief powers of national government were
vested in representative bodies took on an aristocratic complexion.
To the masses the rule of an alien monarch who professed to
champion their interests might easily appear preferable to the rule
of the representatives of a native class. And if this was true
generally, it was especially true when this rule was shared, as in
Leagues, with the representatives of similar classes in other states;
for then local feeling was apt to be outraged as well as popular
feeling. Leagues which, like those of Philip II, Demetrius Poliorcetes, and Antigonus Doson, aspired to include Greeks generally,
lacking as they necessarily did the deliberative organ by which
alone a collective public opinion could be quickly formed, were
bound to be ruled arbitrarily even if they had been ruled by
representative synods and not monarchically. Thus hampered, the
various Leagues attempted at this time in Greece did not secure
enough loyalty from their members, or enough magnitude, or
enough freedom of action, to offset the advantages of monarchy.

Monarchy was accordingly the instrument for building up
territorial states to which the Macedonian age gave the stamp
of its approval. Of its work much was ephemeral, but it itself
was singularly long-lived. Made dominant in Greece by the
Macedonians, discredited temporarily but not destroyed by the
Roman Senate, kings, as the heads of states and not merely of
tribes as in the early Greek monarchies, came into the western
world at this time, there to stay until in our day it has become
possible for big states to be republics. During the two millenniums
and a quarter that intervene between the rise of the Macedonians

and the downfall of the Romanoffs, Hapsburgs, and Hohen-
zollerns, monarchy in some form or other has been the normal
form of political life.

The monarchy which first approved itself in action and lent
its prestige to the whole institution was the national monarchy of
Philip and Alexander. This was home-grown in Macedonia. There
it had the strong sanction of antiquity. Hereditary in the royal
house of the Argeadae it passed, in the event of a disputed succession, to the claimant whom the army favoured. Its basis was
the instinctive loyalty of a politically undeveloped people to their
legitimate head. Its forms were military; and behind the forms
lay the 'fellowship' of the nobles (ἑταῖροι) and commons
(πεζέταιροι) with their king, which lent a spirit of camaraderie
to discipline; for discipline there was, at least after Philip's time—
the stiff discipline of the phalanx, which yet, for all its rigour, left
unimpaired the natural sturdiness of Macedonian character.
Custom served for a constitution. It required the king to draw
near to his person the chief nobles of his realm (as Bodyguards and
Companions), and to assemble at his court their sons (as Royal
Pages), but it left him free to select his civil, military, and diplomatic officials according to his own judgment, to promote or dismiss them, but not to put them to death without the consent of
the army. The army was the people. The right of decision in
matters of policy in peace and war rested with the king, but it was
customary for him to exercise it in a council of his Companions[1].
Large scope was left to kings of strong character. A regency fell
to the nearest agnate in the case of minors. There was no remedy
for adult rulers of weak character.

This kind of monarchy was mobile but not exportable. It
moved with the Macedonian king and army, but wherever it
went it had to accommodate itself to local conditions. In Greece,
where the prevailing sentiment was hostile, the intrusive office
had to be camouflaged. In the surface drift of the age of Isocrates
toward larger Hellenic unity there had been a side current that
was perceptibly monarchical; but the monarch it portended was
an emergency man, a reconciler of factions, a war-lord, the head
of a crusade (see vol. VI, p. 518). The main current in this surface
drift was toward federalism, not monarchy; and however much
statesmen and communities, political theorists and leagues might
try to stem it, the deep drift in Greece, then and thereafter, was
toward the slow disintegration of the *polis* without re-integration
in any political cosmos—toward the making of a world of com-

[1] See vol. VI, pp. 205, 359, and H. Berve, *Das Alexanderreich*, I, p. 30.

paratively isolated individuals, actuated primarily by economic, social, ethical, and religious egoisms, and hence, as the sequel showed, less indisposed to let their government pass into the hands of autocrats. In Greece monarchy stayed as hegemony. The king of Macedon continued the line of paramount *poleis*— Athens, Sparta, Thebes. He was a tyrant, or the prop of tyrants, in so far as he was not a constitutional magistrate. His composite office might be regularized by making a god of him, and this was frequently done until Antigonus Gonatas put a check on it. The transition from a *hegemon* to a king premised more than decay of popular interest in political life. It implied the growth of an active feeling of devotion for the representative of royalty, and of this there is not a trace in third-century Greece. Nor was the decay in urban loyalty an unmixed evil. It reduced particularistic opposition to federalism as well as to autocracy. It betokened despair rather than unwillingness to make personal sacrifices for the commonwealth. On any revival of hope local patriotism flared up anew, whereupon decadence manifested itself in fickleness and indiscipline rather than in lack of courage. For monarchy Greece remained stony ground throughout this period.

It was not Philip's conquest of Greece but Alexander's conquest of Persia that stabilized monarchy in the western world. For it was only thereafter that it became a political necessity. In a realm like Alexander's, as in an empire like Rome's, the territory was too large for any government but a monarchy to control it. Indeed it proved to be too large for a single monarchy. And even if countries so vast as its divisions had not precluded by their very magnitude organization on republican lines, the confusion of their peoples would have done so. Under the Persian monarchy, the inhabitants of Asia, already torn by violence or tempted by hope of gain far from their homes, had become, as later under the Turk, almost inextricably mixed. Iranians, Jews, Babylonians, and Greeks were thus superimposed in many parts upon the indigenous stocks (pp. 177 *sqq.*). The areas without racial or religious intermixture were apt to be remote and inaccessible. Any other kind of state than a monarchy requires some sort of taking counsel together, and where population was so heterogeneous, stratified, and widely dispersed, this was impossible in the state of communications at that time existing. There was thus reason behind the persistence of monarchy in the world conquered by Alexander —reason and, at the time of the conquest, age-long tradition; and reason and tradition taken together would have compelled the conqueror to maintain monarchy there even if he had not been himself a king and the head of a monarchically-minded people; and not only there, but also in the sections into which it became divided.

But what sort of a monarchy should this be? The answer given by Alexander to this question has been described in the previous volume (see vol. vi, pp. 432 *sqq.*): it should assume, he concluded, a different character in accordance with differences in the ideas and customs of the peoples over which it was exercised. That this was a provisional answer is probable. Certainly it was not a definitive one. The Macedonian reaction which followed his death stressed the Macedonian characteristics of the monarchical institution at the expense of the Persian; and the court which evolved in each section retained the institutions noted above as Macedonian—Royal Pages, Bodyguards, and (in place of Companions) an exclusive body of dignitaries graded (ultimately at least) by titles in ranks expressive of the degree of their intimacy with the monarch. From this body, as from the Companions during the reigns of Philip and Alexander, a Crown Council was constituted. Even though the executive posts under the king were multiplied out of all recognition, and the camaraderie of the king with his fellows was affected by changes in the character of his entourage as well as by a general exaltation of the royal office of which the assumption by the monarch of the diadem was the symbol, these familiar institutions sufficed to create the impression that the national kingship had survived. But resting as it did on a king-made aristocracy and not, as in Macedon and in Persia, on a nobility that sprang from the soil, Hellenistic kingship possessed a strongly marked cosmopolitan character. It was a type of monarchy that could be applied in any empire; and it was thus assured of a great future in the long age which separated the destruction of national states in ancient times from the formation of new ones in the modern age. Augustus compromised with it when he recognized the cult of *Roma et Augustus*; and it was Hellenistic kingship (gradually assimilated by Rome in the first three Christian centuries), quite as much as its Persian derivative (brusquely copied by Diocletian), that constituted the most important non-Roman element in the autocracy of the late and eastern empires. It thus formed part of the classical heritage of the Middle Ages and of the Byzantine inheritance of the Renascence.

As we have seen, Hellenistic kingship had Macedonian kingship as its core. It was not only by acquiring an officialdom shot with alien elements that it became a distinct type of government. Something essential to Macedonian kingship had also to be abandoned. For monarchy in Macedon presupposed the presence of a Macedonian nation, or at least of a Macedonian army, and what the Successors had to work with, after the revolt in Greece had forced Leonnatus and Craterus to return home with their troops, was not a nation and a national army, but corps of mercenaries and a Macedonian *diaspora*. And as time passed and Macedon, organized as a separate kingdom, needed all its manpower to maintain its hegemony in Hellas, the Macedonian element in the European stratum of population which the conquest had made dominant in Persia became relatively smaller and smaller. The claim of the garrisons stationed in the new capitals to act as the Macedonian army-nation became a revolutionary manifesto. In these circumstances royal ordinances could not continue to be regarded as affirmations of Macedonian custom, and a new sanction for them had to be sought. For the former subjects of the Persian kings it already existed: the wearer of the diadem was the vice-gerent of the gods—of Ahuramazda, Bel, Amon, as the case might be. But with the shift of the courts from the ancient seats of government (Persepolis, Babylon, Memphis, Thebes) to Seleuceia on the Tigris, Antioch, Alexandria, and Pergamum, the ideas of the priesthoods and the populations of the old capitals ceased to be of much practical importance. The preponderance passed to the Greeks, both those resident in the old cities situated on the coast of Asia Minor and those who migrated thence or from the islands and mainland of Greece to form the nuclei of the new cities in the interior, and especially of the new capitals. It came about, too, and not without design, that both the great eastern monarchies into which Alexander's kingdom was divided had a Greek portion, which, moreover, because of its emigrants, its rulers had imperative reasons to conciliate. In these circumstances the Greeks were bound to have great influence in fixing the form which monarchy was to assume in Asia and Egypt, and especially on points in which, from their political training, they were most deeply interested—its theory and legal basis. Hence in the triune kingship that Alexander had created, with one nature for the Macedonians, one for the Greeks, and one for the Orientals, it was the nature that was formulated in terms of Hellenic thinking which gave character to the whole institution.

III. DEIFICATION

Living men had been deified in Greece before Alexander crossed over into Asia: Lysander by the Samian aristocrats, Dionysius and Dion by their Syracusan partisans, Philip by some of his subjects, and Plato by his scholars. From one point of view the attribution of divinity to a man was deference; or, when construed unfavourably, flattery; and it harmonized with Greek psychology to translate extraordinary endowment of will, intellect, character, persuasiveness, beauty into the sphere of the supernatural, and thus to acknowledge the mystery of strong human personality. Nor did men who were wont to see Aphrodite present in a picture when Paris was represented abducting Helen (to convey the idea that in Helen resided the *dämonische aphrodisische* power of beauty[1]), or Asclepius present in a relief when a physician was portrayed working with a patient, find it difficult to conceive some god or other present in the triumphant progress of Alexander through Asia. But the deification of rulers was a peculiar manifestation of this *theopoetic* faculty in this (if in nothing else), that it was not a sculptor's or a painter's fancy but a solemn act of legislation, and that rulers specifically were its objects.

And indeed there is another approach, likewise in Greek thought, to this, at first seeming, bizarre Hellenistic phenomenon. Looked at from another point of view, that of a legalistic society, the deification of outstanding leaders was simply political justice. The right of men of genius to be above the law was an axiom of Greek political theory[2]. What then was their position to be? The answer was suggested repeatedly by Aristotle. 'If,' he argued in a famous passage of the *Politics*[3], 'there exists in a state an individual so preeminent in virtue that neither the virtue nor political capacity of all the other citizens is comparable with his ..., he should not be regarded as a member of the state at all. For he will be wronged if treated as an equal when he is thus unequal in virtue and political capacity. Such a man should be rated as a god among men.' For a citizen to be uplifted thus above his fellow-citizens, however great his virtues, did not come within the range of theoretical assumption much less of practical politics; but when a foreign ruler appeared, vested with the authority due theoretically to the man of super-eminent ability, a place was ready made for him, and it was a place in the ranks of

---

[1] U. v. Wilamowitz-Moellendorff, *Hellenistische Dichtung*, I, p. 74.
[2] Plato, *Politicus*, 294 A, 296 *sqq.*
[3] III, 13, 1284 *a*; cf. Plato, *Politicus*, 303 B.

the gods. Here, then, in the sphere of politics a special reason existed for the indulgence of what we have called the theopoetic faculty of the Greeks, a reason, moreover, that was operative in epochs of political speculation and advanced constitutionalism like those in which deification of rulers was first established in Greece and first transplanted to Rome.

In the period of enlightenment that followed the age of illumination (see vol. v, pp. 376 *sqq.*), many men viewed gods simply as symbols. From their point of view a ruler who occupied the place of a god might be recognized as one without scruple should reason of state so dictate; and to this sceptical category belonged most of those influential in city-state politics. Others had to be helped by a miracle; nor was this hard to find in the days of anthropomorphic polytheism. When all men were thought to be sprung from the gods in some way and all nobles in a peculiar way, it was credible that Alexander was sprung directly from Zeus, as three authoritative oracles affirmed or were said to have affirmed; and it was in fact on the score of his sonship of Zeus that he requested and received admission into the circle of deities of the Greek cities in 324 B.C. Thus religious objections to the deification of rulers could be overcome among any populace that was content to accept the miracle (vol. vi, pp. 377, 398, 419, 432).

In 323 B.C. Alexander 'departed from among men,' as the official formula ran (Diodorus xviii, 56, 2; *O.G.I.S.* 4)[1]. In other words, he remained a god according to the theory of the dynasty; and was recognized as such by loyalists, but only in the portions of his realm where his sonship of Zeus had been acknowledged, *i.e.* in the Greek cities. Elsewhere, except in Egypt (where every Pharaoh was inevitably the incarnation of Amon and became an Osiris at death), if he received divine honours it was in consequence of an act of posthumous canonization (heroïzation). Even this seems to have been withheld in Macedon, where his claim to divinity seemed to Antipater to be injurious to Philip and blasphemous[2]. In the regions of Asia where a theory of the state had been evolved, Alexander, like the Persian kings whom he had succeeded, was not a god but the chosen of the gods. He was for the Persians a being endowed by the supreme Light-God, Ahuramazda, with his spirit; hence with a peculiar glory (*hvareno*), an indwelling light from which issued a radiance so brilliant as to dazzle ordinary men. But he was not the object of an official cult.

---

[1] For the abbreviations used in references, see p. 865 *sq.*

[2] Suidas, *s.v.* Antipatros; cf. *Gött. Nach.*, *Phil.-Hist. Kl.* 1922, pp. 32, 189; *Arch. Pap.* vii, p. 238.

In Asia deities either were, or were tending to become, cosmic forces, while their worshippers, unlike the Greeks, remained devoutly religious. Hence a Darius was as incapable, almost, of being approximated to Ahuramazda as a Solomon to Yahweh. In Asia there was little soil for deification of rulers to germinate or take root in. And even if it were better established than it is that Persian *proskynesis* involved not merely homage to rank, but also, when rendered to the king, an offering to his *daimon* (*fravashi*?)[1], the rite would imply simply the existence among the Persians of conceptions of the vital element in man (*psyche, genius*) which *mutatis mutandis* were also part and parcel of the Greek heritage of Alexander and the Roman heritage of Augustus. It is not these conceptions but the alteration of them that we have to explain in trying to account for king-worship.

As it was in Greece (Egypt apart) that the deification of rulers originated, so it was there that it was perpetuated. For a whole half-century after Alexander's death no ruler *demanded*, so far as we know, recognition for himself as a god from anybody. But during this interval many Greek communities voted of their own accord divine honours (temples, images, altars, priests, processions, games, sacrifices) to their rulers[2]. What led them thus to worship as gods persons who treated themselves as men? Servility? Hardly. If the Greeks of this epoch had become thus abject, their wars, sieges, insurrections, confederacies, would be beyond understanding. The example of Alexander? Perhaps. But those with whom it should have counted for most—the Successors—did not follow it themselves. What lay behind these repeated acts of deification was doubtless the same motive which led the Samians and Alexander to the idea in the first instance— political convenience and political thought. The same political problem presented itself again and again: the need of finding a legal basis in a constitutional state for an extra-constitutional authority. As kings, Antigonus and his rivals had no right to interfere with a free city; as gods, they had the right to make known their wishes and their worshippers the duty to regard them. On purely scientific grounds states experienced no difficulty in the discovery of new gods or in the recognition of old gods under new names; nor was there anyone to dispute the right of the organized community to adopt new gods once it had discovered them. It had been doing this from time immemorial.

---

[1] L. R. Taylor, *The 'Proskynesis' and the Hellenistic Ruler Cult*, J.H.S. XLVII, 1927, p. 53; *The Cult of Alexander at Alexandria*, C.P. 1927, p. 162.

[2] Vol. VI, pp. 490 *sq.*, 497, 500; below, pp. 92, 101, 202, 702, 712.

Since it was the fact that kings had to be obeyed, deification was a way, consonant with Hellenic feeling, of legalizing absolutism.

All the while that monarchy was becoming stabilized in the world, the development of general ideas was making it easier for city-states in deifying rulers to consult their political convenience with less violence to religious orthodoxy. In this half-century (323–273 B.C.) political thought obliterated more and more completely the distinction between what was human and what was divine. The concept of the ideal wise man, launched on the world by the Cynics, was interpreted pantheistically by Zeno (pp. 239 *sqq.*). A ruler after the Stoic model was in fact a living god as well as a godlike mechanism. Here there was an elevation of the human to the divine. On the other hand, rationalistic ideas, long since disseminated in Greek circles, bore fruit in the doctrine of Euhemerus that the gods and goddesses of cities were simply deceased rulers and benefactors, and religious rites simply commemorative exercises for the dead[1]. Here the divine was degraded to the human. And if gratitude was the essence of worship it seemed ingratitude to withhold it till the recipient was dead.

That rude men like the Macedonian barons who succeeded Alexander were slower in enunciating a right for the power they wielded than the Greek cities that were their subjects is not surprising. As, too, we should expect, they long adhered to what was conventional in matters of religious practice. That a human being, if deserving, might become a hero (*i.e.* a god) after death was a commonplace of Greek religious thinking; and, since founders of city-states had been regularly accorded this honour[2], there was no good reason to refuse it to founders of kingdoms. Hence Ptolemy I and his queen Berenice were canonized by their son and successor as the *Theoi Soteres*, and Seleucus I and Antiochus I by their heirs as Zeus Nicator and Apollo Soter respectively. There was some presumption in the latter identifications, doubtless, but no irreligion, any more than in the worship of Sophocles by the Athenians as the Hero Dexion. The essence of this kind of deification, however, was that it was posthumous. Between it and the deification of the living there was a chasm that could not be crossed, so long as men believed that the gods were supernatural beings, exempt from death. Hence it is an error to assert that the Hellenistic deification of the living was simply an ex-

[1] Cf. the just comment of Cicero, *de nat. deor.* I, 15, 38: quo quid absurdius quam...homines iam morte deletos reponere in deos, quorum omnis cultus esset futurus in luctu?

[2] L. R. Farnell, *Greek Hero Cults*, p. 420.

tension of the Hellenic heroïzation of the dead. In reality it was an irreligious substitute for it; a substitute by which the apotheosis of rulers occurred at or shortly after their accession, and not at their demise. It meant a victory of Greece over Macedon.

Progress from a sporadic urban cult of a living ruler to an official imperial cult was seemingly the work of the Ptolemies; and in it, though much is still uncertain, two steps are clearly recognizable. The first was taken by Ptolemy I, probably on assuming the title of king, in 305 B.C. (see below, p. 113), certainly before 289 B.C., when he instituted in his capital an official state cult of Alexander. The priest, an eponymous magistrate, was a Macedonian or Greek of high station, appointed annually by the crown, and the ritual used was Hellenic, not native. In centring the official worship of his realm in Alexander, Ptolemy I simply sought, in all probability, to distinguish his claim to kingship in the matter of legitimacy from the claims of his rivals; and what was involved may have been nothing but an amplification of a local Alexandrian cult. But this act served as the point of departure for the second step in the development of the imperial cult of the Ptolemies, one that was decisive for the character of Hellenistic king-worship generally. This advance was made at some time between 273–2 and 271–0 B.C.[1] (see below, p. 705) when Ptolemy II and Arsinoe, his sister-wife and consort, already lifted above ordinary mortals through being the children of the 'Saviour Gods,' shared a temple with Alexander as the 'Brother-Sister Gods' in the cult established by Ptolemy I. Thus by his own fiat a living ruler raised himself to a place by the side of the *archegetes* of empire as the divine object of the homage of his subjects, as the extra-constitutional authority whose will was everywhere law—a symbol of the common fealty to one head of diverse elements in the population of the kingdom. And thenceforth the kings and queens of the royal family succeeded, at an unfixed interval after their accession, to an ever-lengthening line of imperial deities so as to constitute a single 'sacred household' (ἱερὰ οἰκία), the source and sanction of the accumulation of laws and ordinances valid in the empire. Then it seemed anomalous that the founders of the dynasty, Ptolemy I and Berenice, should be omitted. Hence they were included at an early date in the circle of divine kings in whose names oaths were sworn, and under Philopator their names were inserted in the dynastic hierarchy in their proper place after Alexander as the 'Saviour Gods,'

[1] Before the death of Arsinoe according to the latest calculation of Beloch, *Griech. Geschichte*, IV, 2, p. 586, n. 1.

although in their lifetime they had not claimed divinity for themselves.

The rôle of Egypt in this transformation of Macedonian monarchy into Ptolemaic god-kingship seems to have been comparatively unimportant. The place of Pharaoh in the religious establishment of the Egyptians was fixed from ancient times by an immutable ritual performed by the priestly class and recorded in sacred pictures and writings on the walls of temples. Two acts are depicted in documents ranging in point of time from the Old Kingdom to the age of the Antonines as requisite for deification according to the Egyptian rite: the divine conception and nativity of the king; and his enthronement. The child predestined for kingship was represented as begotten of the queen by the god Amon, as born with divine assistance, and nourished at the breasts of goddesses. He was thus the son of the gods. He was also their heir. He entered upon his heritage by the ceremony of enthronement. His heritage was spiritual as well as temporal. The gods administered to him *le fluide magique* by which he was endowed with divine 'life,' 'power,' and 'permanence'; he was presented by his divine father to the assembly of the gods and accepted by them as legitimate; he was presented by his earthly father to the court as divinely born and endowed; his royal name was proclaimed. Thus identified and once again given *le fluide magique*, he was formally enthroned by being seated on the thrones of the North and South and invested with the insignia of authority—the double crown with its *uraeus* band, the crook, the sceptre, and the whip; whereupon he symbolically bound Upper and Lower Egypt together and took ritualistic possession of all the lands over which the gods held sway. The ceremony was concluded by the royal ascent to the temple of his divine father, where he was embraced by him and thus reinfused with the fluid of divinity.

By virtue of these rites, which were repeated in all temples daily, and, with more elaboration, on special occasions throughout the year and reign[1], Pharaoh alone of the gods enjoyed direct association with mankind and alone of mortals enjoyed by anticipation during his lifetime the identification with Amon-Re, Horus, and especially Osiris, which Egyptians generally believed they would themselves attain after death through the magical potency of funerary rites. On his death Pharaoh, his career as an earthly god ended, joined the deified dead as one more Osiris— a great one doubtless—in the realms of Osiris, and a new Pharaoh

[1] A. Moret, *Du caractère religieux de la royauté pharaonique.* Cf. E. Norden, *Die Geburt des Kindes,* pp. 75, 118 *sqq.*

took his place as the intermediary between mankind and the gods of the upper and lower worlds. Pharaoh was thus king because he was priest (see vol. II, p. 157), and as priest-king it was in his name that all temples were built and sacrifices offered. Without a Pharaoh the Egyptian religion lacked the essential link between man and the gods; and it is hard to believe that Ptolemy I, on assuming the royal title, did not follow the example of Alexander (see vol. VI, pp. 154 *sqq.*) and become Pharaoh. In any event, Ptolemy II possessed the pharaonic crown-name, as did all his successors, so that, although the pharaonic ceremony of coronation is attested by documents only for the fourth and later Ptolemies, it may also be inferred in some form or other for the second and third, and possibly for the first[1]. Conceivably, in deification according to the Egyptian rite, no account need have been taken of the fact that Ptolemy was a Greek god, just as in the Hellenic deification no account was taken of his identification with Amon, Horus, and Osiris; but Ptolemy willed it otherwise. He had his Greek cult-name—Theos Adelphos, Theos Euergetes, Theos Philopator, as the case might be—added to the Egyptian cult-names as a new and barbarous element in the hierarchy of titles which had constituted since the end of the Middle Kingdom the crown-name of Pharaoh. Except for this and what it entailed in Egyptian worship, the two cults were distinct. They were different in ritual and priestly personnel. They were different in consequences, in that, whereas Pharaoh dropped out of the ritual when dead, the Theoi Adelphoi did not. And they were also different in idea: Pharaoh was not *Law* incarnate (νόμος ἔμψυχος), like the Hellenistic god-king; he was rather the apotheosis of *Life* —the Osiris of the living. The one common factor of the two cults was the god Ptolemy, a single symbol for the profound aspirations of two very different people—of the Egyptians for life after death, and of the Greeks for government according to law. The religion of the Egyptians, as it was presented authoritatively to the *Greek* world by Ptolemy I, centred, not in Pharaoh, but in Sarapis (p. 145); and if Greeks who felt the need sought help at the native shrines, that was their affair.

Though the steps in the development of the imperial cult of the Seleucids cannot be traced, the chances are that the process was completed during the reign of the second Antiochus. The system seems to have arisen, on the one hand, through the normalizing of city cults and, on the other hand, through the creation by the crown of a provincial cult, for the conduct of which the

[1] See, however, E. R. Bevan, *Hist. of Egypt under the Ptol. dynasty*, p. 260.

king appointed annually a high priest of himself in each satrapy
of the empire. In the urban cults the worship of the living monarch (or monarchs) was combined, under the same or (perhaps
later) a separate priest, with that of his predecessors beginning
with the founder of the dynasty; and the same was probably the
practice in the provincial cults, in which, moreover, first the queen
and later other princesses of the royal family participated with a
high priestess of their own. The offices of high priest and
high priestess were positions of great dignity in the imperial
service, appropriate to kinsmen of the king, comparable in this
and other respects with that of the priest of the Ptolemies in
Alexandria. The indications are that there was no articulation
between them and the priesthoods of the cities, since they emanated from different authorities. Unlike the Ptolemies, the Seleucids
did not attach their dynasty to Alexander. They had their own
theory of legitimacy, according to which Apollo stood in the same
paternal relation to Seleucus as Zeus did to Alexander (p. 162, n. 1).
With Seleucus himself they accordingly began their dynasty,
thus making 312–1 and not 323–2 B.C. their epochal year.

The kingdom of Pergamum had no satrapies or hyparchies,
or need of any, until it was awarded the territories of the Seleucids
in Asia Minor in 188 B.C. Hence it shows no trace of provincial
cults or indeed of the normalizing of its numerous city cults.
Otherwise the worship of the Attalids was like that of the Seleucids, with this modification (another consequence, perhaps, of the
tardiness of the dynasty in assuming the regal title and state) that
apparently the dead monarchs were not combined with one
another, or, collectively with the reigning sovereigns, in a single
'sacred household.'

There is much in this king-worship that seems contradictory
and is hard for us to understand. In ordinances the deified
monarchs speak as kings simply and not as gods. It was permissible, not to say usual, for courtiers and others to address the
Ptolemies as gods, and the Seleucids and Attalids by their cult-
names, yet to make offerings to other gods on their behalf as if
they were men. The Seleucids and Attalids had priests and all the
regular apparatus of worship during their lifetime, yet became
theoi only after their 'departure from among men.' The cult-names
are traceable at times to the initiative of dependent political bodies,
but their adoption by rulers must certainly have been the work of
rulers themselves. Official cult-names were apparently reserved
to members of the royal family; and among Seleucid cult-names
was included, by a curious prolepsis, *Theos.* A deified king might

justify a grant of more elaborate worship to his deified 'sister-queen' on the plea that she had been a good wife and a pious woman; and the motive most frequently avowed by cities and leagues for deifying rulers was gratitude for services received. The official cult-names traceable to popular initiative reflected this motive. They were preponderantly either 'Benefactor' (*Euergetes*) or 'Saviour' (*Soter*). The service was regularly a political service such as might be prayed for from a god, rescue from great danger—destruction, oppression, or distress. The 'saving' was the saving of communities from their enemies, not of individuals from their transgressions; and the situation ordinarily looked forward to in the future was 'liberty.'

The truth is that the godhood of these cults was official, not personal. Like a uniform it could be changed by a monarch to suit the occasion. For by the middle of the third century B.C. deification had a history behind it that enabled it at one and the same time to mean different things to different persons. To a king it meant primarily peaceful access to otherwise autonomous communities; to autonomous communities it meant 'liberty'[1]—the supplanting of a 'tyrant' by a god, the continuance in function (with an occasional impulse from on high) of the complex of civic laws by means of which citizens had ruled, taught, moulded, and expressed themselves: the addition simply of another divine symbol of their corporate life. To them the alternative was ordinarily the concentration in the hands of an unlicensed autocrat, or his deputy, of the vast power (political, social, educational) vested in an all-inclusive state, such as the city-state traditionally was. After Demetrius of Phalerum even Demetrius Poliorcetes seemed a liberator: the one imposed his conception of society on Athens, the other his policy alone. To a dynasty, again, deification meant legitimacy, the regularizing of right acquired by the sword. It meant, further, the elevation of the royal family above the ambition of men who had recently been their peers, the strengthening of the rights of sovereigns by fusing them in a single whole with the prerogatives of their divine predecessors, the presentation to subjects everywhere of a symbol round which they might, perchance, rally through religious sentiment since they could not do so through national sentiment. Those to whom the worship of the living seemed impious had understanding for the worship of the dead with which, as the dynastic cults developed, the worship of

---

[1] Cf. P. Freib. 2, ii, 4: ἡ ᾽Αλεξάνδρου θιότης τὸν τῆς ἡγεμονίας ὅρον ἐκτέθιτε. Also A. Rehm, *Milet*, 1, 7 (ed. by Wiegand), p. 295, and J. Kaerst, *Studien zur Entwickelung der Monarchie im Altertum*, p. 7.

the living was craftily conjoined. And if a king was a god as the result of an act based on his being the son of a god, and if on death he simply departed from among men, he must have been a god before he came among men. This conclusion the third-century rulers did not draw. To them, as we have said, their divinity was official, not personal; but they could not prevent others, poets and courtiers through fancy, humble folk and orientals through mysticism, and theorists through logical inference, from drawing it for them. And by the second century some of the kings became so far complaisant to these multiplied suggestions as officially to designate their appearance on the political stage as an epiphany.

In 290 B.C. the Athenians hailed Demetrius as 'a true god, not one of wood or stone.' What they and he understood by a true god was one thing; what Egyptians understood by it was something altogether different; and centuries later Christians would have viewed both these understandings as blasphemous. King-worship altered its forms with alterations in the organization of states, its nature with alterations in the conception of God.

IV. THE LARGE STATE AND THE POLIS

What we call national feeling had attached itself in classical Greece to the city and territory which constituted the city-state. And then, as now, it had helped to strengthen enormously public authority. But even before Chaeronea nationalism was on the wane. It had proved too weak to suppress class aspirations. Already for a long time city-states had had to suffer from the abuse of their aggrandized public authority to the special economic advantage of particular groups; and furthermore, from the formation in their citizen-bodies, notably in small states, of international parties. Yet it was only in comparison with their own past that these national states were ineffective. The ineffectiveness for which Greece paid the supreme penalty in the epoch of Philip sprang from the inveterate defect of nationalism—antipathy of one national state for another, which the existence, already noted, of international parties seems rather to have exacerbated than diminished. The fatal weakness of the Greek city-states as the custodians of civilization was their incapacity in the face of foreign menace to form one all-embracing coalition. A single nation was out of the question without the sacrifice of democracy, and Greece without democracy meant a Greece in which, if it was united in one state, a majority of the inhabitants would have been, as respects self-government, in the condition of Asiatics. National states cannot exceed the areas of national feeling without becoming empires. In Greece national feeling and government by public opinion had grown up together. The limitation of states to territories that were small enough to centre easily and completely in single cities made both possible and inevitable the control of government by public opinion. Any government not so controlled seemed, and was, tyranny, it mattered not whether it consisted of an executive official alone, or of a representative council (*synedrion*), or of both. Hence the expansion of urban nationality into Hellenic nationality was impossible on republican lines except through the formation of an effective Hellenic public opinion, and not only its formation, but its re-formation again and again upon each successive problem of politics. Whatever the chances of attaining this may have been earlier—and they were small indeed—they were utterly destroyed when the area of Hellenism was enlarged by Alexander to include the whole of the Persian Empire; and they remained negligible when, on the division of Alexander's empire, the ambition of Macedon to attach Greece firmly to itself was constantly frustrated by hopes inspired by kings of the East.

The city-states that were least ready to compromise their national points of view were, of course, the greatest states, like Athens and Sparta, in which traditions of power, of having had their own way, were strongest; and when the world had been re-cast in such large patterns that their strivings for leadership became visionary, rather than yield they made obstinate efforts to assert themselves. When these failed—that of Athens in 262–1 B.C., that of Sparta forty years later (p. 708, p. 761)—they tried to withdraw altogether from the common life of nations. Thus even where urban nationalism was most vital the tendency existed to substitute cities for city-states, economic organisms for political organisms, an assemblage of class or individual purposes for a national purpose popularly based and organized. The most notable exception was Rhodes (p. 207 *sq*.; see also vol. VIII).

The chief refuge of republican nationalism in this epoch, when city-states had become too small to promote their interests and defend themselves, was the autonomous federation; and the Aetolian League, and, in lesser degree, the Achaean League, showed that there was a strength in the spirit of nationality, even though it was incorporated in a poor, remote and (despite the geographical elasticity involved in the federal idea) necessarily restricted territory, that made its general decay in the Hellenic world a political catastrophe. Here, too, the concentration of foreign affairs in the federal authority went a certain way to

converting city-states into cities; and even though the federal
authority itself was organized on city-state lines, in this super-state
two essentials of the *polis* were lacking—frequent meetings of a
primary assembly and laws sufficiently inclusive to form a rule
of life for citizens. Much more completely were the *poleis* shorn
of their statehood in the spuriously autonomous federations
(League of the Islanders, Ionians, Ilians, etc.) which were called
into existence by one or other of the god-kings (see below, p. 91).
Since these lacked federal assemblies altogether, and their federal
parliaments (synods) had their executive officers appointed by the
kings, the member-cities were practically municipalities.

The new foundations in what had been the Persian Empire
may have had the outward appearance of city-states and the status
of 'allies.' Assemblies, councils, and magistrates may have gone
through the motions of governing according to bodies of laws
furnished ready-made by the founders; the towns may ordinarily
have possessed territories (partly farmed by citizens and partly by
villagers) subject to their jurisdiction, so that the frontiers of the
state were wider than the limits of the city. The fact remains that
in some, if not all of these cities, since it was to the king and not
to the city that property escheated, urban sovereignty was defective from their foundation, and regal interference at all times
both warranted and imperative (see vol. vi, p. 430). Nor was this
the only practical justification for curtailing urban autonomy. The
king had to have means of exercising authority in his cities, if for
nothing else, for their protection. Hence in some of them (as often
in the Seleucid Empire) imperial officials were installed with or
without garrisons, and in others (as in the kingdom of Pergamum
generally) the highest magistracies were filled from the ranks of
citizens, but by royal appointment. In no case was there any
escaping from the consequences of the fact that the cities were
everywhere embedded in land ($\chi\omega\rho\alpha$) which was administered
directly for or by the crown; or of the theory that the king was one
of their gods. Moreover, the urban complex can seldom have
formed a single civic corporation. Rather, in addition to a body
politic of citizens it must ordinarily have comprised bodies of men
of lesser, or at least different rights, of varying number and magnitude; some in process of assimilation, others, like the Jews,
obstinately recusant, others strong enough, perhaps, eventually
to do the assimilating themselves. And where these *paroikoi*, to
give them their technical name, were disproportionately multi-
tudinous and polyglot, as early in Alexandria and later in Delos[1],

[1] P. Roussel, *Délos, colonie athénienne*, p. 50.

the bodies politic themselves were transformed into privileged social organizations, with atrophied demes and phylae and phratries. They formed but one element in something that did service for an assembly, but since this did not possess a council[1] it was incompetent of independent activity, and government rested with appointed officers alone. The homogeneity of the old city-states was gone. Gone, too, was the general partnership in community-action of large scope, and the training and interest in politics inseparable from it. Such city-states were like modern cities, seats of culture, hives of business, purveyors of refined and unrefined amusements; but lacking two things—safeguarded municipal rights, and a voice in the affairs of the realm of which they formed part.

City-states desired two things which the world situation made it impossible for them to have simultaneously—liberty and protection; and yearning for the former killed gratitude for the latter, so that devotion to a dynasty had great difficulty in gathering strength. Accordingly, cities had usually little preference for one god-king rather than another provided he was philhellene. They yielded readily to every such invader, and when the tide turned they deserted him with equal promptitude. The remedies sought for this oscillation were the fixing of definite frontiers to protectorates and the building up for the territories thus circumscribed of stable administrative services centring in the capitals.

The first of these remedies could not be applied until it was settled that neither should the empire of Alexander remain undivided nor should virtually every satrapy form an independent realm. The logic of events rather than of geography or ethnology excluded both these alternatives; and the outcome of long and disastrous wars was the formation of a continental kingdom based first on Seleuceia and then on Antioch as a capital, of an Egyptian kingdom based on Alexandria, and of a Macedonian kingdom based on Pella, each ruled by a Macedonian dynasty, each with ill-defined land frontiers, all vitally interested in getting and holding against one another, as large a foothold as possible, if not a predominance, in the Aegean Archipelago and its environs, which, already a prey to the conflicting ambitions of its own cities and federations, was thus additionally rent with dissension. The wars which registered attempts to delimit frontiers to protectorates in this debatable region did not produce the desired result. The most that could be achieved was a sort of condominium resting on the possession of strategic posts by each rival power.

[1] Claudius, *Letter to the Alexandrines*, I, 66. (H. I. Bell, *Jews and Christians in Egypt*, p. 24; cf. p. 8. See also *ib.* p. 13, n. 3).

The failure of the city-states in classic times to create a concert of the powers that might have saved Greek civilization was matched by an even more complete failure of the monarchical states in the period of their ascendancy.

The struggles of the monarchies were also grounded in mutual fears and commercial rivalries; and they were prolonged by personal and dynastic animosities. In the light of modern experience their long continuance presents no mystery. But it was none the less catastrophic. Not only did it permit the Gauls to occupy the heart of Asia Minor (pp. 104 *sqq.*), the Parthians to establish themselves across the highways leading from the Near to the Far East of the Asia then known (pp. 159 *sqq.*), and the Romans to incorporate in their empire the Greeks of Magna Graecia and Sicily (chaps. xx–xxi): it also wore down the strength of the three monarchies themselves. The Ptolemies proved unequal to the sustained effort involved in holding the empire in the eastern Mediterranean mapped out by the founder of the dynasty. The Seleucids were forced by the wars which had to be waged on their sea front to denude outlying areas of troops, so that local 'protectors' seemed more capable and, if resisted, more dangerous than they. Thus new philhellene kings founded dynasties within the continental empire in Pergamum (the Attalids) and in Bactria and Sogdiana (the Diodotids), the former to assume the rôle of 'saviour' for the 'cities' in western Asia Minor against the Gauls, the latter to do the like for the 'cities' on the north-eastern frontier against the Scythians and, in the sequel, in North-west India and all that lay between. The interposition of the Parthian kingdom of the Arsacids made re-incorporation of these Far Eastern 'cities' in the Seleucid empire more difficult, but also, from the cities' point of view, more desirable, since otherwise they were isolated from the world of Greeks. The autonomy of the Diodotids under Seleucid suzerainty was the way found out of this difficulty. The suzerainty invoked by the Attalids (when Egypt failed them) to save themselves from the Seleucids and Antigonids after they had saved their protectorate from the Gauls was that of Rome.

National states had had their weaknesses; but one knew, at least approximately, where their frontiers ran. There was also a certain natural limit of size to a federal state, though what that was could only be ascertained empirically: the less democratic a federation, the larger it might become. The Hellenistic monarchies were less happily situated. Their fundamental principle was force, and this could be checked and delimited only by encountering an equal and opposite force. An equilibrium of forces might be achieved, and in a certain measure it was achieved in the course of the third century. But it was maintained by no political principle. Given the power, any monarch might aspire to sovereignty as far as the edge of Hellenism or of 'the inhabited world.' And the situation in the East actually encouraged such aspirations, since any narrower frontiers than these dismembered every *diaspora*, and ethnological lines, long since faint, had been obliterated yet further, as by a new fall of snow, wherever Greeks and Macedonians settled in considerable numbers. Hence the land frontiers between the kingdoms of Alexandria, Antioch, and Pergamum remained vague and shifting. In both Syria and Asia Minor they were at any particular time those laid down in oft-made, oft-broken treaties which merely reflected the situation reached in the fighting in each war.

How the territories of these monarchies were connected up by the web of a governmental system—administrative, economic, fiscal—will be described fully in another place (chaps. iv and v). Egypt was peculiar in that all the land in the valley of the Nile and the Delta was the private property of the Ptolemies (p. 113). This fact served as the starting point for organizing there a system for making state control effective over all private activities for which history has few parallels. An estate rather than a state and managed accordingly, Egypt had much use for overseers and guards and little use for autonomous cities. The Ptolemies yielded readily to the temptation to extend to their dependencies abroad the proprietary attitude engendered at home; but there they had perforce to use *poleis* as the agencies of local government and even to add to their number by founding colonies. The Seleucids did not inherit from their predecessors, as did the Ptolemies from the Pharaohs (p. 114), a divine title giving them ownership of their realm. They recognized the proprietary rights of the 'kings, dynasts, tribes, and cities,' of whose territories their kingdom was mainly formed, and deputed to them most of the work of government. In addition to the officials by which these deputies were supervised, they needed permanent administrators only for the central bureaux in Antioch and for the widespread royal demesne. Their administrative web was thus much less intricate than that of the Ptolemies, and it differed further in that it contained subordinate patterns that centred strongly in the provincial capitals. Entire provinces might be disengaged without disrupting the whole. Pergamum had much the character of a Seleucid province that had gained its independence until in 188 B.C. it became an aggregate of such provinces (see below, vol. VIII).

Through being aliens in conquered lands the Macedonian

dynasties were bound to be assimilated by the Orient and lost unless they could surround themselves by large numbers of their fellow-countrymen. For success in this policy they had to make conditions in their kingdoms as attractive as possible to Greeks and Macedonians without driving the natives to desperation. The methods followed in each realm to secure this end will be described elsewhere (chaps. IV and V). The profession of philhellenism was by no means a pose. Each dynasty was the other's rival. It needed splendour, prestige, and, above all, money and property, with which to fascinate, encourage, and reward Greeks and Macedonians and attach them firmly to the crown. To this necessity of their position, rather than to the love of grandeur or popularity of individual rulers, is to be traced the combination of fiscality and prodigality which seems the cardinal vice of all these states.

Naturally it was the native populations which suffered chiefly from the excessive energy of their masters in raising money; but not exclusively. Even in Alexandria the Greeks had to pay 52 drachmae for the metretes of olive oil, instead of 16–21 as at Delos, because Ptolemy took 34 drachmae in taxes and profit. And enormous though the revenues of Egypt were, from rentals, taxes, monopolies, concessions, customs, tolls, etc., the essential services of the country, like the maintenance of dykes and canals, and the reclamation of marsh and arid lands, transport, the upkeep of warships, were supplied by forced levies of labour, animals, and capital. To take much and give little except by way of favours seems to have been a principle of Ptolemaic finance, and (we may add, though insufficiently informed) of royal finance in general in Hellenistic times.

Unlike the old city-states, or indeed the new cities, the eastern monarchies had to base their administration on professionalism. Republics were able to treat their offices as honours, and it was their aim to train their citizens so highly that they, or at least the well-to-do among them, could take turns in ruling and being ruled. Through love of distinction (*philotimia*), if not through love of country, citizens were found ready to serve the community in the most varied capacities at large personal expense; but even the richest could do this only intermittently. Kings demanded in their administrative services permanency of tenure. Annual change of his subordinates—indeed, any displacement of them except at his pleasure—could not and did not seem reasonable or wise to a life-long chief executive. This consideration would have sufficed for the creation under monarchical rule of a permanent officialdom even without the tendency of the times toward specialization of functions. The principle that a man does a thing best when he has to do nothing else was incapable of being elevated into a general law, as Aristotle saw clearly; but it had validity in science as well as in industry, and the Hellenistic age was scientific and materialistic.

The success of professionalism in the conduct and practice of war also helped this tendency to prevail elsewhere. In matters of statecraft the view became ascendant that 'the cook was a better judge of the dinner than the company to whom it was served.' The new monarchies had to have a paid service, civil and military, with officials and officers, high and low, with ordinary clerks and labourers, common soldiers and sailors, and even in peace time this service was a heavy charge on every treasury. Recruited as it had to be from subjects (Macedonians and Greeks primarily) irrespective of birthplace and condition, it could be kept faithful only by self-interest. Devotion to the crown and professional pride were apparently the exception rather than the rule. Hence salaries had to be supplemented by gifts; and wages, at least in the army, by gratuities. Indeed, the careers which were thus furnished attracted men primarily because of their perquisites—because of the occasions they offered for receiving benefices and the opportunities they afforded for collateral gains. If the king's favour or that of someone more highly stationed than oneself endured, men might advance to places of princely opulence and power, when they would themselves furnish careers to others in their employ or clientage, comparable with those in the service of the crown (p. 116). At the court of the Ptolemies such favourites of fortune were Demetrius of Phalerum, founder of the Museum and benefactor of Athens, Sostratus of Cnidus, to whose munificence Alexandria owed its famous lighthouse, Sosibius the elder, patron of Callimachus, who lauds his 'public spirit and his loyal remembrance of strugglers,' Glaucon and Chremonides, to whom with exile from Athens came in Alexandria 'eminence and responsibility and money-power,' and, in the days when the kings had lost their grip, Sosibius the younger[1], Tlepolemus (see p. 30), and Polycrates the Argive—to mention only a few of those who preceded or followed Apollonius, Philadelphus' all-powerful minister, as the recipients and dispensers of the bounty of Egypt[2].

Nor were there careers only for statesmen and generals. There

---

[1] If Sosibius the elder and Sosibius the younger are not one and the same person, as Beloch maintains (*Griech. Gesch.* IV, 2, p. 589).

[2] For rich magnates at the court of the Seleucids see below, p. 181 *sq.*

were others for engineers and architects, physicians and stewards, business managers of all sorts, and notably scientists, artists, and men of letters. Every king had to be philhellene and every courtier had to ape him. And to be philhellene meant to have, or to show, an interest in the intellectual and aesthetic pursuits which the Greeks had made concomitants of civilization and the Athenians essentials. Without them the new capitals were, and seemed, raw. To make Alexandria and Antioch a new Athens was long an important aim of Ptolemaic and Seleucid ambition—a new Athens and not a new Sparta, for ancient Sparta had been eclipsed in its own specialty by Thebes and Macedon, and the tendency of modern political thinking was no longer socialistic but individualistic. The life desired was a life of diversified culture centring not only in the gymnasium and the stadium but also in the theatre and the college, if we may apply this name to institutes like the Museum at Alexandria, itself a copy of the schools of the philosophers in Athens. Hence kings and courtiers vied with one another and with other kings and courtiers in showering appointments and gifts and invitations upon men of letters and science, commissions and encouragements upon artists of all kinds; and in establishing games and fêtes and pageants that should both add *éclat* to their own society and attract and stimulate talent, as the Great Dionysia and Panathenaea had done, and were still doing.

And they did not lack success. It has been suggested that to take much and give little except by way of favours was a characteristic of royal finance. It is only fair to add that to bestow favours with a bountiful hand was an even more marked characteristic. Soldiers and officials were undoubtedly the chief beneficiaries; but not the only ones. The favour of a king or courtier came to be the hope or mainstay of many a scientist, philosopher, historian; and of many a poet, painter, architect, sculptor, and goldsmith or silversmith. Of Tlepolemus, regent of Egypt at the end of the third century, it is said by Polybius (xvi, 21): 'he spent, nay, to call it by its true name, he squandered, the King's money on all comers—envoys from Greece, troups of playwrights and musicians, and, notably, officers and soldiers in attendance on the Court. For he did not know how to refuse anybody.' Here, then, in the lavishness of kings and courtiers, which was politic at base but impolitic because without bounds, was one of the roots of fiscality.

All that money could do for the material equipment of the royal capitals was done. Alexandria, Antioch, and Pergamum came soon to possess sacred buildings that challenged even those of

Athens and Olympia, while their palaces and mansions surpassed in magnificence anything that Greece had hitherto seen. But these cities lacked the charm of antiquity and were conscious of it. Their kings might import old manuscripts, paintings, statues, and other *objets d'art*. That was well so far as it went. But what America has lost through having no share in the Middle Ages and Renaissance the Hellenistic great-cities lost through having come too late for the Classic Age. And they had yet a greater lack: bodies of citizens influential enough, disciplined enough, cultivated enough, homogeneous enough, to preserve the great tradition at once against the vagaries of artists and the caprices of kings and courtiers. It was easier to re-create the city of the Athenians than their society, for this could not be made, it had to grow, as it *had* grown, after a long period of gestation, in an atmosphere of great freedom and great responsibility. There was no such atmosphere in Alexandria, Antioch, or Pergamum. These cities were poor nurseries of men of eminence. It was not from them but mainly from the old city-states that these sprang. There, in alert and exacting environments, amid memories that challenged and under masters who knew, as often as not with the handicap of straitened circumstances, the minds and hands were trained that did most of the world's best work in science, literature, and art. And when men left home to seek larger opportunities, it was not solely to courts that they travelled.

Athens was still a magnet for talent, and Rhodes became another; and both had talented men of their own. To measure the attraction of courts and republics respectively is difficult. Perhaps the attraction of opportunities was more important: poets and artists sought patronage, philologists libraries, scientists equipment and philosophers freedom—freedom to launch new theories of state and society, freedom to discuss the nature and power of the gods, freedom to doubt; and this they found most abundantly in Athens (chap. vii). And with all the more prospect of permanency because, when the right of philosophers to teach had been forbidden in the reaction that followed Demetrius of Phalerum's attempt to make the city an ideal state on the Peripatetic model, the courts had held this prohibition unconstitutional as contravening the general right of free association. There are individual acts of intolerance recorded of this age as of all periods of the world's history. But it was a favourable circumstance for freedom of thought that within the circle of Hellenism there were still many separate states that were centres of culture, and that it was easier than ever for men who felt oppressed in one to leave it and go to another. Nor need they, if they had grasped the spirit of the new philosophies, change their place: they might make refuge in their own souls, and leave the worry of the world to 'fools.'

But there was a pressure being exerted on men's minds that was more powerful, because more subtle, than downright coercion. Since the conquest of Persia a change of emphasis had come over the values assigned by the Greeks to different kinds of human actions. With greater opportunities for its gratification desire for riches had grown and with the diminution of republicanism desire for civic honour had weakened, as motives for effort. We may trace a less instinctive and steady general sense of beauty. But things of the mind were prized as highly as ever, and not for over two thousand years was so resolute an attempt again made to interpret the universe scientifically. Yet in their dispersion the Greeks had given a multitude of hostages to the Orient, and, with all their pride of race, it is an open question whether they could have withstood the seductive ideals of Asia even if they had been able to repulse the arms of Rome. Be that as it may, the serious *malaise* from which the Greek world suffered on the intervention of Rome was political and military rather than spiritual. The strength of the eastern monarchies lay in their revenues, their weakness in their scanty supply of men of the dominant stock; whereas old Hellas was, comparatively, strong in men and weak in money. So long as the Aegean world was able to keep pouring emigrants into the East, the Macedonian kings there had little difficulty in enlisting recruits for their armies—for the army was the readiest road to preferment; but when the flood subsided and the colonists had settled down in their *nomoi*, *poleis*, and *katoikiai*, they neither would nor could be mobilized to furnish armies equal in numbers and quality to the exigencies of major wars. The new world had thus to turn again and again to the old world for soldiers—and it got mercenaries, to whom success was more important than the cause for which they were fighting. On the other hand, the free cities and leagues of old Greece, drained constantly of their increase of population by the departure of their youth to seek their fortunes in the East, found their development arrested, like rural New England on the opening of the American West. And since the centres of commerce shifted simultaneously to Alexandria, Rhodes, and the coastal cities of the eastern Mediterranean, the European states were unable any longer to back their policies by adequate material resources. The economic forces of the Hellenistic world had been thrown badly out of gear with its man-power when Rome came.

V. COSMOPOLITANISM, INDIVIDUALISM, STOICISM

Awareness of the world as a place in which he might anywhere make his home, if he chose—a place with frontiers unexplored to be sure, but as definite as those of most great states—entered into the every-day consciousness of the Greek in the Macedonian age as never before. The question raised by the Sophists as to whether he should live in it according to his own natural bent (φύσις) or according to the rules laid down by his own political society (νόμοι) was met by Aristotle with the affirmation that the two things were the same—'that by nature man was a *political* animal'; and Aristotle constructed his *Politics* on the foundation, laid, he thought, by history, analogy, and theory conjointly, that political animal meant city-state animal. The question was met by the Cynics—rebels against the discipline and conventions of city-state civilization—by the counter-affirmation that the two things were indeed the same, but that man could live according to his own bent only when all the world was his city: 'that by nature man was a *cosmopolitan* animal.' Both respondents were reformers. In order to enable men really to live according to their own nature Aristotle would remodel the *polis*. For the same reason the Cynics would eliminate it. The past belonged to the philosopher: was the future to belong to the anarchists?

There was much in current happenings to suggest to contemporaries that all political order was indeed crumbling. The city-states were fast becoming subordinate cities. With what authority could they claim to determine the life of their citizens—to educate them in their spirit, to teach them the relative values of human activities, to issue general rules for magistrates to apply to their conduct—when they lacked self-determination themselves? The proof that *poleis* could no longer speak authoritatively to men is that many of them, particularly the new great-cities, did not even make the attempt: they were too disintegrated and their inhabitants were too heterogeneous for that. None the less, the city-state retained so strong a hold on the minds of men even in this the time of its decay as to make it very difficult for anybody, tracing the royal or federal ordinances to their source, to arrive at the idea that by nature man was a *monarchical* or *confederative* animal. The utterances of the super-states were too incoherent to constitute a rule of life. In monarchies they formed simply frameworks (*diagrammata*) in which were set the 'laws' of cities and 'nations'; and in true federations, while formally they were laws, they were thought of as international covenants, and even the Achaean League, though at its acme it was dimly visioned as a new state, was understood as a kind of city-state embracing the entire Peloponnese[1].

In these circumstances, where rules of life derived from the *polis* were becoming obsolete and none were derivable from its substitutes, there was at first a stronger tendency for speculative thinking to re-establish social morality by basing it on class, and especially on an idealization of the castes and the hierarchy of castes that existed, or was thought to exist, in Egypt, India, Judaea, and other eastern countries. But on closer acquaintance these exotic social systems lost their prestige, discredited by the political helplessness of the peoples that lived under them. And the happenings incident to the 'planting of a nation in the new world' unsettled classes in the dominant race both at home and abroad. Abroad the drafts of colonists made by kings for the founding or re-founding of cities were combined with one another, and with immigrants that came individually, in ways that cannot but have blurred social distinctions as well as distinctions of nationality. Nor was there anything socially sharp and distinct in the imperial bureaucracies. At home the rich tended to become richer and the poor poorer—a development that rendered social revolutions chronic, thus furthering mixture of classes[2]. Social confusion was accordingly as pronounced in the Hellenistic world as political.

The only social unit that throve was the 'club,' what the Greeks called generically a *koinon*, the Romans a *collegium*. With private associations of this type the Hellenic world became honeycombed. They arose spontaneously—without any form of state compulsion; and both in this particular and in the complete subordination of the hereditary principle to freedom of choice as the basis for their recruitment, they must be distinguished sharply from the guilds of the later Roman Empire. The occasions for their organization were almost infinitely diverse—the promotion of the lyric and dramatic arts, of new religious cults, of conviviality and mutual support among co-nationals when living abroad, among soldiers in garrison and other professional groups, among classmates in the gymnasium, or simply among friends or neighbours. The spread of these societies may be traced ultimately to changes in economic life; but not directly. Trading and transport companies and syndicates for farming taxes are not to be taken as

---

[1] Polybius, II, 37, 11. 'Its properties,' says Acton (*History of Freedom*, p. 21), 'were imperfectly investigated in theory.' Cf. above, p. 23 *sq.*

[2] W. W. Tarn in *The Hellenistic Age*, p. 108, and below, p. 212.

significant of their nature since they belonged to the world of business partnerships rather than of private associations. Among artisans associations that transcended the fellowship of the quarter or street in which the specific art or craft was practised were rare as yet outside Egypt. Clubs of professional athletes were unknown. The conditions under which merchants and shipmasters, warehousemen and traders did business at home and abroad apparently made the formation of guilds, in the common sense of this term, exceptional, so that when men engaged in these occupations in a given centre united at all, it was usually as one body in a quasi-political assembly or as social groups in the form of ethnic or religious clubs. It may be conceded that at meetings of such clubs more went on than was contained in their records. Since the members had the same vocations, useful information must have been interchanged; and the fact that they occasionally voted honours to external benefactors betrays the existence among them of a sense of corporate interest that may well have been economic at times. But that they issued rules for the conduct of a trade or profession, or used their organization to advance prices or rates or to press claims for special privileges, conforms neither to the evidence nor to the probabilities. The problems peculiar to labour were not open to collective treatment so long as most of the industrial wage-earners were slaves.

Business remained essentially a sphere of individual initiative, and the characteristic thing is rather the number of men that it uprooted from home and city than the growth of co-operative enterprises. Hence the urge to form associations was rarely grounded in strictly economic considerations. Yet it was felt very widely, by women as well as by men, and also, though exceptionally, by slaves. On the evidence available the fact seems to be that private associations were multiplied because they offered the easiest way of escape to a sociable people from loneliness and helplessness in a vast disintegrating world. The super-state was too remote to be real, the *polis* too subject to external control to reward exclusive devotion. Hence the club flourished. But it in turn was too real to enlist ideals strongly. Class and nationality remain as principles of social organization. But, as we have seen, class was blurred at home, while abroad it was tarnished through having become distinctive of natives; whereas nationality, weakened everywhere by the example and influence of denationalized territorial states, was either supplanted by municipalism in the new world or used, and then misused, to mark off the constituent elements of conglomerate cities and armies. What response was political and ethical theory to make to this complication of affairs?

For all its instinctive conservatism Greek thought was a living thing, sensitive to changes of environment; and a masterful thing, set on dominating life. And in the Hellenistic age it had not lost its qualities. The political institution of which it had now to determine more explicitly the theoretical properties was monarchy. In considering this men trained in the Greek schools naturally used the method which had been followed in considering the city-state—the elucidation, with a view to betterment, of the actual by the setting up of the ideal (see vol. VI, pp. 505, 523). The personal qualities of the ideal king had been already defined by Plato and Aristotle; and their definitions were retained and amplified by their successors (p. 113 *sq.*). But the institution itself had to be explored anew. For in order to be ideal monarchy had now to be universal. Once the city-state had ceased to be conceived as self-sufficient, the ideal monarch could not be confined to a single city-state without loss of perfection; nor could he tolerate longer, like the philosopher-king of Plato, the co-existence of ideal monarchs in other city-states. He could suffer no territorial limitation whatsoever. For, the self-sufficiency of the city-state gone, it did not occur to anyone as possible to attribute self-sufficiency to any other *section* of the world. The traditions of monarchy in Persia and Egypt, the example of Alexander and of Antigonus I, and the failure of the Successors to set frontiers to their kingdoms conspired to crush any thought of sectional completeness. Yet without self-sufficiency the government of a section, whatever its form might be, could not be ideal, least of all in an age which, like the Hellenistic, made self-sufficiency the universal test of perfection. Greek theory of monarchy had thus to be one degree further removed from political realities than the theory of the *polis*. It tended to become merged with the theory of the universe in general.

Greek thought was led in this same direction by yet other considerations. It could not fail to respond to the enormous widening of horizon and enlargement of knowledge and interlocking of business interests that had occurred. The way for a larger synthesis was also blazed by the rise of a standard Greek language—the so-called Hellenistic *koine*—and its spread beyond the bounds of the Hellenic world. The effects of community of language and of dialect had been of course overborne in classic Greece by divergence among its states in national and political aims; and the use by Greeks and non-Greeks from Rome to Parthia of the *koine* as the one language of culture meant no more durable interpenetration of aspirations than, for example, the like use of Greek in the Ottoman Empire. But such use did mean that, for the time being at least, men of culture everywhere, irrespective of race, had one further element and agency of exchange in common—a fact which political thinking could not overlook. Nor could it overlook the implications of Alexander's astounding policy of fusing races (vol. VI, p. 431 *sq.*). Be his motive what it may, the projected marriage of Europe and Asia emphasized in unforgettable fashion both the artificiality of the distinctions separating men of one race, language, religion, and culture from those of another, and the significance for social life of their common humanity. The fundamental idea did not die with its author. Rejected by his successors as humiliating to their national pride, it lived on in men's consciousness and fired the imagination of another great dreamer, who, being a Semite by birth and an Athenian by education, was well placed to see in humanity an ideal unity by which to resolve the dualism of his experience.

It thus happened that the political theory of the Greeks leaped at one bound from the reality of the *polis* to the vision of 'the universe of men,' the *oecumene*, without deigning to set foot in passing on the half-reality of the territorial monarchy and the federation. It was, however, a leap of the imagination alone. The framework of the Stoic cosmopolis was filled in, if at all, not by concrete *nomoi* of its own, but by the patchwork fabric of existing institutions. It was not with this 'dream or image of a state' that the mind of Zeno lived. With him, as with his contemporary Epicurus, the *real* thing about which to theorize was no association of men, but its negation—the solitary self-centred individual. With Zeno individualism all but sufficed; with Epicurus it sufficed altogether, at least theoretically. Both of them had more in common in the premises of their thinking with the Cynics than with the older Academicians or the Peripatetics, in that they grounded their systems in the self-sufficiency of the sage in place of the self-sufficiency of the *polis*. The gods they wrote off as limiting factors in the individual's life, Epicurus by a cosmogony which made gods extra-mundane, Zeno by a cosmogony which made gods and men identical in essence. Death was a release, of the Epicurean from everything, of the Stoic from the corruption of the body: in neither creed was it an end to determine human activity. There remained the 'domination of things.' From this the way to freedom led inward—to the refuge of one's own thoughts. The sage's peace of mind (*ataraxia*) came to him, not through existing without pain, disease, hardship, slavery, poverty, humiliations, but through mental capacity to disassociate well-being from externals. From such things as formed the evils of the multitude of men no man could escape, but the wise man would make nothing of them; and from the rush and turmoil and confusion of the life of ordinary men he would seek deliverance by reducing his interests to a minimum. 'Every interest man had in an object,' writes a modern interpreter of Hellenistic popular philosophy[1], 'was a filament, as it were, going out from his heart and attaching itself to that object, so that if the object was unstable and elusive he was pulled miserably after it. The way of freedom therefore was to cut all these strands going out in all directions and attaching to a multitude of objects'—family, state, property, honours and the like.

Unlike the Cynics, neither the Epicureans nor the Stoics were anarchists, though they had nothing positive to offer in the sphere of ordinary politics. The Epicureans needed the state as a shield for their own life, and traced its origin to a contract, or kind of international treaty, between individuals; but it mattered not at all what the state was, and they put 'the saving of the Hellenes' among the valueless things. The life they envisaged as ideal was that of a club, a group of congenial friends like the one in the midst of which their Master lived in the Garden in Athens, unmolested because of its obscurity and inactivity, an earthly replica of the society of the extra-mundane gods and goddesses, a stage, rather than a necessity for the life of subdued pleasure which they made their *summum bonum* (see further below, pp. 232 *sqq.*).

The Garden thus embodied one of the two concepts of society round which men chiefly rallied in the Hellenistic age. The Stoics laid hold of the other—that of a world-order—and made it their own. From the standpoint of their psychology the ideal wise man could not but jeopardize his self-sufficiency (*autarkeia*) if he engaged his interest in politics, but from the standpoint of their ethics he could not but display activity of some sort, be it mental or physical, since they made virtue his *summum bonum*, and virtue meant to all Greeks virtuous action. The solution of this dilemma they found in the sage's refusal to let himself become wrapped up in any particular state or society while accepting with indifference the form of government or station of life in which he was placed. Ὁ σοφὸς πολιτεύσεται: 'the sage will take part in politics,' they

---

[1] E. R. Bevan in *The Hellenistic Age*, p. 83.

affirmed[1], not because of the result to be attained thereby—
that was preordained—but simply because it was in the line
of his duty: like an actor on the stage, he will try to do his part
well.

This unenthusiastic acceptance of civic obligations was consonant with Stoic cosmology. Rather—it would, perhaps, be
more accurate to say—the Stoics accepted a cosmology from which
they could infer that if man lived in harmony with his own higher
nature, *i.e.* virtuously, he at the same time lived in harmony with
the nature of the cosmos. Like man the cosmos was, they held, a
rational animal. Within them both was diffused the heat of life,
due both in man and cosmos to the presence of the divine fire
that was reason. Like the cosmos, again, man was an intelligent
machine. Both ran their set course and perished; whereupon they
released for re-use their portions of the fire, man to the cosmos
after life's brief span, the cosmos, after its great cycle had been
completed, to re-create the imperishable fire from which it had
sprung. All men were thus partakers one with another of the
divine reason, and the sympathy which existed between man and
nature existed necessarily between man and man. From this conception the vertical classification of men into sages and fools (in
the matter of wisdom and folly, as they understood it, there was
no *tertium quid*) had as its necessary complement a horizontal
grouping of them as kinsmen, it being a matter of no consequence
in either case whether they were Greeks or Barbarians, rich or
poor, free or slave. As parts of the cosmos, the sun and the moon
and the lesser bodies that fretted the magisterial roof of the world
with golden fire were, like men, mechanisms and quickened by the
same reason. Theirs was the high office to disclose by the un-
swerving regularity of their movements that this all-pervading
reason was law. There was then one law for all men—the law of
their own nature, or, simply, natural law. But the correlate alike
of one blood and of one law among all mankind was a single universal state, of which naturally the wise and not the fools should
have the governance. Since, moreover, wisdom was teachable and
the sage could not exist without doing something virtuous, he
must needs work for the more complete realization of the state of
his vision. But he must work without fervour. The rôle of the
Stoa was thus to launch the idea of a cosmos that was also a *polis*
at a time when the world had been prepared somewhat to accept
it, by the conquests and policy of Alexander, by the decay of
nations and national loyalties, by the development of an universal

[1] H. von Arnim, *Veterum Stoicorum Fragmenta*, III, 157, 175.

language, and by the groping of mankind after a way of escape from the tyranny of Tyche and the seductiveness of things that did not require the rejection of religion, civilization, and community life. And if, as has been suggested[1], 'the dividing line between the ancient and the modern political theory must be sought, if anywhere, in the period between Aristotle and Cicero,' for this the Stoics were primarily responsible.

The Greek world which Rome presently entered was a world governed more by these new ideas than by the philosophies which were sprung from the Greek city-states. They were of course meaningless to her until she felt the need for them; and, meanwhile, she learned from the Hellenistic world its less admirable traits—to look upon public service as an opportunity for private enrichment; to covet a life of relaxation, luxury, frivolity; to seek happiness by gratifying desires however extravagant or vicious; to evade, as being the affair of professionals, the inconveniences, hardships, and sacrifices of war. But the need came all the sooner because the vices came first. And Rome's need for Stoicism was three-fold: to justify theoretically her dominion over the *orbis terrarum*; to guide her courts in the award of legal rights when political rights did not determine them; and to give her citizens a reason for doing their duty disinterestedly when patriotism proved not enough. The Greek world which the Romans entered was not the world which they idealized; but from it many of the best of them, as well as many of the worst of them, drew their inspiration. Its science they did not understand; its art they did not feel; its mission they frustrated—and then undertook themselves.

[1] A. J. Carlyle, *A History of Mediaeval Political Theory*, I, p. 9.

CHAPTER II

THE COMING OF THE CELTS

I. THE MATERIAL CIVILIZATION OF THE CELTS DURING THE LA TÈNE PERIOD

ABOUT the year 400 B.C. a flood of barbarian invaders crossed the Alps and advanced upon the cities of Upper Italy. These barbarians, whose invasions were to be such a menace to the Mediterranean world, were the Celts[1], whose territories, now so shrunken, extended in the heyday of their glory from the British Isles to Asia Minor. The purpose of this chapter is to describe their early civilization and history and the causes which led to their migrations. The period which mainly concerns us stretches from the sixth to the end of the second century B.C. The preceding phases have been dealt with in vol. II, chaps. II and XXI; while the Celtic invasions of Spain, Italy, Greece and Asia Minor are described in chaps. III, XVI, and XXIV of the present volume[2].

Prior to the second century B.C., we are indebted to archaeological research for the greater part of our knowledge concerning the Celts. To archaeology therefore we must turn, and see what light it sheds on their culture in this still somewhat obscure period.

The Early Iron Age in Central Europe is divided into two epochs: the Hallstatt and La Tène periods, which take their names from the sites where antiquities characteristic of these two cultures were first identified. Hallstatt is situated in Upper Austria, La Tène in Switzerland, at the eastern end of the Lake of Neuchâtel. But the cradle of the La Tène civilization is not to be sought in Switzerland: the region in which that culture unfolded lay farther to the north. Broadly speaking, the La Tène culture was originally a Celtic culture, but this does not imply

---

[1] The word 'Celt,' unless otherwise stated, is used in the sense 'Celtic-speaking peoples' or 'peoples of Celtic nationality,' so far as the word 'nationality' can be applied to a group of barbaric peoples under no central authority. This chapter is only concerned with the Celts of the Continent: the insular Celts are reserved for treatment when, later, they come within the range of written history.

[2] In chapters III and XVII the traditional name for the whole body of these invaders—Gauls—is retained.

that it was shared by all the Celtic peoples in its earliest stages. Later, its influence spread into non-Celtic regions as well.

The credit for having first established the chronological subdivisions of this period rests with Tischler. His scheme has since been modified by others, notably by his compatriot, Paul Reinecke. Below is given Reinecke's most recent chronology, together with those of Schumacher and Déchelette.

Reinecke[1]	Schumacher[2]	Déchelette[3]
La Tène A From the second half of the sixth century into the second half of the fifth century B.C.	La Tène₁ From end of the sixth century to c. 400 B.C.	La Tène I c. 500–300
La Tène B Beginning from the end of the fifth century B.C.	La Tène₂ c. 400–300	
La Tène C Before and after 200 B.C.	La Tène₃ c. 300–100	La Tène II c. 300–100
La Tène D c. 121–15 B.C.	La Tène₄ c. 100 B.C.–A.D. I	La Tène III c. 100–A.D. I

The subdivision of La Tène I into two phases is of considerable importance, but, although accepted by leading German and Austrian archaeologists, it has not elsewhere met with the recognition which, in the opinion of the present writer, it undoubtedly deserves. This is due to a mistaken notion, either that La Tène A is nothing more than the last phase of the Hallstatt period under another name, or that it is a mere transition from Hallstatt to La Tène. On stylistic and typological grounds the first assumption is unjustifiable, and the same applies to the latter, except possibly in eastern Bavaria and Bohemia. The art of La Tène A betrays features that are quite distinct from the art of the periods preceding and following it. Indeed, without recognizing this phase as a separate cultural and chronological entity, one cannot obtain a thoroughly accurate conception of the genesis and development of art in the second Iron Age.

[1] *Bayerischer Vorgeschichtsfreund*, I/II, 1921/2, p. 21 *sq*.
[2] In *Reallexikon der Vorgeschichte*, s.v. Mittel- und Süddeutschland and *Siedlungs- und Kulturgeschichte der Rheinlande*, I, p. 120 *sq*.
[3] *Manuel d'Archéologie*, II, 3, pp. 928 *sqq*.

A brief summary of some of the leading features of Reinecke's phases A–C is necessary in order to give an idea of the material cultures of the Celts[1]. Phase D (Late La Tène) falls outside the scope of the present chapter.

PHASE A, OR THE EARLIEST LA TÈNE PERIOD. The funeral rite is generally inhumation under a tumulus. The most typical weapons are: the short sword or dagger; long swords; heavy, one-edged, curved knives (*Hiebmesser*), often of considerable size; bronze helmets. Horse-trappings and parts of chariots are not infrequently found. The chief objects of adornment are: Certosa, mask- and bird-headed fibulae; girdle-clasps based on the palmette motif or on zoomorphic designs; armlets, torcs and finger-rings of bronze and gold; orange and blue-green stratified eye-beads. The most important series of objects are the imported Greek bronze vessels, which date, in Greece, from the sixth century: beaked-flagons (*Schnabelkannen*), *stamnoi*, round flat dishes with and without (rigid) handles, large bronze cauldrons with iron ring-handles, and the like. Barbaric imitations of the flagons are not unknown. Attic black- and red-figured pottery occurs on a few sites in France and southern Germany. In the west native pottery is best represented in Champagne. It also occurs in the region of Trèves.

The zone covered by the La Tène A culture extends from France to Bohemia, and for the sake of convenience may be divided into a Central, a Western and an Eastern area. The Central area consists of the Middle Rhine region and the adjacent districts, in which the celebrated series of burials commonly known as the 'Chieftains' Graves' are found. Inhumation is the dominant rite in this group of burials, the dead being mostly covered by tumuli. These, with their Greek imports and their gold ornaments, are the richest graves of the whole La Tène A group. It is probable that the La Tène culture first flowered in this region. South of a line through Hagenau, Rastatt, Stuttgart and Ulm, the Late Hallstatt (D) culture persisted down to *c.* 400 B.C. La Tène A, therefore, is not found to the south of this line, nor is it represented in Switzerland. Next in richness to the Middle Rhine area is the Western area, eastern and north-east France. The rich chariot-burials (Somme Bionne, La Gorge Meillet, Berru, etc.) of the Marne and neighbouring districts belong to this phase, but as Reinecke's fourfold division of the La Tène period has

---

[1] Objects characteristic of this material culture will be illustrated in Volume of Plates III (to vols. VII and VIII). What follows is, for the most part, an exposition of Reinecke's views concerning the phases in question.

still to be recognized by French archaeologists, the limits of
La Tène A in the Western area have not as yet been established.
The Eastern group consists of east Bavaria, southern Thuringia
and the western half of Bohemia (particularly the south-west
districts). The more or less contemporary Greek influence, so
strongly reflected in the imports and the native art of both the
Western and Central areas, and in the shapes of the native pottery
of the Western area, had far less effect upon this Eastern group.
The pottery, though distinctive, betrays little connection with
Greece in form, though in decoration an older Greek influence,
derived from Upper Italy, is occasionally to be discerned. The
influence of Upper Italy is far more strongly felt than in the
Central and Western areas. Farther to the east sporadic finds
occur, but most of them, if they belong to phase A at all, date from
the very end of that phase. In La Tène A the potter's wheel
was introduced into Central Europe. But hand-made pottery is
very common in this and the succeeding phase: most of the
Marne pottery (in Phases A–C) is hand-made.

PHASE B is better known as the EARLY LA TÈNE PERIOD. It
reveals a greater uniformity of civilization than the period immediately preceding it. The funeral rite is inhumation, but large
cemeteries of flat-graves take the place of the older and more
isolated tumuli, though in some districts the latter persist. The
greater part of the Marne flat-graves, and the flat-grave cemeteries of the Boii in Bohemia and the Helvetii in northern Switzerland date from phases B and C. The most characteristic weapon
is the (usually) shortish, thrusting sword, with sheath ending in
an open-work or trefoil chape. The most typical objects of adornment are the Early La Tène fibula (with foot bent back till it
touches or nearly touches the bow) and a great variety of armlets
and torcs, among the most characteristic of which are those with
'buffer' and 'seal-top' terminals. Girdle-clasps also occur. In
north-east France we find polychrome and unpainted pottery,
while in Brittany, where painted pottery is not found, vessels occur
with rich curvilinear designs (St Pol-de-Léon and Plouhinec).
All three types seem first to appear in the preceding phase. But
the last named may have survived for a long time, if Déchelette
is right in connecting it with a ware, dating from the latter part
of the La Tène period, found at Glastonbury and other sites in
England[1]. In the Rhine area the pottery is not painted, though
vessels with 'graceful' (*grazierende*) designs are found at Braubach

[1] E. T. Leeds, *Archaeologia*, 1926/7, pp. 230 *sqq.*, would derive the last-
named pottery from the Celts in the western parts of the Spanish peninsula.

and elsewhere. East of the Rhine and Neckar pottery is rare. Compared to A, phase B is very poor in imported bronze vessels. A bucket, decorated with drooping palmettes and tendril motifs, was among the objects in the celebrated find at Waldalgesheim. Another specimen was unearthed in the Gaulish cemetery at Montefortino. These finds show phase B to have been in existence by *c.* 400 B.C. The Italian cemeteries are important: they yield characteristic B objects in association with antiquities of the fourth century B.C., but Hellenistic pottery, and metal work of the third century, are almost entirely lacking. This would show that, apart from certain isolated localities (where it may have lasted longer), La Tène B ended *c.* 300 B.C. According to Schumacher, this stage witnessed a development in agriculture in the low-lying districts of south-west Germany.

The culture of phase B covers a wider area than that of A. It spreads as far east as Budapest, and beyond; we find it in Moravia and to the north of the Central German mountain-chain in Silesia (as far as the Oder), Saxony and Thuringia. These were frontier provinces between Celt and Teuton. It was probably in this period that the Helvetii occupied Switzerland and the Boii and Volcae Tectosages Bohemia and Moravia. But the most important event was the Celtic invasion of Italy *c.* 400 B.C. and their settlement in Cisalpine Gaul (see below, pp. 60 *sqq.*). Towards the close of this fourth-century period Pytheas of Marseilles made his famous voyage. (See below, p. 53 *sq.*)

PHASE C OR THE MIDDLE LA TÈNE PERIOD. In this, as in the preceding period, the predominant rite was inhumation under flat graves. There is no evidence for a displacement of population in Switzerland and the greater part of northern Bohemia: the large flat-grave inhumation cemeteries persist undisturbed into this phase. The same is true for the Marne area. Cremation burials occur, however, both in south-west Germany and the southern half of the East Alpine region, but they are exceptional. The most typical weapons are: long swords, with slightly tapered point and bell-shaped guard (the scabbards often finely decorated, with strangulated and heart-shaped chapes); broad-bladed spear-heads; large oval or oblong shields with 'trigger-guard' bosses. The most characteristic objects of adornment are: the Middle La Tène fibula (with foot *clasping* the bow); a variety of bracelets, among which may be mentioned the type with hollow semi-ovoid or semi-globular protuberances (*Nussarmring*). The band-shaped glass bangle first appears. Torcs are rare. Perhaps the most typical object of adornment is the chain girdle composed of bronze (sometimes of iron and bronze) members decorated with red enamel. It was in this phase that red enamel was first substituted for coral by the continental Celts; the latter was employed in Central Europe from Hallstatt D to La Tène B. Wheel-made pottery becomes more common; the shapes of the vessels sometimes reveal Hellenistic influences. Painted vessels still appear in burials of the Marne group (Montfercaut). But pottery of phase C is rare in this region. Graves of the Middle La Tène period occur in Upper Italy. Phase C was marked by a great expansion of Celtic power to the east and the south-east: the Middle Danubian and Dacian areas, together with Carniola, etc., began to be fundamentally affected by the La Tène culture, while the defeat of Ptolemy Keraunos, the onslaught on Delphi, and the first incursion of Celts into Asia Minor happened in 279–8 B.C. (See pp. 101 *sqq.*) The area to the immediate north of the Central German mountain-chain was abandoned. A topographical study of the different sites reveals that the propensity for agriculture, already manifest among the Celtic peoples in La Tène B, was further intensified in this phase. Classical authors, too, speak of the Cisalpine Gauls as an agricultural people.

Perhaps the chief advance in civilization of the Middle La Tène period was the adoption of currency. If the inferior early coins, forming part of the hoard from Auriol, are really barbaric copies, they were struck by the pre-Celtic inhabitants of southern France, for their area of distribution lies to the south of the Celtic zone. Although, at an outside estimate, the earliest gold staters of Philip of Macedon may have been copied by Celtic peoples prior to his death in 336 B.C., the minting of coins by the continental Celts can hardly have become very widespread before the Middle La Tène period.

The earlier Celtic coins were exclusively imitated from Greek prototypes and a number of the latter have been found in the Celtic area. It is not possible here to allude to more than a few types. If one may generalize, silver predominated at first among the eastern Celts (the middle and lower Danubian regions); in the Western zone gold was common. The first Greek coin to be copied in the West was the gold stater of Philip II, while the silver coinage was based on the later (fourth-century) issues of the Greek colony of Massilia and on those of Emporiae and Rhode. The coins of these three cities were copied by the Celts from the third to the first century B.C. The gold stater, apparently, did not reach the western Celts by way of the Danube; it came from Massilia: the Massiliotes, having no gold coinage of their own, used the

stater of Philip. To the east, the earliest type copied was the silver
stater of the same king. As a rule, the coins were first copied by
the Celts nearest the Greek centres: Celtic coins of the third and
second centuries do occur in south-west Germany, but the
majority date from the first. In Britain minting began roughly
about 100 B.C. Celtic copies of Greek coins which had been
issued one or more centuries earlier are quite common. The extent
of barbarization is such that it is not always easy to recognize the
classic prototype. The Roman denarius was first copied in southern
France at the end of the third century B.C., but farther north not
until the second century B.C. The concave coins known as
'*Regenbogenschüsselchen*' date from phases C and D.

II. THE ART OF THE LA TÈNE PERIOD

The two chief formative elements in the art of the La Tène
period are the survivals of certain Hallstatt influences and the new
influence of more or less contemporary Greek art. The former
reveal themselves in technique and in ornamentation, the latter
for the most part in the ornamentation only. The older barbaric
survivals are geometric in feeling, the new influence of the Greek
art naturalistic. The zoomorphic motifs are mainly derived from
the Greek element, though in the more easterly districts of the
phase A group they must be regarded as survivals of a style
known as the Upper Italian situla art. The influence of plant
motifs, for the most part Greek in origin, becomes more and
more prominent: witness the derivatives, mainly geometric, of the
palmette, the free tendril and other motifs. One should also
mention the scroll patterns with thickened ends (*Fischblasen-
müster*) and the trisceles.

Viewed as a whole, the art of the continental Celts in the La
Tène period may be regarded as a period of gradual decline. It
attains its zenith almost at once—in phase A—but in each succeeding chronological subdivision it becomes more barbarized
and conventionalistic. In the British Isles, this process was reversed, the zenith being reached in the later stages of the La Tène
period. On the continent, the decline was perhaps due to a
falling-off in the number of southern imports, perhaps also to a
corresponding decline in the art of Greece itself. The cradle of
the true La Tène style is probably to be found in the Middle
Rhine region, for here lay the point of contact between the two
above-mentioned formative elements. At all events, it is in this
region that the Greek imports are best represented.

Reinecke was the first to understand the development of La Tène art. He observes that, although in Celtic art of the fifth century B.C. we occasionally encounter fairly faithful representations of Greek types, we find for the most part, both in plant and figural motifs, that a conscious stylizing of the Greek models has taken place. Certain unessential details are exaggerated, others suppressed, while disintegrations and combinations with other motifs are not infrequent. Finally, from these degenerate and barbaric reproductions, new forms arise. By phase C the classical tradition was scarcely recognizable: the art had now become purely Celtic.

Two divergent tendencies have been traced in La Tène art. The first, an inheritance from the Hallstatt period, is mostly in evidence during phase A. It consists in a 'mechanical repetition of congruent motifs,' little regard being paid to the design as an organic whole. The second, due to Greek influence, is found side by side with, and survives this repetitional tendency: the ornamental form—which is often highly complex—is treated as an indissoluble unity, a complex organism. As the La Tène period proceeds, the plant motifs become less representational and more geometric in feeling, though this does not imply that the arrangement of the design was less organic. One important characteristic of La Tène art remains to be mentioned: the practice of embellishing the whole ornamental field with primary and complementary curvilinear patterns (e.g. the helmet from Berru, the scabbard from Lisnacroghera). This entailed the abolishing of the differentiation between design and background, a tendency foreign to Greek classical art of the best period, and one which contributed also to the loss of the originally naturalistic character of plant motifs in Celtic art[1].

It remains to describe the channels through which Greek influence reached north-east and eastern France, and the middle Rhine area[2]. The main route seems to have been Massilia, the Rhône and the Saône, the chief exports from the south being metal vessels, Attic pottery, and wine. The peculiarities of the Eastern La Tène A area have been discussed above, p. 44. The most important route for this region passed over the Brenner. Scythian influence, though possibly of importance later, can hardly have played a part in the genesis of the La Tène style; even for later times, the possibility of a parallel development must be taken into account.

[1] van Scheltema in *Reallexikon der Vorgeschichte*, VII, s.v. Latènestil.
[2] See the forthcoming discussion by the present writer in *Antiquity*.

III. EARLY TRADERS AND CONTACTS WITH THE GREEK WORLD

The first known classical author to mention Celts is Hecataeus of Miletus (c. 540–475 B.C.). His works are lost, but two fragments have survived that are of interest to us. In the first he mentions 'Nyrax, a Celtic city,' but of this Celtic city nothing more is known. In the second he speaks of 'Massilia, a town in the land of the Ligurians (πόλις τῆς Λιγυστικῆς), in the region of the land of the Celts (κατὰ τὴν Κελτικήν), a Phocaean colony.' The truth of his statement is borne out by the evidence of archaeology: the Ligurians, in his day (La Tène A), dwelt in the regions around Massilia, and the territory of the Celts lay to the north of the Ligurian zone. The redaction of the pseudo-Scylax periplus (c. 335 B.C.) mentions the presence in southern France of Ligurians, but not of the Celts. Yet when Hannibal marched from Spain to Italy in 218 B.C., the only peoples mentioned as encountered in southern Gaul are the Celtic peoples (Polybius, III, 40 sq.). Archaeological finds show that they can hardly have conquered that region prior to c. 300 B.C.

After Hecataeus, the next author to mention them is Herodotus. He tells us (II, 33) that the Danube rose 'in the country of the Celts' (ἐκ Κελτῶν) near the town of Pyrene; he then adds that the Celts dwelt beyond the Pillars of Hercules, next to the Cynetes, who were the westernmost people of Europe. These remarks he reiterates in Book IV, 49. Attempts have been made to prove that his second statement (in II, 33) is not essentially connected with his first, and that there may have been another town called Pyrene which was not situated in the Pyrenean area. But on the whole, the facts suggest that Herodotus blundered over the region in which the Danube rises, although he is correct in saying that the source of that river lay in Celtic territory, that there were Celts in the Pyrenean area and that Celtic peoples were already settled in Spain. During the fifth century B.C., the Celts were in possession of all those regions. Timaeus (352–256 B.C.) alludes to the Celts as dwelling by the Ocean (ap. Diodorus IV, 56).

It is highly probable that the Greeks derived their first knowledge of the Celtic peoples from traders. It has been observed, in connection with the second of the two fragments of Hecataeus, that there was a lively trade in Greek bronze vessels and pottery between Massilia and the Western and Central areas of the La Tène A zone, a trade in which the Ligurians of south-eastern France appear to have acted as middlemen; even supposing the

4

Greeks were not in direct touch with these Celtic peoples, they must have learnt of them through the Ligurians[1].

The Greeks also seem to have derived their first knowledge of the more westerly and northern regions, including the British Isles, through commercial channels. It is probable that one of the chief materials in this sea-traffic was tin, though Irish gold may still have been of importance[2]. Much has been written about the Cassiterides ('the tin islands'), but owing to insufficiency of evidence, the definite knowledge which has accrued from these writings is slight. One scholar holds that *kassiteros*, the Greek for tin, is of eastern origin[3]; but it seems more probable that in Arabic, for instance, the word for tin (*kaṣdīr*) was borrowed from the Greek[4]. Arguments for a Celtic origin of the word are also inconclusive. In spite of manifold attempts at identification, we are still unable to localize the Cassiterides. Whatever the origin and first significance of this word may have been, it is not improbable that it came to be used of any source (or sources) in western Europe from which tin was exported to the classic world. The most important of these lay in Cornwall, Brittany, Spain, and the adjacent islands. With the Bohemian deposits which figured largely in trade during the Early Bronze Age, we are not concerned. How great a part Cornwall played in the tin traffic, is hard to say, but there is reason to believe that the ores of this region were exploited in the Bronze Age. Cornish tin was apparently exported *c.* 300 B.C., and it is possible that trading stations were at that time established in Cornwall by Celtic peoples from the western parts of the Spanish peninsula[5]. If, at an earlier date, Cornish tin reached Tartessus, it is probable that the Oestrymnians (see below, p. 771) acted as middlemen in the traffic, for there is no evidence for supposing Cornwall to have been in direct touch with that port. The deposits in Brittany and Spain were apparently worked in very early times, and the Breton tin probably reached Tartessus by sea (see below, p. 771). But, despite recent criticism, this metal may also have come to the south, by overland routes through Gaul, before as well as after 300 B.C.

[1] M. Piroutet, *L'Anthropologie*, XXIX, 1918/19, pp. 215 *sqq.*
[2] There is no evidence of tin being exported from Ireland. See R. A. Macalister, *Archaeology of Ireland*, 1928, p. 55
[3] J. Pokorny, *Zeitschr. für Celtische Philologie*, IX, 1913, p. 164 *sq.*
[4] S. Fraenkel, *Die aramäischen Fremdwörter im Arabischen*, p. 153.
[5] See E. T. Leeds, *op. cit.* pp. 205 *sqq.* It is possible that the tin ores were being worked in Cornwall at the time of Pytheas' voyage (see M. Cary in *J.H.S.*, XLIV, 1924, pp. 167, 174). Cf. also Caesar, *B.G.* v, 12.

Greeks were already in touch with Tartessus during the seventh and sixth centuries B.C. We know from Herodotus that Colaeus of Samos, about the year 620 B.C., chanced by accident upon the port of Tartessus at the mouth of the Guadalquivir, in southern Spain, and brought back a rich cargo, and that the Phocaeans in their long penteconters established relations with that port (vol. IV, p. 352).

Avienus' poem *Ora Maritima* is of great interest in this connection: although written in the fourth century A.D., it is based upon earlier sources. It has been shown that chief among these is a lost Massiliote *Periplus* dating from the sixth century, but Ephorus and other early Greek authors were also employed; while, apart from additions of his own, Avienus seems to have used later Greek sources[1]. In view of the composite nature of the poem, it should be used with caution when chronology is involved, and checked with other evidence. The *Periplus* falls into three parts, one dealing with the navigation between Tartessus and Massilia, another with the Atlantic coasts between Tartessus and the Oestrymnides, while the third gives an account of Ierne, Albion and, apparently, the Frisian coast, an account probably derived by the Tartessians from the Oestrymnians (cf. ll. 113 *sq.* and 130 *sqq.*), which the Massiliotes in their turn derived from the Tartessians[2].

We find a group of names connected with the latter people. Scholars are not in agreement in their identifications. But most authorities are of the opinion that the northernmost Oestrymnis (there are two in the poem, one being situated in the Spanish peninsula) is Brittany. There are two days and nights sail (*duo soles*) between the Oestrymnides and Ireland (l. 108 *sq.*); so the former can hardly be—as some have supposed—the British Isles, which are mentioned under other names in the poem. The Oestrymnides are probably small islands off the coast of Brittany. They are mentioned (ll. 96–8) as being rich in tin and lead[3]. The tin deposits of the Breton mainland we know to have been exploited from a yet remoter period[4]. We are told that the Tartessians traded with the Oestrymnides, l. 113 *sq.*, as later did the Carthaginians (ll. 114 *sqq.*, see below, p. 771).

The *sacra insula* mentioned (l. 108) is undoubtedly Ireland. The name, if one may say so without offence, is probably due to a mistake, the early form, Iwerio, being confused by the Greeks

---

[1] A. Schulten, *Fontes Hispaniae Antiquae*, I, 1922.
[2] *Ibid.* p. 11, and see below, p. 770.
[3] Cf. L. Siret in *L'Anthropologie*, XIX, 1908, p. 143 *sq.*
[4] Daryll Forde, *Man*, XXVI, 1926, p. 136 *sq.*

with ἱερός 'holy.' The *insula Albionum* (l. 112) refers to Great Britain, of which it is the earliest name. This is regarded by some as a pre-Celtic word. It occurs, however, in Celtic sources. In the earlier of these, it is applied to Britain generally; in the later, to the districts north of the Clyde. It survived in the expression 'the Kingdom of Alba' and some authorities hold it to be derived from a Celtic word meaning 'white,' ultimately connected with the Latin *albus*. At all events, its pre-Celtic origin is not proven.

There is an allusion to 'a Northern Liguria' whose inhabitants had been driven out by the Celts (ll. 130–8). This region Schulten places on the Frisian coasts, and he derives the passage from the *Periplus* (see below, p. 771). It is very surprising to find the Ligurians so far north and, until satisfactory evidence of a philological character can be produced in support of this passage, it appears to the present writer safer to regard it as due to some misunderstanding[1]. At all events, we should remember that even if the above passage was derived from the Massiliote *Periplus*, its author probably had the information at second hand from the Tartessians, who learned of it from the Oestrymnians.

Shortly before the end of the sixth century the Straits of Gibraltar fell under Carthaginian control, and the connection of the Greeks with Tartessus and the Atlantic sea route was severed (see below, p. 775). Some regard this severance as the chief cause of the opening of a land-trade across Gaul by the Greeks, and the establishment of such a route they date to the fifth century[2]. Objections to this theory, based upon lack of numismatic evidence, are hardly valid[3]. At the same time, while we have every reason to believe that trade relations at that time extended along the Rhône-Saône route between the Greek colonists and the Celts (with the Ligurians acting as middlemen), it is not so easy to say whether the more westerly route—from southern Gaul to Corbilo (at the mouth of the Loire) and thence to Cornwall—was in use at this particular time or not. In the present writer's opinion, the route from Ictis (in Britain) to the mouth of the Rhône (Diodorus v, 22) may have been opened before 300 B.C. At all events some sort of trade connection between the Greek colonies in southern France and the Marne area was established by 500 B.C.

So far as the Greeks were concerned, the gate to the Atlantic

---

[1] Convincing arguments as to how such an error may have arisen have been advanced by M. Piroutet, *L'Anthropologie*, xxx, 1920, pp. 55 *sqq.*

[2] C. Jullian, *Hist. de la Gaule*, i, p. 410 *sq.* and A. Schulten, *Tartessos*, p. 49 *sq.*   [3] See above, p. 48, n. 2.

was barred by the Carthaginians from the last decade of the sixth
century to the time of Pytheas, and even the latter's voyage was
followed by no immediate resumption of traffic along the old
sea-route. Pytheas of Massilia was the first Greek known to have
visited these islands. His celebrated voyage probably took place
about the years 325–3 B.C. (p. 780). We cannot say for certain
whether its purpose was scientific. Unfortunately his account of
it has perished, but fragments of it are quoted by Strabo, Pliny and
other writers. Polybius and Strabo regard him as a liar and a
charlatan, but time has shown their opinions of him to be ill-
founded. He sailed to Brittany, for he notes that the Ostimii dwelt
on the headland of *Kabaion*, perhaps Pointe du Raz or Pointe
St Mathieu. Some hold that the Oestrymnians of Avienus are to
be identified with the Ostimii of Pytheas, the former being the
corrupt form. Pytheas speaks of an island, Uxisama, which is
alleged to be the island of Ouessant. These identifications are
somewhat hazardous, even though some of the places are mentioned by the geographer Ptolemy: for all we know, the latter may
have attempted to localize names of places ultimately derived from
Pytheas. Pytheas apparently visited the stannaries of Cornwall—
he mentions Belerion (Land's End)—and it is not improbable that
Diodorus' information concerning the route from Ictis to southern
France was derived from him through Timaeus[1]. If Pytheas
sailed eastwards up the Channel to Kent, his otherwise unaccount-
able statement that the latter was some days' sail from *Keltike* is
easily explained. He states that he travelled all over the accessible
parts of Britain, and he would seem to have circumnavigated the
island[2]. We probably owe to him the name Orcas, the northernmost cape in Great Britain (Dunnet Head?).

Most spectacular of all was his report of the remote island of
Thule, which he says was six days sail northward from Britain,
an estimate which favours Thule being 'the island of Scandza'
(*i.e.* Norway), and not one of the Shetlands which are too close.
In view of the mention of the midnight sun, it is not likely that
Pytheas' Thule can be identified with Iceland, as that phenomenon is only visible from one or two points in the extreme north
of that island.

[1] M. Cary, *op. cit.* p. 174.
[2] Pytheas alludes to the British Isles not as Ierne and Albion, but as
Πρεττανικαὶ νῆσοι. This is the earliest Greek form of the word Britain
and it would seem that P-Celts (see vol. ii, p. 33) had invaded this country
by the fourth century, or at all events at a time prior to Pytheas' voyage.

From what has been said above, it is more than probable that the ancients derived the main part of their early knowledge of the Celts from traders and sea-farers, though it is open to doubt if, prior to the time of Pytheas, Greeks were in direct contact with the British Isles.

IV. THE EARLY HOME OF THE CELTIC PEOPLES

The area of differentiation of the Celtic language probably lay in the Upper Danubian region (see vol. II, p. 33). Both archaeological and linguistic evidence testifies to the presence of Celts in that area at an early date, while certain regions in eastern France belong culturally to the Upper Danubian province (Württemberg, etc.)[1]. But did the early Celtic home stretch farther afield?

There is little reason for placing the cradle of the Celtic peoples in Gaul. The origin of the French river-names is against such an assumption. River-names (especially those of the larger streams) are apt to be older than names of towns. In France, many Celtic names of towns are found, very few of rivers; the majority of these last are of pre-Celtic origin. In south-west Germany, Celtic river-names are very common and they also occur, though somewhat less frequently, in north-west Germany. As the Celts seem to have abandoned this latter region at a comparatively early date, the occurrence of Celtic river-names there is not without significance. The evidence of place-names and river-names favours the view that the early home of the Celts lay, for the most part, to the east of the Rhine; and that the greater part of Gaul was not conquered by them until later[2]. How far eastward their territories originally extended, it is not easy to say.

A recent hypothesis[3] deserves special consideration, for it is more comprehensive and coherent than many of those hitherto advanced. The proto-Celts are identified with a people known by their pottery as the zone-beaker[4] people, who inhumed their dead beneath tumuli, and whose territory, at the end of the Stone Age, extended from Central France to Bohemia. From orna-

[1] M. Piroutet, *L'Anthropologie*, XXIX, pp. 444 *sqq. Ibid.* XXX, pp. 78 *sqq.*
[2] The names 'Jura' and 'Doubs' are of Celtic origin. Apart from Alsace-Lorraine, the Franche-Comté and Burgundy seem to be the first regions in France to be occupied by the Celts.
[3] E. Rademacher, *Reallexikon der Vorgesch.* VI, p. 282 *sq.*; *Mannus*, XVIII, 1926, pp. 16 *sqq.*
[4] *I.e.* the late zone-beakers, which were evolved from the West European bell-beakers and the Central German corded ware.

mental features on the bell-beaker ware, the later chip-carving technique (*Kerbschnitt*) was evolved[1]. The development of civilization in the above zone-beaker area advanced practically without interruption until the end of the Bronze Age, when an Alpine people appeared. They brought with them the Urnfield Culture (Hallstatt A), Villanovan forms (destined to have a persistent influence in south-west Germany), the rite of cremation, and the disposal of their dead in large cemeteries of flat graves (or at all events under very low tumuli)[2]. For a time they were dominant over the proto-Celts, but the older population re-asserted itself and finally absorbed its conquerors. Inhumation again became prominent. From this time, once the absorption of the Urnfield Peoples was complete, it is permissible to speak of the population of southern Germany and a large part of France as being Celtic. North of this area, in the Marne district, Belgium, south Holland, the lower Rhine valley and the region to the east of it as far as the Weser, lived a different people, who were only externally affected by the Urnfield Culture and, unlike the majority of their more southerly neighbours, practised cremation. These are regarded as a more backward element which remained proto-Celtic, when the peoples farther to the south had become fully-fledged Celts. In both areas tumulus-burials prevailed. Such, in outline, is Rademacher's theory concerning the early home and pre-history of the Celts.

Although there is much to be said for the theory as a whole, certain points are open to criticism. First, in the light of the distribution of river-names, the original home of the Celts seems to extend too far to the west. On the other hand, a few Celtic mountain-names and river-names do occur in south-west France, the most important of these being Cebennon, the old form of Cevennes (cf. Chevin, the name of a hill in Yorkshire). But these names are very rare, and how far back they take us is hard to say. When these are the names of rivers, they are not those of large streams, such as the Weser and the Rhine (see above, p. 54). In view of this, it is perhaps safer not to identify the proto-Celts with the late zone-beaker peoples, but to regard them as forming an element or elements in the late zone-beaker complex. Second,

[1] The *Kerbschnittkeramik* was the most characteristic ware of the Bronze Age Tumulus Culture (B–D) in south-west Germany. During Hallstatt C this type of ornamentation re-asserted itself.

[2] Iron objects first appear during this period, but they are of such rarity that many authorities allude to Hallstatt A—or the greater part of it—as Bronze Age V or E.

some authorities hold the Urnfield peoples of south-west Germany to be of Illyrian stock. If it is true that *îsarno-*, the primitive Celtic for 'iron,' was borrowed from the Illyrian, it would appear that the Celts and Illyrians were in close contact possibly early in the Iron Age[1]. The second of these objections is not so important as the first, for the nationality of the Urnfield peoples is still an open question, and the Illyrian origin of *îsarno-* is far from being definitely proved.

One fact seems to have been thoroughly established: the continuity of the Lower Rhenish Tumulus Culture. This culture, the result of a fusion between west European, Central-German and purely Nordic elements, developed more or less undisturbed from the end of the Stone Age until towards the close of the Hallstatt Period[2]. Peoples from the Nordic zone (see below, pp. 66 *sqq.*) began to appear in the Lower Rhenish area during the middle Hallstatt phases, and eventually, late in the sixth century, drove the greater part of the older inhabitants to the south and to the west. The period which immediately followed is an obscure one. But the remnants of the Celtic population to the east of the Rhine seem to have mingled with the Teutonic invaders, and from this fusion of Celt and Teuton the Belgic people came into being. There is little evidence for the hypothesis that the language of the Belgae was Germanic. But if the latter spoke some form of Celtic, by Caesar's time at all events, it must at least have shown dialectical differences from that spoken by the Celts (see *B.G.* I, i). During La Tène C, the Belgae began to push westward and, at the end of that phase, succeeded in bringing about the downfall of the four hundred year-old Marne culture. The period *c.* 100–60 B.C. witnessed the gradual penetration of south-eastern Britain by Belgic peoples.

The question of 'Celts' and 'Galatae' is a very disputed one[3]. It has been suggested that the Red Celts conquered the Black Celts, who were the early population, and probably imposed their language upon them (see vol. II, p. 33 *sq.*). If this is true, the Black Celts may not have been Celtic at all. Both from anthropological and linguistic standpoints, it is perhaps safer to dispense with the terms Black and Red Celt: they invite generalizations which, far from simplifying matters, mislead and obscure the true issues.

[1] But see O. Schrader, *Reallexikon der indogerm. Altertumskunde* (2nd ed.), I, p. 235 and G. Kossinna, *Mannus*, VII, 1915, p. 125.

[2] E. Rademacher, *Mannus*, Ergänzungsband, IV, pp. 112 *sqq.*

[3] For the meaning given to 'Galatae' and 'Galatian' see below, p. 57 *sq.*

An examination of the skull-measurements from most of the Culture-groups within the Celtic area reveals the population to have been physically of a very mixed character, and shows that it is impossible to employ such an expression as 'the Celtic race.'

Among the ruling classes buried in the tumuli of Burgundy and Lorraine on the one hand, and the Alaise-Württemberg group on the other, long-headed elements have been detected. The former are orthognathic, the latter prognathic. These elements, which are regarded as intrusive, have been termed proto-Galatian and proto-Germanic respectively[1]. Brachycephalic skulls, however, have been found in both the above groups. The Alaise-Württemberg tumuli often contained the remains of tall individuals. Farther to the east, in Bavaria, brachycephaly seems to have predominated.

The peoples of the Marne culture were a mixed population in which long-headed elements preponderated[2]. Piroutet holds that among the peoples of the Marne culture, there was a Galatian element which came into that region from Normandy shortly before the close of the Hallstatt period, an element which soon grew to be the dominant one[3]. Camille Jullian identifies the Galatae with the Belgae, but some of his arguments are based on a rather too arbitrary interpretation of classical authorities.

The majority of Greek and Roman authors did not clearly distinguish between Celt (in the narrow sense) and Galatian, although among the barbarians who invaded Italy and Greece in the fourth and third centuries B.C., there was a tall, fair element which caught the eye of their southern adversaries and which is mentioned by more than one classical writer. This element many hold to have been Galatian, but in view of the complex physical anthropology of the Celtic-speaking peoples, one should be wary of laying too much weight upon generalizations of this nature[4].

There appears to be no evidence for supposing the Galatae and the Celts to have spoken fundamentally different languages, any more than the Irish and Welsh of later times; indeed, we have little reason to believe the original significance of the terms

[1] M. Piroutet, *L'Anthropologie*, xxx, pp. 69 *sqq.*, a somewhat hazardous identification.

[2] Yet G. Guiart (*Rev. Anthropologique*, 1927) regards the Galatae as being brachycephalic. See the Bibliography.

[3] *L'Anthropologie*, xxix, pp. 240, 242 n., xxx, p. 54.

[4] It is interesting to note, however, that in the Irish Prose Epics the heroes are often described as blonde and tall. But cf. M. Piroutet, *L'Anthropologie*, xxx, p. 62.

'Galatae' and 'Celt' to have been more than northern and southern Celtic-speaking peoples respectively. Diodorus (v, 32), whose account is largely drawn from an earlier source (possibly Posidonius) and Strabo (iv, 189) support this view[1]. Each, doubtless, had its peculiar characteristics, but a merging of the two groups was already taking place at the turn of the sixth and fifth centuries. In some regions it is probable that the Galatae may have asserted themselves at the others' expense. By the fourth and third centuries, this process of fusion seems to have reached a sufficiently advanced state to prevent the classical adversaries of these barbaric invaders of Italy and Greece from clearly distinguishing between the two elements[2]. If Chadwick is right, we find a somewhat analogous case in the Angles and Saxons at the time of their invasion of this country[3].

A passage from Ammianus Marcellinus (xv, 9, 4) remains to be discussed. It is apparently derived from Timagenes who lived in the reign of Augustus. 'The Druids say that a part of the population (of Gaul) was really indigenous to the soil, but that other inhabitants streamed in from the islands on the coast, and from districts beyond the Rhine, having been driven from their old abodes by frequent wars, and occasionally by inroads of the raging sea.' We have here an old native tradition, preserved by a learned priesthood, which as evidence far outweighs the late and largely fictitious Ambigatus story as given in Livy (v, 34, see below, p. 60 sq.). As to the indigenous element, it is not at all unlikely that this was the pre-Celtic population, which had gradually become Celticized, though it is possible that the Druids may have included the Celtic peoples established in eastern France at a comparatively early date under this heading. The reference to the islands on the coast is not easy to explain. Greek writers of the fourth century hint or actually speak of the Celts' proximity to the sea[4]. The reference to part of the inhabitants coming from beyond the Rhine is of great interest, for it shows native tradition to be partly in agreement with conclusions deduced from philological and archaeological evidence: it was mainly from the east of the Rhine that the Celtic-speaking peoples expanded into Gaul.

[1] But see T. Rice Holmes, *Caesar's Conquest of Gaul*[2], p. 311 sq.
[2] In spite of what has been said to the contrary, it is difficult to believe that Polybius used the terms *Keltoi* and *Galatai*, other than as synonyms. The question of P- and Q-Celts and the close affinity between the Celtic and the Italic languages has been dealt with in vol. ii, chap. ii.
[3] *Origin of the English Nation*, chap. iv.
[4] Ephorus (Frag. 132 Jac.); Aristotle, *Nic. Eth.* iii, 9, 7; *Eud. Eth.* iii, 1.

It may be objected that this expansion took place at too remote
a date for it to be remembered by the Druids. While not altogether agreeing with this view, one should remember that a large
migration from the Lower Rhine area to the west and south-west
occurred in the sixth century B.C. (see below, p. 67 *sq.*); the Belgic
invasion of north-east Gaul (also in part from beyond the Rhine)
took place at a still later date; and similar movements occurred in
regions farther to the south. The allusion to Celtic invaders being
driven into Gaul by frequent wars may partly refer to the pressure
upon the Celts caused by the expansion of peoples from the Nordic
zone, whom many authorities regard as Teutonic (see below,
pp. 66 *sqq.*).

V. CELTIC MIGRATIONS

South-western France and the Spanish Peninsula. With
the possible exception of an early invasion of Britain, the first
important movement of the Celtic Migration Period seems to
have proceeded in a south-westerly direction and to have reached
south-west France and the Spanish peninsula in the later part of
the sixth century (see below, p. 67 *sq.*). They probably entered the
latter region through the passes of the western Pyrenees. Our
earliest source for the ethnography of Spain and Portugal is
Avienus' *Ora Maritima*. If the relevant passages are derived
from the Massiliote *Periplus*, Celtic peoples were already settled
in the west and in the highlands of Castile, at all events within
the last quarter of the sixth century (see below, p. 67 *sq.*).

An important contribution has recently been made on the
Celtic invasion of south-west France and the Spanish peninsula[1].
In south-west France we find a group of tumulus-cemeteries extending from the Mediterranean to the Atlantic coasts, especially
on the Ger plateau and the French Pyrenees region. They are not
earlier than the last phase of the Hallstatt period (Reinecke D)
and, in part, probably later. With their *solliferrea*, their peculiar
antennae-hilted iron daggers and certain types of fibulae, they
show marked affinities with a contemporary and somewhat later
culture in Spain, although the burials of this Spanish culture are
not under tumuli. On the other hand, the degenerate types of
Hallstatt pottery yielded by the south-west French group, and,
above all, the burial customs and the structure of the tumuli themselves, bear a most remarkable resemblance to the Hallstatt
Tumulus Culture of the Lower Rhine valley and the regions

[1] E. Rademacher in *Reallexikon der Vorgeschichte*, v, s.vv. Haulzy and
Hügelgräber der französischen Pyrenäengegend. Cf. also Bosch-Gimpera,
Mannus Bibliothek, No. 22, pp. 53 *sqq.*

adjacent to it. Further, Rademacher sees a connecting link between these two groups in the unique and isolated burial-ground at Haulzy (Marne). Déchelette is mistaken in describing the rite in the later graves of this site as inhumation; the burials are cremation burials throughout (cremations under tumuli). The earlier graves (1–69) date, typologically, from the Middle Hallstatt period. The structure of the graves and much of the pottery they contained testify to a migration from the Lower Rhine region. The later graves (70–78) mark the transition from the Late Hallstatt period (D) to La Tène I. They have yielded antennae-hilted daggers which closely resemble a 'post-Hallstatt' Spanish variant of that type of weapon.

These and other phenomena have led Rademacher to believe that, under pressure of peoples expanding from the Nordic area, the Celts in occupation of the north-west German zone moved westward and southward. This pressure began c. 900 B.C., possibly earlier. In the sixth century a great Celtic migration took place from the Lower Rhine region, which, after various vicissitudes, reached south-west France. Here part of the new-comers settled in the districts above mentioned. But the more adventurous elements, crossing the Pyrenees, occupied those regions in the Spanish peninsula of which we have already spoken. Although adopting certain new customs, they remained in contact with their kindred in south-west France, influencing them and being influenced by them in turn. Cut off from the main body of the Celtic world, these 'Spanish' Celts during the fifth and fourth centuries developed what has been termed 'a post-Hallstatt' civilization of their own. This Celtic-Iberian culture is described below in chap. xxiv. It is to be noted that La Tène culture was not well represented in Spain until it had entered upon its later phases.

ITALY. Livy (v, 34) repeats a fairly detailed account of an early Celtic invasion of Italy and the circumstances which led up to it: during the reign of Tarquinius Priscus at Rome, Ambigatus, supreme king of Gaul, found that country to be so over-populated that he summoned his sister's sons Segovesus and Bellovesus; lots were drawn and the former led part of the superfluous population eastward into the Hercynian Forest, while the latter, at the head of a large host, invaded Italy. This is the story, stripped of its details. It has been proved to be a tissue of inaccuracies. Literary and archaeological evidence shows that Livy's dating (c. 600 B.C.) is two centuries too early. With the exception of the Senones, none of the peoples mentioned as comprising Bellovesus' host ever appear to have settled in Italy—the Senones are mentioned in the next chapter as being the *last* band of Celts to settle in that peninsula! Further, we have no evidence for a central authority being established among the Celts at so early a date; while the information given by Livy in this chapter on the political geography of the Celtic world is derived from Caesar's Gallic War and in no way represents the ethnography of Gaul in the fourth—far less the sixth—century B.C. Finally, some scholars regard the names of the principal characters in this chapter as fictitious. It is clear, therefore, that the story told by Livy in practically all its details is historically worthless. We shall see later whether there is a kernel of truth embedded in this mass of anachronisms.

It is difficult to decide by what pass or passes the earlier Celtic invaders of Italy crossed the Alps. Livy, whom as far as details are concerned we have found to be untrustworthy, makes the first invaders come by way of Mont Genèvre in the western Alps[1]. But archaeological finds and references from other classical authors show that the regions to the west of that pass—in fact most of south-eastern Gaul—were Ligurian territory until the third century (see above, p. 49), while the Celtic graves in the western districts of Upper Italy date from the *later* phases of the La Tène period. In view of this we are probably justified in ruling out all the passes of the western Alps from the Col di Tenda to the Little St Bernard, at least so far as the earliest Celtic invasion was concerned.

Before inquiring into the claims of other passes, mention must be made of climatic conditions. In the Early Iron Age, a deterioration of climate set in which considerably affected the higher Alpine passes (those over 6500 ft. high); the glaciers increased and the forest level subsided. Hallstatt and La Tène pass-finds are much rarer than those of the Bronze Age. The two worst periods in this phase of cold wet weather seem to have been *c.* 850 and 500–350 or 300 B.C. The Celtic invasion of Italy took place *c.* 400–390, and thus falls into the second of these two periods.

Livy speaks of some of the early invaders crossing the Great St Bernard[2]. Although 8111 ft. high, this pass does not, like other passes of an altitude over 6500 ft., appear to have been affected by the ravages of glaciers. Finds of the La Tène period have come to light on the Great St Bernard, but they belong to the later phases. This tallies well with a passage in Polybius

---

[1] v, 34 reading, 'ipsi per Taurinos saltus ⟨uallem⟩que Duriae transcenderunt' (Madvig), *i.e.* by Mont Genèvre (6083 ft.) and the valley of the Dora Riparia.

[2] *Ibid.* 35, 'Poenino deinde Boii Lingonesque transgressi.'

(II, 22 *sq*.). He tells us that the Gaesati (a caste of Celtic warriors or mercenaries) (see p. 811), lived 'about the Alps and on the Rhône,' and that they crossed those mountains in 225 B.C. and fought with the Cisalpine Celts against the Romans (p. 812). The phrase 'about the Alps and on the Rhône' points to their being at that time settled in the Swiss canton of Wallis, a region in which finds of the La Tène period occur not infrequently. If they did come from Wallis, it is probable that they crossed the Great St Bernard. But evidence for this pass being traversed by the *earlier* Celtic invaders is at present lacking. There are no signs of any early case of crossing the St Gotthard (6936 ft.).

Whether the Bernardino (6769 ft.) was of importance in this respect cannot be determined. A number of cemeteries occur in the Ticino and Mesocco valleys, dating from the La Tène and ostensibly from the Hallstatt periods. These districts were extremely conservative, different types occurring in the same grave which in other districts would be four centuries apart. In view of this, it is impossible to say whether the graves which are *typologically* of an Early or Middle La Tène character belong *chronologically* to these periods. Reinecke is inclined to assign a late date to the whole group. Until the tangled chronology of these cemeteries has been unravelled, it is difficult to tell whether the earliest invaders crossed this pass or not.

We have little evidence for the routes from Como over the Splügen (6946 ft.) and Julier (7504 ft.) passes being used in the Early Iron Ages. The finds, in this area, are far less numerous than in the Ticino-Bernardino district, and the assumption is that the routes in question were less frequented, possibly on account of their being over 6500 ft. high and consequently more liable to be affected by the deterioration in the climate which is mentioned above.

The chief pass left for discussion is the Brenner, for it is hardly likely that the first Celtic hosts to invade Italy came by a more eastern route. One of the main trade-routes linking Italy with northern Europe went over this pass. It is of a sufficiently low altitude (4495 ft.) to have been unaffected by the above-mentioned change in climate. Some authorities hold that the close connection during La Tène A between Upper Italy and east Bavaria and Bohemia suggests that the Celtic invasion of Italy came from the Upper Danubian region rather than from France. If so, the normal route would have lain through the Tyrol, over the Brenner and down the Adige. Others contend that the dearth of pure Celtic La Tène finds in the Tyrol points to the first invaders not having come by that pass. But this may only mean that their transit through the Tyrol was a rapid one[1]. Reinecke, moreover, sees a hint of a catastrophe having taken place in the Tyrolean area *c.* 400 B.C.: the sequence of bronze hoards comes to an abrupt end, just at the time when the Celts first descended upon Italy. The fact that Venetia was not conquered by the Celts can hardly be used as evidence against their having come by this route: the point at which it debouched upon the Upper Italian plain barely touched the south-western corner of Venetia, the latter being protected from inroads from the north-west by the Alps. Nevertheless, strong Celtic influences made themselves felt at Este from *c.* 400 B.C. onwards, and this fact favours the assumption that the Celts and their Atestine neighbours were in close contact with each other from the time of the arrival of the former peoples in Italy. Finally—perhaps the most important testimony in favour of the Brenner—the earliest Celtic graves (phase B) of Upper Italy are confined to the eastern half of that region.

Of the four passes known to Polybius (*ap.* Strabo, IV, 208) three lie in the west Alpine zone. Although these may have been important so far as local trade was concerned, we have seen that the evidence is against the earlier invaders having come from this direction. The fourth many identify with the Brenner.

Let us turn once more to Livy. It has been recently suggested[2] that the Earliest La Tène population of Bohemia and east Bavaria, etc., was not of Celtic but of the old Illyrian stock, and that the Celts first appeared in those regions at the beginning of phase B. Others hold that the Celts were already in the Hausrück area by the fifth century. Whichever view is adopted, there is every reason to suppose that a change of population took place in east Bavaria, Bohemia and Moravia at the beginning of phase B (400 B.C., or possibly a few years earlier). The new-comers, the people of the flat-grave inhumation cemeteries, were indubitably Celtic and seem to have come from the west. If the latter surmise is correct— seeing that Bohemia and the regions to the east and west thereof lay in the Hercynian area—there is a certain amount of truth in Livy's account; two important Celtic migrations occurred about the same time: one moved eastward into the Hercynian region (Segovesus), the other southward into Italy (Bellovesus). We might argue from the fact that a Celtic people called the Boii

---

[1] Cf. F. von Duhn, *Reallexikon der Vorgeschichte*, VI, p. 292.

[2] O. Menghin, *Einführung in die Urgeschichte Böhmens und Mährens*, p. 97 *sq.*; see also Reinecke, *Bayerischer Vorgeschichtsfreund*, 1925, p. 53.

dwelt both in Bohemia and the Bologna region that these movements to the east and to the south branched out from a common
centre. Where that centre lay, it is hard to determine. Can it
have been Gaul? We must remember that in Livy's day the
centre of gravity among the continental Celts lay in that province,
but at an earlier time it was farther to the east. We know that a
westward drift of Celtic peoples into certain regions in Gaul
happened during the later Hallstatt and earliest La Tène
phases. Is it likely, then, that they retraced their steps so soon?
Perhaps we have a hint of the truth in Appian (*Celt.* 1, 2), who
tells us that a great part of the Celtic invaders of Italy came from
the Rhine.

THE SOUTH-EASTWARD EXPANSION. Although later in time than
the migrations of which we have just been speaking, the south-
eastward movement of the Celts was far greater in extension, for
its ultimate waves spread beyond Europe into Asia Minor. The
first recorded appearance of Celts in Greece was in 369–8 B.C.,
when Dionysius I sent Celtic and Iberian mercenaries to aid his
Lacedaemonian allies against the Boeotians in the Peloponnese
(vol. VI, p. 93). If we can trust Justin (xx, 5), Dionysius first came
in contact with the Celts about twenty years earlier: when fighting
against the Locrians and Crotonians in southern Italy, an embassy
came to him from the Celts who had shortly before sacked Rome
offering to fight for him or to harass his enemies in the rear
(vol. VI, p. 130). In this connection it should be noted that Celtic
graves of the fourth century have been found as far south as Apulia[1].

In 335 B.C., when Alexander the Great made his expedition
against the Triballi—then in Bulgaria—and their neighbours,
the Illyrians, he received deputations from all the Danubian
peoples. It was on this expedition that the embassy came to him
from the Celts of the Adriatic[2]. Unfortunately more precise indications of their whereabouts are lacking. Alexander's expedition against the Triballi and the Illyrians was doubtless undertaken to prevent a repetition of the Triballian irruption of 376–5.
From early in the fourth century, there had been an eastward drift
of Illyrian and other tribes like the Triballi. This drift has been
attributed to the upheaval caused by the arrival of the Celts in
the region of the Save and the Middle Danube, and to their penetration into the lands between the Dinaric Alps and the sea-board
from Istria to the river Narenta[3]. It was possibly from the latter

[1] J. Naue, *Prähist. Blätter*, x, 1898, pp. 49 *sqq.*
[2] Arrian, *Anab.* 1, 4, 6; Strabo, VII, p. 301, see above, vol. VI, p. 355.
[3] G. Zippel, *Die römische Herrschaft in Illyrien*, pp. 34 *sqq.*

region that the Celts came who visited Alexander in 335. But the Celts did not take root in these Illyrian regions[1]: their penetration was purely of a warlike nature, and the native elements soon re-asserted themselves.

Archaeological evidence hardly supports the view that the Celtic occupation of the Middle Danube-Save region happened early in the fourth century B.C. Objects from the counties of Túrócz and Borsód, and the earliest finds from Munkacz, show that roughly about 400 B.C. the Celts had spread along the Upper Danube and beyond into the Upper Tisza (Theiss) area. The objects from Silivaş are cited as evidence for the advance of Celtic bands up the Maros into Transylvania as early as that date[2]. Otherwise, very few objects of a La Tène B character have come to light in Transylvania. Indeed, apart from the finds mentioned above, there appear to be hardly any La Tène sites in this eastern area earlier than phase C, that is to say prior to c. 300 B.C. In the present state of our knowledge, while not denying that Celtic raids happened in Illyria, Pannonia and Dacia during the fourth century or that isolated Celtic communities may have been dotted about here and there, it seems that the eastward drift of Illyrians and Thracians was mainly due to pressure from fugitive peoples, dispossessed of their lands by the Celts, rather than to immediate contact with the Celts themselves. Judging from the finds, it was not till the Middle La Tène period (c. 300–100 B.C.) that the area between the Danube and the Tisza together with the regions to the west and south of it became really Celticized. Dacia, too, began to be fundamentally affected by Celtic culture about this time; and, finally, it was during this phase, in 279 B.C., that the Celtic hosts first appeared in Macedonia and then turned south and attacked Delphi[3]. They were beaten off and soon after suffered defeat and dispersed. Some settled in Asia Minor, some in the Thraco-Illyrian area, while others are reputed to have returned to their old home, see below, pp. 101 sqq.

[1] V. Pârvan in Dacia, I, 1924, p. 46 sq.
[2] V. Pârvan, op. cit. p. 47.
[3] Thanks to their raid on the great Greek sanctuary and their settlement in Asia Minor, we have additional evidence for the physical appearance of the Celts in the Delphic and Pergamene groups of sculpture.

VI. CAUSES OF CELTIC MIGRATIONS

The Celtic migrations which have been described above were doubtless due to more than one cause. Justin (xx, 5, 7) ascribes the invasion of Italy to the quarrels of the Celts among themselves. This appears to be connected with the theory of over-population, referred to in the Ambigatus legend (p. 60). But the over-population theory, though important if applied locally, is apt to be exaggerated. It is far more probable that there was a large warlike element that preferred living by plunder to a peaceful and industrious existence. We find this too among the Teutonic peoples of later times in an even more marked degree, for the latter had little inclination to till the soil, whereas the Celts even during La Tène I (Déchelette) practised agriculture extensively.

The attractions of the south proved a great magnet to these warriors bent on adventure and plunder. But the chief cause was apparently an external one: the pressure upon the Celts of Teutonic peoples. When Caesar arrived in Gaul in 58 B.C., he found that a large body of Teutonic and other invaders had crossed the Rhine in the region of Mainz and Worms and were at war with certain sections of the Gaulish community; a few years later he drove back the Usipetes and Tencteri who had crossed the Lower Rhine and invaded Gaul. Caesar's conquests put a stop to this encroachment upon Gaulish territory of peoples from beyond the Rhine. But there is reason to believe that a process of expansion of elements from this quarter at the expense of the Celtic peoples had a long history behind it.

In southern Sweden and Denmark, at all events from the start of the second phase of the Montelian Bronze Age (c. 1500 B.C.), we find a more or less 'self-contained' and indisputably 'continuous' culture, which, period by period, as the Bronze Age progressed, advanced into the north German area. For this people and their culture the neutral term 'Nordic' is here employed. There is, however, no archaeological evidence in favour of an invasion of the Nordic zone by a people who brought with them the Teutonic language subsequent to 1500 B.C.: indeed from that date, if not before, the evidence all points to the movements of peoples issuing *from* that zone and not entering *into* it.

Three stages have recently been distinguished in which the peoples of this Nordic culture encroached upon the Lower

Rhenish area and north-west Germany[1]: c. 900–800 B.C. they advanced to the west of the Teutoburger Wald and occupied the valley of the Upper Lippe; c. 800–700 they made themselves masters of the right bank of the Rhine as far as the Duisburg region, while, not later than c. 500 B.C., they had not only advanced south to the Siebengebirge but had crossed the Lower Rhine and the Maas and driven the Celts out of that area. A good deal depends upon the chronology of the Harpstedt culture which expanded from the Ems-Weser district to the Rhine and beyond[2]. It is one of the leading features of these Nordic invaders. The influence of this culture upon the Lower Rhenish pottery dating from the transition between Hallstatt C and D (shortly before and after 600 B.C.) is very marked. But it probably originated as early as c. 900 B.C.

There is little reason to doubt that this pressure from the north brought about the downfall of the Lower Rhenish Tumulus Culture. The second of these three stages seems to have caused some displacement in the population of the latter area. At all events, the earlier graves at Haulzy (Middle Hallstatt), both in their structure and the pottery which they contain, indicate a movement from that region. But Haulzy is an isolated phenomenon and these movements did not assume serious proportions until later. In the later graves at Haulzy (Late Hallstatt and La Tène I) and in the La Tène I burials of the Marne culture, we find pottery typical of the Late Hallstatt period in the Lower Rhine region. Just at the time when these vessels first appear in France (Haulzy), the Tumulus Culture in the regions from the Cologne district northward came to an abrupt end, i.e. shortly before the beginning of the La Tène period. The migration from the Lower Rhine into north-east France took place, therefore, a little before 500 B.C. Part of these invaders settled in Champagne, where almost at once they were merged with other elements (from Normandy and, possibly, from the true Celtic area to the south-east); from this fusion, crossed with the Greek influence from southern France, the Marne culture arose. Other elements from the Lower Rhenish area passed on into south-west France, some of them advancing yet farther afield into the Spanish penin-

---

[1] E. Rademacher, *Mannus*, Ergänzungsband, IV, pp. 129 *sqq.* and *Reallexikon der Vorgeschichte*, s.v. Niederrheinische Hügelgräber.

[2] See Stampfuss (*Mannus*, 1925, XVII, pp. 287 *sqq.*) who gives earlier dating for these Nordic movements than Rademacher. But in view of his latest contribution (*Mannus*, Ergänzungsband, V, pp. 50 *sqq.*) it is not altogether clear how far his chronology for this culture should be lowered.

sula. If they abandoned their ancient homes shortly before 500 B.C., their transit through north-eastern and central France must have been rapid indeed, for they seem to have reached Spain before the sixth century had come to a close. But on the analogy of the Vandal invasion of A.D. 406/9, this is by no means improbable. At all events, the Celtic migration into south-western France and the Spanish peninsula was ultimately due to Nordic pressure upon the Lower Rhine.

But part of the Lower Rhine tumulus-peoples were driven southward up the valley of that river. This movement took place at the same time as the above migration to the south-west. It has recently been shown that as the numbers of the population in the Lippe region declined (possibly c. 800 B.C.) there was a marked increase in the population of the Cologne area, while the sudden decrease in the population of the Cologne area which happened at the end of the Hallstatt period was accompanied by corresponding increase in the highlands of Eifel, Hunsrück and Taunus. This was maintained in the latter regions till the advent of the Teutonic peoples in the Middle La Tène period. Farther to the south, the Teutonic menace was mainly felt in La Tène D[1].

The Celts erected fortresses to stem the tide of invasion. The most important of these was the Odilienberg (near Strasbourg), its walls, some six miles long, composed of large blocks of stone joined by oak tenons, enclosing an area of over two hundred acres. As early as the second century B.C. we find Celtic houses in south-west Germany fortified with ramparts—another sign of the turbulence of the times.

But the regions further north seem to have lain deserted for some time. No Celtic finds of the La Tène period have been found north-east of a line from Andernach to Aachen. 'Teutonic finds of an Early La Tène character' occur to the east of the Rhine in the Cologne area, but to the west, they are mainly confined to the left bank of that river. The greater part of Belgium— apart from Eygenbilsen and a few other sites—would almost appear to have been a species of no-man's-land during most of the La Tène period. But this may be due to the unobtrusive character of the graves, poor in tomb-furniture and without tumuli, only a few of which have as yet come to light[2]. In the regions to the east of the Lower Rhine, and perhaps in Belgium too, the Nordic invaders mingled with the remnants of the older population, and from this intermingling the genesis of the Belgic peoples took place (see above, p. 56).

[1] *Mannus*, Ergänzungsband, IV, p. 137 *sq.*   [2] Ebert, *Reallexikon*, I, p. 405.

Such in brief was the march of events on the western boundary of the Celtic and Nordic zones. Let us now turn to the southern frontier of these two provinces which in the Iron Age lay in Central Germany.

It is held by Kossinna that the Harz district, and the region to the east thereof as far as the confluence of the Mulde with the Elbe, was occupied during the Middle and Late Bronze Age by various elements, two of which were Celtic and Teutonic (Nordic), the latter only appearing towards the end of period V[1]. In the Earlier Iron Age (Montelius' Bronze Age VI) these Nordic elements become stronger, and the stone-cist, a form of grave so characteristic of the north, appears. The rite, of course, is cremation. But about 600 B.C. we find a mysterious group of in-humation graves, comparatively richly furnished with objects of adornment: torcs, armlets, ear-rings, pins, girdle-mounts and amber beads. These some regard as evidence for a Celtic invasion; indeed, they seem to have come from districts where the Mehren culture prevailed, southern Eifel and Hunsrück, which were then presumably Celtic. This group of graves occurs both to the north and south of the Harz mountains and stretches as far east as the Mulde region, being best represented in the Halle district. Kossinna regards it as evidence for an eastward thrust of the Celts, at the expense of the peoples of the Nordic group (his *Germanen*). In this region, then, we have two cultures at this period, the Nordic and the Celtic, but they do not seem to have influenced each other.

In the fourth century, we find Celtic peoples established to the north of the Central German mountain-range in Thuringia, Saxony, Upper and Middle Silesia to the south of the Oder. This and the century preceding it were a troubled period for the latter province: not only was it invaded by Celtic peoples from the south and subjected to inroads of Scythians from the east, but about 500 B.C. (or possibly slightly earlier) an invasion from the north took place. The new-comers were the peoples of the Face-Urn and Stone-Cist culture which originated in the region to the west of Danzig about 800–700 B.C., and spread south through Posen into Middle and Lower Silesia. Its peoples are generally regarded as the first Teutons to have invaded the latter province. Owing, doubtless, to the turbulence of the times, the old urnfield civili-zation of Silesia came to a sudden end. Whether the Face-Urn culture lasted in this region later than 300 B.C. is disputed. If it did not, we are forced to admit that Silesia, a remarkably fertile

[1] *Ursprung und Verbreitung der Germanen*, p. 37 *sq.*

region, remained practically unpeopled for about two centuries:
for the Early La Tène culture of Middle and Upper Silesia disappears and the succeeding phase (C) is only sparsely represented.
Reinecke[1] regards the end of the Early La Tène culture in Silesia
as being due to Teutonic pressure and observes that the same
process probably took place in Saxony also. Farther west, the
Celtic population, settled in the Thuringian area during La Tène
B, did not long survive the fourth century: during the third
century, the Teutonic peoples conquered practically all of this
region and beat the Celts back to their last great stronghold, the
Steinsburg, on the Kleiner Gleichberg (near Römhild) which, in
a sense, may be regarded as the key position to southern Germany.
Farther east, about 200 B.C., a fresh Teutonic invasion poured
through the rocky mountain-gorge of the Elbe into northern
Bohemia, the new-comers obtaining a firm footing in the land of
the Boii. This is shown by certain grave-finds at Bodenbach on
the Elbe, which, although revealing a civilization identical with
a contemporary culture to the north of the Erzgebirge, differ
from those of the Middle La Tène inhumation cemeteries of the
Boii[2].

It seems probable, therefore, that the evacuation by the Celts
of the territories to the north of the Central German mountains
happened c. 300 B.C. and was due to pressure from the southward-
advancing Teutons. Indeed, it is not inconceivable that the Celtic
invasion of Greece in 279 B.C. may have been ultimately connected with this pressure. If the latter conjecture prove correct,
it would be an argument in favour of not regarding the Celtic
expansion into Thrace, Macedonia and the Peloponnese as a later
episode of the movement that resulted in the Celtic conquest of
Cisalpine Gaul.

The gradual penetration of south-eastern Britain by the Belgae
(Aylesford culture) which took place c. 100–60 B.C. may partly
have been due to the expansion of the Teutonic peoples on the
continent. But generally speaking, there were few Celtic migrations on a great scale in this later period. The way to the south was
blocked by the Romans who established themselves in southern
Gaul in 121 B.C., and Teutonic aggression prevented movements
to the east. A centripetal tendency asserted itself among the
different Celtic peoples which culminated in the development of
towns and town life. This is also true of the Celtic area east of the

[1] *Wiener Prähistorische Zeitschrift*, 1915, p. 25 *sq.*
[2] *Ibid.* pp. 15 *sqq.* The funeral rite in the Teutonic graves at Bodenbach
was cremation.

Rhine, where Teuton and Roman were soon to prove the upper and nether millstones. By the Late La Tène period (D) the Celts were no longer merely a country people but a town-folk as well. This development of town-life was the greatest contribution toward civilization in western and central Europe during the pre-Roman Iron Ages, and it also explains why the culture of the Late La Tène period exhibits a greater homogeneity than that of the phases which preceded it.

It remains to speak of the influence of climate. The dry warm climate of the Bronze Age was succeeded by a moist cool phase known as the sub-Atlantic Period. Correlations of the geological, botanic and other data with archaeological finds have shown that this phase began c. 850 B.C. It was ushered in by a sudden increase in the rainfall; and c. 500 B.C., a second rainfall maximum was reached. Generally speaking, the peoples of the Nordic culture-province, dwelling as they did in the more maritime regions, were to a greater extent affected than the Celts. It is tempting, therefore, to regard this climate-change as one of the factors which caused the peoples of the Nordic province to expand at the expense of their Celtic neighbours, and it was largely due to this expansion that the Celtic migrations began.

VII. THE LIFE AND CHARACTER OF THE CELTS

Our chief classical authorities for the mode of life and character of the Celts are for the most part late, but it is evident that they drew much of their information from earlier sources that have perished[1].

Judged by their art and their material culture, the Celts, though a barbaric people, attained a relatively high standard of civilization. The same may be said for certain less material aspects of their life. The first mention of Druids is not earlier than about 200 B.C., although Druids were no doubt in existence before that time[2]. By the middle of the first century B.C., they had developed into a highly organized priesthood, and were men of considerable learning, with a knowledge of writing. Poetry was cultivated by the Celtic peoples, though the poems of the continental Celts have not survived. They were probably never committed to writing, but we know them to have been partly didactic

[1] The most detailed accounts are in Diodorus v, 25–32, Strabo, iv and Ammianus Marcellinus, xv, 9–12.

[2] For an account of the Druids see T. D. Kendrick, *The Druids*, p. 74 *sq.*, and below, vol. ix.

and mythological, partly heroic and panegyric. Their religion was polytheistic. Strabo tells us that they held the soul and the world to be indestructible, but that 'fire and water will one day prevail.' There is a striking parallel to the last statement in the Norse doctrine of Ragnarök. It is hard to say whether their belief in metempsychosis was an old one. Some would trace it to Pythagorean influence derived from contact with the Greek colonists in southern France[1]. Attempts have been made to connect the doctrine of metempsychosis among the Celts with the introduction of the rite of cremation—-a rather difficult thesis to maintain. At all events, the rich tomb-furniture in such burials as the earliest La Tène graves of the Middle Rhine area would indicate a belief that the after-life was merely a prolongation of this life, that the chieftains who lie buried beneath those barrows thought that they would

> fight on, fare ever
> There as here.

Our information concerning government and political organization among the Celts earlier than the first century B.C. is mainly confined to literary evidence and is very scanty. We know that a kingly government prevailed among certain peoples, but we cannot say for certain whether kingship was universal or not. From Polybius (II, 21) it would seem that a dual kingship existed among the Cisalpine Boii c. 236 B.C. Whether this is also true for the Gaesati we cannot tell, for the latter seem to have been a conglomeration of mercenaries rather than a definite people. In an age of national migrations the existence of the comitatus— the band of retainers attached to the person of the chief or king— is not to be wondered at: the chief's comitatus in a migrating people formed the nucleus of the new kingdom. The existence of this institution in this period is attested by Polybius (II, 17). We have no evidence for the existence of a central political authority among the Celts; though circumstances or an ambitious king may have brought about alliances between various peoples, such unions were ephemeral. The sense of nationality was not highly developed among the Celts of our period, although Cisalpine Gauls recognized that there was some sort of kinship between them and their Transalpine brethren. Grave-finds in the Celtic area show that, as early as the Hallstatt period, there was a sharp division between the ruling classes and the lower orders, while the Marne chariot-burials and the 'Chieftains'

---

[1] But see Kendrick, *op. cit.* p. 108 *sq.*

Graves' would indicate that, although these chieftains or kings may not have ruled over very extensive territories, they were possessed of considerable wealth. The cessation of the migrations and the development of town-life no doubt led to considerable changes in the political organization.

In warfare, the Celts were noted for their cavalry[1], but they also had large numbers of foot soldiers. The latter are thought to have been drawn from the lower classes and from the subject population. Chariots were also used in warfare, but, as cavalry fighting developed among the continental Celts, they seem to have gone out of fashion. In the British Isles the use of the chariot survived later than on the continent. The chief weapons were the sword and spear; during the Middle La Tène period, the length of the swords rendered them cumbersome and they appear to have been so badly tempered that after a blow they had frequently to be straightened under the foot. Apart from the shield, defensive armour seems only to have been worn by the leaders, indeed the Celtic warrior frequently went naked into battle. Once the novelty of their appearance, their huge stature, strange cries and weapons had ceased to strike terror into their adversaries, the Celts were no match for the trained armies of the Greeks and Romans, though they retained their value as mercenaries.

Prior to the Late La Tène period, stone was not used in domestic architecture. The houses consisted of a single building or a group of buildings; their ground-plans were either round or rectangular. The art of fortification was highly developed, witness the *murus gallicus*, built of stone courses and wooden beams and the structure of the walls on the Odilienberg[2] (see above, p. 68). Although the Celts were great agriculturalists, during the La Tène period they contributed greatly to the advance of industry, which developed further with the rise of towns and town-life in phase D.

All the evidence tends to show that the Celts reached a high level of culture in the La Tène period; and yet, in some respects, they were mere savages. They indulged in head-hunting, in the slaughter of wives, concubines and male dependants at funerals, and they practised human sacrifices. They had a passion for wine; to judge by what Diodorus tells us, their table-manners were disgusting. They had a marked liking for flashy clothes, and for

[1] For the cavalry formation known as *trimarkisia*, see Pausanias x. 19, 11.
[2] A type of structure derived from the Greeks.

bizarre fashions in hair-dressing[1]. We know little concerning the position of women among the Celtic peoples. They appear to have been strong, handsome and ferocious; and were inclined to dominate their husbands. Strabo tells us that 'the labours of the two sexes are distributed in a manner the reverse of what they are with us, but this is a common thing among very many other barbarians.'

The ancients have much to say concerning the character of the Celts. They were given to boasting, prone to flattery, quick to learn. They were capricious but devoid of malice, fond of money but extraordinarily hospitable, great fighters but easily defeated by strategy, truculent and fearless but unable to bear hunger or exposure. They were extraordinarily susceptible to the charms of poetry and from their works we know them to have been artists of a high order. Half civilized, half savage, they lived masterful, passionate lives in an atmosphere utterly remote from what literary men of to-day term the Celtic twilight.

[1] Trews (bracae) were worn by the men, a form of clothing apparently derived from the Teutonic peoples and ultimately of Eastern origin. The introduction of trews among the Teutonic and Celtic peoples is probably to be connected with horse-riding.

CHAPTER III

THE NEW HELLENISTIC KINGDOMS

I. THE YEARS AFTER IPSUS

SHORTLY before the battle of Ipsus (see vol. VI, p. 504) Diodorus' narrative, largely based on Hieronymus, breaks off, and for the eighty years between 301 B.C. and the formal commencement of Polybius' history in 221 no continuous account remains; and large parts of the story have to be reconstructed from inscriptions and from surviving fragments of literary material, often of dubious value. Chronology in particular, prior to Polybius, is an ever-present difficulty, except when an event can be dated by the Delian archons or the eponymous magistrates of Miletus, whose years and succession are certain, or by that great invention the Seleucid Era, which was fortunately used at Babylon[1]; some of the Athenian archon-list is conjectural, scarcely any Delphic archon can be satisfactorily dated, and the Egyptian chronological material is difficult to interpret precisely. A solid deposit of fact is slowly being built up beneath the ebb and flow of conflicting discussion; but it seems proper to warn the reader that this chapter, and more especially chapters VI and XXII, contain of necessity much which can only claim to represent what seems the most probable view at the time of writing.

With Antigonus' death the new kingdoms began to take shape. Cassander's renunciation of possessions in Asia was to

Note. Contemporary historians for the period covered by this chapter were abundant, but have all perished except a few fragments, though Hieronymus' influence probably helped to keep later tradition in a sound path. Of the extant secondary sources, Plutarch's *Lives* of Demetrius (Hieronymus, Duris, and other material) and of Pyrrhus (draws on Hieronymus and Phylarchus amongst others in the Greek part) supply some sort of narrative until Demetrius' death; Justin XVI, XVII, XXIV, and XXV, though quite untrustworthy over details, provide the broken outline of a story throughout; Pausanias in book X gives the Gallic invasion of Greece from a good source overlaid with accretions; Memnon (Nymphis) tells the story of Heraclea Pontica. The rest has to be put together from inscriptions, here numerous and valuable, coins, and literary fragments or notices, here tolerably plentiful; for these see the Bibliography. Genealogical tables of the Hellenistic dynasties will be found at the end of the volume.

[1] At Babylon it ran from 1 Nisan (March–April) 311, in Syria from October 312.

determine the future of Macedonia as again a purely European state. In the partition Lysimachus nominally secured all Asia Minor north of the Taurus, including Cappadocia (for Cassander would certainly not have surrendered his claim on that province to anyone else); Pontus and Bithynia were however independent kingdoms, and many Greek cities still held to Demetrius. South of the Taurus Pleistarchus' kingdom, with its capital at Heraclea on Latmus, renamed Pleistarchea, whose astonishing fortifications have now been traced, was to be only a temporary accident. Seleucus nominally obtained Syria and Mesopotamia; his vast empire stretched in theory from the Hindu Kush and the Jaxartes to the Mediterranean, though Tyre and Sidon remained possessions of Demetrius; he demolished Antigoneia on the Orontes, and built himself a new capital near it, Antioch, named after his father, to mark his return to Aegean politics. Ptolemy, who had not fought at Ipsus, received no share of Antigonus' kingdom; Cassander was hardly his friend, and Cassander's hand can be traced in the assignment of Syria to Seleucus as clearly as in that of Cappadocia to Lysimachus. But during the campaign Ptolemy had occupied Syria south of Damascus and the Lebanon, and Seleucus, who never forgot that he owed Ptolemy both life and fortune, did not insist on its retrocession; but he preserved his claim (pp. 700 *sqq.*).

Demetrius had escaped from Ipsus to Ephesus with 9000 men. Except for various coastal cities in Ionia, Caria, and Phoenicia, he had lost Asia; but he was still supreme at sea, he held Cyprus and the Aegean islands, and was still President of his powerful Hellenic League. He had left Deidameia and part of his fleet and treasure at Athens; from there, lord of Greece and the sea, he hoped to retrieve his fortunes. But his friends in Athens had been overthrown after Ipsus, and envoys from the new government met him in the Cyclades; they restored to him his wife, ships, and money, but explained that to himself their gates were closed. It was a harder blow to Demetrius even than Ipsus; it was the end of his illusions about Greece; all thought of a union of hearts was now dead. He landed at Corinth and found the Hellenic League in ruins; most of the cities not held by his garrisons had repudiated him; that he retained part of the Peloponnese shows that even in 302 he had not trusted entirely to Greek good-will. Cassander possibly helped to break up the League, for during the Ipsus campaign he had invaded Peloponnese; but after a failure before Argos he was apparently recalled by events on the Adriatic, and in attempting to reduce Corcyra, which had been seized by the Spartan Cleonymus during his campaign in Italy, he was defeated by Agathocles of Syracuse, who annexed the island (p. 634).

Demetrius was now little but a sea-king; but he still had friends in Asia, where the Ionian League was maintaining his cause against one Hieron, who had seized Priene as a tyrant in Lysimachus' interest. Between Lysimachus and Demetrius there existed an irreconcilable personal hatred, of which the cause is unknown; Demetrius shipped some mercenaries and sailed to the Dardanelles, to help Ionia and take revenge on Lysimachus. Nothing is known of this war, except that Lysimachus failed to secure Ionia; but in 299 relief came to Demetrius unexpectedly. The victors of Ipsus were already quarrelling; Ptolemy, to safeguard himself against Seleucus, approached Cassander and Lysimachus; Cassander's son Alexander married Lysandra, daughter of Ptolemy and Eurydice, and Lysimachus married Arsinoe, daughter of Ptolemy and Berenice, and sent his Persian wife Amestris away to Heraclea, which he restored to her as compensation; there this remarkable woman made herself a principality, including Tios and Cieros, and founded Amastris. Seleucus saw himself isolated, and offered Demetrius his alliance; he married Stratonice, daughter of Demetrius and Phila, and reconciled him to Ptolemy, who betrothed to him his and Eurydice's daughter Ptolemais. Phila was still alive, though Deidameia was dead; but Demetrius, like Seleucus and Pyrrhus, claimed the old right to two legitimate queens at once, which the other Successors abandoned. He sent Pyrrhus to Egypt as his hostage, together with Deidameia's son Alexander, who lived and died there[1]; but he did not marry Ptolemais, for Ptolemy soon became his enemy again. Pyrrhus then abandoned Demetrius, joined Ptolemy, and married Berenice's daughter Antigone; and Ptolemy took a belated revenge upon Cassander for the Ipsus settlement by restoring Pyrrhus to his kingdom after Cassander's death. Meanwhile Seleucus began to court Demetrius' cities. He had already restored to Miletus the temple statue of Didyma, carried off by the Persians, and he and his wife Apama now encouraged the Milesians to begin rebuilding the temple, for which he and his son Antiochus later sent large gifts, while Antiochus undertook to construct a market hall in Miletus, now excavated[2], whose revenues should go toward the rebuilding. A joint embassy also announced the alliance of Seleucus and Demetrius at Ephesus,

---

[1] On Alexander see E. W. Webster, *C.P.* XVII, 1922, p. 357.
[2] Th. Wiegand, *Milet* I, vii, pp. 31 *sqq.*

and doubtless elsewhere. Demetrius on his side, with Seleucus' privity, attacked Pleistarchus and drove him from his kingdom.

The shifting policies of the Successors since 301, all afraid of each other and unwilling to commit themselves too far, were of advantage to Athens. There both the extreme parties had suffered; many of Cassander's friends, the thorough-going oligarchs, were in exile, while of the democrats Stratocles' following was discredited and his opponent Demochares was in exile also. On Stratocles' downfall after Ipsus a true centre party took shape, composed of the well-to-do of both types, moderate oligarchs and democrats, and came into power; its leaders were Phaedrus of Sphettus, the moderate son of a Cassandrean oligarch, Philippides of Paeania, and Lachares, a friend of Cassander. Their policy was strict neutrality; they hoped that if Athens interfered with no one, no one would interfere with her; and for five years this curious optimism was justified by events. They even disarmed, and substituted for the compulsory ephebe training a voluntary system, which reduced the annual recruits from 800 to 30, generally young men of means who could afford to study arms and philosophy; the franchise was apparently reduced, and election by lot abolished. The success of such a policy depended on Cassander; and after 301 Cassander left Greece alone, and made a treaty with Athens which did not even restore his exiled supporters. The explanation is the fearful exhaustion of Macedonia; Cassander was statesman enough to abandon his policy of conquest in Greece and subordinate personal ambition to the recuperation of his people. He even refused to reinstate his dispossessed brother Pleistarchus, a refusal to which the pleading of his sister Phila on Demetrius' behalf perhaps contributed. But in 297 Cassander died of consumption, and with him died the wisest head in the world's councils; a fresh outburst of fighting followed.

In 296 Seleucus demanded Tyre and Sidon from Demetrius as compensation for allowing him to take Cilicia, and Demetrius in a rage broke off relations[1]. He then sailed to Greece to take up again his project of 302, which Cassander's death seemed to have rendered feasible, whereupon Lysimachus, Seleucus, and Ptolemy renewed their alliance against him; Ptolemy annexed Cyprus and possibly part of Lycia, Seleucus Cilicia, and Lysimachus Ephesus, Miletus (between 294 and 289), and all Ionia and most of Caria; nothing remained to Demetrius in Asia but Tyre, Sidon, and Caunus in Caria. Demetrius himself first attacked Athens, where

[1] Eusebius' story (II, p. 118, Schoene) that Demetrius took Samaria this year connects with nothing else known and seems incredible.

dissensions had arisen between the democrats and Lachares, who was seeking power for himself even before Cassander's death; but some ships were wrecked, his attack repulsed, and he retired into Peloponnese. During his absence Lachares made himself dictator (March 295), Phaedrus consenting to serve under him, and secured Boeotia's alliance and possibly Sparta's; the democrats, who held the Piraeus, then called on Demetrius, who returned, occupied Eleusis and Rhamnus, and blockaded Athens. Lachares showed energy and decision, even stripping the gold robes from Pheidias' statue of Athena, and the city held out gallantly; but an attempt at relief made by Ptolemy failed in face of Demetrius' superior fleet, and in spring 294 Athens, after enduring the extremity of hunger, surrendered; Lachares escaped. Demetrius treated the city kindly, and poured in corn; but though he banished no one and merely restored Stratocles' government, he disclosed a very different policy from that of 307; the days of free alliance were over, and henceforth he would act like Cassander. He not only secured and garrisoned the Piraeus and Munychia, but he built and garrisoned a new fort on the Museum hill; and Athens became a subject town, with foreign troops inside the city wall.

II. DEMETRIUS, KING OF MACEDONIA

Demetrius was still following his father's plan of 307–302, but with a difference; he still meant to lead Greece against Macedonia, but as a subject country, not a willing ally. After taking Athens he attacked Sparta, but was called off by news from Macedonia which promised him a shorter way. Cassander's eldest son, Philip IV, had died of consumption after reigning four months, and Cassander's widow Thessalonice had used the unique influence which, as the last survivor of Philip's house, she possessed with the army to obtain a division of the kingship between her younger sons Antipater and Alexander; Antipater, the elder, who had married Lysimachus' daughter Eurydice and probably had his support, thereupon murdered his mother and attacked Alexander, who turned for help to Pyrrhus and Demetrius. Pyrrhus established Alexander as sole ruler and took five provinces in payment (p. 83); Demetrius came too late, and Alexander escorted him back to Larissa, where he himself was killed by Demetrius' guards; the Antigonid version of the affair was that Demetrius merely anticipated a plot to assassinate himself, but another version, perhaps that of Lysimachus, said that Lysimachus had reconciled the brothers and spoilt Demetrius' opening. Whatever the truth, the leaderless Macedonian army elected Demetrius king, a choice to which the popularity of Phila, the favourite daughter of Antipater the Regent, is said to have contributed. Demetrius now had the country which, in his father's plan, was the indispensable starting-point for the reconquest of Asia.

As such he treated it. Macedonia never had a worse king, and many must have regretted Cassander. The people naturally felt no loyalty to him; but instead of cultivating their good-will, he made himself inaccessible, like an Asiatic despot. They might have pardoned his double diadem (Europe and Asia), or the mantle which portrayed him as the Sun among the stars, or his own portrait on the coinage, a thing unknown in Europe; they could not pardon his neglect of his duties, justice and administration. Above all, they needed peace and he gave them war. That his rule lasted for six years was largely due to the fact that the cautious Lysimachus, who respected Demetrius' generalship, waited till the fruit was ripe. Cassander's son Antipater, his nephew, another Antipater, Alexander's widow Lysandra, all took refuge with Lysimachus, and all Cassander's friends looked to him. He married Lysandra to Agathocles, his son by his first wife Nicaea: he had a pretext for war whenever he chose.

A united Greece would still have been the strongest Power between the Adriatic and the Indus; and, as Demetrius had abandoned the idea of winning over Greece, he spent the years 293–289 in attempting to subdue enough of it to give him a preponderance of strength over the states he could not hope to secure—Epirus, Aetolia, and Sparta—and enable him to reconquer Asia. In spring 293 he mastered Thessaly, and assumed the regular place of a Macedonian king as the nominally elected head for life of the Thessalian League. In spite of its frequent revolts, Thessaly stood nearer to Macedonia than any other country, and must have contained larger pro-Macedonian elements; some Greeks refused to reckon it as part of Hellas[1], while Macedonians regarded it almost as part of Macedonia; not only were the two dialects akin, but almost every Macedonian proper name is common in the Hellenistic Thessalian inscriptions. It may explain why Demetrius founded his name-city on Thessalian (Magnesian) soil. This impregnable fortress, Demetrias, was built on the north side of Pagasae, both apparently being enclosed within one continuous wall[2]; from it the Antigonid kings could keep Greece under observation. It contained the palace and probably the administration

---

[1] Heracleides Criticus, *F.H.G.* II, p. 263.

[2] Probably two walled towns within a common wall, like the four at Antioch.

buildings, and Pagasae became only the commercial quarter and harbour. Cassander had once similarly planned an enlarged Phthiotic Thebes on the Pagasaean Gulf, but Demetrius went further; Pagasae and every Magnesian town from Cape Sepias to Tempe on the Macedonian border became villages of Demetrias, a unique synoecism which in effect made Demetrias a southward projection of Macedonia. Demetrias came to possess a hereditary corporation of herbalists called 'Cheiron's descendants,' with a secret lore, who healed the sick free. Demetrius next received the submission of the Euboean League—if it was not already his—and Chalcis probably became again a Macedonian fortress; he was worshipped in the Euboean cities, and a month named after him. Boeotia first submitted and then rose under the lead of Pisis of Thespiae, once Antigonus' partisan; but Demetrius quelled the revolt, and as Boeotia with its 10,000 hoplites was vital to him he showed clemency, pardoned Pisis, and made him polemarch; but he garrisoned some cities and made Hieronymus the historian *harmost* (governor) over the country, and Boeotia became, like Athens, a subject state; he also acquired Eastern Locris and most of Phocis. As he already held Athens, Corinth, and Megara, he had by winter everything he could hope for north of the Isthmus.

But he was no longer champion of the Greek democracies, as in 302; he now sat in Cassander's seat, and Cassander's friends the oligarchs began to look to him. Though difficult, it was not quite impossible to reconcile parties; Alexander had succeeded in some cities, as Nymphis at Heraclea later (p. 98); and in 294 Demetrius honestly tried to unite the factions at Athens. Though Stratocles was in power, Demetrius won over the moderate Phaedrus, while Stratocles cultivated Philippides of Paeania; and Demetrius then approached the two extremes, the Nationalist democrats and the banished Cassandrean oligarchs. He issued a general amnesty, recalled all exiles, and secured as eponymous archon a strong democrat, Olympiodorus, who, though a Peripatetic, was also a patriot, and in the Four Years' War had defeated Cassander; but, generally speaking, he failed to win the democrats; they would not stomach the recall of the oligarchs, and branded the government, which was really composed of Stratocles' followers and the moderate Centre, as oligarchic; the democrats at Lysimachus' court—Demochares and Lysimachus' friend Philippides of Cephale, writer of comedies, whose lampoons on Stratocles had rendered residence abroad advisable—refused to return under the amnesty, and the democratic opposition of 303 revived. Consequently when in 293 Stratocles died, Demetrius was thrown back upon the moderates, and Phaedrus became leader of the government.

From this time the labels of oligarch and democrat begin to lose their meaning; the real question in most cities was simply, were you for or against the house of Antigonus; and men divided into pro-Macedonians and Nationalists. The kernel of the Nationalist party at Athens was the democratic opposition to Demetrius, but it must have absorbed some moderates; the kernel of the pro-Macedonian party was at first Phaedrus and the moderates, though later the party absorbed the Cassandrean oligarchs. But there was of course some cross-division; the Stratoclean democrats, for instance, were pro-Macedonians. Doubtless there was, as in every self-governing community, an indeterminate body of opinion which might swing either way and transfer power from one party to the other, but there was no longer, as in 301, a separate centre party with leaders; that vanished when Phaedrus joined Demetrius.

In 292 Lysimachus made a mistake; he crossed the Danube, attacked the Getae, and was worn down, like Darius, and compelled to surrender; but the Getic king Dromichaetes released him and secured his friendship. Tradition merely points the moral of the civilized brigand and the noble savage; but in reality Dromichaetes saw the advantage of restoring Lysimachus to ward off from himself a worse danger, Demetrius, who had at once attempted to seize Thrace. During Demetrius' absence, Boeotia allied herself with Aetolia and Pyrrhus, and rose; and at Athens the extreme oligarchs, who had returned in no pleasant temper, conspired with Boeotia's help to overthrow both government and constitution. Phaedrus however frustrated their attempt, and Demetrius on his return found that his son Antigonus had already defeated the Boeotians. He besieged Thebes; Pyrrhus in vain attempted to relieve the city by raiding Thessaly, and in 291, after a brave resistance, Thebes fell. Demetrius only executed ten ringleaders; but he deprived Thebes of autonomy and garrisoned the Cadmea. But the revolt had shown him that, before thinking of Asia, he must reckon with Boeotia's allies, Aetolia and Pyrrhus.

III. PYRRHUS AND DEMETRIUS

The effective history of Epirus begins and almost ends with Pyrrhus the Molossian, who for a time forced his backward country into prominence at the expense of its future. Brilliant

and attractive, Alexander's kinsman must have had some good
points as a king, for he kept his people's loyalty in spite of their
terrible losses in his wars; but he was essentially a soldier, and
lived for war only. Unlike his Macedonian contemporaries, he
cared nothing for the advancement of learning; Epirote literature
consisted of his military *Memoirs*, probably based on his *Journal*,
and an epitome of Aeneas' military manuals made for him by
his minister Cineas. Chivalrous in act, he was unscrupulous in
breaking his word; he had neither ideas nor a connected policy,
and though he could always win battles he never gathered their
fruit; Antigonus Gonatas said of him that (in modern phraseology)
he held good cards but could not play them. His men thought
him a second Alexander; except in military talent, few resembled
Alexander less. Modern Albania claims him, and probably he
had some Illyrian blood; his people at best were only semi-Greek.

Their three tribal Leagues—Molossians, Thesprotians, Cha-
onians—had before 300 coalesced into the 'Epirote alliance,' a
combination of federalism and monarchy under the Molossian
king. The king's power was limited; every year at the holy place
at Passaron he took a fresh oath to the people to rule according
to the laws, while they, instead of renewing their annual oath to
uphold him, could expel him and take another. But, though
federalism ultimately conquered, the rule of the energetic and
popular Pyrrhus much resembled autocracy. He greatly enlarged
the kingdom; Cassander's son Alexander had ceded to him two
Macedonian provinces, Parauaea and Tymphaea, and three vassal
countries, Ambracia, Amphilochia, and Acarnania; he also
acquired Atintania, and soon afterwards Corcyra, Apollonia, and
part of Southern Illyria, thus cutting off Macedonia from access
to the Adriatic. He cultivated Egypt's friendship, and founded
a city Berenikis in honour of his Egyptian wife; but Ambracia,
which he adorned, became his capital. His offerings at Dodona
show that he realized the advantage to Epirus, in Greek eyes, of
containing a great oracle; possibly he modernized its buildings
and founded the festival Naia.

The Aetolian League will be described later (p. 208 *sq.*). This
brave and democratic people had already begun to expand;
between Cassander's death and 292 they incorporated Western
Locris and gained control of Delphi, perhaps through disturbances in Phocis; for though most of Phocis obeyed Demetrius,
Aetolia in her treaty with Boeotia in 292 contracted for herself
and her Phocian friends, possibly a body of exiles settled in her
territory. Her present policy was to maintain the balance of

power by supporting the second state in the peninsula against the first; except when Macedonia was divided, this implied opposition to Macedonia.

Demetrius soon found an opportunity of repaying Pyrrhus for his interference on Thebes' behalf. After Antigone's death Pyrrhus had married Lanassa, daughter of Agathocles of Syracuse, who brought him Corcyra as her dower; but subsequently he married an Illyrian princess, and in 291 Lanassa left him, retired to Corcyra, and offered herself and her island to Demetrius. Demetrius married her and apparently wintered in Corcyra with her; he cultivated Agathocles' friendship, and planned to cut a canal through the Isthmus of Corinth. Pyrrhus prepared for war, and his ally Aetolia excluded all Demetrius' friends, including the Athenians, from the Pythian games of 290; and when in that summer Demetrius made a state entry into Athens with Lanassa as the divine pair Demetrius and Demeter, he found the people greatly excited; a popular song, addressed to himself as the Sun, begged him to put down the new Sphinx who was harrying Greece. He quieted the Athenians by celebrating an opposition Pythian festival in Athens, and in spring 289 invaded and ravaged Aetolia. But the wild country was not seriously damaged; and when, leaving Pantauchus with an army to occupy Aetolia, he entered Epirus, Pyrrhus evaded him, defeated Pantauchus, and compelled Demetrius to evacuate both countries; but when he in turn raided Macedonia, his opponent, though ill, easily chased him out again. Then Demetrius made an inconclusive peace; his rear was no more secure than before, but he was impatient to begin the invasion of Asia.

Demetrius' power, to outward seeming, was great; beside Macedonia, he controlled Thessaly, Athens, Boeotia, Eastern Locris, Phocis, Euboea, Megara, Corinth, Argos and the Argolid, Sicyon, Achaea, all Arcadia except Sparta's satellite Mantinea, and the Island League. These states were frankly his possessions; he taxed the cities, and some were under his governors—he had a *harmost* in Boeotia, a *nesiarch* over the Islands; his money circulated among them, and in many places he was worshipped. Of the independent states, Messene consistently avoided aggression, and Elis would only act in conjunction with Sparta or Aetolia; this left three states as his potential enemies, Greater Epirus, Aetolia, and Sparta. They might raise some 35–40,000 men, half of them Pyrrhus' troops; but Sparta was isolated, and only Pyrrhus actually threatened Macedonia. Against this, Macedonia could give Demetrius 30–35,000 men, and his Greek possessions at least as many; add his mercenaries, and his capable allies, the semi-organized pirates of the Aegean, and it may really be true that his army list, *i.e.* the paper total of troops on whom he might draw, amounted to 110,000 men. On land he was far stronger, on paper, than any other king, and at sea he was supreme; he perhaps controlled 300 warships, while Ptolemy had hardly yet restored his standard number before Salamis, 200, and the navies of Lysimachus, Seleucus, Rhodes, Heraclea, and Byzantium were relatively small. In the autumn of 289 he began his preparations for invading Asia and retrieving the failure of 301 by conquering Alexander's empire. He was already coining freely at Pella and Amphipolis for this purpose; he now built more ships at Corinth, Chalcis, Piraeus, and Pella, and launched among others two galleys of fifteen and sixteen men to the oar, whose speed and efficiency were even more admired than their size.

IV. THE FALL OF DEMETRIUS

Demetrius' shipbuilding revealed his intentions, and Lysimachus, Seleucus, and Ptolemy once more revived the coalition of 302 against him, Lysimachus being the moving spirit; his task was to invade Macedonia while Ptolemy raised Athens. Lysimachus presumably knew on what an unstable basis Demetrius' rule in Macedonia rested, and as he asked no help from Seleucus, whom doubtless he already mistrusted, he may well have felt certain of the ultimate result; but he rather feared Demetrius in the field, so he persuaded Pyrrhus to break his treaty and aid him; Audoleon of Paeonia, another of Pyrrhus' numerous fathers-in-law, also joined the coalition. In spring 288 Lysimachus and Pyrrhus invaded Macedonia from opposite sides. Demetrius was taken by surprise; his fleet was laid up, his mercenaries distributed throughout Greece. He could only call out the Macedonians and hurry to meet Lysimachus, whom he checked before Amphipolis; but his men's temper was unsatisfactory, and on the news that Pyrrhus had reached Beroea they began to desert to Lysimachus. Demetrius left a force at Amphipolis to hold Lysimachus, and turned to face Pyrrhus. But the Macedonians, who thought he had no further chance, went over to Pyrrhus in a body (about September 288); Amphipolis was betrayed to Lysimachus; and he and Pyrrhus partitioned Macedonia, Pyrrhus obtaining the larger share and part of the elephants. Demetrius escaped to Cassandreia; there Phila committed suicide. The reason given is the loss of Demetrius' kingdom; but she had stood by him through every adversity before, and though to modern ideas her life amid his innumerable infidelities must have been a terrible one, no other Hellenistic queen, until Cleopatra VII, took her own life. As tradition praises her as the noblest woman of the age, her death conceals some unknown tragedy, the sadder because, had she lived, she would soon have found rest with her son.

Meanwhile Ptolemy had put to sea; while his battle-fleet watched Corinth, his cruisers under Zeno appeared off Athens some time before July, and on their arrival the Nationalists rose under the lead of Olympiodorus and a young Olympian victor named Glaucon, and overthrew the government; Demetrius' garrison, probably tampered with, did not interfere, and though he held the Piraeus, Zeno provisioned the city from one of the open roadsteads, for which Athens thanked him in the first days of 288–7. Every Athenian now had to decide for Demetrius or the revolution. Demetrius' friends, including Phaedrus, who was hoplite-general, were excluded from office, and new magistrates chosen; election by lot was restored, and the single superintendent of the administration replaced by a board, henceforth the distinguishing mark of Nationalist rule. Demochares and Philippides of Cephale were at once recalled, if indeed they had not already started; they arrived soon after the revolution, and Demochares took the lead in the new government. It began well, for Olympiodorus with some volunteers stormed the Museum fort, a captain of mercenaries, Strombichus, coming over with his men; but it then made the mistake of supposing that there was nothing more to fear from Demetrius; it trusted to its friends the kings, and neglected to raise a proper force, for which Demochares must take his share of responsibility.

Demochares has been alike over-praised and over-abused. He had rendered Athens much service as an organizer in the Four Years War, and he now succeeded in the doubtless necessary task of reducing public expenditure; and for six years his government was to maintain Athens' freedom. But he was a purist in democracy, and would not work with moderate men, whom his circle branded as 'oligarchs'; his provocative oratory made him many enemies; and it is unpleasant to recall that subsequently, despite his hostility to Demetrius, he tried to get Zeno the philosopher to make interest for him with Demetrius' son. He was probably a useful politician of the second rank, conscious that as Demosthenes' nephew he ought to play Demosthenes, but not qualified for the part.

The loss of a second kingdom, the ruin for the second time of his ambition, called out all that was best in Demetrius' very formidable talents. He hurried to Greece; the mercenaries of his garrisons stood by their oath; he secured Boeotia by restoring autonomy to Thebes, and appeared unexpectedly before Athens with a considerable force. Athens was thoroughly alarmed; she had no army ready, and the walls were perhaps out of repair. Messengers were sent to Pyrrhus and Lysimachus for help, but though Pyrrhus started at once it became apparent that Demetrius would take Athens before he arrived; and an embassy of philosophers, headed by Crates of the Academy, was sent out to beseech Demetrius to spare the violet-crowned city in the name of her illustrious dead. It was not an incident creditable to Athens, though it probably relieved Demetrius of some embarrassment; he had never been vindictive, he retained a tender feeling for Athens, and he did not want to squander his mercenaries on fighting Pyrrhus. He granted the philosophers' request, and made peace with Pyrrhus on his arrival, each to keep what he had; each merely wanted to turn elsewhere. Pyrrhus entered Athens, sacrificed, and told the people that if they had any sense they would never again admit a king within their walls; then he hurried back to Macedonia. He did not trust Lysimachus. But Lysimachus as usual was in no hurry; he probably suspected that Demetrius was not yet done with, and that he might yet need Pyrrhus.

And indeed Demetrius did carry out his invasion of Asia, but not as he had hoped; his motive probably, as after Ipsus, was vengeance upon Lysimachus. Ptolemy did not interfere; Demetrius was still powerful at sea, and Lysimachus' troubles would not hurt Egypt. Demetrius left Antigonus as his governor in Greece, and by denuding him of troops shipped 11,000 mercenaries; he landed near Miletus (287), which opened its gates. There he found Phila's sister Eurydice, Ptolemy's divorced wife (p. 96), with her daughter Ptolemais, betrothed to him in 299; the three are probably shown on the Villa Boscoreale fresco, where the sadness of Eurydice's face is haunting[1]. He married Ptolemais, and probably spent some time with her at Miletus, recruiting troops; he then invaded Ionia, perhaps late in 287. Some cities he took, some joined him; Lysimachus' governor put Sardes into his hands. But there were cities that refused to abandon Lysimachus; Demetrius could not take Ephesus, and Priene remained loyal, though attacked, not only by Magnesia, but by the peasants

---

[1] Fr. Studniczka, *J.D.A.I.* xxxviii–ix, 1923–4, p. 64.

on her own territory, the Pedieis; the dread their rising inspired can be measured by the extraordinary present, a crown of 1000 gold pieces, which Priene made to Lysimachus for suppressing it. Ionia was evidently thrown into confusion, but Demetrius' success was only partial; it was probably in this campaign that Lysimachus' general in Ionia, Sosthenes, acquired his reputation.

Then in spring 286 Lysimachus' popular and capable son Agathocles came south with a strong army. Demetrius could not face him, and turned eastward, as Eumenes had once done, hoping to reach Media through independent Armenia and raise the Far East; perhaps he thought of treating Seleucus as Seleucus had treated Antigonus I, and of founding a kingdom in his rear. But Agathocles followed and cut off his supplies; his Greek troops disliked going so far from the sea; he suffered great hardships, lost many men through hunger and plague, and was forced across the Taurus into Seleucus' province of Cilicia; Agathocles closed the passes behind him to prevent his return. Seleucus was at first inclined to welcome Lysimachus' enemy, and sent him supplies; but presently, urged by his experienced general Patrocles, he took fright, closed the Amanus passes, and attacked him instead. Demetrius fought 'like a wild beast cornered'; whatever the odds, he defeated Seleucus in every engagement, captured the Amanic Gates, and opened a way into Syria. Seleucus was at his wits' end, yet he dared not accept Lysimachus' proffered help; men from every quarter flocked to Demetrius' banner, and it looked as if he would yet win a *third* kingdom, and rule Asia from Seleucus' throne in Antioch. Then he fell ill. He had recovered from the loss of two kingdoms, but from the loss of his hand on the helm during those critical weeks he could not recover; he arose to find his army reduced by desertion to a remnant of his own mercenaries. He met his fate face to face; he crossed the Amanus, planned a night surprise of Seleucus' army, which was betrayed, and then attacked him next day and even obtained some success, till Seleucus, bringing up the elephants, dismounted and ran forward bareheaded to the little band of mercenaries who had kept their oath to the end, begging them to abandon their hopeless cause and not force him to kill them. Demetrius escaped, and tried to recross the Amanus, hoping to reach his fleet; but all points were guarded, and finally, starving, he surrendered (285).

V. LYSIMACHUS

Demetrius had made no treaty with Athens before his departure, and the Nationalist government at once prepared to attack Antigonus, who was short of men. Their vital needs were corn and money to hire mercenaries. Audoleon of Paeonia and Spartocus, dynast of the Crimea, sent corn, but Philippides, who in 287 went to Lysimachus, got nothing but compliments. In 286, however, pressed by Demetrius in Ionia, Lysimachus was ready to subsidize any enemy of his; Demochares went himself and obtained 130 talents from him, while Cassander's son Antipater gave twenty talents and Ptolemy fifty. The democracy acclaimed Demochares' services; but they were a confession that Athens could no longer fight without some king's help. Demochares recovered Eleusis by arms, but the government trusted to Lysimachus' gold to recover the Piraeus, and bribed the wrong man, a Carian officer named Hierocles, who informed his commander; a gate was opened as arranged, and the Athenians who entered were cut to pieces. Next year, however, 285, Olympiodorus' Phocian friend Xanthippus, also subsidized by Lysimachus, expelled Antigonus' garrison from Elatea and perhaps freed Phocis, and Olympiodorus himself crowned his services to Athens by storming the Piraeus; and events elsewhere, with Demetrius' captivity, compelled Antigonus to make peace.

Lysimachus had benefited by his foresight in leaving Pyrrhus undisturbed since 288; for in 286 he persuaded him that the treaty under which they had partitioned Macedonia, and which probably provided for mutual defence against Demetrius, must override his later treaty with Demetrius; and Pyrrhus in Lysimachus' interest attacked Antigonus and took all Thessaly except Demetrias. Lysimachus also approached Aetolia, where cities were founded in the names of himself and Arsinoe, while Delphi honoured his general Prepelaus, formerly Cassander's man. But by winter Lysimachus was satisfied that he need no longer fear Demetrius, and began to show his hand; and Pyrrhus, isolated and afraid, turned round and approached Antigonus, who made a secret alliance with him; that Antigonus should join the man who had so injured his father and himself shows alike to what straits he was reduced and what fear Lysimachus inspired. Once secure in Asia, Lysimachus in 285 tore up his treaty with Pyrrhus and invaded Pyrrhus' half of Macedonia, and Antigonus sent troops to aid his ally, denuding his garrisons; but Lysimachus outgeneralled Pyrrhus and corrupted his friends, and Pyrrhus abandoned Macedonia and Thessaly to him without a battle, while Antigonus lost Piraeus and had to make peace with Athens. The Macedonian army elected Lysimachus king; Cassander's son Antipater, who had expected Lysimachus to restore him, apparently protested, whereon Lysimachus, to further his own ambition, put his best friend's son to death. Aeschylus himself could not have bettered the vengeance which was to be taken by Antipater's Furies.

But at present it looked as if Lysimachus were Alexander's destined heir. His power had grown great; he ruled Macedonia, Thessaly (except Demetrias), Thrace, and most of Asia Minor north and west of the Taurus; his Greek cities gave him a navy, and he could turn Antigonus out of Greece whenever he chose. Bithynia indeed under Ziboetes successfully maintained her independence against him, while eastward of Sinope he was cut off by the new kingdom of Pontus, with which he never lived to deal; but in 289 the murder of Amestris by her sons enabled him, in the guise of vengeance for his former wife, to annex Heraclea, which isolated Bithynia and gave him some good ships and a new outlet to the Black Sea; and if Byzantium, independent and wealthy, controlled the Bosporus, anxiety for her territory would prevent her thwarting him. Probably he now made Cassandreia his capital.

Lysimachus may have had less feeling for learning than some of his contemporaries, but Onesicritus wrote at his court, and he perhaps joined Cassander in subsidizing the researches of Dicaearchus the Peripatetic, who in calculating the earth's circumference used Lysimacheia-Syene as base line; and the tradition that he expelled the philosophers from his kingdom may be untrue, for his finance minister Mithres was the close friend of Epicurus and Metrodorus. Lysimachus is represented as harsh and avaricious, but possibly literary tradition, influenced perhaps by Hieronymus' friendship for his Antigonid foes, has been less than just; after Ipsus he released his Athenian prisoners without ransom. Certainly his finances were well managed; beside the land tax, he must have taxed manufactures, for it is said no industry was too unimportant to escape his levies. But he did much to foster trade, and the enormous outburst of striking money in the Black Sea cities, first of Alexander's and then of Lysimachus' pieces, which replaced their local coinages, probably belongs to his reign; certainly at Sinope, which flourished exceedingly, the change has been dated to about 290[1].

---

[1] E. T. Newell, *A.J. Num.* LII, 1918, p. 118.

Possibly he was following out certain indications that Alexander, had he lived, would have turned his attention to the Black Sea, and he hoped to make it his lake; the coins suggest that his relations extended from Sinope round to Odessus, and doubtless the powerful Spartocids of the Crimea were his friends, as they both supported Athens in 288; his expedition against Dromichaetes, which recalls Zopyrion's (vol. vi, p. 394), may have been made on behalf of the Greek cities. He put Alexander's head on his coins and renamed Antigoneia Troas Alexandria; and though he was worshipped himself in Cassandreia, Priene, and elsewhere, it was doubtless his doing that the Ionian League substituted for Antigonus as their official god not Lysimachus but Alexander.

Toward the cities his policy was of course Cassander's; they were subjects, not allies, and he managed the Ionian League (and doubtless the Ilian) through a general, as Cassander had managed the Peloponnese. His policy contained few innovations: he taxed the cities, but so had Athens and Demetrius done; he interfered with their affairs and transferred populations, but so at the end did Antigonus I; he supported tyrants in Priene, Samos, and elsewhere, but Antipater had done the same; if he stopped Callatis coining her local money, it was to replace it by an international issue, like Alexander's. At Ephesus, however, he curtailed democratic government, and replaced the Council by an oligarchic council of elders, to which he apparently gave control of the revenues of the temple of Artemis, heretofore administered by the semi-oriental priesthood; the temple ceased to be a state within the State, and the bee of Artemis vanished from the coinage. His interferences, though often bitterly resented, were not necessarily arbitrary; when, against the people's protests, he moved Ephesus nearer to the sea, it was because the harbour was silting up; but that the people had to pay for the new wall[1] was characteristic of him. But he ruined Cardia by moving the people to Lysimacheia, of which it became a village, and he destroyed Astacus, which the Bithynians had made their capital. The story that he destroyed Colophon is, however, unfounded; what he did was to quash Antigonus' synoecism of Lebedus and Teos, and remove some of the people of Lebedus and Colophon to Ephesus; but both continued to exist as cities. But he had to take Colophon by force, perhaps in 286, and the poet Phoenix wrote a lament on his city's fate. On the other hand, he released

---

[1] For this wall see J. Keil in *Jahreshefte*, xv, 1912, Beiblatt p. 183.

the Scepsians whom Antigonus had settled in Troas and allowed
them to restore Scepsis, and perhaps gave freedom to Thasos[1]
and permitted Miletus to coin; and in 286 some cities refused to
desert him. He built no important new city except Lysimacheia,
though another Lysimacheia occurs in Mysia; but he enlarged
Troas and Ilium by new synoecisms, adorned Ilium, completed
Smyrna, and refounded Antigoneia on the Ascanian lake, most
symmetrical of all Hellenistic cities. He renamed Antigoneia after
his first wife Nicaea, his new Ephesus after Arsinoe, and Smyrna
after his daughter Eurydice; doubtless the ladies were honorary
'founders' and received the taxes as pin-money, though he also
presented Arsinoe with Heraclea. Two of the names went out
of use on his death; but Nicaea's endured for centuries, and is
still perpetuated in the Nicene creed.

But if Lysimachus secured much when Demetrius fell, he did
not secure the sea. During 286 he regained his revolted cities
in Asia, except Miletus, where lay Demetrius' great fleet; Miletus
joined Ptolemy as an ally[2] (though Lysimachus recovered it later)
and the ships loyal to Demetrius moved to Caunus, but Demetrius' Phoenician admiral, Philocles king of the Sidonians, carried
over to Ptolemy the best of the fleet, including the Phoenician
contingents, and therewith Ptolemy also acquired Tyre and Sidon;
Demetrius' dated Tyrian coinage ends with the 287 issue, while
its deterioration exhibits his gradual loss of grip[3]. Ptolemy thus
gained command of the sea without fighting, and with it the
Island League and the prestige of the suzerainty of Delos, where
possibly he dedicated Demetrius' flagship to Apollo[4], as a sign
that the sea had changed hands; he also acquired Thera, while
in 285 Philocles gave him a footing in Caria by capturing Caunus.
Ptolemy temporarily remitted Demetrius' taxation in the Islands,
as was usual with new acquisitions, and the Islanders replaced
the worship of the aforetime Saviours, Antigonus and Demetrius,
by that of their new Saviour, Ptolemy, and honoured Philocles as
their Deliverer. Ptolemy rewarded Philocles by making him
nauarch, *i.e.* admiral and military governor of the Island League,
with powers equivalent to a viceroyalty of the sea; no Asiatic
ever again held such a position in any Hellenistic kingdom.
Lysimachus indeed secured Lemnos, Imbros, and Samothrace;

---

[1] *B.C.H.* xlv, 1921, p. 153, no. 6, as emended by E. Ziebarth in Bursian's *Jahresbericht*, ccxiii, 1927, p. 32.
[2] Th. Wiegand, *Milet* i, iii, no. 139, l. 24.
[3] E. T. Newell, *Tyrus Rediviva*, pp. 14, 21 *sq.*
[4] The present writer in *B.C.H.* xlvi, 1922, p. 473; and see p. 476.

Arsinoe adorned Samothrace with a new temple, and the island worshipped Lysimachus as a Benefactor. But he wanted more than Samothrace; he bided his time, but carefully informed Delos of his goodwill.

Seleucus alone acquired no territory by Demetrius' overthrow, though he recovered Cilicia; but he gained indirectly, for all Demetrius' friends in the cities, and all Lysimachus' enemies, necessarily turned to him, and parties of 'Seleucizers' appeared in Ephesus, and doubtless in every city. In 292, recognizing that he could not govern the Far East from Antioch, he had handed over his wife Stratonice, who had borne him a daughter Phila, to his son Antiochus, and made Antiochus, who as Apama's son was half Iranian, joint-king and governor of the East, an extension of the Achaemenid practice of making a prince of the blood satrap of Bactria. The reason why he gave Stratonice to Antiochus is lost, but the tradition that she objected seems correct; for her numerous dedications at Delos not only show Antigonus' sister to have been a religious woman[1], but reveal the significant fact that she never describes herself as Antiochus' wife. Antiochus' capital was the 'Royal City,' Seleuceia on the Tigris, where Seleucus had settled many Babylonians, Antigonus I having partially ruined Babylon; in 275 Antiochus ended Babylon's civil existence, but Seleuceians were still sometimes called Babylonians (p. 187).

Seleucus received Demetrius honourably on his surrender, and assigned him a residence in a loop of the Orontes, ample, but too well guarded to permit of escape. He indeed spoke of releasing him when Antiochus and Stratonice should come to Antioch; but they never came, and were not meant to come. Antigonus with devoted loyalty offered to cede to Seleucus every city he held and to come himself as hostage if Seleucus would free his father, but Seleucus dared not take the risk of liberating a man still capable of shaking the civilized world; also Demetrius was the one man Lysimachus feared, and the threat of his release could be usefully held over Lysimachus' head. Lysimachus knew this, and in his hatred he offered Seleucus 2000 talents to murder Demetrius. Seleucus rejected the bribe with scorn; and the 'dirty piece of savagery,' as he called it, merely served to deepen the growing distrust between the two kings. Demetrius on his side had managed to send a message to his captains in Greece, telling

---

[1] She rebuilt Atargatis' temple at Bambyce-Hierapolis, and joined a club at Smyrna which worshipped Anubis (Michel 1223); doubtless she saw in them all forms of one deity.

them to trust no orders that purported to come from him, but to treat him as dead and hold the cities for Antigonus. It made Antigonus' position clear. He was no longer his father's lieutenant; he was to act for himself.

VI. ANTIGONUS GONATAS

Antigonus II Gonatas, son of Demetrius and Phila, now about 35, was to be the second founder of the Macedonian monarchy and the first king whom philosophy could claim as her own. The meaning of his nickname Gonatas is unknown; if Greek, it might be 'knock-kneed.' He was a plain, straightforward character, with none of Demetrius' brilliance and few of his failings; probably he owed much to his mother. Moralists were to cite him as proof that the sins of the fathers are not always visited on their children; he himself said that a man was what he made himself. His blunt sarcastic method of speech was often enough turned against himself; he was perhaps the first to remark that he was no hero to his valet, and to call his defeats strategic movements to the rear. But he had the sense of duty which had characterized Antipater and Phila, and the family loyalty which never failed the Antigonids till the half-Epirote Philip V; above all, he possessed a dogged tenacity which never knew when it was beaten. Statesmanship was his by blood on both sides, and he had learnt from the successes and failures of Cassander, Antigonus I, and Demetrius. His tutor had been the Megarian philosopher Euphantus of Olynthus; but his relations with philosophy really centre on Menedemus and on Zeno the founder of Stoicism.

Menedemus of Eretria was a dignified and cultivated man of the world, prominent in Eretria's political life, though scarcely an original philosopher; but he possessed a strong personality and a noble character, and his mocking speech, the terror of evildoers, was often belied by kindly actions. His friends compared him to Socrates; like Socrates, he wrote nothing, but tried to call out what was in his pupils by question and conversation. Eretria was an art-loving city, and Menedemus gathered round him a little circle of literary men—the poets Aratus of Soli and Antagoras of Rhodes, Dionysius of Heraclea, afterwards Zeno's pupil, and the youthful tragedian Lycophron, who wrote a satyrplay *Menedemos* in his master's honour; from it has survived an account of Menedemus' famous suppers, modelled perhaps on Plato's *Banquet*, where the guests had to bring their own cushions, and the conversation, more important than the wine, might be kept up till cockcrow. Antigonus had frequented the circle when

Demetrius ruled Euboea; Menedemus told him his faults, and Antigonus was fond of him and called himself his pupil. We would gladly know more of Menedemus' circle, for it is a pleasing picture; there we can forget war, and even the feud between philosophy and life was hushed in that oasis of peace.

But Antigonus' relations with Zeno went deeper than this; for Zeno had seen a vision of something that transcended peace and war alike, a certainty of the soul that no outward thing could shake. We do not know what it was that, in an Athens full of more immediately successful philosophers, attracted Antigonus to the gaunt Phoenician with the thought-lined face, too shy to lecture, silent where all were talking, outraging men's minds by his impossible demands on their virtue, but with an idea in him that would move the world. Zeno accepted Antigonus as he did the poorest who came; king or beggar was nothing to him. But he became Antigonus' friend; and to Zeno a friend meant a second self. We can hardly figure the relationship between the rough-spoken hard-drinking prince and the retiring ascetic; but Stoicism acted as a tonic on strong natures, and Zeno taught his pupil to be free of illusions and false pride; and the two men had this in common, that each could look facts in the face. Zeno himself kept his independence as absolutely as if his friend had been the simplest citizen, and scrupulously avoided everything that might affix the stigma of partiality to his school; he was respected because he respected himself, and none ever called him a pro-Macedonian. But it is written that with Zeno Antigonus recognized no difference of rank or race, and that his admiration and affection for him knew no bounds; Zeno, so long as he lived, was his inspiration, and Zeno's approval his reward.

Antigonus in 285 was nothing but a commander of mercenaries who held some Greek cities; having no other revenues, he had to tax the cities to pay his troops, which made him unpopular; and as he had no kingdom at his back, and was not a god, his rule rested on force, and he differed from a tyrant only in being pretender to the throne of Macedonia. He had, however, some officers of ability, including his half-brother Craterus, son of Craterus and Phila, whose devotion to him became proverbial, and Hieronymus; the return of the loyal ships from Caunus gave him a fleet; and Aetolia, now that Lysimachus held all Macedonia, followed her consistent policy by informally joining Pyrrhus and himself. Antigonus, however, could hardly rely on the unstable Pyrrhus, who, moreover, was probably occupied in conquering southern Illyria and Corcyra; and at any moment it might suit

Lysimachus to appear in Greece in overwhelming force. Lysimachus, however, as usual proceeded methodically; he spent 284 in reducing Paeonia, where Audoleon was dead, and in 283 invaded Epirus, but incurred much unpopularity through his Thracians plundering the tombs of Pyrrhus' ancestors. It is unknown whether he meant to reduce Epirus and met a rebuff, and also whether he restored Parauaea and Tymphaea to Macedonia or whether this was done by Antigonus after Pyrrhus' death; but he freed Acarnania from Pyrrhus, and, like Cassander, re-established her as Macedonia's informal vassal, ready to stab Aetolia in the back when required. Pyrrhus subsequently made a treaty with her and recruited Acarnanian mercenaries for his Italian expedition (chap. xx).

VII. THE PASSING OF THE SUCCESSORS

In spring 283 Demetrius' imprisonment ended; the most brilliant figure of the age, broken by hope deferred, had drunk himself to death. Antigonus thereon assumed the royal title, and set out to reconquer his father's kingdom; but, as he could not hope to defeat Lysimachus, he began with Athens. Athens had been rejoicing in her recovered freedom, and Philippides as *agonothetes* had celebrated a special festival in honour of Demeter and Kore; but unfortunately the city, amid its gratitude to Lysimachus, had expected him to make an end of Antigonus altogether, and had not prepared for a fresh war. Seleucus, too, who wanted friends for his now inevitable conflict with Lysimachus, turned to Antigonus, and sent back to him Demetrius' ashes; and Antigonus with his fleet met the funeral ship in the Aegean, and brought the remains of the great sea-king in state to Corinth, and thence to his own city Demetrias.

Lysimachus on his side turned toward Egypt; but he played a double game. The long duel in Egypt between Eurydice and her maid-of-honour Berenice had ended (before 287) in Ptolemy repudiating his wife and marrying his mistress; and in spring 285 he adopted as his heir Berenice's eldest son Ptolemy and made him joint-king with himself to secure his succession. Eurydice's eldest son Ptolemy (afterwards called Keraunos, the Thunderbolt), a violent and unscrupulous man, had sought help from Seleucus, who promised to seat him on the throne after his father's death; but Keraunos could not wait, and went to Lysimachus, who always offered asylum to useful pretenders. But when late in 283 Ptolemy I died—the only Successor who died a natural death—and Berenice's son succeeded peacefully as

Ptolemy II, Lysimachus reinsured himself by giving Ptolemy II
as his wife his daughter by Nicaea, another Arsinoe; and Keraunos,
hopeless of reinstatement in Egypt, began to aim at position in
Macedonia. There he found Lysimachus' son Agathocles an
obstacle. Lysimachus' court was a mass of intrigue, with his
wife Arsinoe and Agathocles' wife Lysandra each scheming for
her own children; but the story that Agathocles played Joseph
to Arsinoe's Zuleika, and that Arsinoe took the usual revenge,
is probably untrue; for, speaking generally, the conduct of the
earlier Hellenistic queens was good, and the vast mass of scandal
we possess leaves them untouched. Arsinoe's fault was inordinate
ambition; but this extraordinary woman did not win the devotion
she afterwards obtained from her subordinates without great
qualities, and one of her coin-portraits[1] is beautiful with a remote
and spiritual beauty which has few parallels in Greek art. Undoubtedly the blame for Agathocles' death lies with Keraunos.
For what happened was that Lysimachus, at the height of his
fortune, committed political suicide; the man who had murdered
Cassander's son now murdered his own; he put Agathocles to
death for alleged treason, and massacred his friends. It was the
end of his dream of Alexander's empire. Lysandra escaped to
Seleucus and sought his help, and, though Lysimachus' position
in Macedonia remained strong, disaffection spread in Asia and
large elements rallied to Agathocles' widow; and Keraunos, who
doubtless held high command, could now make himself indispensable to Lysimachus while ingratiating himself with the army.
With Lysimachus paralysed, Athens was left to face Antigonus
unaided. It was beyond her strength. Antigonus captured the
Piraeus, garrisoned Munychia, and by spring 281 starved Athens
into surrender; but he acted with moderation, for he was anxiously
watching events in Macedonia; he garrisoned the Piraeus, but
not the Museum, and was content that his friends came into
power again.

Lysimachus' heavy war-requisitions and his support of certain
tyrants increased the disaffection in his cities in Asia; and in 282
Seleucus, perhaps at their invitation, crossed the Taurus. Philetaerus, the eunuch from Tios who had helped to betray Antigonus I to Lysimachus, now betrayed Lysimachus in turn, and
surrendered Pergamum and the 9000 talents there to Seleucus;
the impregnable Sardes with its treasure was also handed over,
and Seleucus was joined by Lysimachus' enemy Ziboetes of

---

[1] *B.M. Coins, Ptolemies,* Pl. VIII, no. 3.

Bithynia. In 281[1] Lysimachus with the Macedonian army came south to meet him, and in summer the two old men met on the Plain of Koros in Lydia (Korupedion) in the last of the great battles between the Successors; Lysimachus was defeated and killed, and Seleucus, last survivor of Alexander's companions, was left with all Alexander's empire save Egypt at his feet. Arsinoe with her three sons escaped from Ephesus to Cassandreia; Keraunos was captured, and honourably received by the victor.

Seleucus enjoyed his triumph just seven months. He made some attempt to settle Asia Minor; many Greek cities, including Miletus, came over to him, others were 'liberated,' and he sent commissioners to settle their affairs; doubtless, as was usual, he at first remitted Lysimachus' taxes; Priene instituted a Soteria festival to celebrate her release from tyranny, and the prevalent feeling is shown by the drastic laws passed by Ilium and Nisyrus against tyrants. But Samos, where Duris the historian had been tyrant, and possibly Halicarnassus and Cnidus, joined Ptolemy; and at Heraclea, which had bought out Arsinoe's garrison, Seleucus' commissioner was expelled, the exiles recalled, and Nymphis the historian actually succeeded in reconciling all parties, the exiles claiming no compensation and the city voluntarily providing for them; and Heraclea, Byzantium, Chalcedon, Cius and Tios formed the so-called Northern League to maintain their independence, and were joined by the Persian prince Mithridates of Pontus, who defeated the army Seleucus sent against him and took the royal title. Seleucus did not wait to clear up the position. He was longing to end his days on Alexander's throne in Pella; he could claim Macedonia by conquest, though probably he was never legally king, *i.e.* elected by Lysimachus' army. Early in 280 he crossed the Dardanelles; but he had forgotten Keraunos. Keraunos saw that Seleucus would not reinstate him in Egypt and had deprived him of all chance in Macedonia; outside Lysimacheia he stabbed him and escaped into the city. Seleucus' army was leaderless, for his son Antiochus was at Babylon; and Lysimachus' Macedonians welcomed Keraunos as Lysimachus' avenger, and hailed him king. Philetaerus ransomed Seleucus' corpse.

[1] Some—De Sanctis, Ferguson, and most recently A. Jardé, *Les céréales dans l'antiquité grecque*, pp. 170 *sqq.*—have argued for 282. Either date used to depend on combinations; but it is now certain from the cuneiform evidence, conjoined with Rehm, *Milet* i, no. 123, l. 37, that Seleucus died between 30 Nov. 281 and 1 Nisan (*i.e.* sometime in March) 280, which renders 282 for Korupedion impossible; see W. Kolbe, *Syrische Beiträge*, pp. 12–14.

Keraunos had numerous rivals. But Antiochus I was cut off from Europe by the Northern League, with which Keraunos allied himself, thus securing Heraclea's fleet; Lysandra and her children are not again heard of; and Pyrrhus, occupied with his preparations for invading Italy, was accommodating enough to marry Keraunos' daughter and borrow some Macedonian troops. But Antigonus and Arsinoe were more dangerous. Antigonus started for Macedonia in spring 280; but Keraunos met him at sea with the fleets of Lysimachus and Heraclea and utterly defeated him, destroying whatever prestige he possessed. Arsinoe was established in Cassandreia with her mercenaries, ruling what she could for her eldest son Ptolemaeus; and if large elements in Macedonia were loyal to Lysimachus' memory, they might not prefer his avenger to his son, while to take Cassandreia would be difficult. Keraunos tried diplomacy: let Lysimachus' two heirs pool their resources; let Arsinoe marry him and be again queen of Macedonia, and he would adopt Ptolemaeus as his successor. Arsinoe long hesitated, for Berenice's daughter could hardly trust Eurydice's son, but ambition conquered; she gave him her hand, was proclaimed queen, and opened the gates; once inside, he murdered her younger sons, but allowed her to take sanctuary in Samothrace. Ptolemaeus escaped to Illyria, and Keraunos gave Cassandreia to his mother Eurydice.

Antigonus' defeat heralded an obscure war which lasted from spring 280 to autumn 279. Areus of Sparta regarded himself as the equal of any Successor, and struck money with Alexander's types and his own name; and, encouraged by the troubles in Macedonia, he re-formed the old Peloponnesian League in winter 281 to expel Antigonus from Greece; he secured Elis, most of Arcadia, and part of the Argolid, and allied himself with Antiochus, who saw the advantage of playing the part of champion of Greece left vacant by Lysimachus' death, and as such restored Lemnos to Athens. Antigonus naturally allied himself with Antiochus' enemy the Northern League, where Byzantium moreover was his hereditary friend; as the Northern League was Keraunos' ally, Antigonus must have made peace with him, and indeed he had his hands full in Greece. In spring Areus came northward; Argos and Megalopolis expelled Antigonus' garrisons and proclaimed themselves free, though naturally they did not join Sparta, and Argos borrowed money from Rhodes to strengthen her walls; and four Achaean cities—Patrae, Dyme, Tritaea, and Pharae—revolted from Antigonus. Areus got shipping at Patrae and invaded Aetolia; the reason is obscure, but possibly his real

objective was Boeotia, whither Antigonus had withdrawn after his
defeat. Anyhow the Aetolians defeated Areus severely and drove
him out; the four Achaean towns then deserted him, re-formed
the old Achaean League, which had broken up at some period
after Ipsus, and looked to Aetolia for help. But in Athens the
Nationalists overthrew Antigonus' friends; Demochares moved
a decree in posthumous honour of Macedonia's great enemy
Demosthenes, and Callippus son of Moerocles, an extreme
Nationalist[1], was elected general in 279. Before autumn 279
Boeotia and Megara were also free, and Antigonus, who had
probably lost Euboea after Demetrius' fall, now held nothing
but Demetrias, Corinth, the Piraeus, and a few places in Achaea
and the Argolid.

Antiochus himself was detained in Syria by a serious revolt
(p. 701), and sent Patrocles to Asia Minor, where Cyzicus, with
subsidies from Philetaerus of Pergamum, now virtually independent, was upholding his cause against the Northern League.
But Patrocles found that Bithynia, though she had helped Seleucus
against Lysimachus, had no intention of accepting Seleucus'
suzerainty, and his lieutenant Hermogenes was defeated by
Ziboetes, perhaps the old king's last act. He died that winter,
and his son Nicomedes, having murdered all his brothers but
one—another Ziboetes who seized the Chalcedon peninsula—
joined the Northern League and Pontus against the common foe
Antiochus, and presently built himself a capital Nicomedia
facing the site of Astacus. The Seleucid empire was now permanently cut off from the Black Sea; in that vast region Lysimachus would have no successor. Antigonus, seeing that after
Areus' defeat Corinth was in no danger, but also seeing no
opening in Greece, imitated Demetrius, and in 279 sailed to the
Dardanelles to recover what he could in Asia; he joined Nicomedes and threatened Antiochus' fleet. But by autumn 279 the
Gallic invasion made his quarrel with Antiochus seem futile,
and the two kings had sense enough to make a real peace[2]. Their
treaty of friendship—*the* treaty of the age—delimited their
spheres: Antiochus was not to interfere west of the Thraco-
Macedonian boundary (*i.e.* in Macedonia and Greece), or Antigonus east of it (*i.e.* in Thrace and Asia); and Antigonus was to
marry Antiochus' half-sister Phila. Probably they did not formally

[1] His politics: *B.C.H.* xxxviii, 1914, p. 451, no. 1.
[2] The date now depends on the fragment of Philodemus published by
A. Mayer, *Philol.* lxxi, 1912, p. 226, on which see the present writer in
J.H.S. xl, 1920, p. 148. The date is independent of the Athenian archon-list.

abandon their respective claims within each other's spheres, but they agreed not to enforce them; and the treaty stood for generations, a cardinal point of Hellenistic politics. Henceforth no king dreams of ruling Alexander's undivided heritage.

To Egypt the events of these last years were pure gain. The deaths of Demetrius, Lysimachus, and Seleucus had stabilized the sea-power of Ptolemy II without any effort on his part; and in 280 he celebrated the occasion by issuing invitations to all the Greek states to a great festival in Alexandria in his father's honour, which became the pattern of many other festivals. He also emphasized his command of the sea by founding at Delos, where the Islanders worshipped him beside his father, the vase-festival[1] in honour of its gods called the first Ptolemaieia.

VIII. THE INVASION OF THE GAULS

Keraunos spent the rest of 280 in defeating an attack by Lysimachus' son Ptolemaeus and his Illyrian allies, which perhaps blinded him to his real danger. For the migrating Galatae (Gauls), whose movements have been previously traced (see p. 64 sq.), had now come within striking distance of Macedonia; Lysimachus' death seemed to render invasion feasible, and Cambaules had already reconnoitred Thrace. Their attack burst upon Macedonia very early in 279, when Keraunos' Macedonians were in their homes and his mercenaries scattered in winter quarters. The Gauls, whose object was two-fold, plunder and settlement, came in three bodies under different leaders: Bolgius entered Macedonia by the Aoüs pass (see p. 830 n. 1), Brennus, the 'Rede-giver,' overran Paeonia, and Cerethrius invaded Thrace. Their actual fighting men cannot have been numerous; but they brought with them slaves, camp-followers, contingents from conquered Illyrian and Thracian tribes, and trains of waggons carrying their families, household goods, and booty; and they were joined by Macedonia's frontier foemen the Dardanians, whose proffered help Keraunos had declined. Keraunos naturally refused Bolgius' preliminary offer of peace for cash down. But he chose, or was compelled, to meet him without waiting to mobilize; he was defeated and killed, and the Gauls poured into Macedonia with its king's head borne before them on a spear.

Panic followed; the walled towns were safe, as the Gauls did not understand siege-works, but the country lay open to plunder. In Cassandreia a proletarian revolution broke out, led by one

---

[1] A festival which, among other things, provided for the annual dedication of an inscribed vase by a chorus of girls.

Apollodorus; Eurydice's mercenaries joined the mob, and, probably making a virtue of necessity, she surrendered the citadel and was honoured as Liberator, while Apollodorus made himself tyrant and plundered the well-to-do, part of whose property he gave to his followers. The Macedonian army crowned Keraunos' brother Meleager, dismissed him as incompetent, crowned Cassander's nephew Antipater, and dismissed him also forty-five days later with the scornful nickname Etesias, 'King of the Dog-days.' Lysimachus' general Sosthenes then took command, but refused the proffered crown; possibly he intended to crown Lysimachus' son. Bolgius, after plundering his fill, apparently withdrew northward; his force perhaps included the Scordisci, who under Bathanattus founded a kingdom in Serbia, and by their pressure compelled the Illyrians to unite into one state. But Brennus had now entered Macedonia by the Iron Gate (Demir Kapu). Sosthenes fought with him without definite results, but at least prevented him settling, if such were his intention; and in late autumn 279 Brennus too quitted Macedonia, but only to invade Greece. It was Brennus' movements which led Antigonus and Antiochus to make peace.

Greek writers were unfortunately fond of comparing Brennus' invasion of Greece with that of Xerxes, and darken counsel with echoes of Herodotus and equally absurd figures. The number of Brennus' fighting men is unknown; but as 20,000 Gauls held up Asia Minor for years, 30,000 would seem an outside estimate. He advanced through Thessaly, where some land-owners joined him to purchase immunity for their estates, had the Spercheus bridged and left the Thessalians on guard there, and reached Thermopylae. The Greeks holding Thermopylae were some 11–12,000 Aetolians, 10,500 Boeotians, 3500 Phocians, 1500 Athenians under Callippus, 700 Locrians, 400 Megarians, and 1000 mercenaries equally contributed by Antigonus and Antiochus; no Peloponnesians came, as they trusted to Antigonus holding the Isthmus. In view of the jealousy between Aetolia and Boeotia the supreme command was given to Callippus. Brennus made one frontal attack, but saw at once that his half-armed followers, however brave, with no body-armour and no weapons except pointless broad-swords, had no chance in a narrow place against spears; he therefore detached a column, which entered Aetolia through Malis, took and burnt the little town of Callium, and butchered the inhabitants. As he hoped, the Aetolians immediately quitted Thermopylae and hurried home. But the whole of Aetolia, men and women alike, had already risen to

take vengeance; they fought no pitched battle, but the Gauls were
caught in an endless guerilla fight and shot down from behind
trees and rocks; less than half escaped, and the Aetolians had
made the great discovery that Gauls were only formidable at
close quarters. Without the Aetolians the Greeks could still
hold the pass, but the mountain paths were ill defended; and
Brennus, leaving Acichorius in command of the main body,
turned the pass with a flying column, traditionally by the same
route as Hydarnes, though he really started farther westward[1]
(see vol. iv, p. 294). The Greeks got word in time and scattered
to their homes, and Thermopylae lay open to Acichorius.

So far Brennus had shown the qualities of a leader. But he
now made a fatal mistake; he decided to raid Delphi for plunder
with his flying column, though the main Aetolian force was intact
and he himself was ignorant both of its whereabouts and of the
defeat of his other column in Aetolia. When the Aetolian leaders
heard of the fall of the pass and Brennus' objective, they were
faced with a critical decision: were they to save Greece, or their
own Delphi? They chose the course which honour and generalship alike demanded; they detached a few men to organize
resistance at Delphi, and with their main body hurried to meet
Acichorius, who had passed Thermopylae with his unwieldy train
of waggons. Again they fought no pitched battle; but they clung
to his flanks, cut off all supplies, and killed when they could; he
had made little progress before the fate of Delphi was decided.

Beside the Delphians, there were at Delphi a Phocian force
under Aleximachus, 400 Amphisseans, a few Aetolians, and some
men from Magnesia on the Maeander, possibly there on other
business. Brennus reached Delphi in mid-winter, and tried to
storm it; Aleximachus fell in the battle on the wall, but Brennus
was checked and Apollo's temple was not sacked. During the
assault a thunderstorm burst, and the priests from the temple
came down to the defenders and announced that Apollo was
fighting for them; some of the excited warriors afterwards declared that they had themselves seen Apollo manifest in the skies,
shooting down the Gauls; that this became an article of official
belief will surprise no one. Brennus camped for the night outside
the town. That night the Greeks were strongly reinforced, for
Phocis was rising as Aetolia had risen; and at dawn, in a blizzard
of snow-flakes—the 'white maidens' whose help Apollo had
promised—they attacked Brennus' camp with missiles. Against

---

[1] Fr. Stählin, *Das hellenische Thessalien*, p. 204.

arrows the Gauls were helpless, but they stood till Brennus was shot down; then they slew their wounded, took up Brennus, and set out on their terrible retreat through unknown country, unable to see their way in the snow or retaliate on their guerilla foemen. Few struggled back to Acichorius. But the news had travelled faster than they; the Athenians and Boeotians took the field again, and Acichorius turned back. The Aetolians hung on his rear and chased him north with heavy loss to the Spercheus, where his Thessalian allies also fell on him; Brennus slew himself in despair; and the remainder of the Gauls retreated into Macedonia, after being twice annihilated on the way by patriotic Greek historians.

There was no question as to who had saved Greece. The Aetolians had borne the burden of the campaign; they had discovered how to defeat Gauls, and had held back the main body of the enemy single-handed. From this year dates the new importance of Aetolia. Beside statues of her generals, she set up at Delphi her monument of victory, an heroic figure of Aetolia as an armed woman seated on a pile of Gallic shields; the shields themselves were hung on the temple to match the Persian shields taken at Marathon. The Amphictyons instituted at Delphi a festival of the Soteria, the Deliverance of Greece, and rewarded Phocis, who had fought well, by restoring to her the Amphictyonic votes she had lost after the Sacred War (vol. vi, p. 241); and for centuries the hymns of Apollo's temple recalled with triumph the repulse of the barbarians.

We may follow the wanderings of the Gauls to their end before returning to Macedonia. Two tribes, the Tolistoagii or Tolistobogii (? Tolistovagi) and the Trocmi, under their 'kings' Leonnorius and Lutarius, had separated from Brennus before he entered Macedonia, but in 278 had reached the sea. They advanced plundering along the coast to the Dardanelles, but Antiochus' governor refused to let them cross; Leonnorius then went on to Byzantium, where Nicomedes engaged him to attack Ziboetes and brought him over; Lutarius captured some boats and crossed the Dardanelles, and Ziboetes was soon disposed of. Meanwhile a third tribe, the Tectosages, who had been with Brennus in Greece, had followed the others, and also crossed. Their combined forces numbered 20,000 men, with women and children; only half were armed, but Nicomedes armed the others. The whole body was in the service of Nicomedes and his ally Mithridates of Pontus; their business was to worry Antiochus, which they did after their own fashion. They divided the Seleucid

territory into spheres of plunder; the Tolistoagii took Aeolis and
Ionia, the Trocmi the Dardanelles region, the Tectosages, the
last to arrive, the less wealthy interior. Then there fell upon Asia
Minor the horrors which Greece had largely escaped. Literature
supplies only echoes of the great raid: how Themisonium and
Celaenae were, like Delphi, saved by their gods from the 'late-
born Titans' who burnt temples and warred against heaven; how
at Miletus some captured girls slew themselves to avoid worse;
how a girl would have betrayed Ephesus for the Gauls' golden
bracelets, and was crushed to death beneath their weight. But
the inscriptions show that seldom can so few men have created
such a panic. The reason given was their cruelty to prisoners;
but the very different ways in which they were met in Greece and
Asia show that the cause lay far deeper.

In fact in 277 Asia Minor was threatening to break up, and
there was no strong central authority. Mithridates had extended
his kingdom along the coast to Amastris, thus marching with
Heraclea, which had bought Tios; inland he was advancing from
the lower Halys and Iris into northern Phrygia, and the unconquerable Bithynia was seemingly extending into Northern Phrygia
also to meet him. There were probably native dynasts in inner
Paphlagonia, and all Pisidia was independent; Egypt held part of
Lycia, together with Miletus and probably Halicarnassus and
Cnidus (pp. 98, 701). Antiochus was needed everywhere, and he
could not leave Syria. There was no common action against the
barbarians; even the cities of the Ionian League, weary of war
and hampered by Miletus' defection, no longer co-operated.
Cyzicus in 277 fought the Trocmi by herself, with Philetaerus'
subsidies. The Tolistoagii, having failed to seize Ilium, came
down the coast in bands. Arcesilas the philosopher went to
Antigonus for help for his city, Pitane, which Antigonus could
not give. Philetaerus himself consolidated his rule by driving
the Gauls off from Pergamum; Miletus seemingly fought, but
Erythrae and other cities paid ransom to save their lands from
plunder. Priene would neither fight nor pay; she let her lands
be ravaged, until Sotas, a private citizen, hired some men himself,
armed his slaves, and had success enough to attract volunteers,
whereon he met the Gauls fairly and saved many country people
by bringing them within the walls; that he had time to do this
shows that the band which held up Priene took some time to work
through its lands, and was therefore very small. At last, late in
277, Antiochus managed to come; but in 276 Ptolemy's invasion
recalled him to Syria (p. 702), and though he left his son Seleucus

at Sardes, the Gauls apparently continued their operations, for in 275 they were at Thyateira. But that year saw the end of the first great raid; Antiochus defeated them thoroughly (p. 702) and restored his kingdom, and the cities worshipped him as a Saviour.

After this, things quieted down in one way, for Nicomedes and Mithridates settled the Gauls on the territory in northern Phrygia (Galatia) taken from Antiochus, as a buffer against him; but the Seleucids were too fully occupied elsewhere ever to deal radically with the barbarians, and for many years they exacted tribute from the Seleucid kings as a condition of sparing their cities, and a special 'Galatian' tax was raised from the cities to pay it. Galatia was a poor country, but it gave the Gauls what they wanted, strongholds in which to leave their families and booty while they raided. The Tolistoagii settled about Pessinus, the Trocmi about Tavium, the Tectosages between them about Ancyra (Angora); each tribe was normally ruled by four tetrarchs, the 'kings' whom we hear of being merely temporary war-leaders; but the three tribes had a common sanctuary called Drynemetos (unidentified), possibly a circular moot in a grove, where (perhaps later) a joint council of 300 elders tried criminal cases. The Phrygian peasants tilled the land for them, and they increased fast, but did not occupy any towns till much later; for long they kept their native customs, a foreign body which the Seleucid empire could not assimilate, always ready to sell their swords to the highest bidder.

IX. ANTIGONUS, KING OF MACEDONIA

The events of 279 had disorganized Macedonia, and in spring 278 Antigonus invaded the country from Thrace and obtained a footing, but Sosthenes drove him out, probably in spring 277, and he retired again into Antiochus' territory; evidently the memory of Lysimachus was still strong in Macedonia, while a city Sosthenis appears among the Aenianes. The last body of Gauls, that which under Cerethrius had invaded Thrace, now appears on the scene. Their slow progress shows the resistance of the Thracian tribes; but in 277 part of them reached the sea and threatened Lysimacheia. Antigonus, whether by accident or design, was near the city; he met the Gauls, and by a ruse compelled them to fight with their backs to the sea; the god Pan spread his panic terror among them, and Antigonus cut them to pieces. The effect was great, for a Gallic army had never yet been broken in a stand-up fight; it gave Antigonus the prestige

he so sorely needed. He probably entered Macedonia again at
once; Sosthenes was apparently dead, the country in anarchy,
and this time, late in 277 or early in 276, the Macedonian army
elected him king. Greek cities thanked him for his victory, and
Eretria's decree, moved by Menedemus, emphasized the return
of the exile to his home. But the interior of Thrace was lost to
Hellenism; the kingdom of the Odrysae revived, and the rest of
Cerethrius' Gauls, under Commontorius, founded the kingdom
of Tylis, which extended from the Danube to Byzantium, and
for two generations was strong enough to blackmail the coastal
cities; even Byzantium ended by paying eighty talents a year to
secure her territory from plunder.

Antigonus spent 276 in consolidating Macedonia, where there
were three pretenders—Antipater Etesias[1], Lysimachus' son
Ptolemaeus, and one Arrhidaeus, who possibly claimed descent
from Philip III. As however he could not call out the Macedonians, utterly weary of fighting, in a domestic quarrel with the
houses of Cassander and Lysimachus, and dared not waste his
own mercenaries, his ultimate support, he imitated Nicomedes,
and enlisted those Gauls who still roamed the country; once
done, every king enlists Gauls as a matter of course. They disposed of the pretenders for him; Ptolemaeus escaped to Egypt
(p. 703), as did Antipater, who played no further part in affairs.
The Gauls tried to bluff Antigonus over their pay, and failed,
which gave them an added respect for the man who had defeated
their countrymen. But he also had to deal with Apollodorus, of
whose wickedness and nightmare terrors a lurid account remains,
possibly derived from a tragedy of Lycophron's; and Gauls were
useless against the walls of Cassandreia. He turned to Demetrius'
friends the pirates; and, while he was recovering Thessaly, the
arch-pirate Ameinias, afterwards his general, stormed Cassandreia for him. By the end of 276 Antigonus was master of his
kingdom. He did not forget Pan's help; his worship was officially
established at Pella, and his head figured on Antigonus' new
tetradrachms, occasionally wearing the diadem; but none of these
coins can be portraits of Antigonus, if, as seems probable, the
thoughtful face of the young king of the Villa Boscoreale fresco
be his. Apparently too Antigonus instituted a festival of kingship
called *Basileia*, to commemorate his victory; Greek cities sent
religious envoys to him to *some* festival. That winter he celebrated,

[1] For Antipater see now the Herculaneum papyrus, no. 1418, col.
xxxiii[a] (xxiii[a]), published by A. Vogliano, *Riv. di fil.* LIV, 1926, p. 322;
LV, 1927, p. 501; and *P. Cairo Zen.* no. 59019, l. 6.

with much circumstance, his marriage with Phila; his friends
from Athens and Eretria were bidden, and Aratus of Soli wrote
two hymns for the occasion: one praised Pan for his help at
Lysimacheia, which had given Antigonus his kingdom; the
subject of the other was the treaty which had given Antigonus
his bride, and which might do something to give peace to a
distracted world.

By 275 the kingdoms, after all the fighting, had thus returned
to much the shape they had before Alexander. Antigonus ruled
most of Philip's Macedonia, less Thrace. Antiochus held most
of what the Achaemenids had held after losing Egypt and India.
Ptolemy represented Pharaoh, but with greatly increased territory. Macedonia however was relatively much weaker, while
Ptolemy's empire was relatively so much stronger that for a
generation the natural grouping was to be that of Antigonid and
Seleucid in opposition to Egypt. But the principal difference—
a very great one—was that Egypt and Asia were now officially,
and to some extent actually, occupied by a different civilization,
which was extending even into semi-barbarous states like Bithynia.
It illustrates the fact that Alexander's work had primarily been
neither military nor political, but cultural.

CHAPTER IV

PTOLEMAIC EGYPT

I. THE CONDITIONS CONFRONTING THE PTOLEMIES

THE political history of Egypt as one of the new Hellenistic monarchies is set forth elsewhere (see chapters III and XXII). The purpose of this chapter is to sketch the administration, the economic, social and religious life of Egypt during the three centuries which separate the appointment of Ptolemy son of Lagus as satrap (upon the death of Alexander) from the annexation by Augustus. This task is easier than the corresponding study of the Seleucid Empire, for Egypt is comparatively rich in literary, epigraphic, papyrological and archaeological material; but it must not be forgotten that even for Egypt our sources are not really abundant and are most unequally distributed[1]. Literary data are as haphazard as for the rest of the Hellenistic world and are almost confined to the third century B.C.; inscriptions, whether Greek or Egyptian, are poorer both in number and content than in other contemporary countries in which the Greek city-state prevailed as the mould of social life; of the towns and villages of Hellenistic Egypt not one has been systematically excavated—in Alexandria such excavation is impossible—and therefore archaeological material is scanty and scattered; finally, the papyri, whether Greek or demotic, are comparatively few for the Ptolemaic period and the light they throw upon the several centuries and the several sides of life is most uneven. After the reigns of Ptolemy II and III, of which they tell us most, there is a comparative lack of evidence until Ptolemy VIII, and then the light fails us again. Moreover, most of the papyri come from the villages in the Fayûm and reflect the life of Egypt as a whole no more than that of England would be reflected in the official documents and letters of a group of villages in Kent or Somerset. The reader must therefore bear in mind that the generalizations in this chapter are, of necessity, based upon hypothesis and reconstruction. There is no single detail of Egyptian life of which we can claim exact and final knowledge. Every new publication of papyri, every new inscription raises new

[1] For the abbreviations used in the few references given in this chapter see the Bibliography. The other references are to be found in the books and articles cited there on the several topics.

problems and sheds light upon the old, every important aspect of Egyptian life is still, and will long be, under discussion.

The problem which faced the Ptolemies in Egypt was no easy one. A country with strong traditions reaching back thousands of years with a fixed and systematic civilization regulating administration, religion, social and economic life had to be reorganized upon new principles and to new purposes. These new principles and purposes were due to new conditions which prevailed in the fourth century. The political collapse of the Greek *polis* had made Greeks ready to go anywhere and to do anything, to live outside the setting of a city-state. They were willing to go to Egypt and Egypt was ready to receive them. Even in the Saïte period, and still more in the sixty years of independence between the two Persian dominations, Egypt had begun to adapt itself to a new order. The effort to secure its independence compelled it to enter the concert of fourth-century powers and link itself closely with the Greek world, which meant a recasting of its internal life, in fact an incipient hellenization. In this direction, foreshadowing the policy of the Ptolemies, the Pharaohs of the Twenty-eighth to the Thirtieth Dynasties went far. They admitted into Egypt both Greek mercenaries and Greek traders to meet emergencies which had evoked a strong nationalist sentiment, but they failed to solve the problem how to establish an acceptable modus vivendi for the immigrants and the native Egyptians while reserving for the latter political and social superiority.

A second fact which conditioned Ptolemaic policy was that Egypt was part of the short-lived empire of Alexander. For twenty years the first Ptolemy ruled it not in his own name as king but as satrap in the name of the central authority. During that period of chaos and struggle between the claimants for Alexander's heritage, Ptolemy was pre-occupied with the confirmation of his own position in Egypt and the creation of an army and fleet strong enough to secure to him not only independence but also his due share in the affairs of the empire. For him therefore a strong army and fleet was a matter of life and death. And so it remained even in later times when, after the battle of Ipsus (301 B.C.), a so-called balance of power was established in the Hellenistic world, that is, a political order in which the only guarantee of independence was military power and military preparedness. The only army on which Ptolemy could safely rely was an army of Macedonians and Greek mercenaries with a staff of officers schooled in the ancient military tradition of Greece. The technical superiority of such an army had been proved by the campaigns both of Alexander and of the Successors. Contingents of orientals were neither sufficiently trained nor sufficiently loyal for any monarch to use them as the main support of his power or as a counterpoise to Macedonians and Greeks, still less to rely upon them entirely and discard the Greeks. It might have been possible for Alexander, unchallenged master of a world-empire, to educate Persians in the Macedonian art of war, to overcome the resistance of Macedonians and Greeks and to bring about a fusion of races and civilizations. But Alexander was dead, and the Successors, hurried into conflicts, dared not face the long and hazardous experiment of attempting to create an army out of native levies. They were forced to rely upon their Graeco-Macedonian armies and to ensure faithful service and a supply of recruits by giving to their soldiers a position of privilege secured to them as a right.

Besides troops they needed money, and the vast sums demanded by their warlike policies could not be obtained from countries which in the main had not advanced beyond natural economy. The necessary economic reorganization could be directed by none but Greeks and was only made possible by the entry of Greek capital and Greek men of business. These were not in the least likely to be satisfied with a modest position and rights on the same level as the native population. Thus Ptolemy Soter in Egypt and Seleucus in the East, and likewise their successors, were forced to open wide the doors of their empires to the Macedonians and Greeks, both soldiers and civilians, to secure to them in various ways the possibility of living in the new country after the Greek fashion and to guarantee to them privilege and dominance.

The new capital, Alexandria, was the centre of the new social influences that poured into the country. Here dwelt the king with his court, his guards, his general staff and his ministers. In the Museum and the Library the leading intellects of Greece, philosophers, scholars, writers, worked together to lay the foundations of a new epoch (see chap. VIII). Splendid commercial possibilities attracted a host of Greek traders and manufacturers, while the growth of the city as the economic centre of Egypt created a numerous lower middle class, petty traders, artisans and the like and an international proletariate mostly Greek. But in opening their doors to Greeks and Macedonians the Ptolemies did not exclude other peoples. There arose in Alexandria communities of immigrants from the East—Syrians, Anatolians, and above all Jews—in social structure not greatly unlike those of the Greeks and Macedonians. Add to these an ever-increasing native Egyptian element and slaves captured in war or imported from Asia or Africa and it will be seen how heterogeneous was the capital of the Ptolemaic kingdom.

Not less mixed was the population of the 'country' (χώρα as against the πόλις, *i.e.* Alexandria). Ever since Saïte times Greeks had been domiciled in Egypt partly in the Greek cities Naucratis and perhaps Paraetonium, partly in the larger Egyptian towns such as Memphis and perhaps Thebes. Anatolians, Jews and Syrians entered in growing numbers after the Persian conquest together with many so-called 'Persians,' soldiers, officials, tax-farmers and the like. With the coming of Alexander the influx of foreigners increased. Graeco-Macedonian garrisons were posted at the chief strategic points. In southern Egypt Ptolemy Soter founded Ptolemaïs to be a counterpoise to the ancient Thebes as Alexandria was the counterpoise to Memphis. Throughout all Egypt, as will be seen, soldiers were settled on plots of land, and everywhere appeared Greek and Macedonian officials, while in the quasi-cities and villages of Egypt there settled Greek and Oriental traders, artisans and husbandmen.

All this foreign population was of course a mere super-structure. The foundation was still, as it had ever been, the Egyptians. Of the fate of the native aristocracy after Alexander our documents have hardly anything to say. But the temples continued to be the centres of religious life, with their numerous priesthood and its stable organization, with their traditional mode of life going back thousands of years. The land was in the occupation of millions of peasants dwelling in thousands of villages. Handicrafts and trades in the towns and villages remained in the hands of hundreds of guilds of artisans and traders. Although we have no definite statistics there can be no doubt that the native population numbered millions, the immigrants thousands, that the natives had a firmly settled tradition of life, while the immigrants, torn from their own environment, could only slowly and gradually build up a new system under new conditions.

The fundamental problem of Ptolemy I, as of Seleucus in his Empire, and of Ptolemy's successors was to reorganize their Oriental states upon new principles, taking into account the strength and stubbornness of local traditions, the feelings and dispositions of their new subjects, while always remembering that the chief bulwark of their rule and the agents of their policy were not the native elements but the new ruling class in their states, the Greeks, Macedonians and other foreigners.

II. THE FOUNDATIONS OF THE PTOLEMIES' POWER IN RIGHT AND PRACTICE

The Ptolemies' title to Egypt was the right of conquest. It was their 'land won by the spear'; economically, their private estate; and it was entirely within their power to concede their right of ownership either temporarily or permanently to particular persons or groups and corporations. But if their power was to be permanent, they must be sure of the active support or at least of the passive acquiescence of the population. Apart from the fact of conquest and inheritance from Alexander their power needed a legitimate basis and recognition on the part of the army, the Greeks and the Egyptians. As to the army, the Ptolemies were in supreme command of it; the troops were bound to obey them within the limits set by military discipline. Further, as the army was essentially a paid force, the bond was not only military but economic. How strong and permanent the bond, whether military or economic, actually was, is hard to say, for we know scarcely anything of the internal constitution of the army, the rights and obligations of the soldiers and officers, its military discipline, its religion. Officially the regular army claimed, as we shall see later, to be the Macedonian army under the command of the Macedonian king. It was natural that from time to time it should show a disposition to follow Macedonian tradition in taking an active part in the political life of the country, particularly in settling the succession to the throne. Whether this right was at all times enjoyed by the army, or only occasionally in times of trouble and disorder, we cannot tell. This at any rate is beyond doubt, that the army's loyalty rested mainly upon two supports: its economic dependence upon the king and its privileged position in the life of the country.

The same factors secured to the Ptolemies the loyal support of the non-Egyptian immigrant population. The outer expression of this loyalty was the cult of the kings. This cult was founded upon the cult of Alexander, recognized even in the time of Ptolemy Soter as the official cult not only of Alexandria but of the whole Greek population of Egypt, and upon the divine honours rendered unofficially to Ptolemy I and his successors both by their Greek allies and by their Greek subjects (see above, pp. 13 *sqq.*).

But these material and religious bonds between themselves and the Greek population were not enough for the Ptolemies. Like their Macedonian and Syrian rivals they endeavoured to provide their power with a philosophical basis. It is due to no mere chance

that just at this time there appear one after another treatises upon
kingship. Each in their own version, Peripatetics, Stoics and Neo-
pythagoreans, repeat the same theory of the power of one man—
the best; and of the rights and, to a much larger degree, of the
duties of the best man towards the population. This idea was
adopted completely by the Ptolemies. In their own eyes, as in the
eyes of the Greek population, they were 'Saviours' and 'Benefactors,' devoting their cares to the good of their country, promoters
of justice, patrons of the sciences and arts, generous employers and
paymasters of the Hellenes and especially of their soldiers, sturdy
defenders of their country against enemies, courteous and civil in
their daily intercourse with other citizens, devoted worshippers of
the immortals—in a word, true kings and no tyrants. Demetrius of
Phalerum insistently counselled Ptolemy I to steep himself in such
ideas by the careful study of philosophical treatises on the 'kingly
power,' and there is no doubt that this was what Ptolemy Soter
and all his successors gave out as their attitude. We have definite
evidence of this in the idylls of Theocritus, in a lately discovered
political treatise of the third century B.C.[1], in the ethico-political discussion at the banquet of Greeks and Jews described in the Epistle
of the so-called Aristeas[2], and in many phrases and expressions that
occur in the Ptolemies' orders and instructions to their officials.

More difficult was it for the Ptolemies to find a formula for
their power acceptable to Egypt, its priests and its millions of common people. Officially, the Ptolemies were a new dynasty of
Pharaohs. The cult of them as gods and sons of the gods became
part of the official cult as practised in thousands of great and small
temples throughout Egypt. Philadelphus, the second Ptolemy,
already adopted in full the ritual style of Pharaoh (see p. 18 *sq.*).

Philadelphus and all his successors did their best to give to these
ancient forms a real content, so as to become in the consciousness
of the natives the successors of the Pharaohs. History does not
concern itself with what the Ptolemies as men thought of this deification of their personalities—whether they smiled when on the
walls of the temples they saw themselves in the Egyptian ritual
garb with the Double Crown upon their heads. As kings they
took this deification seriously. Who can tell whether even they

---

[1] Kunst, *Berl. Klass. Texte*, VII, 13, ll. 34 *sqq.*; cf. *P. Oxy.* 1611, ll. 38 *sqq.*
quotation from Theophrastus περὶ βασιλείας II (the real king rules by the
sceptre not by the spear). See further the Bibliography.

[2] This letter (of late date, not earlier than the second century B.C.),
Jewish propaganda though it is, reflects the traditional ideas on royal power
firmly rooted in the consciousness of the Ptolemies. See S. Tracy,
III Maccabees and Pseudo-Aristeas: A Study. Yale Classical Studies, I, (1928).

did not feel the glamour of their new subjects' ancient and enthusiastic religiosity; whether they, or at least some of them, did
not almost come to believe that some deep esoteric meaning was
enshrined in the ancient and mysterious religion of Egypt? However this may be, the important thing is that officially they accepted
the Egyptian religion in all its entirety and never attempted to
hellenize or modify it in the least. If some hellenizing of certain
forms in Egyptian religiosity did occur, it came about of itself
as many non-Egyptians became enthusiastic adherents of the
Egyptian gods and created for themselves a hellenized version of
their cult and hellenized forms for their representations.

The bond between the State and religion that had existed in
Egypt from the beginning the Ptolemies did nothing to break;
they even strengthened it, ever seeking to be on the best of terms
with the hierarchy. But, when all was done, the Egyptian population never in its heart identified them with the real Pharaohs and
never recognized Alexandria as the true capital of Egypt. They
continued to regard the Ptolemies as foreigners and to dream of
a national king with Memphis as his capital. Under Ptolemy III
the prophecy of the 'Potter' (as a matter of fact the god Khnum)
speaks undisguisedly of the 'coast town' yielding its pre-eminence
to Memphis and of the return thither of the Good Genius, the
Agathos Daimon[1]. Under Philopator the so-called Demotic chronicle speaks of a 'Heracleopolite who should bear rule after the
foreigners and Ionians.' It was not for nothing that the appearance of these prophecies coincided with active opposition on the
part of the native population and with insurrections, of which we
shall speak later. All this shows that the Egyptians never recognized the Ptolemies as their national kings and never settled
down to be their loyal subjects. Too great was the contrast between
theory and actuality: between the theoretical Pharaohs and the
actual foreign lord, the chief of the intrusive masters who behaved
in Egypt as in their spear-won land.

Ptolemies and Seleucids may have thought that in course of
time fusion by hellenization would come of itself. But in this they
were mistaken. No such fusion occurred. The Greek population
proved unable to hellenize the spirit of the East. Hellenization of
certain forms of life and administration was attained; but in spirit
the new immigrants were gradually assimilated by the ancient
oriental civilization: their general psychology under new conditions assumed a new character neither purely Eastern nor yet
purely Greek (see below, pp. 144 sqq.).

[1] W. Struve in *Raccolta Lumbroso*, p. 280; cf. E. R. Bevan, *Hist. of Egypt*,
p. 240 sq.

III. ADMINISTRATION: EGYPT

In the actual administration of Egypt the Ptolemies never created such a strict and elaborate system as the Romans did later. The king is the owner of Egypt. His chief assistants in the task of administration are for the most part literally the members of his own household with whom again are closely connected their own households and their agents. To draw a definite line between the public and private activities of one of these members of the Ptolemies' household is occasionally no easy matter. Gradually the Ptolemies' household develops into their court, organized partly on the model of the Macedonian court, partly on that of the Persian and Egyptian courts with a whole series of titles, the king's 'kinsmen' (and the men who were reckoned their equals, *isotimoi*), his 'first friends' (and their *isotimoi*), his 'senior bodyguard,' and the merely 'friends of the king': further there are the so-called 'successors' (*diadochoi*) and the purely court officials, carvers, butlers, grooms and such like with an establishment of 'royal pages,' and so on[1]. The same change into 'courts' also gradually happens to the 'households' of the king's nearest assistants and friends. An admirable example is furnished by the complicated organization of the 'household' or 'court' of Apollonius, Minister of finance to Ptolemy Philadelphus, well known to us from the correspondence of his closest assistant Zeno. The court of Apollonius with the secretary and his office, the treasurer, the manager of the household, the managers of the estates, the physicians, the managers of the shipping, the managers of the palaestra, dozens of agents without definite titles, hundreds of servants, free and slaves, among them musicians and dancing girls, all together gives some idea of what the household and court of Ptolemy Philadelphus himself were like; of this some details may be found also in the Epistle of the so-called Aristeas. Such 'courts' dependent on the courts of the Ptolemies were numbered probably at least by dozens.

The chief posts at the Ptolemies' court were naturally held by the men who in the king's name commanded the army and fleet or managed the economic and financial administration. We hear of officers who commanded in war, but the permanent hierarchy of generals and admirals escapes our knowledge; except the existence of a War Minister, the 'Secretary for armed forces,' who dealt with the enrolment and pay of soldiers and the allotment to them of lands. We know more of the organization of the army

[1] As typical cf. the Delian Inscription, Durrbach, *Choix*, no. 127; *S.E.G.* I, 342.

itself, especially in the reigns of Philadelphus, Euergetes I and Philopator. The Royal Guards stationed in or near Alexandria consisted mainly of Macedonians, and the heavy infantry of the line was drilled on the Macedonian model. It was divided into battalions—chiliarchies, numbered first, second, third, and so on. The light infantry consisted of peltasts and hypaspists. There were also separate formations of Cretans, Thracians and Galatians with their national armament and tactics. The cavalry was organized in the same way. There are numbered hipparchies of heavy horse and light cavalry units named after the peoples from whom they were recruited. We hear of Thracians, Thessalians, Medes and Persians. These forces made up the standing army, predominantly Macedonian and Greek in training and tradition.

The one addition which the Wars of the Successors had introduced was the use of squadrons of elephants protected by armour. Most of these elephants were African, and the catching and training of them was organized on a great scale by the Ptolemies, especially by Philadelphus. Side by side with the standing army, forces of mere mercenaries were sometimes taken into service. The native Egyptian militia—the *machimoi*—a survival from the Pharaohs, was in ordinary campaigns relegated to the service of transport. In critical moments they might be used as a reserve, but they were definitely regarded as of inferior value, and, as we have seen, they were not permanently trusted as part of the military machine.

It was therefore the task of the Ptolemies to attract to Egypt and to maintain there a supply of Greeks and Macedonians, bound to themselves by a firm bond of loyalty and interest. In time of war the soldiers of the regular army received pay and rations; what was needed was a retaining fee in times of peace. This was provided by making to them allotments of land (*kleroi*), near which lodgings (*stathmoi*) were provided for themselves and their families, either separate houses or permanent billets on the native population. In peace they followed their own occupations on the land, in wartime they were mobilized and reported in full equipment to their several units. Military service naturally became hereditary; this was encouraged by the Ptolemies, and possibly was made a condition of the assignment of lands. Soldiers of the younger generation were technically called *epigonoi*, 'cadets,' and usually were trained in garrisons. After this, according to the theory which the writer regards as the most probable (the question is far from settled), they passed into the 'cadet' class (*epigone*) and waited for vacancies to enable them to become regular soldiers. A soldier's son might become himself a soldier during his father's lifetime and so become co-tenant of his father's allotment; or he might succeed to his father both as soldier and land-holder. There thus arose a class of soldier-husbandmen (*klerouchoi*, later *katoikoi*), who held the same plot of land from generation to generation. The allotments varied in size according to the arm to which the soldier belonged and to the rank of the soldier, and similar though smaller allotments were assigned to the native militia[1].

This system secured to the Ptolemies the *cadres* of a standing army of trained soldiers, the immense majority Greek or Macedonian in origin, or sufficiently hellenized. They were broken in to military discipline from their childhood, and it was assumed that with their mothers' milk they imbibed the deepest devotion to the dynasty to which they owed their prosperity and their privileged position. The Greeks despised the Egyptians, whose military value was assessed by their smaller holdings, but in a very short time this army of *klerouchoi*, as always happens to soldiers settled on the land, lost their fine fighting quality and caught the spirit of its despised colleagues, the Egyptian *machimoi*. Nor did they remain sufficiently numerous, for as the supply of tilled or untilled land for allotment was exhausted, the size of the allotments was perforce reduced, and it became impossible to attract recruits from abroad. Mercenaries became scarcer and scarcer in the second-century market, and the only resource left to the Ptolemies was to accept for their army more and more of the native populations whose loyalty, as well as their fighting quality, was more than doubtful.

Of the fleet we know less even than of the army. To judge by recently discovered evidence[2], there was a king's fleet as a nucleus, supplemented by hired ships or squadrons, perhaps Egyptian ships with hired Greek crews. Part of the nucleus fleet was built at the king's expense, and sailors and rowers who served on these were Egyptian fellahin and galley-slaves, the marines apparently Egyptian *machimoi*. The remainder of the king's fleet was supplied by the rich men of Alexandria and of Greek and Phoenician cities on the principle of the Greek trierarchy which Alexander had applied during his time in India. We may assume that the trierarchs found crews for these ships, both marines, sailors and oarsmen. Service in the fleet, whether on the men-of-war or

---

[1] New evidence on the assignment of land to the soldiers is contained in *P. Cairo Zen.* 59001, 59132, 59136 and *P. Heid.* 47 and 48.

[2] *P. Cairo Zen.* 59036 and P. M. Meyer in *Klio* xv, pp. 376 *sqq.*; cf. *P. Lond.* 1, p. 60, 3, and the songs of soldiers and sailors, Powell, *Collectanea Alexandrina*, Lyr. adesp., 16–21, pp. 190 *sqq.* and 32, pp. 195 *sqq.*

the merchantmen, whether on the sea or on the Nile, was hard labour in the worst sense for the people of Egypt. It is true that in the second century we find naval *klerouchoi*, but there were also regular press-gangs for the naval service as well as to provide the men sent to catch elephants in the jungles of Central Africa.

Besides organizing both an army and a fleet, the Ptolemies devoted themselves to building up a smooth-working and efficient administration of the country[1]. Of this, as of the army and fleet, the king was head. His power, being doubly divine, was unbounded. His commands had the force of law and he was the one and only authority which issued laws binding upon the whole population of Egypt. In the last resort it was from the king that proceeded those constitutions (πολιτεῖαι) and city-laws (πολιτικοὶ νόμοι) which authorized the few Greek cities of Egypt and the national associations of non-Egyptian communities outside the cities to enjoy a certain amount of self-government. The legislative and regulating activity of the king was quite unlimited. Such petty matters as the enrolment of a young Macedonian in the garrison of a different town from that to which he had been assigned, or the payment of arrears of salary to inferior priests, any trifle just out of the normal, might sometimes come directly up to the king and be settled by his rescript. There was also much use made of personal audiences granted by the king either at Alexandria or on his numerous progresses through the country. In attendance upon the king, both to keep a register of his orders and decisions and to carry on his voluminous diplomatic and general correspondence, there were of course special secretaries with large staffs under them: we can judge how big the secretariate was by the number of secretaries who followed the journeys of Apollonius, Minister of Finance to Ptolemy Philadelphus. We can see from a document in Zeno's correspondence (the assignment of lamp-oil to the members of Apollonius's court, *P. Cornell*, 1) that the secretariate worked by night as well as day. All the king's acts were registered after Alexander's tradition in a special palace journal; a special secretary (*hypomnematographos*) looked after it. Another secretary (*epistolographos*) directed the king's correspondence. His closest assistant in the administration of justice was the Chief Justice (*archidikastes*), whose duties are not at all clear to us. He probably appointed, with the king's assent, the king's justices on circuit who decided matters according to Greek law (*chrematistai*), and the members of the royal courts of justice in various localities, who settled the affairs of the native population (*laokritai*).

[1] For the parallel organization of the Seleucid Empire, see below, pp. 164 *sqq.*

He also, very likely, prepared for the king the cases decided by him as the final court of appeal.

The organization of justice was a most complicated matter in Ptolemaic Egypt. The principle which governed its application was that the law in any given case was not determined by the domicile of the person concerned but by the section of the population to which he belonged. There were special courts and judges, special civil and criminal law for the Greek cities, for the Jewish community, for the Greeks who lived outside the cities, and for the native population. We are ill-informed both as to the organization of these courts and as to their relation to the royal courts of the *chrematistai* and *laokritai*. Nor is it clear how matters were settled when the interests of a member of one section clashed with those of a member of another. At one time the rule was in force that the language of the documents upon which a civil case was founded determined whether it should go before the king's Greek or Egyptian judges and be decided according to one or the other legal system. It was natural that the population should prefer to have its matters decided by the nearest official rather than submit to the complicated procedure of the courts. It is also natural that the one regulating force to which all courts and officials must conform resided in the king's decrees, on the basis of which there gradually grew up something like a unified law.

A most important position both at court and in the general life of Egypt was that of the official in whose hands was the financial administration of the Egyptian state. He had the direction of its economic life and the care of the state-treasury, with its vast revenues both in money and in kind. This great complex of institutions and offices all came under the rather vague name of 'the Royalty' (τὸ βασιλικόν), for, as we have seen, king and state coincided, and there was and could be no distinction between what belonged to the one and what belonged to the other. The man who directed the whole complicated machine of the economic and financial life of the country—and how complicated it was we shall see from what follows—bore the modest title of manager (*dioiketes*). About one of these managers, Apollonius, under Philadelphus, we are well informed: and we know something of the life of one or two of his successors. But it is not easy to distinguish the personal affairs of the *dioiketes* from his official activity. His assistants, his court and his secretariate are equally concerned with the one and the other. Like the king he has a large and complicated secretariate, his own *hypomnematographos*, his own *epistolographos*. Closely mixed up with his work is that of another high official, the so-called 'accountant,' *eklogistes*, who combined in his one person the functions of Controller of Finance and Secretary to the Treasury. He had his agents throughout the country, apparently bearing the Athenian title of *antigrapheus*, controller. Finally, in late Ptolemaic times, yet another high official comes into view, who manages the 'Privy account' (*idios logos*): his business was to keep an account of all the royal income which did not fall under the regular heads, particularly income from fines, confiscations, escheats and such like.

The administration of the country was conditioned by the presence of a ruling and privileged class of foreigners. From the legal and administrative point of view Egypt was divided into the territory of the Greek cities on the one hand, and on the other the so-called 'country' (χώρα), in its turn cut up into nomes (*nomoi*) or departments, each of which was an independent administrative unit. The Greek cities in Egypt were few. The Ptolemies in their settlement policy did not follow Alexander. They did not urbanize Egypt and did not try to do so, evidently recognizing that to urbanize the country would only make its administration more complicated and lessen its financial and military strength[1]. Of Greek cities there were those which existed before Alexander, Naucratis and perhaps Paraetonium. These continued to exist, but we do not know how their life was organized. In Upper Egypt Ptolemy Soter founded Ptolemaïs but this city, owing to its position, played no great part in Egyptian life. It was Alexander's city Alexandria which under Soter became the capital of the country, though it did not really become part of it but remained Alexandria-next-Egypt (πρὸς Αἴγυπτον). This was the city of the future. With dizzy rapidity it became the largest of Greek cities, larger than Athens, Corinth or Syracuse, at least as large as the Seleucid capitals, Antioch on the Orontes and Seleuceia on the Tigris.

From its earliest days its constitution was as complicated as its population was heterogeneous. The basis was the group of citizens of Alexandria who constituted the Greek city (*polis*) of Alexandria. As usual in a Greek city the citizens were divided into tribes and demes. To what degree this part of Alexandria was really governed after the fashion of regular Greek towns we cannot be sure, but many facts tend to show indirectly that the citizen community in Alexandria lived much the life of an ordinary Greek *polis*, as laid

---

[1] On the other hand, in their provinces the Ptolemies, like the Seleucids, practised the opposite policy, and favoured the turning of villages into cities of the Greek type (see *P. Cairo Zen.* 59003 and 59006, probably military colonies in Jewish towns and villages).

down by the city's constitution and a set of city-laws, of which we
have some miserable fragments. Alexandria had its own popular
assembly, its own council (*boule*) and its own magistrates. Among
these latter the exegetes and the gymnasiarch came in more recent
times to have most importance (*S.E.G.* 11, 864). To what degree
the council of the Alexandrians ruled the life of the whole town we
do not know. Most probably its authority was confined to the
affairs of the citizen-community, while the town as a whole was
managed by a governor (*strategos*) appointed by the king. This is
the natural consequence of the fact that in Alexandria the Alexandrian citizens were a minority. Outside their authority stood
the king's palace and everything that went with it, harbour, lighthouse, royal magazines, and probably the bigger temples such as
the Sarapeum. Outside their community stood also the royal army
and the so-called Macedonians and many of the royal officers and,
finally, sundry communities inhabiting Alexandria but not possessing its citizenship; various Greeks, so-called Persians, Anatolians, Syrians, especially Jews and Egyptians. Each of these
groups probably formed a miniature community: of the Jews at
any rate this is quite certain. Under these conditions no decree
of the popular assembly and council of the Alexandrian citizens
could be binding upon the whole population unless of course it
were made so by a special act of the king's. The institutions of
the city, for instance the gymnasium, might and probably did own
landed property on advantageous terms: it is possible that the
Alexandrians had special rights with regard to owning land in a
particular piece of Egypt adjacent to the city, but, as a city, Alexandria had no territory of which it was the independent owner.

What degree of self-government was enjoyed by the group of
non-Egyptians scattered all through Egypt in the so-called cities
(*metropoleis*), and in the villages, we do not know. Ptolemaïs was
a city and as such had Greek self-government and even a certain
shadow of being a sovereign state (in the third century we find
'ambassadors of the king' at Ptolemaïs). But we cannot tell how
much self-government was allowed for instance to the inhabitants
of the former capital Memphis or of the new Graeco-Egyptian
village of Philadelphia in the Fayûm. Nor do we know what
exactly was meant by the so-called *politeumata* of the Cretans,
Boeotians, Lycians, Idumeans, Phrygians and Helleno-memphites.
Their military character is in most cases beyond a doubt: they
seem to have been in some way military societies of men from the
same district with their own local cults and some little power to
manage their own affairs; but the military element certainly did
not survive in all its purity.

Apart from these few islands of non-Egyptian population the 'country' was divided up into nomes, toparchies and villages (*komai*), and was administered by the king's officials. Legally these derived their full powers directly from the king but in practice they were appointed by the higher officials of the Ptolemaic bureaucracy. To draw lines exactly separating the authority of each official from the next is difficult, not only because of the scantiness of our information and the difficulty of following the historical evolution of each office, but because it is probable that no strict and exact distinction of the functions of the different officials had ever been laid down. They were the agents of the king and worked both by the ancient pre-Ptolemaic tradition and on the directions and instructions that reached them from their own superiors or from the king. These instructions (*entolai*), so far as we know, were never codified, but were promulgated one after the other without any definite system and undoubtedly often contradicted each other. The officials also guided their conduct by the directions of more general character that emanated from the king and bore the name of 'laws' (*nomoi*). How complicated was the administrative system of Ptolemaic Egypt may be seen from the story how the young cadet Apollonius was in the days of Ptolemy Philometor given leave to transfer to Memphis. We see how Apollonius in order to establish his position and get his due pay, though he can show an authorization from the king himself, has to run round from one official authority to another, the war office, the treasury, the local authority, while his dossier grows like a snowball. The same complicated procedure may be observed in the practice of the judicial branch (cf. vol. vi, p. 178 n.)

The composition and functions of the staff that administered the different nomes were never permanently settled. We see them changing before our very eyes, though we cannot always discover what was the reason and purpose of these changes. Under Ptolemy Soter, as it seems, there was still preserved the ordinary system of administration which had prevailed in former times and had not been changed in any essential by Alexander the Great. As of old, the head of the nome was the governor, the nomarch, sometimes an Egyptian, in old days almost a feudal *grand seigneur*. In the time of Philadelphus things have changed entirely. Feudal survivals have vanished once and for all. The administration of the nome has been split up and is entrusted to all sorts of officials, all subordinate to the king and his ministers but not to each other. Military business is in the hands of a *strategos*, and he has some judicial authority especially in criminal matters. Under his orders, but not exclusively, is the military police of the nome, its commanders, the *epistatai* and *archiphylakitai*, and the rank and file, the *phylakitai*. Side by side with him is the financial governor of the nome, the *oikonomos*, with unusually wide and varied functions in economics and finance, and alongside with him local *dioiketai* and *hypodioiketai*. With him works the controller, *antigrapheus*, a colleague rather than a subordinate. Nomarchs still exist, but they are no longer anything like governors nor are they supreme, but yet they are not subordinate to the *oikonomos*. The boundaries of their authority are often not the same as those of the nome. Sometimes in one nome, for example, the Arsinoïte, there are several. Their functions are miscellaneous and hard to define. Their chief business seems to be connected with the development of the government land in the nome, and yet this is not altogether outside the competence of the *oikonomos*. All work concerned with statistics, keeping an account of the population, of how the sharing out of land and other real property stands, of the obligations of the population to the state (taxes and forced labour), and the making out of notices as to the taxes due—in a word, all the secretarial and statistical work of the nome, toparchy and village, lies on the shoulders of a series of clerks, the most typical officials of ancient Egypt; the 'royal clerk' (*basilikos grammateus*) established in the chief town of the nome, the *topogrammateus* in the toparchy and the *komogrammateus* for each village.

The collection, transport and storage of the produce paid as taxes and rents was the business of the toparchs and komarchs in each district and village, the elected or nominated representatives of the native Egyptian population. They worked in conjunction with the heads of the government stores (*thesauroi*), who were called 'corn-collectors' (*sitologoi*), and the directors of the local branches of the treasury (*trapezitai*), half-officials, half tax-farmers, who carried out at their own expense various banking operations. Special collectors (*logeutai*) and exactors (*praktores*) co-operated with the above-mentioned officials and also with an array of tax-farmers, middle-men between the state and the tax-payers, peasants, artisans, manufacturers or tradesmen. Special functions in connection with the branches of the revenue that were farmed and with other special branches of the economic life of the state were entrusted to the 'curators' (*epimeletai*). The administration of the nome was in touch with the temples through the *epistatai* who managed the temples and were responsible for the fulfilment of their obligations to the state, being the representatives before the state of the numerous, firmly organized and admirably disciplined Egyptian clergy. On its side the state had a whole series of officials to deal with temple affairs, sometimes these were appointed for a particular purpose: the details unfortunately still escape us.

Finally, on the lowest rung of the administrative ladder stood in hundreds or thousands the guardians of various kinds who had care of dams and canals, of roads, sown crops, vineyards, stores, pastures, cattle and so on; these obligations fell upon the villages, who bore them without enthusiasm as a heavy and hateful burden.

The officials of the Ptolemaic period were not a separate class, they had no professional instruction, received no special education: they were mostly new Greek immigrants (save for the lowest officials, and the police officers, komarchs, *komogrammateis* and *phylakitai*, who might be natives), creatures of some big official, often his fellow-townsmen. They went into the service for the sake of the pay offered by the state and because an adroit and able man might get rich and rise high. In the many fawning petitions addressed by the people to officials they wish them a brilliant career, which was altogether a matter of the king's favour[1]. But the lower offices about the villages were nothing but a burden of heavy responsibility which gave no access either to wealth or a brilliant career.

This sketch of the administration of Egypt is more or less correct only for the third century B.C. At the end of the third and in the second century many changes were introduced but we know very little what they were. The general tendency was towards greater centralization and to a concentration of local power in the hands of the *strategos*, who sometimes also held in his own hands the functions of the financial governor (ὁ ἐπὶ τῶν προσόδων) who had taken the place of the *oikonomos*, an office which had fallen to the second rank. Another novelty in the last two centuries B.C. was the gradual admission to administrative office of the richer and more civilized elements in the native population now superficially hellenized. At the end of the first century B.C. the two tendencies bring about in the person of Egyptian *strategoi* a revival of the old semi-feudal nomarchs of pre-Ptolemaic times. Posts are more and more given to the richer elements in the population. As an official was responsible to the king both with his person and his property it was to the interest of the state to recruit its officials and tax-farmers from the richer class regardless of their origin. Office was not yet a burden but it was getting very near it. Finally, under pressure of necessity, in view of the constant growth of dissatisfaction in the south and the repeated risings, the king was

---

[1] A model official is described in a fragment of an Alexandrian comedy recently published by Crönert, *Gött. Gel. Nachr.*, 1922, pp. 31 *sqq.* Note the epithets φιλοβασιλεύς and φιλέλλην.

forced to unite all Upper Egypt under one governor-general (the *epistrategos*).

IV. ADMINISTRATION. PROVINCES

During the century after Alexander, the period of her greatest prosperity, Egypt under Ptolemy Soter, Philadelphus and Euergetes I, acquired and kept a number of external possessions, what the Romans would have called provinces. The more important and the more permanently connected with Egypt were Cyprus, Cyrene and the Cyrenaica, and the so-called Coele-Syria with Phoenicia and Palestine. Lycia with its valuable forests, Caria with its trade and manufactures (including part of Ionia with Miletus and Ephesus) and a league of Aegean Islands, of which the most loyal were Thera and parts of Crete, for many years formed part of the Ptolemaic Empire; finally, Egypt held for a while part of Thrace with the Chersonese, and Samothrace and for a short time even had a footing in the Peloponnese. The acquisition and loss of these provinces, depending as they did on the international situation and the military successes of the Ptolemies, have been dealt with elsewhere; here must be described, so far as may be, the system applied by the Ptolemies to the administration of their provinces.

Our information is fullest about the government of Cyprus. We know from inscriptions that Cyprus was under a military governor (*strategos*) commanding considerable forces stationed in the various cities of Cyprus and organized in the Egyptian fashion: these were certainly taken from the king's regular Egyptian army. By the second century the Governor has his own powerful fleet probably supplied and equipped by the big coast-towns of Cyprus: and bears the additional title of *nauarchos*. In view of the special economic and political part played by the great and rich temples of Cyprus in the life of the island, the governor bears the third title of *archiereus*, that is head of the priesthood in the Cyprian temples. At certain times, perhaps permanently, a special governor, probably with full military authority (*antistrategos*) has charge of the valuable mines of Cyprus, all of which probably belonged to the state and were worked by it. The cities of Cyprus had never enjoyed the Greek autonomy, so the question of the relations between the cities and the central power did not assume much importance there. The practical masters of the cities were the commanders of the garrisons who gave their orders to the native elected organs of government. The revenues which the Ptolemies drew from Cyprus were undoubtedly enormous. Hence came the copper that Egypt needed so much; here, too, probably were built many ships for the Egyptian navy and mercantile fleet. Of the financial and economic organization of Cyprus we know little. The revenues, at least in the later period, were, according to Polybius (XVIII, 55), collected by the *strategos* and passed on to the Alexandrian *dioiketes*. There is, however, reason to think that what Polybius says is only true of the second century. Formerly in Cyprus as in the other provinces the *dioiketes* had had his agents, *oikonomoi*, *grammateis*, who had charge of the revenues (*P. Cairo Zen.* 59016; *P.S.I.* 505 and 429).

As to the organization of the Cyrenaica during the rule of the Ptolemies we know hardly anything. Here the great problem was to establish a modus vivendi with the ancient Greek city of Cyrene. This modus vivendi was laid down by the newly discovered *diagramma* which is to be placed in the time of Ptolemy Soter (322 or 308 B.C.) In it the king confirms and modifies the constitution of the Cyrenaic league. In the main it is the ancient constitution of Cyrene slightly modified and with certain definite provisions inserted by Ptolemy to secure control of Cyrenaic affairs. Ptolemy reserves to himself certain rights and privileges which naturally follow from his being sovereign over the city: (1) the right to enrol in the tribes certain new citizens, perhaps *klerouchoi* of the Ptolemaic army; (2) the right to insist on the restoration to their rights of exiles who had been Ptolemy's adherents; (3) the appointment of members of the Gerusia; (4) the handing over to Ptolemy of the office of *strategos*; (5) his right to interfere in judicial affairs concerning the former exiles; (6) certain privileges touching the granting of citizenship. Some of these privileges, as that concerning the exiles, were merely temporary, but the right to nominate members of the Gerusia and the right to be perpetual *strategos* were evidently permanent provisions comparable to the rights of the Pergamene kings over the city of Pergamum, and to the constitution of Ptolemaïs in Upper Egypt.

The social structure of Cyrene and the Cyrenaica as described by Strabo (*ap.* Joseph., *Ant.* XIV, 115 *sqq.*) closely resembles that of Alexandria and Egypt. The city has a large non-Greek population, mainly Jewish; side by side with the full citizens and those with limited rights there is a mass of foreigners (metoecs) who are not citizens at all, in part, probably, native Libyans; the population of the 'country' consists of 'husbandmen' (*georgoi*) tilling the land belonging either to the city or to the king; these were also most likely soldiers settled as *klerouchoi*.

The fundamental problem which faced the Ptolemies in the Cyrenaica faced them also in all their provinces where the leading part in the life of the country was played by the Greek cities; in the League of Islanders, the separate Greek islands, Caria, Ionia, Lycia and to some extent in Thrace. To judge by the scanty data available, the Ptolemies showed little respect for the cities' autonomy. Their suzerainty is expressed most clearly by the fact that all the official documents of the Greek cities in the Ptolemies' dominions begin not with the names of the city, its people, council and magistrates, but with the name of the king. Most consideration was shown by the Ptolemies in their treatment of the League of Islanders, a considerable power and well organized, which claimed respect. But even here the Ptolemaic nesiarch is really the dictator of the League: he summons meetings of its deputies, executes the decisions of such meetings, commands the military forces of the League, keeps the seas clear of pirates, collects payments from the members and appoints arbitrators to settle disputes. On the other hand, the Ptolemies during the short time of their supremacy were careful not to interfere in the internal affairs of these island states.

It was quite otherwise with the Greek towns in the mainland provinces. Although their institutions, popular assembly, council and magistrates, continued in being they could decide no single important question without the preliminary consent of the king, that is, of his officials. Besides this the administration was continually interfering with the petty affairs of city life either directly by definite injunctions or indirectly by private letters and instructions. Halicarnassus cannot build a gymnasium without the king's permission. At Samothrace it is for the king and his governor to allow or to forbid the importation of wheat into the island: and the governor has the deciding voice in the question of sharing out the land among the citizens. At Miletus the king assigns land, though apparently not the city's land, at his own good pleasure. Particularly instructive are two letters found among Zeno's papers, speaking of Calynda in Caria. In one, in order to secure a small payment from the city, one of the citizens appeals to Apollonius the *dioiketes* to put pressure upon the military governor and financial officer of the province and through them and also directly upon the assembly and council of the city. The other letter is even more interesting. At Calynda, as in other cities in their provinces, the Ptolemies kept a garrison. The soldiers were billeted upon the citizens and certain landowners were bound to supply fodder for the horses of particular cavalrymen. Evidently this burden was exceedingly unwelcome to the citizens. One of them, a kinsman of Zeno, obtained through him exemption, but on his death his family had to submit to the old exactions. The letter makes an appeal to Zeno who forwards it to Apollonius, asking him to restore the rights which had been taken away from his relations. No protest against this reign of force and continual interference was possible for the cities were at the mercy of the Ptolemaic garrison and its commander. In word the Ptolemies claimed to bring freedom to the Greek cities, in fact they were much less liberal than the Seleucids or even the Antigonids of Macedonia[1].

The most oppressive side of Ptolemaic rule, however, was the consistent and systematic adjustment of taxation to the interests of the central power. Before they passed under one of the Hellenistic monarchies the cities had possessed their own systems of taxation, customs dues, possibly monopolies. It is probable that these systems remained in force with slight alterations, but a part of the city's income was taken for the king's treasury while royal officials controlled the expenditure even of the rest. This supposition agrees entirely with the evidence of lately published papyri and inscriptions. One of these papyri (*P. Tebt.* 8; Wilcken, *Chrest.* 2), which contains extracts from letters addressed by the *dioiketes* probably to the *oikonomoi* of the several Ptolemaic provinces, gives us a general picture of the taxes which on the whole agrees with what we know both of the general character of the royal financial system and of the practice in the several cities. Land-taxes (*phoroi*) and, distinct from them, rents from public property are paid partly in money, partly in kind. The customs are turned to account by the central government and monopolies, for instance in purple and scented oils, are introduced. The same picture is given by an inscription from Telmessus in Lycia. This city was granted by Euergetes to his vassal Ptolemaeus, son of Lysimachus, and the new ruler found his subjects so impoverished by taxation that he was compelled to remit some imposts and lighten others, particularly those on agriculture and cattle-keeping. The tax on gardens and the payment for the right of pasturage are abolished; in the duty on vegetable produce the Ptolemaic system gives place to the less oppressive Seleucid tithe, and various other duties of the same kind are cancelled.

The system by which these various taxes were collected was in principle Greek—the farming method. The tax-farmers were local people, but the taxes were put up to auction not locally but at Alexandria. This is proved by various documents in the Zeno letters (esp. *P. Cairo Zen.* 59037) which show that the picture of an auction of provincial taxes drawn by Josephus in his wonderful story of the farmer of tribute from Coele-Syria (*Ant.* xii, 169 *sqq.*)

---

[1] The papyri bearing on the administration of Caria in the time of Ptolemy II are quoted in Edgar's Introductions to *P. Cairo Zen.* 59037 (Halicarnassus); 59045 and 59046 (Caunus). On Palestine and Syria see pp. 184 *sqq.*

is on the whole accurate. We see how, when the taxes are being put up to auction for a new term, all the best known and richest men of the place go up to Alexandria and with any amount of bribery and intrigue compete against each other at the auction at which the tribute and taxes of the towns are being put up. To judge by the sums quoted in the papyrus just mentioned (*P. Tebt.* 8), the revenues received by the state from the provinces were enormous. The revenues of the Ptolemies in gold and silver were as much the profits of their external trade as of their exploitation of the provinces. Particularly productive were the customs and commercial duties in the coast towns of Coele-Syria, Phoenicia and Palestine (particularly Gaza) and those of Alexandria and Pelusium from goods which came from Syria and Palestine, as we can see from Zeno's correspondence (*e.g. P. Cairo Zen.* 59077, 59093 and 59012).

The local tax-farmers worked under the constant control of the Ptolemaic officials, agents of the *dioiketes* at Alexandria, backed by the garrisons. Their names recur constantly in the correspondence of Zeno, who was himself such an agent in Syria and Palestine. We find them also mentioned in the letters to and from his native region of Caria, Caunus, Calynda and Halicarnassus. One letter is all about supporting some candidate at Alexandria (*P. Cairo Zen.* 59037): probably he wants to get the farming of the taxes: and we can see what a network of intrigues, bribes and lobbying this means. As in Egypt, the agents of the *dioiketes* probably bore the humble title of *oikonomos*; their assistants were termed clerks. But most of his agents are not given a title; a man is just called 'Apollonius' man': this shows us very clearly how the provinces, like Egypt, were regarded as the personal possessions of the several Ptolemies. Parallel with their government work, the agents of the *dioiketes* also carry on his personal commercial business, and they manage to find time for trafficking on their own account: they buy up olive oil, wine, scents, horses, slaves; they make loans to local people; they try to smuggle in their goods without paying the proper duty or getting the proper licences—just the same sort of thing that we find later in the provinces of the Roman Empire.

V. ECONOMIC CONDITIONS. THE RESOURCES OF EGYPT AND THEIR APPLICATION

It has already been pointed out that the permanence of the Ptolemies' power in Egypt and in the provinces, and also of their international position, had as its basis the efficient and systematic utilization of the economic resources of Egypt and the provinces, and the development of their economic life in accordance with new social conditions within Egypt and that country's new position among other nations.

The economic resources of Egypt were indeed very great, but Egypt was far from being economically self-sufficient. Accordingly the development of its economic life was as much a matter of systematically and intensively exploiting its national wealth and arranging for due export of its products as of an unceasing and efficient regulation of its enormous imports. Egypt had always been mainly agricultural, and so it remained under the Ptolemies. A vast quantity of various crops could be produced if the annual Nile floods were skilfully and systematically regulated and the embankments and canals carefully kept up and wisely extended. This regulation, these labours of irrigation and drainage, determined the area which could bear cereals and the amount of the yearly crop. In all this the Ptolemies did a great deal for Egypt, by combining the age-old experience of Egypt with the achievements of Greek skill. It is characteristic that the main direction was in the hands of Greek engineers, with the Egyptian experts working under them. For the Ptolemies the increase in the area of cultivated land and greater regularity in the harvests was a matter of life and death. But for it they could not have found in Egypt space for the new Greek agricultural population without ruining their authority in the eyes of the natives and lessening their economic prosperity. The Ptolemies were thus able not only to assign a share of land to the soldiers and other new settlers, but to offer work and certain subsistence to the ever-growing native population. The risings of the Egyptians in the last three centuries B.C. certainly had economic as well as political and religious causes, as the area of land under cultivation first ceased to grow because every acre was being used that the level of ancient skill enabled them to use, and then began to decrease just because the insurrections and the disorder that went with them brought about a deterioration in the system of irrigation works.

The new lands and new cultivators introduced into Egyptian farming new methods and new branches of agriculture. From time immemorial Egypt had not only produced cereals and fodder for cattle, oil-bearing plants, vegetables, flax and hemp, but had grown many fruit trees, the date palms and vines. The Ptolemaic period increased the area of those plantations, especially vineyards. The Greeks had always been used to growing vines, and on the lands which did not suit crops well and which they accordingly got cheaply, they planted vines. Their experience and skill certainly improved the quality of the wine and brought it within the reach of everybody side by side with the national drink of beer. An attempt was also made to grow the olive. In some places in the Fayûm this attempt was successful, but still Egyptian olive oil remained of second-rate quality, unprofitable to produce, in spite of some protective measures taken by the Ptolemies (p. 139). The correspondence of Zeno who, in the second half of his life, became the manager of Apollonius's great estate at Philadelphia in the Fayûm, shows that the Ptolemies and their ministers and assistants not only took their share in helping the natural development of agriculture and horticulture in Egypt but did their best to stimulate it in every way, introducing new sorts of fruit trees, berries, vines and vegetables. In this they followed the example both of the more enlightened Pharaohs and of tyrants in Greek states. It was thus that the Fayûm quickly changed from marshes and desert into a wide expanse of corn land beyond which, as at the present day, there stretched orchards, vineyards, olive and date groves and vegetable gardens. Nor can we doubt that the same activity was displayed in the region of Alexandria and throughout the whole marsh-lands of the Delta.

A real difficulty for the Ptolemies was the question of timber building, for Egypt has never possessed forests. To import all the wood needed and at a reasonable price, bearing in mind the anterior necessity of making sure of a sufficient supply for the shipyards and for building in Alexandria, was impossible. So of imported timber up-country we hear nothing. The population supplied its needs by the use of old fruit trees (especially date palms, of which not only the stem but the leaves were most valuable material for basket-work, mat and rope-making) and by the systematic use of all space suitable for planting trees, especially the embankments, on which the trees and shrubs served a double purpose, consolidating the banks and supplying new fascines for fresh ones.

Hardly less important for the life of the country was the keeping of cattle and poultry: oxen, cows, sheep, goats, pigs, asses, geese and ducks had ever been the glory and pride of Egypt. In developing cattle-breeding the Ptolemies showed even more initiative than in agriculture. Under their rule the horse was used not only in war but for transportation, and we hear of camels for the first time. They tried also to acclimatize various hybrids; they imported new breeds of sheep and for the first time began to get wool fit for the finer textiles: many new breeds of poultry were introduced. The Ptolemies found Egypt the home of ancient and famous manufactures. Weaving and pottery, particularly the making of glazed ware and bright tiles, leather work and other handicrafts had flourished for centuries, while from all time Egypt had produced admirable unblown glass and exported it wholesale. Her products of decorative stone, especially alabaster, supplied a world-market, while her most famous monopoly was in the production of paper from papyrus. Under the rule of the Ptolemies all these crafts continued to flourish and in the manufacture, for example, of glass and papyrus new devices were introduced. But for the development of agriculture and still more of manufactures Egypt had always needed large and regular imports. She possessed excellent quarries and rich mines of natron and salt, but hardly any metals, apart from a little copper and iron of inferior quality, and hardly any heavy timber. This goes far to explain the perpetual attempts of Egypt before the Ptolemies to conquer Cyprus, Syria, the ports of Phoenicia and parts of Asia Minor. Gold and silver always came to Egypt from outside, partly as bullion from Cyprus, Syria, Phoenicia and Central Africa, partly, under the Persians and later, as coined metal paying for Egyptian agricultural produce, cattle and manufactures. So it was natural that Egypt should from the beginning have sought both to frame her foreign policy in accordance with these facts and to develop her external trade.

The result of this development of trade with Central Africa, Arabia, India, Palestine, Syria and Phoenicia, and also with the countries on the Aegean, Mediterranean and Black seas, was that Egypt from time immemorial had obtained other materials than metal and wood, and these called into existence new branches of manufacture. The splendid level attained in early Egypt by the art of the jeweller and goldsmith, and by the skill of the craftsman in ivory and various imported woods, has often been described. Another ancient speciality of Egypt was the preparation of scents, cosmetics and sweet-smelling oils.

The Ptolemies gave an immense stimulus to the external trade of Egypt. None of the old trade-routes were abandoned and many new ones were opened. Masses of wares of all kinds went in and out through Alexandria and the other ports of Northern Egypt, especially Pelusium, east of Alexandria, on the one side, and through the Red Sea ports on the other. Exports were corn, without which industrial Greece could not exist, linen stuffs, papyrus, glass, objects of ivory, wood, alabaster and precious metals, scents, salves and other cosmetics: imports were wine and olive oil mostly from Syria and Greece, metals from Cyprus and Phoenicia, timber from Asia Minor, horses from Syria and

Palestine, slaves from the East and Greece, gold, precious stones, ivory, precious woods, sweet-scented oils, silk, possibly cotton from Central Africa, Arabia and India. For the encouragement of commerce the Ptolemies kept up the ancient ways across the desert from the quays upon the Nile to the little ports on the Red Sea, which rapidly increased in size. Philadelphus even cleared out and made navigable the canal from the Nile to the Red Sea that Pharaoh Necho had dug and Darius had restored. The Ptolemies were active in furthering the interests of their merchants along the Mediterranean and Aegean coasts. Egyptian trade came to be world-wide in the then sense of the word. The products of Egypt were to be found in China, and in India, in Central Africa and far away to the West: in Northern Africa, Spain, Britain, Gaul, on the Steppes of South Russia and in Central Asia.

Hand in hand with the development of external, as of internal trade went the development of industry. Alongside the old centres of Egyptian industry, with the ancient guilds of craftsmen in the temples of the *metropoleis* of Egypt, Alexandria became more and more, not merely the place where the goods produced in Egypt were accumulated for export, but a centre of industrial production. We have to arrive at this supposition *a priori*, for, strange as it may appear, we have no exact data to guide us. The name 'Alexandrian' borne by certain manufactures on the world-market proves nothing. They came on the market from Alexandria, but they might just as well have been made up-country. However, it is difficult to believe that at Alexandria, to which gravitated masses of raw materials, no industry arose. But we must not exaggerate and think that Alexandrian industry put an end to that of Egypt. Probably we shall never be able to say whether any particular stuff, any particular glass bottle, any particular ivory box or silver vessel was made in the capital itself or in one of the little workshops of the towns and villages of Egypt. Of the weaving industry we do know that the workshops in the temples and throughout the 'country' went on making not merely plain cloths, but dyed and embroidered stuffs, rich carpets and curtains, the famous 'byssus,' even in Ptolemaic times, partly for their own use, partly for the king, that is, for Alexandria and the foreign market. Equally, Mendes continued to be the great centre for the production of myrrh and other perfumes.

On the organization of commerce in Alexandria and Egypt we are ill-informed, particularly as to Alexandria. We know that foreign trade was in the hands both of Alexandrians (we find groups of them organized in societies at Delos and other places) and of foreign merchants. We have some idea how certain big men under the Ptolemies managed their commerce: Apollonius had his own merchant fleet, both for the Nile and for the sea. In Syria, Palestine and Phoenicia he had a number of agents, who bought up for him slaves, olive oil, wine and various other things. All these were dispatched to Egypt, as we see by the documents which speak of paying the import duties. The same was done by many members of his household and presumably by the heads and members of many other great households in Alexandria. It is not likely that Apollonius did all this in the name of the king and for the king's profit, though this is not actually ruled out. Still less can we distinguish how far the agents of Apollonius worked on his account and how far on their own.

As to industry in Alexandria and its organization we know decidedly less. The large importation of slaves into Egypt from Syria and Palestine, the existence of a law forbidding their export, the elaborate legislation about home-born slaves, the existence of a special tax upon slaves, all go to show the importance of servile labour in Ptolemaic Egypt and particularly in Alexandria. For it is hard to believe that all the slaves imported into Egypt were for domestic use in the great households. Apollonius undoubtedly imported slaves for his cloth works at Memphis. If this be so, we may suppose that in Alexandria industry was developed not only by the growth of a large class of small craftsmen, but on the lines already adopted at Athens of establishing rather large factories with numerous hands either slaves or free. But we must admit that this is all guesswork.

We know rather more about the organization of industry up-country. Some branches were only carried on by the state. This is true of the preparation of vegetable oils. All the mills belonged exclusively to the state as did all the raw material, either bought at a forced price from the producer or else received by the treasury as rent from the so-called crown-peasants. There were no temple-mills and no private ones. Labour was supplied by the native population, in return for payment, but it was obligatory to render it for a definite time. The workers were members of the olive-workers' guild; but we do not know whether they were professional olive-workers or ordinary peasants and artisans.

Nor do we know whether the same principle was applied to other branches of industry, but it is quite likely in the case of salt and also in that of natron. Weaving was arranged quite otherwise: the work was done at home by the proprietors of looms. It is possible that the production, sale and buying of linen and woollen stuffs was uncontrolled. But the state had a register of all looms, and their work was strictly supervised by royal officials and contractors. The first obligation of the weavers was to execute orders from the state; for each piece they were paid according to scale. Whether they were allowed also to work on their own account and for the general market we do not know. The temple weavers mostly worked to supply the needs of the temples.

Again, we do not know what branches of industry were organized in the same way as weaving. There certainly were some in which the state did not interfere as much as with oil, salt and stuffs. In these industries it is possible that the state contented itself with taxing the craftsman who might produce what he liked and offer it on the general market without being burdened with obligatory state orders.

We must not think that the Ptolemies in their economic policy and their efforts to develop the resources of the country thought only of their private gain, that is, that their main purpose was to enrich themselves and not the country. Of course their foreign policy and their personal expenses swallowed up enormous sums, but we have no right to suppose that for them the good of Egypt was only a means and not an end. The first Ptolemies devoted much energy to their foreign policy, trying to secure for themselves the first place among the powers of the Hellenistic world: but their success did not tend to exhaust Egypt, on the contrary it strengthened and enriched her. We have seen how great were the revenues received by them from their provinces and how enormously important it was for the development of economic life in Egypt itself that Cyprus, Phoenicia, Syria and Palestine, and parts of Asia Minor were Ptolemaic, that is Egyptian, possessions and that at one time the Ptolemies ruled the Aegean Sea. There is no reason to think that after Soter any of his successors dreamed of restoring Alexander's empire under the sceptre of the Ptolemies and it is far from certain that even Soter sought the restoration of the whole empire. Still less can we impute imperialistic tendencies to the Ptolemies of the last two centuries B.C. They were well content if they succeeded in defending the independence of Egypt against foreign foes.

VI. TAXATION

The economic and fiscal policy of the Ptolemies made its chief aim to establish and confirm the prosperity of Egypt, and there is no doubt that they were genuinely anxious that Egypt should be rich and contented. But it goes without saying that they did their best to make use of this prosperity for the purposes of state. The Greeks had always put the interests of the state a long way first and private interests second. The taxation of the country was therefore heavier than in modern states and on quite a different basis. This basis was partly an inheritance from the past, partly a direct consequence of the conquest of Egypt by Alexander, partly a logical development of the Greek idea of the supremacy of the state and its self-sufficiency. The governing idea was that Egypt, both the country itself and the provinces, belonged to the king and that the king had the full right to use for the purposes of state, that is for the general good, the wealth and strength of the population. On these two premises the whole financial organization of the country was built up.

The Ptolemies both as successors of the Pharaohs and so gods in human form and the sons of gods, and also as persons who held Egypt by right of conquest, were, as we said above, the owners of the whole land of Egypt and all that it contained. From time immemorial, the land had been cultivated by the native population living in the towns and villages. Year after year they would plough this or that plot as crown peasants (βασιλικοὶ γεωργοί) of the crown land (γῆ βασιλική) assigned to this or that village. Owners of this land they had never been and did not consider themselves such. The land belonged to the god and king and its tilling was carried out by the directions of the king and his officials. But as a matter of fact the peasants were bound to the land and the land to them by ties going back hundreds of years. To break these ties was neither in the power nor in the interest of the king. So under the Ptolemies as under the Pharaohs the crown land continued to be ploughed by the crown peasants. Their right to the land was not defined juridically. In Greek terminology they were leaseholders paying to the king rent in money or in kind. But they differed from a Greek leaseholder, in that they were bound to their land and compelled to cultivate it under whatever conditions the state might dictate to them. Still, the state was not really free in defining the conditions. They had been for ever defined by a tradition based upon the experience of centuries and any infringement of the tradition aroused mass resistance: the peasants appeal to God, go off to 'take seat' in a temple, and refuse to work.

The peasants who tilled the land to support the temples and the cult of the gods were upon the same footing. They too laboured for themselves and also for the state. But into their relations with the temples and the priests the Ptolemies brought a great change by cutting the direct connection between the peasants and the priesthood: henceforward the peasants paid their rent not to the priests but to the king's officials; the state in return guaranteed to supply the needs of each temple and its cult. The same reform was introduced in the collection of a special impost upon vine-dressers which formerly had gone to the temple treasuries. From the time of Philadelphus this *apomoira* supported the cult of Arsinoe.

One might think that in this organization which had endured for centuries there was no room for new men and new Greek methods. But the new men, as we have seen, were the real basis of the king's power and strength. Room had to be made for them in Egypt and their life must be arranged upon conditions that they would accept. So a part of their land was granted by the Ptolemies to the new settlers, mainly soldiers of their army. At first probably a certain amount of land reached by the inundation and fit for growing cereals was still at the disposal of the state. This may have been the estates of the great landowners in former times, both natives and foreigners. But these lands would not suffice for long, so new lands had to be found for the new settlers. This explains the Ptolemies' feverish activity in the Fayûm and probably in the Delta to reclaim marshes and desert and turn them into allotments. These were given to the new soldier-settlers for them to hold, but ownership remained with the king and they could enjoy them only as long as they served the state. For the use of the land they naturally made certain payments. One man, however, might do no more than till the land which was flooded every year and was part of the old cultivation; another might have the capital and energy to apply his labour to land which was not suited for raising the ordinary cereals, but good enough, if suitably irrigated, to support fruit trees and vines. Such a piece would then, in accordance with ancient practice both in Egypt and Greece, become his own 'property' (*ktema*) and was his to enjoy so long as he went on keeping up the orchard or vineyard and paid rather heavy dues to the king and the temples. This procedure was open not only to soldiers, but to anyone with the needful capital and enterprise. Besides the soldiers certain officials received grants of land upon much the same conditions. In early days when there was more land than men who wanted it, and when it was desirable to attract private capital and private enterprise to get the land skilfully farmed and brought into good condition, the Ptolemies distributed great tracts to the men immediately about them, high officials and generals. These lands were either free grants (ἐν δωρεᾷ) or held in return for definite services (ἐν συντάξει).

From the land accordingly the state received partly a rent in kind partly dues either in kind or money. The amount of the state revenue was determined by the conditions of each year, that is, the height attained by the river Nile in the yearly inundations: money was also paid in taxes on houses and building lots. Landholders had to divide among themselves certain special taxes both temporary and permanent, and were also subject to certain other special conditions. For example, as the state had the right to buy up the whole crop of oil-producing plants at its own price, and naturally did not wish to take more of the produce than it needed, it regulated the amount of these crops to be sown each year throughout the whole of Egypt. The state also claimed to control the cattle fodder with which land was sown after the cereals had been carried or in the years of 'resting' prescribed by the rotation of crops mostly practised in Egypt. For the right of using this fodder for their cattle the landholders and leaseholders paid definite sums. They also paid fees for the privilege of turning their beasts out on the pastures which were reckoned state property, or for hiring the pastures. Besides these permanent taxes, landholders and people occupied in keeping cattle or transport work paid a separate tax for the right to keep cattle. The state itself owned great droves of oxen and cows, pigs, goats, sheep and geese, which were looked after by special keepers who hired them from the state. There was a tax on slaves, as we have seen; moreover, a special due was paid for the right of plying a particular handicraft. Finally, the whole population except the soldiers and officials paid a poll-tax.

The collection of all these dues required a strict registration of the land, cattle and people, an exact calculation of what was due and an exact account of what was paid. All this was the business of the officers of the nome working in some branches in conjunction with the tax-farmers, who were responsible for the collection and received in consideration of their labour and responsibility a certain percentage of what was collected.

A great income accrued to the state from trade and industry. We have already spoken of the high export and import duties at Alexandria, Pelusium and the other ports of Egypt. These customs were occasionally protective, for example, the high duties upon wine and olive oil. A recently deciphered papyrus found in the Zeno correspondence (*P. Cairo Zen.* 59012) shows that all the imported olive oil paid a very high tariff and was bought up at a fixed price by the state. It was sold on the market at the same artificially high price as the home-produced olive oil. This was a heavy burden on those who were not able to live without olive oil,

i.e. on the Greeks. Moreover it encouraged the Greeks to plant
olive trees, and last but not least it protected the sale of the monopolized native vegetable oils. We have already seen that among
the revenues from the exterior provinces the proceeds from
customs took a high place. There were also internal customs, for
instance on goods imported into the Oases or exported from them,
and on goods floated down the Nile.

Still greater was the importance of revenue from industry and
industrial dues. We have already mentioned that certain raw
products were a state monopoly. These the state further manufactured in its own factories, strictly reserving to special con-
cessionaires the right of selling them. In other branches of industry
the state confined itself to its right of manufacturing the produce
of which it had need for its own purposes (army, temples, export)
in unlimited quantities at its own fixed price in private establishments compelled to work for the state. In certain other occupations, as fowling and fishing, the state, to begin with, claimed for
itself a high proportion, 25 per cent. of the catch. In many cases
the state laid a certain tax on the trade and often reserved to
persons who bought it from the state the right of selling retail.
Variations of these main types were many. Our knowledge is very
far from complete, very unequally distributed and very indefinite.
The state protected itself against loss by employing tax-farmers,
whose property was the state's security. It goes without saying
that for the completion of all legal documents, for the validation
of buying and selling, for succession to an inheritance, the people
paid the state definite dues.

Besides all these payments in money and kind the inhabitants
were obliged to render the state service both in person and with
their beasts. By this forced labour of man and beast two essential
needs of the state were met: the construction, cleaning out and
upkeep of the embankments and canals without which Egypt
could not exist, and transport both by road and water. The whole
population of Egypt had to do its duty by the embankments and
canals. The native population with its beasts of burden had to give
its own labour; the privileged classes could pay to be let off. For
each day's work the state gave pay, but of course at the lowest
possible rate. The question of transport was particularly serious
just after the harvest, when enormous masses of grain and other
produce had to be carted from the fields to the threshing floors and
from there to the nearest store, thence to the river or canal down
which the corn went in barges to the granaries of Alexandria. All
this was impossible without corvée of men and animals: small

distances could be managed with the draught-asses of the land-holders: for greater distances the guilds of owners of beasts of burden were employed. River transport was in the hands of ship-owners or men who hired state barges, but this too called for forced labour of sailors, and men and beasts for towing. Compulsion was also employed by the Ptolemies in getting together labour for the mines and quarries, for great buildings and men to go long expedi-tions to catch elephants. Nor were Liturgies, that is the execution of duties imposed by the state, to be avoided by the privileged class. These duties would naturally be of a special character in accordance with the social position and special knowledge of the men upon whom they were laid. Finally there were requisitions and forced sales of goods to the state at its own price. The movements of the king and his officers, as of the armies and military units, meant requisition of foodstuffs, forced use of ships and beasts of burden, forced labour of the population to put into order the roads and quays, to build rest-houses and the like. Upon definite occasions the Ptolemies expected the population to express their loyalty by complimentary presents (crowns, *stephanoi*).

How much the Ptolemies' budget of receipts and expenditure amounted to we do not know. It was naturally based upon actual money, the stores of gold and silver at Alexandria. These stores were also the foundation of the Ptolemaic monetary system with its abundance of gold and full-value silver. The Ptolemies devoted much attention to increasing their reserves in money and regu-lating currency. At one time they tried to gain for their gold and silver a dominant position in the world-market side by side with the ancient Persian coinage, the coinage of Alexander and the Athenian silver, and in competition with the currency of their rivals the Seleucids. They failed, and the attempt was without any consequences. There is some interest in the attempt of Phila-delphus to make only one currency circulate at any rate in Egypt. In the Zeno correspondence we have a letter from the head of the mint to Apollonius (*P. Cairo Zen*. 59021) reporting on this opera-tion and pointing out some further steps which had to be taken. The main idea was to withdraw from circulation the foreign coins, which were widely current in Egypt, likewise the native ones which were worn and below standard, and substitute for them new full-value money of one definite type. How small was the store of gold and silver in the king's reserves we see from the fact that for this pur-pose the state was forced to establish a monopoly (perhaps tem-porary or limited) in gold and silver, that is, of buying and selling them, or to insist on its exclusive right to buy for melting down.

The Ptolemies began to coin on the Rhodian standard and then went over to the Milesian, that is, the Phoenician. The monetary unit was the silver drachma: both in gold and silver higher denominations were coined, 10, 8, 4 and 2 drachmae. There remained in circulation the high denominations of gold and the 4 drachma-pieces in silver. But the gold and even the silver did not penetrate far up the country: there after old custom they reckoned in copper, and the unit of account—for there was no such coin in existence—was the copper drachma, at first $\frac{1}{120}$, afterwards $\frac{1}{300}$ of the silver one. But even with the help of copper currency it was found impossible completely to put an end to barter in Egypt. The people reckon both in money and in corn, the state itself calculates its receipts and expenses in money and in corn, wine and oil. It is characteristic that the salary of the priests, for instance, is paid not in cash but in oil and corn. The complication of this double method of reckoning, the complication of reckoning in money in view of the fluctuations of the exchange and the concurrent circulation of foreign coins, made any transaction or any business impossible without the help of specialists. These specialists were most indispensable to the state in its transactions with its subjects. Therefore the state treasuries for payments in cash or in kind quickly became banks. By their help it became possible to make payments to the state and to transfer money and corn from one client's account to another. Rich business men had current accounts in other places besides where they lived. More and more the bank and the grain-store became the centres of business life and one of the most popular institutions in the country. But the right to open a bank was in Ptolemaic times strictly reserved to the state alone.

VII. SOCIAL, RELIGIOUS AND INTELLECTUAL LIFE. THE HELLENIZATION OF EGYPT

Socially Ptolemaic Egypt was from the beginning a miscellaneous conglomeration, as is shown above all by the various elements which made up the population of the capital Alexandria, and its 'political' life. Details of life in Alexandria are unluckily little accessible to us. There is no doubt that in the eyes of foreigners and in the eyes of the population of Egypt, Alexandria was the capital of the world, the city *par excellence*: 'other cities,' says a newly discovered early Hellenistic treatise, 'are but the cities of the country round them, compared to Alexandria they are

but villages. Alexandria is the world-city.'[1] Alexandria is described in early Hellenistic poetry, in Theocritus and Herodas,
and in later sources, Strabo, Dio Chrysostom, Clement of Alexandria, *Scriptores Historiae Augustae*, when it had long ceased to be
the capital of the world. The descriptions give us some glimpses of
the topography of the city and we can picture to ourselves the
magnificence of its royal and civic buildings: its harbours and its
lighthouse, one of the wonders of the world, the royal palace, the
Mausoleum of Alexander, the Library and Museum, its wide and
straight streets lit by night, its parks and squares, gymnasia and
palaestrae, theatres and hippodromes, temples and synagogues;
the magnificent Mausolea, both above ground and below, the
villas and gardens in the neighbourhood especially at Canopus.
Unfortunately the miserable remnants of Alexandria under the
modern town give not the slightest general idea of its former
magnificence. Still less do we know of its life, of the life of the
king and his court, the army, the high officials, of the Museum
and Library, the schools, Greek and foreign temples, docks and
ports, workshops and stores.

Some detail or other in a letter or in literature lights up a corner
of the picture, but it is only a corner and only for a moment. We
can see the great celebration of Philadelphus, the magnificent
procession, the soldiers of his army, the statues of the gods, the
animal victims, the marquee for a feast to the multitude; we can
be present at a grand dinner in honour of some foreigners at the
court of Philadelphus, or at an auction of the proceeds of imposts
and tributes from the provinces; we have a description of Philopator's luxurious *dahabieh*, a floating villa; in the letters of Zeno
there passes before us the life of Apollonius's court with its trifling
daily excitements, gossip, tale-bearing, perpetual anxiety about
getting one's pay, perpetual fear of the all-powerful master, all
sorts of queer goings-on. We hear the specialist in mending
knuckle-bones (the best were imported from Syria), proud of his
particular skill, criticizing a set given him to put to rights and
boasting how he worked for that famous Macedonian exile, Antipater, Cassander's nephew, 'the King of the Dog-days' (p. 102),
whose main occupation was evidently playing knuckle-bones. In
an anxious letter from one member of Apollonius's household we
can read between the lines of the fall of the all-powerful minister,
perhaps of his violent death and the confiscation of his property.
In the *Aitia* of Callimachus we have before us a banquet given to

[1] *Berl. Klass. Texte*, vii, 13; cf. A. Körte, *Arch. Pap.* vii, 270 (first
century B.C.).

the stars of scientific and literary Alexandria. In his famous idyll Theocritus lets us into the bourgeois house of one of the townsfolk of Alexandria; we meet his wife, her guest, her child, her slave-girl, and go with them on an excursion through the streets and squares of Alexandria with their crowds of people to the place where there is to be the queen's service in memory of Adonis. From time to time we can be present when the unruly mob of the Alexandrian streets breaks out in riot. But that is all.

We have more information about the 'country,' most of all of the villages and towns of the Fayûm. Zeno's correspondence lets us see new towns and villages arising in that new Eldorado of Ptolemy Philadelphus; the houses and streets, temples and public buildings, being constructed and surrounded with orchards and gardens, new canals being dug, new vineyards and plantations set out. The ruins of Philadelphia have been partly excavated and illustrate what the documents say, still more so the ruins of Theadelphia and of Caranis which is being systematically ex-plored. Here, as in most early Ptolemaic documents, we see the life of the new settlers in the 'country,' Greeks and hellenized aliens from the Aegean basin, but this life stands out against a background of the life of the native population with which it is bound by a thousand links: in still greater degree is this true of life in the old Egyptian towns with a new Greek population, Memphis, Oxyrhynchus, Hermupolis, Syene, Thebes, as far as we know them from Greek papyri.

The chief question which faces the historian who enquires into this life is that of the mutual relations of the two strata of popula-tion in Egypt, the new-comers and the natives, of their influence upon one another, the hellenizing of the natives and the egyptian-izing of the Greeks. There is no doubt that at first the new-comers kept themselves to themselves, putting a barrier between them-selves as masters and the natives. The Greeks brought with them their religion and their cult, their habits and mode of life, their language and their law, their education and mental outlook. There were few towns in Egypt in which these peculiarities of their life lasted long. Local bye-laws preserved even into Roman times the refusal to recognize as valid intermarriage between Greeks and Egyptians. This was the case at Naucratis, probably at Alexandria and Ptolemaïs. But even in these cities the Greek system gradually changed and life on new lines came in. There was the influence of the environment, the separation from the Greek world, isolation amid new conditions. The cities of Egypt were Greek cities only outwardly. Alexandria was essentially the capital of the Ptolemies, a cosmopolitan, commercial, and manufacturing city. The life of a Greek *polis* it did not possess or at any rate only in outer form. It is very possible that under the later Ptolemies even these forms took on a special aspect and even the 'self-government' of the Alexandrian citizens was more and more limited by the close watch and strict control exercised by the king and his court.

This new aspect marks everything that in the life of Alexandria can be called specifically Alexandrian: the newness is not the result of fusion with Egypt or influence from Egypt, but the result of a transformation of the Greek spirit in a new environment, and under new conditions, a creation of new Greeks very little like the old. We do not know much about them, but somewhat is clear to us even with our little knowledge. It is not surprising that in the sphere of religion the purely Greek cults, the city cults, for example, of Zeus, Hera and Poseidon, are not the most conspicuous, though they enjoy official recognition. The real religion of the Alexandrians is partly the worship of the gods of the old homes from which the new inhabitants of Alexandria came, partly, indeed chiefly, the mystical cults of Greece and the East which were now spreading over the whole world: the ancient Eleusinian cult, torn away from Attica, the Eleusino-Orphic mysteries of Dionysus Zagreus, common to all Greeks and even to the whole world, the cult of Adonis so strikingly described by Theocritus and celebrated with the same forms and ritual by the up-country Greeks in the early Ptolemaic period. This mystical streak in the religious life of the Greek *diaspora*, scarcely connected with any particular place, still less with any particular city, but none the less Greek rather than Oriental, explains better than anything else the success of the cult and mysteries of Sarapis. What were the real motives of Ptolemy Soter in introducing the cult of Sarapis as the official cult of his new state side by side with that of Alexander, we do not know. Did he think that he could find in it common ground for the fusion of Greeks and Egyptians in one mass of subjects to one king and worshippers of the king's god; did he wish like Ikhnaton long ago to create a god for his empire, just as Philopator tried the same thing by bringing into prominence the cult of his mystical ancestor Dionysus? We do not know; one thing is clear, this god Sarapis became the true symbol of the new religiosity and the changed outlook of the new 'Greeks' in Egypt.

For the Egyptians Sarapis had been and probably remained their god of the under-world. Osiris under the slightly changed name of the dead Apis became Osorapis, whom they had long worshipped at Memphis. The temple of Sarapis built by the

Ptolemies at Memphis was just such a scene of Egyptian cult as the temples at Thebes, Edfu, Kom-Ombos and the rest. But this Egyptian deity became dear to the Greeks of Egypt as well and took the chief place at Alexandria: scarcely as an Egyptian, rather as a new great mystical god, whose theology and whose ritual were worked out in concert by Timotheus the expounder of the Eleusinian mysteries, and the hellenized Egyptian priest and scholar Manetho, a god in whom were united for the Greek both the ancient Egyptian theological wisdom and all the mysticism of the new Greek religion: the mysticism of Zeus and Pluto, of the Sun and Asclepius, and perhaps even more that of Dionysus Zagreus. For him a consort was found in the equally mystic Isis and her divine son Horus (Harpocrates), who took the place of Anubis, Isis with the thousand names and the limitless mystic power, the apotheosis of maternal love and the personification of the mystic female principle. It is no wonder that this god, concentrating in himself the religious aspirations of the new Greek world, was never an artificial god, a god of politics[1]. Ptolemy Soter did not create him, he only gave him statues, temples and ritual. And to him reached out the souls of believers from all sides.

In a letter to Apollonius (*P. Cairo Zen.* 59034), one of Sarapis's new servants tells the *dioiketes* that the will of his lord Sarapis has caused him to do all he could to raise a temple to Sarapis in his sea-coast home. Such servants of Sarapis, deeply convinced of his divine power, were the cloistered anchorites, Macedonians and Greeks, in the Sarapeum at Memphis. It may be doubted whether the cult of Sarapis went far towards uniting the religion of Greeks and Egyptians. Their views of it were so different. But for the Greeks he became one of the gods who attracted their souls like the Great Mother in Asia Minor, the Sun in Syria, Mithras in Asia Minor, Sabazius in Thrace; this was true not only in Egypt but far outside throughout the new Greek world.

As in the religious life of the Greek population in Egypt, so in every other department Alexandria took the lead. The Ptolemies invited from everywhere the best poets, scholars, architects, sculptors, and set them to work for themselves and their capital (chap. VIII). But can we call what was accomplished at Alexandria typically Alexandrian? Is there a typically Alexandrian stamp upon the poetry of Callimachus, Apollonius and Theocritus, or is it just Hellenistic poetry, the poetry of the time after Alexander, the creators of which happened to live at Alexandria but might

---

[1] We know how his cult arose and developed at Delos: this development has not in it a hint of politics.

have lived at Cos or Miletus or Antioch? The atmosphere of a great cosmopolitan city was not specifically Alexandrian and the peculiarities of the work done by the poets who lived in Alexandria are just the same as those of the poets living elsewhere. No successors were left at Alexandria by the great poets of the third century B.C. Their true successors work in the new capital of the world, Rome, and work in Latin.

Alexandria was closely bound up with science and scholarship. The study of the classics, the history of literature, scientific bibliographies, scientific editions of earlier literature, the whole circle of experimental science, astronomy and geography, the whole circle of applied science, all these without the Library, without the constant support of the state, were in the long run unthinkable. But whether Alexandrian science bears the impress of the Alexandrian spirit is a question not to be solved in the state of our knowledge both of the organization and resources of the Library and Museum, and especially of what they produced more particularly in the second and first centuries. One thing is quite clear: as in the poetry so in the science of Alexandria there was nothing Egyptian.

Still more difficult is it to decide whether there was any Alexandrian art. If by Alexandrian art we mean a new Greek version of Egyptian art as we see it in the statues and statuettes of gods and men, in reliefs, the architecture of temples, in certain examples of decorative painting and mosaic, in certain productions of jewelry and goldsmith's work of the Ptolemaic period, we must of course say that there was. But if that is all, we must also say that Alexandrian art exercised no influence upon the development of Greek art and no new note sounds in it. The style of the neo-Egyptian art did not penetrate into the productions of Greek, Italian, Celtic, even Punic art of the Hellenistic period. A few queer details reached the Greek world, a few motives, especially in decorative art, but that was all.

At Alexandria all the great buildings, sculptures and paintings which decked the capital of the world, have perished. How far we are to look for their reflections in the temples, palaces and villas of later-republican and imperial Rome and Italy we cannot tell: this influence is possible, even probable, but we cannot prove it, just as we cannot prove either the Alexandrian origin even of one of the styles of decorative painting practised at Pompeii, or yet the supremacy of Alexandrian toreutic in the last two centuries B.C. or the Alexandrian derivation of the so-called picturesque Hellenistic reliefs. But of one thing there can be no doubt—the

enormous part that Alexandrian culture played in the life of the
Greeks in Egypt. Pompeii can scarcely be reckoned a copy of
Alexandria, but the Greek quarters of the cities in Egypt and the
new villages of the Fayûm, so far as they were Greek, followed in
the wake of the great capital. If ever one of these last is systematically excavated, we shall gain some idea of Alexandria.

Alexandria did of course give to its population at least a veneer
of Greek. The translation of the Old Testament into Greek shows
that the Jews of Alexandria spoke Greek, as did the majority of
the Egyptians who lived there: but neither the Jews nor the
Egyptians of Alexandria ever became Greek, either in spirit or in
countenance. Was it that the Hellenism of Alexandria was not a
pure solution, or was it that no one ever has been able to change
the Jewish spirit? In externals, however, Alexandria was, and remained right to the very last days of ancient civilization, Hellenic,
to the same extent that, for instance, Chicago has the air of an
English town. If these Neo-Hellenes did not succeed in hellenizing in spirit, even in the Neo-Hellenic spirit, the other inhabitants of Alexandria, still the other inhabitants left no impress upon
the Greeks. If the Alexandrian Greeks were a new type, this was
due to their new environment and new conditions of life.

Was it the same with the Greeks up-country, in the towns and
villages in which they lived?

No doubt the Greeks as the dominant nation tried to organize
their life in the new places à la grecque. As at Alexandria so at any
place where a large number of Greeks lived, we must suppose the
existence of gymnasium and palaestra. The existence of elementary
Greek schools is made palpable by the preservation both of the
boys' exercise books and of the texts they studied. There were also
Greek temples. Baths after the Greek fashion were built. The new
towns also probably had squares lined with colonnades in the
Greek manner and some public buildings in the Greek style. The
Greeks naturally tried to keep together as much as they could,
and preserve the likeness of Greeks. They read Greek books,
listened to Greek music, went to Greek plays and ballets. The
richer men would go in to Alexandria and send their children there.

But the up-country Greeks were living outside the atmosphere
of the *polis*, far more than the Greeks of Alexandria and the other
cities of Egypt. Their daily routine, the whole spirit of their life
was not urban, and so not Greek, and that means half-way to
Egyptian. Like the Egyptians, they were entirely absorbed in
material cares; like them, they were in complete dependence upon
the king and his officers; like them, they were subject to hundreds

of regulations limiting their freedom. The greater part of the people round them were Egyptians. It was hard to find a Greek wife for a Greek soldier, while the Egyptian girls were attractive and ready to hand. Of course in the first generation the children talked Greek and received a Greek up-bringing: without that they would not have felt themselves at home in the privileged class. But they, and still more their children, very likely by a half-Egyptian mother, were already only half-Greek and the Egyptian cast of mind was nearer to them than that of their fathers.

As the dominant class the Greeks made their language dominant. In the affairs of state and law-court it gradually ousted Egyptian. There is no doubt that many Egyptians learnt it. It is possible that certain Egyptians for the convenience of the Greek officials assumed Greek names. But the hellenization of the Egyptian masses went no further. Their life was and remained as of old, and accordingly could not be hellenized. The Greeks generally succeeded in hellenizing 'barbarians,' but not always, only within the definite life of the city-state. This life the Greeks in Egypt lacked. Perhaps too thorough a hellenization would have been scarcely welcome to the Ptolemies. Too sharp was the contrast between the ideas of a Hellene and the subject condition of an Egyptian, however prosperous. So the Egyptians went on living on their own lines.

The Ptolemies never tried to make any change in the organization of the Egyptian priesthood. The priests continued to be divided into the classed and the non-classed priesthood, higher and lower. In every temple as of old there went on being four, after 238 B.C. five classes of priests, a special hierarchy, and we know the Greek titles for them: *archiereis, prophetai, stolistai* (who vested the gods), *pterophoroi* (wing-bearers), *hierogrammateis* (sacred clerks). Besides these were the religious, semi-sacerdotal guilds, serving the cult of the gods and the dead; *pastophoroi* (bearers of shrines), *taricheutai* (embalmers), *paraschistai* (who opened the dead body), and so forth. In every temple the priests of the five classes elected the temple council. Every year delegates of the temples met in congress and not only passed resolutions in the king's honour, but debated long upon their own affairs. What these were we do not know exactly, but there is no doubt they included something besides theology and ritual. It is clear that these synods gave expression not only to what the priests but to what the people were thinking, and were the nucleus about which the Egyptian population of the country gathered.

Into the organization of this population the Ptolemies brought little change. Upon it, upon the centuries-old organization of the *laoi* (folk) rested the whole system of administration and assessment. Every Egyptian belonged to a group and was firmly and permanently bound to it. The cultivator belonged to the group of his fellow-villagers, and could in no wise escape from it: his village was the place where he was registered, it was his 'own place' (ἰδία): without this an exact census of the population was inconceivable. An artisan was a member of his village and of one of the ancient guilds: without this the organization of assessments and monopolies was inconceivable. These guilds, though they had their Greek names, must be strictly distinguished from the Greek associations and clubs, though sometimes the names of one and the other exactly coincided. And all these groups, like the priests, have their own representatives, their own komarchs, their own elders (*presbyteroi*).

Compared with this stable organization, centuries old, how unstable and indeterminate were the institutions of the Greeks once they had lost their own splendid organization—the city! It is not to be wondered at that side by side with the external hellenization of the Egyptians and a more effective hellenizing of the other non-Greek settlers, there goes on a process of egyptianization, not outward but inward, a gradual egyptianization of the spirit of the immigrant population. This first appears in the sphere of religion. Strange as it may seem, no single Greek temple has been excavated in Egypt though they are often mentioned in documents. In the new villages of the Fayûm all the temples excavated have been those either of Egyptian gods or of non-Greek gods egyptianized, *e.g.* the Thracian Horseman-hero. And many of the Egyptian temples were built by Greeks. For the Ptolemies this was a matter of policy. But what about private people? From early times we have dedications by Greeks made to Egyptian gods, but no single dedication by an Egyptian to a Greek god.

At first a more or less pure Hellenism was kept up by an accession of Greeks from abroad. But when this current slackened and then probably stopped, the egyptianization of the people, underneath the Greek veneer, went on more and more quickly. Thracians, Galatians, Syrians were of course more open to it than Greeks. A great stratum of the population comes into being, neither Greek nor Egyptian, spiritual half-breeds. Part of it is recognized as such even by law. Between Greeks and Egyptians there appears a special intermediary group assigned to the *politeuma* of the Persians and enjoying some of the privileges of the Greek population.

In spirit and in outlook, in manner of life and interests the

Greeks approached more and more to the Egyptians: whereas the more the Egyptians got used to these new Greeks the more indisposed they were to put up with their own lack of rights and the others' privileges. The halo round the Greek as a superior being disappears and leaves only hate for the oppressor, the intruder, who is in no way better than the old masters of the country but who holds the best land and the best houses, for whom the Egyptians are forced to work, who orders them about and plunders them, on whose side are the law and authority.

Here lies the explanation why, as soon as the Greeks' halo began to grow dim and fear of them to pass away, the native population, led by the priests, makes one insurrection after another. The first explosion came under Euergetes (p. 717), while, from the day when Philopator was compelled to mobilize Egyptians in the contest with Antiochus, the insurrections became endemic, dying down for a time and then bursting out again.

These risings were doomed to failure, nor did they issue in a second Saïte period in the life of Egypt. Alexandria did not yield her place to Memphis or to Thebes. On the contrary Thebes was destroyed and the proud city turned into five modest villages. It is true that the government did make some concessions. The Ptolemies insist more on their character of Pharaohs in their dealings with the Egyptian priesthood; the priests in their decrees speak rather more in the Egyptian fashion than before, many small temples are given the right of sanctuary (but with the other hand the Ptolemies take strict measures to regulate all right of taking sanctuary), temples are again allowed to own some property, though to what extent and whether with freedom to make use of their revenues we do not know. As to the rest of the population, one decree after another, at the end of each period of serious risings, promises the insurgents amnesty, bids them come back each to his home to start again upon his peaceful labour. These decrees also offer certain compensations, certain relief. But the relief amounts to very little, is concerned with the abuses of officialdom, and absolutely fails to touch the fundamental question of the class of masters and the class of servants.

Next Philopator deluded himself into believing that the fusion of Greeks and Egyptians had now been accomplished, the Egyptians turned into good enough Greeks, the Greeks brought sufficiently to understand and respect the Egyptians, so that all were equally ready faithfully to serve Ptolemy-Dionysus united in the mysteries of the god. When under this delusion Philopator dared side by side with the Greek to set up an Egyptian army, the clashing discord between Egyptians and Greeks broke out in full strength. It appeared that the Egyptians had not been hellenized at all, and the Greeks were not at all prepared to give up half their privileges. The insurrections of the Egyptians had one decisive result. They forced the Ptolemies to take definitely one side or the other. Philopator had paid too dearly for seeking to ride two horses at once. And as a general rule they leant for support on the population of Egypt which in manner of life and education was Greek, of whatever origin the particular families of 'Greeks' might be. Another very important point about the risings is that they largely tended to arrest the process of fusion. The 'Greeks' of Egypt were afraid for their rights, their privileged position, and stood shoulder to shoulder in defence of the king and their privileges. To them rallied the more or less hellenized inhabitants who were neither Egyptian nor Greek by origin, and also many of the upper-class Egyptians who had also become in part Greek. Altogether they got the better of the Egyptians and did not allow Egypt to go back to the days of the Twenty-eighth to Thirtieth Dynasties when the Egyptians were lords of the land and the Greeks their servants.

The Greeks of Egypt—little of the Greek as was left in them— kept their position and defended their special culture, in which the chief elements, but not all, were non-Egyptian. When the Romans became lords of Egypt they relied upon this class and used it as the base of their organization of Egypt. With this class they could find contacts; the Egyptians were and remained alien.

If it is hard to say whether Alexandria, that is the type of Greek that arose in Alexandria, added anything to the store of ancient civilization, it is even more difficult to make out what the up-country Greeks contributed. In their letters they speak of nothing but their family affairs and material interests. They read books of many kinds: but there is no trace of this in their letters, not a single quotation, not a single idea with any tinge of reading. Money, squabbles about money, business, family life on its material side, such are the subjects of the letters. It may be said that papyrus was expensive, it was hard to send letters, nothing could be written but what was absolutely necessary. But that means that nothing that was not material was absolutely necessary for the up-country Greek. Of material things he often writes in the fullest detail. Zeno and his correspondents do not spare paper (supplied by the state): they talk at great length of the tiniest everyday things, but in their letters their intellectual interests do not come out.

To judge by all we read, these Greeks were good managers and for a time improved the economic life of the country: but this improvement did not last. The enthusiasm passed and things went back into the old rut, at least in the matter of agriculture. In the two centuries after Philadelphus we can observe no novelty in cultivation. Then something fresh does come in again with the Romans. Nor can we detect much progress in industry. Creative power steadily wanes in artistic handicraft. Anything at all good one has to date in the third or early second century B.C. Thus creative power was scarcely the property of Egyptian Hellenism: the city had vanished and with it faded creative power.

To sum up, what value shall we give to the Ptolemies' work in Egypt? There is no doubt that the Ptolemies during the first century of their rule created a strong power and a mighty state, increased the productivity of the country and established favourable conditions for the economic activities of their new settlers. They applied great skill to elaborating a system of administering the country and exploiting it economically. On the Egyptian foundation they built their edifice in which all the upper storeys were for the dwelling of strangers and the cellars reserved for the natives.

Like any other strong government capable of defending the interests of the state and securing its country's peace, the Ptolemies established more tolerable conditions of life for the natives than probably had existed under the Persian domination or the latest Pharaohs. But beyond this they gave the Egyptians very little: all their gifts were for the Greeks. It is true that before their time the Egyptians had not had very much. But in earlier times, save for the short dominations of the Assyrians and Persians, they were masters in their own house, servants perhaps but servants of their own gods and their own kings. Now they had become the servants of foreigners. We can see how, in view of this, the increased strictness with which the system of petty and detailed control over the whole life of the population, bound up with the nationalization of production and exchange, was a very heavy burden for the population to bear and aroused intense dissatisfaction. Further, the system necessitated giving officialdom an altogether exaggerated part in affairs, and this worked out particularly badly in Egypt. Even when the government was vigorous and still more in moments of weakness, the abuses and arbitrary action of the officials were really intolerable to the Egyptian population. By the second century B.C. even the life of the Greeks had ceased to be particularly attractive. Perpetual risings made the future uncertain. The state began to exercise pressure even upon the upper class, which came to experience the doubtful blessings of nationalization carried to extremes.

Historians do not issue diplomas or distribute praise and blame. The Ptolemies in Egypt were in a difficult position. They dealt with it as best they could according to their lights, keeping in mind not only their own interests but the good of the country. It is idle to divide the Ptolemies into sheep and goats, good and bad. They all had the same system of government. In foreign policy some were successful, some were not, but this often depended not on their own abilities but on the conditions under which they had to execute their policy. In the task of maintaining the independence of Egypt they succeeded longer than did their enemies and colleagues in their various empires.

Furthermore, it is due to the conscious and persistent efforts of the Ptolemies that products of Alexandrian and Egyptian art and industry spread far and wide all over the civilized and the half civilized world and contributed thus to the spread of Greek art and civilization. Moreover, it is probable that the efficient organization of Ptolemaic administration, finance and economics influenced the neighbouring countries, especially the nascent Roman Empire. Still more interesting is it to note how similar was the financial and economic organization of the Indian empire of Chandragupta and his successors as set forth in the newly discovered political treatise, the so-called *Arthashastra* of Kautilia, to that of Ptolemaic Egypt. We see, for instance, the three state monopolies—oil, salt, mines—and their organization, and the far reaching state-socialism under the rule of 'enlightened monarchs' both in India and Ptolemaic Egypt. However, so long as the date of the *Arthashastra* is controversial we shall not be able to decide whether we have to deal with mere coincidences or with an influence of Ptolemaic Egypt on India of the Hellenistic and the early Roman times.

In internal policy the later Ptolemies had to reap the harvest sown by the early ones, and do so under very difficult conditions, an atmosphere of bitter hostility between the two unequal parts of the population. In that struggle they took the side of Hellenism and saved it. To the country in general, especially to the native population, their behaviour was no worse, maybe rather better than that of the early Ptolemies. Beneath the formal phrases of their amnesties one can feel a true sympathy for the country torn by civil wars and groaning under abuses. Here and there in the edicts of certain emperors this note is heard, but apart from that we pass, with the advent of the Roman governors, to a régime in which the voice of sympathy is dumb.

CHAPTER V

SYRIA AND THE EAST

I. THE EMPIRE OF THE SELEUCIDS, ITS CHARACTER AND DEVELOPMENT

IN 281 B.C. Seleucus I, for some time past the acknowledged king of Syria, Mesopotamia and Iran, added to his Empire most of Asia Minor with its Greek cities and the Greek or hellenized population of its western coast and seemed to have firmly established his authority over it (see above, p. 98). At once, like his predecessors the Persian kings, like Alexander, Antigonus and Lysimachus, he found himself face to face with many problems vastly important and quite insoluble. These problems passed by inheritance to his earlier successors down to Antiochus III the Great, whose unsuccessful struggle with Rome entirely changed the character of the Seleucid Empire and therewith the main lines of Seleucid policy (see vol. VIII).

The Empire of Seleucus I and his immediate successors was an aggregation of many nations and many civilizations. On the Iranian table-land were the various Iranian and pre-Iranian tribes, one in the nationality of the dominant race but infinitely varied in the manner of life of the different nations and tribes: nomads of the steppe, shepherds of the hills, agriculturists, gardeners and vine-dressers—these, together with the great urban centres of trade and administration, made up the eastern third of the Seleucid Empire and had been for the Persian kings the centre and foundation of their power and rule over the remaining parts of their empire. One part of this vast province had attained to a high culture, imperial in character, that of the Persian kings and the Persian nobles: there entered into it the ancient Sumerian and Elamite culture, Babylonian and Assyrian elements, some mixture of Hittite and Aramaean, the basis of life and religion being that of the Iranian tribes to whom belonged the first place in the state: to this cultural province adjoined as it were two wings, on the south-east the region of the Indus and Ganges with its highly developed civilization, and on the north-west the Armenian table-land and the valleys and foothills of the Caucasus with their high civilization made up of Hittite and Caucasian elements and once so flourishing in the kingdom of Van (vol. III, chap. VIII).

The centre of the Seleucid Empire was made up of the former

kingdoms of Babylonia and Assyria, going back thousands of years, and of the lands which depended upon them for their civilization, Syria, the land of Aramaean cities dependent upon the caravan trade, Phoenicia, a land of great trading and manufacturing coast-towns, and Palestine, of which the coast or Philistine region was a continuation of Phoenicia, while the interior or Jewish part went on with the primitive life of shepherds, agriculturists and gardeners under the protection of Yahweh and his temple at Jerusalem. In these dependent regions there was the strangest mixture of old-fashioned Semitic nomad life with the high civilization of Babylon and Assyria, Egypt and the Hittites. The foundations of life in Babylonia were laid on permanent and immutable lines: they might be destroyed but there was no changing them, whereas the adaptable trading and manufacturing towns of Syria and Phoenicia with their mixed population were ready for every novelty. The stability of the new theocratic system in Jewry had not yet been exposed to serious trial. If we can call the eastern third of the empire mainly Iranian, its middle part was predominantly Semitic. The star of imperial Ashur had set, but his successor Ahuramazda had made no attempt to try his strength against Bel, Marduk, Yahweh and the many Ba'alim.

The third or north-western part of the empire, Asia Minor, was even more miscellaneous and the various systems of life made up a more complicated whole. Behind the belt of Greek coast-cities with its Graeco-oriental civilization and Graeco-oriental temples, there lived, on the one hand, in the river-valleys, on the Anatolian table-land, in the Taurus and Anti-Taurus mountains elements going back to the ancient Hittite culture, itself sufficiently mixed, and, on the other, strange new developments, Phrygian Pessinus, Lydian Sardes, Carian Halicarnassus, Lycian Termessus, Cilician Tarsus and so on, and little do we know even now of their complex civilizations and religions.

To build up anything out of this aggregation of tribes, peoples and regions, lacking any mutual connection and naturally tending in different directions, was a hard task, especially for the new lords of the empire, the successors of Alexander. The Persian kings had a solid base in their Iranian subjects who had always been the dominant nation and remained such in spite of the very liberal policy of the Persian kings. Alexander had behind him his own people the Macedonians, and on them and on the glamour of his personality his power was based till the day of his death.

The position of Seleucus I and his successors was far more difficult. After the death of Seleucus it became clear that it was idle to dream of uniting the Seleucid power with Macedon. Such a union was not beyond the bounds of possibility (everything was possible in the fantastic world of Hellenistic politics), but to build a policy upon this vague possibility would have been madness. The facts had to be reckoned with and the facts spoke plainly. Within the boundaries of their rule Seleucus and his successors, as Macedonians and Greeks, had, like the Ptolemies in Egypt, no single part of their empire on which they could rely and dare to use as a basis for their power. They had gained their power by the hands of Macedonian soldiers. As they had not Macedon and Greece behind them, they might have let this handful of Macedonians dissolve in the sea of their Iranian, Semitic and Anatolian subjects, but they did not and could not make up their minds to this experiment. It would have meant exchanging a stable though purely personal rule for the vision of a precarious support by the East at the price of orientalizing dynasty, army and administration. It was simpler and safer to do as did the Ptolemies in Egypt, and rely on the community of interest between the dynasty and the army, the dynasty and the dominant nation of conquerors, the Macedonians and the Greeks. The logical inference from this, an inference probably suggested to Seleucus by his experience and observation in the eastern third of the empire during the first years of his rule, was the necessity, once Macedon and Greece proved to be beyond his reach, of building up a new Macedon and Greece of his own in those parts of the empire which he had best hope of keeping permanently in his power.

In the very first years of the Seleucid Empire it was clear that there was no escaping endless rivalry with the Ptolemies and that there was no chance of getting hold of Macedon, so that to create this new Macedon and Greece in western Asia Minor on the basis of the liberty-loving cities of the coast was against all common sense. It was clear that for the possession of these cities and access to the sea, and likewise for the cities of Syria, Phoenicia and Palestine, there was going to be a long and obstinate struggle (which as a matter of fact never did cease), and accordingly the centre of the state, the military and political headquarters of the kingdom, must be in a region more easily defended, less open to attack, and closer to the eastern part of the empire.

Hence the Seleucid policy, pursued consistently, though hastily, with an enormous expenditure of money and energy, the policy of settling Macedonians and Greeks within the empire especially in its central regions. This settlement was the work of the first two rulers, Seleucus I and Antiochus I. To them was due the Graeco-Macedonian nucleus which secured to the dynasty and empire permanence for more than two hundred years. By them the system was worked out. They had predecessors in Alexander and Antigonus (vol. VI, pp. 429 *sqq.*, 491), but their purpose and the speed with which it was carried out were new.

Their purpose was not only to secure the frontiers and great trade-routes with urban foundations for soldiers and civilians, to plant single islands of Hellenism in the eastern sea, but to create whole regions thickly covered with a network of Macedonian and Greek cities and villages, regular Greek and Macedonian provinces. These settlements were sometimes new centres of population, sometimes ancient towns or villages transformed by a new name and a new social and political life, while into their population a large and powerful group of new settlers was introduced. Communication between these newly settled regions was secured by chains of Graeco-Macedonian fortified cities planted along the chief roads.

These groups of Graeco-Macedonian cities reached from the coasts of the Aegean right through Asia Minor, Syria, Mesopotamia and Babylonia all the way to Bactria and Sogdiana. The first was the Lydian, Phrygian and Carian group in Asia Minor, with its military and administrative centres in Sardes and Celaenae (Apamea Cibotos). The second, still more compact and powerful, stretched from the north end of the Syrian coast (above Phoenicia) along the whole course of the Orontes and its tributaries, along the middle course of the Euphrates and along the Khabur and its tributaries. This was Syria, the heart and kernel of the empire with its political capital Antioch on the Orontes, the military Apamea, and the commercial Seleuceia in Pieria and Laodicea. Babylonia and Susiana were the last group of Greek cities in the western half of the empire, holding the gate to the eastern half and its administrative and military centre. The political and economic capital of this group and the second capital of the empire was Seleuceia on the Tigris. How far Babylonia and Susiana were hellenized we shall discuss later (see pp. 187 *sqq.*). But an attempt, and a not unsuccessful attempt, was made.

To judge by the few scraps of information given by our miserable sources the settlement policy did not stop short at the Tigris: but what was its character in the eastern satrapies we do not know. The purpose of the Seleucids may have been no more than to maintain and strengthen, partly to restore, Alexander's network of colonies along the routes of trade and war, or here again they may have tried to make other great groups of Hellenic cities and villages. This appears the more probable explanation; we have evidence for the existence of groups in Media, Parthia and Ariana, in Persis, and finally in Bactria and perhaps in Sogdiana.

It was on this new Graeco-Macedonian population and on those elements among the natives who were assimilated to it that the Seleucids relied as their most permanent support; and on the whole, as in Egypt, the Graeco-Macedonians faithfully and firmly supported their kings.

The political history of the Seleucids, as set forth elsewhere (see chap. xxii, and below, vol. viii), shows how the empire was gradually pressed back towards its centre. Seleucus I soon failed to dominate Bithynia and Pontus; in the reign of his successor, Antiochus I, Ptolemy Philadelphus extended the power of Egypt in Asia Minor; while the western part of the empire suffered a severe blow when the Gauls seized the centre of the peninsula and Pergamum fell away. Under Antiochus II came the turn of the eastern provinces, of which India was already lost. About 255 B.C. Bactria, too, revolted under Diodotus and gradually asserted her liberty (see below, p. 719 *sq.*); the year 248–7 B.C. marks the Era of Parthia, the sign of its independence. About the same time arose the separate kingdom of Great Cappadocia. Farther west things went better. After the dizzy exploits of Ptolemy Philadelphus the battle of Cos restored the power of Antiochus II in Asia Minor apart from Pergamum. The brilliant victories of Ptolemy III for a long time contracted the boundaries of the Seleucids' empire not in its centre but in Asia Minor: except for the Troad they lost their influence all along its western coast. For a short while both in west and east the old power of Seleucus I and Antiochus I was restored by Antiochus III, but he too had to accept the independence of Pergamum, Bactria and Parthia as accomplished facts. A new epoch in the history of the empire begins with the defeat of Antiochus III by Rome (190 B.C.). Asia Minor was lost for ever. Direct access by land to Greek civilization and to the Greek ports of Asia Minor was for ever cut off. An end was put to all hopes of independent commerce in the Mediterranean supported by a navy: the Syrian merchants were made dependent on the kind offices of Rhodes and of Delos which became more and more a Roman port. It is not surprising that Antiochus III in his latter years, and particularly Antiochus IV with his more able and active successors such as Demetrius I and Antiochus VII Sidetes, henceforward chiefly aim at confirming and strengthening the centre of their kingdom, Syria (to which Coele-Syria and Palestine had been reunited), Mesopotamia and what could still be kept of the nearer parts of Iran.

Their problem was accordingly a double one: to make their kingdom more compact and to resist with this kingdom compacted of Greeks and Semites the pressure of a reborn Iran. There was only one way to attain the first object, the way of Seleucus I and Antiochus I: to extend and confirm the patches of Hellenism by the creation of new Greek cities and the strengthening of the Greek element in the old ones so that the whole kingdom should bear but one stamp, the Greek. To this Antiochus IV and his successors devoted themselves wholeheartedly. They had no reason to think that this course would meet with any invincible obstacles. The experience of the past, the success of their earliest predecessors, allowed them to think that the surface hellenization and urbanization of the new provinces conquered from the Ptolemies, Phoenicia, Coele-Syria, Palestine and Transjordania and the more intensive hellenization of Mesopotamia, Babylonia, Media, Susiana and Persis would give as little trouble as the experiment of hellenizing the Aramaean provinces, Mesopotamia, Kurdistan and Babylonia, and the Iranian Media and Persis under Seleucus I and Antiochus I. After all, in Phoenicia, Coele-Syria and Transjordania the chief work of city-building and hellenization had been already done by the Ptolemies. There was only Palestine left: and even here much had been done in the last years of Ptolemaic rule by the efforts of the house of Tobias, Philhellenes and business men of the regular new Hellenistic type. Relying on the new cities with their Greek appearance, on the hellenized population and on a sensible utilization of the abundant resources of the country, the Seleucids hoped to defend the country against the Parthians, and keep at any rate a part of the Iranian provinces, Media, Susiana and Persis. In this they were mistaken. The hellenization of Palestine failed in spite of heroic efforts. This is to be explained not so much by the desperate resistance of the Jews as by the way in which the successors of Antiochus III had their hands tied. Behind them stood Rome and her consistent and cunning policy of weakening the Seleucids. Rome would not allow them either to break right down the resistance of the Jews, or to weld Syria and Mesopotamia into one whole or to support Hellenism in Mesopotamia against the steady pressure of Iranianism. Not the Maccabees nor the Parthians conquered the Seleucids but Rome. To Rome were due the successes of the Jews and of the Parthians under Mithridates I and Phraates II. The fictitious independence of Judaea was the beginning of a feudalization of Syria and Mesopotamia. Most of the cities both on the coast and inland become independent: in many appear petty princes of local

origin. The same process recurs in so-called Parthian Mesopotamia after the defeat of Antiochus VII Sidetes in 129 B.C. In
the last century B.C. the Seleucid kingdom has come to an end and
Rome herself has to undertake the task of saving Syrian Hellenism
from the Iranians who threaten it from the East and the Aramaeans
who rise up against it from the depths of Syria itself.

II. THE ORGANIZATION OF THE SELEUCID EMPIRE

A. THE KING'S POWER

Seleucus I, like Ptolemy Soter, first drew close his connection
with the country which afterwards became the centre of his empire,
in his case Babylonia, through being its satrap, first after the
agreement of Triparadeisus, and afterwards from 312 B.C., the
time of Ptolemy's victory at Gaza. This is the year from which is
reckoned his Era (from 1 Dius = October for the Greeks; 1 Nisan
= March or April for the Babylonians), which is even now in use
in Syria, and from about this date his oriental subjects began to
call him king long before the other Diadochi had officially assumed
that style. The power of Seleucus and his successors, like that of
the Ptolemies, had two sides to it. In the eyes of his army, his
friends and the Macedonian and Greek inhabitants of his empire,
as well as of Greeks outside, the king's power was personal,
founded upon his personal supremacy and personal qualities and
on the support given by the army and his 'friends.' This gave him
the right to claim that he and his descendants were the lawful
heirs of Alexander. This point of view is quite definitely expressed
both in the probably spurious speech made by Seleucus I to his
friends and troops on the occasion of his son's romantic marriage
and nomination as king of the East and partner in the government
(Appian, *Syr.* 61), and in the decree passed by Ilium in honour of
Antiochus I (*O.G.I.S.* 219)[1]: the honours offered by the city to
Antiochus are based upon his having ensured peace to the cities,
and increased his kingdom, 'thanks mainly to his personal
superiority (ἰδία ἀρετή) and to the devotion of his friends and
troops.' In general, in the eyes of the Greeks, the king, his family,
his 'friends' and his army make up one indissoluble whole, the
holders of power in the empire. This is the *de facto* basis for
the king's power, which rests entirely upon the devotion of his
'friends,' that is his officers in military and civil service, and on the
loyalty of his army, these being assured him as long as he shows
himself worthy of his position and conducts the affairs of state with

---

[1] For the abbreviations used in these references see the Bibliography.

success, so working on behalf of his friends and troops. But side by side with this the Seleucids like the Ptolemies had of course need for another, a higher, philosophic and religious, sanction for their power, a sanction which should make them less dependent on the goodwill of their court and army (see pp. 113 *sqq*.).

No doubt, like the Ptolemies and Antigonus Gonatas, a philosophic sanction was suggested to the Seleucids or formulated for them by the philosophers of the time. An echo of such a formula can be heard for instance in Seleucus I's speech to his army, just mentioned. Explaining the marriage of Antiochus I with his own stepmother he says 'it is not the customs of the Persians and other peoples that I impose upon you, but a *law common to all*, by which that is always *just* which is decreed by the king.' The phrase offers a philosophic justification for the absolutism of the king, as against a historical one, the inheritance of power from Persian kings and Persian tradition. The same search for a higher sanction which should justify their power in the eyes of the Greek and hellenized population of the empire, especially in the eyes of the Greek city-states whose whole nature and tradition revolted against subjection to a king, is to be seen in the gradual process by which the cult of the deceased kings of the Seleucid dynasty and of the living king and queen changed into a state institution. From the days of Seleucus I, certainly from those of Antiochus I (*O.G.I.S.* 219, 26; cf. 227, 6 and 237, 5), the divine descent of Seleucus from Apollo was generally accepted and became part of the royal style[1]. This divine descent made it possible for the Greek cities on their own initiative to set up a cult of the king, as at Ilium (*O.G.I.S.* 212, cf. 219). Further, we may assume that divine honours were paid to Seleucus after his death in cities which he had founded, and that this practice was followed with his successors, until in the time of Antiochus III if not earlier there can have been no Greek city in the Seleucid Empire without a cult in some form or other of the deceased kings and of the reigning sovereign. At some time, not before Antiochus II, order was brought into this chaos and the cult of the kings became a state institution with its own priests and special ceremonies repeated at fixed intervals. In a rescript to the governor of Lydia (*O.G.I.S.* 224, cf. 244) Antiochus III appoints a lady of rank to be high priestess of the cult of Laodice, 'queen and sister,'

[1] Probably declared after the battle of Ipsus by the oracle at Didyma to which, as to the city of Miletus, Seleucus and Antiochus always extended their protection. (*O.G.I.S.* 213, 214; cf. A. Wilhelm, *Neue Beiträge*, VI, 1921, pp. 54 *sqq.*; cf. also *Milet, Erg. d. Ausgr.* I, 7, 1924, no. 193, and M. Holleaux, *Rev.E.G.* XXXVI, 1923, pp. 1 *sqq.*)

in all the temples of the satrapy, and remarks that high priests of his cult exist throughout the kingdom[1]. But the cult epithet of which there was one for each of the Seleucids did not form part of their official style before the time of Antiochus IV Epiphanes.

Such was the royal power of the Seleucids from the point of view of the Greeks. What formula they found for the miscellaneous non-Greek population of the empire we do not know. Over a country in which they were foreigners the Seleucids bore rule by right of conquest. Perhaps, too, like the Ptolemies in Egypt, they tried to assume in the eyes of the natives the forms of their previous kings and gain recognition from the local gods and their priests, but of this we have neither direct nor indirect evidence. In any case the religion and cult of local deities suffered no persecution from them and it is unlikely that they insisted on introducing their Greek cult in the eastern temples. Some form or other of king-worship no doubt already existed in all the eastern temples, for in all eastern monarchies the king played a conspicuous part in the cult of the gods and it is unlikely that his figure disappeared from ritual with the extinction of the legitimate native dynasties. Probably the earlier Seleucids, down to Antiochus III, did not find it necessary to interfere with the affairs of temples and priests. In Babylon and throughout Babylonia masses of business documents, almost all concerned with the affairs of the temples, show that at this time the temples were living their old life with all its peculiarities, worshipping the ancient gods after the ancient forms and using the offerings of the faithful to support their priests and servants.

It is possible that with their expulsion from Asia Minor the Seleucids rather modified their attitude to eastern temples. We hear of repeated cases of Antiochus III and his successors 'plundering' eastern temples, and these, as also the 'plundering' of the temple at Jerusalem by Antiochus Epiphanes, may be regarded as attempts on the part of the later Seleucids to insist on their sovereign right to the possessions of the temple, a right belonging to them as 'the Lord's anointed,' representing the god upon earth. In the difficult times that followed the defeat of Antiochus III by Rome the Seleucids thought they had a right to use for the state the vast resources of the eastern temples. But they had overrated their strength and the degree to which their right had been recognized as religious. Antiochus III was slain after plundering the temple of Bel in Elam. Antiochus IV could not succeed even in penetrating to the very wealthy temple of Nanaia in the same

[1] See further, O.G.I.S. 233, 245, 246.

district. An even fiercer opposition was put up by the orthodox part of the Jewish population, and he was compelled for the first time in the history of the Seleucids to have recourse to religious persecution and perhaps to the forcible establishment of his own cult in Greek forms so as to break down this opposition. The mild policy of Antiochus III towards the temple at Jerusalem was probably the traditional policy of the earlier Seleucids towards eastern temples in general: non-interference with the forms of religious life and the privileges of the priests in return for their loyalty and support.

There can be no doubt that the native non-Greek population of the empire failed to show any particular enthusiasm for the Seleucids. Passive acquiescence was the very utmost that the Seleucids could demand of them. That is why one part after another breaks off so easily: that is why even the centre of the Seleucid power, Syria and Mesopotamia, swiftly turned Aramaean and feudal the moment the central power and the imperial army collapsed. On the other hand, the Graeco-Macedonian population of the central parts, and even of the extremities, was quite loyal, one may even say deeply devoted to the Seleucid dynasty. It felt that the state was its own, that it must stand or fall together with the Seleucids. This comes out very clearly in the difficult times of the second century B.C. The mob of the cities and the army again and again take a hand in the often unsavoury and always sanguinary dynastic quarrels, but when they so interfere and revolt the main reason is always devotion to the dynasty and a desire to support its worthiest representative.

B. THE COURT AND CENTRAL ADMINISTRATION. GOVERNMENT OF THE PROVINCES

Amid this Graeco-Macedonian population the king's family, his court, his highest officials, the officers, armies and fleets play the chief part in determining the king's mode of life. All this must have been much the same for the Seleucids as for the Ptolemies and other Hellenistic dynasties. In all of them there was a strange mixture of Macedonian traditions with those of the oriental monarchies. Among the Seleucids, too, the wives of the kings play a great part in public life, court ceremonial, and policy. But on the coinage the queen's portrait appears later among the Seleucids than among the Ptolemies, not before Demetrius Soter. The succession is governed by the Macedonian and Greek law of inheritance. The king's 'friends' make up his council. There also enter into it other members of the group which surrounds the king, bearing the titles of 'tutor' (*tropheus*), 'comrade' (*syntrophos*), 'kinsman' and 'body-guard.'[1] The king is surrounded by the 'king's pages' and a great number of servants, under the direction of different members of the court, bearing the same titles as at the courts of the other Hellenistic rulers. As usual such titles as Butler, Carver, Chamberlain become purely honorary (see p. 116).

From time to time our sources give us the names of the highest and most influential officials: 'The Minister for Affairs' (ὁ ἐπὶ τῶν πραγμάτων), the head of the royal chancery (ἐπιστολογράφος), finance minister (ὁ ἐπὶ τῶν προσόδων), the financial secretary and quarter-master general, the chief physician. The finance minister managed the so-called *basilikon*, a term which embraced both the state (*i.e.* royal) exchequer and the administration of the king's property, taxation and probably currency. The coinage was mostly produced at Antioch, directed by special officers whose monograms appear regularly on Seleucid coins of this mint. As with the Ptolemies, there were also provincial mints, especially that of Seleuceia on the Tigris: Tyre also issued abundant coinage for the empire. Political and economic conditions governed the coinage of imperial currency in other great towns. The king's privy purse, his 'treasure' or 'money-chest,' had its own guardian called as in other Hellenistic monarchies *gazophylax* or *rhiskophylax*. No doubt there were many more important officials than are mentioned in our scanty sources. The king had his own chancery and archives, doubtless with a special director. The extent and ramifications of the central bureaucracy with its groups of subordinate officials can be only conjectured until it is defined by systematic excavations at Antioch.

Unfortunately the local provincial administration of the Seleucids is little better known to us. The few inscriptions scattered over the whole extent of their empire cannot compare with the thousands of papyri from Egypt. Only systematic excavations in the cities on the edge of the desert where there is hope of finding parchment documents can illuminate this darkness. In the Seleucid empire there was no strong contrast, such as we find in the Ptolemaic, between the country which served as the centre and base of the king's power and the king's dominions oversea. Nor again is there the deep division between the capital, as the Greek

---

[1] It is possible that in some cases these titles have a real basis, *e.g.* that the 'tutor' Craterus (*O.G.I.S.* 256) had really educated Antiochus Cyzicenus, but in the inscription this title appears side by side with others which are merely honorary.

centre of the king's power, and the provinces. In Egypt Alexandria was opposed on the one hand to the 'country' and on the other hand to the dominions (pp. 121 *sqq*.). The Seleucid Empire had a different past and different traditions—the traditions of the Persian kings, especially Darius and his successors, and those of Alexander the Great. The empire, being made up of many nations and many regions, had to be divided into separate administrative units. This division was natural, historical and not artificial, and on the whole was the same as under the Persians and Alexander. To go back to the tradition of Cyrus, who administered the country as a conglomeration of vassal kingdoms under a ruling nation, was impossible. We find a return to this state of things in the Seleucid Empire, as in the Persian, only at the time when it was swiftly and finally falling to pieces. Our information as to how the Seleucid Empire was divided into administrative units and how these units were ruled is extremely scanty and contradictory. But we may assume that under the Seleucids, as under the Persians and under Alexander, the administrative divisions bore the names of satrapies, though the governors with military and civil authority were called not satraps but *strategoi*[1]. Subdivisions of the satrapies were entrusted to subordinate governors, hyparchs and probably meridarchs, while on the other hand the Eastern satrapies or those of Asia Minor were sometimes grouped together under governor-generals. It is almost certain that the *strategoi* commanded the contingents of their satrapies as well as the military police, who were probably recruited from military settlers and had as their main duty the task of assisting the chief financial officer of the satrapy or hyparchy, presumably in the collection of taxes and imposts[2].

The financial administration of the satrapy was concentrated in the hands of a special 'finance officer.' Whether he was subordinate to the *strategos* and hyparch or immediately under the minister of finances in Antioch we do not know. To judge by certain inscriptions the management of the king's property, mostly his lands in the provinces, was entrusted to *oikonomoi* and *dioiketai*. One (*O.G.I.S.* 225, Antiochus II) shows that the *oikonomos* did not receive his orders immediately from the king but from the

[1] Appian, *Syr.* 62, gives the number of satrapies as seventy-two but if we put together the data of historians and inscriptions we cannot make up more than twenty-five. We must assume that Appian has counted as satrapies smaller units more properly called *hyparchiai* in Asia Minor and Media Atropatene, *merides* in Coele-Syria, Phoenicia and Palestine.

[2] *O.G.I.S.* 238, an inscription of Eriza which, though perhaps dating from Pergamene rule, reflects Seleucid administration.

strategos of the satrapy to whom the king gives his immediate
directions. The king's command is executed in accordance with
a special order from the *oikonomos*, by the hyparch. This probably
implies that the *oikonomos* had in his charge the king's lands
throughout the satrapy and that the Finance officer also was subordinated not only to the king but to some extent to the *strategos*
of the satrapy.

Each satrapy certainly had its own capital. The capital of Lydia
was Sardes. It is possible that in the life of Asia Minor Sardes
played an even greater part, that it was the capital both civil and
military of a whole group of satrapies. Here probably was the
royal treasury with branches in the other big towns. Here too was
a central record office under the charge of a special archivist
(*bibliophylax*). Such record offices were scattered over the whole
empire not only in the capitals but in the smaller towns where
there were also branches of the exchequer. So in the ancient Uruk
we find a special state *chreophylakion*, with its chief 'the *chreophylax*
of Uruk,' whose seal bearing the same types as the coins of his
time, the head of the deified king as Apollo, shows that he was a
royal, not a municipal official nor yet a private person like the
'keeper of contracts' in Egypt. At a somewhat earlier period the
same official is found at the capital of Susiana (Seleuceia on the
Eulaeus) and probably at Doura-Europos on the Euphrates[1]. In
Syria and Palestine we have mention of local *thesauroi* (1 Macc.
iii, 29). In the eastern provinces of Mesopotamia and Media, as
we see from the inscriptions of Doura and the Avroman parchments, the Parthians left the main features of the administration
unchanged.

The relation between the *strategoi* and the Greek cities in their
satrapies will be discussed later (pp. 177 *sqq.*). It is very probable
that they had control of all the temples of their satrapies and that
this is why, like the Ptolemaic governors of Cyprus, they were called
archiereis under Antiochus III and later, though it may have been
as chief priests of the cult of the kings. But the use of this title side
by side with that of *strategos* in Syria and Phoenicia only occurs
in one inscription (*O.G.I.S.* 230).

Of taxation in the Seleucid Empire we have little information.
We have, however, every reason to think that it was different in
different parts, being adapted to the economic conditions of each
and determined by very ancient traditions, as was the case in

---

[1] The existence of a *gazophylax* at Doura under the Severi points, in the
opinion of the present writer, to the existence of a separate exchequer there
in the time of the Seleucids.

Egypt. Accordingly we shall treat taxation in connection with our examination of the economic and social life of the different parts of the empire. We may, however, note here that not only the terminology but the leading features of the fiscal system so far as it is known to us were Greek. We do not know whether Greek was the regular language used for documents dealing with provincial government and with the taxation of the natives, but we may perhaps infer that as in Egypt so in the Seleucid Empire Greek was predominantly the official language. On the other hand, the form of documents by which the business of private persons was transacted was probably determined by the nationality of the parties. The contracts found at Doura-Europos are Greek and are drawn according to Greek law, the parties being Macedonian settlers. Those at Avroman are also in Greek: the parties, though of Iranian extraction, were descendants of military settlers probably planted in Seleucid times and undoubtedly largely hellenized. We may, however, observe that in the Parthian period we find Greek and Pahlavi documents existing side by side, a fact which shows that the once hellenized settlers were turning Iranian again. At Uruk, on the other hand, we have many tablets of the Seleucid period, written in the Babylonian language and in cuneiform. They differ neither in form nor contents from documents of an earlier date, yet some of the parties concerned, as their double names show, were either hellenized Babylonians or Babylonized Greeks. But there is reason to think these documents were also transcribed on parchments in Greek (or in Aramaic). Not only is a 'parchment-scribe' often mentioned as a witness, but also there have been found clay *bullae* bearing private or official seals, which were probably appended to parchment documents of this kind.

In any event Greek law with Greek administration penetrated with the Seleucids to countries which had hitherto lived under another system. As in Egypt, Greek law spread from the Greek settlers to the native population. This is definitely proved by the fact that as late as the fourth century A.D. the so-called Syro-Roman Law-Book which fixes the law practised in Syria at that time is founded neither on native law, nor on Roman, but upon Greek. This has recently been made quite clear by the comparison of the rules laid down by the Law-Book for succession *ab intestato* with those of a Hellenistic law on the same subject, a chapter from a first century B.C. copy of the laws of the Macedonian colony, Doura-Europos on the Euphrates, probably the laws given it by its founder Nicanor in the time of Seleucus I[1].

[1] On Doura-Europos see also vol. VI, p. 430 *sq.*

C. THE ARMY AND FLEET

The composition and organization of the Seleucid army are very little known to us. The historians tell us of its size and composition in time of war, some inscriptions and the parchments of Doura and Avroman speak of the composition of the garrisons, and supply some information about the *katoikoi* or *klerouchoi*, the soldier-occupiers of allotments of land, who, as in Egypt were reservists (see pp. 117 *sqq.*).

The standing army was not large, the utmost efforts could not raise more than 70,000 men. This is to be explained by the difficulty of provisioning and moving about a bigger army, the absolute need of recruiting for it only efficient soldiers who really would fight, the necessity of drawing the greater part of the recruits from material upon which the king could rely, that is the military settlers from within the empire, who could be opposed on the one hand to the mercenaries, on the other to the native levies raised mostly from Iranian and Anatolian tribes. Finally, there was the enormous cost of paying and supporting the army.

Unfortunately we do not know what was the pay of a soldier on active service nor that of those serving in garrisons. Cavalry received three times the pay of infantry, mercenaries were probably better paid than soldiers from among the military settlers or than the native levies. The Seleucids had to meet keen competition in hiring mercenaries and even the military settlers might go over to their rivals. Further, the number of experienced officers was limited, and a good officer cost a great deal and was not tied to any particular country. It is thus no wonder that the Seleucids were often unable to find the money for their army on a war footing and had either to seek the help of their 'friends' or utilize temple funds. A highly developed military technique required great expenditure on military bases, arsenals, siege-trains, a remount and horse-breeding department, war-chariots, elephants to be fed and looked after, to say nothing of expenses on the construction and upkeep of naval bases. The main centre of the land forces was Apamea near the chief capital Antioch and not far from great forests which could provide timber; iron and copper probably came down from the mines on the Black Sea. The horse-breeding centre was in Media, a fact which explains the efforts made by the Seleucids to keep that province at all costs and hellenize it as much as possible.

The Seleucid army consisted of cavalry and infantry. The cavalry, as in the Ptolemaic and other Hellenistic kingdoms, besides receiving higher pay, was specially privileged and ranked before the infantry. A letter begins (*O.G.I.S.* 217) 'King Antiochus (III) to the *strategoi,* hipparchs, leaders of the infantry, soldiers and others,' *i.e.* the civil population (?). In time of peace the standing army was divided between the capital, being the station of the king's guard, and the military bases and principal *points d'appui* in the provinces, which were garrisoned. The army on a war footing falls into two parts, the regular cavalry and infantry as against auxiliary units and the corps concerned with special arms. The regular army was nominally composed of Macedonians and was recruited from the Macedonian and Greek population of the empire, mainly from the military settlements both urban and agricultural. In the Macedonian cavalry we hear of the Companions, the Royal Regiment (βασιλικὴ ἴλη) and the so-called ἄγημα. We cannot draw clear lines between these groups. It seems that in the regular cavalry which included the royal guard there was a large proportion of Iranians probably recruited from Iranian military settlers. There was also the heavy cavalry formation of the *kataphraktoi* with man and horse protected by armour. We also have mention of bodies of horsemen called Tarentines (special type of cavalry, each man leading two horses), Scythians, Dahae and Arabs on their dromedaries, the Elephant corps and that survival from the ancient East, scythed-chariots.

The strength of the infantry lay in the Macedonian phalanx and in the Hypaspistae which may have belonged to the king's guard. The light infantry consisted of mercenaries, Greeks, Cretans and men from Asia Minor (Pamphylians, Pisidians, Carians, Cilicians, Mysians), Cypriotes, Thracians, Illyrians and Gauls. Special corps were the slingers (Thracians and Kurds), archers (Mysians, Elymaeans, Medes, Persians) and javelin men (Lydians). So motley was a Seleucid army, and there were doubtless other corps of which our sources do not inform us. The mercenary Greeks and Anatolians were an important source of strength, and after the battle of Magnesia the Romans were careful to forbid the Seleucids to recruit troops within the Roman sphere of influence. It was impossible to cut off entirely the flow of mercenaries, but Rome did put an end to regular organized recruiting outside the boundaries of the Seleucid Empire. But from the days of Seleucus I and Antiochus I the mainstay of the army had been the Macedonians and Greeks settled in great masses within the boundaries of the empire, in Asia Minor, in Syria, in Mesopotamia and Babylonia, in Media, Persis and Elymais. Unfortunately we cannot determine the number of these immigrants. But the fact that the Mace-

donian phalanx at the battle of Raphia numbered 20,000 men, at
Magnesia 16,000, at the review at Daphne again 20,000, that to
these numbers we must add the Macedonian cavalry, the city
garrisons and the military police recruited from the same Graeco-
Macedonian stratum of the population, shows how great must
have been this population which was officially classed as Macedonians and Greeks. It is true that certain native elements soon
began to mingle with this population; no doubt, as the Avroman
parchments show, many Iranians also became military settlers; no
doubt from the time of Antiochus III natives (*e.g.* Jews) were
occasionally recruited as military settlers; but, for all this, the
number of Macedonians and Greeks in the Seleucid Empire must
have been very great. We must assume that military service was
demanded not only of the soldiers who received land from the king
but also of the Greek and Macedonian population of the cities.
But what were the exact duties to the state of either class
unfortunately we do not know.

The evidence for the organization of the *katoikoi* is contained in
a few inscriptions from Asia Minor[1]. The soldiers or officers
resident in any given place were distinguished from the other
Macedonians and enrolled on military lists. Each soldier received
a plot of land (*kleros*) perhaps in free possession but more probably
against some payment. In exceptional cases soldiers received immunity from land tax or tithe on the harvest. The parchments
found at Doura show that the plots of land, of which *katoikoi* may
hold more than one, pass by inheritance, may even pass to women
and may be sold. The rights of inheritance are limited: in default
of heirs within certain degrees the property reverts to the king,
and this may too have happened if the settler failed to fulfil his
various obligations. If this was so then the land always remained
in theory the king's property, but our documents do not prove it.
During peace part of the *katoikoi* serve in garrisons receiving pay,
others may be employed in training or may be cadets (see p. 117),
the remainder cultivate their allotments. From these scattered
facts we can gather what enormous expenditure was involved in
establishing each military settlement. From the accounts of the
refoundation of Lysimacheia and the planting of a Jewish colony in
Asia Minor by Antiochus III we see that not only had grants of
land to be made to the settlers but they must be given *stathmoi*,

---

[1] *O G.I.S.* 229, the sympoliteia of Smyrna and Magnesia on Mt Sipylus,
ibid. 211, of Thyateira, and the Mnesimachus inscription from Sardes
(*A.J.A.* XVI, 1912) which, in the view of the present writer, belongs to the
Seleucid rather than to the Pergamene régime.

houses to live in, and helped to stock their farms and guaranteed, for a time at least, certain immunities from taxation.

The inscription of Mnesimachus at Sardes and the inscription dating from the time of Antiochus II which tell of a sale of lands to Laodice (*O.G.I.S.* 225) give us some idea of the sources from which the Seleucids made good their enormous expenses for the upkeep of their standing army and their military settlements. We know from Plutarch that Eumenes, Alexander's secretary, got money to pay his army by selling to his officers lands formerly belonging to the Persian barons (vol. vi, p. 471). The need of money for the same purpose explains in large part the way the Seleucids disposed of land wholesale to cities, members of their own family, army officers, probably receiving payment even for lands granted as fiefs (ἐν δωρεᾷ). In the Mnesimachus inscription the revenues (in gold) from the lands granted or sold to the officers of the army do not go to the local exchequer but to this and that battalion (chiliarchy). Here the chiliarchy is not a part of the active army, still less is it a division of a satrapy, but rather a definite group of military settlers belonging to such and such a chiliarchy both in time of peace and in war. The money went partly for the needs of the *katoikoi* (*e.g.* the orphans' fund and various sorts of pensions), partly to pay those soldiers of the chiliarchy who were actually on service in garrisons or as military police.

We know even less of the Seleucid fleet. Antiochus III confronted Rome with so imposing a naval force that the Romans found it necessary to put into the peace-treaty a clause confining the sphere of action of the Seleucid fleet to Asiatic waters. There was a special squadron maintained by the Seleucids in the Persian Gulf. But the fleet had no decisive importance for the empire and gained no laurels in war. It co-operated with the active army, protected military transports which carried mercenaries and was a considerable factor in the political and commercial life of the period. How the royal fleet was equipped and maintained we are very ill-informed. It is possible that the system of trierarchies also existed in the Seleucid Empire, that is to say that the ships were built, equipped and maintained by particular groups of individuals. In the second book of the Maccabees (iv, 19 *sqq.*) there is a curious story of how Jason, a candidate for the Jewish High-priesthood, sent three hundred drachmae to Antiochus Epiphanes for sacrifices to Heracles and how his envoys asked that the money should be used for equipping triremes.

It is possible that the general command of the naval bases and the navy itself was in the hands of a controller of the naval ports.

At least Athenaeus who bears that title under Antiochus I not only holds wide tracts of land granted him by the king (*O.G.I.S.* 221, 54) but plays a great part in protecting the Greek cities of Asia Minor against the Galatians (Ditt³. 410, about 274 B.C.). Separate squadrons were under the command of admirals (*nauarchoi*).

D.   THE ECONOMIC POLICY OF THE SELEUCIDS

Our lack of information about the Seleucid Empire, the king's policy and efforts on behalf of it makes us unable to form any definite idea of the objects to which they directed their economic policy. One of the chief items in their revenues, little as we know about it in detail, was undoubtedly the revenue derived from taxes on commerce. The great trade-routes of the ancient world which joined Central Asia, India and Arabia with the Mediterranean, both by sea and by land, passed through the Seleucid Empire. The Ptolemies had to make great efforts to divert part of the Arabian and Indian trade from routes under Seleucid control to routes in their own hands, that is to the Red Sea ports of Egypt on the one side and to those of Palestine, Phoenicia and Coele-Syria on the other. The loss of these last provinces to Antiochus III was undoubtedly a very severe blow to the Ptolemies and made them pay special attention to developing the sea trade between Egypt and India by Arabia. But for the Seleucids the reunion in their hands of the whole Syro-Palestinian coast-line nearly made up for the loss of Asia Minor and its ports, due to the war between Antiochus III and Rome. Control over this coast kept the empire alive. During the first period of the empire's existence, down to the end of Antiochus III's reign, the Seleucids were specially concerned in keeping in their own hands both the sea route from India by the Persian Gulf to the mouth of the Tigris and Euphrates, and the land routes which from China, Central Asia and India crossed the Iranian plateau to Mesopotamia. The ancient trade-routes had been confirmed and regulated by the Persians and taken over from them by Alexander who set his chief colonies all along them: they were not neglected by the Seleucids. Intercourse with India under Seleucus I and Antiochus I, in spite of its having escaped their political control, was constant and lively. We find proof of this in the work of Megasthenes and Daïmachus and their embassies to the courts of Chandragupta and Amitrochates in India, and particularly in the expedition of Patrocles, a close associate of the first Seleucids, who explored the trade route from the Caspian to the Caucasus and Black Sea and collected in his book very valuable information both about the shores of the Caspian and about India, information of which Eratosthenes made use[1]. Still farther penetrated Demodamas of Miletus, 'a general under Seleucus and Antiochus who crossed the Jaxartes and raised altars to the Didymean Apollo' (Pliny, VI, 49). The Seleucids, particularly Antiochus I both before and after his father's death, made very great efforts to hellenize as much as possible Media, Parthia and Ariana, and to restore and support Alexander's principal foundations along the far-eastern trade routes, Alexandria Ariana (Herat), Antiochia Margiana (Merv), Alexandria in Arachosia (Candahar), and Alexandria on the Etymandrus (Helmund). Many cities were founded and maintained by them in north-eastern Iran: we have mentions of Antioch in Scythia and Alexandreschate on the Jaxartes.

The efforts of the Seleucids to maintain permanent connection with the Far East were by no means in vain. Not even the defection of Bactria, and subsequently of Parthia, cut it off. This is proved by the recent discovery in Northern Mongolia of woollen textiles from Syria, and by the strong probability that Hellenistic art exercised direct influence on the development of Chinese art under the Han dynasty. There had been a large import of Greek manufactures into the nearer Iranian countries even under the Persians: under the Seleucids it was a regular thing: witness the Rhodian amphora handles found at Susa. Both the sea trade to India and the chief land routes from the same country and from Central Asia had from time immemorial converged upon Babylonia near the mouth of the two rivers. Here Seleucus I founded the second capital of his kingdom Seleuceia on the Tigris in a situation more convenient and favourable than that of Babylon for concentrating in it the Asiatic trade. But Seleuceia lay too far from Greece and the Mediterranean to be the chief capital of the whole empire. This distinction therefore fell to Antioch on the Orontes with its port Seleuceia in Pieria. Once Antioch was founded, the chief care of the Seleucids was to join their eastern and western capitals by convenient and safe roads, and make this route more attractive and cheaper than the desert route to the ports of Palestine and Phoenicia. They therefore made two chief roads connecting Antioch with the great Mesopotamian roads of the Persian kings; one ran from Antioch to Zeugma on the Euphrates, thence by a bridge to Edessa and Nisibis to join the Persian road that led to the Iranian satrapies, the other also by Zeugma but across the Mesopotamian plain by Anthemusias and Ichnae to Nicephorium

[1] *Cambridge History of India*, I, p. 433.

and so by the great Persian road to Babylon and Seleuceia on the Tigris.

Seleuceia in Pieria never succeeded in attracting a large trade, and the chief outlets of the eastern trade still remained the great ports of Asia Minor; moreover the road through Asia Minor remained the main road from the Seleucid Empire to the Greek world and the Aegean, as the sea route from the North Syrian ports could always be blocked by the Ptolemies. The early Seleucids accordingly paid on the whole most attention to the Persian trade routes through Asia Minor, in which they improved and developed the net-work of roads, securing the chief stations and intersections with Macedonian colonies (see above, p. 158).

The position changed entirely in the latter period of the empire, during the second century B.C. Intercourse with the East, in spite of the Parthian advance, was not interrupted, as is shown by the fact that the finds in Mongolia belong to the last century B.C. There was, however, no longer any reason to prefer the northern routes to the southern. Accordingly the desert route from Seleuceia to the ports of Palestine came to life again, especially when the road along the Euphrates described above was closed to wholesale trade by the plundering practices of the Arab sheikhs who, during the political anarchy of the second half of the second century and the beginning of the last century B.C., had seized the chief points in the Mesopotamian plain. This, and the continual interruptions due to war with Parthia, made the sea route to India by the Persian Gulf and its continuation the desert routes to the ports of Palestine more important. Part of the Arabian trade had always passed through Seleucid territory: witness the large quantity of Arabian sweet-smelling gums presented by Seleucus I and Antiochus I to the temple of Apollo at Didyma (*O.G.I.S.* 214). Now, by a new development, it finally escaped from Ptolemaic control and went either by Petra to Gaza or by Damascus to the ports of Phoenicia, lately fallen into Seleucid hands. Finally, the exclusion of the Seleucids from Asia Minor and the revival of commercial life in Palestine and Phoenicia brought these ports into direct communication with the Greek world and left Alexandria on one side. This explains the lively intercourse between the Seleucids and Delos, Rhodes, and the cities of Greece, and the appearance of large numbers of Phoenician and Syrian traders both at Delos and at the Italian Delos, Puteoli.

How the upkeep of the roads was organized, how they were made safe and what imposts there were upon commerce in the Seleucid Empire we know most imperfectly. The roads, it appears, were, at any rate in Asia Minor, partly the king's highways, partly the charge of cities. In the Pergamene kingdom their upkeep was the duty of the owners of the land through which they passed, and it is quite likely that this rule was taken over from the Seleucids, who had it from the Persians. The Persians too had made for the Seleucids the organization of posts along the king's highways (vol. IV, p. 193).

We do not know whether the Seleucids did much to improve agriculture and manufactures. We have a chance mention that they introduced the cultivation of ammonium and nard into the empire. There can be no doubt that the settlement of large masses of Greek and Macedonian colonists in all parts of the empire must have had its influence in the introduction of Greek methods of agriculture and in the enlargement of the area under cultivation. So the appearance of Greek artisans and manufacturers in the commercial cities brought about a certain hellenization of the goods manufactured, and their export went mainly to countries entirely dominated by Greek taste and Greek habits.

Finally, trade must have been facilitated by the abundance of money coined in the Seleucid Empire. Whereas the Ptolemies began by coining on the Rhodian standard and then passed to the Milesian, that is the Phoenician, the Seleucids adopted and kept almost to the end the Attic standard which was accepted by the other kingdoms of Asia Minor and the Far East. In the world-market Seleucid currency competed successfully with Ptolemaic, but neither of them became world-wide or even drove out of circulation the coins of the Greek cities and of the lesser Hellenistic kingdoms.

III. THE EMPIRE: ASIA MINOR

Asia Minor, with its mountains and mountain-valleys, its steppe-like tablelands, luxuriant river valleys and fertile coastline close-set with admirable harbours open to the north, west and south, had always been a country of contrasts with one façade to the East, another to the West. In its geography, economics, nationality, social structure and civilization, it has from the earliest days of its secular past presented a most miscellaneous conglomerate: the cities of the coast with their developed culture of corn, wine and fruit, with their ever-growing manufactures and commerce; the temples of the coast region and of the interior also great centres of intensive agriculture and cattle-raising, manufacture and commerce; the great estates of the kings and nobles, successively

Hittite, Phrygian, Median, Persian, who lived in fortified burghs and castles, surrounded like the commercial cities with villages of tillers of the soil, ploughmen, vine-dressers and herdsmen, serfs of the king and of the urban aristocracy; the mountain tribes of cattle-keepers and bandits, living their primitive tribal life; such had from the beginning been the social and economic *ensemble* of Asia Minor.

No less diverse were the races: an ancient autochthonous population, invading Hittites and Thracians, certain Semitic wedges, Persians during the time of Persian rule, Greeks in the coast cities, —all these were mingled in Asia Minor. Diverse too was its civilization. Babylonian and Egyptian influences, the mighty Hittite culture and its later offshoots, those of the Phrygians, Lydians, Lycians and Carians mixed with Minoan and Achaean elements, finally the rich and varied Ionian society at once Greek and Oriental, all combine to stamp a special impress of variety upon what we call Anatolian civilization.

This was the general character of the country which the Seleucids took over from their predecessors, though, as we have seen, they never held Bithynia and Pontus, and fought a losing battle for much of the rest (p. 159, chap. xxii). The permanent possessions of the Seleucids were the Troad and the wide belt running along the middle of the peninsula and joining its western coast to the centre of the empire in Northern Syria. The description of the political entity Asia Minor in official documents of the Seleucid period is 'the kings, dynasts, cities and tribes' (*O.G.I.S.* 229, 13). Within the Asia Minor part of their empire the Seleucid kings distinguish between *symmachia*, the territory of their allies inhabited by citizens of Greek states and their subjects, and what they probably called 'royal land' (βασιλική), the territory of the kingdom inhabited by the king's direct subjects.

What the Seleucids and Ptolemies exactly understood by the term *symmachia* is not quite clear to us. Whether it consisted only of the ancient Greek cities with which the kings had definite treaties of alliance or included also the cities founded by the kings themselves and indebted to them for their constitution and laws we do not know. Also we have little information as to the relations between the Seleucids and individual cities. The official policy of all Hellenistic kings, what they proclaimed abroad, as did the Romans after them, was that they protected or restored the cities' freedom. But the fact that they all kept promising this freedom to the cities in their enemies' hands shows that this guarantee of freedom was nothing more than propaganda. The underlying reality was quite different. The degree of freedom and autonomy allowed to the cities by the Seleucids and the other Hellenistic kings was precisely defined by the political situation. The weaker the king, the more need he had of support and sympathy from the Greek city, the more likely he was to refrain from interfering in the city's internal affairs and autonomy and to lower or waive his demands for tribute and imposts.

In any case the king's principle was that autonomy, democracy and immunity from tribute and imposts were the definite gift of the king, and the guiding rule was that the king's will is the highest law and the king's decree overrides any decision of the people. 'The cities under our dominion' is the official term used by the king to define his relations to the Greek cities. And he claims the right to give orders to them when necessary. This rule is recognized by the cities, and they occasionally insert in their resolutions a clause 'if the king shall not make other arrangements in this matter.' With all this the king may show the most courteous consideration for the necessities of the cities, may make them from time to time the most generous presents, as those made by Seleucus I and Antiochus I to Miletus (p. 77), confirm or grant them freedom, autonomy and immunity (Smyrna, Miletus, Erythrae). On the other hand, however, the same Seleucus I and Antiochus I interfere with a high hand in the internal affairs of free cities as readily as Antigonus or Lysimachus, and if their successors do not, it is because of the political situation rather than of their personal dispositions.

The normal position of most of the old Greek cities of Asia Minor within the empire of the Seleucids was that the city preserved its constitution and life ordered after its own laws, but was obliged to obey the king's commands and pay tribute and imposts to the king's treasury. Subjection to the king was most clearly exemplified in the payment of tribute (*phoros*). This is very clearly brought out by the complaints made by the envoys of Antiochus III to Rome and the Roman arrangement that after the battle of Magnesia the cities that used to pay tribute to Antiochus should receive freedom, while those that paid to Attalus should still pay to Eumenes. Most interesting on this point is an inscription of one of the Greek cities on the Hellespont in honour of Corragus, *strategos* of that region (*S.E.G.* II, 663). The inscription probably belongs to the time when the towns of the Hellespont had passed from Antiochus III to Rome and, as having been 'conquered by force of arms' and forced to surrender (*deditio*), had lost all their rights and were afterwards handed over by Rome to Eumenes.

This appears to the present writer to be the right interpretation of the inscription. The position was desperate. The war had ruined both city and citizens, and they were absolutely at the mercy of the conqueror. The king restores to the city what it possessed before: (1) its laws and its 'ancestral constitution,' (2) the temples and sacred plots of land, with money for worship and for administering the city, (3) oil for the young men and (4) all it had before. Further, he confirms the citizens' rights to their holdings of land and to those who had none land is granted from the king's treasury. Finally, immunity from all imposts is guaranteed for three years, extended to five at the request of the governor. Besides all this there are many presents made by the king and personal gifts from the governor.

The inscription shows that under Antiochus III and probably earlier the city had enjoyed freedom and autonomy but paid tribute to the royal treasury, probably not in one single payment made by the city, but separately under various heads. Some of these payments the king returned to the city for the expenses of worship and the like. The treasury also allows a certain quantity of olive oil for the needs of the city's palaestrae and gymnasia. This would suggest that the oil produced in the city's territory passed either all (as a monopoly) or in part (as an impost) into the king's treasury. The private property of the citizens in their own pieces of land is recognized: but side by side with this private land there is in the city territory a considerable amount of royal land. The city as such owns the temples and their lands, but apparently has no other landed property. The same arrangement of imposts may be deduced from the letter of Antiochus I to Erythrae (*O.G.I.S.* 223). The city receives immunity from all tributes and imposts, including a special contribution exacted for the defence of the country against the Gauls. Still this immunity scarcely included freedom from the payment of lump sums as presents to the king, 'crowns' or 'gold for presents.' This probably had to be provided both by cities subject to tribute and those immune from it.

The Seleucids, as we said before, did much towards the urbanization of those regions within the country which were in their possession. Part of their settlements were military colonies, part cities with a civilian population. Of the military colonies some were organized as cities or afterwards attained to that rank, others were villages (*komai*) before the Macedonian settlers came, and remained so. To draw a line between one class and the other is very difficult. The case of Magnesia by Sipylus shows that even ancient Greek cities might be converted into military settlements, and yet keep their old civil population. The colonization of Central Asia Minor by the Seleucids was undoubtedly very intensive: we know the names of not less than thirty Seleucid cities and settlements.

This business of settlements was complicated and expensive. The *modus operandi* is shown us by one or two chance documents. Lysimacheia, which had been the capital of Lysimachus in Thrace, was restored by Antiochus III. For this purpose he summoned together the former inhabitants of the city, some of whom he redeemed from being prisoners of war, invited new settlers, gave them cattle and agricultural implements, and fortified the town at his own expense. Another type of settlement is represented by the story of the foundation of Nysa on the Maeander. Antiochus I created this city by settling in it the population of three neighbouring communities. The town received the privilege of *asylia* afterwards confirmed by Antiochus III. This was the ordinary and frequent method of *synoikismos*. So was created the town of Apollonis under one of the Attalids. The settlers were given a subvention out of the funds of the person who directed the *synoikismos* (Keil and Premerstein, *II. Reise*, No. 113). Finally, the foundation of a purely military colony is illustrated by the story in Josephus (*Ant.* xii, 148) how Antiochus III settled Jewish colonists from Mesopotamia and Babylonia in Lydia and Phrygia. Whether we have to do with a historical fact or with mere fiction and whether the letter of Antiochus to Zeuxis quoted by Josephus is genuine or not (its style is singularly like the letter from the same Antiochus to the city of Amyzon) is immaterial for our purposes. There is no doubt that the letter gives us exactly the normal procedure when the Seleucids founded a military colony. By a resolution of the council of the king's 'friends,' it was decided to settle in some fortified posts where such settlements were especially needed (κατὰ τοὺς ἀναγκαιοτάτους τόπους) two thousand families with their belongings. The settlers were guaranteed autonomy, sites for houses, allotments for agriculture and planting vineyards, immunity from taxation upon their lands for ten years, grain to keep them the first year, support for the representatives of the new communities and a guarantee of their safety—presumably in the form of fortifications. All these measures so closely agree with the reorganization of the town on the Hellespont carried out by Corragus (p. 178 *sq.*) and the procedure at Lysimacheia that we need have no doubt as to their authenticity.

The organization of the new cities is not likely to have differed essentially from that of any Greek city. Each had its constitution granted by the king and the same laws[1]. Whether there was always in the city a representative of the central power, an *epistates*, or only in certain cities and for particular times, as under the Ptolemies (*Inschr. v. Priene*, 37, ll. 134 and 153), we cannot tell. Nor do we know anything of the organization of the military settlements that were not cities.

The new cities arose on lands which the Seleucid kings took over from their predecessors by right of conquest.

But apart from the royal land allotted to cities and military settlements the king had left in his hands enormous stretches of tilled land which had formerly belonged, as we have said, to native or immigrant proprietors and inhabited by the so-called 'king's folk' (*laoi basilikoi*). The centre of each estate was the manor-house or castle of the proprietor (p. 177)[2]. These lands had been even before Seleucid times the property of the king held of him by the Hittite, Phrygian, Lydian and Persian barons. The title of the temples to their lands and serfs was sounder. But even in this case, as the representative of the god upon earth was the king, the land in the last resort was at the king's disposal. Large tracts of land also belonged to the king in the near neighbourhood of the Greek cities. Such for instance was the land given by Ptolemy Philadelphus to Miletus. Such lands are mentioned in inscriptions dealing with their sale or grant to Greek cities, members of the royal family and high officials or friends of the king (pp. 172, 182).

In the years which followed Alexander's death lands were sometimes seized by his officers, but later on the lands were precisely registered and their enjoyment systematized. In their need of cash to pay their army, the Seleucids used to sell some of the lands to the Greek cities, to members of their family, and probably to other persons possessing large sums of money. Rich men were not rare in the Seleucid Empire, mostly in the king's entourage. Hermeias the Carian, the grand vizier of Antiochus III, was rich enough to pay the troops when at the time of Molon's insurrection the king himself lacked the means to do so. Dionysius, *epistolographos* of Antiochus IV, could send to take part in a procession at Daphne a thousand slaves each with a silver dish in his hand worth a thousand drachmae or more. We must believe that Laodice, first wife of Antiochus II, and Aristodicides, the friend of Antiochus I, his admiral Athenaeus and Larichus, their contemporary, and

---

[1] We know this in the case of Antioch in Pisidia (*Inschr. v. Magn.* 80 and 81), Antioch in Caria (*ibid.* 170), Laodicea on the Lycus (Michel, 543).

[2] *Tyrsis* is the Hittite name of such a castle, *Baris* the Semitic, while the Greeks called it *pyrgos*, *tetrapyrgion*, *aule*, *epaulion*, etc.

Mnesimachus of the Sardian inscription were no poorer than those other grandees. The lands that these persons bought became in most cases their private property. Inasmuch as outside the Greek cities fee simple did not exist, one condition of the purchase was that the land must be ascribed to the territory of some city.

Often, however, the lands were granted not in fee simple but as fiefs, perhaps in return for the payment of one lump sum. The best example is perhaps the Mnesimachus inscription in which we see how the practice of granting fiefs exists side by side with the practice of providing officers with allotments, military *kleroi*. Mnesimachus received three estates with three villages and two allotments in the territory of two of these villages. 'When the division took place, Pytheus and Adrastus (probably two officers) received as their separate property (ἐξαίρημα) the manor-house with the serfs' houses round it and gardens near one village, and arable land with gardens and serfs near the other.' It is evident that the legal position of the village and land granted as a fief is different from that of a military allotment but in what the difference consists we do not know. Both pay rent to the king in gold. Both are part of the estate of Mnesimachus and are accordingly mortgaged to the temple at Sardes, possibly to raise the money for the lump sum to the king.

How arbitrarily the Seleucids disposed of lands which they for some reason considered to be theirs, and how greedily their 'friends' pounced upon them although they had only just come into possession of the royal house we can see from the story of the so-called Anaitis, a well-known tract of land on the coast opposite Samos. There were many claimants for it, especially the Samians, at the moment when Antiochus II seized it for a short space. The grandees (ἐνδοξότατοι φίλοι) evidently thought that it was crown land, that is that they might make petition for it. So the officers of Antiochus divided it up without delay and the Samians had to make very great efforts before they could establish their right to it in the king's eyes. This meant a long and difficult embassy which began by missing the king at Ephesus and finally caught him at Sardes (*S.E.G.* 1, 366). During the occupation power was in the hands of a *phrourarchos*, and the distribution of the land was managed by a *dioiketes*.

The chief characteristic of these lands was that they were the territories of villages and that near or in the villages were the fortified manor-houses of the holders of the villages and lands. In the Laodice inscription (*O.G.I.S.* 225) and in an inscription from Magnesia (*Inschr. v. Magn.* 122 d. 4) these manor-houses are called *baris* like the castle of Hyrcanus the son of Tobias in the land of the Ammonites. The inhabitants of the villages (*mandrai*) were no doubt *adscripti glebae* and bound to render the feudal proprietor a certain proportion of the harvest and also probably a certain amount of labour. More exact information as to these obligations is lacking. The technical word for these people was *laoi*. How far besides receiving the rents from these villeins the landholders cultivated their own demesne with the villeins' labour and that of their own slaves we cannot say. The same *laoi*, superintended by the royal *oikonomoi* or *dioiketai*, also tilled the land which remained in the king's possession. Whether there already existed in Seleucid times the custom of letting great tracts of land with their *laoi* we do not know. But when it was embodied in the territory of a city, they went with it and were then numbered with the *paroikoi* or *katoikoi* who had from all time lived on the city territory working on the land which belonged to the citizens. Finally, a similar position, with perhaps some extra obligations, was that of the peasants who tilled the wide-stretching temple-lands.

These temples, as has been said, were a peculiarity of many parts of the Near East. In Asia Minor they are found near the Greek coast cities, in the interior and near the ancient native cities. Even after their priesthood and cults had been in large part hellenized, they kept a certain autonomy. Indeed many of them were never brought into touch with Greek cities at all. Their lands were regarded by the earlier Seleucids as not beyond the king's reach, and were disposed of by the kings as it is shown by their action at Baetocaece and Aezani (*O.G.I.S.* 262, 502). But, as in Egypt, we find that when the dynasty began to fail there was a return to the former state of things. The later Seleucids return their lands and privileges to the temples and many of them once more become the feudal possessions of sacerdotal dynasties. This we see most of all in Syria as the Seleucids had lost Asia Minor before their final stage of weakness.

The ancient Greek cities, the new urban foundations of the Seleucids, temples, royal estates, estates of the royal family and the grandees did not fill up the whole area of Asia Minor. Many tribes living in the mountains and valleys of Lycia, Pisidia, Pamphylia, Isauria and Lycaonia, nominally formed part of the empire, probably paid tribute and supplied soldiers, but for all that continued to live their own independent tribal life, of which we know very little. Finally, from the time when the Persian Empire was falling to pieces Asia Minor had contained petty states, centred in tribes, cities or temples governed by local dynasts of

native or of Greek origin. In the fourth century there were many
of them: the houses of Gongylus and Demaratus, the tyrants of
Aeolis, Atarneus, Zelea and the like, and, most important of all, the
dynasts Hecatomnus and Mausolus in Caria with their capital at
Halicarnassus (vol. VI, p. 210). During the two generations after
Alexander we hear little of these states. But from the time of
Antiochus II they begin to appear everywhere. At Cibyra in
Pisidia there is reigning in 189 B.C. a local dynast Moagetes; Olba
in Cilicia is ruled in the third century by the priest-kings of the
house of Teucer: somewhere in Cilicia there flourishes the house
of Xenophanes. The Pergamene kingdom itself was to spring
from such a state, and finds its closest analogue in the principality
of Lysias, son of Philomelus, a Macedonian, probably descended
from Lysias the general of Seleucus I. Rulers of this house probably founded the cities of Lysias and Philomelium in Phrygia;
and it is possible that one of the line is mentioned by Polybius
(v, 90) under the name of Lysanias, alongside of Olympichus, a
dynast in the region of Mylasa, and Limnaeus whose principality
is unknown.

IV THE EMPIRE: SYRIA, MESOPOTAMIA AND BABYLONIA

Cilicia, Northern Syria and Mesopotamia became, as we have
seen, the centre of the Seleucid Empire and its main support. Here
too the Seleucids inherited ancient traditions and built their Syria
on the foundations of an ancient civilization and a stable social,
economic and religious system. Here too as in Asia Minor, even
more so in fact, they found many great and flourishing commercial
cities, Damascus, Aleppo, Carchemish and the like, many rich
temples with developed agriculture, commerce and manufactures
(the temple of Zeus near Baetocaece, Baalbek, Emesa, Bambyce
Hierapolis and so on), any number of rich and populous villages,
such as were so characteristic of Syria in the later, Roman period,
a number of mountain tribes and of tribes on the borders of the
desert living by their cattle and if occasion served by plunder.

The Seleucid policy in Syria and Mesopotamia has already been
described: it was a steady policy of founding cities and bringing
in Macedonians and Greeks. Syria and Mesopotamia were to be
made a second Macedonia but a Macedonia of cities and fortresses
not of tribes and villages. Seleucus I, Antiochus I and later
Antiochus IV pursued this policy steadily and with energy. To
Seleucus I was due the foundation of the political capital of the

empire, Antioch on the Orontes, its military capital Apamea in Syria and its commercial capitals Seleuceia in Pieria and Laodicea. Round these were scattered dozens of settlements, cities or almost cities, like the group—Larissa, Casiana, Megara, Apollonia and the rest—which Strabo (XVI, 752) describes as near Apamea and assessed along with it.

It is very difficult for us to get an idea of these cities and of their relation to the native population. Their ruins are in part excellently preserved but still await their investigator. What is on the surface belongs to the Roman or Byzantine period, ruins of buildings and inscriptions. The four capitals of the empire were apparently quite new creations; perhaps there were old villages or groups of villages on the sites. Many of the smaller cities were probably equally new foundations. But in many other instances founding a city meant settling Macedonians and Greeks in an already existing and flourishing urban centre or in a town-like settlement closely connected with one of the ancient and powerful temples. We shall only learn something about each of these settlements when at last we begin systematically to explore their ruins.

Equally scanty is our knowledge of the inner organization of the Greek cities in Syria. Even of the capital Antioch, which by the time of Antiochus Epiphanes had grown into an enormous city, we know considerably less than of its Egyptian rival Alexandria. Like Alexandria and like the other cities of Syria Antioch was made up of many nationalities. How the non-Greek inhabitants of the city, Syrians, Jews and the like were organized, we do not know. The Greek part of it was no doubt organized like a Greek *polis* with tribes and eighteen demes, a city council, colleges of magistrates. Colleges of ephebes with their gymnasia and palaestrae, probably with their gymnasiarchs and cosmetae, clubs and associations of various sorts, are known to have existed at Antioch. Some change in this organization was made by Antiochus Epiphanes. As a great admirer of Rome, he not only tried to romanize the civic life of Antioch, introducing tribunes and aediles, but evidently wished to make Antioch not only his Rome, the centre of an empire for himself, as later Rome was for Augustus, but also the metropolis of the other Greek cities of the empire. The cities he founded were to him colonies of the great city in which he was both king and chief magistrate.

The story of Seleuceia in Pieria is very typical: at the beginning of the third century probably its constitution hardly differed from that of Antioch. In 229 B.C. it received freedom from Seleucus II and acts as a free city in its relations with Athens (Ditt[3]. 475). But it is quite characteristic that this very liberty is granted to the city for the second time by Antiochus Grypus in 109 B.C. (*O.G.I.S.* 257).

The only site from which we can gain some idea of the history and constitution of a Seleucid settlement is Doura-Europos on the Euphrates, part of which has been recently excavated by M. Cumont. The town was founded on the site of an ancient Assyrian fortress and perhaps of a Syrian village (see vol. VI, pp. 430 *sq.*, 491). Its first settlers were Macedonians, soldiers. For them there were built houses, civic buildings and temples, the whole surrounded by a strong wall. Inside the town was a citadel occupied evidently by a garrison to protect the town, command the crossing of the Euphrates and keep in order the neighbouring nomads. The land round the town and perhaps the land on the other side of the Euphrates was divided into *ekades* and *kleroi*. Perhaps twenty *kleroi* went to the *ekas*. This was called after the name of the officer who presumably first allotted the *kleroi* among their original holders and was the commander of that group of *klerouchoi*. The *kleroi* kept as in Egypt the names of their original holders and passed by inheritance. Whether the holders paid any impost and what were their obligations in return for receiving a *kleros* we do not know. The mode of descent by inheritance, even to women, was governed by the laws of the city. If direct heirs as provided by law failed the lot again became the property of the king. So likewise in all probability in case of failure on the part of a *klerouchos* to fulfil his obligations to the king.

The group of settlers in the new urban centre was organized as a Greek *polis*. On its foundation it received of the king a constitution and laws. One chapter of those laws, on inheritance *ab intestato*, we have in a later copy upon parchment. The town had its council and its magistrates, a popular assembly is not mentioned, the chief was the *strategos* either elected or nominated by the king. In one inscription of the Parthian period he is also the *epistates* of the city, that is the commander of the garrison. The Macedonians in the city side by side with their political organization retained their religious and social organization based upon the tribe with a division into *genē* at the head of which stood *genearchoi*. In the city there was a bank-treasury and a special official institution for registering and authenticating private contracts; at its head stood a *chreophylax*, probably a state official. Part of his business was to exact the duties imposed on the completion of various kinds of transactions.

The Macedonians undoubtedly from the very beginning shared the town with Syrians, whoever these Syrians may have been, inhabitants of the village which already existed on the site, or traders and artisans who came and settled there. But the fact that one of the oldest temples was dedicated to the local goddess Nanaia, identified with the Graeco-Macedonian Artemis, suggests that important and wealthy Syrians lived in the city from the moment of its foundation. The temple of Nanaia had its own resources and probably its own landed property. A later inscription mentions a special temple-treasurer.

The documents found at Doura are very closely allied to the parchments from Avroman in Media and lead us to think that the conditions under which that province was settled differed little from those in Mesopotamia. It is, however, probable that in Media the military settlers, especially those outside the cities, were not Macedonians or Greeks but Iranians.

South of Mesopotamia lay Babylonia and beyond it Susiana, two important satrapies, governed by strategi. We know rather more of Babylonia than of the other eastern parts of the empire. A few Greek inscriptions, the ruins of some buildings of Hellenistic date and, most important of all, thousands of cuneiform tablets of the same period mostly from Babylon and Uruk have been found. Very few of these have been read and published and even fewer translated, but we can draw certain conclusions about the history of Babylon and Babylonia under Seleucid rule, and, when the tablets scattered through Europe and America are published and translated, we shall doubtless know a great deal more.

From the time of Seleucus I the capital of the Babylonian, or as the tablets call it the Akkadian, satrapy was the royal city of Seleuceia founded by Seleucus I on the Tigris, on the site of the ancient Opis, to be the second or even the first commercial capital of the kingdom. Here lived the Governor-general of the East, under the early Seleucids usually the heir-apparent, with his staff and chancery, his guard and army, also the *strategos* of the satrapy and the *epistates* of the city, the commander probably of the strong garrison. No doubt even in military affairs Seleuceia was of great importance as the base for numerous expeditions to the East and also for the navy on the Persian Gulf. The city had an enormous and heterogeneous population, probably larger than that of Antioch. In it lived a certain number of Macedonians and Greeks, many Syrians and an enormous part of the population formerly in Babylon: there were also a good many Jews. For a time Seleuceia existed side by side with Babylon but under Antiochus I a large part of the population of Babylon was forcibly removed to

Seleuceia and what was left in Babylon, with the exception of the
population of the temples, was condemned to die out by lack of
subsistence. The constitution of Seleuceia was probably on the
same lines as that of Antioch. The Macedonians and Greeks
formed a self-governing *polis* with a popular assembly, a council
of three hundred and a *gerousia*, probably magistrates and everything else that made up a Greek *polis*. The native elements were
quite separate, likewise the Syrians and Jews. In late times the
city, like Seleuceia in Pieria, receives freedom and the right to coin
money.

As to the position of Babylon under the early Seleucids we have
some data. Under Seleucus I the city, as we have said, was not
yet dead. It had a hard time under Antiochus I when it was finally
sacrificed to Seleuceia and in it during the first Syrian war reigned
hunger, sickness and despair: this is clearly described in the
chronicle for 276–4 B.C. The inhabitants of Babylon were little
consoled by the restoration of their ancient temples, E-sagila and
E-zida (vol. IV, p. 13 *sq.*). A little earlier (287 B.C.) the same despair
of Uruk, Akkad, Nippur is heard in a little cuneiform Babylonian
poem. There is also a confused story about certain lands, cattle and
other valuables referred to in the above chronicle and in a copy of
an inscription of Seleucus II on a Babylonian tablet. In 280 B.C. the
land was given by Antiochus I to Babylon, Borsippa and Kuthah
to support their inhabitants, in 276 it was taken back by the king's
exchequer, under Antiochus II it was granted to his wife Laodice
and her sons and by them handed back again to Babylon, Borsippa
and Kuthah; finally under Seleucus II it passed to the temples.
These vicissitudes probably mark the veering of early Seleucid
policy towards Babylon.

A new era in the history of Babylon and the other cities of
Babylonia comes in with Antiochus Epiphanes. An inscription
from Babylon calls him the founder of the city and the Saviour of
Asia. Under him probably the city received a considerable Greek
colony, a theatre and gymnasium were built, Greek *agones* organized, and the new city granted a constitution and laws. From
that time on we find there a *strategos* and an *epistates*. The same
policy of restoration was adopted at Uruk. Many cuneiform
documents mention people with double names, Greek and Babylonian, and speak of their dealings with the still wealthy temples,
of the royal official who kept contracts, and of various imposts
with Greek names paid by the population of the city, a salt monopoly like that in Palestine, a tax on sales (ἐπώνιον) and a tax on
slaves. In the business documents reference is made to the king's

new laws, regulating business relations (a law about *deposita*) and
royal currency: one of them is concerned with the affairs of a
soldier-settler. But it is interesting to notice how fast the old tradition holds. The Greeks take Babylonian names; the forms of
contracts even when the parties or one of them are Greek remain
purely Babylonian; the old Babylonian banks survive. The temples
go on playing the chief part in the economic, social and general
life of the country: the language survives and the ancient cuneiform
writing, though side by side with it Greek becomes the second
official language for business.

Antiochus Epiphanes applied the same policy to the whole
valley of the Euphrates and Tigris. We shall see below that the
same policy dictates his treatment of Palestine. He has come down
to us as a new Seleucus I or Antiochus I, a new city builder
credited with fifteen foundations most of which received his name.
But not one of them is really founded by him, or his creation. In
some cities he strengthens the Greek element; but in most cases
he tries to hellenize ancient oriental cities that had perhaps been
left in peace by his predecessors. He is particularly fond of doing
this in Babylonia: also in Cilicia and in such ancient oriental
centres as Bambyce, Edessa, Nisibis and Ecbatana. This policy
was forced upon him by necessity: the natural hellenization of the
East had come to a standstill, the oriental element had begun to
submerge the Greek, especially in the great and ancient centres
of the East: the Hellenic empire of the Seleucids was threatened
with collapse. Antiochus' attempt was dictated by a desire to
revive Hellenism by introducing into the chief strongholds of
Orientalism a new and fresh Greek element. It was a counsel of
despair. Epiphanes and Hellenism lacked the strength to put it into
execution. His failure in Palestine (p. 159 *sq.*) was not exceptional.
It is unlikely that he really hellenized Babylon. To stop the growth
of Orientalism was beyond his strength.

The further we go eastwards the scantier becomes our information. At Susa de Morgan dug up a few inscriptions, but not all
of them are published. Antioch in Persis with its purely Greek
constitution and a number of other such cities in its neighbourhood (including Susa) are mentioned in an inscription from
Magnesia on the Maeander (*O.G.I.S.* 233), but further eastwards
unbroken darkness reigns. Even the organization of Bactria, its
cities and population, first under the rule of Seleucid satraps and
then under local Greek kings, is absolutely unknown to us.

V. THE EMPIRE: PHOENICIA AND PALESTINE

For nearly a century the Ptolemies ruled almost uninterruptedly the coast of Phoenicia and Palestine: how far their authority extended into the interior behind the Phoenician coast we do not know, probably no farther than the territory of the cities they held. It went deeper into the country towards the south, certainly they held Judaea, Samaria, and Transjordania, and Egypt was probably acknowledged as suzerain by the tribes on the borders of these more or less civilized districts. All these possessions were lost to the Ptolemies after the victory of Antiochus III at Panion (200 B.C.) and the provinces that had been theirs passed for the next century or so to the Seleucids. These only retained effective dominion over them until the middle of the second century B.C.: after this begins the dissolution of this part of their empire. The cities of Phoenicia and the Palestine coast became almost independent, received freedom and *asylia*, and many of them fell into the hands of tyrants (Gaza, Dora, Turris Stratonis, Byblus, Tripolis, Tyre). The same thing happens in the interior, Judaea becomes independent, so too many of the tribes on its borders, in many of the hellenized towns arise dynasts and tyrants (Gamala, Philadelphia, Lysias in Lebanon, etc.). This was partly a reaction of Orientalism against Hellenism: partly the natural result of the political anarchy produced by the joint efforts of Rome and Parthia, unceasingly encouraging dynastic struggles between various members of the house of Seleucus.

In Phoenicia we must clearly distinguish between the district of Aradus and the districts of the more famous Phoenician cities, Tripolis, Byblus, Berytus, Sidon, Tyre and Ake-Ptolemaïs. Of the Phoenician cities the most powerful was Aradus with its large territory on the main land (Peraea) and several dependent cities. Aradus had succeeded not only in slipping out of the hands of the Ptolemies but in establishing its almost complete independence within the Seleucid empire as early as 259 B.C. and finally in 243.

The life of the Phoenician cities under the Ptolemies and Seleucids is little known to us. Zeno's correspondence shows us how close was the intercourse with Egypt and what crowds of Egyptian Greeks there were in Phoenicia: we must remember that the Phoenicia of the late fourth and early third centuries B.C. was hellenized to a comparatively large extent. At that time Phoenicians were quite at home in Greece, in Athens, Rhodes and Corinth, and the Greeks at home in Phoenicia. We need but mention the Sidonian sarcophagi, the strong hellenization of Carthage, the Greek character of most of the Phoenician manufactures at this period. No doubt even in the fourth century there had existed in all the cities of Phoenicia strong and influential groups of Greek settlers and among the nobles it was the fashion to live as Greeks and have a Greek name. The best example of this is Philocles the well-known admiral who served first Demetrius and then Ptolemy Philadelphus (see above, p. 92). Under the Ptolemies this hellenization spread even farther and the cities probably adopted a more or less hellenized constitution which they subsequently retained under the Seleucids. Josephus speaks of the people, council and magistrates of Tyre and Sidon, and the same council and people reappear in the heading of a letter of Tyre to Delphi some time after 125 B.C. We cannot tell whether these bodies only represented the Greeks living in the Phoenician cities (including hellenized Phoenicians) or the whole population of the city, but very probably some new Hellenic form of constitution was introduced under either the Ptolemies or the Seleucids.

The business life of the Phoenician cities naturally went on in its old forms. We know of the existence therein of long established firms, we know too that outside Phoenicia the merchants of the different cities acted at Athens, at Delos and in Italy as compact groups, regular guilds. It is no accident that at Delos the first appearance of these guilds is under the later Seleucids (merchants, shipowners and warehousemen from Berytus, Laodicea, merchants and shipowners from Tyre). This was the natural result, as we have noticed, of the Seleucids' loss of Asia Minor and the freeing of the Phoenician cities from subordination to Alexandria: they were now its keen competitors.

Some interest attaches to the colonizing activity of the Phoenician cities, probably growing under the Ptolemies and producing its effects under the Seleucids. At Marissa in Palestine there certainly existed a colony of Sidonians, for the most part Greeks, with its own self-government and representatives. In the painted tombs of this city, dated about 200 B.C., we have besides Phoenicians many Sidonians with Greek names and a certain Apollophanes who was archon 'of the Sidonians in Marissa.' We must bring this into relation with the well-known exchange of letters between Antiochus and the Sidonians at Shechem (Joseph. *Ant.* XII, 258–264; cf. 2 Macc. vi), in which these Sidonians point out the difference between themselves and the Jews and ask leave to convert the temple on Mount Gerizim into a sanctuary of Zeus.

Such semi-Greeks from the Phoenician cities were probably scattered in groups throughout Judaea and Samaria and were (especially in Jerusalem) powerful advocates of Hellenism. The special part played by Sidon is explained by the importance of Sidon for the life of the whole coast in the fourth and third centuries B.C., especially during the rule of Eshmunazar's dynasty when Dora and Joppa belonged to Sidon and it probably had all the trade of Palestine.

As far back as the time of the Ptolemaic rule, Judaea, that is the city of Jerusalem, its territory and the adjacent district inhabited by the Jews, was surrounded by a ring of 'Greek' cities[1]. Some of those were cities containing a fair number of Macedonian and Greek settlers, military and civilian, some of them ancient commercial cities of the Philistine coast which had developed along the same lines of gradual hellenization as the neighbouring cities of Phoenicia. The chief coast towns were to the south of Ake-Ptolemaïs: Apollonia, Joppa, Azotus, Ascalon, Anthedon, Gaza and Raphia. In Samaria the city of Samaria itself and Nysa Scythopolis had undoubtedly a considerable Greek population. In Transjordania side by side with the native sheikhs and their tribes, a group of towns with a mainly Greek population made up what was afterwards called the Decapolis. The names of Philadelphia (Rabbath-Ammon), Philoteria on Lake Gennesareth (perhaps the same as Gamala), Arsinoe in the valley of the Marsyas, reflect Ptolemaic foundations. On the other hand Pella, Dion, Gerasa (called Antioch in the reign of Antiochus III or IV), Gadara (Seleuceia), Abila (Seleuceia) and a third Seleuceia to the south-east of the waters of Merom are due to the various Seleucid kings.

We know little of the constitution of the coast towns and their relations to the Ptolemies and Seleucids: we cannot tell whether the council of five hundred at Gaza was an ancient institution or a new creation of Ptolemies or Seleucids. In the matter of tribute the coast towns were no doubt in the same position as those of Phoenicia and most of those in Asia Minor. We happen to know that at Ascalon in the time of Alexander Jannaeus (103–78 B.C.) a very prominent place in the town was taken by a tax-farmer; evidently tribute and taxes were farmed by auction (at first at

---

[1] The question of the trustworthiness of 1 and 2 Maccabees and of Josephus, *Antiquities*, and their interrelation will be discussed elsewhere, as also the authenticity of the documents cited in them (see further, vol. VIII). In the view of the present writer these sources are sufficiently based on good evidence to give a picture which is substantially correct.

Alexandria, then at Antioch and finally at Jerusalem) and the sum paid for them went to the state treasury.

Some light is cast on the peculiar arrangements of Transjordania by the correspondence of Zeno. Side by side with the flourishing Greek city of Philadelphia we find a native sheikh (an ethnarch or *strategos* in the later terminology—probably borrowed by the Romans from their Hellenistic predecessors), who is at the same time governor of the district and commander of a unit of Ptolemaic forces. This sheikh lives probably not in the city but in his castle (*baris*); and that of Tobias, Zeno's correspondent, and of his descendants, who played a great part in the history of Palestine in the second half of the third century B.C., has survived to our day in ruins.

In this circle of Greek towns Judaea was undoubtedly a survival of the past, one of those temple states of which there were so many in other parts of the Seleucid Empire. The structure of this temple state with its centre at Jerusalem is fairly well known: the High Priest at its head, his council consisting of the chiefs of the more distinguished clans, the whole set of persons occupied in the cult make up the government and aristocracy of the nation. The population living in Jerusalem and various villages, fortified or open, paid to the temple, that is to the god for the support of the temple, the High Priest, the other priests and the servants, various dues in money or in kind. In the name of his people the High Priest contributed to the treasury, first of the Persian kings, then to that of Alexander, his successors and finally the Ptolemies, a certain sum of tribute. This tribute, of course, was not paid out of the revenues of the temple and the priests, but was a separate exaction from the people. Towards paying the tribute went first of all the special land tax which the High Priest collected from the people for that purpose. Under the Seleucids the Jews paid one-third of the produce of cereals and half the fruits of trees, and there is no reason to think that this high rate of taxation was newly introduced by the Seleucids. It is quite possible that the High Priest paid a special sum to the suzerain for his investiture. For the state to sell priesthoods was usual in the Greek and Hellenistic world. Where the High Priests got the money from we do not know, but we need not doubt that, side by side with the temple treasury and its deposits acting as a state bank for the population, the High Priests had their own treasury too, supplied by taxes for their benefit paid by the population and by the commission that they certainly made as intermediaries between the people and the suzerain king.

Besides those imposts upon the land we have, however, in the letters of Antiochus III and of Demetrius and Alexander Jannaeus mention of several imperial imposts which were specially burdensome to the population. As Antiochus III has to deal with them it is likely that they were introduced by the Ptolemies. These imposts are well known to us; they form part of the royal economy in almost all Hellenistic states. There is the poll-tax, a special poll or income-tax called a wreath (*stephanos*), and finally the salt-tax known to us in Egypt and in Babylonia. This was connected with the king's ownership of salt-mines which were a government monopoly, and took the form of a forced payment for a minimum of salt which was required by every person liable to the tax. These imposts may have been collected by the High Priest or else the state may have farmed them out; but the fact that Antiochus III and Demetrius and Alexander all speak of them separately and that they were particularly unpopular argues that they were probably farmed separately and collected by special contractors and their agents whom the people hated. The same arrangement probably applied to the frontier customs and to imposts upon sales as in Mesopotamia, Susiana, and Babylonia. To these imperial imposts the whole population was subject, including the privileged classes, hence the value which was attached to the grant of Antiochus III freeing from these 'humiliating' pagan imposts all persons connected with the Temple, and afterwards to its extension by Alexander Balas to the whole population of Judaea. But we may assume that later on, perhaps even before Roman times, these taxes were restored to their full former amount.

VI. THE RESULTS OF THE SELEUCIDS' WORK

We have seen that the guiding principle of the Seleucids throughout their dominions was to found cities and to spread Hellenism. To what degree did they really succeed in this aim? Life in the cities of Asia Minor probably was purely Greek. Livy (xxxvii, 54, 22) makes a Rhodian envoy say definitely that it was so in the time of Antiochus III. But he says as definitely that the Greek cities were Greek islands in the sea of a native population untouched by Hellenism. Still more true is this of Syria, Mesopotamia and Babylonia. Posidonius, himself a Syrian Greek, held no high opinion as to the purity of Hellenism among his compatriots. And this diluted Hellenism of the cities was not likely to penetrate very deeply into the thousands of villages with their Semitic population. How quickly the population was turning

Aramaean in the late Seleucid period we see by Doura on the Euphrates. Its Greek and Macedonian settlers still keep their language, their names, their law, their city organization. But their life and religion are, through the women, becoming more and more Aramaean; and, but for the proportion of Greek names, we should not hesitate to see in the benefactors of the temple of Bel in the last century B.C., as represented on its walls, Syrians as pure as are the priests of the goddess pictured side by side with them.

It does not seem that in the province of religion the Greeks exercised any influence at all on the native faith. The Greek names which the population gives to the native deities in Roman times and the semi-Greek forms in which the artisans of the time clothe them, do not in the least prove that Greek religious ideas had really penetrated the mass of the people. In the Greek towns there are of course purely Greek cults and purely Greek temples. But these do not play the chief parts, which fall to the superficially hellenized gods and temples of the natives, Phoenician, Syrian, Aramaean, Arabian. Certain cults in a hellenized form spread over the whole Greek world. The Seleucid Empire contributed to these mystic world-religions in the Hellenistic period the cult and mysteries of Adonis, and, in the Roman time, several hypostases of the one Sun-god, and the cult, partly Iranian, partly Anatolian, of Mithras. But fundamentally all these cults remain oriental and prove not that the East was hellenized but that the Greek world was orientalized. Into Babylonia for instance this external hellenization did not penetrate.

To what did the contribution made by Syrian, Seleucid, Hellenism to the treasure of Greek civilization amount? A few philosophers, born in Syria, one or two historians and geographers, a few men of science, mainly astronomers—Seleucus of Seleuceia who maintained that the sun was the centre of the universe (p. 302) —Meleager of Gadara with his subtle epigrams, Posidonius who spent all his life at Rhodes; this is the sum of what Seleucid Syria gave to the civilization of the world, if we do not count that doubtful contribution to the treasure of ancient learning, astrology. With the exception of Posidonius, who was as little a typical Syrian as the Stoic Zeno, all these Syrians belonged to the second if not to the third class. Equally second or third rate among the capitals of the Hellenistic world is the Seleucid capital Antioch as a centre of artistic, literary and scientific creativeness.

Yet we must not make too little of the part played by the Seleucid Empire in the history of civilization. Whatever we may say, it is only through the Seleucids that the contact between East and West which Alexander had begun lasted for some time, so that Hellenism had full opportunity to try and hellenize the East; and this contact did not merely orientalize the Greeks in the East, it brought many new elements into the development of the Semitic and Iranian East. These elements will make themselves specially manifest in the Roman period and will contribute to the creation of such important phenomena in the history of humanity as Sasanian Persia, early Christian Armenia and Syria, Arabia before Islam; but it was under the Seleucids that the sources of these influences upon the East were opened.

Rivulets of Greek influence spread and filtered a long way into the Middle and Far East: we know so little of the civilization of these parts in Hellenistic times that we can hardly speak of a Hellenistic streak in it; but careful archaeological study of Northern India has shown that the foundations of the hellenizing art of Gandhara must have been laid during the time when the Bactrian kingdom was independent. This is clearly exemplified by the ruins of Taxila now systematically excavated; here we have the ancient Persian influence that made itself so deeply felt in India, but side by side with it undoubted traces of Graeco-Syrian influence coming through Bactria from the Seleucid Empire[1].

A more difficult question is whether there be any Hellenistic influence on the organization of political and economic life in India during the great empire of Chandragupta and his successors, but if there was, the influence was Egyptian not Seleucid (see p. 154). There is, however, good reason to think that the civilization of the Seleucid East was not without influence upon the renascence, coming precisely in the last two centuries B.C., to which China awoke under the Han Dynasty. The rebuilding of the political and economic life of China at this time does not actually indicate any external influence except that of the military system of its Iranian neighbours upon that of China, but in the art of the Han period there are certain elements which can only be explained by the effect of the very lively commerce carried on by caravans through Bactria between Syria and China.

[1] See *Cambridge History of India*, vol. 1, chap. XVIII.

CHAPTER VI

MACEDONIA AND GREECE

I. ANTIGONUS GONATAS AND MACEDONIA

IN becoming king of Macedonia, Antigonus had succeeded to a kingdom likely to test his abilities as a statesman. Since Cassander's death the country had had no enduring government; it had been mutilated, partitioned, tossed from hand to hand, and finally ravaged and reduced almost to anarchy by the Gauls. The first task of any ruler worth the name would be reconstruction; and for that the prime requisite was peace, and peace was not easy to secure. Antigonus had indeed disposed of the various pretenders, but the spirit of faction that made those pretenders was alive, and to win over the adherents of Lysimachus or Antipater time was needed; and whether time would be given depended on Pyrrhus, with whom Antigonus had not yet settled. Still, the spirit of faction was only political, and might be overcome; it had almost ceased to be local or racial. For the Macedonians had become one people, with enough sense of unity to absorb foreign elements, like the Autariatae settled there. They were of mixed blood; for the Macedones, probably an undeveloped Greek tribe akin to the Thessalians, had by conquering Emathia imposed themselves on earlier Anatolian, Illyrian, and Thracian layers of population. The existence of people formerly speaking an Anatolian language can be seen in place-names like Edessa, and in the name of the national weapon, the sarissa; the original name of Pella, Bounomos, is probably Illyrian; many Thracian elements have been traced in the names of places and persons. The country had developed a peculiar pantheon of its own: Thaulos, god of war; Gyga, afterwards equated with Athena; the hunting goddess Gazoria; Zeirene, the Macedonian Aphrodite; Xandos, god of light; Totoës, god of sleep; Darron, god of healing; Aretos, the local Heracles; the mysterious Bedu, the eponymous

Note. Section vi, to 272, depends on Plutarch's *Life* of Pyrrhus; section ix, from 251, on his *Life* of Aratus. For the rest of the chapter we have no ancient narrative at all; the history of the years 272–51 seemingly always depended largely on a single writer, the contemporary Phylarchus, who is lost. The inscriptions, though less informative than in chapters iii and xix, are of primary value; for these and the scanty literary fragments and notices see the Bibliography. For a map of Greece and Macedonia see opposite p. 768.

deity of Edessa, god, now of air, now of water; the Echedorides, nymphs; the Arantides, probably Furies; the Sauadai, water spirits; and of course the Thracian Sabazius-Dionysus. Some of these divinities may be Greek, but some are certainly much older; Gyga, who occurs in Lydia, might be Anatolian; Bedu corresponds to nothing Greek, the name being variously transliterated in compounds; while Thaulos, who in Macedonia became Ares, in Thessaly became Zeus, a fact which seems conclusive. But by the third century the Olympians (of whom Apollo and Artemis were perhaps of old standing in the country) were annexing or superseding the old gods, as Attic Greek was in the cities replacing the Macedonian dialect. Race and religion were fusing into a common type, though later the fashionable Egyptian and Syrian cults obtained a footing; the subordinate princedoms had vanished, and, though some local feeling persisted in Orestis, there was a Macedonian people, whose upper class at least had eagerly assimilated Hellenic culture. Even in the Greek coastal cities men had begun to call themselves Macedonians, and in Thessalonica this was usual, though Amphipolis remained Greek enough to worship Philip V. Cassandreia alone, which represented Olynthus, had perhaps no national feeling; there Cassander and Lysimachus had been worshipped, and for three years it had lain under a proletarian tyranny and had finally been stormed for Antigonus; it may have been disaffected toward his rule, for it can hardly be chance that, alone of the cities, its people never called themselves Macedonians.

Two generations of war, combined with wholesale emigration to the new kingdoms, had weakened the country; it was no longer Philip's Macedonia, and probably could hardly raise 30,000 men. The heaviest loss had fallen on the aristocracy, and Antigonus and his successors often had to employ Greeks in their administration. The people were essentially sound and capable, and, given peace, the country would soon recover; but at present Antigonus only held his throne on condition that he should not call out the Macedonians. As yet he commanded little loyalty; he was king only in default of a better; if he could not give peace, there were others. His real support was his mercenaries, whom he kept distributed throughout the coastal cities. As regards revenue, Macedonia was never a rich country, and had been well plundered by the Gauls. The land tax produced little over 200 talents a year; some Greek cities were better off. This tax was probably, as elsewhere, fixed by tradition to 10 per cent. on the harvest, and though it would rise if wheat rose in price, wheat in

275 had long passed its maximum and was falling back toward the standard price of Demosthenes' time. The silver mines of Mt Pangaeus would assist the revenue, and there were gold mines, though seemingly of small account; but the deposit of alluvial gold which had helped Philip to conquer Greece had been worked out. Macedonia produced timber and pitch besides corn, but had little else to export, and consequently could never do a large trade; so that Antigonus could only substantially increase his ordinary revenue either by developing his State domains like Ptolemy II, of which there is no sign, or by conquering and taxing Greek cities, which was not his policy. As in 275 he can hardly have possessed any reserve, finance must at first have been an ever-present difficulty.

The king was for most purposes the State, and his purse the Treasury; consequently the State domains, the 'King's Land,' were his possession. There was probably no King's Land in Macedonia proper, unless the State owned the forests. For Macedonia had been, and still to some extent was, a kingship of the heroic type; and (whatever the case elsewhere) the natural explanation of the constitutional rights, so jealously guarded, of the Macedonian people under arms is that the kingship had grown out of the nation and not *vice versa*; if so, the king can never have possessed the soil of Macedonia proper, and the Macedonian peasant probably owned his own farm. But in the conquered districts, like Chalcidice or (later) Paeonia and Atintania, doubtless the whole soil became, theoretically, the king's; for in Cassander's reign there was King's Land in Chalcidice. Out of this he gave estates to his friends, and also maintained his military strength by granting lots to settlers. The lot was held on a heritable tenure, the settler paying land tax and rendering military service; probably the king could re-enter for failure to serve, and as grants ended with the king's death[1] it was seemingly customary for a new king to confirm titles, probably on payment of a fine, like the crown tax in Egypt. These military lots must have been in origin inalienable, but were now freely alienable, subject doubtless to the obligation to serve. The king however (as with freehold land in England to-day) still retained the right of escheat, though of little value; there is no sign that he ever granted lands out and out, as the Seleucids sometimes did, for that imported that the land should be joined to some city and become city-land,

---

[1] Grants, like treaties, ended in Macedonia with the king's death because there was no continuity; the crown was vested in the army till they elected or confirmed the new king.

and the position of a city in Chalcidice was hardly that of Ephesus
or Smyrna. The State domains not granted out were cultivated
for the king by tenants or serfs, and produced much corn.

Outside Macedonia proper and Thessaly, which he governed
directly (the latter as head for life of the Thessalian League),
Antigonus, like all the kings, governed his possessions through
generals with military powers; there were two for Greece, one
later for Paeonia, and presumably one each for Atintania and
Chalcidice. Under the generals, or under himself in Macedonia
and Thessaly, were *epistatai*, governors of cities or groups of
cities. In the Greek coastal towns of Macedonia, the *epistates*
or (if he governed several cities) his lieutenant had some control
over the Assembly; a decree of Thessalonica bears at its head
the names of this lieutenant and a board of *harmostai*. As these
cities were also garrisoned, and as part of their old city-lands had
become King's Land (they of course retaining enough to live on),
their autonomy was strictly limited. In Greece proper Antigonus
only employed this system of *epistatai* very exceptionally and
under compulsion of events, and the city Assemblies were never
controlled; probably also Cassandreia was fully autonomous,
and its Assembly uncontrolled, as under Cassander. In Thessaly,
though the cities were governed by *epistatai*, their Assemblies
were uncontrolled, the governor's name never appearing on
decrees; and the same was the case in Macedonia proper. For
one system must have applied there to all the principal cities;
but while Pella (and therefore Beroea) was now an autonomous
city on the Greek model, there was an *epistates* in Beroea (and
therefore in Pella); but as no *epistates'* name occurs on Pella's
unique decree, it follows that the Assemblies of the Macedonian
cities were, like the Thessalian, uncontrolled. Pella dated by
some priesthood and not by Antigonus' regnal year; and the
enacting words of its decree, 'be it decreed by the city,' though
known elsewhere, were the regular formula in some Thessalian
cities, as Gonni and Phalanna,—another instance of the intimate
connection between Thessaly and Macedonia. City Assemblies
therefore were formally controlled only outside Greece and in
districts governed by a general, *i.e.* on a military basis; but, later,
Thessalian cities are found obeying the king's direct orders, even
in domestic matters like grants of citizenship; his headship of
the league was treated autocratically[1]. Antigonus made Pella

---

[1] The boards of politarchs which occur in some Macedonian inscriptions
probably belong after 168, when in some Thessalian cities they also replaced
the traditional boards of *tagoi*.

again the capital and substituted on his coinage its goddess, Athene Alkis, for his father's Poseidon, god of the lost seas. He built Stratonice (Stratoni) near Stagirus, and three Antigoneias, one near Cassandreia and two later in Paeonia (near Tremmik) and Atintania[1], commanding the two great passes into Macedonia. Presumably these Antigoneias were the seats of the generals who governed Chalcidice, Paeonia, and Atintania.

The day of the professional long-service Macedonian army was over, and that army was again a levy of farmers called up when needed; only the guards, and a few Macedonians in important garrisons like Corinth, were permanently under arms. Antigonus' standing force was his mercenaries,—Greeks, Illyrians, and northerners. But Greek mercenaries had to be engaged and paid by the military year (nine or ten months), and expected allotments of land when past service; consequently for war Antigonus regularly hired Gauls from the Gallic kingdoms in Serbia and Thrace, who at first were cheaper and could be discharged when no longer needed. Later the Gaul mastered the market conditions, and Gauls, obviously time-expired mercenaries, were settled in Macedonia. The Bodyguards or Staff, and the Royal Pages, remained as under Alexander. But two other things changed; when, is unknown. In the old heroic monarchy one of the chief bonds of society must have been the 'kin,' and the idea was still not quite dead in Alexander's time, for the army at Opis reproached him for introducing Persians into the 'kin'; but 'Kinsman' ultimately became a mere title, granted by the king. Similarly Alexander's Companions (not the cavalry), last remnant of the king's original retinue, had still ridden with him in battle; but the Companions finally became merely the 'Friends,' again a title, lower than 'Kinsman,' conferred by the king. These formed a council with advisory powers only, but were still useful for filling offices.

The Macedonian people under arms still retained their constitutional powers, those of the old national assembly of the heroic monarchy. But both monarch and people had come under the influence of Greek ideas. Greek writers called the assembly of the Macedonian people in arms to elect a king or try a treason case an *ecclesia*, as though it were the Assembly of an autonomous city; later their rights were to be crystallized under a Greek formula (p. 751). Antigonus himself, saturated with Greek thought, trained by Greek philosophers, and with his principal friends all Greeks, may at first have seemed to the Macedonians

---

[1] Beloch, *Gr. Gesch.* IV, ii, p. 381, makes this an Epirote foundation.

a strange sort of national king; even his royal style was not the
customary 'King of the Macedonians,' but 'King Antigonus, son
of King Demetrius, Macedonian,' possibly a relic of the time
when he had only been a king in exile, with claims upon Asia. He
was of course a national king, constitutionally elected by the army.
But he answered very much to the description of a Successor given
in Stoic literature (Suidas, βασιλεία no. 2); he had found no established succession waiting for him, but had won his kingdom at
Lysimacheia, and could only hold it by administering it well; his
rule was founded on competence, not on birth. He was therefore
anxious to find some unassailable theoretic basis for his kingship.
Ptolemy II found such in being a god. But Macedonian kings,
though worshipped in Greek cities, even in Cassandreia, had
never been gods in Macedonia, and Antigonus was not likely to
break with the national tradition, for Zeno's friend had no fancy
for being a god at all; the hearty snub he administered to some
poet who so addressed him[1] shows that he regarded the thing as
a sham; and apparently he was never worshipped by anyone
anywhere. He therefore sought the basis of his kingship in
satisfying the demands of philosophy. To the Cynics the ideal
king was Heracles, labouring incessantly for mankind; but this
did not take one far, for every king worked hard. Then the Stoics
said that as a king had to account to no one, you needed one who
would know of himself how to conform to the Universal Law;
the philosopher alone was such an one, but, as in real life philo-
sophei were not kings, the philosopher must stand behind the
throne and advise. Antigonus met this by inviting Zeno to
Macedonia; but Zeno, unable to tear himself from Athens, sent
his pupil Persaeus to Antigonus as his spiritual director. But
the Stoics went further. With an eye on Ptolemy, they refused
to approve of a king, however hardworking and enlightened, who
treated the State as his private domain, and taxed his people as
though their goods were his own; the true view was that kingship
was the possession of the State. It was a startling phrase; but its
unknown author was thinking, not of ethics, but of property;
he was suggesting that a king, as opposed to a tyrant, could only
tax his subjects with their consent. Antigonus went beyond this,
for he laid stress on the ethical side of the idea; his son Halcyoneus had been ill-using some subjects, and Antigonus, after
rebuking him, said 'Do you not understand, boy, that *our* kingship is a noble servitude?' It has a very modern ring; for the

---

[1] Plutarch, *Mor.* 360 c: οὐ τοιαῦτά μοι ὁ λασανοφόρος σύνοιδεν.

first time it was now laid down that the king should be the servant of his people. The theoretic basis of the new Macedonian monarchy was to be the duty of service (see p. 114).

II. ANTIGONUS AND HIS CIRCLE

Owing to the inclusion of Athens in his sphere Antigonus could not have set up another intellectual centre in Macedonia, even had he so desired; but, following Menedemus' example, he formed a literary circle of his own; some of his friends came to Pella at his marriage, others appeared later; some spent their time between Pella and Athens. The circle was entirely Greek; the chief Macedonian writer of the time, the epigrammatist Poseidippus of Pella, lived in Alexandria. Poetry, history, and philosophy, in which Antigonus was interested, were all represented; but science, which to a Stoic had no meaning, he left to Alexandria. Aratus was Court poet; beside the marriage hymns (p. 108), he wrote a *Praise of Antigonus* and some poems for Phila; and it was at Antigonus' request that he produced his much-lauded *Phaenomena*, an astronomical poem, which owed its success to its illustration, drawn from the utility of the stars to sailor and husbandman, of the Stoic doctrine that the Supreme Deity *does* care for His children on earth. Other poets of the circle were Antagoras of Rhodes, best known for his beautiful epitaph on his friends Polemon and Crates of the Academy, and Alexander of Aetolia, writer of tragedies and mimes; while Timon of Phlius, the 'Sillographer,' a pupil of Pyrrhon the Sceptic, who wandered into many places besides Pella making money by preaching to men the worthlessness of wealth, almost belongs to the poets, for his name lived through his *Silloi*, an amusing skit on other philosophers written later in Athens. Whether the Craterus who compiled a history of Athens from her inscriptions —a very modern idea—were really Antigonus' half-brother, as tradition asserts, is disputed; but history was worthily represented by Hieronymus, who in old age wrote at Antigonus' court his history of the Successors from the death of Alexander to (apparently) that of Pyrrhus, a history in which he himself had played a not undistinguished part. He was the highest product of the reaction against the rhetorical school; his aim was not effect, but truth. Possibly he was the first historian to trace, in Demetrius, the *development* of character. But he had not the preservative of style, and his work, like much else of the time, was allowed to perish. It has been suggested that his place may be with

Thucydides and Polybius; certainly it is difficult to read those books of Diodorus which very imperfectly reproduce part of his history without feeling that something really great lies behind them.

Philosophy was officially represented by Persaeus, who spent his life in Macedonia, and wrote for Antigonus the usual treatise on Government, and another on the Spartan constitution, showing that Antigonus studied his enemies. But Persaeus was not man enough to take Zeno's place; he became the courtier, perhaps the boon companion; that Menedemus hated him is illuminating. More important were the appearances at Pella of the wandering semi-Cynic, Bion of Borysthenes, the first to popularize philosophy; the resemblance of some of his ideas and sayings to those of Antigonus points to some closer association than we know of. Low-born, perhaps a liberated slave, Bion was a new influence which was to spread far. On the surface he was full of flaws. He could be very vulgar; he could not refrain from displaying his wit, and none escaped its sting—Pyrrhus, Antigonus (who helped him and whom he really honoured), Persaeus, every lesser man; the Diatribe which he perfected—a method of talking with your audience instead of lecturing—easily lent itself to abuse, and he is called a patchwork sophist, who played to the gallery; even his admirer, the great Eratosthenes, accused him of prostituting philosophy. But Eratosthenes also said that all this was merely outer husk; there was a genuine Odysseus under the beggar's rags. We can just distinguish traces of the real Bion, the man who protested against the belief that heaven would visit the fathers' sins on the children, and whose pity for a tortured frog gives a glimpse of humanity towards animals strange at that epoch. There was a power in him that could draw even Rhodian sailors to his lectures; and if he had no new message to men, he forced them to listen to the old ones. And the one connected fragment of his teaching left is simple and manly enough. Not to seek wealth; to realise that happiness depends on yourself and not on circumstances; to do your duty, and be faithful in little as in much. Spread your sails, if you will, to the fair breeze; but should it change, bear without complaint what Fortune sends, and see that, if she strike you down, she strike down a man and not a worm—words which were still remembered in Pella two generations later.

One unique event may also be mentioned here: the Mauryan Emperor Asoka, who was converting Northern India to Buddhism, subsequently sent missions to several Hellenistic kings, including

Antigonus[1]. It is pleasant to let fancy play round the meeting of the Stoic king and the Buddhist missionary; but it is not known if Asoka's envoys reached Macedonia.

III. MACEDONIA AND HER NEIGHBOURS

We turn to the relations of the new Macedonian kingdom with the outer world. Here the most important thing, Antigonus's measures to keep out northern barbarism, is utterly lost; all we know is that he succeeded, but, like Philip V, he must have been perpetually fighting on his northern frontier, though only one doubtful allusion to such a campaign remains. From 276 to 168 his dynasty was to be the shield of Greek civilization, a task which they performed far better than Republican Rome was to do; to their success high tribute was paid later even by their enemies, Polybius and their Roman conqueror Flamininus.

In reviewing Antigonus' relations with Greece two things must be emphasized: Macedonia was now fast becoming completely hellenized, and merely formed another unit of the Greek circle, more powerful than others and rather more mixed in blood; and Antigonus was, first and foremost, the Macedonian king, and regarded things from Macedonia's standpoint, which was that, as a united Greece would be stronger than Macedonia, Greece must not unite against her. Demetrius had sought in Greece a base for Asiatic conquest; Antigonus sought safety for Macedonia. The antiquated idea that Antigonus' object was to conquer as much of Greece as possible has recently been revived, but is quite untenable on the known facts; he possessed a definite conception of something which may be called his sphere, beyond which he did not mean to go. The key of this conception was Corinth; while he held Acrocorinthus, Greece could not unite; and as Corinth safeguarded Macedonia, so he was prepared to do everything necessary to safeguard Corinth. In 275 Corinth was not safe; it had no land communication with Demetrias, Euboea was probably independent, and the sea was Egyptian; but after Pyrrhus' death he established Corinth's communications, and here, for security's sake, he applied Cassander's policy of garrisons. Certainly in 275, beside Corinth, he held another important point, the Piraeus; but the Piraeus was held for Athens' sake, not for Corinth's, and as he wanted Athens in his sphere only as his intellectual capital he did not apply to her Cassander's policy, but revived that of Alexander, which had seemed dead, and left

[1] On Asoka see *Cambridge History of India*, vol. i, chap. xx.

Athens free and ungarrisoned. This then was Antigonus' sphere: Corinth and its communications, for safety; Athens and all that Athens implied, for culture; this and no more. He governed Corinth and the Piraeus, like his other external possessions, through generals; in Corinth his half-brother Craterus, and in the Piraeus the Carian Hierocles, who had proved his loyalty, but in a manner which Athenians could hardly forgive (p. 89).

At Athens, Antigonus' friends had overthrown the Nationalist government after Lysimacheia and seized power; it may have been a spontaneous swing of opinion, for possibly after his victory there was for a time a friendly feeling. The government restored the single superintendent of the administration, and held a specially splendid celebration of the Great Panathenaea of 274, designed to show that their side, no less than the democratic Aetolians, had deserved well of Greece; for this festival Antigonus' partisan Heracleitus of Athmonon adorned the stadium and dedicated to Athena a series of pictures illustrating Antigonus' victory in 'his struggle against the barbarians for the deliverance of the Hellenes.' The government also passed a long decree in Phaedrus' honour, which seems like an answer to Demochares' decree of 280 for Demosthenes; its date is now very uncertain and has even been placed after the Chremonidean war[1], but in the writer's opinion it probably falls soon after 275. Antigonus' relationship to Athens at this time is difficult to define. Athens was called free; she held her own forts, except Munychia and the Piraeus, and sent sacred envoys (*hieromnēmones*) to Aetolian Delphi; and she was not yet, apparently, offering sacrifices for Antigonus, as she did later. 'Suzerain' seems too explicit a word for Antigonus' position; one might suppose Athens was his free ally, but that alliance is never mentioned; perhaps the relationship *was* undefined, and merely illustrated that favourite conception of the time, *Homonoia* or a union of hearts; Athens was the most-favoured city, Antigonus' spiritual capital. But he was behind the government if required, and he held the Piraeus; it was not a position which commended itself to earnest Nationalists. The idea, drawn largely from stage plays, that Zeno's Athens was decadent can hardly be accepted; there was not much decadence about the men who fought the Chremonidean war (p. 707), and Athens was still 'Hellas of Hellas,' the centre of the world's thought. Wealth and power might pass to others; Athens 'alone had the secret of the path which raises men to the heavens.'

---

[1] Beloch in *Riv. fil.* LI, 1923, p. 273.

Demetrius' one-time possessions in Central Greece—Boeotia, Phocis, Eastern Locris—lay outside Antigonus' sphere, and he never sought to recover them. In the Peloponnese the circumstances were peculiar; in 275 he still happened to hold a remnant of Demetrius' former kingdom—Troezen, and some of the seven Achaean towns (Olenus being the seventh)[1] not yet in the Achaean League. He did not withdraw; Macedonian kings were not altruists. But he did not reckon Peloponnese as in his sphere, so he made no effort to recover these towns after losing them, a process completed in 272. Possibly in 275 Craterus could be called his general in Peloponnese; by 271 there was probably nothing south of Corinth for him to govern. The system on which Antigonus afterwards regulated his relations with the Peloponnese, relations conditioned by Sparta's ineradicable hostility to Macedonia, will be considered later (p. 219); but prior to the Chremonidean war he really left the Peloponnese to Sparta; she would not be a danger north of the Isthmus unless Egypt supported her, while Megalopolis and Argos, though independent, acted as a check on her and so in his interest. North of Corinth he possibly had some arrangement with Boeotia, which was not his enemy and was soon occupied with other matters; and as Athens was his friend, and Pyrrhus abroad, he apparently had in 275 only one potential enemy of immediate importance, Aetolia.

There was, however, one Greek city outside Greece sufficiently powerful and energetic to affect his policy: Rhodes. The island city was prospering exceedingly, and her merchants would usually throw their weight upon the side of peace, but she was ready to fight against any aggressor for the balance of power or for a free sea; she was the scourge of piracy, and the skill of her sailors was proverbial. Her government was aristocratic, a limited democracy in which the leading families exercised a steadying influence; and she was to try an extraordinary experiment, a system of food liturgies under which the rich undertook to look after a certain number of poor, possibly one of the reasons of her stability; in Demetrius' siege she had dared arm her slaves. She was the centre of international banking and exchange, and when the city was shattered by the earthquake which in 225 overthrew the Colossus, and a commercial crisis threatened, every Greek-speaking king and many cities came to her aid with lavish contributions in money, kind, and labour, the greatest demonstration

---

[1] *S.E.G.* vol. I, no. 74, with Wilhelm's commentary.

of solidarity which the Hellenistic world ever made. Perhaps her famous maritime code is the only Greek law which ever remained law in a modern state; for some believe that, owing to its adoption by the Antonines, fragments of it were taken up into the Byzantine compilation called '*The Rhodian Sea-law*' and thus reached Venice.

IV. THE AETOLIAN LEAGUE

Aetolia was the parvenu among Greek states; she was backward in culture, and still raided her neighbours. But she had bought her place with her blood; she had never yielded a foot's breadth to Macedonia, and she had saved Greece from the Gauls. As her young men went out freely as mercenaries, her field force was probably not over 12,000; but her mountainous wooded country, with bad roads, few cities, and numerous hill forts, was almost unconquerable. She had no capital, the largest city being her seaport Naupactus; the federal centre was the temple of Apollo at Thermum, which was not a town, but the 'place' where the Aetolians stored their booty and kept their archives. During the Lamian war they were still only a Folk, loosely organized in a cantonal League, or rather Commune, such as was the common inheritance of most states of Northern Greece; but after it they reorganized their League, and began to collect to some extent into towns; the units which composed the third century League were partly towns and partly country districts, whose villages were perhaps grouped round some fort. The towns at first were probably not all autonomous cities, but doubtless such continued to develop throughout the century. The League in 275 was an intensely democratic body; power resided in a primary Assembly, which was open to every citizen; the Assembly was the people, the civil counterpart of the army, the people under arms, from which it sprang. The Assembly met twice a year, before and after the campaigning season (though extraordinary Assemblies are known); the spring session, Panaetolica, was held in different towns in turn, the autumn, Thermica, at Thermum, when the year's booty was stored and the annual officials elected. The Assembly controlled all policy; it made alliances, admitted new members, conferred League citizenship, sent and received ambassadors, elected religious envoys, and decided on peace and war; if the Aetolians had the reputation of being too fond of war, at least war was declared by the men who were themselves to do the fighting. The Assembly also made laws, but these were revised periodically by a board of *nomographoi*. The head of the League was a General elected annually, who was both President and

Commander-in-Chief; re-election was only possible after some years' interval. The officials were a cavalry leader, a secretary, an *agonothetes* to celebrate festivals, and seven financial stewards; there was no admiral, for at sea Aetolia only employed privateers.

The Council consisted of members elected by the League units in proportion to their military contingents, and was meant to sit permanently. It was the Federal court of justice, but otherwise had little power; its function was to keep touch with the officials, and decide such current matters as could not wait till the next Assembly. But, as the League grew, the Council, which ultimately numbered well over 1000, became too large to sit permanently, and during the century it threw up a small committee, called *Apokletoi*, who did sit permanently with the General; as they are never mentioned in inscriptions, they were presumably, like the British Cabinet, unknown to the Constitution. Aetolia never solved the problems inherent in government by mass-meeting; consequently, when the League's subsequent expansion made it impossible for all citizens to attend the Assembly, the *Apokletoi*, with the General, became the real governing body; they took all foreign policy into their own hands, though the Assembly still kept the power of peace and war. As the *Apokletoi* also sat in secret session, the government between 275 and 220 developed from the most democratic into the least democratic in Greece. This evolution accompanied a similar evolution in the character of the Aetolian League, apparently very much for the worse; but it must be remembered that Aetolia produced no historian, and that her later history depends on the very vigorous narrative of an enemy. Art and literature were not Aetolia's strong point; her national dedications at Delphi, with one exception, monotonously reproduced her generals and the Delphic gods; her one active man of letters, the tragic poet Alexander, lived elsewhere. Aetolia's control of Delphi, however, was to be honourable to both parties; under it Delphi led the two movements which so greatly increased the manumission of slaves and the number of 'asylums,' movements which grew in force as the Aetolian control of Delphi became more complete. The numerous statues of Aetolian women dedicated at Delphi probably show that the position of women in Aetolia was higher and more free than was usual in some Greek communities; and of the known third-century poetesses, Alcinoe was an Aetolian, and Aristodama of Smyrna visited Aetolia and recited her epic on the glorious deeds of the Aetolian people in various League cities, where she received high honours.

The Aetolian League had already incorporated Western Locris and Malis, and was to expand greatly between 275 and 220. A country joining the League joined, not as a whole, but as a number of separate cities; hence part of another League, like Acarnania or Phocis, could be detached and taken in. All cities of the Aetolian League remained autonomous as regarded their institutions, territory, and citizenship; but sometimes a city joining assimilated its magistracies to those of the League, and the League alone could coin. A city whose territory adjoined that of the League entered into sympolity with it, that is, its citizens became for all purposes Aetolians,—a considerable attraction as Aetolia increased in power, though possibly some cities joined only to avoid being raided. A city at a distance entered into isopolity, an exchange of citizenships; the citizens of such a city potentially became Aetolians, but their Aetolian citizenship only came into play if they settled in, and (as they had the right to) became citizens of, some city of the Aetolian sympolity. In its expansion the Aetolian League set the example, afterwards followed by Boeotia and Achaea, of a League using its federal citizenship to enlarge its territory. This was a new thing in the world, but the events of 279 had given Aetolia new ambitions; she now aspired to be Macedonia's rival, and felt strong enough to conduct her own policy quite independently of either Macedonia or Egypt.

Her aim was to control the Amphictyonic League, whose peoples she henceforth regarded as her sphere. Amphictyonic judgments would assume a new importance with Aetolia as executive; in 278 the Amphictyons had claimed to impose a decree upon cities not parties to it; and later Aetolia took Amphictyonic judgments into her own hands. Aetolia, it is true, had no Amphictyonic vote; but the Aetolian League exercised the votes of every Amphictyonic people who joined it, the Aetolian Assembly regularly electing their *hieromnēmones*. In 275 the Aetolian League had only three votes, two Malian and one Locrian; but Aetolia had the advantage of controlling the Federal centre, Delphi, and she had persuaded the Amphictyons to give Delphi the two ownerless votes, once Alexander's, which would be cast as she wished. That Delphi was in the Aetolian League, as some think, seems impossible, for then Aetolia must have exercised the Delphic votes; she was really suzerain of Delphi, as Ptolemy of Delos, and she sometimes took upon herself to regulate Delphi's internal affairs, and later planted settlers and kept a civilian governor in Delphi and set up there duplicates of her decrees. Aetolia's intention to control the Amphictyonic League might seem to threaten difficulties with Macedonia, who, by her possession of Thessaly, was also an Amphictyonic power; and Aetolia also had a second aim, access to the Aegean. She had reached the Malian gulf, but had no good harbour there; her ultimate objective was to be Phthiotic Thebes on the Gulf of Pagasae, at present Macedonian, but a possible rival to Demetrias; this would throw her right across Macedonia's communications with Greece. It seemed therefore as if both her aims must ultimately render a collision with Macedonia inevitable. In 275, however, she was still friendly to Antigonus; it remained to be seen if his accession to the Macedonian throne would alter the position.

V. SOCIAL CHANGES IN GREECE

Certain changes which began to affect Greece as a whole between 275 and 217 can only be briefly indicated here. One was a growth in the feeling of humanity and in dislike of war and its laws, natural after the great struggles of the Successors. While Polybius in the second century was to emphasize only the senselessness of material destruction, Phylarchus in the third rebels, with an energy not before seen, against the sale of free captives, however legal; and some cities, even in Crete, bound themselves not to enslave each other's citizens. Under Delphic inspiration, some cities were to attempt to obtain from the Hellenistic world recognition of themselves and their territories both as 'holy,' that is, immune from war as a temple was immune, and as 'asylums,' that is, immune from reprisals or private war; the practical result was perhaps not great, but it shows the trend of men's thoughts. Arbitration begins to increase enormously, and every boundary award is a strangled war; some cities even had treaties to refer all questions to arbitration. Certainly awards were not always observed, but at worst this meant, not war, but more awards; and if some cities seem to spend much time in boundary litigation, arable land was scarce and even a few farms made a difference. In connexion with the spread of arbitration may be noticed the growing system of having all private lawsuits in a city adjudicated by a commission from another city, which tended to approximate the various cities' legal outlook; and as these commissioners only sent to the juries a small residue of cases which they had failed to settle informally, one may almost call it the beginning of an international system of equity. Stoicism had begun to accustom men to the idea of a better treatment of slaves; manumission by will steadily increased, and the time is approaching when the slave will be able to purchase his freedom[1].

There were changes too in the economic position. The centre of the world's commerce had shifted from Greece to Asia, and with the substitution of Rhodes for Athens as the principal trade centre of the Aegean, Athens was becoming definitely poorer; on the other hand Aetolia and some of the islands were growing richer, and, while Corinth maintained her commercial position, other cities beside Rhodes—Delos, Pagasae, possibly Ambracia—greatly improved theirs; Chalcis had the finest market-place in Greece. The great emigration to Asia was over, and a return flow was perhaps already beginning after 250, though some of the Asiatics met with may be liberated slaves. The extinction of various old families at Athens has been traced; but everywhere new men had become wealthy, and things like the number of new festivals, the growth of and immunities accorded to the Dionysiac artists, the spread of social clubs with a member's subscription (*eranoi*), and the fall during the century in the rate of interest, testify to plenty of money. Alexander's release of the Persian treasure had prior to 300 reduced the drachma to half its value, with a corresponding rise in prices; by the middle of the century it had largely recovered, but the effects of the great disturbance remained, the more so as wages had not risen with prices; working men were definitely worse off than in the fourth century, and the gulf between rich and poor had widened, which made for social unrest.

There was as yet no depopulation, but the process was beginning which would lead to depopulation and the introduction of alien stocks: the rich would not, and the poor could not, bring up families of any size. Toward the end of the century, as the inscriptions show, four or five children were extremely rare. A one-child system had become common; beyond that, though two sons (to allow for a death in war) were still fairly numerous, only about one family in a hundred reared more than one daughter. Among seventy-nine couples who settled at Miletus with their children, many young, there were only twenty-eight daughters to 118 sons; there is only one explanation of such figures. Local variations occur, like the frequency of adoptions at Rhodes; but undoubtedly by the latter part of the century the curse of infanticide, especially female infanticide, was becoming fearfully

---

[1] A solitary manumission of this type has however come to light in the fourth century; Ch. Picard, *B.C.H.* XLV, 1921, p. 150, no. 3.

common. Greece was beginning to overdo its secular precaution against hunger.

VI. PYRRHUS

In 275, it is true, Macedonia actually had peace; but conditions were far from being stable. Ptolemy II had already married his sister Arsinoe, who claimed the throne of Macedonia for her son by Lysimachus, Ptolemaeus (pp. 107, 703); and though Egypt made no open move for years, there was now a direct threat to Antigonus. But the actual cause of war was Pyrrhus' return from Italy in the autumn of 275 (p. 653); he came with a grievance, for Antigonus had refused him help against Rome. He brought back only 8000 men and no money; but throughout his life he never lost hope that the next throw of the dice would be the lucky one. In spring 274 he invaded Macedonia with a large army, and the money to raise it can only have come from one quarter; he was subsidized by Arsinoe. Antigonus hired Gauls, but he was in a dilemma; he could neither safely withdraw his mercenaries from the coastal cities nor meet Pyrrhus with Gauls alone; he had to call out the Macedonians, though he knew the danger. Pyrrhus out-manœuvred him and then attacked him while retreating; the Gauls died to a man; the Macedonians refused to fight and went over to the enemy; Antigonus escaped to Thessalonica, and Pyrrhus overran most of Macedonia and Thessaly. The Macedonians' behaviour was quite consistent; Pyrrhus seemed the stronger, and perhaps he would give them peace, if Antigonus could not. But Pyrrhus as usual failed to gather the fruits of victory; he allowed his Gauls to plunder the royal tombs at Aegae in revenge for Lysimachus' desecration of the royal tombs of Epirus (p. 96), and opinion in Macedonia turned against him. He made no attempt to consolidate his conquest; he left his son Ptolemaeus to govern Macedonia, and went home to dedicate his spoils at Dodona. Antigonus began to collect his mercenaries, and by summer 272 had recovered much of the country; Pyrrhus perhaps withdrew Ptolemaeus in 272 because he had to. But Antigonus' overthrow apparently led to the overthrow of his friends in Athens; the Nationalists, with some understanding with Egypt, returned to power and sent envoys to Pyrrhus; it seems also, from the evidence of coins and Macedonian proxenies at Delphi, that Aetolia was on good terms with Pyrrhus, which imports a cleavage with Antigonus; Pyrrhus had probably helped to rebuild Callium, where a statue was erected to him.

But Pyrrhus was already seeking a new adventure. Among his

generals was the Spartan Cleonymus (p. 77), who was unpopular and had been passed over for the kingship in favour of his nephew Areus; he persuaded Pyrrhus to reinstate him. In spring 272 Pyrrhus, leaving his son Alexander to govern Epirus, invaded the Peloponnese with his sons Ptolemaeus and Helenus and a large army, including Macedonian troops. He landed in Achaea, and announced that he had come to free Antigonus' cities; all the Achaean towns which had not yet joined the Achaean League now did so, and that League and Messene sent envoys to Pyrrhus, while Elis joined him; Antigonus, who had lost Troezen, probably retained nothing south of Corinth. But Pyrrhus did not attack Corinth; he marched to Megalopolis, which, though free, opened her gates; she must have guessed that his objective was her enemy Sparta, and so must Sparta, for if Areus, who was in Crete, really returned just in time, he must have already been recalled. Pyrrhus assured the Spartan envoys who met him at Megalopolis that he had no intention of attacking Sparta; but after some delay he entered and plundered Laconia, reached Sparta one evening, and camped, not wishing to enter in the dark. Meanwhile Antigonus saw that it was more important to follow Pyrrhus than to complete the recovery of Macedonia, for Pyrrhus' activities gave no hope of peace; victor or vanquished, he must trouble the world till he died. While Pyrrhus was advancing on Sparta, Antigonus was shipping his troops to Corinth; with him were his illegitimate son Halcyoneus, the old Hieronymus, and his general Ameinias the ex-pirate, who hurried on by forced marches from Corinth with the advance guard. Sparta was Macedonia's secular enemy; but as Pyrrhus had done with Carthage and Rome, so he had done with Macedonia and Sparta; he had driven two consistent opponents into each other's arms. Lack of statesmanship can go no farther.

Pyrrhus' assault on Sparta has given Plutarch occasion for one of the most stirring narratives in the Greek language, but from the military point of view the story, drawn from Phylarchus, is unintelligible; Pyrrhus attacks only at the one point where Sparta is well fortified, and Areus' son Acrotatus, the hero of the defence, is posted at a part of the circuit where there is no fighting. Sparta was apparently surrounded by a palisade and ditch; and during the night before Pyrrhus' attack the women, who had refused to be sent away to Crete, dug a deep trench opposite Pyrrhus' camp and lagered waggons at each end. For two days Pyrrhus assaulted the place with relays of troops, while the Spartan women kept their men supplied with food and missiles; on the second day he almost broke through, and only failed because his horse was wounded and threw him. Then, when the defenders, too few to fight in relays, were utterly worn out, Ameinias arrived and threw himself into the city; the same evening came Areus with 2000 fresh men; and Pyrrhus had lost his chance. A message from Argos then made him clutch at a new hope; he does not seem to have been pursuing any plan which can be understood. The dominant party in Argos, led by Aristippus, was, as always, friendly to Macedonia; their opponents thought to overthrow them by calling in Pyrrhus, who broke camp and started for Argos. On the way Areus ambushed him, and Ptolemaeus was killed; but though Pyrrhus took vengeance for his son he lost time, and on reaching Argos found Antigonus established in an impregnable position on the hills above the town; he challenged him to come down and fight it out, but Antigonus naturally declined to humour him.

The Argive government in alarm begged both kings to retire from Argos, and she would be friendly to both; both agreed, but Pyrrhus at least had no intention of keeping his word, for that night his partisans opened a gate and he poured in troops. But the Argives were roused by the noise and flew to arms, while Antigonus, in response to his friends' request for help, came down to the plain and sent Halcyoneus forward to the city. Pyrrhus himself reached the market-place, but dawn showed him the Aspis full of Halcyoneus' men; he tried to retreat, and was caught in the inextricable confusion of a soldiers' battle in the narrow streets, where he was stunned by a tile thrown on his head by an old woman from a house-top; before he could recover his senses, an Illyrian mercenary of Antigonus' recognized him, hacked off his head, and gave it to Halcyoneus, who galloped away with it and flung it at his father's feet as he sat in his tent with his Council. Hieronymus, who was doubtless there, says that when Antigonus recognized it he struck Halcyoneus with his staff, calling him accursed and barbarian, and then covered his face with his cloak and wept; 'for he remembered the fate of his grandfather Antigonus and his father Demetrius, and he knew not what Fortune might yet have in store for his house.' Pyrrhus' army surrendered; Antigonus received Helenus kindly and sent him back to Epirus, and himself rendered the funeral rites to Pyrrhus' corpse. On the spot where Pyrrhus fell the Argives raised a temple to the goddess Demeter, who, their legend said, had taken a woman's form to slay him.

VII. GREECE AFTER PYRRHUS' DEATH

With Pyrrhus' death Hieronymus' history apparently ended, and with it ends all possibility of a sympathetic understanding of the Macedonian kingdom; henceforth we possess only stories told by enemies, who had not even access to the Macedonian archives; the friends of Macedonia in Greece produced no historian. Antigonus was left master of the situation in the Peloponnese, where his partisans seized power in Megalopolis, Argos and other cities; Sparta could not at once quarrel with the man who had saved her, and had Antigonus desired to recover and garrison his father's possessions, there was nothing to stop him. But he deliberately held his hand; he interfered neither with Achaea's new League nor with Sicyon's re-established democracy; he was anxious to return to Macedonia, and was content that Argos and Megalopolis, the natural checks upon Sparta, were governed by his friends; Craterus, if need were, could support them, as he did attempt to support Aristotimus, a man who seized power in Elis and was soon afterwards assassinated for cruelty. Antigonus probably spent 271 in re-organizing Macedonia. But he had realized that the Egyptian fleet could have prevented him reaching Corinth, had Egypt so desired, and he therefore took Corinth's communications in hand, and as land connection with Demetrias was impossible, he annexed Euboea as an alternative route, perhaps in 270; he garrisoned Eretria, which had to be taken, and Chalcis, which became a third key fortress linking Corinth to Demetrias, and placed them under Craterus' generalship; Histiaea perhaps remained free but in his friends' hands, like Athens and Argos. Perhaps now, perhaps later, he also took Megara and garrisoned Nisaea. These possessions completed his system north of Corinth; except Athens, he was to conquer no more of Greece. Corinth's communications were now well knit up; but the Piraeus remained a separate generalship under Hierocles, as it was held for the sake of Athens, not of Corinth.

A sad story is connected with Eretria's loss of freedom. Before its capture, Menedemus was falsely accused of intending to betray the city to his friend Antigonus, and was exiled. He went to Oropus, where subsequently Hierocles saw him, and thought to please the exile by relating how Antigonus had taken Eretria. But the old man's heart was with the city which he had done so much to render illustrious; he flung at Hierocles the foulest insult he could think of, and went to Antigonus to plead for Eretria's freedom. It is said that Antigonus would for his sake have withdrawn the garrison, but that Menedemus' enemy, Persaeus, dissuaded him; it was perhaps this which made Menedemus say that Persaeus might be a sort of philosopher, but as a man he was the worst that was or ever would be. Menedemus became deeply dejected, and died soon after at Antigonus' court.

Antigonus had also to consider his disturbed relations with Athens and Aetolia. The Nationalists seemingly governed Athens during 271, for late in the year they passed the decree in honour of Demochares which indirectly branded Phaedrus and the moderate pro-Macedonians as oligarchs; but soon afterwards Antigonus' friends regained power, which was all he sought, and Athens became again the most-favoured city; Antigonus used to visit her, and his half-brother Demetrius the Fair, son of Demetrius I and Ptolemais, who was barely sixteen in 270, studied there under Arcesilas, now head of Plato's school, the Academy. With Aetolia, Pyrrhus being dead, Antigonus succeeded in coming to an arrangement. He attached little importance to the Amphictyonic League himself, for he controlled only the seven votes of his Thessalian possessions—two apiece for Thessaly, Magnesia, and Achaea Phthiotis, and one for Perrhaebia; Aetolia and her friends, the little peoples, could therefore outvote him, and he could not afford to send his men to be outvoted. No *hieromnēmones* therefore had gone or were to go to Delphi from his Thessalian possessions. On these considerations his agreement with Aetolia was based; she was to be free to incorporate in her League any Amphictyonic people outside of Antigonus' Thessalian possessions, and to manage the Amphictyonic League; in return she promised Antigonus neutrality while he lived. She publicly emphasized the fact that her engagement was neutrality, not alliance, for Delphi gave honours to Egyptians and Spartans; but she kept her undertaking never to assist Antigonus' enemies, and this treaty formed a cornerstone of his power hardly less important than that with Antiochus.

One result of the treaty was that Aetolia insured herself against Pyrrhus' son Alexander, who now ruled Epirus, by an alliance with Acarnania, lately Epirus' vassal but Macedonia's traditional friend; subsequently, however, for reasons unknown, she turned round, and disgraced herself by aiding Alexander to recover Acarnania and taking as payment Stratus, Oeniadae, and the south-eastern part of the country; Alexander probably governed Acarnania as titular head of the Acarnanian League.

Aetolia's expansion eastward after her treaty with Antigonus was obviously difficult; but in the absence of an established Delphian chronology detailed reconstruction is impossible. Her expansion was apparently disputed by Boeotia's new leader Abaeocritus, with support from Phocis and Achaea, and a struggle ensued for the Locrian seaboard. In 272 Boeotia acquired Opuntian Locris, but lost it again. At some period Phocis had three Amphictyonic votes, that is, she held Epicnemidian Locris; but Aetolia secured one corner of Phocis, and before 261 the four Phocian archons had been replaced by three Phocarchs, modelled on the Boeotarchs, showing that the Phocian League, though with diminished territory, was Boeotia's ally and under her influence. In 261 Phocis was at war, presumably with Aetolia; and about this time no Boeotian *hieromnēmones* appear at Delphi, showing Boeotia also was at war with Aetolia. By this time Aetolia had acquired nine Amphictyonic votes, by incorporating in her League Malis (two), Epicnemidian and Western Locris (two), the Aenianes (two), the Dolopes (one), Doris (one), and part of Phocis with one vote; this number gave Aetolia control of the Amphictyonic body, for of the twenty-four votes the seven controlled by Macedonia were never exercised. Boeotia ultimately secured Opuntian Locris again for good—Opus, Halae, Larymna,—Aetolia retaining Epicnemidian Locris and exercising Eastern Locris' vote. It seems as if this position lasted from the end of the war (? by 258) to 246,—Boeotia and Phocis allies and Aetolia exercising nine votes; but this period is utterly obscure. The noteworthy thing is that all these states conduct their affairs as though Macedonia did not exist, a sufficient proof that Antigonus confined himself to his sphere.

VIII. GREECE AFTER THE CHREMONIDEAN WAR

By the time that the Chremonidean war (p. 705) broke out, Antigonus had definitely secured his position in Macedonia, and could trust the people, who doubtless realized that the war was not of his seeking; when his Gauls mutinied he could use his Macedonian troops to destroy them, and when Alexander of Epirus invaded Macedonia he could not raise the country, and was defeated and driven out again (p. 708). Once Antigonus had won the loyalty of the Macedonians to himself and his house it was won for ever; and even when his line was extinct and his country dismembered, Rome was for long not safe from pretenders calling themselves Antigonids. The war relieved Macedonia of all further danger from Epirus; probably Antigonus now recovered Atintania[1], which had belonged to Cassander, thus severing Epirus from Illyria, gaining access to the Adriatic, and securing the Aoüs pass, by which every western invader entered Macedonia. When he retook Paeonia, also once Macedonian, and secured the Axius pass into Macedonia, is uncertain. After Brennus' invasion one Dropion had reorganized Paeonia as a League, which honoured him as king and founder, a combination of monarchy and federalism on the Epirote model; but he left no successor.

The Chremonidean war worked a considerable change in the Peloponnese. Before it broke out, eastern Arcadia—Tegea, Mantinea, Orchomenus, and Caphyae—had quitted the Arcadian League, which had subsisted since Alexander's time, and joined the Spartan alliance; after the defeat of Areus of Sparta at Corinth, Mantinea apparently rejoined the League, and Areus' son Acrotatus, attempting to recover the city, was defeated and killed by the League's General, Aristodemus of Megalopolis, possibly with Achaean help. Aristodemus, called 'the Good,' was leader of the permanently anti-Spartan democratic majority in Megalopolis, and therefore Antigonus' partisan. Soon after 259 he made himself tyrant of Megalopolis, though a mutilated Arcadian League still existed for a time; he adorned his city with temples and a pillared hall built from Spartan spoils, and his tomb, though a tyrant's, was never disturbed. The leader of the anti-Spartan majority in Argos, Aristomachus, son of Antigonus' partisan Aristippus, also seized power in Argos; he was capable and evidently popular, for he founded a dynasty of which inscriptions remain, a rare event, as a tyrant's name on stone seldom survived his rule; in some places, as Ilium and Nisyrus, its erasure was provided for by a standing law. In 261, as in 272, Antigonus could have recovered his father's possessions in the Peloponnese, but again he refrained; he was content with supporting his friends, the subsequent tyrants of Argos and Megalopolis. Possibly he supported tyrants in three other cities, Orchomenus, Hermione, and Phlius, where tyrants appear later, but every tyrant was not necessarily his man; Abantidas, who in 264 seized power in Sicyon, was Aristomachus' enemy. Neither was every third-century tyrant of one type; there was little in common between Aristodemus, head of the greatest party in his city, and a prole-

---

[1] That Atintania was once Antigonid is shown by Rome's restoring it to Philip V in 205.

tarian dictator like the inhuman Apollodorus at Cassandreia. In supporting tyrants, Antigonus had reacted to an idea of Antipater's; Sparta, with Egypt behind her, had threatened his position north of the Isthmus and had to be held in check for the future, and his tyrants enabled him to do this without wasting his mercenaries on garrison service or unwillingly ruling part of an unwilling Peloponnese himself. Late writers assert that Antigonus, like Antipater, also set up tyrants; but this is doubtful, for Polybius gives it only as what men said, and was perhaps merely quoting a popular saying or song[1]. To support tyrants was morally indefensible, but so were the aggressive wars of the democracies; the difference was that one shocked Greek sentiment, the other did not. In his Peloponnesian system Antigonus was merely doing what seemed politically expedient, without regard to morality; and he paid the inevitable price. The price was Aratus and the Achaean League.

Athens, after its surrender, Antigonus took into his own hands, and proceeded to apply Cassander's policy; like most other kings, he ultimately came back to Cassander. Glaucon and his brother Chremonides (pp. 706 sqq.) were exiled and went to Egypt, where Glaucon became priest of Alexander in 255, and Chremonides commanded an Egyptian fleet (p. 713); but there were seemingly no executions. Antigonus, however, garrisoned the Museum and all the Attic forts, which were placed under the general in Piraeus; he removed the existing generals and magistrates from office, appointed new ones himself, and governed Athens as a subject town through an *epistates*, as Cassander had done through Demetrius of Phalerum; if the Assembly still passed decrees, they were few. Possibly the franchise was limited; but it does not appear that Athens lost the right of coining. The passing of Athens' greatness was dramatically marked by Zeno's death in autumn 261. He was the last survivor of the renowned group of philosophers who for forty years had rendered the city illustrious; what he felt in living through the struggle between his friend and his home none can say. He was a foreigner and the friend of Athens' enemy; but the Athenians honoured him because he was also a noble man. At Antigonus' request they gave him a public funeral; and Antigonus himself, adapting a phrase made current by Zeno's rival Epicurus, lamented that with Zeno he had 'lost his audience.' But only Athens could have paid to the dead the tribute of the beautiful words, touched with strong feeling, which

---

[1] He repeats it twice, II, 41, 10 and IX, 29, 6, each time using ἐμφυτεύειν, apparently unique in this sense.

still remain; the draftsman of the decree for him, after recalling
Zeno's long services to philosophy and the insistence with which
he had preached virtue and self-control to the young, said simply:
'He made his life a pattern to all, for he followed his own teaching.'

Athens did not long remain a subject town; after the peace of
255 Antigonus, secure in the command of the sea (p. 713),
withdrew the Museum garrison and the *epistates* and restored
Athens' autonomy; and she again became the most-favoured city,
governed by his friends in his interest, and able to conduct her
own affairs, like her war with Alexander of Corinth and her
arbitration with Boeotia in 244. But the old relationship was not
fully restored. Antigonus was now definitely suzerain; the pro-
Macedonian government voted him honours and a statue, and
regularly offered sacrifices for 'the king'[1]; and his general in the
Piraeus, now the Athenian Heracleitus of Athmonon, continued to
hold the forts important for naval purposes, Salamis and Sunium,
though Eleusis, Phyle, and Panactum were restored to Athens.
Athens was again Antigonus' spiritual capital; Lycon, now head
of Aristotle's school, was his friend, and when he desired to in-
stitute a birthday feast in honour of his dead son Halcyoneus it
was at Athens he founded it; Hieronymus of Rhodes, the Peripatetic, had the management, and every year the philosophers of
the city, including even the patriotic Arcesilas, dined together
at Antigonus' charges. But with the Chremonidean war Athens
had for the last time played a leading part in the world's politics.
Never again was she to possess real power; her importance
henceforth is purely intellectual.

It was probably late in 253 or in 252 that Antigonus' new-
found sea power was paralysed by the revolt, with Ptolemy's
support, of Craterus' son and successor Alexander, which deprived him of much of his fleet, for Alexander proclaimed himself
king in his generalship, Corinth and Euboea; Eretria honoured
him as Benefactor, and he made Chalcis his capital, where his
wife Nicaea played patroness to the poet Euphorion, an inferior
imitator of Callimachus. War followed between Alexander, aided
by some pirates, and Antigonus' friends, Athens and Aristomachus of Argos, supported by Heracleitus; Heracleitus defeated
an attack on Salamis, but by about 249 Alexander had compelled
both cities to make peace. Antigonus' actions during this war
are utterly obscure; he may have been trying to save some of the
Cyclades from Ptolemy (p. 715). Megalopolis gave him no help,

---

[1] Nothing turns on Athens' name preceding Antigonus' in the sacrificial
formulae, for under Demetrius I either name had come first at random.

for about 252 Aristodemus had been assassinated by two Megalopolitan exiles, Ecdemus and Demophanes, friends of Arcesilas,
who in his classroom had helped to keep alive the spirit of patriotism native to Plato's school. The two were to earn further
fame as 'liberators' at Sicyon and Cyrene (p. 713); but they were
soon overshadowed by the man who in 251 appeared on the stage
which he was for so long to fill.

IX. ARATUS OF SICYON

Aratus of Sicyon is one of the most perplexing personalities in
Greek history. A hero and afraid; an upholder of constitutionalism who broke laws at his pleasure, a political idealist who
allowed a good end to justify the most immoral means; neither
virtuous nor great, but secure in a devotion often denied to the
great and virtuous; inspired by a high idea which possessed his
whole being and gave him amazing success against heavy odds,
and at the end a traitor to that idea and to his whole life's work:
such was Aratus, largely drawn for us by himself.

He was born in 271, son of Cleinias, a democratic leader during
Sicyon's brief freedom. In 264 one Abantidas slew Cleinias and
made himself tyrant; but Abantidas' sister saved Aratus and he
grew up under Aristomachus' protection in Argos, to reward
Aristomachus later by trying to assassinate him. In 252 Abantidas was assassinated, and ultimately one Nicocles, apparently
a partisan of Alexander of Corinth, seized the tyranny. There
were many Sicyonian exiles in Argos, and Aratus, who was now
twenty, capable and athletic, decided that they might overthrow
Nicocles; Ecdemus and Demophanes came from Megalopolis to
help them, and they hired some brigands, from which, it seems,
few districts in Greece were free. Aratus' preparations were
skilfully made, and on a night in May 251, after some exciting
adventures, he surprised and freed Sicyon without bloodshed.
Antigonus at first thought that Aratus might be useful to him,
and sent him twenty-five talents, which Aratus used in freeing
prisoners. He indeed felt that Sicyon, in view of Alexander's
possible enmity, could not stand alone; but instead of joining
Antigonus he united his Dorian city to the League of the eleven
Achaean towns, whose constitution he greatly admired. But an
abortive attempt made by Aratus on Corinth alarmed Alexander,
and he too safeguarded himself by an alliance with the Achaean
League. It was not Aratus' doing, but it placed him officially on
Ptolemy's side, and as Sicyon was full of the troubles that gene-

rally occurred when exiles returned and claimed compensation
for their former property, he decided to seek Ptolemy's help. He
was shipwrecked on the way, but reached Egypt, interested
Ptolemy, and returned with 150 talents, which enabled him to
satisfy all claims.

About 247 Alexander died, and Nicaea took over his kingdom
and mercenaries. Antigonus at once saw a chance of recovering
Corinth; his son Demetrius' wife Stratonice (p. 715) had left
him, and Antigonus sent him to offer Nicaea his hand and the
future queenship of Macedonia. Nicaea fell to the bait; but
though she handed over Corinth, she kept Acrocorinthus, and
without it the city was valueless. The story goes that just before
the wedding, when Nicaea and her friends were on their way to
some festival, Antigonus slipped away unperceived, climbed
Acrocorinthus with his guards, and knocked at the fortress gate;
the dumb-foundered sentry opened it, and Antigonus again held
the key of his system. How he recovered Euboea is unknown,
but he did not restore the great generalship of Corinth; he made
Persaeus the philosopher *epistates* of the city, with a garrison
commander at his side. Certainly Demetrius did not marry
Nicaea. Tricking a woman, even the widow of a traitor, leaves
an unpleasant impression; but the story comes from a source
bitterly hostile to Macedonia. Antigonus recovered Corinth
either in 247 or, at latest, some time in 246, and there is a story
that after it he made another attempt to win Aratus, giving out
that the young man had been disillusioned in Egypt and was
ready to join him; he would receive a warm welcome. But there
was no question of Aratus joining him. His mind was becoming
full of one dominant thought: the Peloponnese must be freed
from tyrants, and he must free it. And to him the worst of all
tyrants was Antigonus.

CHAPTER VII

ATHENS

I. THE SPIRIT OF THE NEW AGE

IN the year that Alexander died in Babylon, two boys in Athens were called up for military service: their names were Epicurus and Menander. In 322 his old tutor, Aristotle, and his enemy, Demosthenes, died also, and in 321 Menander produced his first play, *Orge*. The classical age is over, and a new epoch begins.

So great a change was not of course immediately apparent. Demades described the defeated city as 'not the sea-power of our fathers, but a gruel-guzzling old slattern in slippers[1],' but on the other hand Antigonus called her 'the beacon of the world, whence reputation was transmitted to all mankind[2],' and sixty years were still to pass before she recognized that her days of imperialism and independence were over. Then followed a generation of submission to Macedonian rule, until, in 229, taking advantage of barbarian invasions of Macedon, Athens was able to buy out the foreign garrison of the Piraeus and proclaim herself to the great powers of the Mediterranean as a neutral state, no longer the centre of commerce or even of literary production, but respected for her glorious past and still attracting students to her schools from all parts of the Greek-speaking world, so that Eratosthenes could refer to the number of philosophers contemporary with Ariston and Arcesilas as unprecedented within the compass of a single city[3]. The political history of Athens during this period is described elsewhere (vol. VI, chaps. XIV *sq.*, vol. VII, chaps. VI, XXII *sq.*), but her real importance in the third century lies in the last two manifestations of her genius—the New Comedy, and the new philosophies. These form the subject of the present chapter.

But though politics are not our present concern, the changed political situation profoundly influenced the New Comedy and was the immediate cause of the new philosophies. Both accordingly exhibit certain common characteristics which it is convenient to trace before proceeding to consider each in detail. For instance, in both appear two qualities which are almost unknown in earlier literature—cosmopolitanism and individualism, and the

---

[1] Demetrius, *de eloc.* 285.   [2] Plutarch, *Demetrius* 8.
[3] Strabo I, 15.

two spring from the same source, the conquests of Alexander, which broke down the self-sufficiency and security of the old city-state and 'relieved active men from the ambitions of a military or political career' (Polybius, III, 59). Though the sacred cause of democracy still struggled, with varying success, to maintain itself in Athens, though kings continued in Sparta, the progress of the century marks their steady decline from sovereign states to municipal towns, merged in military empires.

The older citizens learn to think parochially, while the younger, more adventurous spirits go fortune-hunting Eastward Ho![1], whence they return to swagger across the stage in the rôle of *Alazon* or *Miles Gloriosus* and boast of their conquests in love and war. Thus the curtailment of national activities and the removal of the old frontiers forced men to substitute for former loyalties both a greater interest in their own personal lives and a recognition of a common humanity: even the distinction between Greek and barbarian tends to disappear, as no longer corresponding to a real division. It has been usual to credit Stoicism with the discovery and proclamation of the cosmopolitan idea, but while the theory had been preached as early as the Sophists and was practised as generously by the Epicureans, Plutarch[2] seems to be right when he insists that the cause which made it practicable was not philosophy:

After all, the much admired *Republic* of Zeno, founder of the Stoic sect, may be summed up in one main principle: we are not to live nationally or parochially, split up into various groups with private conventions; we are to consider all men fellow-countrymen, and our life and world are to be one— one flock living together in one fold. But while Zeno sketched his philosopher's Utopia on paper, it was Alexander who gave the theory realization.

Aristophanes could never have written the original of Terence's famous line

> homo sum, humani nihil a me alienum puto.

But we find it, or something very like, in Menander—

> No honest man I call
> A foreigner; one nature have we all.   (Frag. 602.)

A third note common to the New Comedy and to the new philosophies, and equally due to the new conditions, is the

---

[1] See for example Terence, *Heauton Timorumenos*, l. 110 *sq.*

[2] Plutarch, *de Alex. virtute, Moral.* p. 329 A. For the Sophists see Antiphon in Diels' *Vorsokratiker*[4], II, p. xxx, Hippias in Plato, *Prot.* 337 C, and the claim attributed to Socrates (Cicero, *Tusc.* V, 108); and for Epicureans Diogenes of Oenoanda, frag. 24, etc. See vol. VI, p. 437, for a somewhat different view.

recognition of the all-but dominant rôle played in human affairs by Chance. The plays reveal, and the new schools presuppose, what the history of Polybius reflects, a background in which almost anything may happen to anybody at any moment[1]. Human endeavour and forethought are for ever being brought to nothing by incalculable and resistless strokes of Fortune, and the odds in favour of disappointment and unhappiness are so great that the wisest man is he who has fewest expectations:

> The favourite of Heaven dies in youth[2].

In short, we are dealing with an age which, like our own, is consequent upon a great catastrophe. Institutions which seemed settled and secure have been destroyed and old landmarks removed, confidence has been badly shaken, unexpected misfortunes have been experienced. And yet life has somehow to go on. We cannot wonder if the literature of the time reflects what has been called 'a failure of nerve,' a lowering of aspiration and withdrawal from high endeavour, a tendency to yield to circumstance rather than strive to control it, and to put safety first.

II. THE NEW COMEDY

Down to the end of the nineteenth century our knowledge of the New Comedy was confined to three sources—the occasional notices of ancient critics, the Latin translations or adaptations by Plautus and Terence[3], and a considerable number of fragments, few of which exceeded ten continuous lines. The first of these raised an expectation which the second entirely failed to satisfy, while the third were too short and disconnected to form the basis of any definite opinion. We hear of five names—Philemon, Diphilus, Apollodorus, Poseidippus and Menander—of whom the last,

---

[1] Compare the famous chapter of Polybius (xxix, 21) with *Ecclesiastes* ix, 1, a passage attributed to the same period and similar political conditions in Alexandria.

[2] Menander, frag. 125—perhaps the best known of his lines, though usually understood in a sense quite different from what seems to have been its original significance. Cf. also frags. 166, 481.

[3] Of the nineteen extant plays of Plautus three are definitely said to have been adapted from Philemon, two from Diphilus and two from Menander. At the end of the *Mostellaria* (1149–51) the slave says to the master whom he has deceived, "If you are a friend of Diphilus or Philemon you can tell them how your servant fooled you. You'll provide first-class material for a comedy." Terence represents the taste of the next generation and is supposed to follow his originals more closely: of his six plays two are translated from Apollodorus and four from Menander. See further, vol. VIII.

neglected by his contemporaries, attained by far the greatest reputation from posterity. Thus Aristophanes of Byzantium praised his realism in the well-known line

> Menander! Life!
> I wonder which of you has copied which?

and Quintilian stated that in his opinion Menander alone, if carefully studied, would suffice to produce all the qualities desired to make a successful orator: 'so complete is his picture of life, so fertile his imagination and command of language, so perfect his adaptation to every circumstance, character and emotion' (x, i, 69). On the other hand, few readers of Roman comedy can have disagreed with Mommsen's verdict, when he complains of their 'tiresome monotony,...the dreadful desolation of life,...the fearfully prosaic atmosphere,...above all the immoral morality.' But, it was argued, these faults were due to the transmitters, not to the originals: the Romans themselves had acknowledged the shortcomings of their countrymen. Aulus Gellius provides an illustration. 'We were reading Caecilius' *Plocium*, with pleasure to all present, and we thought we would read the original by Menander also. Heavens! how flat and dull Caecilius immediately appeared, and what a change after Menander!' and he proceeds to support his judgment with extracts (ii, xxiii, *5 sqq.*) Then, in 1905, at a place near Cairo, appropriately named Aphroditopolis, Gustave Lefebvre found a papyrus containing 1400 lines of Menander, 659 of which belonged to one play, *The Arbitrants* (*Epitrepontes*), so that we have altogether now not quite 4000 lines of his, perhaps one twenty-fifth of what he wrote. No play indeed is yet complete, but we have sufficient material surely to form a judgment. What is the verdict? Undoubtedly our first feeling is one of disappointment. The new fragments exhibit on the whole just those characteristics with which the Latin imitations had made us familiar and which Mommsen had condemned. There is the same narrow range of plot, the same lack of interest in public life or foreign affairs, the same concentration on amatory intrigue with the assumptions that 'all's fair in love' and 'all's well that ends well.' The realism and fidelity to nature, so much admired by antiquity, appear to have consisted more in the skill with which he reproduced the linguistic characteristics of his various types[1] than in psychological observation: his studies of character do not show, so far as we can see, any particular subtlety or depth.

---

[1] P. A. E. F. Le Grand, Κωμῳδία Néα (Eng. trans.), p. 256.

In one of his rapid reviews of previous poets Ovid wrote (*Amores*, I, xv, 17 *sq.*)

> So long as fathers bully, servants lie,
> And women smile, MENANDER cannot die,

and it seems that here, as so often, he laid his finger on the essential.

Feeling therefore free to include in our evidence the Latin plays which have survived as well as the Greek fragments, new and old, we may attempt to summarize very briefly the main features of the New Comedy. As all ancient authorities testified, it has more in common with Euripides than with Aristophanes. The *agon* (vol. v, p. 138), round which the Old Comedy centred, is gone, and so is the chorus: interludes are provided, where necessary, by bands of revellers, 'young men half-seas-over.' The central theme is almost always the love of a young man in good social position for a girl who has none, and his efforts (or rather those of his servant) to conceal his passion from his father. His intentions may or may not be honourable, but it presently transpires that his beloved is a lady after all, who had by one means or other been separated from her parents, and the play ends happily with marriage bells. The main emphasis is laid on youth and the pleasures that money can buy. Married women appear but seldom, and never to advantage, and married life is depicted in the background as very different from the thrills which lead up to it. There is a great deal about eating (not so much about drinking), and cooks and their Art are treated with the frequency and respect due to a popular subject. Secondary types are doctors, philosophers and soldiers, who provide comic relief.

The fragments, especially those of Menander, abound in moral commonplaces, pithily expressed, and in worldly wisdom mellowed by a kindly tolerance of human frailty. So far as they contain a criticism of life, their attitude is Epicurean, not Stoic, and there is no depth of either thought or feeling. One illustration must suffice. It is taken from one of the newly discovered plays, *The Arbitrants*, and occurs towards the end. Smicrines, persuaded that his daughter is being unfairly treated, is on his way to take her from her husband, if necessary, by force, when he meets Onesimus, a slave, who is better informed as to the situation.

> ONES. Do you believe the gods have time enough
> To pay each individual every day
> His wages, good or bad?
>
> SMIC.   How do you mean?

ONES. I'll show you. All the cities in the world
　　　　Are, say, a thousand: thirty thousand souls
　　　　Inhabit each of them. Does Heaven damn
　　　　Or save each of these millions one by one?
SMIC. They cannot have so hard a time as that!
ONES. Then do they take (you'll ask) *no* interest
　　　　In us? We have attached as Resident[1]
　　　　In each his Character, which from within
　　　　Damns one, who chooses to mishandle It,
　　　　And saves another. That's the God for us,
　　　　The source of happiness or misery
　　　　For everyone. If you want happiness,
　　　　Please It, by not behaving stupidly.
SMIC. And so my Character, you atheist,
　　　　Is at this moment acting stupidly?
ONES. It's crushing you.
SMIC. 　　　　　　　　What damned impertinence!
ONES. Well, do *you* think it right to separate
　　　　One's daughter from her husband?
SMIC. 　　　　　　　　　　　　　No one calls
　　　　It *right*. Just now it can't be helped.
ONES. 　　　　　　　　　　　　　You see?
　　　　What's wrong our friend considers 'can't be helped,'
　　　　And nothing but his Character contrives
　　　　His ruin! You are on the brink of crime,
　　　　And now pure Chance has saved you, and you find
　　　　Your difficulties solved and reconciled.

(*Epitrepontes*, 544–569.)

But the dominant impression left upon the mind from a study
of the Greek fragments—and here they differ from the Latin
copies, written a century or more later, when conditions had
changed—is, as has been said, the helplessness of man against the
changes and chances of this mortal life, in which he is at the mercy
of external circumstance and may be ruined in a moment. The
references to the dazzling whirligigs of life and the power
and caprice of Fortune are too common in Menander to be
negligible. Here are a few examples:

In short, you're human. There's no living thing
Is subjected to such a sudden swing
Up to the heights and back to degradation.　　　(Frag. 531.)

　　　　　Fortune observes no rules
In her decisions, and while life endures
No man can boast '*That* fate shall ne'er be mine.' (Frag. 355.)

We live, not as we choose, but as we may.　　　(Frag. 50.)

---

[1] Perhaps a metaphor from the Macedonian garrison in the Piraeus.

> So many cases I have known
> Of men who, though not naturally rogues,
> Became so, through misfortune, by constraint.   (Frag. 604.)

It was in this soil, and to meet this menace, that the new philosophies grew. And so Theophrastus, who succeeded Aristotle, 'is bitterly attacked in the books and lectures of all philosophers'[1] for approving in his *Callisthenes* Chaeremon's line

> Fortune, not counsel, guides the affairs of men.

He had betrayed his cloth, sold the pass, and surrendered to the eternal foe.

III. THE NEW PHILOSOPHIES

The first effect of Alexander's conquests upon thought was to render obsolete and useless those theories of morals and social organization which we consider most typically classical. Aristotle's *Ethics* for example must have seemed out of date almost as soon as its author died. Both to him and to Plato it had been axiomatic that 'good living,' or happiness in the highest sense, was only possible for members of the limited, self-sufficient and self-governing communities to which they were accustomed. 'Man is a political animal,' the individual is intended by Nature to form part of Society, in whose service alone he can find full self-expression, and without which he is 'either a god or a beast' (cf. vol. VI, pp. 519 *sqq.*). But now society as they had known it, the sovereign city-state, had ceased to exist. And many who were not professed students of philosophy, who had taken current institutions for granted and accepted the law and custom of their *polis* as an unquestioned authority, must have felt themselves left without guidance and protection just at the time when life was most difficult and insecure. This bewilderment found its echo in the nihilistic pronouncements of Pyrrhon and of his pupil, Timon of Phlius. They criticized the presuppositions of all other philosophers: for them the only certainty was that there was no certainty. But such a system of thought was scarcely constructive, and can have brought little comfort to spiritual exiles, who required new standards of values and a home where they might be safe from fear of men or fortune.

These philosophy now set itself to provide. The change of attitude may be shown by two quotations. To Plato and Aristotle the origin of philosophy had been a sense of intellectual doubt and perplexity: to Epictetus it is 'a consciousness of one's own weakness and inadequacy.'[2] To Cicero philosophy is 'the art, or guide,

---

[1] Cicero, *Tusc.* v, 25.   [2] Arrian, *Dissertations*, II, xi, 1.

of life,' 'the training, or healing, of the soul,'[1] to Plutarch 'the
only medicine for spiritual diseases.'[2] In other words, metaphysics sink into the background, and ethics, now individual,
become of the first importance. Philosophy is no longer the pillar
of fire going before a few intrepid seekers after truth: it is rather
an ambulance following in the wake of the struggle for existence
and picking up the weak and wounded. To this extent at least
it occupied the place filled by religion to-day, and the post-
Aristotelian schools, like modern churches, made no distinction of
nationality or status or even sex. They offered to all by diverse
ways a road to peace and happiness and a stronghold against the
attacks of Fortune, and tried to construct in 'the Sage' an ideal
character who should be independent of all outward circumstance.

Two systems of thought were pre-eminently successful in
meeting this need. Separated at first sight by a fundamental
difference of standpoint, and appealing, now as then, to opposite
sides of human nature, they had nevertheless certain elements in
common. While the Jews learnt from their political disasters to look
forward to a good time coming, it did not occur to either Epicurus
or Zeno to call in a new world to redress the balance of the old.
Both schools were materialistic, and brought no hopes of heaven
or new revelation of God. They sought rather to make each man a
god unto himself, and preached independence through withdrawal and resignation rather than by conquest. Thus evil is
avoided by Epicurus, denied by Zeno, by neither overcome.

With the details of either system we shall be concerned presently. Let us first contrast the general attitude of each, and note
by what different paths they point to the same goal.

IV. EPICURUS

Epicurus is one to whom tradition has done scant justice.
We have been taught to think of him as a godless scientist and an
immoral pleasure-seeker, whereas in fact he did not deny the
existence of the gods—but only their interference in the affairs
of men—cared nothing for science in itself, and sought not
pleasure, but peace. Born in 341, an Athenian citizen, he lived
with his father Neocles in Samos, until in 322 the family were
expelled with other Athenian settlers from the island by Perdiccas,
and he spent the next fifteen years without a settled home. It has
been suggested[3] that 'he built up his philosophy while helping

---

[1] *De fin.* III, 4; *Tusc.* II, 13; III, 6; v, 5.   [2] *Moral.* 7 D.
[3] G. Murray, *Five Stages of Greek Religion*, p 129.

his parents and brothers through this bad time,' and certainly Epicureanism betrays symptoms of a refugee philosophy. Possessing himself a strong personality, with a genius for friendship, he was the author of a real evangel to many who were in bondage to the fear of death or to that mental disquietude which is produced sooner or later by polytheism. The gospel according to Epicurus has come down to us less imperfectly than its Stoic rival (which is our excuse for allowing it the larger space), and though the three hundred rolls attributed to his pen are lost, including 37 books *On Nature* and the longer summary which is supposed to be the authority followed by Lucretius, we have three letters (or Epistles) preserved by Diogenes Laertius, as well as the poem of his great disciple. These, together with some essays by Cicero and Plutarch and the recently discovered fragments of Diogenes of Oenoanda, enable us to reconstruct it with some approach to completeness. Based on the atomic theory of Democritus (see vol. IV, pp. 576 *sqq.*), to which it added one patent improvement, and an entirely naturalistic interpretation of the Universe, it drew the essential inference that man has nothing to fear—either from the gods, who live in careless bliss, remote from our world, and unconcerned to punish or reward us, or from a life to come, since our souls are as mortal as our bodies, and Death is but a sleep that has no waking. It included as corollaries an explanation of the legendary torments of Hell in terms of this life—for men make their own hell here and now[1], and an account of the evolution of man from savagery to civilization which attributed every step to *natural* development and left no room for the interposition of Divine beneficence: progress *came*, as the undesigned consequence of time and experience; necessity was the mother of invention[2].

Wonderful to relate, no change is recorded in the teaching of the school from the Master's death in 270 till its final disappearance six centuries later[3]. Epicureanism was, it has been said, a secular Church with infallible dogmas[4]. The grosser minds of Rome seized on those sides of it which were most liable to perversion and won for it the infamy associated with the term 'epicure.' But if Roman converts were swine[5], Epicurus himself

---

[1] Lucret. III, 978 *sqq.*; Cic. *de fin.* 1, 60.

[2] Lucret. V, 772–1457; Diog. Oen. frag. 10; Diog. Laert. x, 75.

[3] For evidence of Epicureans in the fourth century A.D. see Usener, *Epicurea*, p. lxxv.

[4] Cf. Martha, *Le poëme de Lucrèce*, 3rd ed., p. 10.

[5] Horace did his Master's reputation no good by avowing himself 'Epicuri de grege porcum' (*Ep.* 1, iv, 16): cf. Cic. *in Pisonem*, 68 *sqq.*

was no swine-herd. To the strength and charm of his character even opponents bore witness, while 'in his lifetime his friends were numbered by whole cities.'[1] In the Garden outside Athens which he bought for his followers women and slaves were made welcome, and little children were among the recipients of his letters. Faithful to his precept 'Live unobtrusively,' Epicureans played no prominent part in politics. But wherever our scanty records of the past enable us to catch a glimpse of them, two things are notable. As an early Society of Friends they did much to develop the more amiable virtues of domesticity in a hard and unsettled age, but they were also always missionaries, waging truceless warfare against superstition, with which their rivals, Platonist, neo-Pythagorean and Stoic, came to terms. In this they were the allies, however unwitting and unwelcome, of the early Christians, with whose unpopularity they had the honour to be associated in a common charge of atheism.

This outline of Epicurus' contribution may be rounded off with three quotations. The first is one of the passages in which Lucretius praises the Saviour who brought life and—mortality to light, and forms the opening of his Fifth Book (1–14, 43–54):

> Who is sufficient, blessed with powers of brain
> Enough to build an adequate refrain
> To match a Truth so wonderful, and those
> Discoveries? Or who is such a lord
> Of language, as may praises fit compose
> For his deserts, who left us such reward,
> Won by the travail of his fruitful brain?
> No *man*, I fancy, born of mortal strain!
>   For should I speak of him as is decreed
> By the known wondrous Truth, He was indeed
> A GOD, who first that way of living taught
> Which now we call Philosophy, and brought
> Life's vessel out of Ocean's storms and night
> Into calm waters and most radiant light.

Then, after a scornful comparison of the legendary labours of the Stoic hero Heracles with the real services rendered by Epicurus to mankind, he continues

> But till the heart is cleansed, what perils must
> We enter then, what struggles of disgust!
> What bitter pangs of passion then divide
> The troubled breast, what terrors! Think of Pride,
> And filthy, wanton Lust: what havoc both
> Occasion! Think of Luxury and Sloth!

---

[1] Diog. Laert. x, 9.

> And shall not he who all these evils quelled
> And from the heart by words, not arms, expelled,
> Though man, be justly reckoned in the line
> Of Gods? Since too with eloquence divine
> The very Gods Immortal he revealed
> And every mystery of life unsealed.

The second is from Lucian's *Life of Alexander*, one of those religious impostors, who, deceiving themselves as well as others, sprang up all over the Roman Empire in the second century A.D. and found in the Epicureans their stoutest opponents:

In this connection Alexander once made himself supremely ridiculous. Coming across Epicurus' *Sovereign Principles*, that noblest of books, which embraces in outline the main points of the Master's wisdom, he brought it into the middle of the market place and burnt it.... The wretch knew nothing of the blessings of which that book has been the cause to those into whose hands it fell, or of what peace, tranquillity and freedom it produces in them, releasing them from fears, phantoms and nightmares, vain hopes and inordinate affections, instilling reason and truth, and truly purifying the mind not with ceremonial rubbish, but with right judgment, truth and liberty.

I have dared to write this in defence of Epicurus, a real saint and prophet, who alone saw and declared the Beautiful and True, and has proved a saviour to those who came unto him. (*Alexander*, 47, 61.)

Lastly, four lines, in Greek twelve words (the *tetrapharmakos*), excavated at Herculaneum a hundred years ago, sum up the Epicurean attitude to life:

> There is nothing to fear in God:
> There is nothing to feel in Death:
> What is good is easily procured;
> What is ill is easily endured.

'Meanwhile,' wrote Sir Thomas Browne, 'Epicurus lies deep in Dante's hell, wherein we meet with tombs enclosing souls which denied their immortality. But whether the virtuous heathen, who lived better than he spake, or erring in the principles of himself, yet lived above philosophers of more specious maxims, lie so deep as he is placed, at least so low as not to rise against Christians, who believing or knowing that truth, have lastingly denied it in their practise and conversation—were a query too sad to insist on.' (*Hydrotaphia*, IV.)

V. ZENO

Very different was the ideal and influence of Stoicism[1].

Its founder, Zeno of Citium in Cyprus, came to Athens as a shipwrecked merchant about the year 314, and after attending the lectures of Xenocrates and Polemon in the Academy and the Cynic Crates he became a teacher himself in 301. 'He used to discourse promenading up and down the Colonnade or "Porch" (*stoa*) of Peisianax, celebrated for Polygnotus' painting of the Persian defeat, and so his followers, who had formerly been called Zenonians, were named Stoics[2].' His native city contained settlers from Phoenicia, and he himself is frequently called a Phoenician, while three of his immediate successors were born at Tarsus, the meeting place of East and West: hence it is perhaps not fanciful to recognize in Stoic teaching some of those characteristics—an intolerance of imperfection amounting to a sense of 'Sin,' an uncompromising idealism, and a demand for resignation before the All-Supreme—which we associate with the Semitic spirit and find later in Islam, but which were new to the thought of Hellas. To Zeno seems to have been due the introduction of the ideas and words of *Duty* and *Conscience*, as well as the distinction of *moral* values, which are absolute, from practical values, which are relative and strictly *indifferent*. He first asserted clearly that the will or intention is everything, and that circumstances are nothing, except as forming material for exercising the will and building character. One thing alone is 'good'—goodness or 'Virtue.'

But just here a curious vagueness appears in the teaching.

The process by which we rise from Nature's first impulse to self-preservation up to the conscious and continuous exercise of virtue is not clearly demonstrated[3], and when we ask what *is* 'Virtue'? a definite reply is not given. It is distinct from the *arete* of Aristotle, it is not this or that; but what is its positive content? 'It is not easy to answer the charge....that, after all, they were merely ascetics; in other words, that their morality not only begins with

---

[1] See further above, pp. 37 *sqq.*, p. 202 *sq.*

[2] Diog. Laert. VII, 5, who makes him 30 at his coming to Athens, a student for another 20 years, and 98 at death (*ibid.* 28), having been head of the school, according to Apollodorus, for 58 years. But he adds that Persaeus, an immediate follower, said that he came to Athens at 22 and died at 72. It is generally agreed to date his death in 261, nine years after Epicurus.

[3] See Cicero, *de fin.* III, 16–22, with commentary in R. D. Hicks, *Stoic and Epicurean*, pp. 77 *sqq.*

the mortification of their passions, but ends there[1].' In their pre-occupation with personal righteousness, their austere attitude towards human nature and their love of terminological distinctions, the Stoics remind us of the Pharisees, and it is interesting to note that Josephus explicitly makes the comparison (*Vita*, 12). Their creed has often been lauded as the noblest embodiment of pre-Christian thought, but it is at best a gospel of Detachment (and as such can be paralleled in Indian ethics), far removed from the gospel of Love. Marcus Aurelius writes of our days as a pilgrimage and a sojourning, but the journey has no goal. We have not even the doctrine of Progress proclaimed by the Epicureans; we may hope for nothing better than the 'final' conflagration, after which the cycle of events will be repeated down to the smallest detail. To the Stoic the world is the best of all possible worlds, but everything in it a necessary evil, including one's fellow-creatures. In Seneca's sermons the slave is a man and a brother, but in practice he and other Stoics seem to have interpreted Brotherhood in the manner of the Elder Brother in the parable. Marcus Aurelius tells himself:

In one respect men are our nearest duty, in so far as we are bound to suffer them and do them good. But in so far as particular individuals interfere with my proper functions, man becomes to me a thing indifferent, no less than sun or wind or beast of the field. (v. 20.)

Even Epictetus, the most lovable of them, warns his hearers:

As on a voyage, when the vessel has reached a port and you go ashore to get water, it is an amusement by the way to pick up a shell or a flower, but your thoughts ought all the while to be directed to the ship, continually on the watch for the captain's call, and when it comes, you must throw all those things away and hasten, that you may not have to be bound and thrown aboard by others: so in life also, if, instead of a flower or a shell, you be given a wife or child, there is naught to hinder you from taking them for your own; but should the Captain call, run to the ship, and leave all that behind. (*Manual*, 7.)

The Stoic paid a high price for his independence and the 'unconquerable soul.' He dare not become sin to deliver others, or poor, that they by his poverty might be made rich. All emotions that might disturb his central calm, all adjuncts within the reach of envious Fortune—pity, love, the fate of others—these must be regarded as of no essential value by the Sage. To render himself invulnerable, he turned his heart into a stone: he made a solitude, and called it peace. It is magnificent, but it is not peace.

---

[1] E. Caird, *Evolution of Theology in the Greek Philosophers*, II, p. 125.

VI. THE OLDER SCHOOLS

Before we proceed to set forth these two new systems in detail, a glance is needed at the older schools. Plato at the Academy was followed by a series of undistinguished moralists, until the headship of Arcesilas, who died in 241, revived its prestige and gave a new turn to its teaching. The change began with his fierce opposition to the theory of knowledge on which the Stoics based their dogmatism. Zeno had taught that of our sense-impressions or presentations (*phantasiai*) some are so 'vivid and striking' as to convey immediate certainty of their truth or of the reality of their objects. Such a presentation he called 'apprehensive' (*kataleptike phantasia*) and defined as one 'stamped or impressed upon the mind from a real object, and representing that object as it is— such as could not come from an unreal object!' To this Arcesilas replied that we have no means of knowing whether a presentation comes from a 'real object' or not, or of distinguishing between true and false sensations: you never can tell.

Next, the Academy seems to have been hoist with its own petard, and the agnosticism, first assumed by Arcesilas for controversial purposes, became his positive belief. Looking back into history, he found the same sceptical attitude in the fountain-head, Socrates, except that Socrates did not go far enough, for he claimed to *know* that he knew nothing. 'And so,' says Cicero, who is inclined to confess himself an adherent of this school, 'Arcesilas declared that nothing could be known—not even Socrates' exception. Everything, he thought, was buried in mystery: neither comprehension nor certainty was possible. It was therefore wrong to assert or assent to any proposition: judgment should be suspended: nothing was more immoral than to let assent or belief outrun knowledge or comprehension. Putting his ideas into practice, he attacked all dogmas and converted most men to his own: finding the arguments on the opposite sides of the same question evenly balanced, they were the more ready to withhold assent from either. This is the New Academy so-called' (*Academica*, I, 45; cf. II, 77). The Academy remained predominantly sceptical for the next two centuries, until Antiochus, who died in 69, produced quite another reading of history and the catholic tradition.

Meanwhile in the Lyceum Aristotle's followers were continuing along the lines which he had prescribed of common research and the historical method. 'While armies sweep Greece this way and that, while the old gods are vanquished and the cities lose their freedom and their meaning,' writes Professor Murray, 'the Peripatetics instead of passionately saving souls diligently pursued knowledge, and in generation after generation produced scientific results which put all their rivals into the shade[1].' In view of the loss of almost all Peripatetic writings, this statement errs perhaps on the side of generosity, but we do know something of the quantity of their output, even if we cannot judge of its quality. The volume of *Problems*, included in the Aristotelian Corpus, indicates the nature and range of their enquiries. Theophrastus, head of the school from 322 to 288, wrote not only the famous *Characters* and treatises on botany and psychology which have survived, but also compiled the first History of Philosophy which seems to have been the main source of the *Placita* ascribed to Plutarch and Aetius; fragments of it remain embedded in the commentaries on Aristotle by Simplicius in the sixth century A.D. Similarly Aristoxenus wrote the history of music, Duris of art, Eudemus of mathematics and astronomy, and Menon of medicine, while Dicaearchus brought geography up to date with a text and map embodying the new knowledge of the East gained by the armies of Macedon. To the Peripatetic school above all we owe the transition from philosophy to a number of specialized sciences. But 'by the middle of the third century its work was over; it had rendered much service to science and much disservice to history[2].'

VII. STOICISM

Turning now to such a detailed account of the new systems as our space affords, we naturally take Stoicism first, as having more in common with the older schools than its rival. Indeed Zeno was accused of having plagiarized his ideas from the Academic Polemon (Diogenes, VII, 25), and Cicero, the earliest consecutive authority that happens to have survived, is fond of discussing the question whether the difference between Stoics and Peripatetics is not one of words rather than of essentials (*de fin.* III, 10, *de nat. deor.* I, 16). The question is complicated for us by our loss of the original authorities. The first three heads of the Porch, Zeno (301–261), Cleanthes (261–231) and Chrysippus (231–206), were all prolific writers, but their works lacked style—Dionysius of Halicarnassus quotes Chrysippus as a typical example of how *not* to write—and dropped out of circulation, so that we have no

---

[1] G. Murray, *op. cit.* p. 145, with additional note on Dicaearchus, pp. 149–152.
[2] W. W. Tarn, *Hellenistic Civilisation*, p. 267.

continuous account of their teaching until we come to Cicero, two centuries later, by which time it had admittedly suffered modification, and no professedly Stoic writings till Seneca: there is no extant Stoic with authority or literary power comparable with the Epicurean Lucretius. It seems however possible to consider Stoicism as an attempt to simplify the views of Aristotle, alike in metaphysics, psychology and ethics. Thus Zeno reduced Aristotle's four causes to two, which appear to be different aspects of one principle, asserted the unity of the soul against Aristotle's distinction of a rational and irrational part, and denied the Peripatetic theory of three kinds of goods, by insisting that there is no good but goodness. But while a historic continuity can thus be traced, it is only fair to repeat that Zeno introduced a moral tone and religious earnestness that transform the whole system.

In their account of the world (physics), the Stoics retained only two of Aristotle's four causes, or, to put it in another way, instead of analysing everything into Matter and Form, they postulated an original Matter and Force. Everything which exists is Matter, but as Force, the Cause, which is creative Reason (*logos*) or God, is eternally present in every part of it, the two principles may be regarded as different aspects of the same reality, though no Stoic writer explicitly identifies them. Hence we have two parallel accounts, one physical, the other metaphysical or theological, of the same Universe.

For the first the Stoics went back to Heracleitus (vol. IV, pp. 554–6). The ultimate reality is Fire, which differentiates itself into air-currents of varying tension (*tonos, i.e.* 'energy'?), upon which the material qualities of things depend—'hardness in iron, thickness in stone, and whiteness in silver' (Chrysippus *ap.* Plutarch *Moral.* 1053 F). But Fire is also Reason or God. Zeno's great originality was the identification of the *logos* of the Socratics —the regulative principle of human thinking and action—with the *Logos* of Heracleitus, to which he gave 'cosmological significance.' The Reason which is in and rules the world is one with the reason in our breasts which governs our lives. Therefore the Law of the Universe is also the law of our own nature, and we can only realize ourselves truly by conforming to the purpose of God, whose service is perfect freedom. Zeus, World-Soul, Creator, Providence, Nature, Necessity or Fate—all are but different descriptions of the same reality. And so the Stoics literally made a virtue of necessity, and Cleanthes, like John Newman, found peace in resignation:

> Lead me, O Zeus, and thou, O Destiny,
>   Lead thou me on.
> To whatsoever task thou sendest me,
>   Lead thou me on.
> I follow fearless, or, if in mistrust
> I lag and will not, follow still I must[1].

Or, as Seneca puts it,

ducunt volentem fata, nolentem trahunt.

Our wills are ours—to make them Thine.

From this followed a cosmopolitanism, which, though not a new idea in the world, found with the Stoics a clearer intellectual basis than elsewhere. 'The universe is like a community composed of gods and men, wherein the gods possess lordship and men are subjects.... And men have fellowship one with another, through partaking in reason, which is natural law' (Arius *ap.* Euseb. *Praep. Ev.* xv, xv, 3). 'Each of us owns two fatherlands, one the country in which we happen to be born, the other an Empire upon which the sun never sets' (Seneca, *de otio*, iv, 1; cf. Marcus, vi, 44, Cicero, *de fin.* iii, 63 *sq.*).

Thus the Stoics retained, what the Epicureans explicitly denied, a faith in the providential government of the world, and therein lay their strength to stand before kings and rebuke oppressors. But this faith cost them a heavy price, in compromising with contemporary superstition and allegorizing traditional mythology, while their attempted explanations of Evil drove them to some very special pleading[2]. The best expression of the metaphysical or religious side of Stoicism is to be found, curiously enough, in two famous stanzas of the Catholic poet Pope:

> All are but parts of one stupendous whole,
> Whose body Nature is, and God the soul;
> That changed through all, and yet in all the same,
> Great in the earth, as in the etherial frame,
> Warms in the sun, refreshes in the breeze,
> Glows in the stars, and blossoms in the trees,
> Lives through all life, extends through all extent,
> Spreads undivided, operates unspent,
> Breathes in our soul, informs our mortal part,

---

[1] Cleanthes *ap.* Epictetus, *Manual* 52. For his longer, more famous hymn in 39 hexameters see the translations by J. Adam, *The Vitality of Platonism*, pp. 119 *sqq.* (also quoted by R. D. Hicks, *Stoics and Epicureans*, pp. 14–16), and by E. V. Arnold, *Roman Stoicism*, pp. 85–87.

[2] See Chrysippus *ap.* Plutarch, *Moral.* 1044 c *sqq.*, and Cicero, *de nat. deor.* ii, 13–22.

As full, as perfect, in a hair as heart;
As full, as perfect, in vile man that mourns,
As the rapt seraph that adores and burns:
To him no high, no low, no great, no small,
He fills, he bounds, connects and equals all.

Cease then, nor order imperfection name;
Our proper bliss depends on what we blame.
Know thy own point: this kind, this due degree
Of blindness, weakness, Heaven bestows on thee,
Submit; in this, or any other sphere,
Secure to be as blest as thou canst bear;
Safe in the hand of one disposing Pow'r,
Safe in the natal, or the mortal hour.
All nature is but art, unknown to thee;
All chance, direction which thou canst not see;
All discord, harmony not understood;
All partial evil, universal good:
And spite of pride, in erring reason's spite,
One truth is clear—Whatever is, is right.

                              (*Essay on Man*, I, ix *sq.*)

In psychology again the Stoics returned to monism. Mansoul is not governed by two chambers—reason and an irrational part—as Aristotle taught, but by reason alone. But reason may make mistakes of partial or hasty vision, and such misjudgment or 'superfluity of impulse' is what is called 'passion.' Thus avarice rests upon a mistaken idea that money is good, pleasure is due to a false opinion of what is really desirable, etc. (Diog. Laert. VII, 110). And *all* passions, not only fear and pleasure, but also pain (which includes pity) and desire (which includes love) are forbidden to the Sage.

But the centre for Stoicism, as for its rival, lay in ethics, and here too Zeno effected a masterly simplification. Aristotle had recognized 'three kinds of goods'—goods of the body, such as good looks and health, and external goods, such as prosperity and friendship, as well as goods of the soul. Zeno on the other hand enunciated the paradox of the unique goodness of goodness. The only thing that matters is that which proceeds out of a man, the purpose or intention within his heart. 'A benefit consists not in the gift, but in the mind of the giver.' 'There can be no right action without right intention' (Seneca, *de beneficiis*, I, vi, 2, *ep.* xcv, 57). Hence of *things*, nothing is 'good' (καλόν) or has moral value (αἱρετόν) but Virtue, for outward circumstances are but material for the will; and no *action* is right (κατόρθωμα) unless proceeding from a good will. No act is right or wrong in itself, and Zeno had no objection in theory to the grossest violations of

convention, as cannibalism, incest or homosexuality[1]. But all acts
not rightly motived are sins (ἁμαρτήματα), and all sins are equal,
since one drowns as surely but one inch below the surface of the sea
as fifty fathoms down. Hence all who have not attained Virtue
remain miserable sinners. 'We have all sinned,...and we shall
continue to be failures to the end of time' (Seneca, *de clementia*,
I, 6). Similarly all things not morally good or bad are 'indifferent'
(ἀδιάφορα)—'such as life and death, good and ill report, pain
and pleasure, riches and poverty, health and sickness, and the
like' (Zeno *ap.* Stobaeus, *eclogae*, II, 90). Happiness depends alone
on Virtue.

Beside this rigid scheme of moral virtues, the Stoics recognized
another standard of relative, practical values, with a second set of
technical terms applying to acts and things. Things 'according to
nature' they allowed to have 'worth' (ἀξία) and called 'preferred'
or 'promoted' (προηγμένα, *producta*): these have no moral value,
but are 'desirable' (ληπτά, *sumenda*), whilst their opposites are
'undesirable' (ἄληπτα, *reicienda*): here the bodily and external
goods of Aristotle were placed. Again it is 'up to' us to perform
certain acts as are appropriate to the occasion, either as being suggested by Nature and contributory to harmonious living or as
admitting of reasonable defence. Such 'obligations' or duties
Zeno termed *kathekonta*, which Cicero rendered *officia*. Under
particular circumstances, we are told, it becomes *kathekon* even
for the Sage, though happy, to make his own exit from life, and
in fact both Zeno and Cleanthes found it unfitting to survive.

It has been held, by ancient as well as modern critics, that the
theory of *officia*, which popularized by Cicero's treatise proved so
attractive to the Roman mind, was an after-thought, forced upon
the original Stoicism as a concession to common sense (Cicero,
de fin. IV, 56; Zeller, *Stoics*, p. 290, etc.). But we are expressly told
that the word *kathekon* was adopted by Zeno himself (Diog. Laert.
VII, 25, 108), and Cicero is careful to make his Stoic spokesman
insist that the two standards do not imply two final standards of
Good (*de fin.* III, 22, 50.) What is the exact relation between them,
or how they can consistently be maintained beside each other, we
are never told (see Plutarch, *Moral.* pp. 1070 A, F), and modern
attempts to fill the gap are only guesswork[2].

[1] Cf. von Arnim, *Stoicorum Veterum Fragmenta*, I, p. 59.
[2] See for example G. Murray, *Essays and Addresses*, p. 100. There does
not appear to be any literary support for these explanations earlier than
Epictetus. But the refinements of Stoicism under the Empire belong to a
later volume.

VIII. EPICUREANISM

Unlike Stoicism, the system of Epicurus admitted neither continuity with previous thinkers[1] nor concessions to criticism, but it was even more direct in its subordination of everything to an ethical point of view. Neither science nor logic (which Epicurus called *Canonic*) was of any interest to him except in so far as either served to secure peace and quietness of mind. In the *epistle to Pythocles* he writes (Diog. Laert. x, 85 *sqq.*):

First then do not suppose any other end to be gained from knowledge of the skies...or from anything else, than peace of mind (*ataraxia*) and firm confidence...for what our life needs is not originality and vain opinions, but to pass our days without alarm.

We must, and can, know the fundamental truth about reality, that it consists of atoms and void and nothing else, but to dogmatize, as the astronomers do, about the causes of particular phenomena is foolish waste of time. More than one explanation is always possible of such mysteries as why the heavenly bodies rise and set or are eclipsed, and we are not in a position to decide between them; but any that is not opposed to observation is good enough, so long as it frees us from fear (*ep. to Herodotus*, Diog. Laert. x, 79 *sq.*)[2].

Above all, leave God out, exempt from responsibility and in the enjoyment of all blessedness. For if this is not secured, all our explanation of the skies will be in vain....Only let superstition be got rid of, as it will be, if we interpret the unknown in true agreement with the known. (*Ibid.* 97, 104.)

And there is one thing worse even than superstition:

It were better to follow the fairytales of gods than to be a slave to the Determinism of the scientists. The one does suggest a hope of appeasing the

---

[1] The debt to Democritus, so clear to critics, was never acknowledged by Epicurus himself or his followers.

[2] Similarly Lucretius, having suggested various causes which *may* account for the rising of the stars, concludes:

> Which of all these is in this world of ours
> The cause, 'tis hard for certain to declare,
> But what in diverse worlds diversely formed
> Is possible throughout the Universe
> Is what I shew, proceeding to assign
> For the stars' motions *reasons more than one*;
> Of which however one must be the cause
> In this world too, but which of these it is
> Our slow advance does not permit to say.   (v, 526–533.)

So also Diog. Oen. frag. 8.

gods by reverencing them, but the other implies a Necessity which is implacable. (*ep. to Menoeceus*, Diog. Laert. x, 134.)

As to the possibility of knowledge, we need not hesitate to trust our senses, for they bring us into immediate contact with reality.

There is a continuous stream from the surface of bodies,...in which the original position and order of the atoms are preserved for a considerable period, even though sometimes they are confused.... The flight of these films (*idola*) through space, if not impeded by any obstacle, takes an inconceivably short time to accomplish any conceivable distance....Our perception of shapes and our ideas are due to some one of these films from external objects invading us,...films which resemble their originals in colour and shape, on a scale accommodated to our sight or understanding.... So too, hearing is produced by a wave proceeding from the object which calls or makes a noise or sound or by whatever means excites audibility....Nor could smell, any more than hearing, have ever effected a response, had there not been certain molecules arising off the object, adapted to excite this particular organ of sense. (*ep. to Herodotus, ap*. Diog. Laert. x, 46–53.)

In this way both the subjectivity of our sensations and undeniable delusions, such as a square tower appearing round from a distance, may be explained. Either the films miss our sense-organ, or they are damaged on the way, or the mind may draw a false inference from them. Sensations in themselves are always true or real—the Greek word is the same: to deny that lands us in scepticism. But with opinions and ideas, which are the work of the mind, the possibility of error begins. These are true only when they have been attested, or at least not contradicted, by experience: we must always wait and see. Finally, our feelings assure us that pleasure is good and pain evil.

Upon this minimum of epistemological theory Epicurus proceeded to build his account of the Universe. Starting from the self-evident laws of Nature, that nothing comes from nothing or can be reduced to nothing, he deduced the existence of an infinite number of invisible, indestructible ($\check{a}\tau o\mu a$) bodies, moving eternally in infinite space. The atoms have three kinds of motion— that due to their own weight, that caused by their collisions with one another, and a third which forms the most original element in the system. It so happens that none of our fragments of Epicurus contain a mention of the famous doctrine of the Swerve, but disciples such as Lucretius and Diogenes of Oenoanda are in agreement with opponents like Cicero and Plutarch as to its existence, though there is not the same agreement as to its explanation. Thus Cicero suggests that Epicurus was 'suddenly struck by the brilliant idea' that a rain of atoms at equal speeds in parallel columns down through space would no more collide than do two lines, and that consequently there would be no Universe produced. And 'so he introduced a pure invention, and declared that the atoms swerved, just the least infinitesimal bit' (*de fin.* I, 19): he also designed by this invention to avoid the determinism of Democritus (*de nat. deor.* I, 69). But the orthodox account seems to have been that this theory, like the rest, was a direct deduction from experience. We know that there is a Universe, and therefore the atoms must have clashed. Further we know that we have freewill, and this quality, like any other, must have its cause in the atoms. Consequently the atoms swerve, and this is not contradicted by experience, for no one can see that they do not! The evidence of Lucretius is decisive:

> Moreover, if all motion is so linked
> That new from old inexorably springs
> Nor atoms swerving give the starting-point
> Of change to burst Determinism's reign
> And break the everlasting causal chain,
> Whence came into the world this privilege
> Of living things, this freedom wrung from Fate,
> By which we move according to our will
> And change our course at undetermined times
> In uncontrolled directions, as we choose?
> (II, 251–260: see the whole passage, 217–224 and 243–250.)

But while the atoms have the property of swerving 'at times and places undetermined,' we must not attribute to them consciousness or design. It was in fulfilment of no plan, but merely through 'fortuitous concourse,' that the worlds have come into being, since in the eternal process of infinite time all possible combinations and permutations must have been effected.

> For certainly it was not by design
> That atoms, gifted with intelligence,
> Arranged themselves in order, or agreed
> Upon the movements to be made by each!
> But that the ever-shifting change and chance
> Of countless numbers through the world dispersed
> Have in the buffetings of countless time
> All motions and all combinations tried
> And such positions finally assumed
> As those which constitute our Universe.
> (Lucretius, I, 1021–8.)

And let us not insult the gods by fathering upon them any concern for our weal or woe.

> For it is certain that the gods enjoy
> An immortality of perfect peace
> Apart and far removed from our concerns,
> Free from all pain and peril, in themselves
> Sufficient, needing naught of human love,
> Whom neither service wins nor passions move.
>
> (*Ibid.* II, 646–651.)

> For, though I knew not what the atoms were,
> Yet from the very workings of the skies
> I dare assert and prove by much besides—
> No God Almighty ever made for man
> A Universe of such imperfect plan.
>
> (*Ibid.* II, 177–181; v, 187–199.)

Evolution has been due to 'Nature' and man's need, to nothing else.

And man himself? The individual consists of a union of body and soul. Both are the result of temporary combinations of atoms, material and therefore mortal. And there is no Heaven beyond the grave—nor Hell. 'Therefore Death, the king of terrors, is no concern of ours, since when we exist, Death is not present, and when Death is come, then we are not' (Epicurus *ap.* Diog. Laert. x, 125). This is the crowning mercy of Epicurus' gospel, and in the 250 lines which conclude his Third Book Lucretius has exhausted human eloquence and power in his earnest endeavour to commend it.

Man therefore finds himself a stranger in a blind world, which is unconscious of his presence and unconcerned for his welfare, and he must make the best terms for himself in his few years that he can. Who will show him any good? Nature herself provides the answer.

Every living creature doth from the moment of birth pursue after Pleasure and delight therein as in the supreme good, and doth reject and so far as may be banish Pain as the supreme evil, and this it doth, being as yet not fallen from innocence, but following the pure and undefiled judgment of Nature. (Epicurus *ap.* Cic. *de fin.* I, 30.)

But what is Pleasure? In two fragments (409 and 67 Usener), continually quoted by his opponents, Epicurus said: 'The source and root of all good is the pleasure of the belly: our subtleties and refinements are reducible to this,' and 'Personally I can attach no meaning to the idea of good, if I take away the pleasures of taste, sex, etc.', but the context (which we have lost) must somehow have modified the grossness of these words, for it is certain that by 'pleasure' Epicurus really meant 'absence of pain'—an identification much ridiculed by ancient critics, but now, it seems, supported by modern psychologists[1]. In the third of the *Articles* or *Sovereign Principles* which his followers learnt by heart, we read that 'the limit of the height of pleasure is the removal of all that causes pain' (Diog. Laert. x, 139), and again in the *epistle to Menoeceus*:

When we say that pleasure is the goal, we do not mean the pleasures of the profligate which consist in sensuality, as some suppose through ignorance or prejudice or wilful misunderstanding, but the absence of pain in the body and of panic in the soul. It is not a succession of banquets and revels, nor enjoyments of boys and women nor of fish and whatever may load an expensive table, that produce the life of pleasure, but a sober calculation which examines the grounds for every choice and refusal and banishes those beliefs through which so much confusion occupies our minds. (Diog. Laert. x, 131 *sq.*)

As for sexual indulgence, 'no man was ever the better for it, and one is lucky if he is not the worse' (*ibid.* 118).

The Stoic Seneca, who loves to quote his sayings, testifies that his teaching 'is pure and upright, and if more closely studied, ascetic. His Pleasure is limited and attenuated, and the condition imposed by us on Virtue, he imposes on Pleasure: he bids it obey Nature' (*de vita beata*, 13). And Lucretius laments the folly of mankind in seeking satisfaction through power and luxury:

> O foolish, blind and miserable men!
> In thoughts how dark, in dangers how profound
> Are all your days consumed! O not to see
> That the demands of Nature are but two:—
> A body guarded and preserved from pain,
> A mind at ease, relieved from fear and strain!
>
> (II, 14–19.)

'Thanks be to the blessed mother nature,' cries Epicurus, 'that she has made necessities accessible and inaccessibles unnecessary' (*frag.* 469).

'Calculation' is necessary, of course, because 'while Pleasure is our first and native good, we do not therefore choose every pleasure. There are many occasions on which we pass over pleasures when the inconveniences consequent upon them are greater, and often we consider pains preferable to pleasures if long endurance of those pains is followed by a greater pleasure' (Diog. Laert. x, 129). Thus intelligence and self-control are needed to secure a balance of pleasure over pain, and it was easy for Epicurus to fit the four classical virtues into his scheme. Not that they have any intrinsic

---

[1] *E.g.* C. S. Sherrington, *The Integrative Action of the Nervous System* (Yale, 1920), p. 255 (quoted by Streeter, *Reality*, p. 57).

merit in themselves, but as means to the procurement of true pleasure they are essential—Wisdom, which expels panic and desire; Temperance, which bids us follow reason, and for the sake of a greater pleasure renounce the less; Courage, to bear such pains as are unavoidable; and Justice, which wins men affection and goodwill from their neighbours, and is always in the end the best policy (Cicero, *de fin.* 1, 42–53).

But of all the devices by which we seek security and happiness, there is no protection like that of Friendship (Diog. Laert. x, 148, *Article* xxvii, etc.). Epicurean friendships were proverbial, and in the simple friendliness of the Society lay, no doubt, its real strength and the secret of its appeal to the world without.

It is easy enough, of course, to criticize Epicurus. He is shrewd but superficial, amiable but indolent: his quietism suggests the charge of 'sour grapes' or lack of vitality, and his exaggerated dread of pain is a mark of decadence. His system can only exist as a parasite upon some over-ripe civilization. The Garden is too small to contain the world, and to enlarge it would require a driving-force which he could not supply and an expenditure of sweat and blood which he would mildly deprecate. His lack of faith and hope cannot be excused by his undoubted charity.

From the first the school was unpopular with the Government, whether at Athens or Rome[1], and despised by the learned (Cicero, *Tusc.* 1, 77), and it has always been compared unfavourably with its rival. But from an age of Science rather than of Faith, and a society which, like his own, has seen its foundations shaken, Epicurus may win better understanding and greater sympathy. The individual who keeps his own door-step clean and shows himself neighbour to other individuals is perhaps a more real benefactor than many eager publicists and big movements. Recent studies, here and in Italy, beginning with Lucretius and advancing to his master, have aroused new interest in the system, and with interest has grown respect. It is even possible that the old verdict may be reconsidered, in accordance with the view expressed by the late Henry Jackson, when he wrote: 'Is not Epicureanism a better philosophy than Stoicism, ἁπλῶς as well as "for poets"? Surely Epicureanism absorbs all the Stoicism that is valuable, and leaves room for something else.'[2]

[1] See W. S. Ferguson, *Hellenistic Athens*, p. 338.
[2] To Professor Platt, 17 April, 1899 (*Henry Jackson, A Memoir*, p. 146).

CHAPTER VIII

ALEXANDRIAN LITERATURE

I. ALEXANDRIA AND ALEXANDRIAN SCHOLARSHIP

THE literary historian who attempts a survey of the century which followed the death of Alexander is handicapped by the fragmentary nature of his material. That writers abounded as never before in the history of Greek literature is proved by the many names that have survived, but only too often these are indeed *nominum umbrae*. Hellenistic Prose paid the price for adaptation to the multifarious demands made upon it as the ordinary medium of expression by becoming slovenly, and in consequence, except for meagre excerpts, has failed to withstand the assaults of time. Poetry—or at any rate that poetry (and it is the characteristic type) which was written by the few for the few—has been more fortunate. But in prose and poetry alike the gifts of fortune have been scanty and capricious. This fact and the exigencies of space compel the historian to thrust certain authors into a prominence perhaps undeserved, and the reader is to remember that by their side were other writers who may well have exemplified with a difference the literary tendencies which these authors represent. All that is possible here is to mark out the main lines, to depict the main figures of Greek literature in the early Hellenistic age.

Alexandria has been called the literary capital of the Greek world in the third century B.C.—and with justice, so long as one remembers that the predominance of a capital does not exclude the existence of provincial centres and even of outlying districts, where possibly some forms of literature flourish more vigorously than in the metropolis itself. At any rate it is true to say that during this period there is practically no form of poetry—except Comedy and certain kinds of moralizing verse—to which Alexandria does not give the tone. By the middle of the century that influence has become so strong that even a poet like Euphorion, who seems to have spent his life in Old Greece and Syria, is as much subject to it as any writer who resided in the Egyptian capital. In prose Alexandria never exerted her authority so strongly. Philosophy remained the speciality of Athens. Though individual philosophers, chiefly Peripatetics, found their way to Egypt, the atmosphere was generally unfavourable to this form of intellectual activity; it is significant that the lectures of Hegesias, the apostle of pessimism, were suppressed by royal decree as detrimental to public morals. Neither apparently were Oratory and Rhetoric of great importance at Alexandria, though a good many school-declamations have turned up of late among the papyri discovered in Egypt. The diminished prestige of Oratory reflects the new political conditions, but even the indirect influence of Rhetoric is least observable in works of Alexandrian origin. It was in fact the technical sciences (geography, mathematics, physics, medicine, natural history, philology) which chiefly engaged the Alexandrian prose-writers.

The long years of war which followed the death of Alexander were less unfavourable to literary production than might have been expected. Poets indeed, except for the writers of the New Comedy at Athens, seem far from numerous; the form of verse most cultivated is the Epigram—a hardy plant, little affected by material conditions. On the other hand some branches of prose are better represented in this period than later, partly because Oratory continued to flourish in the transition period of the Diadochi, and partly because the exciting events of these years and those just past inspired a good deal of historical writing. Literature, nevertheless, had to live from hand to mouth, and it is the great merit of the Ptolemies that, being the first Hellenistic monarchs to establish a stable dynasty, they set the example of providing Letters and Science with a firmer footing. The Greeks were not unaware of their debt to Alexandria, for Athenaeus (IV, 184B) cites with approval the statement that 'it was the Alexandrians who educated all the Greeks and barbarians, when general culture was tending to disappear owing to the continuous disturbances in the age of the Diadochi.' Athenaeus and his authorities may perhaps be considered partial, but the importance of the Ptolemaic patronage of literature may be measured by comparing it with that available at this epoch in other regions of the Greek world.

As regards Macedonia, the circle of Antigonus, described elsewhere (p. 203 *sq.*), was short-lived, and in general the rulers of this kingdom may well have regarded Athens, which was usually under their control, as an adequate representative of learning within their territory. The Seleucids did more for literature. Occasional patronage, such as that of Aratus and Simonides of Magnesia by Antiochus Soter, meant little, but Antiochus the Great established a library at Antioch and put Euphorion in charge. That such encouragement was not in vain is shown a century later by the appearance of Meleager and other poets of the Phoenician school.

But the only dynasty whose interest in Letters is at all comparable with that shown by the Ptolemies is the Pergamene. The patronage of the Arts, particularly sculpture, by the Attalids is well known; they also promoted the cause of literature by inviting scholars to their court and by forming a splendid library. Though there is little to be said for the view that this library tended to concentrate on prose, while that at Alexandria paid more attention to verse, it is true that few of the literary men, whom the Attalids patronized, were poets. The reason lies partly in the fact that Hellenistic Poetry had passed its zenith before Pergamum became important, and partly in the classicist tastes of the dynasty, which, being Greek rather than Macedonian, prided itself on keeping in touch with Athens and particularly with the Attic schools of philosophy. In consequence the most notable figures among the littérateurs of Pergamum are Antigonus of Carystus, sculptor and biographer; Crates of Mallus, the Stoic grammarian; Polemon of Ilium and Demetrius of Scepsis, the antiquarians.

To turn back to Alexandria, ancient authorities are not agreed which Ptolemy, Soter or Philadelphus, founded the Library and Museum, but the undoubted connection of Demetrius of Phalerum with the origin of these institutions strongly supports the claims of the first Ptolemy, since Demetrius fell from favour under Philadelphus. In all probability Soter took the first steps towards the foundation of the Museum and Library round about 290 B.C.

Both institutions continue at Alexandria the tradition of Aristotle. The Museum is clearly modelled on the Athenian schools of philosophy, in particular the Academy and Lyceum. Demetrius, as governor of Athens, had secured the legal existence of the Peripatetic school by organizing it as a religious community formed to worship the Muses. At Alexandria, though the legal necessity no longer applied, the fiction was maintained. Such institutions are conservative, and we may therefore use Strabo's account (XVII, 793 *sqq.*) for times before his own. 'The Museum too,' he says, 'is part of the Royal Quarter; it contains a promenade and arcade, and a large building in which is the common dining-room of the scholars who are members of the Museum. This association has a common fund, and a priest in charge of the Muses' shrine, formerly appointed by the kings, but now by Caesar.' We note that the Museum is definitely under state-control. Alexander had been content to offer a subsidy to the Academy and Lyceum; Soter, who was founding a new institution, naturally retained the direction in his own hands. It is not clear what branches of knowledge were represented by the members.

Strabo speaks vaguely of 'scholars' (*philologoi*); Timon of Phlius, one of the two writers of the third century to mention the Museum (the other is Herodas), refers to philosophers in his caustic verses:

> In the thronging land of Egypt,
> There are many that are feeding,
> Many scribblers on papyrus
> Ever ceaselessly contending,
> In the bird-coop of the Muses.
>
> (*ap.* Athen. 1, 22 D, trans. Sandys.)

Probably 'philosophy' in this connection is to be widely interpreted, and we may fairly assume that a place was found for all branches of scientific research. Strabo says nothing of lecture-rooms or residential quarters, and though lectures were certainly delivered and definite 'schools,' *e.g.* of medicine and mathematics, formed at Alexandria, it is probable that such instruction was given in public halls and the like. The discussions at the Museum were 'for members only.' In short, the nearest modern parallel is such a body as the British Academy, with the not unimportant difference that the members of the Museum were subsidized.

Strabo expressly cites the example of Aristotle as having given the Egyptian kings the idea of forming a library. The collecting of manuscripts was doubtless begun under Soter, but Philadelphus may have been the first to construct the actual library, since, to begin with, the rolls were housed in certain buildings 'in heaps.' The main library was, like the Museum, in the Royal Quarter, but there was also a smaller library near the temple of Sarapis in the south-west quarter of Alexandria. This, known as the 'daughter' library, was founded after the larger one, but not later than the reign of Philadelphus; possibly it contained modern copies for the use of the general public. As to the size of the libraries, the evidence is conflicting, and this is not surprising, since it is seldom clear to what precise epoch our authorities refer and whether they are describing the contents of both libraries or only of the larger. The most credible statement is that of the Byzantine scholar Tzetzes, who says that the outer library contained 42,800 volumes (*bibloi*), while that within the Palace contained 400,000 'mixed' and 90,000 'unmixed and simple' volumes, and adds that catalogues of the books were made later by Callimachus. The last remark seems to justify us in assigning Tzetzes' figures to an early period in the history of the libraries. As regards his distinction between the 'mixed' and 'unmixed' volumes, the most reasonable view is that by the latter are meant papyrus-rolls containing a single work of small dimensions or a section of a larger work (as divided into 'books' by the Alexandrians); the 'mixed' volumes were the bigger and more cumbrous rolls, containing either two (or more) single works of smaller size or several sections of a longer work (not yet divided into 'books'). The number of the 'mixed' volumes was gradually reduced by transcription into rolls of more convenient size and by other methods. This system became general, so that, when Antony presented Cleopatra with the Pergamene library to replace the books burned at Alexandria, we are expressly told that the gift consisted of 200,000 'simple' volumes.

Such sorting-out and division was the first task of the men appointed by the Ptolemies to posts in the Library. Alexander Aetolus and Lycophron of Chalcis dealt with the Dramatists, Alexander taking Tragedy and Lycophron Comedy, while Epic and possibly Lyric Poetry fell to the lot of Zenodotus of Ephesus, who was also the first Chief Librarian. The real catalogue, we have seen, was made by Callimachus. This, his celebrated *Pinakes* in 120 books, included short lives of the chief authors and was divided under at least eight headings, viz. (1) Dramatists, (2) Epic and Lyric Poets, (3) Legislators, (4) Philosophers, (5) Historians, (6) Orators, (7) Rhetoricians, (8) Miscellaneous. A document, discovered some years ago in Egypt[1], appears to give the following succession of Chief Librarians after Zenodotus—Apollonius Rhodius, Eratosthenes, Aristophanes of Byzantium, Apollonius the Eidograph, Aristarchus, Cydas 'one of the Bodyguard.' The last was apparently a purely political appointment by Ptolemy Physcon. Since Zenodotus, Apollonius Rhodius, Eratosthenes, Aristarchus all taught the children of those Ptolemies who were contemporary with them, it is a fair conclusion that the Chief Librarian was *ex officio* tutor to the Royal Family.

To estimate the services rendered to Greek literature by the Alexandrian scholars is not altogether easy. It is their work on the Homeric Poems which is best known to-day, but our present vulgate of Homer is pre-Alexandrian and a comparatively stable text had been achieved before Zenodotus and his successors published their 'editions.' It is probably in regard to Lyric Poetry and the Drama that these scholars have the greatest claims on our gratitude. In the Classical period readers were content with such texts of any author as came their way, and there is little to show that these were too unsatisfactory; they at least gave an intelligible version, though eccentric copies were not uncommon. Still, mere

---

[1] *P. Oxy.* x, 1241. But it is perhaps doubtful how far this document is to be trusted. See especially Beloch, *Griech. Gesch.* iv², 2, pp. 592 *sqq.*

lapse of time was continually corrupting the texts, and the process was accelerated by the decay of the *polis* and the superficial extension of the Greek reading-public; the efforts of Aristophanes of Byzantium at the beginning of the second century to check this degeneration of the texts were not made a moment too soon. It is necessary then to make a distinction between the editions of Homer which were produced by the Alexandrians and the work of these scholars on the rest of Greek literature. The former were not trade-editions (some even doubt if they were published by the author in book-form), but were intended for a small public of pupils and other connoisseurs of textual criticism. This explains why they failed to affect the vulgate, and why uncertainties soon arose in regard to readings and even as to the number of editions. On the other hand the editions of the Lyric and Dramatic Poets were an attempt to provide the general public with a good text and to collect works hitherto only procurable separately; it is this practical purpose which explains the attention paid to punctuation and accents in these editions.

The Alexandrian scholars conceived it their duty in dealing with any author, firstly to establish the text, and secondly to explain the language and subject-matter. The successive editions of Homer by Zenodotus, Rhianus, Aristophanes, and Aristarchus give us the best idea of their methods. This evidence shows a constant advance in critical scholarship. Manuscript material accumulated and the very variety of readings made for caution in conjecture; at the same time with the multiplication of critical signs it became easier for an editor to indicate his opinion. Aristarchus' *Commentaries* on Homer followed the text line by line; special problems were reserved for separate *brochures* which were often polemical. The critical skill acquired in these studies was applied by Aristophanes and his successors to other kinds of Poetry and in a lesser degree to Prose. In Drama and Lyric Poetry the Aristophanic text seems to have won general acceptance, so that later scholars confined themselves mainly to exegesis. After the criticism and exposition of texts came the study of grammar for its own sake, much assisted by Stoic speculations on the origin and development of language. The first Greek Grammar was compiled by a pupil of Aristarchus, Dionysius the Thracian.

II. PROSE

The chief reason for the disappearance of so much Hellenistic Prose is to be found in its lack of attention to style. It was on this count that the so-called 'Atticist' reaction, which began to show its strength about 100 B.C., and found a powerful representative in Dionysius of Halicarnassus, a contemporary of Augustus, pronounced a damning verdict against the chief prose-writers of the period 300–100 B.C. Though later authors continued to draw their material from these writers, the general public was content to know them at second-hand, and in consequence the original works dropped out of circulation and eventually disappeared altogether. Style apart, Hellenistic Prose was subject to two influences, which contrast rather sharply with each other, and it is the failure to bridge this difference which accounts for the second-rate quality of all this literature. The first, that of the Peripatetics, may be summed up as the cult of the 'Memoir' (*hypomnema*), *i.e.* the passion for recording facts as such. This produced on the one hand a large number of reports by first-hand witnesses, but on the other the collections of *Mirabilia*, anecdotes, *et hoc genus omne*, which fill a disproportionate space in the literary activity of the time. The other influence came from Isocrates, and showed itself most plainly in the composition of history. This was treated 'rhetorically,' that is to say, truth was sacrificed for dramatic effect, or facts were perverted to point a moral. Still the ineptitudes of the compilers should not blind us to the fact that there was a good deal of grain among their chaff, and we are certainly not justified in endorsing without reservations the hard words of Polybius about the historians who immediately preceded him.

ORATORY AND RHETORIC: There was no room in the Hellenistic monarchies for the political oration which had been the glory of Demosthenic Athens; even in Old Greece the controversies of the hour found expression in party-pamphlets and tendencious histories, not in public harangues. Ancient critics accepted Demetrius of Phalerum as the last of the Attic Orators, but the most remarkable thing about Demetrius is his versatility. The composer of philosophic dialogues, declamations on imaginary topics, a history of his regency; the collector of fables and apophthegms, must have regarded his public speeches as only one form of his literary activities. An agreeable and flowery manner led critics to apply to his treatment of Oratory the dictum of Eratosthenes regarding Bion and Philosophy: both had prostituted the science with which they were concerned. Demetrius is credited with the

invention of a new type of speech, composed to put the case of a
state as favourably as possible before an all-powerful friend. Such
oratory seems to have been a speciality of the philosophers, as
being the most notable citizens that Greek states could now put
forward on these occasions. Judicial oratory lost the prestige
which it had temporarily acquired. The last orator of this type
whose works were deemed worthy of preservation was Charisius.
An imitator of Lysias, he became in turn the model of Hegesias
of Magnesia, the butt of so much Atticist criticism as the chief
exponent of the Asianic style. This style dominated the only form
of oratory which continued to enjoy undiminished popularity, viz.
the purely epideictic, though traditions of Attic sobriety may have
survived at Rhodes.

The term 'Asianic' covers two quite different perversions of
the classical style. The one is the manner of Hegesias, whom
critics like Dionysius represent as an affected and pretentious
writer in whose works strained metaphors, play upon words, and
false antitheses concealed or failed to conceal an absence of real
thought. He abandoned the periodic style of the Attic school as
involving too great a strain on the concentration of his audience,
and substituted short epigrammatic sentences such as we find so
often in Seneca. It is doubtful if this type of Asianism was so
popular as the other, the bombastic and flamboyant, an example
of which survives in the curious inscription of Antiochus of Commagene from the first century B.C., the very time when all Asia,
according to Cicero, practised this sonorous and rolling oratory.
During the supremacy of the Asianic styles the professional
rhetoricians seem to have troubled little about the principles underlying their art; it was left for philosophers, chiefly Peripatetics
and Stoics, to write on this subject. But some sort of technical
training must have been available for aspiring speakers, and in
the second century an ambitious effort to formulate an *Art of
Rhetoric* was made by Hermagoras of Temnos. Though important
for the technique of oratory, he apparently contributed nothing
to the discussion of style and language. These problems were left
to the critics of Pergamum and Rhodes and the classicist reaction.

History: The writing of history had travelled a long way since
Herodotus and Thucydides, the one the heir of the Epic, the
other himself a man of action and a political thinker as well (see
vol. v, chap. xiv). Apart from Xenophon, the most notable among
Thucydides' successors were Philistus of Syracuse, the historian
of the two tyrants Dionysius, and Cratippus, for whom some
scholars claim the authorship of the important historical fragment

known as the *Hellenica Oxyrhynchia*. Whatever their merits—
and Cicero calls Philistus a 'miniature Thucydides'—neither
writer attracted a large public, but they were followed by two
historians, Ephorus of Cyme and Theopompus of Chios, whose
vogue both in their own age and afterwards was very considerable.
Both men were products of Isocrates' 'workshop,' but their
temperaments were in sharp contrast, Ephorus, according to his
teacher's famous remark, needing the spur, Theopompus the
bridle. The *Hellenica* of Ephorus exhibits several novelties. The
first Universal History produced by a Greek, in the sense that it
embraced the history of all the Greeks from the Return of the
Heracleidae down to 340 B.C., it consisted of thirty Books (the
last added by the author's son), of which each was a unity in
itself. The arrangement was according to subject-matter, with
possibly some application of the annalistic method in the later
Books. Ephorus' reading had been large, and some of the fragments show that he was not devoid of critical sense, but his precept was better than his practice. He made many mistakes in
topography and geography, while the unreality of the harangues
which he inserted into his battle-descriptions became proverbial.

Theopompus was a more interesting, but hardly, it seems,
more trustworthy writer. His earlier work, the *Hellenica* in
twelve Books, probably covered the period 410–394 B.C., thus
continuing the narrative of Thucydides. Considerably more
famous was his *Philippica* in fifty-eight Books. Like Ephorus,
Theopompus had been affected by Isocrates' ideas of national
unity, but, more practically-minded than his fellow-historian, he
applied these ideas to contemporary politics, and grouped his
story round the rise of Macedon, as illustrated by the career of
Philip. Polybius finds fault with Theopompus for his pro-
Macedonian bias; a commoner charge is that of exaggerated
severity in the appraising of character and assignment of motives,
so that Nepos, for instance, calls him *scriptor maledicentissimus*.
In his fondness for psychological analysis he anticipated Tacitus.
The *Philippica* abounded in digressions—among them a description of a completely imaginary land of wonders, called Meropis.
Though he had roved about the world, Theopompus was not
exempt from the pedantry which marks the Isocratean school,
and, like Ephorus, he was weakest when dealing with matters of
fact (for example, battles) which called for a certain amount of
technical knowledge. Still he had the advantage of being contemporary with the events which formed his main theme, and

the loss of his chief work has robbed us of a valuable supplement
to the Athenian account of the Demosthenic age.

Another regrettable loss is that of the *Hellenica* of Callisthenes,
the philosopher of Olynthus; it covered the years 387–357 B.C.,
and comprised ten Books. Callisthenes' earliest work had been
a monograph on the Third Sacred War; his *Hellenica* exhibited
sympathy with the pretensions of Macedon, and it is not surprising to find him accompanying Alexander as the self-appointed
chronicler of his campaigns. His account, entitled *The Deeds
of Alexander*, a work abruptly terminated by his execution (vol.
VI, pp. 398–400), exercised great influence at the time of its
publication, and on the later vulgate about Alexander (*ibid.*
p. 352 n.).

Theopompus and Ephorus set the fashion, and nearly all the
historical works of larger scope written in the early Hellenistic
age betray the influence of rhetoric, the notable names being
Cleitarchus of Colophon, Timaeus of Tauromenium, Duris of
Samos, Phylarchus, and the notorious Hegesias. The most
rhetorical of these is Cleitarchus, whose *History of Alexander*
held the field till Arrian went back to more sober authorities
(vol. VI, p. 352 n.). The leading idea of his work seems to
have been the gradual demoralization of Alexander, intoxicated
by success and Eastern luxury. Cicero cites Cleitarchus as
an example of the rhetorician's privileged mendacity in history.
Timaeus on the other hand was not a professional *rhetor*,
and his great *History of Sicily* must have possessed many good
qualities. The son of a small tyrant driven out by Agathocles,
whom he could never forgive, Timaeus established himself at
Athens and devoted his life to research and writing. Polybius
derides him as a stay-at-home pedant and bookworm, but Timaeus
was something more. His indiscriminate collecting of odds and
ends of information gained him the nickname of 'the old rag
woman,' but not all his material came from books, and the scholars
of Alexandria were quick to recognize its value. For his love of
passing moral judgments he was christened Epitimaeus (the
Censorious) by Istrus. Traces of rationalism which crop up in
the fragments are hard to reconcile with the numerous proofs of
his superstition, for example, his belief in the importance of
coincident dates or his explanation of military disasters as due to
acts of sacrilege by the losing side. Sometimes he appears hardly
serious, as when he says that the fact that Nicias (the man of
victory) was against the Sicilian Expedition portended its failure,
or pretends that Hermes used Hermocrates to punish the

Athenians for the mutilation of the Hermae! These puerilities
seem part of the Asianic style which we find more fully developed
in Hegesias, and, though there is too little material to reconstruct
the latter's *History of Alexander*, one may conjecture that it showed
Timaeus' vices but lacked his virtues.

Duris of Samos, a pupil of Theophrastus, became the tyrant
of his native island about 300 B.C. He was the author of many
works, among them a *Chronicle of Samos*, a *History of Greece* from
370 to 281 B.C. (or later), a biography of Agathocles, and numerous
compilations (*About Laws*, *About Athletic Contests*, *About Painters*).
These last reveal the Peripatetic and prepare us for the similar
works of Callimachus and his school. Duris found fault with contemporary writing of history as deficient in realism (*mimesis*), and
tried to remedy this by exactitude in detail (especially of costume),
emphasis on apparently unimportant particulars, anecdotes about
his characters' private lives and the like. Tragic or pathetic scenes
were his *forte*, and we catch a glimpse of his powers in passages of
Diodorus Siculus and Plutarch, who used him as a source. But
his passion for vividness was greater than his love of truth.
Phylarchus, whose *Histories* covered the period 272–220 B.C.,
gave a lively account of the attempts at reform in Sparta by Agis
and Cleomenes (pp. 739 *sqq.*). As an ardent supporter of Cleomenes, he is denounced by Polybius, who favoured Aratus, and
even Plutarch admits his bias and love of theatrical devices, but at
least he has managed to make his hero stand out sharp and
clear against the background of his time.

With History thus delivered over to Rhetoric, it was a fortunate
thing that men were found who 'had first lived through or played
a part in the thing they wrote, and afterwards wrote down the
thing they knew.' Such were Ptolemy Soter and Aristobulus, the
chief authorities for Arrian's account of Alexander. There were
others, besides these two, who seem to disprove Strabo's sweeping
assertion that all the companions of Alexander preferred the
marvellous to the true, for example Chares of Mytilene, the Royal
Chamberlain; Baeton and Diognetus, Alexander's route-mea-
surers; Nearchus, his admiral. With a larger canvas, but on the
same basis of fact and personal experience, Hieronymus of Cardia,
perhaps the greatest of Hellenistic historians, told the story of the
Diadochi and their successors. His work has vanished, but we
know enough of his personality and of the great advantages which
he enjoyed by having access to the Macedonian archives to suspect
the extent of our loss (p. 203).

Two fields of historical writing much cultivated at this time were the local history and the history of foreign countries. Some authors like Duris and Neanthes, the annalist of Cyzicus, combined local with general history. The accounts of Attic history (*Atthides*), which first appear in the fourth century and culminate in the great work of Philochorus (*ob.* 262 B.C.) were rather chronicles than formal histories. Rich in details on institutions, ritual, and topography, they were ransacked for information by the Alexandrians. The history of Sparta too attracted many students; these were chiefly philosophers, who saw their ideals realized in the Spartan type. Local history had always been popular in the islands and among the Greeks of Asia Minor; the type prevalent there seems to have included a larger element of fiction than that found on the mainland, and the debt of the poets to this source was correspondingly greater. Yet these records were often taken seriously, as is proved by the arbitration of the Rhodians between Priene and Samos, when, besides Theopompus, four Samian and two Ephesian local historians were cited as witnesses, and the evidence of the Milesian chronicle of Maeandrius was rejected as that of a forgery.

Though it is probable that in the various countries which now came under Macedonian or Greek sway the new rulers and their Greek subjects acquired only a very meagre knowledge of the native cultures, still the large number of historical and geographical works dealing with foreign lands shows a certain increase in curiosity. Three countries attracted attention above the rest; Egypt, Babylonia, and India. For Egyptian history the most trustworthy guide was Manetho, high-priest at Heliopolis, who dedicated to Philadelphus an *Aegyptiaca* in three books, based on the hieroglyphic records. A similar history of Babylon dedicated to Antiochus Soter by Berosus, priest of Bel in Babylon, found, though not immediately, a wider public. Comparison of his statements with the cuneiform inscriptions shows that he followed his native sources fairly closely. The great Hellenistic authority on India was Megasthenes, who on several occasions between 302 and 291 B.C. was sent as envoy of Seleucus to the Indian king Sandrakottos. He was a curious observer of lands and peoples, and gave much useful information on the flora and fauna, on the caste-system, and generally on the habits of the natives. Eratosthenes and Strabo denounce him as a liar, but modern scholars, finding his evidence corroborated by contemporary Indian records, are content to charge him with nothing worse than credulity[1].

[1] See *Cambridge Hist. of India,* I, pp. 398 *sqq.*

Autobiographies were surprisingly scarce, and, save for that of Aratus of Sicyon, comparatively unimportant. But if these were rare, biographies were numerous. Under this heading the Greeks included not only the narration of an individual's life, but also the description of national or other types. The third century produced nothing so scientific as Dicaearchus' *Life of Greece*, a history of Greek civilization; for a work of Clearchus of Soli, in which he described the lives of various races and of different types—the glutton, the parasite, and so on—seems to have been marked by all the failings of the later Peripatetics. This school had practically a monopoly of such writing, as of biography proper. The latter starts with the researches of Aristoxenus into the life of Pythagoras, and is continued by Chamaeleon at the beginning and by Satyrus and Hermippus at the end of the third century. These later writers took little trouble to sift the true and false elements in the popular tradition; in fact they often added inventions of their own. Enough survives of Satyrus' *Lives of the Dramatists*, composed in the form of a dialogue, to show that these biographies were intended primarily as light reading. Chamaeleon and the rest concerned themselves with the ancients; it is the exception to find a writer who describes the life of his contemporaries, though the career of such a man as Agathocles provoked a literary warfare soon after his death. But luckily there was one man who thought it worth while to note down his reminiscences of the great men whom he had known. This was Antigonus of Carystus, whose *Lives of the Philosophers*, as excerpted by later authors, is our most valuable source for the intimate life of the third century.

GEOGRAPHY: Alexander's conquests and the subsequent intercourse of the Diadochi with the states lying beyond their boundaries led to a great increase in the geographical knowledge of the Greeks. We have seen the Seleucid monarchy in communication with India. The Ptolemies for their part were naturally interested in the little known lands situated south of Egypt; Philadelphus, in particular, furthered the opening-up of Ethiopia, partly to facilitate his supply of elephants, and partly in order to obtain new medicinal herbs. His agents sent back reports, and the description by his admiral Timosthenes of the harbours of the Red Sea and the Mediterranean was long a standard work. Exploration was no monopoly of the monarchies; mercantile communities sought out new avenues for trade. On the basis of the information thus acquired, and with the help of astronomy and mathematics, Eratosthenes produced his great system of scientific geography.

Among the original explorers three figures stand out more clearly than the rest. Nearchus, who commanded Alexander's fleet on its voyage down the Indus and across the Indian Ocean to the Euphrates, wrote an account of his experiences distinguished by accuracy of observation and sound judgment, as may be seen from his story, preserved in Arrian (*Ind.* 30), of the shoal of whales encountered on his journey (vol. VI, p. 416). Patrocles explored the Caspian for Seleucus I, and was responsible for the mistaken idea that this sea was a gulf of the all-encircling Ocean. Most notable of all, Pytheas late in the fourth century sailed from Marseilles through the Straits of Gibraltar and up the coast of Spain and France to the limits of Britain (see p. 53). Some of the observations attributed to Pytheas may represent the deductions of later geographers drawn from the information which he furnished, but it is beyond doubt that he was possessed of more scientific knowledge than the average explorer of his day. He was the first Greek to note the influence of the moon on the tides, as he was the first to give anything like an accurate account of Britain and its inhabitants. He discovered the existence at least of Thule six days sail northwards from Britain on the Arctic Circle. His travels were recorded in a book called *About the Ocean*, to which Eratosthenes was indebted for much valuable information.

ERATOSTHENES himself is the most characteristic figure of Alexandrian Prose. Born at Cyrene, probably in 276–5 B.C., he was first Callimachus' pupil at Alexandria, and then studied at Athens until he was recalled about 246 B.C. by Euergetes to succeed Apollonius Rhodius as Chief Librarian. His versatility was proverbial and earned him the nicknames of *Beta* and *pentathlos* (the latter because athletes who competed in this kind of contest were not usually first-class in any one branch). Actually his published works embraced poetry, philosophy, grammar and philology, chronology, geography. His writings on the last two subjects were more important than his learned verse or the many dialogues of which Suidas speaks or even his magnum opus on the Old Comedy. In chronology his chief work was his *Chronographiae* in at least nine Books. About a century later his system was adopted by Apollodorus of Athens as the basis of a versified treatise on the subject, and so exerted a lasting influence. Eratosthenes began with the capture of Troy, which he placed in 1184 B.C., and went down to the death of Alexander. It has been doubted whether he claimed absolute truth for his dating of events earlier than 776 B.C., *i.e.* the first Olympian contest for which the names of the victors were preserved; certainly in the fragments he dis-

tinguishes between the mythical and historical periods. For the
earlier period he seems to have chosen the lists of the Spartan
kings as his guide; for the later he adopted the system introduced
by Timaeus of reckoning by Olympiads, and on this subject he
wrote a monograph. The fragments contain some evidence of his
method; thus we find him inferring the priority of Homer to
Hesiod from the difference in their geographical outlook, and
pointing out that Homer must have preceded the Ionian migrations since he shows no knowledge of such things as the
Panionia.

As a geographer Eratosthenes owed his eminence to the fact
that he was no mean mathematician; a method of finding the
sequence of prime numbers was called after him, and he invented
a mesolabe (p. 307). Accordingly, it is not surprising to find him in
correspondence with Archimedes, who as a young man dedicated
one of his works to him. Eratosthenes' most important contributions to geography were contained in two works, a special
treatise called *On the Mensuration of the Earth* and a *Geographica*
in three Books. In the former he calculated the circumference of
the earth to be about 28,000 miles, arriving at this result by means
of observations of the position of the sun at noon in Alexandria
and Syene at the time of the summer-solstice; the close approximation to the correct figure (24,860 miles) has been often admired.
In Book I of the *Geographica* he traced the history of Greek
geography from Homer to the historians of Alexander. His
attitude to the Homeric Question was notable and in sharp contrast with the allegorical interpretation made popular by the
Stoics. Regarding the poems, like all poetry, as primarily intended to charm rather than to instruct, he denied among other
things that it was possible to fix exactly the route of Odysseus'
wanderings. 'To find the route followed by Odysseus' he said,
'you must first discover the cobbler who sewed up the bag of the
winds.' In Book 11 he stated his own views on the shape and size
of the earth, and on the nature and extent of the Ocean. Book 111
gave a descriptive geography of the world in accordance with his
map, on which the *oecumene* or inhabited world was divided by a
line, running from Gades to the middle of Asia, into a northern
and southern half, each of which was cut up into segments. By
this division Eratosthenes restored, while bringing it up to date,
the old Ionian scheme of two continents (Asia and Europe). In
fact, despite his criticism of earlier geographers, it would be a
mistake to regard Eratosthenes as a radical innovator; how far his
theories had been anticipated by his immediate predecessors,

particularly Dicaearchus, remains uncertain, but some of his conclusions did in fact represent a compromise, and it was this weakness that drew down upon him the strictures of a later and more severe scientist, Hipparchus of Nicaea. As treated by the latter and his followers, geography became too technical a subject for the layman, while on the other hand writers like Polybius and Strabo, by their emphasis on its practical utility, unduly minimized the importance of its scientific basis[1].

POPULAR PROSE-WORKS: There was a great demand in the Hellenistic age for books that were intended merely to amuse or were adapted to convey information in not too austere a manner. Even History, as we saw, was affected by this demand; the work of such a writer as Cleitarchus was little better than a historical novel, and the historical dialogues (for example on Peisistratus, on Antipater and Olympias) which have come to light among the papyri show the same tendency to popularization. Philosophy underwent the same process; hence the Diatribe of Bion and the rest, as also the tracts on self-help and good manners, the numerous symposia, the collections of philosophical apophthegms and anecdotes. How far such frames as these were employed for the treatment of non-philosophical themes, is uncertain; we have as yet no Alexandrian equivalent of the *Cena Trimalchionis*, but it is quite possible that Menippus of Gadara, for instance, had anticipated Petronius. Certainly the *Chriae*, *i.e.* the collections of acts and remarks from which a moral could be extracted, had a lighter counterpart in the writings of Lynceus of Samos, the author of an *Art of Shopping* which advised a niggardly friend how to deal with the 'murderous fishmongers'; of letters in which he described to his acquaintances the superb dinner-parties given by the *demi-monde* and visiting royalties at Athens; and of anecdotes and *bons mots* attributed to courtesans and flatterers.

Another much favoured type of compilation was that of the so-called *Paradoxa*, wonders or peculiarities in nature such as strange animals, plants, or rivers. Curiosity about these things becomes more marked from the fourth century onwards. Historians inserted such marvels to add colour to their narrative, while philosophers either tried to explain them scientifically or used them to demonstrate the existence of Providence. Hellenistic collections of *Paradoxa* were many, both in prose and verse; one by Antigonus of Carystus is extant, Callimachus and his pupils wrote others.

Another form of composition which separates itself off from

[1] For Greek mathematics and science in this period see chap. IX.

History in this age and approximates to the novel is Mythography.
Collections of myths were made later for two purposes, either for
use in schools or elsewhere, or occasionally to provide poets with
their subject-matter; in the Hellenistic age a more definitely
rationalizing treatment was in vogue, if we may judge by the
works of Palaephatus and Euhemerus. The latter came from
Messana in Sicily and was employed by Cassander on distant
embassies in the South and East. In his book, *The Sacred List*,
he told how, setting out from Arabia into the Indian Ocean, he
arrived at the three islands of Panchaea, of which the capital was
called Panara. On a golden pillar in the shrine of Zeus Triphylios
at Panara he claimed to have found an inscription which commemorated the deeds of Ouranos, Cronos, and Zeus, formerly
kings of Panchaea. Arguing from this, Euhemerus proposed a
similar origin for the other Greek gods and goddesses; his explanation of Aphrodite as the first courtesan is typical of his
method. The deification of Heracles and Dionysus afforded a
parallel to the development imagined by Euhemerus, but his
disciples (the most famous is Ennius) were much outnumbered
by his critics, among whom Callimachus and Eratosthenes were
the earliest. Euhemerus did not regard all gods as having a
mortal origin; some—for example, the sun, moon, stars, winds—
he explained as personified powers of nature. He seems to have
borrowed some of his ideas from a writer who was slightly earlier,
Hecataeus of Abdera. In a book dealing with Egypt, Hecataeus
described the Egyptians as the originators of civilization, and
commended their political institutions and religious beliefs. His
ideal constitution was apparently a paternal despotism. The
element of fiction was less veiled in another work, *Concerning the
Hyperboreans*, in which he represented this people as living in the
bliss of innocence on an island off north-west Europe, and remarkable for their friendliness to the Greeks.

   The names of other writers of such romances are known to us,
for instance Amometus who described the Utta Kourou of the
Himalaya, Antiphanes of Berga in Thrace (whose birth-place
gave its name to a verb meaning 'to lie like Munchausen'), and
finally Iambulus. The excerpts of Diodorus from the narrative of
the last-named show that Iambulus provided plenty of incident
—some of it perhaps based on actual experiences of himself or
contemporaries—during the course of his story, how he went as
merchant to the Cinnamon country, was captured by pirates and
then by Ethiopians, and turned adrift with other captives on a
ship which eventually reached a Blessed Isle inhabited by amiable

natives. The description of this island, by some identified as Ceylon, of its natural wonders, of its strange and fortunate inhabitants, occupied the greater part of the book. After living there seven years the narrator and his companions were sent away as failing to reach the islanders' high standard of virtue. After suffering shipwreck on the Indian coast Iambulus alone reached Palimbothra, whence he returned to Greece with the assistance of the local king who, like the Hyperboreans, was a philhellene. Though the tendencious element is less conspicuous in Iambulus' romance than in those of Hecataeus and Euhemerus, it is plain that he belongs to the same school of writing. It does not appear that anything on the lines of the later Greek Novel was composed in this age (the earliest example of such literature is the fragmentary *Story of Ninus*, which is thought to belong to the first century B.C.), but no doubt the exercises of the rhetorical schools contained the germ of such works of fiction; in Imperial Rome, as we see from the works of the elder Seneca, some of the themes set to pupils in rhetoric were quite romantic, and the medieval story-teller drew several novels from this source.

III. POETRY: GENERAL FEATURES

While the Prose of the Hellenistic age was a natural development from that of the fourth century, its Poetry, if we except Comedy and the Epigram, exhibits no such continuity of tradition. The Athenians had exalted Drama at the expense of other departments of poetry; it was still written, but the new conditions called for something more intimate, less dependent on popular support. A revival of non-dramatic forms of verse is first visible, about 300 B.C., in the cities along the south-western coast of Asia Minor and on the adjacent islands, the chief figures being Philetas of Cos, Asclepiades of Samos, and Simias of Rhodes. The first two at any rate gathered pupils and associates round them, so that we find Hermesianax of Colophon, Theocritus of Syracuse, and Zenodotus of Ephesus connected with Philetas, while Poseidippus of Pella and Hedylus of Samos (or Athens), slightly junior to Asclepiades, share his society and collaborate with him in the production of a 'Garner of Epigrams.' In those days it was an easy step from Cos or Samos to Alexandria, and while the older poets remained attached to their native soil, the younger usually found their way to Egypt. The coterie-spirit in which they had been bred throve in the atmosphere of the Museum; a remarkable facility of intercourse between men of letters extended these traditions over the Greek world. The poets of this period write for each other and a limited public of cultured amateurs; they form an exclusive society, in which mutual admiration and detraction have every opportunity for display. Poetry itself was becoming more and more a matter of the word written to be read, not heard; authors like Theocritus and Callimachus may have given preliminary recitations of their compositions to a select audience of intimates, but oral delivery before a large public must have been confined to the popular productions recited at city-festivals and similar gatherings, and these were apparently the work of second-rate poets. For the Alexandrians the conditions of literary production were already almost the same as those prevailing later at Rome; they reached their public through the bookseller. Theocritus probably 'published' his pieces separately, and the stray poems were not gathered together till the first century B.C., but a collected edition, arranged by the author, is possible for Callimachus and more than likely for Herodas. Apollonius was perhaps the first writer to publish an epic poem carefully divided into 'books.' These innovations brought with them gain as well as loss, for, while they favoured a 'bookish' and rather artificial poetry, in certain departments—notably Lyric and the Epigram—the writer now enjoyed a liberty of manœuvre previously denied to him.

In form this poetry was marked by a reaction against the standards and fashions of the later Athenian period. This is true even of Alexandrian Drama—or at any rate Tragedy. The members of the once famous Tragic Pleiad at Alexandria seem to have gone back beyond Euripides to Phrynichus and Aeschylus; their versification exhibits archaic strictness, while their liking for historical subjects recalls the *Capture of Miletus* and the *Persae*. The Satyr-play came into vogue again, either as a frame for themes which belonged to Pastoral Poetry, or adapted—as by Lycophron in his *Menedemus*—for playful satire of contemporaries. Of native Alexandrian Comedy we know very little, but its existence seems to be attested by comic fragments found in Egypt which contain references to local officials and institutions; we have further the name of Machon, a Peloponnesian resident in Alexandria, praised by a later poet for having transplanted the spirit of the Old Comedy to the banks of the Nile, a boast not confirmed by the fragments, which smack of the New.

The poetic forms most favoured by the Alexandrians were the Epic, the Elegy, the non-choral Lyric, the Iambus, and the Epigram. In the opinion of most, exact reproduction of the earlier types was neither possible nor desirable. Epic on the grand scale involved difficulties which seemed insuperable; hence the greater number favoured the short epic poem which it is the fashion to call the *Epyllion*, or the looser structure of compositions modelled on the Hesiodic catalogue-poetry and didactic verse. In an earlier age Epic had been confined in the main to narrative, but it is characteristic of the Alexandrians to disregard the frontiers which had previously separated the departments. The *Epyllion* in consequence borrowed some details of treatment from the Elegy and Lyric Poetry, while the Elegy itself, after the example set by Antimachus of Colophon in the fourth century, was chiefly employed for purposes of narrative, though Callimachus at least turned it into a sort of maid-of-all-work. Lyric Poetry, shaking off the trammels of its musical accompaniment—the Alexandrians despised the popular dithyramb, in which sense was subordinate to sound—showed a versatility which is impressive even in the sparse fragments that survive. Old metres (those of Sappho and Alcaeus) were revived by Asclepiades and Theocritus; new metres were introduced and developed, for instance, the Hendeca-syllabic by Phalaecus, the Galliambic by Callimachus. The debt of Horace in his *Odes* to these poets, though we cannot check it, must have been considerable. The *Scazon*, *i.e.* 'limping,' Iambus had been the weapon of the Satirist Hipponax in the sixth century; in this age Phoenix and Callimachus used it for popular fables and to air their views on morals and literature, while Herodas adapted it for dramatic scenes which drew much of their subject-matter from Sophron's Mimes, written in rhythmical prose. Theocritus too, at any rate in his mimes of town-life, owed something to Sophron, but preferred hexameters as his medium. The Epigram, unlike the forms of poetry mentioned above, had been cultivated throughout the period of Athens' literary supremacy; the de-velopment of its two earliest types, the epitaph and the dedication, had been accelerated by the Persian Wars, and in the fourth century the collection of epigrams from the stones into books had paved the way for the book-epigram. In this field the Alexandrians continued the work of their immediate predecessors.

In view of the Hellenistic attitude to Poetry it is not surprising that certain traditional sources of inspiration were closed to these writers. Religion for instance, as a serious motive, plays no part in Alexandrian Poetry. Aratus, it is true, professes the Stoic doc-trine of Divine Providence, but his fellow-poets left such things to the philosophers. Cleanthes' fine *Hymn to Zeus* and the poem of Callimachus which bears the same title have one thing only in common—the fact that they were composed in the same age. For the Alexandrians religion spelt mythology. The Olympians were on the same level as the heroes and heroines of Greek story, interesting figures whose biographies, rich in varied detail, gave the poet excellent opportunities for parading his erudition, but nothing more. Like the heroes they could be reduced to the ordinary scale of bourgeois existence, and this is the favourite method of Callimachus, who, for instance, makes the infant Artemis address Zeus as 'papa,' when she is coaxing him to increase her privileges. Apollonius caught the infection and uses this style in the scene from the *Argonautica*, where Hera and Athene visit Aphrodite to secure her intervention with Eros. The easy manner of Cypris in undress, her reproaches for the tardiness of their call, her complaints about her naughty son recall the Mimes of Theocritus and Herodas. At times, no doubt, and particularly by Apollonius, the gods are treated with more dignity, but the emotion then excited can hardly be called religious.

Yet Callimachus can create a religious atmosphere—or a very good substitute for one. The opening of his *Hymn to Apollo* is effective:

How the laurel branch of Apollo trembles! How trembles all the shrine! Away, away ye sinners! Hark! Phoebus knocketh at the door with his fair foot.... Of yourselves now, ye bolts, be pushed back, of yourselves, ye bars! The god is no longer far away!

Similarly in the 'holy story' of Demeter's starving of Erysichthon, despite the mocking realism—'he ate the race-horse and the war-charger and the cat at which the little vermin trembled'—not everything seems caricature.

Patriotic poetry in the manner of earlier Greece was not to be expected in this age, but cities and peoples were interested in their past. Hence in verse, as a *pendant* to the prose-chronicles, arose the *encomia* of towns and districts, and on a larger scale the tribal epics, of which the most famous was Rhianus' *Messeniaca*, a sort of bandit-romance with Aristomenes for its hero (vol. III, p. 557). A sentimental enthusiasm for their homeland occasionally colours the poetry even of expatriated Alexandrians, such as Theocritus and Callimachus, but the only representative of a sterner patriotism is Alcaeus of Messene, who in the second century assailed Philip V of Macedon with biting epigrams.

If religion and patriotism were too remote, natural science, another possible theme, was perhaps too near. The Alexandrians were not tempted to celebrate the scientific achievements of the colleagues whom they met at the Museum. Aratus is no real exception, for the prose-authors whom he versified belong to the fourth century and his astronomical knowledge was hardly up-to-date. Eratosthenes himself wrote a poem about the stars, but this composition, with its story of the amour of Hermes and Aphrodite, was little more than an *epyllion* staged in the heavens. Other writers of didactic verse chose topics so repellent that their lack of success is easy to understand. A much more gifted poet than Nicander might be excused failure when dealing with 'Antidotes to Poisons' and 'Snake-bites.'

But there was one field of knowledge in which the Alexandrians were intensely interested. This was the record of the Greek nation's infancy, contained in a mass of information—mythological, historical, geographical, religious—which had been handed down from the earliest times, and now, as collected in the great libraries, was accessible to the exploring student. At the end of the fifth century the epic poet Choerilus had complained that the themes of poetry were exhausted; the Alexandrians showed that such despair was premature. Leaving the repetition of Pan-Hellenic saga to others, who foolishly 'cackled in vain against the Chian bard,' they devoted themselves to the poetic treatment of the less-known stories and particularly of the so-called Local Legends, to which the popular fancy of early Greece had given birth in such abundance, but which the literature of the Classical period had scarcely noticed. The purpose of these stories was generally to explain some local custom or ritual or feature of the country-side, and it was this 'aetiological' element which chiefly commended them to the Alexandrians, but it is remarkable that the explanations offered very often traced things back to a love-affair (usually unhappy) between two mortals or between a mortal and a god or goddess. It was for this reason that Parthenius, the teacher of Gallus and Virgil, included so many of these narratives in his collection of 'Tragic Love-Stories,' which is still extant. The material was promising, and with it the Alexandrians might have produced a genuinely romantic poetry, but they were fatally hampered by two defects, excess of learning and lack of heart.

Callimachus in his *Aetia* rebukes himself for almost blurting out a disrespectful anecdote about Zeus and Hera with the words: 'Verily much knowledge is a grievous ill for him that controls not his tongue: surely such a man is like a child with a knife.' The lines furnish an apt comment on the abuse of erudition which characterizes so much Alexandrian Poetry. Had these writers trusted more to their imagination and less to their authorities, had less observance been paid to Callimachus' principle, 'I sing nothing for which I cannot produce evidence,' they would have achieved far greater things. The defect was perhaps inherent. Antimachus, fore-runner of the Alexandrians, had been the first Greek scholar-poet; Philetas and Simias were not unworthy successors. The appointment of poets to deal with the treasures of the Alexandrian Library, which is explained by this tendency, gave fresh impetus to it. Callimachus, Apollonius, Lycophron, all produced works of solid scholarship in prose. As the years pass, the poet yields to the *savant*; Aristarchus, a scholar pure and simple, represents the inevitable conclusion of this development.

While the learned men of letters at Alexandria still wrote verse, it was natural that it should serve to display the fruits of their reading, but in this matter they went far beyond the bounds of good taste. Callimachus' lengthy extract of Cean history from the prose-chronicle of Xenomedes effectually shatters such illusion as has been achieved by the preceding recital of the love-story of Acontius and Cydippe, a tale taken from the same source; Phanocles' lines on the murder of Orpheus possess some charm, but the aetiological excursus on the tattooing of Thracian women is, where it stands, simply ridiculous; even Theocritus sins in this way, when he concludes his story of the infant Heracles and the snakes with the bald list of the demi-god's instructors. In these instances the poet is over-anxious to convey information; in others he teases the reader by concealing it. The vocabulary of Alexandrian Poetry consists largely of 'glosses,' that is obscure words (many of them already obsolete in Homer's day), which Aristotle in his *Poetics* had recommended as an ornament of poetry and which Philetas and Simias had collected into dictionaries. Further, some writers definitely cultivated an enigmatic or riddling style. In the Pattern-Poems, an invention of Simias, written or originally supposed to be written on the object described, as an egg, or a shepherd's pipe, such a form of expression was the rule. The *Alexandra* is one vast riddle; Euphorion affected the same obscurity. Callimachus too does not spare his audience on occasion. Thus in his elegiac *Victory of Sosibius*, he refers to the victor on the strength of his Isthmian and Nemean successes as 'twice-crowned hard by both children, the brother of Learchus and the infant who was suckled with Myrine's milk.' A hard nut to crack without a mythological dictionary!

The Alexandrians have been charged with unrestrained indulgence in sentiment, but their narrative poetry at any rate certainly errs in the opposite direction. Love between the two sexes plays, as we have seen, a great part in such poetry, but the Medea of Apollonius is the only instance of real passion vividly described. Alexander Aetolus, in his *Apollo*, told the story of Cleoboea's guilty love for Antheus, her husband's guest; how, repulsed, she asked the young man to descend into a well to fetch a golden pail which she had dropped there, and then crushed him to death with a heavy stone: after which she hung herself. Alexander's narrative is almost as bald as the summary given above. Even in the more personal poetry of the Alexandrians— Epigram, Lyric, Pastoral—emotional treatment of love between the sexes is the exception. The love-epigrams of Asclepiades are more sincere than those of later poets, such as Meleager, but the artifices of erotic poetry are already there. Only one of Calli- machus' epigrams is addressed to a woman; it is a conventional plaint by an excluded lover. Theocritus' Simaetha in Idyll 11 is a unique figure, and the resemblances with the *Alexandrian Erotic Fragment* suggest that the vividness of Theocritus' picture comes in some degree from contact with the popular art of the Mime set to music. Apart from this, it is only in some epigrams of Callimachus and in certain poems of Theocritus, inspired by their boy-loves, that we find heart-felt emotion expressing itself.

It is well known that the Alexandrians show a greater interest in the life and scenery of the country than their predecessors, and it is claimed that this interest is a natural reaction from the arti- ficial conditions which prevailed in great cities like Alexandria. This claim is confirmed in part by passages such as Callimachus' description of dawn in the *Hecale*:

Come, no longer are the hands of thieves in search of prey: for already the lamps of dawn are shining. The water-carrier is singing his song at the well, and the axle creaking under the wagon wakes the dweller by the highway, and many smithy slaves are tormented by the deafening din.

In such circumstances it was natural for a man to dream of some quiet country-side; contemporary Art made a similar attempt to create a *rus in urbe*, as may be seen from the Campanian wall- paintings. But this is not the whole story. Cos was no metropolis like Alexandria, and even before the Coan school set to praising and mimicking a rustic life, Peloponnesian epigrammatists had sung the charm of landscapes and seascapes. Further, urban existence was no novelty. Athens, not to mention the great cities of Ionia and Magna Graecia, had anticipated Alexandria. The Hellenistic attitude towards Nature can only be explained by a definite change of outlook. Previously condemned as a weakness of the indolent, such emotions were now, in an age which interpreted the civic obligations of the individual far less rigorously, not only pardoned but cultivated. Yet, save occasionally in Theocritus, the lack of variety in these 'idyllic' descriptions renders their sincerity rather suspect.

IV. THE FORE-RUNNERS

Theocritus in his seventh Idyll hails Philetas and Asclepiades as the masters of the new art of poetry. The latter, though he has given his name to several lyric metres, is to-day only appreciable as an epigrammatist. PHILETAS was a writer of wider activities. In verse Suidas credits him with 'epigrams, elegies, and other works.' The fragments vouch for a narrative elegy, the *Demeter*; collections called *Paegnia* and *Epigrams*; an epic poem, entitled *Hermes*, which described Odysseus' sojourn at the court of Aeolus and his intrigue with the Aeolid Polymela. There is more evidence for Philetas than for any other Alexandrian as the author of a body of verse addressed to a woman in the manner of the Roman Elegists. We know the name of his lady-love—Bittis, and we hear from Hermesianax that after Philetas' death the Coans erected a bronze statue of him under a plane-tree, because Philetas had sat there and made verse in honour of Bittis. But we know nothing about the *form* of the Coan's love-poetry. Probably *Paegnia* and *Epigrams* were alternative titles for one work of mixed content, and Philetas' amatory pieces formed part—when collected—of this volume. Though they are written exclusively in elegiacs, there is nothing to prove that the poems were elegies of the Roman type. Simias, roughly contemporary with Philetas (whose life may have extended from about 340 to 285 B.C.), was the author of four Books of 'Various Poems'—Hymns, Epyllia, Epigrams etc.—and a thorough modern in his literary tastes. His metrical innovations were copied at Alexandria, but Rhodes, his birthplace, lay outside Ptolemaic influence, and the *Thebaid* of its poet Antagoras, the flight of Apollonius thither, the opprobrious nickname which Callimachus in the *Aetia* bestows on his critics (he calls them Telchines, the legendary inhabitants of Rhodes) all suggest that the islanders preferred the unfashionable long epic.

HERMESIANAX was slightly younger than the two poets just mentioned. His chief work was the *Leontion*, a narrative elegy in three Books, named after his mistress and actually addressed to her; by this device Hermesianax tried to link together a series of more or less unconnected tragic love-stories, thus imitating Anti-

machus who had consoled himself for the loss of his wife or
mistress, Lyde, by composing an elegiac narrative of 'heroic mis-
adventures' which bore her name. The long fragment cited from
the *Leontion* by Athenaeus (XIII, 597 B) can scarcely be typical of
the whole poem; it comes from the last of the three Books, and is
in fact a summing-up of the power of Love, as exemplified in the
most famous Greek poets and philosophers. The matter is drawn
partly from literary tradition, which had already credited
Orpheus, Alcaeus and Anacreon (rivals for the affections of
Sappho) with affairs of the heart, and partly from history, for
instance the tale of Mimnermus' love for Nanno; but much is
mere invention and silly invention at that. Thus Homer is the
lover of Penelope, Hesiod of an Eoie, eponymous of the heroines
of the Hesiodic *Eoiai*! Like the Peripatetic biographers, Hermesianax met the prevailing demand for personal detail about the
great figures of the past by impudent fabrication.

PHOENIX OF COLOPHON, a contemporary and compatriot of
Hermesianax, was a writer of another stamp; interesting as a link
between Hipponax and the Alexandrians who used the Choliambic
metre, and because he and Cercidas of Megalopolis, who fifty
years later may have excerpted Phoenix' *Iambi* for an anthology
of moralizing verse, are to-day the chief representatives of
Hellenistic Satire. Cercidas and two other versifying moralists
of this age, Crates of Thebes and Menippus of Gadara, were
Cynics, but Phoenix belongs to no definite school. His verse
reflects the man in the street, poor but honest, with a taste for
traditional things and a profound dislike for the *nouveaux riches* of
the time. The lines from his 'chough-song,' supposed to be spoken
by the begging-procession at the house-door, have a pleasant ring:

> I, as I wander over vale and hill,
> Keep my eyes fixed upon the Muses still,
> And be you churl or noble, at your wicket
> More blithely will I sing than any cricket.
>
> (trans. A. D. Knox.)

V. THE GOLDEN AGE

For contemporaries the chief figure in Alexandrian Poetry
was CALLIMACHUS; yet his supremacy was far from being undisputed. If, as now seems probable, Apollonius succeeded Zenodotus as Chief Librarian, Callimachus at the zenith of his career
was faced with the opposition of a man who was officially his
superior. That Apollonius had once been Callimachus' pupil and
that he had laid the works of his teacher under contribution for

his own, only made matters worse. The end came soon after Euergetes' accession (246 B.C.). Apollonius lost his post and left Egypt, an event jubilantly celebrated by his rival at the end of his *Hymn to Apollo*. Though political and social factors played a part in the quarrel, there was of course a literary question involved. Callimachus' dictum 'big book—big evil' is sometimes cited to show that he objected above all to length in a poem. But it is possible that he was protesting more as a cataloguer than a poet, and it is certain that the *Aetia*, measured by the verses that it contained, was a 'big book.' What Callimachus really abhorred was the 'one continuous poem' which dealt at length with a single theme such as the Voyage of the Argo. No poet of the third century, however modern he was determined to be, could quite avoid the 'cyclic' manner, once he was embarked on such an enterprise. Callimachus' own counsel was either to select a single subject of small compass or in works of larger scope to pass rapidly from one story to another. In vigorous polemic he compares his own poetry with the clear note of the cicada, that of his opponents with the noise of asses. 'Let another bray after the very manner of the long-eared beast, but let me be the dainty, the winged one.'

Born about 310 B.C., Callimachus soon migrated from Cyrene to Alexandria, and is first discovered as a schoolmaster in the suburb Eleusis. The Epigrams, which mostly belong to this period, perhaps brought him to the notice of the Court; at any rate he was given some post in connection with the Library. In middle age mainly occupied with the preparation of the *Pinakes*, he was still writing verse at the end of his life under Euergetes. Of the 800 books mentioned by Suidas little enough survives to-day; of the prose we have nothing intact, of the poetry only the Epigrams and Hymns. In five of the latter (Hymn v, the *Bathing of Pallas*, is written in elegiacs) Callimachus follows the model of the Homeric Hymns, but modernizes, invents, and in at least two instances gives a political turn to the whole. The Hymn to Zeus has been described as a pamphlet on the divine right of kings; that to Apollo seems intended to reconcile Cyrene to the overlordship of Euergetes. While devoid of genuine religion, the Hymns abound in brilliant descriptions and highly-coloured pictures: Artemis visiting the smithy of the Cyclopes; Leto seeking a refuge in which to give birth to Apollo, while islands, mountains, and rivers flee from the wrath of Hera; Iris couched like a hound before Hera's throne.

Callimachus' most important poem was his *Aetia* or 'Causes,' a miscellany of information about history, geography, mythology, dictated to the poet by the Muses in the manner familiar to us from Ovid's *Fasti*, but containing personal touches—retorts to criticism, a description of a dinner-party, and the like—not found in the Latin poem. Further, the *Aetia* lacked the connecting-thread which serves to give the *Fasti* an appearance of unity; the author passed from one topic to another as the whim seized him, exhibiting a preference for the primitive and uncouth which explains his acknowledgment (in preface and epilogue) of a debt to Hesiod, from whose *Theogony* he has adapted the revelation made to the poet by the Muses of Helicon. The *Hecale*, an *epyllion* containing about 1000 lines, represents Callimachus' ideal of epic narrative. The heroine was the old woman at whose hut Theseus spent the night before his encounter with the Bull of Marathon. After his triumph Theseus returning to thank his hostess finds her dead and the funeral in progress. The longest episode, the scene in Hecale's hut, illustrates the Alexandrian fondness for realistic pictures of the heroic age; the details of the homely menu, the polite dispute over the single truckle-bed still retain a piquant charm.

The fragments of Callimachus' *Lyrics* show a striking variety of metre and subject. The most imposing is the *Funeral Ode for Arsinoe*, in which the poet abandons his usual tone for one of impressive pathos. The abrupt beginning in which he describes the passage of Arsinoe's soul to the stars, and the later episode where Charis, after her vigil on Athos, reports to the anxious Philotera, Arsinoe's deified sister, that the murky clouds which cover the sky come from the Queen's funeral-pyre in Egypt, where a whole nation mourns its loss, are effective even in their present mutilated condition. The *Iambi* contained tales from folk-lore, such as the *Quarrel of the Olive and Laurel*, which were perhaps too popular to find a place in the *Aetia*, and other matter of a more topical nature. Finally, as semi-official Poet Laureate, Callimachus wrote many elegies of the occasion; the best known is the *Lock of Berenice*, which Catullus (LXVI) has adapted, if not translated.

APOLLONIUS, called the Rhodian but originally of Naucratis or Alexandria, was the only Hellenistic poet of the first rank to be born in Egypt; hence Callimachus compared him to the ibis, an Egyptian bird of uncleanly habits. In several poems on the foundations of cities Apollonius followed the fashion; in his master-piece, an epic running to 5,835 lines, he defied it. As an epic, the *Argonautica* suffers from weakness in characterization and lack of unity. Its hero Jason is a very colourless figure—

the poet's favourite word for him is 'helpless'!—and, except for his achievements in the ordeal of the Bulls and the Earth-born, of less account than several of his crew. Medea is marvellously drawn in Book III, but the Medea of Book IV is the wronged queen of Tragedy, a type of cold resolution that has little connection with the earlier character. The action of heroes and heroine is controlled at every turn by higher powers, either Fate or the Olympians. The lack of unity is not so visible, since Apollonius shows considerable skill in welding together his heterogeneous material (the way in which he conflates the divergent stories of the return is a master-piece of eclecticism), but the epic has no central idea. The geographical and aetiological details clog the narrative, and at times give the poem the air of a 'conducted tour.'

Yet the *Argonautica* has many merits. The most striking is the power of psychological analysis, shown in the portrayal of Medea's love and of the struggle between it and her affection for home and family. There is more of primitive passion in Theocritus' Simaetha, but Apollonius has excellently rendered the first love of a younger and more bashful maid, who, complimented by Jason, 'cast her eyes down with a smile divinely sweet; and her soul melted within her, uplifted by his praise, and she gazed upon him face to face; nor did she know what word to utter first, but was eager to pour out everything at once.' Notable too is Apollonius' treatment of nature and natural phenomena. An epic poet is constantly embarrassed to find ways of indicating the time of day. Apollonius not only avoids repeating himself, but even, making a virtue of necessity, creates pictures of dawn, of dusk, of night, which are remarkable for their intrinsic beauty. In other passages he exhibits a surprising power of seizing the atmosphere of such strange regions as the 'Black Country' of the Chalybes, or the gloomy waste of the Syrtes with the desert behind. Though tarred with the brush of Callimachus, Apollonius was indeed a 'romantic born out of due season.'

In the literary controversy of the third century THEOCRITUS sided with Callimachus; his works reveal the versatility and preference for short poems which the Master inculcated. Born at Syracuse, Theocritus seems to have gone early in life to Cos (whence his grand-parents may have migrated to Sicily in the days of Timoleon), and to have formed one of Philetas' circle there. Soon after 275 B.C. we find him again at Syracuse and soliciting the patronage of Hiero (Idyll XVI). Disappointed here, he was attracted to Alexandria, where he composed the *Syracusan Women* (Idyll XV) and a panegyric of Philadelphus (Idyll XVII), possibly also the fragmentary *Berenice*. But Theocritus was not meant for courts and libraries, and before long he is back in Cos or its neighbourhood, to enjoy for the rest of his life the society which he has so attractively described in his *Harvest-home* (Idyll VII). Some idylls and epigrams belong to this last period of his career, but, with the exceptions mentioned above, the rest of the pieces, including Idyll VII itself, were apparently composed during his first visit to Cos. Idyll XXVIII, written to accompany the gift of a distaff to Theugenis, the wife of the poet's friend Nicias, and a precious illustration of the refinement possible in the social inter- course of these times, may have been delivered when Theocritus called at Miletus *en route* from Sicily to Egypt.

The 'Father of Pastoral Poetry' was no mere pastoralist. Besides the 'bucolic' pieces, his collected works contain examples of mimes, of *epyllia*, of *encomia*; in addition an *epithalamium*, the Aeolic poems in lyric metres, and the epigrams. There is variety even in the *genus*; thus of the two *encomia*, one addressed to Hiero and the other praising Philadelphus, the former is a personal document and draws its inspiration from Classical Lyric Poetry with touches of the Mime and Pastoral; the latter is a rather frigid production on purely conventional lines.

There is little homogeneity in the bucolic poems themselves, save that all (with the dubious exception of Idyll VIII, which con- tains elegiacs) are written in hexameters and in a dialect which may be called literary Doric. Though Theocritus borrowed some conventions (for example, the singing-match, the refrain) from the practice of rustics in all ages, and though he displays much acute observation of country life and manners, it was apparently literary influences which first led him to pastoral poetry. We have noted bucolic motives in Hellenistic epigram and satyr-play; these had been anticipated in the dithyramb of the fourth century. But the chief impulse must have come from Philetas' circle and its cult of love, song, and bucolic masquerade. Theocritus shows this influence in two ways; at times he accepts—with a smile—the affectations of his contemporaries, at others he reacts against the current mode and goes back to the real simplicity of the country- side. Idyll X is the best example of this latter mood. Milon's version of the 'Reaping-song of Lityerses' is certainly taken from life; even Boucaeus' ditty about Bombyca is not beyond the powers of a peasant in love. Next in realism come Idylls IV and V, interesting also for the reminiscences of the poet's youth in Magna Graecia, but these contain topical allusions out of place on the lips of South Italian rustics. In the *Serenade of Amaryllis*

(Idyll III) the tone is different. The amorous goat-herd who prays to be metamorphosed into a bee, who declares Love was suckled by a lioness, and finally threatens to jump over the cliff, is no figure of real life, but a caricature of the love-sick swain of contemporary verse. Theocritus strikes the same note in Idyll XI. Here the character of Polyphemus *amans* lends itself to the poet's jesting, but Theocritus cannot help feeling some sympathy for the distressed giant, and so, while he makes him repeat the usual phrases of love *à la mode*, he also credits him with sentiments which show real passion. In the *Thyrsis* (Idyll I) Theocritus idealizes the folk-story of Daphnis' love and death, a theme already treated by Hermesianax; in the *Harvest-home* the influence of Cos is more obvious. The 'bucolic songs' in which the masquerading goat-herd Lycidas and Simichidas-Theocritus try their powers are actually songs about boy-loves. Their tone of gallantry (so unlike the autobiographic love-poems, Idylls XII, XXIX, XXX) and the erudition, a rare feature in Theocritus, suggest that these songs represent the poet's tribute to his friends' tastes. But the description of a country scene in late summer, with which the idyll ends, comes from the writer's heart:

There we reclined on deep beds of fragrant lentisk, strewn on the ground, and lay rejoicing on newly stript leaves of the vine. High above our heads waved many poplars and elms, while hard by the sacred water from the cave of the Nymphs murmured as it welled forth. On the shady boughs the brown crickets were busy with their chatter, and from far away came the low note of the tree-frog in the thick thornbrake. The larks and finches were singing, the turtle moaned, the yellow bees were flitting about the spring. Everything smelt of the rich summer, smelt of the season of fruits.

To turn to the urban mimes, in the *Syracusan Women*, though a few motives seem traditional (they reappear in Herodas), Theocritus is no mere imitator. Gorgo and Praxinoa are individual and alive; the world in which they move is that of Philadelphus' Alexandria, not Sophron's Syracuse. There is less art in the *Love of Cynisca* (Idyll XIV), but the story of Aeschines' misfortunes is graphic and amusing. The last urban mime, Idyll II, is Theocritus' greatest achievement. The setting, women engaged in magic, is taken from Sophron, but Simaetha, it has been aptly said, is a girl in love, not a sorceress. In Theocritus the witchcraft provides an atmosphere of awe and enables the poet to reveal Simaetha's reactions to her own magic, as she remembers the past. At first indignation masters her, and she cries out on Nature which is at rest, while she is in torment. 'Lo! the sea is silent, and the winds are silent too, but not silent is the heart within my breast.'

Gradually the narrative of her betrayal brings relief; she yields to the spell of the still night; and after one last outburst ends on a note of resignation:

Farewell now, Queen; with blessing, thy car to the Ocean bend
And I will bear my trouble, as I have borne, to the end.
Farewell, thou shining Moon, farewell, companions bright,
You train of Stars that follow the wheels of quiet Night.

(trans. W. Headlam.)

From this masterpiece it is an abrupt descent to Theocritus' *epyllia*, which are interesting but no more than that. In Idyll xiii he tells the story of Hylas in a letter to a friend; in xxiv he depicts a night alarm in a bourgeois family under the pretence of celebrating Heracles' strangling of the snakes; in xxii, which purports to be a hymn to the Dioscuri, he shows his virtuosity by employing a modern style in the first half of the poem, an archaic in the second.

HERODAS, who was possibly a native of Ionia but shows himself well-acquainted with Cos, and may have visited Alexandria, belongs to the same generation as Callimachus (his Mimiambi, *i.e.* mimes written in the Choliambic metre, were composed between 280 and 260 B.C.), but for reasons now obscure he was excluded from the charmed circle of his contemporaries. In his eighth Mime, the *Dream*, he represents his critics as goat-herds; so it seems that he had no sympathy for the devotees of bucolic poetry. Nevertheless Herodas is a child of his age. His pieces are short —they are to Comedy what the *Epyllion* is to the Epic; his metre and dialect (an obsolete Ionic) are archaic. Thus his work was definitely for the elect, and it seems unlikely that the Mimes were composed for recitation on the stage—even of an 'intimate' theatre. They are book-poetry like those of Theocritus. But if the form is artificial, the matter and treatment are ultra-realistic. The most original piece is Mime ii, a speech delivered in a court-of-law by a pander against a ship's captain, whom he charges with assault and the abduction of one of his women. The detailed parody of the conventions dear to Attic Oratory and the naïve impudence of Battarus are exceedingly amusing. Even the pieces which follow traditional lines—for example, Mime i, describing the fruitless visit of the old bawd who tempts Metriche to abandon her absent lover, or Mime vii, in which the cobbler Cerdon bargains engagingly with his female customers—are full of touches drawn from contemporary life. On the other hand Mime iii, the least offensive to delicate ears, makes rather tedious reading owing to the exaggerated complaints of Lampriscus' mother about his

school-boy misdemeanours. In Mime iv, which describes the visit
of two women to the famous temple of Asclepius, situated just
outside the town of Cos, Coccale's admiration for the sculptured
boy ('Why, one would say the sculpture would talk') and for
Apelles' painting ('Look, this naked boy will bleed if I scratch
him') reflects the author's preferences for the life-like in Art; he
joined issue with the idealists in Art as with the idyllists in poetry.

The Golden Age of Alexandrian Poetry lasted some fifty years
only, from about 290 to 240 B.C. Bucolic poetry flourished
spasmodically down to the first century B.C., beginning with the
pseudo-Theocritean *Lovers' Talk* (Idyll xxvii) and *Fishermen*
(Idyll xxi), both of which belong to the third century and are
excellent in their way, and continuing with Moschus, a pupil of
Aristarchus, and Bion of Smyrna, who was born not long before
100 B.C. Moschus' *epyllion*, the *Europa*, is a pleasing work with
a certain plastic quality in the descriptions; Bion's *Lament for
Adonis* and the *Lament for Bion*, written by a pupil, bring an
Oriental colour into Greek poetry. But Theocritus' real successor
is not a Greek, but a Roman—Vergil. In Epic, Euphorion of
Chalcis (*c.* 220 B.C.) attained fame by exaggerating the defects of
his predecessors and plagiarizing shamelessly from their works.
In Catullus' day the Romans admired this unattractive poet for
his erudition, but the fragments of his *epyllia* and other poems,
for instance one in which he collected the most horrible deaths,
recorded in myth and history, in order to terrify a man who had
stolen his goblet, raise no desire for more. On the other hand
Idyll xxv of the Theocritean corpus is a work of considerable
originality, and if not written by Theocritus himself comes from
some early and talented imitator. The subject, Heracles *chez*
Augeas, is treated in three episodes, and the poem has been called
a miniature Heracleid in three 'books'; the pictures of the dogs at
the homestead and of the return of the cattle are particularly
successful, while the anatomical details in the description of
Heracles' slaying of the Nemean lion recall Theocritus' portrait
of Amycus, the giant pugilist, in Idyll xxii, and similar features in
Hellenistic Art. The notorious *Alexandra*, a dramatic monologue
in 1474 tragic iambics, in which the slave appointed to watch
Cassandra reports her prophecies to Priam, is commonly, on
Suidas' authority, attributed to the famous Lycophron, but a later
date—probably about 196 B.C.—seems necessary, in view of the
clear reference (ll. 1226–33) to the Romans as already supreme
on land and sea (see however, p. 653 *sq.*).

Even the Epigram has few representatives in the second

century, though about 100 B.C. it revives in the hands of Meleager and the other Syrians. These copied, but could not equal, the earlier Alexandrians, among whom Asclepiades, Leonidas of Tarentum, and Callimachus had been most successful in this branch. Life in Samos about 300 B.C. under the rule of Duris was a gay affair, and this atmosphere is reflected in the epigrams of Asclepiades, Poseidippus, and Hedylus. They extended the use of the *genre*, employing it for amatory and humorous pieces, which may have been bandied about the dinner-table (like the Athenian *scolia*) before they were published in book-form. Asclepiades and Poseidippus seem often to be capping one another's efforts on the same theme, but each of the three poets has his particular character. Asclepiades is the young man of pleasure, full of wit and fancy and generally in high spirits, though, when gaiety palls, he can cry 'I am scarce twenty-two and yet I am weary of living.' Poseidippus, as befits an ex-pupil of the philosophers, in his sober moments moralizes on life. Hedylus is the satirist of the circle and rails against gluttony and its sequel—gout. These poets contributed more than any others to the transformation of Eros from the somewhat austere youth of earlier times to the mischievous imp who is a commonplace of later Art and Literature, as also to the introduction of the amatory 'topics' which fill so much of Roman Elegy. In style and sentiment they differ widely from Leonidas (*c.* 285 B.C.), whose wandering life was spent in Magna Graecia and Western Greece. Termed with some justice the 'Tramp-poet,' Leonidas gives us a picture of the existence of the common people such as we get nowhere else in Hellenistic Poetry, but his style is disagreeable; the Epigram is no place for verbiage and bombast. Not a few of his epitaphs and dedications seem to be literary *tours de force*, to judge by the improbability of many details in the former and the frequent resemblance of the latter to a tradesman's catalogue.

From Callimachus we have some sixty epigrams. The most conventional are the dedications, many of which were apparently written to order for real use. In the epitaphs there is a strange contradiction. When he writes for clients, Callimachus shows a power of sympathy with bereavement which is the more impressive for the simplicity of the language. Examples are his epitaph on Nicoteles:

Δωδεκέτη τὸν παῖδα πατὴρ ἀπέθηκε Φίλιππος
ἐνθάδε τὴν πολλὴν ἐλπίδα Νικοτέλην.

Ep. XIX. W.-M.

'Here the father laid his twelve-year old son; here Philippus laid his great hope—Nicoteles'; or his consolation for the death of Saon of Acanthus: 'Here Saon of Acanthus, Dicon's son, rests in holy sleep. Say not that the good die:'

Τῇδε Σάων ὁ Δίκωνος Ἀκάνθιος ἱερὸν ὕπνον
κοιμᾶται. θνήσκειν μὴ λέγε τοὺς ἀγαθούς.

Ep. ix. w.-m.

Alongside such epitaphs we find others where Callimachus parodies the usual type and mocks openly at belief. But it is the intimate poems, dealing with the love-affairs, literary tastes, and day-to-day experiences of Callimachus' circle, which give the collection its chief charm. Most of Callimachus' friends are only names to-day, but the most famous of his epigrams, in which he records how in company with Heracleitus of Halicarnassus he 'tired the sun with talking and sent him down the sky' still allows us a glimpse into the scholar's life as men lived it in the third century at Alexandria.

CHAPTER IX

HELLENISTIC SCIENCE AND MATHEMATICS

I. MEDICINE AND SURGERY

IN the fifth century Greek medicine reached its highest level in the work of Hippocrates and his followers (vol. v, p. 380 *sq.*). It was their achievement to see in disease a natural evil to be combated by natural means. They were influenced by the philosophy of their day, though sometimes they resisted its claims, but in time the study of medicine assumed a rather different character. The science of the third century B.C. developed under two powerful influences, the genius of Aristotle and the endowment of research. Aristotle had done much to separate science from philosophy by his differentiation of the various branches of knowledge and by restricting speculation to those subjects which admit it best. Natural history in particular was based upon a large collection of observed facts, with greater attention to detail than previous thinkers had thought necessary. Most in fact of the conditions required for the development of science were recognized, and efforts were made to secure them, although experiment had by no means attained its rightful position. Scope for work on the lines laid down by Aristotle was provided by the endowment of research at Alexandria and other centres. While mathematicians and astronomers were making brilliant conquests of knowledge and speculation, the laborious diligence of students of medicine had the opportunity of doing its special task in the surroundings provided by the Ptolemies and similar patrons of learning. There are no startling discoveries, no illuminations of genius. On the other hand, there is a distinct advance in knowledge of detail, a knowledge made possible by careful and patient observation. Human anatomy in particular was studied with success, and the work done at Alexandria compares very favourably with the crude information and fanciful guess-work that disfigures so many of the treatises in the Hippocratic *Corpus*[1].

In the medical school at Alexandria worked Herophilus the anatomist and Erasistratus the physiologist. We know little about their lives, except that they came from Asia Minor to work at

---

[1] The Hippocratic *Corpus* contains works not only of the fifth, but also of the fourth and third century, together with some writings that are yet later. See the Bibliography.

Alexandria during the first half of the third century, Erasistratus being slightly the younger. Their works are entirely lost, but we can gather a great deal of information from references in Galen, Soranus and Celsus. Modern scholars have been particularly successful in reconstructing an account of the researches of Herophilus. The fact that these two medical men came from Asia Minor suggests that Alexandrian medicine may have been subjected to Eastern influences. Research, however, cannot trace any such influence, nor yet any direct connection with native Egyptian science, although we know this to have been by no means contemptible.

Herophilus was a careful student of Hippocrates, and wrote commentaries on two of the Hippocratic treatises, maintaining the humoral pathology in opposition to Erasistratus. He paid great attention to pulsation, following in the steps of his teacher Praxagoras, who was the first physician to insist on the importance of the pulse, although pulsation was known at least a century before. He used drugs far more than the Hippocratics, regarding them as invaluable helps in the cure of diseases. His anatomical researches centred around the brain, nerves, liver, lungs, and the organs of generation. The brain he regarded as the seat of intelligence, connecting it with the nervous system, of which he was the first to form any clear conception. It is interesting to observe that Herophilus must have dissected animals, because he described the *rete mirabile*, which exists at the base of the brain of animals, but not in human beings. He distinguished 'sensory' from 'motor' nerves, and contributed much to the knowledge of the ventricles of the brain. He distinguished also the *cerebrum* from the *cerebellum* and paid great attention to the cavity in the fourth ventricle. The other anatomical researches of Herophilus are less striking, but he named the *duodenum* and described at some length the *uterus*. Tradition asserts that he conducted *postmortem* examinations, and certainly his work could not have been done without dissecting the human subject. Recent research shows that he used an ingenious instrument to measure the rate of pulses. Here we have one of the earliest efforts—perhaps the first—in the direction of that exact measurement which is the very soul of modern science.

Erasistratus rejected the humoral pathology, substituting for it a doctrine of air or *pneuma*, which he considered to be a vital factor in the physiological processes. It has been well said that this attention paid to air, which goes back at least to Alcmaeon (vol. IV, p. 548), finally resulted in the discovery of oxygen and of the part it plays in supporting life. Erasistratus, however, appears to have regarded the action of *pneuma* as purely mechanical. He improved on the work of Herophilus on the heart and the brain, and distinguished yet more clearly the sensory from the motor nerves. It has even been maintained that the discovery is due to him rather than to his contemporary. In his practice Erasistratus rejected bleeding, substituting for it a low diet, and he used medicines only of the mildest kind, in the latter respect reverting to the Hippocratic tradition. He invented a catheter, but was probably not the first to do so.

Improved anatomy naturally resulted in improved surgery, and the great glory of the Alexandrian school was the invention of new surgical instruments with increased skill in the use of them. Both Herophilus and Erasistratus have been accused of practising vivisection on human beings. The evidence comes from certain passages in Celsus and Tertullian[1], and is therefore by no means contemptible. The Ptolemies are said to have permitted the vivisection of condemned criminals, and no ancient authority doubts the truth of the assertion. Celsus felt that there were ethical arguments on both sides of the question, although he personally regarded the practice as barbarous. It is interesting to observe that a similar charge was brought against certain princes and surgeons of the sixteenth century, but the best historical opinion rejects the stories as based on untrustworthy evidence. Recent historians of ancient surgery do not believe that the Alexandrian surgeons had recourse to human vivisection, and they regard the accusation as a lie manufactured by those who were opposed to dissection of any kind. Even if this view be adopted, it is clear that surgeons against whom such charges were made must have attached great importance to ocular examination of the internal organs; they were, in fact, the real fathers of modern anatomy.

In spite of their comparative freedom from speculation, Galen classes the two great Alexandrian anatomists with what he names the 'Rational,' or, as it is more commonly called, the 'Dogmatic' school of medicine. The essence of Dogmatism is that it values the study of causes of disease, and therefore calls in to aid medicine the kindred sciences of anatomy and physiology. A more complete reaction from speculation came about 280 B.C., when two pupils of Herophilus founded at Alexandria the Empiric school. Empiricism discarded anatomy and physiology, and held that medicine was concerned only with the cure of diseases and not with their cause. The whole duty of the physician was to discover what treat-

---

[1] Celsus, *pref.* and Tertullian, *de anima*, 10.

ment will banish any particular set of symptoms. He was to be guided by personal observation, by instruction from others and by analogy. Empiricism probably did much good by opposing the speculative tendency, always a weakness in Greek medicine, and by investigating the usefulness of many new drugs and remedies.

One Empiric deserves a special notice. Heracleides of Tarentum wrote an apparently excellent work on *materia medica*, containing, as he said, nothing that he had not observed himself. He pointed out the value of opium, both in poultices and in medicines. By calling attention to the proper use of anodynes he prepared the way for the discovery of anaesthetics. He was also an excellent surgeon, as well as a commentator on several Hippocratic treatises. He earns from Galen the commendation that he never preferred his party to the truth. Heracleides was thought until quite recently to belong to the last thirty years of the third century. Recent research working on new evidence makes it extremely likely that he did not flourish until the early part of the first century B.C.

It is noteworthy that the history of medicine, and in particular the critical study of the Hippocratic writings, continued to flourish during the third century. Menon's *Iatrica* is rather earlier, but a long series of writers, whose works have perished, show that the new methods of research adopted at Alexandria did not blind students to the importance of keeping in touch with the work of previous investigators. These writers include Herophilus, his pupil Bacchius, Philinus and Glaucias. Some of this interest was possibly antiquarian, but there is no reason to doubt that there was felt a genuine appreciation of the continuity of science, and of the truth that the past cannot be forgotten without serious danger to the present and the future.

In the Hippocratic *Corpus* are two short works which may perhaps belong to the third century B.C. These are *Precepts* and *Decorum*, both dealing chiefly with what may be called medical etiquette. Their date is indeed a vexed question, but *Precepts* contains passages very similar in language to remarks attributed by Diogenes Laertius to Epicurus, while the ideal physician of *Decorum* bears strong resemblance to the Stoic Wise Man. The Greek of both works shows signs of a comparatively late date, and it is hard to resist the conclusion that they are later than 300 B.C.

During the fifth century philosophy made a strong effort to thrust its method of postulates (ὑποθέσεις) upon the science of medicine, and the Hippocratic work called *Ancient Medicine* attacks those who would assert, for instance, that all diseases are caused by heat, and would accordingly base treatment upon this assumption. So this attempt of philosophy was resisted, because it sought to interfere with the true function of the physician's art. But when philosophers concentrated their attention on moral questions, as happened in the third century, medicine did not try to resist it, because an educated and enlightened morality can do nothing but good to medical practice. In insisting upon the moral side of a physician's work these later philosophers contributed much to the building up of a sound medical etiquette. This etiquette aimed at raising the doctor's ethical standard rather than at defending the business interests of the profession.

Two short sentences, one from the sixth chapter of *Precepts*, the other from the fifth chapter of *Decorum*, well sum up the influence of the later ethical philosophy upon medicine:

> Where love of man is, there also is love of the Art.
> A physician who is a philosopher is a god indeed.

II. BIOLOGY AND BOTANY

Chemistry was to the Greeks rather a collection of trade-secrets than a body of knowledge, 'not a science, but a mystery.'[1] It was to be otherwise with biology and botany. A people that lived so much in the open air and by the sea, and that was naturally so observant and curious, had not failed to notice the ways of birds, beasts, fishes and all manner of plants. Then came Aristotle, who brought system and method, building up and classifying a great body of observations in a series of treatises of which the crown is the *de generatione animalium*. Theophrastus, his pupil, whose interests ranged from the arts of government to the arts of the stone-cutter, did for plants, in his sober way, what his master's greater genius had done for animals. We do not know exactly when Theophrastus wrote his botanical works, *The History of Plants* and *The Causes of Plants*, but, as a garden was his hobby throughout his life, it is not unreasonable to suppose that his researches continued well into the third century B.C. Without the speculative genius of his master, he was both by nature and by education fully competent to apply to plant-life the Aristotelian method. It is perhaps fortunate that Theophrastus was more of a scientist than a philosopher, for it is his patient adherence to observed fact that makes his treatises the best specimens of ancient biological study.

[1] D'A. W. Thompson, in *The Legacy of Greece*, p. 142 *sq*.

Before Theophrastus, plants were studied chiefly for their use, and his chief claim to distinction is that he raised botany to the rank of a pure science. The conception may have been due to Aristotle, but the working out of the idea was left to his pupil. The number of facts collected by Theophrastus is very great, and points to his having used, not only his own observations taken in the garden of the Lyceum, but also data supplied by friends in many parts of the world. Some five hundred different plants are mentioned, and the knowledge displayed is often astonishing, when we remember that as yet the microscope was not and chemistry was in its infancy. The classification of plants is of course unsatisfactory, although the flowering plants are distinguished from the flowerless. The organs of plants are carefully described: root, stem, branch, leaf, flower, seed and fruit being distinguished with notable accuracy if the means of observation at his disposal are taken into account. Nomenclature receives great attention. The non-technical terms *karpos* and *perikarpion* are used in a technical sense, and the zoological word *mētra* is applied to describe the core of any stem. Authorities agree in praising Theophrastus for his acute observation of the phenomena of germination, and also for his clear conception of the distribution of plants as dependent on climate and soil.

That dates are fertilized was known to the Greeks from early times, and Theophrastus describes the process at some length, comparing it to the caprification of figs. The true sexual nature of plants, however, was not yet known. Species, plants and flowers have sex ascribed to them, but generally in a metaphorical sense, 'male' being equivalent to 'barren' and 'female' to 'fertile.'

Dr E. L. Greene, in a thorough examination of Theophrastean botany, draws up a list of seventeen items representing original contributions of Theophrastus to botanical discovery. We cannot be certain that in all cases the originality is made out, but the mere claim proves that in many respects Theophrastus was a pioneer. None, however, of the seventeen items, nor yet the sum of them, can be compared with the outstanding merit of having set forth a scheme of botanical science, free from utilitarian bias and marking out various departments for the guidance of all later investigators.

III. MATHEMATICS CREATED A SCIENCE: THALES AND THE PYTHAGOREANS

The contributions to philosophy of men such as Pythagoras and Eudoxus have been described in earlier volumes of this work, and allusion has been made to their attainments in mathematics and science (vol. IV, chap. XV; vol. VI, chap. XI). In the history of Greek mathematics three periods may be distinguished. The first includes the beginnings of the science and the working out of the elements by Pythagoras and the Pythagoreans. The second begins with the mathematicians, mostly outside the Pythagorean school, who first carried geometry beyond the elements by attacking the famous problems of duplicating the cube, trisecting any angle and squaring the circle, which do not yield to elementary methods, that is, those of the straight line and circle. The third period is associated with Alexandria and includes the age of Euclid (*flor.* 300 B.C. or a little earlier), who taught and founded a school at Alexandria, and his successors, Archimedes and Apollonius of Perga, both of whom studied there. The fact that the greatest monuments of Greek mathematics are the work of these three men makes the present a proper occasion for a more connected survey.

It was through contact with the more ancient civilizations of Egypt and Babylonia that the Ionian Greeks became acquainted with certain elementary facts in geometry and astronomy. Egyptian geometry was mensuration, arising out of the requirements of land-surveying and architecture (vol. II, pp. 215 *sqq.*); Chaldaean astronomy (vol. III, pp. 237 *sqq.*) included a wonderful amount of knowledge accumulated as the result of long-continued observations, coupled with measurement of angles, calculation of times, etc. Working on these things, the Greek genius, by an inspiration unique in the history of the world, first conceived the idea of a *science*. Tradition credits Thales with the first proofs of a few elementary theorems in geometry, *e.g.* that the base angles in an isosceles triangle are equal. What was wonderful was that the idea of proving such things should occur to any one at all; as Kant once wrote, 'A light broke on the first man who demonstrated the property of the isosceles triangle, whether his name was Thales or what you will'; 'from that time the safe way of a science was struck and traced out for all time.' Thales also reduced theory to practice by calculating (1) the height of a pyramid, (2) the distance of a ship from the shore. In astronomy he predicted the solar eclipse of May 585 B.C.

After Thales come Pythagoras and the Pythagoreans. The Pythagoreans, says Aristotle, devoted themselves to mathematics and were the first to advance that science as a study pursued for its own sake[1]. They made geometry a part of liberal education: their *quadrivium* comprised arithmetic, geometry, sphaeric (astronomy) and music. By arithmetic in this classification is meant, not the arithmetic of daily life, but the theory of numbers in themselves. We have seen (vol. IV, p. 547) that Pythagoras discovered that the musical intervals correspond to certain arithmetical ratios between lengths of string at the same tension, 2 : 1 giving the octave, 3 : 2 the fifth and 4 : 3 the fourth. These ratios are the same as those of 12 to 6, 8, 9 respectively, and 6 : 8 = 9 : 12, so that this proportion shows all three intervals. The principle of proportion so established became a uniform principle for all science and notably for medicine.

An easy transition from arithmetic to geometry, from numbers to geometrical magnitudes, was through figured numbers, triangles, squares, etc. marked out by dots. This revealed a law of formation. Three dots were placed in contiguity to one dot so as to form a square, five dots round two sides of that square gave the next square, and so on, showing that the sum of any number of terms of the series of odd numbers beginning with 1 is a square number; to add any odd number to the sum of all the preceding odd numbers (including 1) made one square into the next larger square; hence the odd numbers were called *gnomons*. If the gnomon (odd number) so added is itself a square, we have two square numbers the sum of which is also a square; and from this is easily deduced the general formula (attributed to Pythagoras) for finding three numbers the squares of two of which are together equal to the square of the third. Any triangle with its sides in the ratio of three such numbers is right-angled; hence the rule is connected with the theorem of the square on the hypotenuse, the proof of which Greek tradition uniformly ascribes to Pythagoras. The comparison, again, of right-angled triangles having their sides in the ratio of integral numbers with other right-angled triangles led to the discovery of the irrational or incommensurable. Not only did the Pythagoreans discover that the ratio of the hypotenuse of an isosceles right-angled triangle to one of its other sides

---

[1] The Pythagoreans expressed this idea in their motto σχᾶμα καὶ βᾶμα ἀλλ᾽ οὐ σχᾶμα καὶ τριώβολον 'a figure (proposition) and a platform; not a figure and sixpence.' (Proclus, *Comm. on Eucl. 1*, p. 84). The motto no doubt recalls the story of the pupil who was bribed to learn mathematics by the gift of a triobol for each proposition mastered.

or, in other words, of the diagonal of a square to its side, cannot be expressed as a ratio between integral numbers, but they discovered a method of finding a series of ratios between numbers approximating more and more closely, in fact as nearly as we please, to the value of this ratio, which we write as $\sqrt{2}$.

The Pythagoreans applied their theory of proportion to geometry as well as arithmetic, and to them also is attributed the discovery of the general method in geometry known as the 'application of areas.' The latter in its most complete form is the geometrical equivalent of the solution of any quadratic equation in algebra so far as it has real roots; and this method, with that of proportions, constituted the main resource of Greek geometry for the solution of problems. Another achievement was a proof, by means of the properties of parallels, that the three angles of any triangle are together equal to two right angles; the Pythagoreans could also construct a regular pentagon, and they had some knowledge of three of the five regular solids, the tetrahedron, the cube and the dodecahedron.

Speaking generally, the Pythagorean geometry seems to have covered the bulk of the subject-matter of Euclid's Books I, II, IV, VI (and probably III). The Pythagorean theory of proportion however, being numerical, only applied to commensurable magnitudes; hence, when the irrational was discovered, doubt was thrown on such proofs as depended on proportions, and there are signs that it was considered necessary in various cases to substitute other proofs not so depending.

In astronomy progress was no less rapid. Pythagoras himself is said to have been the first to hold that the earth is spherical in shape. He realised that the sun, moon and planets have a motion of their own in a sense opposite to that of the daily rotation (this he may have learnt from the Babylonians). Later Pythagoreans actually deposed the earth from its place in the centre and made the earth, like the sun, moon and planets, revolve in a circle about the 'central fire'; this first step towards the Copernican hypothesis is alternatively attributed to Philolaus and one Hicetas of Syracuse. Nor were the Pythagoreans alone in this field; it was Anaxagoras who first declared that the moon receives its light from the sun, and Oenopides of Chios first discovered the obliquity of the ecliptic.

IV. SECOND STAGE: HIGHER PROBLEMS. THE IRRATIONAL AND INFINITESIMALS

Hippocrates of Chios (middle of fifth century) belongs to the second period above distinguished (p. 290). Having lost his property, he was reduced to earning a livelihood by teaching. The first known writer of 'Elements,' he also grappled with two of the higher problems. He is said to have reduced the duplication of the cube to the equivalent problem of finding two mean proportionals in continued proportion between two given straight lines; it was in this form that the problem was thereafter solved. He tried also to square the circle. He first proved, it is said, that the areas of circles are as the squares on their diameters; then, with great ingenuity, he squared certain figures bounded by arcs of circles and called *lunes* on account of their shape, hoping thereby to pass to the squaring of the circle. He squared three different lunes and also the sum of a circle and a certain lune; but he failed to square the circle itself because that particular lune was not one of the three which he had squared.

Democritus, the forerunner of modern atomic theory, was in the front rank of mathematicians. He was the first to discover that the volume of a cone or a pyramid is one-third of that of the cylinder or prism respectively which has the same base and height. He wrote on 'irrational straight lines and solids (atoms)' and on 'contact with a circle and a sphere'; these titles, with some remarks of his about contiguous sections of cones, suggest some inkling of infinitesimals.

Hippias of Elis, the sophist, a man of the most varied accomplishments, taught (among other things) geometry, astronomy and music. His theoretical trisection of any angle (cf. vol. v, p. 380) was by means of a higher curve generated by the concurrent motions (one a translation and one a rotation) of two straight lines; the curve was afterwards called *tetragonizousa* (*quadratrix*) because Dinostratus and Nicomedes used it later to square the circle.

Archytas, the friend of Plato, gave the first known solution of the problem of finding the two mean proportionals; he used a striking construction in three dimensions determining a certain point as the intersection of three surfaces, (1) a right cone, (2) a right cylinder, (3) an anchor-ring or *tore* with inner diameter *nil*.

Theodorus of Cyrene, Plato's teacher in mathematics, is associated with Theaetetus in the dialogue of that name as having contributed to the theory of the irrational by proving that, no less than $\sqrt{2}$, the surds $\sqrt{3}$, $\sqrt{5}$...$\sqrt{17}$ are all incommensurable with unity. Theodorus went no farther, but Theaetetus generalized the proof in a theorem afterwards reproduced by Euclid in his Book x. Theaetetus further distinguished two kinds of compound irrational, the 'binomial' and the 'apotome,' as well as the irrational straight line which Euclid calls 'medial,' and proved propositions about them. He also wrote the first theoretical treatise on the five regular solids; one scholium says that he was the first to discover two of the five, the octahedron and the icosahedron. We may assume therefore that for the substance of his Books x and xiii Euclid was greatly indebted to Theaetetus.

Though Zeno of Elea was apparently not a mathematician, it is certain that the statement of his famous paradoxes profoundly affected the later course of Greek geometry. The first two, the *Dichotomy* and the *Achilles*, proceeded on the mathematicians' hypothesis of the divisibility of magnitudes *ad infinitum*, and argued that, on this hypothesis, motion can never begin, and that, even assuming that it can, a swifter motion cannot overtake a slower; the last two, the *Arrow* and the *Stadium*, proceeding on the opposite assumption that continuous magnitudes (lengths and times) are made up of indivisible elements, argued the impossibility of motion on this hypothesis. But Democritus stated a similar dilemma with no less force. Given a cone with a circular base, if we take the very next parallel circular section, 'what,' said Democritus, 'are we to say of the two circles? Are they equal or unequal? If unequal, they will make the cone irregular, with indentations, like steps...; if they are equal, the sections will be equal, and the cone will appear to have the property of the cylinder, as being made up of equal, not unequal, circles, which is very absurd.'

Zeno's arguments were thought to be fatal to the first attempts to square the circle such as that of Antiphon, which was nevertheless on right lines. Antiphon's idea was to take an equilateral triangle or a square inscribed in a circle; then, by bisecting the arcs and drawing chords, to double the number of sides in the inscribed figure, and to continue this process until (as he said) the area of the circle was used up by reason of the sides of the polygon becoming so small as to coincide with the circumference of the circle. No, Zeno would say, this could never happen because the process would never end. The difficulty was avoided by what is known as the 'method of exhaustion' in the form given to it by its discoverer, Eudoxus of Cnidus (408–353 B.C.); for this method only requires that it shall be proved, *e.g.* in the case of the circle and the inscribed polygons, that, by continuing the construction of Antiphon, we can make the inscribed polygon approach equality with the circle *as nearly as we please.*

The 'method of exhaustion' became the one classical method of proving propositions about the content of figures bounded by curved lines or surfaces, although, as we learn from Archimedes' *Method*, the results to be proved might be divined in other less rigorous ways. Eudoxus himself used the method in proving, for the first time, the propositions discovered by Democritus about the volumes of the cone and the pyramid.

By another epoch-making discovery Eudoxus established geometry once more on a secure basis after the shock which it received when the discovery of the irrational showed the old arithmetical theory of proportion to be inadequate. This was the great theory of proportion applicable to all magnitudes commensurable or incommensurable which is expounded in Euclid's Book v; and the famous definition on which the theory is based (Eucl. v. Def. 5) still holds the field (cf. Weierstrass's definition of equal numbers).

In astronomy Eudoxus is famous for his hypothesis of concentric spheres devised to account for the apparent irregularities in the motions of the sun, moon and planets (cf. vol. vi, p. 343). This was, no doubt, his answer to Plato, who had set to all earnest students the problem of showing by what combinations of uniform and ordered movements the apparent motions of the heavenly bodies can be accounted for. Eudoxus' solution was purely theoretical; he imagined, for the sun and moon, a system of three spheres, and for each of the planets a set of four spheres, concentric with the earth, rotating about different axes, and one within the other. The poles about which each of the inner spheres rotates are fixed on the next enclosing sphere. In the case of the planets the effect of the two innermost rotations is to make the planet (fixed on the equator of the innermost sphere) describe, on the sphere of which the zodiac is a great circle, a curve called the *hippopede* (horse-fetter), an elongated figure of eight, which lies along and is bisected by the zodiac circle. This marvel of geometrical ingenuity itself stamps Eudoxus as a geometer of the very first rank.

The same challenge by Plato was also, in all probability, the incentive to the important forward step in astronomy taken by Heracleides of Pontus (*c.* 388–315 B.C.), who declared that the earth rotates on its own axis once in 24 hours, and that Venus and Mercury revolve about the sun like satellites.

The problem of doubling the cube, or finding the two mean proportionals, continued to attract attention. Eudoxus himself is said to have solved it by means of certain curves the nature of which is not known. But his pupil Menaechmus is credited with solutions by means of the intersection (1) of two parabolas, and (2) of a parabola and a rectangular hyperbola; it is inferred that Menaechmus discovered the three conic sections, as is also implied by the line in Eratosthenes' genuine epigram about the problem, which bids us 'not to cut the cone in the triads of Menaechmus.' Menaechmus, we are told, also contributed to make the whole of geometry more perfect. The story about the king who wanted a short cut to geometry, told of Euclid and Ptolemy, is also related of Menaechmus and Alexander in this form: 'O king,' said Menaechmus, 'for travelling about the country there are royal roads and roads for common citizens; but in geometry there is one road for all.'

Aristotle was no doubt less of a mathematician than Plato, but both contributed to the elucidation of the first principles of mathematics. Plato discussed the hypotheses of mathematics and gave certain definitions, *e.g.* of odd and even, 'figure,' and 'straight line'; 'points' he apparently refused to recognize as a separate genus, regarding a point as the 'beginning of a line' or 'an indivisible line,' a view which Aristotle controverts. Aristotle's views on the objects of mathematics have already been mentioned (vol. VI, p. 335). Aristotle also lays down very clearly the distinctions between axioms (common to all sciences) and definitions, hypotheses and postulates (which are different for different sciences, since they relate to the subject-matter of the particular science). He is clear, for instance, that a definition says nothing about the existence or non-existence of the thing defined; its existence has to be proved (save in the case of the unit and magnitude, which alone must be assumed to exist). A postulate, he says, is something which, *e.g.*, the geometer assumes, for reasons known to himself, without demonstration (though properly a subject for demonstration), and without any assent on the part of the learner, or even against his opinion rather than otherwise.

The Peripatetic school, in the person of Eudemus of Rhodes, produced (cf. vol. VI, p. 350) the first *History of Geometry* (in four Books) and the first *History of Astronomy*; a few citations from these works are made by various commentators and other writers, but the loss of the rest can never be sufficiently deplored.

V. ALEXANDRIA: EUCLID, ARISTARCHUS, ARCHIMEDES, APOLLONIUS OF PERGA

After the death of Alexander, Athens remained a centre of study, especially in philosophy; but the headquarters of science and most forms of literature was transferred to Alexandria as the result of the enlightened patronage of the first Ptolemies (pp. 31; 241 *sqq.*). Ptolemy I Soter was himself a historian, and he tried to attract philosophers and writers to Alexandria. Unsuccessful in his invitations to Theophrastus and Stilpo, he received Demetrius of Phalerum at his court and appointed Strato of Lampsacus, the successor of Theophrastus in the Peripatetic school, as well as Philetas of Cos, poet and grammarian, to instruct his son Philadelphus. In his reign (305–283 B.C.) Euclid studied and taught mathematics, and the great Herophilus anatomy, physiology and medicine, at Alexandria. Ptolemy II Philadelphus seems to have been especially fond of natural science and natural history, while the third Ptolemy, Euergetes I (246–221 B.C.), seems to have been interested in mathematics.

Strato, the most original thinker of the Peripatetic school, was not only tutor to Ptolemy Philadelphus; he also taught Aristarchus of Samos. His greatest work was in natural philosophy and earned him the title of 'the physicist.' By his theory of the vacuum in particular he seems to have greatly influenced two branches of science, medicine (through Erasistratus) and pneumatics (through Ctesibius). According to Strato there is in nature no such thing as continuous void, but substances, including air and gases, are made up of molecules, and vacuum exists in the tiny interstices which everywhere separate the molecules, and there only. This is why air is compressible; and this is why light is not only reflected from water but shines through it on the bottom of a vessel. If there were no interstices of vacuum between the molecules of water, and light had to force its way through the water in a vessel full of it, the water would overflow; as it is, the sun's light is partly reflected from the molecules of the water and partly passes through it by the path provided by the interstices. The same constitution of things explains their expansion by heat. Strato discussed the attraction exercised by a magnet, and there is some reason to believe that it was he who first conceived the idea of a connexion between this phenomenon and the shock communicated by the 'electric fish,' the *narke*.

Two mathematicians claim notice before we come to Euclid, though nearly contemporary with him, Autolycus of Pitane and Aristaeus 'the elder.' Autolycus had as a pupil, at Pitane and Sardes, Arcesilas of Pitane (*c.* 315–241 B.C.), who later founded the New Academy (p. 237). Autolycus' treatises *On the Moving Sphere* and *On Risings and Settings* are the only works of any Greek mathematician earlier than Euclid which have come down to us entire. The work *On the Moving Sphere* treats of the geometry of the sphere with special reference to the heavenly sphere and the circles on it which are used in astronomy, and is a tract of the same sort as Euclid's *Phaenomena*, though in form less purely astronomical. Autolycus' work preceded Euclid's, for Euclid makes use of propositions contained in it; further, whereas Autolycus speaks of the horizon as 'the circle which defines (*horizōn*) the visible and the invisible portions of the sphere,' Euclid uses for the first time the single word *horizon*. The form of Autolycus' propositions is like that which Euclid's practice has made classical, showing that the Euclidean type of proposition with its formal divisions was not invented by him but had already taken shape before his time.

Aristaeus 'the elder' is mentioned by Pappus as the author of a work in five Books entitled *Solid Loci*, now lost but extant in Pappus' time. 'Solid loci' meant loci which were conic sections, and were so called to distinguish them from plane loci which were straight lines and circles only. Euclid apparently used this work in writing his own *Conics*; but, as the *Conics* is also lost, we cannot judge of the extent of his obligation. A certain Aristaeus (probably the same person) wrote a *Comparison of the Five Figures* (the regular solids) in which he proved, among other things, that 'the same circle circumscribes both the pentagon of the dodecahedron and the triangle of the icosahedron inscribed in one and the same sphere.' As this interesting theorem is not in Euclid, it has been suggested that Aristaeus' work was not before Euclid when he was compiling Book XIII, but was written later.

Next to nothing is known of the life and personality of Euclid, though the two stories of him are worthy of their subject; these relate how he told Ptolemy that 'there is no royal road to geometry' (see above, p. 296), and how, when a pupil, after the first proposition, asked him 'What shall I get by learning these things?', Euclid called the slave and said 'Give him threepence, since he must needs make money by what he learns.'

Proclus says that he was not much younger than Hermotimus of Colophon (who continued the work of Eudoxus and Menaechmus) and Philippus of Medma or Opus (Plato's pupil), and that he lived under the first Ptolemy (305–283 B.C.) and before Eratosthenes and Archimedes. He taught and founded a school at Alexandria, where, in his turn, Apollonius of Perga studied under his successors. Euclid has, at least in this country, always been so identified with his great work, the *Elements*, that there are probably many persons to whom it has not occurred that Euclid was a man and not a book. Greek writers after Archimedes generally spoke of him as 'the writer of the Elements' (*Stoicheiōtes*) without using his name, while the Arabs tried to make out that, etymologically, Uclides or Icludes meant the 'key of geometry.' No book in the world except the Bible has had such a reign. Accepted from the first as the authoritative treatise on the subject, it superseded all other compilations of Elements. Apollonius, it is true, discussed some of the first principles, *e.g.* certain definitions, and suggested some alternative constructions for problems, but his criticisms and suggestions seem to have fallen flat. The famous fifth Postulate on which Euclid bases the theory of parallels was early recognized as a crux; Posidonius sought to evade the difficulty by a different definition of parallels based on equidistance, and Geminus after him tried to prove the Postulate. Elaborate commentaries were written by two able mathematicians, Pappus and Heron of Alexandria, as well as by Porphyry, Proclus and Simplicius. Theon of Alexandria (fourth century A.D.) produced a new edition with alterations and additions designed to make the language more uniform and the proofs easier to follow. Boëtius is said to have translated the *Elements* into Latin. The book passed to Arabia in the eighth century. The first mediaeval translations, by Athelhard of Bath and Gherard of Cremona (twelfth century), were made from the Arabic, as was also the translation by Campano (thirteenth century), the first to be put into print (Erhard Ratdolt, Venice, 1482).

As Proclus says, what is most to be admired in the book is the selection made by Euclid of the things (definitions, postulates and axioms) to be taken for granted and of the particular propositions which deserve to be called 'elements' as being the most fundamental and of the widest application. The selection and arrangement, as well as many of the proofs, are Euclid's own; for the content of the treatise he laid under contribution every source open to him. We can say, for instance, generally that in Books I, II, IV, VI and probably III he is giving the substance of the Pythagorean geometry, with the contributions of such men as Oenopides and Hippocrates of Chios, while, from hints regarding current proofs of certain propositions found in Aristotle and elsewhere, we can judge of the definite innovations which Euclid himself made in methods of proof and otherwise, *e.g.* in the formulation of Postulate 5. Books VII–IX, on the elementary theory of numbers, including the numerical theory of proportion, must also be largely Pythagorean. Book V, containing the theory of proportion applicable to commensurable and incommensurable magnitudes alike, is all due in substance to Eudoxus, though the form and sequence are probably Euclid's. Book X, on irrational straight lines, is again in substance largely due to Theaetetus, as is Book XIII on the five regular solids. Book XII includes the propositions about the solid content of pyramids and cones which we know to have been first proved by Eudoxus, and these must be connected with the other propositions in which the method of exhaustion is used, namely the theorems that circles are to one another as the squares, and spheres are to one another as the cubes, on their diameters. But here, as everywhere, we see the master-hand in the formulation of the propositions and the logical development of the subject.

Euclid wrote other works not confined to geometry but covering all branches of mathematics as then known. Those which are extant in Greek include:

(1) The *Data*, containing propositions of the same purport as some in the *Elements* but in a form more directly serviceable in problems of construction;

(2) The *Optics*, a kind of elementary treatise on perspective;

(3) The *Phaenomena*, containing propositions in spherical astronomy;

(4) A *Sectio Canonis*, a book on the elements of music, which however is scarcely Euclid's in its present form, though probably based on a genuine treatise by him.

There were other works by Euclid which are now lost. One belonged to elementary geometry and was called *Pseudaria* or *Fallacies*, the purpose of which was to put pupils on their guard against possible pitfalls in geometrical reasoning. More important were three treatises in higher geometry. For what we know of these we are indebted to Pappus. The first is the *Conics*, which roughly covered the ground of the first four Books of Apollonius' *Conics* and, no doubt, like the *Elements*, carried its subject to the limit of what was then known. The second is the *Surface-Loci*. The nature of its contents is not known. The loci in question may have been loci *on* surfaces, as the Greek title implies, or loci which *are* surfaces. It seems clear that conics came into the discussion, for Pappus gives, as a lemma for use with the book, a proposition proving the fundamental property of each of the three conics referred to what we call the focus and directrix, and it is a natural inference that Euclid was aware of this property and assumed it without proof, although it does not appear in Apollonius' *Conics*. The *Porisms*, in three Books, is probably the treatise the loss of which is the most to be deplored. Pappus speaks of the contents of this work in considerable detail, though in a very summary form, and he gives a number of lemmas to it. Important attempts have been made to restore the treatise, notably by Robert Simson and Michel Chasles; but we cannot be sure that any of them have even come near to a solution of the problem. Certain it is that the work belonged to higher geometry and was of considerable scope (Pappus says that it contained 171 theorems).

Aristarchus of Samos, the ancient Copernicus, was known as 'the mathematician,' to distinguish him from the host of other persons of the same name. He was a pupil of Strato, and an observation of the summer solstice made by him in 281–280 B.C. is recorded by Ptolemy; on the other hand, his extant book *On the Sizes and Distances of the Sun and Moon* and other works of his were written before the *Psammites* or *Sand-reckoner* of Archimedes. We gather therefore that Aristarchus lived from about 310 to 230 B.C. Like his master Strato, he wrote on vision, light and colours; but it is as mathematician and astronomer that he is famous. He followed Heracleides of Pontus in attributing to the earth the daily rotation about its axis, but he went farther than Heracleides by suggesting that not only do the planets Mercury and Venus revolve about the sun like satellites (as Heracleides held), but the earth itself, as well as the planets, revolves about the sun, a hypothesis amounting to an anticipation of Copernicus. Our authority for this is Archimedes, who, in his *Sand-reckoner*, says that Aristarchus brought out a book of hypotheses, one of which was that 'the fixed stars and the sun remain unmoved, and that the earth revolves about the sun in the circumference of a circle, the sun lying in the middle of the orbit.' On the other hand, the extant treatise *On the Sizes and Distances of the Sun and Moon* was written from the ordinary geocentric standpoint. This work is a perfect specimen of Greek geometry at its best. Starting from certain assumptions of matters of fact and observation, which are naturally inaccurate as compared with modern results, Aristarchus obtains, by clever and rigorous geometry, upper and lower limits for the measures of (1) the diameter of the moon in terms of its distance from the centre of the earth, (2) the distance of the sun from the earth in terms of the distance of the moon from the earth, (3) the diameters of the sun and moon respectively in terms of that of the earth. He finds, for instance, that, on his assumptions, the distance of the sun from the earth is between 18 and 20 times the distance of the moon from the earth, a much better result than others quoted by Archimedes, who says that Eudoxus made it nine times, and Pheidias, his own father, twelve times. It was for want of trigonometry that Aristarchus could not arrive at definite figures for what are really the trigonometrical sines, cosines, and tangents of certain small angles, but could only find upper and lower limits, just as Archimedes did for the value of π. Archimedes says that Aristarchus also discovered that the arc subtended by the diameter of the sun at our eye is one seven hundred and twentieth part of a complete circle, that is, half a degree. We are told that Cleanthes the Stoic said that Aristarchus ought to be prosecuted for impiety in putting the Hearth of the Universe in motion. As Cleanthes became head of the Stoa in 261 (p. 238), it seems likely that the heliocentric hypothesis was not put forward before that date. Apparently Seleucus, of Seleuceia on the Tigris, (second century B.C.) alone accepted Aristarchus' hypothesis and tried to prove its truth; Hipparchus reverted to the geocentric view.

Conon of Samos was the courtier-astronomer who gave the name *Coma Berenices* to a group of stars in honour of Berenice, the queen of Ptolemy III Euergetes (246–221 B.C.). The story is that Berenice vowed to sacrifice her hair for the safe return of her husband from his campaign against Syria to avenge the death of his sister Berenice; this was soon after Euergetes' accession. When Euergetes actually returned, the queen's tresses were duly cut off and placed in the temple of Arsinoë-Aphrodite, but disappeared, whereupon Conon declared that they had been caught up to the skies and placed as a constellation in the triangle between Leo, Virgo and Ursa Major. Conon must therefore have died after (say) 245 B.C. On the other hand, he died long before Archimedes wrote his book *On Spirals*; for in sending this to Dositheus, Conon's pupil, Archimedes says that many years had passed since Conon's death. Archimedes had been in the habit of communicating his discoveries, before publication, to Conon whom he admired as a mathematician and cherished as a friend. Conon spent a considerable time in Italy where he made his astronomical observations, after which he settled in Alexandria. It was probably there that he made the acquaintance of Archimedes. Conon is said to have left seven Books on astronomy dedicated to Euergetes; he also made a list of the solar eclipses recorded as having occurred in Egypt. In mathematics Conon tried to prove certain propositions about the number of points (at most) in which a conic section may meet another conic or the circumference of a circle; this we learn from Apollonius.

Archimedes of Syracuse, the most original genius among the Greek mathematicians, was born about 287 and was killed, at the sack of Syracuse in 212 B.C., by a Roman soldier who found him intent on a diagram drawn on the ground and was incensed when Archimedes said to him 'Stand away, fellow, from my diagram.' Well-known stories about him tell how he declared 'Give me a place to stand on and I will move the earth'; and how for a long time he kept the Romans at bay by all sorts of mechanical devices which he employed against them. The problem of moving a great weight by a small force he is said to have illustrated, at the request and to the amazement of Hiero, by using a system of pulleys, which he worked himself, to draw up a huge ship with three masts and fully loaded. It was, no doubt, when he was in Egypt that he invented the Archimedean screw for pumping water. But he himself thought nothing of these things, which were merely the 'diversions of geometry at play'; his whole soul was absorbed in pure mathematical research. Hence it was that he caused to be engraved on his tomb a representation of a cylinder circumscribing a sphere with the ratio 3 : 2 which the cylinder bears to the sphere, in respect both of its volume and of its total surface, evidently regarding this as his greatest discovery. This tomb Cicero, when quaestor in Sicily, found in a neglected state and repaired; no trace of it now exists. Cicero also himself saw an astronomical sphere constructed by Archimedes to imitate the motions of the sun, moon and planets; according to Cicero it represented the periods of the moon and the apparent motion of the sun with such accuracy that it would even (over a short period) show the eclipses of the sun and moon.

Heron, Pappus and Theon of Alexandria all cite works of Archimedes which no longer survive. These works therefore still existed at Alexandria as late as the third and fourth centuries A.D. But attention came to be concentrated on two works only, the *Measurement of a Circle* and *On the Sphere and Cylinder*, which were at some time turned from their original Doric into the ordinary language, with alterations designed to make them easier for elementary pupils; the former, as we have it, is not in its original form, and may only be a fragment. The following are the works extant in Greek, arranged as nearly as may be in the order of composition: *On Plane Equilibriums*, Book I, *Quadrature of the Parabola*, *On Plane Equilibriums*, Book II, The *Method* (addressed to Eratosthenes), *On the Sphere and Cylinder*, I, II, *On Spirals*, *On Conoids and Spheroids*, *On Floating Bodies*, I, II (formerly known only in the Latin translation by William of Moerbeke but now in great part recovered in Greek), *Measurement of a Circle*, the *Sand-reckoner*, the *Stomachion* (a fragment). The *Method* was discovered by Heiberg as recently as 1906 in a palimpsest at Constantinople; the end of it is defective, but the beginning is there and it is complete in all essentials. It was from the same MS. that Heiberg was able partially to restore the Greek text of *On Floating Bodies* and the *Stomachion* (a sort of Chinese puzzle).

A *Book of Lemmas* which has come to us through the Arabic is not, in its present form, the work of Archimedes; but some elegant propositions in it may go back to Archimedes, and notably some theorems about figures called respectively *salinon* (salt-cellar) and *shoe-maker's knife* on account of their shape. The famous *Cattle-Problem*, purporting to have been sent by Archimedes to the mathematicians at Alexandria in a letter to Eratosthenes, is a difficult problem in indeterminate analysis leading to enormous numbers.

We have notices by Greek writers of works of Archimedes now lost. (1) Pappus says that he investigated thirteen semi-regular solids, which are contained by equilateral and equiangular polygons but not all of one kind; thus one figure has eight faces of which four are equilateral triangles and four are regular hexagons, another has fourteen faces of which eight are equilateral triangles and six are squares, another has sixty-two faces of which twenty are equilateral triangles, thirty are squares and twelve are regular pentagons, and so on (according to Heron, Plato knew of two of the thirteen solids). (2) Theon of Alexandria mentions a work by Archimedes called *Catoptrica* (theory of mirrors).

The details of Archimedes' mathematics cannot be entered on here; it must suffice to indicate the nature of his work. In the geometrical treatises he stands, as it were, on the shoulders of Eudoxus, measuring the content of curvilinear plane figures and solids by methods which are a development of Eudoxus' method of exhaustion. If we may judge by the examples of the use of this method by Euclid in his Book XII, Eudoxus approached the figure to be measured from below only, inscribing figures more and more nearly approaching it and so 'exhausting' it. Archimedes approaches it both from above and from below, circumscribing successive figures as well as inscribing them, and showing that the final circumscribed and inscribed figures can be compressed, as it were, as nearly as we please, into coincidence with the figure to be measured and with one another. The desired result is, last of all, established by a proof by *reductio ad absurdum*. In many instances Archimedes' procedure amounts to a genuine *integration*, as can be seen by writing down the equivalent of his steps in modern analytical notation; this is so with his investigation of the areas of a parabolic segment and a spiral, the surface and volume of a sphere, and the volumes of any segments of the conoids (paraboloids and hyperboloids of revolution) and spheroids.

But the recently discovered *Method* shows that this was not the way in which Archimedes made his first discoveries in this field. Thus he first discovered that the area of a segment of a parabola is four-thirds of that of the triangle with the same base and height by a mechanical method which it is the object of the treatise to expound. The procedure is to *weigh* countless elements of the figure to be measured against the same number of elements of another figure the mensuration of which is already known. The elements are, in the case of plane areas, parallel straight lines in them and, in the case of solids, parallel plane sections; and it is implied that the figures are *made up of* the infinite number of parallel straight lines or parallel plane sections in the figures respectively, which is very much the view taken by Cavalieri. Hence Chasles could truly say that Archimedes' investigations 'gave birth to the calculus of the infinite conceived and brought to perfection successively by Kepler, Cavalieri, Fermat, Leibniz and Newton.' With regard, however, to the mechanical method, Archimedes is careful to explain that, while it is useful in suggesting results, it does not afford a conclusive proof of them; this has later to be supplied by the rigorous method of exhaustion.

The *Measurement of a Circle* first proves rigorously by exhaustion that the area of a circle is equal to that of a right-angled triangle in which the perpendicular sides are respectively equal to the circumference and the radius of the circle. Archimedes then finds upper and lower limits to the value (π) of the ratio of the circumference to the diameter by inscribing and circumscribing regular polygons of 96 sides, and approximating by sheer calculation to their contours respectively. He assumes as known certain limits to the value of $\sqrt{3}$, namely $\frac{1351}{780} > \sqrt{3} > \frac{265}{153}$, and finally arrives at the well-known result $3\frac{1}{7} > \pi > 3\frac{10}{71}$.

The *Plane Equilibriums* is the first known scientific treatise on the first principles of mechanics. Premising a few postulates suggested by common experience, Archimedes proves the principle of the lever and then finds the centres of gravity of certain figures, a parallelogram, a triangle, a trapezium, and finally (in the elaborate Book II) of a parabolic segment and of any portion of such cut off between the base and any straight line parallel to it.

In the *Sand-reckoner* Archimedes undertakes to prove that, notwithstanding the inadequacy of the ordinary Greek numerical notation to express large numbers, he can, by a certain system developed by him in a separate work called *Principles*, express any number however large, as *e.g.* the number of grains of sand which, on any reasonable hypothesis as to the size of the universe, the universe would contain. The system is one of *orders* and *periods* based on powers of myriad-myriads ($10,000^2$), and would suffice to express any number up to the 80,000 million-millionth power of ten! The number of grains of sand required to fill up a space equal to the universe is, on the hypothesis taken, proved to be less than "10,000,000 units of the eighth order of numbers," which is in fact 10^{63}.

Lastly, Archimedes invented the whole science of hydrostatics. In the treatise *On Floating Bodies*, after an assumption about uniform pressure in a fluid, he first proves that the surface of a fluid at rest is a sphere concentric with the earth. Propositions following prove that, if a solid floats in a fluid, the weight of the solid is equal to that of the fluid displaced, and if a solid heavier than a fluid is weighed in it, it will be lighter than its true weight by the weight of the fluid displaced. Then, after an assumption that a body which is forced upwards in a fluid is forced upwards along the perpendicular to the surface of the fluid drawn through the centre of gravity of the body, Archimedes investigates the positions of rest and stability of a segment of a sphere floating in a fluid either side up, but with its base entirely above or entirely below the surface. Book II goes still farther and investigates fully all the positions of rest and stability of a right segment of a paraboloid similarly floating in different cases according (1) to the relation between the length of the axis of the solid and the parameter of the generating parabola and (2) to the specific gravity of the solid in relation to the fluid.

A younger contemporary of Archimedes was Eratosthenes of Cyrene, with whom, as we have seen, Archimedes had relations. The other activities of this many-sided man have already been described (see above, p. 262 *sq.*); it remains to say a word about his mathematics. He devised a mechanical solution of the problem of finding two, or any number of, mean proportionals in continued proportion between two straight lines. A bronze representation of the contrivance (*mesŏlăbon*, mean-finder) was attached to the pillar which Eratosthenes erected in recognition of his obligation to Ptolemy Euergetes, and on which were inscribed a diagram and short proof of the solution, with an epigram. Eratosthenes wrote a book entitled *Platonicus* which was used by Theon of Smyrna in his work on the mathematics which it was necessary for the student of Plato to know; the *Platonicus* seems to have begun with the story of the problem of Delos and to have contained disquisitions on proportion, the fundamental definitions of geometry and the principles of music. Another work by Eratosthenes *On Means*, in two Books, is included by Pappus, along with works by Euclid, Aristaeus and Apollonius, in the 'Treasury of Analysis.' His device known as the *sieve*, for finding prime numbers, is not very recondite. In astronomy he wrote a descriptive poem *Hermes*, fragments of which remain, and another work which may have been the basis of the Pseudo-Eratosthenic *Catasterismi*.

A school of mechanicians also flourished under the first Ptolemies. Ctesibius, the earlier of two persons of that name, probably lived under Philadelphus and Euergetes I. This Ctesibius constructed engines of war and pneumatic and hydraulic machines, among which Vitruvius mentions a force-pump, a water-clock, etc. Philo of Byzantium, perhaps a generation or so later than Ctesibius, wrote a *Mechanical Collection* in at least nine Books of which the fourth (*Belopoeica*) and a further fragment survive in Greek, while a portion of Book V (*Pneumatica*) exists in a Latin translation from the Arabic. Another extant treatise on engines of war was written by one Athenaeus and is addressed to Marcellus.

Apollonius of Perga, known as 'the great geometer' on the strength of his *Conics*, was born at Perga in Pamphylia, but studied for a long time at Alexandria with the successors of Euclid. He flourished in the reign of Ptolemy Euergetes I (246–221 B.C.). He refers in one of his prefaces to a visit to Pergamum, and he dedicated the fourth and following Books of the *Conics* to King Attalus I (241–197 B.C.).

The *Conics* was originally in eight Books. Of these only the first four survive in Greek, but Books v–vii exist in Arabic; the eighth is lost. Eutocius (*flor.* A.D. 520) edited the first four Books and added a commentary; it is probably to this fact that we owe the survival of both text and commentary. The monumental edition of Halley (Oxford, 1710) includes, besides the Greek text of Books I–IV, a Latin translation of Books V–VII from the Arabic and an attempted restoration of Book VIII.

From the outset we are struck by the remarkable generality of treatment. Before Apollonius' time the three conics were called 'sections of a right-angled, acute-angled, and obtuse-angled cone' respectively, because they were originally produced as sections of right cones of these types by planes always perpendicular to a generator (edge). Apollonius produces all three curves (including the double-branch hyperbola) in the most general way from any one cone (in general oblique). The diameter emerging from the construction is in general not an axis; but the fundamental property is in each case stated with reference to this diameter and the corresponding 'parameter' or 'latus rectum.' Though expressed in the language of 'application of areas,' the property is actually equivalent to the Cartesian equation of the curve referred to any diameter and the tangent at its extremity as axes; the square on the 'ordinate' is stated to be equal to a rectangle of width equal to the 'abscissa' applied to the parameter, but in the case of the parabola the rectangle is *applied* exactly (*parabole* simply) to the parameter, whereas in the case of the ellipse or hyperbola it *falls short* (*elleipsis*) or exceeds (*hyperbole*) respectively by a rectangle of given shape. Hence the names *parabola, ellipse, hyperbola* applied to the conics for the first time by Apollonius. There is something impressive in a treatise which only condescends to notice the principal axes of a conic, as a particular case, so late as I. 52, after it has been shown that the conic has the same property with regard to any diameter and parameter as it has with reference to the pair arising out of the original construction.

Books I–IV are described by Apollonius himself as forming an elementary introduction. They evidently cover much the same ground as earlier treatises (notably Euclid's); only certain propositions in Books III, IV are new, but Apollonius rightly claims to have treated the whole subject more fully and generally than his predecessors. The four Books contain all the well-known ordinate-, chord-, and tangent-properties of the three conics (including the double-branch hyperbola treated as one curve), as well as, in the case of the central conics, the focal properties other than those which bring in the directrix; the directrix does not appear at all; nor does Apollonius mention the focus of a parabola.

Books V–VII are, in Apollonius' own words, more 'by way of surplusage'; they contain in fact highly specialized, and in part very difficult, investigations. Book V is the most remarkable. It deals with *normals* to the conics regarded as maximum and

minimum straight lines drawn to a conic from any point, internal
or external, and apart from their relation to tangents. The Book
is a *tour de force* which must be read to be believed. Not only does
it investigate the number of normals that can be drawn from any
point, but there are propositions in it (all established by pure
geometry) which lead immediately to the determination of the
evolutes of a parabola and a central conic.

Six other works by Apollonius are included by Pappus in the
'Treasury of Analysis.' Only one has survived, and that in Arabic,
On the Cutting-off of a Ratio. The others are *On the Cutting-off of an
Area, On Determinate Section, On Tangencies* (in this the historic
problem of drawing a circle to touch each of three given circles
was solved by elementary methods), *Plane Loci,* and *Inclinationes.*
Apollonius also wrote on (1) the *Comparison of the Dodecahedron
with the Icosahedron,* (2) the *Cochlias* (or cylindrical helix), (3) *Un-
ordered Irrationals.* In a *General Treatise* he apparently discussed
fundamental principles, while in a book called *Ōcytocion* ('quick
delivery') he is said to have found a closer approximation than
that of Archimedes to the value of π. He also had a system for
expressing large numbers based on powers of the myriad; this
may have been a counterblast to Archimedes's system (p. 306
above).

Apollonius was no less distinguished in astronomy. He was
master of (if he did not invent) the theories of epicycles and
eccentric circles as a means of accounting for the movements of
the planets; he may therefore have been the ancient Tycho Brahe
following the ancient Copernicus (Aristarchus).

The classical tradition was kept up for a time by geometers
who are mostly known for one particular achievement. Thus
Nicomedes was the discoverer of the *conchoid* or *cochloid,* a me-
chanically-constructed curve useful for solving higher problems.
Perseus investigated the *spiric* curves, namely certain sections of
the *speira,* one variety of which is the anchor-ring or *tore.* Zenodorus
wrote on *Isometric figures,* the problem being to compare the content of different figures, plane or solid, having equal contours or
surfaces respectively. Diocles, the discoverer of the curve called
the *cissoid,* also wrote on *Burning Mirrors.*

But with Apollonius pure geometry had practically reached the
limit of what it could accomplish unaided. Advance only became
possible after many centuries, when men like Fermat and Des-
cartes showed that the symbolism and methods of algebra could
be used as aids to geometry, and when again in course of time the
calculus increased the resources of the new analytical geometry. The

wonder is, not that Greek geometry could go no farther, but that it could accomplish so much. And it was, after all, the Greeks and notably Apollonius who pointed the way to co-ordinate geometry, while Archimedes actually anticipated the calculus.

VI. HIPPARCHUS

One branch of geometry remained to be developed, namely trigonometry. So far as we know, the first person to make systematic use of trigonometry was Hipparchus, with whom this chapter may suitably conclude.

Hipparchus, the greatest astronomer of antiquity, was born at Nicaea in Bithynia. His date can only be inferred from Ptolemy's references to observations made by him, the limits of which are 161 and 126 B.C. His characteristics were extraordinary modesty and passionate love of truth. The only book of his which has survived is the *Commentary on the Phaenomena of Eudoxus and Aratus* (an early work); what we know of his work apart from this is contained in Ptolemy (who based himself mainly on Hipparchus) and in scattered references by other authors. Hipparchus, we are told, wrote a treatise in twelve Books on straight lines (*i.e.* chords) in a circle, which no doubt included a table of chords (equivalent to a table of trigonometrical *sines*) something like that given by Ptolemy. Ptolemy sets out, in an admirably clear and succinct form, the minimum number of geometrical propositions required for preparing his own table, and these (including the well-known 'Ptolemy's theorem') were doubtless known to Hipparchus.

It remains to indicate briefly the main contributions of Hipparchus to astronomy.

1. His greatest discovery was, no doubt, that of the *precession of the equinoxes*. He found that the bright star Spica was, at the time of his observation of it (129–128 B.C.), 6° distant from the autumnal equinoctial point, whereas he deduced from observations recorded by one Timocharis that Timocharis had made the distance 8°. Now Timocharis made observations of fixed stars (among the first recorded) in 295 and 283–282 B.C.; the interval was thus 166 or 154 years, and the difference of 2° gives for the motion an average of 43·4" or 46·8" a year as compared with the true figure of 50·3757".

2. In a work *On the length of the Year* Hipparchus compared observations of the summer solstice made by Aristarchus in 281–280 B.C. and by himself in 136–135 B.C. and found that, after

the 145 years, the summer solstice occurred half a day and night earlier than it should have done on the assumption of $365\frac{1}{4}$ days to the year; hence he inferred that the *tropical* year contained about $\frac{1}{300}$th of a day and night less than $365\frac{1}{4}$ days. This agrees very nearly with Censorinus' statement that Hipparchus made his cycle 304 years or four times that of Callippus (76 years), but with 111,035 days in it instead of 111,036 (= 27,759 × 4). Counting in the 304 years 3760 months in all (12 × 304 + 112 intercalary), Hipparchus made the mean lunar month 29 days, 12 hours, 44 minutes, $2\frac{1}{2}$ seconds, which is less than a second out in comparison with the present accepted figure of 29·53059 days!

3. Hipparchus improved on Aristarchus' figures for the sizes and distances of the sun and moon, determining the apparent diameters more exactly and noting the changes in them.

4. He accounted for the motions of the sun and moon by the simple epicycle and eccentric hypotheses, but found it necessary, in the case of the planets, to combine the two, *i.e.* to superadd epicycles to motion in eccentric circles.

5. He made a catalogue of fixed stars to the number of 850 or more, distinguishing degrees of brightness and (apparently for the first time) stating the position of each star in terms of co-ordinates (latitude and longitude) referred to the ecliptic.

6. He constructed a globe showing the positions of the fixed stars as determined by him, and made great improvements in the instruments used for observations.

7. He wrote on geography, mainly by way of criticism of Eratosthenes, and emphasizing the necessity of applying astronomy to geography.

The debt of humanity to Hipparchus, and the greatness of soul of the man whose system was practically not improved upon until the days of Copernicus, Galilei and Kepler, cannot be better illustrated than by his motive in compiling the catalogue. He discovered a new star which first appeared in his time, and this set him thinking whether the same phenomenon might not occur at any time, and whether there might not be movement on the part even of the stars which we deem 'fixed'; in making his catalogue, therefore, he 'left the heavens as a sort of heritage to all and sundry' (as Pliny says), in order that it might be easy for posterity to judge, not only whether stars vanish and new ones appear, but whether changes occur in their relative positions, and whether they wax or wane.

CHAPTER X

THE SOURCES FOR THE TRADITION OF EARLY ROMAN HISTORY

I. EARLY MONUMENTS

IT is impossible to hope that fresh discoveries will make any important addition to our knowledge of the early history of Rome, so far as that depends on contemporary documents of which the original text is preserved. The only monument of this kind which has been brought to light is the truncated pillar found by Comm. Boni beneath the lava pavement in the Comitium which is supposed to represent the *lapis niger* marking the site of the tomb of Romulus. This is too fragmentary to permit of restoration, and there is no sufficient evidence for determining its date; but from the fact that the variety of tufa of which it is made is found at Veii it has been argued that it belongs to the period during which Etruscans ruled in Rome, in which case the *rex* whom it clearly names may have been one of the Tarquins. It seems to refer to some religious observance, and we may recall the entry in the Roman calendar QUANDO REX COMITIAVIT, FAS. But we do not need its evidence to prove that there were *reges* in early Rome; and it proves nothing more.

It is true that we possess reproductions, more or less faithful and precise, of certain early documents, handed down to us by literary tradition. A collection of laws ascribed to the Kings (*leges regiae*) relating mainly to religion or to crimes regarded in their religious aspect was current under the name of *ius Papirianum*, which was explained by the supposition that a member of the *gens Papiria*, the first *pontifex maximus* of the free state, had brought them together. The code of the Twelve Tables, to be discussed presently, was also preserved by tradition, and, as Cicero tells us, taught in the school up to his own childhood; and we can reconstruct it in part from the quotations. We also have translations (or paraphrases) of a treaty between Rome and Carthage ascribed by Polybius to the first year of the Republic, and of a treaty between Rome and the Latin league inscribed on a bronze tablet in the Forum, and dated by the name of Spurius Cassius, believed to have been consul in 493 B.C. But the dates of both these documents are matter of controversy (see Chronological Note 1, pp. 859 *sqq.*, and p. 490 *sq.*).

In 36 B.C. the Regia, *i.e.* the office of the *pontifex maximus*, was rebuilt in marble at the instance of Augustus with the spoils gained in Spain by his general Cn. Domitius Calvinus, and on its walls were engraved two lists. The first gave the names of the chief magistrates of the state from the beginning of the Republic, whether consuls, decemvirs, or *tribuni militum consulari potestate*, who gave their names to their year of office, as well as those of the dictators and their masters of the horse, and also of the censors, with the number of the *lustrum* which they performed. The other contained the names of all who had triumphed, with the occasion and the date, beginning with 'Romulus son of Mars,' who celebrated a triumph over the Caeninenses on the first of March. It is not certain when these lists were engraved; the names of Mark Antony and of his grandfather have been erased in the list of magistrates, which must therefore have been made before his defeat at Actium. The list was continued down to A.D. 12; the list of triumphs (in which the names of Antony and his brother were not erased) goes down to 19 B.C. Needless to say, these documents are compilations, made almost certainly by order of Augustus, and, in the form in which we have them, they have no higher claim to credibility than literary works of the same period such as that of Livy. The problem of their sources is a literary problem, and there is no ground for regarding them as a faithful reproduction of an official record kept on behalf of the Roman state. We shall find that they agree with the less trustworthy of the chronological traditions preserved in literary sources.

II. EXTANT HISTORIANS

The narrative of the early history of Rome is only preserved for us in a continuous form in two extant works, both written under Augustus, the *Histories* of Livy and the *Roman Antiquities* of Dionysius of Halicarnassus, and neither of these is complete. Livy, born at Patavium (Padua) in 59 B.C., seems to have conceived the plan of his work about the year 27 B.C., in which year Augustus 'restored the Republic' and found in the historian a loyal believer in the sincerity of his intentions and a fervent sympathizer in his effort to recreate the ancient Roman virtues. When complete, the work carried the story down from the landing of Aeneas to 9 B.C. in 142 books. These were divided for convenience of handling into groups of ten ('decades,' as writers of later antiquity term them); but these did not correspond with any logical divisions of the subject-matter, and the first decade ends abruptly in 293 B.C., whereas 287 B.C. would form a natural break. It follows that as the second decade is not preserved we do not possess Livy's account of the constitutional settlement which terminated the political struggle of the orders. For the lost books we possess only meagre 'tables of contents' (*periochae*); there must also have been somewhat fuller abridgments, as appears from the fragment of such an epitome found at Oxyrhynchus, which deals with events of the second century B.C.[1] Dionysius of Halicarnassus, a Greek teacher of rhetoric and a literary critic who represents to us the severe classicism which endeavoured to maintain the standard of the Attic orators against modern tendencies, came to Rome in 30 B.C. and spent more than twenty years in compiling his *Roman Antiquities*. This work was published in 7 B.C. and covered the history of Rome from its foundation to the outbreak of the First Punic War in twenty books. Of these only the first ten are preserved in a complete form; the eleventh is partly extant, and we have extracts from the rest.

Among extant writers of later date two deserve mention at this point. Appian, a citizen of Alexandria, born about A.D. 90, who had an undistinguished career in the Imperial Civil Service as *advocatus fisci* and obtained the title of *procurator* from Antoninus Pius through the influence of Fronto, set out in A.D. 160 or thereabouts to write a History of Rome on a new principle, describing the wars waged by the Romans in a series of treatises in which the subject-matter is distributed mainly on geographical principles. From the *Wars of the Kings*, the *Wars in Italy* and the *Samnite Wars*, which cover the early period we have only excerpts. Half a century later Cassius Dio Cocceianus, a native of Nicaea in Bithynia, of senatorial family, who was born about A.D. 155 and rose to the consulship, which he held for the second time in A.D. 229 as the colleague of the Emperor Severus Alexander, wrote a History of Rome from its foundation to his own time in eighty books. This work is only preserved in part in its complete form, and the first thirty-five books, carrying the narrative down to 68 B.C., are lost; but apart from excerpts, of which there are a fair number, we possess an *Abridgment of History* made by Ioannes Zonaras in the twelfth century A.D. which is directly based on the original work of Dio in its earlier portions.

Such are the works, dealing at large with the history of Rome, of which substantial remains have come down to us. But we must also take into account the *Universal History* compiled by Diodorus of Agyrium in Sicily. This was a work in forty books under

[1] *P. Oxy.* IV, 668 (printed in Rossbach's Teubner text of the *Periochae*).

the title *Bibliotheke*, which ended with Caesar's expedition to Britain (54 B.C.), and was apparently completed under Augustus, that is, if the colonization of Tauromenium, to which allusion is made in the sixteenth book, took place in 21 B.C. The first five books, which we have in a complete form, deal with the mythical period; of the next five we have only fragments. The ten which follow cover the period from 479–301 B.C., and are fitted into a chronological framework based on the synchronism of Olympiads, Athenian archonships and Roman consulates. Diodorus has little space to spare for notice of the events of Roman history, and under many years only the names of the consuls appear.

In addition we have the meagre epitomes of writers such as Florus, who wrote his two books on the *Wars of the Romans* under Hadrian, Eutropius, whose *Brief Sketch* of Roman history was written in the fourth century, perhaps in rivalry with a similar work by Rufius Festus, and Orosius, a pupil of St Augustine, whose *Historiae adversus paganos*, designed to show that the miseries of his own age were less than those of pre-Christian times, were published in A.D. 417. All of these derive such value as they possess from the fact that they used an abridged version of the lost books of Livy. Such, then, are the immediate sources of our knowledge of the early history of Rome. It is evident that we can only gauge their value by considering what were the sources of information open to them and used by them, and what principles they followed in dealing with those sources. The latter question is of the highest importance; for a compiler whose work is based on that of his predecessors may set forth conflicting evidence in detail and treat it critically, or he may slavishly follow one main authority, or different authorities in different parts of his work. Had the ancient historians of the Imperial age followed the first course, we should at least have been acquainted with the elements of the problems which they were trying to solve: but that was not the way of ancient historians, especially those for whom the writing of history was a rhetorical exercise, nor would critical discussion have been to the taste of the public for whom they catered. Livy does, it is true, from time to time mention some of the more glaring discrepancies which he finds in his authorities; but it is to be assumed that as a general rule he has smoothed out contradictions or selected what appears to him the preferable version. The same applies to Dionysius, who rarely notes variants in the narrative, although he assures us that he spent many years in acquiring Latin and studying the works of the native historians, and mentions some of the more obscure by name.

What then were the sources from which Livy and Dionysius derived the outline of history which each filled in after his own manner? Neither of them, we may feel sure, made original researches into such official documents as may have been accessible. Livy makes a reference to the cuirass dedicated in the temple of Juppiter Feretrius by A. Cornelius Cossus as *spolia opima*, when he had slain with his own hand Lars Tolumnius, King of Veii, and tells us that the inscription proved that the dedicator did not, as the literary tradition said, perform this exploit as *tribunus militum* in 437 B.C., but as consul in 428 B.C. (p. 507 *sq.*). But this information was supplied to him by Augustus, who had secured it from his court antiquaries in order to bar the claim of M. Licinius Crassus, proconsul in 27 B.C., to dedicate *spolia opima* taken from the chieftain of the Bastarnae, by establishing that no precedent existed for such a dedication by one who (like Crassus) fought under the *auspicia* of a higher magistrate. The exception therefore proves the rule. The immediate sources of Livy and Dionysius were literary.

III. THE EARLIER ANNALISTS

Historical writing at Rome dates from the end of the third century B.C., and the pioneers in this field used the Greek tongue. The earliest was Q. Fabius Pictor, a descendant (as his *cognomen* shows) of C. Fabius Pictor, who decorated with paintings the temple of Salus on the Quirinal in 304 B.C. He had taken part in the war of 225–222 B.C. with the Gauls, and was sent on a mission to consult the Delphic oracle in 216 B.C. To judge from the extant references to his work (we can hardly describe them as 'fragments') he dealt with the earliest legends at considerable length, and, as Dionysius tells us, he treated in detail of the events of his own time; the intervening period was more summarily handled. The same was true of his contemporary, L. Cincius Alimentus, praetor in 210 B.C. These writers, in treating of Republican history, arranged their matter by years in strict chronological order, and their works and those of their successors were known as *libri annales*. Two writers of the second century, A. Postumius Albinus, consul in 151 B.C., and C. Acilius, who acted as interpreter for the Greek philosophers who were sent from Athens as envoys to the Senate in 155 B.C., also wrote in Greek. Their works were, however, translated into Latin, and the Latin 'Annals of Fabius' mentioned by Aulus Gellius were in all probability a translation of those of Q. Fabius Pictor and not the work of a later member of his family.

The first historian to employ the Latin tongue was apparently L. Cassius Hemina, who, we are told, was living in 146 B.C. We know nothing of his career, and it is remarkable that he is not mentioned by our extant historians, and is quoted only by antiquarians and grammarians (none earlier than the elder Pliny). Three statesmen of the latter half of the second century B.C., Q. Fabius Maximus Servilianus, consul in 142 B.C., L. Calpurnius Piso, consul in 133 B.C. and censor in 120 B.C., and perhaps C. Sempronius Tuditanus, consul in 129 B.C., wrote Latin *annales*; of these Piso, as the quotations show, exercised by far the greatest influence on later writers. We know nothing of Vennonius, a writer mentioned by Cicero and Dionysius, who probably belonged to the same period.

None of the *annales* so far written was of great length. The first historian to depict Roman history on a broad canvas was Cn. Gellius, whose work extended at least to ninety-seven books in the fifteenth of which events recounted by Livy in his fifth book were described. There is, however, little reason to think that he formed one of the principal sources directly used by our extant writers, for Dionysius generally couples him with Licinius Macer (which probably means that the latter was the immediate authority used), and Livy never mentions him.

We now come to the writers of the first century B.C., in whom we may reasonably expect to find the authorities upon whom Livy and Dionysius mainly drew. We know little or nothing of the personal history of Q. Claudius Quadrigarius (probably not to be identified with the 'Claudius' who translated the Greek annals of Acilius), and as he is not cited for any fact of Roman history earlier than the sack of Rome by the Gauls, his work may have begun from that point. He is frequently quoted by Livy, and his archaic style caused him to be read and cited by the grammarians. His contemporary, Valerius Antias, a *protégé*, as we may suppose, of the Valerian house, treated Roman history on a larger scale; we have quotations up to the seventy-fifth book, and it is evident that Livy treats him as one of his principal authorities, though Dionysius scarcely mentions him. C. Licinius Macer, a democratic politician, who made a premature endeavour to restore the powers of the tribunate in 73 B.C., was praetor shortly after 70 B.C., and was condemned for misgovernment of a province in 66 B.C. by a court over which Cicero presided, wrote a work which both Livy and Dionysius used freely. The form of the references in Dionysius suggests that Macer made use of the work of Gellius: but he also, if his own account may be trusted, undertook research in archives; this raises a serious question to be discussed later. The last of the Republican annalists was Aelius Tubero, a contemporary of Cicero, probably the L. Aelius Tubero who was writing a history in 60 B.C., as Cicero mentions in a letter to his brother, although Livy gives him the *praenomen* Quintus, which belongs to his son, a well-known jurist.

In the above group of writers we must seek the sources of the traditional narrative. The epic poem of Ennius (who came to Rome in 204 B.C. and no doubt had the work of Fabius Pictor before him) is not to be counted amongst the authorities used by the prose annalists: the *Origines* of Cato the Elder, valuable as they were by reason of the fact that their author did not confine himself to Rome, but related the early history of the other Italian peoples, was little used except for the legends of the foundation and the regal period, to which there are some references in Dionysius.

We cannot leave this branch of our subject without mentioning the view held by many scholars that Diodorus drew his statements concerning early Roman history from one of the earlier annalists, perhaps Fabius Pictor, and thus preserves a less vitiated tradition than Livy and Dionysius. It is no doubt true that the imaginative details which seem characteristic of post-Gracchan annalists are comparatively absent from Diodorus; but whether we are to explain this by the antiquity of his source or the brevity of his compilation cannot be determined with any degree of certainty. We are, in fact, quite unable to give a name or a date to the primary source of Diodorus; the second-century annalists cannot be ruled out, but every statement must be considered on its merits, and brevity alone must not be regarded as creating a presumption of accuracy. Diodorus was, no doubt, an indolent compiler who saved himself trouble by copying almost verbally from a single authority, such as Ephorus, and the brief notices of events in Roman history which he inserts from time to time— there are none at all in Books xvII and xvIII—might well have been drawn from a single source; in this case, however, it is most likely that they were taken from a chronological table with synchronisms between Greek and Roman history rather than from one of the Roman annalists, and something might be said for the view that this was the Chronicle of Castor of Rhodes, which was certainly known to Diodorus, and was continued almost precisely to the point at which Diodorus closed his History[1]. It should be observed, however, that Diodorus in a few places (*e.g.* xi, 53; xiv,

[1] See Beloch, *Römische Geschichte*, pp. 107 *sqq.*

102, 116, 117) mentions variants in the Roman tradition, which
he would not have found in Fabius Pictor. In one of his opening
chapters (i, 4) Diodorus tries to convey the impression that he
studied *Latin* writers on Roman history—he talks of *hypomnemata*
preserved from ancient times; but this means no more than the
works of annalists and it is hard to think that the statement (xii,
25) that in 449 B.C. it was enacted that one consul should be
plebeian could be derived from that writer. A passage (xix, 72)
on which great stress has been laid, in which he says that Luceria
was used by the Romans as a base of operations 'until our times'
(ἕως τῶν καθ᾿ ἡμᾶς χρόνων), is explicable if the authority followed
belonged not to the time of the Second Punic War but to the
Sullan period, since Luceria may well have played its part in the
Social War. The expression is in fact suspicious, since Diodorus
purloins a story from Posidonius and says that it occurred 'in
our times' (καθ᾿ ἡμᾶς) and in another passage (also taken from
Posidonius) involves himself in a bad blunder concerning the
Aedui by the use of a similar phrase.

IV. SOURCES USED BY THE ANNALISTS

We must next ask what were the materials upon which the
annalists worked, and how they treated them; above all, to what
extent was their narrative based on official archives. In the *de
oratore* (ii, 12, 52) Cicero says that early historical writing consisted
in 'the drawing-up of year-books' (*annalium confectio*); and that
with this object, 'from the beginnings of the Roman state down to
P. Mucius' (*i.e.* P. Mucius Scaevola, consul in 133 B.C., *pontifex
maximus* in 130 B.C.) the *pontifex maximus* recorded the events of
each year on a tablet which he exposed at his house: these year-
books, he continues, are still called *annales maximi*. In the *de legibus*
(i, 2, 6) he speaks of the *annales* of the *pontifices maximi*, 'quibus
nihil potest esse ieiunius' (so we must clearly read for 'iucundius').
Cato wrote in the fourth book of his *Origines*[1] (which dealt with the
Punic wars) that he did not care to set down 'what is to be found
in the tablet at the house of the *pontifex maximus*,' such as the rise
of food-prices or eclipses of sun or moon: and the only genuine
fragments of the *annales maximi* contain mention of an eclipse
(to which Ennius also referred) and of the portent which occurred
when the statue of Horatius Cocles in the Comitium was struck
by lightning. A note of Servius on the *Aeneid* amplifies the statement made by Cicero in the *de oratore*; the names of the consuls

[1] Frag. 77, Peter.

and other magistrates, he says, appeared at the head of the calendar of each year, and all the principal events 'at home and abroad, by sea or land' were noted with their dates; the whole compilation (ascribed to 'the ancients') was contained in eighty books. It has been inferred from this that P. Mucius Scaevola published these records, which he found in the Regia. It is hard to believe that a work so elaborate could not have been cited by our historians in matters of dispute: but it is not to be denied that records of the kind to which Cato refers existed, and the question must be asked, at what date did they begin? The text of Cicero's *de legibus* is defective and corrupt in the passage relating to the eclipse mentioned by Ennius. Taking the figures inserted by a corrector to be right, it occurred in 'about the 350th year from the foundation of Rome,' and Ennius dated it to the fifth of June. There is no known eclipse which is chronologically suitable, and it is suggested by Beloch that '450th' should be read, and the eclipse identified with that which took place in June, 288 B.C.[1] It must, however, have been the first in the series, since Cicero tells us that astronomers had calculated from it a series extending back to the time of Romulus. Possibly the genuine records began not much before that date, and Beloch conjectures that the reorganization of the pontifical college by the Lex Ogulnia (see below, p. 535) may have furnished the occasion.

A second official record is cited in four passages of the fourth book of Livy. Licinius Macer, he tells us, found in the 'linen rolls' containing lists of magistrates which were kept in the temple of Juno Moneta on the *Arx*, the names of two consuls who held office in 444 B.C., in which year the *Fasti* give a college of three *tribuni militum*. From the same source Macer derived the name of L. Minucius, which appeared as that of a *praefectus annonae* amongst the magistrates of those years: the Minicii or Minucii were a plebeian family who endeavoured to connect their name with the corn-supply of Rome, and this Minucius appears in a rival tradition as an 'eleventh tribune.' It is, however, a suspicious fact that in recording a discrepancy between the traditions with regard to the supreme college of 434 B.C., Livy tells us that Macer and Aelius Tubero both cited the 'linen rolls,' but each for a different pair of consuls. Ingenious suggestions have been made in recent years in order to explain the causes of the uncertainty which existed as to the office-holders of this period and at the same time to save the credit of Macer; but it is hard to believe in

[1] In *Hermes*, LVII, 1922, pp. 119 *sqq.*

the genuineness of these documents. The temple of Juno Moneta, it may be added, dates from 344 B.C.

V. SYSTEMS OF CHRONOLOGY

The systems of chronology set up by the ancient historians of Rome were based partly on synchronisms with the events of Greek history and partly on the lists of magistrates; but there were, as we shall see, great difficulties in accommodating the *data* derived from the two sources.

The synchronisms with Greek history are expressed either in terms of Olympiads or of Athenian archonships, or by means of intervals, and the events whose dates are thus fixed are (*a*) the foundation of Rome, (*b*) the first Republican consulship, (*c*) the sack of Rome by the Gauls. In his first book (1, 74) Dionysius tells us that Timaeus dated the foundation of Rome and that of Carthage in the same year, '38 years before the first Olympiad' (*i.e.* 814 B.C.). How he arrived at this figure it is impossible to say, but it seems fair to conclude that he calculated the date for Carthage and assumed Rome to be coeval. Of the early annalists Fabius Pictor placed the foundation in Ol. 8. 1 = 748 B.C. and Cincius Alimentus in Ol. 12. 4 = 729/8 B.C. Cato placed the same event '432 years after the Trojan War,' *i.e.* in Ol. 7. 1 = 752 B.C., as Dionysius determined the date by the tables of Eratosthenes. Finally Polybius, says Dionysius, gave the year following, Ol. 7. 2 = 751/0 B.C.[1], and the same date is found in Diodorus (VII, frag. 5) and Cicero (*de Rep.* II, 18). The reigns of the Kings covered 244 years according to most authorities[2], and this tallies with Polybius' statement that the first consuls of the Republic took office '28 years before Xerxes crossed over to Greece,' *i.e.* in 508/7 B.C., if his reckoning was inclusive. Dionysius places the first consulship in the archonship of Isagoras (508 B.C.), which is determined by the interval of 120 years between this event and the sack of Rome by the Gauls, which, he says, was 'generally agreed to have taken place when Pyrgion was archon at Athens.' This was in 388/7 B.C., but Polybius definitely states (1, 6) that the Gauls took Rome in the year of the Peace of Antalcidas (387/6 B.C.) and of the siege of Rhegium by Dionysius of Syracuse

---

[1] It has been asserted that he derived this date from the *annales maximi*: but the words of Dionysius prove the exact opposite. He says: 'I was determined not, like Polybius, to say *merely* "I am convinced that Rome was founded in Ol. 7. 2," *nor* to accept the authority of the table of the *pontifex maximus* alone without checking it.'

[2] 240 years are allotted them by Cic. *de Rep.* II, 52 and Solinus 1, 31.

(387 B.C.), and this synchronism is given by Diodorus. It must obviously come from a Greek source and it is most natural to assume that the Sicilian Timaeus is to be credited with it.

These last dates imply that 106 years elapsed between the sack of Rome and the invasion of Italy by Pyrrhus (Ol. 124. 4 = 281/0 B.C.). But the Roman chronologists found that the list of chief magistrates which they had before them did not suffice to fill the gap, and recourse was had to strange expedients in order to make the tally correct. Livy speaks of a five years anarchy (*solitudo magistratuum*) fifteen years after the Gallic invasion, and a mutilated entry in the Capitoline *Fasti* shows that the compiler followed the same view. Diodorus, on the other hand, who gives only one year of 'anarchy,' repeats the names of the magistrates of 391–387 B.C. immediately after the year of the sack. Polybius is not concerned to construct a table of Roman magistrates, but in his excursus on the wars of Rome with the Gauls he counts thirty years between the first and second Gallic invasions, and this could not be filled without some similar expedient. But in the last century of the Republic a further step was taken. Atticus, the friend and correspondent of Cicero, compiled a chronological table of Roman history under the name of *Liber annalis*, in which he placed the foundation of Rome in Ol. 6. 3 = 754/3 B.C.; and the same date was given by Varro, according to Solinus. This result was evidently accepted in official quarters[1], for it can only be with the purpose of raising the earlier dates of Roman history that we find in the Capitoline *Fasti* (or in sources derived therefrom) four years in which dictators and their *magistri equitum* appear as chief magistrates (333, 324, 309, 301 B.C.). Diodorus takes no account of these, and Livy mentions dictators who were appointed in the normal manner in each of the years immediately preceding. The insertions, like the 'five years anarchy,' were evidently an expedient adopted in order to accommodate the list of magistrates to some accepted synchronism. Modern convention has adopted the 'Varronian' dates, and thus in the tables to which we are accustomed 390 B.C. is given as the year of the Gallic invasion[2]. The year of the foundation, however, is generally taken as 753 B.C.; but that is because, with the Capitoline *Fasti*, we only count 119 years between the first consulships and the sack of Rome, rejecting the second college of *decemviri*.

[1] It is worthy of note that it is implied in Velleius Paterculus I, 8.
[2] Throughout this volume the dates of Roman history are given in accordance with the conventional 'Varronian' system. See table facing p. 321.

VI. LISTS OF MAGISTRATES

The list of magistrates, then, was in disaccord with the other *data* which the Romans believed themselves to possess. Can we accept it as genuine in its earlier parts? No great stress need be laid on the fact that no less than *five* consuls are assigned to the first year of the Republic, in order to find room for all the principal characters who figure in the legend of the Tarquins. But it is very difficult to say how much is historical in the Fasti of the fifth century, which in the inscription of the Regia present us with a series of consuls, all possessing *cognomina*, whose descent is indicated by the *nomina* of father and grandfather. If all of these were patrician, it might be hard to say that the list was not based on early records: Beloch has ingeniously reconstructed the pedigrees of the patrician families who appear most often in the Fasti in order to show that there is nothing abnormal in the intervals between the generations, and argues that a forger would inevitably have betrayed himself in such matters. We must remember, however, that the great families of Rome regarded the tradition of their ancestral distinctions as a patrimony to be jealously guarded, and that an intensive study of the principal pedigrees had been carried on in the later years of the Republic. It is worthy of note that Atticus, whose *Liber annalis*, as we saw, may have been, whether mediately or immediately, one of the principal sources of the *Fasti* which we possess, had drawn out the pedigrees of the Claudii Marcelli, the Fabii and the Aemilii, assigning to each member of the family the magistracies which he had held; and the learned editor of the *Fasti* seems to have made full use of these materials. Unfortunately their value, at any rate as regards the early period, is very doubtful. In a well-known passage (VIII, 40) Livy, after citing the discrepant versions which were current regarding the events of 322 B.C., goes on to say:

It is hard to prefer either one version to another or one authority to another. I am of opinion that the tradition has been corrupted by funeral panegyrics and forged inscriptions on busts, each family appropriating to itself by means of mendacious deceptions the credit of exploits and public offices: undoubtedly both the careers of individuals and the public records have thus been thrown into confusion.

Cicero, in the *Brutus* (16, 62), stresses the point as regards funeral orations, which the families preserved as their 'ornaments and monuments.'

'By these panegyrics,' he says, 'the history of our past has been filled with errors; for many things are set down in them which never took place—

imaginary triumphs, multiplied consulships, false descents and passages from patrician to plebeian rank, by which means persons of low degree were, so to speak, injected into an alien family bearing the same name: as though I myself, for example, were to claim descent from M'. Tullius the patrician, who was consul with Servius Sulpicius in the tenth year after the expulsion of the Kings.'

It is to be noted that, while the Capitoline *Fasti* are not extant for this period, and Livy (II, 19, 1) gives the corrupt names 'Servilius Sulpicius' and 'M. Manlius Tullus,' the *cognomina* of both consuls are given by Dionysius, but that of M'. Tullius is 'Longus,' whereas Festus (p. 180, L.) gives 'Tolerinus.' But the lists of this period contain a number of names taken from other families only known to us as plebeian, all duly provided with *cognomina*, which plebeians did not employ in early times: at the head of the list stands L. Junius Brutus, the legendary hero of the Revolution, and we may recall the fact that Atticus provided his supposed descendant the 'Liberator' with a family tree tracing its origin to the first consul.

A striking example of the unreliability of the records is furnished by the Minucii, a family which may perhaps have been in Cicero's mind when he wrote the passage quoted, since according to a tradition mentioned by Livy (IV, 16) a certain L. Minucius 'passed over to the *plebs*' at the time of the sedition of Spurius Maelius and was co-opted as an 'eleventh tribune' (439 B.C.). Now the *Fasti* give 'Augurinus' as the *cognomen* of L. Minucius, consul in 458 B.C., although this was in fact adopted by M. Minucius Faesus, one of the first plebeian augurs elected under the Lex Ogulnia of 300 B.C. An equally remarkable case is that of the supposed consuls of 454 B.C., who appear in the *Fasti* under the names 'Sp. Tarpeius M. f. M. n. Montanus Capitolinus' and 'A. Aternius...Varus Fontinalis.' Cicero and Dionysius ascribe to Aternius and Tarpeius a law fixing the maximum fine which could be levied on an individual without appeal to the people at thirty head of cattle and two sheep. Livy knows nothing of this law, but tells us that Aternius and Tarpeius, 'patricians and ex-consuls,' were co-opted as tribunes of the plebs in 448 B.C. Further light is thrown on the facts by the entry in Festus (p. 268 *sq.*, L.), which tells us that the law concerning fines in cattle was passed by the consuls Menenius and Sestius in 452 B.C., and that 'after coined money came into use a Lex Tarpeia provided that 100 asses should be regarded as the equivalent of an ox and 10 as that of a sheep,' which makes it evident that the law belongs to the fourth century. The entry in the *Fasti* is of course not in this instance due to family claims, since neither Aternii nor Tarpeii are otherwise known; but the *cognomina* betray their late origin, for those of Tarpeius are thinly disguised derivatives from Mons Capitolinus (suggested by the position of the *rupes Tarpeia*), and Fontinalis, for some reason which escapes us, is taken from the *Porta Fontinalis* in the Servian wall at the north-east end of the Capitoline hill. In view of such facts as these it is quite impossible to regard the elaborate Fasti of the early Republic as based on authentic or contemporary records, whether public or private, except in so far as a genuine nucleus may have been expanded by interpolation of names and colleges.

In view of the early history of the constitution we are more especially bound to view with suspicion the names of plebeian *gentes* and the traditions connected with them. Thus, for example, the consuls for the year 487 B.C. are given by Livy as C. Aquilius and T. Sicinius, while the *Fasti* (represented by Cassiodorus' Chronicle) and Dionysius call the last-named T. Siccius. Not only were the Aquilii of later times plebeian, but the names Siccius and Sicinius (which are constantly interchanged) play a part in the legends which clustered round the 'struggle of the orders' on the plebeian side. Cn. Siccius appears as one of the *five* tribunes elected, according to Piso in 471 B.C., and joins with his colleague Duilius in prosecuting Appius Claudius in the following year; the authority followed by Diodorus on the other hand, gave the name of C. Sicinius as one of the *four* tribunes appointed in 471 B.C. The legend of the 'Roman Achilles,' who fought in 120 battles, and received decorations of every kind known to the Romans, the numbers of which are set forth at length by our sources, is told both of 'L. Sicinius Dentatus' and 'L. Siccius Dentatus,' and is brought into connection with the imaginary consulship of Aternius and Tarpeius (see above); but whichever name is assigned to him, he is beyond question a champion of the *plebs*; and the appearance of this gentile name in either of its forms in the consular *Fasti* can only be due to interpolation.

Of the same type is a more famous figure of the early Republic, Sp. Maelius. He derived his name from a fanciful explanation of Aequimelium, a site on the south side of the Capitol where victims for sacrifice were on sale. This, it was said, was the spot where the house of Maelius had stood before it was razed to the ground (*aequata solo*), and its supposed owner became the central figure of a legend, according to which he attempted to win the favour of the populace by largesses of corn and aimed at monarchy, but was slain by the hand of C. Servilius Ahala, whose *cognomen* was interpreted as a form of *Axilla*, with allusion to the fact that he carried under his armpit the dagger with which he killed the would-be tyrant; it is however attributed in the *Fasti* to the consul of 478 B.C. It is fortunate that Dionysius has preserved for us two forms of the legend. The earlier of these, which, as he tells us, was found in the annals of Cincius Alimentus and of Calpurnius Piso, made Ahala a private citizen commissioned by the Senate to slay the would-be tyrant, whereas that which Dionysius himself, together with Cicero (*de senect.* 16, 56) and Livy, prefers, represented him as *magister equitum* to the dictator L. Quinctius Cincinnatus. This dictatorship (like many others) is wholly unhistorical, and was invented in order to give the act of Ahala a semblance of legality, probably by the politicians of the Gracchan period; and a place was found for Cincinnatus in the consular *Fasti* by the chronologist followed by Diodorus between the years 458 and 456 B.C. Further illustration will hardly be needed of the process by which the *Fasti* which we possess were built up as a framework for the legends (usually with political colouring) which were still 'timeless' when the annalists began their work[1]. Whether these had been elaborated by a school of bards whose poems were sung at banquets in early days is a question which it is hardly necessary to discuss: Cicero (*Brutus,* 19, 75) lamented that these songs (which Cato the Elder spoke of as belonging to ancient times) were no longer extant, and we have therefore clearly no right to identify them with the 'ancestral hymns' (πάτριοι ὕμνοι) in which, as Dionysius tells us (I, 79), the Romans still celebrated the life of Romulus and Remus in the hut of Faustulus.

VII. JURISTS AND ANTIQUARIANS

If the literary narratives of early Roman history, and the lists of magistrates which form their framework, thus arouse our suspicions, what shall we say of the works of jurists and antiquarians, based upon the study of legal and other texts? We have in the *Digest* (I, 2, 2) a long extract from the *Handbook* of Pomponius, a lawyer who wrote under Hadrian and the Antonines, which pur-

---

[1] The Register of Triumphs is naturally even less trustworthy than the Fasti and afforded greater scope for invention. Thus we find triumphs recorded in the list which Livy treats as matter of controversy or refuses to acknowledge because not mentioned in the earliest annals, while on the other hand some which are recorded by Dionysius and Livy are absent from the Register. Livy and the Register ascribe to C. Marcius Rutulus a triumph over Privernum in 357 B.C.: Diodorus (XVI, 31) says that in that year Rome was at war with Falerii καὶ μέγα οὐδὲν οὐδ' ἄξιον μνήμης ἐπετελέσθη.

ports to give a historical sketch of the sources of Roman Law and the principal exponents of jurisprudence. He begins with the collection of supposed 'laws of the kings' already mentioned under the title of *ius Papirianum*; his next landmark is the *ius Flavianum*, so called from Cn. Flavius, curule aedile in 304 b.c., who, according to the legend followed by Pomponius, 'stole' the digest of the *legis actiones*, or forms of procedure, made by Appius Claudius Caecus, and published it. 'Not much later,' he continues, 'Sextus Aelius put together other forms of action and issued a book which bore the name of *ius Aelianum*.' Since Pomponius goes on to speak of the *secessio plebis* which led to the passing of the Lex Hortensia in 287 b.c., one would suppose that he placed Aelius at an earlier date; but he is clearly referring to Sextus Aelius Paetus, consul in 198 b.c. and censor in 194 b.c., of whom he tells us in a later section that he was the author of an extant work called *Tripertita*, which contained (1) the text of the Laws of the Twelve Tables, (2) a commentary thereon, (3) the forms of procedure. From a passage in the *de legibus* of Cicero (ii, 23, 59) it appears that Aelius, like other commentators, found the archaic Latin of the Code difficult of interpretation, and it did not cease to attract the grammarians of later times, such as Aelius Stilo, the teacher of Varro, as well as expert jurists such as Ser. Sulpicius Rufus, the friend of Cicero.

In the meanwhile a school of writers, of whom the most famous were the Scaevolae, father and son, both consuls and *pontifices maximi*, had begun to treat systematically of the *ius civile*. P. Mucius Scaevola, consul in 133 b.c., was the founder of the school, and his son Quintus, consul in 95 b.c., made a *Digest* of the *ius civile* in 18 books, which itself became the text for learned commentaries by Sulpicius Rufus and others: Gaius in his *Institutes* refers to a work of his own based on that of Mucius.

As early as the Gracchan period, too, special treatises had been devoted to the various magistracies, their history and functions. Cassius Hemina, the annalist (see p. 317) had written *de censoribus*. C. Sempronius Tuditanus, consul in 129 b.c., wrote *libri magistratuum*, and a quotation from the thirteenth book shows that he concerned himself with the various grades of *imperium*. He no doubt represented the conservative view in politics: on the other side we have Junius Congus, surnamed Gracchanus because of his political affinities, whose work *de potestatibus* is quoted by Ulpian in the *Digest* for a theory about the origin of the quaestorship.

There was no lack of material, therefore, for the study of law and procedure; but with regard to political institutions the case is by no means so clear. In a well-known passage in the *de legibus* (III, 20, 48) Cicero complains: 'We have no system for preserving our laws, and hence the laws are such as our clerks please; we get copies from the booksellers, and we have no public records publicly set forth in writing.' It is easy to believe this. The well-known inscription which contains on one face the Lex Acilia Repetundarum of 123/2 B.C. and on the other the Lex Agraria of 111 B.C. shows that the official copy in bronze was for the sake of economy put to a fresh use when the law ceased to be in force. The idea of preserving it for the purpose of a permanent record never occurred to the Romans. Each magistrate kept his own record of his official acts, and if we may judge by what Cicero tells us in his speech for the poet Archias (5, 9), the greater number showed the utmost carelessness in so doing, even where the claim of a non-Roman to a grant of citizenship was at stake. Dionysius, indeed, informs us that the registers kept by censors were preserved in their family archives as heirlooms; unfortunately, the example which he gives (prefaced by a chronological note in which the era of the foundation of the city is used) refers to a date when, if we are to believe Festus (p. 500, L.), no census took place; and the list of censors contained in the Capitoline *Fasti*, together with the numbered *lustra* which include the four ascribed to Servius Tullius, was evidently a literary compilation.

There existed, no doubt, certain *commentarii*, as they were called, which were handed down by the various colleges of magistrates and priests, and consisted partly in rules and regulations for the conduct of the business of the several offices, partly in reports of cases in which a decision on some doubtful point had been taken by the college. Thus the *libri* or *commentarii* of the *pontifices* are quoted by Cicero for a decision given by P. Mucius Scaevola in 123 B.C., and in the *Brutus* he tells us that the records of the college bore testimony to the outstanding abilities of Ti. Coruncanius. So too the *libri augurales* or *commentarii augurum* recorded decisions taken by the college with regard to the interpretation of *auspicia*, and since these had a direct bearing on the validity of the acts of magistrates and people, they embodied important constitutional doctrines. Cicero, for example, in a letter to Atticus written in 49 B.C., when the validity of the consular elections held by Lepidus was a burning question, writes: 'We (*i.e.* the augurs) have it in our books that not only consuls, but even praetors, may not lawfully be brought into office by a praetor, and that such a thing has never been done: it is unlawful in the case of consuls because the higher authority may not be proposed for election by the lower, in the case of praetors because they are elected to be the colleagues of the consuls, who enjoy a higher authority' (*ad Att.* ix, 9, 3). This instance will suffice to show the importance of the *libri augurales* for constitutional law and procedure; and it is not surprising that in the last century of the Republic, statesmen who held seats in the augural college wrote treatises on the traditions of that body. Such were L. Julius Caesar (consul in 64 B.C.), Appius Claudius Pulcher (consul in 54 B.C.), P. Servilius Isauricus (consul in 48 B.C.), besides Cicero himself and especially 'Messalla the augur,' *i.e.* M. Valerius Messalla, consul in 53 B.C., who was a member of the college for fifty-five years, and from whose work *de auspiciis* Gellius quotes at length to illustrate the doctrine of the *auspicia* as applied to assemblies.

From such sources the antiquarians, encyclopaedists, grammarians and jurists drew largely, and constructed what was no doubt a coherent theory of the Roman constitution. First and foremost, M. Terentius Varro (116–27 B.C.), 'vir Romanorum eruditissimus'[1], whose writings covered the whole field of knowledge, compiled 41 books of *Antiquitates rerum humanarum et divinarum*, 15 *de iure civili* and 25 *de lingua Latina*; of these only Books 5–10 of the last-named survive, from the contents of which, notably those which deal with the terms for Places and Times, we can judge how irreparable is the loss of the remainder. To the following generation belongs the *de significatu verborum* of Verrius Flaccus, a learned freedman chosen by Augustus to be the tutor of his grandsons. He was, as Suetonius tells us, the compiler of the Calendar (with notes) set up at Praeneste—possibly his native town—which is in part extant, and it is likely enough that he was responsible for the *Fasti* and Table of Triumphs engraved upon the walls of the Regia. His encyclopaedic dictionary is lost, but we have a mutilated epitome (interlarded with cheap sneers intended to create an impression of independence) made by Sex. Pompeius Festus in the second century A.D., which survives in a single MS., and a skeleton abridgment of this work compiled by Paul the Deacon towards the end of the eighth century A.D. Festus sometimes gives quotations—all too brief—from the authors used by Verrius Flaccus; besides those named above we meet with L. Cincius, who in addition to lexicographical studies *de verbis priscis* wrote on the Comitia, on the authority of the consuls and the duties of a jurisconsult; with the great lawyers of the Augustan age, Antistius Labeo, the leading authority on

[1] Quintilian, x, 1, 95.

ius pontificium, and Ateius Capito, whose writings (especially the *Coniectanea*) covered a much wider field; and with *grammatici* in the narrower sense, whose main interest was in the explanation of archaic terms of law, civil or ecclesiastical, such as Aelius Stilo and Sinnius Capito.

Of this lost literature only the scantiest fragments remain; the commentaries of Asconius Pedianus, written probably under Nero, on the speeches of Cicero, contain some scraps of valuable knowledge, and we owe a deep debt to Aulus Gellius, whose commonplace book, compiled at Athens under Antoninus Pius and published under the title of *Noctes Atticae*, includes priceless extracts from the writings of Varro and his successors, as well as from those of his own period, such as Laelius Felix, who wrote a commentary upon Q. Mucius Scaevola's *Digest of the Civil Law*. Mention must also be made of the excerpts from the classical jurists contained in the *Digest* of Justinian (we have already had occasion to cite Pomponius) and of the *Institutes* of Gaius, written about the middle of the second century. Later than these are the works of grammarians, such as Nonius Marcellus (fourth century A.D.), commentaries such as that of Servius on Vergil (fourth or fifth century), and the miscellany in dialogue form compiled under the title of *Saturnalia* by Macrobius, of about the same date.

From all these sources we can form some idea of the immense labour of research expended by Roman scholars on the documents handed down by tradition; and we possess, in the works of Cicero's later years, the *de Republica*, written between 54 B.C. and 51 B.C., and the *de legibus*, which was left unfinished, documents which illustrate the jurist's attitude towards Roman institutions; for the first contains a sketch of its growth in the royal period, and the second a schematic outline of the constitution, couched in archaizing language, which, though modified in accordance with Cicero's political ideas, expresses in traditional terms the principles embodied in each of its organs.

What was the value of the material collected and interpreted by the antiquarians, regarded as evidence of the origin and growth of the constitution? The interest of the compilers was practical rather than theoretical, they were concerned with precedent and procedure as a guide to the conduct of business. When Pompey, in 70 B.C., became consul without having passed through the apprenticeship of the minor offices, Varro put together a handbook for his use as chairman of the Senate, and though this was not preserved, the extracts given by Gellius (XIV, 7 *sq.*) from a letter written by Varro on the subject show that it was based on a careful study of constitutional usage. In the *de lingua Latina* Varro quotes at length from documents which lay down rules of procedure in the form of reports (*commentarii*). Thus he finds in the *commentarii consulum* instructions for the summoning of the 'army,' that is to say, the nation in arms in centuriate assembly; the attendant who issues the summons bears the name 'C. Calpurnius.' Greater interest attaches to the 'ancient report of a criminal investigation' which serves Varro as a model for the procedure in capital trials before the people (see p. 446). Here the *quaestor* who conducts the investigation is M'. Sergius, the defendant T. Quinctius Rocus—names which some have supposed to be those of real persons.

These documents deserve the highest respect, and are evidently of considerable antiquity; but what shall we say of the *discriptio centuriarum* or *discriptio classium* 'made by Servius Tullius,' twice mentioned by Festus, once in a quotation from Varro, who seems to refer to the same document as *censoriae tabulae*? We remember that Livy mentions the tradition that the first consuls of the Republic were elected 'ex commentariis Servii Tullii', and recognize in these a similar document. Livy speaks of the *commentarii* of Numa relating to the celebration of public rites; and Cicero, in his defence of Rabirius, complains that the prosecution has unearthed an antiquated procedure 'ex annalium monumentis atque ex regum commentariis.' We are not left in doubt as to his meaning; for Livy (i, 26) recounts at length the institution of *duoviri perduellionis* by Tullus Hostilius in the case of Horatius, giving the text of the *lex horrendi carminis* and the formal utterances of the parties in the suit. This lets us into the secret. The Roman lawyer demanded a historical precedent and an archetypal procedure which was given him in the case of Horatius, just as the Athenian mythmaker traced the jurisdiction of the Areopagus in cases of homicide to the trial of Orestes. The *commentarii regum* were a collection of such documents, and Livy—though no jurist by profession—made such use of them that a large portion of his first book reads like a handbook of *formulae* with their supposed historical settings; some of them, such as the utterances prescribed for the *fetiales*, with their appeal to a personified *Fas* (cf. p. 428 *sq.*), can obviously lay no claim to high antiquity. We should, therefore, not take at their face value the accounts which the Roman antiquarians gave of the origin of institutions; and we must be on our guard against the natural but insidious tendency of a nation of trained lawyers to represent the Roman constitution as the result of an ordered and organic growth, ending in a coherent system based throughout on fixed principles. An examination of the conflicting statements made by our historians will teach us that the legists were at times hard put to it to square their constitutional formulae with awkward facts.

From the above it will be seen how hazardous a task is the reconstruction of early Roman history from what the Romans tell us and how inevitable it is that scholars must disagree in their evaluation of this evidence, and vary in the degree of scepticism with which they approach the statements of the authorities for each separate period. It is not even true that there is a steady improvement in the evidence as we approach the third century, for the gap between the fourth century and the writing of contemporary history is great enough for falsification to creep in even about the most important events, and in constructing the history of each period the Roman annalists were exposed to various temptations. Archaeological discovery can give us evidence which sometimes acts as a touchstone of the truth of the tradition, and as will be seen in the chapters that follow, it is to archaeological discovery that we owe almost all that may be regarded as certain about the beginnings of the city of Rome. But often the stones are dumb and the books speak but do not speak truth. Yet to reject root and branch the statements of the Romans about their early history is to abdicate the office of the historian. Amid much that is false the tradition contains a nucleus of truth, and it is the task of the historian to do the best he can to discover it. There is one factor which cannot be neglected, and that is the possibility of an oral tradition handing down, even though distorted, the memory of great events or persons; for the accretions of fiction may attach themselves to what is true as well as to what is false. But it has also to be remembered that the Roman tradition was a manufactured product rather than a natural growth and we have not the right to say that, though fiction may invade the record of events, we may always claim to have truth of atmosphere. The atmosphere of the first decade of Livy, for example, is evidence for the conceptions formed by men of the Augustan age rather than for the Roman character in the days of the Kings and of the early Republic.

In the following chapters, therefore, will be found an attempt to set forth what may be reconstructed with fair certainty about the history of early Rome down to the point when, with the third century, we reach a period for which our information, if scanty, has the merit of being as trustworthy as that about Greece in the same period.

CHAPTER XI

THE FOUNDING OF ROME

I. THE ORIGIN OF THE LATINS

ROMAN history does not begin at Rome. The genius of the people who rose from the insignificance of Latin villagers to the headship of an œcumenical State lends more than usual interest to the question of their origin; and, though race will not account for national character, the origin of the people is a subject of which we know so much that it cannot be ignored. In spite of the dubious nature of the evidence, which even now is capable of more interpretations than one, knowledge of Italian pre-history has progressed far enough during the last fifty years to establish the truth of at least a few propositions and to show that of the doctrines currently accepted during the nineteenth century some of the most fundamental were false. On dates and details of ethnic relationship precision is misleading and dogmatism wrong; but of such points those which are still at issue belong with few exceptions to the sphere of archaeology, within which the evidence chiefly lies, and their bearing on ethnological conclusions is so remote that for the present purpose they may be ignored.

To the history of Rome the antecedents of the populations found spread over the length and breadth of the Italian peninsula before the full Bronze Age are immaterial. In whatever relation these peoples, or any part of them, may have stood to their palaeolithic predecessors, and whatever cultural differences of a minor kind may be discernible at this time in different parts of the peninsula, it is enough for the present purpose to say that in the Neolithic Age the inhabitants of Italy were a long-headed folk whose unbroken practice in disposing of the dead was to bury them without cremation. The distribution of this people was peculiar. Though to north and south they spread from sea to sea, in the middle zone, for reasons perhaps not unconnected with volcanic activity on the central western coast (see p. 341), their western frontier ran roughly along a line formed by the Arno, the Apennine, and the Liris. In the area to the west of this, traces of their presence are noticeably scarce; and it is precisely in this area, whence the neolithic people seem almost to have been excluded, that the origin of the population is a matter peculiarly germane to the early history of Rome. It is elsewhere, however, that the next development takes place[1].

Not long before the opening of the Bronze Age itself a new element can be recognized in the southern foothills of the Alps. The pile-dwellings (*palafitte*) which first appear are those on the western lakes, but for the general purposes of Italian history they and their authors are not of the first importance. It is in the makers of the rather later *palafitte* to the east, who did not arrive until the Bronze Age had begun, that we should almost certainly see the emergence of the Indo-European stock which formed the basis of the peoples regularly regarded as Italic. This second set of newcomers, who probably reached the Po-valley by way of the Veneto, settled first on the Lago di Garda and other pieces of water in its neighbourhood, but by about the middle of the second millennium they had transferred their building technique to dry land and had produced the *terremare*. The *terramaricoli*, whose remains are found most freely south of the Po between the Trebbia and the Panaro, were a farming people. Of crops they grew wheat, flax and beans, and they had some slight acquaintance with the olive and the vine; of live-stock—besides dogs, cats and poultry —they kept horses, donkeys, oxen, pigs, goats and sheep. But for the present study more significant characteristics of these people are, first, their custom of cremating the dead, which is alien to Italy before the *palafitte*, and, secondly, the peculiar plan on which they laid out their settlements. In this plan there are points of resemblance to certain features of Roman practice which call for closer notice. The familiar *fossa* and *vallum* which surrounded the Roman camp find parallels in the moat and rampart of any *terramara*, and to the intersection at right-angles of the *cardo* and *decumanus* corresponds a similar intersection of the two main streets in these early settlements. Furthermore, it is impossible to overlook the remarkable repetition of details found in the *terremare* in the ideal scheme adopted by the Romans for the delimitation of cities at their foundation. It is true that the Roman practice is assigned by all but the earliest authority[2] to an Etruscan origin, and also that in these days, when the debt of Rome to Etruria is frequently magnified to the greatest possible extent, this assignation is widely emphasized. But it is to be remembered that, small as they may be, there are certain indications, apart from the appearance of something similar in the *terremare*, which casts

[1] See U. Antonielli, *Due gravi problemi paletnologici*, in *Studi etruschi*, I, pp. 11–48.

[2] Cato, who is silent on the subject.

doubts upon an attribution of this Roman custom to any people who entered Italy after the Iron Age had begun. The well-attested use of a bronze plough in the operations which this ceremony involved is suggestive of a survival from times earlier at any rate than the earliest which the Romans called Etruscan; and the *cinctus Gabinus*, which Cato (*Orig.* frag. 18 P.) records to have been prescribed for the *conditores*, points definitely to the Latins and their ancestors. The ritual itself, of which perhaps the best account is given in Plutarch's *Romulus* (11), in later times consisted first in marking out with a plough the limits of an augural *templum*, within which certain first-fruits were buried. To this precisely corresponds the mound, itself surrounded with a trench and having buried in it various objects of religious or magical significance, which normally appears on the eastern side of a *terramara*. In the second part of the ceremony the boundaries of the city itself were traced by another furrow drawn round the *templum* at a distance, and this again the *terremare* anticipate in the *solco rituale* still occasionally preserved at the foot of the encircling rampart.

The events which follow the full development of the *terremare* are still a subject of dispute. Questions of ethnic relationship cannot all be answered in detail, and dates are a matter of spacing between limits which, though themselves approximately fixed, allow wide variations within them. Soon, perhaps even before the *terremare* of the north had reached their full extension, *terramaricoli* and their kin began to spread into central and southern Italy to form, in all probability, the characteristic stratum among the peoples which in historical times are called Italic. For the present purpose, however, the general movement may be ignored and attention concentrated on archaeological evidence which confirms the conclusion naturally to be drawn from the similarities between the practices of the *terramaricoli* and those of Rome, and supports the view that between the *terremare* and Latium the connection was close. At a time which is probably not later than the twelfth century, there appears in Rome and on the Alban hills a people probably to be recognized again, not only in what later became Etruria, but also in a region north of the Apennine between Bologna and the Adriatic. The Iron Age has now begun, and of the groups into which its early remains from Italy naturally fall these three—the Latian, Tuscan and Bolognese (Villanovan proper)—though they are distinct, still hang loosely together and constitute a class to which the name Villanovan in a more general sense may be applied. Their authors, if not actually descended from the *terramaricoli*, as is probable, are at any rate nearly related to them, and they are beyond any reasonable doubt a section of the Indo-European people who, split into subdivisions long enough before to allow their linguistic histories to follow different lines, yet recently enough to keep their material culture recognizably one, did something at least to give their character to those parts of Italy which history knows as Umbria and Latium.

There now appears a complication. In neolithic times the Latin plain had scarcely been occupied by man. Its earliest settlers were the cremators from the north, but these cremators were quickly followed by an inhuming population whose affinities present a problem still unsolved. Their graves appear already on the Alban hills, at Ardea and at Lavinium: but here it is more noteworthy that they are found freely on the site of Rome. The region covered by their remains is one where the Oscan, and to some extent the Umbrian, dialects prevailed, but archaeology shows no evidence that these people marked by their burial rite entered Italy either after, or within a measurable time before, the cremators of the *terremare*. Their language is in Italy something recent; their material culture and their custom of inhumation finds its affinities in the neolithic age from which it seems to be directly and continuously descended. The way in which this people should be described is a matter of some indifference. They may be regarded as Italic invaders, who, as would be natural in a region where the previous inhabitants were strong, took over the customs and culture of the people among whom they settled; or they may be called survivors from the neolithic population with a new language acquired from immigrants who had advanced even farther than the people of the Alban hills. Two points may be stressed with such slight confidence as the existing evidence allows. The first is that the Italic settlers from the *terremare* preserved their own peculiarities most completely in these districts to the west of the Apennine where they were least closely in contact with their predecessors: the second that the inhuming population which is supreme to the south and east of Rome is the population to which the Sabines belonged, and that when the literary authorities speak of Sabine settlement at Rome—a settlement which is amply supported by archaeological fact—they indicate the coming of migrants from this inhuming region to join the pure Italic cremators.

The position may now be summarized. That the first newcomers to Latium at the opening of the Iron Age were Villanovans is almost certain; and it is probable that the links between the Villanovans and the *terramaricoli* were continuous. But if the

Villanovans of Latium are not direct descendants of the *terra-maricoli*, at any rate they are closely akin; and these Villanovans, whatever their precise origin may have been, are the first stratum in the Latin population. Their arrival was followed by that of an inhuming people, who soon looked down on the Campagna from the Sabine hills. And these two peoples in succession occupy the site of Rome. Thus questions about the making of the Roman people take a more definite shape. Apart from speculative theories about the origin of the name 'Aventine,' the evidence available recognizes no element in historical Rome before the cremators from the north. First, the respective contributions of these cremators and their inhuming neighbours must be considered,— which may best be done in connection with the site of Rome itself. And secondly, there arises the more thorny question of the debt owed by the resultant blend to Etruria. This, however, is a later story (see pp. 382 *sqq.*). The next step is to survey the geography of the region in which the Latian Villanovans and the Sabine inhumers are pre-eminent when documented history opens in the seventh century B.C.

II. THE GEOGRAPHY OF LATIUM

The region to which in this section the name Latium will be given is not merely the area wherein archaeology shows traces of the Latian Villanovans—this at present is little more than Rome and the Alban hills—but the district which, according to literary authorities, by some time near the end of the eighth century was in the hands of a people whom we believe, in spite of some mingling with another stock, to be their descendants—the Latins. The advance of these newcomers from their first settlements in the hills down into the plain which is now the Campagna di Roma will most conveniently be discussed later together with the development of fenced villages into walled towns (p. 346). Before that it will be well to leave the course of events and consider some of the greater geographical factors by which events were largely affected.

Forty miles from its mouth the Tiber rounds Soracte, and Soracte may be said to mark the point at which the Tiber valley begins to open out into the broad basin which is the scene of early Roman history. From the summit of Soracte the stage may be surveyed. On the right bank, where the mountain stands, the southern lowlands of Etruria rise slowly up to the distant ridge which once was crowned by the Ciminian forest—a ridge which was Rome's horizon to the north until the last quarter of the fourth

century. On this region Rome for long was forced to turn her
back. It is true that these lowlands are as much a part of the
Tiber basin as the Latin plain itself; and it is true that the evidence
of language, which proves the Faliscans to have been close kindred
of the Latins, is supported by the discovery of characteristic Latin
hut-urns in southern Etruria in suggesting ethnic affinities between the lands on both sides of the lower Tiber. But for purposes of early Latin history the right bank may be ignored,
because from the eighth century at latest until the fourth it was
politically divorced from the Latin plain. We hear indeed tales of
Roman access even in the age of Romulus to the salt-pans north
of the Tiber mouth, and there is evidence that, soon after the
Roman villages became a single city, Rome held a bridge-head
on the farther bank extending in one direction to the fifth milestone towards the coast[1]. But during these centuries, centuries
in which the growth of Rome was given its direction, the whole
of this country, with the possible exception of the merest fringe,
lay under an Etruscan domination so complete that it was counted
hostile territory from which Rome was excluded until the fall
of Veii opened the way for an advance.

It was on the left bank that Rome emerged, and by the con-
formation of the lands on this side the course of history was to
some extent determined. Here the mountains, which opposite
Soracte rise close above the bank, fall back south-eastwards and
leave between themselves and the river a plain which, though
it is broken by the spur of the Monti Corniculani, gradually
grows broader as it approaches the sea. Between the plain
and Italy to the east and south communications lie through gaps
in the southern barrier. Of such gaps there are two, which
divide the chain into three sections and which are to be recognized to-day by the two main lines of railway from Rome to
the Adriatic and Campania. From a point opposite Soracte the
steep escarpment of the Sabine hills runs on unbroken until it
reaches the cleft of the Anio, by which the first of the natural
passages is approached. Here the Via Valeria of the Romans,
along a route now roughly followed by the railway from Rome to
Castellamare Adriatico, led through the mountains to eastern
Italy. On such a road the entrance to the hills is a position of
commercial possibilities as well as of strategic value; and in this
case the entrance was dominated by the site of Tibur, whose early
prosperity thereby is at least in part explained. From Tibur the

---

[1] Dessau, 5048; Strabo, v, 230.

barrier stretches on—here under the name of the Monti Prenestini
—until it drops down to the second of the gaps—the broad *col*
which connects the Sabine highlands with the volcanic hills of
Alba. This *col*, by which the Via Labicana and the more familiar
of the two railways to Naples reach the valley of the Trerus
(Sacco) and so lead down to Casinum and Campania, was one of
the two great avenues from Latium to the south; and, until at
the end of the fifth century the Romans gave military significance
to other sites like Labici, the key to it was Praeneste.

Beyond this lies the third section of the line—the *massif* of the
Alban hills, which on their south-western side end the barrier by
falling gently to the sea. These hills themselves are not impassable;
across their midst lies a shallow depression—the pass of Mount
Algidus—separating the heights of Tusculum from the *mons
Albanus* proper. Through this gap the Via Latina passed, commanded by Tusculum and later by a Roman fort; but, since the
road led nowhere beyond the Alban hills save down to the Via
Labicana, its value was only local, and it is not to be counted
among the natural routes from Latium to Campania. More important by far was the second natural way—the way which ran
over the easy slopes between Aricia and the sea. Here, where
round Ardea the Rutulan country lay, the foothills are so slight
as to give easy access from the Tiber valley to the broad lands
which stretch south from the Rio Torto towards Anxur (Tarracina) until they sink into the Pomptine Marshes. In this region
between the plains to north and south no natural boundary exists.
Geographically they belong to a single whole, and round this gap
between hills and sea much early history was enacted before
geographical and political units became one under the hegemony
of Rome. Along this passage Latin movement from the north
and Volscian pressure from the south combined to produce warlike operations which are a constant feature of Italian history from
the sixth century onwards, until in the fourth Rome finally asserted her authority up to the Liris and beyond.

Such in broadest outline is the geography of the region wherein
Roman history begins; but within the region there were more
peoples to be found than one, and their boundaries did not always
coincide with frontiers provided by nature. To the Latins, who
are the most important section of the population, part of the plain
belonged; but the plain was not their centre, nor was the whole
of it theirs. The kernel of their territory, as tradition and archaeology combine to show, was the Alban hills, round which in course
of time they came to occupy an area stretching north and west

and south for a distance of something like twenty miles. Northwards their frontier ran by the coast to the Tiber mouth; but
across the river, though, as has been said, the population was to
some extent their kin, the Latins with whom Rome had first
to deal held no more than a fringe ending within a mile or two
of the farther bank. From the sea the frontier roughly ran along
the river up to the site of Rome; but soon it turned to the east.
Three miles above the city the Anio joins the Tiber, and there
is reason to believe that Augustus did not act without historical
justification when he made the Anio a boundary between Latium-
Campania, the first of the districts into which he divided Italy, and
Samnium, the fourth. Across the Tiber were the Etruscans; across
the Anio the Sabines; but, just as there was a doubtful strip
beyond the Tiber to which the Latins had some claim, so there
was also beyond the Anio. About twelve miles north of the confluence lay Eretum, and between this and the Anio were Crustumerium, Nomentum, Ficulea and Fidenae; but though Eretum
was always, and though the rest of these cities were sometimes,
described as Sabine, the last four are so often called Latin that
there is no period of Latin history, after the merely archaeological
age, at which it would be safe to deny any kind of Latin occupation on the northern bank. With so much by way of qualification
the Anio may be regarded as the boundary up to the north-east
corner of the Latin region where, probably not far from Varia
(Vicovaro), the territory of Tibur bordered on the country of the
Aequi. South of Tibur, Praeneste was the Latin outpost facing
the Hernici of the Trerus valley; and the *ager Praenestinus* fetches
back to the Alban hills.

It is on the south-eastern slopes of these that the limits of
early Latium are hardest to define. Here lay the *ager Rutulus*;
and though at Ardea, its centre, excavation has shown burials by
inhumation, the presence of these side by side with cremations
both at Rome and in the Alban hills makes it possible to believe
Vergil when he connects the *consanguinei Rutuli* with the Latins,
at least if the connection means no more than that this tract was
early a part of the Latin world. The proposal to derive this people
from the neolithic population on the strength of the termination
of their name is unconvincing[1]; and, though there are slight suggestions of an Etruscan element among them, there is no valid
reason for ascribing this to any other period than that of the
Etruscan advance on Latium which began soon after the middle

[1] Rutuli: cf. Siculi. Appian, *Bas.* 1: for the name 'Turnus' see Schulze,
Zur Geschichte lateinischer Eigennamen, p. 574, n. 6.

of the seventh century B.C. But if Ardea and the *ager Rutulus*
may be included in the Latin area, it is less clear how far east
of this the area extended. Velitrae seems to have been a Volscian
foundation: but, though on these sites too a Volscian dominion
in the fifth century must be admitted, in spite of Livy's approval
it would be unsafe to reject outright the tradition, preserved by
Diodorus and Vergil, which includes Cora and Pometia among
the cities of the Prisci Latini[1]. If this tradition is to be accepted,
Latium passed south of the slopes between Aricia and the sea
down into the plain beneath the Monti Lepini, where Pometia
lay with Cora on the mountain-side above. But in this direction
these two cities must be fixed as the limit of the Latins, if indeed
Latins are to be seen anywhere south-east of the *ager Rutulus*: the
advance to Signia and Norba is not recorded until the end of the
regal period at Rome. Thus the circuit is complete; and though
the frontier is often indistinct, it seems that the stage for the
beginnings of Latin history was set in a region lying round the
Alban hills as far as Praeneste, Tibur, Rome and Ardea, with a
possible extension up to Cora and Pometia towards the south-
east.

III. EARLY LATIUM

At the dawn of the Iron Age the soil of Latium was young.
The country lies on the line of the Italian volcanic system immediately round what, at least until late in the second millennium
B.C., was a centre of formidable activity. Monte Cavo, which
dominates the Latin landscape, is only the most prominent of
some fifty craters to be found in its neighbourhood, and these do
not seem to have become finally extinct until times which are
almost historical. Though the passages (I, 31, 1; XXXV, 9, 3) in
which Livy has been thought to preserve hints of eruptions during
the reign of Tullus Hostilius and again as late as 193 B.C. must be
interpreted otherwise, more valuable evidence is provided by excavation, which reveals traces of serious havoc done not long before
1000 B.C. And though again the suggestion cannot be accepted
that it was the mountain, and not Rome as the Roman annalists
asserted, which was responsible for the destruction of Alba, it is
wholly probable that when the Villanovans arrived they found in
the Alban hills a region which had only recently become habitable
and where, in consequence, there was no strong body of the earlier
inhabitants to dispute possession. However these things may be,
it is certain that Latium had long received at intervals a deep

---

[1] Livy, II, 16, 8; Diodorus, VII, 5, 9; Vergil, *Aen.* VI, 775.

covering of volcanic ash, which at once postponed the age of agriculture and ensured its prosperity when it came. Not until, after the eruptions at length had ceased to be catastrophic, the uppermost stratum of ashes had been overspread by jungle growth and the jungle in turn had formed a surface soil, was Latium ripe for cultivation.

Of the forest in which scattered clearings must have seen the first attempts at agriculture small remains may be recognized in the sacred thickets freely mentioned in literature. As late as the third century B.C., according to Theophrastus (*Hist. Pl.* v, 8, 1 and 3), Latium was renowned for the timber of its beech-woods: but even before the growth of population in Rome began to make heavy calls on the productivity of the surrounding plain Latium was, for those early times, so thickly inhabited, and the need for food must consequently have been so great, that the winning of woodland to cultivation had probably gone far enough for the country fairly to be called agricultural. That the population was large there is sufficient evidence to show. Though it should probably be regarded only as a minimum, the *heredium* of the *bina iugera*, whether ownership was vested in the family or the individual, is so small as to suggest that land was scarce (p. 469). But perhaps the most cogent of the proofs that the inhabitants of Latium were spread thick is to be found in the remains of drainage-works which may be seen from Etruria to the Monti Lepini. Sometimes these works are channels cut in the rock along some slope, at others they are dams of masonry built on a valley-floor to protect some strip of land beside the river-bed; but in all cases alike their purpose seems to have been the preservation of the soil from the destructive torrents in which rain-water came down from the mountain sides. Indications are abundant that in the early days of Rome the Latin climate was wetter than it is at present. Whatever the circumstances of this may have been, whether the evidence of Californian sequoias is enough to prove a rainy age in Latium during the regal period at Rome or whether, as is more probable, the deforestation of the hills has reduced what once was a fertile region to the doubtful value of the Campagna to-day, the rainfall in Latium for the greater part of the last millennium B.C. was more than enough to meet the needs of agriculture. And when food was plentiful the population grew, until at length it became necessary to undertake hydraulic measures on a great scale in order to save for cultivation a few acres here and a few more there.

The corn grown in Latium for human consumption was one of

the coarser wheats which pass under the general name of 'spelt'; but millet seems also to have been used[1], and the *aes hordearium* of the Roman knights suggests that, when the horse appeared, barley was the regular fodder for it, if not for every kind of beast. Yet, though the production of corn was large, it is impossible to believe that, when trade developed, corn was normally available for exportation after the needs of the inhabitants had been met. It was in other forms of wealth that the cost of imports must have been paid. Latin timber has been mentioned already, and to this only few additions can be made. The olive is not among them. Though the wild olive has probably left traces in the *terremare*, Fenestella's tale (Frag. 7 P.) that the tree was unknown to Latium in the time of the first Tarquin finds some support in the Greek origin of *amurca*, *trapetum*, and other words connected with the olive trade. This evidence, which is not unique, suggests the conclusion that the olive reached Latium late and from the south. The vine, on the other hand, came early: on this point Roman writers are agreed, and their agreement is confirmed by the presence of grape-stones, if such they really be, in one of the burials of the Roman Forum. But that viticulture assumed any large dimensions before republican times is by no means certain. In the absence of independent support, tales to the effect that in primitive Latium wine was only used for medicinal purposes[2] might be regarded as no more than edifying anecdotes of moralists who found virtue in the past; but there are other facts which forbid such an explanation. Though the appearance of the Vinalia in the Calendar of Numa proves that the vine had been assimilated by Roman agriculture by the seventh century B.C., the frequent use of cow's milk for ritual purposes in some of the oldest cults is a hint that even after the Latin settlement there may have been a period in which wine had not yet taken the place it afterwards achieved; and again, the taboo placed on wine-drinking by women in historical times[3] seems to show that even then there clung to wine something of the suspicion which forms round innovations. The only other product of the soil which can be assigned with confidence to primitive Latium is the fig, which plays a part in early Roman legend large enough to vouch for its familiarity. But to fruits and crops the Latins added flocks and herds. The history of the goat in Latium is not to be recovered, though the Tomba del Duce at Vetulonia proves its use by the Etruscans, as by the *terramari-coli*. In the *terremare* again the horse is found, but in Latium

---

[1] Dion. Hal. VII, 12, 3.

[2] Pliny, *N.H.* XIV, 88–91.   [3] Plutarch, *Quaest. Rom.* VI.

its connection is almost wholly with war, and its advent late. The
famous taboo which forbade the presence of a horse in the precinct
of Diana at Aricia[1], the prohibition against horse-riding under
which the Flamen Dialis was placed[2], are indications enough of
a time when the horse was a new-comer. On the other hand the
rite of the Suovetaurilia shows the early presence of pigs, sheep
and oxen. From the beginning of the Latin occupation the ox
was probably the draught-beast which it still remains, and the
penalties enacted for its wrongful slaughter are evidence of the
value it possessed. It is not a matter for surprise that oxen and
sheep together were the currency of exchange until a pecuniary
system in the modern sense was introduced.

The social history of early Latium is a subject on which conjecture too often has to take the place of knowledge. When the
necessary evidence is not wholly lacking, it either is the unsupported statement of some Roman annalist or antiquarian, or at best
lies in the surviving institutions of historical times from which the
previous conditions may be inferred with varying degrees of
probability. That the dominant element in the population of
Latium was regarded as ethnically one, even if its unity was the
result of fusion, is clear from the general use of the words 'Latium'
and 'Latini' as well as from the title 'Latiaris' which came to be
borne by the chief of their divinities. On the other hand, there is
evidence no less clear in the whole history of the Latins and their
leagues that at first the ethnic unit was split into political fractions,
of which the origins are not recorded. It is probable that, when
the Italici arrived in Latium, they came in small bands of the kind
which are better seen in the Dorian invasion of the Peloponnese.
These bands, which seem everywhere to have been the earliest
form of social and political organization, preceded the family;
and though in the case of the Latins this must have happened
long before they settled in the Tiber Valley, it was within these
bands, round centres provided by stable sexual relations, that
the family was formed. Such groups, which did not necessarily
all reach their destinations at the same time, each appropriated a
tract of territory, and in course of time by fusion with neighbouring
groups they produced societies large enough to be dignified with
the name of *populus*.

The form of habitation which the people used was preserved
at Rome in the *casa Romuli* of the Palatine and is familiar to us

---

[1] Vergil, *Aen.* VII, 761 *sqq.*

[2] Gellius, *N.A.* x, 15, 3. See also Pliny, *N.H.* XXVIII, 146 and Festus,
p. 71 L.: the last is absurd.

both from the hut-urns which are a regular feature of the early
iron age in Latium and also from their descendants—the *capanne*
(huts) of the Campagna to-day: but how these huts were at first
distributed—whether in clusters or in isolation, each on its own
occupants' estate—is a question to which the answer has been
made a matter of needless controversy. Attempts to prove that
in primitive times the regular grouping of the Italic peoples was
in isolated households or again that it was always in villages are
wholly misdirected. Archaeological facts generally favour the
latter view, but the literary authorities show that both are right:
there is no reason whatever for refusing to believe that practice
varied according to circumstances, and the custom in a particular
district can only be discovered from local evidence. On this point
excavation in Latium and especially on the site of Rome indicates
beyond dispute that here at least, in the days before cities had
grown up, the people lived in villages and not in scattered households. By historical times a *populus* was normally called after the
city to which its several villages had given place, but the recorded
names of the 'Laurentes Lauinates' and of the 'populus Ardeatis
Rutulus'[1] suggest that, before this happened, the peoples had
each borne a name proper to themselves and not derived from
that of their central town. Even at this stage the Latins seem to
have chosen for their villages sites like those on which we find
the cities that afterwards became famous. Advantage of position
undoubtedly was one of the factors which determined that a village
should grow into something more; but, whether the reason was
convenience for defence or that the flat lands needed drainage to
fit them for human habitation, the earliest settlements, like the
cities which succeeded them, are generally to be found on high
ground—either on some knoll in the Campagna or on the slopes
of the surrounding hills.

So far as its initial stages are concerned, the process by which
the early settlers formed themselves into communities of the size
familiar in recorded history is veiled in impenetrable darkness:
it cannot have been long before the eighth century that Latium
first approached a condition of which our authorities allow us to
draw a picture in any kind of detail, and even then the details are
so blurred as scarcely to be worthy of the name. In an age where
smaller groups, in the manner best illustrated by the history of the
site of Rome, were steadily coalescing into larger, no precise
number of *populi* can be true of more than a brief space of time.

---

[1] *E.g.* Dessau, 1371; Cato, *Orig.* fr. 58 P.

Nevertheless, it is from numbers alone that we are able to deduce the dimensions of the political units in Latium at the first stage of which it is possible to speak. The material is scanty. However good their evidence might be—and it varies from excellence to utter worthlessness—the list of eighteen Alban colonies given by Diodorus and the lists, preserved by Cato and Dionysius, of Latin states allied against Rome at the beginning of the fifth century would have no bearing in the age before Rome had emerged[1]. With none but the smallest help from other sources we are left with the catalogues of Pliny. In the course of his description of the eleven regions into which imperial Italy was divided, Pliny (*N.H.* III, 56 *sqq.*) deals at length with Latium, which was the first. The basis of his survey was a document compiled at the order of Augustus, but to this must be added some other source or sources for his information about cities which had disappeared in the early days of Rome. Calculations from Pliny's text are hazardous and the margin of error is wide, but in the upshot the conclusion to be drawn is that some sixty communities, more or less, may have divided among themselves the territory of early Latium. The region which these people shared, exclusive of the doubtful fringes discussed above, covers less than 650 square miles which, split among sixty groups, would provide an average of about 10 square miles for each.

So much is enough to give an indication of the size attained by the Latin *populi* at a time which, although it must be placed several centuries after the settlement, is still the earliest at which their scale can be discerned. It has, indeed, been asserted that the primitive political units in Latium were large and that their disruption was due to Rome; but there can be no doubt that in reality the development was in the opposite direction. Within the territorial units (*pagi*), which were probably the basis of the social structure, the small groups in which the settlers arrived coalesced to form villages, and the villages in turn were merged into still larger organizations which, when they are surrounded by walls of stone, may claim the name of cities. But though it is to be admitted that by the seventh century at latest the centripetal tendency of the population had caused a reduction in the number of settlements over which the Latins had originally been spread, the full city-age cannot be carried back beyond the sixth. By now there is a general agreement that the differences between so-called Cyclopean and polygonal masonry and between the latter

---

[1] Diodorus, VII, 5, 9; Cato, *Orig.* frag. 58 P.; Dion. Hal. V, 61, 3.

and masonry built in regular courses is due not to age but to the varying formations of local stones, which in some cases are laminated in a way which makes easy the cutting of rectangular blocks and in others are not. Stone walls seem to be a development of the sixth century, though it is not to be denied that before then villages may often have been protected with earthworks of the kind which at Rome left traces in the *murus terreus* of the Carinae (p. 356).

The little world which these villages composed remained long in comparative isolation. In culture it was backward; and whether because Latium was poor in the mineral resources which abounded in Northern Tuscany or for some other reason, from the beginning of the Iron Age down to the end of the seventh century B.C. the Latins lagged behind their more favoured neighbours across the Tiber. The date at which Cumae received its first settlers from the eastern Mediterranean, the measure of Cretan influence on Italy, and the visits of Semitic traders from Asia—visits which even north of Sicily were certainly free in the period before the close connection of Etruria and Carthage—are matters which, for all their importance in the general history of Italian relations with the outer world, scarcely concern Latium at all. Latium lay outside the stream of traffic. To the lack of natural wealth by which trade might be attracted was added a lack of harbours. The Tiber, with a current which needed the special favours vouchsafed to Aeneas to make navigation possible for early ships, flowed into the sea through an estuary more valuable for the salt-marshes on either side than for such harbourage as its mud-banks might afford; and even the creeks below the Alban hills seem rarely to have received visitors from the sea. The Latins were not sailors; most of their cities were inland, like Rome; and of such few as were within reach of the coast Satricum alone shows some tardy signs of trade. At the end of the ninth century, when Tarquinii was already feeling foreign influence from Asia, and again a hundred years later when Etruria was learning from Cumae how to write, Latium still kept almost wholly to itself. Even such intercourse as passed by land left Latium untouched, though new wares were coming—we may conjecture from the Etruscan cities—as near as the Faliscan territory. Soon after 700 the first effects of the higher culture begin to appear in the deposits of Latium and of Rome itself. By the middle of the century Praeneste had fallen into Etruscan hands and had become one of the great cities of central Italy, and thereafter Latium slowly enters deeper into the system of commercial relations of which Etruria was the focus, until some time before 600 B.C. the Etruscan period begins in Rome itself.

IV. THE BEGINNINGS OF LATIN UNITY

With the social institutions of early Latium there is no need to deal here at length. Much of our information is of doubtful value at best. When the Roman writers insist on the prevalence of aristocracies in the Latin towns, their account may well be true: but it would be rash to say that their statements rest on any knowledge of the facts and are not rather to be explained as inferences from the patrician control of early republican Rome. Such social forms as are of any relevance to Roman history may best be mentioned in connection with their developments in the religion, the society and the constitution of Rome (chaps. XIII, XIV). In the present place only one feature calls for detailed notice—the various movements towards a Latin federation. The sanctuary of Juppiter Latiaris on the Monte Cavo, whose antiquity as the centre of a widespread Latin cult cannot be doubted, is only one among several high places round which the Latins seemed to have grouped themselves for political purposes. Apart from less important, and probably later, institutions like the common worship of Venus at Lavinium, we hear in particular of various places at which the cult of Diana seems to have been a bond uniting to some degree or other various sections of the Latin population. First, and most famous, is the precinct of Diana at Aricia, but to this must be added another on Mount Corne, in the territory of Tusculum[1], and also the temple on the Aventine whose foundation is ascribed by tradition to Servius Tullius. There can be no doubt that the unions which grew up round these centres of worship were primarily religious in character, but it is no less clear that in some cases at least a common cult led on to a kind of political federation. The early history of the Latin leagues is a subject about which certainty will never be attained, but its relevance to the rise of Rome demands some consideration of the evidence. When tradition places the earliest religious centre of the Latins on the Monte Cavo, tradition is confirmed both by probability and by the results of excavation. It is in every way plausible that the tendencies to a common Latin festival should have been attracted to the shrine whose position dominates the whole Latin region, and archaeology adds support by showing that the Alban hills were the central point of Latin settlement.

[1] Pliny, *N.H.* XVI, 242.

But though round the sanctuary of Juppiter Latiaris some kind of Latin unity developed, the nature of the union and its dimensions are unknown. That it was religious in origin is clear, but how far membership involved any political obligations beyond that of keeping peace during the period of actual celebrations cannot be said with assurance. Certainly there are grave objections to the Roman version that the league was definitely political, with Alba Longa at its head, and that by her conquest of this city Rome herself succeeded to the headship. There is no reason, indeed, to doubt the historical existence of Alba Longa. Tradition is strong in its favour, and the survival of an *ager Albanus* into historical times adds confirmation. But though Alba Longa may be accepted, and though its site may with some confidence be fixed in the neighbourhood of Castel Gandolfo, there are difficulties in the way of believing that so early as the seventh century it was the head of a league which deserves to be called political. It is a minor objection that the cult-centre itself seems to have been in the territory, not of Alba, but of Cabum: Athens might fairly be called head of the Delian Confederacy even before the Confederacy passed from the protection of Apollo at Delos to that of Athena at Athens. But it is more serious that the Roman destruction of Alba does not seem to have conferred on Rome the formal primacy of Latium. That Rome thereafter was a considerable power is probable; but it will be seen that there is reason for believing in a Latin league still free of Roman domination for a considerable time after Alba disappeared. It seems then that by the seventh century the Mons Albanus had become the religious centre of the Latins, but that the extent to which the federation of Latin cities was political and the degree of control exercised by Alba Longa are both easy to exaggerate.

The names and number of the cities which joined in the Latin festival were also vague. Dionysius, indeed, in an account of which much must be rejected (iv, 49, 2), says that towards the end of the sixth century the members of the Alban league were forty-seven; but though the number is plausible, the reference to cities of the Volsci and Hernici in the same chapter makes it impossible to accept this figure for the period of Alba Longa. Nor does the list of Pliny (*N.H.* iii, 69) give any serious help. The thirty or thirty-one 'carnem in monte Albano soliti accipere populi (Albenses)' are apparently only a selection, made from a larger catalogue, of certain peoples who had disappeared by the first century A.D., and the larger catalogue itself is shown by the alphabetic order of the names to be a late compilation. The evidence here is too weak to justify speculation, even if it were worth while. But names and numbers are fortunately unimportant. There is only one point on which our ignorance is to be regretted. Was Rome at this stage counted a member or not?

It is not to be suggested that all the Latin peoples without exception took part in the festival of the Latiar, nor again can it be maintained that the Latiar was the only celebration held in common by a number of Latin communities. Still less will the evidence prove that the sanctuary of Diana at Aricia served as a political centre at the time when the Alban league was purely religious, though it does suggest that Aricia from very early times was a cult-centre widely recognized in Latium. Our first clear information about the Arician league is contained in the inscription preserved by Priscian from Cato's *Origines* (frag. 58 P.), and probably refers to the closing years of the sixth century. Though, as has often been observed, the absence from the list of Signia and Norba, whose foundation is to be placed early in the fifth, proves that the league here in question is very little later than the end of the regal period at Rome, even when the absence of cities like Gabii, Bovillae and Praeneste has been explained by various considerations, the small number of members—who only amount to eight—shows that the political geography of Latium had greatly changed since the days when the Alban festival was celebrated by forty peoples or more. Since that early stage the process of centralization had gone far, and the time required for this development forbids the league of eight to be fixed much before 500 B.C. But if the precinct of Diana entered on a new period of its history as a federal centre towards the beginning of the fifth century, it seems to have served this purpose before.

On the slopes of the Aventine at Rome, looking over what is now the Jewish Cemetery across the Circus Maximus to the Palatine, there stood the most famous of the Roman temples to Diana. By tradition its establishment is regularly ascribed to Servius Tullius, and on the justice of this ascription much depends. It matters nothing what the name of the king responsible may have been, but it is of the first importance to decide whether the regal origin of the temple can or cannot be accepted. The unanimity of tradition carries weight, but in this case it is confirmed. The testimony of Dionysius (x, 32, 4) that in his time the temple contained a fifth-century document—the lex Icilia de Aventino publicando, the date of which was about 456 B.C.—suggests that the temple was in use within a hundred years of Servius; but another of its contents, also mentioned by Dionysius, seems to carry its date still farther back. This was a treaty with the Latins attributed to Servius himself and preserved on a stele. The words in which this stele is described by Dionysius[1] point to an alphabet as early as that found on the *cippus* beneath the *lapis niger*, which on account of the Fidenae tufa of which it is composed may be dated with much probability to the sixth century. If such a date is right, and if the document is more or less contemporary with the Latin treaty, the temple of Diana contained a document of the Servian age and so may well, as tradition asserts, be of that age itself.

The relevance of this dating to the history of the Latin Leagues is due to a consideration first emphasized by Wissowa. Like the sanctuary of Aricia, the Aventine establishment, according to Varro, was a 'commune Latinorum Dianae templum[2],' and at both the *dies natalis* was celebrated on the Ides of August. Even if the probability be neglected that with this cult the nymph Egeria was brought from Aricia to Rome, so much is enough to show the plausibility of the suggestion that the Aventine foundation was a direct imitation of the Arician cult. For its transference to Rome or for its reproduction there political reasons are the most obvious, and they are also the reasons indicated by tradition; but they are only cogent if it can be inferred that the sanctuary of Diana at Aricia was a federal centre of the Latins at the time to which Servius Tullius must be assigned. In spite of the criticisms to which conclusions of this kind have been freely subjected, the inference still seems sound, and in that case it may be said that, whatever other centres at Lavinium, Tusculum or elsewhere had attracted the allegiance of the Latins, in the sixth century Aricia was the focus of a league which could claim importance enough to make its hegemony an object of Roman aspiration. More than this about the early movements towards unity in Latium must rest on conjecture so uncertain that it may be omitted: the later developments will best be discussed with the rise of Rome.

V. THE SITE OF ROME AND THE GROWTH OF THE CITY

On the lower reaches of the Tiber, where the river divides the Latin region from its neighbours to the west, nature has marked out one site before all others for human occupation. The hills of

---

[1] iv, 26, 5, γραμμάτων ἔχουσα χαρακτῆρας ['Ελληνικῶν], οἷς τὸ παλαιὸν ἡ 'Ελλὰς ἐχρῆτο.

[2] *L.L.* v, 43.

Rome, elusive as they may be among the buildings of the modern city, are more than the mere knolls which alone relieve the flatness of the Campagna to the east. The Palatine in particular was a position of outstanding strength. Its summit was broad enough to receive a considerable community behind the protection of its cliffs, and the stronghold it offered was in a peculiarly profitable situation, because it dominated the river at the point where the ford below the Tiber-island offered the easiest of all crossings from the Latin plain to the west. Though it is not to be denied that the earliest settlers were attracted by the defensive value of the hills, it has also to be remembered that in later times, when intercourse across the river had developed and trade was free, both strategic and commercial facts contributed something to the importance of Rome. And when the advantages of the position collected a larger population than the original settlement could hold, other elements in the hill-system provided sites which it was easy to bring within the circuit of a single wall.

To the history of the city's expansion the complicated details of Roman topography are irrelevant; but the main features are essential, and on them the story depends[1]. Fifteen miles in a direct line from the modern coast the Tiber encounters a ring of hills through which it breaks its way. The ring is a rough ellipse, with its major axis running north and south and with its periphery indented on the north-east and south-west sides. The western limits and the south-western flattening are formed by the ridge which from north to south now bears the successive names of Monte Mario, the Vatican, Janiculum and Monte Verde; close below these the river flows. On the other bank, where the city lay, from a point to the north opposite the Monte Mario to another on the south facing the Monte Verde, the eastern heights stretch round in a broad curve, from the line of which spurs project towards the centre. These spurs in order are the Pincian, Quirinal, Viminal, Cispius, Oppius and Caelius, of which the Oppius and Cispius spring from a section of the surrounding plateau which bears Esquiline as its special name. Finally the gap between the Caelius and the Tiber is filled by the Aventine, which lies opposite the Monte Verde and so completes the circuit. Within this ring the Palatine and Capitoline are enclosed. The isolation, which makes these two hills to-day, with the possible exception of the Aventine, the most impressive of all, owes little if anything to the handiwork of man. Though Trajan's engineers undoubtedly cut

[1] See map 6, facing p. 351.

back the southern escarpment of the Quirinal, Boni's excavations
in the Forum Ulpium have produced conclusive refutation of the
theory, which the inscription on the base of the Trajan column was
formerly supposed to confirm, that until the second century A.D.
Quirinal and Capitoline were connected by a *col* so pronounced as
virtually to merge the two hills into a single ridge. About the
Palatine there is no dispute. The only link which joins it to the surrounding heights still remains what it has been since the earliest
Roman times. This is the narrow saddle of the Velia, which runs
from the Oppius to the north-eastern angle of the Palatine and
provides it with a natural approach which is yet narrow enough
to be easy of defence.

In the legends of the city's foundation the rivalry of Romulus
and Remus bulks large. According to the story, when it had been
agreed that augury should decide the disputed primacy, Remus
chose the Aventine for his *templum* and Romulus the Palatine.
The tale serves at least to call attention to the hills between which
the first settlers on the vacant site of Rome would have to choose.
The Capitoline is so small, and its approaches were probably so
inconvenient, that its escape from the attention of early seekers
for a home is intelligible. Of the other eminences, the Palatine
and Aventine alone have claims. They alone stand clear of their
surroundings, and offer no easy access to an enemy from the surrounding heights. These are the natural strongholds of Rome;
but in strength, as well as in convenience of situation, the difference between them is so great that their respective claims
scarcely need examination. The slopes of the Aventine, which are
gradual on all sides except that towards the Tiber, are useless for
defence without the help of an extensive wall. The Palatine, on
the other hand, rises on three sides in formidable cliffs, the height
of which is even now impressive and whose protective value was
greater still before the level of the surrounding valleys was raised
to the extent which excavation has revealed; and beneath these
cliffs, until the Etruscan age, lay the marshes which later on became the Forum, the Velabrum and the Circus Maximus. Except
by such artificial approaches as the Scalae Caci and the winding
ramp at the western end, access to the Palatine was only possible
by the Velia, where the *col* is so narrow that its protection against
attack was well within the capacity of a village of the size which
the Palatine would hold. Moreover, the position of the Palatine
was not less attractive than its natural strength. Though it was
farther from the river than the Aventine, it was the nearest of all
the hills to the ford below the Tiber-island. Thus the ancient

view that on the Palatine the beginnings of Rome should be sought seems to find every confirmation in considerations of general probability.

The summit of the Palatine has an area of roughly twenty-five acres and is divided by a natural depression into an eastern and a western section, of which the former was Palatium proper and the latter bore the name 'Cermalus.' There is evidence to suggest that at first the communities of these two sites were distinct; but though the name 'Cermalus' survived even into imperial times it is clear that the whole population of the hill was very early united. The scarcity of material evidence for primitive occupation must be ascribed in part to the intensity of the use to which the Palatine was put throughout the classical period, at least until the foundation of New Rome; but nevertheless there remains enough to lend archaeological support to the view of the literary authorities. The only authentic burial discovered on the hill itself is an inhumation which cannot be carried back farther than the fifth century, but it is not within the limits of the settlement that its cemetery must be sought. Below the slopes of the Velia on its western side there came to light in 1902 a burial-place whose full dimensions cannot be ascertained: but the fragment exposed beside the temple of Antoninus and Faustina may be assumed to be typical of the whole. In this *sepulcretum* there is a series of cremations, with which the Volcanal near by has plausibly been connected and which show an undeniable affinity with the cremations of the Alban hills. Though the Alban series has deposits which are definitely earlier than the first at Rome, the cremations of the Forum have begun by the close of the second millennium and extend in all probability into the ninth century B.C. at least, and perhaps beyond.

At a date which the evidence both from Rome and from other parts of Central Italy seems to fix in the neighbourhood of 800 B.C. the *sepulcretum* began to receive the dead of a population distinct from the cremators—of a people whose progress towards Latium can be traced in some detail and the mark of whose presence is inhumation of the body unburnt. From the eighth century these inhumations continue till the sixth, when the cemetery was given up for good. With the draining of the low ground north of the Palatine by the *cloaca maxima*, the history of the Roman Forum begins, and in the history of the business centre of the city the graveyard has no part.

Though demonstrative proof is impossible, there is much plausibility in the view which assigns the cremations of the Forum to the early community of the Palatine. The absence of remains on the hill directs the search for a cemetery outside the limits of the settlement itself, and beyond these limits no site is more obvious than one close by the *col* which served to connect the Palatine with the surrounding country. But the identification does not depend on probability alone. In the necropolis of the Forum the priority of the earlier cremations is proved both by the lower levels at which they are found and by the fact that at the time of the inhumation the cremation-deposits had so far been forgotten that at least one of them was broken into by a later grave. The oldest inhumations at Rome are probably to be sought on the Esquiline, but from the Esquiline they spread rapidly round the heights to the Forum and the Quirinal. The striking fact about the deposits on the outer hills is that, whereas inhumations are freely found, traces of cremation, and especially of cremations belonging to a time before the burying people arrived, are extremely rare. From this it may be inferred that when, about the end of the ninth century, the inhuming immigrants reached the site of Rome they found the hills of the outer ring only lightly occupied by scattered stragglers of a people whose main settlement was elsewhere, and whose dead lay at the foot of the slopes north of the later Forum. The problem then is to find the home of these cremators. The festival of the Septimontium preserves the memory of a time, early indeed in the history of Rome, but still one at which seven communities had grown up round the site and which consequently is later the age of the first cremators. Besides the Palatine, the only hills which the necropolis of the Forum might conceivably have served are the Capitoline and Quirinal; but since these two hills, according at least to the most credible of our authorities, were not occupied by any of the seven villages which joined to celebrate the Septimontium, it seems to follow that they cannot claim the first village of all. Thus the Palatine remains, and the consensus of antiquity finds support.

The arguments advanced by those who look for the beginnings of Rome elsewhere are as weak as the suggestion—made in the interests of the traditional account—that the cremating immigrants were attracted to the Palatine by its similarity in shape to the *terremare* of their ancestors. The existence of a *porta Esquilina* at Tibur (Dessau, 6245) cannot be accepted as proof that the earliest inhabitants of Rome lived on the Esquiline, though it may be admitted that our evidence, such as it is, points to the Esquiline as the first home of the later inhuming population. Nor again is the

primacy of the Quirinal to be deduced either from the course of the
Via Salaria or from its association with some of the earliest Roman
cults. That the salt route passed over the Quirinal is admitted;
but farther south it runs close to the Palatine round the eastern
side of the Capitoline. And if inferences are to be made from the
lines of ancient tracks, an argument against the claim of the
Quirinal must be found in the road which led under the south
side of the Palatine along the Vallis Murcia and provided the
earliest communication between these and the Alban hills. To
the final charge against the traditional view—the charge that the
Palatine is not, as might have been expected, the home of the
oldest Roman cults—it is possible to reply by quoting the
Lupercal, the Ficus Ruminalis, the Tugurium Faustuli and the
Casa Romuli. Those who lack the courage to assert that some
historical significance is to be seen in the secondary Casa Romuli
of the Capitoline must at least admit that the Palatine alone can
claim association with the traditional founder of the city. For the
present question, however, the evidence of cult is of little value.
The issue is whether the first settlers on the site of Rome, whose
cremations are found in the Forum, lived on the Palatine or elsewhere. It is admitted that the inhumers who followed them had
reached the outer hills by the end of the ninth century, and unless
it could be proved of the so-called earliest cults that they belonged
not to these inhumers but to their cremating predecessors the
situation of the cult-centres gives no clue to the whereabouts of
the village in which the cremators lived. At present such proof
is not forthcoming.

Apart from some cuttings in the rock which have been interpreted as the pole-sockets of primitive *capanne*, nothing has been
found in the Palatine earlier than the various cisterns and sundry
pieces of wall which may perhaps be dated to the sixth century[1].
The earliest inhabitants probably depended for protection on the
natural strength of the hill, assisted by some small defences,
probably no more than rough earthworks of the kind still
remembered in classical times near the site of one of the Esquiline
settlements[2]. On which summit of the Palatine, if both were not
occupied, the first village was pitched there is no indication to
show, but we may conjecture that before long huts spread over
the whole habitable surface of the hill. This brings us to Roma
Quadrata.

Roma Quadrata was the name of a shrine on the Palatine con-

---

[1] Much later dates have been proposed.   [2] Varro, *L.L.* v, 48.

taining various objects connected with the foundation of the city[1]; but the term was also used to describe the earliest city recognized by tradition, the city whose limits were those of the Palatine hill. The antiquity of this use has been doubted, and it must be confessed that Varro[2] is the best and earliest authority in its favour. But the common criticisms of Varro carry little weight. Whatever date should be assigned to the origin of the ritual conducted by the Argei, the fact that one of their chapels is located 'in Cermalo'[3] does not prove that Cermalus and Palatine had yet to become parts of a larger whole: and the appearance of the Cermalus in Festus'[4] list of eight communities which celebrated the Septimontium is inconclusive because, though suspicion here usually and reasonably falls on the Subura, it is at least possible that in the original form of the document Palatium denoted the whole hill and that Cermalus, which breaks the geographical sequence, should be rejected as the intruder. Varro's evidence is not to be ignored; and in any case Roma Quadrata may be accepted as the name used by him and his followers to distinguish the Palatine settlement at the beginning of the last millennium B.C. from the larger Rome in which it was subsequently merged.

By a date which falls somewhere within the limits of the eighth century, the outer hills had been freely planted with settlements of the inhuming 'Sabines' (p. 336), and the next stage in the history of Rome is marked by the formation of a union, apparently religious in character, to include both the cremators of the Palatine and at least a section of the newcomers. The survival by which the memory of this union was preserved in republican Rome was the festival of the Septimontium; but the evidence for this celebration is so confused that conclusions of historical relevance can only be drawn from it by more or less hazardous conjecture. There is general agreement that the rites of the Septimontium were performed on seven different hills, and it is obvious that from the earliest days of the institution the communities living on these hills must have been in some way connected. But at this point speculation begins. If, on the ground of its lateness, we may ignore the view which sees the seven hills in the seven main heights of classical Rome, and which therefore includes Janiculum in the list, there remains the account preserved in an unsatisfactory form by Festus. According to the passage as it stands, the hills were: Palatium, Velia, Fagutal, Subura, Cermalus, Caelius, Oppius, Cispius; but emendation is clearly

---

[1] Festus, p. 310 L.   [2] *Ap.* Solin. 1, 17.
[3] Varro, *L.L.* v, 54.   [4] p. 458 *sq.* L.

demanded by the presence of eight names instead of seven, if not
also by the fact that the Subura of later times was a valley and
not a hill at all. The means, however, by which these difficulties
of detail are removed do not affect the wider implications of the
passage, which are that the hills of the Septimontium should be
found in the Palatine, and certain spurs of the outer heights
which lay round about the northern end of the Velia, together
with the Velia itself. It is in all ways probable that when Palatine
Rome began to grow into something larger the first stage in the
expansion was a loose union of the Palatine community with
others round about, and as a record of this stage the festival of
the Septimontium may be accepted.

Thus far it is possible to go with tradition; but the further
suggestion that the seven communities formed a single city, and
that Septimontium was its name, must be rejected. It cannot
be doubted that in the late republic, if not before, the word
Septimontium was capable of a local signification, but in this sense
it properly denoted a district and nothing more. Whatever political
or religious ties may have bound the seven villages to one another,
the total lack of evidence for any common system of defence
indicates the essential difference between the Septimontium and
the late Servian City. Individually, of course, the villages may
have been fenced, and it is even possible that the stretch of earth-
work which survived into historical times had originally belonged
to the people of the Subura or the Oppius. But on the nature of
the Septimontium in general nothing need be added to the account
of Varro[1]—rightly understood—that Septimontium was a name
used to denote a certain area at a time in its history before that
area was included in the walls of a later city.

The theory which seems to have won credence in classical Rome
suggests that the enclosure of the Palatine and other settlements
within a single boundary came with the formation of what may
be called the City of the Four Regions. For this development
the evidence is vague and scanty, but attempts to discredit the
Four Regions City as an antiquarian invention have not achieved
success. To the defence of the traditional view arguments based
on religion do not contribute much. From the sites of the cult-
centres recognized in the so-called Calendar of Numa no conclusions about the dimensions of the city can be drawn: for cult-
centres might lie outside the boundaries as well as within. The
cogent case for the City of the Four Regions rests on the *pomerium*

---

[1] *L.L.* v, 41.

of republican times. In its original sense *pomerium* seems to have meant the divine boundary of a city, and since it marked the limits of the area specially protected by the city's gods, Varro is wholly plausible in saying that the *pomerium* properly ran outside, and not inside, the defensive walls where such existed[1]. Thus a *pomerium* which encloses a smaller area than that within the Servian wall must be connected with a city earlier in date than this defensive system. It will be seen that the remains of the Servian defences contain evidence for the extent of sixth-century Rome; and since one large region—the Esquiline—is outside the *pomerium* but inside the sixth-century circuit it seems to follow that the *pomerium* must be assigned to something earlier than the so-called Servian City[2]. In addition to the districts of the Septimontium, the *pomerium* of the Republic included Capitoline, Quirinal and Viminal, as well as certain low-lying districts between the hills, of which the Forum is the most important; and such archaeological material as these districts provide suggests that the origin of this city is to be placed in the seventh century[3].

The choice of a name for this stage of Rome's development is a matter of small importance. 'City of the Four Regions' is a modern label, justified to some extent by the fact that, with the possible exception of the Mons Capitolinus and the Roman Forum, the whole area within the *pomerium* which formed the boundary of the seventh-century city, was divided in republican times between the *regiones Suburana*, *Esquilina*, *Collina* and *Palatina*. The exception is of some interest. If the ritual of the Argei is early, and not an institution of the third century B.C., as Wissowa has essayed to show, Varro's list (*L.L.* v, 45 *sqq.*) of chapels visited by the procession on 16 and 17 March throws valuable light on the city's growth when it suggests that the Capitoline and the low ground beneath it to the east were not included in any one of the Regions. Though a city from which the Capitoline was omitted may be surprising, the explanation of its omission is so obvious as to confirm the suggestion of the evidence. Before the draining of the Forum by the canalization of what later became the Cloaca maxima, the Mons Capitolinus

---

[1] *L.L.* v, 143.

[2] Of an earlier *pomerium* which included the Palatine alone, though it may well have existed, we know nothing. Tacitus (*Ann.* XII, 24) is probably only sketching the course followed in his own day by the celebrants of the Lupercalia.

[3] See J. B. Carter, *Roma Quadrata and the Septimontium*, in *A.J.A.* XII. pp. 172 *sqq.*

was almost worthless, too small to be an independent stronghold and too isolated to be made part of the Quirinal group. Though no certainty can be attained, it is at least possible that in the earliest city the Capitoline had no place and that its inclusion was due to the later kings with whose building activities it is closely associated. Against such inferences from our knowledge of the four regions no objection can be drawn from the fact that the regions bear the same names as the four urban tribes. Whatever the date of the urban tribes, there is no reason to think that the regions drew their names from the tribes and not *vice versa*. It seems then that in the *pomerium* we have evidence for a city earlier than that of the sixth century, and that in the conjectural limits of the regions there is a hint that this first Rome excluded the Capitoline, which may, like the Esquiline, have been added at the time with which tradition at least connects Servius Tullius.

That the City of the Four Regions was protected by more worldly defences than its *pomerium* there is nothing to show. Evidence for a continuous fortification embracing part of the outer heights is wholly lacking until the sixth century brings the wall of Servius. The Servian wall in its final form was an elaborate work which varied in construction according to the demands of the *terrain*. Wherever possible the line gave advantage of position to the defence by following the contours of the hills rather more than half-way up the slopes, and in these sections the wall was the sole protection. But on level ground the works were of a more formidable type, which may be seen in the extant remains south of the Colline Gate. First a ditch was dug, said to have been thirty feet deep and a hundred wide, and next the spoil from this excavation was piled behind it to form an *agger*. Both faces of the *agger* were then supported by retaining walls of which the outer one is built in the same style as the defences on those sections of the circuit where no *agger* is found. The inner wall is of rougher technique. The date of these defences in their final form can be fixed with some assurance. Since the material of the outer wall throughout is tufa from the quarries of Grotta Oscura which lay in the territory of Veii, it has been argued that the construction belongs either to the period of Etruscan supremacy in Rome or to a time after the destruction of Veii, and that consequently it must be placed either in the sixth century or after the beginning of the fourth[1]. To support the later date there is ample evidence, and evidence independent of

---

[1] See T. Frank, *Roman Buildings of the Republic*, p. 114.

all questions about the relations between Rome and Veii. The use of the Roman foot, which had almost certainly not super-seded the old Italic foot when the foundations of the Capitoline temple were laid in the sixth century, points to a date after the foundation of the Republic. The fourth century is indicated in particular both by the forms of the letters used on the blocks as quarry-marks or for some similar purpose, and by a comparison of the structural technique with that shown by fourth-century walls in other Italian cities; and it is in the fourth century that Livy records (vi, 32, 1; vii, 20, 9), not indeed with the lucidity which might be desired, extensive repairs to the fortifications of Rome. There can be little doubt that the Servian wall in its familiar form is a monument of Rome's recovery after the Gallic invasion (p. 567).

The possibility, however, that Livy is right in regarding the works of the fourth century as no more than repairs, and that an earlier wall had stood on the line of the 'Servian' *enceinte*, is by no means to be ignored (p. 563). At various points in the circuit there appear short stretches of masonry whose peculiar charac-teristics point to a different date, and the difficulties of regarding them as contemporary are too great to be seriously weakened by the fact that these fragments are at times worked into the later construction. The materials provide the most significant evidence; for whereas the fourth-century remains are of Veientane tufa throughout, the masonry now in question is uniformly of the local *cappellaccio*. And even if this difference of material did not suggest a difference of date, there would still remain the con-structional technique to show that the wall to which these traces belong was built at least a century before the later repairs were carried out. The smallness of the blocks, whose height is only ten inches or thereabouts against two feet in the restorations, and the irregularity of the courses combine to indicate an origin in the sixth century or the fifth. In the absence of pottery from the foundations of this wall, so far as they have been explored, the material evidence will not authorize a more definite date than this; but it may be said that at present no valid archaeological objection can be brought against the connection of these survivals with the wall ascribed by tradition to the sixth of the kings of Rome. To this stage the addition of the Esquiline, and possibly of the Capitoline, belongs.

Whatever view may be taken of the details related by Livy and Dionysius about the Icilian rogation of 456 (p. 472 *sq.*), the story probably rests on a basis sound enough to justify the conclusion that in the middle of the fifth century the Aventine was still more or less unoccupied. If this is so, the tale that Ancus Marcius added the Aventine to the city becomes incredible, as indeed it always has been in the light of archaeological evidence for the expansion of Rome; and there is much plausibility in the theory that this hill was first included when the Servian defences were re-organized after the Gallic retreat (p. 567). The question of the Aventine and its incorporation affects the interpretation of the *cappellaccio* wall because there are traces of this work on the Palatine which could not easily be assigned to a circuit including the Aventine *massif*. Even if proof were forthcoming that the Aventine formed part of the city as early as the sixth century, it would be possible to connect the Palatine remains with the independent defences which that hill may have boasted even after the coming of the Gauls: but if, on the other hand, the Aventine remained outside the defences until the fourth-century reconstruction, then it is possible to say that the whole series of these *cappellaccio* survivals lie on the trace of the fourth-century *enceinte*, except on the slope above the Vallis Murcia where the line was altered, at the time of the restoration, to take in the last of the Roman hills. With the City of the Four Regions this wall can have nothing to do, because the clearest of all the signs it has left are north of the Baths of Diocletian, at a point where the Servian circuit extends as far beyond the *pomerium* as it does anywhere in its course. For the present, and until more light is won, it would be unwise to rule out the possibility that the first wall of Rome which included not only the Palatine but part of the outer heights was built in the sixth century, and that an extension on the Esquiline, as Livy asserts, together possibly with one to include the Capitoline, was really an achievement of the regal period.

Such were the changes of five hundred years. The Palatine settlement, founded not long before the end of the second millennium B.C., had been joined in about 800 by the younger communities of the outer hills. In the eighth century seven of these had begun the common celebration of the Septimontium, and in the seventh these villages, together with those of the Quirinal and Viminal, with or without the Capitoline, had been merged into a single city lying behind a continuous *pomerium*. Next, possibly in the sixth century, a defensive wall was built which, unless the Capitoline was now for the first time annexed, only deserted the line of the *pomerium* in the north-east, where it was carried forward to enclose a large section of the Esquiline; and finally, in the fourth century, when this wall was renewed, one more addition was made by the inclusion of the Aventine to the south. Thereafter Rome still grew: but when the fourth-century works had saved the city from the menace of Hannibal, the need for defences slowly disappeared, and Rome became something like the open city which it remained until the Alemannic danger produced the fortifications of Aurelian and Probus.

VI. THE FOUNDATION LEGENDS

The legends which grew up round the origin of Rome have so slight a value as evidence for the history of the city that they can claim little space: all that is needed is to make their irrelevance plain. The arrival of the Greeks in the western Mediterranean gradually brought Italy within the ambit of Greek myth, and it is on Greek foundations that the whole saga of early Rome is based. To extend the geographical range of Hellenic legend the most obvious expedient was to continue the tale of the *Nostoi*, and this expedient in the end affected other places in Latium than Rome: Telegonus, for instance, became the recognized founder of Tusculum. The westward progress of Odysseus and Aeneas, so far as details are concerned, may be ignored before the fifth century, when Hellanicus of Lesbos brings Aeneas to the site of Rome to found a city called after one of the Trojan women[1]. From the fifth century, with unimportant changes in its main outlines, the tale was elaborated by the Greeks until soon after 230 B.C., when under the influence of Hellas a Roman literature was coming into existence, it was taken over by Naevius and Fabius Pictor (see vol. VIII).

At this time the fusion of Greek and Latin legend was still imperfect, but although the final version had not yet been evolved, something had been done to meet the most serious difficulty of all. This was chronological. Before the establishment of the Republic in the last decade of the sixth century Roman tradition could tell of nothing more than seven kings—or eight at most; and these were by no means enough to span the gap between the Trojan war and the expulsion of the second Tarquin. To fill the lacuna drastic measures were taken. Aeneas, whose first advent to Latium had been as founder of Rome itself, was shorn of this proud privilege. He might visit the site, indeed, as he does under Vergil's guidance, but for four centuries or so he and his descendants are condemned to drag out a misty existence elsewhere,

---

[1] Hellanicus *ap.* Dion. Hal. I, 72, 2, where the authorship of Hellanicus is rightly accepted by Jacoby (*F.G.H.*, Hell. fr. 84 = *F.H.G.*, Hell. frag. 53).

until the time arrives when Romulus at long last may carry out
the task for which Aeneas originally had come. In the search
for a local habitation to which the waiting progeny of Aeneas
might be consigned it was both natural and appropriate that men
should turn to the hills which dominate the Latin landscape. If
Aeneas had reached Latium too soon, and if, in consequence, the
founder of Rome was to rise from some neighbouring city, no
home could be more suitable than one which lay close to the
greatest of the religious centres in the region. At one time, it is
true, the sanctuary of Juppiter Latiaris seems to have lain within
the territory of Cabum, but it was undoubtedly the proximity
of this establishment which conferred on Alba Longa its prestige.
According to the account which finally prevailed, Alba Longa
was founded by Ascanius, son of Aeneas, who had settled with
his father at Lavinium; and it was at Lavinium that Aeneas
ended his earthly career either by drowning in the river Numicus
or by bodily assumption to heaven after death at the hands of the
Etruscan Mezentius. The choice of Lavinium, the city of the
Laurentes, for the honour of this association does not admit of
certain explanation. Though it would be wrong to say that the
advent of Aeneas to the western Mediterranean was due to his
connection in Greek minds with any locality which could boast
a cult capable of identification with that of Aphrodite, in Greek
mythology the hero's connection with his divine mother was undoubtedly close. Somewhere between Lavinium and Ardea was
what Strabo (v, p. 232) calls a 'shrine of Aphrodite shared
by the Latins' (κοινὸν τῶν Λατίνων ἱερὸν Ἀφροδίτης), and
it is conceivable that therein should be seen the reason for
Aeneas' presence at this particular spot. The cult, however, does
not seem to have been important; and since the date of its origin
cannot be ascertained, it must be regarded as possible that this
was not the cause, but the result, of the connection of Lavinium
with Aeneas. If the worship of Aphrodite at Lavinium was
generated by the presence of Aeneas, Lavinium may be no more
than an obvious stepping-stone between the site of Rome, where
the hero first arrived, and the home of his immediate descendants
—Alba Longa.

No light is thrown on the origins of Rome by the legends of
Hercules, Cacus and Evander, the tenants of the site before
Romulus appears. Hercules is Greek, and though Cacus seems
originally to have been an Italic fire-spirit, he does not enter into
the legend localized at Rome until he has taken on the character
of the Greek Typhoeus. Evander again comes from Arcadia. In
origin he seems to have been a form of Pan, and his translation

to Rome is to be explained by the similarity of name between Pallanteion, the home of his cult near Tripolitza, and the Mons Palatinus at Rome. The theory that the Roman associations of Evander are to be explained in whole or part by his resemblance to Faunus is to be treated with the greatest caution: it depends wholly on the assumption, questioned by Warde Fowler, that Faunus was early involved in the Lupercalia and was consequently recognized in Rome for an indefinite time before the temple on the Tiber-island was built in 196 B.C.

It is only with Romulus that the legends of the city proper rise to importance. In the fifth century, before the presence of Aeneas in Latium had been finally accepted, the foundation of Rome was vaguely ascribed to an eponymous Rhōmos, of whom our earliest mention (Festus, p. 328 L.) is derived from an unknown source through Agathocles of Cyzicus. Rhomos, therefore, was known in Greece by the end of the fifth century; but in Latium this form of the name found no acceptance. Instead, perhaps through familiarity with a name which appears in Etruscan monuments as *rumlna* and in later Latin as Romilius, the Romans chose 'Romulus' as the appellation of their founder. The ancient view that it was Romulus who gave his name to Rome, and more modern suggestions that the legendary ancestor of the Romilii was somehow assigned the honour of the city's foundation, may both be set aside. Romulus indeed may be a form suggested by a proper name common among the early settlers in Latium and its surroundings; but, whatever the word 'Roma' may mean, and whether or not there be any value in the theory that its origin is Etruscan, the Romulus of legend, both in function and in name, is nothing more than eponym of the city. The identification of Romulus with Quirinus, apparently the title under which a deity corresponding to Mars was worshipped by the people of the outer hills, cannot be proved before the Ciceronian age, and is to be explained partly by the ease with which Quirinus could be made eponym of the Quirites and partly by a desire to turn Romulus, whose ancestry was early said to be divine, into a god himself.

In the fourth century the Latin Romulus joins Rhomos in Greece—not indeed as brother but, in the first place, apparently as grandfather[1]. In the third century Rhomos disappears, and in his stead there enters Rĕmus—twin brother of Romulus. Such evidence as survives tends strongly to suggest that at first the

[1] This depends on the correction of 'Rhodius' to 'Rhomus' made by F. Orsini in Festus' report (p. 328 L.) of a passage from the historian Alcimus.

founder of the city was unique, that Rhomos and Romulus are alternatives, and that the connection of both with the choosing of a site is a comparatively late development. In its final form the story contains many details which need not detain us. Akki's rescue of Sharrukîn, the vicissitudes of Moses, and the early adventures of Cyrus the Great are reminders enough that miraculous preservation is a feature in the early life of famous men by no means peculiar to the Greek and Roman worlds. In this case, however, the parallels from Greece are the most relevant, and in Greece the nearest may be found in the tale of Neleus and Pelias. This pair, twin sons of Tyro, daughter of Salmoneus, by Poseidon, were turned adrift on the Enipeus; and, when at length the stream cast them ashore, they were suckled the one by a bitch, the other by a mare. The resemblance here is close enough to suggest that, like most of the speculations current in antiquity about the founders of Rome, the tale of Romulus and Remus in form at least is Greek, but to this it must be added that details such as the choice of a she-wolf for foster-mother and the association with the *ficus ruminalis* are Italian.

The version which makes the two founders twins cannot be shown to have existed before the end of the fourth century. The 'Lupa Capitolina,' a work to be dated about 500 B.C., would be our earliest evidence if it were evidence at all: but it is very doubtful whether this monument in its original form included any children or child. The figures of the twins now to be seen in the Palazzo dei Conservatori are works probably of the Quattrocento, and the view that they are not mere additions, but took the place of children contemporary with the wolf itself, is hard to reconcile with the general design. In the long series of monuments which show the suckling of the twins, the wolf regularly turns its head back towards its haunches, in an attitude wholly unlike that of the Capitoline bronze. Of the Capitoline type no copy or even reminiscence survives; and the difficulty of believing that this should be so if the group enjoyed the fame which would have belonged to one of the earliest sculptured representations of a famous scene, together with the suggestion of the wolf's position that it was not in the act of giving suck at all, compels the conclusion that the bronze is irrelevant to the history of Romulus and Remus in Roman legend. After this, another monument deserves mention because, though it cannot be connected with the twins or even with Rome, it is our first instance in art of the suckling wolf in the familiar pose, and also sound evidence for wolf-children in the tales of Italy. This is the Etruscan *stele* from the Certosa di Bologna, now in the Bologna Museum, which probably belongs

to the first half of the fourth century and shows a she-wolf with
back-turned head giving milk, not to twins indeed, but to a single
child.

If the Romano-Campanian coinage, on which the wolf and
twins appear, belongs to the period of the Pyrrhic war and does
not follow immediately on Rome's entry into Campania (p. 608),
our earliest valid evidence for the story of the twins at Rome is
the monumental group set up by the brothers Ogulnii, when
aediles in 296 B.C. According to Livy (x, 23, 11–12) 'ad ficum
Ruminalem simulacra infantium conditorum urbis sub uberibus
lupae posuerunt'; and, so far as the motive is concerned, probability is on Livy's side, though his account has been disputed.
The view that the Ogulnii meant the two children to symbolize
some dualism—for instance, the partnership of patricians and
plebeians in the priesthoods—and that a misinterpretation of
these figures subsequently gave rise to the story of the twin
founders of the city is hard to reconcile with the fact that less
than a century later the vulgate version of the city's origin found
a place in the *Histories* of Fabius Pictor (frags. *5a*, *5b*, P.). The
dedication may be accepted as our earliest evidence for Romulus
and Remus at Rome; and this interpretation is to some extent
confirmed by the appearance of the suckling wolf on Romano-
Campanian didrachms of the heavy series. It may be assumed
that whatever meaning the type was intended to convey must
have been one easy for the uninstructed to grasp, and it is more
reasonable to see in it a reference to a legend which soon won wide
acceptance than to argue that it indicates some other union which
is not known with certainty even to have been represented in art.

In the first stage of the development Rhomos is alone. In the
second, when Rhomos and Romulus are competing claimants to
the founder's place, the former is slowly ousted by the latter.
And in the third, to those at least who are unmoved by arguments
designed to prove the priority of Remus to his brother, Remus
joins Romulus and the pair are twins. No wholly satisfactory
account of this duplication can be given. The view which sees
in it an attempt to find authority for the collegiate magistracy
of later times fails before the fact that Remus, though brother
of Romulus, is nowhere represented as his partner in rule and is,
indeed, rather a rival aspirant to monarchy. Remus, in fact, is too
little like Titus Tatius for this theory to be true. Nor again is it
easy to agree that the brothers stand for two racial elements in
the population of Rome. It is most improbable that the Romans
of the fourth century desired to emphasize the early distinction
between the cremating and inhuming inhabitants of the city, and

the suggestion that the twins record the reception by the Roman people, already more or less united, of Sabine invaders soon after the foundation of the Republic hangs together with a version of fifth-century Latin history which is by no means proved (see below, p. 495 *sq.*). So far as our scanty information goes it rather points to a simpler conclusion. After Greece had given Rhomos to Rome and Rome had returned him to Greece under the Italian name Romulus, the Greeks found two figures associated with the foundation of the city. By this pair they were reminded of legends in which a part was played by twins, and therefore this relationship between Rhomos and Romulus was established. At Rome, however, Rhomos was not an accepted name. Romulus had already been invented as an alternative, and when the twins reached Italy as Rhomos and Romulus another variant was needed. This was found in Remus—a form which, just as Romulus had been influenced by the name Romilius, was commended by its likeness to the name Remmius or Remnius (cf. Ramnes), if it was not actually modelled thereon.

Thus far the story has been of legends devised by the theorists of Greece to provide some account of Roman origins. The Italian element they contain is small and their historical value is negligible. Of the other tales in which the name of Romulus appears the majority bear either on the constitutional development or on the history of Roman expansion during the regal period, and in these connections they will be mentioned. All that remains for notice here is the Rape of the Sabine Women, with its pendent—the *asylum inter duos lucos*. It was a foible of the Romans—and a foible which has seriously distorted the tradition—to represent their ancestors as rude warriors of the sort which appropriately might found an imperial race, and in this spirit they suggest that the followers of Romulus—the first citizens of Rome—were high-spirited youths moved by a thirst for glory to leave their Alban home. When they were safely settled in the new city, the festival of the Consualia, to which neighbouring peoples had been invited, was chosen as an opportunity for seizing the Sabine women to make good a scarcity of wives. The reasons for this *coup* are variously given. Some said that in their eagerness for adventure the first settlers had come without womenfolk at all, others that it was for newcomers who had taken refuge at the *asylum* that wives were needed, and others again that Romulus indulged in this escapade simply in order to provoke a war. The details do not matter. In outline the story seems to be no more than an attempt by means of legendary history to explain various features of the Roman marriage rite. The tale is conditioned by the military character of the first settlement, wherein women were rare. The choice of Sabines as the victims is made plausible by the early intimacy of this people with Rome. The rape is a supposed precedent for the force put upon a bride before she entered her husband's house—force which probably had its origin in a desire to free her effectively from the magical conditions of the virgin state she was about to lose. The hero Talasius, who appears in the account of Livy (I, 9, 12) and elsewhere, is an antiquarian invention to account for the mysterious cry 'Talassio' raised by marriage processions at Rome. And the choice of the Consualia as the occasion of this affair is perhaps due to one of the two annual celebrations of this festival—that on 21 August—having been a merry-making after harvest, whereat the ordinary rules of behaviour were to some extent relaxed.

The Rape of the Sabines makes an early appearance: there is evidence enough to show that it was accepted by Ennius in the first half of the second century B.C. For this reason it can claim priority to the tale that, in order to increase the population of his city, Romulus founded an *asylum* in the depression between the two summits of the Mons Capitolinus—a tale which cannot be traced back beyond the first century B.C. There is, indeed, no reason to believe that the particular *asylum* here concerned was ever used as such; and, in spite of what Lang admits to be no more than a guess about the *nemus* at Aricia[1], the evidence for sanctuaries of this sort in Italy is so weak that the institution itself, like its name, may well be an importation from Greece. It is a plausible conjecture that, when the idea of an *asylum* had grown familiar at Rome, the erection of such a place was ascribed to Romulus in order that the fugitives whom it would attract might be available to explain the need for women implied by the legend of the rape; and its localization on the Capitoline may well be due, as De Sanctis has suggested[2], to nothing more than the presence there, in a very prominent position, of a *bidental* or some similar enclosure.

Of the early legends no more need be said. The evidence they supply is less valuable for the beginnings of Roman history than for the entry of Rome into the intellectual heritage of Greece. Far more important is the native tradition on which our knowledge of the next subject depends—the history of Rome in the regal age.

---

[1] *Magic and Religion*, pp. 218 sqq.   [2] *Storia dei Romani*, I, p. 220.

CHAPTER XII

THE KINGS OF ROME

I. THE EARLY KINGS

IF the tradition of a regal period at Rome needs confirmation, confirmation is not difficult to find: various considerations unite to prove that beyond all doubt monarchy was one of the early phases in the constitutional development (see below, p. 407 *sq.*). But acceptance of the kingship does not imply belief in the vulgate version of the kings. Of Romulus enough has been said to show that his claims to consideration as an historical figure may be ignored. His successors, according to the received account, are six, to whom Titus Tatius may possibly be added as a seventh; and seven is the greatest number of kings that tradition can produce to cover the whole period of history which Rome may boast before the establishment of a republic at the end of the sixth century. Under an elective monarchy, where men have to win distinction before they can become king, reigns tend to be short, and in such circumstances half a dozen kings can scarcely be expected to account for the government for more than two hundred years. Thus the kings of traditional history will provide at best for less than half the period which elapsed between the first settlement of cremating Latins on the Palatine (p. 354) and the beginning of the Republic; and tradition confesses its consciousness of this hiatus by postponing the foundation of Rome and filling the four preceding centuries with the worthless tales of Alba (p. 363 *sq.*). Towards those of the kings who have some claim to be regarded as historical two alternative attitudes are possible. It may be held that their number is arbitrary, and that, whether these names be those of actual kings or not, they are merely selected as lay figures on whom to father the more outstanding monuments, exploits and institutions of Rome from its origin to the end of the sixth century. Or again it is possible to maintain that the regal period with which tradition purports to deal is in actual fact what the accepted story implies—a short final

Note.—The main continuous sources for the traditions of the seven kings of Rome are Livy I, Dionysius of Halicarnassus, *Roman Antiquities* I–IV (see chapter x), and Plutarch's Lives of Romulus and Numa.

section of Roman history before the foundation of the Republic—
and that the section was one in which Rome was ruled by a series
of six or seven kings, who may even have borne the names which
are preserved.

Romulus stands apart and is wholly a construction, but a number
of considerations combine to suggest that the figures of the remaining kings are built round a kernel of fact. If Romulus be set
aside and with him Titus Tatius, who holds an equivocal position
on the fringe of the king-list but outside it, the kings of Rome run
in an ordered canon which knows no variation. From this it is a
common and valid inference that the canon must have been established before the third century, when the speculations of Roman
historiography began; but the fixing of the list can be carried back
further still. Had it been a creation of the fifth and fourth centuries
it is difficult to believe that no attempt would have been made to
claim regal dignity for some of the great patrician houses which
then were dominant in Rome. Yet in the nomenclature of the kings
there is no hint of a connection with the Fabii, the Valerii and the
rest. It must be admitted, however, that, if the regal names had to
be invented, inventors were not bound to take their ideas from the
names of families famous in their own time. Names might be
significant, like that of Romulus himself, and this would probably
have been the case if their owners were mere fictitious eponyms,
created to be the authors of various features in early Roman history.
But this is not so. To the kings' achievements, to the parts they were
made to play in the traditional history, their names bear no relation.
They are names familiar in Etruria or Rome, though such distinction as was won by the republican namesakes of Numa Pompilius,
Tullus Hostilius, Ancus Marcius and Servius Tullius was late and
rare. It seems then that the list of kings was fixed as early as the
fifth century and that the names which composed the list were neither
invented nor chosen to dignify with regal ancestry men who bore
them in later days. Under such circumstances the conclusion can
hardly be escaped that the names at least are those of figures distinguished in regal times—and, if distinguished, in what capacity
but as king?

The traditional chronology of the regal period is artificial. Details
of the development by which the final version was produced are a
subject which at best is one for speculation; but in outline what
happened is perhaps simpler than some authorities would allow. To
the seven canonical kings, though the first was not historical at all,
theory assigned reigns which together made a period equal to as many
generations; and, since thirty-five years in this case were reckoned

as a generation[1], a date two hundred and forty-five years before the beginning of the Republic was chosen for the foundation of the city and the opening of the regal age. Materials from which to construct a less arbitrary and more accurate chronology are to seek. For chronological purposes the constitutional question about the government of the villages which formed the Septimontium is unimportant: but even if seven kings ruled over seven separate communities they would not belong to that regal period of Roman history as it is generally understood. If it is right to regard the Septimontium as a stage before the city of Rome came into existence, the regal period in the ordinary sense cannot have opened before the City of the Four Regions was formed; and the assignment of the kings to that city is confirmed by another fact. The peculiar position of the Regia, in which it is perverse to see anything but the palace of the kings, has often been noticed: it is not on the Palatine or any other hill but on the lowest slopes of the Velia. The choice of such a site points strongly to a date when settlements on several hills were coming under a single government—that is, to a date somewhere in the seventh century when it seems probable that the villages of Rome were first merged into a city.

Theories which would interpret the kings as in origin gods may be disregarded, if a regal period is accepted at all: even if it were possible, a demonstration that, though Rome had once been ruled by kings, the names ascribed to the monarchs of tradition are really those of deities would at best be unprofitable. In fact, however, the scrutiny to which the evidence has been subjected in recent years leads unmistakably to the conclusion that, so far from it being possible to regard the kings themselves as originally gods, the materials from Rome will not even justify the view that the primary functions of the kingship were priestly and that the king derived his authority from a connection with the gods closer than that of ordinary mortals. Save in the case of Romulus, who only attained to deity by identification with Quirinus, cults of the Roman kings are unknown, and such rare connections with gods as are ascribed to various kings must be put down to republican elaborations of tradition. Nor again is it a happy suggestion that the seven kings personify the seven hills. If Romulus is eponym of the city as a whole, only six kings are left for seven heights, and of the six no one has a significant name of the kind which a personification would naturally bear. By such considerations the suggestion might be refuted, even if De Sanctis had

---

[1] For the generation of 35 years see Thuc. VI, 4, 2; 5, 2, who in his sketch of Greek colonization in Sicily is probably reproducing Antiochus of Syracuse.

not proved to demonstration that no king is ever associated exclusively with a single hill[1].

With that small degree of confidence which is the greatest permissible in early Roman history, the six kings from Numa to the second Tarquin may be accepted as figures named after men who presided over the destinies of Rome from the time in the seventh century when Rome became a city down to the establishment of republican government. But so much by way of concession to the authority of tradition does not involve acceptance of tradition as a whole. In detail the recorded achievements of the kings call for close examination, and when the legendary dross has been rejected the residuum of possibly historical matter will be small.

Consideration of the list in detail may begin with Titus Tatius—so far as our evidence goes, the one unsuccessful candidate for inclusion in the accepted canon. He is in a different position from the six successors of Romulus: for though his statue stood on the Capitoline with those of the other kings[2], he was rejected by historical tradition, and the early scepticism which his rejection implies is confirmed. Unlike the others, Tatius has a name which may be significant. It seems to connect him with the Tities; and though he was familiar as early as the time of Ennius[3], the only part which we know Ennius to have made him play is that of eponym to the tribe. Moreover another of Tatius' functions—to personify the Sabine element at Rome—is not assigned to him with any unanimity, or even by the dominant tradition. The story of the Sabine settlement which won widest acceptance—probably, it is true, less on its historical merits than through the influence of the Claudii—made Attius Clausus the leader of the newcomers and put their arrival at the end of the sixth century (p. 494). And finally the 'equal power' ($\iota\sigma o\psi\eta\phi\iota a$) of Romulus and Tatius, unlike the relation assumed between Romulus and his brother Remus, is suspiciously suggestive of an attempt to find early precedents for the collegiate magistracy. About Tatius, then, the conclusion must be that though his connection with the Sabine immigrants serves at least as a reminder of the undoubted presence in the early population of more elements than one, he cannot be accepted with any confidence as historical. His name and his constitutional position both have the appearance of late inductions made to account for one of the Romulian tribes and to lend the sanction of antiquity to the supreme magistracy of the Republic.

The traditional achievements of the seven Roman kings fall

---

[1] *Storia dei Romani*, I, p. 362, *n.* 4.   [2] Pliny, *N.H.* xxxiv, 23.

[3] Varro, *L.L.* v, 55.

naturally into groups, of which the two largest concern the development of the constitution and the extension of the city's territory. These two are subjects of an importance which justifies separate treatment: in connection with the individual kings only such matters need be mentioned as belong to neither but are still not without significance.

The character of the founder was appropriately bellicose. More pacific institutions, and especially those embodied in the religious system, were ascribed in general to his successor. Numa Pompilius may indeed be the name of a ruler in early Rome, but many of the activities assigned to him are the merest legend. His association with the religious side of public life made him a peculiarly fitting figure for insertion in tales which, however picturesque, bear only on the study of Roman religion. The story which tells how Numa made Picus and Faunus drunk and captured them in order to extract the secret of expiating a stroke of lightning, and how they, unable to give the answer, arranged an interview between Numa and Juppiter himself, in which Numa's part is to protest the Roman horror of human sacrifice, is one which sheds light on the religious workings of the Roman mind; but for Numa, king of Rome, it is no evidence at all. That the story lacks even the slenderest foundation of fact need not be said: but what is not so generally agreed is that, though the story is wholly legend, its attachment to Numa does not prove that Numa himself is unhistorical. The same is true of the relationship between Numa and Egeria—in origin the nymph of a spring close by the sanctuary of Diana at Aricia, who later acquired other functions and also became adviser and even wife of Numa. His connection with this source of inspiration does nothing to authorize punning conjectures that Numa began his career as spirit of the river Numicus: but on the other hand, though Diana of Aricia almost certainly came to Rome before the end of the regal period and though, with Diana, Egeria probably came too, the evidence of the tale is not itself enough to prove that Numa was the king who presided over their introduction.

The main work of Numa, the organization of the religious calendar and of the priestly colleges, is more difficult to interpret. The suggestion that the traditional account of Numa's legislation finds support in the need for a powerful reformer to reduce the pristine authority of a great magician-king to the dignified impotence of the Flamen Dialis fails, unless the history of kingship in Italy is other than we believe. There is no good evidence that kings before Numa were afflicted with taboos so severe as those under which the Flamen Dialis laboured; but, unless a priest-king of this sort existed so late as the seventh century, Numa is not needed to confine him to his priestly functions. Again, it must be admitted that the several sacred colleges and the so-called Calendar of Numa are the results of a slow and natural growth. Of the calendar, which is known to us with certainty from the Fasti, this much is proved by the ease with which three distinct stages of cultural history may be detected in the festivals which compose it. But still there remains the fact that at a certain point—a point early in Roman history when city-life was something new and when deities of such consequence as the Capitoline Triad were still unknown at Rome—the growth was suddenly arrested, and the festivals existing at the time were embodied in a calendar which thenceforward was kept distinct from all later innovations. Here the hand of a legislator is visible, and though the institutions of Numa cannot be accepted as his invention, there is reason to think that during the regal period some individual —almost certainly a king—did concern himself with the religious side of public life in a way which marked a definite stage in its development (see below, pp. 425 *sqq.*).

Among the measures ascribed to Numa more often than to other kings two reforms are marked out by the need for executive action which alone could make them possible. The change in the secular calendar, by which two months were added to the recognized ten[1], is assigned to him; and it is a change which must have needed an author if it were ever made. For long the calendar of ten months lay under grave suspicion, and it must be confessed that the earliest recorded evidence for its existence was a document inscribed in the Temple of Hercules Musarum[2], dedicated in all probability by the father of Q. Fulvius Nobilior, who was one of the consuls in 153 B.C. when for the first time the consular year opened with the month of January. But though his view of its origin may be doubted, the value of Mommsen's warning against its rejection is recalled by Nilsson's demonstration[3] that various primitive peoples used a cycle covering, not the whole year, but only that part of it between the beginning and end of agricultural operations. If the ancestors of the Romans had known something such as this, the introduction of a calendar designed to run continuously, without an annual gap, must have been a memorable reform; and tradition may not be wrong in connecting its memory with Numa.

The second institution which must have had an author and whose

---

[1] Censorinus, *de die nat.* 20, 2.

[2] Macrobius, *Sat.* I, 12, 16; Varro, *L.L.* VI, 33.

[3] M. P. Nilsson, *Primitive Time-Reckoning*, pp. 86 *sqq.* and 173 *sqq. Cf.* H. J. Rose, *Primitive Culture in Italy*, pp. 90 *sqq.*

author Numa is said to have been is the Regia; and in this connection tradition needs special notice. According to the vulgate, Numa, like Titus Tatius whom he resembles in more ways than one, migrated to Rome from the Sabine town of Cures and settled on the Quirinal; but from the Quirinal in course of time he moved to a new home on the lowest slope of the Velia towards the Forum. If Romulus is a legend and Numa is the first historical king of Rome, it is wholly appropriate that he should have built the palace whose position shows it to have been the abode of kings who ruled a united city: in fact the foundation of the Regia is among the most plausible of the activities ascribed to Numa. But the story's strongest claim to attention lies in another aspect. Numa is said to have been of Sabine origin, and the Sabine nature of his name Pompilius, of which Quinctilius is the nearest Latin form, is beyond dispute[1]. Then, again, at Rome his earliest connection is with the Quirinal, one of the outer hills where inhumations are most freely found, and of these burials it has been the work of von Duhn to show the Sabine affinities. Tradition here finds strong support in the evidence of language and of excavation. The question of the Sabine element in Rome will be mentioned more fully in connection with the fifth century (p. 495 sq.); here it will be enough to say that the prominence of a Sabine like Numa Pompilius must not be thought to justify the view that Rome was a Sabine city. Sabine settlers there undoubtedly were; but when a Roman meant 'five' he said *quinque* and not *pompe.

Thus, though much that is recorded of him must be rejected, it would be rash to assert that the figure of Numa Pompilius is without historical foundation. It is true that the function assigned to him by the developed tradition—to supply an author for those institutions whose religious and pacific character made them unsuitable for connection with the warlike Romulus—rendered Numa peculiarly liable to legendary associations. To treatment of this kind he was still subjected in times which are fully historical. The *leges regiae* ascribed to him were a work of which the final compilation was probably not achieved before the Punic wars, and his alleged dealings with Pythagoras led, so late as 181 B.C., to the propagandist hoax which called for state intervention to destroy the Pythagorean 'Books of Numa,' said by some charlatan to have been discovered in the king's tomb on the Janiculum. But in spite of such corruptions the nucleus of tradition about Numa must be retained. If nothing else, the connection of a king with the organization of the State religion is not without plausibility, nor is the assertion that the name of this king was Numa Pompilius.

[1] Pompilius = *Quinquilius; see vol. ii, p. 36, vol. iv, p. 450.

Tullus Hostilius disputes with Numa the establishment of the *fetiales* (p. 429), to which Ancus also lays a much weaker claim. This was perhaps inevitable. For the *fetiales* were a priestly college and therefore appropriate to Numa; but their business was with war, and for this reason they might be given to Tullus who was above all things a warrior—'ferocior etiam quam Romulus.' His main activities are provoked by an Alban invasion and end with the destruction of Alba itself. Such kernel of fact as the story may contain is so deeply encrusted with legend as often to escape the consideration it deserves. The details have to be ignored. The Alban king, C. Cluilius, is eponym of the *fossa(e) Cluilia(e)*. The fight of the three Horatii with the three Curiatii bears every sign of invention: the doubts under which our authorities labour about the side to which each family belonged are not enough to prove an early origin for the tale, nor do the many parallels from Greece—like the duel of Phrynon and Pittacus for Sigeum—strengthen its claim to a place in Roman history. The story of the surviving Horatius is an aetiological effort to explain the *tigillum sororium* and *provocatio ad populum*. And finally the fate of the treacherous Mettius Fufetius, appointed dictator by the Albans when Cluilius was killed, merely points a moral, as does the end of Tullus himself, who perished by a stroke of lightning through trying to meddle with the weather. But when all this is discounted, the Alban war remains; and it will be seen that such a war must be accepted somewhere in the regal period (p. 401 *sq.*). Who led the Roman forces only tradition tells; but there is at least a possibility that here tradition tells the truth. Every parallel suggests that in the Curia Hostilia, the first meeting place of the Roman Senate, we have a monument raised by a man of wealth and influence belonging to the *gens Hostilia*. When, towards the end of the Second Punic War, a small revival in the fortunes of the clan, till then unnoticed in republican history, was begun by the Hostilii Catones, the Curia was already old and Tullus Hostilius had long held his place in the regal list. The name of the building is earlier than the earliest occasion on which its false ascription to a fictitious king would be in place; and since its name almost certainly preserves the record of a man famous in his day, even if Varro (*L.L.* v, 155) did not say that its author was Hostilius the king, the Curia might be accepted as evidence of a sort for his historical existence.

The traditions of Ancus Marcius are contaminated by the achievements of men who bore the name of Marcius in republican times. When Pliny (*N.H.* xxxi, 41) says that the Aqua Marcia, which took its name from Q. Marcius Rex praetor in 144 B.C., owed its inception to Ancus, the falsification is clear; but in other cases detection is more difficult. The activities of Ancus Marcius begin with a war against various cities alleged to have been in conflict with Rome under Romulus and other kings, but in the end they are concentrated on the extension of Roman territory towards the Tiber mouth. The details of regal warfare round Rome can never be recovered, and in the wars of Ancus there is little that need be mentioned. Much may be rejected at once: the tale that the people of the conquered towns were settled in the Aventine is disproved by the absence of inhabitants on that hill in the middle of the fifth century and by its exclusion from the city down to the time of the Gallic invasion (p. 362). But one place, which Ancus alone is said to have taken, must be noticed. Ficana probably stood somewhere near the Monte Cugno, the last hill on the east bank of the Tiber before the salt marsh begins; and this according to tradition was captured by Ancus, who afterwards founded the colony of Ostia and extended his operations across the river to the Silva Maesia. On one point tradition here is wrong. Excavation has shown beyond any reasonable doubt that Ostia was not a regal foundation and had no history before the second half of the fourth century. The basis of the story is a matter of conjecture. Probably it is to be found neither in the fourth-century Etruscan attack on the lower Tiber to which the Roman resistance was led by C. Marcius Rutilus (p. 575), nor in the bold assumption that on the site of Ostia there was a cult of Vulcan which had been among the great religious centres of early Latium. If, as will be suggested, there is evidence to show that before the establishment of the Republic Roman authority and even Roman territory extended to the sea, the war of Ancus with Ficana and his foundation of Ostia may more plausibly be regarded as the traditional account of Rome's southward advance. That such an advance was made is as little doubtful as anything in the regal history, and in the operations of Ancus we have the authorized account of its conduct.

II. ETRUSCAN ROME

Rome under the kings from Numa to Ancus Marcius is to be regarded as a Latin city. That in this period it was Latin and Italic is widely, though not universally, agreed; and to deny that it was a city, for the sake of making the city an Etruscan foundation, is to ignore the plainest evidence for the Italic origin of the kingship and the most central features of the urban constitution. The three remaining kings—L. Tarquinius Priscus, Servius Tullius and L.

Tarquinius Superbus—belong to a phase which in some sense may be called Etruscan.

Wherever the line of division may be drawn, there is every reason for breaking the history of regal Rome into Latin and Etruscan sections. There can be no doubt that for a time the city was under Etruscan control, and that connection with Etruria brought a rapid cultural advance. But the historical significance to be seen in the Etruscan age depends on the way in which the Etruscans are understood. In the present diversity of opinion, though Etruria in general is a subject not to be handled here, a discussion of the Etruscan influence on Rome must begin with a statement of the sense in which 'Etruria' and 'Etruscan' will be used.

The question of Etruscan origins has been treated in a previous volume and it is impossible to discuss the problem a second time at length; here it must suffice to give a bald statement of the conclusions to which the evidence leads the present writer. At the outset it should be said that the necessity for briefness is alone responsible for the appearance of dogmatism on certain points where dogmatism is neither justified nor intended. The literary authorities are divided. Herodotus (i, 94), whose account is often repeated in later antiquity, brings the Etruscans from an early home in Asia: Dionysius (i, 30, 2) regards them as indigenous. To the view of Herodotus archaeology lends no support: the culture of Etruria is Villanovan and does not show the break which would mark the coming of immigrants at any point where, on the Herodotean theory, signs of immigration should be sought. Such external influences as Etruscan culture betrays in the centuries after 800 B.C. are to be explained by contacts developed in the normal course of trade, first with the Phoenicians and later with the Greeks. The linguistic evidence, again, does not offer convincing proof of affinities between Etruscan and any of the languages known to have been used in Asia Minor in the second and first millennia B.C. It is true that the Etruscan population contained a section—and a section of considerable magnitude—which is shown by the evidence both of language and of the burial practice which it revived to have been distinct from the Italic Villanovans; but this section, whose own language is what we call Etruscan, is probably to be regarded as descended from the neolithic inhabitants of Italy[1].

[1] On the Etruscans in general, see vol. iv, chap. xii, where the conclusion is reached that the Etruscan language was introduced into Italy by a ruling caste of pirate-invaders who came from some part of Asia Minor which they called Lydia, and the earliest of whom arrived not later than

For the present study, which is primarily concerned with the influence of Etruria on Rome, a more important question than that of Etruscan origins is the question about the sources of Etruscan culture. It has to be asked whether the civilization of Etruria was, as has often been suggested, brought into Italy ready-made, or whether it was a native Italian growth. The view which insists most strongly on the cultural debt of Italy to the Etruscans is bound up, not only with the theory of Etruscan immigration, but with the account of Herodotus which traces the Etruscans to a region which was in the forefront of civilization at the supposed time of their departure for the west. To illustrate the weakness of such speculations one aspect of the case may be noticed, but an aspect which is typical of the rest. In spite of the arguments which have been based on the ivory tablet found at Marsiliana d'Albegna, it remains as clear as ever that the alphabet used in Etruscan monuments is western Greek, and that, though influences due to contact with Central Greece may be detected, it was learnt in Italy by the Etruscans, in all probability from the Chalcidic colonists of Cumae[1]. The absence of any Etruscan document written in an earlier and different script points straight to the conclusion that the Etruscans did not write at all until they learnt the alphabet from Campania. But if Asia Minor was their home before they set sail for the west, they came to Italy from a region where writing was by no means unfamiliar. Indeed the much-quoted coincidence of the Etruscan 'Tarchna' (Tarquinius) with Anatolian names like 'Tarchon' would connect them, if it were evidence at all, with the Hattic power and its cultural subsidiaries, where the prevalence of writing by the middle of the second millennium is beyond doubt. And the Phaestus disk is reminder enough that cuneiform was not the only script known in Asia Minor. Either, then, the Etruscans did not come from Asia Minor at all, or their wanderings were so protracted that before the end was reached their scribes had died and writing was forgotten. And if this was the case, even were undeniable evidence for their Asiatic origin forthcoming, it would seem that so much of their culture had been shed during the voyage that to speak of these immigrants arriving with a knowledge of the arts which entitled

the period between 1000 and 800 B.C. (*ibid.* p. 394). The present writer, on the other hand, regards the non-Indo-European element in Etruria as indigenous in the sense that they are probably descended from the neolithic inhabitants of central Italy.

[1] For a discussion of the evidence provided by the Etruscan alphabets, see L. Pareti, *Le origine etrusche*, I, pp. 168–182, and for the value of the material from Lemnos, chapter V of the same work.

them to guide a barbarous Italy into the way of civilization is wholly misleading.

It appears that when Tuscany became available for human habitation it received both descendants of the neolithic people and also Villanovans. These two elements blended to form the population of historical Etruria; and, though the material civilization was Villanovan, the other section, which may have been distantly related to the inhuming 'Sabines' of Rome, was responsible both for the language and for the practice of inhumation which finally came widely to prevail in the Etruscan region. In the eighth century, when commercial intercourse with the Phoenicians had begun, the Etruscans began to lead an advance in material progress. By the seventh they had far outstripped their neighbours, and at this time Etruria became the centre from which knowledge of the arts and crafts spread far and wide over the more backward parts of the peninsula. The reason for this development, which probably is also the reason for the attraction of a comparatively dense population to Etruria, is to be found in its natural wealth. The fertility of the country did not distinguish it from other parts of Italy, but in the iron of Elba and the copper of Volterra it had resources which were unique. For Etruria, commercial activities were made easy by the commodities she could supply; and the concentration of trade in this part of the western Italian coast, to the neglect of other regions such as the Latin plain, is adequately explained by the fact on which Plutarch makes Solon insist, 'that those who sail the seas are not wont to take their wares to those who have nothing to give in exchange' (*Solon*, XXII). Natural resources bred commerce, commerce made the trading population rich, and riches generated those tastes which grow with the means to satisfy them. Thus Etruria took the lead in culture; it became a centre from which culture was diffused, and it was to their more accomplished brethren across the Tiber that the Romans owed their introduction to some of the higher arts.

Any account of the Etruscans at present must be given with reserve, and the views adopted here are admittedly no more than those which, in the writer's opinion, accord best with such evidence as is so far available. But, if on the main issue they are not wholly wrong, it follows that 'Etruria' and 'Etruscans' are both terms to be used in a geographical sense. 'The Etruscans' are the inhabitants of a certain area, and 'Etruscan influence' is merely the cultural influence of this area exercised on regions beyond its limits. For the present purposes at least the Etruscans are not to be understood as an ethnic unit; for, though non-Italic people were undoubtedly present in Etruria, if by Italic a branch of the Indo-European stock is understood, the Etruscan culture seems to have grown up in Italy and to owe little, if anything, to the fact that the population among whom it arose contained a non-Italic element.

Since attention was concentrated on the subject by the learned investigations of Wilhelm Schulze, it has been familiar that the personal nomenclatures of Rome and Etruria have much in common. In the monuments of Etruscan epigraphy—which, it must be remembered, stretch from the seventh century B.C. to the first— names freely occur of which the root appears again at Rome (*e.g.* rumlnas—Romilius); and at Rome there are names with terminations which with some reason may be connected with the non-Aryan language of Etruria (*e.g.* Sisenna). But the day has gone when these two classes could be grouped together and explained by the simple supposition of a large Etruscan settlement at Rome. If men at Rome bear names ending in the Etruscan *-enna* and the like, their presence may indeed be the result of immigration: but the appearance of Etruscan names based on a definitely Italic radical is evidence enough that, when the same root appears in the nomenclatures of Etruria and Rome, the explanation is to be sought in the mixture of non-Italic Etruscans, not necessarily with the Romans themselves, but with some of their neighbouring kin (vol. IV, p. 406 *sq.*). A bolder suggestion that the *tria nomina* of the Romans are borrowed from the practice of Etruria—a suggestion which would be important, if it were true—fails when the chronology of the Etruscan evidence is considered; and thus such indications of Etruscan influence in Rome as may be derived from the study of names point at most to nothing more than a certain infiltration from Etruria of newcomers who, in spite of their names, must not even be assumed to have belonged wholly to the non-Italic stratum of the population.

By the beginning of the seventh century the strength and prosperity of Etruria had their natural issue in political expansion. Veii was occupied. Fidenae seems to have supplied a crossing of the Tiber, and with the sudden capture of Praeneste a way was opened by which the Etruscans could reach the rich lands of Campania without encountering such obstacles as might be raised by Rome. By the middle of the century, or thereabouts, the Regolini-Galassi burial at Caere is answered from Praeneste by the Bernardini and Barberini tombs. Rome is straddled by the Etruscans; and though the rich lands of Campania may well have been their chief objective, it is easy to see that Rome was not likely to escape the effects of this envelopment. By their seizure of Praeneste and by their advance into Campania, which cannot be denied even if their numbers were small, the Etruscans enclosed the western section of the Latin plain

in lines which made it an enclave in an Etruscan empire. Such seem
to have been the circumstances in which Rome became a place of
interest to the power across the Tiber.

The personal traditions which may be interpreted as records of
Etruscan lords in Rome may for the present be ignored: to the
question of Rome's cultural debt to Etruria they are unessential.
There is other evidence enough to show Etruscan influence of a
kind. If the tale of an Etruscan settlement on the Caelian is a late
deduction from the name of the Etruscan hero Caeles Vibenna, the
strongest proof that Etruscans were actually present in Rome is to
be found in the name of the street which ran beneath the western
end of the Palatine—the Vicus Tuscus. To this may be added the
names of the Porta Capena—a gate, which does not, however, lead
to the Etruscan (or Faliscan) city of Capena, in the Servian wall at
a point on the Caelian where it is probably following the trace of the
sixth-century defences—and of the Porta Ratumena, the whereabouts
of which is obscure. Both of these names are of interest not merely
because they show formations which may be suspected of definitely
Etruscan origin, but for their connection with building works, in
which it is clear that Etruria gave much to Rome.

More important still is the testimony of religion. An accurate
assessment of the whole Roman debt in religion cannot be attempted
here, but sufficient illustration is provided by the Capitoline Triad
and by the practices of divination (vol. IV, pp. 416 *sqq.*). Even if
Servius[1] did not expressly say that it was the Etruscans who regarded
temples of Juppiter, Juno and Minerva as necessary in every real
city, independent evidence would show that the first Italian home
of this triadic arrangement of deities was Etruria. For instance, the
triple temple recently uncovered at Orvieto almost certainly goes
back to a date at least a century before any influence can have been
exerted there by Rome. Though the origin of the arrangement may
be Greek, and though the deities to whom it was applied in Italy
owed to Greece their anthropomorphic guise, it is clear that the
arrangement itself was received by Rome from Etruria: and its
reception confirms, though it does not compel, the view of tradition
that it was Etruscans actually in Rome who were responsible for
the building of the great temple on the Capitoline. The introduction
of the Triad seems thus to be due, not to spontaneous borrowing,
but to the presence in Rome of a powerful element to which this
particular grouping of gods was familiar. If so, if the cults were to
some extent an alien imposition, it might be expected that the Triad
would be regarded with a certain coldness by the Romans themselves:

[1] *ad Aen.* 1, 422.

and this is the case. Whatever the reason, whether it be that Juppiter retained the prestige of age which he derived from the time when he had been Juppiter Feretrius or not, it is notorious that the temple was always 'templum Iovis Optimi Maximi' and that in his presence the two goddesses faded into something like insignificance.

The testimony of the Capitoline Triad is strengthened by the evidence of augury. The practice of *extispicium*—divination from the entrails of victims—is a late arrival at Rome, probably to be put in the third century; and the *haruspices* who professed it were never admitted to the public priesthood of the Roman people, even though the Emperor Claudius was so far interested in their art as to form them into an *ordo* in A.D. 47. The Etruscan fondness for *extispicium* is undoubted, and the frequency with which *haruspices* had to be summoned from Etruria shows whence it came to Rome; but it cannot be admitted as a legacy of Etruscan occupation in regal times. With augury, however, the case is different. In all probability the Italic peoples, like most early men, had ways of their own by which they sought to gain knowledge of the prospects that the supernatural powers would favour or frown upon their undertakings; and in particular it would be rash to deny that divination at Rome from the flight of birds—the proper and original business of augury—was other than purely Italian. But the developments of the augural system—the magistrate's demarcation of a *templum* in the sky, which in turn was subdivided into *regiones*, and the whole business of augury from lightning, to which alone the *templum* was appropriate —are connected with Etruria not only by the Romans themselves, who include the *libri fulgurales*—whatever their date—in the corpus containing the *disciplina Etrusca*, but also by the independent evidence of the Piacenza liver, which is divided into something like a *templum*, and the bilingual inscription from Pesaro (vol. IV, p. 416 *sq.*, and below, p. 430)[1].

It is to be noticed that the introduction of the Capitoline cult and the adoption of certain methods in magisterial *auspicatio*, together with the consequent augural interpretation, are matters connected with the public institutions, where in particular the influence of Etruscan domination in Rome might be expected. The same is true of a third debt which the Romans are said to have incurred. According to a tradition prevalent in classical times the trappings of office used as their insignia by Roman magistrates were almost wholly due to Etruria. In most cases the derivation cannot be proved, but in one there is evidence which lends colour to the tale. The *fasces* are included with the rest: in particular they are con-

1 Dessau, 4958.

nected with Vetulonia[1]: and at Vetulonia, in the late eighth-century burial called the Tomba del Littore, there was discovered a double-headed axe whose shaft was surrounded by eight iron tubes.

Evidence such as this seems to show Etruscan influence on the public life of Rome, and such influence is wholly compatible with the suggestion that the later kings of Rome were Etruscans. But for the rest a distinction must be made. Thus far the story has been of Etruscan influence which conceivably may be ascribed to the presence of an Etruscan element. What remains may well be nothing more than the result of normal intercourse between Rome and her more progressive neighbours. At this point, but not before, mention must be made of Rome's military debt to Etruria. If it were true, as has often been alleged both in ancient times and in modern, that virtually the whole of the so-called Servian equipment of the soldiers was Etruscan, such borrowing would be a powerful addition to the evidence for the political control of Etruscans at Rome. But the theory cannot be maintained. The metal helmet is not Etruscan but Greek, and the derivation of the metal-tipped *hasta* from Etruria is impossible. Propertius, indeed, may say that the early warriors of Rome (IV, 1, 28)

> miscebant usta proelia nuda sude,

but his words find no support except in a mistaken explanation of the *hasta pura*; and their suggestion about the weapons of pre-Servian Rome are refuted by the steady development of spear-heads from stone to metal which excavation has revealed. Etruscan influence here is as much to seek as it is again in the *clipeus* and the *pilum*. The *clipeus*, like the metal helmet, is Greek. From Greece both of these articles may, indeed, have reached Rome through Etruria; but at most the Etruscans here transmitted isolated ideas, and there can be no question of the Romans at a stroke adopting the whole panoply of their neighbours. In these circumstances we may view with scepticism the suggestion[2] that the Romans adopted from Etruria the solid formation in battle, which was characteristic of Greece.

It is in the arts that the influence of Etruria is most marked—and naturally so: for in the arts a backward stock can borrow freely from people more advanced without violence to those social institutions which men change only with reluctance. Vulca of Veii may well have been summoned to Rome, as Pliny (*N.H.* xxxv, 157) records, to adorn the Capitoline temple with terra-cotta *akroteria*

---

[1] Silius Italicus, VIII, 483 *sqq.*
[2] *Ineditum Vaticanum*, 3. See however below, p. 568.

and to make the cult-statue of Juppiter himself. The frequent discoveries of terra-cotta works at Rome show that by the sixth
century the city was familiar with a form of architectural decoration
common in Etruria; but the origin of this form is clearly Greek,
and its widespread popularity in Italy from Umbria to Campania
casts doubts on the view that the Etruscans were in all cases even
the intermediaries by whom it was communicated to the Italic
peoples. Nevertheless in the terra-cottas of Rome there are suggestions both in the style and in the use of external friezes, which
confirm the hints of literary authorities that Rome at least was here
receiving from Etruria. Moreover, it is clear that some of the
greatest public works in early Rome—the draining of the Forum
and the walling of the city—belong to the period when Etruscan
influence was at its height. Of the *cappellaccio* wall enough has been
said already; and tradition is unanimous in ascribing the Cloaca
maxima to the Tarquins. Though this does not mean that anything
more was done so early than to confine the stream within artificial
banks, the abandonment during the sixth century of the *sepulcretum*
in the Forum for the burial of the dead shows that by then that area
was coming to be of use to the living and so serves to confirm the
traditional account.

Yet in architecture, as in religion and in military equipment,
Etruscan influence on Rome is easy to exaggerate. The allegation
that Rome learnt from Etruria to use the arch rests on no evidence
at all, because in the covered side-drains connected with the Cloaca
maxima Rome can boast true arches which are earlier than anything
of the kind known in Etruria. And again, unless it can be proved
of the lower chamber in the Carcer, not only that originally it was
covered by a cupola, but also that it was built in the sixth century
or the fifth, it must be confessed that Rome seems to have passed
through the Etruscan period of her career without adopting that
method of roofing a circular area which is one of the most notable
features of the developed Etruscan tombs. The influence of Etruria
is desultory: Rome seems to pick and choose in her borrowings.
But there has still to be mentioned the central piece of evidence
which must control every estimate of the part played by Etruria in the
making of Rome. Burials on and round the site of Rome have been
found in plenty; but, possibly with a single eighth-century exception
on the Esquiline, there is none which can be recognized as Etruscan
nearer than the Colle di S. Agata, which is on the Tuscan bank of
the Tiber to the north-west of Monte Mario, and not less than four
miles in a direct line from the Roman Forum. This is the fact which
decides the main issue between those who, by calling Rome an

Etruscan city, imply, if they do not assert, a large Etruscan settlement among the purely Italic population, and those who confine Etruscan influence to such borrowings as a backward people is always prone to make from more progressive neighbours. At Rome the borrowing was probably encouraged by a period of Etruscan government, which left its trace on the public works of the city and the public institutions of the State. But this occupation did not involve any noticeable shift of population from Etruria to Rome. As in architecture the Etruscan forms ignored by the Romans are no less remarkable than those which they adopted, so in religion and in language. The testimony of Latin carries weight by reason, not of the presence of a few odd words which it possibly received from Etruria, but of their fewness. In this connection the essential feature of the language is its immunity from any Etruscan contamination on a scale which would suggest the presence of Etruscans in the city and a long period of Etruscanization. So, too, in religion. Though the public cults give evidence of Etruscan control for a time, the beliefs of the Romans remain singularly unaffected by the gloomy brood of bogies which, to judge from the tomb-paintings which are preserved, bulked ever larger in Etruscan minds.

It would be idle to deny that Rome borrowed from Etruria, but no less idle to represent Roman culture as Etruscan. With the exception of those few cases which can be connected with the presence of Etruscan rulers in Rome, the Roman debt was incurred by casual loans from the more rapidly developed culture which lay across the river. From the seventh century onwards to the fourth, when, according to a tradition preserved by Livy (ix, 36, 3), cadets of the great Roman houses were sometimes sent to Etruria for their education, Rome was picking up hints from her neighbours to the north. But, save for a period in the sixth century, and then only in a political sense, Rome was not an Etruscan city.

One subject connected with the Etruscan age at Rome remains. Etruscan occupation seems to have enlarged the city's political outlook and to have brought Rome into contact with other powers in the western Mediterranean. The question of Roman relations with Carthage is of primary importance, but the appropriate place for its discussion is in the history of Rome's territorial expansion (see below, p. 405 *sq.*).

III. THE LATER KINGS

L. Tarquinius Priscus, Servius Tullius and L. Tarquinius Superbus present problems more difficult, because more detailed, than those raised by their predecessors. The later kings of Rome do

not stand far from the full light of history, and the clearness with
which their outlines can be discerned invites speculation about
aspects which are more dimly visible. The tradition which associates
the Tarquins with Rome is so strong that it might be accepted
without hesitation even if it were not confirmed; and the painting
from the François Tomb of Vulci, once in the Museo Torlonia at
Rome, makes reasonable doubt impossible. Though it is not contemporary with the regal period this monument probably belongs
to the fourth century and is earlier than the age of annalistic invention: so when it shows the fate of Cneᴲe Tar↓unies Ruma↓—
or Gnaeus Tarquinius of Rome—its evidence for the presence of
Tarquins in the city is good[1]. But, if the Roman associations of the
house are clear, agreement has not been complete since the time of
Niebuhr on their Etruscan origin. Though tradition again is strong,
the justifiable suspicion under which one feature of it lies has tended
to bring the rest into unmerited disrepute. The choice of Tarquinii
(Corneto) as the place from which the *lucumo*, known afterwards as
Tarquinius Priscus, should migrate to Rome was rightly recognized
as a mere inference from the identity of name; but to go further and
reject the whole story on the ground that one detail is discredited
implies a method which should have been buried with the nineteenth
century.

In the last section it was suggested that for a hundred years or
more before the foundation of the Republic Rome was included in
the cultural system of Etruria, and that the signs of Etruscan inspiration which can be detected both in the public works and in the
political institutions of Rome point to a period of Etruscan government. In tradition this government is represented by the Tarquins.
On their Etruscan origin the authorities are clear, and independent
evidence supports them. Though Niebuhr was right in saying that
Tarquinius, Tarquitius and the like are Latin names, it is also true
that Tarchu and its cognates are found in Etruria; and there they
appear at a place from which Etruscan influence on Rome might be
expected. Caere is less than half as far from Rome as Tarquinii.
Unless Veii was one of the twelve Etruscan cities, Caere was nearest
of all to the lower reaches of the Tiber: to Caere, according to one
version, the last Tarquin retired: and it is at Caere that a tomb of the

---

[1] For the reading of this text see *C.I.E.* ii, No. 5275, p. 161. The last
four letters of the word Tar↓unies are no longer visible, if they were ever
written. Though the form they give the name is unobjectionable, the only
evidence for them is the reproduction, for which H. Brunn seems to have
been responsible, in Noël Des Vergers, *L'Étrurie et les Étrusques*, Atlas,
plate xxx and p. 24.

Tarquinii still survives[1]. It has been seen already that the isolation
of the Latins ended when, in the middle of the seventh century,
Etruria suddenly stretched southwards from Caere to Praeneste,
and it is in every way probable that this advance of Etruscan culture
had as its political consequence what is recorded as the arrival of the
Tarquins in Rome.

The *lucumo* and his wife Tanaquil drive to Rome in a cart, not
at the head of a great band of settlers but with their own household
at most. Here again tradition calls for respect. The peaceful
character of the arrival might possibly be doubted; but if that feature
is due to the patriotism of Roman annalists, the insignificant number
of newcomers is not. On this point the lack of Etruscan elements in
Latin, and still more the absence of Etruscan graves in Rome, leave
no room for question that the Etruscans in the city were a mere
handful. The nature—and especially the continuity—of their occupation is less certain. Between the two Tarquins stands Servius
Tullius; and Servius, who was generally regarded as a Latin, was
held in high respect by a Rome which certainly was not Etruscan
itself and which showed its dislike for Etruria by a thorough-going
hatred of the second Tarquin and at best a mild tolerance of the
first. The Etruscan affinities of Servius rest on no surer foundation
than the antiquarian guesses of the Emperor Claudius (see p. 391)
and the tale—of a kind which demands no credence because it is
designed to explain his succession to the kingship—that he married
a daughter of the elder Tarquin. Even if this were true, Servius
might still be of Roman birth; but the cogent proof that he was no
foreigner is the veneration in which his memory was held. These
considerations, however, are not alone. The Etruscan tale of Mastarna and the story of Porsenna, which was admitted even in Rome,
suggest that the city was an object of dispute not only between the
Latins and their neighbours across the Tiber but between various
powers in Etruria itself. In the light of such evidence as this, it
would be rash to conclude that throughout the sixth century Rome
was under constant Etruscan control. It may be admitted that
Etruscan culture stayed when once it had come; but if the political
government was really in Etruscan hands for more than the reign
of Tarquinius Superbus, it may well have been for briefer periods,
broken by incidents of which only the faintest traces remain.

The figure of the elder Tarquin is not wholly clear, and in some
cases the details of his career are duplications of tales told about his
more infamous namesake. It has been pointed out by Pais[2] that

[1] See Körte in *J.D.A.I.* 1897, pp. 57 *sqq.*
[2] *Storia di Roma*, ii, p. 153.

the capture of Apiolae[1], with the spoils of which he is alleged to have begun the building of the Capitoline temple, is an anticipation of the second Tarquin's capture of Suessa Pometia, the booty of which he is said to have devoted to the same purpose; and to this it may be added that the personal relations of the two Tarquins, especially with their somewhat enterprising womenfolk, show a marked resemblance. These, however, are no grounds for regarding the first Tarquin as a mere double of the second, nor are they strengthened by such arguments as are often supposed to reinforce them. Both are connected with building operations, with the *cloacae* and the great temple: and Tarquinius Priscus is said to have proposed the walls whose erection is ascribed to Servius. But if it is right to see in the Tarquins the bringers of Etruscan arts to Rome, these tales may be accepted as tradition's indication that the works of public utility which Etruria gave Rome began with the earliest Etruscan influence. They add no cogency to the case for banishing the first Tarquin from the pages of history. The details of his career may often be unsound, but the figure to which they are attached is one that history cannot surrender. Since the Etruscan advance southwards across the Tiber to the Monti Lepini can be fixed at the middle of the seventh century, probability demands what tradition provides—a representative of Etruria in Rome before the latter part of the sixth. Whatever truth may be behind the stories of Tarquinius Priscus and his activities either in war or in constitutional reform—about which little of value can be said (see pp. 403 *sqq.*)—the figure to which this name is attached may be reckoned without hesitation among the rulers of early Rome.

There follows Servius Tullius. Though the sceptics are ready with various theories of his invention, a less daring criticism must admit that the evidence for his existence is stronger than that for any other king's. Here again, as always, various accretions must be removed from the figure presented by tradition before the historical core is revealed. For instance, his servile birth is almost certainly a punning explanation of his name; and the marriage arrangements by which he is made son-in-law of the elder Tarquin are due to speculation which assumed that the Roman monarchy was hereditary. But when such elaborations have been set aside, there remains a king who may be accepted, though not for the reason which often has been found most cogent. On Servius Tullius the Etruscan evidence for Mastarna has no bearing. In A.D. 48 when the Emperor Claudius was concerned to win approval for his intended adlection of various Gallic notables to the Senate, he took

---

[1] Strabo, v, 231.

the opportunity of airing his knowledge of antiquity in the speech preserved both by Tacitus and by the bronze tables now in Lyons[1]. According to the inscription, which contains what is certainly the more faithful of the two extant versions, among other pieces of information the *princeps* announced that Servius Tullius, whose name in Etruscan was Mastarna, originally came to Rome as comrade of a certain Caelus Vivenna, who settled on the Caelian and gave the hill his name. If the identity of Servius with Mastarna could be accepted, fourth-century evidence for his life would be provided by the paintings of the François tomb mentioned above (p. 388). In one panel 'Marce Camitlnas' is seen killing 'Cneᚠe Tar↓unies Ruma↓,' in another 'Macstrna' rescues 'Caile ᚠipinas' from some kind of captivity and cuts through the cords by which his hands are tied; and in a third 'Aule ᚠipinas' does to death a victim whose name is illegible.

If the paintings in the register to which these belong are not wholly unrelated but tell a single tale—as may be inferred from the presence in different groups of the brothers Caeles and Aulus Vibenna—the tale would seem to be that Cneᚠe Tar↓unies of Rome had won some success against an Etruscan community and had taken Caeles Vibenna prisoner, but that Caeles was rescued by his friends after a struggle in which Cneᚠe Tar↓unies was killed. If Mastarna was leader of the rescue party, it would be easy, as De Sanctis has observed[2], for the intelligent antiquarian to guess that Mastarna was the next king of Rome; and in that case Cneᚠe Tar↓unies must be the elder Tarquin—the only one who had a regal successor—and Mastarna the king who followed him—*i.e.* Servius Tullius. The possibility of such an origin would not by itself discredit the identification, if the evidence for seeing a single figure in Servius and Mastarna were good. But it is not. The only authority for this version is the speech of Claudius; and whether Claudius himself is responsible for the suggestion or not, the theory must be regarded as a late invention which does nothing to justify conclusions from the evidence for Mastarna to the existence of Servius Tullius.

The case for the historical character of Servius rests on other foundations. In the first place it must be remembered that his name, like that of all the other kings after Romulus, is not significant and does not proclaim an eponym: rather its use in regal Rome is suggested by the possible appearance of M'. Tullius in the Fasti at 500 B.C. And secondly that the king is not an invented author either of political institutions or of public works is indicated by the variety of achievements which he is assigned. Servius is not connected with

---

[1] *Ann.* XI, 24; Dessau, 212.   [2] *Op. cit.* I, p. 375.

the *centuriae* alone, but also with the city wall and with what is even more important—the Aventine temple of Diana and the treaty with the Latins which it contained (p. 350 *sq*.). The attribution of such diverse activities to a figure whose name betrays no sign of invention is hard to explain unless the figure itself is that of a king who actually ruled in Rome. And the conclusion that Servius belongs not to a myth but to history is strengthened by the liveliness with which his memory was preserved. The contrast between the vague and unconvincing references made by Romans of classical times to the legendary Romulus and their matter-of-fact treatment of Servius is testimony of weight for Servius' claims to be something more than a figment.

To this might be added evidence provided by the Temple of Diana on the Aventine. The early origin of this building, which is always ascribed to Servius Tullius and which boasted a statue said to represent the king, is almost beyond question. Its primacy among Roman sanctuaries of Diana is proved by the way in which the *lex arae Dianae in Aventino* was used as a model for all such establishments; and its high antiquity is suggested by the account which Dionysius (IV, 26, 5) gives of one of the archives it contained. The treaty with the Latins may be assigned to the sixth century (see above, p. 351); and though this fact alone will not fix the age of the temple itself, yet when the antiquity of the building is strongly suggested by other evidence, it adds precision by indicating its connection with sixth-century history. Thus the ascription of the Aventine temple to Servius seems so far right that its appearance belongs to the period in which Servius himself is placed. But the value of the treaty as proof that Servius Tullius once was king of Rome is more difficult to estimate. That the *stele* was forged is unlikely. It is beyond doubt that documents of the sixth century survived in Rome, and it is not easy to see at what later period or for what reason it would have been in Roman interests to invent an agreement with the Latins and foist it upon Servius. If it was genuine, since it seems to have contained no mention of a magistrate's name, it can scarcely have been of republican date; and in that case a regal origin remains. But though it is probable that the name of Servius was mentioned in the treaty, our ignorance of regal documents makes its presence no more than a matter of conjecture. The Aventine temple does not then provide the demonstrative proof that Servius was king which would have been forthcoming if his name had been known to appear in the compact with the Latins; but it does confirm the powerful evidence of tradition by yielding reasons for belief that tradition about the temple was not wrong,

as has often been asserted, in the important matter of its age.
Precisely the same must be said about the Servian *enceinte*, which
in its original form belongs to the sixth century (see above, p. 361),
and the same again about some, at least, of the constitutional innovations of which Servius is made the author. In the last connection more than in any other the king's achievements have been
elaborated: but such elaborations do not affect the historical character
of the figure to whom they are attached. The conclusion remains
unaltered that Servius Tullius was king of Rome during the sixth
century, that he was not a foreign conqueror but a kinsman of the
Latins over whom he ruled, and that his reign was memorable for
constitutional advance, for the fortification of the city and for
various developments in external politics of which the most notable
concerned Rome's position in the Latin League.

The second Tarquin stands apart from his predecessor—'neque
enim ad ius regni quicquam praeter uim habebat, ut qui neque
populi iussu neque auctoribus patribus regnaret'[1]. He is a tyrant,
not set up like the majority of Greek *tyrannoi* by a section of the
people whom he governed, but imposed from outside like the tyrants
thrust by the Persian king on the cities of Ionia. Though it is to some
extent concealed by the patriotic Roman tradition, the army which
he had behind him seems to have played as large a part in the rise of
Tarquinius Superbus to power as it did in the subsequent achievements of his career. The wars, however, are another story; but there
is one document connected with external affairs which is relevant
to the problem of the king's historical character. In the temple of
Semo Sancus Dius Fidius on the Quirinal a treaty between Rome and
Gabii, written on the ox-hide covering of a wooden shield, was still
to be seen in Augustan times[2]. The forgery of this record would be
even harder to explain than that of Servius' treaty with the Latins:
at the earliest time remote enough from the event for falsification
to be possible, the position of Rome was such that tinkering with
the history of her relations with what was then only an unimportant
city of the Campagna would be pointless. The inscription was probably genuine, and the suggestion of the authorities that it contained
the terms of a treaty is confirmed by the place of its preservation.
Its assignment to the second Tarquin shows that it mentioned the
name of no republican magistrate; and if it were an anonymous
relic of the regal age it would not be easy to see why so unpopular
a figure as that of Tarquinius Superbus should have been made
the author of an arrangement which established 'isopolity' between

---

[1] Livy, I, 49, 3.   [2] Dion. Hal. IV, 58, 4; Festus, p. 48 L.

Rome and another city whose friendship undoubtedly was of very early origin. To general probability constitutional considerations may be added in support of the conclusion that in this monument the name of a Tarquinius appeared; and probability again is so far on the side of tradition in identifying him with a king later than Tarquinius Priscus, that the late sixth century is more plausible than any earlier date for an instrument establishing relations so highly developed as those of isopolity. But though the treaty with Gabii goes some way towards confirming the presence of a Tarquin at the head of the Roman state during the latter part of the sixth century, it is on the strength of tradition that his acceptance must ultimately depend.

On two points tradition is so strong that it cannot be set aside. One is that a Tarquin was the last king of Rome: and here tradition is generally believed even by those who regard the two Tarquins as duplications of a single figure. The other is that the last king was forcibly deposed by a revolution which brought the monarchy itself to an end. The story of Sextus Tarquinius and Lucretia and the various other personal details with which the fall of the kingship is embellished may be dismissed at once. In any event they are unimportant, and it is scarcely to be doubted that they are as worthless as the tales transferred to Sextus and his father from the Zopyrus and Thrasybulus of Herodotus. Nor need much attention be paid to the Vulci painting of Cnefe Tarƴunies being done to death by Marce Camitlnas. Since the *praenomen* Lucius given by tradition to both the Tarquins may well have been suggested by their Etruscan title *lucumo*, the fact that the Tarƴunies of Vulci is 'Cnefe' would not be an insuperable obstacle to his identification with L. Tarquinius Superbus. But though Cnefe Tarƴunies was a Roman, it is not certain that he was a king: and if he were a king, there is nothing to prove that he is not the elder Tarquin and that Marce Camitlnas is not performing the function attributed in the Roman version to the shepherds employed by the sons of Ancus Marcius. For a criticism which accepts two Tarquins as kings of Rome it is by no means necessary to see in the Vulci painting an alternative Etruscan version which discredits the Roman story of the monarchy's collapse. Even if this were so, Etruria and Rome would agree that the rule of a Roman Tarquin came to a violent end; and it may be doubted whether the painting necessarily implies that Mastarna succeeded to the kingship in his stead. Another institution, once accepted as evidence for the expulsion of a king from Rome, may be dismissed at once. The view, which finds fullest expression in the *Fasti* of Ovid, that the *Regifugium* of 24 February commemorated the departure of Tarquinius Superbus is wholly untenable. The *Poplifugia* of 5 July, which is clearly a counterpart, cannot be an expulsion of the people; and such slight evidence as is available shows that both festivals alike had a ritual significance, which is enough to refute the commemorative interpretation even though the significance cannot confidently be defined (p. 408).

For the catastrophic end of the monarchy the cogent evidence is to be found in the strength of a unanimous tradition, confirmed by various pieces of independent testimony. At Athens the name *basileus* moved no emotions; and at Athens the kingship had sunk into insignificance through a gradual devolution of its powers. At Rome the name *rex*, at least in any political sense, was held in detestation. Of that there can be no doubt, nor is it possible to believe that the authorities are wholly wrong in recording the early provision of penalties against crimes such as 'regnum occupare, adfectare.' No importance need be attached to the *lex Valeria* on this subject assigned to the first year of the republic; but the cases of Sp. Cassius and M. Manlius Capitolinus rest on a sufficient basis of fact to justify the conclusion that some rule existed in the fourth century, and even in the fifth, by which the capital penalty was imposed for this offence. The testimony of Diodorus is here important, because it can be carried back at least to the middle of the second century, when the Gracchi and the succeeding *principes* of republican Rome had not yet arisen to generate fanatical dislike of monarchy. Marius, Sulla, Caesar and the like undoubtedly stirred up latent horror of a king; but the feeling itself was not their creation. It existed before: and its existence is evidence that the history of kingship in Rome had taken a different course from that which it followed at Athens. Hatred of an institution which has disappeared is not apt to grow stronger with the lapse of time: rather the reverse is true, and the later bitterness against monarchy in Rome suggests feeling so violent at the time of its fall as to be incompatible with any kind of orderly devolution (see below, p. 437 *sq.*).

Moreover, unless it is wholly wrong to see in the last phase of the Roman monarchy a period of direct Etruscan control, a violent end of regal government is made probable by the general course of events in western Italy. The Etruscan advance into Campania, which had begun before the end of the seventh century, was checked and perhaps even repulsed by Aristodemus, tyrant of Cumae, in the last quarter of the sixth. According to the Greek tradition, in 524 B.C. Aristodemus defeated an Etruscan attack on his city. The power of the Etruscans in Campania was not yet broken: it seems indeed to have survived until maritime communications between Etruria and the south were destroyed by Hiero of Syracuse in 474 (vol. IV, p. 390). But some success had been achieved, and it was followed up by an assault on the Etruscan position in Latium. At a date about which our authorities are vague, but which probably was rather before the fall of the Roman monarchy than after it, the Etruscan hold on the hill-country to the south of Latium was weakened, if not destroyed, by the battle of Aricia. The authority for this episode is good. It appears in both Greek and Roman tradition[1]; and though Greek tradition alone asserts that Aristodemus took part in the operations, the view that it was the continuation of a thrust against the Etruscans from the south is confirmed by the failure of even the Roman version to claim that Rome had any share in the achievement. It seems then that the last quarter of the sixth century was a period in which the Etruscans south of the Tiber were being forced back on their base: the age is one in which the Italic peoples were throwing off the political domination of their neighbours across the river, and in such circumstances the catastrophic end of the Tarquins' rule as recorded by tradition is wholly appropriate.

The violent ejection of Tarquinius Superbus cannot seriously be questioned; and this is not the place to discuss, further than has been necessary already, the social and constitutional problems raised by this upheaval (see below, pp. 436 sqq.). However unconvincing may be the arguments advanced to show that the creation of the consulship was, not a result, but the cause of the monarchy's disappearance, the question of the last Tarquin's fate is distinct from that about the circumstances in which the republican government was established. The various narratives are so diverse that details cannot be determined. According to the most prevalent account, Tarquinius was outside the city when the monarchy fell, and of the powers and places from which he is said to have sought help some have a certain interest. His connection with Aristodemus of Cumae is improbable in view of Cumaean policy, and the protection he is made to receive from Octavius (or Octavus) Mamilius of Tusculum is a tale almost certainly generated by the assumption that the name of Tusculum implies an Etruscan population. Again, though the battle of the Silva Arsia is mentioned so often as to deserve some credence, the part played by Tarquinii in the campaign cannot be treated seriously in the absence of evidence that its introduction is due to more than an obvious conjecture. Most worthy of notice, since the discovery of the Tarchnas tomb at Caere, is the fact that Caere is the place for which the exiles set out in the

[1] See De Sanctis, op. cit. I, pp. 450 sqq., for a discussion of the authorities.

account of Livy (i, 60, 2); but in this period of confusion the most important feature of all is the expedition of Porsenna.

On the appearance of Porsenna in Latin history of the years round 500 b.c. tradition is confused. He himself descends on Rome at the invitation of Tarquinius after the *coup d'état*, but it is his son who leads the Etruscans in the battle of Aricia which, if the absence of Rome is evidence that Rome was still under Etruscan control, may be put before the end of the monarchy. The suspicion, to which this vagueness gives rise, that tradition is here unsound is strengthened by the fact that though the attack of Porsenna is placed in the first years of the Republic, the great figures of the earliest Fasti are absent from the Roman side until the days of late elaboration. Instead of men like Publicola and his associates, the mysterious Horatius Cocles, of whom nothing else is recorded, has been cast for the leading part. And, furthermore, since it was only in the fourth century that Rome came into contact with the world beyond the Monti Cimini, not even the peculiar cultural affinities of Chiusi will give plausibility to tradition when it represents Porsenna as *lars* of Clusium. The episode is one on which nothing more is possible than speculation; but of the speculations which have been made the theory of Pais[1] has an attractiveness which entitles it to mention. Porsenna is a name which appears on more Etruscan sites than one: it is connected by Pliny[2] with Volsinii, and possibly by epigraphic evidence with Vulci as well, so that its association with any Etruscan city is not incredible. The narrative of Porsenna's operations points in the direction of Veii: Veii is one of the cities which is said by a less isolated tradition—less isolated because it admits L. Junius Brutus—to have helped in an attempt to restore the Roman monarchy: Veientane activity in the first quarter of the fifth century is assumed by the stories which have their climax in the disaster to the Fabii (p. 504): and finally Veii, in virtue of its position, is the natural place to be chosen as the head-quarters of Etruscan operations against the Latin plain when Rome itself was no longer in Etruscan hands. The details of the history in which Porsenna appears may be ignored: at the outline it is only possible to guess: but of the guesses so far made none is more attractive than that which makes Porsenna stand for an Etruscan attempt, based on Veii, to save so much Etruscan authority east of the Tiber as had not been lost for ever in the Roman wreck.

After so much about the later kings, it remains to consider in what way the evidence makes it proper to regard the government

---

[1] See *Storia critica*, ii, pp. 97 *sqq.*　　　　[2] *N.H.* ii, 140.

of Rome during the period which they represent. Though the
existence of the Vicus Tuscus seems to show the presence of an
Etruscan settlement at Rome, the absence of Etruscan influence
on Latin and the absence of Etruscan burials in or near the city
show that the settlers were extremely few. The Roman population
was a blend of cremating and inhuming peoples, but there is no
ground whatever for the view that ethnically Rome was an Etruscan
city. Culturally, on the other hand, Rome had fallen under the
influence of Etruria before the end of the seventh century, and
throughout the three generations covered by Tarquinius Priscus,
Servius Tullius and Tarquinius Superbus the borrowings from across
the Tiber are wholly intelligible, whether the government was in
Etruscan hands or not. If Servius Tullius built walls in the Etruscan
style, he need be none the less of a Roman for that. Such a view
makes it impossible to use the public works associated with a king
as conclusive evidence to show on which side of the river he had
his origin. To these questions the answers must be sought in tradition. If the elder Tarquin is to be accepted as a separate figure,
distinct from his more tangible namesake, it is hard to decide about
the circumstances in which he won his position at Rome. All that
can be said is that tradition lends no support to the view that he
was king by right of conquest, and that the possibility must not be
ignored that in him is to be seen no more than a native king belonging to a house which either by marriage or by occupation had
come into more than usually close connection with Etruria. Servius
Tullius, who is much more definitely historical than his predecessor,
is shown by the popularity he enjoyed in the tradition of a Latin
city to have been no alien. Nevertheless he lived at a time when
the cultural influence of Etruria was being strongly felt, and his
most famous memorial—if such the *cappellaccio* wall may be called—
is as good an example as any of the way in which sixth-century
Rome was falling into the debt of her neighbours farther north.
Finally comes the chief, if not the only, period of foreign government—the reign of the second Tarquin, of which the most significant
feature is the wholly different tone whereby tradition distinguishes
it from what had gone before. Though Roman patriotism did its
best to dissemble the conquest, the hint of Livy about the Tarquin's
accession and the activities of Etruscan cities after his fall combine
to suggest that he imposed himself on Rome and made it an outpost
of Etruscan power in Latium.

The foreign domination was not without its advantages. Though
the city seems not to have advanced far before the beginning of the
Republic towards the use of stone for the general purposes of

building, the Romans now had access to all the architectural resources of Etruria, whether in the employment of masonry for foundations or in the decoration of a brick or wooden super-structure with terra-cotta. On government too the Etruscan left his mark; but it was above all in the extension of Roman authority beyond its previous limits that the second Tarquin seems to have laid Rome under a serious obligation. In this period Rome had become a political centre of importance, and when the Etruscan had been expelled the Romans found themselves heirs to a political position which was at least an ideal to regain if not a legacy of value at the time. So much may be ascribed to the Etruscans in Rome without it being necessary to group the three final kings together as an Etruscan dynasty. The last Tarquin alone seems to have been Etruscan in a political sense, and with his two pre-decessors he has no more in common than that all three alike belong to times when the culture of Etruria was rapidly pene-trating Rome.

IV. THE SPREAD OF ROMAN AUTHORITY DURING THE REGAL PERIOD

The earliest limits of Roman territory which can still be fixed have been briefly mentioned already. On the right bank of the Tiber, where the ancient Via Campana led close along the river bank towards the coast, the precinct of the deity to whom the title 'Dea Dia' was applied lay at the fifth milestone; and here, during the first three centuries of the Empire, the Arval Brother-hood held celebrations which undoubtedly preserved a part of the primitive Ambarvalia[1]. The inference which may be drawn from this is uncertain: but if, as is probable and as Strabo (v, 230) seems to have thought, the point whereat the Arval rites took place was one which had been visited by the processions of early days, the fifth milestone is fixed as the boundary of Roman terri-tory on the right bank of the river towards the sea. The depth to which this bridgehead extended into the Etruscan country cannot be determined. Probably it included Janiculum and some of the neighbouring heights, and, unless it refers to a later time, it is possible, as Ashby has suggested, that a fragment of evidence is preserved for its dimensions towards the north-west. Though the institution is ascribed by Pliny (*N.H.* xviii, 285) to Numa, the offering of the Robigalia may well be almost coeval with Latin agriculture, and from Verrius Flaccus (*C.I.L.* i², p. 236) we

[1] Dessau, 5048.

know that on 25 April sacrifice to Robigo was made at the fifth milestone on what later was called the Via Claudia. In this direction, too, Roman authority seems at an early stage, if not at the earliest of all, to have reached as far as the fifth milestone and perhaps beyond.

On the opposite bank three points may be fixed. To the north, along the line of the Via Salaria, since Antemnae stood less than four miles from the Forum as the crow flies, Roman territory must have ended only a mile or two outside the *pomerium*. Towards Alba and the east the prominence of the *fossa(e) Cluilia(e)* in the narratives of wars[1] suggests that this channel, again five miles from Rome, was another frontier. And finally, on the Via Laurentina towards the south-east it was still true in Augustan times that to the god Terminus, on 23 February,

sacra videt fieri sextus ab urbe lapis[2].

Such is the scanty evidence for the dominions of the youngest Rome. So far as the clues will serve, they seem to indicate an area of not more than fifty or sixty square miles. In this section it remains to trace, in what detail is possible, the steps by which Roman territory was increased during the regal period to something perhaps seven times as great.

In general the view of tradition about the military operations undertaken by the earlier Roman kings against neighbouring Latin towns is that after conquest the inhabitants of these places became Roman citizens, if they were not actually transported to Rome, and that their lands were added to Roman territory. Beneath this there lies a certain solid foundation, but the details are often suspect and the general tone of the tales as they are told is sometimes misleading. Piecemeal criticism would be unremunerative. Most of the military achievements ascribed to Romulus and the earlier kings, if not mere inventions, seem to be no more than garbled versions of incidents, only vaguely recorded, in the period when the many townships of Latium were slowly coalescing into larger units and when a raid upon neighbouring territory was almost a normal Latin way of occupying the idle months between harvest and the time for sowing. To trace the growth of Roman power it is more profitable to examine such few episodes as can claim some kind of evidence in their support than to consider in succession the long list of razzias accepted by annalists of the first century.

The first, and in some ways the most important, of the military

---

[1] *Cf.* Livy, I, 23, 3; II, 39, 5.   [2] Ovid, *Fast.* II, 682.

operations which calls for notice is the alleged destruction of Alba
Longa by Tullus Hostilius. The existence of Alba cannot be
doubted, and it is no less certain that the city disappeared early,
leaving no more trace behind it than the region known as the *ager
Albanus* and the name, not indeed known before imperial times,
of the Albani Longani Bovillenses[1]. The explanation of this
offered by tradition is that Alba ceased to be as the result of a
war with Rome which is memorable for its association with the
names of Gaius Cluilius, Mettius Fufetius, King Tullus and the
Horatii and Curiatii (p. 377). This account, divested of its personal
embellishments, may be accepted, and it is in accord with such
independent evidence as survives. Since Aricia seems to have been
the head-quarters of the Latin League whose hegemony Servius
Tullius essayed to claim for Rome, it appears that Alban leadership had ceased before the middle of the sixth century. Chronologically, therefore, tradition is credible when it places the destruction in the time of the early kings. Again, tradition is confirmed
in ascribing the fall of Alba to defeat in war by the failure of the
only alternative attempt to explain its desolation in later centuries
—the hypothesis that the city was overwhelmed by an eruption:
of this the impossibility is now beyond question. And finally, the
truth of tradition in making Rome the other party to the fatal
conflict is suggested both by the undoubted tendency of Rome to
intrude into the affairs of this region and by the strong claims
made by several Roman houses to connection with Alba and with
its dependency Bovillae. But though Rome seems to have acquired the *ager Albanus*, the fate of the Alban population is
uncertain. Part of it may have moved to Rome, but in a wholesale
transportation it is not easy to believe. It would be misleading to
maintain that in these early years Rome had devised as a regular
method of dealing with troublesome peoples the policy which in
the third century she applied to Volsinii and Falerii—the method
of compelling them to abandon a strongly-posted city on a hill
and live in some less defensible position lower down: yet there
are indications that Bovillae, which stood by the Via Appia just
at the point where it begins to mount the slope up to Albano,
was in some way the successor of Alba Longa. With both, for
instance, the Julii claim to be associated[2], and at Bovillae there
were cults in later times which purported to maintain some kind
of Alban tradition[3]. Of the status given to Bovillae nothing can
be proved. Its inclusion by Dionysius (v, 61, 3) in his list of Latin

---

[1] Dessau, 6188–9.　　　　　　[2] *Ibid.* 2988.
[3] *Ibid.* 5011 and note; 6190. Cf. Asconius, ed. Clark, p. 40, ll. 16 *sq.*

allies is not enough to show its independence at the end of the sixth century, and more probably it was a village standing on what had now become Roman territory. The remaining question which arises from the fall of Alba—the question of its effect on Rome's relation with the Latin League—must be postponed (see below, p. 405).

Roman aggression under Tullus Hostilius towards the south-east and the Alban hills is followed by a new advance under Ancus Marcius towards the south-west and the Tiber mouth. The only value of the tale that it was Romulus who won for Rome the salt-pans near the site of Ostia is its suggestion that Roman progress towards the sea was made early. The suggestion is easy to accept. The importance which Rome attained before the end of the regal period, her position on the track later known as the Via Salaria and, lastly, the state of affairs revealed by the first treaty with Carthage combine to make probable an account which puts an advance to the coast in the opening phases of Roman expansion and to prove that this advance had been made before the end of the sixth century. Though the foundation of Ostia by Ancus Marcius cannot be maintained (see above, p. 378), in the tale of his campaign against Ficana may be seen a record of the second memorable annexation of territory by Rome.

Of the incidents recorded by tradition in connection with the right bank of the Tiber none calls for serious notice except the acquisition of the salt-pans, which in part at least were north of the estuary. The winning of the region by Romulus is represented as a gain made at the expense of Veii; and, however far short of the coast Veientane authority may have stopped, the tale is plausible to the extent that it agrees with the clear indication of many incidents in suggesting that throughout the regal period Veii was disputing the Roman foothold on the Etruscan bank. In this direction, however, Roman success was small; and, apart from the annexation of a district called the *septem pagi*—the position and size of which are uncertain—and the capture of the Silva Maesia by Ancus Marcius, nothing is recorded except fruitless frontier wars until the time when the three latest Roman kings are made to win something like supremacy in Etruria. The story that Servius Tullius and the two Tarquins imposed their authority on the twelve great cities of Etruria cannot be accepted in the absence of any cogent evidence for Roman interest north of the Ciminian range. Such tales are probably due to exaggeration of Roman success in that outlying region which may be called Etruria Minor—the region which lies between the Monti

Cimini and the Tiber, whose isolation from the rest of Tuscany made its acquisition a possible object of Roman aspiration. That Rome won some victories here before the monarchy fell may be believed. The Etruscan affinities of the second Tarquin are not an objection to such a view. The fate of Etruria in the fourth century is enough to show that the Etruscan cities did not always love one another, and the Etruscan connections of Tarquinius Superbus need not have prevented his policy from being wholly Roman. But Veii stood for the Republic to destroy: and the survival of Veii is enough to show that the tangible results of regal activities on the right bank cannot claim much space in the history of Roman expansion.

The remaining military operations ascribed to the age before Rome began to win hegemony in Latium need only brief consideration. Up stream on the left bank of the Tiber a number of cities are said to have engaged the attentions of Romulus and the elder Tarquin. Romulus himself is made to deal with Antemnae, Fidenae and Crustumerium, as well as with places like Caenina and Medullia of which the sites are uncertain. Tarquinius Priscus goes farther afield: besides doing most of Romulus' work again, he extends his range to Ficulea and Nomentum and even up to the Monti Corniculani, if these are the hills south of Palombara and if that is the district in which Corniculum should be sought. Of all this, however, little can be accepted as evidence for the growth of the *ager Romanus*. That Antemnae was soon annexed is probable, because it lay on the Roman side of Rome's nearest natural boundary to the north—the channel of the Anio. But across the Anio uncertainty begins. Crustumerium and Fidenae lose their independence at the end of the fifth century or the beginning of the fourth, and Nomentum becomes Roman even later. Either then any permanent conquest of these places in the regal period must be denied, or it must be assumed that Rome won them under the kings but lost them for a time during the dark days which followed the foundation of the Republic. Silence of Roman tradition on such a theme would indeed have an intelligible motive: but the silenc is complete, and in such circumstances it is perhaps more prudent to see in these achievements of the kings exaggerations of unimportant wars, if not mere retrojections of later history, than to postulate an episode in the fifth century for which direct authority is wholly lacking. Thus north of the Anio the limits of Roman control at this time cannot be discerned; but it is unlikely that they ran at their farthest more than ten miles beyond the river.

South of the Anio towards the east the evidence is better. Ten miles in a direct line from the centre of Rome, and close by the southern bank, stood the city of Collatia; and when tradition says that the conquest of Collatia by Rome was due to the elder Tarquin there is no reason for doubt. Nothing suggests that the city retained its independence after the sixth century, and the name of Tarquinius Collatinus adds some degree of confirmation to the assertion that it was Roman before the collapse of the monarchy. Collatia lies close to the *ager Tiburtinus*, and it seems that in this region the frontiers of Rome and Tibur marched together. The gap between Tibur and the Roman territory round Alba Longa was filled by Gabii and Tusculum. Both of these remained beyond the pale of regal Rome, but with the former Rome had a close alliance embodied in the treaty ascribed to the second Tarquin, the authenticity of which may be believed (see above, p. 393). Gabii and Tusculum are followed by the Roman possessions on the slopes of Monte Cavo, where Rome must have reached the north-western frontier of Aricia. Between Aricia and Rome the country was continuously in Roman hands, but except in the neighbourhood of the Tiber Rome did not touch the sea. Along the coast her land was flanked by the *ager Rutulus* and the *ager Laurens*, where Ardea and Lavinium led lives of their own.

Such, so far as it can be discerned, was the territory of Rome at the end of the regal period—a territory covering about three hundred and fifty square miles, or more than twice as much as any other Latin state could boast. It remains to consider Rome's efforts to extend her authority over peoples beyond her borders— that is, to examine the history of Rome's intrusion into the affairs of the Latin Leagues.

Of the two schools into which opinion on the history of federal movements in Latium is divided, one holds it possible to trace the steady development of a single league, while the other sees a variety of incipient movements towards unity, about which, except in one or two cases, nothing but their variety can be asserted. If, as is probable, the latter view comes nearer to the truth, schematic histories of the federal development are misleading, and it will be enough to mention the more outstanding organizations of which some record is preserved. It has been seen already that a league had existed with its religious centre on the Monte Cavo, in which Alba Longa may have enjoyed some pretensions to political control, though this control, if it existed, did not pass to Rome on the destruction of that city.

Next, according at least to the grammarian Cincius (*ap.* Festus, p. 276, L.) and Dionysius (iii, 34, 3), there sprang up, immediately on the fall of Alba, a federation which had its meeting-place at the *caput (aquae) Ferentinae*: this was the league with which Rome concluded the *foedus Cassianum* early in the fifth century (see below, p. 487). Thirdly, there is the league of Aricia, which late in the sixth century contained eight powerful members and which Rome in the time of Servius Tullius sought to control, imitating if not supplanting the Arician cult of Diana by a temple on the Aventine (p. 351). Besides the religious worships round which these leagues were centred, various other cults were maintained, if not by the whole Latin people, at least by groups of cities more or less considerable. We may detect a tendency among these federations and groups to become more political and military and less exclusively concerned with cult. The Arician League, at least, had advanced far enough in the direction of political federation for the rights and privileges of citizens in its various states to be set down in writing. More than this the evidence does not permit us to say, and even the existence of any considerable and independent group, meeting *ad caput Ferentinae*, in the sixth century is highly uncertain.

Finally, it falls to consider the Roman advance in this environment during the period of the Etruscan control. The outward sign of Rome's supremacy is to be seen in the building on Roman territory of a temple to Juppiter Latiaris at the spot where the oldest cult common to the Latins had been celebrated in the past. At length the greatness of the Alban League was to be restored; and, though Dionysius (iv, 49, 2) may be inaccurate when he says that forty-seven cities joined this organization, independent evidence shows that at this time Rome was exercising a wide hegemony in Latium. The most important document is the first treaty between Rome and Carthage (for the date of this see chron. note 1, p. 859). Here Rome is revealed claiming some sort of supremacy over the whole Latin coast from the Tiber to Tarracina. Carthage is to refrain from attacks on Ardea, Antium, the Laurentes, Circeii, Tarracina, and other Latins ὅσοι ἂν ὑπήκοοι —a phrase which probably means no more than 'who are associated with Rome[1]'. If this implies, not merely membership of the Latin League, but a separate treaty of alliance with Rome, a well-authenticated parallel is supplied by the case of Gabii, and another —for which the evidence is far less sound—by independent mention of an agreement between Rome and one of the coastal cities

[1] See *e.g.* Dion. Hal. vi, 18, 2.

here in question—Lavinium[1]. In the present place, however, the Carthaginian Treaty is to be noticed, not for the issues which it opens on questions of international law, but for its testimony to the scope of Roman power at the end of the regal period. Though the treaty itself reveals that there were still places in Latium less closely connected with Rome than the cities enumerated in its text, her domination of the sea-board implies that wide control of the Campagna outside Roman territory itself which tradition describes as leadership of the Latin League.

Whether Rome was already in contact with the Aequi[2] and Hernici[3] or not, from the Monte Cavo she looked south-east across the Pomptine Marshes, and her horizon lay far enough away for Circeii and Tarracina, to the former of which a colony is said to have been sent by the second Tarquin[4], to be within her ken. Nearer to the Alban hills stood Pometia, a town which fell early into Volscian hands, if it was not a Volscian foundation. Tradition is wrong in ascribing the destruction of Pometia to Tarquinius Superbus[5]; but it is plausible in suggesting warlike operations during the last years of the monarchy in the region where Pometia lay, and the suggestion of military operations in this region by Etruscans, if not by Etruscan Rome, is confirmed by Cato's mention[6] of fighting between Volscians and Etruscan invaders. It is a region in which Roman interest is implied by the treaty with Carthage, and it is the first region to demand attention after a hold on the Campagna had been made secure. The consolidation of such a hold was the external work of the Etruscan government in Rome. The next step brought Rome face to face with the Volsci; and in the history of Roman expansion the Volsci are the link between the regal period and the Republic. The Volscian problem was raised before the monarchy collapsed, and its solution was delayed for nearly two hundred years; but it was in the early decades of the fifth century that the Volscian danger loomed largest in the affairs of Rome.

[1] Livy, I, 14, 3.
[2] Id. I, 55, 1.
[3] Dion. Hal. IV, 49, 1.
[4] Livy, I, 56, 3.
[5] Id. I, 53, 2.
[6] Orig. fr. 62 P.

CHAPTER XIII

THE PRIMITIVE INSTITUTIONS OF ROME

I. PRIMITIVE MONARCHY

ALTHOUGH the traditions of the Seven Kings of Rome consist largely of fiction, it is beyond doubt that the earliest constitution of the Roman state was a monarchy. Rome, in fact, was never without a king; for the senior in rank amongst the ancient priesthoods was that of the *rex sacrorum*, and in the entries in the calendar which relate to his functions he is indicated by the letter R only, in the formula Q(uando) R(ex) C(omitiavit) F(as)[1]. This fact, and such survivals as the ceremony of the *Regifugium* (to be discussed presently), and the institution of the *interregnum*, as well as the name *regia*, applied to the residence of the *pontifex maximus*, who succeeded to the position of the king as the chief authority in the religion of the State, permit no doubt of the existence in early times of a chief whose title is philologically identical with that of the *rig* of the Goidelic Celts—and, it may be added, the *rāj* of the Aryan invaders of India. The traditions give us no help with regard to the origin of the kingship in Rome and contain little that is trustworthy concerning its history; but they have a negative importance in that they give no hint of a hereditary title enjoyed by a ruling family. In no instance does the succession pass from father to son; and however we interpret the account given by our authorities of the procedure on the demise of the crown, it is implied that the king's power was derived from the expressed will of the community. Here Celtic analogies may be of some help; for it is well known that the office of the *rig* did not necessarily pass from father to son, though the circle of choice was limited within the clan (*tuath*). We cannot, however, furnish definite proof that the successor to the kingdom was selected by anticipation in Early Rome, like the 'Tanist' in Ireland; while on the other hand, it would be rash to argue from the fact that under the Republican constitution the chief magis-

---

[1] The early inscription from the Comitium (above, p. 312) contains the word RECEI (= regi); but as its date is uncertain we cannot be sure whether the monarch or the *rex sacrorum* is meant. The suggestion that the word is the passive infinitive of *regere* is very improbable.

trate 'nominated' his successor (subject of course to the confirmation of his act by the assembled people) that the king had designated the future holder of his powers in his lifetime.

In considering the functions of the *rex* we may set aside the traditions of the Seven Kings, of whom the first is credited with the establishment of civil government and the beginnings of military organization, while the second was recognized as founder of the religious institutions of Rome (p. 374 *sq.*). We shall, however, not be rash if we assume that the *imperium* of the Republican chief magistrate, of which we shall speak more fully later (p. 441 *sq.*), derived its features from the authority exercised by the *rex*. Cicero draws this inference in the passage of the *de legibus* relating to the consulship, which is worth giving in full[1]: 'Let there be two holders of kingly authority and inasmuch as they lead and give judgment and take counsel let them be called leaders, judges, and counsellors; in war let them enjoy supreme power, and obey no man: for them let the safety of the people be the highest law.'

Cicero, it will be noticed, treats the *regium imperium* as comprehending the supreme command in war and the administration of justice in peace: he says nothing of the king as priest. The few facts which we know with regard to the duties of the later *rex sacrorum* do not give a complete picture of the religious functions of the king. The *rex sacrorum* proclaimed the festivals to be observed during each month on the Nones: he offered a sacrifice, probably to Janus, in the Regia, on 9 January; and on 24 March and 24 May he performed some ceremony in the *comitium*, indicated by the entry in the calendar Q(uando) R(ex) C(omitiavit) F(as). Lastly, on 24 February, he took part in the ceremony of the *Regifugium*, which was commonly misinterpreted as commemorating the expulsion of Tarquin. A gloss of Festus (unfortunately much mutilated) shows that Verrius Flaccus rightly rejected this view: he is also the author of the note in the Fasti of Praeneste on the entry Q.R.C.F., in which he controverts the view of those who believed the letters to signify Q(uod) R(ex) C(omitio) F(ugerit), and probably followed Varro, who gives the correct explanation of the letters. It seems certain that the *Regifugium*, like the *Poplifugia* of 5 July, was a 'ritual flight' like that of the priest who slew the ox at the Attic *Buphonia* (vol. II, p. 623), so that the ceremony was one belonging to a stratum of primitive religious ideas. There

---

[1] regio imperio duo sunto, iique praeeundo, iudicando, consulendo praetores, iudices, consules appellamino: militiae summum ius habento, nemini parento: ollis salus populi suprema lex esto (III, 3, 8).

is, however, no trace at all of the conceptions of kingship familiar amongst primitive folk in the Roman institution, nor in fact, amongst the Italic peoples, except in the case of the *rex nemorensis* at Aricia. That the Roman king was originally a god is in no way proved by the fact that the garb of the *triumphator* was assimilated to that of Juppiter the Best and Greatest; and if the king-god of primitive magic has any representative in Rome, he is to be found rather in the *flamen Dialis*, whose precious life was hedged about with a host of taboos, than in the *rex* (p. 426).

II. PRIMITIVE DIVISIONS OF THE PEOPLE

The Romans clearly had little if any direct knowledge of the monarchical constitution; nor is it easy to reconstruct from the material supplied to us by tradition and survival the primitive society over which the *rex* held sway. To begin with the divisions of the people. It was an accepted fact that the system of local tribes which prevailed in historical times did not go back to the beginnings of Roman history. There were, however, three names which were applied to the six senior *centuriae* of the Roman *equites*, viz. Ramnenses, Titienses and Luceres, each being divided into *priores* and *posteriores*. They subsisted as voting-units in the assembly of the centuries and were therefore called *sex suffragia*; and it was a natural conjecture that they represented three primitive tribes. This is not the account given by Livy, who merely says that Romulus enrolled three centuries of horsemen after his reconciliation with the Sabines, and called one after himself, and one after Titus Tatius—the third name defied explanation—and that the number was doubled by Tarquin the elder; but Cicero (*de Rep.* II, 8, 14), who explains the third name as derived from Lucumo, an ally of Romulus, definitely speaks of three tribes, and Varro (*L.L.* v, 55) tells us that the *ager Romanus* was first of all divided into three portions, from which the three tribes took their names. The derivation of *tribus* from *tres* which he implies has been rejected by modern scholars, who connect the word with the Celtic *treb-* (Modern Welsh *tref*), comparing the spelling *trefi-* in one passage of the Tables of Iguvium; but so far as the explanation of the *tribus* as local is concerned, he is likely enough to be right: it was not only the later Roman *tribus* that were territorial, for a district in Umbria is described as *tribus Sapinia* by Livy (XXXI, 2). But that the centuries of cavalry were named after tribes is not thereby proved. According to Varro the three names were explained as Etruscan, by one Volnius (Vol⟨um⟩nius seems a more probable name) who wrote tragedies in Etruscan: and Schulze accepts this, pointing to the Etruscan family names *Titie* and *Luchre*, and explaining Ram-nenses from the stem expanded in the names Ramnius and Ramennius. If this is correct, the tribes (or cavalry-squadrons, as the case may be) would date from the period of Etruscan influence at Rome[1].

Tradition has it that besides the three tribes thirty *curiae* were established by the founder of Rome; and here we are on firmer ground, for these subsisted throughout Republican history as the framework of an assembly of the people which evidently survived from primitive times. The Romans possessed no more characteristic institution than that of the group-vote. When the people were gathered together to hear proclamations or harangues from those in authority, the assemblage was described simply as a *couentio* (later *contio*); thus in the senatusconsultum de Bacchanalibus (186 B.C.) the Senate gives instruction to publish its decisions *in couentionid* on three successive market-days. Varro also tells us that the censors summoned a *conventio* when they were about to perform the ceremony of the *lustrum*. When, however, the will of the people was to be formally expressed in binding terms, the *contio* was dismissed, and those about to vote were marshalled in groups, each of which cast a single vote: the assembly was now termed *comitia*. Messalla expounds the distinction between *comitiatus* and *contio* in a passage from the *de auspiciis* quoted by Gellius (xiii, 16), who summarizes the doctrine in his comment: '*cum populo agere* (*i.e.* in the *comitia*) is to put a question to the people, in answer to which it may by its votes enjoin or forbid, *contionem habere* is to deliver a speech to the people without putting any question.' Now the primitive form of grouping (which must go back to the regal period) is that by *curiae*, described as *comitia curiata* in distinction from later groupings which will be described in due course. The derivation and original meaning of the term *curia* are obscure. The only dialectic variant known to us is *couehriu*, found on a bronze tablet from the Volscian town of Velitrae and possibly as early as the fourth century B.C., and it is suggested that this is for **couirium*, but this is far from certain. It is indeed not unlikely that the word denoted a place of meeting rather than the group itself, for it was applied to the shrines at which the *curiae* performed their sacred rites and to other halls of assembly, such as the senate-house. The *curiae* took part in two festivals belonging to the primitive calendar. The first

[1] For attempts to connect the *augures* with the three tribes see below, p. 429.

was the *fordicidia* or slaying of pregnant cows, one for each of the thirty, on 15 April; the victims were offered to Tellus, and the unborn calves were burnt and their ashes handed over to the Vestals to be mixed with the blood of the 'October horse' and used for the magic of the Parilia on 21 April. Of the other, the *Fornacalia* or Feast of Ovens, ending on 17 February, we have some account in the *Fasti* of Ovid (11, 527 *sqq.*), who tells us that it was held in the Forum, where each *curia* had a place allotted to it; and Dionysius seems to refer to it where he speaks of having seen offerings of cakes and first-fruits on wooden tables of primitive shape in the several *curiae*. Each of them had its *curio*, who presided over its rites, and the *curio maximus*, elected by the people, proclaimed the festival.

It is by no means easy to explain the origin of the *curia* and the part which it played in the political organization of the Roman community. Our Greek authorities, such as Dionysius, equate it with the *phratria*, in order that the three-fold division *gens-curia-tribus* may correspond with *genos-phratria-phyle*, and Laelius Felix, in discussing the principles of grouping in the various *comitia*, said that the *comitia curiata* were those in which votes were cast *ex generibus hominum*. The Romans therefore held that the *curia* was an element in a social and political order based on kinship. It does not, however, seem that they went a step farther and completed the symmetry of the scheme by assigning ten *gentes* to each *curia*; for the obscure passage in which Dionysius speaks of a division of the *curiae* into *dekades*, though Niebuhr interpreted it in this sense, carries little weight: nor (as we shall see) do the ancient authorities connect the normal number of three hundred assumed for the Senate with any such arrangement.

The fact is that the *curia* is the only unit of grouping of whose existence in Early Rome we can be sure. It seems to have been found amongst other Latin peoples, for we find it at Lanuvium, and (as a survival) in towns enjoying Latin right, such as Malaca in Spain, where it takes the place of the *tribus* in Roman *coloniae*: and we shall probably not be far wrong if we regard it as a group of households formed for the purpose of political organization. Symmetrical divisions of this kind are apparently implied in the Tables of Iguvium, where we find *tekvias* (= *decuriae*), *famedias* (= *familiae*), *pumpedias* (= **quincuriae*, cf. the Oscan *pumperiais* at Capua), and though they are artificial, and no doubt often calculated on the basis of round numbers (as were the English 'hundred' and the Welsh *cantref* or 'hundred settlements'), the principle of grouping is likely to have been local. Of the few names of the Roman *curiae* which survive, some, such as Foriensis and Veliensis, lend themselves readily to such an interpretation: the myth which related that Romulus christened his *curiae* after the raped Sabines very probably arose from the name Rapta.

As the earliest assembly of the people the *comitia curiata* was retained throughout Republican history in order to represent the community in its religious capacity. Thus it was summoned in order to witness the *inauguratio* of the *rex* and the greater *flamines*, and also to give the necessary assent of the people to private acts which might affect the due performance of *sacra*, such as adoption by *adrogatio* and the execution of the primitive form of will, of which more will be said later. In this capacity it was summoned by the *pontifex maximus* in Republican times and known as *comitia calata*, and we learn from a remark of Cicero in his speech on the Agrarian Law of Rullus that the formalities were duly witnessed by thirty lictors representing the thirty *curiae*.

It is more important to consider what was the position of this assembly in relation to the *rex*. In historical times the *comitia curiata* was regularly summoned to pass a *lex de imperio*, which formally conferred the *imperium* on the magistrates who had already been elected by the *comitia centuriata*. In the speech quoted above, Cicero explicitly says that the consul, if he has not secured the passing of such a law, cannot undertake military operations, 'attingere rem militarem non licet'[1]. Nor, again, could the magistrate exercise jurisdiction until he had thus been invested with *imperium*; and thus in 56 B.C. the courts were paralysed for a time because Clodius prevented the passing of *leges curiatae*. Lastly, the consul who had failed to secure his *lex curiata* was held to be incapable of holding valid elections for his successor, and on this ground the *comitia* held at Thessalonica in 49 B.C. by Pompey's supporters were not recognized by Caesar's party. At the same time, the formality of assembling thirty lictors and treating them as representatives of the sovereign people was probably not always observed in later times: in a letter of Cicero, Appius Claudius, the consul of 54 B.C., is reported as expressing the view that the passing of the *lex curiata* 'was requisite but not indispensable', 'opus esse, necesse non esse'[2]. Common sense tells us that the ceremony was a survival from a

[1] Cf. comitia curiata quae rem militarem continent, comitia centuriata, quibus consules...creatis (Livy v, 52, 16).

[2] Cicero in a letter of 53 B.C. (*ad Att.* IV, 18, 2) speaks of a corrupt compact made by the consuls of that year with their predecessors, one of the terms of which was that the latter should produce three augurs to swear falsely that a *lex curiata* had been passed for them.

time when the assembly of the centuries did not exist and the *comitia curiata* was the only organ by which the people expressed its will and conferred *imperium* on its rulers. But the accounts which we have of its function in the period of the kings are not so simple. All authorities agree that on the demise of the crown the Senate set up an *interrex*, who held office for five days, and was succeeded by others until the vacant throne was filled, and that this officer proposed the name of the future *rex* for the approval of the people. Livy tells us that the choice of the *populus* received the ratification of the Senate (*patres auctores fuere*). But Cicero in the *de Republica* says nothing of this: on the other hand he states most explicitly that the newly-appointed *rex* took a *second* vote of the *comitia curiata* in order to secure the grant of the *imperium*[1]. It is to be feared that we have in this curious doctrine an unintelligent explanation of the dual vote taken in historical times; the jurist from whom Cicero borrowed it supposed that the vote of the Republican *comitia centuriata* had been substituted for the first of two acts of the *comitia curiata* when that was the only assembly. We, on the other hand, conclude that it was the *comitia curiata* as the assembly of the Roman people which conferred upon the king the *imperium*, but that its choice was preceded by a nomination by the Senate's *interrex* and ratified by the *patrum auctoritas*.

III. THE STRUCTURE OF SOCIETY: PATRES AND GENTES: CLIENTS: PLEBEIANS

In order to explain the part played by the Senate we shall have to go farther afield. The Council of Elders, whose existence in a primitive community we should be obliged to assume, even were it not attested, is described by the term *patres*. Livy, for instance, says that on the death of the king *res ad patres redit* (1, 32); Cicero, putting the matter from the point of view of the state-religion, uses the phrase 'auspicia ad patres redire' (*ad Brut.*1, 5, 4). In the historical period *patres* in this context meant the *patrician members of the Senate only*: Asconius in his commentary on the *pro Milone* speaks of a motion made 'de patriciis convocandis qui interregem proderent.' It was likewise used in this special sense in connection with the *patrum auctoritas*, or act of ratification which (as Livy clearly states) was necessary to validate the election

---

[1] II, 13, 25 (with reference to Numa): quamquam populus curiatis eum comitiis regem esse iusserat, tamen ipse de imperio suo curiatam legem tulit; cf. II, 17, 31 Tullum Hostilium populus interrege rogante comitiis creavit, isque de imperio suo exemplo Pompilii populum consuluit curiatim.

of the king, and which, down to the close of the Republic, was performed on the occasion of every vote of the people, whether in elections or in legislation, although (as will be shown later) it was in time reduced to a bare formality. This is made clear, not only by the passages in which Livy (VI, 42) and Sallust (*Hist.* III, frag. 48, M.) use *patricii* for *patres*, but also by the fact that both Cicero (*de domo sua*, 14, 38) and Livy (VI, 41), in passages which show a striking verbal resemblance, suggesting that they are derived from one and the same juristic source, state that the extinction of the patriciate would mean that no body would remain which could by its *auctoritas* ratify the decisions of the *comitia*. It is a legitimate inference that there had been a time when the Senate was composed entirely of patricians, and that after the admission of plebeians the body of *patres* in the old sense retained certain functions as its exclusive privilege. We are thus compelled to face the question, what was the ground of the distinction between *patres* and *plebs*, and in order to answer it we must examine the structure of Roman society.

In the developed legal system of historical Rome the only recognized holder of rights was the *pater*, or, to use the full expression, *paterfamilias*. He alone possessed juristic personality, and the members of his family could not (apart from legal fictions) own property or sue or be sued in the courts. The *familia* of which he was the head included both persons and things, though there is a trace of some distinction between movable goods (originally 'stock') and the remaining rights (including those over persons) in the phrase *familia pecuniaque*, used by the 'buyer of the *familia*' in the fictitious sale which cloaked a testamentary disposition. The authority of the *pater* was variously described: his wife was said to be under his 'hand' (*manus*)[1], his slaves were in his *dominium*; but the most characteristic expression of his power is contained in the *patria potestas*, which is especially used of the father's authority over his descendants, including the 'right of life and death' (*ius vitae necisque*), which, though rarely exercised in historical times, was never extinguished by law. The execution by Brutus the First Consul of his two sons was the legendary prototype of this extreme manifestation of the father's power over the family, which was only extinguished by his death, when his sons in their turn became *patresfamiliarum*.

Here, then, we have the ordinary use of *pater* in its legal sense as the subject of civil rights. But behind the house-father with his

---

[1] This was probably the general term for authority over persons, since *manu mittere* signifies emancipation from the *patria potestas*.

concentrated authority and indefeasible right of property stood a group with claims which might, in the absence of heirs, be revived at any time. The issue of the *pater* were in the first instance his 'necessary heirs' (*heredes necessarii*, also known as *heredes sui* or 'heirs of his personality'): but in default of such heirs the *familia*, according to the Law of the Twelve Tables—our earliest evidence for the Roman customs of inheritance—was claimed by the 'nearest *agnatus*,' that is to say (since *agnatus* denotes descent in the male line only) the nearest kinsman who could show that his ancestor and that of the deceased had been under the same *patria potestas*. But what if there were no person who could thus trace collateral descent through males? Then, says the Code, 'the *gentiles* shall have the *familia*.' This enactment introduces us to the *gens*, the place of which in early Roman society is not easy to determine precisely. The nomenclature of the Romans was based on the use of a personal name (*praenomen*), selected from a number which was never large, and was so much reduced in historical times that only fifteen were in common use, and the name proper (*nomen*). Of these *nomina*, according to a tract ascribed to Varro, there were 1000 in use, which is perhaps an exaggeration; but they were very numerous, and the same *nomina* are often found both among the Latins and other Italic stocks. The *nomen* denoted the *gens*—indeed a jurist of Cicero's time says quite simply 'gentiles mihi sunt qui meo nomine appellantur.' But it was far from being true that all who possessed the same *nomen* could lay claim to the reversionary rights above mentioned. In Cicero's *Topics* (6, 29), 'definition' is illustrated by the example of the word *gentilis*, the precise meaning of which had been laid down by Q. Mucius Scaevola, doubtless in an authoritative interpretation of the passage above quoted from the Code. Scaevola ruled thus: 'gentiles sunt inter se (i) qui eodem nomine sunt, (ii) qui ingenuis oriundi sunt, (iii) quorum maiorum nemo servitutem servivit, (iv) qui capite non sunt deminuti.' This excludes all freedmen and their descendants, who, though according to the Roman practice they bore the *nomen* of the original manumitter, could lay no claim to a share in his *familia*, though of course his descendants were entitled to claim his succession *ab intestato*. The last limitation excludes other categories of persons. The *caput* of a Roman citizen was the sum of the rights which he enjoyed in virtue of his birth. These the lawyers of historical times defined as 'citizenship, freedom and family' (*civitas, libertas, familia*); and if any one of these were lost for whatever reason the sum was diminished and *capitis deminutio* took place. *Civitas*, for instance, was lost when a

Roman joined another community—even a Latin colony; and *familia* was lost when he was adopted into another family.

Were the reversionary rights, thus limited, the survival of a system of joint-holding in which individual property had not yet emerged? The *gens*, as its name shows, was based on a presumed natural kinship; and the adjectival termination of Latin *nomina* in *-ius* seems to be patronymic, like the -ειος of Epic and Aeolic Greek. It affords a natural ground of comparison with the formation of Goidelic clan-names in Scotland and Ireland by the use of the prefixes Mac- and O' (Ua)-, and however fictitious the theory of common descent may have been, there is nothing improbable in the supposition that when migration gave way to settled life, tracts of land were occupied by *gentes* in the Roman sense, which gradually became disintegrated by the appropriation of cultivated areas to smaller kin-groups. The *familiae* in the common and non-technical use of that word, whose members were distinguished from those of the remainder of the *gens* by the use of an added name (*cognomen*), represent a stage in the dissolution of the clan; the independence of the *paterfamilias* and his highly-developed right of ownership form the term of the process, which has its analogies in the breaking-up of other tribal systems[1].

There is very little direct evidence of joint-holding by the *gens* at Rome. It may be implied in the well-known legend of Attius Clausus, the eponym of the *gens Claudia*, who was said to have migrated from his Sabine home in 504 B.C., followed by a host of kinsmen and dependents, and to have received the Roman citizenship with patrician rank and an allotment of land beyond the Anio which formed the nucleus of the Claudian *tribus* (p. 494). Mommsen inferred the primitive existence of common property in land from the use of certain terms of law. Thus *heredium* is explained by Varro (*R.R.* 1, 10) as 'the two *iugera* allotted by Romulus to each citizen as his hereditary property.' The word was found in the Twelve Tables, and the elder Pliny tells us (*N.H.* XIX, 50) that it there had the sense of *hortus*, whereas *hortus* was used in that of *villa*. Since two *iugera* would scarcely suffice to maintain a family (though according to Livy allotments of this extent were given to the colonists of Anxur in 329 B.C.) it is suggested that the exclusive possession of the plot was supplemented by rights of common tillage and pasture in a wider area. We are of course

---

[1] The Welsh Codes show how the land-holding *gwely* (literally 'bed') was gradually dissolved and ownership in severalty (*priodoldeb*) established itself.

in complete ignorance of the context in which *heredium* was found in the Tables, and can only conjecture that it was the homestead which could not be alienated from the natural heir. Nor can we draw any clear inference from the fact that *mancipium* was the oldest form of conveyance known to Roman law. The 'taking with the hand' which was necessary to transfer the right of property was a symbolical act, just as was the striking of the scales with the ingot of bronze, which represented the payment made. The terms of the bargain, according to the Twelve Tables, were expressed in the words which accompanied the formal ceremony. The theory that Romulus distributed the land taken by right of conquest *viritim* (Cic. *de Rep.* II, 14, 26), shows that the Romans themselves regarded individual property as primitive. In the opinion of the present writer, therefore, the case for extensive joint-holding by the Roman *gens* is not made out[1].

There is better evidence for a religious tie uniting the members of the *gens*, and for the possession by *gentes* of a common place of burial. Ateius Capito mentioned that 'in the sacrifices of the *gens Claudia*' a *propudialis porcus* was offered as a purificatory victim (see Festus, p. 274 L.); and we are told that during the siege of the Capitol by the Gauls one of the Fabii passed unharmed through the enemies' lines to the Quirinal in order to perform the *sacra* of his *gens*. When a member of a *gens* placed himself under the *potestas* of one of another clan, he went through the form of *sacrorum detestatio*; and it was the duty of the *pontifices* to see that the transmission and maintenance of gentile *sacra* were not endangered by adoptions. That the place of worship was the common sepulchre might be inferred from the rule which forbade the burial of non-members *extra sacra et gentem*. We are told that the Claudii were allotted a burial-place at the foot of the Capitol; and Cicero (*de leg.* II, 22, 56) speaks of the *gens Cornelia* as occupying the same sepulchre down to his own time: the well-known grave of the Scipios was of course the property not of the *gens Cornelia* as a whole, but of one of its *familiae*, the Cornelii Scipiones.

The questions must now be asked (*a*) whether the *patres familiarum* of the *gentes* known as patrician formed the citizen body of the primitive Roman state to the exclusion of others, (*b*) whether the *patres* forming the Senate in the regal period directly represented these *gentes*. There was certainly a claim that the rights of *gentiles* belonged to patricians, and to them only. Livy (x, 8) puts into the mouth of Decius Mus a dramatic speech in which he tells the *patres* that they claim 'vos solos gentem habere.' Cicero (*de Orat.* I, 39,

[1] See further below, p. 468 *sq.*

176) mentions a lawsuit between the patrician *gens Claudia* and the Claudii Marcelli, who were plebeians, concerning the right of succession on intestacy to the estate of the son of a freedman of the Marcelli. They claimed the estate *stirpe*, the patrician Claudii *gente*: and from this it has been inferred that the Marcelli, as plebeians, could not form a *gens*, but must base their claim solely on descent. We do not know how the case was decided; and even if we suppose that the patrician Claudii were successful, this would only establish the rule that where patricians and plebeians bore the same *nomen*, the reversionary rights of *gentilitas* belonged to the former only, because it was presumed that the plebeian branch was sprung from a freedman, and thus excluded by the definition cited above.

Certain facts, however, are beyond dispute. In historical times there were true *gentes* which were plebeian. Verres, when praetor, tried a case in which the plebeian *gens Minucia* claimed their reversion to an intestate estate (Cic. *Verr.* 1, 45, 115); and the leading case which established the rule above-mentioned, that strangers might not be interred in the burial-place of the *gens*, concerned the plebeian *gens Popillia* (Cic. *de leg.* II, 22, 55): so too we read of the *gentile Domitiorum monumentum* belonging to the plebeian Domitii. There were, moreover, amongst these several which had the same *nomen* as a patrician *gens*. Cicero, in a letter to his friend Papirius Paetus (*ad fam.* IX, 21), corrects his statement that all Papirii had been plebeian, and in fact advises him to claim no kinship with those *familiae* of the Papirian *gens*, who had a discreditable record, but to link his name with the patrician Papisii or Papirii who played a famous part in early Roman history. No doubt the connection in such cases was often fictitious: as we have already mentioned, the plebeian families of later times imagined a *transitio ad plebem* in order to trace descent from an extinct patrician *gens*. The case of the Marcii is noteworthy. The plebeian *gens* of this name furnished, in the person of C. Marcius Rutilus, the first member of the *plebs* to hold the offices of dictator and censor (his son was the only Roman to be re-elected to the latter office), and, what is more remarkable, a later Marcius actually became *rex sacrorum* and transmitted the *cognomen* of *Rex* to his descendants, although this priesthood was of right confined to patricians. But we also find a Marcius as the third king of Rome. Nor is he the only king to bear a plebeian name, for the historical Pompilii and Hostilii also belonged to the *plebs*. Again, three of the Seven Hills on which the ancient rites of the Septimontium were performed—Cispius, Oppius, and Caelius—

bear names which are those of plebeian *gentes*. It is difficult in view of these facts to believe that Early Rome was a community the citizenship of which was confined to patrician *gentes* only.

This was a theory held by antiquarians at the close of the Republican period. Cincius is quoted by Festus for the explanation of *patricii* as 'those who are now called *ingenui*,' *i.e.* free-born citizens; and this is obviously connected with the absurd derivation of the word from *patrem ciere*—'those who can point to a father.' It means in reality 'those who belong to the class of *patres*'; but *patres* here signifies, not *patresfamiliarum* in general, but the heads of the ruling families. That the long struggle of the *plebs* had as its object the admission to citizenship of a class outside the citizen body there is no evidence at all.

Whatever view the lawyers may have taken, the Roman writers of historical narrative regarded the patriciate as a kind of peerage created in the first instance by the kings. Romulus, says Livy, 'made a hundred senators, either because that number sufficed, or because there were only 100 persons fit to be made *patres*. *Patres*, at any rate, they were called from the dignity of their office, and *patricii* was the name given to their descendants.' When Alba fell and was incorporated with Rome, its *plebs* received the citizenship, but its chief families were added to the *patres* by Tullus Hostilius; six are named, including the Iulii[1]. Tarquinius Priscus added to the *patres* 100, who were called *minorum gentium*; the Papirii, we are told, belonged to this group of 'junior families,' and in Suetonius' *Life of Augustus* we meet with the strange theory that the Octavii were introduced (*adlecta*) by Tarquin among the *minores gentes*, then 'raised to the patriciate' by Servius Tullius, and in course of time 'passed over to the *plebs*.' Even after the fall of the kingdom, it was held, the Sabine *gens* of the Claudii had been co-opted into the patrician body by the Senate; and Livy, in the speech which he puts into the mouth of Canuleius in support of his proposal to permit *conubium* between *patres* and *plebs*, writes thus: 'the exalted rank which most of you, sprung from Alban or Sabine stocks, enjoy not by right of race or blood, but through co-optation into the body of the *patres*, whether by the choice of the kings or, after their expulsion, by the command of the people[2].' It was a convenient theory, for it carried back to the beginnings of Rome the doctrine that the Senate was formed by free 'choice' (*lectio*), as it was in name throughout Roman history, and upon this fact it may have

---

[1] Livy I, 30.   [2] IV, 4.

been based. But, whatever the origin of the theory, it is inconsistent with the doctrine that the *patres* were the only true *cives*. Selection no doubt there was among the *gentes* who settled on the *ager Romanus*; but it was the natural selection which inevitably takes place when a migratory folk takes to settled agriculture.

In the establishment of the supremacy of the *patres* the institution of clientship played a considerable part. A powerful economic group always attracts to itself a crowd of dependents who, in return for protection against the strong arm and grants of land for occupation and cattle for use thereon, render services fixed by custom or agreement. We have little direct information about the relation of the *patroni* and their *clientes* in Early Rome; but that it entailed mutual obligations enforced by moral and even religious sanctions the Romans never forgot. Vergil, in his *Inferno*[1], places beside him who strikes his father the man 'who weaves a net of guile about his client,' and the comment of Servius on the passage shows that the poet had in mind the Law of the Eighth Table, PATRONUS SI CLIENTI FRAUDEM FECERIT SACER ESTO. The client, on the other hand, as we are told by Dionysius, was called upon to assist in dowering the daughter of his patron and in paying his ransom when made captive in war or the fines which he might incur in court. The moral aspect of the relation comes out clearly in the use of the word *fides*: in the Lex Acilia Repetundarum the word *cliens* is not found, but instead we have 'quoia in fide is erit maioresve in maiorum fide fuerint.' It goes without saying that a large body of *clientes* was a source of strength to the *gens*; Attius Clausus and his Sabines, together with their *clientes*, were said to number 5000 souls[2]. Livy writes under the date 468 B.C. 'that the *plebs* in its anger refused to take part in the election of consuls and T. Quinctius and Q. Servilius were chosen by the votes of the *patres* and their clients'; and though the statement may have little claim to credence—and a similar remark about the elections of tribunes is even more suspect—we may infer from it that the struggle between *patres* and *plebs* was not conceived by the Romans as originating in the effort of a depressed class of *clientes* to free themselves from dependence. We must therefore reject the view

---

[1] *Aeneid* VI, 609.
[2] The Fabii who were cut to pieces at the Cremera numbered 4000 in all, including clients, according to Dionysius (IX, 15). These numbers are cited as evidence of what the later Romans thought possible.

that the *plebs* originated from the existence of non-citizen *clientes* in a wholly patrician state.

It is of course clear that, as the older patrician *gentes* suffered the incidents of dissolution and decay to which families, whether ancient or modern, are liable, their clients, while acquiring economic independence, would remain excluded from the privileged class, and join the ranks of the *plebs*. The extinction of the patrician families is a process which can be clearly traced in the Republican period. From the Fasti and narratives of the Early Republic we can compile a list of about seventy such *gentes* (including those only known at a later time as plebeian, whether sprung from clients, or, as they so often claimed, reduced in status by *transitio ad plebem*). From 366 B.C., the date at which the first plebeian became consul, to 179 B.C. only twenty-four of these are represented in the higher grades of the magistrature, and four of them disappear after 287 B.C. From 179 to 55 B.C. the number is eighteen, and from 55 B.C. to the close of the Republic fourteen or fifteen. We shall not be wrong, then, in thinking that the relaxation of the tie of clientship was a substantial factor in the rise of the *plebs*. But the view put forward by Cicero (*de Rep.* II, 9, 16) and others, that the founder of Rome 'allotted' the whole of the *plebs* as clients to the patricians[1], is too narrow. The growth of Rome as a centre of trade and handicraft, and her absorption of the village-communities of the surrounding districts of Latium, inevitably resulted in the growth of the 'multitude' ($pl\bar{e}$-bs = $\pi\lambda\hat{\eta}$-θos) which was excluded by the ruling caste from representation in the Council of Elders and the conduct of the State's relations with its gods, except in so far as the more powerful families in the territories incorporated in the Roman community were admitted on equal terms by the *patres*[2]. The plebeians, therefore, comprise members of *gentes* which had fallen behind in the race for eminence; clients, many of whom had lost their *patroni*; the peasants from neighbouring villages which had been absorbed by Rome and immigrants to the growing city. The *plebs* is a composite body, but Roman by birth or naturalization, and, in the opinion of the present writer, the theory that the

[1] Dionysius (II, 9) says that each was allowed to choose his own *patronus*.

[2] The *cognomina* (borne by some of the patrician families) derived from the names of towns in Latium which had ceased to exist in historical times (*e.g.* Furius Medullinus, Cornelius Maluginensis, etc.) may indicate sometimes the place of origin of family, but can also be explained as showing that lands were acquired by conquest in these regions and occupied by the Roman *patres*.

difference between patrician and plebeian is due to a difference of race is unacceptable, the more so as the Romans seem to have recognized no racial distinction between the orders in historical times[1].

IV. CIVIC RIGHTS OF PLEBEIANS

We cannot deny to the plebeian element in Rome the title of *cives Romani*, although the rights associated with the franchise of later times were not possessed in their entirety by the 'commons.' Those whom the Romans admitted to their citizen body in the later periods of their history enjoyed both private rights and public privileges. The former are summed up in the words *commercium* and *conubium*. Of these the first signifies much more than the right to trade. It implies the right to acquire a title to property, whether in land or in goods, *ex iure Quiritium*, and to defend that title in court by the methods appropriate to the *ius civile*—the law which holds good between citizens. The forms of procedure by which rights of property are acquired and maintained against all comers form the most important part of Early Law, and are jealously guarded by primitive communities against usurpation by strangers; but there is no reason to think that plebeians were ever debarred from their use, though the client who had placed himself under the protection of a Roman *patronus* was represented by him should he sue or be sued. *Conubium* implied the power to contract a marriage with a Roman citizen, the issue of which would themselves be citizens, subject to the *patria potestas* of the father, and inheriting his *familia* in due course. In this respect the rights of the *plebs* were curtailed, since the *patres*, we are told, refused *conubium* to plebeians. They themselves practised a form of religious marriage known as *confarreatio*, so-called from the cakes of spelt (*far*) which were offered to Jupiter. The *pontifex maximus* and *flamen Dialis* were present at the ceremony together with ten witnesses. The dissolution of such a sacramental union (*diffarreatio*) was hedged about with difficulties[2], and was entirely forbidden to the *flamen Dialis*, who, like the holders of other great priesthoods, was required to be sprung from such a marriage. The patricians, who denied community of religion to the *plebs*, naturally declined to contract such unions with those outside the pale.

The forms of marriage which were open to the *plebs* were two: *coemptio*, which, although reduced to a symbolical conveyance, was, as its name shows, derived from the primitive practice of

[1] See, however, above, vol. IV, pp. 466 *sqq.*

[2] Plutarch (*Quaest. Rom.* L) says that 'many terrible, strange and dismal rites' were performed.

marriage by purchase, and *usus*, in which the possession of the wife by the husband was, after the lapse of a year, converted by prescription into ownership. We do not know whether these forms were also used by patricians in early times, though it is impossible to prove the contrary. It is maintained by De Sanctis[1] that *coemptio*, being a survival of savage custom, is the oldest form, and that *confarreatio* belongs to a society—or, as at Rome, to a social caste—which had developed higher religious conceptions. However this may be, it is not to be doubted that plebeian marriages were, in the eye of the civil law, *iustae nuptiae*, and gave to the husband the full rights of *patria potestas*.

In the matter of public rights the *plebs* was in a very different position. The question whether the plebeians exercised a vote in the *comitia curiata* has been debated, but their exclusion from the *curiae* can only be maintained on *a priori* grounds; not only were the *plebs* members of this body in historical times—it is recorded that a plebeian was elected for the first time to fill the office of *curio maximus* in 208 B.C., and of course the thirty lictors who formally cast the votes of the *curiae* in Cicero's day were plebeian —but the Roman historians imply that this was so in the days of patrician ascendancy in the state and even in the regal period. Livy, for example, tells us that Servius Tullius, when he created the new assembly, presently to be mentioned, retained the traditional practice of the kings by giving a vote 'of equal force and right' to all citizens without exception; and Dionysius adds that his reform was undertaken 'because the poor out-voted the rich' in order that the decisive voice might rest with wealth. The proposal made in 472 B.C., according to the annalistic tradition, that tribunes of the *plebs* should be elected in an assembly of tribes and not, as before, in the *comitia curiata*, is described by Livy as one which 'took away from the patricians the power of securing the election of tribunes agreeable to themselves by means of the vote of their clients.'[2] But though the plebeian possessed the *ius suffragii*, he was for ever debarred from holding such offices as may have existed under the kingship and especially from sitting in the council of *patres*.

This leads us to consider the second question which we set out to answer—in what sense, if any, were the *patres* who formed the primitive Senate representative of the patrician *gentes*? There is no suggestion in ancient tradition of the direct representation of each *gens* by its head. As we have already seen, the *curia* is the only group which, in the belief of the Romans themselves, played

[1] *Storia dei Romani* i, 237.   [2] ii, 56, 3.

a part in the political organization of the people; and there was in fact a theory that the Senate was formed in such a way as to give representation to the thirty *curiae*. There is a passage in Festus (p. 290 L.) which states that at a later date (see below, p. 449) the censors were charged with the duty of placing on the senatorial roll *optimum quemque curiati*, and if we write *curiati⟨m⟩*, as several editors have done, we might hold that this continued a previously existing practice; but too much stress cannot be laid on this passage, since it seems very probable that *iurati* should be written, signifying that the censors were put on oath to choose the persons best qualified in their judgment to serve, just as in later times the praetor was bound by a similar oath in empanelling a jury. Again, if the primitive Senate represented the *curiae*, one would expect to find its number divisible by three. Now this was in fact the case in the Republican period, for there is good evidence that the normal number of senators was regarded as 300 down to the time of Sulla. But tradition was unanimous in ascribing to Romulus the formation of a Senate of one hundred only, which is not easily reconciled with the representation of *curiae*, although Dionysius gives an ingenious scheme—derived from what source we know not—according to which Romulus first nominated a *praefectus urbi* to take charge of the city during his absence on campaign, and then gave each tribe the right to elect three and each *curia* nine senators. This smells strongly of the lamp; and the same must be said of the statements made with regard to the increase in the numbers of the Senate. Livy assumes that on the death of Romulus the *interregnum* was organized by the Senate of one hundred, divided into ten *decuriae* (which obviously could not represent *curiae*): but Dionysius tells us (continuing no doubt to copy the same annalist) that after the peace between Romulus and Tatius and the incorporation of the latter's Sabine followers in the state 'the kings' decided to double the number of patricians by the admission of those later called νεώτεροι (clearly for *minores gentes*), and that one hundred additional senators were chosen, *their names being put forward by the curiae*[1]. He is consistent in putting the number of the Senate at 200 when the first *interregnum* took place. Livy's account, on the other hand, is that Tarquinius Priscus added a hundred senators, 'afterwards called those of the *minores gentes*,' while Dionysius makes him raise the number of senators to 300 by his new creations. At all

---

[1] He makes the statement that 'almost all writers of Roman history' agree as to the procedure, but adds that some held that only fifty new senators were created.

events, it is assumed that this was the normal figure in our accounts of the revision of the roll on the expulsion of the kings.

We cannot therefore affirm with any confidence that the Council of the kings was formed by the heads of all the patrician *gentes*—if indeed the *gens* had such an officer, for which there is no evidence —though its members were all of patrician rank. In view of the plebeian names borne by several of the kings and some of the Seven Hills (Cispius and Oppius are derived by Festus, following Varro, from the names of immigrants from Anagnia and Tus- culum), coupled with the fact that the earliest 'rustic' tribes, of which we shall speak presently, are called after patrician *gentes*, it has been suggested that the patriciate was formed by a group of powerful families which succeeded in overthrowing the Etruscan monarchy and monopolizing the government of the newly-founded Republic. But this theory runs counter to all ancient beliefs. The claim of the patricians to be the depositaries of all the traditional knowledge of divine and human law, and especially of the means whereby the *pax deorum*, or the right relation between the Roman state and its gods, could be maintained, was not seriously challenged, as it surely would have been if it had been due to a late usurpation. Thus the Senate was a body of advisers, perhaps selected by the kings, which, in the aggregate, represented the ruling families.

V. RELIGIOUS INSTITUTIONS

Tradition, which ascribed to Romulus the civil constitution of Rome, was unanimous in assigning her religious institutions to Numa. The 'religious experience' of the Romans (to use Warde Fowler's phrase) will be more suitably described elsewhere[1]; but something must be said of the organs through which religion as a function of the state expressed itself. It was characteristic of the Romans that they never possessed a priestly caste, excluded from secular activities, but claiming authority over the conscience and conduct of the individual. Just as the Roman *paterfamilias* was a priest in his own house and was subject to no external control in the conduct of the family rites, so the Roman magistrate per- formed priestly functions, especially that of securing the favour of the gods by due observance of the signs which they vouchsafed before taking any important action, whether in peace or war, on behalf of the state. Nor was the highest civil office incompatible with the tenure of any of the special priesthoods to which the cults

[1] See below, vol. VIII.

of the individual gods of the state were allotted. These *flamines*, as they were called[1], were fifteen in number, and their antiquity is shown by the fact that several of them served half-forgotten divinities of whose nature (and sometimes of whose names) we know little or nothing. Three of them, the *flamines* of Jupiter, Mars and Quirinus, ranked above the rest, and the *flamen Dialis*, of whom we know most, was subject to a formidable series of taboos. He might not ride a horse, nor see an army in battle-array, nor take an oath, nor wear a ring or knots on his clothing, nor do or see done any secular work, nor bare his head even indoors[2], nor go near a dead body, nor eat (or even mention) a variety of things, e.g. a she-goat, a dog, raw meat, ivy, beans. His hair and nails must be trimmed by a free man with a bronze knife and the parings buried under a lucky tree. The use of bronze is clearly a survival from the age when iron was unknown, and the taboos are all capable of simple explanations in accordance with the laws of primitive magic; and we may rest assured that they go back to days much earlier than those of Numa. Beside the single *flamines*, there were the colleges of Salii, the dancing priests of Mars, who had charge of the *ancilia* or shields believed to have fallen from heaven, and sang a hymn the text of which is only partly intelligible to philologists and was meaningless to the Romans of the Empire. There were two such colleges, originally no doubt belonging to distinct communities; we find similar priests in other Latin cities, and it was even held that they were earlier at Tusculum than at Rome. The hearth of Vesta was served by the Six Virgins, the rites of whose cult were simple yet extremely primitive[3].

But all these priesthoods, though essential to the maintenance of the cults which kept Rome in right relation with her gods, were concerned with the ritual which perpetuates—often without the slightest understanding—primitive magic. They exerted no authority over the public or private life of the Roman, and were in fact subject to a certain measure of disciplinary control, exercised by the head of the state religion, the *pontifex maximus*. It has been inferred from the fact that this officer 'took' the *flamen* for the god whom he was to serve, thus freeing him from the *patria potestas* of his father if living, and himself exercised the *patria potestas* over the Vestal Virgins, that he succeeded to the position of the primitive chief, whose sons and daughters tended

---

[1] The tempting equation *flamen* = *brahman* is now disputed.
[2] This prohibition was only relaxed in late historical times.
[3] Warde Fowler's account deserves study (*The Roman Festivals*, pp. 147 *sqq.*)

the sacred hearth of the community and performed the needful rites; but this is quite fanciful. The *pontifex maximus* was the head of an ecclesiastical college the creation of which was ascribed to Numa. Livy tells us that he 'chose Numa, son of Marcius, from the *patres* to be *pontifex*,' and entrusted to him a written statement of all ceremonies, setting forth the victims to be offered, the dates of the festivals, the temples at which they were to be celebrated, and the revenues from which the expenses were to be defrayed. Cicero makes Numa set up *five pontifices*, and as there were four in 300 B.C., when the number was raised to nine by the Lex Ogulnia, it has been supposed that Numa himself was reckoned in by Cicero's authority. The origin of the name provoked fruitless speculation in ancient as well as in modern times. If the obvious connection with *pons* is historical, we must take that word to include all causeways and not merely (as some have suggested) the bridge which connected the pile-village or the *terramara* with the land, and suppose that it was not merely technical knowledge which belonged to the *pontifices*, but acquaintance with the pleasure of the gods in regard to the settlements and migrations of the Italic stocks.

We are here concerned with the functions of this priestly college in historical times, and especially those which affected the life of the state and of its citizens. The Romans possessed from very early times the conception of *ius*, which is wider than that of positive law (*lex*) laid down by authority, and denotes an order morally binding on the members of the community, both human and divine. They distinguished *ius divinum* from *ius humanum*, and the *pontifices* were the natural guardians of the former. They alone could distinguish *fas* from *nefas*, properly that which might be uttered from that which might not; these terms were especially applicable to the utterances of authority, and hence the calendar, which was drawn up by the *pontifices*, distinguished *dies fasti*, upon which, as Varro explains, the praetor might 'utter' his three pronouncements—do, dico, addico—from *dies nefasti*, when the judge was perforce silent. On some few days his power of utterance was restored after certain ceremonies had been duly performed, hence such an entry as Q.S.D.F. = Q(uando) S(tercus) D(elatum) F(as), *i.e.* after the Vestal Virgins had swept out the refuse of the House of the Hearth. In course of time *fas* came to signify in general that which the gods permitted, and eventually the word seems to have acquired the meaning of a sort of code of *ius divinum*, as in Vergil's *fas et iura sinunt* (*Georgics* I, 269). Livy (VIII, 5) puts into the mouth of T. Manlius Torquatus the rhetorical appeal *audite*,

Ius Fasque, and this personification is borrowed from the curious *pastiche* of formulae ascribed to the *fetiales* in his first book.

The border-line between divine and human law is not easy to draw in the matter of crime, which is regarded by the conscience of the community as a breach of the *pax deorum*, entailing an act or offering of expiation (*piaculum*). Sometimes the offender escaped with the sacrifice of a victim: the 'law of Numa' said that 'the harlot shall not touch the altar of Juno: should she touch it, she must let down her hair and sacrifice a female lamb to Juno.' But in graver matters the criminal and his goods themselves formed the expiatory offering. In this case the term *sacer* is used of both; and this puzzled the learned Romans of the late Republic, for, as Aelius Gallus (quoted by Festus, p. 424, L.) says: 'the man who is *sacer* is he whom the people has condemned for crime: and it is not *fas* for him to be sacrificed, but the man who slays him is not condemned for murder.' He is not, that is to say, a victim meet for the gods, who can be slain at the altar; and, in fact, though subject to a taboo which, if observed by the community which has cast him out, would practically cut him off from the means of life, and liable to death at the hands of any citizen, he was nominally left to the power whom he had offended to deal with—except in cases where economic interest was involved like that of the harvest-thief 'whom they ordered to be hanged and slain for Ceres.' Since the *pontifices* were the authority which determined that which was *nefas*, it was they who elaborated the earliest criminal code.

In private law the influence of the *pontifices* was chiefly exerted in connection with the forms of procedure, but as in most early systems of law correct procedure is all-important, the fact that the pontifical college determined the form of words to be used in oaths and binding covenants, as well as in the solemn 'pleadings' afterwards called *legis actiones*, made their influence very powerful. The *sacramentum* which gave its name to the simplest form of *legis actio*, though it came in time to be regarded as no more than a stake deposited by the suitor and forfeited if he lost his case, must, as the name shows, have been in origin a penalty provided in advance for the breach of an oath. The *pontifices*, as we have already seen, summoned the assembly of the *curiae* which gave its assent to such private acts as might affect the maintenance of family *sacra*. The description given by Gellius (v, 19) of the procedure in the solemn form of adoption by *adrogatio* shows that the *pontifices* took their duties in this respect seriously, and Q. Mucius Scaevola, the most famous of the jurists who held the office of *pontifex maximus*, framed an oath which he administered to the adopter before putting the formal question to the *comitia curiata*. The sanction of such rudiments of international law as existed in early times was naturally religious; and in order to satisfy as well as to bind the public conscience a special ritual was performed. In this the *pontifices* did not play a direct part, but a special college of *fetiales*, the origin of which is variously ascribed to Numa, Ancus Marcius and Tullus Hostilius, asserted the claims of Rome, and if they were denied, conveyed the declaration of war with ceremonies described in detail by Livy and others. The formulae which Livy gives suggest a late origin, or at any rate considerable modernization. The *fetiales* also concluded the treaties which put an end to the state of war, and the use of a flint knife in the sacrifice of the victim points to the primitive origin of the ceremony of treaty-making. Though the pontifical college was not concerned here, it was responsible for the solemn formulae of *devotio* and *evocatio* by which the Roman commander sought to win over the gods of the enemy: in a supreme emergency he might 'devote' not only the enemy's person, lands and goods, but his own life in order to secure the victory to Rome.

The origin of the second great priestly college, that of the Augurs, is ascribed by tradition to Romulus. Cicero's account is that Romulus 'co-opted' (presumably in addition to himself) three Augurs, one from each of his three tribes, and that Numa added two more. Livy notes that when the college was raised in number to nine by the Lex Ogulnia of 300 B.C. four patricians were in office, to whom five plebeians were added, and is puzzled by this, since 'the augurs are agreed' that the number must always be divisible by three, in order that the Ramnes, Tities and Luceres may be equally represented—though of course this can only have been achieved by a legal fiction in later times. Their name, as well as the word *auspicium* which denotes their function, shows that the primitive form of divination practised by the Romans was based on the observation of the flight of birds; and this is very natural with a migratory race such as that to which the Italic *populi* belonged. It follows that the use of augury is earlier than the period of Etruscan influence, although, as has been pointed out in the previous chapter, its later development may have owed much to Etruscan practice, especially as regards the observation and interpretation of lightning which was grafted upon the *auspicium* proper (p. 384). There was a compilation known as *Etrusca disciplina*, of which the first part dealt with the specially Etruscan form of divination by examination of the entrails of victims (*extispicium*) practiced by *haruspices*, whom the Romans summoned from

Etruria when necessary, while the second—*libri fulgurales*—treated of lightnings and their interpretation. What we know of its contents—chiefly from Seneca's *Quaestiones naturales*—seems to show Greek influence at work, and it is noteworthy that in the bilingual inscription from Pesaro (Dessau, 4958) *fulguriator* corresponds with the Etruscan *frontac* (cf. βροντή). The same man was also a *haruspex*, but in the inscription he says nothing of augury proper; and it appears that the Etruscans borrowed the Italic *aviekl* when they spoke of auspices.

The object of Roman augury, and of divination in general, was not so much to ascertain the future as to secure that the favour of the gods was with them in the business in hand—to put it bluntly, to 'get the luck on their side.' With this end in view they scanned the heavens for a sign, either such as the gods might vouchsafe unasked (*oblativum auspicium*), or one sent in answer to prayer (*impetrativum auspicium*). The observation must be taken by a person duly qualified, in other words, by one who 'possesses the auspices'; and the sign must be noted and interpreted by a skilled diviner, the *augur*. It would obviously be impossible in practice to ensure that a favourable sign was vouchsafed at the required moment—the opposite might well happen: but such *contretemps* were prevented by two complementary and highly convenient principles of augury, (i) that a bad omen has no application to one who denies that he has seen it—which enables the *augur* to turn a blind eye to unwelcome signs[1]; (ii) that the omen which counts is the omen *as reported* irrespective of its actual occurrence—which enables the *augur* to give the magistrate the assurance which he requires that heaven approves his contemplated action[2]. It is evident that although it was the magistrate who 'had the auspices,' the case in which no magistrate had been duly elected being covered by the principle mentioned above by which 'the auspices return to the *patres*,' the augural college could pronounce an authoritative decision[3] on the question whether the action of a

[1] 'Quod ego non sensi, nullum mihi vitium facit,' says the elder Cato (*ap.* Fest. p. 268 L.). Pliny (*N.H.* xxvIII, 17), in laying down this doctrine, adds: 'quo munere divinae indulgentiae maius nullum est.'

[2] The converse is of course true, viz. that the attention of the magistrate may be drawn to a bad omen which has not in fact taken place by a person qualified to do so. 'The business in hand is brought to nought,' writes Cicero (*de leg.* II, 12, 31) 'if a single augur says "another day."'

[3] It is worthy of note that in the charter of the colony of Urso, founded by Julius Caesar's directions, the augurs of the colony are given *iuris dictio* and *iudicatio* 'in the matter of *auspicia* and all things pertaining thereto' (*Lex Coloniae Genetivae Juliae*, cap. 66).

magistrate was in accordance with or in defiance of the signs vouchsafed, and that this right might be used for political ends.

The machinery of the state religion, then, so far as it was politically important, was controlled by the two great colleges— 'sacris pontifices, auspiciis augures praesunt,' says Cicero (*de nat. deor.* 1, 44, 122)—and was thus in the hands of the *patres*, who were alone eligible. That the practice of augury was prior to any Etruscan influence has already been indicated, and the early establishment of these two colleges with their monopoly of religious authority is an additional argument against the doctrine that the patriciate was a group of families which owed their predominance to a successful revolt against monarchical rule.

VI. MILITARY INSTITUTIONS

The traditions regarding the army of the kings are vague and conflicting. There were, in the organization of the people by centuries, to be described presently, eighteen *centuriae equitum*, and six of those bore the names of the three primitive tribes already mentioned, *Ramnes*, *Tities* and *Luceres priores* and *posteriores*. It was an obvious inference from this fact that they were the primitive units in the mounted force of Rome, and so we find that Livy attributes the creation of the first three to Romulus. His account of the gradual increase in the number of *equites* is confused; 300, he tells us, were added by Tullus Hostilius after the conquest of Alba Longa, while Tarquinius Priscus, having been forbidden by the augur Attus Navius to increase the number of *centuriae*, doubled their strength, 'so that there were 1800 horsemen in *three* centuries[1].' Yet Servius Tullius adds twelve centuries to the existing *six*. Cicero (*de Rep.* 11, 20, 36) seems to make the force, as doubled by Tarquin the elder, 1200 strong; and Festus (p. 452 L.) speaks of the *sex suffragia* as 'added to the tale of the centuries established by Tarquinius Priscus.' But it is more reasonable to suppose that these were the three pairs of *centuriae* named after the primitive tribes, and this was clearly what Livy (1, 36) understood by the 'six centuries' of Tarquinius Priscus. Attempts were naturally made to connect the *equites* with the thirty *curiae*, the theory being that each of these contributed a *decuria* of ten horsemen; but this no doubt is pure speculation[2]. It is certain,

[1] Livy 1, 36; the figure is probable, though the MSS. vary.

[2] Varro, who knew that the tactical unit of the cavalry was the *turma*, explained this (in his usual manner) as for *terima*, because it consisted of three *decuriae* representing the three old tribes!

however, that the earliest name for the force was *celeres*. The foolish etymologies proposed by ancient writers may be disregarded in favour of the plain meaning of the word. As Helbig showed, they are to be regarded as mounted infantry rather than cavalry[1]. Some confusion seems to have existed in the mind of Livy between the *celeres* (whom, together with others, he treats as the bodyguard of Romulus) and the *equites* proper; but other authorities explicitly identify them, and the name survived in the title of the *tribuni celerum*, who officered the force, and were retained (like the *rex sacrorum*) under the Republican constitution with certain religious functions, which (as we learn from the Fasti set up at Praeneste and compiled by Verrius Flaccus) they still discharged under the Empire on 19 March. The office of *tribunus celerum* was regarded by the Roman historians as having possessed very high importance under the kings, and was said to have been held by Tarquinius Priscus, Servius Tullius and (according to one version) by L. Junius Brutus, the founder of the Republic[2]. The infantry, in the theory of the Romans, were termed *milites*, and had their own *tribuni*; and it was natural to derive the name from *mille*, and by an easy transition, to consider the 'levy' (*legio*) as consisting in a force of 3000 drawn in equal numbers from the three tribes; this was the view of Varro, and of course the supposed derivation of *tribus* from *tres* was used to explain *tribunus*. In later times the Greeks translated *tribunus militum* by χιλίαρχος (the word is found for the first time in Polybius) on the ground of the supposed etymology of *miles*[3].

VII. REFORM OF SERVIUS TULLIUS: THE COMITIA CENTURIATA AND THE CENSUS

Roman tradition is unanimous in asserting that Servius Tullius was the author of a reform of the first importance, by means of which the 'nation in arms' was reorganized for military and at the same time for political purposes. The principal assembly of the Roman people in historical times was the *comitia centuriata*, in which the group-vote was cast by centuries. These were not tactical units of the army, nor even muster-rolls from which such units could be drawn: yet the assembly was essentially military in conception and aspect. It is termed *exercitus urbanus* by Varro;

---

[1] *Abh. d. bay. Akad. d. Wiss.* Ph.–Ph. Kl. xxiii, 1905, pp. 265 *sqq.*

[2] Some appear to have regarded the force as under the command of a single officer with this title.

[3] Philologists are not agreed as to the true derivation of this word.

it was summoned by blast of trumpet, and met without the wall in the Field of Mars, and during its sessions red flags were hoisted on the Arx and the Janiculum, which were struck on the tidings, true or feigned (as happened in 63 B.C.!), of an enemy's approach, a fact which points to the antiquity of the institution. After the centuries of *equites*, which voted apart, came those of the 'seniors' and 'juniors,' the latter naturally furnishing the striking force of the army. These were grouped in five *classes* or 'summonings,' graduated according to their equipment. The full panoply of the hoplite—bronze helmet, shield, cuirass and greaves, with spear and sword—was worn by the first class only, the second lacked the cuirass, the third and fourth (according to Livy[1]) had no defensive armour, the last were armed only with slings and stones. Besides these combatants, the assembly contained centuries of armourers, trumpet- and horn-blowers and other unarmed categories, and one formed by the *proletarii*, who had no taxable property and whose only contribution to the commonwealth consisted in their progeny. For the graduation of the *classes*, expressed in a military sense by the difference in equipment, was based on a registration of property, the *census*, which was instituted, according to tradition, by Servius Tullius, and took place, according to the later view (apparently embodied in the *Fasti* of the Regia) four times during his reign.

The Romans believed that Servius was the author of a 'timocratic' constitution somewhat like that of Solon; it was suggested, however, that his object was to prevent the poor from out-voting the rich as they had done in the *comitia curiata*. There is some variation in the details given by our authorities with regard to the ratings of the five *classes*; but they are expressed in *asses*, and range from 100,000 (or 120,000) to 11,000 (or 12,500) of these units. It is not in dispute that the *as*, or 'unit,' was originally one pound of bronze; but the earliest ingots of this weight, bearing the stamp of official guarantee in the types of the Janus head and ship's prow on obverse and reverse, and thus fulfilling the function of a true coinage, are very little earlier than 300 B.C., nor can we be at all certain that our authorities appreciated the fact that the pound of bronze ceased to be the unit of account in the third century B.C., and that the *as* underwent a series of reductions which brought it down to one-twelfth of its original weight. But if (as is quite possible) the qualifications of the *classes* have been translated into terms of a later currency, there can be no doubt that it is an essential part of the scheme that property

---

[1] Dionysius, however, gives them shields and a place in the phalanx.

should be the basis of classification, and furthermore, that the highest class should be given a preponderating influence, since it contained eighty centuries (forty of 'seniors' and forty of 'juniors'), while the second, third and fourth had twenty each and the fifth thirty, so that as there were 193 in all, the votes of the *equites* and the first class sufficed to give a clear majority[1]. Now the property recognized for registration was property in land, and when the *census* was taken, its situation was defined by the *tribus* in which it lay. The censors not only placed a man in the list of his *centuria*, but they enrolled him in a tribe; and the tribe was in origin a division of the *ager Romanus*. Those, then, who attributed the origin of the *census*, and of the centuriate organization which was based thereon, to Servius Tullius, were consistent in ascribing to him the creation of the local tribes which took the place of the three tribes of Romulus with their supposed racial distinctions.

Here questions of some difficulty arise. Tradition ascribes to Servius Tullius the division of the city of Rome into four *tribus* —*Succusana, Esquilina, Palatina, Collina*—which were known as the *tribus urbanae*; but there was evidently much doubt as to his part in the further division of the *ager Romanus* into *tribus rusticae*. Livy states (II, 21) that in 495 B.C. 'the number of tribes at Rome was made twenty-one,' and this is taken to mean that the first seventeen of the 'rustic tribes' were then added to the city tribes of Servius Tullius. Sixteen of these bear the names of *gentes*, most of which are among the leading patrician houses, while others no doubt belong to families later extinct. It has been argued that since (as was pointed out above) plebeian gentile names appear in the list of kings, whereas the tribe-names are patrician, the *patres* represent an oligarchical group which seized the reins of power on the fall of monarchy: but this is a hazardous speculation. The *tribus Lemonia* may, it is true, be called after an extinct *gens Lemonia*; but if this was one of the families which brought about the overthrow of the kings, it is strange that its members do not appear in the Fasti; and as we hear of a *pagus Lemonius*, it is far easier to suppose that the sixteen rustic tribes are named after *pagi*, and that these in turn were known by the principal *gentes* settled therein. Besides the tradition which placed the creation of the 'rustic tribes' in 495 B.C., there was another, which Dionysius ascribes to the earliest of the annalists, Fabius Pictor, according to which Servius Tullius divided the *ager Romanus* outside the city into twenty-six tribes, and a writer of the Gracchan period, Vennonius, went so

---

[1] The calculations of Cicero, in a corrupt passage of the *de Republica*, are slightly different.

far as to ascribe all thirty-five tribes (the last two of which were actually formed in 241 B.C.) to that king. Moreover, there is a passage in Livy (IX, 46) which is so worded that it may be taken to mean that the 'city' tribes were later than the rest[1], and were formed by Q. Fabius Rullianus, censor in 304 B.C., and some modern writers have based theories upon this. The most reasonable view seems to be that the *census*, the centuriate organization, and the creation of twenty tribes[2] are coeval[3].

But this is not to say that the organization of the *comitia* as described by our authorities was the work of a moment. There are traces of a terminology in which one *classis* only, forming no doubt the fully-equipped phalanx, was recognized, the rest of the *populus* being denoted by the term *infra classem*[4]. The tactics implied in the system are at any rate clearly phalanx-tactics; for the view that the army consisted of *equites* alone, fighting in the Homeric manner and followed by a crowd of lightly-armed clients, has little to commend it. What the Romans at any rate believed was that the organization of the nation in arms, *including both patricians and plebeians* (for there is no suggestion that the latter were excluded or even placed in an inferior position), was the work of the later monarchy. That the *comitia centuriata* of Servius Tullius was the legislative organ of the *populus* seems to be the view underlying the statement of Tacitus (*Ann.* III, 26) that Servius Tullius gave his sanction to laws 'which even kings must obey.' That he designed it to fulfil the function of electing supreme magistrates is no doubt a fiction of the constitutionalists; it is expressed by saying that the first consuls of the Republic were elected 'ex commentariis Servii Tullii.' But this carries us beyond the fall of the monarchy, and belongs to the next chapter.

[1] 'Fabius...omnem forensem turbam excretam in quattuor tribus coniecit easque urbanas appellavit.'

[2] The twenty-first, Clustumina, which is the first rustic tribe to bear a geographical name, is called after the town of Crustumerium, which can hardly have fallen to Rome before the conquest of Fidenae, on which see pp. 507 *sqq.*

[3] This implies the rejection of the theory advanced by Neumann that the formation of the rustic tribes reflects a great emancipation of serfs who cultivated the lands of the urban landowners.

[4] This expression was found in a speech by Cato the elder; it is interpreted in the sense that it included those rated at less than 125,000 *asses* by Festus.

CHAPTER XIV

THE EARLY REPUBLIC

I. THE SUCCESSORS OF THE KINGS

THE fall of monarchy at Rome is the subject of a famous legend, the details of which this is not the place to discuss, especially since that part of the narrative which concerns the family of the Tarquins conforms to a type which belongs to poetry rather than history (p. 394). Setting this aside, we find three names associated with the establishment of free institutions in Rome. The first is L. Junius Brutus, whose gentile name was borne in later times by a plebeian family claiming descent from him. He was, according to one version, *tribunus celerum* (p. 432), according to another, *praefectus urbi*, *i.e.* a deputy left in charge of the city during the absence of Tarquinius Superbus on an expedition against Ardea. The second is P. Valerius, surnamed Publicola on account of the services rendered by him to the cause of popular liberty, a member of one of the most distinguished patrician houses of the Republic, whose story no doubt lost nothing in its telling by the annalist Valerius Antias (p. 317). The third is M. Horatius Pulvillus, who plays a more modest but probably a more historical part as the dedicator of the temple of Jupiter Capitolinus, which had been built with forced labour by the command of the second Tarquin. Polybius dates the first treaty between Rome and Carthage (see below, p. 859) 'in the consulship of Brutus and Horatius,' which is evidence for their appearance at the head of the list of supreme magistrates as known to him. In the final form of the legend, however, room had to be found for the other actors, and so we have, as consuls in the Year One of the Republic, first, Brutus and Collatinus, then, on the enforced retirement of the latter, Valerius Publicola, who becomes sole consul when Brutus has been slain in war and passes the laws which guarantee the liberties of the citizen, and is then joined in his office (according to some) by Sp. Lucretius, the father of the heroine of the tragedy of the Rape, and after his death by Horatius, for whom, as we have suggested, a place had to be found on account of his recorded connection with the Capitoline temple.

Whatever view may be taken of the origins of the legend or of the reasons for the introduction of particular names, there can be no question that to the Roman historians it was an accepted fact that upon the abolition of the monarchy a dual magistracy, invested with supreme executive authority, or *imperium*, was called into being. To this magistracy the name of *consul* is given both in our narrative sources and in the Fasti; and it is assumed that throughout Republican history two *consules* were annually appointed, save in the exceptional case of the Decemvirate, created for the purpose of codifying the law, and in the period when (for reasons to be discussed later) the 'consular power' was bestowed by a fiction upon a variable number of *tribuni militum* (pp. 519 *sqq.*). From time to time, however, the authority of the *consules* was overridden by an emergency officer with almost unlimited power under the name of *dictator*—a practice dating from the very first decade of Republican government. The declaration of a state of emergency was the act of the people; the *dictator* himself was nominated by the consul[1]. The first appointment of a *dictator* was made, according to tradition, either in 501 B.C. (Livy) or 498 B.C. (Dionysius), *i.e.* within about ten years from the expulsion of the Tarquins; but Livy himself admits (II, 18) that there was no certainty regarding either the date or the name of the first dictator; and we may add that many of the early dictatorships recorded in the Fasti or *annales* are suspect on various grounds.

This traditional version of the origins of the supreme magistracies of the Republic has been criticized by recent writers. De Sanctis[2] put forward the theory that the decline of monarchy at Rome was gradual and followed a course somewhat similar to that of the constitutional development of Athens. The priest-king of the Republic, he argued, laying stress on the fact that in official documents such as the Calendar he bears the title *rex* without qualification, resembles the Athenian *basileus* (vol. III, pp. 590 *sqq.*) and is the direct successor, with limited functions, of the early kings. Beside him, he thinks, the Romans set up annual magistrates, whose function, like that of the Athenian *polemarch*, was primarily command in war, and this was expressed by the title *praetor* (*prae-itor*, 'leader'). There is evidence that this was the original style of the chief magistrate at Rome. In describing the constitutional settlement of 449 B.C. Livy (III, 55), in the course of a juristic argument to which we shall return later, states that

---

[1] When no consul was in Rome he was nominated by the chief magistrate available; thus Sulla was nominated by an *interrex* in 82 B.C., Caesar by a praetor in 49 B.C. Only once did the people elect a dictator, and that was in the crisis of the Hannibalic war (217 B.C.).

[2] *Storia dei Romani* I, pp. 399 *sqq.*

'at that time the judge was not yet called *consul*, but *praetor*';
while Zonaras, in his abridgment of Dio Cassius, tells us that the
title of *consul* was used for the first time at that date. This suggests
that the term *consul* was not to be found in the Twelve Tables; it
does not occur in the extant fragments, and the title [*prae*]*tor* is a
likely, though not a certain, restoration in a provision relating to
certain claims (*vindiciae*). Festus (p. 249 L. *i.e.* Verrius Flaccus) expressly says, 'initio praetores erant qui nunc consules,' and his
explanation of the phrase *maximus praetor* may be taken to mean that
the augural college distinguished consuls and praetors as *praetores
maiores* and *minores*. Varro (*ap.* Non. *s.v. consulum*) compromises
by the statement that 'idem dicebantur consules et praetores, quod
praeirent populo praetores, quod consulerent senatui consules.'
The Greeks invariably translated *praetor* by στρατηγός (which
disposes of the theory that the *praetor* was a judge who 'went
first,' *i.e.* dictated *formulae* to suitors) and *consul* at first by στρατηγὸς
ὕπατος (later abbreviated to ὕπατος[1]), which has a close, but
probably accidental, resemblance to *praetor maximus*. Finally, the
Roman governor who left the city for his province was saluted as
praetor 'at the gate,' a practice which Festus traces back to the
time when Rome and the Latin league supplied commanders to
the federal forces in alternate years. On the other hand, the title
consul is implied in the *consularis potestas* conferred on the Decemvirs in 451 B.C. and military tribunes from 444 B.C. onwards,
and it appeared on the cuirass dedicated by A. Cornelius Cossus
(p. 507), if we accept that document as genuine. The earliest
extant inscription in which the word occurs is the epitaph of L.
Cornelius Scipio Barbatus (consul 298 B.C.); and the title was used
for the chief magistrate in the colonies of Ariminum and Beneventum, founded in 268 B.C.

Those who reject the belief of the Romans that a dual magistracy with coordinate authority was set up on the fall of the
monarchy propose various reconstructions of the course of constitutional development. De Sanctis, as we have seen, holds that the
powers of the *rex* were limited by the creation of *praetores*, and that
the functions of these officers were gradually specialized and a
gradation of rank established. The *praetor* set up, according to
tradition in 366 B.C., to administer justice was in his view one of
these magistrates, and the creation of a new officer in that year
was wrongly inferred from the fact that the names of such magistrates began to be recorded at that time. This theory of course
entails the rejection of the tradition which makes the Licinio-

[1] Polybius sometimes styles the consul simply στρατηγός.

Sextian laws of 367 B.C., leading to the creation of this praetorship, a landmark in the 'struggle of the orders' (p. 526); and if our records of that settlement are unworthy of all credence, our reconstruction of the earlier history becomes little else than guess-work.

Others have approached the question from a different angle—that of the comparative study of Italic and Etruscan institutions. To begin with the latter, it seems clear that in Etruria each town was governed by a single chief magistrate with the title of $zila\chi$, next in authority to whom was the $marunu\chi$[1]. The league of twelve cities had a $zila\theta$ at its head, as well as a $marunu\chi$. The Latin renderings of these titles are to be noted. At Caere the $zila\chi$ becomes a *dictator*, but the federal officer is known in later times as *praetor Etruriae*. The federal $marunu\chi$ at the same date has become *aedilis Etruriae*. When we turn to the Latin cities, we find that in some, such as Aricia, Lanuvium and Nomentum, the title of the chief magistrate is *dictator*, and we may recall the federal *dictator Latinus*, who, according to Cato, dedicated the grove of Diana at Aricia. Other communities, however, such as the Laurentes Lavinates and Praeneste, were governed by *praetores*, and the tradition represented by Livy and Dionysius speaks of federal *praetores* (in Greek στρατηγοί), of whom, according to the former, there were two when the League embarked on its last revolt against Roman supremacy (p. 590). It may be noted that whereas the annalists speak of a *dictator* as the successor of the kings of Alba, and a *dictator Albanus* survived in historical times with priestly functions, Cato in his *Origines* (Frag. 22 P.) mentions a *praetor Albanus*.

These facts cannot be said to furnish conclusive proof of any theory concerning Roman constitutional development. It may be thought probable that *dictator* was the recognized title among the Latin peoples for a single supreme magistrate, and that *praetor* connoted collegial authority; but we cannot safely proceed further to infer, either that the institution of the dictatorship was copied from Etruria, or that it always preceded the praetorship, especially in Rome itself, as some recent writers have held, or again that where we find it in Latium it betrays Roman influence. Nor are we much helped by a consideration of the political institutions of other Italic stocks. The Oscan title for the chief magistrate is *meddix*, and where more than one *meddix* is found, there seems to be good reason for thinking that the senior (*meddix tuticus* or

---

[1] See vol. IV, p. 412 and n. 1, and Rosenberg, *Der Staat der alten Italiker*, where the evidence for Etruscan and Italic magistracies is collected and examined.

'magistrate of the community') enjoyed higher authority (see below, p. 596 n. 2); but here again it is not legitimate to argue Etruscan influence. Among the Umbrians the title *maro* is clearly derived from the Etruscan *marunuχ*, yet (if we may judge from the case of Asisium) the magistracy was collegial.

Much has been made of the fact that in some communities we find a college of three *aediles*. This is so at Tusculum, at three towns which were under Volscian rule before coming under the power of Rome—Fundi, Formiae and Arpinum—and in the Latin colony of Ariminum. The title is clearly Latin, and it is natural to regard it as borrowed from Rome[1]; but the triple magistracy may be older than the title, and as we find it in *pagi* as well as in cities, it is suggested that it was a widespread 'Italic' institution. This rests on very slender evidence. We shall presently consider the institution of *aediles* in Rome, where, as will be seen, they form no part of the patrician constitution (p. 456).

There is good evidence that the original title of the *dictator* at Rome was *magister populi*—'master of the people'. The term is found in Varro and Festus, and Cicero (*de Rep.* 1, 40, 63) expressly states that he was so designated in the books of the augurs, from which no doubt the rule 'consul oriens magistrum populi dicat' was taken; and throughout Roman history he appointed as his lieutenant and, in his absence, vice-gerent a *magister equitum* or 'master of horse.' This official has been compared with the *praetor iuventutis* found in certain 'Latin' colonies where the chief magistrate appears to have been a *dictator*, and it is suggested that the earliest form of the Republican constitution may have been based on the authority of the *magister populi* and his subordinate, the *magister equitum*, as annual magistrates. This, of course, involves the total rejection of the traditional history with its unbroken series of consuls following on the abolition of the monarchy, and, as a logical consequence, the supposition that the consuls of the early Fasti—possibly down to the time of the Decemvirate—are in reality dictators, with whom the compiler coupled such names of *magistri equitum* as he could recover from family traditions. This would no doubt make it easy to account for the interpolation of plebeian names in the earlier portion of the list, and also (as Beloch has pointed out[2]) for the curious fact that no two of the first decemvirs belong to the same year in the Fasti. It may further be conceded that grave suspicion attaches

---

[1] Fundi and Formiae, at any rate, borrowed the institution of the *interrex* from Rome.

[2] *Römische Geschichte*, pp. 232 *sqq.*

to the names of the dictators recorded by tradition as holding office in the fifth century; and it is remarkable that T. Larcius (or Largius), whom most authorities regarded as the first dictator, is represented as actually consul when appointed, whether in 501 or 498 B.C. (p. 437). Livy, however, says that there was no agreement as to the date of the first dictatorship, and we may well doubt whether the Romans preserved more than the bare memory that the bearer of an unusual name, which disappears from the Fasti in the early days of the Republic, was the first dictator.

Had the dictatorship been the chief *annual* magistracy of early Rome, it is hard to believe that no trace of any tradition to this effect would have survived; and the procedure of appointment, the limited (six-monthly) tenure of the office, and its use for the performance of special functions—as for example the driving of the nail in the Capitoline temple, the holding of elections, and the celebration of *feriae*,—all of which go back to the fourth century, are all consistent with the view that it was from the first an extra-ordinary magistracy. That it belongs to the early days of the Republic may be inferred from its archaic features—the nomi-nation by the consul at dead of night and the fact that the dictator was forbidden to mount a horse.

The attempts of modern scholars to reconstruct the primitive constitution of the Republic on lines inconsistent with the tradition are thus unconvincing; and without committing our-selves to any details of the record (most of which are obviously legendary), we may take the dual magistracy as it certainly existed in the latter part of the fifth century as our starting-point, and consider its main characteristics. In so doing we must remember that the formulation of constitutional doctrines was the work of much later times, when the jurists sought to make explicit the ideas inherent in the institutions under which they lived; at the same time, their grasp of essentials was firm, and the Roman had a natural gift for basing government on simple principles judi-ciously applied to circumstances.

II. THE POWERS OF THE MAGISTRATES

The first feature which claims attention is the concept of *imperium*, or executive authority, which to the Roman always and before all things meant command in war, actual or potential. If he wished to speak of 'authority' in general, he used the word *potestas*, and this was applied to such magistracies as were created for the performance of specific functions when these became differentiated; and so we find that Festus is careful to distinguish those who are *cum imperio*, *i.e.* on whom the people has conferred the *imperium* by name, from others who are *cum potestate* because the people has placed them in charge of 'a piece of business' (*negotium*). The *imperium*, which, it will be remembered, was conferred by a special vote of the assembly of *curiae* (p. 412), belonged to all *praetores* (a college gradually enlarged in number, the two senior members of which were the consuls), to those who temporarily filled the place of the *praetores* (viz. the dictator and his master of horse and the *interrex*), and to the bodies set up when the supreme magistracy was put in commission, such as the Decemvirs and the colleges of *tribuni militum consulari potestate* of which we shall speak later[1]. It was not enjoyed by the censors, aediles or other officials with administrative functions, although, for example, Livy, who was loose in his use of constitutional terms, ascribes it to Commissioners entrusted with the establishment of colonies. On the other hand, by means of the fictions of which the Romans learned to make such effective use, it was conferred upon magistrates whose term of office had expired, and ultimately even on persons who had held none of the qualifying offices, in order to furnish military governors for the overseas territories under Roman sway.

As originally conceived, the *imperium*, though essentially military, carrying with it as it did the supreme command of a nation in arms which was engaged in a constant struggle for existence, was not specialized in function. The holder was empowered to act for the state in every branch of its life. In peace as well as in war he could 'coerce' the private citizen. He was the supreme judge in matters civil and criminal, and the development of law consisted in the gradual circumscription of his originally unlimited power. With the aid of his subordinates, he supplied the modest needs of a primitive community for financial and general administration, and was responsible for the census mentioned above (p. 433 *sq.*), together with the registration of the citizens' property which it entailed.

These tremendous powers, for the wielders of which Cicero, in his ideal Constitutional Statute already quoted (p. 408), lays down the famous rule *Salus populi suprema lex esto*, were subject to limitations definitely understood. In the first place, they were conferred by the people for a limited time. For the ordinary magistracies of state this was one year, a rule which was never

---

[1] The Triumvirs set up in 43 B.C are analogous.

broken[1], though the extension of tenure by the fiction of *prorogatio*, as will be seen, removed the limit as regards command in the field, which might be prolonged 'for the duration' of a war, and came in time to be the normal method of filling provincial governorships, while in the decline of the Republic it furnished great military leaders with a basis for almost monarchical power. If the historians are to be trusted, centuries passed before the year of office was made to coincide with that of the calendar: Livy mentions August 1, May 15 and December 13 as the days on which, at various periods, the chief magistrates entered upon office, not to speak of special dates adopted by resolution of the people or brought about by a series of *interregna*. For the extraordinary office of *dictator* the term was fixed at six months; and the censors, for reasons of administrative convenience, were allowed eighteen months to complete their task. They, however, did not possess *imperium*. No steps were at first taken to prohibit re-election to the annual magistracies; but we shall see that in course of time measures were carried to prevent individuals from acquiring undue influence by continuous or frequently repeated tenure of the *imperium*.

Secondly, the power of the magistrate was limited by the fact that the *imperium* was held in its plenitude by all upon whom it was conferred *in the same grade*, *i.e.* in the early period by both consuls, and later by those *praetores* who were added to the supreme college. This principle of 'collegiality' was a characteristically Roman conception, and its operation was extended to other offices beside those which carried with them the *imperium*. The conception of a board taking its decisions by a majority vote was foreign to the Romans, though in later times we hear of discussions by the priestly colleges and the ten tribunes leading to joint action[2]; and on the other hand, the powers of the magistrate could be exercised without restraint when a vacancy left him without a colleague. The effect of the doctrine of collegiality was that every magistrate could nullify the act of a colleague by the exercise of his coordinate authority—*par maiorve potestas* is the phrase used by Cicero; and the tribunes of the *plebs*, though not magistrates, were by analogy invested with the power of creating

---

[1] The exception which proves the rule is the *prorogatio* of the magistracy of a *praetor* who was discharging censorial functions in 144 B.C. (Frontinus, *de aquaeductibus*, cap. 7), because censors were allowed 18 months to complete their task (see above).

[2] Livy (IX, 46), it is true, speaks of a law forbidding the dedication of a temple without leave of the Senate or of *a majority* of the tribunes.

a deadlock. It speaks volumes for the political sense of the Romans that the possession of the veto by so many officers of state did not lead to the breakdown of orderly government.

In the third place, the relation of magistrate and people subjected both parties to certain limitations. The sovereignty of the *populus* was a cardinal principle of the Roman constitution, and no fiction of democratic politicians. All authority exercised by magistrates or commissioners had its source, as Cicero says (*de lege agr.* II, 7, 17), in the will of the whole people; and we saw (p. 413) how the *imperium* of the kings themselves was conferred by a 'law of the *curiae.*' It is, however, unlikely that in the early days of the free state the people claimed or exercised the right to withdraw the authority which they had granted during the holder's term of office, in spite of the legendary deposition of Collatinus by Junius Brutus in the first year of the Republic. It was left for the revolutionaries of the last century of freedom to 'abrogate' the *imperium* of the magistrate. Moreover, though the *populus Romanus Quiritium* was a sovereign whose will and command were absolute, the expression of that will and command could only be elicited by the convener of the ordered assembly. The genius of the Romans for Law was shown not only in their grasp of Principles but also in their sense of the importance of Forms. It is worth while to quote two striking passages relating to the expression of the people's will. Livy relates (xxxix, 15) that the consuls of 186 B.C., in addressing a gathering of the people on the 'Bacchanalian conspiracy,' said:

It was the will of our ancestors that even you should not come together casually or heedlessly, unless either the flag had been raised on the citadel and the army had been called out for the purpose of an Assembly (*comitia*), or the tribunes had issued notice of Meeting (*concilium*) to the *plebs*[1] or one of the magistrates had summoned you to a Gathering (*contio*, cf. p. 410); and wheresoever a multitude was, there they held that that multitude should have a lawful controller.

Cicero, in his speech for Flaccus (7, 15), puts the conditions more precisely:

Those wise and reverend ancestors of ours refused to allow a Gathering (*contio*) to have any force; as for the Resolutions of the *plebs* or the Commands of the people, it was their pleasure that only when the Gathering had been dissolved and its parts distributed in tribes and centuries and marshalled according to ranks, classes and ages, when many days' notice of the matter had been given and it had been made fully known—then Commands and Prohibitions should be uttered.

[1] This distinction of terms is explained below, p. 451.

It is to be observed that both historian and orator appeal to the wisdom of the ancestors as the ground of the constitutional forms. The *mos maiorum*, in the last resort, is the Law of the Constitution: and a study of the references to it in Latin literature would show that when Cicero wrote in the *de legibus* of the Custom of the Ancestors 'which *then* [*i.e.* in early days] had the force of Law,' he was making a statement capable of a much wider application. The attempt to treat custom and precedent as the sources of binding law may land us in some awkward dilemmas (especially if we are inquisitive as to origins), but this does not alter the fact that a people with a natural gift for orderly government can make them play a part for which written statutes are unfitted.

Custom, then, prescribed that the magistrate who convened an assembly, and he only, should put the vital question, 'Is it your will and command, Quirites?' and if the response was 'Be it as you ask' the result was a *Lex* in the Austinian sense of Law as the command of a Sovereign. Thus the 'right to transact business with the people' was one of the most important privileges of the magistrate, who had the framing of all questions and whose initiative could neither be forced nor challenged.

III. CRIMINAL JURISDICTION: THE RIGHT OF APPEAL

There was, however, one sphere in which the sovereignty of the *populus*, exercised in the manner described, impinged on the *imperium*. This was in the matter of the punishment of crime. In his first book Livy tells the tale of Horatius, sole survivor of the fight with the Curiatii, who slew his sister on his return from battle and was haled before the king. Tullus thereupon said:

'I appoint two men to pass sentence of *perduellio* on Horatius according to Law.' He then issued his instructions. 'Let the two pass sentence of *perduellio*. If he appeals from the two, let him contend by appeal; if they win, let one cover his head and hang him with a rope on a barren tree; let him scourge him within or without the *pomerium*' (I, 26).

The legend is an expression of the principles of Roman criminal jurisdiction in the form of an archetypal case. These principles are that for a crime against the state sentence is passed, not by the chief magistrate, but by delegates appointed by him, and that by the use of the word 'provoco' the citizen may lodge an appeal to the sovereign *populus*, which not only ensures a stay of execution, but converts the judge into a party.

The term *perduellio* is badly chosen in this instance, for Horatius' crime is hardly a case of constructive treason. It should properly be called *parricidium*—a term which, from denoting the murder of a kinsman, soon came to signify man-slaying in general. But this, according to Roman principles, fell within the province of the *quaestores parricidii*, or 'trackers of murder,' officers whose origin was obscure to the Romans of historical times. The name *quaestor* was also applied to the officials who, under the supervision of the consuls, had the management of the state treasury (*aerarium*), the seat of which was in the ancient temple of Saturn. Originally they were two in number, but others were added, in Tacitus' words, 'as business increased'; at least one, for example, was attached to the staff of each provincial governor. It is evident both from the conflicting statements and from the eloquent silences of our authorities that no record existed of the institution of either type of *quaestor*, nor of the relationship between the two. There was a tradition that the office was created by the kings—Junius Gracchanus, as Ulpian tells us, even dated it back to Romulus— and this may well be true. As the *duoviri perduellionis* pronounced sentence upon crimes directly affecting the life of the state, so the 'trackers of murder' dealt with those grave offences which the Romans, at a very early date, removed from the sphere of self-help tempered by composition, and treated as crimes of which the community was bound to take cognizance. Under the Republic these *quaestores* naturally carried out the behests of the consuls, and since differentiation of function was as yet scarcely conceived of, they added to their duties that of keeping the keys of the public treasury.

We may disregard the legend that the financial *quaestores* were the creation of Valerius Publicola, or even of a later date, but the statement of Tacitus (*Ann.* xi, 22) that the consuls at first nominated their subordinates and that popular election to the office dates from the sixty-third year of the Republic (447 B.C.) may contain some truth. We may safely disregard the mention of the *quaestores parricidii* in connection with the trial of Sp. Cassius for attempted tyranny (Livy, ii, 41; Cic. *de Rep.* ii, 35, 60), which would properly be a case of *perduellio*—the converse of the confusion of crimes in the story of Horatius. But we possess a most interesting document preserved by Varro (*L. L.* vi, 90 *sqq.*), under the name of *Commentarium vetus anquisitionis*, which in the form of directions for the conduct of a particular trial prescribes the procedure in criminal cases tried before the people as the result of an appeal by a citizen against a capital sentence. The date of the document is uncertain, but no doubt fairly early; and we see that the *quaestor*, though he summons the *comitia* by blast of horn[1], is obliged to 'send and ask for auspices' from one of the higher magistrates. The principle which underlies this procedure is that by custom the holder of the *imperium* does not himself pronounce sentences which are liable to reversal by the assembly but delegates the function to his subordinate.

It is of course a further question, and not an easy one to answer, what is the basis of the citizen's right to utter the word 'provoco' if his *caput*, that is, the sum of his rights as a member of the *populus* (the loss of which deprives the community of a citizen, and in early times means physical death), is threatened by a magisterial sentence? Tradition has it that, whereas the appeal to the *populus* was allowed by the kings as an act of grace, the first law passed by the assembly of the centuries under the Republic was that proposed by Valerius Publicola, 'that no magistrate might put to death or scourge a Roman citizen in the face of an appeal.' That the procedure of *provocatio* existed in the early days of the Republic is implied in the statement that the Decemvirs were freed from the limitations which it imposed, and that on the restoration of constitutional government in 449 B.C. a law was passed forbidding for all future time the institution of a similar magistracy. Cicero tells us (*de Rep.* II, 31, 54) that the Twelve Tables 'in many laws' provided an appeal 'from every penalty and sentence,' and from a passage in the *de legibus* (III, 4, 11) we gather that, according to their provisions, only the 'greatest assembly' (*maximus comitiatus*) was competent to pass a judgment affecting the *caput* of the citizen. In spite of this a third Valerian law was passed in 300 B.C. which provided what, it seems, had hitherto been lacking, namely, a sanction for the breach of the law by the magistrate. Livy expresses his surprise that this should be couched in the mild terms *improbe factum*, which seem to imply nothing more than moral censure passed on the consul who defies the law. Mommsen suggested that the words meant that his action was to be deemed 'invalid,' and therefore not covered by his privilege of office: since the law had been finally determined before Livy's time by the three Porcian statutes, the meaning of the terms of the Lex Valeria may have been forgotten. But Mommsen strains the words (*improbe fieri* is used of 'unconstitutional' action in a quotation given by Asconius, p. 58, Clark), and we must remember that (as we

---

[1] The horn-blower is also directed to sound a blast before the door of 'that wicked person, T. Quinctius Trogus,' directing him to be present in the Field of Mars at break of day.

shall see) the code of honour, built up by the censors, entailed grave consequences in the breach, and also that recourse could always be had by the accused to the *auxilium* of the tribunes of the *plebs* (see below, p. 456 *sq*.).

It must be added that the right of appeal was limited to the city of Rome, where magistrate and citizen were alike 'at home' (*domi*): beyond the *pomerium*, or more probably the 'first mile-stone,' the magistrate was 'on active service' (*militiae*), and Cicero (*de leg*. III, 3, 6) lays down explicitly 'there shall be no appeal from him who exercises command in the field.' This is not the place to discuss the controversial question of the date at which Roman citizens outside the city were rendered immune from the axe and rods of the *imperator*; Cicero may not be expressing the law of his own day, but approving that of an earlier time. That he is right for the Early Republic we may not doubt. Lastly, Festus (p. 216 L.) tells us plainly that in early times the *magister populi*, commonly called *dictator*, was free from the limitation of *provocatio*, but that this was imposed at a later date: it is commonly assumed that the Lex Valeria of 300 B.C. brought about the change.

IV. THE EARLY REPUBLICAN SENATE

But besides the limitations imposed upon the power of the magistrate by the Law of the Constitution, there was a check which the 'custom of the ancestors' made equally effective. This was the necessity of 'taking advice' before embarking upon action in behalf of the state. We have already mentioned the Council of Elders, or Senate, which dated back to the Regal period, and discussed the question whether it was in any sense representative of the *gentes* (pp. 417 *sqq*.). But it was not until Republican times that it became the principal organ of government and the deliberative body by which Roman policy was shaped. It was the supreme example of a *consilium* or 'body of advisers,' such as the general commanding in the field found in his staff, or the *paterfamilias* in his family council. At the present stage we can do little more than approach the question how this body was formed in the early Republic—a question to which our authorities do not give a very satisfactory answer. It is agreed that upon the expulsion of the Tarquins the ranks of the Senate, depleted by the executions of the tyrant, were refilled by what might be called a 'creation of peers'; but although the details are circumstantial, the authorities differ on important points. In the first place, it was in dispute whether L. Junius Brutus or P. Valerius Publicola was the author of the change; Livy names the first, Festus and Plutarch the second. The latter authorities say that the new senators numbered 164; Livy does not give a precise figure, but says that the tale of senators was made up to 300, and this was certainly regarded as the normal number down to the time of Sulla. The story arose, it seems, from an attempt to explain the formula 'qui patres qui conscripti' used in summoning the senators to meet, where 'patres' is evidently used in the sense of 'patrician senators' explained above (pp. 413 *sqq.*). It is natural therefore that the democratic tradition should make the new members plebeians—the effect being to create at once a plebeian majority in the earliest Republican Senate! Livy, it is true, says that they were chosen 'ex equestri ordine'; but what meaning he attached, or could have attached to this phrase it would be hard to say[1]. A trace of a different tradition is to be found in the statement of Tacitus (*Ann.* xi, 25) that L. Junius Brutus created the fresh batch of patricians known as *minores gentes* (cf. p. 419).

In any case, the creation of new senators is represented as the work of one of the first consuls of the Republic; and the constitutional doctrine was plain—that in early times the supreme magistrate, like the kings before him, had exercised his free choice in selecting the *publicum consilium.* Festus states this positively (p. 290 L.) in discussing the expression *praeteriti senatores* used of those 'passed over' on the revision of the roll. After the expulsion of the kings, he says, the consuls and the *tribuni militum consulari potestate* selected those most closely allied with them, at first patricians, then plebeians also, until the tribunician law of Ovinius was passed, by which it was provided that the censors should enrol in the Senate the best men in every rank[2]. This measure will best be discussed in connection with the first recorded revision of the senatorial roll by censors[3]; in the meanwhile it need only be noted that in the narratives of the 'struggle of the orders' the Senate figures as the stronghold of patrician conservatism, and that the first allusion to a plebeian senator in our authorities is found in Livy's narrative under 401 B.C., where he speaks of the election as *tribunus militum consulari potestate* of one P. Licinius Calvus, 'who had held no previous office, but was a senator of old standing.' It is indeed evident that in the post-decemviral period, when the

---

[1] There were actually some who believed that plebeians had found a place in the Senate of Servius Tullius (Zonaras VII, 9, representing Dio Cassius).

[2] The disputed reading in the following word has been discussed in another context (p. 424).   [3] See below, p. 522.

rise of the *plebs* was making progress, its leaders must have found a place in the Senate.

To the patrician members—*patres* in the technical sense—certain privileges were reserved throughout the history of the Republic. Reference has been made to these above (p. 417). When the term of office of the supreme magistrates expired, and no successor had been duly elected, an *interregnum* followed, and the *patres* appointed an *interrex*, or if necessary a series of *interreges* (for no *interrex* could hold office for more than five days) to conduct elections. What was of far greater importance in the earlier days of the Republic, the *patres* ratified all acts of the assembly, whether in legislation or in elections, and without the *patrum auctoritas* such acts were invalid. The reduction of this act to a pure formality was a landmark in the progress of democracy at Rome (p. 530).

The authority exerted by the Senate over the conduct of government furnished the supreme example of the respect of the Romans for the *mos maiorum*. The first section of the Handbook of Senatorial Procedure compiled by Varro for Pompey was devoted to the determination of those who had the privilege *more maiorum* of convening the Senate. In his speech for Cornelius, as we learn from the quotations of Asconius, Cicero examined at length the conditions under which the Senate, *more maiorum*, took upon itself to quash laws passed by the Assembly either directly or by instruction to the consuls to secure their repeal or amendment. There was, however, no method by which the Senate could compel the magistrate to take its advice against his will; in matters of procedure a new precedent might be made, and we hear that Varro in the Handbook above quoted speaks of a *novus mos* recently introduced with respect to the order in which the opinions of senators were invited by the chairman. In the formula of advice tendered to the consuls, says Donatus, the phrase 'if it shall seem good to them' ('si eis videatur') was introduced. This advice, however, came in practice to have a binding force second only to that of law.

V. PLEBEIAN INSTITUTIONS: TRIBUNES: *CONCILIUM PLEBIS*

The nascent Republic was soon brought face to face with a grave political issue, the solution of which was characteristically Roman and unique in the history of political experiment. This arose from the claim of the *plebs* to a share in the government, which had hitherto been exclusively patrician. We find in historical times a dual system of magistracies and of assemblies, corresponding with the *populus* and the *plebs*, and in careful writers and official documents distinctions of terminology are meticulously observed. The officers of the *plebs*—*tribuni* and *aediles*—have the genitive *plebi(s)* added to their title, and this qualification also serves to distinguish the *aediles* of the *plebs* from those set up at a later date (p. 526) as magistrates of the Roman people. The assemblies of the *populus* were styled *comitia*, those of the *plebs* *concilia*. The people issued commands and prohibitions—*iubere ac vetare* are the words applied to their utterances, which alone were Laws (*leges*) in the fullest sense of the word. The *plebs* could in strict parlance only pass resolutions (*sciscere*) and these were properly described as *plebiscita*.

The theory has been advanced that the distinction between *comitia* and *concilium* was due to the subtlety of the later constitutional lawyers. Its most precise expression is to be found in a definition cited from Laelius Felix, a jurist who lived under Hadrian, by Aulus Gellius (xv, 27). In his commentary on the *Digest of the Civil Law* by Q. Mucius Scaevola (p. 330) Laelius wrote: 'He who orders, not the whole people, but a part thereof, to be present, must give notice, not of *comitia* but of a *concilium*. But the tribunes neither summon the patricians nor can they bring any business before them. And so measures passed on the proposal of tribunes are not, strictly speaking "*leges*," but "*plebiscita*," and these enactments were not binding on patricians until Q. Hortensius as dictator (287 B.C.) carried a law that all citizens (*Quirites*) should be bound by the law (*ius*) laid down by the *plebs*.' This is clear enough, and so we find that in a fragmentary law found at Bantia, which may perhaps belong to 101 B.C., we get the expression 'whatever magistrate shall hold *comitia* or *concilium*,' and the phrase *comitiatus et concilia* is used by Cicero in the *de legibus* (ii, 12, 31). We may therefore take it that the distinction was current in the second century B.C. in formal documents, and perpetuated the eternal severance of *populus* from *plebs*, the whole from the part. The parallel expression *lex plebive scitum* is regular in the texts of Republican laws. It is easy to show that in ordinary parlance and in loose writing the distinction was not strictly observed. There was a strong tendency to use *comitia* in the sense of 'elections,' whether conducted by *populus* or *plebs*—the word is even applied to elective assemblies in non-Roman communities; while *concilium*, as the general word for a 'gathering,' might be, and sometimes was, applied to the assemblies of the whole people. But even Livy, who is very lax in his use of terms, can, if the occasion demands it, express himself with due formality, as is shown by the passage cited above (p. 444). We may therefore conclude that the distinction is ancient, and reflects a real and acknowledged dualism in the Roman state.

What then was the origin of this remarkable dualism? There was no doubt on this point in the minds of the Romans. It came into being, so they believed, as the result of the 'struggle of the orders,' the vicissitudes of which filled the first two centuries of Republican history. This movement, which was only ended by the concession to the *plebs* in assembly of a sovereignty co-ordinate with that of the *populus*, is represented by our historians as inspired in the main by economic motives—land-hunger and the intolerable pressure of debt. We have to be very cautious in accepting the highly-coloured version of events which fills the pages of Livy and Dionysius, and the economic conditions of early Rome, in their bearing on the question at issue, are discussed below (pp. 468 *sqq.*). Briefly, it may be said that the struggle was not brought about by the efforts of a non-citizen class to obtain a footing in the community—*plebs* and *patres* were alike *cives Romani*—nor was it in essence a class-war between 'haves' and 'have-nots'; in the main it would appear to have been a movement on the part of the richer plebeians directed towards the attainment of political privilege, but there were without doubt economic grounds for discontent in early Rome, and the leaders of the movement were ready enough to use them in order to gain support and inspire enthusiasm.

The method employed by the agitators was the *secessio*, a 'general strike' of the *plebs*, which marched out to some point outside the city and withdrew from the life of the community, setting up its own assembly and electing its own officers. Tradition tells of three *secessiones*—in 494, 449 and 287 B.C.[1]. The last is unquestionably historical; and scepticism need not be carried so far as to suppose that others are 'projections' of the latest into the past. Unfortunately there is but a small measure of agreement among our authorities in the details given with regard to the earliest *secessio* and the creation of the college of *tribuni*. Varro has the mysterious statement that tribunes of the *plebs* were so-called because the *tribuni militum* were turned into defenders of the *plebs* in the *secessio Crustumerina*. Crustumerium, an ancient town whose territory formed the *tribus Clustumina*, can scarcely have been incorporated in the *ager Romanus* at so early a date, but without knowing more of the authorities followed by Varro we

---

[1] A fourth, in 445 B.C., rests on the doubtful testimony of Florus, a fifth, in 342 B.C., is only recorded as a variant of the usual tradition.

can offer no explanation. Those who reproduced the common form of the legend disagreed as to the spot at which the *plebs* held its assembly: Piso placed it on the Aventine, but most writers spoke of the 'Mons Sacer,' a transparent designation of the scene where the *plebs* swore the tremendous oath to slay any who should violate the sanctity of their officers. There were grave discrepancies, too, with regard to the number of tribunes created in the original *secessio* and the steps by which it was raised to the ten of historical times. Cicero, in an antiquarian digression which he inserted in the lost speech *Pro Cornelio* delivered in 65 B.C., after alluding to the first *secessio*, and the appointment of two tribunes, goes on to say that 'in the following year ten[1] tribunes were appointed in the *comitia curiata* after auspices had been taken.' The learned note of Asconius on this passage is worth quoting at length, as showing that no reliable tradition was preserved.

Some (he says) record that not two (as Cicero has it) but five tribunes were appointed, one from each of the [Servian] classes. But others give the number as two, in agreement with Cicero; amongst these are [Sempronius] Tuditanus and Atticus, as well as our friend Livy, who also (like Tuditanus) adds that three others were appointed by them as their colleagues. The names of the two first appointed are given as L. Sicinius L. f. Velutus and L. Albinius C. f. Paterculus.

Livy, it should be added, does not agree that Sicinius, the leader of the *secessio*, was one of the two first-named, but places him among the co-opted members of the college. Dionysius couples Sicinius with the shadowy figure of L. Junius Brutus, who is said to have adopted his cognomen by way of aping the First Consul.

The next stage in the development is marked by the 'law' said to have been passed in 471 B.C. by Publilius Volero, which transferred the election of tribunes from the assembly of the *curiae* to that of the tribes—*comitia tributa*, according to Livy. Tribal assemblies will be dealt with presently: in the meantime it should be noted that whereas Piso believed that the number of tribunes was now raised from two to five, Diodorus (XI, 68) says that 'four tribunes were now for the first time elected.' It is not at all clear that he means that no such officers had previously existed, and as his notice of the secession of 494 B.C. (if it ever existed) is lost, it would be highly unsafe to infer either that the tribunate was created by this enactment or that the four tribunes represented

---

[1] The omission of the numeral x, found in two copies, is hardly warranted. Asconius *in Cornelianam*, p. 76, Clark.

the city tribes. The full tale of ten was made up, according to Livy[1] and Dionysius, in 459 B.C. Diodorus is silent, Cicero (as we saw) probably assigned the increase in number to 493 B.C., and it is implied in a fragment of Dio Cassius prior to 458 B.C. Suspended during the government of the decemvirs, the tribunate was restored in 449 B.C.[2]; and Livy tells us that the election of ten tribunes took place on the Aventine under the presidency of the *pontifex maximus*, whose name is given as M. Furius by Livy, but as M. Papirius by Asconius; Cicero merely says that the *pontifex* held the election 'since there was no magistrate.'

The above details have been set out at length by way of exception, in order to make two points clear: the first, that no reliable or consistent record of the constitutional changes of the fifth century B.C. existed at Rome, the second (which is less obvious), that attempts were made by constitutionalists, to whom it was repugnant to admit a revolutionary origin for Roman institutions, to show that the tribunes had on occasion been elected with all the forms prescribed by religion and under the presidency of the chief priest of the state[3].

This tendency is shown in other ways. Nothing is more characteristic of the institution of the tribunate than the inviolability or 'sacrosanctity' of the holders of that office. It is stated by Livy in his account of the restoration of constitutional government in 449 B.C. that a law was then passed providing that any who did violence to the tribunes and aediles of the plebs (amongst others) should be *sacer Iovi*, *i.e.* an outlaw, and this was, according to one view, the basis of their claim to sacrosanctity; but this was strenuously denied, and the inviolability of the officers of the *plebs* was based on the oath sworn by that body to slay any man who should lay violent hands upon them[4]. There is a further question with regard to the *sacratae leges*, which are naturally explained as laws to the violation of which the sanction of outlawry was attached. These two were connected by a tradition, which Festus mentions, with the *secessio* of the Mons Sacer: but the list includes

[1] Livy states (III, 30) that two were chosen from each of the five Servian classes.

[2] For Diodorus' version see below, p. 480.

[3] It was asserted that two patricians, Aternius and Tarpeius, who have been mentioned above, were co-opted as tribunes in 448 B.C.; for the story of L. Minucius see above, p. 324.

[4] The case of the aediles was peculiar. Cato (cited by Festus) says that they were included in the 'ancient oath of the *plebs*': but their claim to inviolability was not admitted in later times.

some which were enactments of the *populus*, if genuine, such as the original Valerian law on *provocatio* (p. 447)[1].

We have thus to be cautious in dealing with the often conflicting statements of our authorities: but it is reasonable to believe that in the main the Romans were right in their account of the origin of the plebeian institutions from a revolutionary act which set up a State within the State. This corporation modelled its organization upon that of the Roman people. In the first place it adopted the group-vote. We may recall the fact that the creation of twenty-one tribes (p. 434) is dated by Livy to the year preceding the first *secessio*. We cannot say that there is a causal connection between the two events: it certainly cannot have been the intention of the patrician rulers of Rome to make it easy for the *plebs* to set up a system of political grouping on a purely local basis, free from the religious associations of the *curiae* and the military discipline (and timocratic arrangement) of the *exercitus urbanus*. But it was the obvious method, and we shall do well to reject the notion that the election of tribunes was first made in the *comitia curiata*.

In course of time the convenience of tribal grouping led to the establishment, alongside of the *concilium plebis tributum*, of *comitia tributa populi*. The direct evidence for the existence of such an assembly, though very clear, is for the most part of much later date. The preambles of extant laws, for example, show that consuls put *rogationes* before an assembly of the *populus* voting by tribes. In 58 B.C., for instance, Cicero's bitter enemies Gabinius and Piso held such *comitia* 'in front of the temple of Castor'[2]; in 9 B.C. the assembly met 'in the Forum in front of the Rostra.' None of the three main functions of a Roman assembly—legislation, elections, and trials on appeal—were outside its competence. The first was, in most important matters, reserved for the *comitia* of the centuries; an early example, however, of legislation by tribes is found in 357 B.C., when the *comitia populi tributa* imposed a tax on the manumission of slaves. This body certainly elected the 'minor magistrates,' *i.e.* those who did not possess the *imperium*; and it is just possible that it was first called into being when the quaestorship was thrown open (447 B.C.). In its judicial capacity it was

---

[1] How hard put to it the purists were when they searched for a strictly constitutional basis for the rights of the *plebs* may be seen from the curious passage in Cicero (*pro Tullio* 5, 47) which speaks of 'an ancient law *concerning the leges sacratae*,' which prescribes that he who smites a tribune shall be slain.

[2] *S.E.G.* I, 335.

restricted to the hearing of appeals against fines levied by the aediles (p. 551)[1].

The *plebs* also followed the practice of the *populus* in restricting the initiative in its assembly to its own magistrates. Its resolutions were elicited by *rogatio*, like the *leges* of the people; and the 'right of transacting business with the *plebs*' belonged only to the tribunes and aediles. In the last-named officers we may probably see another example of the modelling of the institutions of the *plebs* on those of the people: for the two *aediles* who (according to all our authorities) were coeval with the tribunes seem to have borne the same relation to them as the quaestors did to the consuls. The name was explained by the fact that the aediles were wardens of the temple of Ceres, Liber and Libera, in which the *plebs* kept its archives, and there is no valid reason for rejecting this view[2]. According to Livy a law of 449 B.C. provided that copies of the Senate's decrees should be deposited with the aediles. Other functions were afterwards conferred upon these officials, who thus came to play an important part in the municipal administration of Rome.

VI. THE DEMANDS OF THE PLEBS: *AUXILIUM*

What were the primary aims of the uprising of the *plebs* and the formation of a State within the State? Leaving out of sight the economic motives discussed elsewhere, we may say that there were three—to secure protection for the plebeian against the arbitrary exercise of the *imperium*, to obtain a clear statement of the Law and of the procedure by which its remedies for wrong might be obtained, and (in the minds of the leaders) to obtain a share in the government of the State and especially in the *imperium*.

To ensure the first the inviolable tribune was authorized to 'bring succour' (*ferre auxilium*) to any citizen who might call upon him. To this end the door of his house remained open by night and day. Never abrogated throughout the history of the Republic, this 'succour,' though at first (we are told) indignantly rejected by the patricians, came to be a constitutional guarantee of personal liberty, and being used to secure freedom from personal arrest to those accused of crime, it helped (together with the right to go into voluntary exile) to bring about the practical abolition

---

[1] Too much stress should not be laid on the expression *comitiatus maximus* used in the XII Tables (p. 447) as implying the existence of the lesser assembly of the tribes.

[2] Other theories have been mentioned above, p. 440.

of the death penalty, which is such a surprising feature of Republican criminal law[1]. More than this, there was gradually developed out of the right to inhibit the action of the magistrate against the private citizen a general power of veto (*intercessio*), which became one of the most effective elements in the system of checks and counter-checks provided by the Roman constitution. This was in fact an extension of the principle of collegiality explained above (p. 443 *sq.*), though it would not be correct to say that the tribune had a *maior potestas* as against the consul.

If we were to believe the historians, we should have to admit that the plebeian assembly of tribes also acted as a High Court of Justice in the same way as the *comitia centuriata* in capital cases tried on appeal, at any rate until the Decemviral code had restricted that function to the *comitiatus maximus*. But the legends in which this doctrine is embodied are more than suspect. The stories of Coriolanus, whose condemnation in 491 B.C. was, according to Dionysius (VII, 50), the first act of the assembly of tribes[2], and of Kaeso Quinctius in 461 B.C., which was evidently cited (Livy III, 13, 6) as archetypal for the practice of allowing sureties (*vades*) for the attendance of the accused, cannot be treated as historical. We have other cases where the penalty proposed is not capital, but pecuniary. The traditions with regard to fines (*multae*) are conflicting. The right to fine is part of the power of coercion inherent in the *imperium*, but according to our sources it was limited by legislation at a very early date. According to Plutarch, it was Valerius Publicola, the author of the first Law of Appeal, who imposed a limit on the power of the magistrate in this respect: and Gellius implies that a limit expressed in terms of cattle was commuted for a money equivalent by the Lex Aternia Tarpeia of 454 B.C. But the more general view was that it was this law which fixed the *multa suprema*, and that the money commutation dates from a Lex Julia Papiria of 430 B.C. On the other hand Festus (p. 268 *sq.*, L.) mentions the fine of two sheep and thirty oxen as fixed by a Lex Menenia Sestia in 452, and a later Lex Tarpeia which converted it into terms of money. We have

---

[1] We are told by Asconius (*in Milon.* p. 47, Clark) that the bench of tribunes met to consider whether this *auxilium* should be extended to a case of serious violence in 52 B.C. and that one member said that no personal injury suffered by himself would deter him from acceding to the appeal as a matter of principle.

[2] Dionysius speaks of a compromise by which the jurisdiction of the *plebs* was allowed subject to the sanction of the Senate. This is a 'constitutionalist' fiction.

already seen that Aternius and Tarpeius are of very doubtful authenticity. Their law, according to Dionysius, applied to all magistrates, including those of the *plebs*[1]; and we do undoubtedly find that in historical times these officers inflict heavy fines and, if these exceed the maximum permitted to the magistrate by way of *coercitio*, allow an appeal to the tribal assembly of the *plebs*, the procedure being the same as in the capital trials before the people. This privilege, then, was undoubtedly permitted to the magistrates of the *plebs*: but the *populus* reserved for itself the last word if the *caput* of the citizen was at stake. We may, however, anticipate later conditions by stating here that in the middle Republic it was the regular practice in cases of treason, not to revive the institution of *duoviri perduellionis* spoken of above, but to allow and indeed request the tribunes of the *plebs* to conduct the prosecution, for which purpose they were obliged to 'borrow a day of the *comitia centuriata*.'

There could be no better example than this of the political genius of the Romans. Looked at from one point of view the plebeian institutions were revolution made permanent—in spite of all the efforts of constitutional purists to fit them into a scheme of orderly development[2]. But this ceased to have significance as time went on: for it was the habit of the Romans to allow institutions apparently discordant to find their *modus vivendi*, and, as conditions changed, to turn them to practical account in unexpected ways. The dealings of the *populus* with the *plebs* are the most striking instance of this, and when the adjustments were made, revolution was indeed made permanent, but—as will be seen later—it was revolution domesticated.

VII. THE DECEMVIRATE AND THE TWELVE TABLES

The agitation of the *plebs* for the codification of the law is narrated with much detail by our annalistic historians. According to Livy and Dionysius[3] the movement began in 462 B.C. when a

[1] It is noteworthy that though Livy omits mention of the law in its natural place, he says that no sooner had Aternius and Tarpeius laid down their office, than they were fined, one by a tribune, and the other by an aedile—the usual story of the proposer of a law being the first to suffer its penalties.

[2] The most curious of these is the suggestion (Dion. Hal. VI, 89) that the first *secessio* was ended by a *foedus*—a treaty between *plebs* and *populus* made with due ceremony under the conduct of the Fetiales.

[3] There are various discrepancies between their versions which cannot be noted in detail; that of Dionysius as usual has a rhetorical colouring.

tribune named C. Terentilius Harsa promulgated a law providing
for the establishment of a commission of five[1] 'to frame laws
concerning the *imperium* of the consuls,' but was dissuaded from
proceeding further by his colleagues, acting on the request of the
Senate. In the following year the proposal was again put forward,
the principal part in the agitation being borne by a tribune named
A. Verginius; this time, says Dionysius, a commission of ten was
proposed, with power to legislate on the whole field of public and
private law. The struggle over these proposals lasted for several
years, in the course of which the *plebs* secured the passing of the
law converting the Aventine into state-property and that of
Aternius and Tarpeius limiting the powers of the magistrate in
the matter of fines, to which allusion has already been made
(p. 457).

At length, in 454 B.C., three commissioners, Sp. Postumius
Albus, A. Manlius, and P. Sulpicius Camerinus, were sent to
Greece to examine the laws of Solon and other codes (those of
Magna Graecia are mentioned by Dionysius) as a preliminary
step. In 452 B.C. they returned, and a Commission of Ten (*decemviri*) was set up to take the place of the magistrates of the year,
with freedom from the limitation which was involved in the right
of appeal. The names of the ten accordingly appear in our Fasti
as those of the chief magistrates of the year in place of the consuls.
They included the consuls already designated for the year 451 B.C.,
Appius Claudius and T. Genucius (or, as Diodorus has it, T.
Minucius), one of those of the previous year, P. Sestius, who had
supported the measure setting up the Decemvirate, the three
commissioners sent to Greece, and others, 'all of whom,' says
Dionysius, 'had served the office of consul.' This is in fact the
case; for the names of all appear in the Fasti of previous years
except that of T. Genucius, and the 'Minucius' of Diodorus' list
may be correct. All the decemvirs were, according to our authorities,
patrician, and this again is true, except for Genucius. The
Minucii, on the other hand, claimed to have been patrician under
the early Republic; but, as we have already noted, their *transitio
ad plebem* is suspicious, as is also the fact that the *cognomen* of
Augurinus, which is borne both by them and by the Genucii, is
obviously derived from the election of a member of each family to
the augurate when thrown open to the *plebs* by the Lex Ogulnia
in 300 B.C. Efforts have been made to discredit the authenticity
of other names in the list, but the arguments adduced are

[1] It appears from a later passage (Livy III, 31) that they were to be
plebeians.

unconvincing. Had we nothing before us but the remains of the
Code and the list in the Fasti, it would be hard to find reasons for
rejecting the tradition.

But the story does not end here. The Commission of Ten issued
a code inscribed on Ten Tables, and these laws, according to
Livy, who breathes the spirit of legal purism, were submitted to
the assembly of the centuries for ratification; but their work was
not complete, and they brought about the election of a second
commission, of which Appius Claudius was again the principal
member. These again appear in the Capitoline Fasti, and although
there was a slight discrepancy in the lists[1], it is quite clear that
plebeians were included; Dionysius, in fact, notes the names of
three, Poetelius, Duillius and Oppius, and, as T. Antonius Merenda
bears a plebeian name and M. Rabuleius that of one of the *tribuni
plebis* of 488 B.C., it is more than likely that the list was invented
on the assumption that five patricians and five plebeians were
elected.

Unfortunately the conduct of the Second Ten was not such as
might have been expected of a body so constituted. They added
'two tables of unjust laws,' as Cicero calls them, including that
which prohibited the contraction of a valid marriage (*conubium*)
between *patres* and *plebs*; and their oppressive rule was brought
to an end by a revolution which arose out of the unjust judgment
delivered by Appius Claudius in the case of the maiden Verginia,
slain by her father's hand according to one of the most famous of
all legends. There was a *secessio* of the *plebs*, modelled on that of
494 B.C. The Senate dispatched three envoys to negotiate, but
their offices were refused; the *plebs* was, however, induced to
return by L. Valerius Potitus and M. Horatius Barbatus, and
constitutional government was restored after the decemvirs had
abdicated. Livy's account of the proceedings is precise. In a
concilium plebis held in the 'Flaminian meadows' (the site of the
circus Flaminius of later times), over which the *pontifex maximus*
presided, ten tribunes were first of all elected; and one of these,
M. Duillius, then proposed the restoration of the consulship and
of the right of *provocatio*. An *interrex* was then appointed, and
Valerius and Horatius were elected consuls. With the legislative
acts which followed we shall deal presently.

The motives of such precision have been analysed in a previous
section (p. 454), and statements like those just quoted scarcely

[1] Diodorus, who only gives seven names, includes one (that of Sp.
Veturius, one of the commissioners of the preceding year), not found in the
other lists.

claim greater credence than the legend of Verginia. Can we use our other authorities—Cicero and Diodorus—to reach a less garbled tradition? Cicero gives us, in the *de Republica* (ii, 36, 61 *sqq.*), a brief account of the decemvirate. He represents the decemvirs as retaining office for a third year, in which Dionysius alone amongst our authorities agrees with him; and this is not in itself probable. He also omits the name of Appius Claudius—though he gives that of D. Verginius as the father of the maiden: from a brief note by Asconius on his speech for Cornelius delivered in 65 B.C. it appears that he there gave no names, 'because,' as his commentator aptly says, 'it is a matter of common knowledge that the decemvir was Appius Claudius, and the father of the maiden L. Verginius.' Yet it has been seriously argued by Niese that names were first invented for the villain and hero of the piece after 65 B.C., and by Eduard Meyer that at that date Cicero had not yet read the annals of Valerius Antias and Licinius Macer in which they were introduced.

But there is a more serious omission in Cicero's narrative. Not a word is said with regard to the law of Terentilius Harsa, the years of democratic agitation which followed, or the embassy to Greece. Cicero writes as follows with regard to the institution of the Decemvirate:

while the Senate was at the height of its power and the people endured and obeyed, a plan was tried, by which the consuls and tribunes of the plebs resigned their offices, in order that Ten Commissioners with the highest authority, not subject to the right of appeal, might be set up, who should enjoy the supreme *imperium* and codify the law.

The omission of any reference to the embassy to Athens need not be taken as a proof that Cicero had not heard of it; from the *de legibus* (ii, 25, 64) we learn that he was familiar with what was a commonplace in antiquity—the derivation of certain of the laws of the Twelve Tables from the code of Solon. But it cannot be denied that his conception of the Decemvirate as the orderly creation of a patrician Senate is very different from that of the political annalists.

Do we find a trace of a similar version, which ignored the acute phase of the 'struggle of the orders' leading up to the Decemvirate, in Diodorus? It would be hazardous to infer this from the fact that he has no notices of political events at Rome in the years preceding 451 B.C., since he has *no* such notices of any kind in the eleventh book (which begins in 486 B.C.) except those relating to Spurius Cassius' *coup d'état* in 485 B.C. and the election of four tribunes in 471 B.C. He therefore gives us no help; his statement that the last two tables were set up by Valerius and Horatius in 449 B.C. is due to a misunderstanding, and his account of the constitutional restoration is, as will appear, more than suspect.

We shall not, therefore, derive much positive result from the analysis of our sources, and must ask ourselves the question, what may be inferred from the Code itself as to its place in Roman History? We shall not here dwell upon the content of those of its provisions which do not bear directly upon constitutional development and the struggle of *patres* and *plebs*, except to note the strange mixture of archaic provisions, such as the *lex talionis* ('if one breaks another's limb and fails to compound with him, let limb be given for limb') and the prohibition of 'charming away' a neighbour's standing corn, with the recognition of plebeian customs such as freedom of testamentary disposition and marriage by cohabitation ripening in a year's time into prescriptive ownership (*usus*), which, however, could be deferred by the wife's three nights' absence. Nor is this the place to speak of the 'methods of pleading at law' (*legis actiones*) and the regulation of procedure, always a matter of primary importance in early law, which is concerned to substitute formalities for unregulated self-help[1]; these matters were naturally given their place in the opening chapters of the Code. Our purpose is rather to determine the place of the Decemviral legislation in the political history of the Republic.

VIII. THE ROME OF THE TWELVE TABLES

The surviving fragments of the Twelve Tables must be accepted as our primary authority for the opening phase of the struggle between the rival orders at Rome. Their evidence, indeed, for a variety of reasons, has to be treated with caution. It is a matter of comparatively trifling importance that the familiar arrangement of the extant material depends, in all cases other than those in which a quotation is assigned by ancient authority to one or other of the Tables, on the somewhat hazardous assumptions of Dirksen about the methods followed by Gaius in arranging his commentary on the Code. But more serious than this are other facts and possibilities. Some of our information about the terms of the legislation is derived from passages which preserve the words, not of the laws themselves, but of a commentator thereon.

[1] The development of the formal side of Roman Law during the Republic will be described in a later volume.

Elsewhere there is suspicion, more or less strong, that glosses have intruded into otherwise sound quotations. And yet again—whether the explanation be found in a re-writing of the Tables after the Gallic sack of Rome or not[1]—it is difficult to doubt that some of the quotations come from versions of the laws which expressed their meaning in the language of a period later than the turn of the fifth century[2]. But on the other hand the high antiquity of the uncorrupted core is proved by its use of words whereof the meaning was a matter of speculation by the end of the Second Punic War[3]; and though glosses may be detected and modernization of the text admitted here and there, the main body of the fragments and the general setting in which tradition places the Decemviral legislation have resisted criticism with success. The attempt of Pais to assign the laws to the *ius Flavianum* broadcast by Cn. Flavius at the end of the fourth century and that of Lambert to father them on Sextus Aelius Paetus Catus at the beginning of the second may be said definitely to have failed. In this matter the sanity of modern civilians has rendered the study of Roman history a service comparable to that which the legal training of his youth enabled Mommsen to perform in the days when Niebuhr and his school were being carried away by the early successes of their critical method.

With such qualifications the surviving remains of the Decemviral laws may be used as contemporary evidence for Roman history in the middle of the fifth century B.C. Their help is essential in answering questions of detail about the condition of the Roman people when the struggle between *patres* and *plebs* had been in progress for forty years, but their help must be invoked as well in the solution of a more serious problem still—the problem of the nature of the struggle. Even the most callous critic of tradition must admit that the final successes of the *plebs* found expression, at least in part, in enactments of a kind which may be described as constitutional. The magistracy was opened to people who had been excluded so long as office remained a patrician preserve, and in general some greater say in the direction of public affairs was given to that section of the population which did not aspire to office at all. But the extent to which the agitation of the *plebs* drew its strength from economic grievances is a more controversial subject, and a decision between the divergent views

[1] Livy VI, 1, 10.
[2] Compare Pliny, *N.H.* VII, 212 with Gellius, *N.A.* XVII, 2, 10 and Censorinus, *de die nat.* 23, 8.
[3] See Cicero, *de leg.* II, 23, 59.

taken in the last hundred years calls for a glance not merely at
the Twelve Tables but at such evidence as may be gleaned from
other sources for the social and economic condition of the Roman
people in the fifth century.

During the period of the later kings Rome had learnt from
Etruria lessons in the arts of civilization: there had been a rapid
cultural advance, of which the outstanding monument was the
earliest temple of Juppiter Optimus Maximus. But it is difficult
to believe that such public works as this were due to a general
increase of wealth produced either by industry or commerce.
Buildings of any pretension are not known to have been numerous,
and such as are recognized by tradition cannot be regarded as
enough to imply resources greater than might be available in an
agricultural state of the dimensions attained by Rome. There is,
indeed, evidence for industry: the story of the guilds whose
formation is ascribed to Numa[1]—the goldsmiths, carpenters,
dyers, leather-workers, tanners, bronze-smiths and potters—may
be historical or not, but it is at least plausible in its suggestion that
these trades were practised in the city's earliest days. Yet this is
not to call Rome industrial. Domestic production of the manufactured necessities of life does not involve an increase of wealth
through industry unless the manufactures are carried on for
export; and evidence for Roman exports is to seek. For various
reasons at various times Rome has never from its foundation until
to-day been an industrial city. Even in periods like that of the
Gracchi, when production for export would have solved a most
urgent problem, industry failed to appear; and the explanation
of its absence in the second century B.C. goes some way towards
disproving its presence in the sixth. For international trade Rome
was badly placed. She owed something to her position on the
Tiber; but that position was valuable far more for its control of
a crossing of the river than for the access which the river provided
to the sea. The elaborate arrangements described in the eighth
book of the *Aeneid* whereby Father Tiber made easy the progress
of Aeneas to the site of Rome are sufficient reminder that only by
courtesy could the Tiber be called a navigable stream. The silting
at the mouth, which it was left for the Emperors Claudius and
Trajan to evade, made the estuary of little value as a harbour; and
the rapidity of the current rendered the journey to Rome from
the sea a laborious business even for river barges. When the
problem of feeding the urban population made it essential to
bring corn up the river, the difficulties were tackled and over-

1 Plutarch, *Numa*, XVII, 2.

come. But though passing traders doubtless paid Rome an occasional call, the familiar pictures of sea-going merchantmen engaged in general trade sailing regularly up and down the Tiber and using a port beneath the Aventine may safely be dismissed as works of the imagination.

Once the theory of maritime commerce in early Rome has been recognized as an assumption, the remaining evidence for industrial production needs no long discussion. First and most striking is the testimony of the earliest treaty between Rome and Carthage (p. 405 *sq.*). Carthage, as might be expected, is insistent on her commercial domination in those regions which she controlled: Rome, on the other hand, is interested in nothing but her political supremacy. The difference between the attitudes of the two contracting powers is marked, and the conclusion which it indicates is that Rome in her earliest republican days was indifferent to those considerations of marketing which must affect every community with a right to be called industrial. The information to be derived from the first treaty with Carthage is confirmed by the evidence of archaeology; and the archaeological remains, besides helping to disprove the view that Rome at this time was the scene of manufacture for export, throw light on another possible source of such wealth as Rome could boast. Though maritime trade may be ruled out, Rome might still have made profit out of traffic across the Tiber. The connections, already mentioned, which seem to have existed between Caere and Praeneste in the seventh century suggest a way of communication which joined Etruria with the Trerus valley and the south; and it has been seen that, before Rome fell under Etruscan control, this route probably found its way across the Tiber at Fidenae. With the extension of Etruscan authority to Rome, traffic presumably began to pass more freely through the city. It is not wholly impossible that the *portoria* mentioned in the earliest days of the Republic[1] were levied to some extent on goods moving between Campania and the Etruscan towns; but it must be added that such revenues as Rome may have derived from customs-dues certainly came in far larger measure from the salt-way which ran by Rome from the pans by the Tiber mouth to the inland parts of Italy[2]. The service of the archaeological evidence is to show that, whether Rome established a position as *entrepôt* between the regions north and south of the Tiber or not, the volume of trade during the fifth century was so small that revenues derived from the passage of goods through Roman

[1] Cf. Livy II, 9, 6. [2] Cf. Pliny, *N.H.* XXXI, 89.

territory cannot have played any noticeable part in the general economy of the State.

Even in the Etruscan age at Rome, when public works were being undertaken on a scale of some pretensions, neither Rome nor Latium in general shows signs of having been more than remotely affected by the flourishing transmarine commerce which had developed in Etruria and Campania. The finds of imported articles are scarce, and their scarceness justifies two definite conclusions. The first is that Roman industrial production was too slight in bulk to leave that margin for export without which imports cannot be attracted in return; and the second that the volume of trade in articles of foreign manufacture which passed through Rome across the Tiber was too small for it to be possible to see in this trade an explanation of Rome's rise to greatness. But there is more than this. At the end of the sixth century stagnation seems to have come over the commerce of Latium. Intercourse with the external world was broken off and was not resumed for two hundred years. Whatever part industry and commerce may have played in the economy of the region down to the fall of the kingship at Rome, during the first two centuries of the Republic Latium depended on its resources in land; and on agriculture, combined with a limited use of pasturage, its inhabitants had in the main to subsist until the revenues won from empire wrought a certain change.

It need not be supposed that the end of the monarchy brought with it any serious cultural set-back at Rome. The traces of foreign imports in Latium during the sixth century are so slight that at most it was only an incipient trade which the young Republic lost. And not all the gains of the Etruscan age were surrendered. In building, at least, the Republic did something to carry on the traditions of the kings. The regal period left monuments like the temple of Diana on the Aventine and the Capitoline temple itself: but against these the fifth century could set the temple of Saturn, which seems at least to have been completed, if not begun, in Republican times[1], and the temple of the Castores, said to have been dedicated in 484[2]. In both of these cases the archaeological evidence for the date is in general agreement with that of the literary authorities. To them must be added the temple of Ceres, Liber and Libera on the Aventine, the opening of which is placed by tradition in 493 B.C.[3] The temples of Ceres and of the Castores have an interest of their own, as evidence for the

[1] See the facts quoted by Macrobius in *Sat.* 1, 8, 1.
[2] Livy 11, 42, 5.   [3] Dion. Hal. vi, 94, 3.

presence of Greek influence at Rome early in the fifth century. Ceres herself is Italian, but the identification of the three deities housed in her temple with Demeter, Dionysus and Persephone and the fact that the building itself was decorated by two Greek artists—Damophilus and Gorgasus[1]—betrays the hand of Greece, which is certainly also to be seen behind the arrival of the Dioscuri. But such signs, which are by no means alone, that the foundation of the Republic did not withdraw Rome from the influence of Greek culture in southern Italy do not prove that Greeks were brought to Rome by attractions of a commercial kind: the chief value of these monuments is as a reminder that in the art of building at least the young Republic could bear comparison with the monarchy in its greatest days. But though there is no foundation for the tale that fifth-century Rome forgot the arts which she had acquired in the sixth, in face of the undeniable reduction of imports almost to the vanishing point it cannot be maintained that the economic history of the early Republic is a history of industry and commerce. The story is rather one of the way in which Rome exploited her resources in land.

The picture outlined by the surviving fragments of the Twelve Tables is one of an agricultural community. In Dirksen's arrangement of the remains the evidence for the occupation of the people whose custom was converted into law by the decemvirs is to be found more particularly in the seventh and in the eighth Tables, where provisions are made to meet the problems of a rustic population, living apparently in *tuguria* (cottages) and concerning itself with the production, among other things, of corn and wine. The usual difficulties of the countryside—boundaries, surface-water, the upkeep of roads and the like—find recognition; but most noticeable of all is the series of enactments against damage to a neighbour's crops by trespass, arson or by the use of charms. Though the law of the Twelve Tables is clearly the law of a city-state, the society in which it was produced had its main interests in the land. Such is the conclusion to be drawn from the contemporary evidence, and it is round the land that annalistic tradition centres the economic life of fifth-century Rome.

[1] Pliny, *N.H.* xxxv, 154.

IX. LAND-TENURE AND THE DEMAND FOR LAND AT ROME

The history of land-tenure at Rome is a subject of great obscurity, but it is one which is not made more lucid by rejecting the beliefs of the Romans themselves. According to the theory which seems to have prevailed in classical times, Romulus divided the territory at his disposal into three parts, of which one was reserved for public purposes, such as the maintenance of the king and the public cults, one became common land, and the third was divided among the *curiae*[1]. Without pressing the meanings of terms which came to acquire a precise and technical significance, it may be said that of these sections the first can be called *ager publicus*[2], the second *compascua* and the third *ager privatus*. Questions then immediately arise. First it must be asked with what truth a phrase like *ager privatus*, which implies private ownership, can be used in connection with the early history of Rome at all. It has been said already (p. 417) that the Romans themselves believed private ownership of land to have been one of their most primitive institutions, and that in this they were probably right. But private ownership in this connection must perhaps be given a somewhat special sense. Whatever other conclusions may be drawn from the fact that *mancipatio* is the Latin for conveyance and that *mancipatio per aes et libram* was its oldest form, one is that the Romans had passed through a period in which chattels alone, as opposed to property in land and buildings, were capable of alienation. That this was true of the time when the ancestors of the Romans were still nomadic is obvious; but there are indications that the customary rules of property did not change at once when the people began to lead a settled life. Though Varro and Pliny do not agree, this much seems to have been recognized by Cicero, who refrains from making private property *in land* a Romulian institution[3]; and Cicero's view is supported by what is known of the later law about gentile claims to the reversion in cases of intestate succession (p. 417 *sq.*). It must be remembered that the provision, probably included in the Tables, for the acquisition of property in land by prescription after *usus* for two years[4] shows that by the middle of the fifth century the advance towards purely private ownership had gone far; but a possible conclusion to which our evidence may point is that the *paterfamilias*, though for most purposes related

---

[1] Dion. Hal. II, 7, 4.   [2] Cf. *ibid.* III, 1, 4.   [3] *De Rep.* II, 9, 16; 14, 26.
[4] VI, 3. See Cicero, *Topica*, 4, 23 and Gaius II, 42 and 54.

to his land as owner to property, was still affected by the customs of the recent past, in which he had so far been only a trustee for his successors that he was unable to alienate the estate, because it belonged not so much to him as to his family in the first place and, more remotely, to his *gens*. If this were so, the consequences would be important. At Rome, as in Solonian Athens[1], the difficulties of debtors would be aggravated by the fact that the customary law belonged to an age in which land could not be conveyed and therefore could not be mortgaged.

It is now time to ask what fraction of the *ager Romanus* was held in private or quasi-private ownership. The brief account of Dionysius is valuable rather for its description of the classes into which land was divided than for any suggestion it contains about the extent of each. Nevertheless there is evidence enough to make it probable that the amount of land held as family property was not a large section of the whole. The Romans of classical times believed that the *heredium* of their ancestors had been a plot of two *iugera*, which meant approximately an acre and a third or a square on a side of eighty yards[2]. This allotment appears in Plutarch's tale of the Claudian settlement at Rome[3], and Livy records that, when Bola was colonized in 418 and Tarracina in 329, the settlers received two *iugera* each[4]. It is true that the whole story of the *heredium* in early Rome has by some been rejected as a false inference from the grants of land made to colonists like these, but it is perhaps more reasonable to see in such colonial arrangements confirmation of the view that at some time or other they had prevailed in Rome. If the repeated statements about the size of the *heredium* may be accepted, the dimensions call for further notice. In Italy during the fifth century B.C. methods of agriculture were not more advanced than those employed in Victorian England; yet the area of the *heredium* was less than half that of the allotments offered by the land reformers at the General Election of 1886. By itself a strip of two *iugera* was certainly too small to support a family, and in these circumstances it seems necessary to assume that tradition is right in admitting the existence of commons and state-lands on which the holders of these exiguous hereditaments also had certain claims. The commons were presumably open as pasture for their beasts, and of *ager publicus* leased by the community they might be tenants.

---

[1] *Ath. Pol.* II, 2, οἱ δανεισμοὶ πᾶσιν ἐπὶ τοῖς σώμασιν ἦσαν. See, however, above, vol. IV, p. 34.

[2] Varro, *R.R.* I, 10, 2; Pliny, *N.H.* XVIII, 7; Festus, p. 476 L.

[3] *Publicola*, XXI, 6.　　　　　　　　　　[4] IV, 47, 7; VIII, 21, II.

Such seem to be the elements of the situation in which the economic discontents of the fifth century were heard. It has been seen already that the origins at least of the centuriate organization are properly placed by our authorities in the regal age (pp. 432 *sqq.*); and since this organization implies that plebeians as well as patricians were free citizens capable of owning land, the struggle of the orders cannot be regarded as a struggle for the emancipation of serfs (see above, p. 435, *n.* 3). The relations of client and patron have been discussed elsewhere (p. 420): here it is only necessary to recall that, whatever they may have been in detail, they were relations between citizen and citizen, however rich one party may have been and however poor the other. But although even the humblest plebeians were able to hold land, it by no means follows that all of them had the opportunity; nor again can it be assumed that the more fortunate, who had a patch to boast of as their own, were always allowed access to the common land without whose aid they could scarcely hope to make a living. In the story of the coming of the Claudii to Rome Plutarch relates that, while the mass were given two *iugera* each, Publicola assigned twenty-five to their leader, Attius Clausus[1]. The suggestion that the good and great owned twelve times as much as their more humble neigh-bours is not to be regarded as an exaggeration. Thanks to their political predominance, the *patres* could apparently do very much as they pleased. While the estates of the more lowly citizens were kept to the minimum dimensions, the patricians acquired acres which in those days seemed broad. And then again, when rights to use common land were at stake or when it was a question of finding tenants for such *ager publicus* as existed in the fifth century, it was the interests of the patricians alone which were con-sidered. Nonius Marcellus preserves a quotation in which Cassius Hemina[2] records that people were ejected from *ager publicus* because they were plebeians; and though it is impossible to defend the frequent use of this passage to prove that the patricians claimed a legal right to exclude all but their own class from the public land, the historian is probably correct when he implies that in fact this was the end which the oligarchs used their influence to attain[3]. It is not, of course, to be argued either that every member of the unprivileged classes found his family property restricted to the minimum dimensions, or that plebeians were wholly excluded from other kinds of land; but the masses had not enough to meet their needs. Lack of land was a grievance,

---

[1] *Publicola*, XXI, 6.   [2] Frag. 17 P.
[3] Cf. Sallust, *Hist.* I, frag. 11 M.

and the grievance provoked an agitation of which the course must now be noticed.

In the century of revolution which opened with the tribunate of Ti. Gracchus, politicians whose programmes needed land for their execution were in the habit of turning first to the *ager publicus*, and it is to the *ager publicus* that champions of the *plebs* in the fifth century are made to look. The details of their activities as recorded by the post-Gracchan annalists are certainly taken to some extent from the agrarian history of the later Republic; but it is difficult to believe that the whole of an elaborate and plausible narrative, spread over a long series of years, is without any foundation in fact. The extent of *ager publicus* in regal Rome cannot even roughly be determined, nor can it be said what fraction of Roman territory fell into this class. When the age of Roman expansion came, conquest was the chief source from which public land was derived: it was a habit of the Romans, when they had defeated a people in war, to deprive them of territory up to about a third of the whole, and though such acquisitions by no means always remained public land, it was to appropriations of this kind that the growth of the *ager publicus* was due. In earlier days, however, when conquered neighbours were often merged in the Roman body politic, they were apparently allowed to keep their land and the *ager publicus* was not increased. But, in spite of this, it does not follow that our authorities are wrong in supposing that public land was known even before successful military operations began to bear fruit.

The story opens with the *rogatio* ascribed to Sp. Cassius Vecellinus in his third consulship, traditionally placed in 486 B.C. Whether Cassius was three times consul or not may be doubted; and in any case no claim need be made for the precise accuracy of the date. But attempts to disprove his existence altogether or to move him into the fourth century have not achieved success, and Cassius himself may be accepted with some confidence as an historical figure of the early Republic. About the details of his agrarian programme Livy and Dionysius are not agreed, and the accounts of both are rendered highly suspect by the improbable circumstances in which the Latins and Hernici are introduced (p. 492 *sq.*)[1]. No more definite conclusion can be drawn with any plausibility than that Cassius proposed to meet the demand for land by making allotments to individuals from the *ager publicus*. To this it may be added that the measure introduced by Cassius failed to become law. After his account of the *rogatio* Livy goes

[1] Livy II, 41, 1; Dion. Hal. VIII, 69, 3–4.

on to describe the *débâcle* in which the career of Cassius came to its inglorious end, and he fails to record any tangible result of the agrarian campaign; but Dionysius (VIII, 76) preserves a tale that the Senate only stopped the agitation of Cassius and his friends by submitting to the people a proposal of its own to appoint ten commissioners who should review the whole question of the *ager publicus* and decide what parts should be leased to tenants and what should be given as allotments to needy members of the *plebs*. Like many other features in the story, the terms of this resolution are influenced by the history of the Gracchan age, but the suggestion that some step was taken by the *patres* is not improbable. If it is wrong altogether to reject the almost continuous agitation of which our authorities make the third consulship of Cassius the start, it is important to notice the form in which the subsequent demands are put; and the form—more clearly in Dionysius, but to some extent in Livy as well—is that of a complaint that the patricians are refusing to take certain steps to which they stood committed. Though Schwegler has been widely and heavily criticized for his assertion[1] that—perhaps in a modified form—the *rogatio* of Cassius actually became law, it can at least be argued on his behalf that the narratives of the succeeding years imply what Dionysius explicitly records—that some nominal success, if no more, was won by the lacklands at the outset of their open agitation.

Of the thirty years which follow the death of Sp. Cassius thirteen are recorded to have seen proposals that his policy should be carried into effect. The incidents narrated are too trivial to call for notice in detail, and only the outstanding features need be mentioned. Already in 485 the *plebs* began to use its most powerful weapon—the refusal of military service[2]; and by 479 B.C. their demands had so far commended themselves to reasonable opinion that they won support from some of the great patricians, of whom K. Fabius Vibulanus was the first. But in spite of its increasing strength the movement failed to produce a change in the uses to which *ager publicus* was put. There was no general distribution of public land in allotments to the *plebs*, and the most familiar of their successes was one which is scarcely relevant to the agrarian history of fifth-century Rome. Tradition assigns to 456 B.C. the law about the Aventine which is associated with the name of the tribune L. Icilius. According to Dionysius (x, 32, 4) this measure, which was passed as a *lex centuriata* in spite of its tribunician origin, was preserved down to his own time in the temple of

[1] *Römische Geschichte*, II, pp. 478 *sqq.* [2] Dion. Hal. VIII, 81, 3.

Diana; and though he does not claim to have seen the text with his own eyes, it is not likely that he made the grave mistakes which have been alleged about the date of an extant monument. Nevertheless the traditional date of the law cannot be claimed as exact: it is enough to say that at some time about the middle of the fifth century the Aventine was turned over to the *plebs*. But whenever Icilius propounded the measure which bears his name, its passage did little, if anything, to satisfy plebeian claims for agricultural land. Down to imperial times, when it became a fashionable quarter for the well-to-do, the Aventine was the home of the humbler classes, and it was as building land that the hill must have been welcomed by the *plebs* when it was assigned to their use by this so-called Icilian rogation.

X. EARLY ROMAN COLONIZATION

Tradition thus fails to ascribe even the smallest success to the plebeian agitation for the distribution of *ager publicus*. Grants of land to individuals were a feature of later history, and it is perhaps the familiarity of this method in Gracchan times which accounts for its prominence in the traditional narratives of the fifth century. But though the demands for land may not have been met by allotments in the Gracchan style, they were not allowed to go wholly unsatisfied. Early Rome adopted the device on which Gaius Gracchus fell back—the device of founding colonies wherein surplus population could be planted in numbers comparatively large. The foundation of colonies seems to have been a recognized method of finding work for idle hands from the earliest days of the Republic, though its use became more frequent in the fourth century. Colonization served a double purpose. The colonists were sometimes sent out 'praesidii causa[1],' to act as garrison in a Roman stronghold, but a colony—in the fifth century B.C. no less than in the second—was also valuable as an outlet for citizens whom Rome could spare. The economic side of colonial foundations justifies tradition in connecting them with the agitation for allotments from the *ager publicus*. Land assigned to a colony—at least if the colony was a Roman foundation—was land which otherwise would presumably have remained public and so have been subjected to that exploitation by the *patres* against which the long-drawn protest was being made. Whatever may be the value of his authority, Livy[2] is wholly plausible when he says that in 467 B.C. Q. Fabius M. f. Vibulanus

[1] Livy IV, 11, 3.   [2] III, 1, 5; cf. Dion. Hal. IX, 59, 1.

staved off the regular demands for a distribution of public land
by an alternative suggestion that a colony should be sent to
Antium—'ita sine querellis possessorum plebem in agros ituram,
ciuitatem in concordia fore.'

Not all, however, of the Roman colonies alleged to have been
established by the middle of the fifth century can be accepted as
historical. Some, like those at Ostia under King Ancus (p. 378)
and at Fidenae at the end of the sixth century[1] (p. 403), are
probably mere anticipations of later history: others, like Norba[2],
were perhaps the work of the Latin League and not of Rome.
But though the versions of Livy and Dionysius call for criticism,
and though it must be remembered that colonies of Roman citizens
could not be founded beyond the limits of Roman territory, at a
time when colonies were being manned by cities of the Latin
League it is wholly natural that, whatever their political status
(see below, p. 541), colonies should have been started by Rome as
well. Political conditions in the fifth century were too unstable for
outlying garrisons always to hold their posts successfully, and the
capture of a place by Rome in the fourth century is no reason for
denying that she had held it in the fifth. The fighting against
Velitrae after the Gallic invasion does not disprove the story that
Velitrae received a colony in 494[3], nor can the settlement at
Antium in 467[4] be rejected merely because the city was captured
in 346. In the fifty years which followed the end of the monarchy
Rome was small and her outposts were neither numerous nor
widely flung; but their existence is recorded and cannot safely
be denied. And if such garrisons were to be found, however
much military considerations may have been responsible for their
dispatch, the demands which they made on the population of
Rome justify their mention in connection with the social and
economic problems of the age.

XI. THE FOOD-SUPPLY

The tales about the outcry for a distribution of public land
imply not only a selfish exploitation by the *patres* of the resources
of the State but also the presence of a population so large that,
if some people had as much land as they would like, others had
to be content with even less than was adequate to meet their
barest needs. This implication that in the fifth century, as in

---

[1] Dion. Hal. v, 43, 2; 60, 4.   [2] Livy II, 34, 6; cf. XXVII, 10, 7.
[3] Livy II, 31, 4; 34, 6; Dion. Hal. VII, 12, 5.
[4] Livy III, 1, 5; Dion. Hal. IX, 59, 1.

earlier times, the number of inhabitants to the square mile in the Roman region was high finds some support in the records of tradition about the corn supply. The poverty of the humbler classes in a community which had no large export trade wherewith to pay for imported food is revealed, not only by the complaints about the burden of debt which will shortly be discussed, but also in stories that on several occasions it became necessary for Rome to buy corn from abroad. Systems whereby the rich made themselves responsible for the feeding of the poor, or which recognized that the maintenance of the masses was an obligation of the State, were a Hellenistic development of the third century B.C., and it is not to be suggested that Rome in the early years of the Republic had adopted an arrangement like that of the later distribution of corn. But no government, however oligarchical, can afford to hold its hand when a crisis arrives in which the territory under its control does not contain enough food to keep the population alive. There need be no question of permanent allowances to the poor or of distribution at prices below the economic figure; but the duty of seeing that citizens do not starve for lack of food upon the market is one which a government cannot shirk. When certain details derived from later history have been discounted, what remains in the narratives of Livy and Dionysius is an unobjectionable account of state intervention to make up deficiencies of food produced at home by purchases from peoples abroad who had food to spare[1].

The distribution of corn attributed to Servius Tullius[2] may be neglected as probably no more than one of the many measures ascribed to that king for no better reason than the fact that he came to be regarded as the first father of the poor. But tales of famines in the fifth century and of measures taken to relieve them cannot be wholly ignored. The subject is one of a kind about which Cato suggests that records had been kept in the annals of the *pontifices maximi*[3], and the stories themselves are appropriate to the age in which they are put. Though the chronology is too weak for any stress to be laid on the coincidence of famines and wars, it is easy to believe that an agricultural community engaged in almost constant military operations might often find its food-supply—which was never too large—brought dangerously low by invasion or by the interference of army service with work upon

---

[1] Cf. in general Dion. Hal. ix, 25 and Livy ii, 27, 5.

[2] *de viris illust.*, 7, 7; Chron. anni 354, p. 144.

[3] Frag. 77 P., non lubet scribere quod in tabula apud pontificem maximum est, quotiens annona cara....

the land. The value of the traditional accounts must be mentioned again in connection with events which follow the Decemviral legislation; and here it will be enough to notice such earlier incidents as are evidence, not only for the danger of starvation in Rome, but for the directions in which Rome turned when foreign corn was needed to make good the deficiencies of the domestic supply. During the disturbances which marked the first years of the Republic economic as well as political help is said to have come from Cumae, and with Cumae the fertile region of Pometia is joined[1]. But more notable and more familiar than this is the crisis connected with the exile of Coriolanus, when corn is alleged to have been sought so far afield as Sicily[2]. It is true that this affair is the occasion on which Dionysius of Halicarnassus (VII, I, 4) reveals a gross mistake made by the later annalists, who asserted that Dionysius I of Syracuse was the benefactor whom the Roman people had to thank for a service rendered sixty years before his birth; but the blunder belongs to an obvious embellishment of the tale and does not destroy its value as evidence for Roman relations with Sicily in the fifth century.

XII. THE LAW OF DEBT

There remains one other feature of the economic situation to be discussed—a feature which brings us back to the Twelve Tables. This is the prevalence of debt and the demand for a reduction or cancellation of interest. According to Tacitus (*Ann.* VI, 16, 3), it was enacted by the decemvirs that no one should practise usury at higher rates than 'unciarium fenus.' The meaning of this phrase is interest amounting to one-twelfth of the principal, and it is probable that such interest was monthly: the result is an annual rate of 100 per cent.[3] The passage, however, raises difficulties, some of which are grave; but the difficulties are not enough to justify the condemnation of Tacitus as wholly wrong. It must be admitted that words open to such diverse interpretations as 'fenus unciarium' here cannot be quoted from the Tables but are merely used by Tacitus in giving his own descrip-

[1] Dion. Hal. v, 26, 3; cf. Livy II, 9, 6.
[2] Livy II, 34, 7; Dion. Hal. VII, 1–2. For Sp. Cassius in the sequel cf. Livy II, 41, 8.
[3] The view, which has been widely accepted since Niebuhr's time, that 'unciarium fenus' is a description, not of the monthly, but of the annual interest has been heavily attacked by C. Appleton in an article (*Nouvelle revue historique de droit*, 1919, pp. 467–543) which demands the most careful consideration.

tion of the rule which the Tables contained. Yet even if the words purported to be a quotation, they could not be rejected out of hand on the ground that they implied a system of coined money and that coinage was not introduced at Rome till more than a hundred years later. For, though 'uncia' in course of time did indeed become a denomination of currency, the ounce was originally a measure of weight, and weight was a standard of value. The long survival of mancipation 'per aes et libram' implies that this method of counting the payment had been a feature of every sale over a period of time long enough to prevent its abandonment even when the advent of coined money had made it an anachronism.

If this period only ended in the second half of the fourth century, it may be assumed that Rome of the decemvirate was still weighing out lumps of *aes rude* whenever it had business to transact, and to a society in this stage the phrase 'fenus unciarium'—or something which Tacitus might describe in these words—is not inappropriate. But a more serious objection to the account given by Tacitus comes from Livy, who attributes a 'rogatio de unciario fenore' to the tribunes M. Duillius and L. Menenius[1] and so suggests that the law assigned by Tacitus to the Twelve Tables was in fact only passed in 357 B.C.—a date made plausible by the undoubted concern of Roman legislators with the debt problem in the years which immediately follow. The suspicion that Tacitus has made a mistake in his chronology is strengthened by Cato's famous announcement[2]—which reads like a reference to the Tables themselves—that the ancestors of the Roman people held it as a custom and enacted it in their laws that a thief should be mulcted in twice the amount concerned and a usurer in four times. If it only refers to a usurer who tries to charge interest at a higher rate than the highest allowed by law, the passage is not incompatible with the evidence of Tacitus; but it must be admitted that the context gives the impression that Cato believed there to have been laws at Rome which absolutely forbade loans at usury. In the circumstances it seems impossible to accept the view of Tacitus with confidence, and complaints against unconscionable rates of interest cannot be counted among the protests of the *plebs* in the first half of the fifth century.

Rates of interest, however, are a comparatively minor grievance in a crisis caused by debt, especially at a time before currency was in use: in the better-known Athenian history of the Solonian age

---

[1] VII, 16, 1.   [2] *de agri cultura, ad init.*

the grievance is not even mentioned. There the cry was for cancellation of debts and for the enfranchisement of debtors who had
been enslaved; and at the time of the first secession this is alleged
to have been the cry in Rome as well[1]. But our knowledge of the
troubles between borrowers and lenders rests on more solid
foundations than tales like those about Valerius Volusus, Menenius Agrippa and Sp. Cassius. The frequent references in our
authorities to the 'nexi,' the debtors with whose plight the story
is concerned, become credible when the grammarian Cincius[2] and
Cicero[3] combine to show that the Tables themselves[4] contained
regulations about the legal relation called 'nexum.' The paucity
of our information on the law of early Rome makes *nexum* a
subject of much uncertainty, but it may be said in general that
nexum was a contract whereby one party received a loan, probably
at the cost of submitting himself to the pronouncement by the
other party of a formula which entitled the lender in case of
default to seize the person of the borrower without judgment.

In the economic history of Rome *nexum* is important as an
institution whereby debt led to slavery and also as one which
suggests that mortgage played only a small part in the life of the
age to which *nexum* belongs. The remedy of the creditor is against
the body of the defaulting debtor: about distraint on his property
there is something approaching silence. The explanation of this
remains obscure. If it were suggested that encumbered property
is a feature which only appears in a later age, the suggestion
would be supported by what is known of securities in early Rome.
The history of security is one in which the position of the pledger
steadily improves. At first he retains neither *dominium* nor
possessio of the pledge: in the end he may even retain both. Thus
at an early stage in the development the lack of references to
mortgage might have been due to the virtual alienation of their
property by debtors before they reached the point at which it
became necessary to enter on a *nexum*. But against this account
serious objections may be urged. If it were true, by whatever
means—legal or illegal—lenders had appropriated their debtors'
land, there would have been a situation incapable of relief without
a restoration of expropriated farms of the kind which in Athenian
history is ascribed to Solon. Yet at Rome, though the troubles
of the debtors lasted long, they seem finally to have ended without
any such drastic treatment as this. And again there is an indi-

---

[1] Cicero, *de Rep.* ii, 34, 59; Dion. Hal. vi, 83, 4. See Mommsen and
Hirschfeld in *C.I.L.* i[2], pp. 190–1.

[2] Festus, p. 176 L.   [3] *de or.* i, 57, 245.   [4] vi, 1.

cation in the Tables[1] that a debtor might reach almost the last extremity and still be a man of property—a situation difficult to envisage if property of all kinds could be mortgaged. For these reasons it is not wholly impossible that the smallness of the part played by land in these transactions may be due to a partial survival of family ownership which prevented real property from being given as security for debt.

Whatever may be the truth about the debtor's land, it is clear that the remedy of the creditors at any rate in the last resort was against their persons, and that the severity of the remedy was chief among the causes of complaint. Defaulters came wholly into the power of their creditors, who apparently might exact their labour from them or sell them abroad into slavery or even put them to death[2]. The Romans themselves even believed that joint creditors might divide the corpse of the debtor, though they admitted that no case was recorded in which this barbarous right had been exercised[3]. But even if, as is perhaps conceivable, the meaning of the Tables[4] in this detail was misunderstood, the plight of the insolvent debtor remains grievous enough to account for the agitation against the hardness of his lot which is described by the historians and confirmed by the Decemviral legislation.

Thus Rome of the early fifth century seems to have been an agricultural community, settled in a land still perhaps famous for its timber (p. 342) but dependent for its living on what could be extracted from the soil. The age was one of frequent wars which, whether they were waged within the Roman territory or without, contrived to interrupt the work of a population so dense that without continuous labour not even a bare subsistence could be assured, and the result of interrupted labour was distress. The food supply of the community as a whole ran short, the poor were forced to seek assistance from the rich, and finally the difficulties were aggravated by the oligarchic exploitation of those resources in land which were at the disposal of the government. Thus the ground was ready for a class-war. The grievances of the poor against the rich were enough to start a fight, and there is no reason to doubt that these grievances played their part in stirring up the *plebs*. But, as in later times, so in the earliest history of the Republic the leaders of the masses profited more than the masses themselves.

[1] iii, 4.   [2] Gellius, *N.A.* xx, 1, 45–52.
[3] Gellius, *loc. cit.* 52; Quintilian, *Inst.* iii, 6, 84.
[4] iii, 6. For the latest statement of the alternative interpretations, see M. Radin in the *Amer. Journ. of Philology*, xliii, 1922, pp. 32 *sqq.*

Almost from the outset the struggle took a constitutional turn, and the most signal success it brought to the unprivileged was no economic triumph but merely the opening of high office to the great plebeians. Doubtless to the many the Decemviral legislation was a gain. Customary rules were formulated and defined, and in procedure a long step was taken from the primitive practice of self-help to something like a system of justice administered by the State. In the matter of debt itself the rights of the creditor were set out, and the debtor who is *iudicatus*[1], by his appearance beside the *nexus* liable to *manus iniectio* without judgment, seems to indicate a growing readiness of the community to intervene. But though the condition of the humbler citizens was gradually improved, their fortunes are only incidental to the struggle of the orders. The thread which runs through the tale and gives it continuity is the long-sustained effort of the *plebs* to limit the *imperium* and to break down the patrician monopoly of its use.

XIII. THE VALERIO-HORATIAN LAWS

We must now consider to what extent the legislation of 449 B.C. gave satisfaction to the political aspirations of the *plebs*. If we were to read the account of the settlement as given by Diodorus (XII, 25) in one of the few passages in which he deals at length with Roman affairs, without previous knowledge, we should naturally assume that it embraced three cardinal measures: (*a*) that ten tribunes should be chosen with the highest authority of all magistrates within the city, to be as it were the guardians of the liberty of the citizens; (*b*) that one of the consuls of the year should always be patrician, and one chosen from the *plebs*; (*c*) that the tribunes of the year, before going out of office, should appoint an equal number to serve for the ensuing year, on pain of being burnt alive. It is impossible to say from what source this strange version is derived. Its author appears to have thought that tribunes had not previously existed, and Diodorus forgot that he had mentioned them in his entry for 471 B.C. The second law is an anticipation of 367 B.C., and the third a confused reminiscence of the legend of the *novem combusti*, connected in one version with Sp. Cassius regarded as a tribune[2].

Livy's account (III, 55) is much more circumstantial. The laws

---

[1] III, 1 *sqq.*

[2] Val. Max. VI, 3, 2; cf. Dio Cass., *Frag.* 22; a different version was followed by Festus.

passed by Valerius and Horatius were three: (*a*) giving to *plebiscita* the force of *leges*; (*b*) restoring the right of appeal (*provocatio*) which the decemvirs had brought to nought, and providing against the creation of a magistracy not subject thereto; (*c*) restoring the sacrosanctity of the tribunes 'by repeating certain ancient ceremonies after a long interval of time' and adding the legal sanction that 'if any man should do hurt to tribunes, aediles, or *iudices decemviri*, his *caput* should be devoted to Jupiter and his goods sold by the temple of Ceres, Liber and Libera'—*i.e.* the temple which served as an archive for the decrees of the *plebs*. This last text must be of fairly early date, since, as Livy makes clear, its explanation was disputed—both as regards the ground of sacrosanctity and the meaning of *iudices decemviri*. Some hold that consuls and praetors were included under this title: but we can see that it refers to the board known in later times as *decemviri stlitibus iudicandis*, which decided cases where the *libertas* of an individual was in question—such cases in fact as those of Verginia in the legend of the Decemvirate. The consuls, according to Livy, further instituted the practice of depositing copies of the Senate's decrees with the aediles of the *plebs*; and a tribune, M. Duillius, passed a *plebiscitum* prescribing the death penalty for him who should 'leave the *plebs* without tribunes or set up a magistracy not subject to *provocatio*.'

We are not in a position to say how much historical truth is contained in this account: the right of *provocatio*, it will be remembered, was guaranteed by the Twelve Tables and did not need further enactment. But the *plebs* evidently regarded the Consulate of Valerius and Horatius as a landmark in the history of its rise; and we can believe that the Roman people at this date accorded recognition—though not as yet sovereignty—to the new corporation, and gave its officials a definite place in the constitution.

In this respect the most remarkable feature of the settlement was the law which made the decrees of the *plebs* binding on the patricians. Nothing could be more explicit than the statement of Livy on this point:

> Seeing that it was, so to speak, a disputed point of law whether the *patres* were bound by resolutions of the *plebs*, they [the consuls] passed a law in the assembly of the centuries, to the effect that commands uttered by the *plebs* in their tribes should be binding on the people; which law furnished the proposals of tribunes with a weapon of keenest edge.

Dionysius (xi, 45) adds the *Sanctio*, which fulminates sentence of death and confiscation of goods against all who should undo or contravene this enactment.

It is impossible to accept these statements without careful examination. If true, they would imply that as early as 449 B.C. the Roman people delegated the legislative power without reserve to the corporation of the *plebs*, which would then have been able to realize the whole of its aims without let or hindrance. In fact more than a century and a half of political strife lay between the *plebs* and the fulfilment of its aspirations. It was universally agreed that in 287 B.C., as the result of the last secession (to the Janiculum), a plebeian dictator, Q. Hortensius, carried a law to the effect that 'what the *plebs* should command should bind all Quirites.' The terms of the law are given in almost the same words by Pliny the Elder[1] and Laelius Felix; Gaius (*Inst.* 1, 3) says that the *patres* formerly declared that they were not bound by *plebiscita* because they had been made without their ratification, but that by the Lex Hortensia *plebiscita* were 'made of equal force with *leges*,' which is expressed by Pomponius in the words 'it thus came about that the difference between *plebiscita* and *leges* rested in the form of enactment, their force being the same.' The jurists were of course only concerned with the Law of the Constitution as finally established, and it was no part of their task to trace the history of the question. But in Livy we find a law making *plebiscita* binding on the whole people attributed not only to Valerius and Horatius in 449 B.C., but also to the first plebeian dictator, Q. Publilius Philo, in 339. He is credited by the historian (VIII, 12) with two measures, (*a*) that *plebiscita* should bind all Quirites, (*b*) that the *patres* should ratify measures proposed in the *comitia centuriata* before the vote was taken. Of the significance of the second law we have already spoken; there is no reason to dispute the truth of Livy's statement. The first, however, is identical in purport with the laws of 449 and 287, and this triple enactment of the sovereignty of the *plebs* has naturally exercised the minds of modern historians, who have propounded various solutions of the problem.

It has been suggested that the accounts which we possess of the two earlier laws are incomplete, and that some limiting condition has been omitted, *e.g.* that the resolutions of the *plebs*, with or without the approval of the Senate, must go forward to the assembly of the centuries for confirmation; or that the *auctoritas patrum* was required at first, that it was then reduced to a formality, and finally abolished; in other words, that the first law merely

[1] *N.H.* XVI, 37. Pliny is our earliest authority, since we do not possess the narratives of Livy or Dionysius for 287 B.C. He tells us that the law was passed at an assembly in the *Aesculetum*.

recognized the right of the *plebs* to pass ordinances binding upon itself, and that the conditions under which they might become applicable to the *populus* were altered and that finally all restrictions were done away with. In that case it is clear that our authorities misunderstood the purport of the earlier laws.

Others have maintained that Livy was wrong in referring to decrees of the *plebs*, and that the enactments of 449 and 339 B.C. dealt with the powers of the *comitia tributa populi*. For what it is worth, we have the testimony of Dionysius that patricians took part in 'tribal assemblies' (φυλετικαὶ ἐκκλησίαι), but were outvoted by the plebeians and the poor. But Dionysius, who was not capable of grasping the subtleties of Roman Constitutional Law, was not very clear as to the distinction between *comitia populi* and *concilium plebis* (see above, p. 451). In an earlier passage (ix, 41) he distinguishes the *comitia curiata* with *probouleuma* and auspices, from the tribal assembly with neither; we may perhaps excuse the translation of *patrum auctoritas* by *probouleuma* on the ground that in his own time it was given in advance; but the tribal *comitia* certainly had auspices, since Julius Caesar took them in 45 B.C. for the election of quaestors.

There is, however, some reason for thinking that its decrees were not subject to the *patrum auctoritas*; for there is an argument expressed in almost identical language, suggesting a common source, which Livy (vi, 41) puts into the mouth of Appius Claudius, opposing the Licinio-Sextian laws in 367 B.C., and which Cicero himself uses in the speech *de domo sua* (14, 38). Both are speaking rhetorically of the dire consequences which will follow, in the first case, if the highest magistracy is thrown open to the *plebs*, in the second, if the practice of *transitio ad plebem* becomes common. 'Soon,' it is urged, 'there will be no *patres* to give *auctoritas* to the decrees of the *comitia curiata* and *centuriata.*' It seems to be implied that the tribal assembly, which in later times met indifferently as *comitia* and *concilium*, according to the office of its president for the day, was not subject to the *auctoritas patrum*. But nothing could be clearer than the importance attached to the distinction between *populus* and *plebs* in Livy's account of the laws, and it does not seem possible to refer them to anything but a strictly plebeian body.

Radical critics naturally reject the Valerio-Horatian law as a fiction of the democratic annalists, for whom 449 B.C. was a landmark in the history of popular liberties. But we have to face the fact that laws of fundamental importance, such as the *lex Canuleia* permitting *conubium* between the orders (445 B.C.), the Licinio-

Sextian rogations of 367, and the *Leges Genuciae* of 342 (p. 529), were passed by the *plebs* before 339 B.C. It may therefore be best to admit that in 449 a law was passed giving validity to the resolutions of the *plebs*, which the patricians long contended were not binding on them because enacted without their consent, and (as long as they could) disregarded *de facto*: thus, as we shall see, the provision that one consul must be plebeian and the law that the office might not be held twice were in practice disobeyed. Not until 287 B.C. was the *controversum ius* finally made plain by agreed legislation.

CHAPTER XV

ROME AND HER NEIGHBOURS IN THE FIFTH CENTURY

I. ROME, LATIUM AND THE HERNICI AT THE BEGINNING OF THE FIFTH CENTURY

THE opening decades of the fifth century were a period of outstanding importance in Italian history. If republican Rome had been strong enough to retain unimpaired the authority in Latium which had been wielded by the latest kings, the process whereby Italian unity was finally achieved might have been set in motion two hundred years before it actually began. In Italian affairs the first and gravest issue presented after the monarchy

Note. The chief authorities for this chapter are Livy, II–v, 23, Dionysius of Halicarnassus, *Roman Antiquities*, v–x together with so much of bk xi as is extant and the surviving excerpts from bk xii, and the notices of Roman affairs contained in Diodorus, xi–xiv, 102.

In the opinion of the present writer, certain documents of the regal age and of the early Republic survived at Rome into classical times, but the main source on which the Roman annalists had to rely for their knowledge of this period was a body of material preserved by oral tradition in the ancestral tales of the great families and in the πάτριοι ὕμνοι. For the Republic the Fasti are in the main sound from the beginning of the fifth century, and their soundness is proof that even at this early stage public records were kept. The existence of such records makes it possible that the *annales maximi* were based on information set down at the time of the events it described: this cannot, indeed, be proved of the fifth and fourth centuries, but attempts to rule out such a source in the period before 300 B.C. have not been altogether successful. For the external history of Rome in the early Republic, on which tradition is definitely less corrupt than it is on the constitutional development, oral sources continue to be of value.

The author of this chapter believes that the nearest approach now possible to the traditions in their original and uncontaminated form is offered by Diodorus, whose authority is earlier than the Gracchan age and therefore comparatively good. The possibility that it was Fabius Pictor cannot be ignored. Meyer's attempt to show that the source was Latin, though plausible, is perhaps not wholly cogent; but, if his case were proved, there would be much to be said for his proposal to recognize the authority in Cassius Hemina. Whether he be Fabius or Cassius or some other writer, the historian behind the Roman sections in Diodorus here belongs to the early age of Roman annalistic and so commands respect. (See, however, p. 318 *sq.*)

A map, 'Rome and her neighbours,' will be found opposite p. 333.

collapsed was this—Should the fifth century see an extension of Roman influence towards Campania and the south? Or should Rome's political horizon still be fixed along the boundaries of Latium? The question was simple and the answer plain. So far from building still further on the foundations laid during the regal age, Rome was to feel the foundations themselves give way. Instead of winning new conquests outside the Latin region, she was first to lose ground in Latium itself; and the history of her external affairs for a century and a quarter before the coming of the Gauls is a tale of very varied fortune, in which the final gain is small. First, for more than half a century Rome is on the defensive, holding her own indeed, though nothing more. And secondly, after a breathing space of twenty years, comes a brief period of Roman success. Enemies who had lately been an aggressive danger were brought definitely under control: Veii itself was captured: and on two fronts the way lay open for a new advance. Then came the Gauls, and the fulfilment of Rome's promise was again postponed. The achievement of the fifth century was not indeed thrown away, but though its potential value remained, its immediate result was to leave Rome, when gains and losses had been cancelled out, very much where she had stood when the century began.

The troubles of Rome were due in part to the advance of peoples who had hitherto lain outside her ken, but in the first place to a movement in Latium against Roman supremacy. Out of the confusion in which Tarquinius Superbus disappears nothing emerges save the fact that Rome was compelled to meet serious onslaughts from more enemies than one. The evidence does not admit of a detailed narrative, and the suggestion that Porsenna was so far successful as to dismantle the walls of Rome is scarcely more a hypothesis designed to explain the ease with which the city was captured by the Gauls a century or so later (p. 563). Nothing more can be said than that the young Republic defeated all attempts at a monarchical restoration and faced the future under the leadership of an oligarchy whose outlook was definitely Latin. But from the monarchy the government of republican Rome seems to have inherited at least enough of patriotic ambition to cling with such tenacity as it could command to that hegemony in Latium which the kings had at length secured. If the first treaty between Rome and Carthage is rightly dated by Polybius[1], it implies a very natural attempt by the Republic to claim the reversion of that predominant position among the Latin cities

[1] See below chronological note 1, p. 859.

which Rome had shown most clearly during the career of the second Tarquin. The combination, however, of Etruscan efforts to retain a foothold on the Latin bank and of Latin movements against a Rome which was weakened by other commitments soon destroyed the prospect of an easy succession to the legacy of the sixth century.

The first incident after the expulsion of the kings which can be accepted as historical is the struggle between Rome and the Latin cities, which culminated at the battle of Lake Regillus and was ended by the treaty associated with the name of Spurius Cassius Vecellinus. In the period of the Etruscan retreat to the Tiber certain Latin cities seem to have formed combinations whose object was to secure Latium for the Latins. One such union is perhaps recorded by the inscription quoted in a fragment of Cato's *Origines*[1]: *lucum Dianium in nemore Aricino Egerius Laeuius Tusculanus dedicauit dictator Latinus. hi populi communiter: Tusculanus, Aricinus, Lanuuinus, Laurens, Coranus, Tiburtis, Pometinus, Ardeatis Rutulus.* In this document the small number of the members, which suggests that it cannot be earlier than a time when the larger states of Latium had absorbed many of their more insignificant neighbours, combines with the presence of Pometia and the absence of Signia and Norba to indicate a date at the end of the sixth century. Moreover, the omission of Rome from so influential a league may be evidence that the humbling of Rome—an achievement perhaps made possible by the expulsion of the kings—was at least one of the purposes for which the league was formed. But though this organization may well belong to the period of Rome's weakness during the infancy of the Republic, it would be rash to see in it the federation with which the *foedus Cassianum* was concluded. The league which finally compelled Rome to exchange her hegemony for the position of an equal undoubtedly had its headquarters *ad caput (aquae) Ferentinae* (p. 405). Since it must have been under Latin, and not under Roman, control, the long-accepted theory which identified it with a spring near Marino cannot be received; but the search for a more plausible site has reached no definite result. On the whole, in spite of doubts recently expressed, probability favours a location somewhere in the direction of Aricia, though the *aqua Ferentina* cannot reasonably be sought in the *nemus Aricinum* itself. If Livy (II, 38, 1) indicates a point near the track along which the Via Appia was built, his evidence tends against any attempt to find the *caput aquae* on the north side of the Lago di Nemi, where the sanctuary

[1] Frag. 58 P.; *cf.* Festus, p. 128 L.

of Diana lay. Thus if the *aqua Ferentina* and the *nemus Aricinum* cannot be associated, though both may have been within the territory of Aricia, it is unsafe to identify the league once commanded by Laevius Egerius with the great Latin League of the fifth century.

Though most of the cities mentioned in the inscription at Aricia undoubtedly belonged to the federation which met in the *lucus Ferentinae*, it cannot be proved that the union whose members are known from the Arician text was the league which concluded the *foedus Cassianum* and not rather a group of powerful states, formed when the weakening of Etruria seemed to invite a Latin *revanche* and afterwards developed into a larger organization whose headquarters were no longer in the precinct of Diana but at a spring probably not far away. Of the cities named in the dedication, Lavinium, Ardea, Lanuvium, Aricia with Cora and Pometia behind, and finally Tusculum lay in a continuous line round the frontiers of Roman territory from a point near Ostia as far as Gabii. But there the ring was broken, and of the leading powers in the league Tibur alone remained. From the other members Tibur was cut off. Between Tusculum and the *ager Tiburtinus* Labici, Pedum and, above all, Praeneste seem to have stood aloof; nor were Nomentum and Crustumerium enrolled to fill the gap between the western boundaries of Tibur and the river. The evidence for later developments whereby the league was enlarged is too scanty to justify speculation about details. The list of thirty cities, given by Dionysius (v, 61, 3) as those which belonged to a league directed against Rome, is shown to be a late invention by its alphabetical order, by its inclusion of Laurentum as well as Lavinium, and by other indications; but it is clear that all the really formidable opponents of Roman supremacy in Latium are to be found in the list of peoples whose names have been preserved by Cato. They formed the nucleus of the Latin alliance which Rome was called upon to face in the early years of the fifth century.

The traditional account of the struggle between Rome and the Latin states united to throw off her hegemony is heavily loaded with matter which has no right to be regarded as historical. In the whole narrative only two features need be seriously considered—the battle of Lake Regillus and the *foedus Cassianum*. Of the battle it is possible to say little more than that it was fought, that on the Latin side a leading part was played by Tusculum, and that the issue was something less than a complete victory for Rome. Neither of the dates offered by antiquity—499 and 496—

can be accepted with any confidence, because one of these two years, in which the consulship was held by the heroes of the battle—T. Aebutius (499) and A. Postumius Albus (496)—was an obvious choice for later annalists whose passion for precision outran the information at their command. Again, the purely Greek origin of the tale which told how the Dioscuri intervened cannot be refuted, nor can the interest of third-century Rome in Regillus be proved, by the reverse type adopted for Roman *denarii* when the issue of these coins began in 268 B.C. In this context the two horsemen are certainly meant to represent the Penates Populi Romani, and they are without any kind of reference to fifth-century history. But though much of the later Roman account must be rejected as worthless accretion, accretions demand a solid foundation: the tradition of the battle itself would be inexplicable unless some kind of battle had taken place, and without a war between Rome and the Latins the *foedus Cassianum* would scarcely be intelligible. If this treaty can be accepted with the confidence which the evidence seems to justify, it implies a battle in circumstances which tradition ascribes to the battle of Lake Regillus. Treaty and battle hang together, and both may be received. But though a battle was fought, little more about it can be said. The prominence of Tusculum in the dedication of the *nemus Aricinum* lends a certain plausibility to the tale that in the campaign of Regillus Tusculum was prominent. The lake itself is probably to be identified with the Pantano Secco near Tusculum itself, but of the Tusculan general—Octavius (or Octavus) Mamilius—it would be rash to say whether he is historical or not. To this nothing further can be added except that the terms of the *foedus Cassianum* contain a strong suggestion that shortly before the conclusion of that agreement Rome had fought a battle against the Latins with a result rather less glorious than the victory of which the Dioscuri were alleged to have brought the news to Rome.

The evidence for the *foedus Cassianum* is as good as evidence for the early fifth century in Italy can be. Livy (II, 33, 9) makes casual reference to the preservation of its text inscribed on a bronze *stele*, and Cicero (*pro Balbo*, 23, 53) adds that within his own memory this document had stood before the Rostra, where it was an object of common knowledge. Its removal was probably made necessary by Sulla's changes at the western end of the Forum. Dionysius (VI, 95, 2) gives the terms. Between Rome and the Latins there was to be perpetual peace. Neither side was to invite attacks on the other by third parties, or to give unmolested passage through its territory to enemies of the other. If one side were attacked, the other was to give the defence every assistance in its power; and each contracting party was to take half the booty won in such wars as were conducted by both parties together. Suits arising out of private contracts were to be tried within ten days at the place where the contract at issue had been made. And, finally, no alteration in the terms of the treaty was to be admitted without the unanimous agreement of the Latins and of Rome. There is no need to argue at length that the account given by Dionysius is a mere summary and not a complete translation of the treaty; but definite proof of his omissions is perhaps to be found in a passage from a 'foedus Latinum' preserved by Festus (p. 166 L.)—though it is rash, as is often done, to assume that the instrument from which this quotation comes is the *foedus Cassianum*—and in a remark of the grammarian Cincius for which Festus again is responsible (p. 276 L.). From Cincius' somewhat unconvincing description of the way in which a 'praetor' was chosen at Rome in those years when it was Rome's business to supply a commander for the combined forces of herself and the Latins, it is possible to argue that the treaty contained some arrangement which secured annual alternation between Rome and the League in the provision of a generalissimo when such an officer was needed. But though the account of Dionysius is not complete, there cannot be any serious doubt that it is no mere invention but a substantially accurate summary of the text which had still been standing in the Forum three-quarters of a century before he wrote. For its accuracy there is strong evidence in its failure to support the annalists' repeated suggestion that during the fifth century Rome was, not the mere equal ally, but the leader of the Latin League. If his report may be accepted, Dionysius adds another fact. His version, and particularly what it has to say about the distribution of booty 'from wars fought in common' (ἐκ πολέμων κοινῶν), makes it clear that the agreement was no mere domestic arrangement made inside the Latin League to curb the excessive pretensions of Rome, but a treaty between two powers whose independence of one another proves that Rome was wholly outside the League[1].

The date of the treaty has provoked discussions which for the most part add nothing to our knowledge of Roman history. It appears from the passage of Livy that on the *stele* in the Forum the name of a certain Spurius Cassius was mentioned as that of a consul at the time when the agreement was concluded; and,

[1] The juridical aspects of the treaty are discussed elsewhere (p. 549 *sq.*).

according to the Fasti, Sp. Cassius Vecellinus was consul three times—502, 493 and 486 B.C. To the second of these years the treaty is assigned by tradition. Modern speculations which seek to set tradition aside vary over roughly a century in their choice of an alternative date. The limits may be put at 380 and 280 B.C. At the start, all theories advocating a time later than 338 may be dismissed, because from that year onwards no Latin league was in existence with which such a treaty could be made (p. 591 *sq.*). There remain suggestions to the effect that the renewal in 358 by Rome and the Latins of the 'foedus vetustum, quod multis intermiserant annis,' which is recorded by Livy (VII, 12, 7), was really the renewal of a treaty made, not at the beginning of the fifth century, but earlier in the fourth. If it is true to say that during the closing years of the monarchy Rome exercised an extensive authority in Latium, the *foedus Cassianum*, which leaves the Latin cities masters of their own fates, must belong to a period in which Rome's fortunes had sustained a reverse. In spite of the successes which she had lately won against the Volsci, the Aequi and, above all, against southern Etruria, the great Gallic invasion might possibly account for the weakness of Rome at the time of the negotiations with Latium. But when the Gauls arrived, Roman prospects were bright; and the Gallic menace was a somewhat transitory cloud. Though such a date is not wholly inconceivable, the years following the departure of the Gauls are not the most plausible period for a display of Roman humility (see below, pp. 569 *sqq.*). But the most powerful argument against such a reconstruction is the absence of any cogent reason for departing from tradition. Unless the account of early Latium accepted here is wholly wrong, there did exist a Latin league in the fifth century with which Rome might make a treaty. Again, if the view taken above of Roman activities under the later kings is right, early in the fifth century Rome unquestionably did suffer a set-back of the kind which the traditions of Regillus and the *foedus Cassianum* combine to suggest. The fact that the Cassii of later centuries are plebeians is, in the opinion of the present writer, no argument against the appearance of a Cassius in the Fasti about 500 B.C. And finally, though chronological precision is not to be supposed, scepticism cannot be allowed its claim that the Fasti preserve no serious record of the men who governed Rome in the time of Cleisthenes and Themistocles.

The course of events after the expulsion of the kings thus seems to be that for a moment, marked by the first treaty with Carthage, Rome tried to maintain the position she had enjoyed in the time

of Tarquinius Superbus, but that before long the Latin cities
began to combine in an attempt to free themselves from external
control, whether Roman or Etruscan. Between Rome and the
Latin League there followed a war wherein the pretensions of Rome
were so far reduced that she agreed to live outside the Latin
federation and to refrain from attempts at political control. Such
were the circumstances of the *foedus Cassianum*. At that point,
however, matters could not rest. Rome and the Latins alike
were confronted with dangers which gave each party need of
the other's help. Across the Tiber the Etruscans were still an
active menace, and behind the Alban hills Aequi and Volsci were
advancing.

The strongholds of the Volsci in the Monti Lepini were
divided from the Aequian country by the valley of the Trerus,
and in this valley lived a people of uncertain ethnical connections
—the Hernici. Their territory was small, but such few cities as
they could claim had formed themselves into a league of which
the most considerable member was Anagnia. With this league
Rome had perhaps come into contact before the end of the sixth
century, but it was at some time soon after the conclusion of the
foedus Cassianum that Rome and the Latins took the Hernici into
partnership to form a triple alliance. Of the circumstances in
which Rome gained this new support the accounts of Dionysius
and Livy are suspect. Though in detail they diverge, in general
they agree that the Hernican alliance was secured by Sp. Cassius
in his third consulship (486 B.C.) and that it was the outcome of
fighting between the Hernici and Rome.

Livy[1] alone is responsible for the suggestion that part of the
Hernican territory was earmarked for division by the abortive *lex
agraria* which Cassius is alleged to have proposed. In all this it
is difficult to take seriously anything more than the implication
that the treaty with the Hernici was made soon after the *foedus
Cassianum*. Since the terms between Rome and the Hernici were
supposed to be identical with those on which Rome and the Latins
had agreed[2], it was natural to make Sp. Cassius the negotiator
of the second treaty as well as of the first. Though this may have
been the case, it is too obvious an inference, which some annalist
may have drawn, to be accepted with even the slightest confidence.
And again, though their position between Aequi and Volsci—
both of whom at this time were aggressive—may have made the
Hernici anxious for the help of Rome, the suggestion that they
purchased her alliance by a surrender of territory is even more

---

[1] II, 41, 1.   [2] Dion. Hal. VIII, 69, 2.

difficult to believe. With Etruria still pressing her from the north
and with the Volscian danger imminent in the south, Rome was
in no position to drive hard bargains with possible supporters,
least of all when their support could serve so useful a purpose as
that which the Hernici might achieve. To secure a wedge of
friendly country in the valley of the Trerus and so to impede a
junction of Volscian and Aequian forces was too valuable a gain
for Rome to run any risk of its sacrifice. And, finally, the supposed
annexation of Hernican territory is made still less convincing by
the way in which it is connected with the doubtful tale of the
rogatio Cassia agraria.

On the whole it is unsafe to say more than that at some time
soon after the treaty between Rome and the Latins was concluded,
the two parties made a similar agreement with the league of the
Trerus valley. Thus the Roman Campagna was at peace with
itself, and in its Hernican allies it had an invaluable buffer between two of its most dangerous enemies—the Volsci and the
Aequi. Though dangers from north and south at times grew so
great as to call for the united efforts of the three allies on a single
front, geography made it the primary business of the Latins and
the Hernici to deal with the Aequian and Volscian threat, while
Rome's affair was with Etruria. Such was the condition in which
Latium faced its invaders during the fifth century.

II. THE SABINES AT ROME

In the early years of the Republic, from the fall of the monarchy
to the middle of the fifth century, there appear scattered and disconnected allusions to trouble between Rome and the Sabines.
These Sabines were a northern outlier of the great Oscan-
speaking people and they formed a link, running east of Latium,
which joined the main Oscan region to the Umbrian country in
the north. Though there is a narrow strip beyond the Anio which
has some claim to be regarded as Latin from the first, the Tiber
from Orta to Antemnae, and the Anio thence to its upper waters,
may roughly be said to mark the extreme limits of Sabine occupation. It was with the south-western borders of this area that the
Romans found themselves in contact.

The Sabines were a unit only in an ethnic sense. Though they
seem to have thought that the district round Reate had been the
peculiar home of the stock from which they sprang, the communities of which this people was composed were politically disunited. In the progress towards political federation they lagged

far behind neighbours like the Hernici and the Latins, and consequently the danger which they threatened to the Latin plain was slight. When the pressure of population along the central Apennine, which in the end brought the Aequi to the frontiers of Latium, thrust onwards the Sabine communities in its way, the Sabines came in groups so small that Rome found it easy to repel such as were not allowed to settle in Roman territory. It would be unprofitable to examine in detail the whole of such scanty records as are preserved of Sabine movements in the sixty years which follow the establishment of the Republic at Rome; but in the history which begins in 505 B.C. and ends with the defeat of the Sabines in 449 after their victory of the previous year there are two episodes which repay consideration. The first is the arrival of Attius Clausus in Rome. In 505, according to the reckoning of Livy (II, 16), when Rome and the Sabines were in conflict, a section of the Sabine people which preferred peace to war migrated into Roman territory under the leadership of this chief. Attius Clausus, henceforward known as Appius Claudius, was admitted to the patriciate and soon became a leader in the state, and his whole following were granted Roman citizenship and settled on lands beyond the Anio. Such was the advent of the Claudian *gens*. The second is the affair of Appius Herdonius, placed by Livy (III, 15–18) in 460. With a suddenness and lack of preliminaries which recall the mysterious recovery of Sardes by the Persians in 498, Appius Herdonius, with a Sabine army of 2500 men, was found one night in possession of the Capitolium at Rome. In the circumstances which follow, so large a part is played by conflicts between tribunes and Senate, which are woven into the narrative of the agrarian agitation, that the tale is more relevant to the constitutional and economic development than to the history of Rome's relations with her neighbours. At last, however, the Capitoline was stormed, Herdonius was killed, and those of his followers who survived were put to death in ways appropriate to their varying conditions.

These incidents, trivial in themselves, deserve notice for the part they play in a theory which has won wide acceptance, but which, nevertheless, is almost certainly to be rejected. It is the view of Pais[1] that the expulsion of the Etruscans from Latium was the work, not of the Latins themselves, but of Sabine invaders, that Rome was conquered by the Sabines in the first half of the fifth century, and that of this conquest, which was not com-

---

[1] For the fullest statement of his case see *La conquista sabina di Roma verso la metà del V. secolo a. C.* in *Ricerche*: Serie prima, pp. 349–364.

pleted at a single stroke, we have such records as Roman tradition
was prepared to admit in stories like those of Attius Clausus and
Appius Herdonius. The end of this Sabine incoming is said to
be marked by the Roman victory of 449, after which nothing more
is heard of Sabines until the Samnite wars.

Such speculations call for the utmost caution: written history,
language and archaeology alike provide grounds for scepticism.
It would be unwise to deny the possibility that the Roman
version of a foreign conquest of the city was garbled in the interests of patriotic pride; and, if they were unsupported by
independent facts, the accounts given by Livy and his kind might
justly be treated with suspicion. For what they are worth, however, their tale is clear. In the population of Rome there was a
strong element described as Sabine, to which some of the greatest
gentes like the Claudii and Valerii belonged[1], but the presence
of this element was the result of gradual infiltration spread over
several centuries and not of any sudden irruption which would
justify the use of phrases like a Sabine conquest of Rome. Already
in the time of Romulus Titus Tatius is made a Sabine, and later
the same is said, with much plausibility, of Numa; but neither
in the regal period nor in any later age is there the slightest sign
that a Sabine army fought its way to Rome and gained permanent
control of the city. Were there any reason to believe in a catastrophic coming of the Sabines at all, it would be easy, as De
Sanctis has observed[2], to show that it should not be placed in the
years to which it is assigned by Pais. In the first half of the fifth
century the silence of tradition about any such event is confirmed
by the evidence of the Fasti, which show no sudden break in the
control exercised by the great patrician houses such as would have
been the inevitable consequence of foreign conquest. But if this
consideration is enough to cast doubts on the reality of Sabine
immigration on a large scale in the only period in which it has
been claimed to find evidence for Sabine domination at Rome,
other facts suggest that at no time was Rome a Sabine city.
Linguistic indications are as clearly opposed to the suggestion
that Rome was suddenly occupied by a large and permanent
Sabine population as they are to the theory of extensive Etruscan
settlement. Among the Italic dialects the speech of the Sabine
population before it fell under the influence of Rome is definitely
remote from Latin and Faliscan and connected most closely with
the Oscan side of the Osco-Umbrian group. Traces of Sabine

[1] Dion. Hal. ii, 46, 3; Plutarch, *Publ.* i, i.
[2] *Storia dei Romani*, i, p. 220.

influence in the speech of Rome, if they were present, would be easy to detect; but, except in a few personal names like that of Numa Pompilius, there are very few that, in the opinion of the present writer, can be regarded as certain[1]. The conclusion to be drawn about the Sabine element in Rome is plain: whatever its total numbers may have been, it was not enough to submerge the Latin-speaking people. Whether the immigrants were few all told, or whether a gradual immigration finally reached large dimensions, the Sabines came to Rome in a way which allowed them to be absorbed by the existing inhabitants of the site so completely that their language was obliterated.

The view that the Sabines penetrated Rome by slow degrees and over a long period of time finds its final confirmation in the evidence of material remains. The Sabine country falls within the region where in the early iron age the regular method of disposing of the dead still was inhumation; and when the plain of Latium became fit for human habitation it was from the Sabine country and neighbouring parts of the same cultural area that an inhuming people made its way to the homes of the Latins and the Faliscans. This people, it is true, found itself forestalled on the site of Rome by the cremators from the north, but traces of its presence can be recognized in the cemetery of the Forum by the end of the ninth century at latest; and from that time onwards the strength of the inhuming settlement continued to increase until it came to dominate the outer hills. The numbers and importance of this people must not be ignored. The mass of primitive inhumations opened at various spots from the Quirinal to the Esquiline suggests an occupation that was dense, and the fact that this colony provided Rome with one of the most famous figures in the regal canon is indication enough of its importance. There are even signs preserved of the independent lives led at one stage by the communities of this region. The existence of a college of Salii Collini side by side with those of the Palatine[2] and perhaps still more the references to a Capitolium Vetus on the Quirinal[3] may be accepted as memorials of an age when the Sabine immigrants still retained a separate organization of their own. But in spite of the claim to superior antiquity implied by calling the Sabine Capitolium the Capitolium Vetus, when the time came for one or other of the two elements in the population of Rome to assert itself over the whole, it was the cremators of the Palatine and their Latin language which prevailed. Though in some matters the

[1] See, however, above, vol. IV, p. 455 sq., p. 467.
[2] Dion. Hal. II, 70, 1.　　[3] Varro, L.L. v, 158; Martial, VII, 73, 4.

Sabines may have affected the Palatine people, though they certainly clung long to their burial rite and may even have communicated it for a time to some members of the other ethnic *stratum*, it is to the Palatine that we must look for the more powerful element in the days when the Roman stock was being formed. The influence of the cremators may be explained in part by their earlier presence on the site, but the explanation demands the further assumption that tradition is right in holding that the Sabine immigration was spread over three centuries at least and that at no time were its numbers more than the original settlers could absorb. Of a sudden invasion there is no valid evidence, and the incidents recorded between 505 and 449 B.C. are only the closing phase of an infiltration of inhumers from the eastern highlands which had begun even before the regal period itself.

III. THE VOLSCIAN ADVANCE

In the struggle between Rome and Veii the prize of victory was the control of the lower Tiber; but the invasions from the south, which occupied the Latin stage during the first half of the fifth century, were movements of population from the surrounding mountains set in motion by the pressure of economic conditions rather than political attacks on Rome or any other power. Besides the line of the Tiber itself where Rome faced southern Etruria, three distinct zones on the northern and eastern borders of the Campagna became theatres of war before Latium at length won freedom from external interference. Between Tiber and Anio the Sabines advanced; the main thrust of the Aequi was delivered from a base between the Anio and the Praeneste gap; and the passage between the Alban hills and the sea was the natural route of Volscian invasions.

In the sixth century the Volsci descended from the slopes of the Apennine somewhere west of the Fucine Lake towards the coastal plain between Latium and Campania, and already in the times of the Tarquins tradition brings them into conflict with Rome over the possession of Suessa Pometia. If Livy (I, 53, 2) is wrong in his assertion that they were ejected from this place by Tarquinius Superbus, the appearance of the *populus Pometinus* in the dedication of Nemi must be explained by a denial that Pometia had fallen into Volscian hands before the end of the monarchy. That the first contact between the Volsci and Rome has been antedated by tradition is possible, since the most intelligible opportunity for a Volscian advance to the sea is provided by the general collapse

of Etruscan authority south of the Tiber, in which the overthrow
of the Roman kingship is a part. But the anticipation is small.
At latest it was only a few years after 500 B.C. that the invaders
appeared in the district to the south-east of the Alban hills, and
it was at this time that they either founded or occupied the city
which retained its Volscian character as long as any: this was
Velitrae. But Velitrae and Pometia were on the frontiers of the
Volscian region, where resistance from the Latins was inevitable,
and it is to be supposed that farther south, where Volscian control
of Antium and (probably) Anxur on the coast and further inland
of the mysterious Ecetra was alleged, the invaders had already
won a foothold before they attempted an extension to the north.
When the time came for the northward advance to be begun, the
newcomers seem to have encountered opposition strong enough
to deny them any permanent foothold in the Roman Campagna.

According to the traditional account, Velitrae was besieged
and recovered, and the Latin front against the Volscians was
strengthened by the foundation of colonies at Signia and Norba.
The dates and details with which the narratives of these events
are provided can make no claims to accuracy, but the incidents
themselves are plausible to the extent that they mark a successful
Latin stand against Volscian advance at a time when such success
is implied by less disputable evidence. It is not to be doubted
that by the end of the sixth century the Volsci had reached the
coastal plain; and, in bringing them soon afterwards as near the
Latin strongholds as Velitrae, tradition is to some extent confirmed by archaeology. But west of Velitrae they leave no trace,
and the stoppage of their expansion at a point reached soon after
500 B.C. is assumed by everything recorded of their attacks on
Latium during the rest of the fifth century.

Of these attacks the first is the most famous, but it is like the
rest in being recorded, so far as the Campagna is concerned, not
as an enduring conquest of new territory so much as a sudden
raid on the rich lands towards the Tiber. The story of Coriolanus
is one whose outstanding merits do not include any notable contribution to our knowledge of the Volscian wars. That the figure
of Coriolanus contains a kernel of fact is certain, nor is an episode
so curious as the invasion of Latium which he directs likely to be
pure invention. Again, of the elements which constitute the legend
in its latest form some at least are additions belonging so obviously
to other times that they may be discarded without damaging the
reputation of the residue. The hero's refusal to allow the *plebs* a
distribution of corn presented to the state, unless they agreed to

the surrender of their tribunes, is more like fiction of the second century than history of the fifth; and the dedication of a temple to Fortuna Muliebris on the spot where Coriolanus was at length persuaded by his mother to spare his native town is an aetiological figment which needs no comment.

But even when such features have been discarded what remains is difficult to understand. Questions about the name of Coriolanus cannot be answered. Whether he is merely the man or founder of Corioli or the conqueror of that place is an open issue; but, whatever view is taken of the probabilities, the value of his career as evidence for the course of Roman relations with the Volsci is unaffected. If Coriolanus be Roman or if, in spite of his connection with the Marcian *gens*, he be Volscian in origin, the main task of criticism is still to decide whether the campaigns with which he is connected are wholly mythical or not. In this case, unfortunately, decision is made more difficult than usual by the peculiarity which Niebuhr rightly stressed. Like Horatius Cocles, Coriolanus hangs in air. His name does not appear in the Fasti— a fact of which elaborate explanations were evolved; he belongs to a *gens* otherwise unrepresented among the officers of the early republican period; and the *personnel* of his story, at least until quite late times, is as much out of touch with the framework of fifth-century history as Coriolanus himself. Whatever the reasons for which the annalists chose 491 and the following years, they were not good: indeed it is a familiar criticism that few years could be less suitable for a Volscian thrust to the gates of Rome than one immediately after Rome and Latium had composed their differences and agreed to present united opposition to attack. Thus arguments from probability, which would have been available if dates were even approximately fixed, in this case are impossible; and nothing but the outline of the tale remains. At worst it tells nothing, and at best little more than that at some point in the first half of the fifth century the Volscians for a moment penetrated clean across the Campagna to Rome.

Those who believe that legend, however much elaborated, rests on some foundation of fact may perhaps accept the raid on Rome on such evidence as this. But an episode so devoid of permanent results is of the smallest importance: it is another and less famous feature of the story which calls for more regard. The list, given by Dionysius (VIII, 14 *sqq.*) and Livy (II, 39, 2 *sqq.*), of towns which the Volscians are said to have acquired under the guidance of their king Attius Tullius and of Coriolanus is in parts open to grave suspicion: some of the alleged conquests are in regions which the

Volsci held from the time of their earliest descent to the littoral plain, and others are in places where no permanent Volscian occupation can be admitted. But one group of names, among which Labici and Pedum are the most familiar, is marked out from the rest by the way in which it bears on later history. The implication of those conquests, if they are true, must be that the Volscians pushed northwards from Velitrae close along the eastern frontier of Tusculum towards the Aequian country. The significance of such a movement is clear: its effect would be to cut off the Hernici from Latium and to open communications between the Volsci and the active mountain tribes whose front against Latium stretched from the Trerus to the Anio. Though there is no need to insist on any part Coriolanus may have played in this advance, the advance itself may be believed, because in the narratives of wars towards the middle of the fifth century—narratives which are certainly sounder than those of fifty years before—joint action by Aequi and Volsci is regularly assumed. But in this later phase it is the Aequi who take the lead, and with the tale of Coriolanus— a tale whose information about the fifth century is negligible in comparison with the light it throws on the character of the Roman people—the independent operations of the Volsci may be left.

IV. THE WARS WITH THE AEQUI

The mountain homes from which the Aequi advanced on Latium seem to have lain north-west of the Fucine Lake on the country between Carsioli and the Avens. Their southward movement first calls for notice when it has brought them to the line of the Anio, and their progress becomes a serious danger to Latium when they cross the river on a wide front from Tibur to the source. On the right flank the Latins held their own, and, though it was perhaps the scene of fighting, the *ager Tiburtinus* did not pass under any enduring occupation by the enemy. With the left flank it was the business of the Hernici to deal; but about the fortunes of war in this direction, where Rome was only distantly concerned, our information is too slight to justify any confident assertion. It was in the centre that the Aequi won their chief success, and with the centre Roman tradition for the most part is concerned. From the middle Anio they pushed in a south-westerly direction round the borders of Tiburtine territory until they reached the Algidus gap and appeared in Latium at Tusculum. The implications of this progress are clear. There is no need to suggest that it involved a passage through the *ager*

Tiburtinus, and still less to base on this unstable ground speculations about the possibility of Tibur having been in origin an
Aequian foundation. With Praeneste, however, the case is different. Praeneste, unlike Tibur, is absent from the inscription
of Nemi, and it is hard to see how the Aequi reached their position
above Tusculum without encroaching on the Praenestine country.
Under these circumstances, though confidence is impossible, it is
at least not unlikely that the decline of Praeneste from the position
she had held in the seventh century is to be explained by her
passing into Aequian hands after the Etruscans had withdrawn.
And what may be true of Praeneste is no less possible of Pedum
and Labici, where the Aequi perhaps found themselves in contact
with their Volscian friends.

In the detailed story of the Aequian attack the evidence of
Dionysius and Livy, which for the Volscian wars stands virtually
alone, receives support from the more credible testimony of
Diodorus. According to Diodorus (XI, 40, 5) the Romans attacked
the Aequian or phil-Aequian occupants of Tusculum as early as
484 and ejected them from the city. From that time onwards for
thirty years the Aequi seem to have hovered round the Algidus and
won possession, more or less secure, of the places east of Frascati.
The frontier struggles, in which the Latins generally contrived,
with the help of Rome, to prevent the Aequian and Volscian
invaders from debouching on the Campagna, are without interest
or importance until, in a year identified by tradition with 462 B.C.,
a hostile thrust, more violent than usual, produced a crisis which
culminated in the first of the two dictatorships ascribed to
L. Quinctius Cincinnatus.

In spite of its many improbabilities, the brief career of Cincinnatus contains more of value for fifth-century history than all
the detailed stories told of Coriolanus. It must be admitted that
knowledge of dictatorships at so early a stage as this may rest
wholly on unofficial records, if on documentary evidence at all,
and it is not in favour of such claims to the consulship of 460 B.C.
as Cincinnatus can advance that in the *Fasti Capitolini* he appears
only as *consul suffectus*. But Cincinnatus differs from Coriolanus
in two important respects. He belongs to a *gens* which played a
leading part in Rome for a hundred years after the middle of the
fifth century, and the minor figures of his story are wholly ap-
posite to the period in which they are set. In the legend of
Coriolanus the Volscian war is the only important element which
can be accepted as sound; but in the case of Cincinnatus the figure
of the hero himself is at least plausible, as well as the business with

which he is concerned. As always, much of the detail must be rejected. The voluntary exile of his son Kaeso and the forfeiture of the *vadimonium*, together with the conflicts between Cincinnatus himself and the tribunate and his opposition to the *rogatio Terentilia* for the appointment of a commission to define the consular *imperium*, belong to that least credible department of tradition which is concerned with the origin of public institutions. Nor again need much notice be taken either of the picturesque details of the dictator's appointment or of the extraordinary methods of war whereby he succeeds in rescuing the consul's army on the Algidus and definitely defeating the Aequian blockaders. But in spite of this, and in spite of confusions between Cincinnatus and other Quinctii of the fifth century, the figure of the dictator is at bottom historical; and the campaign he conducts in the eastern hills, however much the Roman version may indulge in its habitual exaggeration of the part played by Rome and neglect the Latin share, may be accepted as characteristic of the warfare which went on before the issue between the Aequi and the peoples of the plain was finally decided.

The decision came, according to the Roman vulgate, with the dictatorship of A. Postumius Tubertus in 431 B.C. The similarity between the achievements of Tubertus and those of Cincinnatus is marked, and there was an obvious tendency at Rome to connect their respective careers and to confuse the details. At the outset Tubertus is made father-in-law of Cincinnatus' son, and it is the younger Cincinnatus who names Tubertus dictator. Moreover there was a danger of the circumstances on the Algidus, with which Tubertus was called upon to deal, being assimilated to those that confronted Cincinnatus. Livy (IV, 26, 6–7) records a version, which he rejects, according to which the reason for the dictator's appointment was a consular defeat—a defeat which looks strangely like an attempted duplication of the reverse from whose results L. Minucius had been rescued by Cincinnatus. And again the tactics used on the two occasions have much in common. But in spite of these grounds for suspicion and in spite of other features —one of which, the dictator's sentence of his son to death for a military crime, Livy himself[1] prefers not to believe in the prevailing conflict of opinion—the story is historically valuable. Though Tubertus is otherwise known only as *magister equitum* to Aemilius Mamercus Mamercinus in 434, he bears a name which is not, like that of Marcius Coriolanus, unique in the fifth century. His name, however, and his personal relations do not call for so

[1] IV, 29, 5–6.

much notice as the final relief of Aequian pressure on the Algidus. There is no room for doubt about the decisive victory of the Latin defence at this time. It has rightly been observed that the traditional accounts of the campaign gain authority from the record, remarkable in such a context as this, of the day—16, 17 or 18 June[1]—on which the final battle was fought. The rarity of such precision outside the *Fasti triumphales* shows that details like this were not regular subjects of invention at Rome, and the appearance of so exact a date in the narrative here is not easy to explain unless the date be true. But the most cogent fact in favour of the tale is that a victory such as it relates is manifestly implied by the easy Roman penetration of country which the Aequi had lately held when the well-authenticated Roman offensive is opened soon after 420. For that reason alone it might be agreed that the battle of the Algidus, said to have been fought in 431, is tradition's version of an historical victory which, after a struggle for sixty years or more, finally destroyed the menace of an Aequian advance and freed Latium for good from the danger of occupation by this people and its Volscian allies.

The connection between Aequi and Volsci has been doubted, and it is not wholly impossible that the part which the Volsci are made to play in operations round the Algidus is due to mere confusion. It seems more probable, however, that the connection should be accepted. The story of the Volscian progress to the north, in the region between Tusculum and Praeneste, bears no clear signs of invention; and, if it is sound, Aequi and Volsci must have been in the closest contact. Moreover, the battle of the Algidus seems to have a marked effect on Volscian fortunes. In the late forties of the fifth century Volscian activity round Ardea is freely recorded: the plausible tradition of a treaty made with Ardea in 444—a treaty which had apparently been accessible to Licinius Macer[2]—if not the somewhat dubious colonization of the place in 442[3], suggests serious concern in this quarter, for which the Volsci were almost certainly responsible. But after this the coastal thrust is heard of no more, and the Volscian front in its narrow sense remains quiescent until the Romans pass to the attack. For this cessation of Volscian pressure after 440 B.C. a reason is available in the battle of the Algidus, if that was a conflict between Rome and, not the Aequi alone, but a Volsco-Aequian alliance. In these circumstances it would perhaps be rash to dismiss off-hand the frequent records of Volscian presence

---

[1] Ovid, *Fast.* VI, 721 *sqq.*   [2] Livy IV, 7, 10 *sqq.*
[3] *Id.* IV, 11, 5.

near Tusculum, and the rarer hints of Aequian contingents farther
south.

V. THE ROMAN DEFENCE OF THE TIBER

When Etruscan influence in Latium was destroyed, a revival
of the ancient dispute about the bridge-heads was inevitable. On
the left bank Veii still tried, not without success, to maintain a
hold on Fidenae; and on the other side Rome had to fight for
its rights to Janiculum and its surroundings. The old contentions
for the *septem pagi* and the salt-pans, whose origin was so early
as to gain them a place in the legends of Romulus himself, began
afresh after the Tarquins were expelled. Whatever he may represent, Porsenna already seems to have challenged Rome's claims
on the *ripa Veientana*, as has been said: but for tradition at least
the mists in which Porsenna is enwrapped lift within twenty-five
years, and in the middle eighties of the fifth century there begins
a period of feverish activity on which the information of the
authorities is explicit. Until its closing chapters, the value of the
story is so slight that it calls for no detailed notice. After a few
years of border raiding the Romans were defeated, but in the
following campaign (480 B.C.) the position was recovered by the
notable victory of M. Fabius and Cn. Manlius. Next year, however, the Veientanes won their way to the Janiculum, and in this
crisis the Fabii came forward to save the state. They fortified
a camp on the Cremera—a stream which flowed down from Veii
and joined the Tiber opposite Fidenae—and there in 477, under
circumstances of which the most widely variant versions are preserved, they were virtually annihilated by the Veientanes. Thereupon Rome was actually besieged: but at this point the Etruscan
fortune failed, and in the three more years for which the war went
on Roman success was so consistent that in 474 a peace of forty
years was made.

However doubtful the details of this history may be, its
strategic implications, though they are not stressed or even understood by tradition, deserve ready acceptance. In her disputes with
Rome for control of the lower Tiber and in particular for access
to the left bank at Fidenae, Veii was at a disadvantage. Whereas
Rome, at least after the *foedus Cassianum*, could have had Latium
behind her if there was any question of an Etruscan *revanche*,
Veii was isolated from the centre of Etruscan power. Her position
in the outlying region south of the Monti Cimini made her interests
a matter of indifference to the greater cities of Etruria, and left
her supported by nothing more than the feeble and intermittent

sympathy of Caere. In these circumstances, if Veii was not to antagonize the Latin league, Veientane operations on the left bank of the Tiber were impossible except in the friendly territory of Fidenae; and consequently the fighting is either confined to a narrow region round the lowest course of the Anio or else is wholly conducted on the Etruscan side. In the campaigns themselves the stakes at issue—the bridge-heads—are clearly indicated. After the Veientane dash to Janiculum in 479, the Fabii retort with their block-house on the Cremera—the site of which, somewhere in a direct line between Veii and Fidenae, makes plain its object to deny the Veientanes access to their outpost in Latium.

So far the general scheme of the war is probable enough; but most of the details must be rejected. In the earlier phases movements are on too small a scale for it to be likely that their memory survived from so early a time, and the siege of Rome after the Fabian disaster is suspect for its resemblance to the siege by Porsenna. On the other hand the victory of Fabius and Manlius may well be authentic, and it is impossible seriously to doubt the presence of historical matter in the episode of the Cremera. Because it is not appreciated by tradition, the strategic value of a Roman garrison in this region—a value obvious when the relations between Veii and Fidenae are known—adds probability to the tale. Though in ancient times it was generally overlooked, the plot of the story is more pointed than anything that ordinary invention can boast. And this consideration in its favour is reinforced by a second—that mere fabrication does not normally employ its ingenuity on the excogitation of unfounded disasters. For this reason the affair of the Fabii has a far greater claim to respect than the victory of 480.

Over the details of the defeat it is useless to linger. The recorded accounts show variations, abnormally pronounced, both in the number and circumstances of the victims and on the nature of the Veientane stratagem which compassed their destruction. The latter may be ignored, and on the question of numbers no help can be got from the absurd suggestion that every male member of the Fabian *gens* perished with one exception. In addition to the three hundred odd Fabii who fell, some of the versions[1] include a body of clients, though on a scale so enormous as to make the result less credible than ever. In a case where no kind of certainty can be expected, the view preserved by Diodorus (xi, 53, 6) is as attractive as any. According to this account, Rome and Veii met in the battle on the Cremera, and the Romans

---

[1] See especially Festus, p. 450 L.

sustained a defeat with heavy losses among which three hundred
of the casualties were Fabii. If the three hundred Fabii be understood to mean Fabii and their clients, the numbers become possible:
and if the campaign is interpreted as one between Veii and the
whole Roman state, the difficulty of explaining how Roman
interests came to be committed to the care of the Fabii alone—a
difficulty which all attempts have failed to surmount—does not
arise. If, however, the fight was an incident of ordinary war, it
follows that, for a single *gens* afterwards to have been able to
annex the whole glory and responsibility, the battle—and indeed
the whole campaign in which it occurred—was of too slight an
importance to impress itself permanently on the public traditions.
If such a theory makes in the right direction, the history behind
the Fabian tale is a defeat inflicted on Rome, with notable losses
to the Fabii and their followers, in the course of otherwise undistinguished operations designed to cut the communications between Veii and her crossing of the Tiber. For the rest nothing
calls for notice until an honourable peace is made in 474 B.C.

With peace comes the question of chronology. No argument
for the view that knowledge of this treaty was derived from contemporary documents can be based on the mention of its duration:
the forty years recorded may be merely the result of a calculation
of the interval between the date to which the disaster of the
Cremera was assigned and the year in which hostilities between
Rome and Veii broke out again. Nor again can any weight be
attached to the placing of the Fabian catastrophe in 477. To the
question whether the early fifth century was a period of warfare
between Rome and Veii the Etruscan activities after the Roman
monarchy fell and certain elements in the tradition of the war itself
are enough to justify an answer in the affirmative. If, when the
war itself is accepted, it be asked again whether the traditional
dates are open to serious criticism, the reply must be that in themselves they are plausible and no better can be found. During the
middle of the fifth century Roman operations towards the east
imply a freedom from embarrassment in the west. The Etruscan
attack on the Tiber line must be put either before or after the
worst period of Volscian and Aequian pressure, and between these
alternatives the choice is easy. Five years after, even if not before,
the battle of the Algidus was fought, there has begun an authentic
history of developments along the river which is almost continuous
until Veii falls to Rome. Here there is no room for the Fabii
and their contemporaries; and the earlier date remains, commended not only by the absence of an alternative but by the

support of tradition and by its proximity to the years of Etruscan activity in which Porsenna is the central figure.

The political relations of Fidenae during the first sixty years of the fifth century are a matter of some importance, about which the evidence is bad. Possibly, as Dionysius asserts (v, 60, 4), the city was captured by Rome soon after 500 B.C., but the garrison which T. Larcius is said to have left in possession plays no part in later events and cannot be accepted as permanent. Nevertheless, the implication of this account—that Fidenae was under Roman control until its affairs are heard of again about the time of the battle of the Algidus—is right to the extent that in the treaty assigned to 474 Rome must have insisted that Fidenae should cease to act as a Veientane outpost in Latium; and it may be assumed that throughout the years of peace Fidenate policy was sufficiently free of Etruscan control to give Rome no cause for a renewal of hostilities.

Fidenae is not heard of again until 438. In that year, according to tradition, the city revolted under Veientane promptings and a war began which was ended by a peace concluded in 435. In 426 Fidenae rebelled again, but in the following year a decisive Roman victory imposed another treaty which remained unbroken for twenty years, until the final war with Veii broke out. The operations of 437–435 show suspicious parallels with those of 426–425. In both the dictatorship is held by Aemilius Mamercus and in both the most prominent actor on the Roman side is A. Cornelius Cossus. In the former Cossus is made, as military tribune, to win *spolia opima* after killing Tolumnius, *lars* of Veii, with his own hand; and in the latter he is *magister equitum* to Mamercus in the year of Fidenae's fall. In details at least, if not in essence, the earlier war is a retrojection of the later.

The claims of the second war to be regarded as the original from which incidents were transferred to the first are adequately vindicated by the one certainly contemporary record which bears on the course of these campaigns. According to Livy (IV, 20, 5 *sqq.*), tradition had been unanimous in believing that the *spolia opima* had been won by Cossus as military tribune, until, during his restoration of the temple of Juppiter Feretrius, the Emperor Augustus discovered the linen cuirass stripped from the body of Tolumnius, on which it was recorded that at the time of this exploit Cossus had been consul. The courtly forbearance of Livy to verify the imperial announcement with his own eyes is to be regretted (p. 316); but though the word of Augustus is without confirmation, and though the office held by Cossus had an intimate

bearing on an issue raised when M. Crassus, governor of Macedonia, killed the Bastarnian Deldo, it cannot be thought probable
that Augustus either forged the inscription on the cuirass, or
misreported its effect in order to justify his refusal of Crassus'
claim to have won *spolia opima* on the ground that he did not hold
the auspices at the time. It is unnecessary to do more than
mention the theory that Augustus misread a contraction of the
name 'Cossus' as *consul*. This document may be accepted as conclusive evidence that at the time of his encounter with Tolumnius
Cossus was consul, and his consulship falls in 428. Thus a date
is fixed for the most famous episode in the struggle with Fidenae:
an alternative suggestion of 426, when Cossus was *tribunus
militum consulari potestate*, fails because the assumption that a
holder of this office could be described as 'consul' is inconsistent
with what is by far the most credible explanation of the consular
tribunate. War, then, had been declared by 428; but since
Diodorus (xii, 80, 6) records a tale that a battle perhaps to be
identified with that in which Cossus won his *spolia opima* was
indecisive, there is no reason to carry the peace back three years
from the traditional 425. It seems rather that in chronology, as
well as in other details, the operations assigned to the years
438–435 are an anticipation of events which should properly be
put precisely ten years later. If this is so, the whole tale of the
first war collapses.

If the war is not a mere invention, nothing is known of its
course. There is a certain plausibility in the view that the affair
of 428–425 was duplicated a decade earlier merely on account
of the names borne both by one of the consuls of 437—L. Sergius
Fidenas—and by the dictator whose command is placed in 435—
Q. Servilius Priscus Structus Fidenas. But, though it is possible
that the *cognomen* is not triumphal, its almost simultaneous appearance in two distinct *gentes*—both of which were represented
in high office at the time and both of which continued to use the
name—is best explained, not by their civil connection with
Fidenae, but by the participation of the consul and dictator in
some earlier and less memorable operations against the city. To
this, one other piece of evidence should be added. It is said that,
when Fidenae made common cause with Veii in 438, a Roman
embassy was sent to protest and that at the instigation of Tolumnius
its four members were murdered. The victims of this outrage
were commemorated by statues which, though perhaps removed
for a time by Sulla[1], were apparently still to be seen on the Rostra

[1] Cicero, *Phil.* ix, 2, 4.

in the first century A.D.[1]; and from these statues our knowledge
of their names is undoubtedly derived. This much about these
monuments has withstood all the attacks of criticism; but any
value they might have as support for the earlier war depends
wholly on the presence of some chronological hint in the inscriptions on the base, and the insertion of such information is neither
proved nor even probable.

Thus the history of the last effort made by Veii to recover her
hold on the Latin bank is confined, so far as we can say, to the
years immediately following 428. The war alleged to have broken
out ten years before rests on the evidence of a tradition which is
manifestly contaminated with retrojections, supported, if at all,
only by the *cognomen* acquired by families of the Sergian and
Servilian *gentes*. The second war is undoubtedly historical. Its
beginning must be put earlier than the traditional date, because
it was in 428 that *spolia opima* were won by Cossus; but no objection need be taken to that date regularly accepted for its end.
Precise accuracy cannot, indeed, be claimed for 425; but this
point is certainly near enough to the year when Fidenae finally
passed under Roman control for it to be true to say that the long
defence of Latium against its various enemies was finally brought
to a successful issue when the last quarter of the fifth century
began. On the eastern front the enemy's back had been broken
on the Algidus in 431, and to the west the same thing happened
in 425. The thirty years which followed saw the opening of the
Roman offensive.

VI. THE EASTERN OFFENSIVE

The advance of Rome into Aequian and Volscian regions is
recorded less fully than the offensive on the western front. Unlike the great campaigns which ended with the fall of Veii, the
operations round the Alban hills seem to have been designed to
win ground rather by persistent nibbling than by any single and
decisive victory. This difference in strategy was probably dictated
by the different political conditions among the enemy. In southern
Etruria authority seems to have been concentrated in the hands
of Veii, whereas in the mountains to the east the hostile tribes,
at least after the battle of the Algidus, were probably broken up
into sections which presented no united opposition. Thus the story
of successes between the Tiber and Circeii is an uncoordinated
list of scattered acquisitions from which little, if anything, can

[1] Pliny, *N.H.* xxxiv. 23.

be divined about the scheme of operations. The general truth of
tradition, however, is not in doubt: the incidents which compose
the tale are individually too insignificant to have been invented,
and their broad implication—that by the time of the Gallic attack
Rome had thrust back the Aequi and Volsci until she was in
direct contact with Praeneste—is essential to the understanding
of fourth-century history.

Against the Aequi activity may have begun already by 423,
when C. Sempronius Atratinus was consul, if Verrugo is to be
placed in the Aequian rather than the Volscian sector[1]; but it was
five years later that Rome won her first valuable acquisition by the
conquest of Labici. To this station, important because it could
control the Algidus gap, a Roman garrison was sent. In 415 the
neighbouring city of Bola was taken, and probably about the
same time Carventum was occupied, though our only information
about its fate is Livy's mention (IV, 53, 3) that it was seized by
the Aequi in 410 and subsequently changed hands more than
once. Next year Verrugo was captured, and in spite of some
vicissitudes it remained generally in Roman hands until its revolt
in 394; and to this period also the occupation of Vitellia by a
Roman colony may possibly be assigned[2]. By these small gains
the Aequi were thrust off the outskirts of the plain; and though
the struggle still went on with varied fortunes, in 393 the invaders
lost their hold on Tiburtine territory when they were ejected from
Aeful-um (or -ae)[3]. Rome could now boast that from Tibur to the
Alban hills Latium was protected by a belt of country in the uplands
beyond the frontier whence the Aequi had finally been expelled.

The lands on the coast where the Volsci had settled were richer
than the heights on which the Aequi appeared, and the efforts
needed for their recovery were on a larger scale. The first recorded
move was made from the Hernican region to the north, when
the Volsci were turned out of Ferentinum in 431. Unless the fall
of Verrugo should properly be mentioned here, the next attack
was delivered from the Latin side along the coast. Anxur fell
in 406 and was definitely in Latin hands by 400. Velitrae received a Roman garrison in 404; and by 393, when a colony
was sent to Circeii, the people of Latium had won back almost
everything in the coastal region that had been lost since the time

---

[1] Val. Max., III, 2, 8; VI, 5, 2.

[2] *Cf.* Livy, V, 29, 3. An alternative date suggested by Niebuhr is 395:
cf. Livy, V, 24, 4.

[3] Diodorus, XIV, 102, 4, reading Αἴφλον with Burger for the Λίφλον
or Λόφλον of the *codices*.

of the second Tarquin. The fall of Antium is not recorded, though
it is implied by the conquests on either side; and Satricum too,
though we do not know when it was first recovered, was under
Roman control when it rebelled in 393. Thus in a century or
rather more Latium had retrieved the disasters which the Etruscan
withdrawal had involved, and the Latin power, back once more
in Tarracina (Anxur), was again almost within sight of the Liris
and Campania.

VII. THE CONQUEST OF SOUTHERN ETRURIA

The last phase in the external history of fifth-century Rome is
the offensive movement on the Etruscan front which ended with
the fall of Veii. On the opposite side of the Campagna Rome and
the Latins had already made progress enough into Aequian and
Volscian country to be secure against the danger of serious invasion from the south-east. Along the Tiber valley the capture
of Fidenae—and of Crustumerium, if tradition is wrong in saying
that Crustumerium was finally taken in the earliest days of the
Republic—had deprived the Etruscans of their last hold on the
left bank and had given the peoples of Latium the best of all bases
for operations against the headquarters of the enemy—the city of
Veii. And Rome herself, with a confidence intelligible after her
success in the troubles of the recent past, seems to have been
in a mood to make the most of her advantages. The advance
against Aequi and Volsci may be regarded as no more than
retaliation against unprovoked attacks. The move against Veii, on
the other hand, was different. Veii, indeed, could not complain of
unjustified aggression if war were carried into her own territory;
but, for Rome, the campaign against Veii meant the opening of
a new epoch in her history. When Rome crossed the Tiber and
claimed something more than a bridge-head on the further bank,
she abandoned her natural boundary to the north-west and entered
a region whose limits in the end were found to lie far beyond the
Monti Cimini which lay on the immediate sky-line.

The chronology of the Veientane war is a matter of some
obscurity and small importance. On one point Diodorus and Livy,
the two primary authorities, are agreed—that M. Furius Camillus
was nominated *dictator* in 396 and brought the war to an end by
capturing Veii in the same year. In spite of the elaborations to
which the career of Camillus has been submitted, the date of his
most memorable achievement may be accepted as approximately
right. That Camillus was in command when Veii fell is a fact too

well attested for doubt. As Beloch has observed[1], it is unlikely that he became *dictator* before 403, when he held the office of *tribunus militum consulari potestate* for the first time; and it is certain that the Roman victory over Veii had been achieved before the Gallic incursion, which cannot be put later than 384, if it was not so early as 390 (p. 561). Thus the capture of Veii is appropriately placed between 403 and 386; and if Rome's treaty with the Faliscans—a treaty certainly made after the Veientane war— is rightly assigned to the second consular tribunate of Camillus in 394, the lower limit for the fall of Veii may be fixed, as Beloch fixes it, in the latter year. Thus the familiar date for the conclusion of the war may be believed, with the admission of a possible error amounting at most to a year or two in one direction or the other. The duration of the war is less clear. According to Diodorus (xiv, 16, 5) hostilities and the siege began together in 406; according to Livy (iv, 58, 1 *sq.*) negotiations opened in 407, when the peace of twenty years between Rome and Veii had either expired or at least was running out, but the siege itself was not begun till 406 (iv, 60, 9). Yet though these accounts are not hard to reconcile and though they are consistent with the versions of the preceding history to which they are attached, there remains a suspicion that the ten years duration of the first great siege in Roman history is derived from the accepted story of the first and most famous siege in the recorded history of Greece. The case against tradition is not strong enough to compel its rejection: but the possibility cannot be ignored that the chronology for the outbreak of war was reached by placing a ten years siege before the date accepted for the fall of Veii.

The details of Livy's story are in large part an unprofitable study. Some of the less important features have clearly been produced by duplication; and others, though their origin is obscure, for other reasons are difficult to believe. Minor episodes in the operations may be ignored; but in the narrative of Livy certain major points demand attention. The brief account of Diodorus mentions only two incidents besides the opening and the close of the campaign. One is a successful sortie by the besieged in 402, which in Livy appears twice—in this year and in the year before: the other is the introduction of military pay at the beginning of the war. To this Livy adds another military reform—the first inclusion in the forces of Rome of *equites* mounted at their own expense. The value to be assigned to the suggestions of developments in the Roman army system during

[1] *Römische Geschichte*, p. 304.

the Veientane war is discussed elsewhere in connection with the history of Roman institutions (p. 522). Here it is enough to say that the introduction of pay and the first appearance of *equites equo privato* do not stand or fall together. An increase of the mounted troops is a change of small significance. The provision of pay, on the other hand, is a departure of the deepest meaning. It is the first step of many taken by Rome towards turning an army characteristic of a typical city-state into the army of an imperial people. A citizen-militia, whose members might reasonably be expected to serve for nothing, was enough to carry on the brief border warfare in which city-states were wont to settle their accounts: but the purposes of an empire called for longer and more continuous service than this. Longer service could only be had if the troops were paid; and there is much plausibility in the view of tradition that it was the protracted siege of Veii which first forced Rome to provide her soldiers with more regular and immediate recompense than a share of the booty when victory had been won.

Another feature of the story deserves notice for its reference to the only monument of the Roman triumph which survived, at least in part, to later times[1]. Livy relates that in 398 the waters of the Alban Lake suddenly rose high above their normal level, and that Rome sent a mission to Delphi to ask the meaning of this manifestation. When the envoys returned they brought an oracle which confirmed the utterance made already in their absence by a Veientane seer—that Veii would not fall to Rome until Rome had built an outlet for the Lake. The *emissarium* was thereupon constructed, and when it was complete the forces of Camillus made their way into the citadel of Veii by a gallery bored underground. At the outset of the campaign of 396 Camillus had vowed a tithe of the booty to Delphi, and after the war was over the tithe was sent in the shape of a gold *krater*, which was first captured by the pirates of the Lipari Islands but finally reached Delphi, where it stood in the Treasury of the Massiliotes. The bowl itself was rifled by Onomarchus in the middle of the fourth century during the Sacred War, but the base remained[2]; and since its original purpose was known, it may be assumed to have borne an inscription recording the origin and occasion of the offering which had disappeared. The tale of this dedication is found in several derivative authorities, but their testimony does nothing

[1] Unless Beloch (*op. cit.* p. 302 *sq.*) is right in connecting the *paterae* dedicated by Camillus in the Capitoline temple with the fall of Veii.

[2] Appian, *Ital.* 8.

to confirm the account of Livy. Confirmation is, however, forth-coming from Diodorus; and since it seems that the base long sur-vived, it can scarcely be doubted that Delphi could boast a memorial of the Veientane war.

For the circumstances which Livy narrates, no credence need be claimed. It is scarcely probable that a connection, even of time, existed between the capture of Veii and the *emissarium* of the Alban Lake. The physical features of the site make it improbable that a *cuniculus* played any part in the taking of the city, and it is certain that no trace of such a gallery has so far been found. Moreover, this method of entering a town through a mine is three times recorded of earlier Roman operations against Fidenae. Again, the oracle may be no more than a later invention designed to explain the offering of the *krater*; and similarly the story that the matrons of Rome were rewarded for their public spirit in surrendering their gold ornaments to provide metal for the dedica-tion by the grant of permission to use carriages in Rome[1] is probably an artificial explanation of the way in which the women had come to enjoy a right denied to men. Such elaborations are not surprising in a piece of history whose embellishment was not complete till the Augustan age. Livy himself seems to have been responsible for a final addition—the great speech[2] in which Camillus, after the departure of the Gauls, is made to utter the sentiments which Livy shared with Vergil and Horace on a living issue in the early principate of Augustus. In word Camillus is resisting a proposal to transfer the Roman people and the Roman gods to the site of Veii; in fact his argument is directed against a plan—which public opinion had attributed to Julius and which Augustus was suspected of having inherited from him—to move at least the administrative centre of the Roman Empire to some city in the eastern Mediterranean.

But though many details of the narrative must be rejected as late, the Roman offering to Delphi stands on the solid foundation of the base which seems long to have survived in the Treasury of Massilia. If the offering may be accepted as historical, it deserves notice for several reasons. Not only does it lend support to other suggestions of friendship between Rome and the Massiliotes at least as early as the end of the fifth century, but it confirms in some degree the date for the introduction of the Apollo-cult at Rome which Livy indicates when he says (IV, 25, 3) that the first temple of which we hear was vowed in 433, and above all it throws a ray of welcome light on the nature of the relations which

[1] Livy, v, 25, 8 *sq.*   [2] *Id.* v, 51–54.

existed already by the time of the Gallic raid between Rome and the world of Hellas.

Of the remaining threads in the narrative only one need be followed with any care. From the beginning of the story there are scattered hints that the peril of Veii at length did something to break down the indifference of her neighbours. Livy tells how in 405 the federal council of the Etruscan cities considered the question of declaring a *bellum publicum gentis universae* against Rome, without, however, coming to a decision. Two years later, when the Veientanes appointed a king for the more effective conduct of the war, the council seized upon this as an excuse for officially proclaiming as its policy the attitude of indolent inaction which in fact it had adopted from the first, and to this policy the Etruscans adhered even when in 397, at the crisis of the struggle, a special appeal on behalf of Veii was made by the peoples of Capena and Falerii. Tarquinii alone among the great cities of Etruria made some attempt to hamper the Roman operations by a sudden raid on the territory of Rome in 397; but this, if it is historical at all, was a brief and futile effort.

The explanation of the Etruscan failure to grapple with a danger which threatened far more than the southern fringe of Etruria is something still to seek. Livy may possibly be right in hinting that the cities farther north were already fully occupied by the advent of the Gauls; but, as has often been observed, the Gauls will not account for the passivity of cities on the Tuscan coast, and it is these which might naturally have led a movement for the relief of Veii. Tarquinii may indeed have done a little; but Caere was Veii's nearest neighbour, and the attitude of Caere, if one may argue from Livy's suggestion[1] that Roman forces enjoyed free passage across Caeretan country and from Caere's behaviour at the time of the Gallic raid, was one of actual hostility to the besieged. So far as our evidence indicates any conclusion at all, the conclusion must be that the Etruscans left Veii to its fate through that petty jealousy which seems always to have been Etruria's curse; and in the Veientane war the land immediately at stake was an outlying district south of the Monti Cimini geographically separated from the rest of Etruria by a division so distinct that the risk of a Roman advance farther north may well have seemed too remote to outweigh the temptations of self interest. Livy's story of the decisions taken at the *fanum Voltumnae* may not be strictly true: it is possible that at this time the Etruscan synod was not concerned with political affairs at all. But even if

[1] Livy, v, 16, 5.

this be so, and if it be regarded as absurd to hold that a religious
meeting of representatives from the Etruscan cities might make
an appropriate opportunity for broaching a proposal for common
action in an affair of common interest, the account which Livy
gives of the spirit prevailing in Etruria is probably not far from
fair.

In another quarter Veii sought help with more success. According to Livy, the cities of Capena and Falerii, of which the
latter at least was strong enough to be an ally of the greatest
value, intervened in 402; and from that year onwards they maintained an almost uninterrupted activity until, when Veii fell, they
were still in arms and found themselves obliged to settle a heavy
account with Rome as best they might. The Faliscans, with a
foresight not vouchsafed to the peoples of Etruria to the north,
had recognized the Roman peril even before Fidenae collapsed.
To Fidenae their help had been unavailing, but in 402 it was
transferred to Veii. In that year, together with the Capenates,
they were victorious in a raid of some dimensions; and though their
territory was ravaged by Rome in 401, they were in the field
again by 399. This time they were defeated; but even when their
appeal to the Etruscan council had failed in 397 they were still
able to strike another blow for Veii in the year in which it fell.
After the power of Veii had been broken, the resistance of Capena
and Falerii was overcome with ease: Capena made terms in 395
and Falerii in 394.

Rome was thus left with a broad tract of land at her disposal
on the right bank of the Tiber, and the way in which this land
was treated is a matter of some obscurity. The outstanding feature
of the settlement, which does not seem to have been made until
the Gallic incursion had been repelled, was the creation of four
new rustic tribes on the *ager Veiens* (p. 574). To the seventeen
already in existence there were added the *tribus Stellatina, Tromentina, Sabatina* and *Arnensis*. But, though this much is clear,
the precise extent of the country thus annexed by Rome is doubtful.
If there were evidence enough to show that Capena was included
in the *tribus Stellatina* from its formation, as it certainly came to
be in later times, the territory of Capena as well as that of Veii
would have to be reckoned among the immediate acquisitions of
Rome. Festus (p. 464 L.), however, does not prove the point, and
the suggestions of his mutilated text are too vague to be set
against the authority of Livy. Since Falerii survived to fight two
more wars with Rome, Livy's account cannot be questioned when
he says that in 394 Rome made no more than a treaty with the

Faliscans: and if in this instance Livy's narrative is sound, it may well be right again when it records a similar treaty between Rome and Capena in 395.

Nevertheless, whatever the view about Rome's treatment of Capena which Festus may at one time have preserved, it is not to be denied that the story of Rome's early dealings with the peoples of southern Etruria is open to some suspicion of corrupt anticipations. Two of the twelve Latin colonies which in 209 B.C. declared themselves unable to continue the supply of men and money to Rome were Sutrium and Nepete. That Rome came into contact with these cities soon after the end of the Veientane war is obvious; for their boundaries on the south-west must have marched at least for some distance with those of Veii. There is nothing improbable in the tale of Diodorus (XIV, 98, 5), unintelligible though it is without emendation, that Sutrium somehow engaged Roman attention in 394; but Diodorus (XIV, 117, 4) is less convincing when he refers to it as a colony (ἀποικία) in 390. Livy mentions the colonization of Nepete in 383, and this is placed by Velleius (I, 14, 2) in 373 with Sutrium ten years earlier[1]. Before this, however—in 389 and 386—Livy calls the people of both cities *socii populi Romani*. The plausible arguments of Beloch[2] do not prove his view that neither of these places became a Latin colony before the fifties of the fourth century; but they at least may serve as a reminder of reasons, among which geographical considerations perhaps carry the greatest weight, for doubting the version which holds that Sutrium and Nepete received their later status within a few years of Veii's fall. It may be admitted that with them, as with Falerii and Capena, Rome made some kind of treaty forthwith; but in the culminating episode of the period with which this chapter deals the actual gain which accrued to the *ager Romanus* across the Tiber was probably confined to the territory of Veii itself.

Thus in Etruria Rome stood facing Caere and Falerii; and her next step northward only comes with the period after the Gallic raid. At this point all that remains is to survey the results achieved by Rome between the expulsion of the kings and the fall of Veii. For more than half of the fifth century Rome had been on the defensive, and for that reason her territorial gains had not been commensurate with her efforts. Land had been annexed on the Algidus and in Etruria, but even so the *ager Romanus* had not increased to more than 650 square miles. Against this the cities of the Latin League, which had profited greatly by the foundation

<hr>

[1] See below, p. 569.   [2] *Römische Geschichte*, pp. 305 *sqq.*

of colonies along the coast on land recovered when the Volscian thrust was repelled, could set a thousand square miles or more. Yet, despite the superiority of the acreage they could boast, the Latins were so far from having strengthened their hands against Rome that the fifth century may justly be said to have sealed the doom of the Latin League. Just as the peoples of the Latin plain had owed much in the fight with the invaders of the fifth century to the continuity of their territory and to its central position, so in the domestic affairs of Latium it was to the great advantage of Rome that the *ager Romanus* was an unbroken block of country round whose fringes the members of the League lay scattered. Notwithstanding its extent, after the advance made by Rome into the Aequian country, the League was geographically so badly placed that strong and united action seems to have become impossible. On the north the towns round Tibur were cut off from the rest by the strip of country about the Algidus which Rome had annexed. Tusculum was wholly surrounded by Rome, except on the north where her lands bordered for a few miles on those of Gabii. The great cities between Aricia and the coast had no access of their own to their fellows farther north; and places like Signia, Cora and Norba were mere outposts round the Monti Lepini—garrisons face to face with the Volscians and denied their natural communications with the main body of the League by the resolute refusal of Praeneste to become a member. The League thus lacked cohesion, and the result appears already in the fifth century. The equal alliance between Rome and the Latins collapsed: the arrangements for alternate Roman and Latin command of the allied forces were disregarded: and in affairs which affected the common interests of the region the initiative lay with Rome. The time had not, indeed, arrived for the formal extension of Rome's authority over Latium as a whole; but when Rome was called upon to face the coming of the Gauls she could claim already to have gained effective hegemony of western Italy from the frontiers of Caere and the Monti Cimini in the north to Cape Circello and Tarracina in the south.

CHAPTER XVI

THE MAKING OF A UNITED STATE

I. CONSULAR TRIBUNES

WHILE Rome was winning notable victories over her neighbours, in her domestic politics she had failed to achieve a lasting peace. The *plebs* were not satisfied with the concessions made to them by the settlement of 449 B.C. We now enter upon the period in which their efforts were concentrated upon obtaining access to the chief magistracy of the State. Our narratives of the years which follow bear the stamp of later politics and cannot be trusted in detail. The right to a triumph, claimed by Valerius and Horatius, was contested by the Senate which (according to the custom of the later Republic) reserved to itself the privilege of according this distinction; whereupon a tribune L. Icilius, is said to have 'brought the matter before the *populus*' and established a precedent for the granting of a triumph by the people. In 448 B.C., the patrician ex-consuls Aternius and Tarpeius (on whom see p. 324) are said to have been co-opted as tribunes, a violation of the constitution which provoked the passing of a law by a tribune named L. Trebonius providing that voting by the *plebs* should continue until the college of ten was at full strength[1].

The constitutional struggle became acute in 445 B.C., when a tribune named C. Canuleius proposed to abolish the prohibition of *conubium* between *patres* and *plebs* and at the same time to throw the consulship open to plebeians; and after a bitter dispute —in which Valerius and Horatius took the side of the *plebs*—the Senate allowed the first measure to go forward, presumably to the *concilium plebis*, but in order to defer a surrender on the second point, consented that in place of consuls, three officers (*tribuni militum*) enjoying the authority of consuls (*consulari potestate*) should be elected from either social order—whereupon the *plebs* showed unexampled magnanimity by electing three patricians. Dionysius (xi, 59 *sq.*) goes so far as to say that, by the terms of the law, three were to be patrician and three plebeian[2].

There seems no good reason for rejecting the tradition that the

---

[1] An attempt to co-opt patrician tribunes in spite of this law was, according to Livy (v, 10 *sq.*) defeated by another Trebonius in 401 B.C.

[2] He adds the provision that it should for the future be determined annually by 'Senate and people' whether consuls or *tribuni militum* were to be elected; Livy, however (IV, 12) records that great difficulty was found in inducing the Senate to take up the matter in 441 B.C.

creation of this office was a political compromise; although Livy (IV, 7, 2) read in some of his authorities that these officers were set up because the military operations in prospect were on several fronts, and that they then assumed the authority and insignia of consuls. Hence it has been proposed to connect the number of *tribuni militum* with the growth of the military forces raised by Rome, each *tribunus* implying a levy (*legio*) of 1000 men. This was certainly not what the Romans meant when they spoke, like the Emperor Claudius, of 'the *imperium* put into commission' (*in plures distributum*, Dessau, 212)[1].

In one point, however, the traditional version is open to criticism. If the object of the institution was to circumvent the admission of plebeians to the supreme magistracy, why do not the names of plebeians occur earlier and oftener in the recorded lists? According to Livy (v, 12) the first plebeian to obtain a place in the college was P. Licinius Calvus in 400 B.C. It is not, however, certain that Livy is right; since (whatever he and Dionysius may say) one of the three first elected, L. Atilius, bears a plebeian name, and so does Q. Antonius Merenda, who served the office in 422 B.C., and was evidently akin to the (supposed) plebeian decemvir of 450 B.C. (see p. 460). An entirely different view is taken by Beloch, who thinks *all* plebeian names which appear in the Fasti of the period 444–367 B.C. interpolated, even those included in the four colleges in which plebeians are said to have obtained a majority (400, 399, 396, 379 B.C.), and by drastic manipulation of the lists arrives at the conclusion that the number of consuls (for this he considers to have been their title) was raised to four in 426 B.C. and to six in 405 B.C. In that case the whole story of the 'struggle of the orders' in this phase falls to the ground; and although the colouring is borrowed from the last century of the Republic[2], the main fact does not seem to be a pure invention.

---

[1] Livy (IV, 30), after mentioning the appointment of four tribunes in 426 B.C., says that the event proved how inexpedient the multiplication of commands was from a military standpoint. Consuls were still elected on several occasions. The number of military tribunes, at first three, seems to have been raised to four in 426 B.C. (after a period of consular government) and to six in 405 B.C., and it is possible that these figures may be correlated with the increasing forces put into the field by Rome. There is much variation between the figures as given by Livy and Diodorus, which is generally to be explained by omissions rather than interpolations. We may add that in 362 B.C. a law was passed giving the people the right to elect six of the *tribuni militum* serving with the legions, the remainder receiving their commissions from the consuls.

[2] *E.g.* we read in Livy (IV, 6) of consuls who can get no business transacted in the Senate 'because of the use of *intercessio* by the tribunes'.

II. THE CREATION OF THE CENSORSHIP

One of the most characteristic of Roman institutions dates from the same period as the creation of *tribuni militum* with consular authority. This was the censorship, which embodies the first serious effort to create an administrative department at Rome. According to the account of Livy it was set up in 443 B.C. in order to relieve the consuls, who were engaged in almost perpetual war-fare, of duties which were scarcely consonant with the dignity of their office. The register of citizens had not, in fact, been made up for many years[1]; and in order to carry it out, the consuls who had been appointed in the previous year, when a flaw in the election of the *tribuni militum* had brought about their retirement, and had not held office for their full term, were 'commissioned to hold a *census*'; and hence called censors. Doubts have been cast on this story, since Livy assures us that he did not find the names of these consuls—L. Papirius Mugillanus and L. Sempronius Atratinus—'in the early annals or the rolls of magistrates.' Licinius Macer, it seems, brought them to light from his *libri lintei*, a fact which does not inspire us with confidence; and the authenticity of the treaty with Ardea, in which they appeared as representing Rome, is not above suspicion (p. 503).

It may well be, however, that the names are really those of the first censors, and Livy's hint that the patricians were not sorry to see an increase in the number of 'patrician magistrates' suggests that some compensation was thus given them for the suspension of the consulship. There is no good ground for thinking (with Mommsen) that in 443 B.C. special commissioners were appointed and that a regular magistracy was not set up until 435, when Livy says that the censors of that year—C. Furius Pacilus and M. Geganius Macerinus—'approved' the *villa publica* in the field of Mars and there held the census for the first time. Five years later we hear from Cicero (*de Rep.* II, 35, 60) of a pair of censors who imposed heavy fines in cattle, which were commuted for money on easy terms by the consuls. They are not mentioned in other sources, but the interval of five years was that which in later times —from 209 B.C. onwards, though with exceptions in the period of civil strife—was regarded as normal. Thus Varro speaks of a 'five-year army' (*exercitus quinquennalis*) and the word *lustrum*, which originally denoted the 'purifying' of the numbered host, came to mean the interval between two such acts and in the end a 'five-year period.' It is, however, evident from the records that

[1] Dion. Hal. (XI, 63) says that the census had not been taken since 459 B.C.

there was no fixed interval in early days. In 433 B.C., however, the dictator Marcus Aemilius passed a law fixing the tenure of the office at eighteen months. Livy, who calls the censorship a 'five-year magistracy' in the speech which he puts into the mouth of Aemilius, mistakes the motive of the measure, which was not to reduce the tenure of the office, but to give the censors a sufficient time to perform their ever-growing administrative duties.

The original function of the censors was the registration of citizens and their property—at first only landed property—in order to determine their liability to taxation and military service. Each was placed in the tribe in which his lands were situate, and on these he was assessed to the special war-tax or *tributum* which was levied when the exigencies of the situation demanded it and sometimes treated as a loan and repaid when the treasury was flourishing. Each was also placed in a *centuria*, in which he voted in the assembly. This made it possible for the censor to inflict certain penalties for misconduct. He could 'remove' the citizen from his tribe, and place him in one of the four city wards, where his vote would count for less in the tribal assembly. He could also 'make him a tax-payer,' *i.e.* erase his name from the roll of his *centuria*, so that he was a citizen only for the purpose of paying *tributum* 'for his *caput*[1].' It was related of the dictator who passed the Lex Aemilia that the censors were so enraged by the slight put upon their office that they 'removed him from his tribe, rated him at eight times the value of his property, and made him a tax-payer'! It was further the censor's duty to draw up the list of those liable to cavalry service (*equites*), for which the highest property qualification must have been required; at any rate Livy tells us that when the cavalry force maintained by the State was found insufficient for military needs during the siege of Veii, those who possessed the *census equester* were allowed to serve 'with their own horses.' Newly enrolled citizens, again, were registered at the discretion of the censors, and this act might have political significance, as for example where the status of freedmen was concerned: and since the rule of collegiality applied as between the censors—though they were not 'colleagues' of the consuls and praetors—it was not uncommon for serious differences of opinion to make it impossible for the census to be completed.

It was not unnatural that the magistrates who made up the register of *equites* should be entrusted with the revision of the Senatorial roll; and this highly important function was assigned to them, as Festus tells us, by a Lex Ovinia of unknown date. The

[1] Pseudo-Asconius *in Div. in Caecil.* (Bruns, *Fontes*, Pars II, p. 70).

first allusion which we have to such a revision relates to the census of 312 B.C.; and it is not a little remarkable that so important a constitutional change should have been made by *plebiscitum* at that date. Here was a new field for the exercise of those disciplinary powers which were already in use in the registration of citizens: the censor's will was law and he could strike a senator off the roll without appeal and without being called upon to give account of his action. But here the sound sense of the Romans prevailed, and a 'code of honour' was gradually built up, which served as a model, as time went on, for the praetors, who punished breaches thereof by the withdrawal of certain civic rights and privileges, known as *infamia*. Thus the 'rule' or 'care of manners' (*regimen* or *cura morum*) became the most conspicuous feature of an office which had its origin in administrative convenience. It might be justified by the necessity of expelling unclean elements from the host which was about to be purified by the *lustrum*; it came to find expression in such edicts as that of the censors of 92 B.C. directed against teachers of Latin oratory.

The second great sphere of the censors' activity was connected with the properties of the State and the contracts to which the people was a party. Since their functions in these matters were not part of their original competence they could be and not infrequently were performed by other magistrates, especially the consuls, who were naturally obliged to act from time to time during the intervals when no censors were in office; but normally it was the censors who, according to the common practice of ancient city-states, entered into contracts for the enjoyment of State properties, mines, salt-pans, etc., or rights of fishery (see Festus, p. 108 L.) or pasturage, and generally for the ingathering of revenues (*vectigalia*); and it was they who made allocations (*ultro tributa*) to contractors who executed public works, especially buildings, or made themselves responsible for their upkeep. As watchful guardians of the people's property it became them to resist encroachments and on occasion to inflict fines.

It has already been mentioned (p. 446) that the quaestors were, according to Tacitus, elected by the people from 447 B.C. onwards; and since the office did not carry with it the *imperium*, the *patres* were not vitally interested in the exclusion of plebeians; and when the number of quaestors was doubled in 421, in order that two might manage the business of the Treasury while two others attended the consuls in the field, plebeians were declared eligible, though not without considerable opposition. The plebeian candidates, however, failed to secure election in the following year, and it was not until 409 that three out of the four places were secured by the *plebs*, who (according to Livy's account) considered that a way was thus paved for access to the consulship and the triumph.

III. THE CLIMAX OF THE CONSTITUTIONAL STRUGGLE

The constitutional struggle reached its climax after the Gallic sack. Once more it is difficult to disentangle legend from history, and we must be content with a balance of probabilities. Little need be said of the *coup d'état* of M. Manlius Capitolinus, the hero of the defence of the Capitol, which is placed by our authorities in 385 B.C. According to Livy, Manlius was 'the first of the patricians to become a partisan of the people,' who took advantage of the chronic discontents in the matter of land and debt to arouse a sedition; a dictator was appointed (in the first instance to conduct a campaign against the Volsci) who threw Manlius into prison. After his triumph, however, he resigned his office, and Manlius was released; but in the following year sedition broke out afresh, and Manlius was brought to trial before the people by two of the tribunes, and as he escaped condemnation by the centuries assembled in the Campus Martius by pointing to the Capitol which he had saved, the *venue* was changed, and Manlius was condemned and hurled by the tribunes from the Tarpeian rock. 'But,' adds Livy, 'some authorities have it that he was condemned by *duoviri perduellionis* specially appointed.' We may therefore doubt whether authentic records of the trial, which evidently interested students of criminal law, were preserved: and there is a variant of the tradition, found in a fragment of Dio Cassius, according to which Camillus was made dictator for the fourth time in order to deal with the sedition, which is clearly due to a desire to point the contrast between the two saviours of the State. Livy introduces into his story the so-called *Senatus consultum ultimum*, instructing the consuls to 'see to it that the Republic take no harm,' for which the senatorial party of the Gracchan period were only too anxious to find precedent, and this may serve to date his source.

We now come to the agitation by which the *plebs* at length secured admission to the supreme magistracy. The leading figures are C. Licinius Stolo and L. Sextius, who on their appointment as tribunes in 376 B.C. came forward with a legislative programme which it took ten years of strife to realize. Two of the three laws associated with their names dealt with the economic problems of land and debt, and will be discussed later (pp. 537 *sqq.*): the third provided that the consulate should be restored, and that one consul at least should be a plebeian. According to Livy's story, Licinius was led to raise the issue by the fact that his wife, the daughter of a patrician, M. Fabius Ambustus, felt herself socially inferior to her sister, who was married to a man of her own rank: the details are not to be trusted, but it is fair to draw the inference that inter-marriage between the orders was beginning to weaken the cohesion of the *patres*.

The Senate, however, secured the veto of the eight colleagues of Licinius and Sextius, which prevented the passing of the three laws; this is a trait borrowed from the history of the later Republic, when it was always easy to find members of the tribunician college ready to block an awkward measure. The agitators retorted by putting a veto on all elections save those of plebeian magistrates —how exactly this could be done is not explained; and then followed what Livy calls a *solitudo magistratuum* and Diodorus an ἀναρχία. According to the former authority this lasted for five years, according to the latter for one year only: but the *Fasti* of the Regia, though unfortunately missing for this period, can be shown to have had space for the names of consular tribunes, and some of these are given in a very corrupt form in the handbook whose author is known as the 'Chronographer of A.D. 354.'

The struggle was resumed under constitutional forms in 370 B.C. (when consular tribunes were once more elected), and in the following years, and the number of tribunes opposed to the Licinio-Sextian laws sank to five. At length, in 368 B.C., Camillus was appointed dictator in order to quell the agitation: he appointed as his master of horse L. Aemilius Mamercinus. After threaten-ing drastic measures, however, he resigned his office, 'either,' says Livy (VI, 38, 9), 'because he had been irregularly appointed, as some have stated, or because the tribunes proposed to the *plebs* and the *plebs* approved a resolution, that should M. Furius per-form any act in virtue of his office of dictator, he should be fined 500,000 sesterces.' Livy prefers the former explanation, and says that P. Manlius Capitolinus was made dictator in his place—not however before a vote on the three laws had been taken in the *concilium plebis*, which passed those relating to land and debt, but rejected the admission of plebeians to the consulship, a decision which the proposers declined to recognize. The new dictator appointed as his master of horse a plebeian, C. Licinius, who was related to him and had held the office of consular tribune[1]. A

---

[1] It is evident that Livy does not here identify this Licinius with the popular leader; but in a later book (X, 8, 8) he makes a speaker refer to

compromise seemed to be in sight, but the senatorial die-hards, led by Appius Claudius, a grandson of the decemvir, succeeded in staving off the passage of the Licinio-Sextian laws. The tribunes, however, passed a law increasing the number of commissioners for the regulation of Rites and Ceremonies (*sacris faciundis*) from two to ten, one-half of whom were plebeians. Consular tribunes were then elected for 367 b.c.

The year began with a Gallic inroad, and Camillus was made dictator for the fifth time, with T. Quinctius Poenus as master of horse (p. 572). After his defeat of the Gauls and the triumph which followed, a final struggle ended in a settlement of the constitutional issue by which both parties were the gainers. The *plebs* attained its cherished ambition by the election of L. Sextius as the first plebeian consul. On the other hand, a third *praetor* (without the title of consul) was added to the supreme college, whose function was the administration of justice in Rome and between Roman citizens[1]; and in pursuance of the Senate's decree, the dictator held an election for the appointment of two patrician aediles. It should be added that in the following year (366 b.c.) an arrangement was come to by which these 'curule' aediles should be chosen in alternate years from *patres* and *plebs*. In 365 b.c. a pestilence carried off Camillus, 'the restorer of his fatherland and second founder after Romulus of the Roman stock.'

Such is the account given by Livy of these momentous changes. It has naturally not escaped criticism. The two dictatorships of Camillus are rejected by those who regard all the later notices of his career as accretions to what Mommsen called 'the most mendacious of Roman legends.' In particular, the Gallic inroad of 367 b.c. is rendered suspect by the statement of Polybius (ii, 18) that thirty years passed between the battle of the Allia and the next irruption of the Gauls: even Livy doubts the statement (which he found in the Annals of Claudius Quadrigarius) that the single combat at the bridge of the Anio which gave T. Manlius Torquatus his *cognomen* took place in this campaign and not, as others said, ten years later (p. 572 *sq.*). But the stubborn fact remains that the name of a plebeian appears for the first time in the Consular Fasti in 366 b.c., from which time onwards *tribuni militum con-*

C. Licinius Stolo as the 'first plebeian master of horse,' and the same version is found in Plutarch's *Life of Camillus* (xxxix) and apparently in Dio Cassius (Frag. 29), although it is possible that Dio distinguishes two Stolones, the *magister equitum* and the tribune.

[1] The influence of the praetor on the subsequent developments of Roman Law will be dealt with in a later volume.

sulari potestate are no longer heard of. And it is hard to believe that this stronghold of patrician rule could have been carried except as the result of an intense political struggle. The concessions made to the *patres* by the institution of the *praetor qui inter cives ius dicit* and the 'curule' aediles give no cause for suspicion in themselves. De Sanctis' suggestion that a third praetor had long been in existence we found unconvincing (p. 437 *sq.*), and the same must be said of Beloch's view that a college of four plebeian aediles had existed since the fifth century[1], to which, on account of its growing administrative importance, the patricians sought and obtained admission.

Our information with respect to the internal politics of Rome in the period following the election of the first plebeian consul is unfortunately very meagre. For eleven years the rule that one of the consuls should be a plebeian was strictly observed; but the office was confined to a limited circle. On the patrician side three persons held the consulship twice in the first six years of the period: L. Aemilius Mamercinus, Q. Servilius Ahala and C. Sulpicius Peticus. L. Sextius, the plebeian who first broke the bar, is not heard of again, but two *familiae*, the Genucii and Licinii, monopolize the representation of the *plebs* during the same years. Whether the first was a plebeian branch of the patrician family to which, if the record is genuine, the consul of 451 B.C. and decemvir belonged, or whether the family in question had 'gone over to the plebs', we cannot determine. Our authorities, again, are at variance with regard to the Licinii. The consul of 364 B.C. bears the cognomen Calvus in the Fasti, while Livy identifies him with Stolo, the popular leader: in 361 B.C. the position is exactly reversed. It cannot however be argued that these elections point to a coalition between a group of 'liberal' patricians and the leaders of the plebeian movement, since Q. Sulpicius Peticus, as we shall find, was evidently a conservative.

In the five years following 361 B.C. the *personnel* changes. The patrician consulships alternate between Fabii and Manlii, while on the plebeian side new names appear in the lists. In 360 B.C. C. Poetelius Libo Visolus, in 359 B.C. M. Popillius Laenas, in 358 B.C. C. Plautius Proculus, and in 357 B.C. C. Marcius Rutilus attained the consulship, and it is a remarkable fact that three of

---

[1] *Römische Geschichte*, p. 278. Beloch observes that Zonaras (VII, 17, 6), in his abridgment of Dio Cassius, writes (with reference, as it appears, to 471 B.C.), καὶ τοὺς ἀγορανόμους καὶ τοὺς δημάρχους ἐπηύξησαν. An increase in the number of tribunes was, as we saw (p. 453), assigned to that date by some annalists.

these, together with a *gentilis* of the fourth, C. Plautius Venox, monopolize the plebeian representation down to 340 B.C. C. Poetelius, who was consul for the second time in 346 B.C., and for the third in 326 B.C., is said to have proposed, as tribune of the *plebs* in 358 B.C., a law *de ambitu*, dealing with abuses in connection with canvassing at elections, especially in the markets and other places of meeting outside Rome; Livy gives no details with regard to the practices forbidden, and his suggestion that it was directed against *novi homines*, *i.e.* those belonging to families hitherto unrepresented in the magistrature, sounds like an anachronism, though it is in keeping with Livy's statement that the Senate approved the measure[1]. In fact, however, the highest office was confined to a limited number of families. M. Popillius Laenas and C. Marcius Rutilus both held the consulship four times, and the Plautian *gens* furnished seven consuls in the course of the fourth century. Meanwhile the other high offices of state were gradually attained by plebeians. C. Marcius Rutilus was the first plebeian dictator in 356 B.C., the first plebeian censor in 351 B.C. His *gens* was that to which a king of Rome had by tradition belonged, and it is remarkable that at a later date it even supplied a *rex sacrorum*, from whom the *cognomen* Rex was derived by his descendants.

On the other hand, the patricians succeeded in nullifying for a time the compromise with regard to the consulship embodied in the Licinio-Sextian law of 367 B.C. From 355–343 B.C. there were at least six, and possibly seven, occasions upon which two patrician consuls were elected. In the first of these years there was a sharp struggle, eleven *interreges* being appointed in succession before the tribunes withdrew their opposition. One of these, M. Fabius Ambustus, appealed to the constitutional doctrine laid down in the Twelve Tables, that the last decision taken by the *populus* should have the force of law, and contended that this should apply to elective as well as legislative acts. It is not certain whether two patricians held office in 354 B.C., since the name of M. Popillius appeared, as Livy tells us, in one recension of the Fasti: but no plebeian was consul in 353, 351, 349, 345 or 343 B.C. This fact has led Münzer to suggest that a compromise was arrived at similar to that which governed the election of curule aediles from *patres* and *plebs* in alternate years; but this supposition is unwarranted. However, C. Marcius Rutilus, who, it will be remembered, had been the first plebeian dictator, attained

---

[1] The tradition which ascribes a measure for the relief of debtors to a member of the Poetelian *gens* is discussed elsewhere (p. 545).

the censorship in 351 B.C., in spite of the fact that two patrician consuls were in office.

In 342 B.C., according to Livy's narrative, a constitutional crisis arose as the result of a mutiny of the Roman troops in Campania. We are not concerned with the details of the story, which was told with some variations by other authorities. The mutiny is counted as a *secessio* of the *plebs* by Florus; and the relief of debtors which ended it (p. 544) is discussed elsewhere. As for the grievances of the army, they are said to have been redressed by a *lex sacrata militaris*, an expression which again recalls the earlier *secessiones* of the *plebs*. But Livy adds that 'according to some authorities' L. Genucius, tribune of the *plebs*, carried three laws. The first prohibited the lending of money at interest; the second forbade re-election to magistracies until a ten-year interval had elapsed, as well as the cumulation of offices; the third made it lawful for both consuls to be plebeian. It is difficult to criticise these statements in the absence of other evidence; and reasons are given below for accepting the genuineness of the *lex fenebris*. But the second law, if passed, was certainly not observed, and must be regarded, if historical, as an unsuccessful attempt to break down the domination of the ruling cliques, whether patrician or plebeian. The third law may be looked upon as defining more clearly the qualifications for the supreme magistracy. It is true that it was not until 172 B.C. that two plebeian consuls actually held office; for when, in 215 B.C., M. Claudius Marcellus was elected to the seat rendered vacant by the death of L. Postumius Albinus, and assumed office, he was induced to abdicate because the gods were alleged to have signified their displeasure at the tenure of both consulships by plebeians. On the other hand, it is doubtful whether the election of two *patrician* consuls took place after 342 B.C.; for T. Veturius Calvinus, who was consul with Sp. Postumius Albinus in 334 B.C. and 321 B.C., may (as Mommsen supposed) have belonged to a branch of the Veturian *gens* which had 'gone over to the *plebs*.' It is therefore not to be denied that a law providing that one consul must, and both might, be plebeian, *may* have been enacted in 342 B.C.

The year 339 B.C. supplies another landmark in the constitutional struggle. The consuls of the year were Ti. Aemilius Mamercinus and Q. Publilius Philo. The first belonged to a patrician house which, as we saw, was represented in the Fasti of the years immediately following the Licinio-Sextian legislation; it is noteworthy that in the person of Q. Servilius, consul in 342 B.C., and perhaps identical with the consul of 365 and 362 B.C., the names characteristic of that period begin to recur. The second was presumably descended from the Publilii of earlier Republican history (the first of them appears in the list of tribunes of 471 B.C.), but was destined to bring far higher distinction upon his *gens*. He was named as dictator by his patrician colleague, and as such carried three laws, if Livy speaks truly. The first affirmed (or re-affirmed, if we accept the genuineness of the Valerio-Horatian statute of 449 B.C.) the validity of *plebiscita* for the whole *populus*; the significance of this has been discussed above (p. 482 *sq.*). The second enacted that the *patrum auctoritas* required to give binding force to the legislative enactments of the assembly of the centuries should be given before the voting took place, and thus reduced the only substantial privilege (except that of appointing the *interrex*) left to the patrician members of the Senate to a pure formality. By the third it was provided that one censor at least should be plebeian[1].

Nor did the achievements of Publilius end here. In 337 B.C. he became the first plebeian praetor; he was censor in 332 B.C., when two additional tribes were created; and in 327 B.C., when he was consul for the second time[2], his position as the 'indispensable man' brought about a momentous innovation. 'Pressure was put upon the tribunes,' says Livy, 'to propose to the people that when Q. Publilius Philo's term of office as consul came to an end, he should continue to act as consul (*pro consule rem gereret*) until the operations against the Greeks [*i.e.* those of Neapolis] were brought to a conclusion.' This was the first example of the conferment of acting-rank by vote of the people (hence called *prorogatio imperii*) in order to extend the term of office of a magistrate. Nothing can be more characteristic of the Roman method of solving practical problems of administration than this legal fiction by which a commander was 'deemed to be consul' in order to meet the necessities of warfare without increasing the numbers of the supreme college or sacrificing the principle of the annual magistracy. It will appear in the sequel how that which was in origin an emergency measure became the normal method, not only of conducting warfare in distant theatres, but of administering overseas territories. Furthermore, it will become clear that the assignment of such extended commands fell in practice into

[1] If Mommsen's restoration of the article of Festus, s.v. *Popillia* [sic] *tribus* (p. 264 L.) is right, the *tribus Poplilia* (later *Publilia*) created in 358 B.C. derived its name from the mother of one of the patrician censors of that year, whose names are unknown.

[2] He held two more consulships, in 320 and 315 B.C.

the hands of the Senate and became one of the chief sources of its authority. True, the sovereign right of the people to grant such extensions of the annual *imperium* never fell into desuetude, and was revived in the death-struggle of the Republic. But the language of the historians implies that the Senate was normally responsible for the *prorogatio imperii*. It is worth noting that Livy (who was careful to observe that the practice began in 327 B.C. and to record the procedure employed) writes under the year 307 B.C. that 'the Senate extended the command of Fabius for the following year,' though in a somewhat later case (in 295 B.C.) he tells us that 'L. Volumnius had his command extended for a year in accordance with a decree of the Senate and a resolution of the *plebs*.'

IV APPIUS CLAUDIUS

We next come to an episode which loomed large in the narratives of the Roman annalists—the censorship of Appius Claudius 'the Blind[1]', whose memory was kept green by the great works which bore his name, the 'queen of roads' connecting Rome with Capua, and the first of the Roman aqueducts, which brought a supply of pure water to Rome from springs near the river Anio, between seven and eight miles from the city. The fullest account of his policy as censor is naturally that given by Livy in the ninth book. According to Livy's version the plebeian colleague of Appius, C. Plautius, resigned his office owing to the odium aroused by the revision of the Senatorial roll[2]. This function, as has already been mentioned (p. 522 *sq.*), was imposed upon the censors by a *plebiscitum* carried by one Ovinius, of whom nothing else is known. It has been supposed that this is to be dated shortly before the censorship of Appius Claudius (312 B.C.), the first in connection with which the *lectio senatus* is mentioned by historians, but there is no evidence on the point. Appius Claudius, it seems, placed the sons of freedmen on the roll of the Senate, and the consuls of the ensuing year refused to recognize the list drawn up by him, and summoned the senators previously on the roll. There can be no doubt that the enfranchisement of slaves had become a common practice in Rome, for Livy records that in 357 B.C.

---

[1] The statement of Diodorus (xx, 36) that Appius, after laying down his office, 'pretended to be blind and remained at home' for fear of incurring odium in the Senate, is worthy of record as a curiosity.

[2] Diodorus says (xx, 36) that Appius found in Plautius a subservient colleague.

a tribal assembly summoned by the consul Cn. Manlius at his camp at Sutrium imposed a tax of 5 per cent. on manumissions. To this enactment the *patres* gave their sanction in spite of the irregularity of the procedure, the repetition of which was forbidden by a *plebiscitum*. Almost a century later than the censorship of Appius, Philip V of Macedon, writing to the citizens of Larissa in Thessaly, brings to their notice the liberal policy of the Romans in the matter of extending the full rights of citizenship (including that of holding office) to their manumitted slaves (Ditt.³ 543).

In a later passage (ix, 46) Livy explains the election of Cn. Flavius (of whom we shall presently speak) to the curule aedileship as due to the votes of the *forensis factio*, which had acquired power since Appius, provoked by the scant respect shown to his senatorial roll, had distributed the lower orders (*humiles*) throughout all the tribes. Diodorus tells us that Appius 'gave to the citizen the right to be placed in whichever tribe he chose and to register his property wherever he pleased.' These statements were taken by Mommsen to mean that Appius *for the first time* took account of property other than land in drawing up his citizen-roll; but that is not what our texts say, nor can we suppose that the inhabitants of the city of Rome—many of them men of considerable wealth—were deprived of voting power unless they possessed land outside the walls. A vote in a 'city' tribe, however, naturally counted for less (since the constituency was much larger) than a vote in a 'rustic' tribe, and Appius seems to have sought popularity by a scheme of redistribution. His reform was not of long duration, for though it survived the censorship of 307 B.C., the censors of 304 B.C.—more especially Q. Fabius Maximus Rullianus—removed the *forensis turba* from the registers of the 'rustic' tribes, and (says Livy) 'flung them into four tribes which he [Fabius] called "urban," thus gaining the title of Maximus which his many victories had failed to earn for him[1].' It is clear that Livy's authority, who seems to have thought that the 'urban' tribes had not previously existed, had a confused notion of the situation.

The censorship of Appius was immediately followed by his election to the consulship. According to Livy, he refused in

---

[1] This statement conflicts with that of Plutarch (*Pomp.* 13), who says that Fabius was given the *cognomen* Maximus because he expelled from the Senate the sons of freedmen placed on the roll by Appius; neither account is probable, and Polybius (iii, 87, 6) tells us that the Fabii Maximi derived their *cognomen* from the Cunctator. It is not legitimate, however, to treat the action recorded as taken by Rullianus as an antedating of the Cunctator's restriction of freedmen to the four tribes.

310 B.C.[1] to lay down his office on the expiry of the eighteen months' term allowed by the Lex Aemilia (p. 522), and though a strong protest was made by the tribune P. Sempronius and five of his colleagues, he secured the assistance of three other tribunes and continued to defy the law. According to some annalists, he was still censor when elected in 308 B.C.[2] to the consulship for 307 B.C., in spite of a tribunician veto on the election. His colleague both in this year and in that of his second consulship (296 B.C.) was one L. Volumnius, doubtless one of his henchmen. In 307 B.C. Volumnius was given a command in the field against the Sallentini, and while Fabius Maximus prosecuted the war against the Samnites in virtue of his *prorogatio imperii* (see below, p. 606), which Appius had strongly opposed, Appius remained in Rome. The later phases of his political career will be noticed in due course.

Amongst the sons of freedmen who benefited by the patronage of Appius Claudius was one Cn. Flavius, 'the son of Annius[3],' whose career was of especial interest to jurists. It is agreed by all authorities that he was a *scriba*, *i.e.* a magistrate's clerk or registrar; some said that he served Appius Claudius in this capacity. According to others he was on the staff of the curule aediles[4], and the annalist Piso (frag. 27 P.) told the story that at the *comitia* for the election of aediles for 304 B.C., when votes were cast for Flavius, the aedile presiding[5] refused to permit his candidature, whereupon Flavius resigned his clerkship and was duly elected. Licinius Macer, on the other hand, stated that Flavius had already held the offices of tribune, *triumvir nocturnus* and *triumvir coloniae deducendae*. Pliny the Elder, who tells us that the colleague of Flavius was a certain Q. Anicius from Praeneste, and their opponents Poetelius and Domitius, both sons of consuls, adds that Flavius was elected tribune as well as aedile, which so shocked the conservative aristocrats that they cast aside their gold rings and other ornaments. These and other[6] stories show how

[1] Diodorus places his censorship in this year, and says nothing of his unconstitutional retention of the office.

[2] 309 B.C. is a 'dictator year' inserted by later chronologists (see p. 322).

[3] So the best authorities: *Cn. filius* in Livy (ix, 46) is corrupt.

[4] The *scribae* of the aediles were of a lower grade than the *scribae quaestorii*, from whom the higher magistrates selected their clerical staff.

[5] In later times the consuls presided at the election of the minor magistrates in the assembly of tribes.

[6] The most interesting is that which relates how Flavius dedicated a chapel to Concordia close to the Comitium, in which was a bronze tablet recording its erection 'in the two hundred and fourth year after the dedication of the Capitoline temple.' We cannot, however, infer from this that

little reliance can be placed on any statement regarding the political career of Flavius. All authorities however agree in connecting his name with the publication both of the *fasti, i.e.* the calendar of court-days, and of the *legis actiones*, or forms of pleading at law. Livy says that 'he made public the civil law, which had hitherto lain buried in the secret archive of the *pontifices*, and posted up the Calendar on a tablet in the Forum, so that all might know when proceedings could be taken at law'; and Cicero confirms this in an amusing passage of the *pro Murena*, when he tells of 'the clerk who picked out the eyes of the crows' (or, as we should say, 'cut their claws'). When, however, we examine the statements of our authorities in detail, certain difficulties arise.

To begin with, it did not escape Atticus, on reading the manuscript of Cicero's *de Republica* (in which the publication of the *fasti* was mentioned), that since the Calendar of court-days was included in the Twelve Tables it might seem to be implied that Flavius lived before the decemvirate. Cicero (*ad. Att.* VI, I, 8) replies that (though this was naturally not the case) 'it is supposed' that the table containing the Calendar had been hidden: and that in any case there are 'not a few authorities' for his statement about Flavius. Nor do the texts agree as to the source and occasion of his publication. Pliny says that it was by the advice of Appius Claudius that by means of diligent enquiry he drew up his list of court-days and published it, thereby gaining such popularity with the *plebs* that he was elected curule aedile. Pomponius, on the other hand, in his sketch of constitutional development (*Dig.* I, 2, 2, 7) relates that Appius Claudius reduced the *legis actiones* to writing and that his clerk Cn. Flavius 'stole the book and presented it to the people, who were so delighted with the gift that he became tribune of the *plebs*, senator and curule aedile.' Livy, on the other hand, seems to have thought that it was as aedile that Flavius published both *fasti* and *ius civile*. Perhaps the most that can be inferred from these contradictory accounts is that Flavius was the author of the earliest compendium of Roman legal procedure, a boon to suitors who might easily lose their way in the maze of technicalities characteristic of early law. This *ius civile Flavianum*, as Pomponius calls it, was superseded by the work of Sex. Aelius Paetus a century or more later, and little was known of it or of the personality of the compiler, about whom legend clustered thickly.

The struggle of the orders was now entering upon its final

Flavius drew up a list of magistrates upon which the chronology of Roman history was based.

stage. To the year 300 B.C. tradition assigns two measures of great importance. The consul M. Valerius Maximus passed a law confirming the right of appeal to the people against capital sentences, the import of which has already been discussed (p. 447 *sq.*). A striking victory for the *plebs* was won when the tribunes Cn. and Q. Ogulnius carried a measure in the teeth of conservative opposition, led by Appius Claudius, throwing the great priestly colleges of *pontifices* and *augures* open to the *plebs*. According to Livy, it was proposed that 'inasmuch as there were at the time four augurs and four *pontifices*, and it was desirable to increase the number of priests, four *pontifices* and five augurs should be added to the number, all from the *plebs*.' The names of the plebeians appointed in pursuance of the law are given, and there is no reason to doubt their genuineness: the four *pontifices* (whose *cognomina* are added) are all *consulares* of recent standing. Livy seems however to be mistaken in supposing that the number of *pontifices* was raised to eight: at any rate the lists show that, like the augurs, they were nine in number in the latter part of the third century. The vacancies continued to be filled by co-optation; but the places now filled by plebeians were for the future reserved for the *plebs*. At the consular elections held in 297 B.C. a last attempt was made to secure both seats for patricians. Q. Fabius Maximus was elected on the first vote, and Appius Claudius endeavoured to secure the second place: but Fabius saved the situation by withdrawing his candidature.

The extant narrative of Livy ends in 293 B.C., before the 'struggle of the orders' was brought to an end. We do not know the date of the Lex Maenia, by which, as a logical corollary of the Publilian law of 339 B.C., the *patrum auctoritas* was made a preliminary formality in elections, but as it is not mentioned in the first decade of Livy, and was not yet passed, according to Cicero, in 299 B.C., it must be later than 293 B.C.

The end of the struggle was now at hand: but before we come to the last act of the drama it will be well to review the economic and political changes of the period which this chapter covers.

V. FOOD-SUPPLY, PUBLIC LANDS AND COLONIES

It has been seen already that the legislation of the decemvirs brought with it no immediate relief of economic distress, and it is therefore natural that in the years following 450 B.C. the agitation of the poor was as insistent as it had been since the time of Sp. Cassius. The recorded incidents still fall into three classes, according to their connection with the food-supply, the use of

public land and the law of debt; and of these the first may be
briefly dismissed.

The tale of famines during the second half of the fifth century,
and of the measures taken to meet them, contains only a single
episode of interest: this is the affair in which Sp. Maelius plays
the leading part. The story ran that in 440 B.C. food became so
scarce that the *plebs* was moved to a memorable step: either in
this year or the next a certain L. Minucius was appointed *praefectus annonae*. It was even alleged that his tenure of this office
was recorded in the *libri lintei*[1]. But though he sent missions far
and wide in search of corn, his efforts were rewarded with a
success so slight that a rich plebeian named Spurius Maelius saw
an opportunity for personal aggrandizement, and seized it by
making public distribution of corn which he had acquired in one
way and another with his own resources. The result of this was
to bring down on Maelius the suspicion of aiming at a tyranny,
and he was finally killed in the public interest by C. Servilius
Ahala. The circumstances wherein Maelius met his death, which
are variously recounted, are as doubtful as the evidence for his
life (p. 325 *sq.*); but it is Minucius who calls for closest notice. In
the early Empire the distribution of corn to the populace of Rome
took place in the Porticus Minucia; and from this it would be
tempting to infer that L. Minucius, the *praefectus annonae* of the
fifth century, was an invention based on the association of the
Porticus Minucia with the food-supply. But this is not the case.
The Porticus is not known to have been used for the service of
the *annona* before the principate of Claudius[2]: it was not even
built until 106 B.C. or thereabouts, when M. Minucius Rufus
triumphed over the Scordisci[3]: and yet L. Minucius is already
associated with Sp. Maelius in dealing with the famine of 440/439
by Cincius Alimentus[4], who wrote before the end of the third
century B.C. Thus the most obvious method of proving the *prae-
fectura annonae* attributed to L. Minucius to be an invention of the
annalists completely fails; and the other proofs which have been
attempted are scarcely more successful. Sp. Maelius was certainly
connected with the area called 'Aequimelium' at the foot of the
Capitoline above the Vicus Iugarius; but the view that Maelius
and Minucius were brought together as actors in a single scene
of history because a column or statue, known to have been erected

---

[1] Livy IV, 13, 7.
[2] For the evidence see M. Rostowzew, *Römische Bleitessarae*, Klio,
Beiheft III, pp. 14 *sqq.*
[3] Velleius II, 8, 3; cf. *C.I.L.* I², p. 177   [4] Frag. 6 P

to Minucius, stood near the Aequimelium is far from cogent. The
monument is said once by Livy[1] and twice by Pliny[2] to have been
set up 'outside the Porta Trigemina'; and though the site of this
gate cannot be identified with certainty, in no case can the statue
and the Aequimelium have been less than a quarter of a mile
apart. Thus, however much a fiction Sp. Maelius may be, the
story of L. Minucius seems to have withstood the efforts so far
made to demonstrate its falsity; and in that case it deserves notice
as a reminder that tales of difficulties with the food-supply in
fifth-century Rome cannot all be brushed aside without consideration. Local shortages were familiar in almost every period
of the Empire, and there is no reason to doubt that they were
known in Italy of the early Republic. The remaining crises of the
fifth and fourth centuries need only the briefest mention. When
the famines of 433 and 411[3], like the affair of 491, are made the
occasion of missions to buy grain from Etruria, the *ager Pomptinus*,
Cumae or Sicily, the details may be doubted, though the incidents
to which they are attached may well be historical. And the same
may be said of the troubles in 299, when the situation was supposed to have been saved by one of the Fabii, alleged by Licinius
Macer and Aelius Tubero—wrongly, as it would seem—to have
been Q. Fabius Maximus Rullianus himself[4].

Of the fruitless complaints about the *ager publicus* which abound
in narratives of the later fifth century the majority may be ignored[5];
but it is perhaps worth while to notice the occasion in 424 when,
according to Livy[6], it was proposed to raise money for military
pay by the exaction of a rent from *possessores*. For the rest it is
enough to say that, as was to be expected, plebeian demands were
loudly heard when fresh land was made available by the advance
against the Aequi, by the conquest of Veii and by the final victories against the Volscians ascribed to Camillus. The attempt of
Schwegler[7] to bring the tribunician demands for allotments of
public land into chronological relation with the military successes
which gave Rome her territorial gains, and his suggestion that
the subject of debate after the fall of Veii was not a proposal to
move the whole Roman people thither so much as a plan to
establish large numbers of the *plebs* on Veientane territory, are
perhaps somewhat speculative. But it is not to be denied that a

[1] IV, 16, 2.   [2] *N.H.* XVIII, 15; XXXIV, 21.
[3] Livy IV, 25, 4; 52, 4.   [4] *Id.* X, 9, 10–11; 11, 9.
[5] Cf. Livy IV, 12, 3 *sqq.*; 43, 6; 44, 7; 49, 11 *sqq.*; 52, 2 *sq.*; 53, 4 *sqq.*;
V, 12, 3 *sq.*   [6] IV, 36, 2
[7] *Röm. Geschichte*, III, pp. 164 and 172.

long-deferred satisfaction of the demand for allotments was brought by the rapid expansion of the *ager Romanus* which may be said to have begun with the battle of the Algidus (p. 503). To the year 393 Livy assigns a decision of the Senate whereby part of the region taken from Veii was to be distributed to the poor in plots of seven *iugera*[1]. Diodorus, indeed, suggests four *iugera* as the normal grant[2], and this is probable: a figure so high as seven is perhaps more appropriate to the third century[3]. But there is no reason to doubt that the decision, whatever precisely it may have been, was taken and also carried into effect. About a later proposal, on the other hand, to deal with the *ager Pomptinus* in the same way, Livy is less confident[4]. Though he mentions demands for its distribution in 388 and 387[5] and believes that *quinqueviri Pomptino agro dividendo* were appointed in 383, he only records that they were prevented from acting at the time and says nothing about a later resumption of their operations. But whatever may be the truth about this, it is clear that with the fourth century there came a change in the prospects of the *plebs*. Their demand for a share in the land which had long been public had failed; but when new acquisitions were made, their fortunes improved. Even in the fifth century they may occasionally have profited from colonial foundations, and after the fall of Veii not only was the policy of colonization continued but allotments to individuals were sometimes made as well. At length the poor seem to have established their claim to a share in the public land, and in these circumstances it is intelligible that the regulation of tenure took a place even more prominent than before in the programme of the plebeian reformers.

Among the measures ascribed to C. Licinius Stolo and L. Sextius Sextinus, none has provoked fiercer controversy than that whereby they are said to have fixed a limit to the amount of *ager publicus* which any individual might hold. Two of our authorities —Plutarch[6] and Appian[7]—allege that Tiberius Gracchus in 133 B.C. re-enacted a law which forbade a citizen to occupy more than five hundred *iugera* of public land; but neither of them gives a clue to its authorship, and for their opinion of its date there is no better evidence than the implication, probably to be found in the opening sentences of Appian (*l.c.*), that it belonged to a time after the Roman conquest of Italy. Such a law is mentioned

---

[1] Livy v, 30, 8.   [2] XIV, 102, 4.
[3] See Val. Max. IV, 3, 5; Pliny, *N.H.* XVIII, 18.   [4] VI, 21, 4 *sqq.*
[5] VI, 5, 1–5; 6, 1.   [6] *Ti. Gracchus*, 8, 2; cf. *Camillus*, 39, 5.
[7] *Bella Civ.* I, 8.

already by Cato[1]. The rest of our informants, of whom Varro is the earliest[2] and Livy the most familiar[3], include the measure among the rogations of Licinius Stolo and L. Sextius and thereby place it in the first half of the fourth century. The arguments wherewith Niese[4] sought to show that the law cannot have been passed before the end of the First Punic War are of very varied value, and the weaker of them would be negligible without the support of the more cogent. His view, for instance, that the accounts of Plutarch and Appian should be preferred to that of Livy because they are derived from Posidonius rests on a theory of the common source used by these two writers which was always doubtful and which should now be definitely given up[5]. The one apparently serious objection which he urged against the traditional date is that to set a limit of five hundred *iugera* to holdings of public land implies the existence of public land in quantities far larger than can be admitted at any time in the fourth century. It is assumed that, when it was found necessary to pass the law, there must have been many holdings of dimensions greater than those to be allowed for the future, and even more of smaller size; and it is then alleged that holdings on this scale demand an amount of public land which was never reached before the conquest of Italy. The case, however, is by no means convincing. At the outset it may be suggested that a prohibitory law is no evidence that the abuse against which it is directed has been frequent in the recent past: if holdings of public land were confined for the future to five hundred *iugera* at most, the fact does not justify the conclusion that holdings of larger size than this were already numerous. Again, the assumption that during the regal period and the fifth century Rome had acquired no more than a negligible amount of territory which remained public is not only improbable but directly opposed to the unanimous evidence of tradition: tradition at least is clear that in the fifth century grants of land to colonies and to individual citizens were not on a scale which would account for the whole of the land which Rome appropriated from her neighbours. But it is by an examination of details that the weakness of Niese's case can best be shown; and of these a single example will suffice. The territory won by the conquest of Veii amounted to more than two hundred thousand acres, which in plots of seven *iugera* would provide for about forty-five thousand allottees; and if Diodorus is right in confining

---

[1] *Orig.* frag. 95 e P.   [2] *R.R.* I, 2, 9.
[3] VI, 35, 5.   [4] In *Hermes*, XXIII, 1888, pp. 410–23.
[5] See E. Meyer, *Kleine Schriften*, I, ed. 2, pp. 379 *sqq.*

the grants to four *iugera* each, the number of possible recipients would rise to something like eighty thousand. Even the lower of these figures is vastly in excess of the highest which they can seriously be believed to have attained. If then, as the evidence suggests, less than half the available territory sufficed for the purpose of these grants, it is clear that, when they had been made and when the needs of the surviving Veientane population had been met, in all probability there was still enough land left over as *ager publicus* of the Roman people for its proper use soon to become an object of legislation. It is not to be denied that the great increase of public land, which subsequently served as the main investment for the capital of the rich, came with the second half of the fourth century; but there is no good reason to doubt that by the time of the Licinian-Sextian legislation Rome already disposed of public land enough to make its control a matter of public interest.

Thus the law may be accepted; and it must be noticed as a measure which fostered the prosperity of the poor at the expense of the richer classes, among whom were to be found the great plebeians whose admission to curule office was the outstanding result of the struggle of the orders. But the details narrated of its passage cannot be stressed. Though its application in 298[1] is wholly plausible, the story that Licinius himself was convicted of violating his own law[2] is based on a *motif* so common in the records of early legislators that episodes in which it appears must all be treated with suspicion. But the most serious doubt concerns the precise limit set to holdings of public land. Five hundred *iugera*, with a possible increase in certain cases, was the amount allowed by Tiberius Gracchus, and it is conceivable that from the Gracchan law this figure has been transferred to the enactment of 367. Even in the fourth century holdings of this extent, though large, are not incredible; but it should perhaps be noticed that the weaker manuscripts of one late authority[3] contain just a suggestion that one hundred *iugera* was the original allowance, and not five. On such evidence, however, no conclusion can be based. A measure setting limits to tenancies of public land may be included with some confidence in the legislation of 367, but the nature of our information makes it imprudent to lay stress on the recorded details.

Grants of land, however, and admission to some share at least in the possession of *ager publicus* were not the only means by which a livelihood was found for the needy citizens of Rome. The old policy of colonization was continued, and with a vigour far greater than before. The precise nature of the political relation-

[1] Livy x, 13, 14.   [2] *E.g.* Livy vii, 16, 9.   [3] *de viris ill.* 20, 3.

ship which Rome established between these colonies and herself must remain uncertain; but it should be said that the evidence is by no means conclusive in favour of the theory that down to the re-occupation of Antium in 338 all these foundations—with the possible exception of Ostia, if Ostia be earlier than this—enjoyed Latin rights and were not part of the Roman body politic. It may at any rate be noticed that this is not the view of tradition. The impression given by Livy, Dionysius and Velleius is that in some cases at least, even in the fifth century, Rome posted small bodies of her own citizens in places of strategic value, and that these garrisons retained their Roman citizenship as much as did the inhabitants of the so-called maritime colonies of which Antium was the first. And this impression is strengthened by the way in which certain of the earlier foundations finally emerge into the full light of history as *coloniae civium Romanorum* without any clear evidence being preserved to show that their status had been changed. The issue is one which cannot be decided with confidence, and for the present purpose its decision is unnecessary; but it is probably not far from the truth to say that the colonies of which notices abound in our authorities for the early history of Republican Rome were foundations of varied types. Some may have been outlying fractions of the Roman State and others independent communities, recruited in part from non-Roman sources, which were related to Rome in the same way as cities belonging to the Latin League. Whatever their status, however, two facts are clear. One is that in the founding of these colonies the initiative was in many cases Roman, and the other that colonies of all kinds alike served to ease the economic difficulties of the city and its more immediate neighbourhood by drawing off part of the surplus population.

The details of Rome's colonizing activities and the chronological difficulties caused by the frequent disagreement of our authorities bear most closely on the military history of the time[1]. Here it is enough to say that, after the garrisoning of Ardea in 442 —if that be historical (see above, p. 503)—colonies are recorded during the eastern offensive which opened about 423 (see above, p. 510) and again in the fifteen years which follow the fall of Veii. With the occupation of Setia, which is put by Velleius eight years after the Gallic raid on Rome, there comes a lull for almost half a century until a period of widespread settlement opens with the re-founding of Antium in 338 and the planting of two thousand five hundred men in the Campanian city of Cales in 334. Thence-

[1] See chapters xv, xvii, xviii and xx, and map 12, facing p. 820.

forward colonies are freely founded, and the foundations continue until the period with which this chapter has to deal ends with the dispatch of settlers to Hadria and Sena Gallica, near the coasts of Picenum and Umbria, at some dates between 290 and 283. By this time colonial foundations were to be found at intervals throughout a quadrilateral enclosed by lines running from Sena Gallica to Nepete, thence by way of Pontia and the surrounding islands to Saticula in Samnium, due west of Beneventum, and so through the Apulian city of Venusia back to the Adriatic coast. The effect of the drain caused by these numerous foundations on the economic problem at Rome is difficult to estimate: the number of settlers sent to the various sites is by no means always recorded, and even when the number is known it has to be remembered that settlers were recruited from other sources than the body of Roman citizens. Nevertheless a certain amount of evidence exists in Livy and Dionysius, and from this it may be conjectured without undue rashness that between the decemviral legislation and the dictatorship of Q. Hortensius colonies provided new homes and a means of livelihood for something like fifty thousand people. Not all of these had been Roman citizens before their migration: but the part played by Rome in setting the colonies afoot suggests that the contribution made to their manning by Rome herself was at least large enough for the consequent loss of population to have had a notable effect on the problem of the lacklands and their poverty in the region round the city, where their difficulties were most acute.

VI. DEBT AND THE *NEXUM*

There remain to be discussed the troubles of those who stayed at home—troubles which are revealed in agitations against the law of debt. The advent of a Roman coinage in the second half of the fourth century is heralded by a crescendo of complaint about the current rate of interest and the severity of the penalties imposed on the insolvent. Though its general suggestions are plausible enough, no information of value is to be had from the story of M. Manlius Capitolinus and his championship of the poor against the demands of their creditors[1]; nor again is it necessary to do more than mention the abortive activities which Livy records of the censors Sp. Servilius Priscus and Q. Cloelius Siculus in 378[2]. But with the legislation of Licinius Stolo and his colleague Sextius Sextinus a serious issue is raised. The measures

---

[1] Livy VI, 11, 8 *sq.*; cf. Appian, *Ital.* 9.   [2] Livy VI, 31, 2.

which composed the programme of this pair are our surest clue
to the demands of the *plebs* during the first three decades of the
fourth century; and when it is alleged that they introduced a
proposal to deduct from the outstanding amount of a debt such
interest as had been already paid and to spread the payment of
what remained over a period of three years[1], the tradition has to
be examined with care. The objections urged against the story
are two. First there is the weakness of the evidence, which is
known to have been exposed to corruption, and which even in its
final form lays far less stress on this particular proposal than on
any of the others ascribed to the same occasion. But it must be
observed that debt was a subject on which legislative action of
undoubted authenticity was taken several times in the half-century
which follows, so that the intervention of the plebeian leaders in
this matter would not be inappropriate in the period to which it
is assigned. And the small meed of fame which the measure
achieved is easily intelligible. The measure was in the nature of
a Seisachtheia. It lightened the burdens of people who were in
debt at the time when it was passed, but it was not a law of permanent application designed to change the law of lending in
perpetuity; and there is no need to suppose that a concession of
such ephemeral value would bulk large in the minds of later
generations. The second objection—that the proposal is too
violent in its disregard for the rights of property to be credible
in a society which had yet to learn the lengths to which revolution
may go—is scarcely more serious. The institution of the *mutuum*
—a simple transfer of property on the one condition that the
property or its equivalent shall be transferred back by the receiver
to the lender at some future time—is a reminder that, among the
Romans, loans and interest were not inseparably connected: a
mutuum was a gratuitous loan, and interest could only be ensured
by a separate contract which is clearly alien to the original form
of *mutuum* itself. Thus it need by no means be assumed that a
reduction of interest, especially at a time when rates of interest
were high, was open to the same objections as could be brought
against proposals to tamper with the principal, and in these circumstances the somewhat drastic character of the measure under
consideration are not enough to prove it an invention. The
tradition cannot be rejected; and if it is sound, though the relief
given by the reformers was limited in its application, their concern
with debt is not to be ignored as evidence for the nature of the
grievances felt by their supporters.

[1] Livy vi, 35, 4; 39, 2.

There follows a period of frequent legislation on debt, provoked in all probability by the approaching introduction of a coinage. According to our authorities, in 357 B.C. the maximum rate of interest was fixed—or, if Tacitus is right about the provisions of the decemvirs (see above, p. 476), was fixed again—at 'unciarium fenus' by the plebiscite of M. Duillius and L. Menenius[1], and ten years later not only was this reduced by half, but debtors were again given three years in which to pay[2]. Whether the details of the narrative are true or not, the existence of these or similar laws is confirmed by casual references to prosecutions for their infringement[3]. Besides this, there should be noticed the elaborate attempt made in 352 B.C. to ease the difficulties of the situation by appointing a board of five to advance money from the Treasury to such debtors as seemed to be in trouble, not through irretrievable insolvency, but merely owing to the violence of the pressure put upon them by creditors: in effect the State, which was prepared to be more lenient than the private usurer, took over such loans as were not wholly bad. Though it is perhaps surprising at so early a date, this establishment of *quinqueviri mensarii* cannot be disproved; but there is much less to be said for another measure which has sometimes been ascribed to the same year, 352 B.C. The jurist Gaius[4] mentions a *lex Marcia* which allowed debtors the right of *manus iniectio* against creditors who essayed to charge interest at a rate higher than the legal maximum; but the context in which Gaius refers to this enactment combines with such scanty knowledge as we have of the history of procedure in cases of the kind concerned to make it highly unlikely that Lange[5] was right in connecting it with C. Marcius Rutilius and the quinqueviral board.

Only two other incidents need be noticed, but both are important. At the end of his somewhat unconvincing story about the mutiny of the Roman army in Campania (p. 529) Livy records that according to certain authorities one of its results was the passing of three measures in the interests of the *plebs*[6]. Two of them concern the constitution, but the third is a flat prohibition of loans and usury. The tribune to whom they are ascribed is L. Genucius, a member of a house whose traditional history is brought under some suspicion by the frequency with which Genucii are shown among the first plebeian holders of offices hitherto reserved for the patricians. But the constitutional changes ascribed to 342 B.C. cannot be proved fictitious, and there is at least a certain amount of evidence to suggest that the *lex fenebris* was an expedient

[1] Livy VII, 16, 1. [2] *Id.* VII, 27, 3–4. [3] Cf. *id.* VII, 28, 9 (344 B.C.).
[4] IV, 23. [5] *Röm. Alterthümer*, II², p. 621. [6] VII, 42.

of the kind to which Rome might resort at a time when progress
which was leading to the introduction of currency was making the
plight of the poor even more grievous than it had been before. Besides the statement of Cato[1] mentioned already (p. 477) and the
words of Livy here under consideration, there are passages of
Tacitus[2] and Appian[3] which make it plain that Romans believed
there to have been a time when lending at usury was absolutely forbidden; and to this it may be added that Tacitus supports Livy in
placing the enactment of this veto in the second half of the fourth
century. In these circumstances it is probably prudent to accept
Livy's story as it stands, and to neglect the large variety of alternative interpretations which have been put upon his description of
the law by modern critics. But it is not to be supposed that the
measure was of enduring validity. It may be regarded as a desperate remedy adopted by a community still strange to the working
of currency, and as one bound to be repealed or evaded as soon
as knowledge had made a small advance. Certainly it was no
more in the interests of potential borrowers than of people with
money to lend that loans should be made so far impossible as they
inevitably must be if no interest may be charged.

The remaining episode marks perhaps the greatest success won
by the poor in their struggle against the moneylenders. By a *lex
Poetelia*, or *Poetelia Papiria*, the *nexum* was so deeply changed that
it soon fell into disuse. The date of this reform is doubtful. Livy[4]
mentions it under the year 326, the consulship of C. Poetelius III
and L. Papirius Mugillanus (or Cursor); but it has been thought
that Varro, in a passage which is highly corrupt[5], refers it to the
rather dubious dictatorship of the younger C. Poetelius in 313.
Whatever the precise year of its passage, this law was clearly of
the first importance. It did not, indeed, abolish *nexum* outright;
but it is generally agreed to have insisted that judgment should
be obtained in all cases before execution was carried out. The age
of self-help was over, and its end is recorded by tradition precisely
at the point where its end is to be expected. At a time when the
State was trying to regulate the rate of interest, it was manifestly
undesirable that creditors should retain the right of taking remedy
for default without the cognizance of a magistrate. But in addition
to this there is much to be said for the proposal of Pais[6] to accept
in its natural meaning Livy's statement that thenceforward the
property and not the person of a borrower was to be the security

---

[1] *de agri cult. ad init.*   [2] *Ann.* VI, 16, 3.   [3] *Bella Civ.* I, 54 *ad init.*
[4] VIII, 28.   [5] *L.L.* VII, 105.   [6] *Ricerche*, Serie IV, pp. 44–47.

for his debt[1]. What exactly happened the evidence does not allow us to determine. Certainly personal execution was not completely abolished; for there were circumstances wherein it was possible even in the classical age. But it is not unlikely that the *lex Poetelia* took a final step in the direction of allowing borrowers to give their whole property in security for their debts.

In the century and a half which followed the Decemviral legislation the poor had improved their lot to an extent of which they might be proud. Poverty and debt were still indeed present, and the economic structure of Roman society had not been fundamentally changed. Rome remained an agricultural community, untouched as yet by that commercial revival which reveals itself, for instance, at Praeneste towards the end of the fourth century[2]. But the resources of the State had grown. Land was more plentiful, and the increase of the *ager publicus* was already beginning to produce wider differences of wealth by allowing the rich to acquire large holdings and so to become richer still. Yet at the same time the demands of the poor for a consideration of their claims had not been ignored. Allotments had been distributed; room had been made on the *ager publicus* for the humbler tenant; colonies had been freely founded; and the troubles of debtors had found champions whose efforts were not unrewarded. When the struggle of the orders at long last reached its end, the poor could count their gains with a certain satisfaction. Nevertheless their troubles were not over, and the only issue to which the struggle brought a final settlement was different—the issue raised by the claims of rich plebeians to the high offices of State.

VII. THE NEW NOBILITY

Turning to the political sphere, we see that the struggles, internal and external, of the fourth century, had brought about profound changes in the Roman state. There is no need here to recapitulate the successive steps by which the *plebs* had won access to all the magistracies, and to those priestly colleges which had a political significance. What we must note is the change in the *personnel* of the ruling order, and the emergence of a new plebeian aristocracy. We have already shown how a small group of families for a long time monopolized the representation of the *plebs* in the supreme college; from 340 B.C. onwards the circle was rapidly enlarged. In the first decade of this period representatives of

---

[1] VIII, 28, 9.
[2] Praenestine art will be dealt with in vol. IX in a survey of Italian art.

eight new *gentes* won their way to the consulship; several of these
bear names which recur throughout Republican history, though
two of the most important, C. Maenius and the far greater soldier
and statesman, Q. Publilius Philo, both of whom were impeached
in 314 B.C. in connection with the 'conspiracy of Capua' and
acquitted, left no successors in the Fasti (p. 602). After 331 B.C.
the influx of *novi homines* slackened, but a good soldier could still
win through to the consulship; the Fulvii had their first consul in
322 B.C. and C. Junius Bubulcus, thrice consul and dictator, came
into office first in 317 B.C. P. Decius Mus, son of the consul of
340 B.C., held the first of his four consulships in 312 B.C. He
was evidently no political opponent of the patrician aristocracy,
and was a colleague of Q. Fabius Maximus Rullianus in three
consulships and the censorship. From 307 B.C., however, until
the close of the fourth century, a number of fresh names appear
in the lists, and in the early years of the third, besides members
of the recently ennobled houses, we find (293 B.C.) Sp. Carvilius,
of whom Velleius records that though of equestrian origin he rose,
like Cato and Mummius, to be consul, *triumphator* and censor,
and (290 B.C.) M'. Curius Dentatus, who celebrated two of his
four triumphs at the expense of Samnites and Sabines. It was,
in fact, impossible to exclude from a share in the government a
class which was not merely growing in wealth, but was also
capable of furnishing efficient commanders in the constant warfare waged by the Romans. We cannot, it is true, place implicit
reliance upon the list of triumphs (cf. p. 326); for example, that of
Q. Publilius Philo in 326 B.C. is probably fictitious (p. 595 n. 1).
Still less credence is due to triumphs not recorded in the Fasti,
such as that of P. Decius Mus in 312 B.C. (*de vir. ill.* 26). When
all deductions are made, however, the achievements of the 'new'
men are worthy to be placed beside those of the Fabii, Valerii or
Papirii. Thus the Senate was gradually transformed into a body
representative of the community in which *patres* and *plebs* shared
a common devotion to the 'public cause' (*res publica*).

At this point the question arises whether at this early date the
ruling class had already received substantial reinforcement from
the communities drawn into Rome's orbit during the period of
expansion. In one instance this is undisputed. The Fulvii were
a Tusculan family, and in 322 B.C. L. Fulvius Curvus attained
the consulship, and according to a tradition recorded by Livy
(VIII, 40) and accepted by the compiler of the Acta Triumphorum,
celebrated a triumph over the Samnites. This fact, real or supposed,
was embellished by later tradition, so that we read in the *Natural*

History of the Elder Pliny (VII, 136) that Fulvius was "consul of the rebellious Tusculans[1] and, having changed sides, was immediately invested with the same office by the Roman people, and was the only man who, in the same year in which he was an enemy, triumphed at Rome over those whose consul he had been." Setting this legend aside, we may note that the Fulvii retained the place which they had secured in the governing order: another Fulvius triumphed in 305 and 299 B.C., a third in 298 B.C. Nor were they the only representatives of that town who sought their fortunes in Rome. According to Cicero (*pro Plancio* 8, 19) Tusculum could boast of more 'consular families' than any other municipium, including that of the Juventii, one of whose members, as he tells us in a later passage (24, 58), was one of the first plebeians to be elected aedile[2]. From Tusculum, too, came Ti. Coruncanius[3], the first plebeian *pontifex maximus*, and although his consulship belongs to 280 B.C., his career no doubt began in our period. In the *pro Sulla* (7, 23) Cicero couples with Coruncanius M'. Curius Dentatus in a list of *municipales* who rose to fame in Rome. We have already mentioned Q. Anicius, the aedile of 304 B.C., as a native of Praeneste; and doubtless if we were more fully informed with regard to the holders of offices of lower grade than the consulship, we should find abundant evidence that the expansion of the citizen body brought in its train an infiltration of fresh elements into the governing class.

We cannot, however, go farther than this, and subscribe to the view of Münzer[4], that a number of families from Latin or Campanian cities were encouraged, largely by the patronage of leading Roman *gentes* such as the Fabii, to seek their fortune in Rome and rose to the highest office. To take but one example, the Plautii are not proved to be of Tiburtine origin by the fact that an imposing tomb below Tivoli belonged to the family in Imperial times. Münzer himself points out (p. 44) that the Ficoroni cista bearing the inscription *Novios Plautios med Romai fecid* is 'one of the finest products of Praenestine art' and that

[1] This may have been suggested by the story told in Livy VIII, 37 of the proposal made by a tribune to punish the Tusculans in 323 B.C. for inciting Velitrae and Privernum to revolt.

[2] This fact is in favour of the supposition that Tusculum was incorporated in the Roman state in 381 B.C. (see p. 569).

[3] The learned Emperor Claudius (Tacitus, *Ann.* XI, 24), said that Coruncanius came from Cameria; but this was a Latin village which suffered extinction at an early date.

[4] *Römische Adelsparteien und Adelsfamilien*, pp. 46 *sqq.* Münzer's theories have been carried still farther by Schur (*Hermes*, LIX, 1924, pp. 450 *sqq.*).

the name is common on the gravestones of Praeneste. The case
for tracing the Atilii to a Campanian origin is equally weak.

Outside the circle of those who possessed the *civitas*, whether
complete or limited, stood the holders of what are termed 'Latin
rights.' Under the later Republic the 'Latin name' (*nomen
Latinum*) is applied to a privileged group of allies (*socii*) of Rome.
This group includes several communities in addition to the
members of the old Latin League, dissolved in 338 B.C. That
league had planted colonies as outposts on its frontiers, where it
was faced by hostile neighbours, and Rome, with her genius for
adapting institutions to meet new needs, had continued the policy
and established what were called 'Latin colonies,' *i.e.* colonies
whose status was assimilated to that of the original members of
the League (and *its* colonies), thus divorcing the term 'Latin' from
its ethnic significance and giving to it an abstract, juridical
meaning as connoting a bundle of rights which might be conferred on communities or even on individuals and might or might
not be enjoyed in their entirety. Thus (to say nothing of later
refinements) we hear of *prisci Latini*, the 'old Latin' communities
of the *foedus Cassianum*, and *Latini coloniarii*, 'Latins of colonial
status,' amongst whom (as will be shown in the sequel) there were
grades of privilege.

We can gather something by inference of the personal privileges enjoyed by the members of the old Latin League. The
foedus Cassianum provided for the trial of suits arising out of
contracts made between members of the League in the *forum
contractus*; in other words, the citizen of a Latin town could sue
and be sued in the courts of the other allied cities. When the
League was dissolved, the Romans deprived its members of
commercia and *conubia* 'amongst themselves,' which is rightly
taken to imply that they retained these ties with Rome (Livy VIII,
14). It appears from Cicero (*pro Caec.* 35, 102) that the 'Latin
colonists' of *less* privileged status (and therefore *a fortiori* those
in the enjoyment of full Latin rights) could enter into obligations
in the Roman form of *nexum* and could enjoy the benefits of the
Roman law of succession. It may fairly be concluded that in early
times the Latin right entitled the possessor to use the forms of the
Roman civil law, which was the true significance of *commercium*
(p. 422). *Conubium* means the right to contract a Roman marriage,
the issue of which will be Roman citizens, and subject to the
patria potestas of the father; and it is a natural corollary that the
adoption of Latin by Roman or of Roman by Latin was allowed.

There were, however, other Latin rights besides those which

flowed from admission to the benefits of the *ius civile*. In early times the members of the League possessed the mutual privilege of exchanging their domicile for that of an allied city (*ius migrandi*); and it was only the abuse of this right, which was inevitable as the citizenship of Rome became increasingly attractive, that caused the Romans to restrict it by law and to substitute for it other avenues to Roman *civitas* in later foundations.

Finally, the Latin who came to Rome enjoyed a certain limited voting power in the assemblies of the tribes. Before a vote was taken, an urn was brought in and lots were cast for a tribe in which the Latins present cast their votes; and this curious formality (*sitellae delatio*) persisted throughout Republican history because a usage grew up according to which the *intercessio* of the tribune might be exerted at this point in the proceedings, but no later[1]. Dionysius, it is true, goes much farther than this, and represents the Latins and Hernici as crowding in to Rome to vote (VIII, 72); but his mind was (as so often) confused by Greek analogies, for he was in the habit of using the term *isopoliteia* to describe the relation of the Latin communities to Rome; and this institution, in its developed form, implied[2] the capacity of the individual for exercising full personal *and political* rights in the allied community.

Thus 'Latinitas,' to use the abstract term coined in the age of Cicero, became a convenient stepping-stone to the acquisition of full Roman citizenship; and the accident of its origin from membership in a league was responsible for the anomaly that the Latin communities, even the colonies planted by Rome and mainly peopled by her own citizens, were technically independent and sovereign states, unlike those possessing the *civitas sine suffragio*.

VIII. THE MACHINERY OF GOVERNMENT

We would gladly know more of the process by which the Romans laid the foundations of an administrative system, which the growth of their city made increasingly needful. We have already mentioned (p. 456) the fact that the aediles of the *plebs* played an increasingly important part in municipal administration; and the admission of patricians to the college when the

[1] See the passages cited by Mommsen, *Staatsrecht*, III (I), 397.
[2] As we see from the agreement between Pergamum and Temnos, *O.G.I.S.* 265.

'curule' aedileship was instituted in 366 B.C. implied the recognition of the fact. We cannot, it is true, attach much weight to the legend that in 463 B.C., when a pestilence was raging, the care of the city was entrusted to the aediles of the *plebs* (Livy III, 6); but there may be some truth in the story that in the rebuilding of the city after the Gallic sack the aediles enforced the execution of work towards which the state gave financial assistance. Mommsen suggests that after 366 B.C. the office was remodelled on the analogy of the *agoranomia* in Greek states; and to this we must trace Cicero's definition of its functions in the *de legibus* as the 'care of the city, the corn-supply, the temples and the games.' Food-control in time of famine is assigned to the aediles in the story (apocryphal in itself) of Q. Fabius Maximus' measures in 299 B.C.: the other functions, as making up the traditional competence of the aedileship, are enumerated by Cicero in his allusion to his own tenure of the office (*Verr.* v, 14, 36). It is more important, in relation to the period under review, to note the position assigned to the aediles in the punishment of certain offences by fine, against which an appeal lay to the *plebs* in assembly. These sometimes fall within the sphere of public morals (Livy VIII, 22, x, 31), but the most significant cases relate to the enforcement of the laws against usury and those concerning public land. In 344 and 304 B.C. we hear of the prosecution of money-lenders (in the latter year by Cn. Flavius); and offenders against the Licinio-Sextian agrarian law, whether by *occupatio* or by unlawfully pasturing cattle on public lands, are dealt with in the same way. The *aediles plebis* are specifically mentioned in one case; and, if Mommsen is right, the Popillius who prosecuted Licinius Stolo under his own act held the same office; but the story seems to be a legend of a well-known type.

As was explained above (p. 458), the *plebs* did not, at any rate after the Decemviral legislation, claim to sit in judgment on appeal from its own magistrates in capital cases; but a practice grew up by which the tribunes initiated proceedings—usually by the infliction of a heavy fine—against magistrates or other official persons for political offences, and 'borrowed auspices' from a consul or praetor in order that the assembly of the centuries might pronounce a verdict on appeal[1]. Such, amongst others, were the cases of M. Postumius, *tribunus militum*, who was fined 10,000 *asses* for misconduct in the war with Veii in 423 B.C., of C. Sem-

---

[1] The origin of this procedure is obscure. On the possibility that it was provided for in the Decemviral code see Strachan Davidson, *Problems of the Roman Criminal Law*, i, 178 and Mommsen, *Strafrecht*, p. 1015.

pronius, consul in 423 B.C., prosecuted and fined in 420 B.C., L. Manlius, dictator in 363 B.C., prosecuted by a tribune Q. Pomponius in 362 B.C. for his oppressive conduct of the *dilectus*[1], and L. Postumius Megellus, consul in 291 B.C., prosecuted by two tribunes and fined for defiance of the Senate in his conduct of the war in Samnium[2]. The last case is remarkable because it shows the tribunes acting in the interests of the Senate and foreshadows the changed position of the tribunate in the Middle Republic, which will be more fully discussed in the sequel, being the natural consequence of the process by which the Senate was converted into a council representative of both orders.

Some attempt was made to relieve the regular magistrates of their administrative duties by the appointment of special commissioners: thus in 311 B.C. *duoviri navales* were appointed to take charge of the small Roman fleet. From time to time *duoviri aedi dedicandae* were elected when new temples were built, and the claim of the *plebs* to have a say in these matters seems to have been admitted at an early date; Livy (IX, 46) records that in 304, by the advice of the Senate, it was proposed to the people that no temple or altar should be set up without the authority of the Senate or of a majority of the tribunes, and Cicero (*de domo sua* 49, 127) cites a *vetus lex tribunicia* of unknown date, proposed by one of the plebeian Papirii, which forbade the *consecratio* of temple, land or altar 'without the command of the *plebs*.' Of still greater importance were the commissioners for the allotment of land and foundation of colonies, usually three in number. In the narrative of Livy we hear of them first in connection with the legendary foundation of a colony at Antium in 467 B.C., and the practice was invariable in historical times: the names of the commissioners are rarely given, but we find a plebeian, Kaeso Duillius, amongst the *tresviri coloniae deducendae* for the settlement of Cales (p. 594).

The *plebs*, therefore, had by the close of our period won access for its members to the highest office and taken its share of the

---

[1] Or, according to Cicero (*de Off.* III, 31, 112), 'quod is paucos sibi dies ad dictaturam gerendam addidisset.'

[2] Dion. Hal. XVII–XVIII, 5. The statement that Postumius was condemned 'by all the *tribes*' would indicate that the *concilium plebis* heard the appeal, if we could attach any importance to Dionysius' use of terms. Other famous examples, especially the prosecution of Camillus in 391 B.C., and those of the decemvir Appius Claudius in 449 B.C., and of Q. Fabius Ambustus, one of the envoys who had taken part in the fight with the Gauls at Clusium in 391 B.C. (Livy VI, 1), have been omitted because the legends with which they are connected or (in the case of Camillus) the inconsistencies of the tradition bring them under suspicion.

burdens of public administration. The plebeians formed an ever-increasing majority of the citizen body, as fresh tribes were established on conquered lands and colonies founded which made an outlet for the surplus population of the city, or communities such as Tusculum and some of the Latin towns were merged in the Roman state. Still, however, the *patres* claimed that they preserved the continuity of the Roman Republic with the state of the Kings, especially as the depositaries of religious tradition, though this was rendered nugatory by the admission of the plebeians to the priestly colleges and the reduction of the privileges of the patrician members of the Senate to empty forms. The *plebs* therefore determined to secure finally the recognition of their tribal assemblies as law-making bodies coordinate in sovereignty with the *populus Romanus*. It is much to be regretted that the narrative of Livy is wanting for the last act in the drama. Practically all we know is that which has been said by anticipation on pp. 481 *sqq.* In 287 B.C., as it would appear (though the exact date is uncertain), the question of debt led to a fresh crisis, and was ended by a *secessio*, this time to the Janiculum, and the appointment of a plebeian dictator, Q. Hortensius, who belonged to a wholly undistinguished *gens*, represented in early tradition only by a tribune of 422 B.C. What measures he took for the relief of debtors we are not told; but all historians and jurists agree that he carried a law which finally disposed of the question at issue between *patres* and *plebs* regarding the law-making power by giving to the resolutions of the *plebs* validity for all Quirites.

The solution of the problem was characteristically Roman. It cannot be called logical, for logic demands a single sovereign in a single state. It was eminently practical in the sense that it gave formal recognition to that which practice had proved workable and (to the vast majority of citizens) desirable. It was not too drastic, for it left the ancient organs of the state untouched, and left them to find their *modus vivendi* with those of more recent creation. The Roman was always confident that his institutions could be adapted to the new ends which the course of history constantly reveals; and the following chapters will show that he was justified in his belief. Thus he steered clear of the reefs of *stasis* which wrecked so many a Greek state, and was rendered free to achieve that work of unification in Italy which even the genius of Athens could never bring about in Greece.

CHAPTER XVII

THE GALLIC WARS OF ROME

I. THE EVIDENCE FOR THE PERIOD

THE value of the sources for early Roman history has already been discussed generally in chap. x, but it is necessary to add a few remarks here upon the character of the literary tradition relating to the Gallic Wars in particular and upon the way in which that tradition has filtered down to us[1]. At the outset the historian is hampered by complete lack of contemporary evidence: Gallic sources there were none, the Etruscan have vanished, and there remain no early Roman accounts. Our tradition appears to be derived from two main currents: the first Greek and more especially Western Greek, as represented in the general History of Italy composed by Timaeus of Tauromenium (352–256 B.C.), who gathered up in his synthesis a host of earlier Western writers such as Philistus, Lycus of Rhegium and Aristoxenus of Tarentum, and the scattered notices of Ephorus, Aristotle and Heracleides Ponticus on Rome or on the Gauls. Although all this body of literature has reached us in but meagre fragments, it is reflected in Polybius and in a lesser degree in Diodorus, Dionysius of Halicarnassus, Trogus, and even to some extent in Roman annalistic.

This last is the second main current: of its comparative lateness and of the faults which tend to vitiate it mention has already been made; on this period we need but point out how, for example, the ransoming of Rome was transformed into something more agreeable to Roman pride and the figure of Camillus enlarged to the heroic proportions suitable to a saviour of the state. Of the annalists themselves, such as L. Cassius Hemina, P. Clodius, Q. Claudius Quadrigarius and others, very little has survived, but they can be traced in Polybius, Diodorus, Livy, and Plutarch, who drew extensively upon them, and in a more fragmentary way in Dionysius of Halicarnassus, Appian, Dio Cassius, and others.

First in order of merit comes Polybius, who unfortunately only furnishes a general outline, which can, however, be filled in by Trogus; both these represent, at any rate in part, the

[1] For detailed references to the Ancient sources see the Bibliography.

Greek tradition directly and independently of Roman annalistic tradition. Second comes Diodorus, who appears to follow the older annalistic, and third Livy, Dionysius of Halicarnassus, Appian and Dio Cassius, who introduce elements from later annalistic tradition. But such a classification as this, though useful as a general guide, must not be taken too rigidly; to exclude the later annalistic would, in the opinion of the present writer, be as grave an error in historical method and as damaging to historical truth as a blind adherence to its statements in preference to all others.

But while the literary tradition is imperfect and needs careful handling, much can be gleaned from the auxiliary sciences such as epigraphy, the study of place-names and archaeology. In spite of the late composition of the *Fasti triumphales* and the influence of annalistic upon it, it can sometimes provide a useful controlling factor. The study of place-names, particularly in Cisalpine Gaul, affords us useful indications of the extent of the Etruscan domination at the time of the Gallic invasions. On the cultural side archaeology furnishes valuable information: for example, excavations at Felsina and Marzabotto have revealed what was the manner of life in the Etruscan cities of that region when the storm burst upon them, while the later Gallic cemeteries found at Montefortino, Ornavasso, Soldo, or Bologna throw a flood of light upon the life and habits of the invaders themselves, and the gradual fusion of Celtic and Etruscan civilizations. Lastly, excavations in Rome itself have been of great value: the Palatine and Forum have yielded important indications as to the extent of the city that the Gauls sacked, and the manner in which it was fortified after that disaster. All these pieces of evidence, in addition to the literary sources, lie ready to the hand of the historian of the Gallic Wars.

II. THE GALLIC CONQUEST OF NORTHERN ITALY

In 391 B.C., at Clusium in Etruria, Romans and Gauls for the first time met face to face. This crisis in Roman history, marking as it does the beginning of the long series of Gallic Wars, was the result of two parallel and simultaneous processes: the conquest of northern Italy by the Gauls, and the conquest of southern Etruria by the Romans; and it is these two decisive events that we have first to describe.

Towards the end of the fifth century B.C. the Gauls debouched from the passes of the Alps and entered northern Italy (see above, pp. 59 *sqq.*). For more than a century the greater part of this territory had been in the hands of the Etruscans. Inscriptions and utensils which have been discovered, together with the linguistic evidence of place-names, suggest the approximate limits of their domination. In the plain of the Po this ended roughly where the mountains begin, for the Alps and the Apennines with their foothills were still held by their original inhabitants, the Ligurians. East of the Adige stretched the territory of the Veneti, who had always succeeded in preserving their independence and their original forms of civilization (vol. IV, pp. 441 *sqq.*). Along the Adriatic the coast lay under Etruscan rule from the Po delta as far south as what is now Pesaro.

The advance-guard of the Gauls was formed by the Insubres. Defeating the Etruscans near the Ticino, they captured Melpum and founded what is now Milan. Attracted by their success, other bands of invaders swept in successive waves into northern Italy: the Cenomani under Etitovius settled round Brescia and Verona, the Lepontii between the Simplon and Lake Maggiore, the Libici and the Salluvii on the banks of the Ticino[1]. Henceforth they occupied the whole of Italy north of the Po, with the exception of the territory of the Veneti. The Etruscans retained only the district south of the river, where the possession of their capital, Felsina, and the proximity of their mother-country enabled them in the years that followed to offer a more vigorous and prolonged resistance to the invaders. But new bands of Gauls, the Boii and the Lingones, in turn crossed the Alps and descended upon Italy. They were forced to push on farther beyond the regions occupied by the earlier arrivals. Crossing the Po on rafts, they defeated the Umbro-Etruscans and settled on the right bank of the river in Emilia, between the pass of the Stradella and Ravenna. The Senones, the latest comers of all, became henceforward the spearhead of the Celtic thrust southward: they pushed back the Umbrian population and settled along the coast of the Adriatic from the Utus to the Aesis.

That this advance of the Celtic invaders was not effected without resistance is certain from the archaeological evidence. The funeral stelae of Bologna, historic documents of the first importance, show numerous battle-scenes, in which Etruscans and Gauls are at grips; and the ruins of the ancient Etruscan city laid bare at Marzabotto, where a thick layer of ashes covers the foundations of public buildings and private houses like a shroud, where skeletons are scattered over the soil and piled up in the wells,

[1] These tribes were, in historical times at least, largely Celtic.

and the ground is thick with a medley of Gallic and Etruscan weapons, are still a true and moving memorial of the grim drama in which the Etruscans of the Po were destroyed. Not only was their resistance vigorous: it was also long sustained. In the necropolis of Felsina have been found Attic vases made at Athens about 370 B.C., and such vases could hardly have been buried as funerary offerings until at least fifty years later. Felsina, then, the Etruscan capital, seems to have resisted till the middle of the fourth century B.C., and during this period the extension of its commerce and the luxury of its civilization prove it to have remained at the height of its prosperity. Finally, the archaeological evidence on this point is confirmed and completed by historical tradition. In his *Periplus*, compiled between 338 and 335, the Pseudo-Scylax bears witness to the presence of Etruscans along the Adriatic from Umbria to the southern arm of the Po, which flowed by Spina, while to the north of that line, as far as Hadria, the coast was already in the hands of the Gauls. It seems therefore that the conquest of northern Italy was not completed until two-thirds or three-quarters of a century had elapsed after the moment when, towards 400 B.C., the advance-guards of the great Celtic invasion passed the Alps.

The gradual Gallic conquest of this region may be explained as due to two fundamental causes, the one general, the other particular. In the Po valley, as in other places where the Etruscans were permanently settled, for instance in Campania and Etruria proper, they only formed a minority, a staff, as it were, of officers and technical experts. The bulk of the population remained the original inhabitants of the country, Ligurians in the Alpine foot-hills and the Apennines, Umbrians in the plains of the Po and on the Adriatic coast. The Etruscans were too few in numbers to occupy the whole of the territory with either advantage or safety; accordingly they had concentrated in the urban centres placed where they might command the most important routes of approach and strategic points. Such were Melpum, Verona and Mantua at the foot of the Alpine passes, Parma, Modena and Bologna to the south of the Po along what was to be later the Via Aemilia, and Pisaurum, Ariminum, Ravenna and Adria along the coast of the Adriatic. City-life was for the Etruscans the basis of political administration; and the country, where the original racial elements still predominated, played but an inferior part. Such conditions were essentially favourable to the rapid advance and ultimate success of the invaders.

In the second place, the decadence which overtook all the

Etruscans from the end of the sixth century onwards made its effects felt in Padane Etruria as elsewhere, and its intensity became the greater as the distance from the mother-country, Etruria proper, increased. This retrogression, after the brilliant advance of the preceding centuries which reached its farthest point in the sixth century B.C., shows itself alike in loss of territory and in decline in national character. Political and social upheavals, the reaction of the native population so long suppressed, incessant attacks by neighbouring peoples, the disappearance of the military spirit, the taste for luxury, a general moral enervation, all these are the vital causes which came into play in Padane Etruria, and provided the ultimate explanation of the Etruscans' fall.

The country districts, in which the Etruscan element was small or non-existent, and where perhaps the invader found the original Umbrian population ready to plot against its masters, were the first to be subdued. The towns, on the other hand, where the dominant race had always concentrated and the population was being continually swelled by the arrival of Etruscan refugees from the countryside, offered a sterner and longer resistance, aided at once by the military organization of the Etruscans and by the lack of siege-engines on the side of the attackers. Thus it was that Felsina contrived to hold out until at least the middle of the fourth century and the towns on the Adriatic coast remained in Etruscan hands for yet another twenty years.

The Etruscan domination in northern Italy had been based on two distinct and complementary elements: an Etruscan population, and Etruscan civilization. In comparison with the inhabitants of the plains of the Po, the Etruscan settlers had never been more than a small minority, owing their strength to their military qualities and their superior civilization. In the course of the long struggle against the Celtic invaders they must have suffered severe losses. Some retreated before the uninterrupted advance of the invaders and regained their native Etruria, others, whether of their own free will or driven by superior force, emigrated to the foothills of the Rhaetic Alps, where they re-appear later as an element in the Rhaeto-Euganean population: a large number, probably the majority, who were held back by various ties of interest, remained in northern Italy, and, as in Campania, ended by becoming merged with the conquerors. Nevertheless there is evidence of their influence and power both north and south of the Po for some time after. Mantua, both in institutions and language, retained its character as an Etruscan town for many years. The Etruscan elements which were concentrated round Brescia and Verona still retained their vigour, and in the course of the struggles between Gauls and Romans their decisive influence is more than once reflected in the policy of the new masters of the country, the Cenomani.

So far as the pre-Etruscan populations were concerned the Gauls refrained from a policy of extermination. The Ligurians were pressed back into the two mountainous zones of the Alps and the Apennines—at the beginning of the Empire the Gaul ruled the plains, the Ligurian the mountains. Sometimes they were assimilated and a process, analogous to that which produced the mixed race of Celtiberians in Spain, the Celto-Greeks in Asia Minor, and the Celto-Scythians in the plains of eastern Europe, produced a Celto-Ligurian people in the maritime Alps. There remained only the Veneti. Sheltered behind the deep waters of the Adige, they succeeded in defending their independence against the Gauls as they had done before against the Etruscans. In 390 B.C. and again in 302 B.C. history shows them at war with the Cisalpine Gauls.

The conquest of northern Italy by the Gauls raised a second problem, a problem of civilization. The two cultures, Etruscan and Celtic, that of the conquered and that of the conquerors, were face to face. The former was infinitely the richer and more brilliant: but, of necessity, it had suffered from the blow which had broken Etruscan domination in the plains of the Po. The Gauls brought with them from the north the civilization of the second Iron Age, known as La Tène, which is exactly that revealed by the Gallic cemeteries in northern Italy immediately after the conquest (see above, chap. ii). These barbarous nomad warriors, ever seeking adventure, had no method of exploiting the soil except by stock-breeding. Thus, the process of their settlement in Cisalpine Gaul still presents a phase of instability and flux: it is at this period that bands of robbers from this region, now become the centre of Italian Celticism, spread over the rest of the peninsula ranging as far as the shores of the Ionian Sea and pillaging practically the whole of Italy. But presently the natural richness of the fertile plains of the Po, and the sight of the agricultural wealth realized by the Etruscans, attracted them towards cultivation of the soil: they settled down, and thanks to their inborn adaptability, one of the fundamental characteristics of the race, became skilful farmers. Polybius, who visited the country half a century after its conquest by the Romans, was deeply impressed by its agricultural riches.

The luxurious, seductive civilization of the Etruscans, which

flourished chiefly in the towns, soon attracted the Gallic aristocracy who with all the enthusiasm of their race eagerly adopted
its products. Of this the tombs of certain Gallic cemeteries,
built after the conquest, provide in their lowest strata full and
reliable evidence. Such are the necropolis of Filottrano, near
Ancona, of the second half of the fourth century B.C., and that
of Montefortino near Arcevia in the territory of the Senones,
which belongs to the end of the fourth and the beginning of the
third century. Here are arms and equipment, in particular the
iron helmet bequeathed by the Etruscans, side by side with the
sword introduced by the Gauls: utensils and ornaments, collars,
bracelets, mirrors, scent-bottles, combs: household appliances,
such as bronze tools, candelabra and basins, and finally pottery, in
fact, all the products of a wealthy refined society, bearing witness
to the force and variety of the influence exercised by Etruscan
civilization on the conquerors.

But two points should be noted. First, this influence does not
appear uniform throughout northern Italy. On the very borders
of Etruria, in eastern Emilia and on the Adriatic shore, it is
strong: but it grows weaker as the distance increases from the
source of this civilization, and the Gauls north of the Po preserve
far more of their original traditional culture than the other
invaders. This fact is seen in its most striking and concrete form
if we compare two series of Gallic cemeteries; on the one side
those of Bologna, Filottrano and Montefortino, the last two in
the Senones' territory, on the other that of Ornavasso (second
century B.C.), in the province of Novara among the Lepontii, or
that of the Soldo near Alzate in Brianza which belong to the same
period. In the second place, archaeological discoveries in the
region of Bologna prove that the influence of Etruscan civilization
grew steadily less and less as the reminders of the past became
effaced. Under Etruscan rule, the town had held the chief place
and it was from the towns that civilization radiated over the
countryside: with the Gallic conquest the countryside once again
comes into its own. The Cisalpine Gaul which the Romans conquered and Polybius described has become a land of peasants,
and it was not until the Romanization of the country that the
characteristic civilization of the Mediterranean area made its
victorious re-entry.

III. THE GALLIC CATASTROPHE

While the Gauls, once the conquest of the Po valley was complete, were pushing forward to the south, Rome after the fall of Veii had continued her advance to the north (see above, pp. 516 *sqq.*). Capena and Falerii, recognizing the Roman menace, had leagued themselves with Veii. Their ally fell in 396 B.C., and their own turn came swiftly. Capena fell in 395, and the next year, after the campaign of Camillus, Falerii was forced to recognize the supremacy of Rome. Sutrium and Nepete soon followed suit. This time the great cities of central Etruria abandoned their egoism and their indolence and were stirred to the depths. But Volsinii, the holy city of Etruria, was subdued in 391 and forced to sue for peace, which Rome granted to her in the form of a twenty years' truce. These victories had a repercussion even on the eastern and southern frontiers of Latium, where the Aequi and Volsci after several defeats ceased from hostilities. By the conquest of southern Etruria, the Roman State acquired the natural frontier of the Ciminian forest and the hills by Lake Sabatinus: and the occupation of the two strong points, Sutrium and Nepete, 'barriers against Etruria and gates to Rome' as Livy vividly describes them, henceforward safeguarded her territory from hostile attack on the north. The circle of her international relations was growing: immediately after the capture of Veii, the Senate dedicated, as we have seen, a gold *krater* at Delphi, and entered into friendly relations with the people of the Lipari Islands (p. 513 *sq.*). This first appearance of the name Roman in Greece and on the coasts of Sicily is significant. The insignificant city of the fifth century has grown wings: a new epoch is beginning. At this moment, an unforeseen event, the disaster of the Gallic invasion, was suddenly to lay low the edifice that she had built. At one blow Roman authority was again reduced to the critical position from which only a century of desperate fighting had rescued her.

It was the year 391 B.C.[1] One day without warning a band of Gauls—30,000 according to Diodorus—under a leader whom history calls Brennus, crossed the Apennines and appeared before the Etruscan city of Clusium. Who were these Gauls and what was their object? To the first of these questions the most trust-

---

[1] According to the conventional Roman chronology the taking of Rome was in 390—according to the Greek chronology, which Polybius in particular follows, in 387–386 B.C. See above, p. 321 *sq.*

worthy account, that of Polybius, gives no precise answer: yet he seems to suggest that they were not Gauls who were already established in the north, but Celts from beyond the Alps. The tradition of the annalists, which is already reflected in Diodorus, makes them Senones. To reconcile these two versions, it is possible to assume that they were Senones reinforced for their raid by other Celtic elements. What did they seek? Tradition says land, but this is open to doubt. At the moment, the conquest of northern Italy by the Gauls had only been in progress a short time, a few decades at most; the number of immigrants could hardly have been so great that the land available in Cisalpine Gaul had already proved insufficient. In all probability, the appearance of the Gauls before Clusium was no more than an incident in one of the raids in search of plunder and ransoms, raids which for more than half a century the Gauls inflicted repeatedly upon the whole of Italy.

However that may be, the people of Clusium offered resistance; but the Etruscan league, either powerless or indifferent to their own interests, deserted them, just as, at the time of the Roman invasion, they had deserted Veii and the other towns of southern Etruria. Clusium, therefore, appealed to Rome, the city which, by the beginning of the fourth century, had become the leading power in central Italy. While refusing all military intervention, Rome sent envoys to negotiate with the enemy and to offer mediation. There is no doubt that in this situation she intended to play her part of mediator in good faith, but the envoys sent upon this delicate task could not have been worse chosen. They abandoned the strict neutrality which was essential to their mission, and fought side by side with the men of Clusium: one of them, even, during an engagement, killed a Gallic chief. The Gauls might have broken off negotiations; instead they contented themselves with demanding reparation, but because of the high position of the culprits it was refused. Accordingly, raising the siege of Clusium, which in view of their lack of skill and of siege-engines would inevitably have turned into a long blockade, they marched on Rome.

The band of raiders lacked organization and proper military science: their strength lay in their love of adventure, their ardour, their instinct for attack. What resistance had they to meet? The military power of Rome, against which they were to be pitted, contained two distinct elements: the fighting qualities of the army, and the defensive possibilities of the city. The army was a citizen militia, organized on the basis of the century, which with all its inherent virtues and defects had reached its final development. On the other hand, the defences of Etruscan Rome, which after the unification of the city had depended on a vast *enceinte*, the wall of Servius Tullius, had not survived the fall of the monarchy[1]. During the long-drawn crisis of the fifth century, old local separatism had reappeared; the several hills became more and more independent at the expense of the ancient unity. Consequently, the defences of Rome at the beginning of the fourth century were no more than a series of isolated forts, coinciding with the various hills, of which the most solid and the best fortified, the citadel of the Capitol, served as a keep. There was, then, a citizen army, with considerable sources from which to recruit—for the whole population of the city might be mobilized —but unwieldy, difficult to manœuvre and often badly commanded; and behind this living rampart lay an open city with the Capitoline citadel as its last stronghold. Such, in its two fundamental elements, was the military organization which the Gauls marching on Rome were to meet.

The distance from Clusium to Rome is some eighty miles, or four days' march: the road follows the valley of the Tiber, the easiest of all routes for an invader. The Gauls with the extreme mobility which always marked their raids swept down it like a torrent. Historical tradition, in which legend figured largely, does at least faithfully reflect the panic caused by the march of the Gauls. Their numbers[2], their masses of cavalry, their lack of discipline, their primitive equipment, the ferocity of their war-cries—all combined to strike terror into the Romans. Livy (VII, 24) makes the consul M. Popillius Laenas say, forty years later: 'You are not facing a Latin or a Sabine foe, who will become your ally when you have beaten him: we have drawn our swords against wild beasts, whose blood we must shed or spill our own '— 'in beluas strinximus ferrum; hauriendus aut dandus est sanguis.'

Anxious to palliate the defeat that followed, Roman historians have endeavoured to throw the blame either on circumstances, such as the lack of time, or on their commanders who had not the wit to make the dispositions which the danger demanded. But there was time to mobilize the allied contingents—according to Plutarch—and with these the Romans had 40,000 men, which made them numerically almost equal to the enemy: and, second,

---

[1] See, however, for a somewhat different view, pp. 358 *sqq.*

[2] Diodorus gives their number now as 70,000. This is an obvious exaggeration due to a variant account, or based on the assumption that the Gauls had called on their kinsmen to reinforce them.

it must be recognized that the defensive line of the Allia on the left bank of the Tiber, covered on the one flank by the river and on the other by the lower spurs of the Crustumian mountains, was strategically as judicious a choice as possible. Actually, the effect of surprise was the supreme weapon in the hands of the Gauls; in the event it played its full part. On 18 July on the battlefield of the Allia, a little tributary on the left of the Tiber above Fidenae, the present Fosso della Bettina, the Roman army broke in confusion. The larger part crossed the Tiber and took refuge in Veii, the remainder fled to Rome. Rome's first line of defence, the field-army, was broken[1].

To dispute the invaders' entry into Rome, an open city, was out of the question. The population abandoned the lower quarters of the town and scattered over the various hills. The remains of the army with the civic authorities occupied the last stronghold, the citadel on the Capitol. The Gauls arrived before Rome according to Polybius three days later, on the same evening according to the more probable statement of Livy. The next day they entered the city unresisted, plundered and burnt it, if not wholly—here perhaps tradition exaggerates when it says that the destruction was complete, though the use of wood for houses which was customary at this period would have made it easy,—at least in part. With the exception of the Capitol the devastation was general. These are the certain historical facts; the rest is little more than legend.

Modern archaeological discoveries, which have laid bare traces of this devastation at two points in the city, the Forum and the Palatine, fully confirm the historical account. The Palatine, which, like the other hills, at the beginning of the fourth century had only the remnants of fortifications, fell before the attacks of the Gauls, and the excavations of 1907 have revealed clear traces of the fire that destroyed it. That sacred corner of the city where the most ancient relics of the primitive town were piously preserved, the Casa Faustuli, the Auguratorium, the Curia of the Salii, the Fifth Sanctuary of the Argei, was laid waste. From that time onwards no trace was left of the earlier buildings except the layer of ashes and rubbish which have been laid bare in the course of excavation. In the Forum the invaders defaced all the monuments, in particular the pyramid bearing an archaic inscription which was discovered in 1899 beneath the famous *Lapis Niger*. After the departure of the Gauls the Romans piously kept these venerable relics, and later, to guard them from all future violation,

[1] For the controversy as to the scene of the battle, see the Bibliography.

protected them with a covering of black flagstones, which was renewed in the fourth century A.D.: this is the paving which modern excavations have revealed.

The Capitol alone, the last stronghold, held out, thanks to its natural situation. Ardent as ever and impatient to end the enterprise, the Gauls sought to force a decision. They attacked by day and by night—once only baffled by the famous intervention of the geese on the Capitol—until, after repeated failures, they resigned themselves to a siege which lasted seven months. At last famine overcame the defenders and, at the end of their resources, they proposed to treat. The Gauls asked for nothing better. Decimated by the lack of provisions and the fevers of summer, and threatened in their own Cisalpine Gaul with an invasion by the Veneti, they accepted the offer, and the Romans ransomed their city and their territory[1]. As soon as the treaty was fulfilled, the invaders departed, though not entirely unhindered, for in the course of their retreat some of their bands were attacked by Roman troops from Caere and above all from Veii, and suffered losses. This account was humiliating to the national pride, and Rome, when she became a great power, read it with shame: it is not surprising therefore that in the annalists it has been replaced by another version. There is no definite denial of the buying-off of the enemy, but it is claimed that Camillus, coming up at the precise moment of the payment, broke the agreement and, sword in hand, cleared Roman territory of the invaders. The few local successes won over the Gauls, at Ardea and elsewhere, made the reversal of tradition, if not probable, at least plausible. The brutal truth, however ungrateful to Roman national pride, is that the Gauls returned home without great loss and with their booty intact.

Besides the material damage which it caused and the heavy blow to Roman prestige, the Gallic invasion produced a final consequence which was still more important and lasting: the thunderbolt of the Allia seems to have been the signal for the downfall of the power of Rome in central Italy. It is a repetition, after a hundred years interval, of the crisis provoked in 509 by the fall of the Etruscan dynasty (p. 487). Livy's description of the main features of the crisis must be as true as it is vigorous.

But they had little time to sit still devising the means necessary to restore the State after so grave a disaster. For, on the one side, old enemies, the

[1] Diodorus XIV, 116, and Livy V, 48 set the ransom at 1000 pounds of gold, a sum more probably dictated by later Roman pride than possible for Roman resources at the time.

Volscians, took up arms and sought the final destruction of the Roman name: on the other merchants brought news that all the chiefs of the Etruscan peoples had met together at the Temple of Voltumna and were leagued together for war. Lastly, there was a further cause for fear: for news came of the rebellion of the Latins and the Hernici, who since the battle of Lake Regillus, that is for nearly a hundred years, had never faltered in the fidelity which bound them to Rome. Such were the alarms which sprang up on every side, while it was clear to all that the Roman name was menaced not only with the hate of her enemies, but also with the scorn of her allies. In these circumstances it was resolved to entrust the defence of the State to the auspices to which it owed its rescue, and to appoint dictator M. Furius Camillus (VI, 2).

IV. THE RE-BUILDING OF ROMAN POWER

Once the Gauls had withdrawn from the scene, the whole edifice of Roman power in central Italy had to be built up again, and for a task of this magnitude two things were needed: the right men and the right programme. Supported by the patriotism of her citizens and favoured by fortune, Rome, in the half-century which followed the Gallic invasion, succeeded both in discovering her leaders and in realizing her programme.

The great figure of the epoch, although by virtue of his previous career he already belonged to the past, was the conqueror of southern Eturia, Camillus. A man of ideas and a man of action, for five and twenty years he personified the national recovery. The highest offices of the state were heaped upon him again and again. Before the Gallic invasion he had already been censor, military tribune three times, and dictator; after the invasion he was again three times military tribune, four times dictator, several times interrex: although these last figures, given by tradition, are not altogether above suspicion. Under his guidance the Roman army underwent a complete transformation; and when the new weapon was forged and tested, he used it to defeat in turn all the enemies of Rome, Gauls and Etruscans, Volscians, Aequi and rebellious Latins alike. His reforms and his victories re-established the supremacy of Rome and safeguarded her future. When he died, in 365 if we may trust tradition, Livy, in devoting to his honour a magnificent funeral oration, did no more than pay the debt of his nation to the man who saved her. By his side stood three men who are worthy of special mention; T. Quinctius Cincinnatus appears as military tribune in 388 and 384 and dictator in 380, C. Sulpicius Peticus as consul in 364, 361, 355, 353 and 351 and dictator, and C. Marcius Rutilus as consul in 357, 352, 344 and 342 and dictator. Then in the next generation there is another line of great generals, among whom two men, both heroes of the Gallic Wars, may claim an honourable eminence, T. Manlius Torquatus, consul in 347, 344 and 340, and M. Valerius Corvus, consul in 348, 346, 343, and 335.

After the men, the programme of reform. The collapse of 390 had been both military and political; and accordingly the reforms were aimed at the army and the administration. From the military point of view the capture of Rome had taught a double lesson. First, Rome could not without perennial danger remain an unfortified city in the midst of open enemies or doubtful friends. Second, the Roman army of the fifth century, despite the reforms introduced at the time of the siege of Veii, was not capable of holding the field in open fight against their new and terrible enemy, the Gauls. On the morrow of the crisis of 390, the government of Rome took the necessary measures to find the most satisfactory solutions to these two problems, the one of fortification, the other of tactics.

One of the strongest points of Rome's policy was, now as ever, the realization that to obtain a satisfactory solution of her problems she must dispose of them in order of urgency. She treated the problem of fortification like all others. To deal with the most pressing needs, the first step was to restore the defences of the Palatine and protect the sacred hill from further violation. The excavations of 1907 have revealed the fact that fragments of wall, long attributed to the era of the Kings, are in fact no older than the re-building carried out immediately after the Gallic invasion (p. 360 sq.). But the great achievement which gave to republican Rome her armour of defence was the restoration of the rampart of Servius Tullius, a restoration which was completed towards the middle of the fourth century. Here too, during the past few years, archaeological research has provided important and trustworthy evidence. This powerful wall, over seven miles long, which was also one of the results of the Gallic Wars, provided Rome with the final solution of her defensive problem. There remained the forging of a weapon of offence: and this too was soon achieved by the military reforms of Camillus and of the generals trained in his school.

The military organization, condemned by its complete collapse in 390, was the traditional timocratic arrangement of classes. This system had saved the authority of Rome during the crisis of the fifth century: but it no longer met the needs of war on the grand scale, nor matched the altered conditions of the new situation. Rome had saved herself from disaster by buying off her enemies: but she knew well that the Gauls might return and she realized also that her hegemony in central Italy could only be regained by a complete and widespread military re-organization. To find soldiers was easy: the centuriate system, brought to its fullest development before the Gallic invasion, provided sufficient effectives. What was all-important was to improve their efficiency. This involved reform and to achieve this in organization, in armament and in tactics, the Roman government, with the fear of the Gauls ever before its eyes, concentrated all its energies.

Tradition attributes to Camillus a large share in this reform: and even if he was not the sole author—for another of the great leaders of the period, C. Sulpicius Peticus, also played a part[1]— there is little doubt but that his was the main inspiration. The military re-organization entailed two fundamental innovations. First, for the principle of arrangement by census was substituted that of arrangement by age, consequently by individual capacity and experience: the heavy infantry, the real legionary troops, are henceforth disposed in three lines, *hastati*, *principes* and *triarii*, the younger men in advance, the older in reserve; the light infantry, the *velites*, on the other hand retained its previous system of recruitment strictly based on the census, and men continued to be drawn from the last two classes. Second, for mass-tactics, modelled on the use of the phalanx which, in the opinion of the present writer, was inherited from the Etruscans, was substituted a less rigid formation, manœuvring by maniples: for only thus was it possible to attain the suppleness and elasticity necessary to make head against the offensive power and the mobility of the Gauls. A further modification of tactics, relative to the discharge of the javelin, was introduced in 358 by the dictator C. Sulpicius. Finally, the armament of the troops underwent corresponding reforms suggested by the struggle against the Gauls: thus, a helmet of iron was substituted for the leathern casque, the shield was strengthened with strips of bronze, and the pilum was modified by the addition of a shaft of soft metal. The Roman army emerged from this programme of reform restored and rejuvenated. The weapon of revenge was ready: in half a century of savage struggles the Gauls and the other adversaries of Rome in turn were to prove its value to their cost on the battle-fields of central Italy.

[1] It is however possible—in the absence of decisive evidence—to adopt the view that the military reform did not reach its conclusion until the period of the Samnite wars. See below, pp. 596, 601.

The programme of reform, which in the minds of all the statesmen of Rome was to culminate in the national restoration, was finally completed by a double series of political measures. In the first place, to guard against all subsequent defection, reconquest was quickly followed by the resumption of the system of colonies. New Latin colonies were founded, two in the south, in Volscian territory, Satricum in 385 and Setia in 382, and two in the north in Etruria, Sutrium and Nepete in 383 (see p. 517). The second measure was an innovation of capital and decisive importance for the future of the state. The conception of enlarging the victorious city by the granting of civic rights to the vanquished, under the new form of *municipium*, was at once original and fruitful. It was first applied to Tusculum in 381; with the dissolution of the Latin League in 338 the system became general (p. 591).

On the morrow of her disaster, Rome did not flinch before the double programme of military and administrative reform necessary for her recovery. Nor did she fail to discover the men capable of leading her armies to victory. And yet despite prodigies of energy, it was fully forty years before she regained the authority which she had enjoyed. There is nothing surprising in this fact if account be taken of the dangers, external and internal, which during this period she found herself called upon to face. The Gallic invasion had destroyed the prestige of Rome and for forty years the Gauls returned again and again to trouble her borders. Latins, Etruscans, Aequi, Volscians, finally Hernici made war upon her until, as a century before, not only the greatness but the very existence of the state was imperilled. At home the struggle between the two orders, risen to fever-heat, delayed and more than once paralysed the progress of national recovery (see chap. XVI). It was not until 367, if we may accept the tradition, that the passing of the Licinian laws mitigated, if it did not end, the bitterness of the conflict. Under these conditions, if there be any cause for wonder, it is that after such total ruin, in the midst of so many and such grave dangers, complete restoration was finally achieved. The miracle of Rome in the first half of the fourth century was only possible because of the determination of her government, the energy of her leaders and the patriotism of her citizens. Once more, and not for the last time, the spirit of Rome was a revelation to others and to herself.

V. GALLIC INCURSIONS

The wars which follow over more than half a century, with the struggle against the Gauls as their centre, are extremely inco- herent for several reasons. The armies of Rome are fighting on several fronts: events are confused with each other, and to this tangle the unreliability of historical tradition adds the final com- plication. According to Polybius, during the thirty years which followed the capture of Rome, that is to say, according to the chronology which he uses, from 387 to 357, the Gauls remained at peace with Rome. This interval gave Rome a breathing-space in which to re-organize her forces and settle the question of Latium. The invaders reappeared in 357 and advanced as far as Alba: the Romans, caught unawares, and with no time to mobilize the allied contingents, did not dare to march against them. Twelve years later, that is in 346 or 345, the Gauls returned to the attack: but this time the Romans were forewarned: reinforced by their allies they marched against them and offered battle. The Gauls, at variance among themselves, fled in panic by night and regained their country in disorder. Finally after another interval of thirteen years, with the growth of Roman power before their eyes, they signed a truce which was to last thirty years, until the end of the fourth century (see below, p. 609).

Livy certainly multiplies the invasions by the Gauls beyond reason, though he gives a very circumstantial account of them as well as of the subsidiary wars. According to him, Satricum was four times captured and Velitrae was repeatedly besieged. The duel of T. Manlius Torquatus with the Gaul is duplicated, in 367 and 361. The annalistic tradition both multiplies the number and increases the importance of the Roman victories. The last element of confusion is the difference between the Greek and Roman chronologies. In this quicksand of doubt, where truth in detail is beyond our reach, the task of the historian is to disen- gage the basic facts and shed light on the general trend of events.

The Gallic invasion of 390 had two main consequences, the one direct—the inauguration of a long series of Gallic wars— the other indirect—the rebellion of the allies or subjects of Rome and a recrudescence of activity among her traditional enemies. Consequently the history of the recovery of Roman prestige during the first half of the fourth century B.C. contains two parallel chapters: on the one side is the story of the Gallic Wars, on the other, the subjection of the revolted nations. For the sake of clearness it is advisable to present them as two successive and distinct pictures.

Although the taking of Rome by the Gauls has always been particularly famous in history, it was in reality no more than a local episode in the course of the Celtic invasions of the Italian peninsula. Episodes of this kind, towns held to ransom, were beyond all doubt, common. Herein lies the explanation of the fact that the departure of the Gauls after the capture of Rome was followed, after an interval, by a series of renewed invasions. Tradition, in so far as it concerns the general history of Italy in the fourth century, is certainly weak and unreliable: but there are nevertheless certain scattered indications which throw light generally on the character and sequence of these often repeated attempts. In northern Italy the Gallic invasion had assumed the form of immigration in mass and stationary settlement; but in peninsular Italy we have no more than transitory raids leading to no lasting settlement.

These irruptions assume two different and at the same time complementary forms. First there are the more or less substantial bands, similar in fact to that which raided Rome in 390: such bands, under commanders of their own nationality, are merely inspired by a lust for plunder. Avoiding the fastness of the Apennines, which was sufficiently defended by nature, these plundering expeditions moved down the two corridors of the western and eastern coasts. By these, the natural routes of penetration into southern Italy, they march on the one side through Etruria, Latium and Campania, where some elements may have found a temporary settlement, and on the other through Apulia. One band of plunderers, returning from such a raid, was attacked by the inhabitants of Caere allied to Rome and completely routed. The second form taken by the Gallic invasions of the Italian peninsula was the appearance of Gauls in the guise of mercenaries. This phenomenon was not peculiar to Italy, but is to be detected throughout the Mediterranean world from the fourth to the end of the second century. Dionysius the Elder, the tyrant of Syracuse who dreamed of supremacy in southern Italy and on the Adriatic coasts (see vol. vi, chap. v), used the Gauls for the development of his policy and the realization of his far-reaching designs. In 368–7 B.C. he sent them to the help of Sparta and his son, Dionysius the Younger, made use of them in his conflicts with the Veneti. In central Italy, the peoples who had revolted from Rome, notably the Latin cities of Velitrae, Tibur and Praeneste, hired troops of Gauls as mercenaries, thus offering them opportunities of establishing in the very heart of Italy centres of political intrigue and military *points d'appui* from which their raids received fresh impulse. It is in this double character of raiding bands and of mercenaries in the service of her enemies that Rome had to face the Gauls and withstand their renewed attacks during the second third of the fourth century B.C.

During a long period, according to Polybius' account thirty years, according to Livy twenty-three, history makes no mention of any conflict between Rome and the Gauls. The reason for this unhoped-for respite lay in the difficulties experienced by the Gauls; according to Polybius there were dissensions among themselves and struggles with the Alpine peoples: according to Strabo they were at war with the Etruscans and the Umbrians. If we may trust Livy's account, which, on this point as on so many others, must be accepted only with the most distinct reserve, the Gauls suddenly reappeared in 367 and pitched their camp in the neighbourhood of the city, on the banks of the Anio. For the fifth time Camillus was raised to the dictatorship. One account assigns to this occasion the curious duel in which T. Manlius Torquatus killed a Gaul of enormous stature and spoiled him of his collar in view of the two armies. Livy prefers to put this particular episode six years later, but he mentions a battle fought in the neighbourhood of Alba in which the victorious Romans slew several thousands of the barbarians and captured their camp. Those that escaped for the most part made their way back to Apulia. In 366 there was a rumour that the Gauls in Apulia had rallied: for a moment there was a fear that the invasion of Roman soil might be repeated: but nothing came of it and the Gauls remained quiet for five years. In 361, a Gallic army marched on Rome and pitched its camp three miles from the town on the Via Salaria beyond the bridge of the Anio. The Romans under the leadership of the dictator, T. Quinctius Poenus, occupied the left bank of the river, covering Rome. The two armies strove for the possession of the bridge: and this is the occasion to which Livy attributes the episode of the duel between T. Manlius Torquatus and the Gaul. It did not come to a battle: the victory of the Roman caused the retreat of the Gauls who regained the territory of Tibur, their ally, and passed on into Campania.

The next year, in 360, they returned, this time too, according to Livy, at the invitation of the inhabitants of Tibur, and they laid waste the territory of the Latin allies who had remained faithful to Rome, Tusculum, Alba and Labici. Taking into account the different chronologies of Polybius and Livy, this seems to be identical with Polybius' invasion of 357, the first, according to him, since the capture of Rome. On this occasion the Gauls advanced as far as Alba, unopposed by the Romans, who did not dare to venture out against them. Livy's account of the events that followed is different from that of Polybius. In face of the danger Q. Servilius Ahala was made dictator (Rome's great leader, Camillus, having been dead some years); near the Colline Gate he crushed the invaders who, as before, retreated on Tibur. The Consul C. Poetelius Libo pursued them, and, despite the intervention of the Tiburtines, who sallied out to their assistance, drove them back into the town. In 358 there was a fresh invasion: the Gauls penetrated into Latium as far as the outskirts of Pedum. The dictator C. Sulpicius Peticus, one of the best military commanders of the period, refused an engagement and temporized in the hope of exhausting the enemy. But the Roman army demanded to be led out to battle, and Sulpicius gave way. The Gauls suffered a crushing defeat.

This victory of 358 won for Rome only a respite, and eight years later Latium was once more invaded by the Gauls. The Roman army, under the consul M. Popillius Laenas, marched to meet them. The Gauls attacked the Romans while they were fortifying their camp, but suffered a repulse and took refuge on the Alban Mount. The next year, in 349, the Gauls were driven out by the rigours of winter, and descended to ravage the plain. The Roman army gave battle but the issue was doubtful, and the invaders retired to their camp. Left sole consul by the death of his colleague, Camillus' son, L. Furius Camillus, entrenched himself in the Pomptine marshes and waited till weariness overtook his adversaries. Finally, a battle was fought during which, according to tradition, took place the episode of M. Valerius Corvus and the famous intervention of the raven. Again the defeated Gauls took their flight through the territory of the Volsci and the remnants of their army regained Apulia. Polybius mentions no battle during this period but merely a stampede of Gauls who in face of the Roman troops were panic-stricken and fled back into their own country. The fact remains that whether they were defeated or only fled, they did not reappear for some time. Towards 332–331, a treaty was concluded between Rome and the Senones which, for a time at least, ended the long struggle.

VI. THE WARS OF ROME WITH HER NEIGHBOURS

The repression of the revolts fomented in central Italy by Gallic intervention falls into four main series of events: in the north the restoration of Roman authority in southern Etruria: in the east the defeat of the Aequi and Hernici, to the south the crushing of the Volsci and the conquest of part of their territory, and finally, the achievement that produced the most important result of all, the renewal, in a still stronger form, of Roman preponderance in Latium.

In southern Etruria the effect of the Gallic invasion had been, if not the total loss of the territory won at the beginning of the century, at any rate a series of separatist movements, such as the insurrection of Fidenae. Here Rome promptly re-established her authority. There are several reasons which explain the ease with which this task was performed: the movement of secession had not been general, the fall of Veii made the task considerably simpler, and finally, Sutrium and Nepete, the two great border citadels, stood firmly by Rome. Fidenae was recaptured and sacked, and Rome victoriously restored her northern frontier. But, on this occasion, taught by experience, Etruria did not allow the work to be accomplished without offering a vigorous resistance. In 389, according to the account of the annalists, a strong army of Etruscans laid siege to Sutrium. The town appealed to Rome, but help arrived too late, and it was forced to surrender. Camillus lost no time in recapturing it: the Etruscans were cut to pieces and either surrendered or fled. In 388 Rome entered on war with Tarquinii, one of the great cities of independent Etruria, and two Etruscan strongholds, Cortuosa and Contenebra, were captured. The next year, southern Etruria was partially annexed to Rome, and four new tribes were made, the *tribus Stellatina* in the territory of Capena, *Tromentina* in the territory of Veii, *Sabatina* in the region of Lake Bracciano, and *Arnensis* in the country between Rome and Caere, north-east of the mouth of the Tiber. From this moment the conditions previous to the Gallic invasion were completely and definitely restored on the northern frontier.

But this settlement, which confirmed the permanent character of the Roman occupation, soon alarmed the great towns of central Etruria, henceforward neighbours of Rome and anxious for the maintenance of their independence. Several among them, in particular Tarquinii, again took up arms. In 386 the Etruscans once more threatened Nepete and Sutrium. They captured the first, thanks to the complicity of the anti-Roman party, and they were on the point of seizing the second, when the relieving army arrived under the orders of Camillus and his colleague, P. Valerius, commanding in the capacity of military tribunes. The two towns were recaptured and the Etruscans retired into their own country. The inhabitants of Nepete who had proved unfaithful to the Roman cause fell under the lictors' axes. Finally, as we have seen, the establishment of two Latin colonies at Sutrium and Nepete secured the frontier and consolidated what had been achieved.

But, despite these brilliant successes, the era of armed resistance on the part of the Etruscans was not at an end. In 359, the inhabitants of Tarquinii invaded Roman territory and laid it waste. In the following year they defeated the consul, C. Fabius Ambustus, and massacred 300 Roman soldiers whom they had taken prisoners. In 357, Tarquinii made an alliance with Falerii, and in 356 the whole Etruscan federation came in to support them. The dictator C. Marcius Rutilus beat the Etruscans and drove them back into their own country. In the following year, Sulpicius Peticus, for the third time consul, took the offensive, invading and ravaging the territory of Tarquinii. Hostilities continued and the war was waged without pity, and neither side shrank from the massacre of prisoners. In 353, Caere itself, Rome's old ally, threatened in its turn, made an alliance with Tarquinii; it was defeated and sued for peace which Rome granted in the form of a hundred years truce.

Finally, in 351, Rome resolved to end these ceaselessly recurring campaigns once and for all. She launched a double offensive against Tarquinii and Falerii and this time her success was complete. Following the example of Caere, Tarquinii and Falerii sued for peace and were accorded a forty years truce. 'Thus,' concludes Livy, 'Rome found herself relieved of the burden of two threatening wars.'

On her eastern frontier, Rome had to deal with two mountain peoples, the Aequi and Hernici. One after the other she attacked them and gained the victory. In 389, Camillus crushed the Aequi at Bola, and took the town by assault: in the following year, the Roman army marched victoriously through the country. The attack upon the Hernici, at first postponed by reason of the Etruscan War, was launched in 386. Allied to the Latins and to the Volsci, the Hernici were beaten on two occasions, in 386 by Camillus, in 385 by the dictator A. Cornelius Cossus. For twenty-three years they remained peaceably in their mountains, whither Rome, beset with numerous difficulties, was careful not to pursue them. Finally in 362, Rome resolved to finish with them and declared war. The operations began badly, the consul, L. Genucius, was surprised in an ambush and killed, but the dictator Appius Claudius lost no time in avenging this set-back by a great victory. In 361, the two consuls, C. Sulpicius Peticus and C. Licinius Stolo, captured Ferentinum, one of their principal towns. In 360, the consul, M. Fabius Ambustus, defeated them afresh, and finally two years later, after the victory of the consul C. Plautius Proculus, the Hernici asked for peace. They were re-admitted to alliance with Rome, doubtless, like the Latins themselves, on less favourable terms than in the past.

Still more bitter and prolonged were the wars against the Volsci, the most obstinate and implacable foes with which Rome had to deal in the first centuries of her history. The anti-Roman reaction was headed by Antium and Satricum, assisted by the Latin colony of Velitrae. To remove the menace it was not sufficient to defeat them: Rome could never be free of them except at the price of a veritable war of extermination. In 389, the Volsci took the offensive and advanced as far as the territory of Lanuvium, in the heart of Latium; Camillus defeated them at Markion, according to the text of Diodorus[1] (Livy gives *ad Maecium* near Lanuvium)[2]: he forced the breast-work of felled trees behind which they were entrenched and ravaged their country. In 386, in coalition with the Hernici and Latins, they were again beaten by Camillus, now military tribune, at Satricum: the town was taken by assault and the Volsci surrendered. Camillus was already intent upon laying siege to their capital Antium, when he was called away by the war in Etruria, and the project was postponed until a more favourable time. In 385, supported by contingents of Latins and Hernici, and also by the Latin colonists of Velitrae, the Volsci made a supreme effort, only to suffer a crushing defeat at the hands of the dictator A. Cornelius Cossus. A colony of 2000 Roman citizens was planted at Satricum with the task of keeping in check the vanquished enemy. In 383, it was resolved to parcel out the lands of the Pomptine marshes, but pestilence interrupted the undertaking and prevented its execution. In 382, in alliance with Praeneste, the Volsci captured the colony of Satricum by assault. But their success was shortlived. In the next year Camillus, military tribune for the sixth time, overwhelmed them after a hard-fought battle. In 379 they renewed the campaign and attacked the

[1] XIV, 117.   [2] VI, 2, 8.

Roman army which was commanded for the moment by two incompetent military tribunes, P. and C. Manlius. They captured the Roman camp, and it was only the tenacity of the Roman soldier that prevented this set-back from turning into disaster.

In 378 Rome planned a converging attack upon the Volsci; two armies invaded their country, the one under the military tribunes, Sp. Furius and M. Horatius, to the west, by the coast, the other, under Q. Servilius and L. Geganius, to the east, by the mountains. The country was methodically pillaged and laid waste: the trees were cut down, harvests burnt, cattle driven off. In 377, the indefatigable Volsci appeared again under the walls of Satricum: a Roman army under P. Valerius and L. Aemilius crushed them, plundered their camp and drove them back on Antium. The lack of the necessary equipment prevented the Romans from undertaking the siege of the town, but, a quarrel arising between the Volsci and the Latins, the Antiates were driven to surrender. In 358, by an operation analogous and parallel to that which she had carried out twenty-nine years earlier in southern Etruria, Rome annexed the Pomptine plains, and formed there two new tribes, the Pomptina and the Poplilia. Decimated and exhausted, the Volsci were forced to stand by and watch this menacing expansion of Roman power. But their passion for independence and their hope of revenge were not yet quenched. In 348 the war re-opened, a war to the death which found its consummation in 338 with the downfall of the Antiates and the final submission of the Volscian people (p. 590 sq.).

Finally, the Romans had to face the task of re-establishing their hegemony in Latium. The Gallic invasion had had as its last and most serious consequence the ruin of what Rome had achieved by generations of effort in the heart of Latium. The ancient pact of alliance was broken: separatist tendencies had arisen, and even though there had not been a unanimous rising in arms against Rome, such as that which followed the expulsion of the kings, yet Tibur and Praeneste, the two most powerful cities in that region, proud of their ancient glory, had endeavoured to form separate confederations for their own advantage. The Latin colony of Velitrae supported the movement, and the rebels could count besides on the co-operation of Rome's enemies, traditional enemies like the Aequi and Volsci or new enemies like the Gauls. Fortunately for Rome, the movement of secession was not general. Tusculum, apart from an equivocal attitude in 381, which however was only momentary, together with the body of southern Latin towns, Ardea, Aricia, Lanuvium, Lavinium, Cora, Norba, Setia and Signia, remained faithful to the cause of Rome, and thus provided her armies in Latium with the bases of operation, political and military, which were indispensable to her arms and to her statecraft.

The stubborn war which continued for thirty-five years between Rome and the Latin towns falls into two successive phases. At first the Latins, who were later to be supported by the mountain peoples to the east and by the Volsci, carried on the struggle alone against the state of Rome. In 386, and in the next year reinforced by the Volsci and the Hernici, they were defeated by Camillus and the dictator A. Cornelius Cossus. In 382, the Praenestines, in conjunction with the Volsci, captured the colony of Satricum. In 377 the allied armies of the revolted Latins and Volsci were overwhelmed near Satricum by the consular tribunes P. Valerius and L. Aemilius. The defeat was followed by a quarrel between the vanquished; the Antiates surrendered, while the Latins retreated homewards.

The second period opened with the Latins conscious of their impotence and with little hope of victory. The seceding cities, among which the Roman tradition expressly mentions Velitrae, Tibur and Praeneste, called in the Gauls and made use of them as mercenaries against Rome. In 360, the Gauls, defeated by the dictator, Q. Servilius Ahala, near the Colline Gate, sought refuge at Tibur, whose inhabitants sallied out to their aid. The defeats of the Gauls and even more, perhaps, the behaviour of the Gallic auxiliaries, which gave as much trouble to their allies as to their enemies, finally sealed the fate of Latium. Nevertheless for some years the Latins resisted bitterly. In 358, defeated and discouraged, Latium was driven to accept the renewal of the old treaty of Spurius Cassius (pp. 487 *sqq.*), with a certain number of new provisions imposed by Rome after her victory, provisions which henceforth secured the political and military leadership of the federation to Rome. In the same year the annexation of the Pomptine plains definitely shut off Praeneste from all access to the sea. By 354 the separatist cities had surrendered one by one: Tibur resumed its position in the federal league, Nomentum, Pedum, even Praeneste herself, were forced by the inexorable pressure of Roman arms to enter the league. This is the final collapse. After half a century of severe trials, Rome was definitely victorious in Latium as elsewhere.

The Gallic Wars of the first half of the fourth century B.C. mark only the beginnings of a struggle which continued in years to come. In the great war of Italian independence Rome was to find herself again faced by the Gauls, where at Sentinum, the decisive battle which sealed the fate of Italy, Celtic contingents were to play their part (see p. 612). They appeared yet once more on the eve of the Second Punic War, on the battlefield of Telamon (p. 812) and, a few years later, in Hannibal's ranks. The implacable duel between the two nations, Latin and Celtic, did not end until the conquest of the Gauls by Caesar. But this first act of the struggle, lasting over half a century, had a fundamental effect on the destinies of Rome and the development of her power.

It is true to say that all the great events which mark the history of Rome during this period, whether victories or defeats, appear as the direct or indirect results of the Gallic invasions of Italy. It was the invasion of the Gauls which, by splitting the Etruscan forces and distracting their attention to the north, made it possible for Rome in the early years of the fourth century to conquer Veii and southern Etruria. It was the invasion of the Gauls which brought about the collapse of Rome in 390, with the important effects which that catastrophe had upon her existence as a great power. Finally it was the invasion of the Gauls which during the period of recovery was always, whether in the background or the foreground, the dominant preoccupation and the ultimate concern of the Roman government. But above all, and this is the consequence that should most be remembered, the Gallic invasions are a decisive factor in the marvellous development of the Roman State at the end of the fourth and the beginning of the third centuries B.C., a factor operating in two directions—material and moral. On the material side, the disaster of 390, brought about by the invasions, gave rise to the great military and political reforms from which Rome, tested and proved, emerged better armed and more powerful. On the moral side, the duration of these invasions, the ravages which the Gauls caused over almost the whole of Italy, inflicting as much injury on their allies as on their adversaries, the impression of terror which they spread everywhere in their course, all contributed, in a form already real though still vague, to the efflorescence of the sentiment of Italian unity. In the very midst of the numerous and heterogeneous races who shared the soil of the peninsula, the invaders prepared the way for acquiescence in unification under Rome. On both these grounds, the general principle which underlies all the greatness of Rome—the principle of Italian unity—should in its elementary form, the unity of central Italy, be directly ascribed to the influence of the Gallic Wars.

The unification of the Italian peninsula was the work of the period that follows: but by the middle of the fourth century important progress had already been made. With her domain of over 2500 square miles, including her own territory and that of her allies, Rome had become the most powerful state in central Italy. She had more than regained, this time never to lose it again, the territorial and political position which she held at the beginning of the fourth century. To the north, southern Etruria had been reconquered, organized and partially annexed, in the form of tribes, to the Roman state. In the east and south, the Aequi and the Volsci had been crushed and reduced to insignificance. The Latin-Roman federation, destroyed after 390 by the action of the allies, had arisen again from its ashes; but Rome no longer took part in it on terms of strict equality. Thanks to her victories she exercised a preponderance which she had never known in the past. Finally, the annexation of the Pomptine plains prepared the way for the encircling of Latium, which, some years later, was to end in the permanent annexation of Campania.

For Rome, the atmosphere was clearing: wider horizons, a wider perspective for the future were opening out before her eyes. In 354, she concluded her first treaty with the Samnites, and six years later, in 348, she signed a treaty with Carthage, two diplomatic acts of capital importance, the first opening the era of her great Italian policy, the second that of her great Mediterranean policy. After the severe struggles of the Gallic Wars, Rome, from the middle of the fourth century onwards, began to harvest the fruits of her exertions.

CHAPTER XVIII
THE CONQUEST OF CENTRAL ITALY
I. THE ROMAN TRADITION

THE preceding chapter has described the recovery of Rome from the Gallic disaster. We have now to trace the events which secured to Rome dominance in central Italy. The issue was placed beyond doubt. When the period ends, the Latins had ceased to be equal allies, the Samnites to be equal rivals or enemies, the Gauls were no longer a danger, and the Greeks only waited for a master. So much is certain. But the historian is ill served by the records of these stormy times. Apart from the scanty notices found in Diodorus, the fragments of Dionysius of Halicarnassus, of Dio Cassius and of Appian's *Samnite Wars*, and the entries in the *Fasti triumphales*, he has nothing but the account in Livy[1], and, since Niebuhr, few will deny that there is much in Livy's narrative that is not true. The fact that the later annalists added much, some true, some false, to the jejune records which served as the earlier stratum of Roman history-writing needs no further proof (see chap. x): what concerns us here is to discover what forms are taken by the admixture of the false in the external history of this period, so that we may endeavour to isolate and remove it.

The period is one in which the new nobility of office was rising to power. Since 366 B.C. plebeian nobles had the right to be consuls and to be independent commanders of armies in the field. But the older patrician houses, above all the Fabii, had not lost their prestige; and when in the next three centuries the Roman annalists composed the history of this period they had to satisfy the claims of the new pride of the new nobles and the old pride of the old. Both old and new nobles held office; it was an age of wars; and it hardly can have seemed invention to attribute to these magistrates victories which they ought to have won. One partial check is the list of triumphs, which, for the latter part of the period at least, may rest on some kind of official records. Any Roman victory of this period described in the literary sources which is not attested by the *Fasti triumphales*, must be suspected as fictitious, unimportant, or really a defeat transmuted by the alchemy of family pride. Real victories may be duplicated, either

---

[1] VII–X. For detailed references see the Bibliography.

by reason of alternative attributions to members of a family or poverty of imagination on the part of fabricators. And yet it is naïve to deny the possibility that in the shapeless warfare of repetition to which Roman campaigns were often reduced, a son might imitate his father in defeating Samnites or Etruscans, or even, in two consulships, win two victories on the same border. For Roman wars in this period had intervals of what was little more than border-warfare, in which small victories with small if any results were not uncommon, and towns were taken or retaken with a casual frequency. But here if scepticism may remove something that is true, it removes little that is other than unimportant.

A further source of falsification is patriotism and the civic pride born of prosperity. The Samnites were tough enemies who exacted from the Romans the homage of mendacity. Defeats which could not be denied, which were perhaps preserved by the enemies of the defeated generals, are hastily repaired by resounding victories which we have the right to suspect. The enemies of Rome are thought of as rebels or treaty-breakers; or if the Romans are the aggressors, Rome has on her side either the spirit or the letter of the bargains which she seems to break. And finally, there are the exaggeration of numbers, the use of conventional battle-pieces to describe battles, the precipitate of old or recent hostilities between noble families, and the dramatic and ethical instinct of historians whose pre-occupation was to point a moral or adorn a tale.

Such are the motives and methods of falsification which most affect the tradition even of this period, which approaches the light of contemporary record, and statements which lie beyond their scope claim especial attention and may often be a touchstone of truth. The *elogia* of the Roman nobles did preserve true details, as of the capture of obscure towns, and when these are mentioned in the tradition we may give them some credence, but it is to be remembered that the exploits may be wrongly assigned to the several stages of a general's career. Sometimes, too, it is not possible to discover where the places were. A Roman general may even by the destruction of a town have destroyed the one means of evaluating his exploit. Acts of state, as treaties, are not lightly to be disregarded, for the record of them for this period may have been preserved by contemporary archives. Roman magistrates used their houses as their offices, and the archives of the great nobles could eke out the scanty records of the state. Equally authentic may be the notices of the founding of colonies which, serving as they did the ends of strategy, are landmarks in the progress of Roman arms. Finally, a study of the terrain and of the strategical problems solved in other wars in central Italy, may indicate the probable effect of operations, though they tempt us to attribute to the Roman Senate too logical and too far-reaching aims. Strategy which has to rely on local knowledge rather than on the use of maps, is apt to be fumbling at first, and at last traditional rather than imaginative.

II. THE GROUPING OF POWERS

By the middle of the fourth century, as has been said above, the horizon of Rome was widening, and we have to review the grouping of powers in the Italian peninsula at this moment. Forces beyond the control, often perhaps beyond the knowledge, of the Romans had been unconsciously preparing the way for Rome's hegemony of Italy. In the first half of the fifth century the richest and most formidable peoples in Italy were the Etruscans and Greeks. It is true that Rome and the Latins had asserted their independence of Etruscan political influence, but the Etruscans had found more than compensation in the mastery of the country between the Apennines and the Po. The Greeks of Sicily, with little to fear from the Carthaginians after the crowning mercy of Himera, had only to find union among themselves and to join hands with their kinsmen in Magna Graecia to make themselves masters of the southern half of the peninsula. But, as we have seen, the Greeks could not unite, they found no great leader, and their opportunity passed unused. In the second half of the fifth century the expansion of the Italic peoples of the Apennines thrust the Greeks back upon the defensive and robbed the Etruscans of their last remnant of power south of the Tiber.

The cause of this great movement of the Sabellian peoples was beyond doubt the progressive over-population of the mountain country, which found its remedy in the strange practice of the *ver sacrum*, by which dedicated bands of emigrants left their homes to take to themselves the homes of others. The early stages of this process escape our knowledge. We may see its by-products in the raids on Latium of the Aequi, who were both impelled and weakened by the greater movements behind them. The set of the movement was southwards. In the north and north-west, the military skill of the Etruscans held their plains intact; in the east the sturdy Picentes could maintain themselves and their civilization which from the sixth century onwards was enriched by imports from the Greeks of southern Italy. Their pugnacity, attested by the weapons which fill their graves[1], did good service

[1] Randall-MacIver, *The Iron Age in Italy*, pp. 105 *sqq.* and *Antiquity*, ii, pp. 144 *sqq.*

to Italy in resistance to the Gauls. Picenum was the *glacis* of the Italian defences. But they were no less and for far longer a check on a northern Sabellian advance. Rome and Latium were screened by their neighbours, and the Sabellians pressed on southwards from glen to glen until they found themselves within reach of the fertile plain of Campania. Here was an ancient population, known to the Greeks as Ausones, enjoying a civilization planted there by the Etruscans and by the Greeks, especially of Cumae, who since Hiero's victory in 474 B.C. had been undisputed masters of the coast (vol. v, p. 148). The Etruscans had no longer the sea-power nor the ambition to re-assert themselves in the south, and the Syracusans were immersed in Sicilian politics. In 445 B.C. Capua was taken by the Sabellians to whom the Greeks gave the name of Ὀπικοί—Oscans, and in 428, Cumae, the oldest Greek settlement in Italy, met the same fate[1]. Neapolis, the offshoot of Cumae, alone remained to shelter Cumaean refugees and to stand for Hellenism. Thus there was interposed an Italic barrier against any Greek advance northwards in western Italy. Content with their conquest, the Oscans in Campania turned aristocrats, learned the use of cavalry, and, played upon by Greek influences and Etruscan traditions, rapidly absorbed the civilization which they found waiting for them.

A further stage in the Sabellian progress was the occupation by the Lucanians of what the Greeks called Oenotria: the area dominated by the Lucanians is roughly bounded by the Silarus on the north, the Bradanus on the east, and by a line drawn west of Thurii on the south. The coasts of this region were, in the main, still held by the Greeks of Posidonia, Pyxus, Scidrus, Laus, and, on the south-east, Metapontum, though they probably lost most of their territory and sometimes their independence. As in Campania, so here, though in less measure, the Sabellians absorbed the culture which they found, a culture which, like that in Apulia, borrowed largely from the Greeks.

By 390 B.C. the Lucanians had formed a league which was encouraged by Dionysius I in order to weaken the Greek cities of southern Italy (vol. vi, p. 128). That opportunist tyrant secured the safety of Hellenism in Sicily by sacrificing the future of Hellenism in Italy. Magna Graecia was left to find a leader in

[1] Diodorus, XII, 31; XII, 76, under the Archon-years 438/437 and 421/0 = Varronian 445 and 428. Livy, IV, 37; IV, 44 gives Varronian 424 for the fall of Capua, 421 for the fall of Cumae. The effects of the Sabellian conquest of Cumae are reflected in the cessation of its silver coinage and the absence of Greek pottery of the next 50 years in the tombs excavated there.

Tarentum, whose tortuous policies sought to protect herself from the barbarians by alien adventurers and from alien adventurers by ingratitude. The natural allies of the Greeks were the Daunians of Apulia who had to guard their plains from these new invaders, but their old fears of Tarentum restricted them to a fairly successful defence. The remaining peoples of the south, in Calabria and Bruttium, had little political significance, save that in the second half of the fourth century the Bruttians began to press hard on their Greek neighbours. See vol. VI, pp. 127 *sqq.*, 299 *sqq.*

Meanwhile the southern Apennines had once more filled up with Sabellians, who now formed the loose confederation which the Romans called the Samnites. The extent of the Samnite league about the middle of the fourth century is marked out by the *periplus* of the pseudo-Scylax. It stretched across the width of the peninsula touching the sea on the west between Campania and Posidonia (Paestum), on the east a strip of coast from Garganus 36 hours sail northward. Thus it included the north of Apulia and the canton of the Frentani. Their kinsmen of the Lucanian league were independent of it, as were the Oscans of Campania and the lesser Sabellian tribes of the high Apennines, the Paeligni, Marsi, Marrucini, with their outliers the Vestini. Much remains to be done in the discovery of the civilization which they enjoyed, but it is roughly true to say that these lesser Apennine peoples lagged behind the dwellers in Latium and the south and still more behind the Campanians and the Etruscans[1]. With slight economic resources they could not attract to themselves the wares of the more advanced peoples. Politically weak, they lived isolated from each other, offering little inducement to a conqueror, possessing little power to make conquests. With the Sabines and the Umbrians they form what may be called a neutral area in central Italy.

In the north, the invasion of the Gauls had broken the Etruscan power beyond the Apennines, and even when their raids were intermitted they remained an incalculable danger against which the states of central Italy had to find protection. Thus Rome and the Samnites, recognizing the presence of a common enemy, had made an alliance in 354 B.C. whereby it would seem they agreed to respect the allies of each other. As the Gallic pressure became less severe, each of the two contracting powers found secondary reasons for maintaining their alliance, the Romans in the incipient movement of secession among the Latins, the Samnites in the complicated politics of southern Italy. There is no reason to credit the Samnites with any profound policy, and the Roman

[1] See v. Duhn, *Italische Gräberkunde*, pp. 557 *sqq.*

Senate were more noteworthy for a clear realization of what lay before their doors than for any far-sighted designs. But once the alliance had served its primary and secondary purposes, it was almost inevitably bound to turn to enmity or rivalry, for the natural sphere into which both peoples might extend their power most profitably was the Campanian plain. In the generations covered by this chapter Rome solved the problems that presented themselves, and in their solution attained predominance in central Italy, and built up most of the great federation which was soon to control the whole peninsula.

III. ROME AND THE LATINS.

In 358 the Latins had acquiesced in a renewal of the treaty which bound them to Rome, accepting for the moment the *fait accompli* of Roman predominance (p. 578). The Volscians, it is true, were not entirely subdued, and remained a possible ally for any Latins who might attempt secession. They had been driven off most of the plains which lay to the west of them, and the Romans had settled there the two tribes Pomptina and Poplilia. On the other hand, the raids of the Gauls, as has been said, had made for the spirit of Italian solidarity. Rome, the martyr and defender of the Italic peoples, had the moral advantage of having withstood the Gauls instead of using them, as had some of the recalcitrant Latins (p. 571). The alliance of Rome with the Samnites in 354 B.C. set a barrier which protected the peoples of central and southern Italy from the Gauls, even if it was to end in their subjection to one or other of the two high contracting powers.

Finally, in 348 B.C. the Romans made a treaty with Carthage, which revived in a modified form the agreement made more than a century and a half earlier[1].

The pre-occupation of Carthage was to preserve her monopoly of trade in the western Mediterranean, especially in Spain (p. 777), and the Senate, faced by pressing political problems nearer home, was prepared to sacrifice the slight interest which Rome possessed in overseas trade and the larger interests of her ally, Massilia. In return for the Roman acceptance of exclusion from these waters the Carthaginians renounced any intention of gaining a foothold in Latium and recognized it as the Roman sphere of interest. The treaty reveals the Roman intention to secure the permanent control of the coast from the Tiber to Tarracina and was a threat to Antium, which was at once a home of pirates and an outlet for the Volscians. The threat was soon translated into action. Two years

---

[1] See below chronological note 1, pp. 859 *sqq.*

after the treaty the Romans made war on the Volscians, and M. Valerius Corvus, the most notable Roman general of the day, celebrated a triumph over the Antiates, the Volscians and the men of Satricum. We may agree with the Roman annalists in suspecting that this was a preventive war intended to weaken the Volscians before the Latins were able to give help or ready to receive it[1]. The treaty reveals more than this intention; it appears to revive the claim to dominate Latium which Rome had successfully asserted in the closing years of the regal period (p. 405). Ten years before the treaty a movement of the older and more powerful Latin cities to break away from Rome had failed, but a new conflict was inevitable as it became more and more clear that Rome intended to be not the leader but the mistress of Latium. It is true that the terms which refer to Italy, as given by Polybius (III, 24), are elusive, whether because of the silences of the historian, who is chiefly concerned to stress the rights claimed by the Carthaginians, or because the Roman Senate preferred formulae of which their power would be the interpreter. But we may suspect that the Latins saw in it a treaty made for them and about them in which their interests were at once neglected and threatened.

Thus Roman ambitions and anxieties combined with Latin fears to govern the course of the Republic's policy. To judge by later events, the Latin element in some of the so-called Latin colonies was gaining the upper hand, and by the year 343 the Latins are found pursuing a military policy of their own independent of Rome. The older annalistic tradition ascribes to this and the next year an internal crisis at Rome which was probably both political and economic, though we have few details that we can trust (p. 529). This crisis may well have given the Latins freedom of action to prepare for the movement of secession which soon followed. In one quarter Rome might feel secure, that is, in the north. The southern Etruscans kept the treaty of 351 B.C., and in 343 Rome turned her forty years truce with Falerii into a definite pact of alliance. This shows that Rome was preparing to face her dangers to the south. It is equally clear that it was not in the interest of Rome to do anything which would dissolve her treaty with the Samnites and augment a present danger.

[1] The taking of Sora on the Upper Liris and the victory over the Aurunci attributed to the year 345 (but not reflected in the Triumphal Fasti) are apparently an anticipation of the events in 314, when also a Sulpicius was consul, except that the success over the Aurunci was attributed to L. Furius Camillus to provide a victory to justify his vow of a temple to Juno Moneta, which was in fact probably to celebrate the repulse of the Gauls (p. 573).

It is at this point that the Roman tradition[1] interposes a First Samnite War which Rome is alleged to have fought in order to protect the Campanians, who by surrender (*deditio*) to Rome made themselves in the nick of time part and parcel of the Roman state. The details of this war as given in Livy notoriously abound in military improbabilities, but that fact does not of itself prove that no war happened, nor is it safe to deduce from the silence of Diodorus that the war was not recorded in the older annalistic tradition on which he drew, for he is capricious in selecting for record incidents of Roman history. It is true that when later he does speak of Romans fighting Samnites[2], his phrasing suggests that he is describing the first war which Rome waged against that enemy, but his methods of historiography hardly entitle us to press that deduction very far. But, once suspicion is aroused, it is impossible to evade the thought that the whole story attributes to Rome uncharacteristic folly and is inconsistent with other elements in the Roman tradition which seem less open to question. That Rome should have chosen a moment when she was embarrassed by well-founded suspicions of the Latins to break with the Samnites for the *beaux yeux* of the Campanians, whose loyal support she did not win by her intervention, argues political folly only equalled by the military foolhardiness of fighting a war in Campania with no sure communications between Rome and her armies. If the war is fictitious, a motive for the invention can readily be found in the desire to provide Rome with a moral justification for her dealings with Campania in the Latin War. At that time, as we shall see, Rome granted to the Campanians *civitas sine suffragio* and a generation which conceived of that as a penalty might well seek to prove ingratitude as the crime. The argument that there must have been a war of Romans and Campanians against Samnites, as otherwise there would be no Roman-Campanian connection to be broken when the Campanians joined the rebellious Latins, is a *petitio principii*, for this connection may be as fictitious as the war which led to it. Certainty is impossible, but respect for the artificial Roman tradition about this period should not compel a cautious critic to postulate folly in the Romans, blindness in the Latins, a short memory for benefits in the Campanians and a short memory for injuries in the Samnites. If this war is eliminated, the tradition presents us with what

[1] *Fasti triumphales*; Livy VII, 29–VIII, 2; Dion Hal. XV, 3; Appian *Samn.* 1; *Oxyr. Chronicle* (P. Oxyr. I, XII).

[2] In XIX, 10, under his year 317/6 B.C. = Varronian 318. Ῥωμαῖοι μὲν ἔννατον ἔτος ἤδη διεπολέμουν πρὸς Σαμνίτας.

follows, a narrative which is probably true and certainly credible, and to that narrative we may now return.

In 343 B.C. the Latin armies were already in the field, though apparently not yet prepared to challenge Rome directly, but according to a statement in Livy (VII, 38, 1) which deserves credence so long as no good reason can be discovered for its invention, they attacked the Paeligni. A successful advance in the Apennines would drive a wedge between Rome and the Samnites without bringing either power directly into the field. The internal troubles at Rome, which a direct attack might have ended, presumably prevented any counterstroke, but subsequent operations suggest that the Latin enterprise had little success[1]. To meet this threat the Romans drew closer their bond with the Samnites by renewing in 341 B.C. the treaty of 354 and by making it clear that they did not regard the territory of the Sidicini south of Latium as covered by it from a Samnite attack. The result was that the Sidicini appealed to the Latins, and a Latin army marched across the Samnite border. Thus the Latins gained one ally and very soon added to themselves another, the Oscans of the league of Capua; and the remainder of the year 341 was spent in preparations for a war against Rome and Samnium.

The forces were not unequal. The Latins were long used to match man for man with Rome, the Volscians and Sidicini were hardy men of the hills, while the Campanians—for so the Romans called the league of Capua—could bring into the field besides the infantry of their populous cities cavalrymen mounted on the spirited little horses which are depicted on their funeral monuments. But they were less formidable than they seemed to be, for the recruiting agents of Carthage and Sicilian tyrants had for nearly a century drained Campania of its more adventurous soldiers. On the other hand, Rome had enjoyed a respite from serious wars and had in the Samnites formidable allies. But the attention of these last was in part distracted by the enterprises of the Spartan king Archidamus in southern Italy (p. 640), and,

---

[1] According to Livy (VII, 42–VIII, 1), the Volscians of Privernum raided the territory of Setia and Norba, were repulsed by the consul of 341, C. Plautius, and saw their city taken, garrisoned, and then restored to them. This is almost certainly an anticipation of the event of 329 B.C. (p. 594) when C. Plautius was also consul with the same colleague as in 341. Livy's statement that two-thirds of the Privernate territory was annexed plainly belongs to the latter year and leads up to the formation of the tribe Oufentina in 318. See De Sanctis, *Storia dei Romani* II, p. 273 and Beloch, *Römische Geschichte*, p. 390 To both of these works this chapter is repeatedly indebted.

besides, there was between the Roman nobility and the democratic Samnites little sympathy. Their alliance had first been
against the Gauls: that danger was past for the time and the
natural antagonism of plain and hill was likely to make them
enemies so soon as they ceased to be allies.

The struggle was short but severe. The Latins, according to
Livy (VIII, 4), demanded full Roman citizenship and a half share
in the government of Rome. The whole narrative seems to be a
rhetorical retrojection of the antecedents of the Social War and
it is more probable that the Latins declared their intention of going
their own way or of asserting the ancient equality of their League
with Rome. Whatever the demand, it was refused and war was
declared. In the spring of 340, while one consul Decius Mus
presumably covered Rome[1], his colleague T. Manlius marched
through the country of the Paeligni and joined hands with the
northern Samnites. The junction which the Latin expedition of
343 had sought to make impossible was now a fact. The allied
army marched down the Liris, met the forces of the Latins and
their allies in the plain near Suessa Aurunca, and defeated them
in a great battle at Trifanum[2]. The patriotic Roman tradition has
reduced the Samnites to the rôle of spectators, but we need not
doubt that they played their share in achieving victory. The fruits
of victory were gathered by the Romans. They hastened to make
a separate peace with the Campanians, offering them very favourable terms, which the nobles of Capua, who perhaps had already
intrigued with Rome and behaved badly in the battle, were willing
enough to accept. Rome had thus anticipated her allies in
gaining control of the fertile plain of the Volturnus and could
leave to them a less valuable prize, the Sidicini. The Latins and
Volscians, reduced to their own resources, resisted for two more
years, but in 338 the leaders of the northern group of Latin towns,
Pedum and Tibur, were defeated by L. Furius Camillus, while his
colleague C. Maenius crushed the southern Latins and the
Volscians in a battle south of Antium. Antium itself was forced to

[1] The *devotio* of Decius is probably an anticipation of that of his son or
grandson, made plausible by the absence of his name from the Triumphal
Fasti. But his absence from the triumph may be due to his absence from the
battle, and it seems imperative for the Romans to have kept an army to
oppose a possible Latin advance northwards. See Beloch, *op. cit.* p. 373 *sq.*

[2] Diod. XVI, 90, 2; Livy, VIII, 8, 19; 11, 11; Dion. Hal. xv, 4. *Fasti
triumphales.* The two battles in Livy may be due to a confusion between
Vesuvius and Monte S. Croce. See Beloch, *op. cit.* p. 373, who, however,
is inclined to put the decisive battle near Capua, as does Dionysius.

surrender and the prows of its small fleet adorned the Comitium at Rome. The arms and diplomacy of Rome had triumphed, and she turned to consolidate her position against a conflict with her Samnite allies, who had served her turn and were now to be her dupes or her enemies.

IV. THE NEW ROMAN POWER

In the settlement which followed the Latin War Rome had three main objects, the first to render impossible a second concerted Latin rising while leaving unimpaired the fighting strength of her old allies, the second to reduce the Volscians finally to harmlessness, the third to attach to herself by strong bonds of common interest the Campanian communities and the people of the coast-road south from Latium.

To the achievement of these objects of high policy desire for revenge or for land were strictly subordinated. Rome indeed behaved with that calculated moderation which inspired her sagacious leaders *parcere subiectis*. The Latin colonies, Ardea, Circeii, Setia, Signia, Norba, Sutrium and Nepete, which had no ancient tradition of independence, were left as they were. Tibur and Praeneste, both strong cities, were mulcted of some territory but otherwise retained their alliances with Rome. Cora remained formally an independent ally of Rome as before. By a yet bolder stroke of enlightened self-interest Rome conferred her complete franchise on Lanuvium, Aricia, Nomentum and Pedum, which became integral parts of the Roman state[1]. The same right was conferred on Tusculum, unless it had already been granted in 381 B.C. (p. 569). Thus the Roman state received an access of full citizens, and, before a generation had passed, a Tusculan noble, L. Fulvius, attained the Roman consulship (322 B.C.). It was annexation, but annexation to privileges as well as to burdens. In 332 two new tribes, Maecia and Scaptia, were formed in Latium. The old Latin cities and Latin colonies which were not thus granted citizenship were deprived of *commercium* and *conubium*[2] with each other and of the right of concerting political action. Although the ancient common worship of Juppiter Latiaris on the Alban Mount and the Feriae Latinae continued, the congresses at the Caput Ferentinae were ended. On the other hand the peoples of these communities retained *commercium* and *conubium* with Roman citizens, who now composed the half of Latium.

The Volscians were held back in their hills by the sending of

---

[1] See Beloch, *op. cit.* pp. 377 *sqq.*
[2] For the rights included in *commercium* and *conubium* see above, p. 422.

Roman colonists to Antium and to Satricum. The anti-Roman leaders in Velitrae were driven into exile and their lands confiscated for the benefit of Roman settlers who retained their citizenship. But Velitrae did not become wholly Roman and, not long after, was still using a Sabellian dialect. For the moment these measures seem to have sufficed, the more, perhaps, as action against the northern Volscians might have brought the Roman armies near the middle Liris, which was debatable ground between Latium and the Samnites. The Hernici, farther north, appear to have remained quiescent or on the side of Rome, but they had ceased to be of great importance.

Finally, it remained to bind fast to Rome the coast peoples south of Latium and the towns in the lower Volturnus valley. Livy (VIII, 14) declares that the people of Fundi, Formiae, Capua, Cumae and Suessula were granted the Roman citizenship *sine suffragio*, i.e. without the rights of voting or holding office in the Roman state. There is no cogent reason against accepting this statement, which most probably goes back to an official record. The limitation of the franchise would have little meaning for most of these people, and though they were involved in wars without the power of deciding about them, this was at least balanced by the fact that Rome could not leave them to the mercy of their mountain neighbours. Livy (VIII, 11) says that the Capuan Knights received the full Roman franchise, but this is possibly a confusion with later events, and the Roman Fasti show no certain instance of a Campanian noble holding office at Rome during the century which followed this settlement (p. 548). The burdens of citizenship were light enough. To judge from the wars which followed, the Campanian levies both of foot and horse were usually left to their own management, and inscriptions show that Capua continued to be an Oscan city governed by its own Oscan magistrates. And yet, if a Capuan or a Formian went to Latium, he found himself in enjoyment of all the private rights of a Roman citizen.

Despite the wars which followed the adhesion of the Campanians to Rome, they gained in security. On the paintings which adorned their tombs we have evidence of the luxurious variety of their lives. We see gaily dressed cavaliers—mounted hoplites or light cavalry—with their plumed helmets and cloaks, going out to war or returning on victory with the spoils of their enemies dangling from their lances. Their womenfolk are depicted sitting among luxurious gear, spruce, dignified and house-proud. At funerals they had combats of gladiators who wore the characteristic armour of the mountain Samnites and were probably

prisoners of war. While the origin of gladiatorial fights may be
Etruscan it is at least probable that the custom reached Rome by
way of Campania. They bought and imitated Greek vases, but in
their tomb-paintings we see an art which rapidly became truly
'Oscan', national in character, more realistic than the Greek, un-
tainted by the cruelty and gloom which at this time dominated the
art of Etruria. The Roman tradition saw in the Campanians
luxurious weaklings, but after all, during decades of social intercourse Campania repaid its debt to Roman strength by helping
to bring some brightness into the lives of its protectors. The
Appian Way was to bring Campanian civilization near to Rome as
well as Roman legions near to Capua. The true Italian vein of
humour which the Romans did not lack was reinforced from
Campania. If Etruria must be credited with the sophisticated professional performer of mime or music and perhaps with the biting
satire of the Fescennine songs, it is Atella in Campania that gave
its name to the more good-humoured farces in which the young
Romans found vent for their high spirits. The manufactures of
Campania reached the Roman market and made good many deficiencies of Roman industry and, by the time of the elder Cato,
supplied tools for Roman agriculture. We must not exaggerate
their prosperity—the heyday of Pompeian prosperity was not
yet—but it cannot be doubted that the adhesion of Campania to
Rome brought at least material benefit to both.

In practice then there was between Rome and the Campanians
a connection giving rather more security but rather less freedom
than an alliance, yet sufficiently resembling an alliance to carry
with it no stigma of inferiority, and this experiment of Roman
statecraft was justified by its results[1]. Some land, perhaps the
estates of anti-Roman notables, was confiscated and used for
citizen settlements, in which Campanians could share, and it is
possible that special rights were granted to the loyal Capuan
aristocrats. The league of which Capua had been head was dissolved in the larger unity of the Roman state so that inhabitants
of Cumae or Suessula now had the same rights as those of Capua.
Not long afterwards (332) the people of Acerrae were also made
cives sine suffragio. Such was the group of states bound to Rome

---

[1] The Romans may have had a further motive, viz. to bring Campania within
the scope of the treaty that bound the Samnites to respect Roman territory;
this may be reflected in Livy's account of the alleged deditio of Capua in 343.
It is also possible that the manager of their policy was Q. Publilius Philo,
consul 339, who was active in Campania in 327 and 315–4 and was attacked
by his enemies on the momentary apparent failure of the policy in 314 (p.602).

by old and new ties of sentiment or interest, at the head of which Rome made her bid for the hegemony of central Italy.

V. ROMAN POLICY AND THE SAMNITES

Rome now controlled a long strip of territory which at several points was dominated by hills which might harbour enemies. During the ten years which followed the defeat of the Latins, the Romans were concerned to find means of protection. To secure the Capuan plain from attacks from the country of the Sidicini, they established in 334 a strong colony at Cales, thus putting a limit to Samnite expansion in that quarter. The Samnites might have intervened to prevent this, but they were kept busy by the enterprise of Alexander of Epirus. Their forbearance was ill-rewarded, for when the Samnites and Lucanians suffered a defeat at Posidonia, the Romans hastened to come to an agreement with Alexander which bound them to friendly neutrality and removed the danger that the king and his Greek allies would attempt to advance north into the Campanian plain (see below, p. 640).

The next step for Rome was to master the Volscian hills which looked down on the Pomptine plain. Accordingly, in 329 the armies of the Republic were sent against Privernum, the town was taken, its walls destroyed and, as at Velitrae, the leaders of the anti-Roman party were exiled beyond the Tiber. Privernum was granted the Roman franchise *sine suffragio*, and part of its territory was confiscated. Some ten years later, in the interval of peace which followed the Caudine disaster, this was constituted a Roman tribe, the Oufentina. In the same year, 329, a Roman colony was planted at Tarracina (Anxur) to hold the coast road where it passes by Lautulae, the Thermopylae of southern Latium. Perhaps as preparation for the attack on Privernum, the Romans allied themselves with Fabrateria (Vetus), the modern Ceccano, in the Trerus valley and possibly with Frusino on the high ground to the north of it. This brought the Romans close to the Samnite border and to the north-western end of the fertile plain of the middle Liris. Here was at once the possibility of annexation and of the further protection of the Roman possessions, and in 328 B.C. the Romans founded a colony at Fregellae, which blocked the north-western entrance to this plain.

The course of Roman policy is clear and consequent, but in the next year it was diverted by a crisis in Campania. West of Capua lay the strong Greek city of Neapolis, which a century before had received the refugees from its parent Cumae when that city fell into the hands of the Oscans. To Neapolis Cumae had been the 'old city' and it may be conjectured that the refugees formed a section of the population which was locally known as the 'old citizens,' *Palaeopolitai*. Within the city grew up two opposed parties, with one of which the 'old citizens' were identified, and these two parties found support, the one in Capua the other in the Oscan town of Nola. The latter won the upper hand, and a garrison of Samnite mercenaries was introduced into Neapolis to support the *régime* of the 'old citizens' party. The result was friction with Capua, which in 327 called on Rome for help; this was promptly given. While one consular army covered the siege, the other under Q. Publilius Philo blockaded the town. It was too strong to be taken by storm and could not be starved while the sea was open. The siege dragged on into the next year and Publilius Philo was continued in office as proconsul to conduct it. The choice was wise, for Publilius seems to have been a diplomatist, and intrigue was to solve the problem. But this diplomatist proconsul was the first of a long line of proconsular soldiers destined to serve and finally to end senatorial government. The Romans might have sought naval help from their allies the Carthaginians but may have shrunk from bringing them into a strong city. Under pressure of the siege and perhaps of this possibility the government of Neapolis passed into the hands of the pro-Romans Charilaus and Nymphius, who tricked the Samnite garrison into evacuating the town and then surrendered it to the besiegers. The Romans made an ally of Neapolis, which remained faithful to her new protectors. The Capuans had no cause to complain, and Capua and Neapolis prospered side by side for a century[1].

We may now, on the eve of the great Samnite War, review the military problem imposed on Rome by the nature of her enemy and of her enemy's country. The Samnites had developed an art of war well suited to their hills. They did not fight in phalanxes but in smaller bands, perhaps the model of the Roman maniple as a tactical unit. Their weapons were a short stabbing sword or (possibly later) a falchion and the heavy casting spear, the pilum. They carried a large shield, oblong or oval, and wore a greave on the left leg to protect themselves from their shields as well as from the enemy. The greater part of Samnium proper is ill adapted to

[1] The account in Livy (VIII, 22–3; 25–6) seems to be derived from a Roman annalist working on a Greek historian or tradition. What appears to the present writer certain is that the city which the Romans besieged is the city with which they made the alliance, *i.e.* Neapolis; that officially no such city as Palaeopolis existed, though the name may once have been used by Neapolitans of Cumae as a city and *Palaeopolitai* of refugees from Cumae as

cavalry, and the strength of the Samnites lay in their footsoldiers, who combined the mobility of light troops with a steadiness which matched that of the Roman legionaries. To face these formidable mountaineers the Romans opposed an army which manœuvred in close formations. The Romans had no cavalry proper but rather mounted infantry. In the open country the Romans were competent enough, and doubtless they had learnt from the great disaster at the Allia[1]. But the fact that they took so long to subdue the Aequi and Volscians, although they defeated them when they could intercept them on the plains, suggests that the Roman army was not well adapted for mountain warfare. They had numbers on their side, and their alliance with the Campanians gave them cavalry to which they added new formations of their own. They could thus make headway on the plains against the valour of the Samnites, though not even there was the fortune of war constant.

The military problem was affected by the political organization of the Samnites. In Campania the Sabellians had become city-dwellers; in Samnium itself they lived mainly in villages with scattered strong places like Aufidena, the one Samnite site that has been thoroughly excavated. The evidence of the few inscriptions that survive from Samnium proper suggests that each glen had as ruler a *meddix* or *meddix tuticus*[2] (= *judex populi*). They were so far banded into a league as to seem to the Romans a political unity, and we must assume that at Bovianum Vetus or Aesernia representatives met in council under the presidency of the *meddices*. Some kind of central organization there must have been. Once the league decided to go to war, the heads of the cantons chose a generalissimo whose powers were absolute until the campaign ended. He might be re-elected or succeeded by another chieftain.

individuals. The triumph of Q. Publilius Philo ('de Samnitibus Palaeo-politaneis') (=de S. et P.). is fictitious, because he was not a regular magistrate in 326 and had not won a victory in the field. Therefore the word 'Palaeo-politaneis' does not come from an official Roman document and the whole phrase represents the romanizing of an informal Greek phrase which conveys the essentials of the situation.

[1] See p. 568. In the view of the present writer, however, the Romans learnt the use of the pilum from the Samnites in the course of the war that follows, rather than earlier, and with the pilum adopted more flexible formations in the field.

[2] The appearance of a second *meddix* at Capua is presumably due to the fact that Capua was a great city; there is no good evidence for assuming a greater and a lesser meddix in each of the Samnite cantons. Beloch's theory that the title *meddix tuticus* was reserved for the chief officer of the Campanian league is refuted by Rosenberg.

The very looseness of this league deferred, though it rendered certain, the Roman subjugation of the country. It deferred it because the Romans had no sufficient objective—no real capital at which they could strike a mortal blow. Nor could they detach glen from glen because of the patriotism with which the Samnites clung to their national cause. For in the mountains of Samnium was a sturdy stock not enervated by luxury or weakened by the recruiting of mercenaries from amongst them, and while men of their race, once out of sight of their mountains, were fickleness itself and changed paymasters without hesitation, in their native glens the Samnites were inspired by a passionate devotion to their country which in moments of peril fused the scattered cantons into a nation of heroes. Not even the large population of Latium could provide settlers to cover the country with a network of colonies, and in the tangle of mountains not even the keen glance of the Romans could discover points of decisive strategic value.

The task of the Romans was first to meet the Samnites in the plains and break their military prestige, next by the planting of fortresses to make good the defence of Latium and Campania, and then either to make peace or, if a lasting peace proved unattainable, to carry fire and sword through the glens of the Apennines until there were too few Samnites left to be a danger. To achieve this they had to isolate Samnium and attach to themselves the neighbouring peoples who would help the Roman armies to break into Samnium from every side. The hope of the Samnites was to win resounding successes which would embolden the jealous and the defeated to rise against Rome, or to entrap the Romans before they had adapted their military technique to this terrain. The course of the war which followed showed how hard a task the Romans had set themselves, and more than once, it seemed as if it was beyond their power. But time is on the side of the big battalions, and in the end Rome was victorious.

VI. THE GREAT SAMNITE WAR: THE FIRST PHASE

The first phase of what is traditionally called the Second Samnite War ended in disaster and in a bad peace for Rome. Few details of the first years of war appear to the present writer to deserve belief. In the year in which Neapolis admitted the Romans they completed their operations on the Samnite border by capturing the two towns Rufrium and Allifae which command the middle Volturnus valley. There is no record of victories in the field, and we may conjecture that it was not until the next year that the Samnites were ready for serious warfare. The Romans knew that in Apulia they might find allies, and about this time they allied themselves with some at least of the Apulians. The problem was to gain contact with these allies, and that could only be through the tribes north of Samnium. Continuous communication through Samnium itself would only be possible when victory had already been won, whereas the route farther south through Lucania was long, and an attempt to go that way would convert the Lucanians into active allies of their Samnite kinsmen, and force Oscan Nola out of the neutrality which she seems to have preserved throughout most of the war. It is true that Livy declares that the Romans made an alliance with the Lucanians, but this is apparently only to make possible a fine story, borrowed from Greek literature, of its breaking. Rome accordingly turned her attention to the central Apennines and in 325 the consul D. Junius Brutus won a victory in the country of the Vestini while, presumably, his colleague stood on the defensive in Latium or Campania. The Samnites retorted by an attack which caused the Romans to appoint L. Papirius Cursor dictator with Q. Fabius Rullianus master of the horse, and the dictator won a victory and earned a triumph. The other details in Livy are plainly modelled on the events of the Second Punic War. If we content ourselves with this victory, we must put it at an unknown place, Imbrivium, and suppose that that detail came from some *elogium* of Papirius or of Fabius.

The remaining achievements with which the Romans are credited in the three years that follow are more than suspect, and even aroused doubts in the mind of that honest man of letters Livy. The *Fasti triumphales*, it is true, credit Q. Fabius with a victory over the Samnites and Apulians in 322 B.C. which may mark an extension by arms of Roman influence in Apulia, and Appian records an abortive Samnite attack on Fregellae which may have been rendered possible by this dispersion of Roman forces. It is, however, more than possible that these victories found their way into the tradition as a foil to the disaster of 321. All else recorded for these years deserves little belief—least of all the alleged revolt of Tusculum—, and the variants given by Livy show how much this phase of the war was the sport of rival traditions.

In 321 B.C. the consuls were T. Veturius and Sp. Postumius, and they concentrated both consular armies in Campania at Calatia. The reason for this is not at first sight clear. It may be that they anticipated a renewal of the Samnite attack on Fregellae and proposed to counter it by a march through the south of Samnium. This, apart from the devastation of the country, would by its success strengthen the Roman influence in Apulia; Fregellae

might be trusted to hold out, and the Latin fortresses would protect Rome and Latium. But the Samnites had this year chosen a
general, Gavius Pontius, whose subtlety was greater still. He saw
to it that the Roman consuls received news that the Samnite main
force was in Apulia. The news, if true, meant that a forced march
by the most direct route might enable the Romans to bring the
enemy to battle in the plains of Apulia with the Romans between
them and their mountains. One great victory might end the war.

But the news was false. The Samnite army had concentrated in
Western Samnium, and when the consuls pushed on their way
with sanguine improvidence they were entrapped in the narrow
valley which led from Saticula to Caudium[1]. The army was doubtless marching light and intending to live upon the country, and,
after failing to break out of the trap, it was starved into surrender.
The Samnite commander dictated a peace which seemed sufficiently to secure to his nation all that they were fighting for, and
took 600 Roman knights as hostages for the acceptance and
maintenance of the treaty by the Roman Senate. The defeated
army was disarmed and forced to admit its discomfiture by passing
beneath a ritual 'yoke' of spears. This blow to the military prestige
of Rome was doubtless dictated by policy more than by insolent
triumph. The terms of the peace were that the Romans should
withdraw their garrisons from places which the Samnites claimed
as their own, and pledge themselves not to re-open the war.

The Senate, even if it was possible to re-arm their troops at
once, had no sufficient motive to refuse the peace, the more as that
would have meant the death of the hostages drawn from the
noblest families of Rome. Doubtless the shrewd elders who guided
Roman policy did not despair of their statecraft, and believed that
revenge would be sweeter for a slow ripening. Those who discern
in the Samnites the last champions of Italian freedom have
denounced their failure to complete their victory. But the Sam-

---

[1] The scene of the disaster has been endlessly disputed. There are three
possibilities. The plain of Caudium between Arpaia and Montesarchio is too
large and has too many exits, the pass between Arienzo and Montesarchio is
too small to include an army even of only two legions in column of march
and—more important—is too visible from the Campanian plain to make
possible the preparation of so elaborate a surprise. There remains the valley
between S. Agata de' Goti and Moiano which fits the account in Livy fairly
well and is on a direct route from Calatia to the heart of Samnium. If this is
the scene of the disaster, we need not be surprised that the Via Appia later
avoided it. The Romans may have neglected Saticula (near S. Agata) and
found out to their cost the unwisdom of doing so. This view was first
advanced by Cluverius in 1624.

nites, unconscious of their historic mission, had no reason to believe that Rome was the destined mistress of all Italy or that, if need be, their mountains would not again bring to defeat the slow-moving Roman legions. Beyond that, their ideas of policy did not extend. We may suspect that the desultory fighting of the last generation both in central and southern Italy had kept their population stationary or reduced it until the control of the upper valleys of the Liris and the Volturnus met their needs. The peace was made and kept. The house of one of the consuls, Veturius, relapsed into obscurity for the century, the other, that of Postumius, survived this defeat as it survived others which it brought upon the Roman arms. Publilius Philo, the Fabii, and Papirius Cursor patiently prepared to fight another day.

VII. THE GREAT SAMNITE WAR: THE SECOND PHASE

The Caudine peace lasted for five or six years. It is true that as early as the next century Roman pride disguised the fact by making the Senate denounce the peace at once and inflict on the Samnites defeat after defeat. This fiction was then elaborated by details taken from the Roman behaviour in 136 B.C., after C. Hostilius Mancinus had been entrapped in Spain. But when we have relegated to their proper years the Roman victories assigned to 321, 320 and 319[1] and to their proper century the elaborate shams and morals which adorn the alleged evasion of the capitulation, we are left with Rome not wholly inactive. While the Samnites occupied Fregellae, and presumably the upper valley of the Volturnus, the Romans strengthened themselves in Apulia and made sure of their connection with it. This activity did not contravene the Caudine peace, and the Romans did nothing which infringed upon the immediate interests of Samnium. In 318 B.C., Teanum in Apulia and Canusium gave hostages to Rome, and in 317 the consul C. Junius Bubulcus took Forentum[2]. The Romans were also able to continue the organization of their extending civic boundaries. In 318 the settlers to whom lands had been assigned north of Campania and in the land taken from Privernum were made into two new tribes, Falerna and Oufentina. During the previous twenty-five years the area occupied by Roman citizens with full or partial rights had trebled, and the military resources of Rome were increased until we may suppose that in place of the two

[1] In particular, those of Papirius and Publilius from 320 and 319 to 315 and 313.

[2] The taking of Nerulum is anachronistic, and may be transferred to the year 277, when also a C. Junius was consul and active in that region. Beloch, *op. cit.* pp. 402, 465.

legions which, with allied contingents, had been the regular field-army of Rome, each of the consuls might command two legions besides the Campanian troops. If we are right in supposing the pilum to have been originally a Samnite weapon, we may assign to this period its introduction into the Roman army and a tactical reform which provided a more flexible manipular formation suitable to the mountain warfare in which the Romans had hitherto proved unsuccessful[1]. For it was the Roman practice to learn from their enemies and to better the instruction.

By the year 316 the Romans felt themselves strong enough to renew the war, and the Samnites must have become aware of the net which their enemies were drawing round them. It is not impossible that they had tampered with the loyalty of the Campanians. The Roman disaster at Caudium must have made a profound impression on the people of Capua who saw the return of the defeated army, and Roman consciousness of this may be reflected in the dispatch of *praefecti* to Capua and Cumae in 318. For it is probable that the legal duties of these officers were a later growth, and that their first duty was to watch the interests of Rome. In 316, when the storm of war was about to break, the league of Nuceria south of Capua abandoned the friendly neutrality which it had shown to Rome and declared itself the ally of the Samnites.

The Romans, meanwhile, were planning to send a colony to Luceria to form a nucleus for their power in Apulia. They elected as consuls their two most trusted leaders, L. Papirius Cursor, whose task it was to cover the founding of the new colony, and Q. Publilius Philo, who by arms and policy was to hold the Roman Campania which may have been his own creation. This wide dispersal of the Roman forces gave an opening to the unknown strategist who now directed the Samnite forces. While Papirius was marching towards Apulia and Publilius was besieging Saticula so as to block one gateway into the Campanian plain, the main enemy force broke through by Sora into the valley of the Liris. The Romans hastily raised an army of reserves and put at the head of it a dictator, Q. Fabius Rullianus, who had made his name as a general seven years before. He marched south and met the Samnites at Lautulae where his army was defeated and Q. Aulius, his master of the horse, was killed. It was an inauspicious moment in the career of the greatest soldier of the Fabian house, and the historical activities of his family have done their best for him by giving him a new master of the horse in C. Fabius (who, having served his turn, disappears from history) and by attributing to him an immediate victory.

[1] See, however, above, p. 568.

The fact is plain: one Roman army was in Apulia, another under Publilius Philo was hard beset in Campania, a third had been defeated in a battle which seemed to confirm the verdict of Caudium. There was a movement of secession from Rome northwards as far as Satricum, southwards into Campania. But the Latins held by Rome, and L. Papirius, who had forced the surrender of Luceria which the Samnites had garrisoned, probably hurried back to cover Rome itself[1].

When the campaigning season of 314 opened, the initiative lay with the Samnites, and they apparently intended to operate in Campania where Capua itself was on the verge of secession. The moment was critical, and Rome had recourse to a veteran soldier, C. Sulpicius Longus, who won a great victory at Tarracina[2] in which the Samnites lost rather more than 10,000 men, if we may accept the not impossible figure given by Diodorus. In Capua the anti-Roman party won the upper hand just too late, and the presence of a victorious Roman army brought the city to repentance. The leaders were executed and Capua remained faithful to Rome for the next hundred years. The story in Livy (IX, 26) that the Romans showed their alarm by impeaching Publilius Philo among others is perhaps a fiction, for the procedure suggests the late Republic, but it is true that the end of his long career was clouded by partial failure.

During the next two years the Romans were busy strengthening their shaken power in the south. The Aurunci, whose loyalty was suspect and whose land was needed, were visited with massacres until their name vanished from the earth. A Latin colony was planted at Suessa. Satricum, which had rebelled, was reduced and the ringleaders of the revolt were put to death. This probably happened in 313 B.C. when L. Papirius was consul; though the event and the triumph for it have been promoted to his earlier consulship, 319 B.C., to make one of the victories of the fictitious war of revenge (p. 600). In the same year (313) Fregellae was recaptured, and in the next the town of Sora on the Samnite border.

---

[1] It has been suggested that this garrison was exchanged against the hostages surrendered by Rome in 321, but it is also possible that they had been restored when the terms of the Caudine Peace had been duly executed. A withdrawal of Papirius to cover Rome is perhaps indicated by the fact that the projected colony at Luceria was not definitely established until 314.

[2] Livy's account of these operations implies that the victory was somewhere in the region of Campania. The mss of Diodorus XIX, 76 give περὶ κίναν πόλιν, for which Burger ingeniously suggested περὶ ταρακίναν πόλιν, and this is widely accepted. Diodorus' narrative may however imply that the Roman victory was far from Capua, and, if so, Niese's suggestion of Pinna (in the country of the Vestini) may be right.

It is true that the capture of this town is assigned also to 314, but it is improbable that the Romans could or would have attacked it until after they were re-established at Fregellae. The eastern entrance of the middle Liris valley was guarded by a strong colony at Interamna (312). Farther south, Calatia and Nola[1] were captured and made allies and the defence of the Campanian border was strengthened by a colony at Saticula. The coast road to Campania was protected by a colony on the island of Pontia, and the Romans made a beginning with the Via Appia, which was destined, as it progressed, to mark the several stages in the conquest of southern Italy.

Rome was now stronger than when she began the war in 326 B.C. In 311 we read of the election of 16 military tribunes by the people, which implies a normal annual levy of four legions, presumably over and above the Campanian formations. In the same year were first appointed *duoviri navales* to be responsible for the tiny fleet which met Rome's immediate needs. It is possible that the establishment of this small fleet had been the occasion of the sending of a colony to Ostia, of which the fortifications belong to the second half of the fourth century. The first recorded action of this squadron was inauspicious, an abortive landing at Pompeii to harry the territory of Nuceria (310 B.C.).

VIII. THE ROMAN ADVANCE IN CENTRAL ITALY

The expansion of Roman power southwards and the maintenance of it in the face of the Samnites had been made at least easier by the fact that for a generation Rome had not to meet enemies on her northern and north-eastern borders. But now the position became menacing though at the same time full of promise, and Roman policy took a wider range. The strategy of attacking Samnium on the west from southern Latium and Campania and on the east from Apulia had compelled Rome to divide her forces and expose herself to dangerous attacks. Now that Campania was secure from anything more serious than raids, the Romans sought to gain a firmer hold on central Italy so as to be able to operate against Samnium from the north and east while keeping her armies within reach of each other. This new offensive strategy had its defensive side, for by it the Romans might prevent their actual enemies in the south and their potential enemies in the north from joining hands.

To the north of Rome lay the Etruscans, beyond the Apennines the Gauls, to the north-east of Rome the Umbrians, the Sabines

---

[1] Livy (ix, 28, 6) also mentions Atina, which may be a mistake for Atella. See De Sanctis, *op. cit.* ii, p. 325 n. 2.

and the remnant of the Aequi, beyond them the Praetuttii and Picenum; then came the group of central Italian peoples, Marsi, Vestini, Marrucini, Paeligni and Frentani, with whom Rome had made alliances or conventions which allowed her armies to march round to Apulia. But these tribes were kinsmen of the Samnites and also within reach of pressure from them which became more severe as the Samnites sought less and less to advance south-westwards. Thus the Roman hold upon them was precarious until it was confirmed by the establishment of strong centres of Roman influence and by victories in the north of Samnium.

The next decade was to witness a Roman defensive towards Etruria concurrent with a steady advance in the Apennines of central Italy.

After the taking of Rome by the Gauls the southern Etruscans had sought to undo what Rome had done in establishing a defensive frontier north of the Tiber (pp. 574 *sqq.*). But their efforts had been in vain. Sutrium and Nepete had weathered the storms that beat against their walls, and the old Roman alliance with Caere and new alliances with Tarquinii and Falerii covered whatever of the frontier was not protected by the Monte Cimini, which seemed an impassable barrier to troops. With characteristic prudence Rome did not annex either Tarquinii or Falerii but kept them as buffer-states and as hostages for their kinsmen's good behaviour. So long as Rome was not too deeply pre-occupied elsewhere, the Roman legions could be in southern Etruria long before the Etruscan cities could join forces against her. A few Roman agents, the friendships of Roman aristocrats for Etruscan lucumos[1], would give early information. Beyond that, Rome cared little about Etruria, and the Etruscans, who had reached an unworthy and pessimistic decadence, reflected in the decline of their art which becomes gloomy instead of jovial, had enough to do with the Gauls, who must have seemed a far more dangerous enemy than Rome. But the Gauls gradually ceased from troubling, and as the treaties of Rome with the southern Etruscan cities came near to running out, these cities preferred to look to their kinsmen for help rather than to trust Rome, which was daily becoming more powerful and more dangerous to her neighbours.

We are told that as early as 312 B.C. rumours reached Rome of danger from Etruria which led to the appointment of a dictator and that in 311 all the Etruscans except the people of Arretium appeared before Sutrium. One of the consuls, Aemilius Barbula, was sent to relieve the town; according to one tradition he could

[1] The Volumnii at Rome were apparently of Etruscan origin, and the Cilnii of Arretium were friends of Rome.

do no more than fight a drawn battle, according to another, he enjoyed a triumph over the Etruscans. It is probable that the whole story is a fiction and that Aemilius' triumph was invented to gratify his family and his drawn battle to explain why it was that next year the Etruscans appeared before Sutrium in full force. The first real conflict between Rome and the Etruscans probably belongs to the year 310. The movement was a complete fiasco. While the Etruscans lay outside Sutrium one of the consuls, Q. Fabius, marched boldly through the Monte Cimini and won a victory which apparently brought to the head of affairs the pro-Roman party in the several Etruscan cities. Treaties were made with Cortona, Perusia and Arretium; in the next year (308)[1] the alliance with Tarquinii was duly renewed and a Roman army brought Volsinii to terms.

Unsuccessful as had been this Etruscan movement, it had not unimportant results. It revealed in Q. Fabius Rullianus a bold strategist and it brought Rome into touch with the Umbrians, whose country lay along the flank of Etruria. We need not believe the story of the wide détour made by Fabius far into the Apennines—which, after all, are not the Ciminian hills—, but there is no reason to doubt that about this time Rome found useful allies in Camerinum in the north-east, and Ocriculum in the south-west, of Umbria. On the other hand, the distraction of Roman attention and the need for keeping considerable forces to counter a danger so near at hand delayed the progress of Roman arms in the other theatres of war. During 312 and 311 the Romans had been active in the country of the Marrucini, where they captured Peltuinum[2], and in northern Apulia, though in the latter year the consul C. Junius Bubulcus got himself entangled in the mountains of northern Samnium. He extricated himself and later dedicated a temple to the goddess of Safety for what may have been an escape rather than a victory. In 310 B.C. the Romans were apparently on the defensive, and the consul C. Marcius, though credited with the capture of Allifae, barely held his own on the western borders of Samnium. Failure in the field brought out the mythopoeic faculty of the Roman annalists. L. Papirius Cursor is made dictator in order to win a victory at Longula which seems to be no more than an anticipation of his son's triumph at Aquilonia in 293 B.C.[3] Nor need we scruple to deprive that excellent soldier of a victory in Etruria at that historical battlefield Lake Vadimo, a

---

[1] The Varronian year 309 is a 'dictator year' (see p. 322) and is a chronological interpolation.

[2] If we may accept Pais' emendation of Diodorus' Πολλίτιον.

[3] Beloch, *op. cit.* p. 412.

victory which was apparently invented too late to be added in the *Fasti triumphales* to his alleged success over the Samnites.

It is possible that the settlement with the Etruscans was hastened by the need of maintaining Roman influence among the tribes to the north of Samnium. For in 308 a Samnite army appeared in the country of the Marsi. Fabius, who had been sent with his army to make good the failure of the infant Roman fleet at Nuceria, was recalled to face this threat and was continued in his command as proconsul for the next year. The consul L. Volumnius operated in northern Apulia while his colleague Appius Claudius chafed inactive at Rome. In 306 B.C. the Romans were ready to open a new offensive against Samnium from the north-east, but they were hindered by a war with the Hernici, their ancient allies. A generation before, the Hernici had remained neutral or helped Rome in the war with the Latins, and since that time they had played a useful part as a barrier between the Samnites and Latium. The recent expansion of Rome had brought them no profit, and they could not well hope to remain independent when Rome triumphed. Part at least of their communities, with open help from the Samnites and secret encouragement from their neighbours, the Aequi, rose in arms. Sora and Atina, the towns which lay between them and Samnium, were taken. But Aletrium, Ferentinum, and Verulae stood aloof, and C. Marcius, hastily recalled from Apulia, marched into their country. Anagnia, the chief city, was taken, receiving the Roman *civitas sine suffragio*, and the towns which did not join the movement were made allies of Rome. The stronghold of Frusino which looks down on the Latin Way was forced to surrender and mulcted of part of its territory. We may assume that the Samnites were active in supporting the Hernici, and Marcius' colleague was left to win easy victories in Apulia and to ravage the east of Samnium.

The power of Rome in central Italy was shaken, and in the next year the Samnites had as allies those of the Hernici who were still in arms and their neighbours, the Aequi and the Paeligni. Apart from an abortive raid in Campania, this region was the main theatre of war. There was hard fighting and one of the consuls fell in battle, but M. Fulvius Curvus, who took his place, won a victory over a Samnite army which tried to relieve the town of Bola[1] in the country of the Aequi. The submission of the Hernici

---

[1] Diodorus xx, 90. This is presumably the place mentioned elsewhere (also as πόλις Βῶλαι) by Diodorus xiii, 42; xiv, 117 and in the parallel passages of Livy (iv, 49 and vi, 2) called by that name. Here the later tradition followed by Livy promotes it to be Bovianum.

was made complete by the fall of Arpinum; Sora was recaptured, and the taking of Cerfennia[1] marked the collapse of the resistance of the Paeligni. In 304 the Romans crushed the Aequi and negotiated with the Samnites, sword in hand. The Samnites, disheartened by their failures, too pessimistic about the present, too optimistic about the future, made a peace which left them with their ancient frontiers almost intact but freed the hands of Rome to complete the fortification of her power in central Italy. The war had given to her Sora and Atina to bar the Samnites from the upper Liris, Allifae and Saticula to cover the Volturnus from north and east. The Roman consul, P. Sulpicius, was granted a triumph to mark the Roman victory. The Samnites had not made submission—they had made a miscalculation. After six years of peace Rome so far completed her mastery of the country that lay between Samnium and Rome's northern enemies that only for one moment, at Sentinum, could the Samnites raise a coalition to challenge her progress towards the domination of Italy.

One possibility remained, that the Greeks of southern Italy would realize that Rome was a greater menace to their political power than their old Oscan enemies and make common cause with them. But the Greeks were not even united among themselves and were concerned with nearer dangers and ambitions, with the plans of Tarentum and Cleonymus and Agathocles (chap. xix). Unaided, their material forces were no longer a match for Rome and if they were to find a master, it was better to fall into the hands of Rome than be a prey to Samnites and Lucanians. Neither Cleonymus nor Agathocles, a Syracusan tyrant hampered by the hostility of Carthage, was the man to raise Magna Graecia to a last effort to dominate Italy, and the day of Pyrrhus was not yet. If need be, Rome could get help from Carthage which had seen Etruscan ships of war assisting her enemy Agathocles and believed that her interests were best served by sowing disunion among the Greeks of the West. In 306 B.C. her treaty with Rome was renewed and it is possible that she gave to the Republic, as to Metapontum, her friend in southern Italy, financial assistance.

It is commonly asserted that Roman coinage began in the second half of the fourth century B.C. This is probably true of the *aes grave*, the bronze moulded pieces of one pound weight which, as true coins, took the place of the bronze for barter, the *aes rude*. The *aes grave* bore the stamp of a ship's prow, and this has been connected with the setting up on the Roman Comitium of the prows of the Antiate galleys taken in 338 B.C. (p. 591). But this

---

[1] Diodorus xx, 90. Σερεννία. Cerfennia is proposed by Mommsen, *C.I.L.* ix, p. 348.

connection, in itself hazardous, appears to give too early a date in
relation to other issues of the kind in central Italy, and it seems
more probable that this step was not taken until about the closing
decade of the century[1]. Not earlier and possibly a generation later
is the inception of the so-called Romano-Campanian silver coinage
which bears the legend ROMANO or ROMA. On one side of some of
the earliest of these silver coins appears the horse's head which
was a badge of Carthage, and the deduction has been drawn that
we have here silver struck with Carthaginian help at a time when
it was in the interest of Carthage to strengthen Rome's finances.
The most notable occasion is the treaty between Rome and
Carthage at the time of the Pyrrhic war but the shadowy treaty of
the two states about 306 B.C. must not be forgotten. Somewhat
in favour of the later date is the marked resemblance between the
head of Apollo on a bronze coin of Beneventum (after 268 B.C.) and
that on some of the earliest of the 'Romano-Campanian' didrachms, a resemblance which suggests that the two series were
struck in the lifetime of the same artist[2]. But the numismatic
history of Italy and of the Greek mints of Magna Graecia has not
yet reached sufficiently certain results to enable the historian to
say with confidence how long before, or how soon after, the year
300 B.C. Rome first had the use of silver currency for trade both
with her Italian and Greek neighbours. The important date is later,
the year, 268 B.C., when Rome first struck the silver denarius which
soon became the symbol and instrument of Rome's hegemony in
Italy (see below, p. 663).

IX. THE LAST CRISIS

The Romans now turned to the consolidation of their position.
A strong colony was sent to Sora, and the *civitas sine suffragio* was
conferred on Arpinum and Trebula, apparently Trebula Suffenas
in the country of the Aequi. The war with the Aequi was convenient, for it justified the annexation of territory on which in
304 B.C. were planted the colony of Alba Fucens and in 302 the
colony of Carsioli. Six thousand colonists were sent to the first,
four thousand to the second, a sufficient proof of their strategic

---

[1] See E. A. Sydenham, *Aes Grave*, pp. 24 *sqq.*

[2] H. Mattingly, *Num. Chron.* 1924, p. 81 and *Roman Coinage*, pp.
6 *sqq.* Another series of the 'Romano-Campanian' didrachms bears a bearded
head of Mars which recalls the head of Leucippus on coins of Metapontum
which are to be set late in the fourth century. In these coins, too, Carthaginian connections may be discovered (see Giesecke, *Italia Numismatica*,
p. 180). The imitation of the Leucippus head suggests that the Romano-
Campanian didrachms of this type are not earlier than 300 B.C.

importance. It is possible that the founding of Carsioli did not pass off peaceably and that C. Junius Bubulcus, a good soldier, was made dictator to crush local resistance. Binding alliances were made with the Vestini, the Marsi, the Paeligni, the Marrucini and the Frentani. In Etruria the Cilnii, who ruled in Arretium and had been driven out by a revolution, were restored by Roman intervention. In the north of Apulia a Roman force was given the credit for the ejection of the Spartan Cleonymus from that coast (see below, p. 641). Thus far the Romans had achieved security near home, but there was a danger in the north. As we have seen, the raids of the Gauls had ceased and, a generation before this time, a treaty with the Senones gave Rome security. But new bands of Celts had crossed the Alps and roused their kinsmen from the agricultural life into which they were settling. For the moment these were at war with the Veneti, but Rome hastened to make an alliance with the Picentes in order to block a southern advance of the Gauls along that line (299 B.C.). They might hope that the Etruscans, for their own sake, would help to keep the Gauls north of the Apennines.

Between Etruria and Picenum lay the country of the Umbrians and the Sabines. The Umbrians had suffered from the Gauls, who had taken the strip of Umbrian coast on the Adriatic; at the crisis of 225 B.C. they counted no more than 20,000 men (p. 811). Their geographical position made the country useful to Rome as a barrier between her northern and southern enemies, and at the same time ensured the destiny of its unorganized population as subject either to the Gauls or to Rome. In the south of Umbria Rome was already allied with Ocriculum, in the north with Camerinum. A clear policy was marked out for Rome, to extend her influence until there was no danger of a Gallic advance through Umbria or of Umbrian defection to her enemies. It was a race which Rome almost lost, but the first stage in her progress is marked by the taking of Nequinum and its transformation into the Roman colony of Narnia. The strategic importance of Narnia is that it guards the point where the ancient road which was to be the Via Flaminia crosses the river Nar[1]. It is conceivable that the

---

[1] Livy x, 10, 5. *Fasti triumphales*. The triumph of M. Fulvius is given as 'de Samnitibus Nequinatibusque.' The 'Samnitibus' is probably derived from his successes in 305. This explanation seems preferable to the supposition that by 'Samnitibus' is meant Sabines. Stephanus of Byzantium cites as from Dionysius XVIII (which covered these years) the statement that Narnia was 'a city of the Samnites' (Ναρνία πόλις Σαυνιτῶν). According to the same authority Dionysius in the previous book described Nequinum as a city of the Umbrians (Νηκονία πόλις Ὀμβρικῶν), as indeed it was. Stephanus is apparently unaware of the identity of Nequinum and Narnia and his state-

statement in Livy (x, 13) that in 298 the Romans sent a colony to Carsioli, if it is not a mere duplication of the foundation of 302, conceals an advance yet farther north to Carsulae. The advance does not necessarily imply Roman control of the southern part of the Sabine country, as the military route would go by way of Falerii, which seems to have been used at this time as a Roman *place d'armes*. At the same time we can well believe that some of the Sabine communities feared for their independence, and, as they found themselves becoming a mere enclave among Roman allies and subjects, looked for an opportunity of striking a blow before it was too late.

In the meantime Rome was busy consolidating her gains of territory elsewhere by the formation of two new tribes, the Aniensis carved out of the territory of the Aequi, the Teretina in the valley of the Trerus composed largely of the land taken from Frusino. These tribes were made in 299 B.C., but in that year the Romans found themselves distracted by the northern danger. The Gauls had swept down into Etruria, to be met not by a sturdy resistance but by the suggestion that farther south they would find Roman territory to ravage. Several of the Etruscan cities joined with them and their forces crossed the Roman frontier and then quickly retired again to quarrel among themselves about the booty they had made. We may suspect that Etruria suffered more from the passage of the Gauls than Rome from their hasty plundering, but the mere news that the Gauls were on the warpath meant anxiety in Rome and aroused new hopes wherever Rome was feared. If the day of the Allia came again Rome's neighbours would know better how to profit by her misfortunes.

Meanwhile the Samnites, perhaps in the belief that Rome would concentrate all her strength on her northern borders, saw an opportunity of gaining control of Lucania, which had taken the side of Rome, so far as it had taken any side at all, in the struggle that had just ended. Agathocles of Syracuse was on the point of landing in Italy, and it may have seemed an opportunity to anticipate his possible enterprise (p. 635). But Rome accepted the challenge with alacrity. War was declared, and L. Cornelius Scipio Barbatus, one of the consuls of 298, marched through the south-western corner of Samnium, taking Taurasia and Cisauna, and forced the pro-Samnite Lucanians to give hostages for their fidelity to Rome. This achievement, which his epitaph enlarged

ment about Ναρυία may do Dionysius injustice and be a false deduction of his own from the attribution to Fulvius of a victory over the Samnites as well as the taking of Nequinum. It is a fair assumption that in this attribution Dionysius would agree with Livy, both using later annalists.

to a claim to have subdued all Lucania, was doubtless made possible by a vigorous attack launched against the north of Samnium by his colleague Cn. Fulvius. He struck at Bovianum Vetus, the old centre of the Samnite league, defeated an army that came against him, and took the town and its northern neighbour Aufidena. The strategic value of Roman control of the northern tribes was demonstrated, and Fulvius returned to enjoy a well-earned triumph. Livy, it is true, attributes to Scipio operations in Etruria, but as these do not appear in his epitaph they were, if historical, unimportant or inglorious. The Etruscans are added to the Samnites by the *Fasti triumphales* in the entry of Fulvius' triumph, but this may be no more than an anticipation of his operations in that region three years later. It is clear that any hopes of an immediate Gallic attack on Rome had come to nothing, and the Samnites were exposed to the full pressure of the Roman armies.

This time Rome was determined to make an end. Her two ablest generals, Q. Fabius Rullianus and P. Decius Mus, were elected consuls for 297 and during this year and the next they led their legions to destroy village after village in the Samnite glens. They even wintered in Samnium, thus preventing the herds and flocks from coming down to the lower pasturage. We may suspect that the Samnites had suffered severely in their defeat before Bovianum and were not able to face the Romans in a great pitched battle. But as Decius and Fabius, now proconsuls, were occupied in the east and south of Samnium, where they took Murgantia, an unknown Ferentinum, and Romulea, the Samnites saw a possibility of joining hands with the northern enemies of Rome. Before the year 296 was out the danger was realized. The consul Volumnius was recalled from Campania, where he had repelled one of the occasional raids on which the Samnites ventured, to reinforce his colleague App. Claudius in the south of Etruria, who, if we may believe his family's record of his achievement, had been engaged with Etruscans and Sabines. It was the fate of the Claudii to be often overblamed, and rarely overpraised, and it may be that there is some truth in the record and that Sabines on the Etruscan border had taken the field on what they may have believed to be the winning side.

The Romans faced their dangers undaunted. Q. Fabius and P. Decius the consuls, on whose well-tried skill rested the hopes of Rome, knew or divined that the Samnites had planned to break through to the north and join hands with the Gauls beyond the Apennines. Thence they might advance into Etruria, gathering allies as they went, or they might strike direct at Rome itself. The problem of this alternative approach on Rome was to be recurrent in the history of the Republic. It was solved by leaving reserve forces to cover Rome and to be ready at the right moment to advance into Etruria, while the two consuls with the main field-army were to prevent the junction of the Gauls and Samnites or, failing that, to fight a battle at once. Near the natural point of junction lay the allied city of Camerinum, a rallying point for Roman friends and a base for Rome's armies in northern Umbria. The Romans arrived almost too late. The Samnites had joined hands with the Gauls and defeated the Roman advance guard near Camerinum. But Fabius and Decius were close at hand and a few days later near Sentinum on the north-eastern slopes of the Apennines was fought a great battle which decided the destiny of central Italy.

It was the supreme test of the reformed Roman army which met the furious onslaught of the Gauls and the stubborn valour of the Samnites. One consul, P. Decius, gave his life to steady his troops and the legions stood firm; at last the tide of battle turned against the confederates. The great coalition collapsed, the Gauls retired, and the remnant of the Samnites broke away south and, after losing part of their troops in the country of the Paeligni, regained their mountains. Q. Fabius made a military promenade through Etruria, where L. Postumius and Cn. Fulvius had performed their task of making good the Roman border, and returned to Rome to celebrate a triumph over Samnites, Gauls and Etruscans. The triumph was well deserved. Decius, who fell, has remained the hero of Sentinum, but we may fairly suppose that the true architect of victory was Fabius. His march through the Ciminian forest fifteen years before had revealed in him something more than a conventional strategist, and we may credit him with the bold decision to defend Rome and dispute the possession of Etruria on the farther side of the Apennines.

There is no need to abandon Polybius (II, 19) and to believe with Livy that the Romans were faced by any considerable force of Etruscans or Umbrians as well as Gauls and Samnites. A few Umbrians may have joined the Samnites after their success near Camerinum but doubtless most of them welcomed the passage of a Roman army marching to fight the Gauls. Nor need we suppose that the Etruscans marched to Sentinum and then returned to Etruria because the Roman reserve armies invaded their country, still less that the consuls at Sentinum were in close touch with their lieutenants near Rome and ordered their advance while they themselves delayed a battle until the Etruscans had retired. To fight and win a battle when that battle was fought against such enemies was achievement enough for any general and any army. But among those that fell was a strategist who can rival Fabius, the Samnite Gellius Egnatius, who had conceived and brought so near to triumph the grandiose scheme of saving his country's cause by this great coalition. Two hundred years later the last throw of the Samnites for freedom was to be lost when a Sabellian army was crushed not far from that very spot as it sought to force its way into Etruria.

Many historians have lamented the issue of Sentinum and seen in the Samnites the martyrs of Italian freedom. But if the legions had been broken, what future was there for Italy but centuries of disunion, or precarious domination by a mountain people devoid of political instincts, whose virtues ended where their neighbours' lands began?

X. THE FINAL VICTORY

Fate had declared for Rome; it remained to break down the last resistance of the Samnites and to complete the Roman command of central Italy. The Gauls and northern Etruria might wait, and a peace for forty years was granted to Volsinii, Perusia, and Arretium. The Samnite raids into the Falernian plain were checked by the planting of colonies at Minturnae and Sinuessa on the Appian Way. One of the consuls of 294, L. Postumius, was sent to prepare an advance into Samnium from Apulia, but suffered a reverse; his colleague M. Atilius was employed in Etruria, where doubtless his army strengthened Roman diplomacy. One reason for the comparative inactivity of Rome may be found in the record of a plague which visited the city, but we can well believe that the strain of the year of Sentinum had for the moment sapped even the energy of Rome.

In 293 the Romans put out a great effort against the Samnites. Q. Fabius had fought his last battle, and the consuls for the next year were L. Papirius, the son of Fabius' old colleague and rival, and Sp. Carvilius, whose career was destined to be linked with that of Papirius. The details of the campaign which followed are difficult to elucidate. Livy's account (x, 38–46) is as follows.

A Roman army had been left at Interamna on the river Liris at the close of the preceding year. Carvilius took over this force and marched against Samnium, taking Amiternum from the Samnites. After laying waste Samnite territory, he next appears before Cominium. His colleague Papirius raised an army at Rome and, after taking Duronia, had reached Aquilonia, and the two consuls are described as being within reach of each other. One or both of them had ravaged the territory of Atina. The main body of the

Samnites faced Papirius at Aquilonia, which is described as if it was not far from Bovianum, presumably Bovianum Vetus. These names present a series of geographical problems. It is improbable that there was any other Amiternum than the Sabine town on the river Aternus, a river which does not find a namesake in Samnium. If the text of Livy is sound, we must either suppose that Carvilius, having an army ready for action, marched north through a corner of Samnium to wrest Amiternum from the Samnites before he turned south again towards his main objective, or fall back on the hypothesis rendered improbable by the explicitness of Livy, that his army had wintered not at Interamna on the Liris but at Interamna Nahars in the Sabine country. Further, we have to choose between the known Aquilonia (Lacedogna) and Cominium Ocritum, both in the far south of Samnium, and a Cominium east of Sora, attested by the survival of the name in medieval times, together with an Aquilonia assigned without any direct evidence to a site near Aufidena in the Sagrus valley. In favour of these shadowy places is the alleged nearness to Bovianum, the possible nearness to Atina and the statement that after Aquilonia Papirius next attacked Saepinum. The mention of Duronia does not help us, for although the name has been conferred on the village of Civita Vecchia near Boiano (Bovianum Undecimanorum), the identification is far from certain.

Of one thing, however, we may be sure. Papirius defeated the Samnites in a great battle which completed the work of Sentinum. This exploit inspires Livy to one of the most brilliant narrations in Latin literature. Bands of Samnites had sworn an oath to die rather than give ground but at last they broke before the steady valour of the Romans led by the young Papirius who in the heat of the battle vowed to Jupiter, not a temple as other generals, but the first draught of wine when the day was won.

Papirius marched to Saepinum and thence to Rome, while his army was quartered on the lower Liris. Carvilius is then described as besieging Velia, Palumbinum, the site of which is unknown, and Herculaneum, but these operations should more probably be assigned to his second consulship in 272, when the Romans were active in that region (p. 655). He is also credited with exploits in the south of Etruria, where he attacked an unknown place Troilum and made a truce with the Falisci, who were said to be in arms, but these exploits may be no more than an anticipation of his operations in the next year as lieutenant of D. Junius Brutus. The main effort of Rome was against Samnium and the consuls earned the triumphs 'de Samnitibus' which they received.

If we assign to 292 B.C. the Roman settlement with Falerii, we

may be content to see in the story of the defeat of the consul
Q. Fabius Gurges, and his subsequent victory with his father's
help, a pious fiction, helped out by details from the Second Punic
War[1], which anticipated with advantages his victory over the
Samnites, Lucanians and Bruttians in 276 (p. 656). The comparative inaction of Rome may be explained by the continued
presence of the plague. It is precisely at this point that the mythopoeic tradition of the Fabian house does most to obscure the course
of events, and the final defeat of the Samnites seems to be due to
L. Postumius Megellus, consul in 291 B.C., whom the Senate
succeeded in depriving of a triumph, and to a greater man, M'.
Curius Dentatus, consul in 290. With this last victory, which
earned for Curius a triumph, the Samnites at last were brought to
acknowledge defeat, and the full power of Rome was set free to
act against her neighbours, the Sabines.

Some modern scholars have advanced the hypothesis that the
Roman annalists or their sources had freely confused Sabines and
Samnites, sometimes using 'Samnites' for Sabines. It is true that
the word 'Sabine' might, to an etymologist, include 'Samnites,'
and it is also true that Greek annalists may have used the name
of the Samnites they knew to describe any of the Apennine peoples;
and in this Roman annalists may here and there have followed
them. But there is no decisive evidence of the confusion, and in
the only year in which it is certain that important operations were
conducted against both Samnites and Sabines the consul of that
year is credited with two triumphs, one against each of them. The
theory that what is called the Third Samnite War (298–90 B.C.)
was mainly conducted against the Sabines appears to the present
writer to be *a priori* improbable. The Sabine country proper can
hardly have been a danger to Rome. Under the early Republic
the Roman frontier had been advanced nearly as far as Eretum.
The one considerable piece of flat country, the plain north of
Reate, was not yet drained, and we may fairly assume that during
the fifth century the institution of the *ver sacrum* and the impulse
of adventure had gone far to reduce the population. The sober
home-keeping remnant had for a century at least been good
neighbours to Rome and there is linguistic evidence to suggest
that much of the Sabine country was already in part latinized. The
various Sabine towns with their *octoviri* as magistrates appear to
have had no close union, and had they been formidable, we may
take it that Rome would not for so long have brooked a danger
near their very gates.

[1] In which Q. Fabius Maximus acted as legatus to his son. Livy xxiv,
44. Claudius Quadrigarius, frag. 57 P.

But now that Rome had learnt the value of a strong barrier to keep apart the peoples of the north and the south of Italy, the independence of the Sabines must be ended. It is possible that the Roman advance in Umbria had seemed to some Sabines a menace and that the march of Carvilius to Amiternum was to forestall or to crush a pro-Samnite movement. Now, in 290 B.C., Curius led the Roman legions into the Sabine country and the whole people was incorporated into the Roman state as *cives sine suffragio*. The alleged wholesale expulsion of Sabines followed by confiscation and distribution of lands among Roman citizens is inconsistent with what seems to be the Roman policy, and probably is part of an annalistic fiction which tried to make of Curius a forerunner of the Gracchi[1]. It is more probable that the Sabines were left in possession of their lands, and that Rome took no more than the plain reclaimed later by the draining of the *Campi Roseae*. What Rome needed at this moment was trusty soldiers and these they found in the people who in their tradition had played a part in the earliest growth of Rome. The continued presence of the Sabines in their country is attested by the characteristic personal names ending in *-edius* which persisted in this region[2]. Before a generation had passed the Sabines received the full Roman franchise, while they retained in local self-government some traces of their own older institutions.

With this act of statesmanship this chapter in the story of Rome's advance to the mastery of Italy finds its natural conclusion. The extension of Roman power south and north of this central block of territory and the organization of the great Italic federation of which Rome was now the unchallenged leader will be described later. By arms and diplomacy, by statecraft—sometimes cynical, sometimes generous, always prudent—the new and old nobility of Rome had learnt to repair defeats and to use victories; and during a period of willing and unwilling concessions to the plebeians, the Senate had earned the right to retain the control of high policy and to stand for the very spirit of Rome.

---

[1] T. Frank, *On Rome's Conquest of Sabinum, Picenum and Etruria*, Klio XI, 1911, p. 367.

[2] A. Schulten, *Italische Namen und Stämme*, III, Klio III, 1903, p. 235.

CHAPTER XIX

AGATHOCLES

I. THE RISE OF AGATHOCLES

WHILE, as we have seen, the Romans were steadily extending their power throughout central Italy, the western Greeks were, in the main, intent upon the affairs of their own microcosm which extended from Tarentum to Carthage. Towards the end of the fourth century B.C. their history almost merges into that of Sicily, and the history of Sicily into that of its most remarkable tyrant, Agathocles. The story of this ruler is one long series of paradoxes, and the greatest paradox of all is that a career like his should have been possible within living memory of Timoleon (vol. VI, pp. 285 *sqq.*). At the death of this great peacemaker Sicilian politics appeared at last to have been stabilized. The ravages of previous warfare had been repaired by the influx of 60,000 settlers from Greece—the last swarm of colonists which the Greek homeland sent forth to the West; and a further increase of man-power accrued to the Siceliotes from the hellenization of the native Sicels, which was now almost complete. The Greeks thus still had ample resources to repel foreign attacks; and their Carthaginian neighbours and rivals, warned by their own failure at the Crimisus, and by Alexander of Macedon's resounding victories in the East, showed no disposition to renew their assaults. Under these conditions the era of tranquillity which Timoleon had introduced should have been of long duration. But not even Timoleon could rid the Siceliotes of their besetting sins, the jealousy which their cities bore against each other, and the reckless violence of their party strife. Not that he had neglected to take precautions against the resurgence of these evils. He had drawn together the Greek cities in a general alliance, and he had set a happy precedent when he gave to the Sicel town of Agyrium the franchise of Syracuse— a method of annexation which Rome was at that time pursuing

Note. The continuous sources for this chapter are Diodorus XIX–XXI, 13 and (on a much smaller scale) Justin XXII–III. The chief subsidiary source is Polyaenus V. All our extant sources appear to derive mainly from Timaeus, who was a Sicilian and a hostile contemporary of Agathocles. A good deal of anecdotal material has been incorporated by them from another contemporary but less trustworthy writer, Duris of Samos (p. 258 *sq.*).

with conspicuous success in Italy (p. 591). He had expelled sundry petty despots who could never have provided their subjects with a stable government, and in Syracuse he had carried out extensive reforms. Of the constitution which he imposed upon the Syracusans there is little to be said: presumably he did not revive the radical democracy which had proved but a fostering-ground for tyrants, but since he did not deprive the Syracusan Assembly of its fundamental powers of electing officials and of holding political trials, it is clear that he did not play into the hands of any narrow oligarchy. Nevertheless in this part of his work Timoleon was least successful, and his failure at this point was the prime cause of the misfortunes which befel the Siceliotes between his death and the Roman conquest.

The first attack upon the new order at Syracuse came from a section of the citizens known as 'the Six Hundred.' These were not an officially constituted body, as their round number might suggest, but a self-appointed coterie of intriguers who were recruited from the wealthier classes and perhaps represented the older inhabitants as against the newcomers introduced by Timoleon. Their primary purpose no doubt was nothing more than to monopolize office and seats on the city council by the usual methods of the electoral caucus; but their leaders, Heracleides and Sosistratus, were bent on setting up a close oligarchy, and where intrigue failed they were not averse from using force. Under the continued leadership of such men Syracuse would no doubt have relapsed into the state of disorder in which Timoleon first found it, and would have involved the other Siceliote towns in a similar confusion. But in the race for power Heracleides and Sosistratus were beaten by a rival who once more, like Dionysius I, riveted his power in 'chains of steel.' This competitor, whose name was Agathocles, was for some thirty years the most outstanding figure in the western Mediterranean, and it is round his personality, which dominated the history of Magna Graecia, that the rest of this chapter will be written.

Like other tyrants of Syracuse, Agathocles was not a native of that city. He was born in 361 B.C. at Thermae, a Greek town in the Carthaginian province of Sicily, where his father Carcinus, an exile from Rhegium, had taken up residence. Agathocles' adventures began almost at the hour of his birth, for his father cast him out to die, but his mother smuggled him into the house of her brother, where he spent his early childhood. Tradition declared that the reason for his exposure was a dream which warned his parent that he would grow up to be a scourge of all Sicily, but this legend is plainly no more than a replica of the story of Cypselus, the first tyrant of Corinth: the real cause was more probably the commonplace one of poverty. At the age of seven Agathocles was received back by his father and learnt the potter's craft: in later life his adversaries cast this menial pursuit in his teeth, but he ever professed himself proud of the skill of his thumb. In 343 B.C. he followed his father and his elder brother Antander to Syracuse, where Timoleon at that time was making a call for settlers, and, being now eighteen years of age, was enrolled as a citizen. Antander evidently found favour with the junta of the Six Hundred, for he was presently elected General. Agathocles was befriended by a wealthy citizen named Damas, whose widow he subsequently married. But in spite of his patron's exertions, and of the distinction which he gained in two minor campaigns against Aetna and Acragas, he did not rise beyond the rank of Chiliarch (Captain of a Thousand).

About 325 B.C. he served on a larger expedition which was sent to assist Croton against the Bruttians (see p. 634 *sq.*), and again displayed great gallantry; but Heracleides and Sosistratus, who no doubt had visions of Agathocles growing above their heads, used their influence to rob him of his just reward. Impatient of remaining a mere Chiliarch, Agathocles now took to political intrigue. Just as Marius at Rome turned upon the nobles who stood in the way of his promotion, so the Syracusan upstart impeached Sosistratus in the Assembly on the ground of aiming at tyranny. But far from carrying his point, Agathocles had the tables turned upon him, for the self-same charge was used by Sosistratus against him and his adherents to drive them into exile. After this encounter Sosistratus proceeded in effect to prove the truth of his opponent's accusations. In the wake of the fugitives he sent a military force to cut them up, and for the future he maintained a mercenary troop of the usual miscellaneous character to enforce his ascendancy. This was the beginning of the most sanguinary civil war in Sicilian history.

Agathocles escaped with the remnants of his followers to southern Italy and for a time led an aimless life of adventure. He broke into Croton, only to be driven out; he took service with the Tarentines, but incurred their ever active suspicions and was dismissed; he turned pirate and preyed upon Syracusan shipping. His chance came presently (*c.* 322 B.C.), when Rhegium was attacked by his old enemies Heracleides and Sosistratus. With a scratch force of broken men he went to the rescue and at one blow secured the liberty of Rhegium and his own reinstatement in Syracuse. In this city the news of the fiasco at Rhegium

brought about a revolution: Heracleides and Sosistratus now
took their turn of banishment, while Agathocles was recalled.
But the oligarchic refugees were not content to wait upon Providence. In preparation for a forcible return into Syracuse they
proceeded to stir up all the old feuds between cities and nations
which under Timoleon had been laid to rest. Among the independent Greek cities they made allies of Gela, and probably
also of Acragas; more ominous still, they enlisted a Carthaginian
force. Thus the warfare of factions broadened out into a *bellum
omnium contra omnes*: once more Sicily was thrown into the
melting pot.

In the ensuing warfare (*c.* 321–319 B.C.) Agathocles served the
Syracusans well. At Gela he displayed his characteristic re-
sourcefulness by drawing off a column which had been trapped
in the streets of the town after an abortive attack. In 319 B.C. he
was appointed 'general plenipotentiary in command of the
fortified positions in Sicily,' and thus appeared to have won at last
a free field for his talents. But under the threat of a new Punic
war the Syracusans took the further precaution of calling in a new
champion from Corinth. This second Timoleon, whose name was
Acestorides, was more bent on diplomacy than upon war, and
thus came into conflict with Agathocles, against whom he
renewed the charge of plotting a tyranny. For a second time
Agathocles was expelled from Syracuse: according to a story
which should be received with caution he only escaped assassination by finding a slave to impersonate him. But his departure
was soon followed by that of Acestorides, who made peace with
Carthage and left the party of Sosistratus and Heracleides once
more in possession of Syracuse (318 B.C.). Thus it was a case
of 'as you were,' except that since 322 B.C. the conflict was no
longer confined to Syracusans or to Greeks.

During his second exile Agathocles went no further than
Morgantia, an inland Sicel town which like many of its kind
stood under Syracusan suzerainty and had been exploited under
the régime of the Six Hundred. From the discontented cities he
gathered an army strong enough to blockade Syracuse, and thus
overawed the oligarchs into receiving him back. On his return he
swore a solemn oath of loyalty to the constitution and received
appointment as 'strategus and guardian of the peace' (317 B.C.).
It appears as if Agathocles' opponents this time acted in good
faith and agreed to share their power with him, rather than risk
a further revolution. But Agathocles was determined not to set
out on his travels again, and to secure himself he now definitely

aimed at acquiring the tyranny which he had long but perhaps unjustly been suspected of coveting. Having procured a commission for some petty war in the interior he collected a composite force from his former Sicel allies and from the Syracusan rabble, and with these fought a one-day war against the rival faction. His first attack fell upon some forty leading men of the Six Hundred, whom he decoyed into the presence of his troops and promptly executed. This swift stroke was followed by a prolonged *battue* in the streets, during which all those of the opposite party who did not jump the walls were cut down. Agathocles justified this slaughter to his troops by pretending that he was but anticipating a plot of his adversaries; but the absence of organized resistance on their part makes it more probable that they were the victims of an unprovoked aggression. On the other hand there is no reason to believe that Agathocles ordered a wanton and indiscriminate massacre from a mere love of cruelty. Having thus cleared the field of his antagonists, he took the usual last steps in the despot's progress. He challenged popular allegiance by pretending to abdicate his generalship, and when the Assembly dutifully begged him to remain in office he stipulated that he should not be hampered with colleagues. Thus he rose to the position of 'General plenipotentiary,' the same as Dionysius I had occupied during his long rule, and under this title he governed Syracuse for the next twelve years (316–304 B.C.).

II. THE SICILIAN WARS 316–310 B.C.

In Syracuse Agathocles consolidated his power by courting popular favour. He promised and no doubt carried out a redistribution of confiscated estates; he put on a disarming air of bonhomie and cultivated a reputation for good-natured drollery. We do not know how far he preserved the constitution, but at any rate he continued to strike coins of a republican type. It is alleged that he dispensed with a body-guard, and this may be so far true that he relied on citizens, not on foreign mercenaries, for his protection.

Elsewhere in Sicily Agathocles' usurpation was the signal for fresh coalitions against Syracuse. The refugees from that city rallied to the number of five or six thousand, under the leadership of Sosistratus: of Heracleides nothing further is heard. The émigrés won the sympathies of the other Greek towns, which no doubt remembered that tyrants of Syracuse had a way of becoming lords of Sicily. But this gave Agathocles a pretext and indeed a partial justification for proceeding to conquer his neighbours: like Dionysius I he could pretend that Syracuse was not safe so long as the surrounding cities remained potential enemies. Accordingly in 315 B.C. he opened his campaign with two assaults upon Messana, both of which miscarried. In 314 B.C. the three most important of the free cities, Acragas, Gela and Messana, replied by a joint invitation to a roving Spartan prince named Acrotatus to organize a coalition army against Syracuse. Acrotatus presently arrived at Acragas, bringing with him a small fleet from Tarentum. His force both on land and on sea must have been a fair match for that of Agathocles, but it was never put to a test. The Spartan generalissimo, whose standard of discipline may have been unsuited to Sicilian troops, created nothing but discontent, and when he endeavoured to stifle the ill-feeling by murdering Sosistratus, the leading refugee from Syracuse, he had to decamp to escape stoning. The allies, now left without any sort of a leader, patched up a peace with Agathocles, in which they recognized Syracusan suzerainty and reserved no more than autonomy for themselves. In the following year the tyrant respected the peace-treaty so far as to confine his operations to the lesser towns, of which he carried an unknown number. In 312 B.C. he renewed his attack on Messana, which was now left unsupported and gave in. Like every town which fell into Agathocles' hands, Messana had to surrender the Syracusan refugees and their supporters for execution. Thus the safeguarding operations of the Syracusan despot left him master of half Sicily: of the more notable towns outside the Carthaginian province only Acragas and Gela remained to be eaten up.

But at this stage Agathocles became involved with a new enemy who drew out all his powers. As we have already seen, the renewal of warfare of factions and cities in Sicily had been a signal of action for the Carthaginians.

True enough, Hamilcar, the Punic governor of Sicily, was not bent on an active war policy. Though he came to the assistance of the Syracusan oligarchs in 321–319 and again in 317 B.C., he preferred the rôle of a mediator to that of a combatant, and it was through his good offices that Agathocles returned to Syracuse after his second exile. It can scarcely be true that he subsequently lent Agathocles some African troops to abet his act of usurpation, for the usurper had no need of these; but at the negotiations of 314 B.C. he resumed the part of honest broker, and he apparently left Agathocles a free hand to conquer the independent Greek cities. But the conduct of affairs was eventu-

ally taken out of his hands and committed to a more vigorous
successor. The Carthaginian home government could afford to con-
done Hamilcar's half-measures so long as the Greeks counter-
acted each other in their war of factions; but they could hardly
fail to take alarm when Agathocles had concentrated power in his
hands and was reuniting the Siceliotes under his dominion, for
these proceedings, as in the case of Dionysius I, might well be the
prelude to a consolidated attack upon the Punic possessions in
Sicily. During Agathocles' second campaign against Messana
in 315 B.C. the Punic Senate sent an envoy to remonstrate with
Agathocles for upsetting the general settlement of Timoleon;
after the third and successful attack of the tyrant upon the same
city in 312 B.C. they definitely broke with him. Suspecting
Hamilcar of something worse than incompetence, they passed
a secret vote upon him, which however was never carried into
effect, for at this juncture Hamilcar died or took his own life;
and they transferred his command to another Hamilcar, the son
of Gisgo, whose actions better befitted a bearer of that name.

After the capture of Messana Agathocles advanced upon
Acragas, but found a Punic squadron of sixty sail at hand to
assist in the defence. Whether from lack of crews or of funds, the
Syracusan despot at this time and for long after had no fleet that
could cope with the Carthaginians, and for the moment he drew
back. After a desultory campaign in the interior he reappeared
on the south coast and endeavoured to force a battle with a
Carthaginian army which had meanwhile taken a position on Mt
Ecnomus (Mte S. Angelo or Cufino, near Licata), a point equally
convenient for watching Acragas and Gela. The enemy, who were
awaiting reinforcements, refused to be drawn, and the main action
was postponed to the next year.

In 311 B.C. the Carthaginians sent a large expeditionary force
to Sicily. A considerable part of this army and no less than sixty
warships suffered destruction in a storm. Nevertheless by the
time that the contingent from Acragas and the Syracusan refugees
had joined hands with him, the Carthaginian commander,
Hamilcar son of Gisgo, disposed of some 45,000 men and thus
had the advantage of numbers. While Hamilcar re-established
his camp on Mount Ecnomus, Agathocles prepared a base for
himself at Gela, which appears at this time to have been ob-
serving a benevolent neutrality. He entered the town by surprise,
and when resistance was offered he cleared the way by a general
massacre. He next advanced to the line of the river Himeras
under Mount Ecnomus and was encouraged by his success in a

casual skirmish to make a sudden onslaught on the enemy's main position. The Syracusan forces tried again and again to break into the Punic camp, but before they could establish their footing they were caught in the flank and rear by a Carthaginian corps which suddenly moved up from the sea coast. It is uncertain whether these were freshly landed reinforcements from Carthage, or, as seems more likely, a division of Hamilcar's army which had been saved up for some such surprise. In any case, their entry into action threw Agathocles' men into a rout. The Syracusan horse, instead of covering the retreat, rode for safety, and the infantry were left to be cut up by the pursuing Carthaginian cavalry. According to a credible estimate Agathocles lost 7000 men to the enemy's 500 (June 311 B.C.). Beaten from the field, the Syracusan ruler had now to prepare his city for a siege. He succeeded in gathering in the harvest before Hamilcar closed upon him, but in the meantime the Carthaginian general made overtures to Agathocles' dependent allies in Sicily and won them over in quick succession, despite the tyrant's drastic precautions against their defection. Agathocles attempted to make one further stand, presumably in the Anapus plain near the Olympieum, but was driven back into Syracuse, which was now blockaded by land and sea (311–310 B.C.).

III. THE AFRICAN CAMPAIGN 310–309 B.C.

In the summer of 310 B.C. the situation in Syracuse became critical. Supplies were giving out, and there was no prospect of the Carthaginian siege being broken, as in the days of Dionysius I, by reinforcements from overseas or by pestilence within the Punic camp. Agathocles' only chance was to create a diversion, and it is his chief distinction as a general that he realized this and had the nerve to act upon it. Just as Hannibal in 211 B.C. broke away towards Rome in order to relax the pressure upon Capua, so the Syracusan tyrant made a sudden pounce on Carthage. Though such a raid could not give him a permanent foothold in Africa, he had reason to hope that it might alter the whole course of the war. At best the Carthaginians, who had never experienced invasion and were quite unprepared for it, might fall into a panic and buy off Agathocles on his own terms; at worst they would have to withdraw forces from Sicily, for with their unaided home levies they would be no match for the seasoned Greek troops.

It was essential to Agathocles' plan that his movements should be swift and unforeseen. Rather than lose time in reorganizing his navy, he decided to take the risk of sailing under inadequate escort. Of men and money he did not require a large supply: mobility counted with him for more than numbers, and once landed in Africa he could rely on making the war pay for itself. His chief difficulty lay in the reluctance which the siege-stricken Syracusans felt against exactions however modest, whose object Agathocles would not and could not divulge. The tyrant, however, coerced recalcitrant taxpayers with wholesale executions and confiscations, and he heartened his bewildered troops by reading a favourable omen into a solar eclipse which befel on the day after his departure (on August 15th, 310 B.C.), too late to deter him and early enough to betoken trouble for Carthage.

The stars certainly fought in their courses for the Syracusans. Just as their fleet had left harbour, by a happy chance the attention of the Carthaginian blockade squadron was distracted between the outgoing armada and an incoming convoy of corn-vessels, with the result that the city was replenished and Agathocles stood out safely to sea[1]. On approaching Africa he was at last caught up by the pursuing Carthaginians, but not in time to prevent his landing, which was safely effected near the Hermaean promontory (Cape Bon), some 70 miles from Carthage. Sacrificing everything to speed, Agathocles burnt his fleet, abandoned his base, and started on the first and last Greek Anabasis into Africa. The invaders' route lay through a plain where the high state of cultivation excited their wonder, as in later days it astonished the troops of Belisarius. The intervening towns lay open and unprotected, and no resistance was offered to Agathocles until a levy en masse of the Carthaginian city population was sent out to meet him.

On the first news of Agathocles' landing the rumour spread in Carthage that he must have destroyed Hamilcar's forces in Sicily and sunk his fleet before he could venture to sail for Africa. But Hamilcar's ships presently arrived from the Hermaean cape with a more reassuring version of events, and the Carthaginian Senate now prepared to crush Agathocles. A citizen army, 40,000 strong, was at once enrolled and marched out to offer battle to the invader. Against this force Agathocles could only muster 3500 Syracusans and 10,000 mercenaries. The troops did not believe that they

---

[1] A recent calculation of the path of the afore-mentioned eclipse makes it practically certain that Agathocles sailed along the north coast of Sicily, not by the more usual southerly route. This helps to explain his success in eluding the Carthaginian fleet. See C. Schoch in *Sirius*, 1926, pp. 248–50.

could win, but Agathocles reckoned up the odds differently and accepted the challenge. His confidence was justified, for the scratch Carthaginian levy fought like amateurs. The most serviceable division, led by a general named Hanno, made a hasty charge on its own account, but was fought to a standstill and broke into flight after losing its leader. The other Punic wing never became fully engaged, for its commander Bomilcar drew it back when Hanno got into difficulties. It is not certain whether Bomilcar, who was a personal rival of Hanno, deliberately played false in this action, or whether he prudently but vainly attempted to disengage his corps before the rout became general. In any case, the entire Punic force was swept off its feet, and but for the fact that its line of retreat to Carthage was a short one it would no doubt have suffered very heavily from Agathocles' pursuit.

The war now entered a critical stage, for the lost battle threw Carthage into a panic. The fires of Moloch, which of late had not been kept burning brightly, were now fed with a holocaust of two hundred children of the noblest families. Such demoralization might seem a prelude to surrender, but with characteristic tenacity the Carthaginians pulled themselves together and prepared to carry on the war. Agathocles thus lost his chance of rattling the enemy into a speedy peace; but he achieved his primary purpose of drawing the Punic siege force away from Syracuse, and for the time being he gained a free hand for himself in Africa. His next move was to put pressure upon Carthage by cutting off its food supplies. To this end he established a fortified post near Tunis, some fourteen miles from Carthage, so as to keep the city under observation, and he set out to occupy the fertile lowland along the east coast of Tunisia. In the course of these operations he captured some two hundred towns and villages, including the ports of Hadrumetum and Thapsus, and repelled a Carthaginian sortie against Tunis. Not the least hopeful feature of the campaign was the readiness of the native Libyans to greet him as a deliverer from their Punic taskmasters. At the end of 310 B.C. Agathocles had apparently obtained a firm foothold in Africa.

It was probably in the ensuing winter that Agathocles took two new steps which indicate that he was thinking of expanding his campaign into something more than a raid. He established and fortified a naval base at Aspis, some twenty miles south of the Hermaean cape, thus securing a permanent line of communications with Sicily. Furthermore, he offered an alliance to a former officer of Alexander named Ophellas, whom Ptolemy I of Egypt had appointed as a semi-independent viceroy of Cyrene (vol. VI, p. 467).

Disclaiming the intention of keeping any part of Africa for himself, Agathocles offered to leave Ophellas in possession of any Libyan territory which they might jointly conquer. In view of the eventual breakdown of this project it is difficult to decide whether the Syracusan ruler had definitely resolved to substitute a Greek for a Punic dominion in Tunisia: indeed it is not certain whether in the long run Ophellas might not have proved a less source of anxiety to him than the Carthaginians. But after the campaign of 310 B.C., when the prospect of a final victory over Carthage opened to Agathocles, it is not surprising that he should have taken the necessary steps to secure this victory without thinking out its after-effects. To Ophellas at any rate the bargain seemed a good one, for he proceeded to send out recruiting officers to Greece and to prepare an expeditionary corps equal in size to Agathocles' force.

In the spring and summer of 309 B.C., previous to the arrival of Ophellas at the scene of war, the balance of power began to swing back against Agathocles. Reinforced from Sicily, the Carthaginians had now the nucleus of an efficient field force. But the most significant change lay in the incipient rally of the Libyans to the Punic side, as they discovered that the requisitions of their new deliverer were as burdensome as the imposts of their former oppressors. One Libyan 'king' who had joined Agathocles came to open blows with him; other native tribes sent contingents to Carthage when required. Agathocles henceforth had difficulties in raising fresh contributions, and the pay of his troops fell into arrears. In the middle of the campaign a mutiny broke out which the general was only able to quell by a threat of suicide, and although the bluff succeeded for this once, his hold on the army remained precarious. Under these conditions the Carthaginians temporarily recovered the initiative. In the early part of 309 B.C. they laid siege to the Greek camp at Tunis and made several up-country expeditions for the reconquest of disloyal natives. In set battle they were still no match for the invaders, for they lost several encounters and were driven off from Tunis; but on balance they regained lost ground.

The war entered upon a new phase in the autumn of 309 B.C., when Ophellas completed a tedious march across the desert of Tripoli and joined hands with Agathocles. On closer acquaintance the two Greek captains quickly repented of their bargain. Before Ophellas' troops had finished resting Agathocles fell out with his ally, murdered him, and incorporated his army. In seeking to explain this strange turn of events we may dismiss the idea of premeditated treason on either side. Agathocles, it is true, pretended to Ophellas' men that he had merely anticipated a treacherous attack by their leader, and on this assurance he gained their allegiance. But for either captain to bank on the success of such an excuse for a deliberate piece of perfidy would have been the height of folly: either of them might have provoked the followers of the murdered man to open hostility or to a separate agreement with Carthage. The most probable explanation is that Ophellas, who had claimed Agathocles' son Heracleides as a hostage, would not meet the Syracusan on terms of equality, and that the latter on the spur of the moment planned a very risky coup which by sheer good luck ended well for him.

The quarrel with Ophellas prevented Agathocles from profiting by a simultaneous crisis in Carthage. The Punic general Bomilcar, whose suspicious conduct in the great battle of 310 B.C. we have already noticed, attempted in autumn 309 B.C. a revolution similar to that which had made Agathocles master of Syracuse. In a dispute between a Carthaginian general and his government it is always difficult to say which side first showed disloyalty to the other, and in the present instance we do not know whether Bomilcar had any grievances or was led on by sheer ambition. But whatever the merits of his case, he found no popular support, and when he let loose his chosen troops on the streets of Carthage he met with a desperate and successful resistance. Overwhelmed by numbers, Bomilcar capitulated and was put to death. Henceforth the Carthaginians kept their ranks closed, and Agathocles lost what chances he ever possessed of breaking down the Carthaginian 'home front.'

IV. THE AFRICAN CAMPAIGN 308–307 B.C.

After 309 B.C. the war in Africa entered upon a new phase. It was no longer being fought in defence of Sicily, for in the meantime the Punic offensive in that island had been definitely abandoned (see p. 632). The question arises, did Agathocles still entertain the project of permanent Greek conquests in Tunisia, such as he had suggested to Ophellas, or did he fight on with some other object in view, for example, in order to obtain cessions of Carthaginian territory in Sicily? As we have seen, the Syracusan ruler declared to Ophellas that he had no permanent interests in Africa, and it is likely enough that he was more bent on consolidating and extending his power in Sicily than on making acquisitions overseas. On the other hand, he was now again in a position to bring pressure to bear upon Carthage, for by the incorporation of Ophellas' army he had nearly doubled his effectives, and after Bomilcar's revolution the Carthaginians, though freed from internal dissension, were unable for a time to risk any actions in the open field.

Accordingly in 308 B.C. Agathocles resumed the operations by which he had planned to blockade Carthage. Without let or hindrance from the Carthaginians he attacked the Phoenician ports on the northern seaboard of Tunisia. Utica, the largest of them, offered a stout resistance, but was eventually carried and subjected to a fearful carnage; Hippou Akra (Bizerta) surrendered after a defeat at the hands of an improvised Syracusan war-fleet. After seizing these positions Agathocles was well placed for intercepting the supplies which still came to Carthage from Sardinia and the western part of Sicily. In addition, he made fresh conquests in the interior, but the extent of these cannot be defined. Thus the cordon round Carthage was being tightened, and it is likely that the Syracusan tyrant could soon have dictated his terms of peace had he continued to conduct his campaign in person. But adverse news from Sicily induced him to leave Africa for the time being. In summer or autumn 308 B.C. he sailed away with a small portion of his army, leaving his son Archagathus in command.

Agathocles' departure at first made little difference to the campaign. Under an officer named Eumachus the Greeks made a bold and successful foray into southern Tunisia, and in the ensuing winter the shortage of supplies in Carthage became serious. In 307 B.C., however, the tide turned with amazing suddenness and swept the Greeks right out of Africa. The blame for this falls chiefly on Archagathus, who sent out Eumachus once more to the inland regions, no doubt under the impression that the Carthaginians would again not venture out. Under the stimulus of a failing food supply, however, the enemy decided to risk a new campaign in the open and sent out a force of thirty thousand men in three divisions, each of which set itself to recover one zone of the lost territory. Archagathus' plain duty now was to hold his troops together and to join hands with Eumachus before engaging in any serious action. Instead of this, he left Eumachus to fend for himself and sent the remainder of his field force in three flying columns to bring the Carthaginians to battle. Like their commander-in-chief, the divisional generals played into the enemy's hands. One of the three columns, led by a certain Aeschrion, lost 4000 men in an ambush; Eumachus on his homeward march was similarly trapped and sustained double that number of casualties. The remnant of the Greek forces were now barely able to hold their base near Tunis.

In summer 307 B.C. Agathocles returned to Africa. With the help of a flotilla from Etruria which had unexpectedly come to his aid he had defeated the attenuated Carthaginian squadron off Syracuse and for the moment was master of the seas. With the reinforcements which he brought he could still number 12,000–15,000 Greek or Italian troops and 10,000 Africans, and with these he at once attacked the Carthaginian fortifications above Tunis. Such instant action was no doubt the only means of pulling the match out of the fire, but it was a desperate venture, and luck was against him. His Libyans held off from the assault, and the Greeks not only were driven off but were tumbled downhill with heavy loss. The victory of the Carthaginians was marred by a fire which burnt out their camp in the ensuing night, and by a disastrous encounter with some of Agathocles' Libyans, who were stealing across to the Punic side but in the dark were taken for enemies, and after a confused scuffle drove the Carthaginians back to their city in a wild rout. But the Greeks also sustained heavy losses in a night action with an errant Libyan division—probably not the same as fell in with the Carthaginians—and in any case they were too demoralized to offer further resistance. Agathocles, realizing that all was lost, and probably fearing that his disgruntled troops would hand him over to the Carthaginians, secretly escaped and left them to make such terms as they could with their enemies. The soldiers first avenged their betrayal by murdering Agathocles' sons, including Archagathus, who had started out with his father but lost touch with him; thereupon they capitulated on easy terms. A few desperate men fought on in fortified posts which were soon carried by the Carthaginians; of those who had surrendered many took service with their former foes.

The Anabasis of Agathocles thus ended in a ludicrous fiasco, and its absconding chief cuts a sorry figure beside Regulus, the first Roman invader of Africa, who stayed with his defeated troops and served Rome best in captivity (see below, pp. 681 *sqq*). Yet the Greek general's venture achieved its first and most important purpose of safeguarding his position in Sicily. In 306 B.C. the Carthaginians tamely agreed to a peace in which they bound themselves to stay behind their old frontier line in Sicily, the river Halycus, and to pay a small indemnity in corn and money. Moreover, Agathocles had once for all discovered the weakest point in the Punic armour. Realizing this, he prepared towards the end of his life for a re-

sumption of the war. With a view to cutting off the supplies of
Carthage from overseas he expended his time and money on a new
fleet of two hundred warships, thus proving that he now aimed at
attempting a regular siege of Carthage. He did not live to carry
out this scheme, and after his death the Carthaginians took advantage of fresh feuds among the Greeks to extend their foothold
in Sicily; yet his efforts had not been wholly wasted. Agathocles'
Anabasis, like that of Xenophon, prepared the way for other and
more decisive attacks.

V. SICILIAN AFFAIRS 310–304 B.C.

The first news which the besieged Syracusans received of
Agathocles after his departure to Africa came from Hamilcar,
the commander of the investing army. They were informed that
Agathocles' force had been destroyed, and as proof they were
shown the salvaged bronze bow-pieces of his burnt galleys.
This announcement was coupled with an offer of peace which
assured the personal safety of Agathocles' partisans. In view of
the seemingly conclusive evidence of the tyrant's fate his elder
brother Antander, who had been left in charge of the city, was
disposed to capitulate. But an Aetolian officer named Erymnon,
whom Agathocles had prudently appointed to advise Antander, induced him to hold out pending confirmation of Hamilcar's message.
The Punic ruse was exposed soon after by a dispatch-boat which
·had been built by Agathocles and brought the news of his first
great victory through the enemy's blockade. To atone for his
diplomatic failure, Hamilcar made a surprise attack on the landward fortifications of Syracuse while its population was crowding
to the harbour to meet Agathocles' messenger; but the garrison
had remained at its post and drove him off. Soon after this double
reverse Hamilcar was required to send 5000 men to Carthage,
and on the land side at least the siege was relaxed. Agathocles'
hold on the city was further strengthened by the expulsion of
a large number of faint-hearted or disloyal citizens who had
clamoured for surrender on hearing of Hamilcar's offer.

In 309 B.C. Hamilcar returned to Syracuse with a larger army
than before. His numbers were swelled by a corps of Greek
refugees collected by Deinocrates, a prominent opponent of
Agathocles whom the despot by a special favour had dismissed
unscathed at the time of his usurpation. The Carthaginian
general evidently intended to sit out the blockade this time, for
he brought an unwieldy supply column with him. While his

force was stumbling through the defiles of the river Anapus near the south-western edge of the Epipolae plateau, a Syracusan force which had been thrown forward to Fort Euryalus at the apex of the plateau swooped down upon it and put it to utter rout. Hamilcar was captured and executed by the Syracusans.

From this blow the Punic forces in Sicily never recovered until after Agathocles' death; the rest of the fighting which is described in this chapter was conducted between the rival armies of the Siceliote Greeks. With the Carthaginians out of action, and Deinocrates' corps cut adrift, the Syracusans had a chance of recovering their lost dependencies such as Agathocles himself would scarcely have missed. But Antander let the occasion slip, and the initiative in Sicilian affairs passed for a season to the city of Acragas, which now undertook to unite the lesser Siceliote towns in a league of liberty directed alike against Carthaginians and Syracusans. Under their general Xenodicus the Acragantines made an excellent start: they expelled a Punic garrison from Gela, secured Camarina and Leontini against Syracusan attempts at reconquest, and won over other towns in the interior (309–308 B.C.).

It was probably due to Xenodicus' sweeping successes that Agathocles paid a flying visit to Sicily (summer or autumn 308 B.C.). His absence from Africa proved fatal; his presence in Sicily did little good. Before his arrival the Syracusans had at last marched out in force against Xenodicus and under a general named Leptines had defeated him so heavily that the Acragantines withdrew their troops and left their allies to fend for themselves. But these found a new and more able champion in the Syracusan émigré Deinocrates, who had been left without a base or a policy since the death of Hamilcar, but now rallied the minor Greek cities and raised a considerable field force from them, for which his former Punic allies perhaps supplied the funds. Agathocles, who had meanwhile landed in Sicily and eventually joined hands with Leptines, achieved no more than the recapture of some minor towns, and when Deinocrates' new levies took the field he tamely fell back on Syracuse (308–307 B.C.).

Before he could prepare for a fresh campaign Agathocles received signals of distress from Africa. He first made Syracuse safe by wholesale executions among a fresh mass of suspects, and then sailed away with heavy drafts for his African army. After his departure Leptines promptly won a fresh success which finally put Xenodicus out of action and left the field free for the Syracusan forces and the corps of Deinocrates. Leptines' campaign however was but a brief interlude before Agathocles' final return

from Africa (summer or autumn 307 B.C.). His arrival in Sicily
was marked by two further atrocities for which the usual excuse of
political necessity could not be offered. In Syracuse he avenged
the death of his sons by murdering all the relatives of his African
soldiers. In the allied city of Segesta he imposed a heavy war
contribution, and when this was not promptly forthcoming he
applied the most revolting tortures to the rich and sold the poor
into slavery. These wanton barbarities suggest that Agathocles
was losing his judgment as well as his prestige. At this stage his
own partisans began to desert to Deinocrates, who now appeared
more than ever to have the whip-hand in Sicily. But with characteristic buoyancy the Syracusan ruler recovered his nerve and
utterly defeated Deinocrates in a diplomatic duel. By concluding
peace with the Carthaginians he deprived Deinocrates of such
support as he had received from that quarter, and acquired from
them a stock of provisions and money sufficient to reconstitute
his field force. At the same time he kept Deinocrates in play by
offering to surrender Syracuse and all his other possessions in
Sicily, except the two small towns of Thermae (his native place)
and Cephaloedium. While Deinocrates was pressing his apparent
advantage and haggling over the surrender of these last two
positions, Agathocles rallied his forces and sowed mistrust among
Deinocrates' supporters, who began to accuse him of protracting
the war for his personal advantage.

In 305 B.C. Agathocles once more took the field and in spite of
his inferior numbers engaged Deinocrates in battle. During the
action part of Deinocrates' forces deserted; the rest were thrown
into disorder and capitulated on an offer of easy terms. Despite
his promise Agathocles killed off one whole division of his
adversaries—presumably his inveterate foes the Syracusan oligarchs; but he spared the life of Deinocrates for a second time
and indeed had his assistance in the remaining stages of the war.
All that now remained for the victor to accomplish was the reduction of some outstanding towns. Of these capitulations
nothing is known, except that at Leontini he perpetrated yet
another massacre. In the western end of the island the Carthaginians according to the recent convention retained the towns of
Selinus and perhaps also of Heraclea; all the remaining Greek
cities, with the possible exception of Acragas, definitely acknowledged the authority of Agathocles, whose dominions now became
as extensive as those of Dionysius I had been. But Agathocles
was not content with the title 'ruler of Sicily' by which Dionysius
had become known to the Greeks (vol. vi, p. 118). Following the

example of the Diadochi, he assumed the title of king and struck coins in his own name, though without his portrait (*c.* 304 B.C.). The fifteen years of his reign were as quiet and uneventful a period for the Siceliotes as those of his tyranny had been stormy.

VI. AGATHOCLES AND SOUTH ITALY

While Agathocles was waging his brilliant but indecisive war against the Carthaginians, the Romans were slowly but surely defeating the Samnites (see above, chap. XVIII). In this twenty years' conflict the Italiote Greeks might well have played an important and even a decisive part, if they had intervened with their united strength; and it is almost certain that they would have seized their opportunity, if they had still been under the vigorous leadership of Alexander of Epirus. But after that monarch's death their history is purely a passive one, for they only figure as a prey of the native Italic tribes and of Greek 'protectors' from other regions.

In 303 B.C. the Tarentines called in Cleonymus the Spartan, who achieved little (p. 640 *sq.*); next came Agathocles. The king of Sicily appears in general to have followed the Italian policy of Dionysius I. He was at some pains to secure the approaches to the Straits of Messina and made occasional forays further afield, but he did not attempt any extensive conquests and achieved no permanent results. His most startling success took place *c.* 300 B.C., when he disputed possession of Corcyra with Cassander and carried it after a decisive naval victory. His object in this adventure was perhaps little more than to test the fleet which he was preparing for eventual use against the Carthaginians, for a few years later he gave the island away as a dowry to his daughter Lanassa on the occasion of her wedding to king Pyrrhus of Epirus. But a story which is told against him, that he acted in collusion with native Italic pirates from Calabria, suggests that he may have taken a passing interest in Corcyra as a station for levying toll upon the trade to the Adriatic and South Italy. Within a few years Corcyra passed from Cleonymus to Demetrius Poliorcetes and from him to Cassander, Agathocles, Pyrrhus, and back again to Demetrius, an experience surely unparalleled in that island's eventful history.

Agathocles maintained a more permanent interest in the Bruttian peninsula. Unlike their Lucanian neighbours, the Bruttians were not drawn into the Second Samnite War, and *c.* 325 B.C. the Greek city of Croton had to ask Syracuse for aid against them. Agathocles, as we have seen (p. 619), took part in the Syracusan relief expedition. Shortly afterwards he reappeared before Croton as an exile and made a vain attempt to capture it on behalf of a democratic party which the Syracusan leaders Heracleides and Sosistratus may have helped to turn out on the previous campaign. The democrats eventually reconquered the town and came to terms with the Bruttians (c. 317 B.C.) but were afterwards betrayed by their own leader Menedemus, who made himself tyrant. Soon after 300 B.C. Agathocles presumed on his friendship with Menedemus to make a treacherous attack upon Croton, but only carried it after a formal siege which ended in the usual carnage. This ill-deserved success however was balanced by two unsuccessful wars against the Bruttians. Called in against them by Tarentum, he landed in Italy (c. 298 B.C.), but lost some 4000 men in a night surprise. In a later campaign (c. 295 B.C.) which he conducted with a force of more than 30,000 men, he began by losing his fleet in a storm; he thereupon conquered the Greek town of Hipponium and overawed the Bruttians into a capitulation; but he lost his labour soon afterwards, when the Bruttians fell upon his garrison, recovered their hostages, and perhaps took Hipponium for themselves.

Of Agathocles' relations with Rhegium, which he had befriended in his early days (see p. 619), nothing is known, but it is probable that he allowed it to remain an independent ally. It is not unlikely that Agathocles entertained relations with Rome, but the nature of these is uncertain. In any case we can hardly suppose that he took upon himself to protect the Italiote Greeks against the Romans, for his assistance was hardly yet required and probably not desired. From Etruria, as we have seen (p. 630), he derived some timely naval aid; but we do not know with which of the Etruscan cities he was in league. Like Dionysius I, Agathocles made much use of Campanian mercenaries. One of these Campanian bands made itself notorious after his death by seizing the town of Messana and helping to set the Romans and Carthaginians by the ears (pp. 667 sqq.).

In the last years of his reign Agathocles had no longer anything to fear from his Siceliote subjects, but he ceased to be master in his own household. Of the sons of his first wife, the widow of his patron Damas, Archagathus and Heracleides, and probably also Agatharchus, had been killed by his troops in Africa. The children of his third consort, a step-daughter of Ptolemy named Theoxena, were mere infants at the time of his death. By his second wife, Alcia, he had a son and a daughter.

The daughter, Lanassa, was successively wedded to Pyrrhus and Demetrius Poliorcetes, with both of whom in turn Agathocles had friendly but distant relations. The son, Agathocles II, was destined to succeed to the kingdom, and Demetrius undertook to guarantee the succession. But Archagathus II, a son of the king's eldest child, took offence at being thus passed over and killed the heir apparent. Agathocles did not long survive his son, and the rumour spread that Archagathus had poisoned his grandfather; but according to a modern diagnosis the old king's death was due to cancer of the jaw (289 B.C.). By his final disposition Syracuse received back its liberty, but after twenty-seven years of autocracy it proved quite unable to reinstate a free government at such short notice, to retain control over the other Siceliotes, or to hold Carthage at arm's length. Within a few months of his death Agathocles' life-work was mostly undone.

VII. CONCLUSION

The history of the Siceliote and Italiote Greeks from 330 to 289 B.C. may be summed up as a movement in a circle, at a time when a neighbouring nation was making rapid progress. Their position in 289 B.C. was much the same as in 330 B.C., except that in the intervening wars they had uselessly depleted their man-power, and this is as much as saying that in the race for supremacy in the western Mediterranean they had been definitely left behind. The blame for this, so far as it can be cast upon one man, rests mainly on Agathocles. In the history of this tyrant the most outstanding feature is the almost endless series of massacres which marked the earlier part of his rule. Although no doubt ancient writers exaggerated the number of his victims and did him injustice when they described him as a Satanic wretch who piped and danced unto his victims before leading them to death, yet it is clear that his executions were vastly in excess of what might have been condoned on the score of political necessity. Moreover the loss of life thus entailed was not made good, as after previous periods of revolution in Sicily, by fresh immigration from the Greek homeland. From a political standpoint the worst charge against him is that he was a mere opportunist who lived by improvisation and had no fixed policy. His usurpation, his descent upon Africa, his campaigns in Italy all appear to have been the products of a hasty resolve; and his kingship, though marred by no atrocities, was not distinguished by any constructive statesmanship such as the Leges Hieronicae of that later and greater king, Hiero II. But as a soldier Agathocles achieved a work of more lasting importance than the story of this chapter, taken by itself, is likely to suggest. Though his actions were mostly on a small scale and often unsuccessful, he was clearly far more than a guerrilla chieftain. His expedition to Africa marks him out as a leader of true strategic insight, and if it did not bring a Greek victory, yet it was in effect a fatal Punic defeat, for it showed the way to the ultimate conquerors of Carthage. The first and chief of these, Scipio Africanus the Elder, virtually acknowledged his indebtedness to Agathocles, when he declared that this ruler and his predecessor Dionysius had been the world's greatest men of action and had known best how to mingle boldness and discretion. This praise of Agathocles may appear extravagant to us, yet in one respect it does less than justice to him, for however inferior he may have been to Dionysius as a war minister, he clearly surpassed the elder tyrant in the higher attributes of generalship, imagination and quick resolve. Lastly, if we blame Agathocles, we must equally censure the Siceliote Greeks for their failure to uphold the settlement of Timoleon, to stabilize their municipal constitutions and to federate their city-states. Their incompetence in this respect rendered possible the despot's rule and indeed almost justified it, for it is doubtful whether his sway was any more wasteful of lives or injurious to Greek interests than the chaos of contending cities and factions which it superseded.

CHAPTER XX

PYRRHUS

I. ROME AND MAGNA GRAECIA

AT the end of the Third Samnite war, in 290 B.C., Rome had created a safety barrier between north and south by annexing Sabine and Praetuttian territory to the city, and planting Latin colonies at Hadria and at Castrum Novum to guard the Adriatic littoral. The utility of this barrier was demonstrated when in 285 the Gauls for the sixth time crossed the Apennines in search of land and booty. The Senones of the Ager Gallicus, the tribe which had sacked Rome a century before, led in this raid, but when we remember that Brennus was at the same time marching toward Macedonia and that several Celtic tribes were on their way to Asia Minor we may suppose that the driving force came from the pressure of migrating peoples behind the Alps (p. 65). The Senones first besieged Arretium with a view to detaching it from the Roman alliance. Caecilius Metellus, the consul of 284, marched up to relieve Arretium, but was slain in a battle which cost Rome more than half the military tribunes and thirteen thousand men. The news of this defeat spread rapidly and caused some of the Samnites and Lucanians, as well as the Etruscans of Vulci and Volsinii (Orvieto), to repudiate their treaties. But the rebels could no longer effect a union of forces, nor did the Senones, who were feared by their neighbours, find any allies near at hand. Manius Curius, elected to complete the term of Metellus, sent envoys to the chiefs of the Senones to treat for the return of prisoners. When these envoys were treacherously slain, the Roman army marched into the Ager Gallicus and defeated the Senones, pursuing them without mercy and driving them completely out of the country. A citizen colony was planted at Sena above Ancona to act as a garrison until Rome should decide what to do with the vacated territory.

Note. Plutarch's Life of Pyrrhus, though late, is the only continuous account. This seems to give the story as it was shaped by Fabius Pictor and Ennius, but Plutarch also drew upon Greek historians who were contemporaries of Pyrrhus (p. 259). Livy's epitomes, XII–XV, Appian's brief fragments (*Samn.* III, 7–11) and those of Dio Cassius (Bks IX, X, with the epitome of Zonaras, VIII, 2–6) reveal the influence of later Roman annalists. Justin's epitome, XVIII, 1–2, and the fragments of Diodorus XXII, 6–10, seem to be based upon older Greek sources, but they are too brief to be of much use. See the Bibliography. For this and the following chapter see maps 7 and 8.

The neighbouring Gallic tribe of the Boii now took up the quarrel and marched far enough south to connect with contingents of the Etruscan cities which were in revolt. Cornelius Dolabella, the consul of 283, met the united forces at Lake Vadimo, south of Volsinii, routing them completely. Nevertheless, the Boii advanced again the next year, having called out every able-bodied man of the tribe. Defeated again, they now sued for peace, and the Romans, having no concern for affairs in the Po valley and deeply committed in Etruria and southern Italy, were eager to make peace. Of the Senones we hear no more in Italy; since Caesar later found a tribe of these people in central Gaul (Sens) it is probable that they migrated thither after their defeat. The Etruscan cities of Volsinii and Vulci held out for two more years, when they surrendered a part of their territory and entered the Roman federation.

In the south the news of these raids had encouraged some of the Samnites to rise again, and even the Lucanians who had for a while been Rome's allies. The Latin colony of Venusia, planted on their common border in 291, stood as an ever-present reminder of Rome's growing power. The Lucanians had for a century been pushing southward against the cities of Magna Graecia. This drive had probably not been caused merely by the natural growth of a prolific people; the Lucanians were being pressed on by their Sabellian cousins who, farther north, were being driven on by the Gauls of the Ager Gallicus and the Po-Valley, as they in turn were crowded down by the constantly oncoming hordes from the seething areas of central Europe. In fact the turmoils that had involved the Etruscans, Latins, Campanians and Greeks one after the other during the last hundred years, were merely repercussions of the great folk-migrations beyond the confines of Italy. Rome had come out of the resulting scrimmage better than the rest because she alone had discovered the solution. While the Etruscans had fallen through lack of unity, the Campanians had survived with diminished power by weakly accepting dependence, and the Greeks, jealous and unarmed, had relied upon unloyal mercenaries, Rome had faced her foes, and organizing a federation of neighbours, had taken the initiative and slowly advanced a barrier of safety till a solid defensive wall had been erected along the northern Apennines.

To settle with the Lucanians now meant the adoption of a definite policy toward the Greek cities to the south with which the Lucanians had kept up a desultory warfare for a century. Rome's customary procedure was to make alliances with common combatants in the rear of her enemy. In the present instance this policy would be the more reasonable since Rome's long friendship with Massilia and Neapolis gave her a good name among the Greeks. That she had already made some overtures of the kind seems likely, for we hear that the people of Thurii had honoured a Roman tribune with a statue and golden crown (apparently in 285) for proposing some measure of assistance in their favour against a Lucanian invader.

By the third century the Greek cities of the south had long since passed their vigour. In the preceding century Dionysius I had nearly wrecked Rhegium, Hipponium and Caulonia and had weakened the flourishing cities of Locri, Croton, and Thurii (vol. VI, chap. V). The Bruttian and Lucanian barbarians had therefore found several cities quite powerless to withstand them. During that century they seized Posidonia, Laus, Tempsa, Terina and Hipponium. On the western coast only Rhegium, now rebuilt, and Velia survived. On the south coast the flourishing commercial city of Tarentum had assumed a protectorate over the league of Italiote cities which had its seat at Heraclea, but her policy of hiring mercenary kings and troops to fight their battles proved disastrous. First Archidamus of Sparta had come, but he fell in a battle with the barbarians in 338. Four years later Tarentum bargained with Alexander of Epirus, an uncle of the great Alexander of Macedon. Defeating the Lucanians and Bruttians, he restored Heraclea, Consentia and Terina. Ambitious to establish an empire in the south, he even entered into friendly relations with Rome, and it is probably this treaty, made in conjunction with Tarentum and the Italiote league, that pledged the Romans never to sail east of the Lacinian headland. It is not a plausible assumption that Rome would have agreed to such a clause after the foundation of Luceria in 314, but before the Samnite wars Magna Graecia was an unknown world to them. Alexander, however, quarrelled with his employer when his own ambitions became known, and he moved the headquarters of the league to Thurii, where it would be under his own control. When therefore he had to meet the barbarian hordes again he received no aid from Tarentum, and in the defeat of his forces he was slain (330). For a generation the Tarentines held their own against the Lucanians; then, needing help, they invited Cleonymus of Sparta to lead them (303); he too came in the hope of empire. There followed the usual imbroglio: since Metapontum refused to send him a contingent Cleonymus entered the town, exacted a heavy penalty, and abused and insulted the citizens. The Greeks deserted him and he was defeated by the barbarians and compelled to depart. Livy states that the defeat was due to Rome. This, though somewhat startling, is by no means impossible, for the Lucanians had aided Rome in the Samnite war, just now coming to an end, and their allies had a right to expect aid in return. Certainly the Romans, who had recently planted a colony at Luceria south of Samnium, could hardly have looked with favour upon Cleonymus' ambitions to establish an empire in Italy.

Failing to learn from all these experiences Tarentum next invited Agathocles of Syracuse. He operated, though with little success, against the Bruttians c. 298. Some two years later he treacherously seized the friendly city of Croton, frightened the Iapygians into a promise to keep the peace, and c. 295 liberated Hipponium and forced the Bruttians to accept terms (see p. 635).

A decade after the departure of Agathocles we find that the Bruttians had again captured Hipponium, and Thurii was being threatened by the Lucanians. Three years before the Thurians had, as we have seen, received the moral support of Rome (see above, p. 640). Since they had usually suffered misfortune at the hands of the mercenary kings who had been summoned to Italy by the rival city of Tarentum, they now appealed not to Tarentum but to Rome for aid and a garrison. Fabricius, the consul of 282, accordingly came to their relief. The Tarentines, who looked upon themselves as protectors of the Greek cities, were deeply offended, and the Romans probably knew enough of southern politics to surmise that there might be trouble. Indeed, the very fact that it was a tribune who first advocated the cause of Thurii at Rome implies that the slow-moving senate had hesitated to enter upon a new far-reaching venture, and that the young democratic leaders—the plebeian assembly attained sovereign powers only in 287—took matters into their own hands and overrode the senate. It is significant throughout this war that the senate was inclined toward peace and that plebeian leaders like Fabricius and Manius Curius, and the Claudii who acted with them, bore the brunt of the fighting and negotiating.

II. TARENTUM: THE COMING OF PYRRHUS

Shortly after the relief of Thurii, a Roman fleet of ten ships anchored before the harbour of Tarentum. This is the first time we hear of Roman war-vessels in these waters, and we do not know why they were there. They had perhaps been sent to support Fabricius before Thurii and were now cruising on a tour of inspection, as Appian (*Bell. Samn.* 7) implies, or perhaps, as

Mommsen surmises, they were on their way to the three colonies recently planted on the Adriatic coast. The Tarentines, reminded of the old treaty that excluded Roman ships from their waters, attacked the Romans, sinking four ships and capturing one. Such an improvident assault could only have been caused by a storm of ungovernable anger at Rome's intervention in their sphere of influence. It could hardly have been due to fear of an attack upon their strongly fortified harbour, which would have been impossible with only ten ships, or to anger at the mere formal infraction of an old treaty on this very occasion, a treaty which could not be other than obsolete as soon as Rome had established her three harbours on the Adriatic. To be sure, Rome was under obligation to bargain for a revocation, but it is likely that her statesmen were by now quite oblivious of the terms of the treaty which had been made in the first instance with a foreign king when Italy presented a wholly different complexion. The animus in the act is revealed by the fact that the Tarentines immediately marched upon Thurii and forced the Roman garrison to withdraw.

Rome at once sent envoys to demand reparations for her losses and those of Thurii. That she did not demand anything more, or fix terms that would establish her power in the south, is again a revelation of the senate's attitude, for it was the senate's province to conduct such negotiations. The envoys were insulted and sent back without satisfaction. The senate then instructed the consul Aemilius Barbula, who was operating in southern Samnium (281), to march with his army to Tarentum and repeat Rome's demands. The Tarentines had meanwhile bargained with Pyrrhus the king of Epirus for aid, but, now quite frightened, placed their government in the hands of one of the nobles friendly to Rome with instructions to reach an understanding. Before he succeeded, however, the first contingent of 3000 Epirote troops arrived with the king's envoy, Cineas, who succeeded in raising a counter-revolution, and Tarentum decided upon war.

Pyrrhus was now about forty years of age and at the height of his reputation. By inheritance and temperament a fit chieftain of primitive and courageous mountain tribes, he was by accident of intermarriage a relative of the Great Alexander. Lured into nebulous ambitions by this fatal propinquity he was constantly driving into adventures which taxed his resources and his staying powers. Courageous and reckless, a magnetic leader of men, a very skilful tactician—Hannibal called him his master—he might well have changed the course of Rome's advance had he compre-hended the world outside of Epirus as well as he knew his own people, and had he possessed an endurance in facing adversity equal to the exuberance of his temporary outbursts of optimism. When he left his native mountains his behaviour at times suggests that of some viking chieftain running amuck in a Renaissance city. He had twice lost and twice gained his throne, the second time by a dastardly murder of the kind that seems not to have been incompatible in his world with certain exacting rules of chivalry. By engaging bravado, by intrigue, and by many well-planned marriages he had united Epirus and extended its boundaries from Leucadia well into Illyricum. Lanassa, the daughter of the powerful Agathocles, had brought him Corcyra as her marriage portion. He had even seized the throne of Macedonia and held it for a few weeks. Cheated of his high hopes there however he was glad to try his fortune in Italy[1]. To be sure he pledged himself to depart as soon as he had relieved Tarentum, but his contemporaries who knew him did not take his promises seriously, for they expected him to build himself an empire in the West as had Alexander in the East. In view of Tarentum's previous record in hiring kings we need not suppose that the promises exacted were very precise. In his later conferences with Rome he seems to have felt bound only to respect the autonomy of Tarentum.

As we have seen, the consul of 281, Aemilius Barbula, had no instructions to capture Tarentum. His mission was merely to frighten the city into granting restitution and signing a treaty of peace. For this purpose he invaded Tarentine territory and devastated as he saw fit, taking care however to spare the property of those who were known to favour peace with Rome. Unsuccessful in his mission, he departed before Pyrrhus' arrival, going back to his former field of operations farther north. Pyrrhus, with the aid of Tarentine transports, came over early in the spring of 280 with a well-trained army 25,000 strong, including 3000 horse and 2000 archers. He also brought with him twenty elephants, from which much was expected, for the Romans had never met these beasts in battle. A thorough drill-master, he summoned the Tarentines to enter his army, and when he found them indifferent, he closed the theatres and the gymnasium and compelled them to drill. While he was training his forces, the new consul of 280, Valerius Laevinus, marched down through central Lucania planting garrisons in the Greek cities which had thrown in their lot with Rome. We are not given a list of them but we hear later of such garrisons stationed at Rhegium, Locri, and Thurii.

---

[1] On the earlier career and character of Pyrrhus see above, pp. 82 *sqq*.

III. THE WAR AND PEACE-PROPOSALS

Early in the summer the opposing armies met on the Siris river near Heraclea. The story of this battle and the subsequent events comes to us largely from late Greek historians who had drawn upon both Greek and Roman sources. It is unusually dramatic, but not on that account as untrustworthy as the ubiquity of anecdote might imply[1]. The whole account had first been given by Hieronymus of Cardia, a contemporary, who, though not friendly to Pyrrhus, had written with a scrupulous regard for the facts. On the Roman side Fabius Pictor and Ennius first wrote the story as they heard it from survivors or found it told in Timaeus. Strange as it may seem, it is the Roman tradition which goes farthest in picturing the chivalry and generosity of Rome's antagonist. This peculiarity, which one finds only too infrequently in Roman history, becomes especially patent in Plutarch's biography of Pyrrhus where the story of the Roman war, drawn largely from Roman sources, presents a more engaging personality than the beginning and end of the biography, which rest upon Greek sources. The explanation seems to be that Ennius, whose Annals became the favourite schoolbook of Rome's youth for two centuries and influenced historical tradition more than any other book, had portrayed Pyrrhus with great sympathy and had told this story very fully and effectively. Ennius in fact was himself a Messapian, the grandson of one of the princes who had probably served as officer under Pyrrhus. He had heard the story of that war told as a household tale. This fact then accounts in some measure for the fullness of details and the colour, which, in this instance, are not signs of apocryphal invention. Ennius, following a custom of his day, versified history, but the rules of this literary *genre* did not permit of wilful insertions; he tells as effectively as he can what he has heard and read. We may infer, however, that in this instance his portrait is somewhat too sympathetically drawn. If we had the Greek story in its purity from Hieronymus—Diodorus is too fragmentary, and Justinus too recklessly condensed to give us any conception of what it was—we should probably have the order of events as presented with a fair degree of congruity by Plutarch, Livy's epitome, and Zonaras, though the story would be more soberly told and with less friendly sympathy for both of the contestants.

Pyrrhus was in no great haste for battle. His Italian allies had boasted of having more than three hundred thousand men avail-

[1] See Judeich, in *Klio*, 1925, p. 1, also *Class. Phil.* 1926, p. 314.

able for the war, but none of these had as yet appeared. It seems that the consul of the preceding year, instead of going home for the winter as was usual, had camped in the vicinity of Venusia just to prove to the Samnite and Lucanian rebels that their services might be needed at home. It was the Roman consul Laevinus who took the initiative, crossed the Siris and forced a battle. For the first time the Roman legions met the solid Macedonian phalanx, and every legionary armed with a sword had to face five spear-points. The Romans, with two citizen legions, about 8000 men, and probably about twice that force of allies, fairly matched the enemy in numbers, but, having a thinner, longer line, could threaten the enemy's flanks if only the first charge could be blocked. It has been remarked with surprise that Pyrrhus did not employ his elephants in the orthodox fashion, which was, as with the modern tank, to make breaches here and there in the line of the enemy. He rather stationed them on his wings to frighten the Roman cavalry that might presumably circle his short and compact line. He had no fear that his heavy phalanx would not take care of his centre. If he could shatter the Roman wings and strike terror in their cavalry, his own well-trained horse would be able to circle the legions and attack from the rear. And his plan succeeded. It is noteworthy that Hannibal, who considered Pyrrhus a master of tactics, employed his horse and elephants in this same manner at the battle of the Trebia, the only contest in Italy in which he had elephants.

The Romans were finally driven off the field with a loss of 7000 men, but Pyrrhus also lost 4000 and these would be more difficult to replace. His frank acknowledgment of what his victory had cost him passed into a proverbial phrase which is still current. At Dodona Pyrrhus recorded his victory in a modest inscription which has been found. It reports a gift to the god by 'Pyrrhus the Epirote and the Tarentines'—no others are mentioned—of booty taken from 'the Romans and their allies' (Ditt.[3] 392). According to Ennius a dedication to Zeus at Tarentum scrupulously mentioned his losses as well as his gains. On the Italiote Greeks his victory made a strong impression. Croton swore allegiance to him, Locri dismissed its Roman garrison of 200 men which he permitted to return home, and Rhegium, which seemed also on the point of veering, was saved from his control only by the brutal massacre of its prominent citizens and the seizure of the town by its lawless Campanian garrison, an act of treachery which Rome later punished in the interest of her good name among the Greeks.

Presently Pyrrhus made a dash toward Rome. Like Hannibal, who later mistook the Roman federation for a conglomeration of unwilling subjects ready to fall away at the first excuse, he supposed that Campania and the northern Samnites would abandon the Roman alliance at his approach. But Capua and Neapolis refused him admittance, the Samnites did not flock to his standard and Coruncanius the other consul, having speedily completed his work in Etruria, made peace with Vulci and Volsinii and came to the relief of the city. The walls of the city were manned for defence, and for the first time men without property were recruited for army service. Pyrrhus, deceived in his expectations, turned back when only forty miles from the city, retreated southward and decided if possible to end by compromise a war which proved to be more tedious than he had expected. He had never been a man of patience. Earlier in Macedonia, later in Sicily, before Sparta, and in his final campaign at Argos, he was similarly impatient of delay. His successes were always won by surprises. Elated to unbounded hopes by a favourable turn of events, he could accomplish amazing prodigies of heroism, but he showed no endurance when plans failed. Overquick despair was his most effective enemy. Finding that he had underrated his task, he sent Cineas to Rome with offers of peace. He was ready to give up his prisoners and end the war if Rome would make peace with Tarentum, promise autonomy and liberty to the Greeks, and surrender what she had taken from his present allies including the Samnites, Lucanians, and Bruttians. This doubtless would mean at least the withdrawal of the colonies of Luceria and Venusia. Following the custom of Oriental courts he also sent with Cineas an abundance of gifts to be presented to the noble ladies of whatever courtly society he might find. This assumption that Rome resembled Alexandria reveals his utter lack of information. The Romans, who had not dealt with royal servitors before, naïvely assumed that they were being bribed and rejected the gifts with a satisfactory display of dignity.

There was however a strong peace party in the senate. The old nobility could hardly have had great enthusiasm for a war which had been induced by a plebiscite contrary to all the customs of the *mos maiorum*. We need not suppose that the peace party was ready to grant Pyrrhus' terms in full. The surrender of the lines established by the Second and Third Samnite Wars could hardly have been considered. But the subjection to Rome of all the south, including Greek cities, with which the Senate had always been traditionally on friendly terms, must have seemed unwarranted.

Now that the barrier of the Rubicon was firmly established, Italy was secure. The fact that Pyrrhus had offered terms implied that he wished to have peace, and a compromise satisfactory to the Romans might be attainable. But while the discussion was in progress, the aged Appius Claudius, who despite his patrician rank acted as his family had traditionally done with the plebeian coterie, was led into the chamber and rebuked the senators roundly for entertaining offers from a victorious enemy still on Italian soil. His speech, still circulated in Cicero's day, was the most ancient record of a public address that Roman archives preserved. He convinced the wavering Senate, and overtures of peace were rejected, but Fabricius, who could be trusted not to re-open the discussion, was sent to offer a ransom for Roman prisoners. The prospect of slavery beyond the seas was not pleasant to contemplate. However, Pyrrhus saw no advantage in a bargain which would prolong the war when he needed peace far more than gold. Since Cineas had reported that the Senate, like an assembly of kings, was very jealous of its dignity, and their haughty representative Fabricius was there to demonstrate the fact, he thought a lofty gesture in his best manner might win for him what Cineas' rhetoric and gifts had failed to get. The dignity of his answer lost nothing in the lines of Ennius who represents him as saying: 'I did not come to bargain: let us settle our dispute on the field of battle. As for your prisoners take them as a gift from me.' It seems that Fabricius received them on the understanding that they should be returned unless peace were made. The gesture had its effect, though not immediately; the next year, after a second defeat, Fabricius was sent again, as we shall see, and this time with instructions to open negotiations for peace.

During the winter Rome trained new armies and in April 279 sent forth both the new consuls, P. Sulpicius and P. Decius Mus, the son of the consul who fell at Sentinum. Two consular armies with the usual allied contingent of about twice the legionary force would amount to about 40,000 men. Now that Pyrrhus had received respectable contingents from his allies, his forces were at least equally strong. This time he decided that the shortest road was not the most expeditious—Campania had proved too well riveted to Rome. By following the Adriatic coast northward and threatening the Latin colonies of Luceria and Venusia there was some hope of liberating Samnium and thus bringing Rome to terms. This Rome had foreseen. The consular armies met him east of Venusia on the banks of the Aufidus near Asculum in a rough and wooded region where the phalanx, cavalry and ele-

phants would not have advantageous ground for effective action.
The king alternated the companies of his phalanxes with Samnite
and Lucanian maniples, either to attain a longer line with which
to face the enlarged Roman army or to make a more flexible line
in rough country. The elephants were again posted on the wings.
The battle lasted all day without a decision. Early next morning,
the king seized the fords of the river and chose a position better
suited to his customary tactics. This time the solid phalanxes
pushed the legions back, then the elephants were sent in to open
the breaches in the legions and the light-armed troops wedged in
to complete the wreckage. The Romans however managed to
regain and hold their fortified camp and Pyrrhus again left the
field with a costly and indecisive victory, unable to advance further.
The Romans had lost the consul, Decius, and 6000 dead on the
field, but Pyrrhus no less than 3500, and he himself had received
a wound which, though not serious, added to his impatience.

Pyrrhus in fact was not only weary of the undertaking but he
now knew that the Celts had made vacant the throne of Macedonia,
and were threatening Aetolia and his own boundaries (p. 101 *sq.*).
He regretted ever having left Epirus for others to profit from such
a crisis. And now to add to his perplexities he had received an
invitation from several Sicilian cities to come to their rescue against
the Carthaginians who had been threatening since the death of
Agathocles to subdue the whole island. The king saw the opportunity for making himself like Agathocles, his father-in-law, a
powerful tyrant of a Greek empire in Sicily, and thought that he
might well succeed where Agathocles had failed and become the
conqueror and ruler of Carthage as well.

The Romans probably did not hear of these perplexities, but
the fact that Pyrrhus again withdrew to Tarentum and did not
follow up his victory might evidence a willingness to offer better
terms than those of the preceding year. Accordingly, during the
winter 279–8, before the inauguration of his second consulate,
Fabricius again visited Pyrrhus and a tentative agreement was
drawn up. Just what these terms were is not clear in the confusion of our accounts, but Plutarch's version that Pyrrhus would
be satisfied if only the independence of Tarentum were safeguarded seems reasonable enough when we consider his eagerness
to depart. Cineas went to Rome to represent the king in the discussion, for the terms of peace must be satisfactory to the Senate
and ratified by the people. We are told that Fabricius actually
agreed to a preliminary draft which was to be made the basis of
the discussion.

IV. CARTHAGINIAN POLICY: PYRRHUS IN SICILY

Meanwhile, however, a Carthaginian admiral, Mago, had hurried to Rome to prevent peace if possible and to induce the senate to keep Pyrrhus engaged in Italy. To make his words all the more impressive he had come with his whole fleet of 120 ships. Carthage had much at stake. She had just decided to take advantage of the civil war in Syracuse in order to gain possession of the whole island. The fleet had been manned to block the Great Harbour. The desire of two centuries seemed to be attainable if only Pyrrhus could be kept away for a few months more. How much of his secret fears and purposes Mago revealed we are not told; he probably concealed them as best he could. Nor does the treaty, which was finally agreed upon, betray many of these secrets. It says nothing of the funds that Mago gave for a continuance of the war, the silver which Rome now coined and stamped with the horse's head of the Punic arms. It exacts no promise from Rome to help Carthage if she is attacked. The Senate was hardly so foolish as to make a binding defensive alliance with Carthage when there was good evidence that the war was nearly over. The treaty, which has so often been rewritten by modern scholars to suit their hypotheses, is after all readily understood without emendations. It reads in Polybius (III, 25) 'If either signatory shall make a treaty with Pyrrhus he shall make a stipulation that he may aid the other in whichsoever country is attacked. Whichever one may need help, the Carthaginians shall provide the ships for transport and for attack, but each shall provide the pay for its own men. The Carthaginians shall also aid the Romans by sea if need be, but no one shall compel the crews to land against their will.'

What had Rome to win by such a treaty? All that she most needed; silver coins with which to pay the expenses of her southern allies and keep them encouraged, and a fleet which could block Tarentum's harbour. As a result, Pyrrhus could be besieged effectively and starved into submission. If Pyrrhus on the other hand chose to go to Sicily, the treaty cost Rome nothing; for she was under no promise to participate in Sicily and presumably would not unless at a later day she chose to keep the enemy at a distance, in which case free transports were provided. Mago, though he had not received as much by the agreement as he might have wished, had kept Rome from making peace and had secured one reservation in the first clause which was likely to prevent Pyrrhus from making a hasty settlement with Rome.

Pyrrhus could not wind up affairs in Italy at once; there was a chance that he would not go to Sicily at all, especially as the phrasing of the treaty suggested that there might be a secret promise of definite aid in Sicily as well. The document reveals shrewd thinking on the part of both negotiators.

Cineas had to go back empty-handed. Mago sailed to Syracuse to blockade that harbour, transporting on his way 500 Roman legionaries as far as Rhegium, who were sent apparently to surprise the mutinous Campanian garrison of that city and restore it to Rome's alliance. The surprise attack failed and Rome had to postpone the punishment till she could muster a sufficient force. For the rigorous prosecution of the war Rome chose two well-tried consuls for 278, the very two who had been colleagues in the relief of Thurii in 282, Fabricius and Aemilius Papus[1]. They marched into the enemy's country, but Pyrrhus, now busily engaged in making his contracts with Sicilian envoys and preparing his fleet, did not stir, nor was it time for Fabricius to invest the strongly fortified city before the arrival of the promised fleet. For the moment we hear only of the famous story—which is at least traceable to very early sources—of how an Epirote traitor promised Fabricius in return for gold to rid him of his opponent by poison, and how the Roman general, refusing to consider the offer, sent the treasonable letter to the king. The incident is wholly in character with the somewhat ostentatious rectitude of that day's rustic nobility; a hundred years later a Roman general would doubtless have torn up the missive and thought no more about it.

The Roman consuls spent a part of the summer winning other tribes and towns that had given aid to Pyrrhus. An incidental remark in Cicero indicates that it was Fabricius who at this time secured for Heraclea its favourable alliance 'of equality' with Rome which left the city autonomous and immune from the burden of military levies. It was one of the few cities which in the year 89 did not desire to exchange its position for the Roman franchise. That winter, according to the Roman triumphal fasti, Fabricius celebrated a triumph over 'Lucanians, Samnites, Tarentines and Bruttians.' The next summer, after Pyrrhus' departure for Sicily, the consul Junius must have continued the work of pacification, for on his return he triumphed over 'Lucanians and Bruttians.' What was more important, Croton and Locri dismissed their Epirote garrisons under compulsion and accepted Roman control during this year. That these cities are not men-

---

[1] For the consular Fasti of 278–267, see *Not. d. Scavi*, 1925, pp. 376–381.

tioned with the barbarians in the triumphal records seems to indicate that it was Rome's policy not to subject Greeks to the same treatment as barbarians.

When in the autumn of 278 Pyrrhus set out for Sicily, that island was in a state of anarchy. Agathocles' power had kept the Carthaginians to the western end of the island, but after his death in 289 his mercenary army of Campanians had seized and sacked Messana and the adjacent territory which they were now ruling, and unscrupulous 'tyrants' had established themselves in several of the Greek cities with the result that the Carthaginians made ready progress eastward at several points. While Pyrrhus was in Italy, Sosistratus, the tyrant of Acragas, was besieging the Syracusan tyrant, Thoenon, and had in fact blockaded him on the island of Ortygia. The Carthaginians, believing this an opportunity to gain supremacy over the whole island, sent a fleet of 120 ships to attack the city. Then, fearing that Pyrrhus might make peace with Rome and turn his attention to Sicily, they had sent Mago to Rome, as we have seen, to reach some agreement which might keep Pyrrhus busy where he was. The Punic attack, however, brought the two Greek combatants to their senses. They united against the common enemy and with other Greeks sent a cry for help to Pyrrhus, promising to accept his overlordship and to place all their forces at his disposal. Pyrrhus had learned enough about Sicily and Agathocles' successes through his former wife Lanassa to entertain the hope that he might win dominion over the whole of Sicily and perhaps also over Carthage. He therefore sent Cineas ahead to secure written promises, he planted a strong garrison in Tarentum as well as in the other Greek cities, and with some 10,000 troops sailed by way of Locri for Sicily. At Tauromenium and Catana he was greeted with enthusiasm and given troops; landing at the latter city he marched upon Syracuse where he was admitted and given the forces of the two tyrants. The Carthaginian fleet sailed away while the rulers of the Greek cities met in conclave at Syracuse and proclaimed Pyrrhus king of Sicily and generalissimo of the Greek forces. His army quickly rose from ten to thirty thousand men so that the Carthaginians did not venture to oppose him.

He proceeded to drive out the Punic garrison which held Enna and was soon welcomed to Acragas, Heraclea, Selinus, Halicyae, and Segesta. He took the strong fort of Mt Eryx by storm and captured the fort of Heirkte which commanded Panormus (Palermo). There was now only Lilybaeum left in Punic hands, and this was well-nigh impregnable from land and could be captured by sea only after a successful naval battle. When, therefore, the Carthaginians offered to surrender the rest of the island provided Pyrrhus would leave them that city and sign terms of peace, he was inclined to do so. The Greeks, however, shamed him into staying to complete his work. After a brief campaign against the Mamertines, in which he confined them within the city of Messana, he tried for two months to take Lilybaeum by storm. Since this could not be done, he decided to man an adequate fleet with which to destroy the Punic sea power, invest Lilybaeum by sea and invade Africa. To the Greeks this would entail contributions of ships, rowers, and money in a venture which seemed to them very hazardous. As there was already some discontent with Pyrrhus on account of his severe demands, his disregard of the native magistrates, and his preferential treatment of his own Epirote officers, rumours of mutiny were frequent. Sosistratus suddenly withdrew with his forces to Acragas depriving Pyrrhus not only of soldiers but of a city of military importance. Pyrrhus, fearing that Thoenon would also withdraw, had him slain. Misfortune betrayed the king into other acts of cruelty which only caused new revolts and several cities openly invited Punic and Mamertine garrisons. Meanwhile the Carthaginians received reinforcements and now had courage to face the reduced Epirote army. Pyrrhus, if we may believe Justin's sole authority, again came off the victor but, unwilling to face the task of reconquering the rebellious island, he used the opportunity to embark and sail away. It was now the spring of 275; he had wasted over two years in Sicily.

The Punic fleet attacked him as he crossed to Italy, destroying more than half of his ships, and the Campanian garrison of Rhegium, aided by a Mamertine force, beset him on his march causing heavy losses. The city of Locri he took by a ruse and punished severely the members of the pro-Roman party who had caused the revolt two years before. Here, being in need of funds, he robbed the rich temple treasure of Persephone, an act of sacrilege to which he later attributed his continued misfortune in Italy until he in some measure made restitution. Croton was also retaken from the Campanians of Rhegium who had seized the city two years before.

V. THE END OF THE WAR

On reaching Tarentum the king gathered what forces he could and advanced boldly northward. For three years the Roman armies had been forcing the Samnites and Lucanians to submission group by group so that he now found no barbarian contingents to aid him, and his Epirote army had suffered heavy losses. But it was known that the two Roman consuls were separated, that Manius Curius, who had been operating in Samnium, was guarding the passes of the eastern road near Malventum (Roman Beneventum), while Cornelius Lentulus seems to have been stationed in Lucania on the central Italian road. He struck out quickly against Curius and, aware of the inferiority of his numbers, he tried to gain a high position over his enemy by a night march. Losing time in the dark, however, he did not quite reach his objective by daybreak. Thanks to this brief delay, Curius had time to deploy his troops, and with great effort he repulsed Pyrrhus' attack and captured several of the elephants. The other consul was now near at hand, and Pyrrhus, seeing that an attack of the united Roman forces would mean disaster, withdrew to Tarentum as hastily as he had come. He stationed a guard of Epirotes in the strong fortress of Tarentum under the command of Milo and his own son Helenus, whose presence was to suggest that he would return with reinforcements as soon as possible to succour the city. Then—probably in the autumn of 275—he embarked as quietly and quickly as he could his pitiful remnant of eight thousand foot and five hundred horse, less than one-third the force with which he had come six years before[1].

The defeat of Pyrrhus directed the attention of the whole Hellenic world toward Rome, for in the East Pyrrhus had been considered a possible empire-builder like Alexander. He had in his youth fought with distinction at Ipsus, had been the governor of Greece appointed by Demetrius Poliorcetes, had married the daughter of Ptolemy Soter in Egypt and with Ptolemy's aid had secured his ancestral throne in Epirus, then had revealed his ambitions by seizing the throne of Macedonia and had finally announced his intentions to win the West from Tarentum to Carthage. And suddenly an unknown barbaric tribe of Latins had driven him back home. Who could the Romans be? Ptolemy Philadelphus, the most powerful monarch of the East, who comprehended the great significance of the event, sent envoys (273) to Rome to establish a record of friendship and Rome replied in kind. The Alexandrine court-poet, Lycophron, who may well have met the Roman envoys and learned from them the traditional stories of Rome's foundation, inserted in his *Alexandra* a reference to the descendants of Troy who were destined in the West to

[1] For the rest of Pyrrhus' career see above, pp. 213 *sqq.*

balance the wrongs of Priam's city[1]. Rome was now in fact a world-power.

Rome had decided that the federation must now be consolidated, and that all misunderstandings throughout Italy left at loose ends during the great peril must be composed in case Pyrrhus returned with reinforcements. The Samnite league, which had proved most troublesome, was broken apart. A wide strip of territory was seized along the river Calor, cutting the Hirpini and Pentri off from the rest of Samnium. Separate settlements were made with these tribes, and a large Latin colony was sent into the severing strip and planted at Malventum, the site of the recent victory. Since the name had an ill-omened sound the colony was called Beneventum. A century later the mountainous district round it was given to two Ligurian tribes of north Italy. Samnium was now at last thoroughly pacified, but the territory of the main tribe comprised only about half as much land as it had before the Samnite wars began. The population still numbered over 300,000, since the census of 225 B.C. records 77,000 able-bodied men of forty-five years and under. The Lucanians suffered less, but they were deprived of the territory of Paestum which still contained some of its Greek population. This city became a 'Latin' colony in 273. In the census of 225 the Lucanians enrolled 33,000 men for active service so that the total population of the tribe was probably over 150,000.

Croton and Locri entered the federation once more. These cities had suffered much during the war. Croton for instance had accepted a Roman garrison before or during 280 but had seceded to Pyrrhus after his first victory. In 277, when Pyrrhus was in Sicily, the consul Rufinus took the town and restored the garrison, but within a year the Campanian rebels at Rhegium captured the city and plundered it. Then Pyrrhus returned, drove out the Campanians and placed his guard there. After his departure in 275, the city again passed into Roman hands, though we are not told how. We hear that in the Hannibalic War it had only 20,000 inhabitants. Locri's misfortunes had been equally severe. The precise terms of Rome's alliance with these Greeks are not known, but at any rate we may not infer from incidents belonging to the Hannibalic war that Rome stationed garrisons in the towns at the time. The coins of Locri which belong to the period of her restored alliance bear the legend πίστις (Faithfulness), which implies a status of considerable dignity in the league. Indeed, there is reason to think that the conventional figure of Dea Roma on

[1] See, however, above, p. 281.

early Roman coins was adopted from these pieces. At a later date, after Rome had instituted a navy (probably in 267), we hear that all of these Greek cities are *socii navales*, that is, they are not called upon for regular military contingents, but provide a certain number of ships fully equipped and manned for the federal navy. What the precise requirements were we are not told. On one occasion, however, Rhegium, Velia, and Paestum together are said to provide ten ships of war; on another, during Rome's war with Perseus, Locri sends two triremes, Thurii four, and Rhegium one. Their position in any case was always more favourable than that of the other allies who had to supply forces nearly every year for military service. And since their people were traders they gained much from Rome's rising prestige in days to come. Unfortunately they suffered severely again during the Second Punic War for ten years when Hannibal devastated southern Italy.

What settlement was made with the Bruttians, who had so long harassed the Greek cities, we do not know, except that Rome confiscated half of their forest land, thereafter farming out the timber and pitch which was extensively used by the Greek ship-builders of the coast towns. The coins which continued to be issued by the Bruttian league imply that it possessed some degree of autonomy, and this remained until after the Second Punic War when, in punishment for their adhesion to Hannibal, many of the Bruttians were deprived of their civil rights. Gradually, then, this conglomeration of diverse peoples down in the cul-de-sac of Italy, fugitive aborigines and Oenotri, migrant Siculi from across the straits, runaway Lucanians and Greek slaves, merged into the stable population of the empire.

In 272 Rome finally undertook the siege of Tarentum in earnest, sending the consul, Papirius Cursor the younger, to complete the work. The city was already divided, one part favouring Rome, the other, while hostile to the Epirote garrison, still refusing to open the gates to Papirius. Finally the garrison, coming to no terms with the citizens, surrendered the fortress to the consul and sailed off. Rome did not treat the city as one captured by force, but accepted it as a *socius navalis* though not with full autonomy, and captives must have been taken since we happen to know that Livius Andronicus, Rome's first writer of tragedies, was as a child brought in captivity to Rome from Tarentum. Furthermore, a Roman legion was permanently placed in the citadel, not presumably to guard the city alone but to protect the whole of southern Italy. Tarentum was then the most important city of the south and possessed a very strongly built fortress commanding the harbour. This was the first standing garrison created by Rome. In late sources we hear that a Carthaginian fleet appeared in the harbour just before the surrender of the fortress, but sailed away upon learning that Rome had taken possession. When Roman writers later summed up the list of Punic treacheries, this act was generally cited among them in the belief that Carthage had intended to seize the city. That Polybius does not mention it in discussing the causes of the Punic war indicates that the interpretation given to the act by later writers was not in vogue in his day. Nor is it a plausible hypothesis that Carthage was ready to risk a war with Rome for one isolated harbour in Italy. The probabilities therefore are that the Carthaginian admiral had in all good faith appeared in obedience to the last clause of Mago's treaty to discover whether his assistance was needed in the blockade of the harbour, and that he departed upon being notified that it was not.

For the present the peoples of Apulia and Messapia, which had helped Pyrrhus and Tarentum, were disregarded, but a few years later, in 267–6, Rome's consuls marched through the region exacting written promises of allegiance. At Brundisium, which had an excellent harbour on the Adriatic, land was taken for a colony which was planted twenty years later and given the 'Latin' status. The census of 225 shows that the Apulian and Messapian coast was rather thickly inhabited during the third century, presumably crowded by people who had given way before the Lucanians during the preceding century. The potential military strength was reckoned at 66,000 able-bodied men. During the Hannibalic War much of this region became waste land.

In 270 the mutinous garrison of Campanians at Rhegium was also disposed of. Soon after their arrival, this force of four thousand men had seized the city in emulation of the Mamertines of Messana, and had murdered and plundered at will. The next year they had prevented Rome's attempt to take the town by surprise, and later had driven the Roman garrison out of Croton and sacked that city. Now the consul, Cornelius Blasio, took the city by storm in a desperate battle in which most of the garrison fell. Some three hundred survivors were captured, brought to Rome, scourged and beheaded in the Forum. The city was handed back to its inhabitants and added to the list of *socii navales* with full autonomy. If the one trireme provided for the fleet in 171 represents Rhegium's regular treaty obligations, it is not surprising that the city proved to be one of Rome's staunchest allies during the Hannibalic War.

There was also much unfinished work to be done farther north. In 273 the Latin colony of Cosa was settled on land that may have been secured for the purpose from Vulci by the treaty of 280. In the same year a deferred dispute was settled with Caere with a loss to her of half her territory. This seems to be the district in which the maritime colony of Castrum Novum was planted nine years later, when the war with Carthage called attention to the importance of the coast line. In order to indicate the northern boundary below the Rubicon, a large Latin colony was sent in 268 to Ariminum at the extreme end of the Ager Gallicus which had been cleared fifteen years before. But this colony differed from those founded heretofore in that its citizens were not privileged to marry Romans or to attain Roman citizenship by registering residence in Rome. The purpose of these restrictions was apparently to stop migration to Rome and to keep the colonists where they were sent, for Ariminum was unattractively near the Gauls. From this time on, it seems, the new type of Latin colony invented for guard-duty at Ariminum was regularly employed.

In the same year the Fasti record triumphs over the city of Sarsina in Umbria (near the Ager Gallicus) and over the Picentes. Excavations have revealed traces of a Gallic settlement at Sarsina so that we may infer that the war was a last act in clearing out the Senones[1]. As for the Picentes we may hazard the conjecture that they had during the last few years crossed the Aesis to resettle the Ager Gallicus from which the Gauls had long ago driven them, and which was now Roman *ager publicus*. If so, they may have resented the colonization of Ariminum. This strange people, probably non-Indo-European (vol. IV, p. 445), which had since the Stone Age succeeded in retaining their territory against all invaders until the Celts came, must for a century have been very uncomfortably packed, for archaeologists have found abundant evidence that their former territory extended from the Rubicon to the Praetuttian fields before the Senones drove them southward. If Rome now refused them the chance to re-occupy their lost territory, which many still called Ager Gallicus *in Piceno*, we may well understand a revolt from the treaty of 299. The struggle must have been bitter, for Rome ended it by herding off a group of them to the hills behind Salerno and Paestum on territory previously taken from the Lucanians. Asculum was the only one of their cities that received a treaty of alliance. On the land vacated by the emigrants a Latin colony was later (in 264) settled near the coast at Firmum. Rome now had five colonies of about 3000

[1] Von Duhn, *Italische Gräberkunde*, p. 189.

families each on the Adriatic coast. In the same eventful year of 268 Rome elevated the Sabine tribes from half to full citizenship by granting them the franchise. This was a full recognition of their capacity to participate with the Romans in the governing of the unwieldy federation, but it must not be forgotten that in return Rome received much-needed assistance in the filling of her own legions year by year.

The period of settlement ends with a strange episode of which ancient historians seem to have known all too little. The Etruscan aristocracy of Volsinii had in the course of the Samnite wars freed their 'slaves' so as to enroll them in their army which was then fighting Rome. These 'freedmen' had now gained control of the city, were instituting a democratic government and, as Zonaras has it, they had seized all the magistracies, made themselves senators and intermarried with their former owners. What we seem to have in this account is a liberation of serfs and the consequences thereof, for the Etruscan princes had long ago reduced the Italic folk to serfdom in many cities (vol. IV, p. 413). That the account is hazy is probably due to the fact that the Latin language had no designation for the serf. The narrative goes on to say that in 265 the aristocracy appealed to Rome for aid against their oppressors, but the rabble, hearing of this appeal, tortured and slew some of the lords and banished the others. The Romans however granted the request, stormed the city and razed it. They built a new city on the lake (Bolsena) for the lords and such of their serfs as were loyal to their masters. Apparently the aristocratic government and the former landlord system were again put into force. Whether the ex-serfs retained their freedom and accepted tenancies from the landlords, or were completely reduced to slavery in the war we are not told. When we find that the census of 225 records only 54,000 men serving as soldiers in the whole of Etruria and the Sabine country we may suspect that in many cities of the former serfdom had led to slavery rather than to freedom. By Cicero's day at any rate we no longer hear of serfdom in Etruria. Had the Romans realized the fact that these serfs were descended from the same ancestry as the Latins they might have advocated a more liberal policy and in the end Etruria would have possessed a healthier body of citizens.

VI. THE ROMAN FEDERATION

The Roman federation now extended the whole length of Italy from Ariminum and bore the character which it retained until the Social War secured citizenship to all the inhabitants of the peninsula. At this time the territory of full citizenship included Latium, a small portion of Etruria from below Caere and Mt Soracte, then a wide corridor across the peninsula including the Sabines and Praetuttians and a few maritime colonies. The inhabitants of this region could doubtless all speak Latin, since the Sabine dialect had been (Vol. iv, p. 448) latinized, and the bulk of the population of Veientane Etruria were of Italic stock like the Latins and had not been under Etruscan domination much longer than the Romans. The territory of citizenship without franchise included Caere on the north, the coastland on the south as far as Neapolis and inland with an irregular boundary line extending about as far as Sora and Arpinum. These peoples were doubtless learning the Latin language especially in camp and in trade and were considered to be candidates for full citizenship at an early date. Intermarriage with Romans was legal, property rights were under Roman law and Roman judicial prefects held court in these regions, though their municipal governments were otherwise undisturbed. There should be included under Roman territory some strips of land which the Romans had taken as public property but not yet colonized, apparently for want of settlers, a large part of the Ager Gallicus, a part of Picenum, of Umbria, and of lower Etruria between Caere and Vulci.

The so-called Latin colony continued to be the chief device for garrisoning strategic points; including the original colonies of the Latin league there were some twenty-eight of these. The method adopted was to confiscate a portion of arable territory which was fertile enough to attract settlers at points which needed protection and possessed a strong site readily fortified. The colonists would serve as a garrison in time of need and were also liable to army service in the league forces at times when they could safely be called from home. The official language of such colonists was Latin, but the presence of foreign inscriptions in many of them proves that the settlers, drawn as they were from several of the allied states, might to some extent at least be more at home in Oscan, Greek, or Etruscan. These colonists seem to have had the rights of intermarriage and of property-holding with Romans and, at least up to the time of the foundation of Ariminum, they were readily accorded citizenship in Rome by residence in the city. But restrictions were later imposed upon them chiefly because the colonial governments complained that it was difficult for them to provide their military contingents when their citizens were permitted to take up residence at Rome and change their citizenship. Their magistrates, however, *ipso facto* received Roman citizenship and this privilege was never questioned. A glance at the map will show that by 264 these settlements had been founded mainly in order to surround Samnium and to protect lower Etruria and the Adriatic coast with cities friendly to Rome: about Samnium are found Interamna, Suessa, Cales, Saticula, Beneventum, Venusia, and Luceria; in lower Etruria, Nepete, Sutrium, and Cosa; on the upper Adriatic, Ariminum, Castrum Novum, Firmum and Hadria (see map 12, facing p. 820).

The rest of the Italian tribes and cities were allied to Rome by a great diversity of treaties similar only in the fact that, while such allies had local autonomy and were not subject to tribute to Rome or the league, they were under contract to contribute a contingent to the army which was under the command of a Roman consul. Although these treaties were in the form of alliances of mutual defence and Rome was always quick to respond if the allied territory was invaded—on the Gallic border for instance—the federation now was bounded by sea and mountains so that few wars were apt to arise because of disturbances on the boundary of an ally. Furthermore, all neighbours recognized Rome's supremacy in the league so that, when disputes arose, the discussion was carried on at Rome and not in some allied city. Hence, from the time of Pyrrhus onwards it was seldom, except in theory, a question of mutual defence.

The diversity in the status of the allies was due to several causes: partly to the circumstances attending their entry, whether by voluntary adhesion as in the case of Neapolis, or by subjection after a war as in the case of Samnium; partly to the cultural status of the ally—Rome had always admired the Greek cities of Italy, and was apt to invite their goodwill; partly to the nature of the allied government. It has been noticed, for instance, that in Etruria and Umbria Rome preferred to see the larger tribes broken up into smaller units. This was doubtless in part due to the prudent principle of *divide et impera*, for Gallic raids would be far less dangerous if Etruria were not inflammable as a whole. But this is not the sole reason. In both Etruria and Umbria strong cities had long existed with separatist loyalties so that responsible united action was difficult to secure. In neither was any treaty of the whole league very dependable. Fractions would secede in times of danger. It was therefore essential that the treaties be signed with the fractions. Hence, while Rome did not disturb religious associations and leagues in Etruria and Umbria, she did insist upon having her treaties signed by the individual cities. Among the Sabellian tribes, however, which had not yet developed strong urban units and where the tribes of villagers presented responsible governments, there was far less segregating. Only in Samnium, where the Frentani, Hirpini and Pentri readily fell into separate groups, did Rome apply the device of severing. The Samnite tribe thus trimmed down was accepted as a unit, and so were also the mountain tribes that went under the names of Marsi, Marrucini, Paeligni, Vestini, Frentani, and Lucani. Finally, it is to be noticed that religion, language, and custom counted for something in determining the status of allies. The Sabines, whose customs and language most resembled the Roman, were among the first to attain the franchise, while the strange Etruscans, whose language has not yet yielded interpretation, and who, even when they adopted Italic gods, Tuscanized their names, were not hurried into close union. After the first experiments citizenship was not extended in Etruria till the Social War, and no colonies were planted in the heart of their country. Indeed, in the early days, though it was Rome's custom to make her alliances for all time, her treaties in this region had always been made for a limited term of years. The Romans apparently felt that this people would not readily be assimilated.

The question has often been raised why, now that Rome's imaginary walls extended to the Adriatic, the representative principle of government was not adopted in order to facilitate the effective participation of people who lived so far away. We may assume that the possibility was discussed from time to time, for at the very beginning of Rome's expansion the Latins had asked to be represented in the Roman Senate, and again during the Punic war a similar proposal was made by Carvilius, a Roman senator. It is doubtful whether the people of Rome would have had much patience with this proposal. The town-meeting was an old Latin institution, one of the most sacred; direct participation of every citizen in the meeting which decided whether there should be war or peace seemed an unquestionable right. History seemed also to have proved the adequacy of this government. When hordes had poured in from the north, tribes within had quarrelled and ambitious tyrants had invaded from the south, other tribes and cities had proved ineffective, but the Roman assembly advised by the Senate had alone followed the prudent course, taken up arms for any sacrifice, and organized their neighbours for steadfast defence. The federation of the whole of Italy seemed a miraculous feat. Why change a government which had accomplished that? Again, it seemed well that those nearest the city, who spoke the language, who worshipped and thought as the Romans did, should for the sake of united action control the government. Sabines of the Adriatic coast, Etruscans of Caere, Ausonians and the rest might in time bring into a representative parliament a predominant number which would destroy unity of purpose and create an ineffective government when, to control the vast federation, decision and speed were necessary. We may also suppose that the recent victory of the principle of popular sovereignty debarred the acceptance of the representative idea. It was naturally assumed that a representative group would form a body like the Senate, and it was the Senate which the assemblies had had to curb for over two hundred years. It was only in 287 that the complete victory had finally been won by which the people could, if they desired, override the Senate on any question of legislation and administration and make their own decisions. A representative Senate would become as conservative as the old one had been, for in the society of that day the landed nobility with their broad estates and many clients would win the seats in the Senate as surely as they now won the elections to the magistracy. And if such a parliament displaced the primary assembly, the struggle of centuries would apparently be lost. Such must have been the feelings of the Romans when the question was raised. It must be admitted that the primary assembly still deserved the confidence it expected and that a change would have been unwise until the federation was far more unified in language and custom than it was in the third century.

When the federation had finally been safely organized, Rome devised a currency which might be adequate for the needs of her citizens and their trade with their associates. The Roman government had always been laggard in providing coinage, partly because her agricultural people cared little for trade and had had no part in maritime commerce, partly because the government needed but little currency since magistrates gave their services without salaries, and soldiers, till the fourth century, provided their own armour and horses and served without pay. Although the Etruscans, the Campanians, and the Greeks had been coining money from the fifth century onwards, it was only after the Latin War that Rome issued any coins, and these were mostly bronze one-pound *asses* and some fractional pieces. During the Samnite and Pyrrhic wars Rome had needed silver coins for purchases made in Campania in the south, but Campanian and southern cities which had old mints provided these coins under contract[1]. Such coins, while bearing the legend ROMA or ROMANO, were issued in weights

[1] See, however, above, p. 608.

usual in the south and corresponded to the Greek *drachma*. There had been much trouble in keeping the Roman bronze pieces properly adjusted to them. The first Roman bronze *asses* had been issued in one-pound pieces, but in time the weight diminished successively to a third, a fourth, and finally to a sixth of a pound. The probability is that this reduction had been due to an effort to adjust the amount of metal used to the changing market value of bronze at a time when wars cut off the supply and increased the demand. This theory rests upon the observation that Rome in 268 and again in 217 observed market values carefully in adjusting the bimetallic system and also upon the fact that, since the bronze pieces were very crudely moulded, counterfeiting would at once have resulted unless the maintenance of intrinsic values had been an essential consideration in their coinage.

But simply because a varying market had been followed through the Pyrrhic War, the restoration of peace-prices after the departure of Pyrrhus made the old bronze pieces obsolete. Hence Rome in 268, deciding to sever official connections with the silver *drachma* currency and to strike a Roman coin to which an adequate Roman bronze currency could be attached, adopted a two-ounce bronze piece as the basis for a new currency. Since silver was now valued at 120 times bronze—and with peace throughout Italy values were not apt to shift much—a silver piece worth ten *asses*— a convenient unit—would weigh one sixth of an ounce, which proved to be a convenient size as well, and this was called the *ten-piece* or *denarius*. Fractional coins were also made, the *quinarius* or *five-as* piece, and the *sestertius* (semistertius) worth two and a half *asses*. The last, being too small for convenient use, did not remain long in circulation, though later when the decimal system was shattered by equating the denarius with sixteen *asses*, the imaginary *sestertius* became the unit of accounts because fours can be reckoned more conveniently than sixteens. Since Rome had accumulated considerable silver during the wars, she now issued a large amount of denarii from her new mint in the city, and also established mints at some of the far distant Latin colonies for the issue of both silver and bronze. Campanian cities, accustomed to the native 'victoriati,' were allowed to continue coining these which passed at the market value of silver according to weight. Some of the Greek cities of the south also continued for a season to issue their own coins until the Roman denarius came into general use throughout the federation. Since these coins eventually had to compete with the standard denarius and were then valued according to their weight, there was no profit in continuing their mintage and the non-Roman mints of Italy all ceased coining silver before the Hannibalic War.

The Roman government, despite the Hortensian law which gave the plebeian assembly an absolute right to legislate without the participation of the Senate or the consuls, continued in practice to be an aristocracy. The centuriate assembly, a conservative body in which the voters of the first class controlled elections, continued to choose the magistrates, and thus indirectly the Senate as well. To be sure, the necessity of electing into the consulship one plebeian every year was constantly bringing new blood into the senate, but the electors chose conservatively and with great care. Only nine new plebeians attained the office in the twenty-six years under discussion, and none of these could be accused of radical tendencies. The others belonged to families that had already attained to the higher nobility since the year 366. It is true that a plebiscite accorded aid to Thurii and thus brought on the Pyrrhic War, but there is not a hint of the flood of legislation and constitutional changes that might have been expected from the plebeian insistence upon the acceptance of the Hortensian measure. In fact there is no record of any purely legislative measure passed by either assembly during the twenty-five years following that drastic reform. Either the plebeians were now satisfied with the assurance that popular sovereignty had been recognized in case of future need, or the Senate had decided to take the warning and, making friends among the tribunes, to retain its power by inviting them into the Senate for consultation. There is at least one illuminating instance of such co-operation. When the traitorous Campanians of Rhegium had been captured, their punishment was decided upon by the plebeian assembly at the advice of the Senate. The Senate, therefore, continued to govern the state and the federation as before, to determine the policies of the generals, to decide upon the objective of each campaign, to receive legations and discuss with them offers of peace and of alliance, and to define the changing status of each member of the federation.

CHAPTER XXI

ROME AND CARTHAGE: THE FIRST PUNIC WAR

I. CARTHAGE

DURING the Pyrrhic War the farsighted policy of Carthage had revealed itself at Rome when Mago accompanied his request for an alliance with a gift of gold and a demonstration of force. And the guarded phrases of the treaty which Rome granted (p. 649) proved that the senators were suspicious of their new friend. The friendship was not to last long. The city of Carthage was probably larger than Rome and was certainly wealthier. Her actual territory was not extensive, containing, besides rough pasture land, only about six hundred square miles of arable soil (see below, p. 682). But Carthage was then probably the most prosperous commercial and industrial city of the world. She carefully kept for herself and her allies a monopoly of the trade in her colonies and trading posts, and these were many. There were several in Southern Spain, including Gades, and they tapped the resources of the richest part of the peninsula; the Punic posts on the coast of North Africa, from Tripolis to beyond Tangiers, attracted the more profitable barter of some three million Moors and Numidians; five colonies exploited the resources of Sardinia, and the tithes of more than half of Sicily went to Carthage.

The ruling nobles of Carthage were largely rich merchants and manufacturers who saw to it that the state maintained a navy powerful enough to enforce embargo acts, protect the trading posts and prevent pirating in the western Mediterranean. The people of the city were the more prosperous because they had no military duties to call them away from their lucrative occupations. Mercenaries were hired and subject peoples conscripted for the army and navy, and the expenses were paid from the tribute exacted from their subjects. But commerce and industry were not the only sources of private wealth. The arable land, though

Note. Polybius, I, based upon Fabius Pictor and Philinus, is the only trustworthy source for the main narrative. The fragments of Diodorus XXIII, XXIV, the brief notices in Appian (*Sic.* 1–2), the fragments of Dio Cassius, XI (with Zonaras' Epitome, VIII, 8–17), Livy's epitomes, XVI–XIX, and Cornelius Nepos' *Hamilcar* add but few facts of importance. See the Bibliography.

not extensive, was generally held by rich landlords, and Punic planters were rapidly penetrating far into Numidia. Hanno's expedition to Theveste during the First Punic War shows that these landed proprietors were powerful enough to force the government into a policy of territorial expansion at a time when the commercial party needed all possible resources to hold the sea and the Sicilian sea ports.

The constitution of the city was not remarkably unlike Rome's. It had attracted the attention of Aristotle (*Pol.* II, 11) because of its aristocratic provisions and its stability. The regal form, so customary in the East, had never been adopted, because Carthage began life as a colony; and pure democracy, for some reason, never found favour among Semitic peoples. The magistrates were two "judges" who held office for but a year. Like the Roman consuls, these *suffetes* had to be men of property. Carthage however had an advantage over Rome in that skilled generals could be elected for long terms to direct the armies in time of war. Hence her armies were often led by far better tacticians than were Rome's. At Carthage also the great Council was the regular lawmaking body, and proposals were not submitted to the popular assembly except in case of decided disagreement. It consisted of about three hundred men who held their seats *ex officio*. A committee of thirty of its members seems to have been an inner deliberative and advisory body of much importance. Carthage, then, was a timocracy with two excellent safety valves, on the one hand a popular referendum which prevented democratic explosions, on the other a centralization of executive power in wartime to provide efficient generalship.

Where the Carthaginian government differed most from the Roman was in its manner of ruling and employing its subjects and allies. Rome professed to be the leader of a large federation of free allies and associates, who, though providing contingents for the federal army, were not subject to a humiliating tribute. Carthage not only commandeered troops from the Phoenician colonies and from the nomad tribes of Africa but exacted a fixed annual tribute from the former and a heavy percentage of the annual crop—from twenty-five to fifty per cent.—from the latter. If these sums, as has been estimated, amounted to 12,000 talents per year, her revenues must have been about twenty times as much as Athens drew from her league in her most prosperous days. Obviously Carthage could face the costs of a large navy far more easily than the Roman state which could tax only its own citizens. But the advantages did not all lie with Carthage. The troops provided by the subject peoples who went into battle with memories of heavy grievances against their ruler were not very enthusiastic soldiers, and the mercenaries would probably have fought better in attacking towns that afforded booty than in facing bare armies of legionaries. In a word, the First Punic War proved to be a test of staying powers between a federation of autonomous peoples and a wealthy city which employed strangers or conscripted subjects to fight for her.

II. THE ALLIANCE WITH THE MAMERTINES

Rome's army had not yet returned from Volsinii when the Mamertines of Messana asked for admission into the federation and a protecting garrison (264 B.C.). Rome after a long debate consented, thereby becoming involved in a war with Carthage that lasted twenty-four years. The exigencies of this war, by which Rome extended her influence over cities not independent, as in Italy, but already subject to the imperial control or ownership of Carthage or of the king of Syracuse, converted Rome gradually into an imperial state. The conquest of Sicily, therefore, marks the end of the consistent policy, adhered to for eighty years, of building a confederation of related states. In Sicily Rome found and adopted old Asiatic ideas of territorial sovereignty which involved provincial domination, standing armies, and the exaction of tithes. It is not to be assumed that when the question was first presented the Senate believed a war inevitable, much less that a conquest of Sicily or an acquisition of subjects was considered a possibility, and yet the invitation of the Mamertines seemed so full of hazard that the debate proved inconclusive and the senate refused to decide the question. It was the assembly (whether the plebeian or the centuriate is not known) that finally accepted the offer.

Conditions in Sicily had long been highly critical. When in 276 B.C. Pyrrhus had made himself obnoxious to his Greek subjects in Sicily, several cities had revolted to Carthage and others had gone over to the Mamertines. Carthage soon regained control of western and central Sicily while the Mamertines mastered all the north-eastern angle as far as Halaesa. It will be remembered that the Mamertines had formerly been mercenaries whom Agathocles had enlisted in Campania and Bruttium and that on his death in 289 they had treacherously occupied Messana, murdered its leading citizens, and forming their own government had set out to shape a tributary empire in that part of the island (p. 651). Hiero, elected strategus of Syracuse soon after Pyrrhus' departure, was also attempting to build an empire in emulation of Dionysius I and Agathocles, for he knew that only by success in war could he impose himself upon Syracuse as 'tyrant' for life. Hence he had refused to recognize the legitimacy of Mamertine rule in Messana on the pretext of their usurpation of fifteen years before, in reality, however, because they were less dangerous than the Carthaginians as foes from whom to make conquests. His first encounter with them resulted in a defeat—brought on intentionally, according to the Sicilian version, in order to rid himself of mutinous mercenaries—but after a few years he marched northward again, captured Halaesa and Tyndaris and finally completely defeated the full force of the Mamertines on the Longanus river. Thereupon he was elected king by his people. This seems to have been in 265, though the date is uncertain. Hiero hoped to take Messana and become master of the whole eastern part of the island, but the Carthaginian admiral Hannibal, who lay with his fleet off the Liparaean islands watching Hiero's advance, saved the city by throwing in a Punic garrison with the consent of the Mamertines. The Carthaginians, who had so long fought for the control of Sicily, naturally did not wish their ambitious rival to seize the harbour which commanded the Sicilian straits. Hiero, who despite the flattering assurance of the poet Theocritus was not yet ready to match his strength with Carthage, returned home in disappointment, and the Carthaginians to strengthen their position proceeded to seize and garrison Tyndaris as well.

The Mamertines were grateful enough for their present salvation but were far from intending to keep the garrison and become Punic subjects. Since, however, their army had been almost completely destroyed on the Longanus, they feared that they would not be able to preserve their autonomy by means of their own resources alone. Some advocated an attempt to reach a formal understanding with Carthage which would acknowledge their autonomy under a protectorate; others favoured an alliance with Rome on the same basis as that of Rhegium, holding that since the Punic garrison was there by their consent, they were at liberty to ask it or compel it to depart. The latter course was decided upon, and envoys were sent to Rome with the proposal. The Roman senators, who knew something of Sicily because of the Pyrrhic War, soon comprehended that the question might well be more complicated than it seemed. They probably did not suppose that Hiero would attack again, for he had been very friendly in 270 when he had offered the services of his fleet against Rhegium, and he had not only fought the Carthaginians in the days of Pyrrhus but had been grievously offended by the Carthaginian entry into Messana.

There was a reasonable possibility, however, that the Punic garrison would not depart at the request of the Mamertines or that it would receive orders from home to hold the fort at all costs. It is likely that the strongest deterrent in the minds of well-informed senators at Rome was the fear that acceptance would eventually result in a war with Carthage.

Polybius, who gives a good but brief account of this war, cannot be relied upon for a full expression of Roman views, for he had at hand in this portion of his history only the account of Fabius Pictor, who, half a century after the event, repeated some of the arguments of the nobles opposing the measure. According to this version the senators fully realized the importance of saving Messana from Carthaginian domination but were deterred by the moral consideration that the Mamertines were brigands whom it would be a disgrace to accept as allies. The reasons for agreeing to the alliance were indeed cogent. The time-honoured policy of Carthage had been to establish a *mare clausum* and a monopoly of trade wherever possible. Rome had good reason to know this, for she had been compelled in two treaties with Carthage to recognize the policy in Africa, southern Spain, and Sardinia. If such a monopoly had not as yet been established in the Punic cities of Sicily, it was wholly due to the fact that the land-routes of Sicily could not be controlled; it was apparent, however, that, the moment Carthage gained mastery of all Sicilian ports, the same embargo would be declared there as in Sardinia. To be sure, the senators were not directly interested in trade, but indirectly the question would soon concern the southern members of Rome's federation, since the closing of Sicilian ports to free trade would in time compel the Greek allies of the south, who were trading folk, to desire closer connections with Carthage in order to save their commerce with Sicily. While Punic vessels could enter their ports, they would be denied entry into Sicilian ports, and the resulting economic pressure might induce them to invite Punic garrisons into their cities and to revolt from Rome. Their disaffection would be enhanced by the presence of the Punic fleet in the straits, which could block them as effectively as it had the Straits of Gibraltar for two centuries. Even Rome's navy cruising to her southern and Adriatic ports might some day have to sail around the whole of Sicily in order to reach its destination. In fact it is difficult to see how the Senate could have hesitated, as we are told the Roman Senate did, on this occasion.

The moralistic argument against the alliance was probably not the most important objection. The Mamertines, in seizing Messana, had committed a crime which all their neighbours execrated, and Rome had punished with extreme severity its own Campanian troops who had similarly taken and sacked Rhegium. But the crime of Messana was now twenty-five years past, committed when Rome had no interest below Neapolis, and probably was not even reported at Rome; and the *status quo* at Messana had been recognized in treaties by Carthage and several Greek cities even in the days of Pyrrhus. That Hiero had withheld recognition was hardly due to a higher morality—since he had vaulted into power by an act no less questionable—but rather to an intention to enlarge his dominions northward. Ancient states were perhaps not quite as ready as modern ones to recognize statutes of limitations in international affairs, but much could be forgotten in one generation even then. Apparently Fabius Pictor, in reporting senatorial debates, enlarged upon an argument which, though not urged very seriously by wiser statesmen, seemed later to shield timidity and myopia under a cloak of respectability. Events had lost their relation in perspective and men no longer remembered that between 289 and 264 Rome had become a world-power and many wars had been fought.

The senators' aversion to the alliance could hardly be summed up in one sentence, for mixed motives were at work. They certainly remembered that a similar appeal from Thurii—granted by the assembly—had led to a perilous contest with Pyrrhus. In this new venture, if Carthage declared war, the struggle would probably be even more severe and prolonged, since Carthage was very rich and could presumably continue to hire mercenaries longer than Rome's recently enrolled allies would care to fight. Moreover, the war would be fought in Sicily or Africa and could hardly be determined without control of the seas: and Rome had not one battleship while Carthage kept a fleet of a hundred and twenty quinqueremes that scoured the western Mediterranean. Even if it were merely a question of Messana, Carthage might— granted that the Roman army could be ferried across the straits— blockade Messana by sea and land and starve it into disgraceful submission. If the war continued beyond Messana, Carthage with the control of the sea could bring reinforcements to the island at will, whereas Rome's army might be cut off by Punic cruisers in the straits. In case of even greater success Pyrrhus's failure to take the stronghold of Lilybaeum without a blockading fleet was not an encouraging object lesson. Certainly Rome was not ready for a contest with a great sea power.

It is also reasonable to suppose that the aversion of the old aristocratic clique to the policy of expansion which had not only strengthened the democratic assembly but had elevated a large number of war heroes into the Senate and consulship worked as a strong if tacit deterrent. Ever since the Caudine Forks the assembly had been able to exercise the ultimate right to ratify declarations of war and terms of peace. Moreover, twenty-three years before this time, the Hortensian law had been passed giving the plebeian assembly power not only to ratify, but to take the initiative and dispose of any business of state regardless of the Senate. The advance of the theory of popular sovereignty had been marked by the elevation into the senate of a number of new men like Curius, Fabricius, Decius, Marcius, Publilius, Junius, Fulvius, and Caecilius. A new war would inevitably raise a group of new officers and politicians who would impress the people as worthy of magistracies. After all, when war began, it was the senate which had to face the responsibility of directing the campaigns, providing the means, and taking the blame for mistaken policies while denied the ultimate decision if the people chose to interfere. It is therefore not difficult to comprehend why the senators were divided on the question.

Polybius does not say which assembly passed the measure, but since it was a tribune who had taken the initiative in the Thurian alliance and since Polybius' account implies that the Senate did not participate in the final decision, it is perhaps safe to assume that the democratic leaders who had elevated the plebeian assembly by means of the Hortensian law were still in political control. Polybius, in explaining the action of the assembly, says that the people had been wearied by recent wars and were convinced by the military leaders not only of the danger of having a Punic garrison near the straits but also of the advantages that would accrue to Roman citizens through the alliance, and that they therefore approved. What could these advantages have been? Presumably not those of a possible war, for they 'were weary of wars.' Nor were they looking for more land; there was public land in Etruria as well as the Ager Gallicus awaiting distribution, and every new colonization cheapened land values for the Roman voters. Nor is it plausible that the question of winning tribute from new possessions entered into the discussion. The Roman people had never exacted tribute from subjects, and any suggestion that Sicilian grain might after the war be brought to Rome to compete with their own in their only market—thirty-one of the thirty-five tribes were rural—would hardly have been greeted with applause.

At any rate the question before the assembly was not whether or not there should be a war, but whether or not there should be an alliance with Messana. If the people were war-weary, such an alliance could be advocated as an insurance against further wars, since it would prevent Carthage from gaining a bridgehead against Italy. Furthermore every new ally added strength to the federal forces, thereby lessening the quota of the citizen army. There can of course be little doubt that the officers who persuaded the people to vote entertained suspicions and hopes which they did not express. They must have seen the strategic importance of Messana and the necessity of blocking Punic advance; they probably also felt quite certain that war would result and presumably they were not wholly averse to it, since military glory and triumphs were prizes worth winning at Rome.

The Sicilian historian, Philinus, asserted that the alliance was a breach of an old treaty with Carthage which specifically denied Rome the right to enter Sicily, as it denied Carthage the right to enter Italy. Polybius (III, 26) explicitly denies the existence of such a treaty. Both historians are fairly trustworthy, but perhaps historical criticism is reasonable in holding to the principle that a correction after discussion and examination is to be given more weight as evidence than a simple statement. It would seem that Philinus had drawn hasty inferences from the treaty of Mago, which implied that the Carthaginian fleet might aid Rome against Pyrrhus without landing its crew, while if Rome's army aided Carthage in Sicily, transports should be provided for its return (see above, p. 649). The careful phrasing of those clauses seems to justify the inference that a mutual fear of permanent acquisitions was felt at the time and that provisions had been made against plausible pretexts for attempting to acquire territory, but Polybius is probably correct in saying that, so far as treaties were concerned, Rome broke no agreement in making an alliance with Messana.

After the assembly had voted to make the alliance, it devolved upon the Senate to take up the awkward task of carrying out its mandate. A consul must be sent to negotiate and he must have sufficient forces to give weight to his words. Much would depend upon the temper and tact of the consul. The lot ominously fell upon Appius Claudius, a cousin, it seems, of the blind censor who had supported the war party against Pyrrhus. Since it would take time to mobilize his two legions and to march four hundred miles to Rhegium, he designated a relative, C. Claudius, who was military tribune, to sail down to Messana at once with an expeditionary force in order, if possible, to announce Rome's decision and to garrison the town. The tribune found the straits patrolled by

Punic cruisers that tried to block his entry into the harbour. But he succeeded in making his way through them with but a slight loss of ships. It seems that the commander of the Punic fleet had orders to avoid open warfare, for he returned the captured ships with a warning that Carthage claimed these waters as *mare clausum*. The Mamertines, emboldened by the tribune's presence, now rid themselves of Hanno and his garrison by threats of force. Hanno, it appears, had received no command from his government to remain against the consent of Messana, and being a subordinate officer he dared not risk a hostile act. That he was more scrupulous than was desired he soon discovered when Carthage ordered his execution for betraying the state's interest. There are several instances on record where Punic officers lost their lives by guessing incorrectly in emergencies of this kind.

Carthage, learning what had happened—a few days would suffice for a message to reach Africa—determined if possible to recover Messana. An army was immediately sent to Sicily under the command of one of her most trusted generals, Hanno the son of Hannibal. Landing at Lilybaeum, he marched by way of Agrigentum (Acragas) where he made a firm alliance with the city and left a garrison. Then he came to an agreement with Hiero—he must have brought a treaty with liberal terms from home—and both marched upon Messana with their full forces. Hanno pitched his camp north-west of the city; Hiero encamped some distance away to the south. The two had been at enmity too long to begin to fraternize at once.

III. THE CROSSING TO SICILY: ALLIANCE WITH HIERO

Meanwhile Appius Claudius had arrived at the straits with his two legions. Transports were provided by Rhegium and the neighbouring *socii navales*. Had Hanno been ordered to prevent his crossing at all costs, he could probably have done so, but there had been no declaration of war as yet, and there was a possibility that even after the entry of Appius, Messana if carefully blockaded might be starved into a friendly attitude. Appius succeeded in getting his troops across by night, and having gained this advantage he began negotiations with both generals. To Hiero particularly he made friendly overtures assuring him that Rome desired to retain his goodwill. When negotiations failed—and a Claudius could not be expected to exert himself strenuously for peace—he attacked, choosing Hiero's camp first as being the weaker. The attack was not a complete success. Hiero saved his camp, but suspecting his ally of treachery in not patrolling the straits, having learned also of Rome's friendly instructions, and having experienced the force of the legionary attack, he withdrew that night to the hills and presently retreated to Syracuse. Claudius was somewhat weakened by his strenuous attack, but learning of Hiero's retreat he at once turned upon Hanno. Again he failed to reach his objective though he caused much damage to the enemy. Hanno at least concluded that, deserted by Hiero, he could not successfully invest Messana. Hence he too withdrew to find a safer and more favourable ground for the contest.

Claudius now marched southward, first storming Echetla, a fort not far from Leontini that marked the eastern limits of the Carthaginian empire. Taking this fort, he advanced directly upon Syracuse, hoping to intimidate Hiero into the desired alliance. An attack upon the splendid fortifications of Syracuse would hardly be feasible with his forces nor could a siege be profitable so long as the harbour was open. Since no offers came from Hiero he withdrew to Messana, and leaving his garrison there for his successor, he returned to Rome. Despite his vigour in relieving Messana he was strangely enough not granted a triumph and it was one of his successors who won the honorary cognomen of 'Messalla.' It is a conjecture—but a plausible one—that the Senate's displeasure was due to his failure to secure peace. Instead of an alliance to ensure the peace of Italy the senate had to face two wars on difficult ground with well-armed foes. Prospects seemed rather unpromising at Rome, and the people elected to the consulship men quite outside the Claudian circle, M' Valerius and M' Otacilius, a plebeian of Samnite stock. Of Appius Claudius Caudex, 'the log,' we hear no more.

In 263 both consuls were sent to Sicily with four legions and a full contingent of allies, probably 40,000 men all told. The situation was serious in the extreme. No definite policy regarding the future of Sicily seems however to have been shaped as yet. The immediate task of compelling the enemies to recognize the alliance and sign a peace agreement was enough. Hence no fleet was built; during the year pledges of freedom were given to several cities which left them for all time outside the federation, and the alliance with Hiero, when made, was for the brief term of fifteen years, a very unusual feature in Rome's treaties. We may safely infer that the Senate had not yet envisaged the conquest of Sicily, but we may be equally sure that the necessity of planting garrisons, consolidating gains and making agreements with Sicilian cities forced the question into prominence before the year was over.

The first task was to overcome Hiero. The consuls marched directly into Syracusan territory and stormed the frontier fort of Hadranum under Aetna. Quick success and a demonstration of force met with a speedy response. A large number of cities under Punic and Syracusan rule sent offers of submission, among them Halaesa, far off on the north coast, Centuripa, Catana and Tauromenium, cities circling Aetna. The first two became free cities. Tauromenium was presently given back to Syracuse, and Catana, whatever her status in 263 B.C., became after the war a tribute-paying city. Now the road lay open to Syracuse, which was at once invested and attacked. It is difficult to see how the Romans expected to take the city without control of the sea. But the memory of Hiero's faint-hearted retreat from Messana justified the attempt, and this calculation proved to be well-founded. Hiero in fact soon found that his subjects disliked fighting on the side of their secular enemy, and so he decided to secure as favourable terms as possible by negotiating quickly. It was agreed, subject to ratification by the assembly, that in return for an alliance of fifteen years and an indemnity of one hundred talents (twenty-five to be paid at once, the rest in fifteen instalments) Hiero should be recognized as king of Syracuse and of most of the territory which he had conquered during his brief reign. This was to include the cities of Megara, Leontini, Acrae, Neetum, and Helorum— a semi-circle about Syracuse with a radius of about thirty miles— and also Tauromenium which lay high on the plateau between Messana and Catana. The inclusion of this city implies that Rome had as yet not considered the question of holding Catana in the league. It seems that Hiero was not required to supply any ships during the war—naval warfare was not yet contemplated—and the grain which he sent from time to time was apparently purchased or given voluntarily. These terms were ratified by the Roman people, who were glad to have this enemy, who possessed much corn-land, converted to friendship.

To the Romans this seemed a great gain, but a more generous treaty would probably have been a good investment. Pyrrhus, for instance, who had proclaimed the 'liberation of the Greeks' as his programme, had been rewarded immediately by the submission of every city in which Greeks were a strong element of the population. In consequence his advance as far as Eryx had been a triumphal procession. Rome was still to find many friendly offers, since the free status of cities like Halaesa and Centuripa gave her a good name, she had not yet imposed tithes as was the custom of Carthage and Hiero, and her legions were kept under stricter discipline than were the unruly mercenaries of her foes. Nevertheless the treaty with Syracuse, the chief Greek city of Sicily, was proof that Rome had not come as liberator. The gates of Sicilian cities were not henceforth to swing open to the Romans with quite the same ease as before.

On his return home Valerius, though he had won no great victory on the field of battle, was granted a triumph by the senate 'over the Carthaginians and Hiero, king of the Sicilians' and was honoured with the cognomen 'Messalla.' So much more highly was his diplomatic victory valued by the Senate than Claudius' overhasty resort to arms. In addition he was permitted to have a wall of the senate-chamber painted with a battle-scene representing himself as a victorious hero. This was the first of the banal war-museum murals that Rome acquired, but far from the last. We may suppose that Valerius had been shown similar frescoes by Hiero at Syracuse, modelled upon the famous battle-scenes of Alexander the Great, and that the king provided the artist. In the succeeding years of this war, Hiero's beautiful city gave many a visiting Roman officer a lesson in art and manners, destined before long to transform Rome and its people.

Valerius left but two legions in Sicily over the winter, for the Senate had decided that, with one enemy disposed of, the difficulty of provisioning troops so far away from home demanded a reduction of forces. However, during the winter news reached Rome that Punic officers were vigorously recruiting mercenaries among the Celts and Ligurians of North Italy and that troops were concentrating at Agrigentum. Hence both the consuls of 262, L. Postumius and Q. Mamilius, the latter a plebeian of obscure family, were dispatched with about forty thousand men. Two old Hellenized cities under Punic rule, Segesta and Halicyae, sent them assurances of friendship. Segesta, as Vergil remembers, claimed descent from Aeneas' refugees, and since the Sicilian historian Timaeus had recently recorded the same pedigree for the Romans the envoys came with excellent recommendations, which flattered the Romans and won complete freedom for Segesta and new favours in succeeding years. Halicyae secured the same status. It looks as if the Senate had not yet formed a definite policy respecting Sicily.

IV. SIEGE OF AGRIGENTUM. THE NEW ROMAN FLEET

The Carthaginian general, Hannibal, had wisely decided to take his stand at Agrigentum. This city had a strong wall enclosing an area overlarge for its diminished population of 50,000 inhabitants. Greek though it was, its situation facing Africa had always invited Punic traders, and Carthaginian customs and cults had entered there as early as the days of Phalaris (vol. IV, p. 355). That Carthaginian relations were still very strong is proved by the stubbornness of its citizens in resisting the terrors of famine and fire during the siege. Hannibal was not ready to fight a pitched battle: the mercenaries being recruited in every land had not yet arrived, but at Agrigentum he could presumably hold Rome at bay till he was ready for battle. The consuls arrived about June, harvested the Agrigentine crops, though not without many costly skirmishes, and then began the siege. A double line of deep trenches was dug about the whole city to protect the besiegers from attacks from within and without—for the relieving forces were expected. After five months the city was near exhaustion, when Hanno at last arrived from Africa with a formidable army of 50,000 foot, 6000 horse and 60 elephants. His troops were, however, not yet trained, and consisted of incongruous masses of barbarians fighting for pay and caring little for success in a battle unless the goal were some city to plunder. Indeed Hanno very much desired more time, but distress signals from the city came more insistently day by day. He therefore seized the Roman base of supplies and blocked the roads so that the Romans also were reduced to low rations. It was Hiero who eventually ran the blockade and brought food to the Romans.

This double siege had continued for two months, when Hanno felt constrained to offer battle in order to relieve the city. He was defeated with heavy losses, escaping to Heraclea with less than half his army. For his failure he was deposed from his command and heavily fined. The Romans however had suffered so severely in the battle that they were unable to prevent the escape of Hannibal's garrison from the city. The day after their escape the Roman army entered, sacked the defenceless town and sold its inhabitants into slavery. This had been the time-honoured custom in Sicily after long sieges, among Greeks as well as Carthaginians, and most Sicilian cities had suffered similar experiences in the past; but since the Romans had hitherto made a distinction between Greek citizens and foreign garrisons, such an example of terror could hardly have been expected. The immediate effect was to frighten some wavering cities into acquiescence. Time, however, proved the act wholly imprudent. A stubborn hatred displaced goodwill, and henceforth Rome had to fight for every advance and guard her gains with wasteful garrisons. In fact the following year the Romans made no progress, though the Punic forces had been badly shattered, and the Punic fleet won several coast towns back to their old allegiance. The consuls who captured Agrigentum received no triumph on their return home.

When the capture of this city brought no confession of defeat and Carthage merely substituted a better general, Hamilcar, for Hanno, the Senate, as Polybius informs us, decided to master the whole of Sicily. In view of the situation, which the Senate now well comprehended, this decision could only mean that Rome had determined to rule subject peoples and therefore had frankly adopted from her foes the policy of imperialism from which Sicily had already suffered too severely. As we have seen, the army made no progress in 261, while the Carthaginians won back several cities. Their fleet even ravaged the coast of Italy. The senate accordingly—since Sicily was to be the prize—determined to build a fleet and clear the seas. Rome had as yet no war-vessels and it is not probable that any of her *socii navales* had ever owned a quinquereme, the standard battleship which had only recently been introduced into western waters and of which the Carthaginians had a great number. The Mediterranean is too tranquil for reliance upon sails, and since success in naval warfare depended largely upon driving force in ramming, three banks of oars did not provide adequate power against ships of five banks. As a model the Roman shipwrights took a Punic vessel which had grounded in the first skirmish of 264; not that Hiero might not have provided a model, but the Punic ships had been proved and tested by the most expert seamen of that day and were presumably the best. A hundred quinqueremes and twenty triremes were ordered to be ready in two months. Doubtless hulls were laid down at Ostia, Antium, Naples, and some of the seaports of south Italy. Simultaneously more than 30,000 rowers had to be found and trained. Rowing in quinqueremes required much skill. Some of these men could be provided by the *socii navales*, but most of them seem to have been hardy Italian peasants, and these had to be given a hurried training in skeleton ship-frames fitted with benches. There was another serious difficulty in that sea-captains skilled in the rapid manœuvring of ships in battle were not to be found, and Roman legionaries could not well be turned into marines overnight. To give the soldiers some semblance of a land battle, long cranes were fitted with grappling spikes that could be swung and dropped on the enemy's deck so as to pin the ship fast and hold it while the marines boarded and cleared it. This device, called a 'raven' in soldier slang, was probably supplied by some of Hiero's shipwrights, for it had been used at Syracuse by the ill-starred Athenian expedition in the days of the Peloponnesian War (vol. v, p. 307).

In the spring Cornelius Scipio sailed southward with the lumbering fleet while Duillius, the other consul, took charge of land operations. At Messana Scipio, hearing that the city of Lipara was disposed to join the Romans, sailed off with twelve ships to negotiate for its surrender. While he was anchored there, a small Punic fleet arrived and captured the consul and his squadron. Cornelius, who seems at this time to have received the appropriate cognomen of Asina, was taken to Carthage as prisoner. The other consul, Duillius, now took command of the fleet and sailed to encounter the enemy who were harassing the coast near Mylae. The Carthaginian admiral Hannibal, superior in strength by nearly thirty ships, and having experienced crews, expected an easy victory, but to his surprise the cranes dropped and held his ships fast at the first onset. The Romans swept the decks and disposed of more than fifty ships. The rest fled in dismay. Duillius at once sailed westward and landed in time to relieve Segesta which was being besieged by Hamilcar and in the last stage of distress. At the news of the naval victory the joy at Rome was unbounded. In the Forum a column of victory was raised to Duillius bearing rams of captured vessels and a fulsome inscription with all the honours voted the successful general. The still existing fragment of a copy of this inscription is now in the Capitoline Museum. It records how Duillius was the first Roman to fight on the high seas and how he conquered in battle the whole Punic fleet commanded by Hannibal the dictator, capturing with their crews one septireme and thirty quinqueremes and triremes and sinking many more. The un-Roman rhetoric of the elaborate phrasing is another evidence of the fact that the consuls campaigning in Sicily were successfully learning the manners and customs of the Greeks.

The Punic fleet, however, was not yet wholly destroyed and Rome did not have the courage to attack Africa. Hence, while one of the consuls of 259, Aquilius Florus, went to Sicily to watch Hamilcar, Cornelius Scipio, a brother of Asina, sailed for Corsica and Sardinia, whither Hannibal had gone presumably to organize raids against the Italian coast. After taking Aleria in Corsica, as his epitaph records, he made for Olbia, the northernmost Punic port of Sardinia, but dared not engage the enemy who was now reinforced. It was his successor of the next year, Sulpicius, who, apparently possessing a stronger force, again assayed a naval battle. Hannibal was forced to beach his ships and abandon them; and his men, disgusted with his futile leadership, crucified him.

Meanwhile in Sicily Hamilcar was proving himself a more worthy opponent. In 259 he won at Thermae the first battle to the credit of Punic arms against the Romans, and advancing eastward rapidly he seized the strong hill town of Enna in the centre of the island and got possession of Camarina far to the south-east. The Punic advance was so threatening that Aquilius Florus had to remain in Sicily during the winter to strengthen Roman garrisons and counteract the diplomacy of the shrewd enemy. Since the situation was perilous, and one consul was now in command of the fleet, Aquilius continued in command of his troops as proconsul while the consul of 258, Atilius Calatinus, brought up new forces. Acting together, the two drove Hamilcar back toward his base at Panormus (Palermo), offering battle which he dared not accept, and now stormed Mytistratus, the Punic stronghold of the central road, which had resisted a seven months siege after the fall of Agrigentum. The walls of the city were destroyed and the inhabitants sold into slavery. After these Roman successes Hamilcar was confined behind a line running from Heraclea to Panormus and the Romans found it possible to eject most of the Punic garrisons east of it. Enna gave in quickly; Camarina was stormed and severely punished.

The year 257, the eighth of the war, began with the assurance that the situation was in hand, but that was all. In Sicily the line had not advanced far beyond Agrigentum and it required a consular and proconsular army, some 50,000 men, to keep Hamilcar in check. To advance farther meant attacking difficult positions like Panormus and Lilybaeum. As for the navy, it had destroyed the Punic fleet which operated from Sardinia, but it had not been able to land enough marines to take possession of Sardinia, and, important as the possession of that island seemed, Rome had for the present to leave it in Punic hands. During the year Cornelius Blasio in Sicily had the aid of the preceding consul, now proconsul, but made no progress. However, the other consul, C. Atilius Regulus, who had command of the fleet, made a dash upon Melita, devastated the island and gathered much booty. He seems to have been training his crews and marines for the more daring enterprise of the coming year. Returning to Sicily he found the refitted Punic fleet off Tyndaris, and sinking eighteen ships came off with enough success to win a triumph. This was Rome's third naval victory. Indeed one of the surprises of this war was that the Romans, who knew nothing of seamanship before it and were wholly helpless before storms, won six of its seven naval battles, and did so against a naval power that had controlled the western Mediterranean for centuries.

V. REGULUS IN AFRICA

Now that the sea had lost its terrors, it was decided to invade Africa and thus withdraw the enemy from Sicily and if possible compel the Punic government to make peace. The Punic fleet had had less than a hundred ships at the last encounter, but it was probably known that Carthage was building new quinqueremes in haste. To meet a possible fleet of two hundred or more successfully and at the same time to provide a convoy for the transports that were to carry 500 horse and an army's food-supplies for a winter would require a navy such as Rome had never heard of. Polybius puts the Roman fleet at 330 ships. If his number is correct, we may assume that it included about 250 battleships, largely quinqueremes, and about eighty transports. These war vessels were of course not very large, being made to carry little except the 300 rowers and 120 marines, but they had to be built strong and firm to withstand the impact of ramming ships. To hold 300 oarsmen on five banks the vessel must be over 150 feet long and have at least five feet of freeboard. The beam was as narrow as was consistent with safety, probably not over 30 feet. The cost of such a fleet can hardly be estimated, but the drain on the slender public purse of that day can be imagined when we know that the oars alone cost more than a million sesterces. A hundred thousand men drawn largely from the Italian allies and the Roman proletariat would barely suffice for the crews, while the 250 battleships required at least 25,000 marines. The soldiers who were to remain in Africa, 15,000 in number, doubtless served as marines during the crossing. The Punic fleet though not encumbered with transports was about as strong in battleships. There is no doubt that both sides had withdrawn part of their forces from Sicily to man these enormous fleets and that the rest were entrenched where they were to await the contest on the sea and in Africa.

In the summer of 256 the Romans sailed southward under the command of L. Manlius Vulso and M. Atilius Regulus who had succeeded his relative, C. Atilius. Off Cape Ecnomus on the southern coast of Sicily they met the Punic fleet under Hamilcar and Hanno whom they had faced before at Agrigentum. The Romans advanced in wedge formation, protecting the transports at the base of the triangle by a covering line of battleships behind. They readily broke through the Punic line which stood only one ship deep, with the result, however, that as they moved on they were completely surrounded on all sides by the lithely manœuvred

ships of the enemy. However, in the battle which followed, ship
by ship, the Romans again used the 'ravens,' grappling and
boarding as at Mylae. Then, driving the Carthaginian right wing
off in flight, they penned up the left wing against the shore and
took fifty ships, having sunk thirty others. The Roman loss was
twenty-four sunk. The victors mended their ships, which consumed much time, added the fifty captured ones to their fleet and
sailed on to Africa. The Carthaginians who had escaped with
some 170 ships, repaired home to defend their capital.

The Romans disembarked at the nearest landing point, Aspis
(Roman Clupea), about three or four days' march from Carthage,
stormed the town and devastated the Punic estates of the region
while waiting for further orders from the senate. Repairing
damages had taken time, and, with a large force in Carthage,
which was well fortified, any attempt to storm the city before
winter was not possible. Furthermore the region of Aspis was
hardly a suitable place in which to provision 100,000 rowers and
numerous prisoners during the winter, and the convoy would be
needed at Rome to carry men and provisions in the spring. The
Senate, therefore, ordered one consul to remain with 15,000 men
and his cavalry force of 500, retaining also forty ships as a safeguard in case of disaster. The rest were ordered to return. Doubtless the returning fleet carried a goodly force of fighting men
against a possible sally of the Punic fleet from Carthage. It was
Regulus to whom fell the lot to remain. The Carthaginian generals
chosen for the defence of the city were Hamilcar, who came from
Sicily with another 5000 men, Hasdrubal and Bostar.

At this time the territory of Carthage was not large. It probably
did not extend farther westward than Dougga nor beyond Zag-
houan southward. Her great strength lay in her commerce at her
African trading posts and in her tribute-paying subject allies,
many of whom had territories fully as large as her own. On the
north were Utica and Hippo, while on the Libyphoenician coast
lay the thriving cities of Hadrumetum, Leptis Minor and Acholla,
and farther off on the Tripolitan coast were Sabratha, Oea, and
Leptis Magna. The last named[1], for instance, paid Carthage a
daily revenue of one talent not long after this war. Had these
cities been severed from Carthage and assured independence and
immunity (and they were too heavily taxed to be loyal) Carthage
would have suffered severely in revenue and in naval supplies.
Furthermore Punic landlords had for some time been acquiring

[1] Livy, xxxiv, 62, 3, may however mean the Tripolitan district of which
Leptis was the chief city.

lands and estates far up along the Bagradas valley in Numidia, so that a prudent general might have done much to cripple Punic resources by offering protection to the Numidian tribes that were eager to regain their possessions. It is apparent, therefore, that the campaign was well planned in that the Roman forces were landed between Carthage and the richest subject cities, and advanced upon Carthage from the rear (see map 8, facing p. 617).

Regulus at once marched toward Carthage but found his way blocked at Adys (Uthina). While he was besieging the city the Carthaginian army marched up to its relief. With their vast superiority in available forces and especially in cavalry and a large array of elephants—they had the marines of two hundred ships and five thousand veterans besides the manhood of Carthage—it would obviously have been wise for them to await the Romans and offer battle in the plains. But eager to relieve Adys, where many of their wealthy citizens had their homes, they advanced into the hills. As a result Regulus was able to strike at them on unfavourable ground. He defeated them with ease, capturing their camp. The remnants withdrew toward Carthage while Regulus marched on unhindered to Tunis where he pitched his camp for the winter.

Oversanguine because of his two victories, Regulus completely neglected his opportunities. The Numidians, oppressed by heavy tribute, were only too glad to revolt at his approach and they so devastated the Carthaginian plains that the city suffered much from lack of food. Yet Regulus made no effort to enlist them, though he had but 500 horse, and cavalry was indispensable in flanking movements, since the strong Punic line of elephants was sure, if well directed, to break the force of the attacking legions. So hopeful was he of completing his task before the spring, when new consuls would come to succeed him, that he announced his readiness to receive offers of peace. Carthage gladly took up negotiations, but found the Roman terms too severe. The late historian, Dio Cassius—never very trustworthy for the history of the Republic —gives what he calls the items of Regulus' demands. These terms seem preposterous since they include not only the surrender of Sicily and Sardinia, an annual tribute besides full indemnity for the cost of the war, but also a complete surrender of sovereignty. It is difficult to believe that any Roman could ask Carthage to accept a position far inferior to that of Tarentum. However, all the actions of Regulus show that he had little comprehension of the situation in Africa, and Dio's account may be correct, and, as such, a fair commentary on the consul's stupidity. Had he invited the co-operation of the Africans and then asked for a light indemnity and the surrender of Sicily and Sardinia, he might have succeeded and ended the war. Carthage had just lost two disastrous battles and was suffering severely from Numidian incursions.

At this juncture a troop of Spartan mercenaries arrived at Carthage, and with them an officer, Xanthippus, who proved to be a good drill-master. By his convincing bearing, his engaging qualities, and his thorough knowledge of tactics he inspired confidence and was given a high position at headquarters. In a short time he re-organized the Punic army and led it out on the plains of the Bagradas before Regulus could advance from winter quarters to invest the city. Xanthippus, having formed his men in solid phalanxes, according to the best Greek tactics, placed a hundred elephants in front of them and four thousand horse on the wings. Regulus, fearing the elephants, likewise massed his maniples many lines deep, but this only made them the easier victims of the trampling feet. Had he read the tacticians he might well have drawn thinner lines, as Scipio did later at Zama, thus enabling him to open lanes through which to drive the beasts to the rear. As it was, the elephants ploughed into his massed men, broke the lines and left them an easy prey to the oncoming phalanx. Meanwhile the strong Punic cavalry had cleared both wings and circled in on the rear. Only two thousand Romans escaped to Aspis. Regulus and five hundred men were captured. The rest were dead.

But this was only the beginning of Rome's disasters. The fugitives at Aspis held out successfully against attack but dared not sail off for fear of the Punic navy. Meanwhile at Rome a splendid fleet of 350 ships had been fitted out for the purpose of dispersing the Carthaginian fleet and blockading the city's harbour while Regulus besieged it by land. Though the news of the consul's disaster probably reached Rome before the fleet sailed, orders to proceed were nevertheless given. The investment of Carthage would have to be postponed, but the Punic navy must if possible be destroyed and the stragglers must be rescued. The consuls of the year, Aemilius Paullus and Servius Fulvius, were in command. They found the Punic fleet, recently enlarged, awaiting them off the Hermaean promontory not far from Aspis, but defeated it with ease, taking 24 ships[1] with their crews, an exploit for which both consuls were voted triumphs and one at least a *columna rostrata* like that of Duillius. Embarking the refugees at Aspis, they sailed directly for home, skirting the dangerous southern coast of Sicily, since the enemy was still in

[1] Diodorus, XXIII, 18. Polybius says 114, but since the Romans had 364, including the captured ships at Pachynus, he is probably in error.

command of most of the harbours of the west and north. Off Camarina, however, a terrific gale dashed them against the rocks scattering wreckage and corpses as far as Cape Pachynus. Of the 364 ships only 80 weathered the storm. Polybius knew of no greater calamity at sea. If the crews perished with the ships—and those rescued could not have been many—we must assume a probable loss of about 25,000 marines and 70,000 rowers; and since free men were then generally used as rowers it would appear that nearly fifteen per cent. of Italy's able-bodied men went down in that disaster.

The Romans set their teeth, raised their taxes, ordered two hundred new quinqueremes to be ready in three months and somehow found 80,000 men for the naval campaign of 254. And such things were done by a state whose census of citizens, including the unfranchised class, fell below 300,000. The two consuls who had fought so well at the Hermaean promontory were not blamed for the loss of the fleet but were kept with the navy for another year. Perhaps it was assumed that they at least had acquired some knowledge of seamanship.

Carthage had cause to rejoice at this turn of fortune, but was still far from victorious. Hamilcar had to employ a considerable force that year in punishing the revolting Numidians, and it required more time to rebuild a fleet at Carthage than at Rome. Hasdrubal, to be sure, was sent to Sicily with a large herd of elephants since these had proved so effective against the Romans before Tunis, but there was little use in risking an open battle while the best troops were operating in Numidia. Hence Carthalo, who had chief command in Sicily, generally kept on the defensive, taking the aggressive once only to make a dash upon the ill-starred city of Agrigentum, which he captured and burned to the ground. The Romans succeeded better. With a formidable fleet on the seas and considerable land forces the two new consuls, Atilius Calatinus, who was now re-elected, and Cornelius Asina, who had been ransomed and somehow regained his reputation, aided by the two experienced ex-consuls, dashed upon Panormus which had long been the Punic headquarters in Sicily, invested it by sea and land, and after a series of tireless attacks took the city. Such of the inhabitants of the inner city as could produce two hundred drachmas each were permitted to redeem themselves at that price. Thirteen thousand who could not, presumably slaves, were carried off as captives. Panormus became one of Rome's chief army posts during the rest of the war, and after the war was given independence and immunity from obligations. This fact would seem to indicate that a large part of the inhabitants had co-operated with the Romans.

This success was of far-reaching importance. Cities like Tyndaris which had long before desired to revolt to Rome had not dared to do so because the Carthaginians had taken hostages from them. In the loss of Panormus these hostages seem to have gained their liberty. At any rate, Tyndaris, Solus, Petra, and several other towns immediately rid themselves of their Punic garrisons and joined Rome.

The Punic possessions in Sicily were now restricted to a few coast cities of the east: Heraclea, Selinus, Lilybaeum and Drepana, with Thermae on the north isolated and of little use. To besiege these places might take years of costly effort, so it was again decided to strike into Africa, if only to entice the natives to revolt and to cut into the Carthaginian revenues. The new consuls of 253, Servilius and Sempronius, accordingly sailed for Africa, aiming not directly at Carthage but at the rich Libyan cities of Tripolis. However, through lack of knowledge of the coast, a number of ships stranded on the shallows in the Syrtes and the venture was given up. In making for Italy the fleet was wrecked by a storm off Cape Palinurus with another loss of 150 ships and a large part of their men.

VI. STALEMATE BY LAND AND SEA

The Senate was discouraged. The navy, though successful in nearly every battle, seemed helpless before the wind. It was decided to revert to the slower and safer method of tiring out the enemy in Sicily, though the process must be tedious, for the troops refused to face the elephants and a siege of the ports was hopeless without a fleet. Accordingly during the next two years nothing was accomplished except the capture of the unimportant town of Thermae.

But early in 250 Hasdrubal took the aggressive. Knowing that the Romans were exchanging forces and that the new consuls had not yet arrived, he marched upon Panormus and tried to draw the retiring consul Caecilius Metellus out to battle. Caecilius, however, warily dug his trenches near the city walls, and refused to be enticed beyond them. Finally, by a show of timidity which was real enough, he lured the attacking party, led by the charging elephants, up to the very trenches, where the beasts became confused and turned on their own men. A quick sally on Hasdrubal's flank succeeded. The Carthaginians were routed, leaving sixty elephants with not a few of their Indian mahouts for the Romans to send home to amuse the public. Hasdrubal's army was nearly destroyed and what was more important the dreaded elephants had lost their power of terrifying. Hasdrubal was recalled and put to death, and Adherbal sent out in his place. Finding it inconvenient to garrison the low-lying Selinus, the Carthaginians now moved its inhabitants to Lilybaeum, and destroyed its dwellings and walls. The imposing temples were plundered and left standing in desolation to await the earthquakes that finally shattered them.

The new consuls of 250 were both tried men, C. Atilius and Manlius Vulso. They advanced on Lilybaeum to attempt finally the assault of the chief port of the enemy, and for this purpose they also brought a new fleet of 240 warships that had been built at leisure. With their four legions, marines, and crews, they had at least 100,000 men. Within the walls were the inhabitants of Lilybaeum and of Selinus, a mercenary garrison of 10,000 Gauls and Greeks, and another 10,000 recruits brought from Africa. At Drepana Adherbal had a considerable fleet which was not yet ready for battle but which aided the city by skilful blockade-running. The Romans put into service all the arts of siege which they had learned from the Sicilians: building walls and equipping them with stockades and battering-rams, constructing moving towers filled with soldiers and catapults to be raised by inclined viaducts up to the city walls, driving mines deep under the ramparts till they were stopped by countermining from within. To block the harbour they would fill boats with rocks and sink them in the channel. But despite months of most strenuous efforts the besieged always raised new walls as the old ones fell and finally on a stormy day succeeded in burning down most of the siege-works. The Romans then had to dig themselves in and wait. Lilybaeum withstood the siege to the very end of the war, eight years later.

The new consuls of 249, P. Claudius Pulcher and L. Junius Pullus, came with orders to drive hard. Claudius, impatient for results, secretly led off his best soldiers and manned the ships hoping to surprise the Punic navy under Adherbal at Drepana. But in his haste he let his ships get caught in confusion at the mouth of the harbour. Nearly a hundred ships were lost. Fortunately they were so near the beach that the loss of men was not quite in proportion, but twenty thousand were among the missing. Despite all its losses by storm at sea, this was in fact the only serious defeat the Roman navy sustained during the war. By this time the Romans had learned certain Punic customs: they recalled Claudius and condemned him to pay a fine of 12,000 denarii.

Junius fared even worse. It was his task to carry supplies

to Lilybaeum, for the siege promised to be long, the number of men engaged was very large, and food could not be requisitioned in Sicily except at high prices without endangering good relations. Junius had been given 120 fully-manned ships with which to convoy his 800 transports. Not knowing of the disaster at Drepana and wishing to make haste, he sent a part of his convoy ahead under his quaestor. Adherbal, learning of their approach, sent Carthalo with a large fleet to meet them. This skilful admiral encountered the first division near Phintias and forced them to anchor with considerable loss near the rough coast, then proceeding to meet the second division he drove them likewise to seek refuge. Then as a storm was approaching he put out into deeper water and rounded Pachynus in safety while the winds and waves completely shattered the whole Roman convoy. Again Rome was without a navy and the year had cost her almost as much as the disasters of 254. The Senate had to establish a caravan of wagons and pack animals to haul food the whole length of Sicily to the hungry army besieging Lilybaeum.

Junius reached Lilybaeum with only two ships, but set out at once to retrieve his honour. There was naturally no use in trying to take the city without ships to block the harbour, and half his force would suffice to carry on the siege by land. With the rest he marched upon Drepana, and taking possession of Mt Eryx behind the city he cut all the roads from Drepana, so that the troublesome Punic cavalry might be restrained from devastating the open country. And now at least the two ports that Carthage still possessed on the island were closed off from the rest of Sicily. The venture was wise, but Junius was presently captured in a sally, and a dictator was named at Rome to complete the work of this disastrous year. Junius later returned to Rome apparently by the exchange of prisoners carried out two years later, and to escape the condemnation that had befallen his colleague he committed suicide.

Rome was near bankruptcy and exhaustion. The census of 247 B.C. shows that during the twenty years just passed the citizen list had fallen 50,000, or seventeen per cent., instead of rising some twenty per cent., the normal increase to be expected in peace times. The allied states had of course suffered equally. Taxes had reached the limit of endurance and it was impossible to find money with which to build new ships. And there was danger that if a call were issued for new crews the allies might be driven to revolt. They had discovered that the casualties of the new crews were even higher than those of the legions and that the apparently simple task of sitting on protected benches, *sedantes atque sudantes*, as Naevius says, might prove very perilous under the command of unpractised Roman admirals. Already at least five hundred fully manned vessels of war and a thousand transports had gone down. At this juncture the Romans might have been expected to ask for terms of peace, but the old tradition, recalled by the blind Appius Claudius, still held firmly: Rome negotiated only after victories. But that the people were determined to have a breathing space is clear from their re-electing to the consulship for the year 248 the slow-goers of 252, C. Aurelius and P. Servilius. Nothing was expected of these men but that they should hold the line with as few losses as possible, and this is all they did.

Nor were the Carthaginians active during the year except for some feeble raids by Carthalo along the Italian coast. The explanation lies perhaps in a temporary party change at Carthage, for during this year we hear that Hanno 'the Great,' who later appears repeatedly as an opponent of the Barcids, was operating far inland in Numidia, and that he captured Theveste, the farthest point to which Punic conquests ever extended in Africa. In later history this Hanno seems to represent the landed nobility of Carthage, who were more interested in exploiting an African agrarian empire than in foreign conquests which benefited the mercantile classes at the price of high taxes on land (p. 666). If this be the explanation, we can understand why at this time the Punic fleet did not take advantage of its control of the seas.

It was apparently at this turn of events that Carthage sent a commission to Rome to offer an exchange of prisoners and if possible open negotiations for peace. Rome had the advantage in the number of captives, and for the excess Carthage offered to pay a ransom. According to Sempronius Tuditanus, who seems wholly trustworthy, the prisoner Regulus was sent with the commission in the hope that he would plead for the exchange. The story—which inspired Horace's stirring ode—goes on to relate how Regulus refused to urge the exchange since it would weaken the morale of the Roman army, and for this action he was somehow brought to his death. From Punic sources we have some confirmation of the tale, for Diodorus reveals the fact that Regulus died in captivity 'from neglect' before the exchange could be effected, and that his wife upon hearing of this avenged her wrath upon Bodostar, a Punic hostage at Rome[1]. The incident is at least significant of a desire for peace on the part of a strong group within the Punic government.

[1] See *Class. Phil.* 1926, p. 311.

This is also the year in which Hiero's treaty with Rome expired. The King had been a loyal friend, had frequently harboured Rome's shattered ships in his great port, and had helped the armies with grain on at least two occasions when rations were running low. A treaty of friendship for all time was now offered him, and since the first indemnity which had been collected in instalments had now been fully paid, he was henceforth free from all burdens. It is also probable that some territory was added to his kingdom, since we find later that Herbessus belonged to him and that he colonized and erected public buildings at Agyrium. It would seem that he now possessed at least a fourth of Sicily and that the richest part. He spent the rest of his life—more than thirty years—in furthering commerce, agriculture, and the arts. That he comprehended the full meaning of the *pax Romana* is evident from his subsequent gift of all his machines of war to the island of Rhodes.

In 247 Carthage, eager for a more effective campaign, chose as general Hamilcar Barca, a young man of vigour, daring and some ingenuity. He refused to waste his time in resisting the besieging armies at the two ports, attempting rather to work from the rear of the enemy. An attack on Locri in Italy failed except for the damage caused by a raiding party through the fields of the region. Rome refused however to be drawn off from her grip on western Sicily. Italian towns were left to the protection of their own garrisons, and new colonies were planted along the coast: first Alsium, a small citizen garrison below Caere, and soon after Fregenae, between Alsium and Ostia. These were doubtless placed here in order to prevent the enemy from landing troops within striking distance of Rome. Then in 246 a Latin colony was placed at the port of Brundisium in case Hamilcar should succeed in taking the Greek ports of the south.

Hamilcar failing in his attacks upon Italy and having no Punic harbours left in Sicily that gave free access to the country, effected a landing west of Panormus, seized the mountains behind the city (whether the towering Mte Pellegrino or Mte Billiemi to the west represents the ancient Heirkte, is not known), whence he could threaten the besieging armies in the rear and possibly draw off Roman forces to the defence of Panormus as well. While the site was being fortified and a harbour built for his fleet, he made new raids upon the Italian coast as far as Cumae. The Romans continued to elect inexperienced men who spent the year learning the art of war only to be replaced as soon as they had acquired the elements. No new navy was built, but letters of marque were

issued to those who cared to venture out as privateers in the few
war vessels remaining, and indeed one raid upon Hippo (Bizerta)
resulted in the capture of considerable booty.

VII. THE FINAL EFFORT

In 244 since Hamilcar had not succeeded by raids or threats
in drawing off the Roman besieging parties, he drove a wedge
between Drepana and the fort of Mt Eryx, hoping to lock in the
besiegers and if possible cut off their supplies. He got possession
of the mountain without, however, driving away the besiegers;
and Rome, convinced now that Hamilcar was too good a soldier to
outwit on land, decided once more to subdue the Carthaginian
fleet so as to make the blockade of the ports effective. Unfortunately there was no money in the treasury and taxes could not be
raised to a higher rate. Hence it was decided that the wealthier
men of the state should make the necessary contributions in proportion to their wealth with the understanding that if Rome were
victorious the moneys advanced should be paid back. Since the
Senate adopted the measure and the members of the Senate were
doubtless those upon whom the burden fell heaviest, one ought
perhaps to say that the senators imposed upon themselves a heavy
loan repayable in case of victory. It seems to be the only instance of
this kind of government loan in Roman history, though crews of
rowers were secured by a similar scheme in the Second Punic War.

The fleet thus built consisted of some two hundred war vessels
with a large number of transports to carry supplies to the army.
For this navy, since former ones had suffered so severely from
storms, a new type of vessel was chosen, modelled on a light and
swift blockade-runner which had been captured at Lilybaeum a
few years before.

In the summer of 242 Lutatius Catulus sailed with the fleet to
Drepana. Strange though it seems, the great Carthaginian fleet
was not there to meet him. It was lying idle at home. Polybius
holds that the Carthaginians did not think that the Romans would
contest the seas again and therefore did not keep their warships
manned. Perhaps this is true, but it does not explain why no one
had discovered that Rome was rebuilding a fleet, nor why the
ships were not anchored within reach of Hamilcar. When the
Carthaginian fleet finally arrived it was badly undermanned
with raw recruits, for it had been planned that Hamilcar and his
soldiers should be taken on board before the battle. All this one
can explain only on the supposition that the party in control at
home had ceased to give hearty support to the army and was throw-

ing the burden of the war upon Hamilcar and his mercenary troops. No fleet appeared that autumn or winter, and the Punic garrisons in Sicily were reduced to very low rations. In March 241, finally, Hanno was sent with supply-transports convoyed by the full Punic navy. Catulus was awaiting his approach at the Aegates islands. When the enemy convoy approached he drew up his line across their course in front of the harbour of Drepana, ready for battle though an unfavourable gale was blowing against him. The battle was brief and decisive. The Romans took seventy ships and sank fifty more. Hanno escaped, but was, of course, crucified. The starving garrisons of the enemy were now at Rome's mercy, for they could not last out till another fleet was built.

Carthage gave Hamilcar full powers to end the war on the best terms he could secure. He had the good fortune of dealing with a consul far more intelligent than Regulus, and though the negotiations were protracted—Hamilcar absolutely refused to surrender deserters—it was finally agreed, subject to ratification by the Roman people, that friendship should be established on these terms: the Carthaginians were to evacuate Sicily, to give up all prisoners without ransom, and to pay in twenty annual instalments the sum of 2200 talents; the allies of both parties were to be secure from attack by the other, neither party was to impose contributions or enrol soldiers in the dominions of the other nor to form alliances with the allies of the other. In other words, Rome would receive about enough by way of indemnity to pay the cost of Lutatius' fleet, and in addition the surrender of the two garrisons that were near the starving point. The Roman people were naturally dissatisfied and decided to send a committee of ten to secure more favourable terms. The commissioners went to Sicily and entered into negotiations, but were themselves convinced that Hamilcar was a man of determination who would prolong the war if need be. They succeeded in adding a thousand talents to the indemnity, apparently in cash so as to make some immediate payment to those who had built the fleet on credit; they also reduced the term of the payments to ten years. This Hamilcar could readily grant, for even then the annual payments would be more than covered by the revenues which Carthage drew from her subjects in Tripolis alone. As for the rest, the commissioners added some clauses to the treaty which laid no burden upon Carthage not already implied in the terms but which would do something to satisfy the Romans, namely that the islands between Sicily and Italy (the Lipari, already in Roman hands) should belong to Rome, that Punic war-vessels should not sail in Italian waters, and that Carthage should not recruit mercenaries in Italy. These terms the Roman people accepted, and the First Punic War came to an end.

This war had lasted long enough to test the staying powers of both combatants and to reveal the strength and weakness of both. In strategic skill and intelligence there proved to be no great difference between them—it discovered no great general on either side—but the resources of the two powers differed in that Carthage matched her great wealth against Rome's superiority in men. Carthage might have been expected to produce superior generals, since her constitution permitted long terms in the supreme command whereas Rome's did not, and Punic officers had learned the art of war in Sicily where the best tactics of the Aegean world were known, while the Romans had shaped their army and strategy in warfare with inexpert Italian country folk. During the war the Punic generals displayed no little ingenuity in defending besieged cities, but they failed to plan far-reaching campaigns, to build up an effective striking force, to reveal any notable capacity for strategy, and indeed to win the loyalty and confidence of their troops.

They were, to be sure, severely hampered by having to operate with mercenary troops. Carthage, though rich in subject-allies, had chosen to exact from them a heavy tribute in gold rather than, like Rome, to retain them as autonomous partners capable of contributing men to a common army. And her citizens had long since decided to relieve themselves of military burdens by hiring mercenaries by means of the tribute derived from subject cities. Only once during the war, when Regulus threatened the walls of Carthage, were the citizens mustered for service, and that time, skilfully drilled by the Spartan Xanthippus, they acquitted themselves well; but as soon as the immediate danger to the city was over they returned to civil life. The mercenaries of Spain, Liguria, Gaul and Greece, good fighters though they were, proved inconstant and untrustworthy under their command. We constantly hear of large bodies of two or three thousand men deserting to the enemy at critical moments. Hannibal's later success with similar material proves that this need not have been if the generals had won the confidence of their men as Hannibal did. It is a significant fact that the Punic forces won no important engagement in the open field during the twenty-four years of this war except on the plains before Carthage. Near the end Hamilcar acquired a striking reputation by his dogged resistance, but even he did not trust himself to take a bold offensive and carry the war back to central or eastern Sicily. To be sure, he arrived too late, and his government did not give him wholehearted support, but the fact that he also suffered severely from the desertion of troops would seem to indicate a lack of the qualities essential in a great general.

The failure of the Carthaginian navy is equally surprising. With the strongest fleet on the seas, and with naval experience gained through centuries, the Carthaginian admirals lost six out of seven of the naval battles, despite the fact that the Romans had never possessed a quinquereme before this time, and very few Romans had ever set foot on shipboard. Roman success is not here to be attributed to the use of borrowed Greek sailors. Rome with characteristic caution had refused to trust the recently acquired *socii navales* or to impose upon them the burden of providing ships. In fact the treaties signed with them at a time when the Romans had not yet thought of a navy required so small a contribution of ships that their contingents were almost negligible. The helplessness of the Roman pilots whenever a storm arose is evidence enough that experienced Greeks were not being employed, and that the silence of Polybius regarding Greek aid is sincere. The fleets were built, manned, and officered by Romans. But, as Polybius makes evident, the victories were not won by skilful manœuvring or brilliant generalship but by dogged determination on the consuls' part and splendid courage on the part of the soldiers who served as marines—not to mention the advantage derived from the unwisdom of Punic generals and the timidity of their hired crews.

Roman generalship seldom proved more capable than that of the Carthaginians. The war on land as well as on the sea was of a kind new to the Romans, and the consuls did not remain in office long enough to learn how to cope with the problems presented by it. The manipular legion, weak in cavalry, trained only for straightforward fighting, untaught in the strategy of surprise and flank movements, was not well adapted to meet the phalanx, the mass of elephants and the strong troops of Numidian horse. Yet we hear of no serious attempt to alter or adapt the tactics of the army. That so few of the consuls met defeat is surprising. For what they lacked in experience and intuition they seem to have compensated by determination and courage. The hopeless attack of Regulus before Carthage with a mere handful of men reveals to what lengths their stolid confidence could carry them, a confidence not only in themselves but in the staying qualities of their men as well. It was, in fact, the Italian rank and file that won the war. The mainstay of the army consisted of the property-holding citizens of Rome who comprehended that the war was their own contest. And the allied contingent proved equally trustworthy, for they too were conscious of their share of the responsibility in the federation. Had that federation been held together merely by compulsion and fear it could not have survived this war. The allied troops would have betrayed the consuls in battle and the cities would have withheld their contingents. Rome's success proved for the first time that a great power could be built upon the well organized co-operation of many autonomous peoples if the cementing force were an intelligible community of interests. Certain it is that Rome's victory was due to the sturdy qualities of the Roman legions and Italian troops, and to the founders of the federation who a century before had evolved a government which could make effective use of this man-power.

VIII. THE EFFECT OF THE WAR ON ROME

The most important result of the war was the eventual acceptance of a non-Roman theory of ownership in subject territory from the former sovereigns of Sicily, a theory that was destined when fully formulated to change the entire conception of government of the Republic. We need not suppose that the Senate considered all the implications of their decision; perhaps the only question discussed was whether or not to collect a tribute in Sicily, as Carthage had done in the western portion and the Syracusan tyrants in the cities subject to them. The Romans had conquered most of Sicily by arms but they had already admitted Hiero and the Mamertines to alliances of the old type, and had accepted several cities as free and equal *amici* during the first two years of the war. The rest of Sicily, about half of the island, was ordered to pay annual tithes to the Roman quaestor, according to a system which will be discussed in a later chapter (xxiv). Within a few years it was also discovered that the collection of tribute necessitated the institution of a court and an executive, and a praetor was therefore assigned to the island with an army empowered to represent the sovereign state. From this time onwards, Rome's territorial acquisitions extended the boundaries not of a confederation but of an empire subject to Rome.

Upon the constitution of the city the effects of the war were not as marked as one might expect. Long wars in the past had usually elevated new war heroes into the senate and consequently into the nobility, and this war was no exception. The Mamilii, Otacilii, Aquilii, Atilii of Calatia, the Aurelii and Lutatii owed their rank to the First Punic War, and other plebeian families long in obscurity, like the Duillii, Caecilii and Fulvii, came back upon the stage. But the war did not create a powerful military family as other wars had done before. The senate did not allow itself to be overshadowed. Consulships were distributed with remarkable evenness and there were relatively few instances of iteration. Of the forty-eight consuls, twelve held the office a second time, two or three extended their services into a second year, though not with certainty as proconsuls; no consul held office a third time. It is apparent that something like a senatorial *esprit de corps* was powerful enough to effect such control at a time when the state's highest interests would have been served by generals of long experience. On the other hand, the even senatorial restraint does not demonstrate a decided weakening of the assemblies. One might expect that the intricate problems of a foreign war would so constantly call the administrative Senate into action as to enlarge its scope and power at the expense of the now sovereign assembly. It is true that the Senate's activities increased with the enlargement of the field of operation. However the facts that new men rose to power so readily, that the old patrician families did not gain any noticeable distinctions, and that at the end the assembly retained the right to ratify and even exerted the right to call for a revision of the terms, demonstrate clearly enough that while the Senate's field of action was enlarged, the aristocracy had not quite gained the dominating influence during this war that it did in the Second Punic War.

The influence of the war upon Roman life and custom must have been very great. When one remembers how in the recent war young men returned from the continent after a few campaigns filled with French phrases, habits and ideas, one naturally turns to the new literature of Rome to see whether it may not reveal the effects of this great experience. We must assume that almost all able-bodied citizens of Rome who, group after group, passed through the prime of manhood during this quarter-century saw service in Sicily. The sons of landowners made up the mainstay of the four legions, of the marines and the many garrisons placed in Sicilian cities, and since the period of service was then usually about six years, few could have escaped. Since a vast transport system had to be maintained and a large number of workmen were used in the siege operations and in the manufacture of arms the proletariat of the city also took their turn. This explains how it is that Naevius and Plautus could in their comedies make the freest use of Greek puns, jokes, oaths, and colloquial expressions with the assurance that the audience would comprehend them.

While out foraging or prowling for food the soldiers had learned
the meaning of words like *harpagare, phylaca, apage, mastigia,
colaphus,* and perhaps we may add *gynaeceum*; words of the market-
place like *danista, trapezita, chrysos, drachuma, mina, marsuppium*
are very numerous, and of the drinking bout even more so: *cadus,
cyathus, propinare, thermipolium* and *crapula,* to record a few; and
Greek military terms like *machaera, catapulta, strategus,* and *techina,*
not to mention colloquial expletives like *evax, attatae* and *euge,*
show that the Roman soldier fought by the side of his Greek
allies. The Greek scenes of saucy slaves and intriguing parasites,
of *hetaerae,* and of the *balineum,* transferred bodily to Rome, did
not picture actual Roman life, but they portrayed a life with which
the Romans had become familiar in Sicily, and because of this
familiarity they were destined the sooner to enter the staid and
peaceful city. To what length imitation might go, we can see in
the accompaniment of 'flute and torch' granted as a special honour
to Duillius by the senate—'a distinction never given before.' It
has been plausibly suggested that Duillius had observed some
after-dinner *Komos,* perhaps ordered by Hiero in his honour, and
that he naïvely carried the outlandish custom home.

But the Roman drama itself both in its form and its contents
sprang out of Sicilian associations. Excellent Greek dramatists
were then still writing for the stage, and not the least among them
was Sosiphanes of Syracuse. Performances not only of new plays
but of the classic writers were constantly given in the cities where
Roman soldiers were stationed or visited on their furloughs.
Hiero, who was still building theatres in his cities, was invited to
Rome to see the games immediately after the close of the war,
the year when Livius produced the first play staged at Rome, and
Naevius, who wrote most of the Roman comedies of the next
thirty years, had campaigned in Sicily. It is noteworthy that the
Greek tragedies which at first found greatest favour at Rome belonged to the Trojan cycle, a reminder of the fact that in Sicily the
Romans had constantly been flattered with suggestions concerning
their descent from Aeneas and the Trojans. The very form of the
plays with their substitution of *cantica* for choruses seems to
suggest Sicilian performances in which the expense of the chorus
had to be considered. It was the Trojan story also which occupied
a large part of Rome's first epic, the *Bellum Punicum* of Naevius.
The story was, to be sure, written in the native Saturnian verse,
but the fact that it was composed in metre points to the influence
of the national epics so popular in Hellenistic literature at this
time. It is therefore to the observations made during this war that

the Romans were indebted for the amazing outburst of production in tragedy, comedy, and epic during the period immediately following.

In other fields of art similar influences must have been at work, though the evidence has largely been obliterated by time. We have mentioned the boastful fresco on the walls of the senate-chamber painted in honour of Valerius, the first Messalla, and the columna rostrata of Duillius with its rhetorical inscription in Greek style. A generation later, as the Scipionic inscriptions show, the Romans had gained poise and wrote their epitaphs with a native dignity. When the excavators have finally disclosed the remains of the many temples erected at Rome during and after the war—to Janus, Spes, Fides, Honos, Flora and the Tempests —we shall doubtless find that Greek architecture, observed and studied in Sicily, wrought as thorough a revolution in this period as did the other arts.

In time it also became apparent that Rome's victory over Carthage would lead to closer political associations with the more sophisticated world of the Aegean. The Greeks were so concerned with their own affairs that they generally missed the true significance of what had occurred in the West, but here and there a wiser statesman added the facts of this victory to the impressions gained in the Pyrrhic War and concluded that Rome would some day have to be reckoned with. The Romans, on the other hand, came to learn through the increasing exchange of embassies that they were parvenus in the region of international politics as in the arts of civilization. They had too high a regard for the *mos maiorum* to abandon tradition lightly and sit down humbly as the devoted pupils of the East, but they observed thoughtfully, and during the next generation, as will be seen, they learned not a little about the state-craft of the Hellenistic monarchies.

CHAPTER XXII

THE STRUGGLE OF EGYPT AGAINST SYRIA AND MACEDONIA

I. INTRODUCTION: THE FIRST SYRIAN WAR

THE period covered by this chapter exhibits the normal grouping of the three great Powers as a state of hostility, often passing into war, between Egypt on the one hand and Seleucid Asia and Macedonia on the other, Egypt at first being most definitely the aggressor in both spheres; but it is not certain that Macedonia and Asia were ever allies, except in the Second Syrian War. Obscure as the details often are, the general tenor of events is clear: the period opens with Egypt, supreme at sea, aiming at something like the empire of the Aegean and its coasts; she ultimately secures much of the Asiatic and Thracian seaboard, but loses the sea to Macedonia and is finally herself threatened with invasion by the Seleucid. As regards Macedonia, the Ptolemies believed that a strong Macedonia, dominating Greece, would be a danger to their rule in the Aegean, and their policy was to stir up trouble for Macedonia in Greece by posing as the champions of Greek freedom; they never employed their own land-forces in these wars, but attacked Macedonia by sea and by subsidizing her enemies in Greece. Asia, on the other hand, they attacked by land or sea or both, as occasion served, but the principle, if any, involved in these wars is obscure; though commonly called the Syrian Wars, they were, prior to 221, fought rather for the control of the coast of Asia Minor than because of the Syrian question.

Note. For the first five sections of this chapter we have no connected historical narrative, except at two points: the Babylonian chronicle concerning Antiochus I in section I, and the Gurob papyrus in section V; but these cover little ground. For section VI Justin XXVII gives an account of the brother-war, which has to be used in default of better. Our evidence is the numerous contemporary inscriptions, Greek and Egyptian, and Babylonian documents, supplemented by coins, monuments, scattered literary notices, and contemporary poetry (see the Bibliography). For sections VII and VIII we have a fairly good secondary narrative in Polybius V, 31–87, controlled at one point by the Raphia stele; for Egypt he probably used the contemporary Ptolemaeus of Megalopolis; for the Seleucids his source is unknown, but there were Greek writers at the court of Antiochus III.

It has been suggested that they were really wars for the eastern trade; but this suggestion would require very definite qualifications. Down to 221 the Ptolemies were not threatened in their possession of Tyre, the head of the great Seleuceia-Damascus route from India and the East, even if they fought for the Marsyas valley partly to strangle Seleucid Damascus; while, in spite of their ephemeral success in 246, they could not seriously hope to deprive the Seleucids of the alternative routes from Seleuceia to northern Syria and Asia Minor, though the struggle in Ionia was perhaps partly a fight for the head of these routes, which connected at Apamea in Phrygia and reached the sea at Ephesus and Smyrna. Doubtless one object of the Ptolemies was markets and revenues —the control, for instance, of the wool trade of Miletus; but it looks as if these wars were primarily wars for power, initiated by the dynastic ambition of Ptolemy II. The age considered such wars legitimate; but they ultimately did harm to Egypt, and they helped to prevent the consolidation of Seleucid rule in Asia, a rule which had many meritorious aspects, and to bring about the set-back which the brilliant civilization of the third century was ultimately to undergo. That century, in fact, never secured the leisure to establish its civilization as firmly as it might have done; the Hellenistic world had already fallen a victim to itself before it fell a victim to Rome.

The coalition treaty of 303 against Antigonus had assigned all Syria to Ptolemy I, but Ptolemy had sent no troops to Ipsus, and in the subsequent partition of Antigonus' kingdom Syria had fallen to Seleucus; that is, the victors treated the assignment to Ptolemy in 303 as conditional upon his helping to fight Antigonus. But in 301 Ptolemy had occupied Syria south of the Lebanon and of Damascus, including Palestine, together with Phoenicia south of the Eleutherus[1], except Tyre and Sidon, which he acquired in 286 from Demetrius; and the Ptolemies apparently claimed that in 282 Seleucus, as the price of Egypt's neutrality in his war with Lysimachus, had confirmed their title to Phoenicia and southern Syria, in which they included both Palestine and Coele-Syria in the narrow sense[2], i.e. the Marsyas or Massyas valley with the Lebanon and Anti-Lebanon, and Damascus. It had been the policy of every strong Pharaoh thus to safeguard Egypt

[1] The Eleutherus was certainly once the boundary, and this seems the only possible date.

[2] Coele-Syria, which does not mean Hollow Syria, was sometimes used of all southern Syria; possibly it was the name of the Ptolemaic province (Kahrstedt, Syrische Territorien, p. 20 sq.), which would include Palestine.

by pushing out the frontier into Syria. The Seleucids on the other hand continued to claim all Syria down to Egypt, including Phoenicia, under the partition of 301. This was the Syrian question.

So long as Seleucus I and Ptolemy I both lived, there was bond enough between them to prevent a conflict; and when after Seleucus' death the first of the long series of wars broke out, it actually started, not in Syria, but with the aggression of Ptolemy II in Asia Minor. Ptolemy I had in 309 acquired some places in Caria and Lycia, but had lost them again in 306 (vol. vi, p. 499). Whether Egypt's first permanent acquisitions in Lycia were made by Ptolemy I in 295 when he took Cyprus from Demetrius (p. 78), or by Ptolemy II after 280, cannot be said: but in 285 Ptolemy I took and retained Caunus in Caria, and Miletus at some time became his 'ally,' probably in 286, when he secured Demetrius' fleet there (p. 92); but Miletus subsequently became Lysimachus' again, perhaps on his daughter's marriage to Ptolemy II (p. 97), and on his death in 281 it passed to Seleucus, for his son Antiochus I became eponymous magistrate in 280.

Down to 280, therefore, Egypt had not interfered with Seleucid territory; for neither Lycia nor Caunus had ever belonged to Seleucus. But once Seleucus was dead, Ptolemy II became aggressive; he recognized Keraunos as king of Macedonia, which Antiochus claimed, and by 278 he was in possession of Miletus—how, is unknown—and restored to her a long-lost piece of territory which must have become King's Land; clearly, if he took King's Land from Antiochus, it meant war. Antiochus, however, in 279 was in no position to resent anything which Ptolemy did; he was still at war with Antigonus and the Northern League (p. 99), and perhaps already faced by the revolt in the Seleucis, the very home-land of the Seleucids on the Orontes, where the rebels at some time apparently held Apamea and all the elephants there; and though in 279 he made peace with Antigonus (p. 100), a peace in which fear of Ptolemy's aggression may conceivably have been a factor, in 278 Nicomedes brought the Gauls over to help the Northern League (p. 104), and Antiochus' difficulties grew worse. Apparently he had made peace with the Northern League before 276, for no more is heard of it, and Seleucid policy was henceforth friendly to Pontus; but this peace made no difference to the Gauls, who were completely out of Nicomedes' control. Probably 277 was the worst year of the Gallic terror in Asia Minor; but though Antiochus mastered the revolt in the Seleucis that year, he was not able to leave Syria till winter[1].

He and his eldest son Seleucus, whom he had made co-regent in 280, wintered at Sardes, but he was not fated to deal with the Gauls as yet; for in spring 276 Ptolemy's troops invaded Coele-Syria and took Damascus and the Marsyas valley. Antiochus, leaving Seleucus to guard Asia Minor, recrossed the Taurus, defeated the invaders and drove them out, and retook Damascus. Syria occupied him throughout 276, and he wintered there; but it may have been in autumn 276 that his land forces in Asia Minor and his fleet invested Miletus; he presumably had an open sea, for he could send his sister Phila to Pella (p. 108), and the powerful Egyptian fleet was doubtless supporting Ptolemy's Syrian campaign. It was probably in 275 that the Egyptian admiral Callicrates of Samos, who had succeeded Philocles after 278, raised the naval investment of Miletus; but the pressure by land was severe, and Ptolemy after his defeat in Syria could only write to the Milesians exhorting them to stand firm and saying that he would *try* to defend them; while in 276 and 275 the god Apollo became Miletus' eponymous magistrate, a regular sign of trouble. Whether Antiochus failed to take Miletus, or took it and lost it again in Eumenes' war, is unknown. But about March 275 his troops from Babylon had reached Syria, preceded a month earlier by twenty elephants which, during the Gallic terror of 277, when he had lost the elephants at Apamea, he had ordered the general of the Bactrian satrapy to obtain from India; and when in April or May he crossed the Taurus, he took these elephants with him. He counted on the fact that elephants were deadly against men who had never met them before, and they justified his confidence; though only sixteen were battle-worthy, he defeated the Gauls in the so-called 'elephant victory,' now seen to have been a considerable and well-calculated success, and by the end of 275 he seemed at last, after an astounding display of energy, to have reached smooth water; it was now that Ilium praised him for giving peace to the cities and restoring his kingdom to an even more glorious condition than after Ptolemy's defeat, and honoured him, as did other cities, as Soter, the Saviour,

---

[1] On the evidence for this and the following paragraphs see the writer in *J.H.S.* XLVI, 1926, p. 155. Mr Glanville has kindly supplied the writer with a translation of the material parts of the Pithom and Saïs steles. The latter (Steindorff, *Urkunden*, II, p. 75) does not refer to Ptolemy's enemies, as would appear from Wiedemann, *Rh. Mus.* XLVIII, p. 391; but Antiochus' fleet is well attested otherwise.

for his defeat of the Gauls. Soter later became his cult-name; but the Gallic trouble was not ended, though it perhaps changed its character (p. 106).

Antiochus, as he deserved, had won the first round of the war. But where Ptolemy and the Gauls had failed, a woman was to succeed. Ptolemy's sister Arsinoe (II), widow of Lysimachus and Keraunos, had not remained long at Samothrace (p. 99); she had returned to Egypt, and was again intriguing for power. The ultimate result was that Ptolemy repudiated his wife Arsinoe (I) on the ground of conspiracy against him, and married his sister; he adopted as his son her son by Lysimachus, Ptolemaeus, and she adopted his eldest son by Arsinoe I, afterwards Ptolemy III. Ptolemaeus, driven out of Macedonia by Antigonus in 276 (p. 107), was governing Miletus some time in 275; Ptolemy's reason for adopting him was doubtless that, as Lysimachus' son, he had hereditary claims in Ionia which Ptolemy could utilize, and probably partisans. It is possible that Ptolemy's marriage with Arsinoe was in 277, and that it was her ambition which led to the invasion of Syria in 276; but it is far more likely, from Ptolemaeus' movements, that it took place late in 276[1] or early in 275, a date which would indicate the reason for this much-discussed step, which had nothing to do with Egyptian custom. For, though the idea of the marriage was doubtless Arsinoe's, Ptolemy must have had some strong reason for marrying his full sister, knowing how repugnant it must be at first to Greek sentiment, and the reason may have been his defeat in 276; despite his ambition and political ability—for he was a man of affairs and no mere dilettante—he did not understand fighting and never led an army himself, and he needed her brain and will-power to manage the war which he himself was losing, as he lost the Second Syrian War when she was not there to help him. Certainly by the end of 275, perhaps earlier, Arsinoe had taken the war into her strong hands. She was not merely queen, but co-ruler, with her head on the coinage; like her mother, she wore the diadem; and opposition to her marriage not only died out as soon as her ability made itself felt, but that marriage was presently glorified as the counterpart on earth of the 'sacred marriage' of Zeus and his sister Hera in heaven.

Antiochus was supposed to be intending to invade Egypt in

[1] In any case the celebration of the Ptolemaieia described by Callixenus, which preceded Arsinoe's marriage, is the *first* one, in winter 279–8, as one would expect from its magnificence. The marriage dates the celebration, not *vice versa*.

274; and he secured as an ally Ptolemy's half-brother Magas, governor of the Cyrenaica, who married Antiochus' daughter Apama and declared himself independent; but whether he took the royal title is more than doubtful. In 274 Magas himself started and, owing to a mutiny of Ptolemy's Gauls, nearly reached Alexandria; but the Libyan Marmaridae, doubtless subsidized by Arsinoe, rose in his rear and compelled him to return, and the Gauls were isolated on an island and destroyed; while later in the year Arsinoe ensured Antigonus' non-interference by subsidizing Pyrrhus against him (p. 213). But Antiochus never started to support Magas, if such were his intention; he was held fast in Asia Minor, for Callicrates' fleet, well-furnished with transports and mercenaries, was sent to attack his key-province of Cilicia and compel him to fight for his communications between Antioch and Sardes, while pirates were hired to ravage all his coasts; perhaps the Gauls again harried his rear. Perhaps at the same time some Arabs, whether instigated by Antiochus or not, raided Egypt from the desert; for in Athyr (January) 273 Ptolemy and Arsinoe were at Heroopolis and he took counsel with her for 'the protection of Egypt against the foreign peoples there[1]'; by 269 a protecting canal and also a wall had been constructed. Egypt in 274 made extensive conquests along the coast of Asia Minor, but it cannot be said if it was in 273 or 272 that Antiochus had to make peace. He managed to hold eastern Cilicia; but Ptolemy's possessions at the peace embraced the western half beyond the Calycadnus, where a Philadelphia and an Arsinoe appear: the eastern coast of Pamphylia, with Phaselis and perhaps Aspendus; most of Lycia south of the Milyad, where Patara became another Arsinoe; and, in Caria and Ionia, Caunus, Halicarnassus, Myndus, Cnidus, and (probably) Miletus. In the Aegean, beside Samos, Thera and the Cyclades, Ptolemy held Samothrace, which perhaps Arsinoe brought him as her dower, and Itanus in Crete. In Syria he retained or reconquered the Marsyas valley, and though Damascus remained Seleucid he acquired Aradus and Marathus, making all Phoenicia Egyptian. Magas again acknowledged his brother's overlordship. It was a great success for Egypt.

The years from 272 to 270, when on July 9th Arsinoe died, were golden years for the Egyptian monarchy. Alexandria was fast growing in material magnificence and intellectual achievement: Theocritus produced his panegyric on Ptolemy as the greatest and wealthiest of kings, master of 13,333 cities; and

[1] This visit therefore had nothing to do with Antiochus.

Callimachus in his *Hymn to Delos*, perhaps written at Arsinoe's request for the Delian Ptolemaieia, prophesied that Ptolemy would rule the world from the rising to the setting sun. The Island League set up a statue of Callicrates, Viceroy of the sea like Philocles, and at Samos some one honoured him jointly with the king and queen, an unique event for a subject. But Arsinoe, 'Lady of Abundance' and 'Lady of Victory,' who had taught Egypt how to use her fleet and had turned failure into triumph, was honoured, both in life and after death, as few women have been. She had a throne-name like a king; her statue stood among those of the Ptolemies before the Odeum at Athens, and beside that of Ptolemy II (both dedicated by Callicrates) at Olympia. Many streets in Alexandria, many cities round the Aegean, bore her name; legend gave her a statue carved from Red Sea topaz, and planned for the Arsinoeion a magnetic room where an iron figure of her should float free in mid-air, like an immortal. An immortal she became. In every native temple she stood beside the immemorial gods of Egypt and shared the adoration of their worshippers; to Greeks she was the goddess Philadelphos, lover of her brother, like Hera, queen of heaven; among her cult-names were Hera's own, and her cult spread beyond Egypt throughout the island world. After death she became Aphrodite and Isis; in the official worship of the dynasty[1] she had her own place and priestess apart; chapels rose to her in Alexandria and Delos, and Callicrates built a temple at Zephyrion to her as Aphrodite Zephyritis, celebrated by the poet Poseidippus. But what the men who served her really thought about her was perhaps best shown by the nesiarch Hermias, Ptolemy's Resident in the Islands, who shortly after her death founded at Delos the vase-festival[2] Philadelpheia in honour of the gods of Delos and the new deities, Ptolemy II and Arsinoe; while in the dedication on the vases Ptolemy's name came last, Arsinoe's came first of all, taking precedence even of Apollo himself.

II. THE CHREMONIDEAN WAR

The death of Pyrrhus in 272 (p. 215) greatly strengthened Antigonus' position; and it became clear that, if a strong Macedonia were really a threat to Egypt, his progress must be checked. Arsinoe, however, aimed higher than merely checking Antigonus; she had herself been queen of Macedonia, and she wanted the Macedonian throne for her son Ptolemaeus, who as Lysimachus'

---

[1] See above, p. 17.   [2] See above, p. 101, n. 1.

heir had a workable claim[1]; possibly she dreamt of reconstituting for him Lysimachus' empire. Doubtless the combination which was now formed against Antigonus was her doing, for her cult-name Chalkioikos suggests relations with Sparta; and though the attack was not launched till after her death, it is expressly stated that Ptolemy was following her policy, though one may believe that, had she lived, the war would have been fought differently. The scheme actually adopted was to attack Antigonus by means of a powerful Greek alliance, supported by Egypt. There was indeed a risk that Ptolemaeus, once king of Macedonia, might adopt the Macedonian standpoint of hostility to Egypt; and it was probably to meet this that Ptolemy, when war was certain (267), made him joint-king with himself, in which capacity he was to rule Lysimachus' former possessions, including Macedonia, just as Antiochus I when joint-king with Seleucus had ruled the far East.

Though after 271 Antigonus' friends again governed Athens, the Nationalists, who desired complete independence of Macedonia, were still the strongest party in the city, and it was easy for Egypt to gain their support; for, as Athens depended on imported corn, and as there was practically no source of supply which was not controlled by, or which could not be cut off by, either Macedonia or Egypt, they could not attack Macedonia, as they longed to do, without being sure of Egypt's help. An Egyptian embassy visited Athens, and various philosophers, including Zeno, were collected to meet them at dinner; that the talk was vehemently anti-Macedonian is shown by one envoy asking Zeno, who sat silent, what he should say about *him* to Ptolemy; Zeno replied 'Tell him there is one man in Athens who knows how to hold his tongue.' By August 267 the pro-Macedonian government was overthrown and the Nationalists came into power and allied themselves with Egypt; their leaders were Glaucon son of Eteocles, prominent in the revolution of 288 (p. 86); his younger brother Chremonides, a pupil of Zeno's and the mainspring of the cause; and Callippus, who had commanded at Thermopylae against the Gauls (p. 100, n. 1). Egypt had secured the alliance of Sparta, where Areus' power and ambition had been increased by his share in Pyrrhus' overthrow, and Sparta brought with her Elis and Achaea; and Athens sent an embassy, which included Glaucon and Callippus, to try to secure Arcadia. In this they failed; but eastern Arcadia—Tegea, Mantinea,

---

[1] Probably too as Cassander's heir, if Berenice had really been Cassander's niece; P. Maas, *Riv. fil.* v, 1927, p. 68.

Orchomenus and Caphyae—broke away from the Arcadian League and joined Sparta; Phigalea also joined.

In September 267[1] Chremonides moved the resolution which was in effect the declaration of war. The preamble, after alluding to the great deeds of Athens and Sparta together against the Persians, stated that the same evil days had again come upon Greece at the hands of men (Antigonus is not named) who were attempting to destroy the laws and the ancestral constitution of each city, and that King Ptolemy, following the policy of his father and his sister, was resolved to free Greece; it was then decreed that there should be alliance between Athens and Sparta with her allies, so that all Greeks might be of one mind together and might with good courage fight shoulder to shoulder with King Ptolemy and each other against those who had wronged and broken faith with their cities, and so save Hellas. It is a ringing document, which conceals the fact that, in the event of success, Athens would merely have become a dependency of Egypt. But the alliance was insufficient for its purpose; Boeotia and Aetolia were neutrals friendly to Antigonus, while Argos and Megalopolis adhered to him; and he held the Isthmus.

Antigonus had not desired war, but he had no option. In spring 266 he invaded Attica in force, while Areus came northward with the Peloponnesian army. The Egyptian fleet, under its new admiral, the Macedonian Patroclus, Callicrates' successor, who had been Alexander-priest in 270, took station at a little island off Cape Sunium, long known as Patroclus' Camp, whence it could command the Saronic Gulf; its advanced base was Poiessa in Ceos, renamed Arsinoe. Antigonus was too weak at sea to interfere. Patroclus however had apparently no troops, and could only worry Antigonus' communications; but he told Areus that if he would attack Antigonus he would land his crews and take him in rear. But Antigonus' brother Craterus, his general in Corinth, had fortified lines across the Isthmus, which Areus could not pass; and Patroclus did not ferry Areus' army across and turn Corinth, as Cassander had once done, probably because Antigonus controlled every possible landing-place. Antigonus himself advanced through the Megarid to meet Areus; but his Gauls mutinied, and though he destroyed them his operations were paralysed, and in autumn both Areus and Patroclus went home. Areus returned next year, 265, and Antigonus defeated and killed him in a hard battle outside Corinth,

[1] More usually dated 266. But Areus died in 265; see the writer in *J.H.S.* XL, 1920, pp. 150 *sqq.*

in which probably Antigonus' son Halcyoneus also fell; and the Peloponnesian alliance broke up, Achaea seceding and Mantinea rejoining the Arcadian League. What Patroclus was doing is unknown. Perhaps Ptolemy really had small desire to destroy Antigonus for Ptolemaeus' benefit; one can only guess at the use to which Arsinoe would have put that powerful fleet, properly supplemented with mercenaries, along the Macedonian coast. Patroclus took Methana in the Argolid, which Egypt held for a century, and renamed it Arsinoe; his only other recorded action is that, having presumably captured Antigonus' supplies, he sent him a present of fish and figs, the food of the rich and the poor, which Antigonus told his Council meant that they must get command of the sea or starve. The king did not forget.

Ptolemy's bad management enabled Antigonus to deal with his enemies piecemeal. Alexander of Epirus had been engaged after his father's death in a struggle with Mitylus of Illyria, but had finally defeated him and had kept Pyrrhus' Illyrian possessions; fortunately for Antigonus, it was not till after Areus' death, probably in 264, that he entered the war and overran part of Macedonia. Antigonus had to quit Greece, but was apparently soon able to leave matters to his home defence force, nominally commanded by Demetrius, his son by Phila, now thirteen, who defeated Alexander and drove him out. By 263, if not earlier, the Egyptian fleet was diverted to Asia Minor, and Athens was left to maintain the struggle unaided, for the attempt of Areus' son Acrotatus in 263 or 262 to recover Mantinea (p. 219) would hardly affect Antigonus, who was now able to bring his strength to bear on Athens. One story remains of the end of the city's days as a leading Power; the aged poet Philemon, who could remember Demosthenes and who died during the siege, saw in a dream nine maidens leaving his house, and when he asked them whither they went the Muses replied that they must not stay to witness the fall of Athens. The city held out to the uttermost, but was starved into surrender by the end of 262; and in 261 Ptolemy and Antigonus made a shortlived peace[1]. The consequences of this war to Greece are dealt with in chapter VI.

---

[1] This peace, and that of 255 (pp. 713, 862), are attested by two of the yearly Delian choragic inscriptions, *I.G.* XI, iv, 114 and 116. The mention of real events in such formal annual lists was common: *e.g.* Ditt.[3] 241, ll. 37, 66, 71, 81, 119 (accounts of the Delphian *naopoei*); *Musée Belge* XV, 1911, p. 256, col. 1, l. 9 (an archon-list from Tenos); Rehm, *Milet* I, 123, ll. 1, 38 (the list of aesymnetae at Miletus); and *I.G.* XII, 5, 898, on which see A. Wilhelm in Ἐπιτύμβιον *H. Swoboda dargebracht*, pp. 336, 343 *sq.*

III. THE WAR OF EUMENES

What was passing in Asia during the Chremonidean war is most obscure, and it is not known if Antiochus was trying to help Antigonus. As Apollo was eponymous magistrate at Miletus from 266 to 263 there was evidently trouble; either Antiochus was trying to retake the city, if it was Egyptian, or else Ptolemy did take it if it was Seleucid. Internal difficulties had arisen in the Seleucid house, for some time before April 266 Antiochus removed Seleucus from the co-regency and replaced him by his second son Antiochus. In 263 Ptolemy found a new ally in Eumenes, who that year succeeded his uncle Philetaerus as dynast of Pergamum, and marked his accession by founding, under Ptolemy's shield, the vase-festival Philetaireia at Delos. Though Philetaerus (p. 97) had become in fact independent, ruling the lower Caïcus valley with Pergamum's port of Elaea, he had always maintained a proper attitude towards Antiochus; he probably acknowledged him as suzerain, and put the head of the deified Seleucus on his coins. But Eumenes—commonly called Eumenes I, though he was never king—desired an acknowledged independence, and initiated what was to be the regular policy of his house, opposition to the Seleucid and alliance with Egypt, a state which Pergamum was in many respects to imitate. As an enemy of the Seleucids, Pergamum was useful to Egypt; but perhaps an economic reason for Ptolemy's support may also be detected. Egypt, being a great sea-power, needed much pitch; but the Syrian supply was seemingly small, and the Hellenistic world was really furnished from Macedonia and from Mount Ida in the Troad; the Idaean pitch-collectors had their own traditional lore and method of preparation, which differed somewhat from the Macedonian. It seems that Antigonus, by means of export licences and probably duties, raised or lowered the price of Macedonian pitch to a city according as that city was in Egypt's sphere or his own; and Antigonus and Antiochus between them could make Egypt pay heavily for pitch in peace, and perhaps cut her off in war-time. It would therefore be a boon to Egypt if some friendly state like Pergamum could obtain a share in the control of Idaean pitch; and Eumenes' foundation of Philetaireia under Ida suggests that at some time he did manage to obtain such a share.

In 263 Eumenes entered the war, and Antiochus, some time before April, restored Seleucus to his position as co-regent; before December Seleucus was dead. A late tradition makes

Antiochus execute him for treason; coins exist which point to an attempt on his part to set up an independent kingdom, probably in Babylonia. Whatever events lie behind the bare facts, Antiochus must have been badly hampered in prosecuting the war. Evidently by 263 Patroclus' fleet had been diverted to Asia; and by 262 Egypt was in possession, not only of Miletus, but of the coveted Ephesus, which was also placed under Ptolemaeus' governorship, and of the Carian coast between Miletus and Halicarnassus; while Eumenes, having with Ptolemy's help raised a large army of mercenaries, defeated Antiochus in 262 near Sardes, established his independence, and enlarged his principality, which by 261 embraced both sides of the whole Caïcus valley from source to sea, with a long strip of coast, including Pitane and Atarneus, and extended south-eastward almost to Thyateira. About now, too, the Persian Ariarathes successfully established an independent kingdom in Seleucid Cappadocia. Between October 262 and April 261 Antiochus died. A man of unknown personality, overweighted by perpetual wars and disturbances in an unwieldy empire, he had somehow managed to do much for the spread of Hellenism in Asia, and as a founder of cities he was inferior to Alexander alone; how he found time for all he did is a mystery. He was succeeded by his younger son as Antiochus II.

IV. THE SECOND SYRIAN WAR

Antiochus II began his reign as a ruler of energy; in our untrustworthy literary sources he figures as a drunken sot, but a contemporary inscription reveals a king who, drunkard or not, seemed genuinely anxious to deal fairly by the Greek cities, and was ready to order his friends to restore city land in their possession to its rightful owners. The peace of 261 was short-lived, and in the ensuing war Antiochus and Antigonus, who both had a heavy score to settle with Ptolemy, certainly co-operated; but though it was apparently waged on a great scale, how it started is unfortunately unknown. This is the most obscure decade of an obscure time; a narrative cannot be given, and one can only indicate various events and the result, the success of the allies.

Though victorious in the Chremonidean war, Antigonus had not damaged Egypt herself; she was still secure in her command of the sea and the mobility it gave. But Demetrius had once ruled the seas; and Antigonus' desire to recover his father's domain had been sharpened by Patroclus' taunt. Naturally therefore he used the peace of 261 to create a new fleet. Through his principal naval base, Corinth, he would learn from Syracuse the details of the fleet Rome was building; but his own adventure was more audacious than Rome's. For at one period Ptolemy's navy-list apparently numbered over 300 warships, many so large that the average power of the whole may have been that of a quinquereme, an average never attained by Demetrius or Rome, and he controlled Phoenicia, which had supplied Demetrius' best vessels; even allowing for possible exaggerations, the odds were great, for analogy, both of territorial resources and tradition, shows that Antigonus could not hope to equip much over the equivalent of 100 to 120 quinqueremes.

But he had one advantage. Corinth, like Syracuse, had always had her own traditional method of sea-fighting; while Athens and Phoenicia had preferred speed and manœuvring for the ram, they had believed in grappling and boarding with heavier if slower vessels; and as Rome learnt from Syracuse, so Antigonus must have learnt from Corinth. And once a Macedonian fleet could board, the battle was over; no marines at Egypt's disposal would stand against Macedonians. That Antigonus relied on boarding is shown by his famous flagship. All large warships were now cataphracts, *i.e.* the ship's sides were carried up to the deck over the rowers to protect them from missiles; this ship probably had also an upper deck over the boarding troops, with similar protection for them, just as Demetrius' siege machines had protected their crews. If it be correct that timber enough for some fifteen quadriremes was built into her, and that her motive power nevertheless, in relation to that of a quadrireme, only bore the ratio 9 : 4 (presumably nine men to an oar), she may have been slow[1]; Ptolemy, like Demetrius, had vessels of far higher ratio. The story that before her battle parsley, the victor's crown at the Isthmian games, sprouted on her poop, and that after it Antigonus changed her name to Isthmia, indicates that she was built at Corinth and named Corinthia; she was in some sense the predecessor of Hiero's more extraordinary Syracosia.

In Asia the war possibly began with Ptolemaeus' revolt. He realized that with Egypt's failure against Antigonus his chances of the crown of Macedonia were over, whether Ptolemy had at the peace formally abandoned his claim or not; but he thought that Lysimachus' son might still have prospects in Ionia, and in 260, at Ephesus, he rose against Ptolemy. Antiochus welcomed the rising and sent him some Thracian troops, and he was

---

[1] Possibly, however, she had more oars. There is no evidence.

supported by his commander in Miletus, the Aetolian Timarchus; that year Apollo again became eponymous magistrate of Miletus, and Timarchus boldly captured Samos, one of Egypt's naval bases, naturally when the fleet was at sea. But Ptolemaeus could not maintain himself; the Thracians murdered him, possibly in conjunction with a rising of Seleucid partisans, and Antiochus recovered Ephesus (259). Timarchus then made himself tyrant of Miletus and plundered the people, but Antiochus, who had brought up his eastern troops, put him down early in 258; he recovered Miletus, where his wife Laodice was honoured, and subsequently took Samos, drove Egypt out of Ionia, and restored to the cities freedom and autonomy; the grateful citizens named him 'the god,' a sign that his position as regards these his free allies was now that of Alexander, and that his footing in them depended solely on his divinity. Ptolemy's ally Eumenes of Pergamum could not help him, as he had to deal with a revolt of his kinsman Eumenes, which must belong to this war and was possibly inspired by Antiochus; and at some period his mercenaries mutinied. Antiochus subsequently expelled Egypt from Cilicia and Pamphylia, recovering all that his father had lost in those provinces; but Lycia he did not take, and seemingly Egypt held her possessions in Caria. However he took Samothrace and various places in Thrace, and even threatened Byzantium; but Heraclea reinforced the Byzantine ships with her powerful fleet, and Antiochus let them alone. In Syria Antiochus took all Phoenicia north of Sidon, and gave Aradus freedom, to which Seleucus II subsequently added very substantial privileges. In the Asiatic sphere, Antiochus had secured full revenge for Ptolemy's attack on his father.

In Greece one solitary fact is known: Antigonus executed the Athenian historian Philochorus for treason. There must therefore have been a rising at Athens; probably he now exiled the remaining leaders of the war-party, as it never appears again. In Africa however events gave him an opening. Magas of Cyrene died about 259, leaving a daughter and heiress of fourteen, Berenice, whom on his death-bed he betrothed to the future Ptolemy III. But though there was an Egyptian party in Cyrene, the large Nationalist opposition, led by the young queen-mother, Antiochus' sister Apama, which desired independence, offered the throne to Antigonus' half-brother, Demetrius the Fair; as he too was a grandson of Ptolemy I through his mother Ptolemais (p. 87), it was hoped that the Egyptian party would accept him. Demetrius came, and was made king; a possible interpretation of the Cyrenaic League coins with the monogram DEM, combined with Eusebius' statement that he founded a new kind of monarchy, is that he formed the Cyrenaica into a federal League with himself head for life, precisely the relationship of the Antigonids to Thessaly. Doubtless this antagonized the Egyptian party, while he also alienated Berenice (though there is nothing to show he was betrothed to her) by a love-affair with her mother, who hoped again to be queen; finally he was assassinated with Berenice's privity, tradition says in 258, but probably some years later. Party strife followed, and in or after 251 the Nationalists invited the famous 'liberators,' Ecdemus and Demophanes (p. 222), who 'preserved' the country's freedom, *i.e.* reorganized the League. But at some time before Ptolemy III received his cult-name Euergetes he recovered the Cyrenaica, Euhesperides at least having to be taken; Euhesperides was renamed Berenice, Teucheira Arsinoe, and Barce replaced by Ptolemaïs, and Ptolemaic hostility to the dead League was exhibited by Ptolemaic regal issues being often over-struck upon League coins[1].

But apparently the decisive event of the war took place at sea. Antigonus and Antiochus had secured the alliance of Rhodes, who, though normally Egypt's friend, regarded Ptolemy's continued aggression as a menace to the balance of power; her fleet, though small, was the best in the Aegean. Early in the war the Egyptian squadron covering Ephesus, commanded by the Athenian exile Chremonides, was defeated by the Rhodian admiral Agathostratus, who then helped Antiochus to recover Ephesus (259); and at some time the main fleets of Egypt and Macedonia, the latter commanded by Antigonus in person on his flagship, met off Cos. Cos was fought during the Isthmian games; and 258 seems more probable than 256[2], for some of Antiochus' successes presuppose that Egypt was crippled at sea. Though heavily outnumbered, Antigonus won a complete victory, which gave him command of the sea and ended the chance of the Aegean becoming an Egyptian lake. In 255 Ptolemy made peace; a story remains that his ambassador Sostratus of Cnidus, architect of the Pharos lighthouse at Alexandria and of the hanging porti-

---

[1] Ptolemy's *diagramma* to Cyrene (S. Ferri, *Alcune Iscrizioni di Cirene*, no. 1) cannot belong here, where Ferri placed it, for the constitution it exhibits succeeds a narrow oligarchy of 1000, which certainly was not the League. Fr. Heichelheim, *Klio*, xxi, 1927, p. 175, dates it 308–7; it is clearly fourth-century, possibly 322. See also E. S. G. Robinson, *B.M. Coins, Cyrenaica*, p. xvi, n. 2; Th. Reinach, *Rev. Arch.* xxvi, 1927, p. 1; and above, p. 127.   [2] See chronological note 2, p. 862 *sq.*

coes at Cnidus, obtained better terms from Antigonus by an apt quotation from Homer (*Iliad* xv, ll. 201–3)[1]. Ptolemy ceded to Antigonus the Islands of the League, but kept Thera, afterwards Egypt's base in the Aegean—perhaps the concession made to Sostratus. Antiochus doubtless secured his conquests by joining in the peace. Some have supposed that he continued at war with Ptolemy till 252, but this seems impossible; for had Antigonus deserted him in 255, their good relations must have ended, whereas in 253 his sister Stratonice married Antigonus' son Demetrius (p. 715).

Antigonus at once emphasized before the world the recovery of his ancestral heritage, the sea, by building the portico on Delos which bore his name; there too he set up a monument which carried his pedigree sculptured in marble, fifteen statues of his ancestors, while Delos set up a statue of his queen, Phila, and the Island League one of Agathostratus. But most of the commemorations of his success centre on his flagship, which before the battle he had vowed to Apollo in the event of victory. He issued a new set of tetradrachms, as after Lysimacheia, bearing on the obverse the head of the Corinthian Poseidon, god of the Isthmia's home port, and on the reverse the Delian Apollo seated on her prow. The ship itself he dedicated to Apollo on Delos—a thing as unique as had been Arsinoe's honours in her day—and probably housed it in the building, recently discovered, which Ptolemy I had erected to house Demetrius' flagship, thus using his vow to release his father's vessel from the servitude of its dedication by an enemy, an act of filial piety which would accord with his character. But if a recent theory be well-founded[2], he raised a finer monument than porticoes or coins; he imitated Demetrius, who after Salamis had set up a statue of Victory standing on a ship (see Vol. of Plates ii, 10, *k*), by setting up, on what had been Arsinoe's own island, one of the world's masterpieces, the winged Victory of Samothrace, who must have borne in her upraised hand the Isthmian victor's crown. Antigonus' wars, once so real, are to-day dreary and dead; but they may have left behind for us one

---

[1] 'A noble heart will relent.' But it implies also that, though Antigonus was now Poseidon, Ptolemy was still Zeus.

[2] Fr. Studnickza, *J.D.A.I.* xxxviii–ix, 1923–4, p. 125. If the statue be Rhodian work (J. Hatzfeld, *Rev. Arch.* xv, p. 132; G. Dickins, *Hellenistic Sculpture*, p. 46) set up by Antigonus on Antiochus' island (where the Mysteries ensured wide publicity), it connects with the triple alliance against Ptolemy and would be the answer to the splendid temples dedicated by Arsinoe and Ptolemy II on Samothrace.

thing which cannot die, that glorious figure of the goddess with the sea-wind sweeping through her draperies as she alights on the prow of his great galley.

V. THE THIRD SYRIAN OR LAODICEAN WAR

In 253 Antigonus founded two vase-festivals at Delos, the Antigoneia in connection with the dedication of his portico that year, and the Stratoniceia, instituted on behalf of Stratonice, to celebrate the marriage of his son Demetrius with Stratonice, Antiochus' sister[1]. He did not much longer enjoy his sea-command undisturbed; late in 253 or in 252 Ptolemy instigated or supported the revolt of Alexander of Corinth (p. 221), which deprived Antigonus of his naval bases in Greece, Corinth and Chalcis, and probably of the squadrons there, and left him partially crippled. What happened at sea is obscure. Possibly in 250 Antigonus still held Delos; and though Ptolemy recovered the island in 249, when he founded the vase-festival called the second Ptolemaieia, the Island League broke up about this time, which suggests that Antigonus managed to retain certain islands, and that Ptolemy's success at sea was perhaps somewhat indeterminate.

In Asia, however, Ptolemy secured a diplomatic triumph: about 253 he brought Antiochus over to his side. Antiochus had married his cousin Laodice, daughter of Achaeus, a younger brother of Antiochus I; she had borne him two sons and two daughters, but she was a masterful woman, and Ptolemy succeeded in buying him outright for a younger wife and a large sum of money; he was to marry Ptolemy's daughter Berenice and receive a dowry which became proverbial, with the understanding that the kingdom should go to Berenice's son. On Ptolemy's part it was a master-stroke; but why Antiochus agreed is incomprehensible. He sent Laodice and her children away to Ephesus; Berenice came to Phoenicia by sea late in 253 and the marriage took place the next year; she bore Antiochus a son, and by 250 it looked as if Egypt had more than recovered by gold what she had lost by the sword.

But Ptolemy's plans were spoilt by three deaths. Alexander of Corinth died about 247, and by 246 Antigonus had recovered Corinth and his ships (p. 223). Antiochus, on the known evidence,

---

[1] Antigonus' sister Stratonice is now known to have died in October 254, F. X. Kugler, *Sternkunde*, II, ii. (2), p. 440; and as ὑπὲρ Στρατονίκης shows this Stratonice was alive, the festival dates the marriage.

may have died any time between October 247 and April 246;
but unless the expedition of Ptolemy III was not till 245, which
seems very unlikely, he must have been dead by the end of
247. Ptolemy himself died in January 246, and his eldest son
succeeded as Ptolemy III; he married Berenice of Cyrene, and his
later cult-title Euergetes, the Benefactor, may refer to the union
of the two countries. At Delos he founded on his accession the
vase-festival called the third Ptolemaieia, and the Delians erected
a statue to him; but he soon had to think of other matters.

As soon as Antiochus was dead a conflict broke out between
the rival queens. Laodice naturally fought for her son's inheritance; she was strong in Asia Minor, where her brother Alexander
was general of the Lydian satrapy, and her eldest son, now about
nineteen, was there proclaimed king as Seleucus II; but the story
that Antiochus on his death-bed was reconciled to her and named
Seleucus as his successor, though possible, reads like propaganda.
Berenice had support in Antioch, where some generals favoured
her; some cities too believed her son to be the rightful heir, and
her friends naturally spread the time-honoured story that Laodice
had poisoned Antiochus. An Egyptian force from Syria or
Cyprus came to her support, and took the seaport of Seleuceia in
Pieria, the garrison perhaps declaring for her; the governor of
Cyprus then entered Seleuceia with a squadron and himself went
on to Antioch, where he had a royal reception from generals,
magistrates, and people, and saw Berenice, to concert measures
with her. Part of a report remains written in his name and based
on his official *Journal*; in it he calls Berenice his 'sister,' and some
believe that he was Ptolemy III himself. Certainly a subordinate
must have given the queen her title[1]; but Ptolemy III was not
governing Cyprus, which moreover had always been a younger
brother's province; most likely the writer was his brother Lysimachus[2]. To isolate Laodice and secure 1500 talents intended
for her, Lysimachus sent the Egyptian force on to Cilicia, where
it captured Soli and the money; the general of the satrapy,
Aribazus, was killed trying to reach Laodice, and ultimately
Egypt held the whole province. What happened meanwhile in
Antioch is obscure, but obviously the strength of Laodice's party
had been miscalculated; Lysimachus' account of his reception
there reads like an apology after the event, and his virtual banishment to Upper Egypt later may suggest a failure to retain suffi-

---

[1] Ἀδελφὴ βασίλισσα in Syria (*O.G.I.S.* 219, 224) just as in Egypt.
[2] A. G. Roos, *Mnem.* LI, 1923, p. 629.

cient force in the capital. Laodice's party rose, and somehow
Berenice and her son were murdered.

These events come down to spring 246, when Ptolemy III
started for Antioch with the land army and the African elephants
his father had trained, leaving his wife Berenice to dedicate a lock
of her hair for his safe return; the Alexandrian astronomer Conon
had the good fortune to discover that lock in the heavens, and as
the constellation *Coma Berenices* it still figures in our star-atlases.
Ptolemy met with little resistance in Syria, for both cities and
officials were distracted between the rival factions, and none
knew who was the legitimate king. It seems probable that
Berenice's women really did manage to conceal her death and
her son's till Ptolemy arrived, and that he kept up the useful
fiction; he was thus not a foreign invader, but the champion and
representative of the rightful heir. His own record of his campaign claims that he conquered all Asia up to the borders of
Bactria; Egyptian scribes subsequently added Armenia, Thrace,
and Macedonia, this last being a very typical amplification of his
later occupation of Abdera (p. 719); by Jerome's time he had
frankly conquered almost all Asia, thus fulfilling Callimachus'
prophecy of Ptolemaic world-rule[1]. What he undoubtedly did do
was to go to Seleuceia on the Tigris and receive the adhesion of
the generals of the eastern satrapies by sending them letters in
Berenice's name. He appointed a general over the eastern satrapies, and went home again with his plunder; he never crossed
the Taurus. His own account supports the tradition that he was
recalled by a rising in the Delta; possibly, once his concealment
of Berenice's death broke down, he found the excuse useful. His
'conquests' were probably little but a parade through countries
where his claim to represent the legitimate ruler was not challenged; but he must have left strong forces in Cilicia and Syria.

The war that followed was early known as 'Laodice's war';
she must at first have been the driving force, though the young
Seleucus soon showed himself competent. In 245 the tide turned;
the deaths of Berenice and her son were known, and the issue was
clear to all: it was Seleucus or Ptolemy. The Greek cities, grateful
for the freedom given them by Antiochus II, rallied to his son;
Seleucus began to collect an army, and got a Greek fleet to sea.
A vivid picture remains of Smyrna, about 244, working heart
and soul for the king in complete freedom; she was almost more

---

[1] The prayer in the model petition, *P.S.I.* v, 541, that Ptolemy III may
rule the whole 'inhabited earth,' is probably only the old Egyptian formula,
the model being for native use.

than an ally, for she had power in Seleucus' name to make promises entailing expenditure by his treasury. He married his
sister Laodice to Mithridates of Pontus, with a slice of Phrygia
as dower, and his sister Stratonice to Ariarathes of Cappadocia,
and thus secured these rulers as allies. In the spring of 244 he
crossed the Taurus, and the Egyptian rule, except along the
coasts, collapsed as quickly as it had arisen; he recovered the
east, and most of Seleucid Syria, and his later cult-name was
Callinicus, the Victorious. An attempt to invade southern Syria
was however defeated, and he returned to Antioch; subsequently
an Egyptian force besieged Damascus, but he was able to relieve
it. The end of the war saw the old boundary in Syria itself re-
established, though Egypt kept Seleuceia in Pieria and all
Phoenicia.

At sea Seleucus was less successful, his fleet being destroyed
by a storm; but there the matter had for a moment passed into
other hands. The action of Antiochus II in joining Egypt in
253 had put an end to the long co-operation, tacit or express,
between Antigonid and Seleucid, and nothing suggests that in
246–245 Antigonus was Seleucus' ally; Seleucus would have to
guard his own coast if he could. But by 246 Antigonus had recovered Corinth and his fleet, and the 'Old Man' saw his chance
of repaying Egypt for her support of Alexander of Corinth and
of regaining Delos. Either in 246 or spring 245 he appeared in
the Aegean in force; off Andros he defeated the Egyptian fleet,
which was watching Corinth, and recovered Delos and many of
the Cyclades, though Egypt kept Thera. His joy at the recovery
of Corinth now found its complement in the two vase-festivals
which in 245 he founded at Delos to celebrate his victory; in one,
the Paneia, the vases were dedicated to his patron Pan, who had
doubtless helped him at Andros as before at Lysimacheia; the
other, the Soteria or Festival of Deliverance, honoured the Saviour
gods, that is, all gods whatsoever who had aided him to victory.
Probably Egypt never actually made peace with him, for beside
her alliance with the Achaean League in 243 (p. 734) she subsidized Aratus for very many years; but as regards fighting
Andros was final; Egypt never again challenged Macedonia on
the water, and the Antigonids held the command of the sea till
they allowed their fleet to decay and left the Aegean without
a master.

But Andros did not of course annihilate Egypt's great navy;
and while Seleucus was recovering northern Syria, Egypt had
used her sea power to transfer the war to her old battle-ground,

the coast of Asia Minor, where circumstances were favourable
to her (p. 720). Ephesus was betrayed to her by the Seleucid
commander, Sophron; Miletus joined her as an ally; she took
Samos (before 243); an Egyptian governor is found in Priene.
By 241 Egypt held southern Ionia, where Lebedus was renamed
Ptolemaïs; but the north—Smyrna, Erythrae, Clazomenae, probably Teos, with Magnesia on the Maeander and Colophon inland
—remained Seleucid. Eumenes secured a small extension of
territory. Egypt retained her former possessions in Caria and
Lycia, where Telmessus suffered in some fighting, and probably
regained some places in Pamphylia; she lost eastern Cilicia again
except Soli, Mallus, and Seleuceia, but retained the western part.
Northward of Ionia Ptolemy considerably extended his power;
Chios found safety under Aetolia's shield (p. 733), but he took
Lesbos (if it was not already Egyptian), Samothrace, possibly
Abydos, the Thracian Chersonese with Lysimacheia and Sestos,
the Thracian coast with Aenus and Maronea, and Cypsela on
the Hebrus, where he executed the dynast Adaeus. At some
period, probably after Antigonus' death, his general in Thrace,
as the coins show[1], also occupied Abdera, which according to the
treaty of 279 was Macedonian, not Seleucid. In 241 Seleucus
made peace. Ptolemy III now held a stronger position along the
eastern and northern coasts of the Aegean than Ptolemy II had
had in 272; against that, he had lost the command of the sea to
Macedonia and therewith (though he still held Methana) the
possibility of effective interference in Greece[2].

One thing this war really settled: the Far East was definitely
lost to the Seleucids. Antiochus II had had no son old enough
to govern in Babylonia, and neither he nor Seleucus II had time
to attend to the east. The great Bactrian-Sogdian satrapy had
always been somewhat detached in feeling, and under Diodotus,
Antiochus' general of the satrapy, it secured independence, in
the tradition about 250; the coins however prove that Diodotus'
assumption of independent rule was a gradual process, and it is
not certain that he ever took the crown[3]; his son Diodotus II was
king some time before 227. Ambition apart, Diodotus believed
that resistance to the perpetual incursions of nomads could be
better organized from Bactra than from Antioch. About the
same time one Arsaces, chief of the Parnoi, a nomad tribe, prob-

---

[1] H. von Fritze, *Nomisma*, III, p. 28, does not regard Imhoof's attribution as certain, but has not noticed Egypt's claim to 'Macedonia.'
[2] The story that Rome offered Ptolemy help has been disproved.
[3] *Cambridge History of India*, I, p. 437.

ably Iranian, invaded Parthia, killed the Seleucid general Andragoras (probably not the Andragoras of the coins) and secured Astauene; after his death his brother Tiridates, who called himself Arsaces II, conquered Hyrcania and Parthia (before 227) and established the Parthian kingdom, whose rulers dated their Era at Babylon from 1 Nisan (March–April) 247.

VI. THE WAR OF THE BROTHERS: ATTALUS I

At some time during the struggle waged by Seleucus II in Syria against Ptolemy he made over Asia Minor north of Taurus to his brother Antiochus, nicknamed Hierax, the Hawk, not as co-regent, but as an independent king, an extraordinary step which could only have been the result of sheer necessity. Tradition says that Laodice exacted it as the price of help from the troops in Asia Minor, but much of the tradition about Laodice is untrustworthy. Obviously however there was some form of revolt, which helps to explain the speed of Ptolemy's conquests along the coast. But once peace with Ptolemy freed his hands, Seleucus attempted to recover Asia Minor, where Ptolemy perhaps supported Antiochus in order to weaken the Seleucid empire. It is not known that Laodice took any part in this war, though she was alive in 236[1]. Seleucus successfully invaded Lydia, and detached several cities, including Smyrna, from his brother, but could not take Sardes. Next year he attacked Mithridates, who was aiding Antiochus, and Antiochus allied himself with the Gauls of Galatia and came to Mithridates' aid; near Ancyra a battle was fought between the brothers in which Seleucus' army was cut to pieces by the Gauls and he with difficulty escaped over the Taurus. Antiochus strengthened himself by marrying a daughter of Ziaelas of Bithynia, and some time before 236[1] a peace was made between the brothers by which Seleucus abandoned Asia Minor north of Taurus to Antiochus.

This war threw Asia Minor into confusion, and allowed little independent dynasts to grow up, as Olympichus in Caria, the line of Moagetes in Cibyra, and others; about Philomelium in Phrygia the Macedonian family of Lysias was already established. It also encouraged the Gauls to hope for the overthrow of settled rule. Whatever their virtues—bravery in the men, chastity in the women, love of freedom in both—the Gauls were still only destroyers, enemies of that civilization for which the Seleucid

[1] Babylonian tablet published by C. F. Lehmann-Haupt, *Zeits. f. Assyriologie*, VII, p. 330. Mr Sidney Smith has kindly supplied a translation.

line stood; and Antiochus' alliance with them, a different thing from employing Gallic mercenaries, was very like treason to the higher purposes of Hellenism. Another ruler saw his chance of seizing the place vacated by the Seleucid prince. Eumenes of Pergamum had died childless in 241, and had been succeeded by his nephew Attalus, son of his brother Attalus and of the Seleucid Antiochis, Laodice's sister; the ambitious Pergamenes were now allied to the older dynasty, and Antiochus and the younger Attalus were first cousins. Attalus' wife Apollonis, daughter of a plain citizen of Cyzicus, was a notable woman; she took no part in politics, but became celebrated for her goodness and virtues; like Cornelia, mother of the Gracchi, her pride was in her four sons, whom she had trained to such mutual harmony that the younger ones could enter the presence of the eldest armed, apparently a rare phenomenon outside the Antigonid house.

It seems that every state in Asia Minor, even the Seleucids, had long been paying tribute to the Gauls to exempt their lands from plunder; and some time before 230 Attalus issued his challenge for the vacant position of champion of Hellenism in Asia Minor by refusing to pay the tribute. The Gauls still maintained their original spheres of plunder (p. 105), and the tribute of Aeolis belonged to the Tolistoagii; this tribe at once attacked Attalus, but were defeated by him on his frontier near the source of the Caïcus. They then applied for help to the Tectosages and to Antiochus; and Antiochus became the ally and instrument of the Gauls in order to overthrow a hellenized state. The allies penetrated as far as the temple of Aphrodite before the walls of Pergamum, where Attalus completely defeated them, and after his victory took the title of king. After their defeat the Gauls broke with Antiochus and isolated him by killing his father-in-law Ziaelas, whereon Attalus took a thorough revenge; he defeated Antiochus in three battles, one in Hellespontine Phrygia, one in 229 at Koloë in Lydia, and one at Harpasus in Caria— that is, he cleared the sea-provinces systematically from north to south; Ptolemy had probably transferred his subsidies to him as being his hereditary friend and likely in his turn to weaken Seleucus. By 228 Attalus had driven Antiochus eastward and brought under his own rule all Seleucid Asia Minor north of the Taurus. In commemorating his victories he emphasized the defeat of the Gauls alone and treated his success as that of Hellas over barbarism; few kings have advertised themselves better. At Athens, on the north wall of the Acropolis, he set up four groups of statuary, two mythical and two historical; the battle of Athenians and Amazons balanced that of Athenians and Persians, while the battle of the gods with the Titans found its counterpart in that of Attalus with those whom Callimachus called 'late-born Titans,' the Gauls; the implication that Attalus (though never officially deified) was in truth a god on earth could not well be missed. On his great monument of victory on the terrace of Athena's temple at Pergamum stood a wonderful series of representations in bronze of his triumphs; the dying Gaul of the Capitol, immortalized by Byron as the 'dying Gladiator,' and the group of the Gaul who has killed his wife and is stabbing himself, are marble copies, probably contemporary, of single figures. This war gave an impulse to a new school of realism in sculpture; but the artists of the monument have caught, beneath the rugged rough-hewn exterior of the Gauls, something of the pathos of the race of the losing battle.

It may have been in 227 that Antigonus Doson of Macedonia invaded Caria (p. 752). For fifty years Macedonia had not interfered in Asia, and Doson's expedition seems so strange that some believe it never took place at all. But it stands in line with the Carian expeditions of Cassander and Philip V, and the evidence for it seems sufficient; as Doson was extending his influence at sea beyond that of Gonatas and Demetrius II (p. 752), he may have been trying to draw a cordon across the Aegean to keep Egypt away from Macedonia; apart from her aid to Athens in 229 (p. 749) and her subsidies to Aratus, her occupation of Abdera, which brought her unpleasantly close, was a direct challenge. Doson took some places in Caria, and some Macedonians appear in the Miletus proxeny-lists, but events in Greece soon recalled him, and his conquests were not held; possibly he ceded them to Ptolemy in 223 to detach him from Cleomenes (p. 761).

Attalus had had a free hand in 228, because Seleucus was engaged in an attempt to recover Parthia from Arsaces II, which failed owing to troubles in Syria. In 227 Antiochus, driven out of Asia Minor, made a compact with his aunt Stratonice, the divorced wife of Demetrius II who was living in Antioch, to overthrow Seleucus and seize the whole kingdom; possibly he promised to marry her if successful. She raised a rebellion in Antioch, while Antiochus invaded Mesopotamia and forced Seleucus to quit Parthia. Ultimately Seleucus drove him out, recovered Antioch, and executed Stratonice; but he died in summer 226 before he could deal with Attalus. Antiochus, now

a mere adventurer, had various wanderings and escapes, till some
Gauls in Thrace ended his useless life.

Seleucus was succeeded by his son Alexander as Seleucus III
Soter; he sent his younger brother Antiochus to govern Babylonia,
and his uncle Andromachus to recover Asia Minor from Attalus;
Andromachus was aided by the dynast Lysias, but Attalus was
consistently victorious, captured Andromachus and sent him to
Egypt, and instituted a festival of victory (Nikephoria). Seleucus
then crossed the Taurus himself; in Phrygia he was assassinated
(summer 223), but his popular general Epigenes got the army
home safely. Andromachus' son and Seleucus' cousin Achaeus,
nominated by Seleucus to govern Asia Minor, at once took
control; he was an able man and some expected him to seize
the crown, but he proclaimed Antiochus king, punished the
murderers, and returned to his province. There he attacked
Attalus, drove him back within the limits of Pergamum itself, and
by 220 had recovered the whole of Seleucid Asia Minor.

VII. ANTIOCHUS III

In 221, two years after Antiochus' accession, Polybius' history
begins, and at last we enjoy a connected narrative. Antiochus III,
whatever his character in later life, displayed in his earlier years
both capacity and energy, with a fair measure of generosity and
sense. His contemporaries were to give him the Oriental title of
Great King, occasionally bestowed upon Antiochus I and Ptolemy
III; by Polybius' time he was 'The Great.' But at his accession,
though he had governed for his brother in Babylonia, he was a
comparatively inexperienced boy of eighteen, overshadowed by
the reputation of his cousin Achaeus and dominated by the im-
perious Carian Hermeias, whom Seleucus III had made minister
'for affairs'—that is, in effect, vizier. Antiochus entrusted Asia
Minor to Achaeus, for no other course was possible, and, as the
east could be properly governed only from Seleuceia, and no
member of the royal house was available, he delegated certain
powers to Molon and his brother Alexander, generals respectively
of the Median and Persian satrapies; probably he revived the old
general command over the eastern satrapies, which Seleucus I
had replaced by government by the crown prince. A divided
authority might seem less dangerous; but in fact Alexander
merely followed Molon's lead.

But an ambitious governor who was not a Seleucid was as
dangerous as no governor at all, and within a year Molon, with

Diodotus' example before him, was in open revolt; should fortune be favourable, Media-Persis could support an independent kingdom as well as Bactria-Sogdiana or Parthia-Hyrcania, especially if it embraced Babylonia. A weak force sent against him achieved nothing, and he occupied the wealthy district of Apolloniatis along the Tigris, assumed the diadem, and in autumn 222 took winter quarters at Ctesiphon opposite Seleuceia, his main objective. Antiochus' Council next spring (221) was divided[1]; the popular general Epigenes urged him to attack Molon in person, while Hermeias advocated that the king should invade southern Syria and send a general against the rebel. Epigenes' advice had ultimately to be taken; southern Syria and Palestine, though valuable, could not compensate the loss of Babylonia. But though Polybius represents Hermeias as self-seeking and all but disloyal, there are hints of a background hidden from us; Egypt was probably trying to win Achaeus, and possibly Hermeias and Ptolemy's minister Sosibius were engaged in a diplomatic duel, and Hermeias was afraid to let Antiochus quit Syria and leave Egypt a free field. Hermeias had his way, and the Achaean Xenoetas was sent against Molon, while Antiochus, who in the winter had married Laodice, daughter of Mithridates of Pontus, later in the year invaded the Marsyas valley. He was held up, however, by the strong fortresses of Brochi and Gerrha, dominating the southern outlet of the valley, where Ptolemy's general Theodotus of Aetolia was in command.

Xenoetas was joined by some loyal governors, and crossed the Tigris to attack Molon. Both commanders displayed a high degree of military incompetence, but Molon recovered himself sufficiently to surprise and destroy Xenoetas' army; following on his victory he took Seleuceia and secured Babylonia and Chaldaea, though Diogenes of Susiana successfully held Susa against him. He then conquered Parapotamia[2] as far north as Doura-Europus on the Euphrates, and was besieging Doura on the Tigris in Mesopotamia when Antiochus appeared. Xenoetas' defeat had made it inevitable that Antiochus must himself take command; he abandoned the invasion of Syria and concentrated his army at Apamea. But he was short of money, as no revenue was coming

---

[1] The council must be before Euergetes' death (p. 726); and the natural solution of the crux in Polybius v, 42, 4 is that Polybius, who has been talking about Philopator, has forgotten that for a moment he is back in Euergetes' reign.

[2] For its position see F. Cumont, *Fouilles de Doura-Europos*, 1926, p. xxv; U. Kahrstedt, *Syrische Territorien*, p. 49.

in either from Asia Minor or the east, and some unpaid troops
mutinied; and Hermeias seized the opportunity of offering to
pay the men himself if his rival Epigenes were left behind.
Antiochus had to agree, and Hermeias presently procured Epigenes' murder; but the incident led to a revolt in Cyrrhestice,
probably Epigenes' own province, which lasted into 220. In
December Antiochus reached Antioch-Nisibis, and early in 220
he crossed the Tigris, marched down the eastern bank, and
raised the siege of Doura. On the news that Antiochus had come
in person Molon began to experience trouble with his army; for
his best troops, the Graeco-Macedonian settlers, were loyal to
the Seleucid house. He gave battle as the less dangerous alternative; but the wing that faced Antiochus went over when it saw
him, and Molon and his brothers slew themselves to avoid torture.
It is regrettable that the Seleucids, who in many respects deserved
well of civilization, should have adopted oriental methods of
dealing with rebels, even though their subjects expected them.
Molon's corpse was ostentatiously crucified; otherwise Antiochus
showed clemency, and when Hermeias began killing and tor-
turing the leading men at Seleuceia he managed to stop the savagery
and reduced the fine imposed upon the city from 1000 talents to
150. Having settled the satrapies, and rewarded Diogenes with
Media, Antiochus crossed the Zagros and compelled Artabazanes
of Aderbaijan, possibly Molon's ally, to acknowledge his suzerainty—an extension of his power, since this dynasty had long
been independent. Antiochus' friend and physician Apollophanes now took the risk of suggesting to him that he might
govern better without Hermeias; and as Antiochus felt the same,
Hermeias was carefully assassinated, whereon the women of
Apamea murdered his wife and family—a horrible incident, but
not without parallels in Greek history.

Late in 220 Antiochus returned to Syria; but his absence had
produced results in Asia Minor which rather justify Hermeias.
Achaeus had seemingly been loyal, though both Egypt and Molon
had probably made overtures to him; but in 220 he thought
Antiochus might never return home, and he set out to join the
rebels in Cyrrhestice and seize Antioch and the crown. But he
too, like Molon, had miscalculated the feeling among his men;
he assumed the diadem at Laodicea in Phrygia, but when the
military colonists in his army guessed that they were marching
against Antiochus they mutinied, and he had to take refuge in
the expedient of attacking some Pisidian tribe instead. Though
Antiochus now knew he was disloyal, he also thought it safe to

let him alone; and in fact down to 217 Achaeus was fully employed in Asia Minor. A strange position thus arose: Antiochus
invaded Egypt in comparative security with a powerful rebel in
his rear because that rebel's troops would not march against him,
thus enabling him to take (as yet) no official notice of the fact
that he had really lost Asia Minor.

Achaeus during this period conquered the Milyad, not previously Seleucid, and part of Pamphylia, where Egypt had lost
any hold she had; but he failed in an attempt on the powerful
semi-Greek city of Selge in Pisidia, though Selge ultimately had
to buy peace for 700 talents. He was also interested as Byzantium's ally when Rhodes in 219 declared war on her for levying
tolls on merchantmen passing through the Dardanelles in order
to pay her tribute to the Gauls of Tylis (p. 107), a war in which
Rhodes and her ally Prusias of Bithynia compelled Byzantium
to re-establish the freedom of the Straits. With Achaeus thus
occupied, Attalus, champion of Hellenism against the Gauls,
brought over from Europe a new tribe of Gauls, the Aigosages,
and with their aid began to recover from his disasters; he won
over or took a number of cities, among them Cyme, Myrina,
Phocaea, Teos and Colophon, wrested some territory from
Achaeus' generals, and by 217 was strong enough to be again a
threat to Achaeus. The Aigosages subsequently ravaged the
Dardanelles region on their own account, till Prusias destroyed
them.

VIII. THE FOURTH SYRIAN WAR

The energy which had characterized the early years of Ptolemy
III had hardly been maintained. Some fanciful portraits have
been drawn of this king as the greatest of the Ptolemies; in fact,
little is known about him beyond the bombastic account of his
Asiatic 'conquests.' Eratosthenes' friendship may speak well for
him; he remitted some taxes during a famine; and after 241
Egypt enjoyed the blessing of twenty years of peace, for he confined his military activities to subsidizing Aratus and Cleomenes
in Greece and probably Hierax and Attalus in Asia. But the long
peace, which depended on the difficulties of Egypt's rivals,
revealed much weakness in his rule; for though he did a little to
foster those difficulties, he let Pamphylia slip from his hands,
endured Doson's attack on Caria, and abandoned Cleomenes as
his father had abandoned Athens; Egypt maintained her ancient
repute as a 'broken reed.' Above all, the once powerful land
army was allowed to decay; and when in 221 he died—perhaps

in July, certainly by October[1]—Egypt was no longer a military power.

He was succeeded by his eldest son, Ptolemy IV Philopator, whom Polybius represents as a worthless person, given up to wine and women; but the picture needs qualification. Philopator was a lazy man; but his heavy face, like a peasant's, looks neither weak nor vicious. He neglected foreign affairs because he thought he had nothing to fear from the two boys, Antiochus III and Philip V, who now ruled in Syria and Macedonia; but if one smiles at his temple to Homer and the plays he wrote, or at his monstrous warship, with a power-ratio to that of a quinquereme as 40 : 5, which cannot have been of practical use—though he showed taste in his house-boat, a superb villa mounted on a barge for excursions on the Nile—his enthusiasm for the worship of his ancestor Dionysus may stand on a very different footing. He must have learnt from his tutor Eratosthenes that other races beside Greeks were of the human brotherhood; and very possibly, deceived by the current identification of Dionysus' name Sabazius with the Jewish Sabaoth, he thought of uniting Jews and Greeks in Dionysus-worship as Ptolemy I had tried to unite Greeks and Egyptians in the worship of Sarapis; and as Sarapis, being Osiris-Apis, could also be equated with Dionysus, Philopator may have dreamt a dream, no unworthy one, of a universal religion which, while promising immortality to its initiates, should reconcile the three chief races in his composite empire. He perhaps made certain approaches to the Egyptians; a cameo portrays him as crown-prince with the attributes of Horus, and he was possibly crowned at Memphis in Egyptian fashion; but if he really tried to introduce Dionysus into Judaea, the Jews took a thorough revenge by blackening his memory. His later years, when he was dominated by his new mistress Agathoclea and her brother Agathocles, doubtless exhibited much evil; but at first his palace-life may have meant art and dreams of a world-religion rather than mere debauchery. But he was undoubtedly a negligent ruler, and he left the government to Sosibius of Alexandria. If Sosibius be the man for whom Callimachus wrote the *Victory of Sosibius*, he had in youth been a famous athlete; by 246 he was important enough to be honoured at Delos, and by 241 he was perhaps finance minister (*dioiketes*). As a criminal he takes high rank; to render Philopator's throne secure he murdered that monarch's mother Berenice, his uncle Lysimachus, and his

---

[1] See chronological note 3, p. 864.

brother Magas; and after Cleomenes' death (p. 762) he uselessly murdered the wives and families of Cleomenes' followers. But he was faithful to his master; and when the crisis came his strength and courage served his country better than the virtues of a weaker man might have done.

Philopator's abdication of his duties naturally made Antiochus think that the time had come to wrest southern Syria and Palestine from Egypt. In spring 219 he attacked Seleuceia in Pieria; some officers there were accessible to bribery, and the strong seaport was soon in his hands. Theodotus, who had held Brochi and Gerrha against him in 221, but who considered that a subsequent attempt made on his life by his government was an inadequate reward for his services, was ready to join him; and Antiochus, without waiting to secure the Marsyas valley, fought his way across the hills to the coast, whereon Theodotus handed over to him Tyre and Ptolemaïs (Acre), with forty warships, and entered his service. But south of Mt Carmel Antiochus was held up by the fortress of Dora (Tantura), supported by Ptolemy's general in Syria, the Aetolian Nicolaus. Nicolaus however was too weak to risk a battle, and had Antiochus masked the fortresses in his path and marched on Pelusium Egypt lay at his feet; but he let himself be deceived by a report skilfully spread by Sosibius that the Egyptian army was holding Pelusium in strength, and agreed to a four months truce. He left Theodotus to govern his new territory, returned to Seleuceia, sent his army into winter quarters, and sat down to await the expected negotiations for the surrender of Palestine.

There was no Egyptian army, but Sosibius, having realized that, in spite of Achaeus, Antiochus meant business, intended to make one; and he was ably seconded by Agathocles, whatever his subsequent misdeeds. They brought from Greece the best mercenary leaders that money could procure, men who had fought under Demetrius II and Doson and knew the Macedonian tradition; the settlers in Egypt were called up, mercenaries hired, and a vast camp formed near Alexandria and kept as secret as possible; there the Greek leaders worked hard at training their troops. But, even so, they were far short of Antiochus' numbers; and Sosibius, perhaps at Ptolemy's instigation, took the critical step of enlisting native Egyptians. No native had ever borne arms since Gaza in 312; but there had once been a warrior class in Egypt, though under the Saïtes it had been largely of Libyan (Berber) descent (vol. III, p. 308). Sosibius however took any likely man without regard to class, and enrolled 20,000 natives

in the phalanx, who counted as Egyptians, though some may
perhaps have been of Berber blood (see however vol. vi, p. 158).
After much delay his envoys reached Seleuceia; they discussed
the Syrian question at great length, and, when that gave out, the
equally contentious question of the inclusion of Achaeus in the
peace; finally they discovered that they had no powers to settle
anything. Meanwhile the army drilled.

By spring 218 Antiochus had seen through the negotiations,
and recalled his troops. Sosibius reinforced Nicolaus, and trusted
that the fortresses would hold Antiochus for a time; every month
gained was valuable. Still Antiochus did not march on Egypt,
but began methodically to reduce southern Syria. Whether he
was welcome there is uncertain. The rule of the early Ptolemies
in Palestine has sometimes been represented as a golden age, and
certainly Polybius says the common people favoured Egypt, but
about 200 the aristocratic author of *Ecclesiastes* drew a very
different picture: the land was full of the tears of the oppressed,
and the dead happier than the living; Ptolemy's spies were so
ubiquitous that a bird of the air would carry the matter. Whether
this can be referred back to 218, or whether it really was the
result of Ptolemy subsequently trying to introduce Dionysus-
worship into Palestine, may be doubtful; but probably there was
in any case, as later, a Seleucid party among the aristocracy, and
seemingly Ptolemy had to quell a rising after Raphia. Antiochus
took the land route through Phoenicia, accompanied by his fleet
under his admiral Diognetus. At the Plane-tree pass between
Berytus and Sidon Nicolaus met him, supported by the admiral
Perigenes with an Egyptian squadron; after a hard fight by land
and sea Antiochus captured the pass. He did not wait to besiege
Sidon, but struck inland from Ptolemaïs; Philoteria on the Sea
of Galilee and Scythopolis (Beisan) both surrendered, which
gave him Galilee, and he reduced the strong Gadara and other
cities beyond Jordan, while some Arab tribes joined him; but
the impregnable Philadelphia (Rabbath-Ammon) delayed him
till he took it by cutting off the water supply. He left a force to
hold it and another to occupy Samaria, and returned to Ptolemaïs
to winter. Some Ptolemaic leaders had deserted to him, including
Ptolemaeus son of Thraseas, who with Andromachus of Aspendus
had been appointed to lead the phalanx.

In 217 Antiochus advanced to the frontier town of Raphia,
south of Gaza. He had 62,000 foot, 6000 horse, and 102 Indian
elephants; some of his light-armed were inferior material, but
his phalanx, composed of European settlers, was 20,000 strong,

and was supported by 10,000 picked men of every nationality armed as hypaspists. The Egyptian army numbered 50,000 foot[1], 5000 horse, and 73 African elephants; the phalanx comprised 5000 Greeks and 20,000 Egyptians, and there were 6000 hypaspists, of whom half were Libyans; Sosibius himself, though not young, took Ptolemaeus' place as phalanx-leader beside Andromachus. Whether the Greeks formed separate battalions of the phalanx, or whether the important ranks, the two front ones and the rearmost, were Greek and the rest Egyptian, cannot be said. In this crisis of the State, Ptolemy, like many another voluptuary, played the man; he took command, and his command was not to be a nominal one. He was accompanied by his popular young sister Arsinoe, subsequently his wife, who had dedicated a lock of her hair for victory and who won her tragic crown in the battle. The Ptolemaic leaders were too confident merely to hold the river line; they advanced through the desert to meet Antiochus.

South of Raphia the two huge armies faced each other, each having the phalanx in the centre, the other infantry on either wing, and cavalry on the two flanks; Ptolemy, with Arsinoe beside him, commanded his left wing, facing Antiochus, while before him forty African elephants were opposed to sixty of Antiochus' Indians; both kings had their hypaspists under their own command. Ptolemy offered battle, which after some delay Antiochus accepted on June 22nd; and as he approached, Arsinoe rode along the Egyptian front, exhorting the men to strike hard. Ptolemy's right wing drove Antiochus' left off the field, but on his left his elephants gave way; the Indian elephants fell on his hypaspists and broke the line, and Antiochus, riding round from the flank, completed the rout of the whole wing. Young and keen, Antiochus threw generalship to the winds and thought only of pursuit. But Ptolemy extricated himself from his flying cavalry, rode to his centre, which, like Antiochus', had not yet been engaged, and put himself at its head; and the two great masses of heavy infantry, with both flanks uncovered, met face to face to decide the day. Then the long year's drill told; Antiochus' Graeco-Macedonian phalanx broke before the shock of the Egyptians, better trained and unexpectedly fighting under their king's lead; and Antiochus got back in time to join the

---

[1] Polybius, v, 79, says 70,000, which many writers accept. But he has certainly counted the Egyptians twice over (v, 65), as Mahaffy saw; for, with a Greek phalanx of 25,000, Raphia could not have been a native victory. The confusion arose from Sosibius replacing Ptolemaeus.

universal flight to Raphia. Thence he hurried to Antioch, fearful of being caught between Ptolemy and Achaeus. But Ptolemy used his victory with moderation—some said slackness; he let Seleuceia go and only took back southern Syria, Palestine and Phoenicia, and Sosibius went to Antioch to sign the treaty of peace. Andromachus was rewarded with the Syrian governorship, and the army with 300,000 gold pieces. Ptolemy himself, accompanied by Arsinoe, now his wife, campaigned in Syria and Palestine for four months to complete their reduction, was overwhelmed with honours in many cities, and then went back to his old life in the palace at Alexandria.

Great personal triumph as was the victory for Sosibius and his king, it had another side, its effect on the native population of Egypt. To them it meant that, where Greeks had given way, they had stood; their Greek rulers, unable to meet Antiochus alone, had called on them to save Egypt, and they had saved her. Down to 217 the Graeco-Macedonians had governed an inferior race; from the day of Raphia the Egyptian element begins to reassert itself against the Greek. Native risings started the year after; and the priests lost no time in issuing their challenge. They met in synod to decree honours for Philopator, as they had once done for his father, but, unlike Ptolemy III, Ptolemy IV no longer figured in their decree as a Greek king; to his name was now attached, in a Greek document, the orthodox list of titles drawn from the Egyptian religion which was proper to a native Pharaoh.

CHAPTER XXIII

THE GREEK LEAGUES AND MACEDONIA

I. ARATUS AND THE ACHAEAN LEAGUE

IN this chapter a continuous narrative can again be given, though the preoccupation of our authorities between 245 and 221 with Peloponnesian affairs, important as these were, rather tends to throw the history of these years out of focus. The growth of federalism in Greece meant that many cities now preferred increased security as against the monarchies to unrestrained sovereignty; and noteworthy features of the time were that the two principal Leagues, the Aetolian and Achaean, now used their federal citizenship to expand to the utmost, incorporating cities of old renown, and that the federal and monarchic principles reacted on each other: while Federalism overthrew the Epirote monarchy and actually influenced the Macedonian, most Leagues tended to come under single heads, thus constituting a middle term between Monarchy and City. Indeed in the Achaean League Aratus became little less a 'monarch' than any Antigonid king in Macedonia; and though Aratus' power was both obtained and exercised under different forms, nevertheless the Antigonid was as definitely the leader elected by the one people as the Sicyonian by the other.

In 245 B.C. the struggle in Central Greece (p. 218) was renewed (or culminated), and the Aetolians were strong enough to invade Boeotia. Achaea, as before, supported Boeotia, but Aratus crossed to her aid too late; she was decisively defeated by the Aetolians at Chaeronea, Abaeocritus was killed, and Aetolia was left arbiter of Central Greece. This defeat was for Boeotia what

Note. The narrative material for this chapter as regards Greece (not Macedonia), though secondary, is fairly good. Plutarch's *Life* of Aratus (based on Aratus' *Memoirs* but using Polybius) gives the point of view of the Achaean League, his *Lives* of Agis and Cleomenes (based on Phylarchus but using Aratus) that of the Spartan revolution; these cover the story to 221. Polybius formally starts in 221, and books IV and V, 1–30 and 91–105, give the War of the Allies at minute length; but in book II, 40 to end, he gives a fairly full preliminary sketch of the history of the Achaean League to Sellasia. His main source is Aratus, but he uses also the Achaean archives, oral traditions current in Philopoemen's circle at Megalopolis, and Phylarchus. The inscriptions also are helpful.

the Chremonidean war was for Athens; she never again played a leading part in politics. Aetolia did not break up her League or incorporate her cities, but made that League her ally; next year an Aetolian city, Lamia, was arbitrating some private disputes between Boeotians and Athenians. The elimination of Boeotia enabled Aetolia to acquire all Phocis with both Phocian votes, making ten in all, and possibly Opuntian Locris. She incorporated the first oversea member of her confederation by entering into isopolity (vol. VI, p. 507) with Chios, thus obtaining a naval station in the Aegean; and as nine votes sufficed for control of the Amphictyons she gave Chios her tenth vote. Acting through the Amphictyons she replaced the existing Soteria by a new and greater quadriennial Soteria, conducted by her own *agonothetes*, and obtained from the Greek world recognition of this new monument of her defeat of the Gauls, a skilful move, for it implied also recognition of the legality of her position at Delphi. So far, however, she had admitted her limitation to the Amphictyonic sphere by making Chios an Amphictyonic state, but she soon began to aim further, and used her friendship with Elis, which tradition made her colony, to expand down the west coast of the Peloponnese; by 241 she had entered into isopolity with Phigalea, once Elis' possession, and about 240 she brought Messenia indirectly into her system through isopolity between Messenia and Phigalea. She aimed also at securing Epirote Acarnania; Alexander of Epirus was dead (? c. 240), and his widow Olympias, who was ruling Epirus for her two young sons, applied for help to Macedonia and offered Demetrius her daughter Phthia. But this incident probably belongs to 239; certainly Aetolia made no actual move while Antigonus lived. The story that Rome ordered Aetolia to leave Acarnania alone is a later invention (see below p. 823).

In 245 Aratus was elected General of the Achaean League; he was not yet 30, but there is no evidence that the General had to be. Thenceforth he held the Generalship every other year, while in the intervening years until 235 his influence was paramount. The war with Aetolia occupied his first generalship; but in his second, in 243, he embarked seriously on his scheme of freeing the Peloponnese. His effectiveness is shown by his going straight to the heart of the position; the Peloponnesian tyrants depended on Antigonus, and the keystone of Antigonus' system was Corinth; he rightly decided that if he could secure Acrocorinthus the system would ultimately fall to pieces. So far there had been no hostility between Antigonus and the Achaean League since Alexander's death, and Antigonus' men went and came peacefully between Corinth and Sicyon. Among them were four brothers, Syrians, who had stolen some of Antigonus' money and came to Sicyon to exchange the Macedonian pieces; Aratus bought their help, and one of them, Erginus, became his lieutenant in his various unofficial enterprises. By their aid he got into Corinth one night with 400 picked Achaeans; a series of fortunate accidents enabled the little force to dispose of the Macedonian commander; Aratus scaled Acrocorinthus, and after a stiff fight forced his way at dawn over the fortress wall, and the sun rose on a free Corinth. It was an amazing feat of arms. The Corinthians gathered in the theatre to hear the news; Achaean troops held the stage, and Aratus came forward in his armour, weary and war-stained, and stood awhile in silence, leaning on his spear, amid the wild enthusiasm of the people. He then persuaded the Corinthians to join the Achaean League, and gave them the keys of their city; they had not handled them for nearly a century. He had set right a great wrong, and to do so he had done a great wrong himself; a declaration of war was obligatory in Greek law, and he had broken the law of nations and attacked a friendly state in time of peace.

Antigonus' system in Greece, though it lingered on for years, had received its death-blow, as both men knew; and Antigonus was too old to rebuild it. In his anger he too put himself in the wrong; he accepted an invitation from Aetolia that they should jointly conquer and partition Achaea. But when his anger cooled, he declined thus to stultify his life's policy, and left Aetolia to act alone. The Achaeans garrisoned Acrocorinthus, and Aratus secured Megara, Troezen, and Epidaurus for the League, and in view of the danger from Aetolia obtained Egypt's alliance, and Ptolemy III was made nominal commander-in-chief of the League. It was a compliment only; but the League's hostility to Macedonia was useful to Ptolemy, and he gave Aratus an annual subsidy. Egypt's friend Sparta also joined the alliance from fear of Megalopolis, where the normal anti-Spartan majority had again recovered power, probably when Antigonus regained Corinth, and its leader Lydiades had made himself tyrant. Early in 242 Aratus invaded Attica, hoping that Athens would join the League; but the Athenians made no sign, and his attempt to take Salamis failed. For some reason unknown the Aetolians did not move till 241; then they came south through Boeotia, and Aratus, General for the third time, and Agis of Sparta joined forces at Corinth to meet them. But Aratus, who distrusted Agis as a revolutionary, decided against fighting, and withdrew his men, though they cursed him for a coward; and Agis naturally went home again. The Aetolians passed the Isthmus and took and sacked Pellene; then, when they were scattered and plunder-laden, Aratus attacked and defeated them. To allow the enemy to plunder his fill and then attack him when in disorder was a recognized manoeuvre in current tactical manuals[1]; and Aratus at once regained his influence with the League, though the disgust of the people of Pellene at being used as bait was to show itself later. Aratus' life was to be full of similar incidents—failure in the field, followed first by indignation in Achaea, and then by complete recovery of his influence when he faced the Achaeans; evidently he could sway a massed audience at his pleasure.

After the Aetolian defeat Antigonus accepted the situation and made peace with Achaea (winter 241). But peace made little difference to Aratus, and he used the spring of 240, when he was still General, in attempts upon Athens and Argos. He tried to surprise the Piraeus, and was repulsed; this breach of international law excited such indignation that he laid the blame on Erginus, which nobody believed: Erginus could not call out federal troops. Aratus then marched on Argos, hoping that the city would join him, since Aristomachus had been killed by his slaves. But no one moved; Aristomachus' son Aristippus had succeeded him, and the people were content. This second attack in peace-time was too much for the Achaeans, and when Aratus' year expired they properly submitted the offence to the arbitration of Sparta's friend Mantinea, who awarded Aristippus thirty minae, a trifling sum which must have represented compensation for material damage only and not for the breach of international law; possibly the arbitrators regarded the tyrant as outside all law, though he was also leader of the democratic and anti-Spartan majority in Argos, who had just refused to overthrow him when success was certain. Aratus then accused Aristippus of planning his assassination. It is possible enough; Aratus had once planned to assassinate his father, and Aristippus must have regarded Mantinea's award as the farce it was.

II. THE CONSTITUTION OF THE ACHAEAN LEAGUE

The Achaean League was now becoming an important state, and its constitution, for which high rank has been claimed among federal constitutions, must be described. It was a League of cities united in a sympolity (vol. VI, p. 507), with a common federal citizenship; any larger agglomerations that joined were,

[1] Aeneas Tacticus XVI, 5–8.

as in Aetolia, normally broken up into their component parts;
thus Pegae and Aegosthena, though villages of Megara, became independent units when Megara joined the League. The
citizenship of the city maintained itself alongside that of the
League; the cities kept their own internal powers and law-courts,
and the League did not arbitrarily interfere; all private law was
outside the League's competence, and a citizen of one city did
not acquire private rights in another without a special grant; the
cities did not in any sense fuse. A city could inflict even exile or
death on its own citizens for offences against itself; but offences
against the League were subject to federal judgment. The cities
also kept their own constitutions; but some cities possessed magistracies so nearly resembling those of the League (a phenomenon
also found occasionally in other Leagues) that the remodelling of
their magistracies may conceivably have been, not merely imitation, but a condition of membership; a good example is Megara,
which on joining the Achaean League substituted *demiourgoi* for her
strategoi, and when subsequently transferred to Boeotia, replaced
the *demiourgoi* by polemarchs. All foreign policy was reserved for
the League; no city could send or receive ambassadors, make
treaties, or wage war; a real service done by the Greek Leagues
was that each prevented war between its own cities. A city could,
however, offer its services as mediator to other states. Every
citizen's military service was due to the League alone, and he
paid the League's property-tax, though apparently his city was
responsible for its collection. There was identity of weights,
measures, and coinage throughout the League; but, unlike Aetolia
and Boeotia, the local mints coined concurrently with the federal,
the bronze coins of each city bearing both the city's name and the
League's. The religious centre was the temple of Zeus Amarios
at the federal capital Aegium.

The League officials, elected annually, consisted of a General
(substituted in 255 for the original two), ten *demiourgoi*, a secretary,
treasurer, and admiral; the elections at this period were held in
mid-winter at a mass meeting of all citizens, called *archairesiai*,
and the new officials entered office in May. The General was both
civil and military head of the League, and could be re-elected
every alternate year. The ten *demiourgoi*, corresponding in number
to ten Achaean cities, were also due to a re-organization carried
through after 273 and before the eleventh city, Olenus, joined
the League, and seem copied from the fifteen *demiourgoi* of the
Arcadian League as re-organized before 300; they formed with
the General a governing Board (*synarchiai*), which transacted

current business and represented the League in its intercourse with other states. A board of *nomographoi*, representing the cities in proportion to population, revised the laws. Any citizen of any League city could be elected to any office.

As the League's written constitution has not survived, its institutions have to be reconstructed from incidental notices given by its distinguished citizen Polybius. Unfortunately he was too familiar with those institutions to trouble to explain them, while, like many Greeks, he does not use technical terms with modern precision; the result is that the nature of the Achaean Assembly and the Achaean meetings is one of the most difficult problems in Greek history. That Assembly did not, like the Aetolian and (so far as it went) the Macedonian, originate in a gathering of the people under arms; it was a thing made by the cities that made the League, so there is no *a priori* guide to its nature. Again, the Council, in Aetolia of little importance, bulked so large in Achaea that we are reminded that some Leagues—Boeotia in the fifth century, and the Ionian, Island, and Panhellenic Leagues—had no primary Assembly at all. The size of the Achaean Council early in the second century is illustrated by Eumenes' offer of 120 talents, the interest of which was to pay the members at their meetings. If we suppose three annual meetings of three days each and interest at 8 per cent., then, taking the usual indemnity of one drachma a day, the Council would number over 6000 members; this may be too high, but it was certainly very large, and quite unlike any other Council known.

For the League meetings Polybius has two names, *synodos* and *synkletos*, and there were certainly two types of meeting corresponding to the two names; but he may not always use *synodos* in its technical sense. In that sense, the *synodos* was the regular meeting fixed by the constitution; there were two, one immediately after the autumn equinox, and one about April, before the end of the official year. Some have believed that there were two other regular *synodoi*, one early in June and one in late July or August; but the few cases alleged occur either in the War of the Allies or the First Macedonian War, and as that in June 218 was certainly an extraordinary meeting summoned at Philip's request, it seems more probable (and nothing forbids the supposition) that every *synodos* outside the regular two was an extraordinary meeting. There has been much argument as to whether a regular *synodos* was a meeting of the Council alone or whether it also included every citizen over 30 years who liked to attend; except for one passage (IV, 26, 7), Polybius is frankly ambiguous. The present writer's opinion is that a regular *synodos* was a meeting of the Council (and officials) alone; otherwise the distinction of *synodos* and *synkletos* is meaningless, and Polybius does once (IV, 26, 7) definitely identify the autumn *synodos* with the Council. The explanation may be that the *synodos* had originally been the Achaean Assembly, limited in some way, which subsequently absorbed, and became, the Council[1]; this would account for the Council's great size. The *synkletos* was the general Assembly of the League, composed of the Council, officials, and all citizens over 30; it met only when summoned by the *synarchiai*. This Board could summon extraordinary meetings as and when it chose, but every extraordinary meeting was not necessarily a *synkletos*; it could undoubtedly call an extraordinary meeting of the Council alone. It seems probable that Polybius sometimes calls an extraordinary meeting a *synodos* without specifying, or perhaps at the distance of time knowing, whether that meeting comprised only the Council or the citizens over 30 also; this assumption would unravel much of the confusion.

The Council was composed of delegations from the several cities in proportion to population. Some such form of delegation was known on the Councils of various Greek states, but never in the Assemblies; so far then as the system could be called representation, the Achaean League had advanced much further than any other Greek state, owing to its Council having in effect almost become the League Assembly. But whether the delegations were chosen by election or lot, and what chance of representation there was for minorities, are things unknown.

League affairs were, generally speaking, the business of the regular *synodos*, *i.e.* the Council, which decided foreign policy, received and sent ambassadors, and conferred federal citizenship; in its hands were the relations between the League and its cities, arrangements to arbitrate disputes between cities, federal justice, and military and financial administration; possibly it could admit a new member. Outside its competence were the declaration of war, and new treaties and alliances, which had to be referred to a *synkletos*. A *synkletos* could not initiate business, but could only decide matters referred to it; and as such matters had usually been discussed in the *synodos*, a *synkletos* was really a mass referendum on particular questions. The two regular *synodoi* always met at Aegium; a *synkletos*, or an extraordinary meeting, could be summoned in any city. The danger of a *synkletos* being swamped by the population of the city where it assembled was met by the

[1] This suggestion is Br. Keil's (see Bibliography).

vote being taken, not by heads, but by cities; but whether each city had one vote, or whether votes were proportional to size, cannot be decided. Apparently the *synodos* voted in the same way.

The Achaean League, then, had a sufficiently democratic constitution; the balance was fairly held between the Federal authority and the constituent cities, and the difficulty of the mass meeting was overcome by *some* degree of representation. It was less democratic than Aetolia in 275, but more so than Aetolia in 220. Its obvious shortcomings were three. War was declared by the men over 30, so that many of those who had to fight had no voice in the decision; in this respect it was behind Aetolia. The president was commander-in-chief, whether he had military ability or not; but this was common to most Greek Leagues. Finally, the expense in time and journeys involved in being a member of the Council must have confined membership to the comparatively well-to-do. Indeed, the League's worst defect apparently was that, the Council being for many purposes the Assembly, it rather weighted the scales on the side of the well-to-do, which told heavily in its conflict with Sparta; at the same time, the preponderance of a few wealthy men had by 220 become more marked in the Aetolian League than it ever was in the Achaean.

III. AGIS IV OF SPARTA AND REFORM

We must now turn to the city which was to be the Achaean League's enemy, Sparta. When in 244 B.C. the young Agis IV, not yet twenty, ascended the throne as Eurypontid king and social reformer, he found Sparta fallen on evil days. Aristotle had indeed drawn a gloomy picture of Sparta in his time—the decay of the Spartiate body, the accumulation of wealth in comparatively few hands, the neglect of the common meals; but the amount of hard fighting which Sparta had done since points to some exaggeration in his sketch, while in his insistence on the uselessness of Spartan women he probably voiced his own prejudices against woman's freedom. But an even darker picture of things at Sparta in 244 was drawn by the contemporary historian Phylarchus, a passionate partisan of Cleomenes and the revolution; one might suspect him of darkening the background to throw his hero into brighter relief, but a comparison with Aristotle, and such analysis as is possible of the economic position of the poor in Greece, leave little doubt of his substantial accuracy; the tendencies noted by Aristotle had merely worked themselves out to their logical conclusion. Phylarchus' figure for the Spartiate body, 700, may be

too low, but is generally accepted; doubtless it was very small.
The old land-system of lots was in ruins, and all the land belonged
to the comparatively few rich men, who had abandoned Spartan
habits and become luxurious; there were many poor men who had
lost their land, and consequently, under the Spartan constitution,
their citizenship; the common meals were deserted, as the rich
would not and the poor could not participate; and very many were
loaded down with debt[1]. What had happened can be traced; the
money which successful wars, or mercenary service in Egypt and
Asia, had once poured into Sparta, and which had enriched individuals, not the State, had been invested in land, since there was no
outlet in trade or manufactures. But the class of large landowners
thus formed were themselves not a homogeneous body; some were
still wealthy in money, but others had only their land, which they
had mortgaged to the former class in order to live up to the rising
standard of luxury. The poor, of course, had as usual run into
debt merely to live at all; for one of the strangest phenomena of
the earlier part of the third century is that while prices, as previously noted, had risen enormously, wages, compared with
Demosthenes' time, had actually fallen; the position of the poor
was desperate in many places beside Sparta. A king of Sparta in
244, if he wanted to think, had plenty to think about; and there
were three main lines of thought which might affect Agis.

The first was the threat of social revolution due to the economic
position. It was nothing new; still in the fourth century civil
strife had usually been a conflict between two ideas of government, democracy and oligarchy, rather than between rich and
poor as such. But in the third century internal troubles were more
and more becoming risings of the 'have-nots' against the 'haves';
such apparently was the revolution at Cassandreia which ended
in Apollodorus' tyranny, such some at least of those troubles in
the islands which had to be settled by the intervention of Egypt
or Macedonia. The social revolution had now a formal programme
under four main heads: abolition of debts, equal division of land,
confiscation of personal property by and for the people, i.e. the
State, and liberation of slaves to support the revolution. The constitutions of the Panhellenic Leagues of Alexander and Demetrius
had each contained provisions for using the full force of the League
to crush social revolution in any League city; and to many a well-
to-do Greek, Macedonia had long seemed the natural bulwark of
law and order. But conservative thinkers had always regarded

---

[1] There was really no such thing in Greece as a rich man, or luxury, in
our sense; the words are used throughout relatively to Greek standards.

Macedonia's enemy Sparta as the true type of Greek stability; what was Sparta going to do?

The second was philosophic. To philosophy, the class state had died with Aristotle; the ideal of Zeno, and of that great unknown called Iambulus, was a human brotherhood, a state without rich or poor, without classes and consequently without dissensions, where men should live in equality and concord, and love one another as they had done in a state of nature before wealth and war came into the world. Certainly Zeno's successors were emphasizing that equality was only theoretical; you could not make men, or their circumstances, *alike*; nothing could prevent some seats in the theatre being better than others. But the watchwords remained: equality, abolition of class war, concord—the famous *Homonoia* or union of hearts. Alexander and Demetrius had tentatively tried to introduce it into practical politics, and failed; might not a king of Sparta, on other lines, succeed? For just as conservatives looked to Sparta, so did all who dreamt of a better world; for had not Sparta once been the nearest approach to the ideal nature-state of their dreams, and Spartans a band of brothers, with no private property and equal lots of land—even if only a military brotherhood camped amid conquered Helots, who presumably were not anybody's brothers? It is startling indeed to find Polybius, the orderly conservative thinker, in his description of Sparta's past, using, consciously or unconsciously, the very phraseology of Iambulus.

Last comes this same tradition about Sparta's past. It was a literary invention of the fourth century, partly derived from the division of land which obtained in new colonies and cleruchies, but still an invention; for there never had been, in historical times, an equal division of land at Sparta, and there had always been rich and poor. But the common meals and training, which were a fact, had helped to foster the idea, and certainly in 244 many people believed it. The idea was that all the land had originally belonged to the Spartan State, which had allotted it among the citizens, not exactly as property, but only to enable them (since the lots were cultivated for them by Helots) to devote their time unhampered to military training. All Sparta's troubles, it was supposed, like those of the Old Testament Jews, were due to back-sliding; she had fallen away from her old ideal; but might not a king of Sparta restore it, and in restoring it cut away the ground from beneath the social revolution and carry out the dreams of philosophy?

These were the lines of thought already in men's minds that

converged on the personality of Agis. Agis was primarily a
Spartan patriot, and desired a conservative reformation which
should restore what he believed to have been Lycurgus' Sparta.
Possibly he had military ambition—he kept extremely good discipline in his army—and he had seen what a source of strength
the military allotment had been to the Macedonian kingdoms.
He may perhaps have dreamt of himself as Plato's philosopher-
king in action. Some have called him a saint; doubtless he really
was a noble and single-hearted man, who may have felt sincere
sympathy for the poor. Those who wish may call him a Socialist,
as he did intend to nationalize the land; but as he must have known
Stoic theories through Zeno's pupil Sphaerus, who was at Sparta,
his leaning was more probably towards Stoic Communism, which,
unlike modern Communism, aimed primarily at abolishing class
war, a horror which Greek thinkers had seen too much of in
practice to idealize. With social revolution as such he cannot, as
a Spartan king, have felt any sympathy; if he succeeded, he would
render it unnecessary, assuming always that no one cared about
Helots. But the restoration of Lycurgus' Sparta in fact entailed
division of the land; and as Agis could not usefully distribute
mortgaged land, or distribute land at all to men burdened with
debt, he had to envisage the cancellation of all debts, the State
having no money to pay them; and so this conservative reformer
was driven to adopt the two main proposals of the social revolution.
As to the other proposals, he did not intend to confiscate personal
property, and freeing Helots was out of the question; they were
the very basis of Lycurgus' institutions. Even the Stoics never
advocated emancipation, for in their eyes slavery affected only the
body, and was immaterial when the poorest slave might be a king
in his own soul

Agis' first converts were the wealthy ladies of his own family;
and he won the support of the young, and of a few men of weight,
who felt Sparta's decadence. The landowners were divided; those
who were burdened with mortgages or debts, led by Agis' uncle
Agesilaus, urged Agis on for their own purposes; the wealthy
were uncompromisingly hostile. Their leader, the other king
Leonidas, Cleonymus' son, is represented as entirely self-seeking;
but the father of Cleomenes and Chilonis, who gave his son
Sphaerus for tutor and secured the devotion of such a daughter,
was perhaps less unworthy than he is drawn. Agis' friend Lysander
obtained election as ephor, and through him Agis laid his proposals before the Council of Elders: all debts were to be cancelled;
the Spartan land proper was to be divided into 4500 lots for

Spartiates, and the outer lands into 15,000 lots for Perioeci; as there were not 4500 Spartiates, the roll was to be filled up from Perioeci and selected metics in sympathy with Spartan institutions. The proposed inclusion of metics excited great interest in Greece, for some might even be Asiatics[1]. The people were easily won over, Agis and his family putting their land and their own fortunes at the disposal of the State amid much enthusiasm; but the Council by a majority of one rejected the proposals. Thereon Lysander impeached Leonidas, who took sanctuary; the ephors removed him, and made king in his place Chilonis' husband Cleombrotus. But Lysander's year now expired, and the reactionaries secured the next ephorate, reinstated Leonidas, and impeached Lysander. As the ephorate was all-powerful, Agis' young followers cut the knot by removing the ephors, and a new board was appointed, headed by Agesilaus; but there was no bloodshed, Agis saving Leonidas' life and sending him to Tegea.

But Agesilaus was merely using Agis for his own ends. He persuaded the inexperienced young king, against his better judgment, not to carry out both his proposals concurrently, but to cancel debts first; this was done, and Agesilaus and his party, once freed from their mortgages, had no intention of surrendering their lands. Chance favoured them; Sparta's ally Aratus applied for help against Aetolia (241), and the ephors sent Agis north with the army (p. 734). During his absence Agesilaus played the tyrant and alienated the people, already disillusioned at not receiving the promised land; Leonidas came back with some mercenaries and recovered power; and when Agis returned, he saw that he must fight or fail. He decided not to fight, and took sanctuary, together with Cleombrotus; as tradition says he was sure of his army, it means that he preferred to die rather than kill his fellow-citizens. He was taken by a trick and murdered, together with his mother and his grandmother Archidamia, the heroine of Pyrrhus' siege; all died like Spartans. Cleombrotus was saved by Chilonis' pleading, and exiled. Cleomenes' sister furnishes the noblest portrait of a woman since the heroines of Euripides; when Cleombrotus helped to overthrow Leonidas she left her husband and shared her father's misfortunes; when her father in his turn threatened Cleombrotus, she left him and took sanctuary with her husband, whose life she saved and whose banishment she shared; exile with her, says Plutarch, were better than kingship without her. Many supporters of Agis were also exiled. His friend Hippomedon, Agesilaus' son, went to Egypt

[1] Alexander of Aetolia, *Anth. Pal.* VII, 709.

and was given high office; but most went to Aetolia, who undertook their restoration as a means of furthering her own influence.
Aetolian troops coming through Messenia presently invaded and
plundered Laconia with impunity; and though they failed to reinstate the exiles, their inroad revealed to Spartans the weakness
of Leonidas' restored régime.

IV. THE WAR OF DEMETRIUS II WITH THE LEAGUES

The year following Agis' death saw the death of Antigonus
(early in 239). He had outlived all his contemporaries and most
of their sons; he was known as The Old Man. He had had much
success in his chequered life; he had restored Macedonia to her
fullest boundaries, had regained at Andros the command of the
Aegean, and so won the confidence of his people that nothing
could now overthrow his line but overwhelming force. But he
had ended with a failure; he had lost Corinth. One city only; but
a bridge with its keystone withdrawn has only lost one stone;
like the bridge, his system in Greece was doomed whenever the
strain should come. His son Demetrius II succeeded, and on his
accession (if not before) married Phthia (p. 733); their eldest son[1],
afterwards Philip V, was born in 238. His marriage meant that
he undertook to prevent Aetolia depriving Epirus of Acarnania;
and as Aetolia's arrangement with Antigonus ended with his
death[2], a collision between Macedonia and Aetolia seemed inevitable. In the Peloponnese, as Demetrius upheld his father's
system, Aratus' intention of freeing the Peloponnese was bound
to bring about a collision between Macedonia and Achaea. The
Aetolian and Achaean Leagues therefore formed an alliance, which
included also Aetolia's allies, Boeotia and Elis.

The obscure war between Demetrius and the two Leagues
probably broke out in 238. Boeotia naturally quitted Aetolia,
joined Demetrius as an ally, and again secured Opuntian Locris;
and that part of Phocis which before 245 had been Boeotia's ally
also joined Demetrius and became independent again. Demetrius
apparently lost Atintania, which appears to have been independent
in 230; but Aetolia failed to secure Acarnania. As against Aetolia,
therefore, Demetrius re-established much the same position that
obtained before Boeotia's defeat in 245. It is true that Aetolia's
Amphictyonic vote was not, apparently, diminished; but even if
the Delphic archons could be certainly dated, stress can no longer

[1] That Philip was the son of Phthia, not of Chryseis, appears from
contemporary inscriptions; see the writer in *C.Q.* XVIII, 1924, p. 17.

[2] As did every treaty with a Macedonian king; see p. 199, n. 1.

be laid on this, for it seems that Aetolia, once she had a country's vote, now claimed to retain that vote so long as she held any fraction of the country, or even sheltered a substantial body of its exiles who could act in her favour; the vote was her method of perpetuating her claim to lost territory, and Demetrius was not interested in Amphictyonic votes, while no *hieromnemon* could appear at Delphi against Aetolia's wishes. Between 238 and 233 Athens' territory was frequently ravaged by the Achaeans and perhaps by Aetolian privateers. But in the Aegean Demetrius was still master; he was suzerain of Delos (where he founded a festival on his accession), Ceos, and probably many of the Cyclades, and Delos had close relations with Thessalonica; he even went farther afield than Antigonus, for in 237, through an alliance with Gortyn and her allies, he obtained a footing in Crete, heretofore the preserve of Egypt and Sparta. He founded one city, Phila near Tempe; but the war with Aetolia at first left him little opportunity to attend to the Peloponnese, where his cause was really maintained by Argos, to whom he sent a few troops by sea. Nothing is heard of Megalopolis, though its tyrant Lydiades must have been Demetrius' partisan.

Aratus, though he periodically ravaged Attica, paid most attention to Argos. After more than one unofficial attempt to surprise the city, he invaded Argolis in force in the summer of 237; Aristippus met him, and Aratus threw away victory by losing his nerve and breaking off the battle. As he refused to renew it because the enemy outnumbered him, and as Aristippus cannot have maintained anything approaching as many mercenaries as would outnumber the Achaean army, of at least 10,000 men, we see once more that the tyrant had large support from the Argives. Aratus persuaded Cleonae to join the League and there celebrated a rival Nemea in opposition to Argos; but he disgraced himself by breaking the Nemean truce, capturing some performers at the Argive Nemea, and selling them as slaves. Next year the Achaeans took Heraea. Aristippus waited till Aratus' next Generalship (235 b.c.), and then tried to recover Cleonae; but Aratus secretly collected troops, slipped into Cleonae unobserved by night, and at dawn flung open the gates and surprised the enemy. Aristippus was defeated and killed, but Argos itself was saved by his brother Aristomachus with Macedonian help. Whatever condemnation some of Aratus' methods deserve, one cannot help feeling sympathy and even admiration for a man who, knowing that he was afraid in a pitched battle, and knowing that others knew it, still never gave up but always fought again, frequently retrieving his errors. Aratus' psychology became a common topic of discussion in the schools; the information that remains points to his weakness being some uncontrollable nervous affection; he was not a coward at heart[1]. His inner life must have been a terrible conflict; it may explain some of his misdeeds.

The victory of Cleonae showed that the Achaean League might become formidable, while Demetrius' power to help his friends seemed doubtful. Lydiades of Megalopolis began to reconsider the situation. He was an ambitious and noble-minded man; he was rather afraid of Aratus, while he envied his position as chief magistrate of a free commonwealth. He laid down his tyranny under an amnesty, joined Megalopolis to the League (235), and became an Achaean citizen and a popular hero; the north and west of Arcadia followed Megalopolis' lead and also joined. Lydiades was elected General for 234, and for six years alternated with Aratus; his popularity was a threat to Aratus' unique influence, and Aratus, who was jealous, intrigued against him, opposed him in the Assembly without, it is said, much success, and suggested to the Achaeans that the cuckoo might some day become a hawk again. More important probably was the change in the League's position created by the adhesion of the 'Great City.' Mercantile Corinth had fallen into line, but Megalopolis was too important and virile a community to become merely an Achaean town; she had her own traditional policy of hostility to Sparta, and the question promptly arose, would Megalopolis follow the policy of the League or would she compel the League to follow the policy of Megalopolis; for the moment Lydiades took office he proposed to attack, not Argos, but Sparta. Aratus secured the defeat of the project. In one way Lydiades was right; had he been successful, there would have been no Cleomenes, and the League would not have become a Macedonian dependency. But these things could not be foreseen; and on what was known in 234 wisdom lay with Aratus. Lydiades persuaded Nearchus, tyrant of Orchomenus, to abdicate under an amnesty as he had done, and Orchomenus joined the League, perhaps unwillingly; for to secure itself the League gave allotments there to Achaean settlers, who were forbidden to alienate them for twenty years. Mantinea also joined, probably the same year.

It was evident that if Demetrius were to retain any footing in the Peloponnese he must act vigorously. In 233 he was able to send a sufficient force, and his general Bithys defeated Aratus thoroughly at Phylacia (locality unknown), to the delight of

---

[1] Cf. *Report of the War Office Committee of Enquiry into 'Shell-shock,'* London 1922, pp. 139 *sqq.*

Athens, who rewarded Bithys with citizenship; the Achaeans were paralysed, and did not move again till Demetrius died. Mantinea and Orchomenus now quitted the Achaean League and with Tegea and probably Caphyae joined the Aetolian, which thus acquired most of eastern Arcadia, a district which had learnt to act independently in the Chremonidean war. As an Achaean city took an oath never to secede, this strange step can hardly have been taken without the Achaean League's concurrence; perhaps it was intended to compensate Aetolia for her losses in Central Greece in the common cause. But Aetolia was now quite safe, for Demetrius' hands were full in the north. A powerful tribe or confederacy, the Bastarnae, now definitely proved to have been Gauls, not Germans[1], were migrating southward, and either they or the Scordisci broke the Illyrian Autariatae and other tribes and drove the fragments to join Dardania, greatly increasing Dardania's strength. The Dardanians, of Illyrian blood, were a brave and semi-barbarous people about the upper Axius (Vardar), who proverbially washed only thrice in their lives, at birth, marriage, and death; they could put a large force into the field, their heavy infantry being armed like Macedonians[2] and accompanied by light-armed slaves. Their king Longarus now invaded Paeonia, and Demetrius allied himself with Agron of Illyria, who had recovered much of the southern Illyrian districts formerly conquered by Pyrrhus and had consolidated a powerful kingdom (p. 827).

V. THE TRIUMPH OF FEDERALISM

Meanwhile Olympias' son Pyrrhus II, king of Epirus, died, and was succeeded by his brother Ptolemaeus. Under him Epirus' constitution broke down; the majority desired a republic, and there was civil war. The revolution was probably supported, if not engineered, by Aetolia, since her enemy Demetrius supported his brother-in-law Ptolemaeus; but Demetrius was fully occupied elsewhere, and the republicans triumphed; Ptolemaeus was killed, Olympias died of grief, and the last member of the great Pyrrhus' house, his granddaughter Deidameia, though she renounced her claim to the throne, was barbarously murdered by the Ambracian mob at the very altar of Artemis (? 235). The new republic allied itself with Aetolia; but Macedonia's friend Acarnania proclaimed herself independent, and restored her ancient League, but under a single general. The Aetolians invaded

---

[1] A. Bauer, *Wien S.B.*, CLXXXV, 1918, Abh. 2. See however vol. II, p. 38.

[2] *Lindian Chronicle*, C 127 *sqq.*, with Wilhelm's readings, *Wien. Anzeiger*, 1922, Sonderabdruck, p. 28.

Acarnania and besieged Medeon, but Agron at Demetrius' request sent a fleet which rescued the city (autumn 231). Next spring, Agron being dead, his widow Teuta sent out a large force which defeated the Epirotes, took the federal capital Phoenice, and broke up Pyrrhus' Epirus; Ambracia entered into isopolity and alliance with the Aetolian League and Amphilochia joined it, while Athamania declared itself a kingdom under Amynander; and Epirus, now reduced to a federation of its original three tribes, under three generals, left Aetolia and allied itself with Illyria, which also acquired Atintania, Epirus' ally in the war (see pp. 831 *sqq.*).

In spring 229 Demetrius died, after a severe defeat by the Dardanians, who occupied Paeonia; his heir was a boy of nine. Confusion followed; the Dardanians invaded Macedonia; and all Macedonia's enemies saw their opportunity. Aetolia struck at once; though she did not recover independent Phocis, she incorporated Thessaly and Achaea Phthiotis, including the coveted Thebes, where she settled some Aetolians; by 228 she had doubled her territory and reached her greatest expansion on the Greek mainland. She was now firmly set across the peninsula from sea to sea, anchored as it were at either end by her two recent acquisitions, Thebes on the Gulf of Pagasae and Ambracia on the Ambracian Gulf; and in either sea she had outposts, bound to her by isopolity and alliance, in the Ionian sea Cephallenia, in the Aegean Chios and (now or later) Ceos, and Vaxus (Oaxus) in Crete. She apparently had 15 Amphictyonic votes, and presently gave two to Cephallenia and Ambracia. Western Peloponnese was in her system and she held part of Arcadia, while Rome had freed her from any fear of Illyria (p. 834 *sq.*). She regarded herself now as Macedonia's equal.

Athens recovered independence in 229. Her leading man was now the wealthy Eurycleidas of Cephissia, a member of the pro-Macedonian government, who as military steward had raised a subscription to protect Attica against Achaean inroads and get in the crops in safety, and as *agonothetes*, perhaps in 230, had spent seven talents on reviving the Dionysia and large sums to bring the ravaged land back into cultivation. On Demetrius' death he led a movement, probably instigated by Egypt, to secede from Macedonia, and approached Diogenes, commander of the Piraeus garrison, who, seeing no prospect of support, agreed to hand over the Piraeus on payment of 150 talents to satisfy his mercenaries. The movement shows that the pro-Macedonian party in Athens was as dead as the Nationalist; in fact, there were now no parties there at all; a few would have joined Achaea, but the great majority had only one object, peace. Aratus hurried to Athens, hoping to secure her adhesion; but Athens' past forbade her becoming a unit in a League, while she had no mind to play buffer-state for Achaea against enemies from the north. Aratus, with his great success elsewhere, could afford to take the rebuff graciously; he made amends to Athens for his attacks by subscribing twenty talents to the fund for Diogenes, and left her alone.

Athens found the money somehow; the Thespians and Thebans raised subscriptions which they lent to her through their cities, and she pawned her official copies of Aeschylus, Sophocles, and Euripides to Ptolemy III for 15 talents. Diogenes was paid, and handed to Athens the Piraeus and all the forts (228). In his honour were founded the festival Diogeneia and the gymnasium called the Diogeneum, which became a centre for the Athenian ephebes; his seat, with the inscription 'Of Diogenes the Benefactor,' still stands in the Dionysiac theatre. Eurycleidas and his brother Micion took the lead in the new government; finance was again administered by a board, but conjoined with a military steward; they restored the walls of Athens and the Piraeus, and strengthened the harbours. But they really relied on international forbearance; and the Greek states readily recognized Athens' freedom, for the harmless and historic city was an object of general friendliness. Men from the new Hellenistic capitals, excellently planned in rectangular blocks, with broad streets and wide vistas, came to regard Athens as we may some mediaeval town; she was a place to visit, with her narrow winding alleys and antiquated houses, her air of bygone greatness, her glorious temples of an older day. Eurycleidas dedicated a new precinct to The People and the Graces (*Charites*), whose worship proclaimed Athens' gratitude (*charis*) to the world for its kindness; he and his family were perpetual priests, and there Ptolemy III and probably Diogenes were also worshipped. In the precinct stood an altar of Aphrodite, goddess of love, with the inscription 'Leader of the People,' typifying that once Imperialist people's goodwill to all men; it recalls the place of Love in Zeno's world-wide Utopia.

In the Peloponnese Aristomachus abandoned the now hopeless struggle to maintain himself. After Demetrius' death, but before May 229 B.C., he had been ready to entertain a proposal made by Aratus that he should, like Lydiades, abdicate, and join Argos to the League; but Lydiades, who was General, naturally desired the credit of bringing Argos over, and himself introduced Aristomachus to the Achaean Assembly. Aratus thereon procured the rejection of Aristomachus' proposal; but after Lydiades had quitted office, and he was himself General, he welcomed him; Argos joined the League, and Aristomachus abdicated under the usual amnesty and was elected General for 228 instead of Lydiades. The episode throws an ugly light on Aratus' attitude toward Lydiades and its repercussion on the League's policy. Following Aristomachus' example, the tyrants of Phlius and Hermione also abdicated and their cities joined the League; in spring 228 Aegina joined, and Aratus took Caphyae; and when in May 228 he went out of office, he had his heart's desire: there was no longer a tyrant in Peloponnese, or any trace of Macedonian influence; there was in fact no tyrant left in Greece.

This was the highest point which the Achaean League ever reached; later it was to embrace more territory, but at present it contained none but willing citizens, and was also a fully independent federation, for its nominal alliance with the now inactive Ptolemy III, and Aratus' Egyptian subsidy, hardly affected its policy, whatever might have happened had there been a strong king reigning at Alexandria. It gave its members good government; and the defects that were to ruin it—lack of proper military training, and the bias of its constitution in favour of the well-to-do —had not yet fully revealed themselves. Aratus had the right to be proud of his work, for his work it was, carried through in the face of what at first looked impossible odds. But the territory of the League suggests one peculiar reflection. It embraced Achaea, Sicyon, Corinth, Megara, Argos, the Argolid and the coastal cities, Aegina, Megalopolis and the larger part of Arcadia; and, except Aegina, all these countries had for long been the sphere of the Macedonian; they had been part of the empires of Cassander and Demetrius I, and comprised the cities in which Antigonus Gonatas had maintained his system. Their use to the Antigonids had been to hold in check the free districts, primarily Sparta, and struggles with Sparta had been the history of the League's principal cities; and the League was, in this aspect, only the old pro-Macedonian opposition to Sparta under a new name and constitution, as events were soon to show. It is said that Aratus, his ambition achieved, now aspired to a greater work, the unification of the whole Peloponnese in his League. It was a natural aspiration, but a vain one. History gave warrant for the overthrow of tyrants; it gave none for the belief that Sparta could ever be brought to join Argos and Megalopolis.

Thus the federal movement had triumphed, though partly by the grace of Dardanian barbarism. Gonatas' system was dead, and Macedonia held nothing south of Olympus but Demetrias,

Euboea, and some Cyclades. Only two Greek-speaking kingdoms remained in the peninsula; and the impact of victorious
federalism upon Macedonia and Sparta must now be traced.

VI. ANTIGONUS DOSON

Demetrius had apparently named as his son Philip's guardian
his cousin Antigonus, called Doson (another nickname of unknown meaning), son of Demetrius the Fair (p. 712); probably
he promised Demetrius to secure Philip's future succession. The
trouble in Macedonia called for a man, and the army must have
confirmed Antigonus' guardianship. Antigonus III was a statesman; he understood the victories federalism had won, and was
prepared to make in Macedonia such concessions to the new
spirit as a Macedonian monarch might; he also understood that
a name may sometimes pass for a thing. We gather dimly that
he presently came into conflict with the army; the result was a
bargain. They elected him King; but Macedonia became 'The
League[1] of the Macedonians.' It seemingly gave the people no
new powers or rights; but it meant that their jealously-guarded
ancestral partnership with their king was now formally recognized, and crystallized under a name borrowed from the terminology of Greek Federalism; the unwritten quasi-constitution of
Macedonia was, so to speak, reduced to writing, and found expression both in Antigonus' acts of state, done by 'King Antigonus
son of King Demetrius and the Macedonians,' and later in Philip V's
bronze coinage inscribed 'Of the Macedonians' and in the statue
of him set up at Delos by the Macedonian League; while the
Macedonians were to appear as members of Antigonus' Hellenic
League (p. 759), since Antigonus alone was no longer the Macedonian State, as Philip II, Alexander, and Demetrius I had been
when they formed their Leagues of Corinth. It seems that Phthia
had pre-deceased Demetrius, and his new wife Chryseis had
adopted Philip; Antigonus now kept his promise to Demetrius
by adopting Philip as his son and successor and marrying his
'mother' Chryseis. Like Cassander, Antigonus was a consumptive.

Antigonus first drove out the Dardanians and recovered southern
Paeonia, but not Bylazora, which commanded the pass into
Paeonia from Dardania. During 228 he recovered much of
Thessaly, and took his place as head of the Thessalian League,
while Epirus became his ally. With Aetolia he succeeded in re-

---

[1] Better 'Commonwealth'; but unless the same word (League) be used
for κοινὸν throughout, the connection of ideas is obscured.

newing the arrangement Gonatas had made and secured her
neutrality, but to obtain this he had to abandon to her all Achaea
Phthiotis and part of Thessaly; her League now seemingly included Limnaea, Gomphi, Tricca, and possibly Pharsalus, that is,
parts of Thessaliotis and of Hestiaeotis; she controlled all the
roads over or round Othrys into Malis, and cut off Macedonia
from access to Greece by land. That he conceded so much to obtain Aetolia's neutrality shows that she had not been much damaged
by Demetrius II. In 227 Antigonus made his obscure expedition
to Caria, directed against Egypt (p. 722). In the Aegean he was
suzerain of Delos and some Cyclades, extended his authority to
Cos and Nisyrus, and made treaties with Eleutherna and Hierapytna in Crete, but he neglected the fleet; by 220 it had largely
rotted away, and most of the Aegean was masterless. He made
no attempt to regain anything in Greece, and even specifically
recognized Athens' independence; his policy before 224 is as
little known as his personality[1]. But his reign saw a dramatic
clash of principles and causes in the Peloponnese.

VII. CLEOMENES III OF SPARTA AND THE REVOLUTION

Agis' death left Leonidas all-powerful at Sparta, and he ruled
unconstitutionally without a colleague. But he at once made a
mistake. Agis had left a young widow, Agiatis, gentle, beautiful,
and wealthy; to obtain her fortune, Leonidas, in spite of her resistance, married her to his young son Cleomenes. The result was
one of the rare love-stories of Greece; Cleomenes fell in love with
his wife, and she, recognizing that her marriage was not the boy's
fault, and moved by his sympathy for herself and Agis, converted him to Agis' ideas, to which he was perhaps already pre-
disposed; for Sphaerus was his tutor, and the treatise he wrote
for him on the Spartan constitution doubtless portrayed Sparta's
history as Agis had understood it. Cleomenes III, on his enemies'
admission, was a born leader. He was a high-minded man, but
harder and stronger than Agis, not so single of purpose, and
intensely ambitious; doubtless he desired to make his people
happier, but he took up reform partly with the ulterior object of
so strengthening Sparta that his ambition should have scope.
He saw why Agis had failed, and realized that he could only carry
reform by force; and a Spartan king, who in peace had little
power, could only secure force in one way, through war. He came

[1] Some see his portrait in the diademed heads of Pan on the Antigonid
tetradrachms. But the features vary, and none suggest a consumptive.

to the throne in 237, when Leonidas died, but he made no move till in 229 Macedonia seemed impotent; then he deliberately provoked Achaea by obtaining the ephors' permission to enter the Belbinate, a district in dispute between Sparta and Megalopolis, where he fortified a post. It is not denied that he sought war with Achaea as the only way of carrying through his reforms, even if those reforms were partly a means to another end; and the quarrel was fanned by the Aetolians, who decided to retire from their Arcadian cities, Tegea, Mantinea, Orchomenus and Caphyae, but ceded them, not to Achaea, but to Sparta, thus driving in a Spartan wedge between Megalopolis and Argos; perhaps Aetolia was becoming alarmed at Achaea's expansion and regarded Sparta as a promising counterpoise.

Aratus, although he attempted unsuccessfully to surprise Tegea and Orchomenus, had no desire to endanger his League's prosperity by open hostilities with Sparta, while the ephors, who distrusted Cleomenes, recalled him; but in spring 228 Aratus, by taking Caphyae, forced them to send out Cleomenes again. In May 228 Aristomachus succeeded Aratus as General; he wholeheartedly desired to attack Argos' secular enemy, and the League at once declared war; it was, however, during 228 confined to border incursions, Cleomenes having only a small force and Aratus straining his influence to hold back Aristomachus; the two armies did meet at Pallantium near Megalopolis, but Aratus managed to prevent a battle. In 227, however, when Aratus was again General, Cleomenes, who had now recruited mercenaries—his real object —was better equipped, and early in the season he defeated Aratus at Lycaeum near Megalopolis, but Aratus as usual recovered himself by surprising and capturing Mantinea; as the majority there was normally pro-Spartan he tried to safeguard the city for the League by giving citizenship to metics and introducing Achaean settlers, hardly a likely method of reconciling Mantinea to League membership.

In view of this setback Cleomenes procured the recall from exile of Agis' brother Archidamus to share the kingship, hoping thus to win over the Eurypontid partisans; but Archidamus was murdered by those who had murdered Agis. It has been proved, if proof be needed, that this was not Cleomenes' doing[1], though his own position was too precarious to enable him to punish the murderers. But he bribed the ephors for a chance to avenge the loss of Mantinea, and at Ladoceia near Megalopolis encountered Aratus with an Achaean force, Lydiades commanding the cavalry.

[1] E. von Stern, *Hermes*, L, 1915, p. 554.

Cleomenes' advance-guard was driven in, and Aratus, who was outnumbered and meant to act only on the defensive, then stopped the Achaean advance at a protecting water-course. But Lydiades disobeyed the order to halt and went on with the cavalry alone; he was defeated and killed, and the Achaean phalanx, disordered by the flying horsemen, was driven in rout from the field. Cleomenes showed what was in his mind by covering Lydiades' body with his purple and sending it to Megalopolis; so had Alexander acted towards Darius. Lydiades' death was his own fault, for he had disobeyed orders, and a commander-in-chief is entitled to fight his battle his own way; but the Achaeans blamed Aratus for not supporting him, and refused to vote him further supplies. But Cleomenes was no longer thinking of Aratus. He left his citizen troops in camp, hurried back to Sparta with his mercenaries, turned out the ephors, killing four of them and ten supporters who fought, exiled 80 of their principal followers, and was sole master of Sparta at a cost of 14 lives, one of the quickest and cheapest revolutions known.

He spent the winter of 227 in re-establishing, as he supposed, Lycurgus' Sparta. He abolished the ephorate as being a later usurpation unknown to Lycurgus and transferred its powers to himself, though possibly he created a new board, the *patronomoi*, to exercise civil justice. The council of elders, being Lycurgan, was only shorn of power and perhaps made an annual magistracy. Debts were abolished and the land divided as Agis had proposed, but the Spartiate lots were made 4000 instead of 4500, the Spartiate body being filled up with Perioeci and approved metics. The common meals and the rigorous Spartan training of the young were restored; here Sphaerus usefully co-operated. These reforms concentrated all power in Cleomenes' hands, and gave him also a strong citizen army, which he re-armed in Macedonian fashion; but just as his land allotment, with the necessary surveys, cannot have been completed for some time, so the reconstitution of the army was perhaps not carried through till Egyptian subsidies became available. He probably built the wall round Sparta of which stone foundations remain, and possibly struck a new coinage with the unaccustomed type of Apollo of Amyclae and his own head—a strong handsome face, if it be his. His panegyrist says that he kept his army free of women and camp-followers, and that his own way of life was the pattern of simplicity; it may well be so, for to one of his overmastering ambition material luxury might mean little. In his new Sparta a majority supported him; but he could not reconcile the wealthy who had opposed Agis, though in dividing the land he set aside lots for the 80 exiles, whom he promised to recall later; like Demetrius I, he meant to imitate Alexander's recall of his political opponents. Probably too some adherents of the Eurypontids remained his enemies; and as the Lycurgan constitution required two kings, and he dared not recall another Eurypontid, he crowned his brother Eucleidas. It was unconstitutional, and gave a handle to those who called him a tyrant; but Sphaerus would doubtless have said that on the contrary he had overthrown a tyranny, a state of things incompatible with that Universal Law to which all, from king to peasant, owed obedience.

The revolution at Sparta greatly affected the Peloponnese. Cleomenes thought that he had been restoring Lycurgus' constitution; the people elsewhere thought that he was carrying out social revolution, and the hopes of all who found this world a hard place began to centre on the brilliant young king. But he affected more than the common people; one of the governing class in Sparta's enemy Megalopolis—Aratus' friend Cercidas, who had Cynic leanings—is actually found preaching philanthropy and exhorting his fellows to heal the sick and give to the poor while they had time, otherwise the social revolution might be upon them and their wealth be taken away. Possibly Cleomenes even affected Boeotia, represented as now sunk in slothful materialism; for though debts were not cancelled they practically ceased to be recoverable, and Polybius blames one Opheltas for using State funds to help the poor. Indeed, had Cleomenes been content to make peace with the willing Aratus and devote himself to the internal betterment of Sparta it does not appear what could have prevented his revolution being permanently successful; in a little country like Laconia the necessary periodical revision of the lots should have been feasible, as Diodorus (v, 9) says it had been at Lipara. But he was in the grip of his ambition; and he was dreaming, not of peace for Sparta or of social reform elsewhere, but of the hegemony of the Peloponnese, perhaps of Greece, and of playing Alexander in a new League of Corinth. There was indeed to be a new League of Corinth, but not under Cleomenes; he was to be forestalled by Antigonus, the rival who, men said, had 'Alexander's own Fortune.'

VIII. CLEOMENES AND ARATUS

So far the driving force of the war had been Megalopolis, whose territory alone had suffered. But Cleomenes now made war differently; in 226 B.C., after again ravaging Megalopolis' lands, he retook Mantinea, where his partisans murdered the Achaean colonists and he re-established the old constitution, passed north and took Lasion, which he restored to his ally Elis (who had joined Sparta in 229), invaded Achaea itself, and at Hecatombaeum near Dyme inflicted a crushing defeat on the Achaean army. The Achaeans, weary of following Megalopolis to disaster, resolved upon peace, and Cleomenes offered to restore land and prisoners in return for the headship of the Achaean League; doubtless he meant to be General for life, as Antigonus was of Thessaly, and to make the League the kernel of his new confederacy, with Sparta playing Macedonia's part. Probably, had he met the Assembly, they would have granted his demand; but he fell ill and had to return to Sparta, and Aratus procured the rejection of the proposal, though many favoured it. But without allies the League lay at Cleomenes' feet; even Ptolemy now transferred his support and subsidies to Cleomenes, as being more likely to hold Macedonia in check. Aratus should have been General for 225, but he refused election, and was ill spoken of for failing his country in her need; his partisan Timoxenus was elected. But the reason of his refusal was that he desired to carry out certain negotiations in a private and not an official capacity. For after Hecatombaeum he had already in spirit made the great betrayal; he, whose life's work it had been to drive the Macedonian out of the Peloponnese, had decided to bring the Macedonian back. He took advantage of the fact that the revelation of Cleomenes' ambition had made Megalopolis—even Cercidas—careless of the means employed to thwart him, and that the dominant party there had always been friendly to Macedonia; and at his instigation two Megalopolitans, Cercidas and Nicophanes, with permission of the Achaeans, approached Antigonus.

It is easy to condemn Aratus, and to say, as some said at the time, that he ought rather to have joined Cleomenes against Macedonia; but how many in his place would have surrendered their position in the League they had made to a younger and hostile rival? Polybius says he was afraid of Aetolia joining Cleomenes; perhaps he knew more than he relates, but, to judge from his narrative, Aetolia's neutrality since 228 had been unexceptional. The truth seems to be that Aratus had lost his hold of the masses; they were turning to Cleomenes, who to them meant land for all and no debts; and what weighed heavily with Aratus and his supporters among the well-to-do was fear of social revolution, against which Macedonia had long been the obvious bulwark (p. 740). Many cities too of the Achaean League had once looked to Macedonia as their suzerain and protector, and there were, as the event showed, strong parties ready to join her again. These reasons amply explain, though they may not excuse, Aratus' action. But one further consideration arises. The man was desperate; in a few months at most all must inevitably be lost; one dare not from an armchair judge too hardly a man struggling blindly with his back to the wall. Some men in Aratus' position would have defied fate and gone down fighting; but he was not of that mettle.

Antigonus too had his ambitions, and he saw that he might utilize the Greek dread of social revolution to regain, by one diplomatic stroke, the position in Greece for which his predecessors had often had to fight. He proffered help, but on terms: the cession of Corinth. The Achaeans could not yet bring themselves to sacrifice a League city, and Aratus, who did not want to take more responsibility than he could help, procured the rejection of the offer by the Assembly. But when in spring 225 Cleomenes moved out from Sparta, the League began to break up; he hardly needed to fight. Every discontented element—men who disliked Aratus, men who hoped to make themselves tyrants —saw its profit in joining him, but the decisive thing was the attitude of the masses; they thought that what Cleomenes had done at Sparta he would do elsewhere, and that there would be a new world. An unexampled wave of revolutionary enthusiasm swept the League's territory; except Megalopolis and Stymphalus, all Arcadia joined him or was easily secured; at Cynaetha the revolution went through and the land was divided. Even one Achaean town, Pellene, expelled the Achaean garrison and went over, its revenge on Aratus for having sacrificed it to the Aetolians in 241. Cleomenes also secured Phlius and almost surprised Sicyon itself; but the League conferred special powers on Aratus, and he mastered the disaffected in his own city. Cleomenes' greatest gain was Argos. Here the popular majority had normally been pro-Macedonian, but the masses had also been prone to revolution, as witness the famous 'cudgelling' (vol. vi, p. 88); possibly the artisan clubs with strange names were really old. As between Macedonia and the revolution, the Argive populace, led by Aristomachus, ex-General of the League, elected for revolution; it is noteworthy that Aristomachus' niece[1] afterwards married a revolutionary, Nabis of Sparta. With their help Cleomenes mastered this important city during the Nemea without bloodshed, and again summoned the League to elect him General, on

[1] A. Wilhelm, *Wien. Anzeiger*, 1921, p. 70.

terms that they should jointly garrison Acrocorinthus; again Aratus procured a refusal. Cleomenes then secured Hermione, Troezen, and Epidaurus, and approached Corinth; and the Corinthians rose and joined him (winter 225), though the Achaean garrison saved Acrocorinthus.

Corinth's defection removed the difficulty of ceding it to Antigonus; but the League, now reduced to Megalopolis, Sicyon, Stymphalus, Megara, and ten Achaean towns, made a last effort. Megara was directed to save herself by joining Boeotia; a special meeting convened at Sicyon then made Aratus dictator[1], with a Sicyonian bodyguard, a form of one man rule which naturally modified the constitution and involved the suspension of the Generalship; consequently no General of the League was again appointed till after Sellasia, though possibly Aratus' powers had to be, and were, annually renewed. But his efforts to secure help from Aetolia and elsewhere had no success. Cleomenes meanwhile drew lines round Acrocorinthus and besieged Sicyon; but the city, under Aratus' command, was still holding out when the date of the spring meeting (224) arrived. Aratus slipped out and reached Aegium by sea; and the Achaean Rump passed the fateful vote to accept Antigonus' terms. Cleomenes at once raised the siege of Sicyon, and fortified lines across the Isthmus, connecting them with his circumvallation of Acrocorinthus. Aetolia, anxious about her neutrality, now courted Ptolemy III and set up statues of him and his family; to this time may also belong her friendship with Attalus I of Pergamum, who at some time before 220 fortified Elaus for her and perhaps built his portico in Delphi to celebrate his Gallic victory (p. 721). Athens, for the same reason, instituted a festival in Ptolemy's honour, and created a thirteenth tribe, Ptolemais, while retaining the two Macedonian tribes.

IX. CLEOMENES AND ANTIGONUS[2]

Antigonus had come south through Euboea, Aetolia having enforced her neutrality and forbidden him passage through Thermopylae; by early summer (224) he was in the Megarid, where Aratus joined him, having appointed Timoxenus to com-

---

[1] Plutarch, *Aratus*, 41: *Strategos autokrator*. This was the form, with a bodyguard, under which the tyrants Gelon (vol. IV, pp. 370, 372) and Dionysius I (Diodorus, XIII, 94, 95) had acquired and held power in Syracuse; Polybius uses it as equivalent to the Roman dictator, III, 86, 7; 87, 6; 103, 4. See further vol. IV, p. 155; VI, p. 116; (Sir) A. J. Evans in Freeman's *History of Sicily*, vol. IV, pp. 211 *sqq.*; H. Swoboda, *Staatsaltertümer*, pp. 84 *sqq.*

[2] On the chronology of this section see chronological note 3, p. 863 *sq.*

mand the Achaean troops in his absence. Antigonus' attempt however to pierce the Isthmus lines failed. But military success could not prevent Cleomenes' cause being already lost; for the masses everywhere had learnt that he had no intention of introducing a general social revolution, and in their disillusionment they were ready to abandon him as quickly as they had joined him. A deputation from Argos so informed Aratus; and while he with 1500 of Antigonus' men made for Argos by sea, Timoxenus marched the League troops thither behind Cleomenes' back, and Argos changed sides. The danger to his communications made Cleomenes' lines untenable; he evacuated them and hurried to Argos, while Antigonus occupied Acrocorinthus. For a moment Cleomenes recaptured Argos, but Antigonus was hard on his heels, and he had to abandon the city and fall back to cover Sparta; to crown his misfortune came news of his wife's death. Antigonus occupied Argos, where Aristomachus was justly enough executed for treason; all Argolis joined him; and at the autumn meeting at Aegium he finally constituted the new Hellenic League which he had already begun to form.

For the last time in Greece Alexander's policy of free alliances was revived; Antigonus' League recalled the Leagues of Alexander and Demetrius I, but it was no longer a League of cities; conformably to the spirit of the age, it was a League of Leagues. The members were the Macedonian and Thessalian Leagues, and Antigonus' allies the Leagues of Achaea, Boeotia, Epirus, Acarnania, Euboea, and non-Aetolian Phocis; Boeotia included Megara and Opuntian Locris, and Macedonia included Magnesia, *i.e.* Demetrias. Antigonus' League had no federal income, and the constituent states had to confirm a declaration of war and (contrary to the provisions of Demetrius' League) suffered no penalty if they refused cooperation; the new League was thus less centralized than that of Demetrius, though Antigonus may have had many of Demetrius' powers. Though powerful, the Hellenic League was not Panhellenic; beside Sparta, it did not include Aetolia, her friends Elis and Messenia, or Athens; and it could not, like the older Panhellenic Leagues, meet at the Panhellenic festivals, for Aetolia controlled Delphi and (through Elis) Olympia. In fact, Greece was definitely split in two. But it restored Macedonia's influence in Greece, for its members could not conduct an independent foreign policy. Antigonus' proclamation later that he was not at war with Sparta but only with Cleomenes shows that a primary business of his League was to crush the social revolution. The Hellenic League's delegates met at Aegium and elected

Antigonus commander-in-chief; he wintered at Corinth and Sicyon, and Aratus took part in Sicyon's worship of a Macedonian king.

In 223 Antigonus invaded Arcadia, took Tegea, and advanced to the Laconian border; but Cleomenes' strong garrison in Orchomenus threatened his rear and compelled him to turn and take the place; a counterstroke of Cleomenes against Megalopolis failed. The smaller Arcadian towns joined Antigonus, but Mantinea resisted. He stormed the town and abandoned it to Achaean vengeance for the settlers murdered four years before (p. 756), a vengeance which brought much disgrace on the Achaean name; for, besides executing the guilty, they razed the 'Lovely City' and sold the entire surviving population as slaves, a horrible law of war which had apparently been falling into disuse. Aratus must bear his share of blame. Having secured Arcadia, Antigonus in September retired to Argos with his mercenaries and sent his Macedonians home to winter; like every Macedonian king, he spared them all he could. Cleomenes' inactivity during the summer possibly means that he was re-arming his troops; he also freed and armed a small body of Helots, for which there was precedent, but the story that he obtained 500 talents by selling 6000 Helots their freedom may be doubted, for next year he was short of money, despite Ptolemy's subsidies. But once the Macedonians had gone, he struck hard; he surprised and captured Megalopolis itself. Most of the people escaped, and he offered them their city again in return for their alliance; the young Philopoemen persuaded them to refuse, whereupon Cleomenes plundered and razed the city in revenge for Mantinea, while next spring (222) he ravaged Argos' territory up to the walls. Antigonus was helpless and the moral impression was considerable, but in reality Cleomenes, possibly from lack of money, only illustrated once more, as Leosthenes had done before Lamia (vol. vi, p. 457), the weakness of Greek warfare as compared with Macedonian: Greeks never now possessed, or made, siege-trains.

By June 222 the Macedonians had returned, and Antigonus collected his forces for the invasion of Laconia. He had some 28,000 men, including beside mercenaries 13,000 Macedonians, about 9000 League troops, and 1600 Illyrian allies under Demetrius of Pharos, a Greek who was now powerful in Illyria (p. 844). Cleomenes, who had raised 20,000 men, was outnumbered; his only chance was skilful use of the ground. Antigonus approached from Tegea, and Cleomenes occupied a position in the middle Oenus (Kelephina) valley north of Sellasia; but exactly where he stood cannot be satisfactorily established from

Polybius' account[1], though the battlefield was near his home. It is impossible also to reconcile the contradictions in our accounts of the battle; but as these go back to three sources—Aratus, who if there was not in action; Philopoemen (probably), who drove his immediate opponents right off the battlefield; and some person unknown on Cleomenes' side—honest discrepancies are inevitable. The political situation, however, shows that on the main point Spartan tradition (Phylarchus) is right and Megalopolitan tradition (Polybius) wrong: Cleomenes charged because he meant to charge and not as a forlorn hope. For the situation was that Antigonus had induced Ptolemy III to abandon Cleomenes (p. 722) and Cleomenes was short of money to pay his men; both commanders therefore desired a decision, Antigonus because it was necessary to destroy the army of the revolution, and Cleomenes because victory was his only chance; he could no longer afford a war of manœuvre, and he had obviously resolved not to stand a siege in Sparta, doubtless through fear of treachery by the opposition, though by the irony of history a brief siege would have saved him, owing to Dardania's intervention.

Cleomenes' position bestrode the Oenus valley; he himself with his phalanx, 6000, and 5000 mercenaries and light-armed, held a palisaded position on Olympus, a sloping hill on his right; his brother Eucleidas with 6000 Perioeci occupied a detached hill, Euas, on the left; in the valley between were some 3000 men. The right was the striking force, the centre and left being really flank guards. Antigonus did not wish to turn the position, even if he could, and could not pierce the centre, commanded from either flank; his decision, after long reconnoitring, to attack Euas seems an obvious one. On his left he himself commanded his phalanx, 10,000, and 5000 mercenaries; in the centre were his 1200 horse, which included the Achaean cavalry under Philopoemen, and a few allies, including 1000 Megalopolitan exiles under Cercidas; his right apparently was in two columns, the inner led by 1000 Acarnanians, the outer composed of the Illyrians and the 3000 Macedonian Bronze Shields, successors of Alexander's hypaspists.

The battle was probably fought early in July. In the night Antigonus' right established themselves under Euas; at dawn the Acarnanian column began the ascent, while the Illyrian column, invisible to Eucleidas and hidden by Euas itself from Cleomenes, turned the hill and ascended from the flank. The Acarnanian column drew the defenders' attention; Cleomenes' centre also attacked it, and Philopoemen charged without orders and drove

[1] For this controversy see the works cited in the Bibliography.

the centre off; Antigonus commended him with a smile, for it was not the real operation. The real striking force, the Illyrian column, surprised and completely defeated Eucleidas, uncovering Cleomenes' flank. Meanwhile on Olympus the mercenaries engaged each other; but before the Illyrians came into sight, and while Eucleidas still stood his ground, Cleomenes called in his mercenaries, Antigonus following his example, and the Spartan phalanx, overthrowing their palisade, lowered their lances and charged magnificently down the slope. The fire of their attack drove Antigonus' phalanx back a considerable distance; meanwhile Euas fell. Whether their effort wore itself out, or whether they were threatened on their now uncovered flank, cannot be said; certainly the two phalanxes lost contact. Antigonus then reformed his Macedonians in close order and attacked in turn; numbers and experience overbore the gallant resistance of the Spartans; after heavy loss they broke, and all was over. Spartan kings died on a lost field; but Cleomenes and some friends escaped to Gythium, where a ship lay ready to take them to Egypt; he had made beforehand his pathetic decision that death was too easy, and that, whatever the obloquy, he must live for Sparta. For three years he ate out his heart in exile, waiting for the help which Egypt never gave; then he and his friends, virtually prisoners, rose against Ptolemy IV (219), tried and failed to raise Alexandria, and finally slew each other, leaving their wives and families to be murdered. History must regret that Cleomenes had not died with his Spartans at Sellasia.

Thus, after many centuries, Sparta was taken. Antigonus was not vindictive; but the ephorate was of course restored (the kingship remaining in abeyance), many of Cleomenes' men lost their land, and Sparta became an ally, perhaps a member, of the Hellenic League; Antigonus appointed a temporary governor to superintend the transition, and dedicated his spoils at Delos. He garrisoned Orchomenus, and Heraea on the Elean frontier; otherwise he re-established the Achaean League and enlarged it by the addition of Tegea, and as there was trouble between rich and poor over the rebuilding of Megalopolis he nominated one Prytanis as lawgiver; but the troubles continued till 217, when Aratus settled them by appointing Cercidas, who could perhaps see both sides, to make fresh laws. The Achaean constitution was restored, and Aratus refounded Mantinea as Antigoneia; there and in many other cities Antigonus was worshipped as Saviour and Benefactor. But much of this took place after Antigonus' return to Macedonia; for hardly was Sellasia fought when a

Dardanian[1] invasion called him home. He defeated the Dardanians, but his exertions brought on haemorrhage of the lungs; though not immediately fatal, it was his death-warrant. He lived for a year, and made all arrangements for Philip's succession; he sent him to visit Aratus and study the affairs of Greece, appointed Apelles his guardian, and filled all offices with men he thought he could trust. He died in autumn 221, aged 42, a loss alike to Macedonia, whose power he had restored, and to Greece, where, except at Mantinea, he had on the whole used that power with moderation and equity.

X. THE WAR OF THE ALLIES

No Macedonian king for a century had come to the throne amid such high hopes as the seventeen-year old Philip V. Nature had endowed him with many qualities: ability and resource, a regal presence and an amazing memory, daring and skill in war, and great personal charm. He was fond of recalling his relationship, on his mother's side, to Alexander; and few perhaps guessed that beneath the surface lay Alexander's temper without Alexander's control, and a cruelty long foreign to the Antigonids. But for the present he was ready to follow in Antigonus' steps; and it was Aetolia's fault, not his, that his first years were occupied by the meaningless struggle between the Macedonian and non-Macedonian halves of Greece called the War of the Allies (commonly known as the Social War). Aetolia had loyally kept her arrangement with Antigonus, and, though friendly with Ptolemy III, had not moved to save Cleomenes; but after Antigonus' death she thought that she could act as she chose: Philip was only a boy. She had invented a method, not unknown afterwards to Elizabeth of England, whereby private citizens made war while the government remained at peace, ready to adopt or disown their proceedings as seemed expedient; and the present war was brought about by two Aetolian citizens, Dorimachus and Scopas, who played much the part which Drake was to play against another Philip. Possibly Philip still for awhile controlled Delos (where he afterwards dedicated the spoils of the war) and certain islands; but the growing anarchy in the Aegean, even before Antigonus' death, had been Aetolia's opportunity, and her corsairs harried any island unless she had granted it immunity, a grant she had previously made to Delos, Ceos, Chios, Tenos, and Mitylene, and was in 219 to make to Athens.

[1] Niese, *Gesch. der griech. und maked. Staaten*, II, 347. See however below, p. 843 n. 1. Polybius says Illyrians.

Dorimachus was Aetolian governor in Phigalea. His privateersmen wanted occupation, and he let them raid Phigalea's ally Messenia; and when Messenia protested, he and Scopas with Cephallenian ships ferried an Aetolian force over to Achaea, through which it marched plundering to Phigalea and thence raided Messenia afresh. Messenia applied for help to Achaea, who, angered by the violation of her territory, agreed; Aratus, General-elect for 220, took the seals five days before he should, sent the Aetolians an ultimatum, tried to cut them off from return with an inadequate force, and was badly defeated near Caphyae; but the indignation in Achaea as usual subsided when he addressed the Achaeans. The Aetolian spring Assembly (220) disavowed Dorimachus and Scopas to the extent of declaring that Aetolia was at peace with Messenia, but they also resolved to fight Achaea if she interfered; and the government made no attempt to prevent Dorimachus and Scopas, with a large force, raiding Arcadia and burning Cynaetha. The Achaeans secured Messenia's admission to the Hellenic League, and then called on Philip for help; he summoned the delegates of the Hellenic League to Corinth, and all came with bitter complaints of Aetolian raids and sacrilege. Philip did not want war, and understood that his allies meant to utilize him as the instrument of their vengeance, but he stood by his covenant, and the congress passed a war resolution: all territory taken by Aetolia from any of the allies since the death of Demetrius II must be restored; every city that had joined the Aetolian League under compulsion was, in the time-honoured formula, to be again free, ungarrisoned, and self-governing; and Aetolia was to surrender her control of the Amphictyons and restore to them the temple at Delphi. Philip then gave Aetolia another chance: he would hear anything they had to say in their defence, but, failing that, the responsibility for war would rest with them. The Aetolian reply was to make Scopas General (September 220). The allies ratified the resolution, though Epirus was half-hearted and Messenia intimated that she could not fight while Aetolia held Phigalea.

Several things beside his obligations to the Hellenic League were influencing Philip. His two advisers were pulling him different ways. Aratus had been through deep waters, which had left their mark; henceforth he plays the honourable part of upholding Philip's better nature and encouraging him in the constitutional path. Apelles greatly desired power for himself; he also desired that Philip should abandon Antigonus Doson's policy, return to that of Cassander, and treat the Greeks as subjects, not allies; but he failed to guess that Philip was stronger than himself. But more important to Philip than these things was Rome. The Roman conquest of Illyria and acquisition of Atintania had definitely cut off Macedonia from the Adriatic (see below, p. 839); also Teuta's husband had been Macedonia's ally, and Doson can have had no love for Rome. Philip did not want war in Greece till he saw what would happen in the West; for Doson's friend Demetrius of Pharos and the Illyrian Scerdilaidas had just broken the treaty with Rome (p. 847), and Demetrius was privateering in the Aegean, presumably in Macedonia's interest. Hence Philip was disinclined to commit himself too far; he gave Aetolia a second chance, and when trouble arose in Sparta and Apelles advised him to wipe the city out he properly replied that, provided she kept her obligations as an ally, her internal affairs were not his business.

War began in the spring of 219 B.C. with Scopas invading Macedonia, taking and razing Dium, and burning the porticoes and offerings in the temple precinct. Greek laws of war pardoned much; but to touch sacred things was outside all law, and considered unpardonable. In Sparta the Cleomenists had murdered the pro-Macedonian ephors and appointed a new board, who naturally allied themselves with Aetolia; they hoped for Cleomenes' return, but on the news of his death (spring 219) they restored the kingship and set up as kings Agesipolis and Lycurgus, the latter not a Heraclid; and in Aetolia's interest Sparta and Elis declared war on Achaea. Sparta had been so weakened that Lycurgus could only undertake border raids, but Elis provided Aetolia with a good base and ample supplies. The division in Greece even extended to Crete, where some towns were fighting against Cnossos' supremacy; the west of the island joined Philip, while Cnossos and her friends supported Aetolia. Philip on his side at present only proposed to defend his allies while sparing his Macedonians. He had in spring entered Acarnania through Epirus; but Rome sent a punitive expedition against Demetrius of Pharos (p. 848 *sq.*), and for half the season Philip marked time and waited on Rome's actions. He restored to Acarnania her seaport Oeniadae, and took Ambracus, a fort covering Ambracia; but he made no attempt to take Ambracia and cut Aetolia off from the Adriatic. In summer Demetrius, defeated, fled to Philip (p. 851); and Philip, who now knew that Rome would be fully employed with Carthage, returned home to attend to Dardania. He ordered Larissa, which had suffered from famine and was partly depopulated, perhaps by the exile in 228 of Aetolia's partisans, to fill up her citizen body with metics, that her lands might be cultivated;

the reasons he gave show that he had studied Roman methods. Meanwhile the Aetolians ravaged Achaea from Elis with such impunity that Dyme, Pharae, and Tritaea refused to pay the League's taxes and hired mercenaries for themselves instead, Tritaea raising money by selling citizenships; it illustrates the lack of grip which now characterized the Achaean League. In September Dorimachus succeeded Scopas as Aetolian General; he raided Dodona, and burnt the porticoes and offerings in the temple precinct.

The first round had gone to Aetolia; and Philip, relieved of anxiety as regards both Rome and Dardania, saw that an autumn campaign in Peloponnese was necessary. He took only a small force, but soon straightened things out; he defeated and ravaged Elis, took the strong border city of Psophis and joined it to the Achaean League, gave the Achaeans back Lasion, and methodically reduced all Triphylia, including Phigalea, in six days; he kept Triphylia himself and appointed a governor, a triumph for Apelles. He wintered at Argos, and there it became evident that, like Alexander, he would have trouble with his generals. Apelles was pressing him to treat Achaea like Thessaly, i.e., to declare himself perpetual head of the Achaean League; he refused, but Apelles in his name improperly influenced the Achaean elections against Aratus, and one Eperatus was elected General. That Apelles wanted to train the incompetent Achaean troops and prevent Achaea being merely a source of weakness to Philip was natural, but he made the mistake of attacking Aratus personally, and Philip did Aratus justice; and when Eperatus failed to provide supplies, Philip wisely supported Aratus whole-heartedly, with the result that a special Achaean meeting called in June 218 voted liberal subsidies. Apelles then conspired with Megaleas, the state secretary, and Leontius, commander of the Bronze Shields, to hamper Philip in every way short of open revolt.

Philip had decided that, if he was both to fight Aetolia and defend Achaea, he must move by water; he collected what ships he and Achaea possessed, procured some Illyrian vessels, and taught his Macedonians to row. He then attacked Cephallenia, Aetolia's naval base, but failed to take Pale through the treachery of Leontius. Leontius then sought to waste time in Messenia; but the Aetolians had invaded Thessaly, and Philip decided on a counterstroke. He landed at Limnaea in the Ambracian Gulf, was joined by the Acarnanians, and set out on a forced march for Thermum, Aetolia's federal centre, which had never yet seen an enemy. With the Macedonians guarded on all sides by less important troops he surprised Thermum and sacked the store-houses; great booty was taken, and 15,000 stand of arms burnt. He then took a step so remote from his previous acts in the war that, whether or not suggested by Demetrius of Pharos, it probably furnishes the first indication of his periodic lack of control; he avenged Dium and Dodona by burning the porticoes and offerings in the temple precinct. It was human, but fatal. He had been waging a limited war, with one eye on Italy and one on peace; he had not attempted to cut Aetolia off from the Adriatic, or to force Sparta and Elis into his Hellenic League. He evidently thought of reconciling Aetolia, as Doson had done; at one stroke he now made reconciliation impossible. With great skill he got his army and booty back to Limnaea intact, after a difficult rearguard action in the dangerous pass along Lake Trichonis; he then made for Corinth at full speed, summoned the Achaeans, and within a fortnight of leaving Thermum stood under the walls of Sparta, a feat regarded as impossible. He plundered Laconia scientifically, drove in Lycurgus, and camped with impunity outside the city; more he did not do; he was only warning Sparta as he had warned Aetolia.

On his return to Corinth, Rhodes and Chios tried to mediate, and he professed himself ready for peace. This brought the con-spiracy against him to a head; Megaleas entered into treasonable correspondence with Aetolia, Leontius raised a mutiny in the army, and Apelles, who had secured many governors of cities, came to Corinth with a great retinue, as though power were already his. But the boy of twenty had only been waiting for the tortoise to put its head out. He talked plainly to the troops, who were essentially loyal; his general in the Peloponnese, Taurion, stood by him; he arrested and executed Apelles and Leontius, while Megaleas committed suicide; like Alexander, he had no more trouble.

But these had been three of Doson's trusted men; he wanted to show the Macedonians that they could do as well without them, and to show Aetolia that she had better make peace. In spring 217 he collected an enormous siege-train, and having first drawn Dardania's teeth by recapturing Bylazora, he set out from Larissa to wage real war; though his ladders proved too short to take Melitaea, whose lofty walls commanded the road over Othrys, he reached his objective, Phthiotic Thebes, by another route and reduced the strong city without a hitch by operations worthy of Demetrius the Besieger. It was Aetolia's anchor on the Aegean and her base for invading Thessaly and Macedonia; under the resolution of the Hellenic League in 220 it reverted to himself as part of Macedonian Thessaly. He sold the Aetolian settlers, but the Thebans were allowed to settle at Thronium in Aetolia; he colonized the place with Macedonians, and renamed it Philippopolis. Apparently he next meditated entering Phocis and attempting Delphi, which Aetolia had garrisoned; but at the Nemea a courier brought him news of Hannibal's victory at Trasimene. Peace now was vital, for he wanted his hands free for events in Italy; and he took advantage of a fresh mediation by Rhodes, Chios, Byzantium, and Egypt to approach Aetolia. Aetolia was ready; instead of a boy she had met a man; also there was a party, led by Agelaus of Naupactus, which, though originally desirous of war, now wanted peace on more honourable grounds than expediency. Philip summoned the delegates of the Hellenic League to meet him, and at Aetolia's request crossed and encamped near Naupactus, where peace was quickly made (about August 217), each side to retain what it had. The war had shown that, though the Hellenic League had held together, it was no match for the independent half of Greece unless Philip intervened; while the war party in Aetolia were now Philip's irreconcilable enemies for ever.

But the conference of Naupactus is notable for this, that it saw a last vain appeal made for Hellenic unity against the barbarian. Agelaus' famous speech is substantially genuine, otherwise Polybius would never have put it into the mouth of one of the hated Aetolians. Pointing to Italy, Agelaus said that, instead of fighting each other, they ought to thank heaven if by all taking hands, like men crossing a river, they could save themselves from the barbarian who, whether Rome or Carthage won, would certainly threaten Greece, and he appealed personally to Philip to treat the whole Hellenic world as his kin; if he desired scope for his energy, let him be ready to fight the victor of Italy in the common cause; with prudence he might reach any height. But Greeks he must let be; 'for,' said he, 'if the cloud rising in the west once overspreads Greece, we shall, I fear, no longer play the games which now like children we play together; rather shall we be praying to the gods to give us back the chance of fighting and making peace with each other when we choose, and even of calling our very quarrels our own.' For the moment he produced some effect. He was elected General and during his year kept Aetolia in the strait path; while Philip, now the 'darling of Hellas,' attracted such widespread goodwill that even the turbulent Cretans ceased fighting each other and the whole island voluntarily joined him. But it was a delusive gleam, the last shaft of sunlight beneath the lowering cloud. In five years' time Agelaus' countrymen were to be again fighting Greeks, and their ally was to be Rome.

CHAPTER XXIV

THE CARTHAGINIANS IN SPAIN

I. EARLY SETTLEMENTS IN SPAIN

IN volumes III and IV we have seen how Greek colonization had, for a moment, transformed the Western Mediterranean almost into a Greek Lake. While the main effort had been concentrated in Sicily and South Italy, the bolder Phocaeans in the seventh century B.C. had pushed farther afield along the Ligurian coast to found Massilia, down the east coast of Spain to found Hemeroscopium, near Denia, and on the south coast to Maenace (east of Malaga); these three being the most westerly Greek colonies. With good reason Bias of Priene could advise the Ionians, when threatened by Persian encroachment, to found in Sardinia a state where they would be free to develope (vol. IV, p. 117). But now a competitor entered these seas from the south. About 600 B.C. Carthage spread her empire over the north coast of Africa, thus staking out her claim to the hegemony of the Western Mediterranean. Strife was inevitable between Hellenes and Barbarians, and the Carthaginians found in the Etruscans allies whose interests were at one with their own in their common hatred of the Greeks.

Carthage made the first move in the struggle under the leadership of a rich, able, and warlike general, Malchus, who carried on the war in Sicily and Sardinia, where it was continued after his death by a succession of generals of the house of Mago. And the Barbarians were materially assisted by the subjugation of the Ionian states in Asia to Persia. Finally in 535 B.C. a sea-battle took place at Alalia on the west coast of Corsica between the Phocaeans who had established themselves there some twenty years earlier and the allied Carthaginians and Etruscans. Tactically the battle was a victory for the Phocaeans, but its actual results were entirely in favour of the Barbarians, since almost the entire Phocaean fleet was destroyed or disabled, and the Greeks evacuated the island. Alalia marks the end of the brilliant Phocaean thalassocracy in the Western Mediterranean (vol. IV, pp. 356 *sqq.*).

But the setback would not have been so decisive if the Phocaeans had not lost their mother-city to the Persians and there-

with their base for westerly colonization. The struggle of the
Barbarians against the Greeks spread over the whole Greek
world, led in the east by the Persians and in the west by the
Carthaginians and Etruscans, exactly as later the so-called
Peloponnesian War was a world-war whose battle grounds were
alike in the East—in Hellas and Asia, and in the West—in
Sicily. On the Barbarian side the war was waged with the
greatest savagery; Phocaean prisoners were stoned to death.
After Alalia the two allied powers hastened to make use of their
victory. The immediate prize, Corsica, the Carthaginians resigned to the Etruscans, since they had no interests in this island,
which by its geographical position belongs to Italy. But Sardinia
from now onwards was held by the Carthaginians in undisputed
possession. From Sardinia it is less than two days sail to the
Balearic Isles off the east coast of Spain. Hence Spain was the
next object of Carthaginian imperialism.

Spain, especially Andalusia, was in consequence of its mineral
wealth one of the most coveted lands of the ancient world. And
the Carthaginians may have believed that they had a real historical
claim to it, since the Tyrian colony at Gades had founded a
Spanish dominion after subduing the unwarlike Tartessians
(c. 800 B.C.?). Later, after the fall of Tyre, in the first half of the
seventh century, the Tartessians succeeded in freeing themselves,
and under the long rule of the far-famed King Arganthonius
'the silver man' their city enjoyed a final period of brilliance
from 620–540 B.C. The Phoenician towns Gades, Malaca,
Sexi, Abdera, were not threatened, but the Phocaeans enjoyed
commercial preference in their trade with Tartessus. Arganthonius had maintained friendly relations with them, and they
founded the colony Maenace on the south coast.

II. SPAIN IN THE GREAT AGE OF TARTESSUS

A very trustworthy picture of conditions in the Iberian peninsula and the empire of Tartessus is preserved in a description
of a coasting voyage (*Periplus*) by a Massiliote sailor written
about 520 B.C.[1] The voyage was made from Massilia to Tartessus
and back, and the sailor describes the return journey with the
enhanced accuracy of a second view. The detailed description
begins at Tartessus, or rather at the mouth of the Tagus, which
was connected with that city by an overland trade-route. A

[1] See A. Schulten, *Avieni Ora Maritima* in *Fontes Hispaniae Antiquae*,
I, 1922, in which is a map of Spain to illustrate the *Periplus*.

short introductory account deals with the coast lands from
Brittany to Tartessus, the tin trade-route; for this metal was in
demand for the manufacture of the beautiful Tartessian bronze
which was exported as far as Greece. It was mined on the coasts
of Brittany and the group of tiny islands adjacent. But the
Periplus makes mention also of lands lying farther north; for
in Brittany (Oestrymnis) the tribesmen told the Tartessian sailors
of their adventurous voyages in boats made of sewn hides to
Ierne (Ireland) and to the North Sea coasts, whence the Ligurians
had been pushed out by the southward pressure of Celtic tribes
moving along the coast. In this latter region the Oestrymnians
probably found amber, the gold of the North. The mention of
Ierne and Albion is the most ancient reference to the British
Isles.

The return journey of the Tartessians was made from Brittany
to the west coast of France, at that time still inhabited by Ligurians; then to the north coast of Spain passing C. Venus (C.
Higuer) and C. Aryium (C. Ortegal), thence to the west coast of
Spain, the island of Saturn (Berlenga) and C. Ophiussa (C. Roca).
Ophiussa is the most ancient name of the Iberian peninsula; like
other names in -*ussa* it belongs to the dialect of the Phocaeans, the
trade-allies of the Tartessians. Off C. Roca the sailors heard
stories of the wild Dragani, a Ligurian people, who lived on the
north coast of Spain; and of Cempsi and Saefes who were probably
Celts. For during the sixth century the Celts had occupied the west
of the peninsula and the central highlands, previously held by the
Ligurians, the oldest known inhabitants of Spain. C. Cempsicum
(C. Espichel) got its name from these Celts. Between C. Espichel
and the Guadiana lived the Cynetes, probably a Ligurian tribe,
who were known to Herodotus as the most westerly of all.
Between the Guadiana and the Hiberus (Rio Tinto) dwelt the
Iberians, a part of the great stock which had spread far and wide
over the peninsula giving it its name. Next we find Tartessians
at the river Tinto, for here the boundaries of that state began,
and her domains stretched as far as C. Nao on the east coast. In
the middle reaches of the Guadalquivir there were the Ileates and
in the higher reaches the Etmaneans.

The first tribe in Tartessian territory was the Cilbiceni between the Guadalquivir and the Guadiaro. On the coast came
next the Liby-phoenicians, Phoenician colonists from Tyre who
had been subjects of Tartessus since about 700 B.C. The Mastieni
occupied the interior as far as C. Palos. Their town was called
Mastia and lay on the site of the later Cartagena. Between C.

Palos and C. Nao there were the Iberian Gymnetes. The boundary of Tartessian territory seems to have been C. Nao. Then northward from C. Nao as far as the Pyrenees there were several tribes, amongst which the names are known of the Indigetes (in the gulf of Rosa) and the Ceretes (in the eastern Pyrenees). And also north of the Pyrenees there were more Iberian tribes, in particular as far as Oranus (now Lez near Montpellier), where the Ligurians began. On the plateau above the Jucar and Guadalquivir dwelt the Berybraces, a Celtic stock like the Cempsi and Saefes in the West.

Thus at the time of the *Periplus* while the empire of Tartessus embraces all Andalusia and Murcia between the Guadalquivir and C. Nao, Celts inhabit the highlands of Castille and the West, and 'Iberians' the north-east coast. But the Cilbiceni and Mastieni in the south must also count as Iberians, since this name is found also between the Guadiana and Tinto rivers. It is clear that the Iberians, immigrants from Africa, had pushed along the south and east coasts and northwards as far as the Pyrenees, whereas the Celts had occupied the central plateau and the West. Traces of the Ligurians are still to be found in the 'Ligurian Lake' on the lower Guadalquivir, apart from the Ligurian Dragani on the north-west coast, and the Cynetes in the north-east.

This great southern empire of Tartessus is a remarkable phenomenon. It is the one great political creation not only of Spain at that time, but in Spain throughout ancient history. Indeed in culture it stood very far above the barbarism of the wild Celtic and Iberian tribes. The racial affinities of Tartessus are a riddle. One wonders whether they were an Iberian stock civilized by early contact with Phoenicians and Greeks; or whether they should not be regarded as an entirely foreign element, colonists from the East, perhaps from Asia Minor (or Crete).

Tartessus, or as the Phoenicians called it Tarshish, the capital of the empire, lay at the mouth of the river of that name (the Baetis) and possessed a rich and ancient culture shown both in material and intellectual achievements. The source of her wealth was vast deposits of minerals in the Sierra Morena, which as far back as 2000 B.C. had been worked by unknown previous inhabitants, 'the Pre-Tartessians'; even at that time it had already been developed into the most important metal industry of the West. The bronze of Tartessus won world-wide fame and found its way into the treasuries of Olympia[1]. Trade went hand in hand

[1] Pausanias VI, 19, 2–4. See Schulten, *Tartessos*, p. 25, n. 4.

with industry, partly in the passive form of commercial dealing with merchants from the East, first Tyrians and later Greeks, and in part actively in voyages to Britain for tin and even to the west coast of Africa for gold and ivory. In the sixth and fifth centuries, there was in Andalusia under the influence of the Greeks a highly developed art. It is known to us in the reliefs of Osuna, in the statues of animals like the lions of Corduba and Bocairente, and the statues of 'Cerro de los Santos,' while perhaps the finest example is the 'Lady of Elche' (vol. of Plates I, 294). The bronzes and the artistically painted vases are of high merit, for in this department also the Tartessians knew how to learn from Greek models and then to manufacture their own ware. Tartessus is credited with a literature of ancient origin and high development. It boasted high antiquity—six thousand years, so it was claimed—and consisted of histories, epics, and laws, written in metrical form. Architecture too was important; there were stone temples and town walls of ashlar masonry (Castel Ibros). One art alone was neglected, the art of military defence against foreign attack. Such were the peace and culture into which the Carthaginians broke, bringing the law that might is right.

III. THE CARTHAGINIAN CONQUEST

After their conquest of Sardinia the Carthaginians reached the Balearic Isles. But it was not till later that they succeeded in getting any firm foothold on them. The capital of the island of Minorca, the town of Mago (to-day Mahon) is clearly named after a Mago, but it is probably the later general of that name who captured it in 206 B.C. The Balearic Isles kept their autonomy, but supplied the Carthaginians with their famous slingers. On the other hand they succeeded completely in winning the neighbouring island, Ebusus (Ibiza), which had already been visited by the Phoenicians and which now became Carthaginian[1]. From Ibiza it is only a day's sail to the east coast of Spain. In the south the inhabitants were subjects of Tartessus, but in the north there were free Iberian tribes. The trade had been the monopoly of the Phocaeans, who had founded here their colony of Hemeroscopium, and of the Massiliotes.

[1] On the few Phoenician finds on the island of Plana, which lies off the harbour of Ibiza, see Vives, *Estudio de arte cartaginesa*, p. 15. According to Timaeus *ap*. Diod. v, 16 the Carthaginians colonized Ibiza 160 years after the founding of Carthage, *i.e.* about 650 B.C., but the archaeological finds appear only to extend back into the sixth century.

Whether there had been wars earlier, about 600 B.C., between Massilia and Carthage is doubtful[1]. But now after the battle of Alalia, the Massiliotes seem to have made a successful resistance, since we see that the Carthaginian empire in Spain only reached as far as Cartagena and C. Palos, which proves that Massilia remained in possession of the north half of the east coast[2]. It appears that Massilia even had extended her zone of influence. For in the Periplus, Hemeroscopium and C. Nao rather than C. Palos are mentioned as the boundaries between Tartessus and the Phocaeans. While an understanding was reached with the stout Massiliotes, and C. Palos was accepted as marking that frontier, the Carthaginians succeeded in conquering the whole empire of Tartessus which stretched from a point south of C. Nao to the river Guadiana.

Unfortunately we possess hardly any direct reference[3] to the collapse of Tartessus and the Carthaginian conquest. But the fact is certain. For in the first treaty between Rome and Carthage, that of 508 B.C.[4], Carthage, as mistress of Spain, prohibits the Romans and their allies from sailing in those waters; and further Polybius (II, 1, 6) tells us that Hamilcar in 237 had to 're-conquer' Andalusia, which shows that Carthage must have held it before, and lost it.

There is, further, one remarkable piece of evidence for the struggle and the Carthaginian victory over Tartessus. The Massiliote *Periplus*, which gives the latest evidence for Tartessus, mentions a trade-route from Maenace, which as a Phocaean colony was closely bound by friendship to Tartessus, over the mountains

---

[1] Thucyd. 1, 13 Φωκαῆς τε Μασσαλίαν οἰκίζοντες Καρχηδονίους ἐνίκων ναυμαχοῦντες. The use of the present tense οἰκίζοντες would seem to show that war must be dated near the time of the colonization of Massilia about 600 B.C. (Gsell, I, 424) whereas the notices of Massiliote victories in Justin, XLIII, 5, 2 and Pausanias, X, 8, 6 may refer to the later time.

[2] In the second treaty between Carthage and Rome 348 B.C. (see p. 777). A further argument that C. Palos was the northern limit of Carthaginian power is the fact that Massilia was able to found two colonies between C. Palos and C. Nao, namely Alonis (Benidorm) and Lucentum (Alicante), see below, p. 780.

[3] Unless Strabo, III, p. 149, οὗτοι (οἱ Ταρτήσσιοι) γὰρ Φοίνιξιν οὕτως ἐγένοντο ὑποχείριοι, refers to the Carthaginians rather than the earlier subjection of Tartessus to the Phoenicians about 800 B.C. The converse of this confusion would be in Justin, XLIV, 5, 1 which has 'Carthaginienses' and not 'Phoenices' in a passage which treats of the struggle of the Phoenicians against Tartessus. See Schulten, *Tartessos*, p. 18.

[4] On the date of this treaty see further chronological note 1, p. 859.

to that city in five days, and farther to the mouth of the Tagus. The voyage by sea from Maenace to Tartessus takes no more than three days and is much easier than this route through wild mountain country, which must therefore owe its existence to the closing of the sea-route through the straits by the Carthaginians. Here, then, we have a glimpse of the struggle between Carthage on the one hand, and Tartessus and Maenace on the other. For the Carthaginians must have first blocked the straits in order to obtain the monopoly of the trade with Tartessus, and then, when the men of Maenace, undaunted, devised a land-route to Tartessus, the Carthaginians blockaded that city on the landward side as well. Thereupon, the traders of Maenace pushed on their route to the Tagus mouth so as to be able there to buy the tin of Brittany from the Tartessians. As a result of this, Carthage proceeded to extreme measures and destroyed first Maenace and then Tartessus in the closing years of the sixth century.

Further evidence of the destruction of Tartessus can be found, in the opinion of the present writer[1], in the description given by Athenaeus (*ap*. Vitruvium, x, 13) of the taking of a fort near Gades and then of Gades itself. By Gades must be meant Tartessus (a confusion which is not uncommon), for the historical Gades was a Phoenician town which must have been a more or less willing ally of Carthage. The mention of the fort, too, suggests Tartessus, for that city could only be besieged after the capture of the stronghold of Geron which commands the mouth of the Guadalquivir. The destruction of Tartessus and Maenace was complete: even their names were blotted out, for in later times Gades was generally substituted for Tartessus and Malaca for Maenace, a fact which also suggests that Gades succeeded to the trade of Tartessus, Malaca to that of Maenace.

With the destruction of Tartessus Carthage became mistress of a wide empire stretching from the Guadiana to C. Nao and inland to the Sierra Morena. The rich valley of the Baetis was a valuable acquisition; and still more valuable was the mineral wealth of the mountains—gold, silver, copper and iron—upon which had been founded the wealth and greatness of the ancient industrial and merchant state. But perhaps even more valuable was the access to the Atlantic and the monopoly of the tin trade which now passed from Tartessus to Carthage. For hundreds of years the Tartessians had sailed to Brittany; they were bold

---

[1] *Op. cit.* p. 44. For the position of Geron on the Salmedina cliff, see *ibid.* pp. 19, 21, 45, 85 and *Arch. Anz.* 1922, p. 43.

sailors like their friendly rivals, the Phocaeans. The Atlantic
had almost become a Tartessian lake, now it was to be Carthaginian. It must have been very soon after the destruction of
Tartessus—and not in 480 B.C. or later, as has been supposed—
that two famous voyages of discovery took place; Hanno's voyage
to the west coast of Africa, which had hitherto been the private
preserve of the Tartessians, and that of Himilco to the tin-lands
of the North. Of Hanno's explorations we have his own account[1];
we only know the fact of Himilco's voyage[2] and one fragment
describing the terrors of the ocean which has been inserted in
the early *Periplus* in Avienus (ll. 380 *sqq.*; 406 *sqq.*). The outlet
to the Atlantic by the straits of Gibraltar was henceforward
closed to all foreign shipping, and in order to frighten away any
alien ships the Carthaginians spread abroad those exaggerated
reports of the terrors of the Atlantic, long calms, shallow reefs,
floating wrecks, fogs, and mountainous seas, which gained the
greater credence because they haunted even Greek literature.

The Pillars of Hercules, once the proud symbol of the unsealing
of the outer ocean, became the 'non plus ultra' of Greek voyaging
and it is with this meaning that they four times appear in Pindar[3].
Ships were allowed to sail as far as the two tiny islands in the
straits, Paloma and Peregil, where a very ancient cult of Heracles,
that is, of the Phoenician Melkart, was celebrated; but the voyage
was only allowed for the purpose of making offerings, in ships
which had left their cargoes behind in the harbour of Maenace
near the Isle of the Moon, and directly the offering was completed,
the ships had to return. The Carthaginians did not even allow
their allies, the Etruscans, to pass through and forbade them to
settle at Madeira[4]. But the bold Massiliotes determined, now
that the tin route by the straits of Gibraltar was blocked, to open
a land-route to the Atlantic; and, by treaties with the Celtic
tribes, they were able to use the waterways of the Loire and Seine
and imported the tin direct from the mines, without the Carthaginians being able to prevent them (vol. IV, p. 123).

[1] *Geogr. Graeci Min.* I.   [2] Pliny, *N.H.* II, 169.

[3] *Ol.* III, 44; *Nem.* III, 21; IV, 69; *Isth.* III, 31. For the reflection of
these events in later Greek literature see *Tartessos*, pp. 51 *sqq.*, and the present
writer's chapter 'Die Säulen des Herakles' in Jessen's *Die Strasse von
Gibraltar*.

[4] Diodorus (V, 20), using Timaeus, who obviously based his evidence on
Pytheas. The discovery of Madeira by the Phoenicians is related here;
and perhaps by Phoenicians the Carthaginians are meant. At any rate,
even if Madeira had earlier been the monopoly of Tyrian trade, it was now
certainly claimed by the Carthaginians as their own.

IV. THE FIRST CARTHAGINIAN EMPIRE IN SPAIN

After the conquest of the Western Mediterranean, the Carthaginians appear to have consolidated the position they had won by treaties with the states with whom they were brought into contact. To one of these treaties we may refer the fixing of C. Palos and Mastia as the boundary between Carthage and Massilia[1]. That the boundary was drawn here is plain from the facts that the Massiliotes were able in the fifth century to found two new trade marts north of C. Palos, and that in the second treaty between Carthage and Rome 'Mastia in Tarsis' is fixed as the boundary for Rome and her allies, by whom in this neighbourhood Massilia alone can be meant. It is surprising that the Carthaginians did not claim the coast as far as C. Nao, the boundary of the Tartessian empire, but only as far as C. Palos. It would seem that after the fall of Tartessus Massilia, which earlier ruled only as far as C. Nao, pushed forward to C. Palos. We may further assume that a treaty was made also with the Etruscans closing the ocean to them, and it is possible that a reference to it is to be found in the *Politics* of Aristotle (III, 9, 1280 *a*, 36).

The only one of these treaties that survives is that with Rome, the first of those cited in Polybius (III, 22). It is dated 508 B.C. and it fits well the time and conditions immediately after the Carthaginian conquest of Southern Spain. For while the Romans are permitted under prescribed conditions to trade in Sicily, Africa, and Sardinia, the route beyond C. Farina, which is the route to Spain, was completely forbidden. And this is still more definitely laid down in the second treaty of 348 B.C.[2], in which the further definition is made that they are not to sail along the Spanish coast beyond C. Palos. If a ship should be driven by storm into the Spanish waters, then it might only put into port for the purpose of repairs and the purchase of what was needed for these repairs, or for a thank-offering. And lastly, it must set sail home again after five days. The wording of this clause exactly corresponds to that which was laid down for the

---

[1] Lenschau in *P.W.* *s.v.* Karthago, col. 2226, makes Justin, XLIII, 5, 2, refer to this treaty: (Massilienses) Carthaginiensium quoque exercitus... saepe fuderunt pacemque victis dederunt; cum Hispanis amicitiam iunxerunt; but the passage fits much better the decline of Carthaginian power in Spain after 340 B.C.

[2] See chronological note I.

offerings on the two tiny islands of the Gibraltar straits and the
formula about immediate return is the same[1].

About the relations of the old Phoenician towns on the south
coast of Andalusia, Gades, Malaca, Sexi, and Abdera, with Carthage we know little. They must have submitted to Carthage's
hegemony more or less of their own accord, like the Libyphoenician towns in Africa. Gades preserved its long-standing
precedence and enjoyed a privileged position, rather like Utica.
The other three towns also kept a certain measure of autonomy;
they were called the Bastulo- or Blasto-Phoenicians after the
Iberian tribe in the middle of whose territory the towns lay.
Gades was the capital of the new Spanish empire and, as we have
seen, the successor of Tartessus. The site of Tartessus itself
remained empty and deserted, and very soon the sand dunes
covered it from view, so that the Greeks had only a faint idea of
where it had lain. The same fate befell Maenace though Artemidorus about 100 B.C. was still able to recognize its ruins.

Carthage took over from Tartessus the suzerainty over the
native Iberian tribes of Andalusia—the Cilbiceni between the
Guadalquivir and Guadiaro, and the Mastieni who extended
from the Guadiaro to Mastia. The wild Iberian tribes of the
east coast, the Indigetes, the Gymnetes, and the Celts of the
highlands were not disturbed by the change of masters. They
were however poor and warlike, and very ready to use the
strength of their right arm in return for good gold in the service
of Carthage. Indeed, after the Africans, they were the best
soldiers of Carthage, and appear in her armies first at the battle
of Himera 480 B.C. and then in the wars between Carthage and
the Greek towns of Sicily from 409 B.C. onwards.

But Spain did not provide Carthage with soldiers alone. The
Sierra Morena was extremely rich in metals, particularly silver,
so that Hannibal later obtained daily from a single mine at
Baebelo 300 pounds of silver. Even in Roman times the silver
mines of Cartagena, although they had been mined for hundreds
of years, produced twenty-five thousand drachmae a day. And
besides the mountains were rich in gold, copper, and iron. The
salt-fish pickling industry of the Andalusian coastal towns,
especially Gades, produced masses of salt-fish which the Carthaginians exported far and wide, even to Greece and beyond. From
the esparto grass of the east coast they manufactured ropes for

---

[1] Avienus 360: deo litare, abire festino pede; Polyb. III, 22, 7: πλὴν ὅσον
πρὸς πλοίου ἐπισκευὴν ἢ πρὸς ἱερά. ἐν πέντε δ᾽ ἡμέραις ἀποτρεχέτω.

their ships. The rich valley of the Baetis produced oil, wine, and corn, the mountains wood and pitch. Not only was Spain herself rich, she was the key of the wealth of the Atlantic lands, since she watched over the straits of Gibraltar which gave access to them. The men of Gades now, like the Tartessians earlier, sailed in search of tin to the isles of Brittany and to England, and brought back cargoes of gold and ivory, etc. from the west coast of Africa.

The supremacy of the Carthaginians and Etruscans in the West founded by the battle of Alalia was severely shaken by the defeat of the Carthaginians at Himera in 480 B.C. and of the Etruscans at Cyme six years later (vol. IV, p. 381; vol. V, p. 148). However, the empire in Spain was hardly affected by these disasters. Here the Carthaginians ruled unchallenged for more than two centuries, until, after 260 B.C., their power began to decline. Unfortunately we possess an almost negligible amount of literary evidence about this first Punic empire in Spain and the archaeological finds are also poor[1]. The oldest objects found in the necropolis of Gades go back into the sixth and fifth centuries, and are therefore to be classed rather as Phoenician, as for example the well-known sarcophagus with carving in relief representing a priest. These are then followed by Carthaginian objects, ornaments, vases and the like.

The same is true of the fine gold ornament of a lady found near Caceres[2]. At Ibiza only the rough clay figures from the Isle of Plana are Phoenician, everything else is Carthaginian. The oldest objects discovered in the Punic necropolis at Puig es Molins on Ibiza, which has yielded ornaments of every kind and provides, next to Carthage itself and Tharros, the richest finds of Carthaginian art, date from 500 B.C. and the same is true of the finds of Carthaginian ivories from the Iberian graves of the Carmona district. On the other hand the Carthaginian amulets and scarabs from the Iberian town of Villaricos on the south-east coast are not earlier than the end of the fifth or the beginning of the fourth century.

Besides Carthaginian objects, Greek imports—vases and so on —are found in Ibiza and in Villaricos. They must have arrived here through Carthaginian middlemen, because since 500 B.C. the Greeks had no longer been able themselves to trade along

---

[1] Cf. P. Bosch, *Arqueologia preromana hispanica* (Appendix to Schulten, *Hispania*), p. 183.
[2] J. R. Melida, *Tesoro de Aliseda*.

these coastlands which were now in Carthaginian possession; still less could they penetrate into the interior, where in many native Iberian towns Greek objects are found beside Carthaginian, as for example at Galera in the province of Granada. Of Carthaginian houses and buildings nothing is known; the only inscription is one at Villaricos on the south-east coast. Massilia in the fifth or fourth century B.C. founded, close to the ancient Phocaean town of Hemeroscopium on the east coast, two new colonies between C. Palos and C. Nao. One was Alonis, the other perhaps that known to the Greeks as 'Akra Leuke,' the later Lucentum of the Romans (modern Alicante). These foundations show that Massilia's sphere of influence began north of C. Palos and that the Carthaginians recognized C. Palos as the boundary of her suzerainty (see above, p. 774, n. 2).

In the fifth and fourth centuries we have no direct testimony about the Carthaginian empire in Spain, but only a few indirect scraps of evidence which show clearly the closure of the straits of Gibraltar. The oldest pieces of evidence after the *Periplus* are Pindar, and Scylax of Caryanda; the latter estimates the width of the straits at seven stades when it is in reality seventy, an error which illustrates the ignorance of the Greeks about the Spanish seas due to the Punic 'mare clausum' policy. Equally significant is Herodotus' ignorance of the Atlantic lands, for example of the tin islands well known earlier to the writer of the *Periplus*. Euripides like Pindar says the Pillars of Hercules are the limits of navigation. Euctemon gives accurate information on the closure of the straits and Damastes repeats Scylax' error about their breadth. Plato too, says that the Pillars are the limits of sailing and his Atlantis is perhaps an imaginative picture of the happy lot of Tartessus. In the fourth century B.C. further evidence for this same fact of the 'mare clausum' is given by Isocrates, and Pseudo-Scylax who narrates the terrors of the Atlantic, and lastly by Aristotle.

Alexander the Great is said to have envisaged the liberation of the West from the yoke of Carthage and the opening up of the straits, but when the great conqueror and discoverer died his bold plans sank with him into the grave[1]. If such plans there were, it seems to the present writer not impossible that the voyage of discovery which Pytheas of Massilia (p. 53) undertook about this time may have had some connection with them. Unfortunately we do not know when exactly the voyage took place. It was however before Dicaearchus, a pupil of Aristotle's

[1] See, however, vol. VI, p. 423.

who wrote about 320 B.C. and attacked Pytheas. Pytheas was in
Gades, which proves that his voyage was undertaken with the
consent of the Carthaginians. They may perhaps have hoped
from his discoveries to gain new land for colonies. It is possible
to assume that it was the weakening of the Carthaginian power
in Spain, which began after 348 B.C. (see below), which made
this voyage possible, but the closure of the straits continued much
later even in the third century B.C., when the earlier Spanish
empire had long been lost. This voyage which Pytheas made
from the west coast of Spain along the shore of Gaul to Britain,
and even farther northwards, dispelled for a moment the night of
ignorance about these lands of the outer ocean, but very soon,
owing to the narrow-mindedness of Greek geographers who
charged Pytheas with flat lying, darkness descended again (see
above, p. 53 *sq.*; p. 262).

After the long silence of tradition from 500 B.C. onwards the
first new information is the treaty of 348 B.C. between Carthage
and Rome recorded in Polybius (III, 24). The clause which
concerns Spain runs: 'On the far side of the "Fair Promontory"
(C. Farina) and Mastia in Tarsis the Romans and their allies
are neither to trade nor to found cities.' While the first treaty
had only forbidden sailing along the African coast, now they
were no longer to pass south of Mastia (Cartagena) and C. Palos.
Thus both routes to Andalusia and the straits were now closed,
since ancient navigation was entirely confined to coasting and
there were only two routes, the one along the African and the
other along the Spanish coast. In 348 B.C., therefore, the empire
of Carthage was as firm as a rock and it was still in existence
just before the First Punic War, since Polybius (I, 10, 5) attests
the existence of the Spanish province. But between 264 B.C.
and 237 B.C. it must have been lost, since, as we have seen,
Hamilcar had to re-conquer Carthaginian Spain. Unfortunately
we do not know exactly when the loss took place. In any event,
the attack came from the Massiliotes, whose power was at its
height in the fourth and third centuries B.C., and who seem to have
strengthened themselves by an alliance with the Iberians.

Although Carthage must have lost her empire, perhaps as far
as Gades, she retained command of the sea, at least sufficiently
to prevent any ship in the third century B.C. passing through
the straits, as Eratosthenes expressly says. The loss of Spanish
possessions was more particularly felt in the reduction of Carthage's financial resources, now that she no longer controlled the
silver mines. This would explain the fact that in the closing

stages of the First Punic War the Carthaginians were in financial straits, and after the war they failed to pay their mercenaries. But the general who crushed the Mercenary Revolt with mailed fist (p. 803) also recovered the Spanish province and extended it by conquests—Hamilcar Barca. He landed in 237 B.C. with a small army at Gades which still remained Carthaginian, and from that base began the re-conquest.

V. THE IBERIANS

There had been great changes in Spain since the writing of the Massiliote *Periplus*. For at that time, about 520 B.C., the central highlands and west of Spain were entirely occupied by Celts with some traces of Ligurians, whereas the Iberians were confined to the south and east coasts. Now however the Carthaginians found Iberians also on the highlands and in the west; for example in New Castille on the Sierra Morena the Oretani (Orissi, Oretes) and the Olcades whose exact locality is not known; on the Tagus near Toledo the Carpetani; in Old Castille the Vaccaei round Salamanca; on the upper waters of the Douro and Tagus the Celtiberi, that is, Iberians inhabiting what were earlier Celtic settlements. On the east coast now between C. Palos and C. Nao the Contestani occupied the territory of the wild Gymnetes; round Valencia lived the Edetani, whose name is borne by the prince Edeco; beyond them as far as the Ebro Ilercavones related to the Ilergetes (round Ilerda); near Tarragona the Cessetani with their town Cissa; as far as Barcelona the Laeetani; on the upper Llobregat the Lacetani; on the gulf of Rosas the Indigetes; along the foot of the Pyrenees the Bargusii and Andosini. In short, the Iberians had pushed forward from the east coast into the central highlands.

Possibly this shifting of population is to be connected with the irruption of Gallic tribes into Provence, for in consequence of their pressure the Iberians north of the Pyrenees may have been compelled to retreat across the mountains, and, since the east coast was already occupied, to find new homes in the highlands previously occupied only by Celts[1]. The mixture of Celts and

---

[1] It was formerly held that the Iberians were the earliest stratum of population in the highlands, but the present writer has demonstrated that they did not enter this region until the fourth century at earliest. This proof from the ancient sources is strengthened by the researches of P. Bosch who has shown that Iberian pottery does not appear in the highlands until the fourth century. This date is given by Greek vases found with it.

Iberians produced the wild Celtiberians, who were in their essential characteristics Iberians but had assimilated many Celtic traits. The highlanders were the most warlike section of the Iberians and at the same time the poorest and most savage. Whereas the tribes of the east coast were steadily subdued, though some of them only after stubborn resistance as for instance at Saguntum, the Carthaginians only succeeded in reducing the most southerly of the highland tribes. Meanwhile the Celtiberians continued to boast of their independence and only succumbed to the Romans after long resistance, as witness the siege of Numantia. But bravery could not make up for their lack of political cohesion. Like their kinsmen in Africa the Iberians showed a disinclination for subordination and discipline.

Among them the political unit was not, as among the Gauls, the tribe, but each single town or fort[1]. Some of the very small castles could only have held a clan of 50 to 100 persons. But even these formed an independent political and economic unit, a miniature state, like the clan 'castella' in Africa. Even the smallest castles were strongly fortified. Apart from their personal names people were called after their clan, as for example 'Madicenus Vailicom' which stood for 'Madicenus' of the 'Vailo' clan. The only government which the Iberians would tolerate was that of the council of the oldest heads of families which corresponds to the 'jemāʻa' of the Berbers. Only among the most civilized tribes of the south and south-east do we find kings, but their powers were probably very small. Only temporarily and in the direst need would several states consent to form a league which elected a chieftain to lead them. And this weak bond was at once broken after a war, in fact often even during a war, especially after a disaster. It is true that round a popular leader a band of *soldurii* (in Latin *devoti*) would collect who took an oath not to survive him. But amongst the Iberians we cannot speak of any national feeling such as inspired and unified the Gauls under Vercingetorix. They were content to be recruited as mercenaries both by the Carthaginians and by the Romans and to fight against their own tribesmen, earning without scruple to-day Carthaginian pay, to-morrow Roman. On the other hand, separate states or castles made the most desperate resistance to attack (Saguntum, Numantia, Astapa and Calagurris), often having recourse to cannibalism in order to hold out

[1] The following account is applicable chiefly to the Celtiberians and Lusitanians, and is based on Strabo and Diodorus, who used Polybius and Posidonius.

longer. Sometimes the clans engaged in war would concentrate in a single town or tribal refuge, as for example the Duero-tribes in Numantia, the tribes of the Jalon valley in Contrebia and Segéda. In general the Iberians avoided pitched battles; their strategy and tactics were those of guerrilla warfare, in which the people and the country fought together against invaders. They made use of the fact that the mountains everywhere were split into deep ravines to lay ambushes, and they wore out the enemy by the poverty of the land, the lack of water, the great distances, and the sparse population. Viriathus and the Roman Sertorius were masters of this warfare; but Hannibal also used ambushes at Trasimene and Gereonium with consummate skill, adopting the kind of warfare in which his African and Iberian troops had been trained.

The Iberians were armed after the fashion of the Berbers: they carried several spears for throwing, the *solliferreum*, entirely of iron; the *falarica*, a wooden shaft with long thin iron point[1], and a very small round shield, the *caetra*, after which their light-armed troops were called *caetrati*; and, in addition, a dagger. Besides these national weapons there were heavy-armed troops with the long Celtic shield and the sword of the late Hallstatt type also borrowed from the Celts (see p. 43). This was the famous 'Spanish sword' later adopted by Rome. Helmet and coat of mail were seldom worn. These heavy-armed troops were called *scutati*. Common also was the use of the falchion which is found in Hellas and is perhaps the descendant of the curved knife of the Bronze Age. There were slingers of extraordinary skill, particularly the Balearic islanders, and the same weapon is still common amongst the herdsmen of Andalusia. The Iberians were superb horsemen and the same warrior could fight, now on horseback, and now on foot. The mount was the native wild pony, small and unimpressive, but very fast and hardy, and wonderfully sure-footed in the mountains. Like their horses the men were small and lean, but speedy, tough, and able to subsist on the smallest rations, as the poverty of the land made necessary.

As a result of this poverty, farming was little developed, and there was far more grazing than agriculture. This was the cause of the laziness which, after the lack of political organization, was the chief characteristic of the Iberian race. Poverty bred rapine, especially amongst the Lusitanians. Often farming was entirely left in the hands of the womenfolk. The Iberians made very

[1] In the opinion of the present writer, the *falarica* is the model for the Roman pilum. See however above, pp. 568, 596 n. 1.

little use of the mineral wealth of the country for the purposes
of trade, but they knew how to forge from the excellent iron,
especially from Moncayo (in the province of Soria), magnificent
weapons which provoked the admiration of the Greeks and the
imitation of the Romans. Of other industries amongst the highlanders there is little trace, except for pottery, which under
Greek influence attains some merit. They painted their vases
chiefly with geometric designs, but also drew plants and animals;
their drawing of the human figure was childish. There is no
evidence of any other art and naturally no signs of any literature.
Only the Tartessians had any literature, and they were probably
not Iberians. In general their manner of life was savage; they
washed their bodies and teeth in urine and dwelt in mud huts or
hovels scooped in the sides of hills. As has been said, they often
resorted to cannibalism in the stress of a siege.

Amongst the Lusitanians the houses still preserved the form
of the oldest type of circular straw hut, but amongst the eastern
tribes the house was as a rule oblong with two or three rooms.
In Numantia and the small towns of the province of Teruel the
houses were on the street, and the town was formed by one or
two long streets cut sectionally by cross streets, a planning which
shows clearly Greek influence. The furniture was poor; prominent were vast pitchers and stone troughs let into the floor,
which were used either for washing purposes or for collecting
the urine (for we are told that it was not used fresh). They slept
on the floor. Public buildings seem not to have existed, though
there may have been a council house for the sittings of the elders.
The staple food was flesh and the national drink *caerea*, a kind
of beer made from wheat, which the Celtiberians had learnt to
make from the Celts, amongst whom it was called *cerevisia*.
Besides this there was a kind of mead, though it was only drunk
amongst the tribes of the east coast. Their clothing was made
from black sheep's wool; it consisted of a close fitting jersey,
gaiters, and the famous *sagum*, a mantle of black wool which the
Romans adopted. Their heads were swathed in a kind of turban,
or else they wore a leather cap. The women wore over a veil or
head-dress an early form of the mantilla; this is in fact what 'the
Lady of Elche' wears. They laid great importance upon slimness
of stature and fixed limits for waist measurements which ought
not to be exceeded. Bright-coloured garments were commonly
worn by the women on the east coast.

They seem in general to have burnt their dead. The ashes
were placed in an urn, and the dead man's arms were laid along-

side; the grave was marked by a tombstone, and these were arranged in long rows, as for instance in the Celtiberian (or perhaps Celtic) necropolis of Aguilar. The highlanders, according to tradition, exposed the bodies of their dead to be devoured by the birds, and this perhaps explains the absence of any necropolis at Numantia. Their religion was a worship of natural phenomena, especially of the stars and the moon, which they celebrated on the nights of the full moon with dances. Dancing, indeed, was very popular amongst all the tribes, particularly the war-dance. Their musical instruments were flutes and horns—clay horns have been found at Numantia. Besides the stars, springs, rivers and mountain tops were worshipped and other local spirits. Human sacrifice was widely practised and divination was performed from the entrails. Of animals from the earliest times the bull had been the chief object of veneration, just as to-day it is the favourite animal of the Spaniards. Yet despite all their savagery, the Iberians did not lack fine qualities, above all, the devotion of soldiers to their chieftain and their gratitude towards foreign conquerors who treated this proud people with courtesy (Hasdrubal, Scipio, Tiberius Gracchus, Sertorius), and lastly their hospitality. Such then were the Iberians about 250 B.C.

VI. THE RE-CONQUEST OF SPAIN

In 237 B.C. Hamilcar landed at Gades. The falsified Roman tradition derived from Fabius Maximus affirms that he conquered Spain on his own initiative against the will of the Carthaginians[1]. This is of course absurd, since every patriot must have rejoiced in his successes, and without state aid he could never have undertaken the enterprise. His first objective was the re-conquest of Spain, but behind this lay his real purpose, war with Rome. On the eve of his arrival in Spain he made his nine-year-old son Hannibal swear eternal hatred to Rome. But when he landed at Gades he could only really rely on the support of this town and at the most three other Phoenician colonies on the south coast (Malaca, Sexi, Abdera). The whole of the south and east of Spain had to be re-conquered.

Hamilcar is said to have fought with Tartessians, Celts and Iberians. The 'Tartessians' were the inhabitants of the former Tartessian kingdom, the country of Andalusia, which had been Carthaginian for a time, the Iberians were the tribes of the east

---

[1] See the Bibliography to the chapter.

coast north of C. Palos, and the Celts, mercenaries who formed the army of the unwarlike Tartessians, are either real Celts who inhabited the central plateau and the west coast (see above, p. 782) or the Iberians who after 300 B.C. were forced into that region, the 'Celtiberians' who are referred to by Livy (xxxiv, 17 *sqq.*, 195 B.C.) as mercenaries of the Turdetani, the name given to the Tartessians. Their total strength is given as 50,000, perhaps an exaggeration; their leaders were Istolatius and Indortes, two names which occur nowhere else. We are told that Hamilcar incorporated in his army the Celts he captured and that he put their leaders to death with great cruelty. After subduing the Tartessians, Hamilcar transferred operations to the east coast and reduced the Iberians north of C. Palos, pushing forward the boundary of the Carthaginian province as far as C. Nao. In the middle of this district, between C. Palos and C. Nao, he built on the steep, rocky hill of Alicante a bulwark of the new domination; its place was later taken by New Carthage. While he was besieging the town of Helice (perhaps Ilici, the modern Elche), on the river Vinalapò (the Alebos) south-west of Alicante, and the King of the Orissi or Oretani (an Iberian tribe near Castulo) was advancing to relieve the city, Hamilcar met his death by drowning in the river. This occurred in 229/8 in the winter, the only season when the Spanish rivers are full of water.

In 231 B.C. the Romans sent an embassy to Hamilcar whose conquests had disquieted them. The Romans had indeed themselves no interests in Spain, but the Carthaginians had overstepped their old boundary line with Massilia at C. Palos, and Rome was concerned as an ally of Massilia. Hamilcar gave the clever answer that he was only engaged in fighting the Iberians in order to get sufficient money to pay to Rome the war indemnity. Rome had at the time to be content with that, but it was clear that any further Carthaginian encroachment would meet with a Roman veto. By his reconquest of Spain Hamilcar had performed a service of lasting value to his country. The material resources of Spain in silver and man-power were a complete offset to the loss of Sicily and Sardinia, and the moral effect of the conquest weighed still heavier in the balance. The star of Carthage was once again in the ascendant.

Hamilcar's successor Hasdrubal avenged his death by leading a punitive expedition into the territory of the Orissi, whose twelve towns he reduced, with the result that the Carthaginian dominion was extended as far as the upper Guadiana. The Iberians of the east coast were won over by diplomacy, for

Hasdrubal contracted a marriage with the daughter of an Iberian prince. He founded New Carthage on the site of Mastia, which had presumably been destroyed by the Carthaginians. This city, the modern Cartagena, was better placed than Alicante to keep in touch with Africa, because it was nearer and possessed a magnificent harbour, the best on the east coast of Spain, indeed one of the best harbours in the world. Moreover, while Alicante lay beyond the old boundary of C. Palos, and so provided evidence of aggression, New Carthage lay within the old frontiers. But Hasdrubal was most unwilling to confine himself within these limits; on the contrary, we hear that he was recognized as king by all the Iberian tribes. That probably meant that his power did not extend beyond the tribes on the coast with their immediate neighbours, but still it gave evidence of a great increase in the sphere of Carthaginian domination. It must have been by drawing largely on the Iberians that Hasdrubal's army was now raised to 50,000 foot and 6000 cavalry. This increase of power alone enables one to understand why in 226 B.C. the Romans sent an embassy with the demand that Hasdrubal should not cross the Ebro. For this demand proves that all the tribes south of the river had already joined Carthage. It was in fact a very considerable concession by Rome, and can only have been forced upon her by the difficulties of her position at home. Polybius says that Rome deliberately avoided a conflict with Carthage now, because her struggle with the Gallic tribes of North Italy was still in progress. And very possibly the Carthaginians undertook not to give any support to the Gauls. Massilia can hardly have welcomed these Roman concessions, for she lost finally as a result of them her three colonies[1] which Hasdrubal had perhaps taken and destroyed, but she was forced to put up with it.

The Carthaginians accepted Rome's offer and established themselves strongly on the frontier line of the Ebro, thus concluding the famous but much disputed Ebro Treaty of 226 B.C. It was later asserted at Rome that Saguntum was specifically excepted in the treaty. But Polybius (ii, 13, 7) says expressly that there was no mention in the treaty of the rest of Spain, from which it follows that Saguntum cannot possibly have been referred to. All that is proved is that Saguntum, presumably soon after the Ebro treaty[2], asked for an alliance with Rome, and that Rome

---

[1] Hemeroscopium, Alonis and Alicante.

[2] Polybius iii, 30, 1. 'Several years before the time of Hannibal,' *i.e.* before 221 B.C. For a somewhat different account of these negotiations which sets the Roman alliance with Saguntum *c.* 231 and makes the Ebro

acceded to the request. But this does not mean that the Ebro treaty was annulled; it is rather an infringement of it by Rome. In this way the Carthaginians had step by step won back and extended their Spanish empire: first as far as C. Nao, and then up to the Ebro river.

VII. HANNIBAL: THE CHALLENGE TO ROME

When Hasdrubal in 221 B.C. was struck down in a private quarrel with a Celt, Hannibal at the age of twenty-five succeeded to the command of the Spanish armies of Carthage. Hasdrubal owed his successes chiefly to his diplomatic skill in handling the Iberian tribes; Hannibal pursued the warlike policy of his father Hamilcar, and at once assailed the tribes of the inland plateau. His first attack was made upon the Olcades[1]. Hannibal took their capital, called Althia or Althaia by Polybius, but Cartala by Livy—possibly two separate towns were taken. Neither name is mentioned elsewhere. The root Cart-, which appears in Cartala, is found also in Cartima and Carteia and other Iberian place-names.

The winter of 221–220 B.C. Hannibal spent at New Carthage. In the spring of 220 B.C. he once again moved against the highland tribes. He attacked first the Vaccaei (on the middle waters of the Douro), and Salmantica (now Salamanca). And since it was on the return journey that he first came into contact with the Carpetani, he must have avoided them on his outward westerly march by keeping to the north edge of the Sierra Morena and then following the later road Emerita-Salmantica to Salamanca. The town was captured by surprise, but a second town Arbocala (east of Zamorra on the Douro) was only taken after a long siege. On his return march along the Segovia-Titulcia road across the southern Guadarrama, he was attacked on the Tagus, east of Toledo, by the Carpetani, who were assisted by the Olcades and fugitives from Salmantica. He succeeded, however, in defeating them, and by this victory the Carthaginian domination on the Tagus was founded. But when the ancient sources say that the Carthaginian empire now included the whole of Spain as far as

treaty the limiting of Carthaginian armed advance northwards rather than the acceptance of a sphere of influence, see below, p. 809.

[1] Their name only appears once again, amongst the Iberian contingents which Hannibal sent to Africa before his march into Italy. It occurs here next to the Tartessians, Mastieni, and Oretani. It would be natural therefore to look for the Olcades near the Oretani somewhere in the regions of the upper Guadiana.

the Ebro, it must be remembered that this statement only holds
good of its lower waters; the brave Celtiberian tribes of the upper
Tagus and the upper Douro remained immune from attack.

The winter of 220–219 B.C. Hannibal again spent in New
Carthage. In the spring of 219 B.C. he proceeded with the conquest of the east coast. His first objective was Saguntum, which,
situated upon a high, rocky, and inaccessible acropolis, was
important for the control of the east coast. He found a *casus belli*
in a frontier quarrel between the inhabitants of Saguntum and
the Turdetani. The Turdetani, including the old kingdom of
Tartessus, occupied the coastal regions as far as C. Nao, or even
the Jucar. And C. Nao or the Jucar had been settled as the
frontier between them and Saguntum. As successors of the
Tartessians the Carthaginians had the right to support them in
their quarrel with Saguntum. This opportunity Hannibal seized.
In their distress the inhabitants of Saguntum had recourse to
Rome, and Rome turned a favourable ear to their request for
help, although support of Saguntum infringed the Ebro treaty,
which allowed the Carthaginians to subdue all the land as far as
the Ebro. Consequently Hannibal and the Carthaginians were
perfectly entitled to take no notice of Rome's protest. If Rome
really demanded, as Polybius reports, that Hannibal should
relinquish Saguntum because it was an ally of Rome, and that
he should not cross the Ebro, Hannibal could answer that Rome's
alliance with Saguntum broke the Ebro treaty, that he was still
far from crossing the Ebro, or on his part from doing anything
contrary to the treaty. Even so, Rome looked on quietly at the
siege of Saguntum, although during the eight months she had
ample time to send help.

Saguntum lies upon a steep plateau joined to the surrounding
hills only on the west; the plateau is about 1000 yards long, but
only 110 to 130 yards broad, and at that time three-quarters of
a mile from the sea, though to-day it is 3 miles, the difference being
due to the alluvial soil brought down by the Palancia. It was an
Iberian town and belonged to the Arsetani, from which the
Romans deduced an affinity with the Latin Ardea, just as they
derived the name Saguntum from the Greek Zacynthus. Hannibal had invested the city and after eight months blockade took
the town by storm from the one accessible side, the west, in the
autumn of 219 B.C. When a Roman embassy protested at
Carthage and declared war, failing the surrender to them of
Hannibal, the Carthaginians could begin the conflict with clear
consciences. For Hannibal had succeeded in putting the Romans

diplomatically in the wrong. Then in the spring of 218 he set off for Italy.

Several Spanish place-names preserve the memory of Hannibal's campaigns in Spain: Portus Hannibalis, a harbour on the peninsula of C. St Vincent near Lagos, Insula Hannibalis near Palma in Mallorca, Scalae Hannibalis, a hill named Mongò shaped like a staircase descending down to the sea at Estartit on the east coast of Spain. Besides these place-names the watch towers built by the Carthaginians in Andalusia were called 'turres' or 'speculae Hannibalis.' Further, the natives in later times pointed to silver mines which Hannibal had opened up and one particular mine Baebelo, which they said had produced 300 lbs. of silver daily in his time. Like Hasdrubal his predecessor, Hannibal took a Spanish wife, a lady from the city of Castulo. His influence in Spain was not entirely extinguished by the Punic War. At least the great revolt of the Turdetani which broke out in 191 B.C. was apparently instigated by him, since it took place at exactly the same time as the outbreak of the war between Rome and Antiochus, in which Hannibal too had a hand.

The Carthaginian empire in Spain embraced in 220 B.C. first of all the whole Baetis valley, what is to-day Andalusia and Granada, as far as the Sierra Morena. Next was included part of the south-west coast about as far as the Tagus, since in this district (Alémtego) is situated Portus Hannibalis, and Carthaginian armies are several times mentioned on the west coast. Then on the east coast it comprised all the littoral as far as the Ebro (Murcia and Valencia). On the other hand, the Carthaginians held no more of the interior plateau of Spain than the south-eastern part together with the land of the Oretani in the Mancha who had been subdued by Hannibal; the Olcades, Vaccaei, and Carpetani had been attacked but not conquered. But the warlike highland tribes provided the Carthaginians with mercenaries so long as the war in Spain went in Carthage's favour, though later they turned more and more towards Rome. The most loyal and trustworthy element of the Carthaginian dominion was formed by the Phoenician towns: Gades (the capital), Malaca, Sexi, Abdera, to which must be added the Phoenician inhabitants on the south and south-east coasts, the Bastulo-phoenicians (p. 778). These inhabitants of the south and south-east coasts alone were bound to the Carthaginians by the tie of race. The inhabitants of the interior were in the south the Tartessians or Turdetani, in the south-east Iberians (Edetani, Ilercavones and the like). The Turdetani were unwarlike and easy to dominate. But much less trustworthy were the Iberians of the east coast and it was here that the later defection began. The Phoenician towns kept their autonomy, and the tribes and towns of the Tartessians and Iberians continued to be ruled by their princes, after whom many of them took their names.

It is impossible to make an estimate of the population in Spain under Carthaginian rule; but it is clear that only the Baetis valley with its hundreds of towns and villages was thickly populated; the rest was for the most part mountainous country with few inhabitants. The capital of the empire since Hasdrubal was New Carthage, a large and strongly fortified town, which was also the naval harbour with dockyards, arsenals and factories. Near by lay the silver mines—the most valuable Carthaginian possessions in Spain, which have already been described (p. 778). It was their loss which made the fall of New Carthage in 209 B.C. so mortal a blow. For arms there were the Spanish metals, worked with the unrivalled skill of the Iberian smiths, and for the tackle of the ships the esparto grass of the east coast provided raw material. In this way Spain was for Carthage, as Posidonius says, 'an inexhaustible treasure store for empire[1].'

[1] *Ap*. Strab. III, 147 (*F.H.G.* III, 273).

CHAPTER XXV

ROME AFTER THE CONQUEST OF SICILY

I. SICILY: TAXATION

AFTER his brilliant victory at the Aegates islands in 241 and the successful negotiations with Hamilcar (p. 692*sq*.), Lutatius Catulus remained in Sicily for some months as proconsul, and with the aid of his brother, who was consul that year, took possession of the towns that still had Punic garrisons, disarmed the natives and established a Roman government. It had been agreed at Rome that the Sicilians were to be autonomous in their local governments but that, except where definite privileges had been granted them, they were to pay a tax of a tenth of their produce to the state. For the supervision of tax-collecting a quaestor was stationed at Lilybaeum. But obviously where subjects are to be taxed, there must also be some governing official and an adequate police force. Whether the appropriate executive powers were at first bestowed upon the quaestor or whether some consular legate was sent to the province in the early days we do not know. It was not till fourteen years later that a definitive form of provincial government under a resident praetor was established.

The immediate tasks of importance were to find a practical system of tax-collecting, to classify the cities of Sicily with reference to their obligations, and to establish suitable governments in towns like Lilybaeum, Drepana, and Agrigentum that had been taken from Carthage. It was no small task to collect, verify, and codify the treaties and promises of immunity, alliance or friendship that had from time to time been given to various cities by Roman consuls in return for adhesion to the Roman cause.

Details regarding the original classification are lacking, but we may make reasonable deductions from the data that we have for the period after Syracuse and her several subject cities were included in the province, that is after the Second Punic War. From the tithe-paying portion of Sicily we have first to exempt the kingdom of Hiero, or about one-fourth of the island. Since 248

Note. There is no continuous source for this period except Zonaras' brief Epitome (VIII, 17–20) of Dio Cassius XII. Polybius (II, 21–36) gives a good account of the Gallic War taken from Fabius Pictor. The methods of governing and taxing Sicily must be deduced from scattered statements in Cicero's Verrine Orations. The rest of the story must be derived from incidental references. See the Bibliography.

Hiero had had a treaty of alliance like those of Italian allies, the only difference being that he was under no formal obligation to provide a specific contingent of men in case of war. Messana was also an ally, subject, like Rhegium, to the upkeep of one war vessel. We may add that after the fall of Syracuse two of Hiero's cities, Tauromenium and Neetum, were added to this class, although Syracuse herself then fell to the rank of a tithe-paying city. We must also place in a separate class five fortunate cities which were free and immune from obligations. This immunity, which had been promised by Roman consuls, continued to be respected by Rome though not confirmed by treaties. Four of these cities, Halaesa, Centuripa, Segesta and Halicyae, had secured their favourable status during the first two years of the war, since they adhered to the Roman cause at a time when the senate had not yet conceived of the idea of mastering Sicily. This immunity, however, was to be a personal privilege of the citizens of the respective towns and be recognized only within the territories concerned. If any other Sicilian or even a Roman should rent land within a free district, he became subject to the tithe. We have in fact the name of a Roman senator in Cicero's day who paid a tax on his lease at Segesta while the natives were immune. The purpose of this restriction is obvious: special privileges were meant only for those, and the descendants of those, who had risked their lives by joining Rome's cause at a very perilous time. The fifth city of the list, Panormus, was taken by storm twelve years after the others had become 'friends' of Rome, and we are not informed why it secured favourable conditions; but we may perhaps suppose that a pro-Roman party within had aided in the speedy capture and that the city was afterwards placed in their hands, and assigned to the privileged class as a reward.

These two classes of allied and immune cities constituted about one-half of the island in the early days of the province, and since Rome seems not to have confiscated any public land here until 212, the other half was apparently subjected to the payment of tithes. This of course applied to harvested crops, and since they could not readily be collected upon pasture land, the tax there took the form of an equivalent in money (*scriptura*), payable annually on each head of grazing stock. The principle of the single tax on land was quite reasonable, since Sicily was largely an agricultural country, and as the export of a tenth of the crop to Rome increased the value of the rest, the burden of the tax may be considered to have distributed itself fairly equably over the non-rural population as well. There was in addition the usual harbour tax levied on all exports and imports at the ports under Roman supervision, and the collection of this was farmed out to contractors at Rome. It was placed at five per cent. and served for revenue only.

The collection of the tithe from subjects was of course a complete innovation for Rome. If carried out directly it would require a vast civil service: if farmed out by contracts let at Rome, as were the port dues, it might lead to endless bickerings, and it is doubtful whether at this time companies had been organized at Rome with sufficient capital to perform the work. Rome wisely adopted outright the plan which Hiero had elaborated in the minutest details in his portion of the island, a plan which had advantages over Punic methods in that it was trusted by the natives because it provided safeguards against peculation and was set out in a language which both Roman officials and the natives comprehended. According to this plan it was the duty of the city magistrates every year to take a census of all the farmers of the district (that is, the actual farmers, whether renters or owners), recording both the complete acreage (*professio jugerum*) and the acreage of each crop actually under cultivation, with the amount of seed-corn used (*professio sationum*). These records were signed under oath and penalty and were made with extreme care, so that the contractor who wished to bid for the year's collection of any city could, after consulting the records and estimating the condition of the growing crops, form a fair calculation of how much he dare offer. He could then with reasonable safety go before the Roman quaestor on the day of the auction of contracts and make his bid. His offer was on the basis of $10\frac{2}{5}$ per cent of the crop in kind, the fraction to serve as his wage. The contract was let to the highest bidder, native or Roman, provided his financial responsibility was approved. The cities were encouraged to make bids for their own contracts so as to protect the general interest as well as to save the wage, and they frequently availed themselves of this right. There is no instance on record of a tithe contract let in Sicily to any agent of a Roman *societas*. Perhaps the law was so drawn as to exclude these firms, but it is more probable that since the contracts were let in small lots the profits were not sufficiently tempting. The contractor who had won a bid was required to reach an agreement with each farmer before a certain day as to the amount of the tithe, and if the two failed to agree on the estimate, the settlement must be made at the threshing-floor where disputes could be decided by an actual measurement of the grain. To safeguard the farmer, who might be an ignorant peasant, the precise form of the agreement was prescribed. The farmer signed a promise to deliver the amount found due, the contractor signed a statement that he accepted that amount as satisfying his claim, and both signed receipts for the documents they exchanged. Finally, the contractor deposited copies of all the documents with the city magistrate, who was then bound to see that the farmers of his district delivered the amount due.

This is not all, but it is sufficient to show that the Lex Hieronica was explicit enough to satisfy even Sicilian Greeks that no frauds were to be perpetrated against them. It also shows that Hiero was a ruler who deserved the high esteem in which his subjects held him. For despite many attempts to find the source of this law in the Ptolemaic revenue codes, the credit still seems to belong to Hiero. It is true that Ptolemy's code seems to be the earlier one, also that Hiero had close commercial relations with Alexandria and probably knew of the Ptolemaic code, but the similarities between the two consist only in the obvious terms that must necessarily recur in all taxation laws, while the basic principles and the underlying spirit differ completely.

That Rome adopted Hiero's method rather than Punic ones was fortunate for the Sicilians, if we may judge from the reputation which Carthage had in Africa, and it speaks well also for the intentions of the first Roman commission which had the task of organizing Sicily. Certain it is that Sicily fared far better than did Asia a century later under a looser plan devised by the Gracchi. The time came—in the late Republic—when Sicily was also cruelly exploited, but the thieving of Verres, from which even Rome suffered, was not due to the financial devices of the Lex Hieronica but must be attributed directly to the Roman praetor who abused his magisterial authority.

The burden of the tax was not considered a heavy one, for a seventh or a fifth was not unusual in ancient taxing, and there were Roman investors who found it possible to rent lands in Sicily and make a profit after paying both rent and tax. Certainly the tithe had been exacted over a large part of Sicily for nearly two centuries. In a country often hurt by droughts, payment in kind had the advantage over a fixed money payment in that the tax rose and fell with the crop. It also saved the Sicilian from the necessity of hurrying a part of his crop to the market at the time of lowest price; and finally this part, instead of being thrown upon his market, was removed to Rome so that the rest proportionately increased in value. This latter fact was so well recognized by the Romans that when in the next century they from time to time bought a second and third tenth of the Sicilian crop, they reckoned their new purchases at a higher price.

The amount collected annually in the early days of the province we do not know, but in Cicero's day, when several cities of Hiero's kingdom had been added to the decuman group, the tithe amounted to about 750,000 bushels annually, or three million modii. A low price was at that time about two shillings the bushel[1] (three sesterces per modius). If the crop was so good in the third century, we may assume that the annual tithe on the smaller area then Roman would have been about half a million bushels and the tax burden on the arable land of Sicily would have amounted to about £50,000—not a large amount for a population of about a million souls. It is difficult to comprehend why the Roman farmers did not object to having this amount of grain thrown upon their only market every year. Had there been serious objection they would probably have demanded that the Sicilians should pay their tribute in cash, as the Romans were compelled to do. The only reasonable explanation for the silence of the Roman farmers is that in the vicinity of the city cereal culture had already begun to give way to olive and vine culture and to pasturing, so that Rome could absorb the Sicilian supply and sell whatever surplus remained after provisioning her army without glutting the market.

It would be interesting to know what the Senate considered the legal status of its tithe-paying subjects in Sicily. In Hadrian's day the jurists spoke of the provincial soil as actually owned by Rome and of the tithe-payers as renters of Rome's land. That theory of sovereignty we find extensively held particularly by the Ptolemaic and Seleucid kings of the third century (see pp. 113, 181), but even they hesitated to apply it to autonomous Greek cities, and it is difficult to believe that Hiero had adopted the doctrine in Sicily since his subjects were Greeks and he made no claim to theocratic autocracy. It is not probable that Rome proclaimed ownership in the soil at the time of taking possession. We may even doubt whether Rome was then aware of such a theory, for hitherto Rome had never claimed ownership over conquered territory except the definite plots which were actually declared *ager publicus*. Without attempting to comprehend the abstract principles, the Senate, bent on practical results, left all the native Sicilians in undisturbed possession, recognized the deeds and leases then in force and simply took over the annual revenues that the former sovereign had collected. It may be that certain

[1] Or in terms of modern purchasing power about 6 shillings.

Carthaginian official residences in Lilybaeum and Panormus fell to the Romans in full possession, but, except for such minor properties, Rome seems not to have acquired any *ager publicus* until 212, when Hiero's royal domains at Leontini and some confiscated estates at Syracuse raised the question of public ownership. In later years the succession to Punic national mines in Spain and to royal estates, forests, and mines in Macedonia and Asia called for legal interpretation, and finally some jurist read into Roman law the Oriental theory of sovereignty. However, we are not yet able to say when that occurred, and it was probably long after the formation of the first province, indeed probably after Augustus.

II. SICILY: ADMINISTRATION

With the local governments of the several cities Rome did not interfere, but an official with large executive powers was needed to assume the responsibility for peace and order in such newly conquered land. In 227 the assembly at Rome began to elect four praetors annually in order to employ one in Sicily and one in Sardinia, and from that time on, the praetorial government continued until the custom was adopted of employing a propraetor. Roman praetors were in theory colleagues of the consuls and, as such, had frequently commanded armies. They had also supervised the finances of their military quaestors and had had charge of the courts of justice at Rome. This office therefore combined the functions that were particularly called for in Sicily. During the term of his office a praetor exercised in theory almost royal authority; but his power was restricted in that his term was short, and he was aware that he could be impeached for maladministration at its expiration. Furthermore, Sicily now had peace, so that there was for a long time no occasion for the exercise of military authority except to look after the legion stationed there; and since the city governments were autonomous and possessed their own courts, the praetor's judicial duties were limited to cases in which one or both litigants were Roman citizens. And even in such cases his powers were later circumscribed by the fact that the jury panel which he appointed must consist of fellow-citizens of the defendant, whether Sicilian or Roman.

On the whole, Rome apparently endeavoured to choose the more liberal practices in vogue at home and in Sicily for the political and financial administration of her new subjects. Time proved, however, that the Roman theory of strong magistrates was a dangerous one to follow in the government of subjects so far away from tribunician supervision. When this fact was discovered, the Roman assembly tried to remedy the defect not by limiting the governor's powers, but by setting up a special court in which provincials might air their grievances. However, it was an expensive undertaking for poor subjects to carry their cases to Rome, and hence, though we know of several instances of mal-administration, we are not surprised to hear that no governor was publicly accused by the Sicilians before Verres, and against him charges were not brought till his plunder reached the skies.

As we have noted, the cities continued to rule themselves, and to issue coins as before; in fact, a dozen cities which had not coined in the past now began to issue their own money. They doubtless felt a certain local pride in acquiring an equal status with their former superiors and a sense of security in the firm peace. No more would the devastating armies of Carthage and of the Syracusan kings, which had fought backwards and forwards across the island for two centuries, raze their city walls. The local governments were usually of the democratic type, and the Romans were at this time so thoroughly committed to the theory of popular sovereignty that they could hardly have wished to change them. It is only later, when Rome herself became more of an aristocracy, that envoys who were asked to rewrite the charters of Halaesa, Agrigentum, and Heraclea reveal a tendency to advocate aristo-cratic forms. In general the primary assembly ruled the town, and the *boule* was in many places a closed corporation with little power except to confer dignity upon its members. To be sure, the pax Romana removed questions of large moment, so that the primary assembly also lost its importance, and then the *boule* somewhat increased its activity, since the sovereign power in its perfunctory dealings with the cities preferred to confer with the smaller and more respectable body. But of direct interference in the form of the governments in Sicily we do not hear. Finally, despite re-strictions upon the right of land-holding in Segesta, we hear of no case in which Rome circumscribed the natural rights of the Sicilians or attempted in any way to break up their community of interests. To the Segestans, their long-lost cousins (p. 676), the Romans accorded special treatment. Segesta not only became 'immune' but also was granted a large accretion of territory including the possession of Mt Eryx with its important temple. When the Senate decided that foreigners, whether Sicilians or Romans, should not have the privilege of buying land there, and that they must pay tithes when they rented within the boundaries of Segesta, the purpose was to safeguard the land and the privileges for the Segestans.

Roman rule in Sicily, however, was not drawn on the lines of an eleemosynary institution. Rome did not pretend to govern subjects for charity. On the other hand her rule was beneficent, at least until the time when her own government at home became a disgrace. Even the war, long as it had been, had brought little suffering to the Sicilians except at the far western end of the island. Peace of course put an end to the oppressive tyrannies and the odious exactions of Carthage. The tax-gathering that followed was meticulously managed for more than a century, and the praetors of that period were of Rome's best. So carefully were they limited by law in their behaviour that they could not so much as buy a slave in Sicily except to fill a vacancy in their staff of servants. Sicily prospered materially. The servile war of the next century, while an indication of slackness on the part of some governor, is proof also of the fact that a large number of farmers had grown very wealthy and possessed great estates, and these owners were natives. No Roman or Latin colony was planted in Sicily before Augustus' day, and relatively few Romans possessed land there before the time of Verres. Unfortunately the over-encouragement of cereal culture by ordering at a fair market price a second and often a third tenth of the produce for the supply of the Roman dole resulted in an over-production of wheat year after year which finally exhausted the chemicals in the soil which are required by cereals; and by the time of Augustus Sicily was compelled to give her land a long rest.

III. ITALY AND ROME

In the Italian federations which had been so heavily burdened with levies during the last twenty-four years, Rome now had to make various readjustments. For some crime committed against Rome's tribunes, the city of Falerii, perched with apparent security upon the high cliffs of the Treia, was swiftly punished. Both of the consuls of 241 marched upon the town with the full forces that had just come back from Sicily, and in a campaign of six days took the city, disarmed the natives and ordered them to leave their homes and to rebuild them on the plains three miles away from their stronghold. A half of their territory was confiscated. Since Rome's alliance with Falerii dated from 293 it is probable that at its expiration in 243 the Faliscans had refused to renew it in order to escape the yearly conscription. When one considers how extensive the federation was, how recently it had been formed, and how costly in men the association with Rome had recently proved, it is amazing that Falerii was the only allied city that rebelled against Rome's orders. On the new site the Faliscans were permitted to build an enclosing wall which, constructed largely upon level ground, would not be likely to withstand Rome's engines in case of a second revolt, but would serve to protect the town against Gallic incursions. A large part of this wall is still standing. The temple of Juno was left intact, but the divinities of the other two temples were evoked and given temples at Rome.

Among the administrative measures of this year we must record the planting of a Latin colony at Spoletium. This city lay in lower Umbria behind Falerii and on the road that led to Ariminum, Rome's frontier post on the edge of the Gallic territory. The colony was doubtless to serve important military purposes.

During the same year, in payment for their loyal services during the war Rome gave the Sabines and Picentes two wards in the centuriate assembly, *i.e.* the tribes Quirina and Velina. Their ballots would now have full value in this assembly, whereas hitherto their voters, coming in small numbers from distant homes, had been lost in the larger groups. With the addition of these two wards Rome now had thirty-five in all, and that number was never increased.

A far more important change was the reform of the centuriate assembly. This happens not to be dated, but it is generally assumed that the censors of 241 who added the two tribes also brought about this reform. Hitherto the wealthiest men, consisting of the eighteen centuries of knights and eighty centuries of the first class, had had a majority of the votes, since the other four classes had had only 20, 20, 20 and 30 votes respectively (p. 434). In the new plan the knights retained their eighteen votes, and it is probable that the five votes of the artisans and proletariat were also retained, but the five classes were somehow equalized. Furthermore, the voting groups within each class were divided by tribes so that the territorial principle received some recognition. Hereafter, for instance, the relatively small group of first-class voters that came from the Velina tribe on the Adriatic had as much importance as the larger group of first-class voters belonging to the Poplilian tribe near Rome. The procedure of the elections is not clear, for the loss of the second decade of Livy leaves us with only meagre information about internal matters, but it is generally supposed that each of the five classes was divided by tribes into thirty-five groups and that each of these groups again fell into two groups of 'juniors' and 'seniors' as before, thus making $5 \times 70 + 18$ (knights) $+ 5 = 373$ voting groups[1]. At the elections one group out of the first class was chosen by lot

[1] On the vexed question of the details of this reform see the works cited in the Bibliographies to this chapter and chapters x–vi, B. 7.

to cast the first ballot. Thereafter the knights and the five classes voted in order until a majority of the 373 votes had been reached, when voting was discontinued. Property still counted for something, since the propertyless—a class which increases in number with the growth of cities—were given but one vote. In what other ways the principle of timocracy was recognized we cannot say, since we do not know what the property qualifications of each class were. Presumably they did not remain as before, since in the old system the property-rating was adapted to a very primitive economy and there were now many wealthy landowners. At any rate, our sources assume that the change was in the nature of a democratic reform. One conservative principle, however, was preserved, since the 'seniors', men over forty-five—who would naturally be a minority—had as many votes as the 'juniors'. The new plan, therefore, like its predecessor, shows respect for age and property, but it no longer gives control of the assembly to men of wealth.

Had this reform been brought about by a democratic contest within the assembly, as were most of the liberalizing changes in the constitution, we should probably have some record of the battle in our sources. Since we have none—the epitome of Livy's Book Twenty does not record it—we may assume that it was a censorial measure carried out by virtue of the censors' power to enrol voters where they saw fit. It is probable therefore that the censors re-organized the centuriate assembly in order to make it more popular and thus, if possible, invite favour away from the radical tribal assembly. Obviously the centuriate assembly, presided over by consuls, would even now be a safer body in which to introduce bills than the plebeian body presided over by young tribunes. If this was the purpose of the reform it must be admitted that the measure was not a great success. The important legislation of the following period is found in plebiscites. However it is not unlikely that the tribunes might some day have transferred the election of consuls, praetors and censors to the tribal assembly had not the centuriate body been re-organized. The fact that the important magistrates continued to be elected in the more conservative body is doubtless due to this revision.

IV. CARTHAGE AFTER THE WAR

After the close of the Punic war relations between the governments of Rome and Carthage were very friendly. Carthage was then in a death struggle with her rebelling mercenaries, whereas Rome could well afford to be generous after her victory. But this is not the whole explanation. Of greater importance is the fact that Carthage, having repudiated the leadership of the Barcid war faction, had now accepted the policy of Hanno, who advocated the acquisition of a land empire in Africa rather than the maritime commercial exploitation which had incurred the hostility of the Greeks and Romans. It would seem that Hanno represented the landed nobility rather than the commercial classes, and that he favoured friendship with Rome. Carthage not only deserted Hamilcar but decided to disregard the promises of bounties which Hamilcar had made to his troops at critical moments of the war. The mercenaries rebelled, of course; and in addition the Numidians and Libyans, who feared the imperialism of the party now in power, gave them strong support. The 'Truceless War' that resulted is described in all its horror by Polybius. The Roman Senate, with nothing to fear from its weakened enemy, desiring in fact to see a friendly faction in the ascendancy in Africa, did much to aid the threatened state. Being warned that Italians were selling food and arms to the rebels, the Senate, after securing the release of the offending traders who had been caught, forbade further commerce with them, while sending grain to the hard-pressed city of Carthage; then bought up at public expense the Punic captives that were to be found in Italy, gave them back as a gift, and, annulling for the time a clause of the recent treaty, permitted Carthage to hire troops in Italy. Presently when the Punic mercenaries stationed in Sardinia revolted from Carthage, slew their officers, and in fear of the natives asked Rome to take possession of the island, Rome refused. Again when Utica, deserting Carthage, joined the African revolt and offered to accept Rome as sovereign, Rome remained loyal to the recent treaty and refused. Had Hamilcar then been the controlling statesman in Carthage, there is little doubt that Rome would have behaved differently.

Hanno however mismanaged the war to such an extent that in its second year Hamilcar was again given a command over a part of the Punic forces, and in the third year a temporary reconciliation was brought about between the two generals with Hamilcar the dominant force. From this time on Carthage began to make steady progress against the rebellion. But meanwhile the Senate began to veer away from its generous course. In 239 B.C. Carthage felt strong enough to send a force to Sardinia in an effort to recover that island, but the troops revolted, killed the general in command and joined the mutineers. The next year, however, the rebellious troops were attacked in force by the natives and now

for a second time asked Rome to take possession of the island.
This time the Senate, 'contrary to all justice,' as Polybius well says,
decided to accept the invitation. The Senate could perhaps advance
the pretext that since Carthage had lost the island two years before
and had failed to recover it the following year, Rome was not
violating the treaty that forbade attacks upon or alliance with
Punic subjects. Indeed Rome had such manifest interests in the
possession of this island, which lay outstretched so near the Italian
coast, that this interpretation has been condoned by several
modern historians. However, it is apparent that the diplomatic
usage of the day did not excuse the act. Polybius, well-versed in
international custom, did not spare words in condemning it, and
the Romans later, feeling that excuses were demanded, busied
themselves in manufacturing explanations. They weakly alleged,
for instance, that Sardinia was one of the islands lying between
Sicily and Italy surrendered by the treaty of 241. They also stated
that Carthage had first broken a treaty by capturing Italians who
carried contraband to Africa—a dispute which had already been
amicably settled. It is interesting to note that the diplomatic
discussion of that day seems to have been silent both about the
length of time that Carthage might reasonably have been allowed
in order to win back her lost island, and about the position of
Sardinia with regard to Rome's sphere of interest and of safety.

Rome fitted out an expedition to take possession; Carthage
served notice that she had not abandoned the island, and began to
man her fleet to anticipate her rival. Rome, hearing of the preparations and claiming that they were directed against her, declared war. Carthage offered to arbitrate but Rome refused.
Carthage, completely worn out, could only ask for terms of peace,
and for these she paid the indemnity imposed of 1200 talents and
surrendered all claim to Sardinia. With Sardinia went Corsica as
well, though the latter island was not mentioned in the treaty.
Apparently Carthage had made no effort to recover that island
since Scipio took its principal harbour, Aleria, twenty years before (p. 679), and saw no point in raising the question of sovereignty now. By any standard Rome's last act of declaring war
left no room for excuses and did much to raise up a lasting
enmity in Carthage; and this enmity strengthened Hamilcar's
party, destroying the influence of the faction which preferred
peace with Rome and confined its ambitions to Africa.

During the next six years, according to the later annals, there
were many battles and skirmishes in Sardinia and Corsica. The
ancient barbarians inhabiting these islands, descendants of the

warlike builders of the picturesque *nuraghi* (vol. ii, p. 583 *sq.*), had
on the whole been left to their own devices by the Carthaginians,
who had been satisfied to hold possession of the port towns and
barter with the natives. The Romans, however, had a different
conception of what overlordship could mean. Trade and barter
did not interest them, and nominal sovereignty over barbaric tribes
without explicit and formal treaties was a thing quite incomprehensible to them. Furthermore, Rome had now learned in Sicily
that possession might mean a lucrative tribute to the sovereign.
So the Roman governor sent his envoys to the various tribes with
treaties of submission which he asked them to sign. When the
signatures were not forthcoming, he advanced with his troops and
compelled submission, sometimes at a heavy cost to his army.
In 235 Manlius, in 234 Carvilius, in 233 Pomponius, all Roman
consuls, triumphed over Sardinian tribes, and in 231 the consul
Papirius triumphed over the Corsi—so seriously did the Senate
take the task of subjugating a harmless people who did not even
comprehend why the Romans were there. In 227 the two islands
were made into a province like Sicily and a fourth praetor allotted
annually to take charge. Tithes were henceforth collected here as
in Sicily, and from all the tribes, for none had gained immunity
through friendly act or speedy submission.

V. NORTH ITALY: FLAMINIUS

About the time that the Senate decided to take Sardinia,
skirmishes with the Ligurians beyond the Arno are first reported.
These mountaineers were then a large nation extending from the
Alps of Upper Savoy, through the Apennines as far as Arretium,
holding therefore the whole of the Italian coast beyond the Arno.
The Etruscans, now members of Rome's federation, had long
before seized the Arno valley and taken possession of Pisa and the
arable region beyond up to the Apennine foothills, but during the
third century, when the Etruscans were too weak to protect their
boundaries and the Romans were too busily engaged to lend them
support, the Ligurians had come back as far as the river. Greek
writers of the third century speak of Pisa and the Arno as Ligurian.
We have no information regarding the causes of Roman operations
there, but we may suppose that the Senate had determined to bring
back the Arno and at least Pisa within the territory of the federation. At any rate we find a few years later that Pisa is a friendly
Etruscan port and is being used by Roman generals as a point of
departure for Corsica. It is not unlikely that the Senate also
planned to carry the line some thirty miles farther back so as to

secure a natural boundary in the Apennines, for in 236 the consul Lentulus is said to have stormed some forts in the mountains. But this may simply have been a demonstration of strength. At any rate no serious effort to gain the foothills was made till after the Hannibalic War, when the acquisition of Spain proved the need of possessing a safe road along the Ligurian coast toward the new province.

In the city the democratic ferment which had made possible the reform of the centuries was still at work. That reform is perhaps to be credited with the elevation of a new group of plebeians to the consulship, for instance the two Pomponii (in 233, 231), Poplicius Malleolus (232), Apustius (226), and in bringing back to prominence the families of Papirius (231) and Aemilius Lepidus (232), for a long time in obscurity. About this time the censors (probably Atilius and Postumius in 234), in response to the democratic dislike of freedmen, significantly enrolled all freedmen and their sons in the four city tribes, thus limiting their influence at elections. It cannot be said that the freedmen were as yet a large or incongruous element. The captives of the Italian wars were of course Italic people, of the same stock as their masters. This was true even of those taken in Etruria (see p. 658), though most of them now spoke the Etruscan language. Of Greeks very few had been captured in the Pyrrhic War, and those were of excellent antecedents. The captives taken in the Punic War had later been given back by Rome. Among their slaves the only people that the Romans ranked inferior to themselves were the Sardinians, who had recently been brought to the block at Rome in large numbers, but these were considered fit only for hard labour and would not be able to gain their freedom in any large numbers. The resentment, therefore, that crops out in the new decree was probably due not to a political or social fear but rather to the dislike of the poorer citizens for slaves who had cheapened their labour. The segregation of the vote remained as a beneficial safeguard in the second century when hordes of slaves were bought in the Aegean. It was a measure to which Cicero later attributed the salvation of Rome's political institutions.

Another act of even greater significance for the present was the distribution of the Ager Gallicus in small lots to Roman citizens. A daring tribune of 232, C. Flaminius, carried the measure in the plebeian assembly against the most strenuous opposition of a large group of senators and without consulting the Senate. As explanation of this opposition we hear only that the Senate considered it a measure which began 'the demoralization of the people,' and incited the neighbouring Gauls to believe that the Romans desired their territory, and hence directly caused the

Gallic invasion of 225. We may suppose that there were other reasons as well. The senators might well have insisted that the government was not prepared to forgo the revenue which the rental of the tract brought, also that individual settlement by citizens was not a sound method, partly because it disregarded the rights of the allies, partly because it provided no sound political and social centres. The land belonged not to Rome but to the federation, and the only just method was to settle it by 'Latin colonies' like Ariminum in which all shared, and which provided not only healthy municipal centres but also compact garrisons in a frontier area. Lastly we may well believe that many senators disliked to lose the lucrative leaseholds on these public lands.

There is no doubt that the plebiscite disregarded allied rights and that the method of settlement was unwise, but the charge of demoralization, though probably brought, could not have been taken very seriously then, when the Romans still remembered that it had been a recognized policy of their ancestors to build up a sound stock of Roman and Italian soldiers by distributing conquered land in small lots to farmers. It is likely that the charge had been repeated under stress of great excitement in the Gracchan days, when it was pointed out that Tiberius Gracchus harked back to the precedents set by Flaminius. The criticism that the action excited the anger of the Gauls also seems unjustified in view of the fact that the Gallic raid came seven years later. Indeed the Gauls had already threatened Ariminum in 236, and vacant lands were as much of an incitement to raids as settled ones. It would be easier to believe that the Gallic threat of 236 was to some extent one of the arguments for sending Roman colonists to the support of the frontier post. The truth is that the hatred against Flaminius rose to such a pitch that he never received his due in Roman history, for the writers of the early period were all of the senatorial party. And we may well believe that this hatred was not so much due to the distribution of the land as to the fact that Flaminius in his legislation disregarded the Senate and the recently reformed centuriate assembly and brought his measure directly before the plebeian body. This procedure not only proved that the more conservative organ had failed to regain its standing by the reform, but also that the Senate was in serious danger of losing its control over such purely administrative questions as the disposal of the public land. We should add that the demand for land at this time did not prove to be very great. Gracchan landmarks have been found in this region which show that considerable areas were not taken for distribution at the first settlement.

While discussing such democratic measures, we may perhaps

be permitted to anticipate slightly and mention the Claudian plebiscite of a few years later—the date is not certain—which Flaminius alone of senators supported. This law prohibited senators and their sons from owning sea-going ships of more than three hundred amphoras capacity (about 225 bushels). Livy's comment is that lucrative occupations did not befit senators, an observation which is wholly credible and to be expected from a Cisalpine historian. Yet it is doubtful whether the tribunes who proposed the bill were especially concerned about decorum. Perhaps some senators had been lured by the new opportunities of trade with Sicily and Sardinia, and it was feared that private interests might warp their judgment in public affairs, or that business might entice them away from regular attendance upon the Senate. Such were apparently Julius Caesar's reasons for re-enacting the rule during his consulship. The consequences of the law were not wholly desirable. The senators on the whole obeyed and invested their surplus in land. Doubtless farmers who wished to go to Picenum could now sell their lands near Rome at a better price, but the law restricted the interests of Rome's states-men too much. Roman legislation continued to disregard the claims of trade and industry and to overvalue landed property. The senators began to exploit the *ager publicus*, refusing to dis-tribute it till compelled to, and the agrarian mind comes to domi-nate even international questions. We hear later of another restriction, which is usually considered to be a clause of the same law, prohibiting senators from taking state contracts. This mea-sure, however, designed to keep the state contractor out of politics, was sound and might with advantage have been applied to the knights a century later.

VI. THE GALLIC PERIL

We have noticed that even before the distribution of the Ager Gallicus the Gauls looked with longing upon the land which their brothers had lost south of the Rubicon river (p. 807). We hear of skirmishes as early as 238, though not from reliable sources. It is not unlikely that some of the Gauls had drifted back there while Rome was too busy in Sicily to take notice of them, and that the trouble was due to an effort to clear the region again. If we may believe Polybius there was no threat of a war till 236, when some of the Boian chieftains, without consulting their people, secretly invited Transalpine tribesmen to come and aid them in an attack upon Ariminum. When these warriors began to appear, Rome became alarmed and sent an army north to the defence of the colony. However, the invasion came to nought. The Boian populace, recalling the stories of the terrible punishment meted out by Cornelius Dolabella and Manius Curius forty-five years before, refused to march, and their refusal resulted in a civil war within the tribe which put an end to all thoughts of an invasion. The Romans, secure in the hope of peace within their borders, closed with due solemnity the portals of Janus.

Some years after the settlement of the Ager Gallicus, the Boii again began to plan an invasion. We are told by Polybius that Rome was then much concerned about Punic designs in Spain, fearing a renewal of the war with Carthage, and that because of the threat on her Gallic frontier she made a hasty agreement with Hasdrubal in Spain in 226. This question has already been discussed from the Carthaginian side (p. 788 *sq.*), and it can be mentioned here only so far as it concerns Rome's immediate policies. After the Truceless War (237) Hamilcar, contrary to the wishes of Hanno's party, had secured the command in southern Spain, where he set himself to restore Carthaginian power (see above, pp. 786 *sqq.*) He did not, however, limit his ambitions to this objective, but advanced northward, subdued tribe after tribe, and as he acquired booty built up and trained an army. Rumours soon came to Rome that he was training the army for a war of vengeance upon Rome. Whether or not this was true— the most reliable of the early historians believed it—we can comprehend why the tales were so quickly borne to Rome. Massilia, Rome's oldest Greek ally, whose trading posts on the eastern coast of Spain were being made useless by the Punic advance in the rear, doubtless kept up an effective propaganda at Rome. If Hamilcar conquered the whole of Spain, a large part of Massilia's commerce would disappear; if he should cross into Gaul and cut the trade-route of the Garumna river, the easiest approach to the Atlantic would be severed. Induced by tales thus well-inspired, Rome sent envoys to confer with Hamilcar in 231. With ready wit Hamilcar told the envoys that he was only engaged in winning enough booty for Carthage to pay her annual indemnity to Rome. The envoys made no answer, but seem to have taken the occasion to form an alliance with Saguntum, a good trading post which was still free. Since Rome had no trade on the seas at this time we may reasonably suppose that it was her ally Massilia rather than Rome herself who was primarily concerned in keeping this port open. Hamilcar died in 229 and was succeeded by his son-in-law, Hasdrubal, who continued to advance in Spain even more successfully than his predecessor.

In 226 Rome heard of the threatened Gallic invasion. Since the Gauls were then recruiting in the Transalpine region above Massilia, the news may have come from her trusted ally, who continued to complain of Punic advances in Spain. Hasdrubal was now near the river Ebro. If he crossed that, the two Massiliote colonies of Emporiae and Rhode would be helpless, for their trading routes into the interior of Spain followed the river. In view of Massilia's part in the war that followed—it was the Massiliote fleet which played the important rôle in the first naval battle—we must assume that Rome came to a complete understanding with her ally about this time. Rome's envoys, at any rate, met Hasdrubal in 226 and expressed their concern. Hasdrubal was probably innocent of any untoward ambition, and to allay needless fears consented to sign an agreement that he would not cross the Ebro with an armed force. The treaty, then, was in the first instance meant to protect the interests of Massilia and in the second to allay fears at Rome. It is probable that the three parties concerned signed the treaty as was done in a similar instance later when Rome aided Massilia against the Ligurians. Since this treaty does not explicitly grant Hasdrubal any definite return for the restrictions imposed upon him, it has been frequently assumed that Rome tacitly surrendered her alliance with Saguntum and that the document marked the Ebro as the boundary line of their respective 'spheres of influence.' This assumption disregards the fact that Rome had never as yet shown any inclination to assume vague responsibility over spheres of influence, having invariably confined herself to definite alliances, and it is also to be noticed that the Ebro was very far from the Arno river, Rome's northernmost boundary line. Hasdrubal's *quid pro quo* was in fact the assurance that extravagant fears of him would now be allayed both at Massilia and at Rome, and that he could proceed with the conquest of Spain without further interference. Nothing was, or needed to be said about Saguntum, since there was enough unconquered territory in Spain for generations of expansion without touching that city. That Hannibal would later regard Saguntum as a dangerous port of entry for the enemy when he decided to march against Rome, was quite beyond the range of Hasdrubal's immediate plans.

Relieved of anxiety about Spain, Rome now set about to meet the dreaded enemy on her northern frontier. At this time the Po Valley was thickly settled by the Celts who had been coming in, horde after horde, for about two hundred years. The strongest tribes were the Taurini (around Turin), the Insubres (in Lombardy and Piedmont), the Cenomani (between the Po and Lago di Garda), the Boii (south of the Po from Bologna to Piacenza), and the Lingones (north of the Ager Gallicus). The lower reaches of the Po for about fifty miles were marshy, frequently flooded, and contained few settlements. Venetia was inhabited by an old non-Celtic folk that had many customs in common with the Romans, claimed kinship with them and remained on friendly terms throughout the Gallic wars (vol. IV, pp. 441 *sqq.*). Among the Celtic tribes, the Cenomani and some minor groups had also signed treaties of friendship and remained at peace throughout the war. A few years after the Roman settlement of the Ager Gallicus below Ariminum, the strongest tribes, the Boii, the Insubres, the Lingones and the Taurini, formed a league of Celts for the purpose of attacking Rome. Envoys were sent over the Alps to invite the aid of bands called Gaesati (lancemen) who were accustomed to hire themselves out as mercenaries. They were told of the ease with which Rome had been taken long ago by the Senones (p. 564), and the wealth and available booty of the city were invitingly described. Large bands accepted the invitation, and the Celts were able to form an army of 50,000 foot and 20,000 horse and chariots, as well as to station strong forces along their frontiers against a possible invasion by the Cenomani and Veneti whom the Romans had induced to arm. This was in 225 B.C.

The Romans, who had not forgotten the sack of Rome, were thoroughly alarmed, for their enemy, if united, could muster two or three hundred thousand men. They took a census of all the available land forces throughout Italy, and the allies, as fully terrified as the Romans, responded quickly. The census of this year, probably the first made for all Italy, is one of the most valuable documents of the Republican period that has survived[1]. The citizens amounted to 250,000 foot and 23,000 horse. This number included both active and defensive forces, 'seniors' as well as 'juniors', as we see by referring to the regular census of 234. The allies, who counted only the soldiers available for army duty, that is the 'juniors', listed about 350,000 of these. The most important of the allied contingents were the following: the Umbrians, who numbered 20,000; the Etruscans and Sabines (the latter being *cives*), 50,000 foot and 4000 horse; Latins, including Latin colonies, 80,000 foot and 5000 horse; Samnites, 70,000 and 7000; Messapians and Apulians, 50,000 and 16,000; Lucanians, 30,000 and 3000; allied Sabellic tribes, 20,000 and

[1] It is cited by Polybius (II, 24) to show the resources of Rome which Hannibal had to face later.

4000. The Bruttians and Greek socii are not reported, but the Veneti and Cenomani actually sent 20,000 men across the border for guard duty. The lists give a fair idea of Italy's population south of the Rubicon at this time. Since males over seventeen may be estimated as constituting about thirty-five per cent. of the free citizen population of Rome and the Ager Romanus, we may assume a citizen population of about 800,000 souls. In estimating the allied and Latin population there is less certainty. If we add the probable number of 'seniors', Bruttians and *socii navales* to the 350,000 listed, we may count upon about 600,000 males over seventeen years of age or a free population of about 1,700,000. The sum total of citizens and allies for Italy south of the Rubicon was therefore about 2,500,000. The present population of the same region is about six times that number.

To meet the expected attack Rome sent two consular armies north, each consisting of four legions of citizens (20,800 foot and 1200 horse) and 30,000 foot with 2000 horse of the allies. Besides these a reserve force of 20,000 Roman foot and 1500 horse with allied contingents of 30,000 foot and 2000 horse guarded Rome, while the Umbri, Veneti and Cenomani policed the frontier. One consul, L. Aemilius Papus, led his army to Ariminum, since the first attack was expected there, while a praetor watched the central Etruscan roads[1]. The other consul, Atilius Regulus, was unfortunately detained in Sardinia. The Gauls did not attack Ariminum. They broke through the mountains, probably above Bologna, escaping even the forces of the praetor, and marched southward as far as Clusium, loading their wagons with booty. Both of the Roman armies started in pursuit, but the Gauls doubled on their tracks, enticed the praetor into battle before the consul arrived and slew six thousand men. Aemilius appeared, however, in time to rescue the remnants of the praetor's army, and the Gauls concluded that they ought to bring their booty home to safety and recruit new forces before meeting so large an army. To avoid being caught between the frontier guards and the consul, they decided to march westward toward the sea and follow the coast-road up to the mountains. Closely followed by Aemilius, they reached the sea near Orbetello and started northward, when to their surprise they met at Telamon the forces of Atilius, who had been recalled from Sardinia and was marching Romewards from Pisa. For once the Roman intelligence service operated efficiently; both consuls soon learned what the situation was and were able to co-operate in encircling the enemy army.

[1] See map 7, facing p. 581.

The Gauls formed in two lines back to back, the Boii and Taurini facing Atilius' legions, while the Gaesati and Insubres met the attack of Aemilius. Atilius himself took charge of the combined cavalry forces, and before the main battle was joined, succeeded in driving off the horse of the enemy, though at the sacrifice of his own life. With the defeat of the Gallic cavalry, the victory of the legions was a foregone conclusion, but the Celts, completely hemmed in, fought with unusual endurance. Forty thousand were slain, among them being one of the chieftains, King Concolitanus. The other chieftain took his own life. Ten thousand prisoners were captured[1]. The Romans too had suffered heavily, but Aemilius nevertheless marched north and raided the territory of the Boii before he returned home to celebrate his triumph.

The great dread of invasion was over for the present. But the Romans decided that they had had enough of Gallic raids, that Italy must have a safe frontier, that there could be no peace with the Cisalpine Gauls until they were completely subjected. Their objective was not to be attained for many years, but the task was at least begun with vigour. Both of the consuls of 224, Fulvius and Manlius, marched into the Boian country with large forces, and despite rains and pestilence succeeded in subduing the Boii, who signed an agreement to keep the peace—an agreement which they broke as soon as Hannibal crossed the Alps a few years later.

The consuls of 223 were Furius Philus and Gaius Flaminius. The latter, who had incurred the hatred of the Senate when tribune and who was too strong a personality to take second place, determined the campaign. His task was obviously to attack the Insubres, and he had the choice between crossing the Po below the friendly Cenomani, where however the river was wide and time would be consumed in building an extensive pontoon, or marching farther up toward Clastidium and crossing a narrower river in the face of the enemy. He chose the latter course, though at some cost in men. Finding his way blocked by strongholds like Acerrae, he made a detour through the friendly country of the Cenomani in order to attack from an exposed side. Somewhere below Bergamo he found the enemy. Leaving the contingent of the Cenomani behind, for he preferred to trust his fate to his own tried soldiers, he—with more bravado than wisdom—burned his bridges behind him and attacked. It is said that the Senate, terrified by omens, had sent letters demanding his return and abdication, and that he, suspecting the contents of the letters, had

[1] Some of the votive offerings dedicated by the Romans on the battlefield have been found: *Mus. Arch. di Firenze*, 1912, Tav. 104–6.

laid them aside unopened till after the battle. The story is plausible in view of the Senate's hatred of the man. The Insubres had an army of fifty thousand, probably the equal of the consular forces, but they were quickly defeated. Ancient historians give the entire credit of the victory to the valour of the legions and the skill of the tribunes, criticizing the general for his recklessness in placing his army in a desperate situation. At Lake Trasimene Flaminius later showed that he lacked skill in strategy, and the criticism is probably just, but some credit is due to the officer who could inspire his men with such personal devotion as could this hero of the rank and file.

After the victory he opened and read his summons to return and lay down his command, but despite the warnings of his colleague he remained for some time in order to compel the enemy to send envoys to Rome with offers of peace. Notwithstanding the opposition of the Senate, Flaminius, together with his colleague, was voted a triumph by the devoted populace, after which both abdicated, thus permitting their successors to enter office in March, a month earlier than had been customary.

The Senate refused to listen to any Gallic offers of peace short of unconditional surrender, and the new consuls of 222, M. Claudius Marcellus and Cn. Cornelius Scipio, invaded the Insubrian territory. The Gauls had in the meanwhile secured the aid of 30,000 Gaesati from the valley of the Rhône. The Romans laid siege to Acerrae, north of Piacenza. In order to raise the siege if possible, the Insubres attacked Clastidium, south of the Po, where the Romans had left their stock of supplies in friendly country. Marcellus marched to the relief of this city with all the horse and light armed troops. During the clash of cavalry forces the Gallic chieftain, Virdumarus, challenged Marcellus to personal combat. Roman generals had long ago abandoned the duels of the heroic age, but they still were wont to lead their men and at times engage in the contest. Marcellus, though over forty-six years of age, when Roman soldiers usually were retired from active service, could still trust his arm. Piercing his enemy's armour with a thrust of his lance, he unhorsed the barbarian and overcame him. The incident was later made the subject of an historical play written by Naevius, the first of its kind to be produced at Rome. Marcellus easily put the enemy to flight, re-crossed the river and joined Scipio, who had meanwhile taken Acerrae. The two consuls advanced upon Mediolanum (Milan), the chief city of the tribe, and stormed it. The Insubres now surrendered without conditions, gave up some territory on which the colony of Cremona was presently planted, and pledged themselves to keep the peace. Thus Cisalpine Gaul was conquered—or so it seemed at the time. Unfortunately for the Celts and for Italy, the invasion of Hannibal invited them later to revolt, which resulted in a long series of wars at the end of which few Celts outside of the Cenomani remained below the foothills of the Alps.

There was still the north-east corner of Italy, a strip of Histrian coastland between the Veneti and the Julian Alps, where the peninsula seemed exposed to danger. The Senate, determined to be thorough, sent the consuls of 221 to this place to demand the submission of all the tribes as far as the mountain passes. An excuse—for this seemed to be necessary in the Senate's conception of international affairs—was available in the pirating expeditions that some of these people engaged in. The work was completed in 220.

VII. ROMAN POLICY

Rome had now reached her natural boundaries. To be sure, a large area of barbaric Ligurian territory lay within the limits, and Rome made no effort for the present to plant forts at the Alpine passes, but at any rate raids were not likely to be organized within the peninsula, nor could an enemy be invited from beyond the Alps without incurring the danger of speedy punishment. Two Latin colonies were at once organized as guards for the Po region and planted in 218. Placentia was placed at the far end of the Boian territory, while Cremona was placed north of the river on Insubrian land. Three thousand men were sent to each and given the same status as the colonists of Ariminum.

In 220 there was also a renewal of trouble with the Illyrians, whose buccaneers had first been subdued nine years before (p. 834). This war came at an unfortunate time, for it kept the two consuls of 219 engaged in the Adriatic during the year that Hannibal attacked Saguntum. His decision to risk an invasion of Italy at that time was doubtless due to Rome's preoccupation with the Illyrians. Had these two able consuls, Aemilius Paulus and Livius Salinator, been at home to give force to Rome's warnings regarding Saguntum, the Hannibalic War might well have been fought to a speedy completion in Spain.

In surveying the petty border wars of this period it would be interesting to find a consistent external policy actuating the Senate or the popular leaders. The seizure of Sardinia and the war with the Illyrian pirates are at times credited to groups interested in commerce. Flaminius has been called an imperialist who carried Rome's standards beyond the Po in the interest of a land-hungry population. A very recent theory finds in the whole period a conscious and consistent drive on the part of an astute Senate toward natural boundaries[1]. However, though an interest in territorial expansion is to be assumed in the large body of small farmers represented in the latter years by the democrat Flaminius, and an appreciation of the value of defensible borders may safely be postulated in senatorial action, Rome seems throughout the period to have met immediate situations with practical remedies and without definitely outlined policies for the far-off future.

The supposed mercantilistic policy may be dismissed at once. There is no evidence that the Romans traded in the Ionian sea at this time. Other Italians and Greeks resident in Italy did, and the suppression of the Illyrian pirates benefited them, but we may doubt whether the Senate was ever deeply stirred by the wrongs done to allied merchants. It is more probable that in the case of the Illyrians the incentive was an appeal to Rome's dignity and self-respect. The seizure of Sardinia, a harsh answer to the ascendancy of the anti-Roman faction in Carthage, can best be attributed to misplaced political nervousness. Nor is there any tangible evidence of imperialistic expansion in the wars with Liguria and the Gauls. In the recovery of the Arno valley the Senate revealed its characteristic habit of scrupulously guarding the frontiers of the federation. The Senate's conferences and bargains with Hamilcar and Hasdrubal in Spain are best explained as efforts to allay the overstrained fears which Massilia had consciously nurtured for the protection of her own interests. To interpret them as an attempt to establish a Roman sphere of influence in Spain is wholly to misunderstand Rome's methods and motives[2].

After the Gallic raid of 225 we are compelled to recognize a determination on the part of the Senate to subjugate Italy as far as the Alps in order to acquire a defensible frontier and to put an end to Gallic raids; but such a policy is not apparent before that. Had the Romans contemplated subduing northern Italy after the raids of 236, they would hardly have closed the portals of Janus with so much circumstance in 235. In any event, this Gallic war was not begun by Rome but by the Gauls. When forced to act, the Senate continued it into the enemy's territory after the victory at Telamon, by sending the consuls of 224 to

---

[1] E. Meyer, *Die römische Politik vom ersten bis zum Ausbruch des zweiten punischen Kriegs*. Kleine Schriften II, pp. 375 *sqq.*, and E. Täubler, *Die Vorgeschichte des zweiten punischen Kriegs*.

[2] See further on the character of Roman policy at this time p. 856 *sq.*

subject the Boii, by directing Flaminius beyond the Po in 223, and by refusing to consider peace overtures until the Insubres surrendered unconditionally to Marcellus and Scipio in 222. In this war it would be incorrect to single out Flaminius as the directing force on the ground of his democratic leanings. His campaign was a part of the whole advance and in no respect more aggressive than the campaigns of the several aristocratic leaders. That the Gauls were left in possession of their country, except for those whose lands were needed for two frontier colonies, would seem to indicate that land hunger was not the motive force. At any rate, we cannot conclude from the wars of these three or four years, wars imposed by the enemy, that success in the contest with Carthage had incited Rome to formulate a consistent policy of expansion, supposedly traceable in all her acts from 241 to 218. Throughout the period we are not aware of any controlling person at Rome who could have imposed a definite dogma for a long series of years. There was no continuing 'foreign office.' The consuls held their command for one year, there are few instances of iteration, and as the Senate itself was constantly changing with the entrance of new members, the attitude of the Senate changed as well. As usual, the Roman government was opportunist.

VIII. THE ROMAN CONSTITUTION

Rome in theory continued to be the democracy that had been created by the Hortensian law of 287 (p. 553), but in fact the plebeian assembly had little to do but elect the tribunes and the plebeian aediles. During the period under consideration Flaminius, against heavy opposition, brought it into action to secure the distribution of the Ager Gallicus and to limit the commercial activities of the senators. That was of very great importance as a demonstration of what the assembly could do. And in 223 the plebeians also voted Flaminius a triumph when the Senate had refused him one. But after that we hear of no other plebiscites except that of Metilius, which defined what cleansing materials the laundries must use on various textiles. To such harmless activity the Senate could hardly take exception. The centuriate assembly was liberalized, but this was presumably in the interest of the nobles, who would naturally prefer to have a legislative body that, while acceptable to the populace, would be presided over by the consuls. And this assembly also found few occasions to vote except at elections. In 229, after the murder of a Roman envoy by the Illyrians, it was called upon to declare war, but in this case there could have been no difference of opinion (p. 832 sq.).

It also voted war against Carthage in 218, when the quarrel had been carried by the Senate to the point where war was the only issue possible. But the seizure of Sardinia and the recovery of the Arno valley seem to have been considered administrative acts wholly within the competence of the Senate; and the same body felt free to direct the invasion of the Po valley and determine the ultimate limits to which the Gallic war should be carried when once the Gauls had begun it. We are not told that the centuriate assembly in this case ratified the treaty. Since the assembly had not declared war, it may be that they were not called upon to close it. In a word, during this time the primary assemblies hardly ever expressed their will in any direct legislation.

The magistrates, elected by the assemblies, and the Senate, made up of ex-magistrates and therefore indirectly representative of the people, carried on the affairs of state. The consuls, while as powerful as ever in the field, were gradually being deprived of independence and leadership by the strong class-consciousness that pervaded the Senate, and by constitutional customs which in legislative activity compelled them to act with and through the Senate and the more conservative assembly. Flaminius, for instance, carried several radical measures to completion while tribune and later as censor; but during his consulship he found that he was expected to be the executive of the Senate's orders. The urban praetor and the praetor peregrinus (an office instituted in 242), by their yearly revision of the praetor's edict, largely removed the need of legislation in the field of civil and criminal law[1]. The latter particularly, by his contact with non-Roman customs, was able to bring new living elements into Roman law. The date of 242 marks an epoch in the history of jurisprudence. The other two praetors exercised such full powers in their provinces in consultation with the Senate that legislative interference in what one might call colonial affairs did not appear for a long time.

The censors retained the broad powers that they had held since Appius Claudius (p. 531), but kept generally on good terms with the Senate. They seem to have interpreted the Ovinian law as essentially restricting their choice of senators to ex-magistrates. We hear of no abuse of their great censorial powers. How far they could carry their functions into the legislative field in emulation of Appius Claudius is shown in the drastic reform of the centuriate assembly—doubtless carried out with the concurrence of the Senate—and in the restriction of the freedmen to the urban wards. Since such acts had so direct a bearing on the very meaning of

[1] For the further development of Roman Law under the Republic see vol. ix.

citizenship, one might have expected the 'sovereign' people, who had struggled so hard for the passage of the Hortensian law, to claim competence in this field. If the democracy did not let itself be heard on such questions, it had little right later on to cry out that the senators and magistrates had usurped its powers. Plebeians had long been eligible for the high office of censor, but since the elective assembly had been conservative the change had had small effect. After the reform of the assembly, however, a popular favourite like Flaminius, distrusted by the Senate, could gain the office. He became censor in 220. We do not hear that he abused his charge by way of paying off old scores against his political enemies, but he did use its large powers in a characteristic way. He let contracts for a highroad to Ariminum, that is to the colonies which he planted contrary to the wishes of the Senate, and he also ordered the construction of a new circus in the campus for the use of a new series of games to be called the Ludi Plebeii. The *patres* apparently had to follow custom and assign the funds.

The Senate, therefore, practically governed Rome and the federation. We need not assume that it deliberately set itself against the spirit of the Hortensian law, or that it hampered independent magistrates. In its organization, its composition and its availability, it had every advantage and, with the growth of Rome's business, silently gained power and esteem during peace as well as war. The senators, since they were ex-magistrates, were experienced judges, officers, and administrators. As men of note they had large personal followings, and as men of wealth and leisure they had time to devote to their work. They were ready for consultation every day. The body was small and could deliberate, and the spirit of *noblesse oblige* demanded that they deliberate without yielding to ulterior motives. They determined the diplomatic action that led to war or peace, and often when war was necessary manœuvred the enemy into the declaration, so that it need not even be submitted to the people; the Senate was of course consulted by the consuls, who were also members, as to what forces should be summoned and paid for, and what the objective of the campaign should be. When peace was offered, the Senate could even delay negotiations till satisfactory terms were secured. When territory was acquired, it usually determined what disposition should be made of it. There were at this time probably fifty allies inscribed on Rome's list, and, if a dispute arose with any of them, it was the Senate that heard the legations and decided the issues. There was a constant stream of administrative questions which the Senate discussed and settled without the knowledge of the Roman people.

We have for the first time in Roman history some reliable information regarding the personal traits of several of the senators. The type of man that appears most frequently in the Ciceronian epoch has already emerged, and there is but little variety. When the pontifex Caecilius Metellus, the hero of Panormus, died in 221, his son in a funeral oration spoke at length of his father's ideals and endeavours. He had striven for the highest offices of state, for wealth honourably attained, for the respect of the community won by deeds of valour and counsels of wisdom, and he had desired a family of many children to survive him. That these purposes should be so candidly avowed is as significant as their content. Fabius Maximus Cunctator belonged to the same school. A stubborn conservative, he bitterly fought the reforms of Flaminius in the interests of the aristocratic constitution. Though scrupulous in every religious observance, he did not hesitate to employ the augural lore, of which he was master, in the defence of those interests. Always ready to take the command against Hannibal when others had failed, he was too prudent to be lured into traps, and yet lacked the versatility and speed of intellect to outwit his brilliant opponent on the field of battle. Marcellus, the hero of Clastidium, seems perhaps a trifle more aggressive, but only because his opportunities were more varied. He had no patience with strategy, always leading his men straight into the fight at fearful cost. He was religious enough to vow temples to the gods, but too eager for battle to observe auguries that might postpone the fray. When he captured Syracuse, works of art, human beings and gold all went into the same heap of booty, though he regretted, even if he failed to prevent, the death of Archimedes whose mechanical skill at least he had learned to respect. He delighted in leading his men into battle, accepted with alacrity the Gallic chieftain's challenge to single combat, and fell at last in an ambuscade because he insisted on conducting his reconnoitring parties in person. From such men Rome could hardly expect brilliant or creative achievements, but they were in any case trustworthy counsellors of a people who insisted upon the ancient right of self-government. It was of men like these that Ennius wrote

Moribus antiquis res stat Romana virisque.

With such men in control there was little need of legislation. They preferred to feel their way through new problems by practical means rather than to use their imagination in plotting possible solutions beforehand. They trusted administrative experience to

adapt the constitution and judicial practice to new needs. The
people knew that the assemblies could be called if the senatorial
machine failed to operate with efficiency, and that for the present
seemed to suffice. And so year after year Rome by acquiescence
became more and more an aristocracy. For the present the Roman
people fared well; the question was whether with its growing
power the aristocracy could retain its perspective and its high
level of achievement.

CHAPTER XXVI

THE ROMANS IN ILLYRIA

I. THE EARLY RELATIONS OF ROME WITH THE GREEK WORLD

IT has already been shown how easy it was at all times for Greek influences to find their way to Rome, and how in the course of the third century, after the submission of Tarentum, the annexation by the Romans of three-quarters of Sicily and their consequent relations with the Syracusan monarchy, these influences became increasingly active and fruitful (pp. 696 *sqq.*). At that period the coming to Rome of many Greeks gave rise to a widely extended knowledge of the Greek language: the most enlightened part of the Roman public, the higher social strata which furnished the personnel of government, learnt to admire ancient Greek literature, and the Latin Muse made its first tentative essays, translations or imitations of Greek originals or Greek models (see below, vol. VIII). But it is a remarkable fact that while the literary forms in which Greek thought was embodied received a more and more enthusiastic welcome at Rome, the group of countries to the east of Italy, where lay the principal seats of earlier and later Hellenic culture, continued to be entirely outside the sphere of Roman political action.

The contrary has often been maintained. If we could accept the conjectures of certain modern historians; if, like them, we could give credence to certain Roman traditions of late date, it would appear that the Senate early adopted an 'Eastern' policy, the effects of which were felt as far as Rhodes, Asia, and Egypt. But criticism cannot countenance these conjectures and traditions. The supposed 'Treaty of Friendship and Commerce,' which according to Droysen the Romans had concluded with Rhodes in the year 306, is wholly imaginary, and owes its origin merely to

Note. The chief source for the narrative of this chapter is Polybius II, 8–12; III, 16–19; IV, 16, 6–9. His account, incomplete or inexact on some points but on the whole entirely trustworthy, is generally held to be based on Fabius Pictor (see p. 664 n.), but cannot be derived exclusively from him. Appian (*Ill.* 7–8) and Dio Cassius (frags. 49, 53; Zonaras, VIII, 19, 3–7; 20, 11–13), influenced by the later annalists, add some details which are either highly suspect or plainly fictitious. Of the Livian account only insignificant fragments have survived.

a late alteration in a passage of Polybius (xxx, 5, 6)[1]. The 'friend-ship and alliance' which the Republic is alleged to have formed with 'King Seleucus (?),' on condition that he exempted the town of Ilium from all tribute, has no authority other than the mention made of it in a document which is certainly apocryphal (Suet. *Claud.* 25). Even less credible is that offer of military aid which the Senate, according to Eutropius (III, 1), made to Ptolemy III when he was at war with 'Antiochus,' an offer declined by the king of Egypt. One only of the facts asserted by the Roman traditions can be retained as authentic. About 273 B.C., from motives which re-main obscure, Ptolemy Philadelphus took the initiative in sending an embassy to Rome, in consequence of which amicable relations were established between the Roman People and the Alexandrian Court. The addition made by the annalists—that this action on the part of Philadelphus resulted in the conclusion of an agree-ment (ὁμολογία), or of a treaty uniting Rome and Egypt—must be held extremely suspect; in any event, as subsequent history shows, this agreement cannot have had any political character.

Moreover, it would be very remarkable if the Republic had gone to the trouble of having an 'Eastern' policy while it was still without a policy which could properly be called 'Hellenic.' And it is certain that for a long period the Senate showed no inclination to enter into political relations with the peoples and cities of European Greece. The alliance which the Romans are alleged to have made, about 266, with Apollonia (on the Illyrian coast) is directly disproved, as we shall see later, by the history of their first war with Illyria (p. 834). Justin (XXVIII, 1, 5–2, following Trogus) asserts that, about 239 (?), acceding to the entreaties of the Acarnanians, the Roman government attempted, though without success, to intervene on their behalf with the Aetolians, who had invaded their territory. Even if a fact, this attempted intervention, not spontaneous in origin and abandoned by the Senate the moment it encountered resistance from the Aetolians, would be an event of very small significance. But among the many reasons which lead us to consider it imaginary, there is one which appears decisive. We owe to Polybius the valuable infor-mation that, prior to the last quarter of the third century B.C.—more precisely, prior to 228—no Roman embassy had ever set foot in Greece. There is no justification for casting doubt on this categorical statement. It is, accordingly, the best possible proof of the prolonged indifference of Roman ruling circles towards the

[1] See Beloch, *Griech. Gesch.*[2] IV, 1, p. 290, n. 2; Holleaux, *Rome, la Grèce et les Monarchies hellén.* p. 30 *sq.*; Täubler, *Imp. Romanum* I, p. 204 *sq.*

Greek States, and of the absence of any desire on their part to make these States the object of their political aims.

We are here struck by an interesting contrast. As is shown in turn by the enterprises of Archidamus, Alexander I of Epirus, Cleonymus and Pyrrhus, a long succession of Greek rulers were ready enough to turn their ambitions towards Italy; while Rome, on the contrary, though mistress of Italy, and, in virtue of her domination of Magna Graecia and Sicily, a Hellenic power, held aloof from Greece proper. Her victories had as their consequence the mutual isolation of the two peninsulas, and politically the narrow channel of the Straits of Otranto appeared to sunder two different worlds. More than ten years after making peace with Carthage, the Roman State did not yet reckon among its 'friends' a single city on those western shores of Greece which lay so close to Italy; and it was not until 228—according to the statement which we owe to Polybius—that, in consequence of special circumstances which we shall have to indicate later, the Senate at last deigned to accord official recognition to Athens and Corinth. It is, then, clear that, contrary to what has been arbitrarily asserted, Greece had no irresistible attraction for the Romans of that day, despite their tincture of Hellenism. The fact is that the Greece which commanded the admiration of the contemporaries of Livius Andronicus and Naevius, and of which they were beginning to appreciate the charm, was the Hellas which was revealed to them by her ancient poets, a Greece wholly ideal and embodied only in its literature, having nothing in common with the Greece which existed feebly in their day.

Thus the first rapid progress of Hellenism at Rome remained without influence on the external conduct of the Republic. But although, until shortly before the end of the third century b.c., there was no political bond between Rome and Greece, an ancient and active maritime trade had brought Italy into permanent relations with her Greek neighbours. It was the need to punish offences against Rome in connection with this trade that finally forced the Senate to direct its attention and its activity for the first time towards these regions.

II. ILLYRIAN PIRACY

Among the ancients the Adriatic had from the earliest times a sinister reputation; at Athens, in the fifth century, 'to sail the Adriatic' was a proverbial phrase meaning 'to undertake a dangerous venture.' From the earliest times, piracy had had free play in these waters, and this profitable career had been assiduously followed by the inhabitants of the eastern shore. For this coast, with its deep indentations, the double and sometimes triple range of islands which lie along the greater part of it, and the labyrinthine channels which wind between the islands, offered an incomparable base of operations for the exercise of their industry, and an inaccessible place of refuge from pursuit. *Illyrii, Liburnique et Histri*, writes Livy, *gentes ferae et magna ex parte latrociniis maritimis infames*. Of kindred origin, all belonging to the Illyrian race—which was distributed, as is well known, over the region bounded by the Eastern Alps, the Adriatic, the Acroceraunian mountains and two rivers, the Morava and the middle Danube—the Histrians, Liburnians, Dalmatians and the Illyrians proper (to the south of the foregoing) were all accustomed to build vessels of the same distinctive model, with lines specially adapted for speed. These were the famous *lembi*, precursors of the future *liburnae* of the Romans. They were small galleys, *caïques* of low free-board, with only a single bank of oars, but roomy enough to accommodate fifty men or more besides the crew; they had no ram, but tapered to a pointed prow. In these vessels, which they handled, whether under sail or oars, with extraordinary skill, the corsairs put to sea, swooping down on merchantmen and carrying devastation from coast to coast.

At the beginning of the fourth century Dionysius the Elder had attempted to curb their activities. Desiring to create a maritime empire, he endeavoured to open up the Adriatic fully to Syracusan trade, a project which involved its pacification. Resuming the colonial enterprises which had been interrupted since the close of the seventh century, he founded, or helped to found, the Greek cities of Issa, Pharos and Corcyra Nigra on the islands of the same names; and on the mainland the stations of Epetium and Tragyrium as dependencies of the Issaeans. The Illyrians, watched by the Syracusan squadron posted at Issa, were for a time held in check (see vol. VI, p. 129 *sq.*). But although Dionysius II made some show of continuing the work, the designs of the great Tyrant scarcely survived him. Abandoned by the Syracusans and receiving no help from the Greeks of Greece, the new colonies exhausted their resources in defending their independence against the barbarians, for the most part without success. The Adriatic continued, as before, to be delivered over to the Illyrians, and piracy, like an endemic disease, continued to be its scourge. Nevertheless, so long as Macedon under Philip and Alexander the Great made its tutelary influence felt upon the seas, and again, when Cassander, Agathocles and Demetrius successively occupied the entrance to the Straits of Otranto, and, still later, when Pyrrhus and his son Alexander II extended their authority over the seaboard from the Corinthian Gulf beyond Dyrrhachium (Epidamnus), we may well believe that the evil, confined within its ancient limits, did not extend very far into Greek waters. But, towards the close of the reign of Alexander II, the power of Epirus declined, while in Macedonia, Antigonus Gonatas, occupied in maintaining his domination over Greece and more and more drawn towards the Aegean by the necessity of resisting Egypt there, had been obliged to withdraw his attention from the western seas and had lost the great naval station of Corinth (pp. 221, 715). The pirates were now able to show themselves more enterprising, and it was probably in the second half of the third century that the Illyrians began to make a habit of infesting the Ionian Sea, ravaged periodically the coasts of Elis and Messenia, and even pushed their incursions as far as Laconia. Moreover, during the same period certain political changes had come into effect on the southern half of the eastern shores of the Adriatic which resulted in rendering their inhabitants more formidable to the Hellenes.

The inhabitants of these regions had originally, and for a long period, been divided into independent nations or tribes, each with its own sovereign ruler. To the south, the most important of these peoples in the fifth and fourth centuries were the Taulantini, whose king, Glaucias, ventured to resist Alexander, fought with Cassander, took Pyrrhus under his protection, and, whether as enemy or ally, made his power felt among the neighbouring Greek cities, Dyrrhachium, Apollonia and Corcyra (vol. VI, pp. 486, 500). A little after 250 these divisions had disappeared—we do not know precisely since when. A vast Illyrian State had been constituted, governed by one sole monarch whose sovereignty was recognized by the local dynasts, the heads of tribes or cities (πολιδυνάσται).

The origins of this State and the history of its formation are unknown. It would appear, however, that the work of unification which gave rise to it was accomplished by the powerful tribe of the Ardiaeans. Under the pressure of the Celts, who were moving down into the Balkans, the Ardiaeans seem, in the course of the fourth century, to have arrived on the right bank of the Naro, opposite the island of Pharos, to the south of the territory occupied by the Dalmatians. Then, without abandoning this settlement, they apparently spread along the coast, mainly in a southerly direction, in such strength that they imposed their authority on all the peoples of Southern Illyria. At the time when the Illyrian kingdom is first mentioned, in 231, the following appear to have been its limits. To the north, beyond the Naro it included at least a part of Dalmatia; its centre was in the neighbourhood of the Bocche di Cattaro and of the lake of Scutari. The fortress of Rhizon and the town of Scodra, the modern Scutari, were the royal residences. To the south the region conquered by Pyrrhus had been recovered, and the Illyrian State, stretching beyond the Drilo (Drin), bordered on the territories of Dyrrhachium and Apollonia; it included, in particular, to the east of Dyrrhachium, the tribe of the Parthinians. Naturally the islands off the coast became its maritime dependencies. Of all the Hellenic colonies of the fourth century Issa alone, and with the greatest difficulty, had succeeded in preserving its freedom.

The existence of a strong and compact Illyrian State on the northern frontier of Greece was necessarily a menace to the latter. One of its principal consequences was the organization of piracy on an extensive scale by the fostering care of the royal power. It continued to be exercised by individuals acting independently, but it also took on a public character and became a national industry. From time to time, when more ambitious expeditions were afoot, the *lembi*, drawn from all parts of the country, assembled *en masse* at the royal summons and formed powerful flotillas. An Illyrian navy was thus created, capable of warlike enterprises, powerful enough to attempt not only pillage but conquest.

III. ILLYRIA UNDER AGRON AND TEUTA

Between the years 240 and 229, in the reign of Agron son of Pleuratus and the subsequent regency of his widow, Queen Teuta, the kingdom of Illyria enjoyed its most glorious period. At the moment when he becomes known to history, Agron had an infant son named Pinnes, whose mother, Triteuta, had not the status of a wife. The Illyrian chief Scerdilaidas, who becomes so important in the sequel, was, it is believed, a brother of the king. 'Agron,' says Polybius, 'had a stronger army and navy than any of his predecessors.' Circumstances gave him the opportunity of turning them to account. The Illyrians had, indeed, to the eastward troublesome neighbours, their brothers by race, the Dardanians (p. 747), the untamed inhabitants of the high valleys of the Axius, the Margus and the Strymon, who were constantly encroaching upon their frontiers. But on the south there was no one to stand in their way, and the contemptible naval weakness of the Greek states left the sea completely open to them. It was long since Corcyra had had a fleet; the Aetolians had never had one; the Achaeans had only ten ships of the cataphract type (see above, p. 711), the Acarnanians only seven. On land Agron had nothing to fear from the Epirotes or the Macedonians. After the death of Alexander II (c. 240) the Epirote kingdom, assailed by the Aetolians, had been reduced to beg for help from Macedonia and had grown steadily weaker (p. 744). It was at this period, it would seem, that Agron was able to recover without difficulty the Illyrian territories formerly annexed by Pyrrhus. And before long the fall of the Aeacid dynasty (c. 235) still further hastening the decadence of Epirus was to mark the end of its historic rôle (p. 747). As for Macedon, the traditional enemy of the Illyrians, any idea of interference on its part was out of the question. Demetrius II, the son of Antigonus Gonatas, had other cares to occupy him. For nearly ten years he had been obliged to fight almost without intermission against a coalition of the Aetolians and Achaeans, and, in addition, to carry on a war, in which he was in the end unsuccessful, against the Dardanians (p. 747). In this extremely critical position, far from picking a quarrel with Agron, he had three good reasons for coming into closer relations with him: Agron, like himself, was at enmity with the Dardanians; it was not without considerable satisfaction that he saw Elis and Messenia, countries friendly to Aetolia, fall a prey to the pirates; finally, in the decadence into which the Macedonian navy had fallen the Illyrian forces could at need operate in its place against the Aetolians.

This is precisely what happened, in 231: the novel spectacle was seen of a king of Macedon having recourse to the good offices of a king of Illyria, and this prepared the way for the event which revealed to Greece proper the military vigour of the Illyrians. The Aetolians, wishing to compel the Acarnanians, who were on friendly terms with Demetrius, to enter their League, laid siege to Medeon, on the south-east of the gulf of Ambracia, and pressed the siege so vigorously that the town was on the point of falling. Prevented by the Dardanian war from giving aid himself to the besieged, Demetrius turned to Agron. In return for a subsidy Agron sent to the help of Medeon 100 *lembi* carrying 5000 fighting-men. No sooner had the Illyrians disembarked than they fell upon the Aetolians, who, completely defeated, were obliged to raise the siege, leaving behind them large numbers of prisoners, all their baggage and ample booty (Oct. 231). If we remember that since their defeat of the Gauls, the Aetolians had claimed, and had been generally accorded, the reputation of being the most warlike of the Greeks, we can imagine the consternation caused by their defeat.

Agron died immediately after his triumph which he had celebrated, it is said, by feasting to excess. Teuta succeeded him as guardian of the child Pinnes (*c.* winter 231 B.C.). Influenced by the 'friends' of the dead king, elated with pride at his success, she was eager to equal it; in any case it was certain that under her regency the Illyrians would not cease to be 'the common scourge of the Greeks.' Had they contented themselves with being the scourge of the Greeks only, their piracies might have continued indefinitely; but they made themselves also a scourge of Italian commerce. Herein lay Teuta's danger. Polybius relates that mariners setting sail from Italy towards the east often fell victims to the Illyrian pirates—and indeed, it could not have been otherwise. From the moment when these pirates, already the terror of the Adriatic, extended their range towards the south, the main sea-route across the Straits of Otranto from Italy to Greece was constantly either blocked or threatened. It became impossible for merchants sailing from Brundisium or from Hydrus to traffic safely with the trading stations which were dotted along the Hellenic seaboard, from Dyrrhachium to Corcyra, or to make the voyage to Corinth and the Piraeus. It may even have been that the towns and countryside of Southern Italy had to endure the hateful visitations of the *lembi*. The strange thing is that such a state of affairs was allowed to continue; that the Romans, all-powerful on the seas since the defeat of Carthage, and possessing a formidable navy, with a strong base at Brundisium since 246, did not promptly put an end to so intolerable a situation. They could have cleared the Straits with a gesture, but they seemed in no hurry to make it. To the repeated complaints of the seamen the Senate turned a deaf ear. Was it from reluctance to use the forces of the State in the interests of private persons? Or from indifference to maritime commerce? Explain it how we may, this inaction is an indication that Rome did not readily turn her attention to events east of Italy, and that she was not greatly concerned at the fact that economic contact with Greece was becoming more and more difficult. And this would be quite inconceivable if Rome had already cherished, as has been asserted, the definite purpose of bringing Greece under Roman influence. But the very impunity which the Illyrians enjoyed had the effect of increasing their audacity to such a point that the patience of the Romans was at last exhausted.

Teuta, when once she had become regent, lost no time in showing herself a worthy successor of her husband. In the spring of 230 B.C. she assembled a fleet and army equal to those of Agron, Scerdilaidas commanding the army, which numbered 5000 men. The fleet had orders to sail for Elis and Messenia, but its commanders had been directed to 'consider as enemies any countries which they encountered.' Consequently the pirate fleet made its first stop at Epirus, under pretext of revictualling, and treasonably, with the complicity of the Gallic mercenaries who formed its garrison, seized Phoenice the capital of the country; the whole population, whether freemen or slaves, were made prisoners. The Epirote army, hastily mobilized, hurried to the rescue, but the approach of Scerdilaidas, who, coming by land, invaded Epirus by the 'passes of Antigoneia' (the famous gorges of the Aoüs to the north-west of its confluence with the Drinus)[1], compelled it to divide its forces. While a part of the troops went to meet Scerdilaidas, the main body, halting in the neighbourhood of Phoenice, allowed itself to be taken unawares by the Illyrians who were occupying the town, was routed, and put to flight. Thus at the first encounter the Epirotes lost more than half their forces. The victors, issuing from Phoenice, then laid waste the plain, while Scerdilaidas, having cleared his path, marched to join them. Caught between the two invading armies, the Epirotes in their distress invoked the aid of the Aetolians and Achaeans. A combined Achaeo-Aetolian army advanced as far as Helicranum[2], whereupon the united forces of the Illyrians marched to offer battle. At this juncture disturbances which had arisen in Illyria—the rebellion and defection of certain tribes who had gone over to the Dardanians—compelled Teuta hastily to recall the whole of her forces. The Illyrians in retiring made a truce with the Epirotes; they restored Phoenice and gave up, on payment of ransom, the freemen whom they had made prisoners, but they carried off the rest of their booty, which was very great.

This expedition of the Illyrians produced in Greece profound uneasiness—and not without reason, for Epirus had been all but conquered. Who could tell whether, once they vanquished the Epirotes, they would not have dealt in like manner with their allies and have repeated at Helicranum their exploit at Medeon?

---

[1] The exact position of the 'gorges' or 'passes' of the Aoüs was determined in 1858 by the explorer Gautier de Claubry, a member of the French School at Athens. See E. Isambert, *Itinéraire descriptif...de l'Orient* (Paris, 1873), p. 861 *sq.*

[2] Perhaps N.W. of Delvinon, Philippson, *Thessalien und Epirus*, Taf. 4.

The best proof of the terror which they inspired was furnished by the Epirotes themselves immediately after their deliverance. Judging themselves insecure, and fearing a new invasion, they abandoned their alliance with Aetolia and Achaea, and along with the Acarnanians besought Teuta to accept them as allies. The queen demanded as the price of her consent the cession of Atintania, the central part of the valley of the Aoüs, which placed in her hands the valuable passes of Antigoneia. Thus in the summer of 230 Illyria definitely dominated Epirus and Acarnania, and, as masters of Atintania, the barbarians commanded two routes by which they could reach the heart of the Greek countries. Half a century before the Greeks had known the Gallic peril; now came the Illyrian.

IV. THE FIRST ROMAN WAR WITH ILLYRIA

But in reality the Illyrians were the dupes of their own good fortune. Their victory in Epirus was to be the first step towards their ruin. After the capture of Phoenice, some Illyrians, encountering 'a number of Italian merchants,' had treated them even worse than usual; not content with robbing them, they had made prisoners of many, and had even put some of them to death. If Teuta knew anything about this escapade, she no doubt regarded it as of small importance; but therein she was mistaken. In Italy, and also at Rome, so fierce a storm of anger broke out that at last the Senate was obliged to act. It took care, however, to do nothing precipitate. If it had been inspired by warlike sentiments it could have sent a squadron overseas immediately, but it confined itself to diplomatic action. It did no more than send to Illyria an embassy to demand reparation for the past and guarantees for the future.

For the moment, however, all went well with Teuta. Her troops on their return had promptly subjugated the insurgent tribes who had gone over to the Dardanians. Internal peace being thus restored, the queen, delighted at her recent successes, was fully determined to pursue her policy of conquest abroad. She now proposed to annex those Greek cities, whether insular or continental, which, while near neighbours of Illyria, were not yet under her sway—Issa to the north, Corcyra to the south, and, on the coast, Dyrrhachium and Apollonia. Issa was the first to be attacked; Teuta in person proceeded to lay siege to it. It was at this moment that she received the visit of the Senate's envoys, C. and L. Coruncanius (autumn 230).

The parties to this controversy were so vastly unequal that it might well have seemed that the weaker must hasten to grant all that the stronger demanded. However ill-informed we may suppose her to have been, Teuta must have had some idea of the power of Rome, nor could she have been ignorant either of Rome's victory over Carthage or of the strength of the Roman navy. But she cherished a strange delusion—a delusion, however, which at this epoch was shared by all the inhabitants of the eastern shores of the Adriatic and the Ionian Sea. Since the Romans had always hitherto abstained from sending their fleets into those seas, she persuaded herself that they would never do so. Her reception of the envoys was therefore ungracious and haughty. She told them indeed that she would see to it that the Illyrians should not publicly undertake any enterprise against the Romans; but in the same breath added that the laws of the country did not permit the sovereigns of Illyria to forbid to their subjects the private exercise of piracy. She thus gave them to understand that the outrages of which the Romans complained were the act of private persons, that she was not responsible for them and that it was not for her to repress them—a sufficiently impudent declaration, since the expedition to Epirus had had in the eyes of all a public character. It is true that she had not the power to forbid the Illyrians to range the seas; to do so would have been to risk her crown. But she could have offered to conclude with the Romans a treaty of *asylia*—such as was customary among the Greeks—which would have guaranteed the inviolability of Italian commerce. She did not, however, deign to consider such a solution. Irritated by her attitude and her language, the younger of the envoys, L. Coruncanius, retorted, it is said, that 'the Romans would find means of compelling her to reform the Illyrian laws.' A statement 'justified in itself,' says Polybius, 'but untimely.' Thereupon the wrath of the queen blazed up and the negotiations were broken off.

The situation was not yet hopeless; but there followed an act that was irreparable. As the envoys were on their way back to Italy pirates started in pursuit, attacked them, and killed L. Coruncanius. Was this done by the queen's orders? At Rome no one doubted it; what the truth was, we cannot say. But the mere fact of the murderers being Teuta's subjects involved her in responsibility. As a matter of fact she accepted it *le cœur léger*. She expressed no regret to the Senate, she made no attempt whatever to exculpate herself; thus justifying all their suspicions. In view of this, no other course was open to the *patres* than to

avenge by force of arms this outrage upon the majesty of Rome.
It has been repeatedly asserted that the Illyrian war was premeditated by the Senate. An examination of the tradition
preserved by Polybius, a tradition in all essentials worthy of belief,
absolutely disproves this theory. It was Teuta who by her blind
obstinacy rendered this war inevitable. If she had shown herself
reasonable, or, still more, if Italian merchants had not been
murdered in Epirus, no one can say how long it would have been
before a Roman fleet crossed the Straits.

Strange as it may appear, there is still further proof that
Teuta apprehended no action on the part of the Romans. In the
spring of 229 some months after her interview with the Roman
envoys she renewed her aggressive enterprises with still greater
boldness. Demetrius II, the powerful ally of the Illyrians, on
whose support she had presumably counted, had been heavily
defeated by the Dardanians (summer 230 ?) and had died not
long afterwards (c. March–April 229). As his successor was a
mere child of nine years, his death left Macedonia exposed to
the gravest dangers. These were, it might have seemed, serious
blows for Teuta, but her audacity was not daunted. While still
carrying on the siege of Issa she sent into southern waters a
flotilla still more numerous than that of the previous year. The
prize she had now in view was the island of Corcyra—which
happened to be one of the stations most frequented by Italian
seamen. After an attempt—which all but succeeded—to take
Dyrrhachium treacherously by surprise, as they had formerly
taken Phoenice, the Illyrians fell upon Corcyra in full strength
and laid siege to the town. In their extremity the Corcyraeans,
in common with the Apollonians and Dyrrhachians, sought help
from without. But the remarkable thing is that they did not
address their appeal to the Romans—a clear indication that even
after the passages between the latter and Teuta, no one in Greece
foresaw their armed intervention. Like the Epirotes in 230, the
Corcyraeans and their neighbours appealed to the Aetolians and
Achaeans, whose naval weakness was nevertheless well known.
Their request was granted. The Achaean fleet—it numbered
ten ships of the line—having on board an Achaeo-Aetolian force
set sail in haste for Corcyra. But near Paxos it encountered
the Illyrians, reinforced by seven warships of the Acarnanians,
coming to oppose it. The barbarians, lashing their *lembi* four
abreast, waited till the enemy bore down on them, and then
attacked by boarding. Their victory was complete; four Achaean
vessels were taken, a fifth was sunk; the Achaean fleet was at one

blow reduced by half. Left without succour, Corcyra capitulated
and admitted an Illyrian garrison. The victors then, turning
northwards again, laid siege to Dyrrhachium (summer 229).

It was at this moment that the Romans, whom all had left out
of account, came into action[1]. They were commanded by the two
consuls. Cn. Fulvius Centumalus with 200 warships—if the
number is not exaggerated—made straight for Corcyra in order
to raise the blockade. He arrived too late, but treason came to
his aid. The Illyrians who had been left in Corcyra were under
the leadership of a Greek of Pharos named Demetrius, who, it
appears, ruled his native island under the suzerainty of Teuta.
Knowing that he had incurred the suspicions of the queen and
dreading disgrace, above all judging it vain to resist the Romans,
he hastened to go over to their side, offered his services to Fulvius,
and delivered up to him the town which had been confided to his
charge, along with his own troops. Being thus rid of the Illyrians,
the Corcyraeans at the instance of the consul gladly made an act
of surrender (*deditio*) to their deliverers. Guided by Demetrius,
the Roman fleet then appeared before Apollonia, where the
consul L. Postumius Albinus, arriving from Brundisium, disembarked the land army, 20,000 foot and 2000 horse. The
Apollonians, like the Corcyraeans, surrendered at discretion[2];
and a like success awaited the Romans at Dyrrhachium, before
which the consuls next appeared. The Illyrians were besieging
the town; but what could their *lembi* do against the Roman armada?
The besiegers retreated in disorder and the inhabitants hastened
to make submission to Rome. Their example was promptly
followed by the two neighbouring barbarian peoples—the Parthinians and the Atintanes. Up to this point the expedition had
been a mere military promenade. Received by the Greeks with
open arms, the Romans had, by the mere terror they inspired
and without striking a blow, wrested from Illyrian domination
the whole eastern shore of the Straits of Otranto. That in fact

---

[1] According to Beloch (*Griech. Gesch.*[2] IV, 1, p. 664 *sq.*; IV, 2, pp. 262, 637)
the Roman expedition is to be placed in the year 228. That is not possible.
This expedition followed immediately on the battle of Paxos. Now, at the
time of the battle of Paxos the Achaeans and Aetolians were still allied (Polyb.
II, 9, 8), which was no longer the case in 228. The alliance was broken off and
the Aetolians became unfriendly towards the Achaeans before the beginning
of hostilities between Achaea and Cleomenes; that is to say, before April 228
(Polyb. II, 45, 1 *sq.*; 46, 1–3). The battle of Paxos and the arrival of the
Romans in Illyria are therefore both events of the summer of 229.

[2] This *deditio* of the Apollonians is a sufficiently clear proof that they had
no 'treaty of alliance' or 'friendship' with Rome as some scholars have supposed.

was their objective. They had no intention of penetrating into the heart of the enemy's country and making conquests in Central Illyria. On land, the legions do not seem to have advanced far north of the Drilo (Drin). By sea, the fleet, convoying the army, sailed as far as Issa, which Teuta was still besieging. As at Dyrrhachium, the Illyrians vanished at its approach. The queen, accompanied only by a few faithful followers, fled to Rhizon; and the Issaeans surrendered to the Romans. The latter took possession of Pharos (the inhabitants of which were well treated, out of regard for Demetrius), and doubtless also of Corcyra Nigra; they then made descents upon various points of the neighbouring coast and took several towns. In some cases the operations were attended with difficulty; at Noutria[1] they lost a considerable number of men, several legionary tribunes and one of the two consular quaestors. This check suggested prudence; returning to Dyrrhachium the consuls regarded the expedition as at an end. One of them, probably Postumius[2], returned to Italy with the greater part of both the sea and land forces (autumn 229); Fulvius, retaining only 40 ships, wintered in Illyria.

He waited in the expectation that Teuta would make her submission. She at length did so in the spring of 228. By the treaty which was then concluded she renounced all claim to the districts, islands or towns taken by the Romans, bound herself to pay them a war-indemnity in annual instalments, and undertook that the Illyrians would never send more than two *lembi* at a time, and those unarmed, beyond Lissus, the town which henceforth marked the southern limit of maritime Illyria. This last clause, the most important of all, ensured the safety of Hellenic waters and of the crossing between Italy and Greece, and showed clearly what had been the purpose of the war.

The Romans divided their conquests into two parts. Demetrius, their new ally, received the price of his services: Pharos, his hereditary domain, was of course restored to him, and, with several other islands and places on the neighbouring seaboard which had been taken from the Illyrians, was formed into a petty State (a *dynasteia*), over which he exercised sovereignty by the permission of Rome. The Romans placed this enemy of the Illyrian monarchy on its flank to keep an eye upon it and to hamper its activities. It was their intention that he should be to

[1] The position of this place is unknown and its name may not be correctly transmitted in the MSS of Polybius.

[2] See De Sanctis (*Storia dei Romani* III, I, p. 297, n. 89, *fin.*), who is no doubt right in assuming an error in Polybius (II, 12, 1–2).

Illyria what Masinissa was later to Carthage and Eumenes to Syria and Macedonia. As for the islands of Corcyra and Issa, they did not give them up any more than the territories on the mainland which had fallen into their hands at the beginning of the campaign.

We have now to indicate the extent of these territories, so far as our insufficient information permits (see map 14). To the north they terminated in the neighbourhood of the town of Lissus; to the south, bounded by the Acroceraunian range and the Chaonian mountains, they bordered on the portion of Epirus which lies to the north of Phoenice, thus corresponding to the western part of central and southern Albania. In addition to the hilly country which rises to the east of Dyrrhachium, they included the whole of the low plain formed by the alluvial deposits of three rivers, the Genusus, the Apsus and the Aoüs, and the group of hills which dominates this plain on the south[1]. Towards the south-east the conquered territory extended along the valley of the Aoüs to its confluence with the Drinus, and probably along that of the Drinus also. To the east it was bounded by the mountainous country, inhabited by the Dassaretae, from which the Genusus and the Apsus debouch into the plain; on this side it was contiguous, in its southern half, with western Macedonia, its frontier passing close to the Macedonian town of Antipatreia. The whole of the districts which remained in the hands of the Romans formed a coastal strip of not less than 120 miles with a breadth which varied from 20 to 40 miles. Among the native inhabitants may be mentioned: behind Dyrrhachium, the Parthinians; to the south of Apollonia, the Bylliones, who, like the Parthinians, were of Illyrian origin; the Atintanes in the central part of the valley of the Aoüs and perhaps in that of the Drinus also. In addition to the Hellenic cities on the coast, Dyrrhachium and Apollonia, with which may be reckoned Aulon (Valona) and Oricus, there were several towns of mixed barbarian and Greek population, such as Dimale (or Dimallum), of unknown site but certainly near Dyrrhachium, Byllis, commanding the right bank of the Aoüs where it issues from the mountains; farther to the south, Amantia; Antigoneia, near the gorges of the Aoüs, a little below its confluence with the Drinus.

All these districts were, after 229, permanently under a Roman protectorate. Juridically the inhabitants counted as *dediticii* enjoying *libertas precaria*. Such was, in particular, the position of the Parthinians and Atintanes; and also of the Greek cities which

[1] The plain is that of Muzhakhia, the hills the *massif* of Malakastra.

had submitted to the consuls—Corcyra, Apollonia, Dyrrhachium, Issa and the rest. The inhabitants of these cities and the barbarians of the surrounding country had not the status of *socii Populi Romani*; nor on the other hand were they precisely subjects: they paid no tribute and no Roman agent resided among them; but though allowed free self-government, they remained in entire dependence upon the Republic. The Romans reserved to themselves, in particular, the right to demand from them, if need be, military and naval contingents; as they had in fact done in the winter of 229–8. The Greek cities which had become vassals of Rome gave later constant evidence of fidelity and devotion; obviously they had no cause to complain of their new condition.

To sum up. The Roman expedition had neither the purpose nor the result of destroying, or even of diminishing considerably, the kingdom of Agron and Pinnes. The Illyrian State lost only the most southerly of its possessions, its principal insular dependencies, and a few points on its northern seaboard. But on the west it was henceforth flanked by a neighbour who threatened to be dangerous, Demetrius of Pharos; and to the south the Romans had established themselves indirectly but effectively along its frontier.

V. THE ROMANS AND ANTIGONUS DOSON

This first establishment by Rome of a foothold on the eastern shore of the straits is a great historic fact, the repercussions of which were to be extremely important; but we must not exaggerate the advantages derived from it by the Romans nor misrepresent its character by an arbitrary interpretation of events.

It is commonly repeated that after imposing their protectorate on Lower Illyria the Romans found themselves masters of the Adriatic in the same sense that they had been masters of the Tyrrhenian Sea since the annexation of Sardinia and Corsica (p. 804). It is a patent exaggeration, and those who fall into it are misled by a false analogy. Masters of Corsica, Sardinia, the north of Sicily and the islands scattered between Sicily and Italy, the Romans completely encircled the Tyrrhenian Sea, they held it by the possession of all its coasts; it was thenceforth merely a Roman lake. But, on the contrary, as masters of Corcyra and Lower Illyria they held only the southern end of the Adriatic where it enters the Ionian Sea; they possessed only the key to it. We have to take into account, it is true, that their alliance with Demetrius and their suzerainty over the Issaeans placed under

their protection the middle region of the Adriatic, lying between
Pharos, with the seaboard east of it, and that part of the Italian
coast where lay the colonies of Firmum, Castrum Novum and
Hadria. But it must not be forgotten that, from the mouth of the
Naro to Lissus, the whole coast continued to be outside their
control. And still more completely independent of them was the
northern part of the seaboard, from Cape Diomede to the peninsula of Histria. In these conditions it is idle to speak of a Roman
'domination' of the Adriatic. It is obvious that the Dalmatians
(those of them at least who were not subject to the Illyrians), the
Liburnians and the Histrians did not feel themselves affected by
the expedition of 229, and that piracy continued to flourish in
the lower part of the Adriatic.

It has moreover been asserted that in setting foot for the first
time on the Hellenic peninsula the Romans were only obeying
their ruling passion of Imperialism. The truth is that, just as
their war with Teuta had had no other cause than the repeated
provocations of the Illyrians, so their establishment on the
further side of the Adriatic was no more than the natural completion and the necessary corollary of their victory. It was a good
thing no doubt to have forbidden the defeated enemy to extend
his expeditions southward; but little confidence was to be placed
in the oath of the barbarians who doubtless were eager to break
the treaty which had been forced upon them. This treaty, the
outcome of her efforts, Rome must be able to enforce. Hence
the necessity to hold, on the farther side of the sea, a base of
operations where she could in case of need—if the treaty was
menaced—moor her ships and disembark her troops, and also
to have, in the same region, clients united to her by the closest
bonds of dependence, ready to aid her efforts, to receive and
revictual her troops, and even to reinforce them with an auxiliary
militia. Moreover it was the Romans who would henceforth
be responsible for the policing of the Straits; a task which they
could only carry out if they had constantly at their disposal some of
the maritime towns on the eastern shores. They must be able in case
of need to place their guard-ships at Dyrrhachium or Apollonia.
Finally, it was necessary to isolate the kingdom of Illyria from
its new Greek allies, the Epirotes and the Acarnanians. In
declaring themselves the protectors of the coastal region from
Lissus to Epirus which the Illyrians had abandoned, but could
not cease to covet, they were only taking a necessary precaution.

But it is possible that they were the more disposed to take this
precaution against the Illyrians because it was a precaution also

against the Macedonians. For the moment, no doubt, the latter
were not formidable. After the death of Demetrius II, his cousin
Antigonus Doson, who became regent for his young son Philip,
had been confronted with a most difficult situation (p. 748). An
invasion of the Dardanians and a rising in Thessaly instigated by
the Aetolians (not to speak of the general defection of the cities
in the Peloponnese which were dependent upon the Macedonian
monarchy) had for a year past (229–228) kept him fully occupied
—and this was probably the reason why he had not attempted to
assist Teuta. But it was quite possible that better days might be
in store for Macedon; might not its kings, once so powerful
upon the sea, again become so? At Rome men had not forgotten
the adventure of Pyrrhus fifty years before. Possibly they considered it wise to seize the chance of preventing its recurrence,
holding that Italy would always be exposed to danger from the
east so long as an enemy fleet could set sail for her shores from
the ports of Lower Illyria, or lurk at Corcyra. They may have
argued that the Macedonians cast longing eyes both upon those
ports and upon the island, and that it would be best to take the
present opportunity of putting these places out of the reach of
this potential enemy.

To credit the Romans with these considerations—not wholly
unlike those which had formerly determined them to occupy
Messana (p. 672)—to suggest that in their dealings with Illyrian
affairs they had in mind the placing of an obstacle in the way of
Macedonia, is no more than a conjecture, and is open to question.
But it is beyond question that their method of settling these
affairs did actually place such an obstacle in Macedonia's way, and
that Antigonus Doson found himself unable to accept the situation. For him, of course, as for all his predecessors, the Illyrian
coast was on the west what the Thracian coast was on the east—
a necessary dependency of the Macedonian kingdom. Macedonia
must, as a matter of course, have access to the Adriatic, and equally
as a matter of course, Dyrrhachium and Apollonia, former conquests of Cassander, and Corcyra, formerly held by Demetrius
Poliorcetes, must return to the possession of their successors. In
brusquely declaring themselves masters of these towns, in establishing themselves, with insolent *sans-gêne*, on the flank of Macedonia and hemming it in upon the west, in raising, as Pyrrhus
had done, a barrier between it and the sea, the Romans had,
whether intentionally or not, taken advantage of her present
powerlessness to infringe grievously her historic rights and thwart
her traditional ambitions. And, worst of all, had not Macedonia

some grounds for believing herself to be threatened? Was it good that the mouths of the valleys of the Genusus, Apsus and Aoüs, which led from the coast into Macedonian territory, and the passes of Antigoneia, the key to the line of communication between the Kingdom and Epirus, should be in the hands of the Romans? Moreover, we have to take into account the fact that Antigonus felt keenly the defeat of the Illyrians, allies of his house. He was furious at not having been able to defend them, and he had lost in them useful auxiliaries against Aetolia. Finally, beyond doubt, he was bitterly chagrined at seeing strangers—and barbarians at that—usurp the proud rôle, so long sustained by the Macedonian princes, of protectors of Hellenism against the barbarism of the north. For a host of reasons the Roman victory and its consequences must have been odious to him, as indeed they were. For the moment, occupied as he was with more pressing tasks, no other course was open to him than to leave the Romans to do what they would; but they must reckon with his lasting enmity. Out of the Illyrian question there thus arose for the Romans a Macedonian question; their expedition of 229 and establishment on the eastern Adriatic coast had the direct effect of creating between them and Macedon a necessary antagonism. They appear to have had some consciousness of this. Contrary to what courtesy would seem to have demanded, no Roman embassy was dispatched to Pella; it is probable that they judged any understanding with Antigonus to be impossible. But was not this ignoring of them, this treatment of them as non-existent, likely to constitute for the regent and for his ward, the young Philip, an unforgettable affront?

But if the Romans after their victory over Teuta neglected to enter into relations with Macedon, on the other hand—for the first time in their history—they came into official contact with Greece. Although—and the fact is significant—the two peoples who were their nearest neighbours, the Epirotes and the Acarnanians, allies of the Illyrians and on friendly terms with the Macedonians, were not favoured by a visit, yet, no sooner was peace concluded than the consul who had remained in Illyria sent a mission to the Aetolians and Achaeans. His representatives explained to them the course of events which had led to the war and forced the Romans to cross the sea, briefly related the incidents of the expedition, and read the treaty which had been imposed upon Teuta; in short they directed their efforts to justifying the intervention of Rome and emphasizing its happy results, thus affecting by a flattering deference to seek the approval of the two great Greek Confederacies. However courteous this action may have been, it placed a rather severe strain upon Hellenic *amour-propre*; for the vanquished of Paxos could not fail to be humiliated by the contrast between Roman might and their own weakness. But they swallowed their mortification, and loaded the Romans with laudatory resolutions. And in fact they were sincerely delighted to be rid of the Illyrian nightmare. A little later (probably still in the year 228) the Senate decided to send ambassadors to Corinth and Athens, where Roman envoys had never before appeared. There, too, their welcome was extremely cordial. The Corinthians, as a signal mark of favour, decreed the admission of the Roman people to the Isthmian Games. This was, in principle, to declare them members of the Hellenic community; though, for all that, the Greeks continued to look on them as barbarians.

The peoples and cities to which the Romans sent missions in 228 had this one thing in common, that they were hostile to Macedonia. The Achaeans and Aetolians had, as we have seen, leagued themselves together against Demetrius II; the Aetolians had lately raised Thessaly against Antigonus, and the Achaeans had annexed the last possessions of the Macedonians in the Peloponnese. Fifteen years earlier, the Corinthians, thanks to the fortunate *coup-de-main* of Aratus, had shaken off the Macedonian yoke; and the Athenians had freed themselves from it in 229, the very year of the Illyrian War (pp. 748). It would be natural enough, therefore, to attach great significance to the friendly demonstrations on the part of the Romans towards these peoples. One might well argue from them that the Romans deliberately designed to unite themselves closely with the Hellenic enemies of the Antigonids and that, taking advantage of the prestige and popularity which the services they had rendered to the Hellenes had brought them, they intended to pursue in Greece, as the Ptolemies had done and were still doing, an anti-Macedonian policy.

It must be admitted that such a policy would have been rational, and even that it would have been the logical sequel of their conduct towards Macedon. Since the latter had inevitably become inimical to them, they might well have sought to weaken her by supporting and inciting against her the enemies with whom she had already to reckon among the Greeks. One cannot help imagining how extreme would have been the peril of the Macedonian State if the Romans in 228 had supported the Aetolians. But in fact the Romans do not seem to have conceived the idea of this preventive policy, and in any event they made no attempt to put it into practice. There is no indication that anything in the nature of negotiations took place between the consular envoys and the Achaean and Aetolian Leagues. It was no more than an exchange of diplomatic courtesies. Similarly, though senatorial envoys presented themselves at Corinth or Athens—the chief centres of Hellenic commerce and as such peculiarly interested in the security of the seas—it was only to notify them formally of the useful task which the Romans had accomplished in Illyria. Corinth was not at that time an independent city but a member of the Achaean League, and therefore the diplomatic mission to her could not have had any direct political purpose. As regards the Athenians, the Roman tradition which reports that they contracted a treaty of friendship with the Romans and even conferred *isopoliteia* and the right of admission to the Mysteries upon them *en bloc*, owes its origin to later events and is quite unworthy of consideration. The Romans immediately after their victory over the Illyrians formed no real connection with the Greeks: they did no more than make themselves known to them. They remained indifferent to the struggle of the two principal Greek states with Macedonia; they had, in fact, no Hellenic policy.

The astute and energetic Antigonus Doson was thus left free to settle matters with his enemies unhindered by outside interference. He extricated himself from his difficulties with admirable address. Before the end of 228 when he took the royal title (p. 751), Macedonia, in spite of the great territorial sacrifices which the war in Greece had cost her, had become sufficiently strong again for the Aetolians to be contemplating uniting themselves with her at the same time as with Sparta against the Achaeans, and for Aratus to conceive the idea of using her against Cleomenes. The sequel is known: scarcely seven years after the insult which Rome had put upon him, Antigonus had acquired in Corinth an incomparable naval base if he should wish once more to build up a navy, had reconstructed the Hellenic League, which ranged seven Greek peoples under his hegemony (p. 759), had reduced to a state of dependence the Achaeans who had come under his protection, had inspired a wholesome dread in the Aetolians, crushed Cleomenes, the sole adversary who was capable of making head against him, and humiliated the Spartans, who had been forced to become his allies—he had, in short, restored the Macedonian monarchy to the height of political and military importance.

This great change in the posture of events could not but be prejudicial to Roman interests. Nevertheless they allowed it to come about unhindered; they did nothing to embarrass Antigonus[1]. It is true that the years which followed their Illyrian expedition were full of dangers and pre-occupations. The Romans felt hanging over them the menace of a vast invasion from the Gauls (p. 810); at the same time they discovered, somewhat late, that a Carthaginian Empire was being built up in Spain— a formidable support to Carthage in the event of a new war with Rome (p. 787); and naturally they were apprehensive of concerted action on the part of these two enemies. They had in these circumstances to negotiate in haste with Hasdrubal, with a view to staying Punic expansion at the line of the Ebro (treaty of 226), at the same time that they were making immense preparations to meet the expected onset of the Gauls. The latter were crushed at Telamon, and the Romans, taking the offensive, proceeded to the conquest of Cisalpine Gaul (p. 813). But this was a long and arduous task; it cost them three years of constant fighting and strenuous effort (224–222). Their armies were fighting on the Po when the king of Macedon made his descent upon the Peloponnese (223). Since they were so fully occupied in the north of Italy, we cannot greatly wonder that they failed to take then in Greece the action which they had omitted to take in 228, and abstained from working against Antigonus by giving, for example, some help to Cleomenes. It is, however, quite possible that they never thought of doing so; that, too little interested in eastern affairs, they did not clearly perceive that Antigonus, once he had Greece at his feet, might become a menace to them in Illyria. It is at all events strange that they did not keep a more

[1] We must at this point, however, take account of a hypothesis of Droysen. At the time of the battle of Sellasia, which, throughout this chapter, is dated 221 B.C. (see p. 863), Macedonia was invaded by Illyrian raiders, and the invasion certainly assumed a serious aspect, for Antigonus returned in great haste from the Peloponnese to repel it (Polyb. ii, 70). J. G. Droysen (*Hist. de l'Hellén.* iii, p. 584, n. 1; French trans.) observes that the invaders certainly cannot have belonged to the party of Demetrius of Pharos (see p. 763), and asks whether the Romans had not a hand in the affair. In this case we should have here a first example of the aggression directed later, at the instigation of the Romans, by Scerdilaidas against Philip V (see below, p. 855). But the hypothesis is unnecessary. Those of the Illyrians who were hostile to Demetrius and enemies of Macedonia had no need to be incited by the Romans to attack the latter. And, moreover, if the Romans had in 221 actively interfered in the affairs of Illyria, it would be very difficult to explain why they had not provided by appropriate defensive measures against the attacks with which Demetrius was threatening their possessions.

watchful eye upon Illyrian affairs and were not more concerned to make sure that the situation did not take a turn to their disadvantage. They were to pay a heavy price for their lack of vigilance.

VI. THE REBELLION OF DEMETRIUS OF PHAROS

There was one man upon whom the Romans should have kept watch, and as close a watch as might be,—the adventurer Demetrius of Pharos, whom they had seen transform himself in a few hours from a vassal of Teuta to a servant of their own, and whom they had made, perhaps imprudently, the representative of their interests as against the Illyrian kingdom. It would have been well for this dubious character to have felt the eyes of the Romans constantly fixed upon him, and in truth it would have been easy enough to keep him under surveillance. It would have sufficed to dispatch, from time to time, a few quinqueremes into the Adriatic. The precaution would have been the more desirable because, almost immediately after the events of 228, the power of Demetrius in circumstances of which we have no exact knowledge, whether with or without the goodwill of Rome, had much increased. According to some traditions of doubtful value Teuta had either abdicated or died soon after her disaster and the guardianship of Agron's son, the child-king Pinnes, had then passed to Demetrius, who had married Triteuta, the mother of Pinnes (p. 827). What is in any case certain is that Demetrius had rapidly become something quite different from what the Romans had made him. He was far from remaining the mere dynast of Pharos and a few islands and seaboard districts in its vicinity. Ill-informed as we are about the internal situation in the Illyrian kingdom between 228 and 220, we at least see clearly that two personages—who treat with one another, it would seem, upon an equality—were then preponderant: one was Prince Scerdilaidas, whom we already know, the other was Demetrius. Their authority was exercised, we may infer, in different parts of the kingdom.

How would the Pharian use this new access of power? Would he be content to remain the devoted client of the Republic? Placed between Rome and the reviving power of Macedon and in such close contiguity to the latter, would he not incline to her if he thought to find his profit in that direction? These were questions on which the Senate would have done well to make up its mind, with a view to intervening in good time and to good purpose if the protégé of Rome appeared to be assuming too great an independence. But it does not appear that the *patres* took measures to inform themselves of the dispositions of Demetrius; they do not seem even to have kept up any regular relations with him.

This carelessness had its natural consequences. Antigonus Doson did not follow the Senate's example in losing sight of Illyrian affairs. Faithful to the traditions of his predecessor Demetrius II, one of his main pre-occupations was to resume close contact with Illyria, to bring her once more under the influence of Macedon and so to keep the Romans in check until he should be able to act directly against them. He therefore entered into relations with the Pharian and endeavoured to attach him to himself. We cannot tell what methods he employed, what alluring hopes and promises he held out[1], but there is no doubt that soon after 225 Demetrius was entirely won over. From 223 onwards he showed himself a very zealous ally of Antigonus; he accompanied him into the Peloponnese at the time of his war with Cleomenes, brought to his support an auxiliary corps of 1600 Illyrians and himself took an active and glorious part in the battle of Sellasia (p. 760). The attitude of Macedon and Rome to each other, their latent antagonism was such that it was impossible to serve the one without injuring the other. By his open alliance with Antigonus, Demetrius in effect broke with the Romans, indeed became their enemy. That he took so lightly so grave a decision, that he had not a more lively dread of the anger of Rome, is certainly strange. No doubt he counted, should the Romans endeavour to punish him, on the support of the king of Macedon. But so long as the war with Cleomenes lasted, that is to say until the summer of 221[2], Antigonus could have done nothing to help him. And the war which the Romans were at this time successfully waging against the Cisalpine Gauls did not of course deprive them of the use of their fleet. How was it that Demetrius while campaigning in the Peloponnese had no

---

[1] Nevertheless we may venture on the following conjecture. It is certain that there was in Illyria a party hostile to Demetrius and Scerdilaidas (Polyb. III, 18, 1: οἱ ἀντιπολιτευόμενοι; V, 4, 3), probably the same party which, under Teuta, had risen against the royal authority (II, 6, 4; 8, 5, see above, p. 830). We can well imagine that in order to gain the upper hand of his opponents, Demetrius had need of the good offices of Antigonus, who would offer them the more readily because the rebellious Illyrians were also hostile to Macedon (cf. Polyb. II, 70; above, p. 843 n. 1). In this connection should be noted the promises of assistance made in the winter of 220–219 by Philip V to Scerdilaidas (Polyb. IV, 29, 2; cf. V, 4, 3).

[2] Or till the summer of 222, if Sellasia was fought in 222 (chronological note 3, p. 863).

fear that a squadron sailing from Brundisium or Ancona might operate against Pharos? That is a question which the historian is bound to ask. The answer is to be found, primarily, in what we know of the character of Demetrius, a man bold to excess, as Polybius tells us, and, moreover, lacking in judgment and incapable of reflection—in short a reckless gambler with fortune. But another thing which goes far to explain his conduct is the conduct of the Romans themselves after their defeat of Teuta— the apparent indifference which they then displayed towards events in Illyria, their neglect to make their authority felt. Never seeing them, imagining them to be so paralysed by the anxieties of their struggle with the Gauls and the advance of the Carthaginian power in Spain, so beset by difficulties that they had neither the leisure, the means nor the will to intervene in the east, the Illyrians ceased to fear them, and relapsed into the same false security into which Agron and Teuta had fallen years before.

That seems to have been Demetrius' state of mind. And in fact for a long time events appeared to justify him. The Romans did not call him to account for his alliance with Antigonus; up to 220 they left him a free hand, and they would perhaps have continued to do so, had he not, emboldened by their long forbearance, rashly thrown down the gauntlet. The death of Antigonus, some months after the battle of Sellasia, had deprived him of his powerful protector—an event as fateful for him as the death of Demetrius II had been for Teuta. The new king, Philip, was a mere stripling of seventeen, and his youth and inexperience were at once a cause of alarm to his allies and an encouragement to the enemies of Macedon. Already the most ardent of these, the Aetolians, were showing themselves violently aggressive; their bands had descended upon Messenia and treated it like a conquered country. Thereupon the Achaeans thus contemptuously defied had been forced to cross swords with them, but, defeated at Caphyae (p. 764), had found themselves reduced to sue for aid to Philip and the Hellenic allies (August 220). Moreover, there could be no doubt that at Sparta the anti-Macedonian and anti-Achaean party, that of Cleomenes, was working to regain the mastery. Thus to all appearance the young king, obliged to defend his allies in the Peloponnese, would soon be plunged into grave difficulties, from which he would have hard work to extricate himself. In these circumstances, how could Demetrius hope to receive any great assistance from him? Everything, it might have seemed, combined to counsel prudence, to dissuade him from irritating the Romans further. Nevertheless he chose this very moment to revolt openly against them. He challenged them by two successive acts of aggression. First, he invaded some of the territories which were under their protectorate, induced or compelled some of the tribes to cast off their allegiance, and took several towns, one of which was the powerful city of Dimale. Then, as if to show that he had no more fear of Rome at sea than on land, he impudently violated the treaty of 228, which had prohibited not only the subjects of Teuta but all the Illyrians from sailing on armed expeditions south of Lissus. Uniting with Scerdilaidas and combining their two flotillas—90 *lembi* in all— he proceeded to attack Pylos in Messenia (*c.* August 220). Then, when the attack failed, and Scerdilaidas, having hired out his troops to the Aetolians, had gone with them to ravage Arcadia (p. 764), he doubled Cape Malea and ranged the Aegean, pillaging or holding to ransom the Cyclades until the Rhodians, the recognized protectors of maritime commerce, forced him to put about and fly towards Greece. Thus the Illyrians again began freely to infest Greek waters: Demetrius was treating the work accomplished by the Romans as though it had never been—the days of Agron and Teuta seemed to have returned.

But, like Teuta, the Pharian had tried the patience of the Romans too far. The legions had not crossed the sea in order that, nine years later, barbarian Illyria should rise up before Italy more insolent than ever. Rome had not set her foot on the eastern shore of the Straits to let herself be driven out again so soon, and by a traitor. The Senate awoke—late enough, it is true—to the fact that, as things were going, the whole of Lower Illyria, including the Greek cities on the coast, was in imminent danger of falling into the hands of Demetrius. This must be prevented at all costs. And the more so as before long affairs with Carthage might well take a turn for the worse. In the autumn of 220, the Roman government, at length responding to the appeals of the Saguntines, who were menaced by Hannibal, had decided to take that city under their protection and forbid the Carthaginians to touch it. An embassy was about to start to make known its wishes, first to Hannibal and then to the Carthaginian Senate (see vol. viii, chap. ii). If this effected nothing, would it not be necessary to have recourse to arms? And in that event would it be a good thing that the eastern shore of the Straits of Otranto should be in the power of Rome's enemies? Would it be a good thing that a Punic fleet might find open to it the harbours of Apollonia and Dyrrhachium, where it could lie in safety and keep watch upon Italy? The idea of a possible understanding between Carthage and Demetrius could not fail to present itself to the mind of the *patres*, an idea the more alarming because, behind the Pharian, they saw the shadow of the Macedonian. A recent happening had been decidedly significant. On his return from the Cyclades, flying before the Rhodians, Demetrius had taken refuge at Cenchreae; and, forthwith, Taurion, Philip's general in the Peloponnese, had entered into relations with him, had had his *lembi* transported across the Isthmus, and had used him as an auxiliary against the Aetolians who were returning from Arcadia. Thus friendly relations, open and avowed, between the Macedonian government and Demetrius continued even after the latter had risen against Rome. A little later another fact which could not be ignored by the Romans must have served still further to arouse their suspicions. In the winter of 220–219 Philip went in person to Illyria to confer with Scerdilaidas. This visit, the precise purpose of which was not known till later (p. 851), must have seemed a very suspicious proceeding. What business had the king of Macedon with the man who was, after Demetrius, the most powerful of the Illyrian chiefs, and who had just joined the latter in infringing the treaty of 228? It was evident that Philip was much more interested in Illyria than was at all desirable.

Such a condition of affairs called for a prompt remedy. It was time and more than time to look after the interests of the Romans oversea, to re-establish the authority of the Republic over the whole of Lower Illyria and to crush Demetrius, thus depriving Macedon of a dangerous tool. By a fortunate chance, in September 220 Philip and the Allies had declared war against the Aetolians (p. 764). Then the expected revolution had broken out at Sparta; the Cleomenists, the friends of Aetolia, had seized power by a *coup de force*. Philip, it seemed, was going to have his hands so full that he would not be able to lend assistance to the Pharian. Demetrius, like Teuta, would be left to face the Romans alone.

VII. THE SECOND ROMAN WAR WITH ILLYRIA

In the campaigning season of 219—exactly ten years after their first expedition—the Romans set out for Illyria again. As in 229, the fleet and army were commanded by the two consuls, L. Aemilius Paullus and M. Livius Salinator, a proof of the interest which was taken in the enterprise. The exact strength of the forces under their orders is not known, but there can be no doubt that they were considerable. L. Aemilius, to whom was entrusted, it would seem, the entire direction of the land operations, must have had under him the normal consular army of about 20,000 foot and 2000 horse. Rash as Demetrius was he did not carry his recklessness so far as to imagine that he could cope with the Romans in the field. Informed of their impending attack he prudently decided to fight them from behind walls. He hoped in this way to play for time; the memory of the check suffered by the Romans at Noutria presumably confirmed him in this hope (p. 835). If the war was protracted, it was possible that Philip, having disposed of the Aetolians, might intervene to aid the Illyrians; or again that the Romans, should a decisive rupture with Carthage occur, might have to oppose the latter with all their forces and consequently to give up their hold on Illyria. And, in fact, shortly before the departure of the consuls, Hannibal, disregarding the prohibition of which the Senate's envoys had notified him, had begun the siege of Saguntum (spring 219), an action which might give rise to the gravest complications. If, as is probable, the Pharian received prompt advices regarding the news from Spain, he must have drawn favourable auguries from it. As the centres of his resistance he chose two large towns which he put into a good state of defence: in the south, on the mainland, Dimale; to the north, Pharos, his island capital. Dimale, well fortified, abundantly provisioned, strongly garrisoned, appeared to him impregnable. He himself retired into Pharos, which he rightly judged to be particularly threatened; he had assembled there a small army of 6000 picked men, the flower of his troops.

But if Demetrius was flattering himself with the hope of dragging out hostilities, the Romans desired the exact opposite. Disquieted by Hannibal's audacity and regarding, henceforth, war with Carthage as almost inevitable, they were in a hurry to be freed from danger in the rear in order to face, if need be, an attack from the west. They must dispose of the Pharian with the utmost dispatch. They acted accordingly. Never was a campaign more speedily carried out. Since Apollonia and Dyrrhachium remained faithful to them, they were able to disembark their troops at one or other of these places, and thence to advance against Dimale. Aemilius attacked it with such energy that he carried it within seven days. He had calculated that the fall of the 'impregnable town' would paralyse its neighbours and break the courage of the partisans of Demetrius. He had reckoned rightly. The cities and tribes which, whether willingly or under compulsion—generally the latter—had fallen away from Rome, all hurried to surrender at discretion. He treated them with politic leniency, abstained from punishing them, and contented himself with placing them once more under the authority of the Republic. The situation created in 228 was restored in a moment.

Affairs in the south having been thus brought to order, the consuls sailed for Pharos. Of great natural strength, well-provided with munitions and supplies and held by 6000 stout-hearted defenders, the town was fitted to sustain a protracted siege. But a protracted siege was just what the Romans were determined to avoid; for them it was all important to draw the garrison into the plain and then overwhelm it by weight of numbers. Aemilius succeeded in this by one of the simplest of stratagems. Reaching the island of Pharos by night, he secretly disembarked the greater part of his army in a wild and remote tract of country, where the soldiers could remain concealed in the cover afforded by some woods. The next morning he himself, with only twenty ships, which had the remainder of the troops on board, made for the principal harbour of the island. Demetrius, believing that he had before him the whole strength of his enemies, hastened to the harbour to prevent them from landing, and summoned to his aid, little by little, almost the entire garrison of the town. Then the Roman troops which had disembarked the previous night, issuing from their hiding-place, succeeded in reaching unobserved a steep hill which lay between the harbour and the town, and occupied it in strength. They thus cut off the retreat of the Illyrians. Demetrius saw his danger; facing about, he endeavoured to dislodge the Romans posted on the hill. But before he could overcome their resistance, the others, from the harbour, having completed their disembarkation, fell upon his rear. Repulsed in front, assailed in rear, the Illyrians broke. Some, though doubtless very few, succeeded in reaching the town, the remainder scattered through the island. Demetrius, seeing that the game was lost, had thenceforward no thought but for his own safety. He had, to be prepared for all eventualities, secretly fitted out several *lembi* which were moored at an out-of-the-way part of the coast. During the night he got on board and put to sea. The town of Pharos, thus left without defenders, fell at the first assault, and Aemilius proceeded to dismantle it.

The news from Spain, where Hannibal was vigorously prosecuting the siege of Saguntum, did not permit of any long delay on the part of the consuls. The defeat and flight of the Pharian and the taking of his capital marked for them the end of the war.

They stayed only to determine the fate of Pharos and the other localities left under the authority of Demetrius in 228. These it seems were put upon the same footing as the towns and districts which ten years before had passed under the protection of Rome. Then, towards the end of the summer, they returned to Italy, taking with them as prisoners some of the household (οἰκεῖοι) of Demetrius, who had fallen into their hands. Shortly after their return, Saguntum fell. The second expedition to Illyria, more rapidly completed even than the first, had lasted but a few months.

VIII. PHILIP V AND ROME AFTER THE SECOND ILLYRIAN WAR

Perhaps, indeed, it was too quickly ended. It was no doubt a brilliant success, but it was incomplete. The Romans had not penetrated into Upper Illyria in 219 any more than in 229, and it remained a free field for Macedonian enterprise. They had punished Demetrius, but Scerdilaidas, who had been almost equally guilty, and had rendered himself particularly open to suspicion by his recent relations with Philip, had gone free. Was it not probable that he aimed at becoming a second Demetrius? In any event he was about to show that the defeat of the Pharian had by no means intimidated him. Nor had it intimidated the king of Macedon. After escaping from his island, Demetrius had fled to Acarnania to join Philip, who had just taken Oeniadae from the Aetolians and was proceeding to attack the Dardanians (p. 765). The king at once welcomed him with open arms and invited him to come to Macedon. He thus declared himself, in defiance of the Romans—who were still in Illyria—the protector of the traitor who had incurred their just anger. And before long it was known that he was making Demetrius his chosen companion, the most influential of his counsellors, thus having constantly about him a passionate enemy of Rome, eager to stir him up against her if indeed he needed it. Furthermore, in the spring of 218, while he was besieging Pale, a city of the Cephallenians, who were allies of the Aetolians, 15 lembi sent from Illyria by Scerdilaidas came to reinforce the Macedonian fleet. That was the result of the intrigues which the king himself had carried on in Illyria in the winter of 220–219 (p. 848). He had then, in contempt of the treaty which forbade the Illyrians to appear south of Lissus, persuaded Scerdilaidas to lend him, at a price, his aid against the Aetolians at sea. What is notable is that the arrangement held good in spite of the new Roman expedition. The treaty of 228, first violated by Demetrius and Scerdilaidas together, was violated afresh by the latter within a year of the chastisement inflicted on Demetrius, and, this second time, it was violated at the instigation of Philip.

Thus the consuls had hardly returned from their campaign when one of the two principal opponents of Rome in Illyria had become the intimate friend of Philip, and the other his active auxiliary. A conjunction of circumstances rendered the king's openly manifested hostility towards the Romans a matter of especial gravity. About April 218 the *patres*, in reply to the taking of Saguntum, had declared war on Carthage. If during this war Philip should be free to act as he chose, there was little doubt that he would endeavour to make common cause with the Carthaginians, and it was certain that he would take advantage of the difficulties of the Republic to attack Roman Illyria. Fortunately for Rome, he had not at the moment liberty of action; his struggle with Aetolia and Sparta was keeping him fully occupied. It was to the interest of the Romans that they should keep him occupied as long as possible. But were they fully conscious of this evident interest?

Since the end of 219, the stripling of seventeen, whose youth had provoked the scorn of his enemies, had shown the most brilliant military talents. His crossing of the Peloponnese and conquest of Elis, in the middle of winter, then his lightning campaign of 218, the sudden blows which he had delivered almost at the same moment in north and south—the sack of Thermum and the invasion of Laconia—had revealed in him marvellous agility and boldness in strategic movement (p. 767). At the pace at which he was carrying on the war, there was reason to believe that it would soon be over; as a matter of fact, at the end of the second campaign the Aetolians, losing courage, were disposed to treat. This was a moment at which Roman intervention in their favour would have been highly opportune. It was because he was unopposed at sea that Philip had been able in 218 to pass so swiftly from one end of Greece to the other, everywhere taking his adversaries by surprise. Nevertheless he possessed no more than a dozen warships of the cataphract type. If even a small Roman squadron had appeared in Greek waters, the face of affairs would doubtless have been changed. Without the command of the sea, forced to protect his coasts and those of his allies against descents of the enemy, he would have found it very difficult to prosecute with the same vigour his land war against the Aetolians and

Spartans. The naval resources of the Romans and their maritime superiority over Carthage were so great, that they could, it would seem, have easily afforded to detach a squadron to oppose Philip. Later, in 214, under pressure of necessity they sent, it is said, fifty warships to Illyria; it is certain that from 212 onwards they maintained, for a series of years, twenty-five in Greek waters. Is it not probable that these twenty-five warships would have been available in 217? One cannot help being surprised that the Romans made no effort to come to the aid of the Aetolians—as though they had failed to observe that the latter, by the mere fact of being the enemies of Philip, became the natural allies of Rome.

No doubt this inaction may be naturally enough explained by the anxiety aroused in Italy by Hannibal's unexpected invasion and the first reverses of the Roman arms. It can well be imagined that at so grave a moment all the thought and all the efforts of the Senate were concentrated upon the Carthaginians; that they were averse from the idea of new war, and that they dreaded to weaken themselves by sending any forces, however restricted, into the eastern sea. But it is very possible that the *patres* persuaded themselves that there were no good grounds for intervention in the affairs of Greece: a defeat of the Aetolians would have no consequences for the Republic, and as Rome had never been the declared enemy of Philip, he would not dream of attacking her. If this was their view, if they believed that they could avoid having Philip as an enemy simply by not making war on him, they were completely mistaken.

Philip's fixed idea, which, inherited from Antigonus, was fostered, not suggested, by Demetrius, was to deliver Macedon from the dangerous neighbour whose proximity she had endured since 228, to wrest Lower Illyria from the Romans, ousting them from it permanently, and, to this end, to fight and conquer them even, if need be, in Italy itself. Rome, the object alike of his hatred and his admiration, whose power he knew and whose history he had studied, Rome, which he liked to set up as an example (witness his letter to the Larissaeans)[1], was ever present to his thoughts. Should the chance of acting against the Romans present itself, he was resolved to seize it. He had been obliged, to his regret, to involve himself in the Aetolian War, thus condemning himself to be the impotent witness of the disaster of Demetrius, as Antigonus had been of that of Teuta; but by his dazzling and constant successes and the discouragement into which he had

---

[1] Dittenberger, *Sylloge*,[3] 543, iv. See also p. 532.

thrown his enemies, he had secured to himself an easy withdrawal from it at his chosen moment. This moment was not long in coming. When he received the news of Hannibal's victorious march, it can be well imagined what hopes awoke in him. While the Romans remained indifferent to events in Greece he followed events in Italy with anxious vigilance. Couriers sent from Macedon to the army in the field kept him informed of them from day to day. If, at the end of June 217, he threw himself with ardour into a new campaign against the Aetolians, this was due, Polybius tells us, to the fact that he was still in ignorance of the disaster at Trasimene. The news reached him about the middle of July at Argos when he was attending the Nemean Games, and his decision was immediately taken. He resolved to bring hostilities to an end forthwith, having asked counsel of no one but Demetrius, whose opinion, he knew, was in agreement with his own, and he made overtures of peace to the Aetolians. His purpose was, the moment that war was ended, to turn all his energies against his powerful enemies at this propitious moment when their fortune was trembling in the balance. Patched up in haste while the impression of the first great victory of the Carthaginians was still fresh, the Peace of Naupactus, which owed its origin to Philip, was a peace directed against the Romans.

IX. SCERDILAIDAS' ATTACK ON PHILIP

The Romans had done nothing either to prevent or delay the peace. As in 228 and 221, so now they had made no effort to prolong the Hellenic War by giving support to the adversaries of Macedon and had remained aloof from Greece. But it does seem that at the moment when peace was about to be concluded, they suddenly had an inkling of the danger, and feared the use which Philip might make of his recovered liberty, and for the first time judged it advisable to raise difficulties for him. Thence arose presumably the events which followed in Illyria at the end of the summer of 217.

The Illyrian chiefs were instability itself and changed sides with amazing facility. We have seen this exemplified in the Pharian; Scerdilaidas was no less an adept. Successively allied with the Aetolians (220), and with Philip (218), he broke with the king, alleging that Philip had not paid him sufficiently for his services, and began to engage in piratical enterprises at his expense (c. June 217). Before long he acted still more audaciously on land. Just as Philip was bringing the peace negotiations at

Naupactus to a close, his frontiers were violated at two points. In Pelagonia, Scerdilaidas took the town of Pissaeum of which the site is unknown; but it was more especially against western Macedonia that he directed his attacks. He attempted the conquest of the valley of the Apsus, one of the three principal routes from the east into Lower Illyria. Several towns situated in this valley or in its neighbourhood fell into his hands, among others the important town of Antipatreia. If we reflect that the invaded districts marched with territory under the authority of the Romans, who must have desired to see them taken from Philip; that, moreover, once he had become the king's enemy it was to Scerdilaidas' interest to stand well with the Romans, and that it would be a strange thing if he had dared, without their approval, to take possession of the hinterland of their territory; and finally, that a little later (winter of 217–216) he became openly their ally, we can hardly doubt that there was an understanding between them and him, and that they had encouraged him to attack Philip. But at the moment when it took place, the attack of Scerdilaidas could be no more than a vain adventure, for he had no chance of making head against Philip, who, once peace was re-established in Hellas, could use his forces where he would. On his return to Macedonia it did not take the king long to bring him to reason. Not only did Philip retake from him all, and more than all, the territory he had seized along the Apsus, but in addition, he made some useful gains at his expense elsewhere, notably, several places in the neighbourhood of Lake Lychnidus. He thereby secured to himself possession of the upper valley of the Genusus; thus two of the three natural routes which led into Roman territory came under his control, and Macedonia thenceforward marched no longer with the southern half only of this territory but with about two-thirds of its whole length[1]. In a word, the most obvious result of Scerdilaidas' enterprises was that Philip became a more inconvenient and a nearer neighbour than before. In loosing him on Macedon so late the Romans made a false move. They ought to have set him in motion when the war was at its height in Greece, in order to add a new enemy to those which Philip already had on his hands. But the Romans did not concern themselves about the Hellenic War; they were loth to interfere in the affairs of Greece, and this reluctance gave Philip his chance to interfere in the affairs of Italy.

[1] See map 14 facing p. 825.

X. CONCLUSION

The history of the Illyrian wars does not, it must be admitted, give us occasion to observe in the Roman authorities either that aggressive ambition or that clearsightedness and consistency in the conduct of foreign affairs, or that love for and skill in political intrigue which have often been attributed to them.

The first of these wars, which has sometimes been regarded as the execution of a premeditated plan of expansion, was, for anyone who considers the facts without prejudice, no more than a piece of maritime police work, which had long been necessary, but had been unduly postponed by the indolence of the Senate. Even then it was only tardily executed under the pressure of sudden and unforeseeable accidents, and was not carried one step farther than was absolutely necessary. And though, after this war, the Romans did establish themselves on the eastern side of the Straits of Otranto, it was primarily, perhaps only, in order to secure that their victory should not have been won in vain.

Moreover their Illyrian enterprise was far from being one of their chief pre-occupations, and it is a mistake to see in it the starting-point of a deliberate and consistent overseas policy directed towards the largest aims. To assume this is to forget that the energetic intervention in 229 was succeeded by nine years of inaction and heedlessness during which Roman interests in Illyria were so imprudently neglected that, in order to avert the dangerous consequences of this negligence, a second war became inevitable.

It has been maintained that the Romans hastened to take advantage of their success in Illyria to develop their political action in Greece. This is very far from the truth. Though, on the occasion of the first war, they did at last make themselves officially known to the Greeks, the *rapprochement* had no real significance. They had no thought of contracting 'friendships' in Greece. And this is a strange thing. For since their Illyrian protectorate must make, and indeed had made, Macedon their enemy—an enemy who might become dangerous—it was highly important for them to take precautions against this danger. To keep Macedon in check they had an instrument ready to their hands. Yet they seem never to have thought of making use of this instrument and of opposing a part of Greece to Macedonia. Alarmed, and with good reason, in 219, they thought they had done enough when they had struck down Demetrius of Pharos.

But this easy victory brought no final settlement, and left them exposed to the revenge of the Macedonian.

The establishment of a Roman protectorate over Lower Illyria, an event of an entirely novel character, was bound by its reactions to oblige the Republic to follow new political paths. The logic of events was to compel the opening of a new chapter in the history of its relations with foreign powers. It is noteworthy that the Senate does not seem to have been fully conscious of this, or to have appreciated clearly the gravity of its action in 229–228. It had neither estimated its scope nor calculated its consequences. It was not, as will be seen later, until 212 that it decided to adopt, under the pressure of a danger which it had allowed to grow formidable before its very eyes, the Hellenic and anti-Macedonian policy which circumstances henceforth imposed upon it; it was only then that it sought in Greece auxiliaries against Macedon. This tardiness is a sufficient indication that Rome was not as yet drawn towards the Greek world by any strong impulse of ambition.

Nevertheless, only thirty years after the second Illyrian War, Rome found herself controlling not only Greece proper, but even Hellenic Asia Minor. How this surprising state of affairs came to pass will be related in due course in volume VIII. But an examination of the circumstances of its accomplishment will show that even then the leading motives of the Romans were far from being those of aggression and desire for domination.

CHRONOLOGICAL NOTES

1. THE DATE OF THE FIRST TREATY
BETWEEN ROME AND CARTHAGE

The purpose of this note is merely to state in briefest summary the main reasons for which the version given by Polybius of the first treaty between Rome and Carthage has been accepted in the text of Chapter XII. But, though no attempt will be made to discuss the whole early history of the relations between the two cities, the evidence for their course down to the Pyrrhic War must be noticed. The chief authorities are three—Polybius, Diodorus and Livy.

Polybius, in his review of the connections between Rome and Carthage before the First Punic War, mentions three treaties. The earliest (III, 22) he assigns to the first year of the Republic, the consulship of L. Junius Brutus and M. Horatius; and the date is made still more definite—if the words are not an interpolation—by the statement that this was twenty-eight years before the crossing of Xerxes to Europe. According to his reckoning, the date is thus either 508 or 507 B.C. The second treaty (III, 24) is undated. And the third (III, 25) is placed κατὰ τὴν Πύρρου διάβασιν. Of these three instruments Polybius gives what purport to be accurate reports, if not *verbatim* reproductions; and to these he adds comments of his own which in several cases call for notice. In the first place he announces that the texts of these agreements were still preserved in his own time ἐν χαλκώμασι παρὰ τὸν Δία τὸν Καπετώλιον ἐν τῶι τῶν ἀγορανόμων ταμιείωι (III, 26, 1). But secondly he goes on to say that the ignorance of these documents displayed by Philinus of Agrigentum—the contemporary historian of the First Punic War—must not be a matter for surprise, ἐπεὶ καθ' ἡμᾶς ἔτι καὶ Ῥωμαίων καὶ Καρχηδονίων οἱ πρεσβύτατοι καὶ μάλιστα δοκοῦντες περὶ τὰ κοινὰ σπουδάζειν ἠγνόουν (III, 26, 2). And thirdly he claims that in his transcript of the *first* treaty he has done his best to overcome the difficulties of its language—καθ' ὅσον ἦν δυνατὸν ἀκριβέστατα διερμηνεύσαντες ἡμεῖς ὑπογεγράφαμεν. τηλικαύτη γὰρ ἡ διαφορὰ γέγονε τῆς διαλέκτου καὶ παρὰ Ῥωμαίοις τῆς νῦν πρὸς τὴν ἀρχαίαν ὥστε τοὺς συνετωτάτους ἔνια μόλις ἐξ ἐπιστάσεως διευκρινεῖν (III, 22, 3). From these observations two conclusions seem to emerge. One is that these treaties had become familiar in the lifetime of Polybius himself, and therefore probably in connection with the Third Punic War. The other is that the first treaty was recorded in much more archaic language than that of its successors.

Next is Diodorus. So far as our knowledge goes he only recognized two treaties between Carthage and Rome. Under the consulship of M. Valerius (Corvus) and M. Popillius (Laenas IV), which may be placed with some assurance in 348 B.C. although the chronological system of Diodorus brings these consuls down to the Attic year 344/3, he says Ῥωμαίοις πρὸς Καρχηδονίους πρῶτον συνθῆκαι ἐγένοντο (XVI, 69, 1). The second treaty mentioned by Diodorus appears in an excerpt dealing with the Pyrrhic War (XXII, 7, 5). The source behind Diodorus has been discussed already[1]. If

[1] See above, p. 485, note.

it was Fabius Pictor, no more need be said. If, on the other hand, Meyer were right in his suggestion of Cassius Hemina, it would have to be remembered about Cassius that, whether he survived to see the fall of Carthage or not, the title which he is said to have given his treatment of the Second Punic War—"Bellum Punicum posterior" (Priscian VII, 69: Keil, *Gramm. Lat.* II p. 347)—shows that his narrative had been carried down to the end of the third century before the final attack on Carthage was delivered.

Thirdly there is Livy. The earliest mention of a treaty between Rome and Carthage comes under the year 348 B.C. with the words "et cum Carthaginiensibus legatis Romae foedus ictum, cum amicitiam ac societatem petentes uenissent" (VII, 27, 2). Next, in 306 B.C., Livy says "et cum Carthaginiensibus eodem anno foedus tertio renouatum legatisque eorum, qui ad id uenerant, comiter munera missa" (IX, 43, 26). And finally in the Epitome of Book XIII, among the references to 279–8 B.C. occurs the sentence "cum Carthaginiensibus quarto foedus renouatum est." On the Livian evidence two comments may be made. Though Livy is silent about any earlier treaty, he does not say that the arrangement of 348 was the first to be concluded between the two cities: the only explicit support which Diodorus finds on this point comes from Orosius (III, 7, 1), who puts in the word "primum" on his own initiative and for the rest adds nothing. The second point is that it would probably be rash to press the phrases 'tertio' and 'quarto renouatum' to mean *renewed* a third and a fourth time: they may well signify no more than that a treaty was renewed by agreements which were the third and fourth in order of time, with the original treaty reckoned as the first.

Only one other authority need be mentioned—and that to indicate his irrelevance. Although Mommsen pointed out their futility at least so long ago as 1858[1], various attempts have even since been made to discredit the evidence of Polybius, Diodorus and Livy on the ground that in all cases their accounts are incomplete. At most they recognize three treaties, whereas it is said that in reality there were six. The basis of this assertion is a fragment from the fourth book of Cato's *Origines*[2] which contains the words 'deinde duouicesimo anno post dimissum bellum, quod quattuor et uiginti annos fuit, Carthaginienses sextum de foedere decessere.' But six breaches of treaties do not involve six separate treaties to be broken. As Mommsen observed, 'für die Zahl und Folge der Bündnisse, für die man die Stelle oft benutzt hat, folgt daraus gar nichts.'

With the treaty of 279–8, of which all three authorities were aware, there is no need here to deal (see above, p. 649): but the second treaty of Polybius, though it belongs to the fourth century, is more relevant. If the second treaty, to which Polybius does not assign a date, could be identified with the second treaty mentioned by Livy, it might be placed in 306 B.C. with some assurance. But this is made difficult by a variety of considerations. In the first place, the treaty whose date is in question according to Polybius was only the second one made between Rome and Carthage, whereas Livy's version of what happened in 306 is 'foedus tertio renouatum.' But secondly there are even stronger arguments against any year late in the fourth century. In the text of the second treaty as Polybius gives it, notwithstanding the interpretation put on Pol. III, 24, 6 by Täubler, Rome is clearly assumed to be still no

---

[1] *Römische Chronologie* (ed. 1), p. 275 n. 9.   [2] Frag. 84 P.

more than a Latin power, without interest either in the Tuscan coast or in the coast of Campania. Now even if the alliance with Capua and its partial enfranchisement not later than 338 (p. 592) did not bring Campania within the Roman sphere, and even if it is disputed at what point in the Samnite Wars this extension of Rome's horizon may be said to be complete, the construction of the Via Appia by Appius Claudius Caecus in the censorship which certainly was ended by 308 shows that the limits of Rome's interests had advanced far beyond Tarracina by the beginning of the last decade in the fourth century. For this reason it appears that the second treaty of Polybius cannot well be later than 310 B.C. and is probably earlier by at least as many years as Rome had become a Campanian power before that time. From the opposite direction too a certain degree of confirmation is to be had: the indifference of Rome to Etruria is easier to understand before the victory of Q. Fabius Maximus Rullianus in 310 (p. 605) than after it. Thus, when a choice has to be made between the year 306 for the second Polybian treaty and a date somewhere in the forties of the fourth century, the latter appears preferable; and, though Livy records the presence at Rome of a Carthaginian mission in 343, the simplest course to follow under the circumstances is to identify the second treaty of Polybius with the first of Diodorus and Livy and to place it in 348.

Between the second treaty of Polybius and the first the differences are marked. The language of the second appears to have given no trouble, whereas the first could only with difficulty be understood. In the first there is no mention of Spain, whither Carthage penetrated during the first half of the fourth century: in the second Spain appears. And, finally, by denying Romans the right to trade in Africa (and Sardinia)—a right which by the first treaty was allowed—the second implies either a marked change for the worse in Rome's ability to secure fair terms for herself or so considerable a development of Roman commercial activities as to have raised fears at Carthage which did not exist before, or possibly both. These facts, and more particularly the linguistic peculiarities of the first treaty on which Polybius insists, suggest that the interval between it and the second was long. Even if the second treaty could be brought down to 306, it would be hard to accept any date in the fourth century as early enough for the first; and if the second treaty belongs to 348, its predecessor must be carried so far back as to make the first year of the Republic as plausible as any alternative.

The evidence by which Polybius felt himself justified in associating the earliest agreement with this particular year need not be discussed in detail. It should, however, be said that to this question the form of the treaty is irrelevant. Even if Täubler is right in arguing that it was drafted in what is supposed to be the Carthaginian style, as an oath without mention of date or personal names, nothing is more probable than that some indication of the responsible Roman officers was recorded on the copy kept in the Capitoline temple. The possibility that Brutus and Horatius Pulvillus were actually mentioned raises questions about the earliest Fasti which this is not the place to examine. It is enough to say that the period in which the treaty is put by Polybius can claim plausibility, and further that within this period a date immediately upon the fall of the kingship is most likely. For the first treaty between Rome and Carthage has every appearance of being no more than an adaptation of something which had originated between Carthage and the Etruscans. It seems to be part of the Etruscan legacy to Rome, and a part on which Rome—not herself at this time really a commercial power worth the name—had to enter at once if she was to enter at all. And further, the implication of the document—that at the time of its composition, while the interests of Carthage were in trade, those of Rome were mainly political— agrees perfectly with the situation between the fall of the monarchy and the *foedus Cassianum*.

Such questions of minute chronology, however, do not affect the value of the treaty as a clue to Roman aspirations. If it is not wholly wrong to accept from Polybius the sixth-century date, the document shows Rome, soon after the fall of the monarchy, claiming as her sphere of interest the Latin region down past Ardea and Antium along the Pomptine Marshes to Circeii and Tarracina.

H. M. L.

2. THE DATE OF THE BATTLE OF COS

The possible limits for this battle are now greatly narrowed. (For previous discussions see the Bibliography p. 882.) The Lindian Chronicle C, ll. 97 *sqq.*, shows that the king against whom Rhodes fought was Ptolemy II; and as the exiled Chremonides commanded for Ptolemy (Polyaenus v, 18), the date is after 261, the year of the peace which concluded the Chremonidean War (*I.G.* xi, ii, 114). But Rhodes could not have gone to war with her friend Egypt if Egypt's sea-power had already been broken, and the Lindian Chronicle shows it was *not* broken, for Rhodes at the start was very anxious; therefore Cos cannot be *before* the peace of 261. (The view which connects Cos with the Chremonidean War neglects these considerations and follows a mistaken dating and interpretation of Rehm, *Milet* i, iii, no. 139, on which see A. Rostagni, *Poeti Alessandrini*, p. 374, and the writer in *J.H.S.* xlvi, 1926, p. 158.) As to the inferior limit, Antigonus' portico on Delos, non-existent c. 260, already needed cleaning in 248 (F. Courby, *B.C.H.* xxxviii, 1914, p. 296); therefore Cos had been fought some considerable time before 248. G. Glotz' argument from the price of pitch at Delos, which is valid, also puts it before 250 (see his table, *Rev. E.G.* xxix, 1916, pp. 284–5); had we the lost prices between 268 and 250 the battle could be dated exactly. These considerations, together with the Antigoneia and Stratoniceia founded in 253, render it now almost a certainty that Cos belongs to the Second Syrian War, where K. J. Beloch and W. S. Ferguson have placed it. That war began after the peace of 261 and ended with the peace of 255 (*I.G.* xi, ii, 116); and as Cos was fought during the Isthmian games, the possible years are 260, 258, and 256. The last is unlikely, as Antiochus' successes rather suppose an Egypt crippled at sea. Probably the war *did* begin in 260; but, seeing Rhodes' anxiety at first, 258 seems more probable for the decisive battle. In *P.S.I.* v, no. 502, l. 24, dated 258–7, Zoilus an *oikonomos* was busy πρὸς τῇ τῶν ναυτῶν ἀποστολῇ, which *might* refer to a conscription to try and make good the disaster. But it may not refer to the war-fleet at all; cf. *P.S.I.* iv, no. 332, l. 16 (257–6).—Fresh confirmation of the peace of 255 is now furnished by a new papyrus dated in 254: H. I. Bell, *Greek sightseers in the Fayûm in the third century B.C.*, Symbolae Osloenses, fasc. v, 1927.—The trierarchy in force at Halicarnassus in 258–7 (*P. Cairo Zen.* 59036; see U. Wilcken in *Raccolta Lumbroso*, p. 92) has no bearing on the year of the battle; it might equally well be before or after, since Ptolemy did not lose Caria. **w. w. t.**

3. THE DATE OF THE BATTLE OF SELLASIA

Whether the date of Sellasia, on which the chronology of the Cleomenic War depends, was 221 or 222 is a very old debate, but still vigorous; and M. Holleaux, who formerly (*Mélanges Nicole*, Geneva 1908, pp. 273 *sqq.*) upheld 222, now accepts 221 (see above p. 843, n. 1), while the writer has felt constrained to adopt 222. The question is perhaps, on present materials, insoluble, for there is no way of reconciling *all* the evidence; I can only indicate here the main arguments and my reasons for adopting 222. The support for 221 is the list of Achaean *strategoi*, best given by A. Boethius, *Der argivische Kalender*, and Polybius' statement (II, 70, 4) that after Sellasia Antigonus was present at the Nemea, which were held in the uneven years and therefore in 221; objections are that Polybius (IV, 35, 8) says that in spring 219 Sparta had been kingless σχεδὸν ἤδη τρεῖς ἐνιαυτούς (while if Sellasia was *c.* July 221 the period was about one year eight months), and that it is difficult to make the known events fill up the time to July 221. I tried the experiment of reading Polybius like a new text, merely noting time indications, and was convinced that *he himself* wrote in the belief that Sellasia was 222; his 'nearly three years' confirms this. What he believed, however, though a strong argument, is not conclusive; and there remains the question of the Achaean *strategoi* after May 224, when Timoxenus' (first) year expired. We have two indications: Polyb. II, 52, 3, when Corinth revolted from the Achaeans the Corinthians gave orders τῷ μὲν Ἀράτῳ στρατηγοῦντι καὶ τοῖς Ἀχαιοῖς to leave the city, and II, 53, 2, when Cleomenes lost Argos the Achaean troops marched thither μετὰ Τιμοξένου τοῦ στρατηγοῦ. Boethius, as those who support 221 must do, takes both phrases to mean 'General of the League,' which they *ought* to mean; consequently in his chronology Aratus was General of the League May 224–3, Timoxenus May 223–2, Antigonus' Arcadian campaign was 222, Sellasia 221. But the attempts made to work out the Achaean constitution from Polybius' indications, and the various names he uses for the governors of the Seleucid satrapies, have proved that he is *not* precise in his use of technical terms; both phrases therefore *may* refer merely to *de facto* commands, and as to the second there seems to be evidence. For too little attention, I think, has been paid to Plutarch, *Aratus* 41: after Corinth revolted, a meeting at Sicyon (the locality shows it was a special meeting) made Aratus dictator (see p. 758). While this office lasted, there could be no General of the League. Now in Boethius' scheme Timoxenus was General of the League, and therefore responsible for Achaean policy, when Antigonus recaptured Argos and Aristomachus was executed; but Polybius II, 60, 2 places the responsibility for Aristomachus' death, not on Antigonus and Timoxenus, but on Antigonus and *Aratus*; Aratus then was still dictator, and Timoxenus 'the general' merely an officer in a *de facto* command. The dictatorship must have lasted till after Sellasia. This view, which I think is new, would settle the question of the *strategoi* and leave only one difficulty, the Nemea; and I would sooner suppose that, owing to the

CHRONOLOGICAL NOTES

war, the Nemea of 223 were held in 222 (as those of 195 were shifted to the autumn, and the Panathenaea of 278 omitted altogether), rather than suppose that the whole basis of Polybius' account, *viz.* Sellasia in 222, was a false belief on his part. Another arrangement of the Achaean *strategoi*, to suit 222, has recently been suggested by K. J. Beloch, *Griechische Geschichte*, vol. IV, ii, pp. 219 *sqq.* Both Beloch and Boethius only give Aratus 16 Generalships, while the tradition gives him 17 (Plutarch, *Aratus* 53); the view I have taken, that he was *strategos autokrator* (dictator) in 224, 223, and 222, does give him 17.

It will be seen that my reasons are not of a nature to preclude anyone from holding that Polybius had no such belief as I suppose, that Aratus' dictatorship was a brief one, that Polybius II, 60, 2 refers only to personal advice given to Antigonus by Aratus, and that Boethius' list of *strategoi* is valid and (with the Nemea) the deciding factor.

But the evidence from Egypt for Euergetes' death (Bibliography C 5, p. 887) has also to be considered. Cleomenes was in Egypt for some time before Euergetes died (Plutarch, *Cleomenes* 32), and Euergetes' death in 221 is certain; the question is the month. Of recent studies, that of Ernst Meyer (1925; written earlier) makes it October; but I myself cannot accept the bases of his reasoning (see *C.R.* XL, 1926, p. 86). Starting from a sound basis, Beloch in 1924 concluded about August and in 1926 about early July. If he be right, *cadit quaestio*; Sellasia was 222. But a papyrus, apparently still unpublished, is mentioned by E. Cavaignac (*B.C.H.* XXXVIII, 1914, p. 18) as dated in Xandikos-Epiphi of 26 Euergetes = September 221 on Beloch's scheme; and one cannot say what may yet come to light. Egypt may finally prove that Sellasia was 222, or may leave the question still open; it cannot of course prove 221. (G. De Sanctis, *Riv. fil.* LV, 1927, p. 489, accepts Beloch's Egyptian chronology as certain that 222 is correct. C. C. Edgar, *Zenon Papyri* I, 1925, p. vii, also supports Beloch's chronology.)   W. W. T.

LIST OF ABBREVIATIONS[1]

Abh.	Abhandlungen.
Abh. Arch.-epig.	Abhandlungen d. archäol.-epigraph. Seminars d. Univ. Wien.
A.J.A.	American Journal of Archaeology.
A.J. Num.	American Journal of Numismatics.
A.J. Ph.	American Journal of Philology.
Ann. Serv.	Annales du Service des antiquités de l'Égypte.
Arch. Anz.	Archäologischer Anzeiger (in J.D.A.I.).
Ἀρχ. Ἐφ.	Ἀρχαιολογικὴ Ἐφημερίς.
Arch. Pap.	Archiv für Papyrusforschung.
Ath. Mitt.	Mitteilungen des deutschen arch. Inst., Athenische Abteilung.
Bay. Abh.	Abhandlungen d. bayerischen Akad. d. Wissenschaften.
Bay. S.B.	Sitzungsberichte d. bayerischen Akad. d. Wissenschaften.
B.C.H.	Bulletin de Correspondance hellénique.
Berl. Abh.	Abhandlungen d. preuss. Akad. d. Wissenschaften zu Berlin.
Berl. S.B.	Sitzungsberichte d. preuss. Akad. d. Wissenschaften zu Berlin.
B.M.I.	Greek Inscriptions in the British Museum.
B.P.W.	Berliner Philologische Wochenschrift.
B.S.A.	Annual of the British School at Athens.
B.S.R.	Papers of the British School at Rome.
Bursian	Bursian's Jahresbericht.
B.V.F.	Bayerischer Vorgeschichtsfreund.
C.I.E.	Corpus Inscriptionum Etruscarum.
C.I.L.	Corpus Inscriptionum Latinarum.
C.J.	Classical Journal.
C.P.	Classical Philology.
C.Q.	Classical Quarterly.
C.R.	Classical Review.
C.R. Ac. Inscr.	Comptes rendus de l'Académie des Inscriptions et Belles-Lettres.
Ditt.[3]	Dittenberger, Sylloge Inscriptionum Graecarum. Ed. 3.
D.S.	Daremberg et Saglio, Dictionnaire des antiquités grecques et romaines.
E. Brit.	Encyclopaedia Britannica. 11th Ed.
F.G.H.	F. Jacoby's Fragmente der griechischen Historiker.
F.H.G.	C. Müller's Fragmenta Historicorum Graecorum.
G.G.A.	Göttingische Gelehrte Anzeigen.
Gött. Nach.	Nachrichten von der königlichen Gesellschaft der Wissenschaften zu Göttingen. Phil.-hist. Klasse.
Harv. St.	Harvard Studies in Classical Philology.
Head H.N.[2]	Head's Historia Numorum. 2nd Ed. 1912.
I.G.	Inscriptiones Graecae.
I.G.[2]	Inscriptiones Graecae. Editio minor.
Jahreshefte	Jahreshefte d. österr. archäol. Instituts in Wien.
J.D.A.I.	Jahrbuch des deutschen archäologischen Instituts.
J.E.A.	Journal of Egyptian Archaeology.
J.H.S.	Journal of Hellenic Studies.
J.I. d'A.N.	Journal International d'Archéologie Numismatique.
J.P.	Journal of Philology.

[1] For Abbreviations for names of collections of Papyri see the Bibliography to chapter IV.

J.R.A.S.	Journal of the Royal Asiatic Society.
J.R.S.	Journal of Roman Studies.
Klio	Klio (Beiträge zur alten Geschichte).
L'Anthr.	L'Anthropologie.
Mnem.	Mnemosyne.
Mon. Linc.	Monumenti antichi pubblicati per cura della R. Accademia dei Lincei.
Mon. d. I.	Monumenti antichi dell' Instituto.
Mus. B.	Musée belge.
N. J. f. Wiss.	Neue Jahrbücher für Wissenschaft und Jugendbildung.
N.J. Kl. Alt.	Neue Jahrbücher für das klassische Altertum.
N.J.P.	Neue Jahrbücher für Philologie.
N.S.A.	Notizie degli Scavi di Antichità.
Num. Chr.	Numismatic Chronicle.
Num. Z.	Numismatische Zeitschrift.
O.G.I.S.	Orientis Graeci Inscriptiones selectae.
Phil.	Philologus.
Phil. Woch.	Philologische Wochenschrift.
P.W.	Pauly-Wissowa's Real-Encyclopädie der classischen Altertums- wissenschaft.
P.Z.	Prähistorische Zeitschrift.
Rend. Linc.	Rendiconti della R. Accademia dei Lincei.
Rev. Anthr.	Revue Anthropologique.
Rev. Arch.	Revue Archéologique.
Rev. E. A.	Revue des études anciennes.
Rev. E.G.	Revue des études grecques.
Rev. H.	Revue historique.
Rev. N.	Revue numismatique.
Rev. Phil.	Revue de philologie, de littérature et d'histoire anciennes.
Rh. Mus.	Rheinisches Museum für Philologie.
Riv. fil.	Rivista di filologia.
Riv. stor. ant.	Rivista di storia antica.
Röm. Mitt.	Mitteilungen des deutschen arch. Inst., Römische Abteilung.
S.B.	Sitzungsberichte.
S.E.G.	Supplementum epigraphicum Graecum.
St. Fil.	Studi italiani di filologia classica.
Wien Anz.	Anzeiger d. Akad. d. Wissenschaften in Wien.
Wien S.B.	Sitzungsberichte d. Akad. d. Wissenschaften in Wien.
Wien St.	Wiener Studien.
W.P.Z.	Wiener Prähistorische Zeitschrift.
Z. d. Sav.-Stift.	Zeitschrift d. Savigny-Stiftung f. Rechtsgeschichte (Romanistische Abteilung).
Z.N.	Zeitschrift für Numismatik.

BIBLIOGRAPHIES

These bibliographies do not aim at completeness. They include modern and standard works and, in particular, books utilized in the writings of the chapters. Many technical monographs, especially in journals, are omitted, but the works that are registered below will put the reader on their track.

The works given in the General Bibliography for Greek and Roman History are, as a rule, not repeated in the bibliographies to the separate chapters.

The first page only of articles in journals is given.

GENERAL BIBLIOGRAPHY

I. General Histories of the Hellenistic Age

Beloch, K. J. *Griechische Geschichte*. Vol. iv. Ed. 2. Berlin-Leipzig, 1925–27.
Bevan, E. R. *The House of Seleucus*. London, 1902.
Bevan, E. R. and Mahaffy, J. P. *A History of Egypt under the Ptolemaic Dynasty*. London, 1927.
Bouché-Leclercq, A. *Histoire des Lagides*. Paris, 1903–7.
—— *Histoire des Seleucides*. Paris, 1913.
Cardinali, G. *Il Regno di Pergamo*. Turin, 1906.
Cavaignac, E. *Histoire de l'Antiquité*. Vol. iii. Paris, 1914.
Droysen, J. G. *Geschichte des Hellenismus*. Ed. 2. Gotha, 1876–.
Fergusson, W. S. *Hellenistic Athens*. London, 1911.
—— *Greek Imperialism*. London and New York, 1913.
Freeman, E. A. *A History of Sicily*. Oxford, 1891.
Gercke, A. and Norden, E. *Einleitung in die Altertumswissenschaft*. Ed. 2. Leipzig and Berlin, 1914.
Holleaux, M. *Rome, la Grèce, et les monarchies hellénistiques au IIIᵉ siècle av. J.-C.* (273–205). Paris, 1921.
Holm, A. *Geschichte Siciliens im Altertum*. Leipzig, 1870.
—— *Geschichte Griechenlands*. Berlin, 1886–.
Jouguet, P. *L'Impérialisme macédonien et l'hellénisation de l'Orient*. Paris. 1926.
Kaerst, J. *Geschichte des Hellenismus*. Ed. 2. Leipzig. Vol. i. 1917. Vol. ii. 1926.
Meltzer, O. *Geschichte der Karthager*. Berlin, 1879–1913.
Niese, B. *Geschichte der griechischen und makedonischen Staaten*. Gotha, 1893–1903.
Niese, B. and U. von Wilamowitz-Moellendorff. *Staat und Gesellschaft der Griechen und Römer*. Ed. 2. Berlin, 1923.
Tarn, W. W. *Antigonos Gonatas*. Oxford, 1913.
—— *Hellenistic Civilisation*. London, 1927.
Wendland, P. *Die hellenistisch-römische Kultur*. Ed. 3. Tübingen, 1912.

II. General Histories of Rome

(See also Bibliography to Chapters x–xv, xviii, B, 1)

Cavaignac, E. *Histoire de l'Antiquité*. Vol. iii, *La Macédoine, Carthage, et Rome*. Paris, 1914.
De Sanctis, G. *Storia dei Romani*. Vols. i–iv, 1. Turin, 1907–23.

Frank, T. *A History of Rome*. New York, n.d.
—— *Roman Imperialism*. New York, 1914.
Heitland, W. E. *The Roman Republic*. 3 vols. Ed. 2. Cambridge, 1923.
Homo, L. *Les Institutions politiques romaines*. Paris, 1927.
—— *L'Italie primitive et les Débuts de l'Impérialisme romain*. Paris, 1925.
Ihne, W. *Römische Geschichte*. Ed. 2. Leipzig, 1893.
Mommsen, Th. *Römische Geschichte*. Vols. I–III. Ed. 2. Berlin, 1856–7. (English translation by W. P. Dickson. New York, 1895.)
Piganiol, A. *La Conquête romaine*. Paris, 1927.
Rostovtzeff, M. *A History of the Ancient World*. Vol. II. Rome. Oxford, 1927.
Wagner, W. *Rom: Geschichte des römischen Volkes und seiner Kultur*. 1ote Auflage, neubearbeitet von O. E. Schmidt. Berlin, 1923.

III. WORKS OF REFERENCE, DICTIONARIES, ETC.

Daremberg et Saglio. *Dictionnaire des antiquités grecques et romaines*. 1877–1919. (D.S.)
Encyclopaedia Britannica. Ed. 11. Articles on Greek and Roman History. (E. Brit.)
Gercke, A. and Norden, E. *Einleitung in die Altertumswissenschaft*. Ed. 2. Leipzig and Berlin, 1914. Ed. 3: part appeared.
Lübkers Reallexikon des klassischen Altertums. Ed. 8. Berlin, 1914.
Mommsen, Th. and Marquardt. *Handbuch der römischen Altertümer*. Ed. 2. Leipzig, 1876–88.
Müller, Iwan. *Handbuch der klassischen Altertumswissenschaft*. Munich, various dates. (Handbuch.)
Pauly-Wissowa-Kroll. *Real-Encyclopädie der classischen Altertumswissenschaft*. Stuttgart, 1893 (in progress). (P.W.)
Roscher, W. *Ausführliches Lexikon der griechischen und römischen Mythologie*. Leipzig, 1884 (in progress). (Roscher.)
Sandys, Sir J. E. *A Companion to Latin Studies*. Ed. 2. Cambridge, 1913.
Stuart Jones, H. *A Companion to Roman History*. Oxford, 1912.
Whibley, L. *A Companion to Greek Studies*. Ed. 3. Cambridge, 1916.

CHAPTER I

THE LEADING IDEAS OF THE NEW PERIOD

The ancient evidence for the topics covered by this chapter and the modern works upon them are cited under the relevant headings in the bibliographies to chapters XII and XIII in volume VI, and to chapters III, VI, XXII, XXIII and chapters IV, V and VII in this volume.

See especially bibliography to volume VI, chapters XII and XIII, section G; and in this volume, the bibliographies to chapters III, VI, XXII, XXIII, section II, B 10, 13; chapter IV, sections B 1, 3, 4, 6, 10, 11; chapter V, section B 1; and chapter VII.

The following works of a more general character, or dealing with more theoretical topics, may also be cited:

Bauer, A. *Vom Griechentum zum Christentum.* Ed. 2. Leipzig, 1923. p. 49.

Bickermann, E. *Beiträge zur antiken Urkundengeschichte.* 1. Arch. Pap. VIII, 1927. p. 216.

Breccia, E. *Il diritto dinastico nelle monarchie dei successori d'Alessandro Magno.* Beloch's Studi di storia antica, IV, Roma, 1903.

Carlyle, A. J. *A History of Mediaeval Political Theory.* Vol. 1. Ed. 2. Edinburgh and London, 1927.

Farnell, L. R. *Greek Hero Cults and Ideas of Immortality.* Oxford, 1921. p. 420.

Goodenough, E. R. *The Political Philosophy of the Hellenistic Kingship.* Yale Studies 1 (1928).

Haussoullier, B. *Inscription grecque de Suse* in Anatolian Studies presented to Sir W. M. Ramsay. Manchester, 1923. p. 187.

Herzog-Hauser, G. Art. *Kaiserkult* in P. W. Supplbd. IV, col. 806.

Kaerst, J. *Zum hellenistischen Kaiserkult.* Geschichte des Hellenismus. Vol. II. Ed. 2, 1926, p. 376.

Laqueur, R. *Hellenismus.* Akademische Rede. Giessen, 1925.

Lietzmann, H. *Der Weltheiland.* Bonn, 1909.

Mewaldt, J. *Das Weltbürgertum in der Antike.* Die Antike, II, 1926, p. 177.

Moore, G. F. *Judaism.* Cambridge, Mass., 1927.

Moret, A. *Du caractère religieux de la royauté pharaonique.* Annales du Musée Guimet, XV, 1902.

Nock, A. D. *Notes on Ruler-Cult.* J. H. S. XLVIII, 1928, p. 21.

Norden, E. *Die Geburt des Kindes.* Leipzig-Berlin, 1924.

Otto, W. *Zum Hofzeremoniell des Hellenismus* in Ἐπιτύμβιον H. Swoboda darge-bracht, p. 194.

Pfister, Fr. Art. *Epiphanie* in P. W. Supplbd. IV, col. 306.

Poland, F. *Geschichte des griechischen Vereinswesens.* Leipzig, 1909.

Rehm, A. *Kultgesetz des römischen Volkes und der Roma.* Wiegand's Milet, I, 7, p. 290.

Roussel, P. *Les cultes égyptiens à Délos du IIIe au Ier siècle av. J.-C.* Nancy, 1916.
—— *Délos, colonie athénienne.* 1916.

Schmidt, W. *Geburtstag im Altertum.* Giessen, 1908.

Scott, K. *The Deification of Demetrius Poliorcetes.* A. J. Ph. XLIX, 1928, p. 137.

Stöckle, A. Art. *Berufsvereine* in P. W. Supplbd. IV, col. 155.

Tarn, W. W. *Hellenistic Civilisation*. London, 1927.

Taylor, L. R. *The 'Proskynesis' and the Hellenistic Ruler Cult*. J. H. S. xlvii, 1927, p. 53.

—— *The Cult of Alexander in Alexandria*. C. P. xxii, 1927, p. 162.

Weber, W. *Der Siegeszug des Griechentums im Orient*. Die Antike, i, 1925, p. 101.

Weinreich, O. *Antikes Gottmenschentum*. N. J. f. Wiss. ii, 1926, p. 633.

Wendland, P. Σωτήρ. Zeitschrift f. d. neutestamentliche Wiss. v, 1904, p. 335.

—— *Die hellenistische-römische Kultur*. Ed. 3. Tübingen, 1912. p. 123.

Wilamowitz-Moellendorff, U. von. *Hellenistische Dichtung in der Zeit des Kallimachos*. Berlin, 1924. i, 68.

Ziebarth, E. *Das griechische Vereinswesen*. Leipzig, 1896.

CHAPTER II

THE COMING OF THE CELTS

I. Ancient Literary Sources

Ammianus Marcellinus, xv, ix–xii.

Avienus, *Ora Maritima* (ed. A. Schulten, Barcelona, 1922 = Fontes Hispaniae Antiquae, 1).

Caesar, *De Bello Gallico.*

Diodorus Siculus, v, 21–32.

Pliny, *N.H.* iii, 31 *sqq.*, 133 *sqq.*; iv, 105 *sq.*; xvi, 249 *sqq.*; xxiv, 103 *sq.*; xxix, 52 *sqq.*; xxx, 13.

Polybius, ii, 17 *sqq.* and iii.

Ptolemy, *Geography*, ii, 7 *sqq.*

Strabo, iv.

For other references see Appian, ἐκ τῆς Κελτικῆς; Aristotle, *Nic. Eth.* iii, 7, 7; Arrian, *Anab.* i, 4, 6; Athenaeus, iv, 34 and 37; Diogenes Laertius, *Vitae*, Intro. 1 and 5; Ephorus, *F.H.G.* i, frag. 43 = 132 Jac.; Hecataeus of Miletus, *F.H.G.* i, frags. 19–22 = 53–6 Jac.; Herodotus, ii, 33 and iv, 49; Justin, xx, xxiv–vi, xxxii; Livy, v, 33 *sqq.*; Lucan, i, 450 *sqq.*; Maximus Tyrius, *Diss.* ii. 8 (Hoheim); Polyaenus, viii, 7, 2; Pseudo-Scylax, *Periplus* (C. Muller, *Geogr. graec. min.* i, 25 *sqq.*). On Pytheas of Massilia, for passages from classical authors see W. Dinan, *Monumenta hist. Celtica*, i, 54 *sqq.*; for bibliography, C. Jullian, *Hist. de la Gaule*, i, 1908, pp. 415 *sqq.* and M. Clerc, *Massalia*, i, pp. 399 and 414 footnotes.

II. Modern Works

Arbois de Jubainville, H. *Cours de Littérature celtique.* i–xii. Paris, 1883–92.

—— *Les Premiers Habitants de l'Europe.* Paris, 1894.

—— *Les Celtes depuis les Temps les plus anciens.* Paris, 1904.

Beltz, R. *Die Latènefibeln.* Zeitschrift für Ethnologie, xliii, 1911, pp. 664, 930.

Bertrand, A. *Nos Origines: La Gaule avant les Gaulois.* Ed. 3. Paris, 1891.

Bertrand, A. and Reinach, S. *Les Celtes dans les vallées du Pô et du Danube.* Paris, 1894.

Brehm, B. *Ursprung der germanischen Tierornamentik* in J. Strzygowski's Der Norden in der bildenden Kunst Westeuropas. Vienna, 1926.

Cary, M. *The Greeks and ancient Trade with the Atlantic.* J. H. S. xliv, 1924, p. 166.

Chadwick, H. M. *Some German River-names* in Essays and Studies presented to W. Ridgeway. Cambridge, 1913.

Chantre, E. *L'Age du Fer dans le Bassin du Rhône.* Paris-Lyons, 1880.

Childe, V. G. *The Aryans.* London, 1926.

Clerc, M. *Massalia.* Vol. 1. Marseilles, 1927.

†Couissin, P. *Les Armes gauloises sur les monuments....* Rev. Arch. 1927, i, pp. 138, 301; ii, p. 43.

Coutil, L. *Sépultures et Mobilier funéraire des Lexovii, Essuvii, Viducasses et Baïocasses.* Bulletin de la Société Normande d'études préhistoriques, xi, 1903, p. 147.

Déchelette, J. *Manuel d'archéologie préhistorique.* ii, 1–3. Paris, 1910–1914. (Important, though in certain points somewhat out of date.)

† Works marked † came into the author's hands too late to be utilized in the writing of this chapter.

Déchelette, J. *La Collection Millon.* Paris, 1913.

Dinan, W. *Monumenta historica celtica.* London, 1911.

Dottin, G. *La Religion celtique.* Paris, 1904.

—— *Manuel pour servir à l'étude de l'Antiquité celtique.* Ed. 2. Paris, 1915.

—— *Les anciens Peuples de l'Europe.* Paris, 1916.

Ebert, M. *Reallexikon der Vorgeschichte.* Berlin, 1924 (in progress).

Favret, L'Abbé P. *Le premier Age du Fer en Champagne.* Soc. archéol. Champenoise, 1925.

†—— *La Nécropole hallstattienne des Jogasses.* Rev. Arch. 1927, I, p. 326; II, p. 80. (An important contribution showing that many types regarded by Déchelette and earlier authorities as "primitive La Tène I" are definitely late Hallstatt.)

†Feist, S. *Germanen und Kelten in antiken Überlieferungen.* Halle, 1927. (But see F. Koepp in G.G.A. 1928, p. 201, and L. Schmidt in Phil. Woch. 1928, no. 6, col. 174.)

Forrer, R. *Die Heidenmauer von St Odilien.* 1899.

—— *Reallexikon.* Berlin and Stuttgart, 1907.

Gams, H. and Nordhagen, R. *Postglaziale Klimaänderungen.* Geograph. Gesell. München, XVI, 2, 1923.

Götze, A. *Die Steinsburg bei Römhild.* P. Z. XIII–XIV, 1921–2, p. 19.

Goury, G. *L'Enceinte d'Haulzy et sa Nécropole.* (Les Étapes de l'Humanité, I, ii.) Nancy, 1911.

Grenier, A. *Les Gaulois.* Paris, 1923.

Guiart, J. *La race galate.* Rev. Anthr. XXXVII, 1927, p. 214. (No attention paid to the prehistoric material.)

Hamy, E. T. *Les premiers Gaulois.* L'Anthr. XVII, 1906. (Useful for physical anthropology only.)

Hörnes, M. and Menghin, O. *Urgeschichte der bildenden Kunst.* Vienna, 1925.

Holmes, T. R. *Caesar's Conquest of Gaul.* Ed. 2. Oxford, 1911. pp. 257–340. (A valuable résumé.)

Joulin, L. *Les Celtes...dans le sud de la France.* Rev. Arch. 1918, I, p. 74.

Jullian, C. *Histoire de la Gaule.* I. Paris, 1908.

Kendrick, T. D. *The Druids.* London, 1927.

Kossinna, G. *Die illyrische, germanische und keltische Kultur der frühesten Eisenzeit.*

—— Mannus, VII, 1915, p. 87. Nachtrag, ib. XI–XII, 1919–20, p. 415.

—— *Ursprung und Verbreitung der Germanen.* Vol. I. Berlin, 1926.

Leeds, E. T. *Excavations at Chun Castle, in Penwith, Cornwall.* Archaeologia, LXXVI, 1926–7, p. 205.

Lindenschmidt, L. *Altertümer unseren heidnischen Vorväter.* Mainz, 1864–1911. Articles by Reinecke and Schumacher in vol. V.

Macalister, R. A. S. *The Archaeology of Ireland.* London, 1928.

Mahr, A. *Die La Tènezeit in Oberoesterreich.* Mitt. der prähist. Kommission, II, 3. Vienna, 1915.

Menghin, O. *Einführung in der Urgeschichte Böhmens und Mährens.* Reichenberg, 1926. See also Hörnes.

Merhart, G. *La Tènefunde aus Tirol.* W.P.Z. XIII, 1926, p. 65.

Moreau, F. *Collection Caranda.* St. Quentin, 1877–94.

—— *Table générale de l'Album Caranda.* Paris, 1908.

Morel, L. *La Champagne souterraine.* Rheims, 1898.

de Mortillet, G. *Musée préhistorique.* Paris, 1881.

de Navarro, J. M. *Massilia and Early Celtic Culture,* in Antiquity (forthcoming).

Niese, B. *Zur Geschichte der keltischen Wanderungen.* Zeitschr. f. deutsches Alterthum, XLII, 1898, p. 127.

Pârvan, V. *Considérations sur les Sépultures celtiques de Gruia.* Dacia, I, 1924, p. 35.

Pârvan, V. *Getica, o Protoistorica a Daciei.* Bucarest, 1926. (With French résumé.)
—— *Dacia.* Cambridge, 1928. p. 127.
Peake, H. *The Bronze Age and the Celtic World.* London, 1922.
Piroutet, M. *Le premier Age du Fer dans les dépts. de Jura et Doubs.* L'Anthr. xi, 1900, p. 369.
—— *Contribution à l'étude des Celtes.* L'Anthr. xxix, 1918–9, pp. 213, 423; xxx, 1920, p. 51.
Piroutet, M. and Déchelette, J. *Découverte de Vases grecs dans un Oppidum hallstattien du Jura.* Rev. Arch. 1909, i, p. 193.
Pothier, Général, *Les Tumulus du Plateau de Ger.* Paris, 1900.
Rademacher, E. *Chronologie der germanischen Gräberfelder in der Umgebung von Köln.* Mannus, xiv, 1922, p. 187.
—— *Niederrheinische Hügelgräberkultur.* Mannus, Ergänzungsband iv, 1925, p. 112.
—— *Kerbschnittkeramik.* Mannus, xviii, 1926, p. 14.
Reinach, S. *Catalogue illustré du Musée...au Château de St Germain.* ii. Paris, 1921. (See also Bertrand, A.)
Reinecke, P. *Zur Kenntnis der Latènedenkmaler der Zone nordwärts der Alpen.* Mainzer Festschrift, Mainz, 1902. (An epoch-making study.)
—— *Zu den Grabfunden von Bodenbach a. d. Elbe.* W.P.Z. ii, 1915, p. 15.
—— *Chronologische Übersicht.* B.V.F. i–ii, 1921–2, p. 21.
—— *Örtliche Bestimmung geographischer Namen.* (ii.) B.V.F. v, 1925, p. 19.
—— *Erste La Tènestufe (A) in rechtsrheinischen Bayern.* Ib. p. 49. (See also Lindenschmidt.)
†Schranil, J. *Slavische Grundriss.* Berlin, 1927–8. p. 211.
Schulten, A. *Tartessos. Ein Beitrag zur ältesten Geschichte des Westens.* Hamburg, 1922.
Schumacher, K. *Eine alte gallische Wandersage.* Mainzer Zeitschr. ii, 1907, p. 16.
—— *Gallische und Germanische Stämme....* P.Z. vi, 1914, p. 230.
—— *Beitr. zur Besiedlungskunde des Hunsrücks der Eifel,* etc. P.Z. viii, 1916, p. 133. (See also Lindenschmidt.)
—— *Kultur und Siedlungsgeschichte der Rheinlande.* i. Mainz, 1921.
Siret, L. *Les Cassitérides et l'Empire colonial des Phœniciens.* L'Anthr. xix, 1908, p. 128; xx, 1909, p. 129; xxi, 1910, p. 281.
Smith, R. A. *British Museum Guide to Iron Age Antiquities.* Ed. 2. London, 1925.
Stampfuss, R. *Vordringen der Germanen zum nördlichen Niederrhein.* Mannus, xvii, 1925, p. 287.
—— *Zur Nordgruppe der Urnenfelderkultur.* Mannus, Ergänzungsband v, 1927, p. 50.
Tackenburg, K. *Neue schlesische Funde der frühgermanischen Zeit.* Breslau, 1922.
Tischler, O. *Über Gliederung der La-Tène Periode.* Correspondenz-Bl. der deutschen Gesellschaft für Anthropologie, Ethnologie und Urgeschichte, 1885, p. 157.
Ulrich, R. *Gräberfelder in der Umgebung von Bellinzona.* Zürich, 1914.
Viollier, D. *Sépultures du second Age du Fer sur le plateau suisse.* Geneva, 1916.
Vouga, P. *La Tène.* Monographie de la station. Leipzig, 1923.
Zeuss, C. *Die Deutschen und ihre Nachbarstämme.* (Reprint.) Heidelberg, 1925.
Zippel, G. *Die römische Herrschaft in Illyrien.* Leipzig, 1877.

CHAPTERS III, VI, XXII, XXIII

THE HELLENISTIC KINGDOMS, GREECE AND MACEDON, THE STRUGGLE OF EGYPT AGAINST MACEDON AND SYRIA, THE GREEK LEAGUES AND MACEDONIA

I. Ancient Sources

1. Contemporary with some part of the period

(*a*) *Official documents.*

Letters and rescripts of Lysimachus, *O.G.I.S.* 12, 13; Seleucus I, *ib.* 214; Antiochus I or II, *ib.* 223, 242; Antiochus II, *ib.* 224, 225; Seleucus II, *ib.* 227; Eumenes I, *ib.* 266; Ptolemy II, Rehm, *Milet* 1, no. 139; Ptolemy III, *I.G.* xii, iii, 327; Demetrius II, Ditt.³ 459; Philip V, *ib.* 543.

The Adulis inscription of Ptolemy III, *O.G.I.S.* 54.

Dedications of Attalus I, *O.G.I.S.* 271 to 279; Antigonus Gonatas, *I.G.* xi, iv, 1095, 1096; Antigonus Doson, *ib.* 1097 =Ditt.³ 518; Arsinoe II, *I.G.* xii, viii, 227; Ptolemy II, *ib.* 228, cf. *B.C.H.* xlix, 1925, p. 244.

The Gurob papyrus, *P. Petr.* ii, 45 + iii, 144 (in Mitteis and Wilcken, ii, B 7, below; see W. Crönert in *Raccolta Lumbroso*, Milan, 1925, p. 441)[1].

Decrees of the Greek cities and Leagues, accounts and dedications (see 3, below).

Coins (see 4, below).

Egyptian priestly decrees: the Pithom and Mendes steles (G. Steindorff, *Urkunden des aegyptischen Altertums*, vol. ii, nos. 20 and 13); the Canopus decree, *O.G.I.S.* 56; the trilingual stele relating to Raphia (see ii, B 7, below).

Asoka's Rock Edict no. 13 (*Corpus Inscr. Indicarum*, i, 48, Oxford, for Government of India, 1925).

(*b*) *Literary texts*[2].

Timaeus, *F.H.G.* i, 227, 228; Phylarchus, *ib.* pp. 334–7, 339, 341, 343, 345–53, and *ap.* Athen. 583 A *sq.*; Hieronymus of Cardia, *F.H.G.* ii, 453, 455; Duris, *ib.* p. 476; Demochares, *ib.* p. 419; Craterus, *ib.* p. 622; Ctesibius, *ib.* p. 631; Euphantus, *F.H.G.* iii, 19; Sphaerus, *ib.* p. 20; Aratus of Sicyon, *ib.* pp. 21 *sqq.*; Deinias, *ib.* p. 26; Callixenus, *ib.* pp. 55 *sqq.*; Ptolemaeus of Megalopolis, *ib.* pp. 66 *sq.*; Hermippus, *ib.* pp. 44, 48; Satyrus, *ib.* p. 164 *sq.*; Antigonus of Carystus *ap.* Athen. 419 E *sqq.*

Marmor Parium, ed. F. Jacoby, Berlin, 1904.

Epicurus' letters: H. Usener, *Epicurea*, frs. 101, 102, 139, 148–51, 194, Leipzig, 1887; Pap. Herculan. 1418, col. xxxª (xxª) (A. Vogliano, *Riv. fil.* liv, 1926, pp. 322 *sqq.*, lv, 1927, p. 501).

Teles: περὶ αὐταρκείας, περὶ φύγης, περὶ πενίας, περὶ ἀπαθείας.

P. Cairo Zen. 59019, 59242, 59251 (C. C. Edgar, *Zenon Papyri*, Cairo, 1925, 1926); P. Edgar, 63 (*Ann. Serv.* xx, 1920, p. 201).

Apollonius' letter of 21 Sept. 254 (H. I. Bell, *Symbolae Osloenses*, fasc. v, 1927, p. 1).

Letter of Diocles (P. Collart and P. Jouguet, *Raccolta Lumbroso*, p. 131).

P. Frankfurt 7 (H. Lewald, *Heidelberg S.B.* 1920, Abh. 14).

Theocritus, xvii (with scholia).

---

[1] For list of Papyri collections see the Bibliography to vol. iv.

[2] The fragments of certain of the historians here mentioned are also to be found in the already published volumes of F. Jacoby's *Fragmente der griechischen Historiker*.

Callimachus: *Hymn to Delos* (with scholia); *Coma Berenices* (*i.e.* Catullus, 66); *Death of Arsinoe*; *Victory of Sosibius* (?); epigram 37.

Lycophron, fragments of *Menedemos* (Nauck, *Tragicorum Graecorum fragmenta*, ed. 2, Leipzig, 1889, pp. 817, 818).

Poseidippus, Epigrams 1–3 (P. M. Schott, *Posidippi Epigrammata*, Berlin, 1905).

Hiller v. Gaertringen, Fr., *Historische griechische Epigramme* nos. 87–104, Bonn, 1926.

Anyte, *Anthologia Pal.* vii, 492.

Leonidas of Tarentum, *ib.* vi, 130; ix, 25.

Damagetus, *ib.* vi, 217.

Alexis, frs. 111, 244 (Th. Kock, *Comicorum Atticorum fragmenta*, ii, 336, 386, Leipzig, 1880).

Phoinikides, fr. 1 (*ib.* iii, 333).

Demetrius Comicus, fr. 1 (*ib.* iii, 357).

Cercidas, *Meliambi*, fr. 4 (J. U. Powell, *Collectanea Alexandrina*, pp. 203 *sqq.*, Oxford, 1925).

Hermocles, *Ithyphallus* (*ib.* p. 173).

Elegiac fragment on the Gallic invasion (*ib.* p. 131).

A Babylonian chronicle concerning Antiochus I in 276–274 (S. Smith, *Babylonian Historical Texts*, London, 1924).

Babylonian tablet referring to Laodice and her sons (C. F. Lehmann-Haupt, *Zeitschr. für Assyriologie*, vii, 330).

(*c*) *Historical monuments.*

Attalus' monument of victory at Pergamum. Antigonus' portico and the building called 'des Taureaux' at Delos. The Aetolian trophy at Delphi. The Victory of Samothrace (?). Many statue bases, etc. (See ii, B 8, below.)

(*d*) *Portraiture.*

The frescoes of the Villa Boscoreale may reproduce contemporary work. Otherwise portraiture depends on the coins; the numerous extant portrait-statues are generally of doubtful attribution.

2. Secondary[1]

Plutarch, *Lives* of Demetrius, Pyrrhus, Aratus, Agis, Cleomenes, Philopoemen; also Pelopidas 2.

—— *Moralia*: 11 A, 119 CD, 126 E, *182* C *7* and *8*, *182* F *17*, *183* B *2* to *183* E, 184 A and C, 216 D, *219* A 9, 240 B, *250* F to *253* F, 330 E, *360* C, 458 A, 475 C, 486 A, 489 AB, *504* A, 508 C, 508 D–F, 511 A, 530 C, 531 EF, 534 C, 545 B, 555 B, 561 C, 562 F, 633 B, 676 D, *736* F, 754 B, 830 C, 972 C.

Polybius, i, 6, 5; ii, 37 to end; iv, i–v, 105; ix, 28, 29, 34; x, 22; fr. 73 (154).

Diodorus, xxi frs. 1, 2, 7, 9, 11–15, 19, 20; xxii, 3–5, 9, 11, 12; xxv, 18; xxvi, 7–9; xxxi, 19 (5).

Justin, xv, 4, 23 *sqq.*, xvi, xvii, xxiv–xxviii, xxix, 1, xxx, 1, and Trogus' *Prologues* to these books.

Strabo, iv, 187; vii, 316, 326; viii, 376, *385*; ix, *436*; xi, 515; xii, 544, 563, 565–7; xiii, 593, 597, 604, *623–4*; xiv, 640, 644, 646, *652–3*, 666, 669; xvi, 738, 749–50, *754*.

Livy, xxxii, 5, 9 and 22, 10; xxxv, 26, 5; xxxviii, 16.

Appian, *Prooimion* 10, *Syriaca* 57–66, *Illyrica* 7.

---

[1] In this section and the next, where a number of references not in historical order are given to some writer or collection of inscriptions, those most important for these chapters are in italic figures, e.g. *182* C *7* and *8*.

Memnon, *F.H.G.* III, pp. 529–38; Porphyrius, *ib.* pp. 695–711, 716–19, 725–6; Agatharchides, *ib.* pp. 192, 194, 196 *sq.*; Aristodemus, *ib.* pp. 310 *sq.*; Heracleides Lembos, *ib.* pp. 168, 171; Baton, *F.H.G.* IV, p. 350; Carystius, *ib.* p. 358; Hegesander, *ib.* pp. 415–16, 418, 421; Pythermus, *ib.* p. 488; Heracleides Criticus (*sub nom.* Dicaearchus), *F.H.G.* II, p. 263; Poseidonius, *ap.* Athen. 234 B = Jacoby, II A, p. 255; Moschion, *ap.* Athen. 209 E.

Pausanias, I, 1, *3–13*, 16, 25, 26, 29 (1); II, *8*, 9, 21; III, *6*; IV, 29, 35; V, 5; VII, 3, 5, 7; VIII, 8, *10*, 27, 30, 32, 35, 49; IX, 7; X, 15–16, *18–23*.

Aelian, *V.H.* II, *20*, 41; III, 5; IV, 1; VII, 14; IX, 9, 26; XIV, 41, 43.

Polyaenus, II, 28, 29; III, 7, 16; IV, 6 (nos. 1, 3, 17–18, 20), 7, 9, 12, 14–17, 20; VI, 5–7; VII, 25, 35; VIII, 49, 52, 57, 68.

Frontinus, I, 5, 11; II, 5, 10; III, 2, *11*; 3, 7; 6, 7.

Pliny, *Hist. Nat.* II, *162*; IV, 10; VI, 31, 49, 58; VII, 53, 208; VIII, 176; XXXIV, *148*; XXXVI, 68, 83; XXXVII, *108*.

Lucian, *Macrobii*, 216; *Pro lapsu in salutando*, 734; *Zeuxis*, 846 *sqq.*

Fragment of (?) Phlegon, *Chronica* (A. S. Hunt, *P. Oxyr.* XVII, 1927, no. 2082).

Suidas, *s.v.* Antigonus, Aratus, Βασιλεία, Euphorion, Galatai, Philemon, Philochorus, Simonides Magnes.

Stobaeus, *Florilegium*, VII, 20; XLIX, 20; LIV, 46.

Stephanus, *s.v.* Ἄγκυρα, Antigoneia, Arsinoe, Demetrias, Ephesus, Pella, Phila, Philadelphia, Ptolemais, Stratonicea.

Pollux, I, 82.

Sextus Empiricus, *Adversus Grammaticos*, 293, 662.

Malalas, *Chronographia*, VIII, cols. 308–20 = *F.H.G.* IV, pp. 468 *sqq.*

Diogenes Laertius, *Lives* of Menedemus, Arcesilaus, Bion, Lycon, Demetrius of Phalerum, Zeno, Cleanthes, Timon.

Stoic literature: H. v. Arnim, *Stoicorum veterum fragmenta*, I, nos. 1–44 (life of Zeno), 435–62 (Persaeus), 620–30 (Sphaerus), Leipzig, 1905.

Philodemus, περὶ τῶν φιλοσόφων, four historical fragments: *Apollodor's Chronik*, ed. Jacoby, Berlin, 1902, pp. 363, 375; A. Mayer, *Phil.* LXXI, 1912, p. 226. Usener, *Epicurea*, p. 133, fr. 101.

Lives of Aratus of Soli, nos. 3, 4, 5 (E. Maass, *Commentariorum in Aratum reliquiae*, Berlin, 1898).

Ptolemy's Canon of Reigns.

Eusebius, *Chronica*, ed. A. Schoene, *Eusebi Chronicorum libri duo*, Berlin, 1875 and 1876: vol. I (book I from the Armenian version, in Latin, with parallel Greek extracts, here largely Porphyry), cols. 231–53, 263–4, App. I A, cols. 13–16, I B, cols. 27–9, III, p. 56, IV, cols. 90–92, VI (*Excerpta Latina Barbari*), pp. 221–3; vol. II (book 2, Jerome's Latin version parallel with the Armenian and Greek versions, the latter here largely from Syncellus), pp. 118–22.

Hieronymus (Jerome); beside the foregoing, see J. K. Fotheringham, *Eusebii Pamphili Chronici Canones*, 1923, pp. 209–16.

Paean Delphicus, I (Anonymous) and II (Limenius); Powell, *Collectanea Alexandrina*, pp. 141 *sqq.*

Fragment of a hymn to Arsinoe-Aphrodite, *ib.* p. 82.

Daniel xi, with Jerome's commentary.

3 Maccabees i.

Josephus, *Antiq.* XII, 125.

3. References for the Greek inscriptions

I.G. II², *640–845*, 861, 1132, 1217, 1225, 1270, 1272, *1280*, 1281, 1285–7, *1299*, 1303. Add *I.G.* II, 3, nos. 1291, 1367–9, 1371, together with accounts and dedications for this period in *I.G.* II, 2 and 3, and supplements to these in *I.G.* II, 5.

—— IV, *427, 750, IIII*, 1419.

—— v, i, *458*, 1122; ii, 299, 300, *344, 419*, 534.

—— VII, *1*, 5, 6, 188, 279, 297–8, 507, 3166.

—— IX, i, *97, 98*; ii, 3 (?), 62, *517*.

—— XI, ii. The Delian inventories in this volume are now continued in *Inscriptions de Délos, Comptes des Hiéropes, Nos.* 290–371, by F. Durrbach, Paris, 1926. The list of offerings runs on throughout. For the dated vase-foundations the most important are nos. 287, 298, 313, 320, 366. Historical notices: 114, 116, 146 a l. 70, 290 l. 130.

—— XI, iv, *514, 542, 559, 563*, 566, 631, *649*, 664–6, 680, 694, *1036–8, 1042–3, 1052–3, 1073, 1095–8, 1102, 1105–10, 1124–30*, 1215.

—— XII, i, 6, 25; ii, *15*, 498, *513*; iii, 204, *320, 327–8, 464–7*; v, 7, *264–6, 444, 481* (see p. 317), 526–7, *532–3*, 570 (see p. 331), *1004, 1008, 1061, 1065–6, 1069*; vii, 13, *221–3, 263–4, 506*; viii, *150, 156, 227–8*; ix, *207*, 212.

S.E.G. I, 74, 187, 360, *363–4, 366*; II, *9*, 10, *257–8*, 261, 263, 339, *512*; III, 89, *93–4*, 98, *100, 122–3*.

Ditt.³ 361–534, 543.

O.G.I.S. 10–80, 211–30, 233, 245–6, 264–80, 312, 335, 724–7, 730, 744–5, 748, 765, 773.

S.G.D.I. 3611 (=*B.M.I.* II, 247), 5043, 5104 a, and under the several countries.

Michel, *Recueil*, 1223, and generally under the several countries.

B.M.I. IV, ii, 1042.

Four decrees, in Diogenes Laertius, II, 142 and VII, 10, and [Plutarch], *Decem Oratorum vitae*, 850 F–851 F.

Delphi. This great mass of inscriptions, part of which appeared in *S.G.D.I.* II, is now being collected in *Fouilles de Delphes*. Most of them only affect these chapters through their bearing on the Delphic chronology (see II, C 2, below). Probably all yet published which furnish historical material for this period will be found in Ditt.³, Pomtow's *Delphische Neufunde* (see II, C 2), and the relevant articles in this bibliography.

The following are also material:

Blinkenberg, C. *Die Lindische Tempel-chronik*, C. XXXVII, XL, XLII. Bonn, 1915.

Breccia, E. *Antiquités découvertes à Maamourah*. Bull. Soc. Arch. d'Alexandrie, VIII, 1905, p. 110, no. 2.

De Sanctis, G. *Note di epigrafia ellenistica*, II. Atti Acc. Torino, XLIX, 1913–14, p. 684.

Doublet, G. *Inscriptions de Crète*. B.C.H. XIII, 1889, p. 47, no. 1 (see *A.J.A.* XI, 1896, p. 583, no. 67, and *S.E.G.* I, 416).

Durrbach, F. *Choix d'Inscriptions de Délos*. Paris, 1921. I, 1, nos. 14–57.

Ferri, S. *Alcune Iscrizioni di Cirene*. Berlin, 1926. No. 1.

Goldman, H. *Inscriptions from Halae*. A.J.A. XIX, 1915, p. 445, no. 3.

Graindor, P. *Inscriptions grecques*. Rev. Arch. VI, 1917, no. 30.

Halbherr, F. *Epigraphical researches in Gortyna*. A.J.A. I, 1897, p. 188, no. 17.

Heberdey, R. *Forschungen in Ephesos*. Vienna, 1912. II, nos. 1, 3, 20. (On 1 see M. Holleaux, *Rev. E.G.* XXIX, 1916, p. 29, and on 20 Ch. Picard, *Rev. Phil.* XXXVII, 1913, p. 86.)

Hiller v. Gaertringen, Fr. *Inschriften von Priene*, nos. 11, 14–18, 24, 37. Berlin, 1906.

Homolle, Th. *Inscriptions de Delphes: Pisis de Thespies.* B.C.H. xxiv, 1900, p. 170.

Kalinka, E. *Tituli Lyciae*, ii (*Tituli Asiae Minoris*, ii, 1). Vienna, 1922. Nos. 1, 158–61, 262.

Keil, J. *Ephesische Bürgerrechts- und Proxenie-dekrete.* Jahreshefte, xvi, 1913, p. 237, no. iii c (see p. 243).

Keil, J. and v. Premerstein, A. *Bericht über eine zweite Reise in Lydien.* Denkschriften Wien. Ak. Wiss. liv, 1911, Abh. ii, p. 14, no. 19.

Kern, O. *Die Inschriften von Magnesia am Maeander.* Berlin, 1900. Nos. 36, 44, 46, 53.

Picard, Ch. *Fouilles de Thasos* (1914 *et* 1920). B.C.H. xlv, 1921, p. 153, no. 6. (See E. Ziebarth in Bursian, vol. 213, 1927, p. 32.)

Plassart, A. and Blum, G. *Inscriptions d'Orchomène d'Arcadie.* B.C.H. xxxviii, 1914, pp. 447, 451, 454, 472 *sqq.*

Soteriades, G. Ἀνασκαφαὶ ἐν Θέρμῳ. Ἀρχ. Ἐφ. 1905, p. 91, nos. 1, 9, 10.

Vollgraff, G. *Novae Inscriptiones Argivae.* Mnemosyne, xliii, 1915, p. 365 A and B; xliv, 1916, p. 219.

Wiegand, Th. *Siebenter Bericht über Milet und Didyma.* Berlin, 1911. Nos. 68, 69.
—— *Milet*, i, iii. Das Delphinion in Milet. The inscriptions, by A. Rehm, nos. 43, 99, 123–4, 138–9, 141, 158. Berlin, 1914.
—— *Milet*, i, vii. Der Südmarkt. The inscriptions, by A. Rehm, nos. 193 a, 194. Berlin, 1924.

Wilamowitz-Moellendorff, U. von. *Nordionische Steine.* Berl. Abh. 1909, ii, p. 18, no. 5.

Wilhelm, A. *Beiträge zur griechischen Inschriftenkunde.* Vienna, 1909. Nos. 43, 62, 64, 95.
—— *Neue Beiträge zur griechischen Inschriftenkunde.* Vienna 1911–15. i, nos. 4, 7; iii, no. 21; iv, p. 60, no. 2.
—— *Zu griechischen Inschriften und Papyri.* Sonderabdruck, Wien. Anz. 1922, p. 7, no. ii, 2; p. 28, no. 3.
—— *Attische Urkunden*, iii, x–xvi. Wien S.B. vol. ccii, 1925, Abh. v.

Zolotas, G. I. Ἐπιγραφαὶ Χίου ἀνεκδοτοί. Ἀθηνᾶ, 1908, p. 195, no. 6.

The unique decree of Pella (Tarn, *Antigonos Gonatas*, p. 184) is not yet published. The unpublished treaty between Pyrrhus and Acarnania (E. Ziebarth in Bursian, vol. clxxxix, 1921, p. 9) is apparently lost.

4. Coins

(See generally Head, H.N.; and Hill, G. F., *Historical Greek Coins*, 1906)

(a) Lysimachus.

Imhoof-Blumer, F. *Lysimachos*, in Corolla Numismatica. Oxford, 1906.
—— *Eurydikeia.* Jahreshefte, viii, 1905, p. 229.

Milne, J. G. *The autonomous coinage of Smyrna.* Num. Chr. 1923, p. 1.

Müller, L. *Die Münzen des thrakischen Königs Lysimachos.* Copenhagen, 1858.

Newell, E. T. *The Alexandrine coinage of Sinope.* A.J. Num. lii, 1918, p. 117.

(b) Antigonids.

Gaebler, H. *Zur Münzkunde Makedoniens.* Z.N. xx, 1897, p. 169. (Philip V.)

Newell, E. T. *Tyrus rediviva.* New York, 1923. (Demetrius I.)
—— *The coinages of Demetrius Poliorcetes.* London, 1927.

Pick, B. and Gaebler, H. *Die antiken Münzen Nordgriechenlands.* Berlin, 1898 and 1906. (Philip V.)

Seltman, C. T. *A synopsis of the coins of Antigonus I and Demetrius Poliorcetes.* Num. Chr. 1909, p. 264.

Six, J. P. *Monnaies grecques, inédites et incertaines.* Num. Chr. 1894, p. 297. (Nos. xviii, Demetrius II, and xix, Alexander of Corinth.)

Studniczka, Fr. *Imagines Illustrium.* J.D.A.I. xxxviii–xxxix, 1923–4, p. 57. (Gonatas and/or Doson.)

Svoronos, J. N. Ἠπειρωτῶν...νομίσματα κοπέντα ἐν Μακεδονίᾳ ἐπὶ Πύρρου. J.I.d'A.N. xiii, 1911, p. 121.

(c) *Ptolemies.*

Fritze, H. von. *Die autonomen Münzen von Abdera.* Nomisma, iii, 1909, p. 28.

Kahrstedt, U. *Frauen auf antiken Münzen.* Klio, x, 1910, p. 261.

Koch, W. *Die ersten Ptolemäerrinnen nach ihren Münzen.* Z.N. xxxiv, 1924, p. 67.

Poole, R. S. *The Ptolemies, Kings of Egypt.* British Museum Catalogue. 1883.

Robinson, E. S. G. *Cyrenaica.* British Museum Catalogue. 1927.

Schubart, W. *Die ptolemäische Reichsmünze in den auswärtigen Besitzungen unter Philadelphos.* Z.N. xxxiii, 1921, p. 68.

Svoronos, J. N. Τὰ νομίσματα τοῦ Κράτους τῶν Πτολεμαίων. Athens, 1904–8.

(d) *Seleucids.*

Babelon, E. *Les rois de Syrie, d'Arménie, et de Commagène.* (Catalogue des monnaies de la Bibliothèque Nationale.) 1890.

Gardner, P. *The Seleucid kings of Syria.* British Museum Catalogue. 1878.

Imhoof-Blumer, F. *Zur Münzkunde der Seleukiden.* Num. Z. 1913, p. 171.

Macdonald, G. *Early Seleucid portraits.* J.H.S. xxiii, 1903, p. 92; xxvii, 1907, p. 145.

Newell, E. T. *The Seleucid Mint of Antioch.* New York, 1918.

(e) *The Greek Leagues.*

Caspari, M. O. B. *A survey of Greek federal coinage.* J.H.S. xxxvii, 1917, p. 168.

Clerk, M. G. *Catalogue of the coins of the Achaean League.* London, 1895.

Gardner, P. *Catalogue of the Greek coins in the British Museum.* Thessaly to Aetolia, 1883, and Peloponnese, 1887.

Hill, G. F. In *Num. Chr.* 1921, p. 12: federal coin of Psophis.

Imhoof-Blumer, F. *Monnaies grecques.* Paris and Leipzig, 1883.

Wace, A. J. B. *A hoard of Hellenistic coins.* B.S.A. xiv, 1907–8, p. 149. (Cleomenes.)

Warren, J. L. *An essay on Greek federal coinage.* London, 1883.

Weil, R. *Das Münzwesen des achäischen Bundes.* Z.N. ix, 1882, p. 199.

II. Modern Literature[1]

A. *On the sources*

The general works of Bury, Christ-Schmid, Croiset, Susemihl, Wachsmuth, Wilamowitz. (See Bibliography to chap. viii.)

Hense, O. *Teletis reliquiae* (with prolegomena). 2nd ed. Tübingen, 1909.

Maass, E. *Aratea.* (Vol. xii of Kiessling and Wilamowitz, Philologische Untersuchungen.) Berlin, 1892.

Schulz, F. F. *Quibus ex fontibus fluxerint Agidis, Cleomenis, Arati vitae Plutarcheae.* Berlin, 1886.

---

[1] Articles dealing with single inscriptions which can be found in Dittenberger or *I.G.* are as a rule not given here.

Stagl, R. *Plutarch in Verhältnis zu seiner Quelle Polybios in der Vita des Aratos.*
Vienna, 1904.
Wilamowitz-Moellendorff, U. von. *Antigonos von Karystos.* (Vol. IV of his and
Kiessling's Philologische Untersuchungen.) Berlin, 1881.

B. *Historical*

(For general histories see the General Bibliography)

1. Antigonids

Arvanitopoullos, A. S. Δημητριὰς-Παγασαί. Ἀρχ. Ἐφ. 1914, p. 264.
Baege, W. *De Macedonum sacris.* Halle, 1913.
Beloch, K. J. *Demetrias.* Klio, XI, 1911, p. 442.
Bettingen, W. *König Antigonos Doson von Makedonien.* Weida i. Th. 1912.
Costanzi, V. Δημητριακὸς πόλεμος in Beloch's Saggi di storia antica. Rome, 1910.
—— *Studi di storia Macedonica sino a Filippo.* Annali Univ. Toscane, XXXIII, 1915.
Dareste, R., and others. *Recueil des Inscriptions juridiques grecques,* II, p. 116. Paris,
1898–1905.
De Sanctis, G. *La ribellione d'Alessandro, figlio di Cratero.* Klio, IX, 1909, p. 1.
Delamarre, J. *L'influence macédonienne dans les Cyclades au IIIᵉ siècle av. J.-C.*
Rev. Phil. XXVI, 1902, p. 301.
Gianopoullos, N. Παγασαὶ-Δημητριάς. Ἀρχ. Ἐφ. 1914, p. 90; 1915, p. 83.
Glotz, G. *L'histoire de Délos d'après les prix d'un denrée.* Rev. E.G. XXIX, 1916,
p. 281.
Holleaux, M. *Remarques sur une inscription de Thessalonique.* Rev. E.G. X, 1897,
p. 446.
—— *Sur un passage de la vie d'Aratos par Plutarque.* Hermes, XLI, 1906, p. 475.
—— *Dédicace d'un monument commémoratif de la bataille de Sellasia.* B.C.H.
XXXI, 1907, p. 95.
Kolbe, W., reviewing Tarn, *Antigonos Gonatas.* G.G.A. 1916, p. 433.
Perdrizet, P. *Voyage dans la Macédoine première.* B.C.H. XVIII, 1894, p. 416 (see
B.C.H. XXI, p. 161).
*Robinson, E. S. G. *Quaestiones Cyrenaicae.* Num. Chr. 1915, p. 249.
Sokolow, Th. *Alexander Krateros' Sohn.* Klio, III, 1903, p. 119.
Studniczka, Fr. *Imagines Illustrium.* J.D.A.I. XXXVIII–XXXIX, 1923–4, p. 57. (The
Villa Boscoreale frescoes.)
*Tarn, W. W. *Antigonos Gonatas.* Oxford, 1913.
—— *Philip V and Phthia.* C.Q. XVIII, 1924, p. 17.
*Tillyard, H. J. W. and Wace, A. J. B. *The history of Demetrius the Fair.* B.S.A.
XI, 1904–5, p. 113.
Walek, T. B. *Drieje Upadku Monarchji Macedónskiej.* Cracow, 1924. (History
of the Antigonids from 228, in Polish, with a French summary.)
Wilamowitz-Moellendorff, U. von. *Antigonos von Karystos.* Berlin, 1881.
Wilhelm, A. *Königin Phthia.* B.P.W. 1912, p. 314.

2. Ptolemies

Bell, H. I. *Notes on early Ptolemaic Papyri.* Arch. Pap. VII, 1924, p. 17.
Bevan, E. R. *A history of Egypt under the Ptolemaic dynasty.* London, 1927.
Blum, G. *Princes hellénistiques, I: Ptolémée IV Philopator.* B.C.H. XXXIX, 1915, p. 17.
Bouché-Leclercq, A. *Histoire des Lagides.* Paris, 1903–7. Vols. I and IV.
De Sanctis, G. *La Magna Charta della Cirenaica.* Riv. fil. LIV, 1926, p. 145.
Fritze, M. *Die ersten Ptolemäer und Griechenland.* Halle, 1917.

* See below, p. 891 *n.*

Heichelheim, Fr. *Zum Verfassungsdiagramma von Kyrene.* Klio, xxi, 1927, p. 175.
Holleaux, M. *Décret du peuple de Délos en l'honneur de Sosibios d'Alexandrie.* Rev. E.A. xiv, 1912, p. 370.
Kolbe, W. *Die griechische Politik der ersten Ptolemäer.* Hermes, li, 1916, p. 50.
Perdrizet, P. *Le fragment de Satyros sur les dèmes d'Alexandrie.* Rev. E.A. xii, 1910, p. 234.
Prott, H. von. *Das ἐγκώμιον εἰς Πτολεμαῖον und die Zeitgeschichte.* Rh. Mus. liii, 1898, p. 460.
Reinach, Th. *La charte ptolémaïque de Cyrène.* Rev. Arch. xxvi, 1927, p. 1.

3. Seleucids

Bevan, E. R. *The house of Seleucus.* London, 1902.
Bouché-Leclerq, A. *Histoire des Séleucides.* Paris, 1913–4.
Corradi, G. *Di Seleuco e della questione della Celesiria.* Atti Acc. Torino, xlvi, 1910, p. 585.
—— *La fine del regno di Seleuco Nicatore.* Riv. fil. xliv, 1916, pp. 297, 409.
—— *L'Asia Minore e le isole dell' Egeo sotto i primi Seleucidi.* Riv. fil. xlviii, 1920, p. 161; l, 1922, p. 20.
Haussoullier, B. *Études sur l'histoire de Milet et de Didymeion.* 1902.
Holleaux, M. *Le décret des Milésiens en l'honneur d'Apamé.* Rev. E.G. xxxvi, 1923, p. 1.
Lehmann-Haupt, C. F., on *Seleucus' Macedonian kingdom.* Klio, v, 1905, p. 244; vii, 1907, p. 449; ix, 1909, p. 248.
Reuss, F., on the same. Rh. Mus. lxii, 1907, p. 595; Klio, ix, 1909, p. 76.

4. Lysimachus

Ghione, P. *Note sul regno di Lisimaco.* Atti Acc. Torino, xxxix, 1903–4, p. 619.
Hicks, E. L. *The Ephesian Gerousia.* B.M.I. iii, p. 74. Oxford, 1890.
Hünerwadel, W. *Forschungen zur Geschichte des Königs Lysimachos von Thrakien.* Zürich, 1900.
Keil, Br. Κόρου πεδίον. Rev. Phil. xxvi, 1902, p. 257.
Picard, Ch. *Éphèse et Claros.* Paris, 1922.
Possenti, G. B. *Il re Lisimaco di Tracia.* Turin, 1901.

5. ' Ptolemaeus son of Lysimachus '

De Groot, A. W. *Ptolemaios der Sohn.* Rh. Mus. lxxii, 1917–18, p. 446.
Holleaux, M. Πτολεμαῖος Λυσιμάχου. B.C.H. xxviii, 1904, p. 408.
—— *Ptolemaios Epigonos.* J.H.S. xli, 1921, p. 183.
Pridik, A. *Der Mitregent des Königs Ptolemaios II Philadelphos.* Acta et Commentationes Universitatis Dorpatensis, v, 1924.
Stern, E. von. *Ptolemaios 'der Sohn.'* Hermes, l, 1915, p. 427.
(These will give full references to the older literature.)

6. Attalids and dynasts

*Cardinali, G. *Il regno di Pergamo.* Turin, 1906.
*—— *La genealogia degli Attalidi.* Mem. della R. Acc. dell' Ist. di Bologna, vii, 1912–13, p. 177.
Ferrabino, A. *La guerra di Attalo I contra i Galati e Antioco Hierace.* Atti Acc. Torino, xlviii, 1912–13, p. 707.
Holleaux, M. Λυσίας Φιλομήλου. Rev. E.A. xvii, 1915, p. 237.
—— *Un nouveau document relatif aux premiers Attalides.* Rev. E.A. xx, 1918, p. 9.
Meyer, Ernst. *Zum Stammbaum der Attaliden.* Klio, xix, 1925, p. 462.

*Reinach, A. J. *Les mercenaires et les colonies militaires de Pergame.* Rev. Arch. xii, 1908, p. 174.
Wilhelm, A. *Kleinasiatische Dynasten* in Neue Beiträge zur griechischen Inschriftenkunde, i, p. 48. Vienna, 1911.

7. The wars of Egypt with Macedonia and Syria (see also B 1, above)

Cardinali, G. *Della terza guerra Siriaca e della guerra fraterna.* Riv. fil. xxxi, 1903, p. 431.
—— *Ancora intorno alla terza guerra Siriaca.* Riv. stor. ant. x, 1906, p. 501.
Corradi, G. *Nota sulla guerra tra Tolomeo Euergete e Seleuco Callinico.* Atti Acc. Torino, xl, 1905, p. 805.
Costanzi, V. *La battaglia di Andro.* Riv. fil. xxxvii, 1909, p. 516.
—— *Il dominio egiziano nelle Cicladi sotto Tolomeo Filopatore.* Klio, xi, 1911, p. 277.
Courby, F. *Note sur la date du Portique d'Antigone à Délos.* B.C.H. xxxviii, 1914, p. 296.
De Sanctis, G. *Contributi alla storia del impero Seleucideo.* Turin, 1912. (Reprinted from Atti Acc. Torino, vol. xlvii.)
—— *Per la storia di Mileto.* Atti Acc. Torino, xlix, 1913, p. 1220.
Durrbach, F. *Choix d'inscriptions de Délos* i (1). Paris, 1921.
Ferguson, W. S. *Egypt's loss of sea power.* J.H.S. xxx, 1910, p. 189.
Gauthier, H. and Sottas, H. *Un décret trilingue en l'honneur de Ptolémée IV.* Cairo, 1925.
Holleaux, M. *Remarques sur le papyrus de Gourob.* B.C.H. xxx, 1906, p. 330.
—— *L'anonyme du papyrus de Gourob.* Rev. E.A. xviii, 1916, p. 153.
*Kahrstedt, U. *Syrische Territorien in hellenistischer Zeit.* Berlin, 1926.
Koch, W. *Ein Ptolemaeer-krieg.* Stuttgart, 1923.
Lehmann-Haupt, C. F. *Die griechisch-römische Geschichtsschreibung im Lichte altorientalischer Quellen.* Festschrift d. Ak. Historikerklubs in Innsbruck, p. 69. Würzburg, 1923.
—— *Vom pyrrhischen und ersten syrischen zum chremonideischen Kriege.* Ἐπιτύμβιον H. Swoboda dargebracht, p. 142. Reichenberg, 1927.
Mahaffy, J. P. *The army of Ptolemy IV at Raphia.* Hermathena, x, 1899, p. 140.
Meyer, Ernst. *Die Grenzen der hellenistischen Staaten in Kleinasien.* Zurich-Leipzig, 1925.
Mitteis, A. and Wilcken, U. *Grundzüge und Chrestomathie der Papyruskunde I, ii, no.* 1. Leipzig-Berlin, 1912.
Pozzi, E. *Le battaglie di Cos e di Andro.* Turin, 1912.
Rehm, A., on no. 139 in Wiegand's *Milet,* i, iii. Berlin, 1914.
Roos, A. G. Λαοδίκειος πόλεμος. Mnem. li, 1923, p. 262.
Rostagni, A. *Poeti alessandrini.* App. vii: Il dominio tolemaico nella Ionia. Turin, 1916.
Schoch, P. *Kallikrates* 7c in P.W. Supp. Band, 1924.
Smith, S. *Babylonian Historical Texts.* London, 1924.
Spiegelberg, W. *Beiträge zur Erklärung des neuen dreisprachigen Priesterdekretes zu Ehren des Ptolemaios Philopator.* Bay. S.B. 1925, Abh. iv.
Tarn, W. W. *The battles of Cos and Andros.* J.H.S. xxix, 1909, p. 264.
—— *The dedicated ship of Antigonos Gonatas. ib.* xxx, 1910, p. 209.
—— *Nauarch and Nesiarch. ib.* xxxi, 1911, p. 251.
—— *The political standing of Delos. ib.* xliv, 1924, p. 141.
—— *The first Syrian war. ib.* xlvi, 1926, p. 155.
—— *Polybius and a literary commonplace.* C.Q. xx, 1926, p. 98. (Raphia.)

Wilamowitz-Moellendorff, U. von, reviewing Rehm's Delphinion inscriptions in *G.G.A.* 1914, p. 65.
—— *Der Feldzugsbericht des Ptolemaios Euergetes.* Hermes, XLIX, 1914, p. 447.

8. Historical Monuments

Bieńkowski, P. R. von. *Die Darstellungen der Gallier in der hellenistischen Kunst.* Vienna, 1908.
Bohn, R. *Altertümer von Pergamon.* Vol. II: Das Heiligtum der Athena Polias Nikephoros. Berlin, 1885.
Couchoud, P. and Svoronos, J. *Le monument dit ' des Taureaux' à Délos.* B.C.H. XLV, 1921, p. 270.
Dickins, G. *Hellenistic Sculpture.* 2nd ed. Oxford, 1920.
Hatzfeld, J. *Démétrius Poliorcète et la Victoire de Samothrace.* Rev. Arch. XV, 1910, p. 132.
Homolle, Th. and Holleaux, M. *Exploration archéologique de Délos,* V: Le portique d'Antigone, by F. Courby. Paris, 1912.
Pontremoli, E. and Collignon, M. *Pergame.* Paris, 1900.
Reinach, A. J. *Un monument Delphien. L'Étolie sur les trophées gaulois de Kallion.* J.I.d'A.N. XIII, 1911, p. 177.
Studniczka, Fr. *Imagines Illustrium.* J.D.A.I. XXXVIII–XXXIX, 1923-4, p. 125. (Victory of Samothrace.)
Tarn, W. W. *Le monument dit 'des Taureaux' à Délos: a note.* B.C.H. XLVI, 1922, p. 473.

9. The Gallic Invasion

Anderson, J. G. C. *Exploration in Galatia cis Halym.* Sect. xii. Galatian Civilisation. J.H.S. XIX, 1899, p. 312.
Couissin, P. *Les armes gauloises sur les monuments grecs, étrusques et romains.* Rev. Arch. XXV, 1927, pp. 138, 301; XXVI, 1927, p. 43.
Garofalo, P. *Observations sur les Galates ou Celtes d'Orient.* Rev. E.G. XIII, 1900, p. 450.
Jullian, C. *Histoire de la Gaule.* Paris, 1908. Vol. I.
Pottier, E. and Reinach, S. *Fouilles dans la nécropole de Myrina; éléphant foulant aux pieds un Galate.* B.C.H. IX, 1885, p. 485.
Reinach, A. J. *Documents nouveaux pour l'histoire des Gaulois d'Orient.* Rev. Celtique, 1909, p. 47.
—— *Les Gaulois en Égypte.* Rev. E.A. XIII, 1911, p. 33.
—— *Nikératos d'Athènes.* Mélanges Holleaux. 1913. p. 233.
—— *La mort de Brennus.* Monuments Piot, XXI, 1913, p. 173.
Reinach, S. *L'attaque de Delphes par les Gaulois.* C.R. Ac. Inscr. 1904, p. 158.
Segre, M. *La più antica tradizione sull' invasione Gallica in Macedonia e in Grecia* (280–79 *a. Cr.*). Historia, I, 1927, 4, p. 18.
Soteriades, G. Ἡ τῶν Γαλατῶν ἐπὶ τὴν Αἰτωλίαν ἔφοδος τὸ 279 πρὸ Χρ. καὶ ἡ πόλις Κάλλιον. B.C.H. XXXI, 1907, p. 177.
Stähelin, F. *Geschichte der kleinasiatischen Galater.* 2nd ed. Leipzig, 1907.
And articles in *P.W.* 1910 on Galli (Niese) and Galatia (two) (Bürchner, with full bibliography, and Brandis).

10. The Leagues

(a) Generally.
Busolt, G. *Griechische Staatskunde,* part II. 3rd ed. by Swoboda. Munich, 1926.
Fougères, G. *Koinon* (κοινόν) in D.S.
Francotte, H. *La polis grecque.* Paderborn, 1907.

Freeman, E. A. *History of Federal Government in Greece and Italy.* (2nd ed., with appendices, by J. B. Bury.) London, 1893.

Keil, Br. *Griechische Staatsaltertümer* in Gercke-Norden, Einleitung in die Altertumswissenschaft, III. 2nd ed. Leipzig, 1912.

Kornemann, E. Κοινόν in P.W. Suppl. 1924.

Lipsius, J. *Beiträge zur Geschichte griechischen Bundesverfassungen.* Berichte sächs. Ges. d. Wiss. L, 1898, p. 145.

Schönfelder, W. *Die städtischen und Bundesbeamten des griechischen Festlandes.* Weida i. Th. 1917.

Swoboda, H. *Die wichtigsten griechischen Bundesstaaten.* In Hermann's Lehrbuch, XVI, part 3 (Staatsaltertümer). Tübingen, 1913.

—— *Zwei Kapitel aus dem griechischen Bundesrechts.* Wien S.B., CXCIX, 1924, Abh. 2.

Szanto, E. *Das griechische Bürgerrecht.* Freiburg i. Br. 1896.

(b) The Aetolian League.

Holleaux, M. *Sur les assemblées ordinaires de la Ligue aitolienne.* B.C.H. XXIX, 1905, p. 362. (See Klio, VII, p. 294.)

Plassart, A. *Remarques sur divers décrets de la Ligue étolienne récemment publiés.* B.C.H. XXXIX, 1915, p. 127.

Roussel, P. *Les épimélètes aitoliens à Delphes.* B.C.H. L, 1926, p. 124.

Salvetti, C. *Ricerche storiche intorno alla lega etolica.* In Beloch's Studi di storia antica, II. Rome, 1892.

Soteriades, G. Ἀνασκαφαὶ ἐν Θέρμῳ. Ἀρχ. Ἐφ. 1900, p. 161.

Stählin, Fr. *Die Phthiotis und die Friede zwischen Philippos V und die Aetolern.* Phil. LXXVII, 1921, p. 199.

Swoboda, H. *Studien zu den griechischen Bunden.* Klio, XI, 1911, p. 450.

—— *Die ätolische Komenverfassung.* Wien St. XXXIV, 1912, p. 37.

Wilhelm, A. Δογμὰ Αἰτωλῶν ὑπὲρ Μυτιληναίων. Ἀρχ. Ἐφ. 1914, p. 84.

(c) The Achaean League.

Caspari, M. O. B. *The Parliament of the Achaean League.* Eng. Hist. Rev. XXIX, 1914, p. 209.

De Sanctis, G. *Le assemblee federali degli Achei.* Riv. fil. XXXVI, 1908, p. 252.

Ferrabino, A. *Il problema della unità nazionale nella Grecia, I. Arato di Sicione e l' idea federale.* Florence, 1921.

Klatt, M. *Chronologische Beiträge zu Geschichte des achäischen Bundes.* Berlin, 1883.

Niccolini, G. *La confederazione achea.* Pavia, 1914.

Niese, B. *Beiträge zur Geschichte und Chronologie des Hellenismus,* I and II. Hermes, XXXV, 1900, p. 53.

Swoboda, H. *Studien zu den griechischen Bunden.* Klio, XII, 1912, p. 17.

(d) Other Leagues.

Caspari, M. O. B. *The Ionian Confederacy.* J.H.S. XXXV, 1915, p. 173.

Holleaux, M. *Un décret du Koinon des villes de Troade.* Rev. E.G. IX, 1896, p. 359.

—— *Dédicaces nouvelles de la confédération Boeotienne.* B.C.H. XIII, 1889, p. 1.

—— *Note sur un décret d'Érétrie.* Rev. E.G. X, 1897, p. 157. (Boeotia.)

Kazarow, G. *De foederis Phocensium institutis.* Leipzig, 1899.

Larsen, J. A. O. *Representative Government in the Panhellenic Leagues.* II. C.P. XXI, 1926, p. 52.

Lenschau, Th. *De rebus Prienensium.* Leipziger Studien, XII, 1890, p. 111. (Ionian League.)

Monceaux, P. *Fastes éponymiques de la Ligue thessalienne,* chapter ii. Rev. Arch. XII, 1888, p. 198.

Swoboda, H. *Zur Geschichte von Akarnanien*. Klio, x, 1910, p. 397.
Tarn, W. W. *The Arcadian League and Aristodemos*. C.R. xxxix, 1925, p. 104.

11. Athens

Chapouthier, F. *Note sur un décret inédit de Rhamnounthe*. B.C.H. xlviii, 1924, p. 264.
De Sanctis, G. *Contributi alla storia Ateniense della guerra Lamiaca alla guerra Chremonidea*. In Beloch's Studi di storia antica, ii, p. 1. Rome, 1893.
—— *Revisioni V: Il dominio macedonico nel Pireo*. Riv. fil. lv, 1927, p. 491.
—— *Lacare*. *ib*. lvi, 1928, p. 53.
Ferguson, W. S. *Athenian politics in the early third century*. Klio, v, 1905, p. 155.
—— *Researches in Athenian and Delian documents*. Klio, viii, 1908, p. 338; ix, 1909, p. 304.
—— *Hellenistic Athens*. London, 1911.
Francotte, H. *Les finances des cités grecques*. Liége-Paris, 1909.
Haussoullier, B. *Demos* in D.S.
Johnson, A. C. *Studies in the financial administration of Athens*. A. J. Ph. xxxvi, 1915, p. 424.
Lehmann-Haupt, C. F. *Zur attischen Politik vor dem chremonideischen Kriege*. Klio, v, 1905, p. 375.
Otto, W., reviewing Ferguson, *Hellenistic Athens*. G.G.A. 1914, p. 633.

12. Sparta

(a) Historical.

Bux, E. *Zwei sozialistische Novellen bei Plutarch*. Klio, xix, 1925, p. 413.
De Sanctis, G. *Questioni politiche e riformi sociali*. Riv. Internaz. di scienze sociali, iv, 1894, pp. 50 and 229.
Kazarow, G. *Zur Geschichte der sozialen Revolution in Sparta*. Klio, vii, 1907, p. 45.
Niccolini, G. *Questioni intorno al re di Sparta Cleomene III*. Beloch's Saggi di storia antica, p. 1. Rome, 1910.
Pöhlmann, R. von. *Geschichte der sozialen Frage und des Sozialismus in der antiken Welt*. 3rd ed. by Fr. Oertel. Munich, 1925.
Stern, E. von. *Kleomenes III und Archidamos*. Hermes, l, 1915, p. 554.
Tarn, W. W. *The social question in the third century*. In The Hellenistic Age, by J. B. Bury and others. Cambridge, 1923.
Wace, A. J. B. *Excavations at Sparta: the city wall*. B.S.A. xii, 1905–6, p. 284.

(b) The battle of Sellasia.

Delbrück, H. *Geschichte der Kriegskunst*, i. 3rd ed. Berlin, 1920.
Ferrabino, A. *La battaglia di Sellasia*. Atti Acc. Torino, liv, 1918–19, pp. 751, 811.
Kahrstedt, U. *Nachlese auf griechischen Schlachtfeldern*. Hermes, xlviii, 1913, p. 286.
Kromayer, J. *Antike Schlachtfelder*. Berlin, 1903. Vol. i, p. 199.
—— *Sellasia*. B.C.H. xxxiv, 1910, p. 508.
Lammert, E. *Die neuesten Forschungen auf antiken Schlachtfeldern in Griechenland*. III. N.J. Kl. Alt. xiii, 1904, pp. 195, 252.
Loring, W. *Some ancient routes in the Peloponnese:* D. J.H.S. xv, 1895, p. 25.
Roloff, G. *Problemen aus der griechischen Kriegsgeschichte*. (Historische Studien, Heft 39.) Berlin, 1904.
Soteriades, G. Τὸ πεδίον τῆς ἐν Σελλασίᾳ μάχης. B.C.H. xxxiv, 1910, p. 5.
—— *Anti-Sellasia*. B.C.H. xxxv, 1911, pp. 87, 241.

13. Miscellaneous

Beloch, K. J. Μιθρῆς. Riv. fil. LIV, 1926, p. 331.

Corradi, G. *Gli ultimi Aeacidi.* Atti Acc. Torino, XLVII, 1911–12, p. 192.

De Sanctis, G. *Epigraphica.* Riv. fil. LIII, 1925, p. 63.

Dussaud, R. *Topographie historique de la Syrie antique et médiévale.* Paris, 1927.

*Holleaux, M. *Rome, la Grèce, et les monarchies hellénistiques au IIIe siècle av. J.-C.* (273–205). Paris, 1921.

Jardé, A. *Les céréales dans l'antiquité grecque.* 1925.

Klotsch, C. *Epeirotische Geschichte bis zum Jahre 280 v. Chr.* Berlin, 1911.

Lenschau, Th. *Jahresbericht über griechische Geschichte* in Bursian-Kroll's Jahresbericht for 1907 (years 1903–6) and 1919 (years 1907–14).

Reinach, A. J. and others. *L'Hellénisation du monde antique.* Paris, 1914.

*Rostowzew, M. *Studien zur Geschichte des römischen Kolonates.* Leipzig-Berlin, 1910.

Schubert, R. *Geschichte des Pyrrhus.* Königsberg, 1894.

Stählin, Fr. *Das hellenische Thessalien.* Stuttgart, 1924.

Tarn, W. W. *Hellenistic Civilisation.* London, 1927.

Tscherikower, V. *Die hellenistischen Städtegründungen von Alexander dem Grossen bis auf die Römerzeit.* Leipzig, 1927.

Walek, T. B. *Ueber das aitolisch-akarnanische Bündnis im III Jahrhundert.* Klio, XIV, 1915, p. 468.

Wiegand, Th. *Milet,* III, ii. Die Befestigungen von Heracleia am Latmos, by Fr. Krischen. Berlin and Leipzig, 1922.

Wilamowitz-Moellendorff, U. von. *Staat und Gesellschaft der Griechen.* 2nd ed. Leipzig and Berlin, 1923.

—— *Hellenistische Dichtung in der Zeit des Kallimachos.* Vol. I. Berlin, 1924.

C. *Chronology*

1. The Athenian Archons

Beloch, K. J. *Die attischen Archonten.* Griechische Geschichte, 2nd ed. 1927, vol. IV, ii, p. 52.

—— Φαῖδρος Σφήττιος. Riv. fil. LI, 1923, p. 273.

De Sanctis, G. *Revisioni. I. Gli Arconti ateniensi del sec.* III. Riv. fil. LI, 1923, p. 167.

Ferguson, W. S. *The Athenian archons of the third and second centuries before Christ.* Cornell Studies in Classical Philology, X. Ithaca (New York), 1899.

—— *The priests of Asklepios.* Berkeley, 1906. Reprinted with additions, 1907.

—— *The Athenian calendar.* C.P. III, 1908, p. 386.

Johnson, A. C. *The creation of the tribe Ptolemais.* A. J. Ph. XXXIV, 1913, p. 381; XXXV, 1914, p. 79.

—— *Attic archons from 294–262 B.C.* C.P. IX, 1914, p. 248.

—— *Notes on Attic inscriptions. ib.* IX, 1914, p. 417.

—— *Notes on Athenian Chronology. ib.* XIX, 1924, p. 67.

Kirchner, J., reviewing Ferguson, *The Athenian archons.* G.G.A. 1900, p. 433.

—— *Zu den attischen Archonten des III Jahrhunderts.* Hermes, XXXVII, 1902, p. 143.

—— reviewing Ferguson, *The priests of Asklepios.* B.P.W. 1906, col. 980, and 1908, col. 880.

—— reviewing Kolbe, *Die attischen Archonten. ib.* 1909, col. 844.

—— *Archon Euthios.* Berl. S.B., 1918, p. 142.

—— *Table of archons* in I.G. II², 1.

Kirchner, J. *Zur Chronologie der attischen Archonten des 3. Jahrhunderts v. Chr.* Phil. Woch. 1924, col. 869.

Kolbe, W. *Zur athenischen Archontenliste des III Jahrhunderts.* Festschrift für O. Hirschfeld, p. 312. Berlin, 1903.

—— *Die attischen Archonten von 293/2–271/0.* Ath. Mitt. xxx, 1905, p. 73.

—— *Die attischen Archonten von 293/2–31/0 v. Chr.* Berlin, 1908.

—— *Archon* Εὔθιος. Phil. lxxiv, 1917, p. 58.

Mayer, A. *Die Chronologie des Zenon und Kleanthes.* Phil. lxxi, 1912, p. 211.

Tarn, W. W. *Telokles and the Athenian archons of 288/7–262/1 b.c.* J.H.S. xl, 1920, p. 143.

Walek, Th. *Nouveaux archontes athéniens du IIIᵉ siècle.* Rev. Phil. xlviii, 1924, p. 5.

2. The Delphic Archons

Beloch, K. J. *Die delphische Amphiktionie im III Jahrhundert.* Griechische Geschichte, 2nd ed. 1927, vol. iv, ii, p. 385.

—— *Appunti di cronologia delphica del secolo III.* Riv. fil. lii, 1924, p. 192.

Bourguet, E. *Monuments et inscriptions de Delphes.* B.C.H. xxxv, 1911, p. 456.

De Sanctis, G. *Areo II re di Sparta.* Atti Acc. Torino, xlvii, 1911–12, p. 267.

Homolle, Th. *Fouilles de Delphes.* Vol. iii, fasc. 1 by E. Bourguet and fasc. 2 by M. G. Colin. 1909–13.

Johnson, A. C. *Problems in Delphian Chronology.* A. J. Ph. xxxix, 1918, p. 145 and xl, 1919, p. 286.

Klaffenbach, G. *Zur Geschichte von Ost-Lokris.* Klio, xx, 1925, p. 68.

Pomtow, H. *Neue delphische Archontentafel des 3. Jahrhunderts.* G.G.A. 1913, p. 143.

—— *Delphische Neufunde.* Klio, xiv, 1915, p. 265; xv, 1918, p. 1; xvii, 1921, p. 190; xviii, 1923, p. 259.

Roussel, P. *Remarques sur la chronologie des archontes de Delphes au IIIᵉ siècle av. J.-C.* B.C.H. xlvii, 1923, p. 1.

—— *La fondation des Sotéria de Delphes.* Rev. E.A. xxvi, 1924, p. 97.

Sokoloff, Th. *Die delphische Amphiktionie.* Klio, vii, 1907, p. 52.

Walek, T. B. *Die delphische Amphiktyonie in der Zeit der aitolischen Herrschaft.* Berlin, 1911.

3. The Delian Archons

Homolle, Th. *Les archives de l'intendance sacrée à Délos.* Paris, 1887.

Durrbach, F. *La chronologie des archontes Déliens.* B.C.H. xl, 1916, p. 298.

—— *Introduction* to I.G. xi, ii.

Schulhof, E. *Fouilles de Délos, Inscriptions financières.* B.C.H. xxxii, 1908, p. 83.

—— *Quelques questions de chronologie délienne.* Mélanges Holleaux. 1913.

4. Seleucid (Babylonian) Chronology

Kolbe, W. *Beiträge zur syrischen und jüdischen Geschichte.* Berlin-Stuttgart-Leipzig, 1926.

Kugler, F. X. *Von Moses bis Paulus.* Münster i. W. 1922.

—— *Sternkunde und Sterndienst in Babel.* Vol. ii, part 2 (ii). Münster i. W. 1924.

5. Ptolemaic Chronology and the Date of Sellasia

Badolle, M. *La date d'avènement de Ptolémée IV Philopator.* Rev. Phil. xlii, 1918, p. 109.

Beloch, K. J. *Zur Chronologie der ersten Ptolemäer.* Arch. Pap. vii, 1924, p. 161; viii, 1926, p. 1.

Boethius, A. *Der argivische Kalender.* Upsala, 1922.

Bouché-Leclerq, A. *Histoire des Lagides*, IV, 1907, App. I.

Cavaignac, E. *La chronologie égyptienne au IIIe siècle avant J.-Chr.* B.C.H. XXXVIII, 1914, p. I.

—— *Le calendrier ptolémaïque sous Philadelphe et Évergète.* Revue belge de philologie et d'histoire, II, 1923, p. 447.

Edgar, C. C. *On the dating of early Ptolemaic papyri.* Ann. Serv. XVII, 1917, p. 209.

—— *A further note on early Ptolemaic chronology. ib.*, XVIII, 1918, p. 58.

—— *A chronological problem.* Recueil Champollion, p. 119. Paris, 1922.

Ferrabino, A. *La cronologia dei primi Tolemei.* Atti Acc. Torino, LI, 1915–16, p. 343.

Grenfell, B. P. and Hunt, A. S. *Hibeh papyri I, App. I and II.* 1906.

Holleaux, M. *La première expédition d'Antiochus-le-Grand en Koilé-Syrie.* Mélanges Nicole, p. 273. Geneva, 1905.

Lesquier, J. *Sur deux dates d'Évergète et de Philopator.* Arch. Pap. IV, 1907, p. 284.

—— *Papyrus de Magdola.* (Introduction.) Paris, 1912.

—— *Les nouvelles études sur le calendrier ptolémaïque.* Rev. égyptol. II, 1920, p. 128.

Meyer, Ernst. *Untersuchungen zur Chronologie der ersten Ptolemäer auf Grund der Papyri.* Leipzig and Berlin, 1925.

Smyly, J. G. *The revenue years of Philadelphus, Euergetes and Philopator.* Hermathena, XXXII, 1906, p. 36.

Sokoloff, Th. *Das jährliche Nemeen-fest.* Klio, V, 1905, p. 219.

CHAPTER IV

PTOLEMAIC EGYPT

A. Ancient Sources

1. *Literary Texts*

For the literary sources for the period covered by this volume see the Bibliography to chapters III, VI, XIX, XX, Part I, sections 1 and 2, to which add

Pseudo-Aristeas letter (ed. Wendland, no. 2).

See S. Tracy, *III Maccabees and Pseudo-Aristeas. A Study.* Yale Class. Studies, 1928.

2. *Inscriptions*

For the inscriptions which are evidence for the general history of Egypt during the period covered by this volume see the Bibliography to chapters III, VI, XIX, XX, Part I, section 3.

Breccia, E. *Iscrizioni Greche e Latine.* Catal. gén. des ant. ég. du Musée d'Alexandrie. Cairo, 1911.

Milne, J. G. *Greek inscriptions.* Catal. gén. des ant. ég. du Musée du Caire. Cairo, 1905.

Preisigke, F. *Sammelbuch griechischer Urkunden aus Aegypten.* Berlin, I, 1915; II, 1918–20; III (by Fr. Bilabel), 1926 (papyri, ostraka and inscriptions).

Strack, M. L. *Die Dynastie der Ptolemäer.* Leipzig, 1897 (epigraphical appendix). Cf. his epigraphical reports in *Arch. Pap.*

The newly found inscriptions are mostly published in the *Annales du Service des Antiquités de l'Egypte,* in the *Bull. de la Soc. arch. d'Alexandrie* and in the *Monuments de l'Égypte gréco-romaine publiés par la Soc. arch. d'Alexandrie* (vol. I, 1926).

3. *Papyri*

Reports on new papyri and on books and articles dealing with papyri may be found in the *Arch. Pap.* (by U. Wilcken), in the *J.E.A.* (by H. I. Bell), and in *Aegyptus* (by various Italian scholars). On the juridical papyri see the reports of P. M. Meyer in *Z. d. Sav.-Stift.*

Here follows a short list of the most important publications which contain papyri of the Ptolemaic period.

P. Amh. B. P. Grenfell and A. S. Hunt. *The Amherst Paypri.* II. Oxford, 1901.

P. Bad. Fr. Bilabel. *Griechische Papyri, veröffentlicht aus den badischen Papyrussammlungen.* II, IV. Heidelberg, 1923–4.

B. G. U. *Aegyptische Urkunden aus den Museen zu Berlin.* Griechische Urkunden, I–V, 1895–1919; VI, 1922; VII, 1926.

P. Bour. P. Collart. *Les papyrus Bouriant.* Paris, 1927. (Nos. 9–12, the Theban revolt of 88 B.C.)

P. Cairo Zen. C. C. Edgar. *Zenon Papyri.* I, II. Catal. gén. des ant. ég. du Musée du Caire. Cairo, 1925, 1927. Cf. C. C. Edgar, *Selected Papyri from the Archives of Zenon,* Ann. Serv. 18–24 (Nos. 1–111). The papyri of the correspondence of Zeno have been published also in *P.S.I.,* Vols. IV–VII, in *P. Corn.* and by Fr. Bilabel, in F. Preisigke, *Sammelbuch,* III, nos. 6707–6820. Scattered papyri of the Zenon correspondence which came to light after the publication of Bilabel: H. I. Bell, *Raccolta Lumbroso*, p. 13; *Symbolae Osloenses*, 1927, p. 14. W. L. Westermann, *Mem. Amer. Acad. Rome*, VI, 1927, p. 147.

P. Corn. W. L. Westermann and C. J. Kraemer. *Greek Papyri in the Library o, Cornell University.* New York, 1926.

DIKAIOMATA. *Dikaiomata, Auszüge aus alexandrinischen Gesetzen herausgegeben von der Graeca Halensis.* Berlin, 1913.

P. Eleph. *Elephantine-Papyri*, bearbeitet von Rubensohn, mit Beiträgen von Schubart und Spiegelberg. Berlin, 1907. (Special volume of *B.G.U.*)

P. Fay. B. P. Grenfell, A. S. Hunt and D. G. Hogarth. *Fayûm Towns and their Papyri.* Oxford, 1900.

P. Frankf. I. H. Lewald. *Griechische Papyri aus dem Besitz des Rechtswissenschaftlichen Seminars der Universität Frankfurt*, Sitz. Heid. Ak. ph.-hist. kl. 1920, 14.

P. Frankf. II. H. Lewald. *Aus der Frankfurter Papyrussammlung*, Z. d. Sav.-Stift. XLII, 1921, p. 115.

P. Freib. *Mitt. aus der Freiburger Papyrussammlung*, I–II. Heid. S.B. 1914, 2 Abhandlung (Ptolemäische Kleruchenurkunde, herausgegeben von M. Gelzer).

P. Freib. 12–38. J. Partsch and U. Wilcken. *Mitteilungen aus der Freiburger Papyrussammlung*, 3. Juristische Urkunden der Ptolemäerzeit. Abh. der Heid. Ak. d. Wiss. philos.-hist. kl. 7, Heidelberg, 1927.

P. Gen. *Les Papyrus de Genève.* Transcrits et publiés par J. Nicole. 1. Geneva, 1896–1906.

P. Giss. *Griechische Papyri im Museum des oberhessischen Geschichtsvereins zu Giessen*, im Verein mit O. Eger herausg. und erkl. von E. Kornemann und P. M. Meyer. 1. Leipzig, 1910–12.

P. Giss. bibl. H. Kling. *Griechische Papyrusurkunden, Mitt. aus der Papyrussammlung der Giess. Universitätsbibliothek.* 1. Giessen, 1924.

P. Grad. *Griechische Papyri der Sammlung Gradenwitz*, herausg. von G. Plaumann. Heid. S.B. 1914, Abhandlung 15.

Gradenwitz, O., Preisigke, F. and Spiegelberg, W. *Ein Erbstreit aus dem ptolemäischen Aegypten.* Strassburg, 1912.

P. Grenfell I. *An Alexandrian Erotic Fragment and other Greek Papyri chiefly Ptolemaic.* Ed. by B. P. Grenfell. Oxford, 1896.

P. Grenfell II. *New Classical Fragments and other Greek and Latin Papyri.* Ed. by B. P. Grenfell and A. Hunt. Oxford, 1897.

P. Gur. J. G. Smyly. *Greek Papyri from Gurob.* Dublin, 1921.

P. Hal. See DIKAIOMATA.

P. Hamb. *Griechische Papyruskunden der Hamburger Stadtbibliothek.* Herausgegeben und erklärt von P. M. Meyer. 1. Leipzig, 1911–24.

P. Hib. *The Hibeh Papyri.* Ed. by B. P. Grenfell and A. Hunt. 1. London, 1906.

P. Kairo dem. W. Spiegelberg, *Die demotischen Papyrus.* Catal. gén. des Ant. ég. du Musée du Caire. Cairo, 1908.

P. Leyd. G. Leemans, *Papyri graeci Musei Antiquarii.* 1. Leyden, 1843.

P. Lille. *Papyrus Grecs publiés sous la direction de P. Jouguet avec la collaboration de P. Collart, J. Lesquier, M. Xoual.* I, II. Paris, 1907–27.

P. Lille dem. H. Sottas, *Papyrus démotiques de Lille.* Paris, 1921.

P. Lond. *Greek Papyri in the British Museum.* Catalogue with Texts. I, 1893 and II, 1898, ed. by F. G. Kenyon; III, 1907, ed. by H. I. Bell and F. G. Kenyon.

P. Louvre. *Notices et Extraits des Manuscrits grecs de la Bibliothèque impériale.* XVIII, par Brunet de Presle. Paris, 1865.

P. Magd. See P. Lille, II. Cf. P. Jouguet, *Raccolta Ramorino*, Milan, 1927, p. 381.

P. Meyer. *Juristische Papyri*. Erklärung von Urkunden zur Einführung in die juristische Papyruskunde von P. M. Meyer. Berlin, 1920.

P. Oxyr. *The Oxyrhynchus papyri*, Parts I–XVII. Ed. by B. P. Grenfell and A. Hunt. London, 1898–1927. Also cited as Oxyr. Pap.

P. Paris. See P. Louvre.

P. Petrie. *The Flinders Petrie Papyri*. With transcriptions, commentaries and index. I, II. Ed. by the Rev. J. P. Mahaffy. Dublin, 1891, 1893. III. Ed. by the Rev. J. P. Mahaffy and J. G. Smyly. Dublin, 1905.

P. Rein. Th. Reinach. *Papyrus grecs et démotiques*. Paris, 1905.

Revillout, E. *Mélanges etc. de l'ancienne Égypte*. Paris, 1895.

R. L. or Rev. Laws. *Revenue Laws of Ptolemy Philadelphus*. Ed. by B. P. Grenfell. Oxford, 1896.

P. Rev. Belge de phil. et hist. IV. M. Hombert, *Quelques papyrus des Collections de Gand et de Paris*, Rev. Belge de Philologie et Histoire, IV, 1925, p. 633.

P. Ryl. *Catalogue of the Greek Papyri in the John Rylands Library, Manchester*. II. Ed. by M. Johnson, V. Martin and A. Hunt. Manchester, 1915.

Schubart, W. *Griechische Papyri, Urkunden und Briefe vom 7. Jahrh. v. Chr. bis ins 8. Jahrh. n. Chr.* Bielefeld, 1927.

P. S. I. *Pubbl. della Soc. It. per la ricerca dei Pap. Greci e Latini in Egitto*. Pap. Greci e Latini. I–VIII. Florence, 1912–25.

P. Strassb. F. Preisigke. *Griechische Papyrus der Universitäts und Landesbibliothek zu Strassburg*. I, II. Leipzig, 1912, 1920.

P. Tebt. *The Tebtunis Papyri*. Part I. Ed. by B. P. Grenfell, A. Hunt and J. Goodspeed. London, 1907.

P. Tur. A. Peyron. *Papyri graeci Regii Taurinensis Musaei Aegyptii*. I, II. 1826–27.

U. P. Z. U. Wilcken. *Urkunden der Ptolemäerzeit*. I. Berlin, 1922–4.

P. Vat. Angelo Mai, *Classicorum auctorum e Vaticanis codicibus editorum*. IV, V. Rome, 1831, 1833.

Witkowski, S. *Epistulae privatae graecae*. Ed. 2. 1901.

4. Ostraka

Gardiner, A. H., Thompson, H. and Milne, J. G. *Theban Ostraka*. Oxford, 1913.

Preisigke, F. *Die Prinz Joachim Ostraka*. Strassburg, 1914.

Tait, J. G. *Greek Ostraka in the Bodleian Library at Oxford and various other collections*. I. Oxford [1929].

Wilcken, U. *Griechische Ostraka aus Aegypten und Nubien*. I, II. Berlin, 1899.

NOTE. Important new evidence on which are based some points in this chapter will be found in Papyrus 703 (instructions of a *dioiketes* to an *oikonomos* of the time of Euergetes I), in the forthcoming Vol. III of the Tebtunis Papyri.

B. MODERN LITERATURE[1]

1. General Works

Bevan, E. R. *A History of Egypt under the Ptolemaic dynasty*. London, 1927.

Ferguson, W. S. *Greek Imperialism*. London, Boston, and New York, 1913, p. 149.

Jouguet, P. *L'impérialisme macédonien et l'hellénisation de l'Orient* (Évolution de l'Humanité). Paris, 1926. p. 273.

Kaerst, J. *Geschichte des Hellenismus*. II, 2. Leipzig, 1926.

[1] See also the works marked with an asterisk in the Bibliography to chapters III, VI, XXII, XXIII, and the whole of the following sections in that Bibliography: I, 4 (c); II, B. 2 and 7, II, C. 5.

Lumbroso, G. *L'Egitto dei Greci e dei Romani.* Ed. 2. Rome, 1896.
Reinach, A. et Jouguet, P. *L'hellénisation du Monde antique.* Paris, 1914. pp. 212, 309.
Schubart, W. *Einführung in die Papyruskunde.* Berlin, 1918.
—— *Aegypten von Alexander dem Grossen bis auf Mohammed.* Berlin, 1922.
—— *Von der Flügelsonne zum Halbmond.* Leipzig, 1926.
Tarn, W. W. *Hellenistic Civilisation.* London, 1927.
Wilcken, U. und Mitteis, L. *Grundzüge und Chrestomathie der Papyruskunde.* I–II. Leipzig-Berlin, 1912.

2. *Pre-ptolemaic Egypt*

Ehrenberg, V. *Alexander und Aegypten.* Beihefte zum Alten Orient, VII, Leipzig, 1926.
Lefebvre, G. *Le tombeau de Pétosiris.* Cairo, 1924.
Luys, E. *Vie de Pétosiris, grand prêtre de Thot à Hermupolis-la-Grande.* Brussels, 1927.
Mallet, D. *Les premiers établissements des Grecs en Égypte.* Paris, 1893.
—— *Les rapports des Grecs avec l'Égypte de la conquête de Cambyse à celle d'Alexandre.* III. Cairo, 1922.
Montet, P. *Notes sur le tombeau de Pétosiris.* Rev. Arch. 1926, p. 161.
Schur, W. *Zur Vorgeschichte des Ptolemäerreiches.* Klio, XX, 1926, p. 270.
Wilcken, U. *Alexander der Grosse und die hellenistische Wirtschaft.* Schmollers Jahrbuch, XLV, 1920, p. 45.

3. *The Power of the Kings and the Royal Cult*

Herzog, R. *Herondea.* Phil. LXXXII, 1926, p. 53.
Kornemann, E. *Die Geschwisterehe im Altertum.* Mitt. der Schlesischen Gesellschaft für Volkskunde, XXIV, 1923, p. 17. Cf. Klio, XIX, 1925, p. 355 and F. Cumont in *C. R. Ac. Inscr.* 1924, p. 53, and in *Doura-Europos,* 1926, p. 377.
—— *Die Satrapenpolitik der ersten Lagiden.* Raccolta Lumbroso, Milan, 1925, p. 235.
Otto, W. *Zum Hofzeremoniell des Hellenismus,* Ἐπιτύμβιον H. Swoboda dargebracht, Reichenberg, 1927, p. 194.
Pfeiffer, R. *Arsinoe Philadelphos in der Dichtung.* Die Antike, II, 1926, p. 161.
Plaumann, G. Art. *Hiereis,* section V, in P.W. col. 1424 (with bibliography).

For the attitude of the Egyptians towards the Ptolemies see an article by W. Reitzenstein on 'The potter's oracle' in *Studien der Bibliothek Warburg,* VII, cp. *P.S.I.* 760, 982 and Struve, *Das Töpferorakel,* Raccolta Lumbroso, p. 280.

4. *Religion and Temples*

Glotz, G. *Les fêtes d'Adonis sous Ptolémée II.* Rev. E. G. XXXIII, 1920, p. 169.
Kornemann, E. *Aus der Geburtsstunde eines Gottes* (Sarapis). Mitt. der Schlesischen Gesellschaft für Volkskunde, XXVII, 1926, p. 1.
Latte, K. *Religiöse Strömungen in der Frühzeit des Hellenismus.* Die Antike, I, 1925, p. 146.
Otto, W. *Priester und Tempel im hellenistischen Aegypten.* I–II, Leipzig-Berlin, 1905–8; cf. M. Rostowzew, *G.G.A.* 1909, p. 603.
—— *Aegyptische Priestersynoden in hellenistischer Zeit.* Bay. S. B., 1926, 2, p. 18.
Perdrizet, P. *Terres cuites d'Égypte de la collection Fouquet.* Paris-Nancy, 1921.
Schubart, W. *Hellenismus und Weltreligion.* Neue Jahrb. für Wissenschaft und Jugendbildung, II, 1926, Heft 5.
Spiegelberg, W. *Beiträge zur Erklärung des neuen dreisprachigen Priesterdekretes zu Ehren des Ptolemaios Philopator.* Bay. S.B. 1925, 4.

Spiegelberg, W. und Otto, W. *Eine neue Urkunde zu der Siegesfeier des Ptolemaios IV und die Frage der ägyptischen Priestersynoden. Ib.* 1926, 2.

Vogt, J. *Die griechisch-ägyptische Sammlung E. v. Sieglin.* II. Terrakotten. Leipzig, 1927.

Weber, W. *Aegyptisch-griechische Götter im Hellenismus.* Groningen, 1912.

—— *Die aegyptisch-griechischen Terrakotten.* Berlin, 1914.

Wilcken, U. *Urkunden der Ptolemaeerzeit.* Berlin-Leipzig, 1922. Einleitung, B, Das Serapeum von Memphis, p. 7 (with full bibliography on Sarapis).

—— *Zu den 'syrischen' Göttern.* Festgabe für A. Deissmann. Tübingen, 1927.

Woess, F. von. *Das Asylwesen Aegyptens in der Ptolemäerzeit und die spätere Entwicklung.* Munich, 1923. Cf. C. F. Lehmann-Haupt, *Klio,* XIX, 1925, pp. 217, 504; and U. Wilcken, *Arch. Pap.* VII, 1925, p. 288: the question of the κάτοχοι of Sarapis, with bibliography.

—— 'Ασυλία. Z. d. Sav.-Stift., Röm. Abt. LXXVI, 1926, p. 32.

Zielinski, Th. *La Sibylle* (Christianisme, 4). Paris, 1924.

5. *Army and Navy*

Breccia, E. *Un nuovo πολίτευμα pseudo-etnico.* Bull. de la Soc. arch. d'Alex. V, 1923, p. 119.

Cohen, D. οἱ ἔξω τάξεων. Mnem. LVII, 1926, p. 82.

Engers, M. *Politeuma.* Mnem. LVII, 1926, p. 157.

Grote, K. *Das griechische Söldnerwesen der hellenistischen Zeit.* Weida i. Th. 1913.

Heichelheim, F. *Die auswärtige Bevölkerung im Ptolemaerreich.* Klio, Beiheft 18, 1925 (on the ἐπιγονή, with bibliography).

Holleaux, M. *"Ceux qui sont dans le bagage."* Rev. E. G. XXXIX, 1926, p. 355 (ἀποσκευή).

—— Ἡγεμὼν τῶν ἔξω τάξεων. Rev. E. G. XXXV, 1922, p. 198.

Lesquier, J. *Les institutions militaires de l'Égypte sous les Lagides.* Paris, 1911.

Ruppel, W. *Politeuma,* Phil. LXXXII, 1927, p. 269.

Segré, A. *Note sul πολίτευμα e l' ἐπιγονή in Egitto.* Aegyptus, III, 1922, p. 142.

Wilcken, U. *Zur Trierarchie im Lagidenreich.* Raccolta Lumbroso, 1925, p. 93.

See further, F. Bilabel's comments on P. Bad. IV, 1, 47 and 48; M. Gelzer's comments on P. Freiburg 7; cf. J. Lesquier, *Rev. E. G.* XXXIV, 1921, p. 359, P. Meyer, *Jurist. Pap.* p. 186, and H. Lewald's comments on P. Frankf. I, 7.

6. *Administration*

Biedermann, E. *Studien zur ägyptischen Verwaltungsgeschichte. Der βασιλικὸς γραμματεύς.* Berlin, 1913.

Breccia, E. *Ann. Serv.* VIII, 1907, p. 62.

Calderini, A. Θησαυροί, *Ricerche di Topografia e di storia della pubblica amministrazione nell' Egitto Greco-Romano.* Studi della Scuola pap., IV, Milan, 1924.

Engers, M. *De Aegyptiorum κωμῶν administratione qualis fuerit aetate Lagidarum.* Groningen, 1909.

—— *Observationes ad Aegypti pertinentes administrationem qualis aetate Lagidarum fuit.* I. Mnem. XLV, 1917, p. 257 (ἐπιστάται φυλακιτῶν). II. *ib.* XLVII, 1919, p. 146 (de Nomarcha).

Hohlwein, N. *Le stratège du Nome.* Musée Belge, XXVIII, 1924, pp. 125, 193; XXIX, 1925, pp. 6, 85, 257.

Kunkel, W. *Verwaltungsakten aus spät-ptolemäischer Zeit.* Arch. Pap. VIII, 1927, p. 169.

Martin, V. *Les Épistratèges.* Geneva, 1911.

Maspero, H. *Les finances de l'Égypte sous les Lagides.* Paris, 1905.

Oertel, F. *Die Liturgie, Studien zur ptolemäischen und kaiserlichen Verwaltung Aegyptens.* Leipzig, 1917.

Piotrowicz, L. *Stanowisko nomarchow w administracji Egiptu w okrasie greckoryzmskin.* (With a summary in French.) Posnan, 1922.

Rostowzew, M. *Geschichte der Staatspacht in der römischen Kaiserzeit bis Diokletian.* Phil. Suppl. Leipzig, 1902.

Spiegelberg, W. *Der Stratege Pammenches.* Zeitschr. f. Aegyptische Sprache, LVII, 1922, p. 88.

Steiner, A. *Der Fiskus der Ptolemäer.* Leipzig, 1914.

7. *Law and the Administration of Justice*

Caldara, A. *I connotati personali nei documenti d'Egitto dell' età greca e romana.* Studi della Scuola pap., IV, 1924.

Collomp, P. *Recherches sur la chancellerie et la diplomatique des Lagides.* Strasbourg, 1926.

DIKAIOMATA. See above, A 3.

Gradenwitz, O. *Das Gericht der Chrematisten.* Arch. Pap. III, 1906, p. 22.

Hasebroek, J. *Das Signalement in den Papyrusurkunden.* Heidelberg, 1921.

Kiessling, E. *Die Aposkeuai und der prozess-rechtliche Stellung der Ehefrauen in ptolemäischen Aegypten.* Arch. Pap. VIII, 1927, p. 270.

Kreller, H. *Erbrechtliche Untersuchungen auf Grund der graeco-aegyptischen Papyrusurkunden.* Leipzig, 1919.

Meyer, P. *Juristische Papyri.* Berlin, 1920.

Mitteis, L. *Reichsrecht und Volksrecht in den östlichen Provinzen des römischen Kaiserreiches.* Leipzig, 1891.

—— *Römisches Privatrecht bis auf die Zeit Diokletians.* I. 1908.

Partsch, J. *Die griechische Publizität der Grundstücksverträge im Ptolemäerrechte.* Festschrift O. Lenel, 1921, p. 77.

Semeka, G. *Ptolemaeisches Prozessrecht.* I, II, Munich, 1913.

Sethe, K., und Partsch, J. *Demotische Urkunden zum ägyptischen Bürgschaftsrecht vorzüglich der Ptolemäerzeit.* Abh. d. sächs. Ges. d. Wiss., ph.-hist. Kl. XXXII, 1920.

Taubenschlag, R. *Das Strafrecht im Rechte der Papyri.* Leipzig, 1916.

—— *Die ptolemäischen Schiedsrichter und ihre Bedeutung für die Rezeption des griechischen Rechts in Aegypten.* Arch. Pap. IV, 1907, p. 1.

Waszynski, St. *Die Laokriten und das κοινὸν δικαστήριον.* Ib. V, 1908, p. 1.

Weiss, E. *Griechisches Privatrecht auf rechtsvergleichender Grundlage.* I, 1923.

Wenger, L. *Ueber Papyri und Gesetzrecht.* Bay. S. B. 1914, 5.

Zucker, F. *Beiträge zur Kenntniss der Gerichtsorganisation im ptolemäischen und römischen Aegypten.* Phil. Suppl. XII, 1.

8. *The Cities and the Villages*

Bell, H. I. *Alexandria.* J.E.A. XIII, 1927, p. 171.

Boak, A. E. R. *The University of Michigan's excavations at Karanis:* 1924–5. J.E.A. XII, 1926, p. 19.

Breccia, E. *Alexandrea ad Aegyptum.* Bergamo, 1922. (With excellent bibliography.)

—— *Monuments de l'Égypte Gréco-Romaine.* I; I, Le rovine e i monumenti di Canopo; 2, Teadelfia e il tempio di Pneferos. Bergamo, 1926.

Grenfell, B., Hunt, A. and Hogarth, D. G. *Fayûm towns and their papyri.* London, 1910. Introduction.

Jouguet, P. *La vie municipale dans l'Égypte romaine.* Paris, 1911.

Plaumann, G. *Ptolemaïs in Oberaegypten*. Leipzig, 1910.

Rink, H. *Strassen- und Viertelnamen von Oxyrhynchus*. Diss. Giessen, 1924.

Rubensohn, O. *Aus griechisch-römischen Häusern des Fayûm*. J.D.A.I. xx, 1905, p. 1.

Schmitz, H. *Die hellenistisch-römische Stadtanlagen in Aegypten*. 1921.

Smith, E. Marion. *Naukratis, a chapter in the history of the hellenization of Egypt*. Wien, 1926 (Journ. of the Soc. of Orient. Research, x, p. 117).

Viereck, P. *Philadelpheia*. Leipzig, 1928. Morgenland, Heft 16.

Viereck, P., und Zucker, F. *Papyri, Ostraka und Wachstafeln aus Philadelphia im Fayûm*. B.G.U. vii, 1926, Einleitung, p. 1. (Die Ruinen von Philadelphia.)

NOTE. New and important information on slave-labour in Alexandria will be found in *Pap. Columbia*, 480 (third century B.C.), to be published by W. L. Westermann, a διάγραμμα of the king, based on a chapter of the πολιτικοὶ νόμοι of Alexandria, regulating the taxes to be paid by buyers and sellers of slaves.

9. *The Provinces*

Cohen, D. *De magistratibus Aegyptiis externas Lagidarum regni provincias administrantibus*. 's Gravenhage, n.d.

Edgar, C. *Comments on Zenon Pap*. Cairo (see Sources), nos. 59003–59011 and 59075, 59076. (Palestine, with full bibliography.)

Ferri, S. *Alcune Iscrizioni di Cirene*, Berl. Abh. 1926, no. 5. Compare also, on this question, G. de Sanctis, *Riv. fil.* iv, 1926, p. 145 and in the forthcoming Volume of *Riv. fil.*; F. Heichelheim, *Klio*, xxi, 1927, p. 174; Th. Reinach, *La Charte ptolémaïque de Cyrène*, Rev. Arch. xxvi, 1927, p. 1; and U. Wilcken, *Zu der epidaurischen Bundes-stele vom J. 302 v. Chr.* Berl. S.B. xxvi, 1927 (Nachtrag zu S. 285).

Harper, G. M. *A Study in the commercial relations between Egypt and Syria in the third cent. B.C.* A.J.Ph. xlix, 1928, p. 1.

Meyer, E. *Die Grenzen hellenistischer Staaten in Kleinasien*. Leipzig, 1925. p. 43.

Tscherikower, V. *Die hellenistischen Städtegründungen von Alexander dem Grossen bis auf die Römerzeit*. Phil. Suppl. xix, 1. Leipzig, 1927. p. 182.

10. *Economic Conditions*

Boak, A. E. R. *Irrigation and population in the Fayûm*. Geographical Review, xvi, 1926, p. 353.

Chwostow, M. *Studies in the history of exchanges in the period of the Hellenistic monarchies and of the Roman Empire*. I. History of the Oriental commerce of Roman Egypt. (In Russian.) Kazan, 1907.

—— *Organization of industry and commerce in Greek and Roman Egypt*. I. The textile industry in Greco-Roman Egypt. (In Russian.) Kazan, 1907.

Collart, P. et Jouguet, P. *Petites recherches sur l'économie politique des Lagides*. Raccolta Lumbroso, 1925, p. 109.

Fitzler, K. *Steinbrüche und Bergwerke im ptolemäischen und römischen Aegypten*. Leipzig, 1910.

Grenfell, B. *Revenue Laws of Ptolemy Philadelphus*. Oxford, 1896.

Leaf, W. *Classics and Reality*. In Proc. of the Class. Assoc. xviii, 1922, p. 20. (Banking.)

Lumbroso, G. *Recherches sur l'économie politique de l'Égypte sous les Lagides*. Turin, 1870.

Mitteis, L. *Trapezitica*. Z. d. Sav.-Stift., Röm. Abt. xix, 1898, p. 198.

Preisigke, F. *Girowesen im griechischen Aegypten*. Strassburg, 1910. Cf. Arch. Pap. iv, 1907, p. 95.

Reil, Th. *Beiträge zur Kenntnis des Gewerbes im hellenistischen Aegypten.* Leipzig, 1913.

Reinach, Th. *De la valeur relative des métaux monétaires dans l'Égypte des Ptolémées.* Rev. E. G. XLI, 1928, p. 110.

Rostowzew, M. *Studien zur Geschichte des römischen Kolonates.* Leipzig, 1910.

—— *The foundations of Social and Economic life in Egypt in Hellenistic times.* J.E.A. VI, 1920, p. 161.

—— *A large estate in Egypt in the third century B.C.* Madison, 1922.

Schnebel, M. *Landwirtschaft im hellenistischen Aegypten.* I. Munich, 1925.

Schubart, W. *Die ptolemäische Reichsmünze in den auswärtigen Besitzungen unter Philadelphus.* Z.N. XXXIII, 1921, p. 68.

Segrè, A. *Misure egiziane dell' epoca tolemaica, romana e bizantina.* Atti d. R. Acc. di Torino, 54 (1918–19). Cf. Aegyptus, I, 1920, pp. 159, 318.

—— *Circolazione tolemaica e pretolemaica.* In Egitto, Riv. Ital. di Num. XXXIII, 1920.

—— *Circolazione monetaria e prezzi nel mondo antico ed in particolare in Egitto.* Rome, 1922.

—— *Metrologia e circolazione monetaria degli antichi.* Bologna, 1928

Smolka, F. *Inwiefern waren die Ptolemäer Merkantilisten?* (In Polish.) Eos, XXVI, 1923, p. 72.

Westermann, W. *The development of the irrigation-system of Egypt.* C.P. 1919, p. 158.

—— *Land-reclamation in the Fayûm under Ptolemies Philadelphus and Euergetes I.* *Ib.* 1917, p. 429.

—— *The uninundated lands in Ptolemaic and Roman Egypt.* *Ib.* 1920, p. 120.

—— *The Greek exploitation of Egypt.* Political Science Quarterly, XL, 1925, p. 517.

—— *Egyptian agricultural labour under Ptolemy Philadelphus.* Agric. History, I, July 1927, p. 377.

Wilcken, U. *Punt-Fahrten in der Ptolemäerzeit.* Zeitschr. f. äg. Sprache, LX, 1925, p. 86.

—— In *Berl. S.B.* 1927, p. 53. (Sea-loan contracted for an expedition to the Somali coast.)

On the irrigation-system of the north desert of the Fayûm new information has been supplied by Miss Caton-Thompson. See *The Egyptian Gazette*, Feb. 28, 1928, and *The Times*, April 17, 1928; cf. *Ancient Egypt*, 1926, p. 1.

11. *Art and Social Conditions.*

Bell, H. I. *Hellenic culture in Egypt.* J.E.A. VIII, 1922, p. 139.

—— *Juden und Griechen im römischen Alexandreia: eine historische Skizze des alexandrinischen Antisemitismus.* (Alte Orient, Beiheft 9.) Leipzig, 1926. (With full bibliography.)

—— *Greek Sightseers in the Fayûm in the Third Century B.C.* Symbolae Osloenses, V, 1927, p. 14; cf. M. Rostovtzeff, *Greek Sightseers in Egypt*, in J.E.A. XIV, 1928, p. 13 and P. Cairo Zen., 59247.

Bendel, P. *Qua ratione Graeci liberos docuerint, papyris, ostracis, tabulis in Aegypto inventis illustratur.* Münster, 1911.

Bickermann, E. *Beiträge zur antiken Urkundengeschichte.* I. Der Heimatsvermerk und die staatsrechtliche Stellung der Hellenen in ptolemäischen Aegypten. Arch. Pap. VIII, 1927, p. 216.

Calderini, A., Untersteiner, M., Accordi, O. e Volani, N. *Ricerche etnografiche sui papiri greco-egizi*, Studi della Scuola pap. III, 1920, p. 1.

Calderini, A. e Mondini, M. *Repertorio per lo studio delle lettere private dell' Egitto greco-romano*, Studi della Scuola pap. II., 1917, p. 109.

Calderini, A. *Lettere private nell'Egitto greco-romano.* Milan, 1915.
—— *Pensiero e sentimento nelle lettere private greche dei papiri,* Studi della Scuola pap. IV, 1917, p. 9.
Curtius, L. *Die antike Kunst.* Berlin, 1923.
Deissmann, A. *Licht vom Osten.* Ed. 4. Tübingen, 1923.
Edgar, C. C. *Records of a village club.* Raccolta Lumbroso, 1925, p. 369.
Ghedini, G. *Di alcuni elementi religiosi pagani nelle epistole private greche dei papiri,* Studi della Scuola pap. II, 1917, p. 51.
Grassi, T. *Musica, mimica e danza secondo i documenti papiracei greco-egizi,* Studi della Scuola pap. III, 1920, p. 117.
Jouguet, P. *Les Lagides et les indigènes égyptiens.* Revue belge de philologie et d'histoire, III, 1923, p. 419.
Kenyon, F. G. *The library of a Greek of Oxyrhynchus,* J.E.A. VIII, 1922, p. 129.
Lawrence, A. W., *Greek Sculpture in Ptolemaic Egypt,* J.E.A. XI, 1925, p. 179.
Luckhard, F. *Das Privathaus im ptolemäischen und römischen Aegypten.* Giessen, 1914.
Majer-Leonhard, E. Ἀγράμματοι *in Aegypto qui litteras sciverint qui nesciverint ex papyris graecis quantum fieri potest exploratur.* Frankfurt a. M., 1913.
Mondini, M. *Lettere femminili nei papiri greco-egizi,* Studi della Scuola pap. II, 1917, p. 29.
—— *Lettere dei soldati.* Atene e Roma, XVIII, 1915, p. 241.
Oldfather, Ch. H. *The Greek literary texts from Greco-Roman Egypt.* University of Wisconsin Studies in the Social Sciences and History, IX, Madison, 1923.
Preisigke, F. *Antikes Leben nach den ägyptischen Papyri.* Leipzig, 1916.
San Nicolò, M. *Aegyptisches Vereinswesen zur Zeit der Ptolemäer und Römer,* I–II. Munich, 1913, 1915.
—— *Zur Vereinsgerichtsbarkeit im hellenistischen Aegypten.* Ἐπιτύμβιον H. Swoboda dargebracht, Reichenberg, 1927, p. 255.
Schmidt, K. Fr. W. *Das griechische Gymnasium in Aegypten.* Halle, 1926.
Schubart, W. *Die Griechen in Aegypten.* Leipzig, 1927. Beiheft z. Alten Orient, p. 10.
—— Οἰκογένεια. Raccolta Lumbroso, 1925, p. 49.
Vogt, J. *Die griechische-ägyptische Sammlung E. v. Sieglin.* III. Terrakotten. 1927.
Ziebarth, E. *Aus dem griechischen Schulwesen.* Ed. 2. Leipzig, 1914.
—— *Aus der antiken Schule.* Ed. 2. Leipzig, 1913.

12. *Egypt and India.*

See generally *Cambridge History of India,* Vol. I, and the following:

Brelocz, B. *Kauṭalīya-Studien.* I. Das Grundeigentum in Indien. Bonn, 1927.
Hildebrandt, A. *Altindische Politik.* Jena, 1926. (G. Fischer.)
Jolly, J. *Staatliches und soziales Leben in India.* (Licht des Ostens.) 1922.
—— *Über die alte politische Literatur Indiens und ihre Bearbeiter.* Zeit. f. vergl. Rechtswissenschaft, XLI, 1925, p. 305.
Meyer, J. J. *Das Arthaçastra des Kautilya.* Leipzig, 1925.
—— *Ueber das Wesen der altindischen Rechtsschriften und ihr Verhältnis zueinander und zu Kautilya.* Leipzig, 1927.
Sarkar, B. K. *The political institutions and theories of the Hindus.* Leipzig, 1922.
Stein, O. *Megasthenes und Kautilya.* Wien S.B. CXCI, 1922, p. 5. Cp. W. Otto in *Phil. Woch.* 1927, p. 1217.

CHAPTER V

SYRIA AND THE EAST

A. ANCIENT SOURCES

1. *Literary Texts*

For the literary sources for the general history of Syria and the East during the period covered by this volume see the Bibliography to chapters III, VI, XXII, XXIII, Part I, sections 1 and 2.

For Palestine and Phoenicia the books of Maccabees and Josephus are especially important.

2. *Inscriptions*

For the inscriptions which bear on the history of Syria during the period covered by this volume see Bibliography to chapters III, VI, XXII, XXIII, Part I, section 3. An inscription of 119/8 B.C. recently found at Delos (soon to be published by P. Roussel in *B.C.H.*) gives a list of ephebes and other young men. Most of these young men appear by the *ethnica* to be of Syrian origin.

For a full list of Greek inscriptions found in Mesopotamia and Iran:

Cumont, F. *Fouilles de Doura-Europos* (1922–1923). Paris, 1926. pp. 452–4.
—— *Inscriptions grecques de Suse*. Mémoires de la Mission Archéologique de Perse, XX. Mission Susiane.

For Greek and Aramaic parchments of Doura:
Cumont, F., *ib.* p. 281.

For Greek and Pahlavi parchments of Avroman:
Minns, E. H. *Parchments of the Parthian period from Avroman in Kurdistan*. J.H.S. XXXV, 1915, p. 22.
Cowley, A. *The Pahlavi document from Avroman*, J.R.A.S. 1919, p. 147; cf. L. Mitteis, in *Z. d. Sav.-Stift.*, Röm. Abt. XXXVI, 1916, p. 425, and H. S. Nyberg, in *Le Monde Oriental*, XVII, 1923, p. 182.
Meyer, P. *Juristische Papyri*. 1920. p. 120.

For Babylonian cuneiform contracts and other private documents of the Seleucid and Parthian periods:

(1) *From Uruk.*
Oppert, J. et Menant, J. *Documents juridiques de l'Assyrie et de la Chaldée*. Paris, 1877. p. 291.
Schroeder, O. *Kontrakte der Seleukidenzeit aus Warka*. Vorderasiatische Schrift-denkmäler der St. Mus. zu Berlin, XV, 1916. (56 tablets.)
Clay, A. *Babylonian Records in the Library of J. Pierpont Morgan*. I, 1912 (Nos. 88 and 98); II, 1913, p. 19 (52 tablets); IV, 1923, p. 52.
Fossey, C. *Études assyriennes, XL. Vente d'esclaves*. Journal Asiatique, 1922, p. 40.
Boissier, A. *Babyloniaca*, VIII, 1924, p. 27.
Winckworth, C. P. T. *A Seleucid Legal Text*, J.R.A.S. 1925, p. 655.

(2) *From Babylon and other places.*
Strassmaier, J. N. *Arsaciden Inschriften*. Zeitschr. f. Assyriologie, III, 1888, p. 129.
Schrader, E. *Keilinschriftliche Bibliothek*, III, 136; IV, 313.
Kohler, J., and Ungnad, A. *Hundert ausgewählte Urkunden aus der Spätzeit des babylonischen Schrifttums*, 1911, Nos. 89–100.

San Nicolò, M. and Ungnad, A. *Neubabylonische Rechtsurkunden.* Leipzig [1929]; see San Nicolò, *Die Stellung der Keilschrifturkunden in der vorasiatischen Rechtsentwicklung* in Z. d. Sav.-Stift., XLVIII, 1928, p. 21.

B. Modern Books[1]

1. *General Works*

Chapot, V. *Les destinées de l'hellénisme au delà de l'Euphrate.* Mém. de la Soc. d. Ant. de France, LIII, 1902, p. 209.

Erdmann, M. *Zur Kunde der hellenistischen Städtegründungen.* Prog. Strassburg, 1883.

Grote, K. *Das griechische Söldnerwesen der hellenistischen Zeit.* Jena, 1913.

Jouguet, P. *L'Impérialisme macédonien et l'hellénisation de l'Orient* (Évolution de l'Humanité). Paris, 1926. p. 403.

Kornemann, E. *Zur Politik der ersten Nachfolger Alexanders des Grossen.* Vergangenheit und Gegenwart, XVI, 1926, p. 333.

Lammens, H. *La Syrie. Précis Historique.* I, II. Beyrouth, 1921.

Lehmann-Haupt, C. F. Art. *Satrap* in P.W.

Meyer, E. *Blüte und Niedergang des Hellenismus in Asien.* Berlin, 1925.

Radet, G. *L'Empire des Séleucides* (323–64 avant J.-C.). Journal des Savants, XI, 1913, p. 300.

Rostowzew, M. *Geschichte der Staatspacht.* Phil. Suppl. IX, 1902, p. 356.

—— *Studien zur Geschichte des römischen Kolonates.* Leipzig, 1910. p. 240.

Tarn, W. W. *Hellenistic Civilisation.* London, 1927.

Tscherikower, V. *Die hellenistischen Städtegründungen von Alexander bis auf die Römerzeit.* Phil. Suppl. XIX. Leipzig, 1927.

Wilcken, U., und Stähelin, F. Arts. *Antiochus* and *Seleucus* in P.W.

2. *Asia Minor*

Asboeck, A. *Das Staatswesen von Priene in hellenistischer Zeit.* Munich, 1913.

Buckler, W. H., and Robinson, D. M. *Greek Inscriptions from Sardes,* A.J.A. XVI, 1912, p. 11.

Clarke, J. T., Bacon, F. H., and Koldewey, R. *Investigations at Assos.* Boston, 1902–21.

Clerc, M. *De rebus Thyatirenorum.* Paris, 1893. (New edition in Greek by Zakas, Athens, 1900.)

Diest, W. von. *Nysa ad Maeandrum.* J.D.A.I. Ergänzungsband. Berlin, 1913.

Dörpfeld, W. *Troja und Ilion.* Athens, 1902.

Hasluck, F. W. *Cyzicus.* Cambridge, 1910.

Haubold, P. *De rebus Iliensium.* Leipzig, 1889.

Heberdey, R. *Forschungen in Ephesos.* I–III Vienna, 1906–23.

Holleaux, M. *Inscription trouvée à Brousse.* B.C.H. XLVIII, 1924, p. 1.

Humann, C. *Magnesia am Maeander.* Berlin, 1904.

Humann, C., and Puchstein, O. *Reisen in Kleinasien und Nord-Syrien.* Berlin, 1890.

Judeich, W. *Kleinasiatische Studien.* Marburg, 1892.

Kornemann, E. Art. *Domänen* in P.W., Suppl. IV.

Lavedan, P. *Histoire de l'architecture urbaine.* Paris, 1926.

Leonhard, R. *Paphlagonia.* Berlin, 1915.

Merle, H. *Geschichte der Städte Byzantion und Kalchedon.* Kiel, 1916.

Meyer, Ernst, *Die Grenzen der hellenistischen Staaten in Kleinasien.* Leipzig, 1925.

[1] See further the works in the Bibliography to chapters III, VI, XXII, XXIII which are marked with an asterisk, and the whole of sections I, 4 (*d*); II, B. 3, 4 and 7, C. 4 of that Bibliography.

Oberhummer, R., und Zimmerer, H. *Durch Syrien und Kleinasien.* Berlin, 1899.
Oertel, F. Art. *Katoikoi* in P.W.
Pontremoli, E., and Haussoullier, B. *Didymes; fouilles de 1895–96.* Paris, 1904.
Radet, G. *De coloniis a Macedonibus in Asiam cis Taurum deductis.* Paris, 1892.
Ramsay, W. M. *The historical Geography of Asia Minor.* London, 1890.
—— *The Cities and Bishoprics of Phrygia.* I, II. Oxford, 1895–7.
—— *Studies in History and Art of the Eastern provinces of the Roman Empire.* London, 1908.
—— *Anatolian Studies presented to Sir William Mitchell Ramsay.* Ed. by W. H. Buckler and W. M. Calder. Manchester, 1923.
—— *Asianic elements in Greek Civilization.* London, 1927.
Rayet, O., and Thomas, A. *Milet et le golfe Latmique.* Paris, 1880–5.
Robinson, D. M. *Ancient Sinope.* Baltimore, 1906.
Swoboda, H. Art. *Rome* in P.W. Suppl. IV.
Westermann, W. L. *Land registers of Western Asia under the Seleucids.* C.P. XVI, 1921, p. 12.
Wiegand, Th. *Milet: Ergebnisse der Ausgrabungen seit dem Jahre* 1899. Berlin, 1906.
Wiegand, Th., and Schrader, H. *Priene: Ergebnisse der Ausgrabungen und Untersuchungen in den Jahren 1895–1898.* Berlin, 1904. (Third volume forthcoming.)
Wilhelm, A. Wien S.B. 1920, p. 40. (On the city of Amyzon.)
Ziebarth, E. *Zum samischen Finanz- und Getreidewesen.* Z.N. XXXIV, 1924, p. 356.

3. Syria, Phoenicia, Mesopotamia and Babylonia

Bouchier, E. S. *A short History of Antioch.* Oxford, 1921.
Butler, H. C. *Publications of an American Archaeological Expedition to Syria, 1899–1900.* I–IV. 1904–5.
—— *Archaeological Expeditions to Syria in 1904–5 and 1909.* Three divisions. 1907–16.
Chapot, V. *Séleucie de Piérie.* Bull. de la Soc. d. Ant. de France, 1906, p. 149.
Cultrera, M. *Architettura ippodamea.* Memorie dell' Acc. dei Lincei, XVII, 1924, p. 357.
Cumont, F. *Études syriennes.* Paris, 1917.
—— *Fouilles de Doura-Europos (1922–3).* Texte et Atlas. Paris, 1926.
Dobiaš. *Séleucie sur l'Euphrate.* Syria, VI, 1925, p. 253.
Dussaud, R. *Topographie historique de la Syrie antique et médiévale.* Paris, 1927.
Eisler, R. *Zeitschr. d. Deutsch. Morgenl. Ges.* LXXVIII, 1924, p. 61. (A Phoenician trading company.)
Fleming, W. *The History of Tyre.* New York, 1915.
Förster, R. *Antiochia am Orontes.* J.D.A.I. XII, 1897, p. 104.
Gerkan, A. von. *Griechische Städteanlagen.* Berlin and Leipzig, 1924.
Honigmann. Art. *Seleukeia* (Pieria) in P.W.
—— *Historische Topographie von Nordsyrien im Altertum.* Leipzig, 1923.
Koldewey, R. *Das wiedererstehende Babylon.* Ed. 3. 1925. (Eng. trans. 1914.)
Lammens, P. H. *La Mecque à la veille de l'hégire.* Mélanges de l'Université Saint-Joseph de Beirout, IX, 1924.
Sachau, E. *Reisen in Syrien und Mesopotamien.* Berlin, 1883.
—— *Am Euphrat und Tigris.* Leipzig, 1900.
Sarre, P., and Herzfeld, J. *Archaeologische Reisen im Euphrat-Tigris Gebiet.* I–IV. 1920.
Schroeder, O. *Das Pantheon der Stadt Uruk in der Seleukidenzeit.* Berl. S.B. 1916, p. 1180.

Strack, M. *Seleukeia und Ktesiphon.* Der Alte Orient, XVI, 2 and 3.
—— Art. *Seleukeia am Tigris* in P.W.
Syria. Revue d'art oriental et d'archéologie. I–VII. (1919–26.)
Watzinger, G., and Walzinger, K. *Damaskos, die antike Stadt.* Wissenschaftliche Veröffentlichungen des deutsch-türkischen Denkmalschutzkommando, IV, 1921.
Wilhelm, A. *Wien. Anz.* 1922, p. 11. (Tyre and Delphi.) Cf. Bequignon, V., and Laumonier, A., *B.C.H.* VII–XII, p. 306 and p. 483. (Tyre and Teos.)
Zingerle, J. *Heiliges Recht.* Jahreshefte, XXIII, 1926, Beiblatt, p. 6. (Temples and Villages.)

NOTE. Important excavations have been recently carried out by Perdrizet and Seyrig at Seleuceia in Pieria. A full report will be published soon by the Haut Commissariat of Syria. An excavation has also been started on the site of Seleuceia on the Tigris by a German Expedition.

4. *Palestine*

Bevan, E. R. *Jerusalem under the High Priests.* London, 1904.
Dickey, S. *The constructive revolution of Jesus.* New York, 1924.
Dussaud, R. *Les Arabes en Syrie avant l'Islam.* Paris, 1907.
Felton, J. *Neutestamentliche Zeitgeschichte.* Eds. 2 and 3. Regensburg, 1925.
Guthe, H. *Die griechisch-römischen Städte des Ostjordanlandes.* Das Land der Bibel, II, 5, 1918.
Hölscher, G. *Palästina in der persischen und hellenistischen Zeit.* W. Sieglin, Quellen und Forschungen zur alten Geschichte und Geographie, No. 5, Berlin, 1903.
Jeremias, J. *Jerusalem zur Zeit Jesu.* I, II. Leipzig, 1923, 1924.
Kolbe, W. *Beiträge zur syrischen und jüdischen Geschichte.* R. Kittel, Beitr. zur Wissenschaft vom Alten Testament, Berlin, 1926.
Macalister, R. A. S. *A century of excavations in Palestine.* London, 1925.
Meyer, E. *Ursprung und Anfänge des Christentums.* II. Berlin, 1921.
Meyer, M. A. *History of the City of Gaza.* New York, 1907.
Motzo, B. *Saggi di storia e letteratura giudeo-ellenistica.* 1925.
O'Leary, De Lacy. *Arabia before Mohammed.* London, 1927.
Reisner, G. A., Fisher, C. S., and Lyon, D. G. *Harvard Excavations at Samaria.* Boston, 1924.
Schlatter, A. *Geschichte Israels von Alexander dem Grossen bis Hadrian.* Ed. 3. Berlin, 1925.
Schürer, E. *Geschichte des jüdischen Volkes im Zeitalter Jesu Christi.* II. Ed. 4. Leipzig, 1907.
Täubler, E. *Tyche.* Historische Studien, Leipzig-Berlin, 1926. (v: Staat und Umwelt. Palästina in der hellenistisch-römischen Zeit.)
Thomsen, P. *Kompendium der palästinischen Altertumskunde.* Tübingen, 1913.
—— *Die lateinischen und griechischen Inschriften der Stadt Jerusalem.* Leipzig, 1922. (Zeitschr. d. Deutschen Palästina-Vereins, 1920–1.)
—— *Die Palästina-Literatur.* IV. Leipzig, 1927.
Vincent, H. *Jérusalem. Recherches de Topographie, d'Archéologie et d'Histoire.* I. Jérusalem antique. Paris, 1912.
Volkmann, H. *Demetrios I und Alexander I von Syrien.* Klio, XIX, 1925, p. 373.
Willrich, H. *Urkundenfälschung in der hellenistisch-jüdischen Literatur.* Göttingen, 1924.

CHAPTER VII

ATHENS

GENERAL HISTORIES AND WORKS OF REFERENCE

Bevan, E. R. *Hellenistic Popular Philosophy* in The Hellenistic Age, pp. 79–107. Cambridge, 1923.
—— *Later Greek Religion.* (The Library of Greek Thought.) London, 1927.
—— *Stoics and Sceptics.* Oxford, 1913.
Brochard, V. *Les Sceptiques grecs.* Ed. 2. Paris, 1923.
Caird, E. *The Evolution of Theology in the Greek Philosophers.* Vol. II. Glasgow, 1904.
Heiberg, J. L. *Naturwissenschaft und Mathematik im klassischen Altertum.* Leipzig, 1912.
—— *Ancient Science.* Trans. D. C. Macgregor. Oxford, 1922.
Hicks, R. D. *Stoic and Epicurean.* London, 1910.
Leisegang, H. *Hellenistische Philosophie.* Breslau, 1923.
More, P. E. *Hellenistic Philosophies.* Princeton, 1923.
Murray, G. *Five Stages of Greek Religion.* Oxford, 1925. pp. 103–152.
Reymond, A. *Histoire des sciences exactes et naturelles dans l'antiquité gréco-romaine.* Paris, 1924.
Tarn, W. W. *Hellenistic Civilisation.* London, 1927.
Zeller, E. *The Stoics, Epicureans and Sceptics.* Trans. O. J. Reichel. London, 1880.

STOICISM (ANCIENT)

Texts

von Arnim, H. *Stoicorum Veterum Fragmenta.* 3 vols. Leipzig, 1903–5.
Hicks, R. D. *Diogenes Laertius* VII. (Loeb Library.) London, 1925.

Modern Works

Arnold, E. V. *Roman Stoicism.* Cambridge, 1911.
Davidson, W. L. *The Stoic Creed.* Edinburgh, 1907.
Murray, G. *The Stoic Philosophy* in Essays and Addresses, pp. 88–106. London, 1921.
Stock, St G. *Stoicism.* London, 1908.

EPICURUS

Texts and Translations

Bailey, C. *Epicurus.* Oxford, 1926. (A companion volume of critical essays is promised.)
Bignone, E. *Epicurus.* (Fragments, with Italian translation.) Bari, 1920.
Ernout, A. *Lucrèce: commentaire exégétique et critique.* Paris, 1925.
Hicks, R. D. *Diogenes Laertius* x. (Loeb Library.) London, 1925.
von der Muehll, P. *Epicurus, epistulae tres.* Leipzig, 1923.
Solovine, M. *Épicure.* Paris, 1925.
Usener, H. *Epicurea.* Leipzig, 1887.
Vogliano, A. *Nuove lettere di Epicuro e dei suoi scolari.* Bologna, 1928. (Appeared too late to be used for this chapter.)

Modern Works

Atanassiévitch, X. *L'Atomisme d'Épicure*. Paris, 1927:
Guyau, M. *La Morale d'Épicure*. Paris, 1878.
Taylor, A. E. *Epicurus*. London, 1911.
Wallace, W. *Epicureanism*. London, 1880.

LATER EPICUREANS

(a) Lucretius

Giussani, C. *Studi Lucreziani*. Turin, 1896.
Martha, C. *Le Poëme de Lucrèce*. Paris, n.d.
Masson, J. *The Atomic Theory of Lucretius*. London, 1884.
—— *Lucretius, Epicurean and Poet*. London, 1907.
Munro, H. A. J. *Lucretius*. Vol. II: Explanatory Notes. Ed. 4 finally revised, with an introductory essay on the scientific significance of Lucretius by E. N. da C. Andrade. London, 1928.

(b) Diogenes of Oenoanda

William, J. *Diogenis Oenoandensis fragmenta*. Leipzig, 1907.

NEW COMEDY

Texts and Translations

Kock, T. *Comicorum Atticorum fragmenta*. 3 vols. Leipzig, 1880.
Allinson, F. G. *Menander*. (Loeb Library.) London, 1921. (This ed. contains a very full bibliography, to which the reader is referred for further details.)
Koerte, A. *Menander*. Leipzig, 1910.
Van Leeuwen, J. *Menandri fabularum reliquiae*. Leyden, 1919.
Waddell, W. G. *Selections from Menander*. Oxford, 1927.

Modern Works

Legrand, P. A. E. F. Κωμῳδία Νέα. Trans. James Loeb. London, 1917.
Lumb, T. W. *The New Menander* (in New Chapters in the History of Greek Literature, ed. Powell and Barber, pp. 66–98). Oxford, 1921.

CHAPTER VIII

ALEXANDRIAN LITERATURE

A. GENERAL LITERATURE

Beloch, K. J. *Griechische Geschichte.* Vol. IV, 1, pp. 400–539 and vol. IV, 2, pp. 557–599. Ed. 2. Leipzig-Berlin, 1925–7.

Bethe, E., Wendland, P. and Pohlenz, M. *Einleitung in die Altertumswissenschaft.* Vol. I, 3. (*Griechische Literatur.*) Ed. 3. Leipzig-Berlin, 1927.

Birt, T. *Alexander der Grosse und das Weltgriechentum.* Ed. 2. Leipzig, n.d.

Bury, J. B., Barber, E. A., Bevan, E. and Tarn, W. W. *The Hellenistic Age.* Ed. 2. Cambridge, 1925.

Christ, W. v. *Geschichte der griechischen Litteratur.* Vol. II, 1. Ed. 6. Munich 1920.

Croiset, A. and M. *Histoire de la littérature grecque.* Vol. v. Paris, 1899.

Mahaffy, J. P. *Greek Life and Thought.* Ed. 2. London, 1896.

Powell, J. U. and Barber, E. A. *New Chapters in the History of Greek Literature.* Oxford, 1921.

Rohde, E. *Der griechische Roman und seine Vorläufer.* Ed. 3. Leipzig, 1914.

Sandys, J. E. *A History of Classical Scholarship.* Vol. I. Ed. 2. Cambridge, 1906.

Susemihl, F. *Geschichte der griechischen Litteratur in der Alexandrinerzeit.* 2 vols. Leipzig, 1891–2.

Tarn, W. W. *Hellenistic Civilisation.* London, 1927.

Wendland, P. *Die hellenistisch-römische Kultur.* Ed. 3. Tübingen, 1912.

Wilamowitz-Moellendorff, U. v. *Die Kultur der Gegenwart, die griechische Literatur.* Ed. 3. Leipzig-Berlin, 1924.

B. SPECIAL WORKS

(See also on the several authors the articles in *P.W.*)

1. *Prose-Writers*

Oratory and Rhetoric:

Blass, F. *Die griechische Beredsamkeit in dem Zeitraum von Alexander bis auf Augustus.* Berlin, 1865.

Norden, E. *Die antike Kunstprosa.* 2 vols. Leipzig, 1898.

History:

Bury, J. B. *The Ancient Greek Historians.* London, 1909.

Geography:

Berger, H. *Geschichte der wissenschaftlichen Erdkunde der Griechen.* Ed. 2. Leipzig, 1903.

Gisinger, F. *Geographie* in P.W., Supplementband IV. Stuttgart, 1924.

Tozer, H. F. *A History of Ancient Geography.* Cambridge, 1897.

2. *Poets*

Cessi, C. *La poesia ellenistica.* Bari, 1912.

Couat, A. *La poésie Alexandrine.* Paris, 1882.

Knox, A. D. *The First Greek Anthologist.* Cambridge, 1923.

Körte, A. *Hellenistische Dichtung.* Leipzig, 1925.

Legrand, Ph.-E. *La poésie Alexandrine*. Paris, 1924.

Mackail, J. W. *Lectures on Greek Poetry*. Ed. 2. London, 1926.

Reitzenstein, R. *Epigram und Skolion*. Giessen, 1893.

Rostagni, A. *Poeti alessandrini*. Torino, 1916.

Symonds, J. A. *Studies of the Greek Poets*. Vol. 2. Ed. 3. London, 1920.

Wilamowitz-Moellendorff, U. von. *Hellenistische Dichtung in der Zeit des Kallimachos*. 2 vols. Berlin, 1924.

Wright, F. A. *The Poets of the Greek Anthology*. London, 1925.

C. Texts and Commentaries

1. *Prose*

The fragments of many of the writers mentioned in this chapter are collected in Müller, *Fragmenta Historicorum Graecorum*, 5 vols. Paris, 1841–70. Ephorus, Philochorus, Phylarchus, Theopompus, Timaeus are in vol. 1; Berosus, Clearchus, Cratippus, Demetrius of Phalerum, Duris, Hecataeus, Hieronymus, Manetho, Megasthenes, Patrocles in vol. 11; Aratus of Sicyon and Neanthes in vol. 111. The new collection by F. Jacoby (*Die Fragmente der griechischen Historiker*, Berlin, 1923–) is not yet complete, but vol. 1 contains Euhemerus; vol. 11 A, Cratippus, Duris, Ephorus, Neanthes, Phylarchus; vol. 11 B, Aristobulus, Baeton, Callisthenes, Chares, Cleitarchus, Diognetus, Hegesias, Nearchus, Ptolemy, Theopompus. The *Hellenica Oxyrhynchia* is printed in vol. 11 A of Jacoby's work, and has been edited, along with the fragments of Cratippus and Theopompus, by B. P. Grenfell and A. S. Hunt (Oxford, 1909), also by E. Kalinka (Leipzig, 1927). The fragments of Eratosthenes dealing with geography are collected in H. Berger, *Die geographische Fragmente des Eratosthenes* (Leipzig, 1880); those concerned with chronology are to be found in the Didot *Herodotus* (Paris, 1844). Satyrus' Life of Euripides is printed in H. v. Arnim, *Supplementum Euripideum* (Bonn, 1913).

2. *Poetry*

For the poets mentioned in this chapter whose works are only extant in a fragmentary condition—viz. Philetas, Simias, Antagoras, Hermesianax, Phoenix, Cercidas, Cleanthes, Rhianus, Eratosthenes, Alexander Aetolus, Phanocles, Euphorion—as also for the *Alexandrian Erotic Fragment*, see J. U. Powell, *Collectanea Alexandrina* (Oxford, 1925).

CALLIMACHUS. Hymns and Epigrams only, U. v. Wilamowitz-Moellendorff (ed. 4, Berlin, 1925); Hymns, Epigrams, and Fragments, O. Schneider (*Callimachea*, 2 vols. Leipzig, 1870–3). For the new fragments see R. Pfeiffer, *Callimachi Fragmenta Nuper Reperta* (ed. maior, Bonn, 1923): for the latest additions *Oxyrhynchus Papyri*, vol. XVII (London, 1927). See also the edition of Callimachus (Hymns, Epigrams, and a selection of the fragments) by E. Cahen (Paris, 1922), which contains a French translation and introductions besides the Greek text.

APOLLONIUS RHODIUS. *Argonautica*, R. C. Seaton (Oxford, 1900); R. Merkel (2 vols. Leipzig, 1854); with commentary, G. W. Mooney (Dublin, 1912); Book III, with introduction and commentary, M. M. Gillies (Cambridge, 1928). Other poems: *Collectanea Alexandrina*.

THEOCRITUS. U. v. Wilamowitz-Moellendorff (ed. 2, Oxford, 1910); with commentary: R. J. Cholmeley (ed. 2, London, 1919). Compare also PH.-E. Legrand, *Étude sur Théocrite* (Paris, 1898); id. *Bucoliques Grecs*. I. *Théocrite* (Paris, 1925), II. *Pseudo-Théocrite, Moschos, Bion, Divers* (Paris, 1927), an edition which contains a French translation and introductions besides the Greek text.

HERODAS. With commentary: J. A. Nairn (Oxford, 1904); with commentary and translation: W. Headlam and A. D. Knox (Cambridge, 1922). See also the edition of R. Herzog (Leipzig, 1926), which contains a German translation, introductions, and short notes besides the Greek text, and that by J. A. Nairn and L. Laloy (Paris, 1928), which contains a French translation and introductions besides the Greek text.

ARATUS. E. Maass (Berlin, 1893).

NICANDER. O. Schneider (*Nicandrea*. Leipzig, 1856).

EPIGRAMMATISTS. F. Dübner and E. Cougny, *Anthologia Palatina* (3 vols. Paris, 1864–1872–1890); H. Stadtmüller, *Anthologia Graeca* (three volumes only published. Leipzig, 1894–1899–1906). Compare also Viscount Harberton, *Meleager and the other poets of Jacobs' Anthology* (Oxford, 1895). For particular poets see—P. Schott, *Posidippi epigrammata collecta et illustrata* (Berlin, 1905); J. Geffcken, *Leonidas von Tarent* (Jahrb. f. kl. Philol., Suppl. 23, 1896); A. Hauvette, *Les Épigrammes de Callimaque* (Paris, 1907).

LYCOPHRON: *Alexandra*. E. Scheer, Text (Berlin, 1881), Scholia (Berlin, 1908); C. v. Holzinger, Text, German translation, and notes (Leipzig, 1895).

D. Translations

Callimachus and Lycophron: A. W. Mair; Aratus: G. R. Mair, London, 1921.
Apollonius Rhodius: R. C. Seaton, London, 1912.
The Greek Bucolic Poets: J. M. Edmonds, London, 1912.
The Greek Anthology: W. R. Paton, 5 vols. London, 1916–18.

All these are in the Loeb Classical Library, with the Greek text opposite the translation.

Compare also—for Apollonius Rhodius, the verse-translation of A. S. Way (Temple Classics, London, 1901); for the *Alexandra*, G. W. Mooney, *The Alexandra of Lycophron* (London, 1921); for Theocritus, A. Lang, *Theocritus, Bion, and Moschus* (Golden Treasury, London, 1906): J. H. Hallard, *The Idylls of Theocritus translated into English Verse* (ed. 2, London, 1901): A. S. Way, *Theocritus, Bion, and Moschus translated into English Verse* (Cambridge, 1913): and the translations in W. Headlam, *A Book of Greek Verse* (Cambridge, 1907); for Herodas, H. Sharpley, *A Realist of the Aegean; being a verse-translation of the Mimes of Herodas* (London, 1906).

CHAPTER IX

HELLENISTIC SCIENCE AND MATHEMATICS

A. Sections I–II

1. *Ancient Authorities*

Hippocratic *Corpus*, *Precepts* and *Decorum*.
Theophrastus, *De historia plantarum* and *De causis plantarum*.
References in Galen to Herophilus and Erasistratus given in J. F. Dobson's articles cited below.

2. *Modern Works*

Allbutt, Sir T. Clifford. *Greek Medicine in Rome*. London, 1921.
Dobson, J. F. *Herophilus of Alexandria*. Proc. Roy. Soc. Med., London, 1925.
—— *Erasistratus*. Proc. Roy. Soc. Med., London, 1927.
Gossen, art. *Herophilos* (4) in P. W.
Greene, E. L. *Landmarks of Botanical History*. Washington, 1909.
Hort, Sir A. *Theophrastus, Enquiry into Plants*. London, 1916.
Marx, K. F. H. *Herophilus*. Karlsruhe, 1838.
Singer, Charles. *Greek Biology and Greek Medicine*. Oxford, 1922.
—— *The Evolution of Anatomy*. London, 1925.
Wellmann, M. Art. *Erasistratos* (2) in P. W.
Withington, E. T. *Medical History from the Earliest Times*. London, 1894.

B. Sections III–VI

1. *Ancient Texts*

Friedlein, G. *Procli Diadochi in primum Euclidis elementorum librum commentarii*. Leipzig, 1873.
Gregory, D. *Euclidis quae supersunt omnia*. Oxford, 1703.
Halley, E. *Apollonii Pergaei conicorum libri octo et Sereni Antissensis de sectione cylindri et coni libri duo*. Oxford, 1710.
Halma, N. Κλαυδίου Πτολεμαίου Μαθηματικὴ Σύνταξις. *Composition mathématique de Claude Ptolémée, traduite pour la première fois du grec en français . . . par* M. Halma, *et suivie des notes de* M. Delambre. 2 vols. Paris, 1813, 1816. (Reprinted 1927, J. Hermann, Paris.)
Heath, Sir T. L. Aristarchus *On the Sizes and Distances of the Sun and Moon* (in *Aristarchus of Samos, The Ancient Copernicus*. Oxford, 1913).
—— *Euclid in Greek*. Book 1. Cambridge, 1920.
Heiberg, J. L. *Apollonii Pergaei quae graece exstant cum commentariis antiquis*. 2 vols. Leipzig, 1891–3.
—— *Archimedis opera omnia cum commentariis Eutocii*. Ed. 2, 3 vols. Leipzig, 1910–15.
—— *Ptolemaei Syntaxis mathematica*. 2 vols. Leipzig, 1898, 1903. Vol. 3 (*Ptolemaei opera astronomica minora*). Leipzig, 1907.
Heiberg, J. L. and Menge, H. *Euclidis opera omnia*. 8 vols. Leipzig, 1883–1916.
Hultsch, F. *Autolyci de sphaera quae movetur, de ortibus et occasibus libri duo*. Leipzig, 1885.
—— *Pappi Alexandrini collectionis quae supersunt. . . .* Berlin, 1876–8.
Manitius, K. *Hipparchi in Arati et Eudoxi phaenomena commentariorum libri tres*. **Leipzig, 1894.**

2. *Translations and Editions*

Archibald, R. C. *Euclid's Book on Divisions (of Figures), with a restoration based on Woepcke's text and the* Practica Geometriae *of Leonardo Pisano.* Cambridge, 1915.

Besthorn, R. O. and Heiberg, J. L. *Codex Leidensis* 399, 1. *Euclidis elementa ex interpretatione al-Hadschdschadschii cum commentariis al-Narizii.* Copenhagen, 1893–1910.

Curtze, M. *Anaritii in decem libros priores elementorum Euclidis commentarii.* Leipzig, 1909.

Halley, E. *Apollonii Pergaei de Sectione Rationis libri duo....* Oxford, 1706.

Heath, Sir T. L. *The Thirteen Books of Euclid's Elements translated from the text of Heiberg with Introduction and Commentary.* Ed. 2. 3 vols. Cambridge, 1926.

—— *The Works of Archimedes, edited in modern notation....* Cambridge, 1897.

—— *The* Method *of Archimedes.* Cambridge, 1912.

—— *Apollonius of Perga, Treatise on Conic Sections, edited in modern notation....* Cambridge, 1896.

Manitius, K. *Des Ptolemäus Handbuch der Astronomie.* 2 vols. Leipzig, 1912–13.

3. *Modern Works*

Gow, J. *A Short History of Greek Mathematics.* Cambridge, 1884.

Hankel, H. *Zur Geschichte der Mathematik im Alterthum und Mittelalter.* Leipzig, 1874.

Heath, Sir T. L. *Aristarchus of Samos, The Ancient Copernicus, a History of Greek astronomy to Aristarchus....* Oxford, 1913.

—— *A History of Greek Mathematics.* 2 vols. Oxford, 1921.

Heiberg, J. L. *Mathematik und Naturwissenschaften im klassischen Altertum.* (English translation by D. C. Macgregor. Oxford, 1922.)

Hultsch, F. Arts. *Apollonius of Perga, Aristarchus of Samos, Archimedes, Astronomie, Autolykos, Eudoxos, Eukleides,* etc. in P.W.

Loria, G. *Le scienze esatte nell' antica Grecia.* Milan, 1914.

Rehm, A. Arts. *Hipparchos* and *Konon* in P.W.

Zeuthen, H. G. *Die Lehre von den Kegelschnitten im Altertum.* Copenhagen, 1888, 1902.

—— *Geschichte der Mathematik im Altertum und Mittelalter.* Copenhagen, 1896.

CHAPTERS X–XVI

THE HISTORY OF ROME TO THE FALL OF VEII AND THE STRUGGLE OF THE ORDERS DOWN TO THE DICTATORSHIP OF Q. HORTENSIUS

A. I. Ancient Authorities

1. *Inscriptions*

Corpus Inscriptionum Etruscarum. Lipsiae. Vol. i, 1893–1902. Vol. ii, 1907– (in progress). Supplementi fasc. i, 1919–21.

Corpus Inscriptionum Latinarum. Berlin. Vol. i. Inscriptiones Latinae antiquissimae ad C. Caesaris mortem. Editio altera. 1893–1918. Vol. xiv. Inscriptiones Latii veteris. 1887.

Dessau, H. *Inscriptiones Latinae Selectae.* Berlin. Vol. i, 1892; vol. ii, i, 1902; vol. ii, 2, 1906; vol. iii, i, 1914; vol. iii, 2, 1916.

Conway, R. S. *The Italic Dialects edited with a grammar and glossary.* 2 vols. Cambridge, 1897.

Zvetaieff, P. *Inscriptiones Italiae inferioris dialecticae.* Moscow, 1886.

Acta Fratrum Arvalium rest. et ill. G. Henzen. Berlin, 1874.

2. *Legal Documents*

Iurisprudentiae anteiustinianae reliquias editione sexta edd. E. Seckel et B. Kuebler. Lipsiae. Gaii Institutionum commentarii quattuor in vol. i, 1908. Pauli Sententiarum ad filium libri quinque in vol. ii, fasc. i, 1921.

Digesta, recognovit T. Mommsen, retractavit P. Krueger in *Corpus Iuris Civilis,* vol. i. Editio stereotypa quarta decima. Berlin, 1922.

Bruns, C. G. *Fontes iuris Romani antiqui,* septimum edidit O. Gradenwitz. Tübingen, 1909.

Girard, P. F. *Textes de Droit romain.* Ed. 5. Paris, 1923.

Rotondi, G. *Leges publicae populi Romani.* Milan, 1912.

3. *Literary Sources*

Peter, H. *Historicorum Romanorum Reliquiae.* Leipzig. Vol. i (ed. 2). 1914. Vol. ii. 1906.

Appiani Historia Romana. Lipsiae. Vol. i. Ed. L. Mendelssohn. 1879. Vol. ii. Ed. L. Mendelssohn: editio altera correctior curante P. Viereck. 1905.

Sexti Aurelii Victoris Liber de Caesaribus, praecedunt Origo gentis Romanae et Liber de viris illustribus urbis Romae rec. F. Pichlmayr. Lipsiae, 1911.

M. Porci Catonis de agri cultura liber ed. G. Goetz. Lipsiae, 1922.

Censorini de die natali liber ed. F. Hultsch. Lipsiae, 1867.

Chronographus anni CCCLIIII ed. T. Mommsen in *Monumenta Germaniae Historica, auctorum antiquissimorum tom. IX.* Berlin, 1892.

M. Tullii Ciceronis de re publica librorum sex quae supersunt rec. C. Pascal. Turin, n.d.

Diodori Bibliotheca Historica ed. F. Vogel. Vol. i, 1888; vol. ii, 1890; vol. iii, 1893; ed. C. T. Fischer, Vol. iv, 1906; Vol. v, 1906. Lipsiae.

Diodors römische Annalen bis 302 a. Chr. samt dem Ineditum Vaticanum heraus-gegeben von A. B. Drachmann. Bonn, 1912.

Dionysi Halicarnasensis Antiquitatum Romanarum quae supersunt ed. C. Jacoby. Lipsiae. Vol. I, 1885; vol. II, 1888; vol. III, 1891; vol. IV, 1905. Supple-mentum indices continens, 1925.

The Annals of Quintus Ennius edited by E. M. Steuart. Cambridge, 1925.

Sexti Pompei Festi de uerborum significatu quae supersunt cum Pauli epitome ed. W. M. Lindsay. Lipsiae, 1913.

A. Gellii Noctium Atticarum Libri XX ed. C. Hosius. 2 vols. Lipsiae, 1903.

Titi Livi ab urbe condita rec. R. S. Conway et C. F. Walters. Oxford. Tom. I: libri I–V. 1914. Tom. II: libri VI–X. 1919.

Pauli Orosii Historiarum adversus paganos libri VII ex recogn. C. Zangemeister. Lipsiae, 1889.

C. Plini Secundi Naturalis Historiae Libri XXXVII ed. C. Mayhoff. Lipsiae. Vol. I, 1906; vol. II, ed. 2, 1909; vol. III, 1892; vol. IV, 1897; vol. V, 1897.

Plutarchi Chaeronensis Moralia rec. G. N. Bernardakis. Vol. II. Lipsiae, 1889. (*Aetia Romana* (*Quaestiones Romanae*) on pp. 250–320.)

Plutarchi Vitae Parallelae recc. C. Lindskog et K. Ziegler. Lipsiae. Vol. I. (2 parts), 1914.

Polybii Historiae. Editionem a L. Dindorfio curatam retractavit T. Büttner-Wobst. Lipsiae. Vol. I, 1882; vol. II, 1889; vol. III, 1893; vol. IV, 1904; vol. V (indices), 1904.

C. Sallusti Crispi Historiarum Reliquiae ed. B. Maurenbrecher. Fasc. II: Fragmenta. Lipsiae, 1893.

Strabonis Geographica rec. A. Meineke. Lipsiae. Vol. I, 1895; vol. II, 1877; vol. III, 1898.

Valerii Maximi Factorum et Dictorum Memorabilium libri novem iterum rec. C. Kempf. Lipsiae, 1888.

M. Terenti Varronis de lingua latina quae supersunt rec. G. Goetz et F. Schoell. Lipsiae, 1910.

M. Terenti Varronis Rerum rusticarum libri tres ed. G. Goetz. Lipsiae, 1912.

Vellei Paterculi ad M. Vinicium libri duo ed. R. Ellis. Oxford, 1898.

II. Criticism of Authorities

Frank, T. *Roman Historiography before Caesar*. American Historical Review, XXXII, 1927, p. 232.

Kornemann, E. *Der Priesterkodex in der Regia und die Entstehung der altrömischen Pseudogeschichte*. Tübingen, 1912.

Niese, B. *De annalibus Romanis observationes*. Marburg, 1886.

Nitzsch, K. W. *Die römische Annalistik von ihren ersten Anfängen bis auf Valerius Antias*. Berlin, 1873.

Peter, H. *Wahrheit und Kunst: Geschichtsschreibung und Plagiat im klassischen Altertum*. Leipzig, 1911.

Rosenberg, A. *Einleitung und Quellenkunde zur römischen Geschichte*. Berlin, 1921.

Schwartz, E. Arts. *Diodoros von Agyrion* and *Dionysios von Halikarnassos* in P.W. V, col. 663 *sqq.*, 934 *sqq.*

Sigwart, G. *Römische Fasten und Annalen bei Diodor*. Greifswald, 1906.

Soltau, W. *Die Anfänge der römischen Geschichtschreibung*. Leipzig, 1909.

Wachsmuth, C. *Einleitung in das Studium der alten Geschichte*. Leipzig, 1895.

III. Chronology

Costa, G. *I fasti consolari romani dalle origini alla morte di Giulio Cesare.* 2 vols. Milan, 1910.

—— *L'originale dei fasti consolari.* Rome, 1910.

Ginzel, F. K. *Handbuch der mathematischen und technischen Chronologie.* Vol. II. Leipzig, 1911.

Holzapfel, L. *Römische Chronologie.* Leipzig, 1885.

Kahrstedt, U. *Zwei Beiträge zur älteren römischen Geschichte,* Rh. Mus. LXXII, 1918, p. 258.

Kornemann, E. *Der Priesterkodex in der Regia und die Entstehung der altrömischen Pseudogeschichte.* Tübingen, 1912.

Kubitschek, W. *Grundriss der antiken Zeitrechnung* in I. Müller's *Handbuch der klassischen Altertumswissenschaft.* Munich, 1927.

Leuze, O. *Die römische Jahrzählung.* Tübingen, 1909.

Matzat, H. *Römische Chronologie.* Berlin, 1883–4.

Mommsen, Th. *Die römische Chronologie bis auf Cäsar.* Ed. 2. Berlin, 1859.

Pais, E. *Fasti triumphales populi Romani.* 2 vols. Rome, 1920–3.

Peter, C. *Zeittafeln zur römischen Geschichte.* Halle, 1882.

Schön, G. *Das capitolinische Verzeichniss der römischen Triumphe.* Vienna, 1903.

—— Art. *Fasti* in *P.W.*

—— *Die Elogien d. Augustusforums und der Liber de viris illustribus urbis Romae.* Cilli, 1895.

—— *Die Differenzen zwischen der capitolinischen Magistrats- und Triumphliste.* Vienna, 1905.

Seeck, O. *Die Kalendertafel der Pontifices.* Berlin, 1885.

Unger, W. *Römische Chronologie* in I. Müller's *Handbuch der klassischen Altertumswissenschaft.* Ed. 2. Munich, 1892.

B. Modern Works

1. *General Histories*

The lists which follow are intended, not to survey the whole field of modern literature on early Roman history, but to indicate works to which the writers of the chapters desire to acknowledge their indebtedness and those wherein references to other publications may conveniently be found. The following may be mentioned in addition to those enumerated in the General Bibliography. The indispensable histories for the study of early Rome are those of Schwegler and De Sanctis.

Beloch, K. J. *Römische Geschichte bis zum Ende der Republik* in Gercke and Norden, *Einleitung in die Altertumswissenschaft,* III², Leipzig, 1914, pp. 160–209.

—— *Römische Geschichte bis zum Beginn der punischen Kriege.* Berlin, 1926.

Bloch, G. *La République romaine.* Ed. 2. Paris, 1922.

De Sanctis, G. *Storia dei Romani.* Vols. I and II. Turin, 1907.

—— *Per la scienza dell' antichità.* Turin, 1909. pp. 303–531.

Hartmann, L. M. *Ältere römische Geschichte* in *Weltgeschichte in gemeinverständlicher Darstellung,* herausgegeben von L. M. Hartmann, vol. III, pp. 1–55. Gotha, 1919.

Lange, L. *Römische Alterthümer.* Vol. I. (Ed. 3.) Berlin, 1876.

Lewis, Sir G. Cornewall. *An Inquiry into the Credibility of the Early Roman History.* 2 vols. London, 1855.

Meyer, E. *Geschichte des Altertums.* Vol. II. Stuttgart, 1893. pp. 484–532; 707–15; 808–14. Vol. V. Ed. 3. Berlin, 1921. pp. 132–49.

—— *Zur älteren römischen Geschichte* in *Kleine Schriften,* vol. II. Halle, 1924. pp. 286–307.

Mommsen, T. *Römische Geschichte.* Vol I. Ed. 13. Berlin, 1923.
—— *Römische Forschungen.* Berlin. Vol. I, 1864; vol. II, 1879.
Neumann, K. J. *Die hellenistischen Staaten und die römische Republik.* In *Welt-geschichte,* herausgegeben von J. von Pflugk-Harttung, vol. I. Berlin, n.d. pp. 355–89.
Niebuhr, B. G. *The History of Rome,* translated by J. C. Hare and Connop Thirlwall. Cambridge. Vol. I, 1831; vol. II, 1832; vol. III, 1851.
—— *Lectures on the History of Rome,* edited by Leonhard Schmitz. Vol. I. Ed. 2. London, 1850.
Niese, B. *Grundriss der römischen Geschichte.* 5te Auflage, neubearbeitet von E. Hohl. Munich, 1923.
Pais, E. *Storia di Roma.* Rome, 1926. Vol. I. *Le fonti—l'età mitica.* Vol. II. *L' età regia.*
—— *Storia critica di Roma durante i primi cinque secoli.* Rome. Vol. II, 1915; vol. III, 1918.
—— *Histoire romaine,* I. *Des origines à l'achèvement de la conquête.* Paris. Fasc. I, 1926, Fasc. II, n.d.
—— *Ricerche sulla Storia e sul Diritto pubblico di Roma.* Rome. Serie I, 1915; II, 1916; III, 1918; IV, 1921.
Schwegler, A. *Römische Geschichte.* Tübingen. Vol. I, 1867; vol. II, 1856; vol. III, 1858.

In sections 2–6 and 8–9 of this bibliography works are grouped, so far as possible, in the order in which they become relevant to the texts of the chapters concerned.

2. *Geography, Ethnology and the Historical Topography of Latium and the Site of Rome*

von Hofmann, A. *Das Land Italien und seine Geschichte.* Stuttgart-Berlin, 1921.
Nissen, H. *Italische Landeskunde.* Berlin. Vol. I. *Land und Leute.* 1883. Vol. II. *Die Städte.* 1902.
Ashby, T. *The Roman Campagna in Classical Times.* London, 1927.
Tomassetti, G. *La campagna romana.* Rome. Vols. I–II, 1910; vol. III, 1913; vol. IV (G. and F. Tomassetti), 1926.
von Duhn, F. *Italische Gräberkunde.* Erster Teil. Heidelberg, 1924.
Peet, T. E. *The Stone and Bronze Ages in Italy.* Oxford, 1909.
Antonielli, U. *Due gravi problemi paletnologici.* Studi etruschi, I. 1927, pp. 11–48.
—— *Appunti di paletnologia laziale.* Bullettino di Paletnologia italiana, Anno XLIV (1924), pp. 154–92.
Randall-MacIver, D. *Villanovans and Early Etruscans.* Oxford, 1924.
—— *The Iron Age in Italy.* Oxford, 1927.
Holland, L. A. *The Faliscans in Prehistoric Times.* Rome, 1925.
Pinza, G. *Monumenti primitivi di Roma e del Lazio antico=* Mon. Linc. XV. 1905.
—— *Monumenti paleoetnologici raccolti nei musei Comunali.* Bullettino della Commissione archeologica comunale di Roma, XL, 1912, p. 15.
Antonielli, U. *Sepolcreto laziale della 'Riserva del Truglio' nel Pescolaro.* N.S.A. 1924, p. 429.
Pinza, G. *Le vicende della zona esquilina fino ai tempi di Augusto.* Bullettino della Commissione archeologica comunale di Roma, XLII, 1914, p. 117.
Piganiol, A. *Essai sur les origines de Rome.* Paris, 1917.
Carcopino, J. *Virgile et les origines d'Ostie.* Paris, 1919.
†Adams, L. E. W. *A Study in the Commerce of Latium from the early Iron Age through the sixth century B.C.* Bryn Mawr Dissertation. Menasha, Wis. n.d.

Graffunder, P. Art. *Rom* in P.W. i, A, col. 1008 *sqq.*

Homo, L. *La Rome antique: histoire-guide des monuments de Rome.* Paris, 1921.

Jordan, H. *Topographie der Stadt Rom im Alterthum.* Berlin. Vol. i, 1, 1878; vol. i, 2, 1885; vol. i, 3 (bearbeitet von Ch. Huelsen), 1907; vol. ii, 1871.

Richter, O. *Topographie der Stadt Rom.* Ed. 2. Munich, 1901.

Stuart Jones, H. *Classical Rome.* London, 1910.

Carter, J. B. *Roma Quadrata and the Septimontium.* A.J.A. xii, 1908, p. 172.

Wissowa, G. *Gesammelte Abhandlungen zur römischen Religions- und Stadtgeschichte.* Munich, 1904. pp. 230–52 (*Septimontium und Subura*).

Merrill, E. T. *The City of Servius and the Pomerium.* C.P. vi, 1909, p. 420.

Besnier, M. *L'île tibérine dans l'antiquité.* Paris, 1902.

Merlin, A. *L'Aventin dans l'antiquité.* Paris, 1906.

Frank, T. *Roman Buildings of the Republic: an attempt to date them from their materials.* American Academy in Rome, 1924.

Graffunder, P. *Das Alter der servianischen Mauer in Rom.* Klio, xi, 1911, p. 83.

3. *Religious Evidence for Social History*

Beckmann, F. *Zauberei und Recht in Roms Frühzeit.* Münster Diss. Osnabrück, 1923.

Fowler, W. Warde, *The Religious Experience of the Roman People.* London, 1911.

—— *The Roman Festivals of the period of the Republic.* London, 1899.

Nilsson, M. P. *Primitive Time-Reckoning.* Lund-Oxford, 1920.

Rose, H. J. *Primitive Culture in Italy.* London, 1926.

—— Introduction to *The Roman Questions of Plutarch.* Oxford, 1924.

Wissowa, G. *Religion und Kultus der Römer.* Ed. 2. Munich, 1912.

4. *The Etruscan Influence on Rome*

Dennis, G. *The Cities and Cemeteries of Etruria.* 2 vols. Ed. 3. London, 1883.

Ducati, P. *Etruria antica.* 2 vols. Turin, 1925.

Fell, R. A. L. *Etruria and Rome.* Cambridge, 1924.

Meyer, E. *Geschichte des Altertums.* Vol. ii, 1. Ed. 2. Berlin, 1928. p. 556, n. 2.

Modestov, B. *Introduction à l'Histoire romaine; l'ethnologie préhistorique, les influences civilisatrices à l'époque préromaine et les commencements de Rome.* Paris, 1907.

Müller, K. O. *Die Etrusker.* Neubearbeitet von W. Deecke. 2 vols. Stuttgart, 1877.

Noël Des Vergers, A. *L'Étrurie et les Étrusques.* Paris. 2 vols. 1862–64, and atlas, 1862.

Pareti, L. *Le origini etrusche. i. Le leggende e i dati della scienza.* Florence, 1926.

Randall-MacIver, D. *The Etruscans.* Oxford, 1927.

Schuchhardt, C. *Die Etrusker als altitalisches Volk.* P.Z. xvi, 1925, p. 109.

Minto, A. *Marsiliana d'Albegna: le scoperte archeologiche del Principe Don Tommaso Corsini.* Florence, 1921.

Grenier, A. *L'alphabet de Marsiliana et les origines de l'écriture à Rome.* Mélanges d'archéologie et d'histoire, xli, 1924, p. 3.

Dall' Osso, I. *Una nuova visione di Roma primitiva.* Nuova Antologia, vol. 232, Nov.–Dec. 1923, p. 350.

Nogara, B. *Dell' influenza esercitata dall' Etruria sulla civiltà e nell' arte romana.* Dissertazioni della pontificia accademia romana di archeologia, Serie ii, vol. xi, 1914, p. 123.

Coussin, P. *Les armes romaines.* Paris, 1926.

Schulze, W. *Zur Geschichte lateinischer Eigennamen.* Berlin, 1904.

5. *Foundation Legends and the Regal Age*

Carter, J. B. Arts. *Romulus, Romos, Remus* in Roscher, *Ausführliches Lexikon der griechischen und römischen Mythologie*, vol. IV, cols. 164–209.

Kretschmer, P. *Remus und Romulus*. Glotta, I, 2–3, 1908, p. 288.

Rosenberg, A. Art. *Romulus* in P.W.

Carcopino, J. *La louve du Capitole*. Paris, 1925.

Stuart Jones, H. (ed.). *A Catalogue of the Ancient Sculptures preserved in the Municipal Collections of Rome: the Sculptures of the Palazzo dei Conservatori*. Oxford. 1926. Text, pp. 56–8; plate no. 17.

Barbagallo, C. *Il problema delle origini di Roma da Vico a noi*. Milan, 1926.

De Sanctis, G. *La légende historique des premiers siècles de Rome*. Journal des Savants, N.S. Année 7, 1909, pp. 126 and 205. Année 8, 1910, p. 310.

Dyer, T. H. *The History of the Kings of Rome*. London, 1868.

Jordan, H. *Die Könige im alten Italien: ein Fragment*. Berlin, 1887.

Seeley, Sir J. R. *Historical Examination of Livy, Book I* in Livy, *Book I*, ed. J. R. S. Ed. 3. Oxford, 1881.

Körte, G. *Ein Wandgemälde von Vulci als Document zur römischen Königsgeschichte*. J.D.A.I. XII, 1897, p. 57.

De Sanctis, G. *Mastarna*. Klio, II, 1902, p. 96.

6. *The First Treaty between Rome and Carthage*

On this subject the reader should consult the histories enumerated in the General Bibliography and in section B 1, and also the works marked with a † in sections B 2 and B 8. In addition to these the following may be mentioned.

Costanzi, V. *Sulla cronologia del primo trattato tra Roma e Cartagine*. Riv. fil. N.S. III, 1925, p. 381.

Gsell, S. *Histoire ancienne de l'Afrique du Nord*. III. Paris, 1920. pp. 67–71.

Mommsen, T. *Die römische Chronologie bis auf Caesar*. Ed. 2. Berlin, 1859. pp. 320–25.

Strachan-Davidson, J. L. *Selections from Polybius*. Oxford, 1888. pp. 50–72.

Täubler, E. *Imperium Romanum*. Vol. I. Leipzig, 1913. pp. 254–76.

7. *The Constitution*

The following works may be mentioned in addition to those enumerated in the General Bibliography:

Bandel, F. *Die Dictaturen der römischen Republik*. Breslau, Diss. 1910.

Beloch, K. J. *Der italische Bund unter Roms Hegemonie*. Leipzig, 1880.

Binder, J. *Die Plebs: Studien zur römischen Rechtsgeschichte*. Leipzig, 1909.

Bloch, G. *La plèbe romaine*. Paris, 1911.

—— *Les origines du sénat romain*. Paris, 1883.

Botsford, G. W. *The Roman Assemblies from their origin to the end of the Republic*. New York, 1909.

Costa, E. *Storia del diritto romano pubblico*. Ed. 2. 1920.

De Boor, C. *Fasti censorii*. Berlin, 1873.

De Francisci, P. *Storia del diritto romano*. Vol. I. Rome, 1926.

Gelzer, M. *Die Nobilität der römischen Republik*. Leipzig-Berlin, 1912.

Greenidge, A. H. J. *Roman Public Life*. London, 1901.

Kornemann, E. *Zur altitalischen Verfassungsgeschichte*. Klio, XIV, 1914, p. 190.

—— *Die Beamtendreizahl in Italien*, Klio XIV, p. 494.

Leifer, F. *Die Einheit des Gewaltgedankens im römischen Staatsrecht.* Munich-Leipzig, 1914.

Leuze, O. *Zur Geschichte der römischen Censur.* Halle, 1912.

Meyer, E. *Kleine Schriften.* Ed. 2. 2 vols. Berlin, 1924.

—— Art. *Plebs,* in Conrad, *Handwörterbuch der Staatswissenschaft.* Ed. 2. Jena, 1910.

Mommsen, T. *Gesammelte Schriften.* 8 vols. Berlin, 1905–13.

—— *Römisches Staatsrecht.* Ed. 3. Leipzig, 1888.

—— *Römisches Strafrecht.* Leipzig, 1899.

Munzer, F. *Consulartribunen und Censoren.* Hermes, LVII, 1922, p. 134.

—— *Römische Adelsparteien und Adelsfamilien.* Stuttgart, 1920.

Neumann, K. J. *Die Grundherrschaft der römischen Republik, die Bauernbefreiung und die Entstehung der servianischen Verfassung.* Strassburg, 1900.

Niccolini, G. *Fasti tribunorum plebis.* Pisa, 1898.

—— *Sui comizi romani.* Atti d. Soc. Lig. de Sc. e Lett. 1925.

Oberziner, G. *L'origine della plebe romana.* Leipzig, 1901.

Pacchioni, G. *Dalla monarchia alla repubblica* (Atti della reale Accademia delle Scienze di Torino, LX).

Rose, H. J. *Patricians and plebeians at Rome.* J.R.S. XII, 1922, p. 106.

Rosenberg, A. *Der Staat der alten Italiker.* Berlin, 1913.

—— *Studien zur Entstehung der Plebs.* Hermes, XLVIII, 1913, p. 359.

—— *Untersuchungen zur römischen Centurienverfassung.* Berlin, 1911.

—— *Zur Geschichte des Latinerbundes.* Hermes, LIV, 1919, p. 113.

—— *Die Entstehung des sogenannten 'foedus Cassianum' und des lateinischen Rechts.* Hermes, LV, 1920, p. 337.

Schur, W. *Fremder Adel im römischen Staat der Samniterkriege.* Hermes, LIX, 1924, p. 450.

Soltau, W. *Ueber Entstehung und Zusammensetzung der altrömischen Volksversammlungen.* Berlin, 1880.

—— *Der Ursprung der Diktatur.* Hermes, XLIX, 1914, p. 352.

—— *Zur römischen Verfassungsgeschichte.* Phil. LXXIII, 1914, p. 504; LXXV, 1916, p. 232.

—— *Der Dezemvirat in Sage und Geschichte.* Z. d. Sav.-Stift. XXXVIII, 1917, p. 1.

Strachan-Davidson, J. L. *Problems of the Roman Criminal Law.* 2 vols. Oxford, 1912.

Täubler, E. *Untersuchungen zur Geschichte des Dezemvirats* (in E. Ebering's *Historische Studien,* vol. CXLVIII). Berlin, 1921.

—— *Tyche; Historische Studien.* Leipzig, 1926.

Willems, P. *Le Sénat de la république romaine.* Ed. 2. Paris, 1885.

—— *Le droit public romain.* Ed. 7. Louvain, 1910.

8. *Rome and her Neighbours in the Fifth Century*

Beloch, J. *Der italische Bund unter Roms Hegemonie.* Leipzig, 1880.

†Gelzer, M. Art. *Latium: politische und staatsrechtliche Verhältnisse* in P. W.

Rosenberg, A. *Zur Geschichte des Latinerbundes.* Hermes, LIV, 1919, p. 113.

—— *Die Entstehung des sogenannten Foedus Cassianum und des latinischen Rechts.* Hermes, LV, 1920, p. 337.

Nitzsch, K. W. *Quellenanalyse von Livius II, 1–IV, 8 und Dionysius Halicarnassensis V, 1–XI, 63.* Rh. Mus. XXIII, 1868, p. 600; XXIV, 1869, p. 145; XXV, 1870, p. 75.

Burger, C. P., Jr. *Sechzig Jahre aus der älteren Geschichte Roms 418–358* in *Ver-handelingen der Koninklijke Akademie van Wetenschappen*. Afdeeling Letter-kunde. Twintigste Deel. Amsterdam, 1891. pp. 1–244 (particularly pp. 60–87, 99–144, 156–60 and 180–206).

Richter, O. *Die Fabier am Cremera*. Hermes, xvii, 1882, p. 425.

Dessau, H. *Livius und Augustus*. Hermes, xli, 1906, p. 142.

9. *Economic and Social Conditions in Early Rome*

Beloch, J. *Die Bevölkerung der griechisch-römischen Welt*. Leipzig, 1886.

Binder, J. *Die Plebs: Studien zur römischen Rechtsgeschichte*. Leipzig, 1909.

Bloch, L. *Soziale Kämpfe im alten Rom*. Ed. 2. Leipzig, 1908.

Cavaignac, E. *Population et Capital dans le monde méditerranéen antique*. Strasbourg, 1923.

Frank, T. *An Economic History of Rome*. Ed. 2. Baltimore, 1927.

Oliver, E. H. *Roman Economic Conditions to the Close of the Republic*. University of Toronto Library, 1907.

Toutain, J. *L'économie antique*. Paris, 1927.

Maschke, R. *Zur Theorie und Geschichte der römischen Agrargesetze*. Tübingen, 1906.

Mommsen, T. *Lex agraria a.u.c. DCXLIII, ante Chr. 111* in *Gesammelte Schriften*, i, pp. 65 *sqq.*

Niese, B. *Das sogenannte licinisch-sextische Ackergesetz*. Hermes, xxiii, 1888, p. 410.

Allen, W. F. *Niese on the Licinian-Sextian Agrarian Law*. C.R. iii, 1889, p. 5.

Cardinali, G. *Studi graccani*. Genoa, 1912.

Neumann, K. J. *Die Grundherrschaft der römischen Republik, die Bauernbefreiung und die Entstehung der servianischen Verfassung*. Strassburg, 1900.

Schwarze, (E. T.) K. *Beiträge zur Geschichte altrömischer Agrarprobleme (bis 367 v. Chr.)*. Diss. Halle a. S., 1912.

Soltau, W. *Die Aechtheit des licinischen Ackergesetzes von 367 v. Chr.* Hermes, xxx, 1895, p. 624.

Taeger, F. *Untersuchungen zur römischen Geschichte und Quellenkunde: Tiberius Gracchus*. Stuttgart, 1928. (Anhang: pp. 112–16.)

Vančura, J. Art. *Leges agrariae* in P.W.

Voigt, M. *Ueber die bina iugera der ältesten römischen Agrarverfassung*. Rh. Mus. xxiv, 1869, p. 52.

Weber, M. *Die römische Agrargeschichte in ihrer Bedeutung für das Staats- und Privatrecht*. Stuttgart, 1891.

Weiss, E. Art. *Grundbücher* in P.W. Supplementband iii, col. 848 *sqq.*

—— Art. *Kollektiveigentum* in P.W.

Ernst, V. *Die Entstehung des deutschen Grundeigentums*. Stuttgart, 1926.

Pais, E. *Serie cronologica delle colonie Romane e Latine dall' età regia fino all' Impero.* Parte prima: *Dall' età regia al tempo dei Gracchi*. Memorie della R. Accad. dei Lincei: Classe di Scienze morali etc. Vol. xvii, fasc. viii. Rome, 1924.

Cardinali, G. Art. *Frumentatio* in De Ruggiero, *Dizionario epigrafico di antichità romane*. Vol. iii. pp. 225 *sqq.*

Rostowzew, M. Art. *Frumentum* in P.W.

Girard, P. F. *L'histoire des XII Tables*. Nouvelle Revue historique de droit français et étranger. Année 26, 1902, p. 381.

Lambert, E. *Le problème de l'origine des XII Tables*. Revue générale de droit, 1902, pp. 385–421, 480–97; 1903, pp. 15–22.

—— *La question de l'authenticité des XII Tables et les annales maximi*. Nouvelle Revue historique de droit français et étranger. Année 26, 1902, p. 149.

———

Billeter, G. *Geschichte des Zinsfusses im griechisch-römischen Altertum bis auf Justinian*. Leipzig, 1898. (Especially pp. 115–62.)

Radin, M. *Secare partis: the early Roman law of execution against a debtor*. A.J.Ph. XLIII, 1922, p. 32.

Huschke, P. E. *Über das Recht des Nexum*. Leipzig, 1846.

de Zulueta, F. *The Recent Controversy about Nexum*. Law Quarterly Review, Vol. XXIX, 1913, p. 137.

Appleton, C. *Contribution à l'histoire du prêt à intérêt à Rome. Le taux du "fenus unciarium"*. Nouvelle Revue historique de droit français et étranger. Année 43, 1919, p. 467.

———

Giesecke, W. *Italia Numismatica: eine Geschichte der italischen Geldsysteme bis zur Kaiserzeit*. Leipzig, 1928.

Grueber, H. A. *Coins of the Roman Republic in the British Museum*. 3 vols. London, 1910.

Mommsen, T. *Histoire de la Monnaie romaine*, traduite par le Duc de Blacas. Paris. Vol. I, 1865; vol. II, 1870; vol. III, 1873; vol. IV, 1875.

Haeberlin, E. J. *Aes grave: das Schwergeld Roms und Mittelitaliens einschliesslich der ihm vorausgehenden Rohbronzewährung*. Frankfurt a. M., 1910.

—— *Zum Corpus numorum aeris gravis: die Systematik des ältesten römischen Münzwesens*. Berlin, 1905.

Mattingly, H. *Roman Coins from the Earliest Times to the Fall of the Western Empire*. London, 1928.

—— *The Romano-Campanian Coinage and the Pyrrhic War*. Num. Chr. 1924, p. 181.

Sydenham, E. A. *Aes Grave: a Study of the cast Coinages of Rome and Central Italy*. London, 1926.

CHAPTER XVII

THE GALLIC WARS OF ROME

A. Ancient Sources

Appian, Frag. of, *Celtica* and *Italica*.
Dio Cassius, Fragments of books VI and VII. (Abridgment in Zonaras, VII, 22–8.)
Diodorus Siculus, XIV, 96–XVI, 45. (The notices on Roman history are collected by Drachmann in *Kleine Texte*, no. 97.)
Dionysius of Halicarnassus, *Antiq. Rom.* XII–XV.
Ineditum Vaticanum. Edited by H. v. Arnim (in Hermes, XXVII, 1892, pp. 118–30), § 3 (Roman army in fourth century B.C.).
Justin, *Hist.* VI, 6, 5; XX, 5, 4–10; XXVIII, 2, 2–6; XXXVIII, 4, 7–8; XLIII, 5, 8. (Abridgment of Trogus.)
Livy, V, 24–VII, 28.
Plutarch, *Life of Camillus*, CC. IX–XLIII.
Polyaenus, VIII, 7, 2.
Polybius, I, 6, 2–4; II, 14–18; II, 22, 4–5.

B. Modern Works

(See also the General Bibliography)

(a) On the Sources

(See also the Bibliography to Chaps. X–XVI, A II)

Mommsen, Th. *Römische Forschungen*, II, Fabius und Diodor, pp. 221–90. Berlin, 1864–1879.
Nitzsch, K. W. *Die römische Annalistik, von ihren ersten Anfängen bis auf Valerius Antias.* Berlin, 1873.
Pais, E. *Fasti Triumphales populi Romani.* Rome, 1920. (I, Introduzione, pp. 5–6, 43–9.)
—— *Ricerche sulla storia e sul diritto pubblico di Roma.* Rome, 1918. (II, Fasti Consulares.)
Peter, H. *Zur Kritik der Quellen der älteren römischen Geschichte.* Halle, 1879.
—— *Die Quellen Plutarchs in den Biographien der Römer* (pp. 17–28, Camillus). Halle, 1868.
Schwartz, E. Articles in P.W.; *Appianus* (II, 216–37), *Cassius Dio* (III, 1684–1722), *Diodoros* (V, 663–704), *Dionysios* (V, 934–61)
Sigwart, G. *Römische Fasten und Annalen bei Diodor.* Klio, VI, 1906, p. 341.
Soltau, W. *Die Anfänge der römischen Geschichtsschreibung.* Leipzig, 1909.
—— *Livius' Geschichtswerk, seine Komposition und seine Quellen.* Leipzig, 1897.

(b) General Works

Arbois de Jubainville, H. d'. *Les Celtes depuis les temps les plus anciens.* Paris, 1904.
Bertrand, A. and Reinach, S. *Les Celtes dans les vallées du Pô et du Danube.* Paris, 1894.
De Sanctis, G. *Storia dei Romani.* Turin, 1907–. II, pp. 146–91 246–61.

Ducati, P. *Etruria antica.* Turin, 1925.

Grenier, A. *Bologne Villanovienne et Étrusque.* Paris, 1912.

—— *Les Gaulois.* Paris, 1923.

Homo, L. *L'Italie primitive.* Paris, 1925. Especially pp. 188–213.

Jullian, C. *Histoire de la Gaule.* Paris, 1908. i, pp. 289–96, 369 *sqq.*

Körte, G. and Skutsch, F. Art. *Etrusker* in P.W.

Meyer, Ed. *Geschichte des Altertums.* Esp. vol. v, pp. 132–60.

Mommsen, Th. *Römische Forschungen.* ii, Die Gallische Katastrophe, pp. 297–381.

Niese, B. *Die Chronologie der gallischen Kriege bei Polybios.* Hermes, xiii, 1878, p. 401.

Pais, E. *Italia Antica.* Bologna, 1922. i, pp. 31–60; ii, pp. 351–61.

—— *Ricerche sulla storia e sul diritto pubblico di Roma.* Rome, 1915–21. i, pp. 367–97.

—— *Storia critica di Roma.* Rome, 1913–20. ii, pp. 76–8, 436–83; iii, pp. 3–24, 35–92, 271–323, and Appendix i, "a proposito del incendio gallico," pp. 377–81.

—— *Storia dell' Italia antica.* Rome, 1925. i, pp. 115 *sqq.*, 193 *sqq.*

(c) Archaeology, Antiquities, Topography, Celtic and Roman

(See further the Bibliographies to Chaps. ii and xi)

Bianchetti, E. *I sepolcreti d' Ornavasso.* Atti d. soc. d. arch. e belle arti per la provincia di Torino, vi. Turin, 1898.

Couissin, P. *Les armes romaines.* Paris, 1926. Esp. pp. 177 *sqq.*

Déchelette, J. *Manuel d'archéologie préhistorique celtique et gallo-romaine.* Paris, 1908–14. ii, 2; ii, 3, especially pp. 1087–1100, on the Celtic burials in N. Italy, and the Bibliography, p. 1097.

—— *Montefortino et Ornavasso.* Rev. Arch. 1902, i, pp. 245–83.

Delbrück, H. *Geschichte der Kriegskunst im Rahmen der politischen Geschichte.* Ed. 2. Berlin, 1908. i, 235–46.

Ducati, P. *Le Pietre funerarie felsinee.* Mon. Linc. xx, 1911, p. 387.

—— *Guida del museo civico di Bologna.* Bologna, 1923.

Gamurrini, G. F. *Iscrizione latina arcaica scoperta nel Foro Romano.* N.S.A. 1899, p. 151.

Ghirardini, G. *La situla italica primitiva studiata specialmente in Este.* Mon. Linc. ii, 1893, pp. 161–252; vii, 1897, pp. 5–200; x, 1901, pp. 5–292.

Graffunder, P. *Das Alter der servianischen Mauer.* Klio, xi, 1911, p. 83.

—— Art. *Rom* in P.W. cols. 1008–30.

Grenier, A. *Bologne Villanovienne et Étrusque.* Paris, 1912.

Marquardt, J. and Mommsen, Th. *Manuel des antiquités romaines.* Paris, 1891. xi, Organisation militaire, pp. 20 *sqq.* (=*Römische Staatsverwaltung*², ii, 321.)

Pinza, G. *Monumenti primitivi di Roma e del Lazio.* Mon. Ant. xv, 1905, p. 746.

Schulze, W. *Zur Geschichte lateinischer Eigennamen.* Abh. d. königl. Gschaft. d. Wissenschaften zu Göttingen, phil.-hist. Klasse, Neue Folge, v, Berlin, 1904.

Vaglieri, D. *Roma. Nuove scoperte nella città e nel suburbio.* N.S.A. 1904, p. 43.

For a general survey of the evidence for Rome see further, L. Homo, *Rome antique,* Paris, 1921, especially pp. 6–9, 34–5, 84–8, and H. Kiepert and Chr. Hülsen, *Formae urbis Romae antiquae,* ed. 2, Berlin, 1912 (especially the articles on *Palatium, Lapis Niger, Murus Servii Tullii*), for bibliography. For a plan of the Palatine see the *Rilievo planimetrico e altimetrico del Palatino eseguito dagli allievi della Scuola d'applicazione per gli ingegneri,* Rome, 1903, in N.S.A. 1904, pp. 43–6.

(*d*) The Battle of the Allia

The identification of the Battle of the Allia has given rise to many investigations, and both the left and right bank of the Tiber have their partisans.

1. *The Left bank.* This view is supported by the text of Livy, v, 37: 'at the twelfth milestone from Rome,' '*qua flumen Allia, Crustumerinis montibus...defluens...haud multum infra viam Tiberino amni miscetur.*' The account in Diodorus is confused and seems to imply a conflict on both banks.

The following writers pronounce for the view that the battle was fought on the left bank:

Kornemann, E. *Die Alliaschlacht und die ältesten Pontificalannalen.* Klio, xi, 1911, p. 335.

Kromayer, J. *Drei Schlachten aus dem griechisch-römischen Altertum*, Abh. d. Sächs. Akad., phil.-hist. Kl. xxxiv, 1921, no. v, p. 28. (A detailed study with map.)

Richter, O. *Beiträge zur römischen Topographie*, I. Alliaschlacht und Serviusmauer. Prog. Prinz Heinr. Gymnasium, Berlin, 1903, iii, *Die Alliaschlacht* ib. 1907.

Sigwart, G. *Römische Fasten und Annalen bei Diodor.* Klio, vi, 1906, p. 341.

Thouret, G. *Über den gallischen Brand.* N.J.P. Suppl. Bd. 1880, p. 93.

2. *The Right bank.*

Hülsen, C. and Lindner, P. *Die Alliaschlacht.* Rome, 1890.

Laqueur, R. *Diodors Bericht über die Schlacht an der Allia.* Phil. Woch. 1921, col. 861.

Meyer, E. *Die Alliaschlacht.* Apophoreton zur 47 Vers. deutscher Philologen und Schulmänner, Berlin, 1903, p. 137.

Besides the account in Livy, the best account of the battle which has come down to us, the left bank has practical reason to commend it. The Romans were concerned to defend their city; it was therefore the logical course to post themselves not on the right bank, where the Tiber itself already afforded a serious line of defence, but on the left bank where this natural defence is lacking.

CHAPTER XVIII

THE CONQUEST OF CENTRAL ITALY

I. Ancient Sources

(a) Inscriptions

Dessau, 1, 53, 54.

Fasti Consulares: *C.I.L.* 1, 1, ed. 2, pp. 81 *sqq.* Also E. Pais in *Ricerche sulla storia e sul diritto pubblico di Roma II.* Rome, 1918.

Fasti Triumphales: *C.I.L.* ib. pp. 168 *sqq.* Also Ed. E. Pais, Rome, 1920–3.

The Oscan Inscriptions of Campania, Samnium, etc., are collected in R. S. Conway's *Italic Dialects,* Cambridge, 1897, vol. 1.

(b) Literary

Appian, frags. of *Samnitica.*

de viris illustribus, 26–34.

Dio Cassius, frags. of bks. VII–VIII. (Boissevain, 1, pp. 90–110.)

Diodorus Siculus, XVI–XX. The notices on Roman History are collected by A. B. Drachmann in Lietzmann's *Kleine Texte,* no. 97, Bonn, 1912.

Dionysius of Halicarnassus, frags. of *Antiq. Rom.* XV–XVIII.

Ineditum Vaticanum. Hermes, XXVII, 1892, p. 118. Appended to Drachmann, *op. cit.*

Frontinus, *Strategemata,* passim, esp. 1, 2, 2; 6, 1–2; 8, 3–4; II, 4, 1–2; 7, 11; IV, 5, 15.

Livy, VII–X; *per.* XI.

Orosius, III, 8–22.

Pliny, *N.H.* VII, 136.

Zonaras, VII, 25–VIII, 1.

II. Modern Works

1. *General Political History*

(See also the General Bibliography)

Beloch, K. J. *Campanien.* Ed. 2. Breslau, 1890.

—— *Der italische Bund unter Roms Hegemonie.* Leipzig, 1880.

—— *La conquista romana della regione sabina.* Riv. stor. ant. IX, 1904, p. 269.

—— *Römische Geschichte.* Berlin, 1926. Esp. pp. 352–450.

Binneboessel, P. *Quellen und Geschichte d. zweiten Samniterkrieges von Caudium bis zum Frieden* 450 u.c. Halle, 1893.

Borman, E. In *C.I.L.* XI.

Bruno, B. *La terza guerra sannitica.* (Beloch's Studi di Storia antica, VI.) Rome, 1906.

Burger, C. P. Jr. *De Bello cum Samnitibus secundo.* Haarlem, 1884.

—— *Neue Forschungen zur aeltern Geschichte Roms,* I, II. Amsterdam, 1894, 1895.

——*Der Kampf zwischen Rom und Samnium bis zum vollständigen Siege Roms um* 312 *v. Chr.* (= Verhandl. der kon. Akad. van Wetenschappen te Amsterdam, N.R. II, 2.) Amsterdam, 1898.

Costanzi, V. *Osservazioni sulla terza Guerra Sannitica.* Riv. fil. XLVII, 1919, p. 161.

Frank, T. *On Rome's conquest of Sabinum, Picenum and Etruria.* Klio, XI, 1911, p. 367.

Gelzer, M. Art. *Latium* in P.W.

Kaerst, J. *Kritische Untersuchungen zur Geschichte des zweiten Samniterkrieges.* Jahrbücher f. Class. Phil. Suppl. 13, 1884, p. 725.

Kaiser, B. *Untersuchungen zur Geschichte der Samniten.* Progr. Pforta, 1907. (See *Woch. f. Klass. Phil.* 1907, col. 1141.)

Klimke, C. *Der zweite Samniterkrieg.* Königshütte, 1882.

Mommsen, T. In *C.I.L.* ix and x, 1.

Münzer, F. *Römische Adelsparteien und Adelsfamilien.* Stuttgart, 1920.
    See further Münzer, articles in *P.W.* on Romans of this period under their *gentile* name.

Philipp, . Arts. *Samnites* and *Sabini* in P.W.

Pirro, A. *La seconda guerra sannitica.* Salerno, 1898.
—— *Le origini di Napoli.* Rome, 1905–6.

Rosenberg, A. *Der Staat der alten Italiker.* Berlin, 1913. pp. 15–50.

Schur, W. *Fremder Adel im römischen Staat.* Hermes, LIX, 1924, p. 450.

Soltau, W. *Wie gelang es Rom 340–290 vor Chr. Italien zu unterwerfen?* N.J.P. XLII, 1896, p. 164.
—— *Rom und die Italiker.* N.J. Kl. Alt. xxv, 1910, p. 721.

Spaeth, J. W. Jr. *A Study of the Causes of Rome's Wars from 343 to 265* B.C. Diss. Princeton, 1926. (Includes a useful bibliography.)

Täubler, E. *Imperium Romanum,* I. Die Staatsverträge und Vertragsverhältnisse. Leipzig, 1913.

Weyer, G. A. *Die staatsrechtlichen Beziehungen Kapuas zu Rom (343–211 v. Chr.).* Diss. Bonn, 1913.

2. Military, topography, etc.

Cluverius, P. *Italia Antiqua.* Lugd. Bat. 1624. pp. 1196 *sq.*

Cocchia, E. *I Romani alle forche Caudine.* Atti della R. Acc. di Napoli, xiv (1889/90), 2, p. 39.

Kromayer, J. *Drei Schlachten aus dem griechisch-römischen Altertum.* Abh. d. Sächs. Akad., phil.-hist. Kl. xxxiv, 5. Leipzig, 1921. (Includes discussion of previous views and bibliography.)

Kromayer, J. and Veith, G. *Schlachten-Atlas zur antiken Kriegsgeschichte.* Röm. Ab. 1. Leipzig, 1922. With text.
—— *Heerwesen und Kriegführung der Griechen und Römer* in J. Müller's *Handbuch der klassischen Altertumswissenschaft,* IV, 3, 2. Munich, 1928.

Meyer, E. *Das römische Manipularheer, seine Entwicklung und seine Vorstufen.* Kleine Schriften, II, Halle, 1924, p. 193.

Nissen, H. *Der Caudinische Friede.* Rh. Mus. xxv, 1870, p. 1.

Stürenburg, H. *Zu den Schlachtfeldern...in den Caudinischen Pässen.* Prog. Leipzig, 1889. (Not accessible to the present writer; see Kromayer above.)

    For the sites of towns, etc., see H. Nissen, *Italische Landeskunde,* and Beloch, *Röm. Geschichte,* together with the text of Kiepert. For the Roman army see further the Bibliography to chapter xvii.

3. Civilization, Coinage, etc.

v. Duhn, F. *Italische Gräberkunde,* Heidelberg, 1924. pp. 437–458, 533 *sqq.*

Frank, T. *Economic History of Rome.* Ed. 2. London, 1927. pp. 69 *sqq.*

Giesecke, W. *Italia Numismatica:* eine Geschichte der italischen Geldsysteme bis zur Kaiserzeit. Leipzig, 1928.

Haeberlin, E. J. *Aes Grave: das Schwergeld Roms und Mittelitaliens einschliesslich der ihm vorausgehenden Rohbronzwährung.* Frankfurt a. M. 1910.
—— *Zum Corpus numorum aeris gravis: systematik des ältesten römischen Münzwesens.* Berlin, 1905.

Mariani, L. *Aufidena, Ricerche storiche ed archeologiche nel Sannio settentrionale.* Mon. Linc. x, 1900, 226.

Mattingly, H. *The Romano-Campanian Coinage and the Pyrrhic War.* Num. Chr. 1924, p. 181.

—— *Roman Coins from the Earliest Times to the Fall of the Western Empire,* pp. 1–55. London, 1928.

Randall-MacIver, D. *The Iron Age in Italy.* Oxford, 1927. pp. 105–144.

—— *Fore-runners of the Romans,* 11. Antiquity, 11, 1928, p. 133.

Samwer, K. and Bahrfeldt, M. v. *Geschichte des älteren römischen Münzwesens.* Vienna, 1883.

Schulten, A. *Italische Namen und Stämme,* 111. Klio, 111, 1903, p. 235.

Sydenham, E. A. *Aes Grave: a Study of the cast Coinages of Rome and Central Italy.* London, 1926.

—— *The Roman Monetary System,* 1. Num. Chr. 1918, p. 155.

Weege, F. *Oskische Grabmalerei; Bewaffnung und Tracht der Osker.* J.D.A.I. xxiv, 1909, pp. 98, 141.

CHAPTER XIX

AGATHOCLES

A. Ancient Sources

Diodorus Siculus, xix–xxi, 13.
Justin, xxii, xxiii, 1–2.
Polyaenus, v, 3.
Polybius, i, 7, 82; vii, 2, 4; viii, 12; ix, 23; xii, 15; xv, 35.

B. Modern Works

(See also the General Bibliography)

Evans, A. J. *The Horsemen of Tarentum*. London, 1889.
Freeman, E. A. and Evans, A. J. *History of Sicily*. iv. Oxford, 1894. Chap. xii and Appendices vii and viii.
Giesecke, W. *Sicilia Numismatica*. Berlin, 1923. pp. 83–95.
Gsell, S. *Histoire de l'Afrique du Nord*. iii. Paris, 1920. pp. 25–66.
Holm, A. *Geschichte Siciliens im Altertum*. ii. Leipzig, 1874. pp. 219–65.
—— *History of Greece*. Eng. Trans. iv. London, 1898. pp. 164–73.
Meltzer, O. *Geschichte der Karthager*. i. Berlin, 1879. chap. v.
Niese, B. *Geschichte der griechischen und makedonischen Staaten*. i. Gotha, 1893. pp. 417–86.
—— Art. *Agathokles* in P.W. i, cols. 748–57.
Pais, E. *Storia critica di Roma*. iv. Rome, 1920. pp. 310–35.
De Sanctis, G. *Per la Scienza dell' Antichità*. Turin, 1909. pp. 141–206.
—— *Storia dei Romani*. ii. Turin, 1907. pp. 344–79.
Schoch, C. *Sirius*. 1926. pp. 248–50. (On the eclipse of 310 B.C.)
Schubert, R. *Geschichte des Agathokles*. Breslau, 1887.
Tillyard, H. J. W. *Agathocles*. Cambridge, 1908.

CHAPTERS XX and XXI

PYRRHUS: ROME AND CARTHAGE; THE FIRST PUNIC WAR

I. Ancient Sources

Appian, frags. of *Samnitica* and *Sicula*.
Cornelius Nepos, *Hamilcar*.
Dio Cassius, frags. of bks ix–xi.
Diodorus Siculus, frags. of bks xxii–xxiv.
Dionysius of Halicarnassus, *Antiq. Rom.*, frags. of bk xx.
Ennius, *Annales*.
Eutropius, *Breviarium*.
Fasti Consulares and *Acta Triumphorum*. C.I.L. i². Berlin. A new fragment of the Fasti for 278–267 b.c. is published in *Notizie degli Scavi*, 1925, pp. 376–381.
Florus, *Epitoma*, i.
Frontinus, *Strategemata*, passim.
Historicorum Romanorum fragmenta. Peter, H. i. Ed. 2. Berlin, 1913.
Ineditum Vaticanum. (Von Arnim.) Hermes, xxvii, 1892, p. 120.
Justin, *Epitoma Pompei Trogi*, xviii.
Livy, *per.* xii–xix.
Naevius, *Bellum Punicum*.
Orosius, *Historia adv. Paganos*, iv.
Plutarch, *Life of Pyrrhus*.
Polybius, i, ii.
Strabo, *Geographica*.
Zonaras, *Epitome*, viii.

II. Modern Works

(See also the works cited in the General Bibliography)

Beloch, K. J. *Griechische Geschichte.* iv². Berlin, 1925.
—— *Römische Geschichte*, i. Berlin, 1926.
Carcopino, J. *La Loi de Hiéron et les Romains.* Paris, 1919.
Cary, M. *The Early Roman Treaties with Tarentum and Rhodes.* J.P. xxxv, 1920, p. 105.
—— *A Forgotten Treaty between Rome and Carthage.* J.R.S. ix, 1919, p. 67.
Cichorius, E. *Die Fragmente historischen Inhalts aus Naevius' Bellum Punicum.* Römische Studien. Berlin, 1922. pp. 24–58.
De Sanctis, G. *Storia dei Romani*, ii, iii. Turin, 1907–16.
v. Duhn, F. Art. *Kelten* in Reallexikon der Vorgeschichte. Vol. vi, pp. 287 *sqq.*
Eliaeson, E. *Beiträge zur Geschichte Sardiniens und Corsicas im ersten punischen Kriege.* Upsala, 1906.
Frank, T. *Economic History of Rome.* Ed. 2. London, 1927.
Gsell, S. *Histoire ancienne de l'Afrique du Nord.* Paris, 1914–28.
Holm, A. *Geschichte Siciliens.* Leipzig, 1870–98.
Judeich, W. *König Pyrrhos römische Politik.* Klio, xx, 1926, p. 1.
Kromayer, J. *Antike Schlachtfelder.* iii. Berlin, 1912.
Lenschau, T. Art. *Hieron II* in P.W.

Leuze, O. *Die Kampfe um Sardinien und Korsica im ersten punischen Kriege.* Klio, x, 1910, p. 406.

Meltzer, O. *Geschichte der Karthager.* II. Berlin, 1896.

Meyer, P. *Der Ausbruch des ersten punischen Krieges.* Berlin, 1908.

Münzer, F. *Römische Adelsparteien.* Stuttgart, 1920.

Niese, B. *Zur Geschichte des pyrrhischen Krieges.* Hermes, XXXI, 1896, p. 481.

Pais, E. *Storia critica di Roma.* IV. Rome, 1920.

—— *Ricerche sulla Storia di Roma.* II. Rome, 1916.

—— *Storia della Sardegna e della Corsica durante il dominio romano.* Rome, 1923.

v. Scala, R. *Der pyrrhische Krieg.* Berlin, 1884.

Schermann, M. *Der erste punische Krieg.* Tübingen, 1905.

Schubert, R. *Geschichte des Pyrrhus.* Königsberg, 1894.

Tarn, W. W. *The Fleets of the First Punic War.* J.H.S. XXVII, 1907, p. 48.

CHAPTER XXIV

THE CARTHAGINIANS IN SPAIN

A. Ancient Sources

(a) Primary

Sosylus. Bilabel, *Die kleineren Historikerfragmente*, 10.

(b) Secondary

Appian, *Iberica*.
Diodorus Siculus, xxv, 9.
Justin, xliv.
Livy, xxi.
Polybius, i–iii.
Valerius Maximus, *passim*.

Note. Of the contemporary sources, Silenus and Sosylus (Carthaginian) and Q. Fabius Pictor (Roman), we have nothing save a papyrus fragment of Sosylus. Of the secondary sources, Polybius is the most important: we possess his complete narrative down to 216 B.C., and fragments—sometimes fairly extensive—for the period after; he appears to have used both Silenus and Fabius, and follows the latter in his judgment upon the Saguntine question. The only continuous narrative is offered by Livy: his chief source for Spain is Coelius Antipater (who drew on Silenus and Fabius); but he also uses the later annalistic, including Valerius Antias, from whom he takes his exaggerated figures. Other authorities, such as Diodorus, Appian (*Iberica*), and Dio Cassius are based on the later and unreliable annalistic (see E. Schwartz in P.W. *s.vv. Diodorus*, col. 688 *sq.*; *Appianus*, col. 218 *sq.*; *Cassius Dio*, col. 1694 *sqq.*).

On these sources generally see De Sanctis, *Storia dei Romani*, iii, 2, pp. 166 *sqq.*, 355 *sqq.*, 638 *sqq.*, Meltzer-Kahrstedt, *Geschichte der Karthager*, iii, pp. 143 *sqq.*, and particularly Klotz' article *Livius* in P.W. xiii, 815. The evidence for the wars in Spain will be found in the forthcoming volume iii of *Fontes Hispaniae Antiquae* by Schulten, Barcelona.

B. Modern Works

(See also the General Bibliography)

(a) General

Gsell, S. *Histoire ancienne de l'Afrique du Nord*. i–iv. Paris. Vol. i, 3rd ed. 1921. ii and iii, 1918; iv, 1920.
Meltzer, O. *Geschichte der Karthager*. Especially vol. iii (by U. Kahrstedt). Berlin, 1879–1913.
Schulten, A. *Numantia*. 1. Munich, 1914.
—— *Sertorius*. Leipzig, 1926.
—— *Tartessos*. Ein Beitrag zur ältesten Geschichte des Westens. Hamburg, 1922.
—— Art. *Hispania* in P.W., also articles in same encyclopaedia by Hübner and Schulten on Spanish towns and tribes.
Schulten A. and Bosch, P. *Fontes Hispaniae Antiquae*. (F.H.A.) Vol. i. Avien Ora Maritima. Berlin, 1922. Vol. ii, 500 B.C.–Caesar, ready. Vol. iii in preparation.

(b) Special Topics

1. Tartessus

Schulten, A. *Tartessos* (see above).
Bosch, P. *Vorgeschichte der iberischen Halbinsel*. P.Z. 1924, p. 128.
Carpenter, R. *The Greeks in Spain*. Bryn Mawr, 1925.
Hennig, R. *Von rätselhaften Ländern*. Munich, 1925.

2. Massilia and her colonies

Jullian, C. *Histoire de la Gaule.* I, pp. 383 *sqq.*
Schulten, A. *Tartessos.* p. 46.
——— *Ampurias.* N.J. Kl. Alt. XIX, 1907, p. 334. (Cf. also Garofalo in *Bolet. de la real Acad. de la Historia,* XXXV, 177.)

On Pytheas, see bibliography to chapter II.

3. Carthage and the West

(See *Tartessos,* pp. 44, 45, 47, 48, 51)

Vives, A. *Estudio de arquelogica cartaginesa. La Necropoli de Ibiza.* Madrid, 1917.
Schulten, A. *Die Inseln der Seligen.* (The discovery of Madeira.) Geogr. Zeitschrift, 1926, p. 229.
Meltzer, O. *Gesch. der Karthager.* I, pp. 158 *sqq.* (Conquest of Spain; cp. Gsell, *op. cit.* I, pp. 420 *sqq.* and Lenschau in P.W. *s.v. Karthago,* col. 2225.
Mair, G. *Der karthagische Admiral Himilko.* Pola, 1899. (Cp. *Tartessos,* pp. 45 and 48, and W. H. Schoff, *The Periplus of Hanno,* Philadelphia, 1913.)

For the history of Hamilcar and his successors in Spain, see De Sanctis, *op. cit.* III, I, pp. 405 *sqq.,* Gsell, *op. cit.* III, pp. 130 *sqq.,* and Meltzer-Kahrstedt, *op. cit.* II, pp. 397 *sqq.*

4. The Iberians

Schulten, A. Art. *Hispania* in P.W. col. 2014; *Numantia,* I, pp. 179 *sqq.* and *Sertorius.* (Cp. also *Numantia,* I, p. 92, and the archaeological evidence as collected by Bosch in P.Z. 1924, p. 128.)
Sandars, G. *The Iberian Weapons.* (Cp. *Numantia,* I, 209, and Gsell, *op. cit.* II, p. 371.)
Bosch, P. *El Problema de la cerámica ibérica.* Madrid, 1915.

See also the works referred to in the bibliography to vol. II, chapter XXI.

5. The Celts in Spain

Schulten, A. *Numantia,* I, pp. 91 *sqq.*
Bosch, P. *Kelten und keltische Kultur in Spanien.* Mannus, XXII, 1922, p. 53. Cp. F. P. Garofalo in *Revue Celtique,* XXI, 1900, p. 200, and Schulten, *Tartessos,* p. 30, and the bibliography to chapter II.

6. Romans and Carthaginians in Spain

(See also the Bibliography to chap. XXV)

For the first Romano-Carthaginian treaty see the Appendix. On the Ebro treaty and the question of Saguntum:

De Sanctis, G. *Op. cit.* III, 41, especially p. 428.
Gsell, S. *Op. cit.* III, 136.
Täubler, E. *Die Vorgeschichte des zweiten punischen Kriegs.* Berlin, 1921.
Meyer, E. *Untersuchungen zur Geschichte des zweiten punischen Kriegs.* I. *Der Ursprung des Kriegs und die Händel mit Sagunt.* Kleine Schriften, II. Halle, 1924, p. 333.

For references to places named after Hannibal:

Mela, II, 89, III, 7.
Pliny, *N.H.* II, 187, III, 78, XXV, 169, XXXIII, 96.

CHAPTER XXV

ROME AFTER THE CONQUEST OF SICILY

I. ANCIENT SOURCES

Cicero, *Verrinae*, especially Act. II, Lib. III.
Corpus Inscriptionum Latinarum. I. Berlin, 1893–1918.
Dio Cassius, XII.
Diodorus Siculus, XXV.
Fasti Triumphales Populi Romani. Ed. E. Pais. Rome, 1920.
Historicorum Romanorum fragmenta. Peter, H. I. Ed. 2. Berlin, 1913.
Livy, *per.* 20.
Orosius, *Historia adversus paganos,* IV.
Plutarch, *Life of Marcellus.*
Polybius, II.
Sosylus, *a fragment.* Wilcken, in Hermes, XLI, 1906, p. 107, and Bilabel, *Die kleineren Historikerfragmente,* 10.
Strabo, *Geographica.*
Velleius Paterculus, *Historia Romana,* bk I.
Zonaras, VIII.

Incidental references in Appian, Ennius, Eutropius and Valerius Maximus.

II. MODERN WORKS

(See also the works cited in the General Bibliography)

Botsford, G. W. *The Roman Assemblies from their origin to the end of the Republic.* New York, 1909.
Carcopino, J. *La Loi d'Hiéron et les Romains.* Paris, 1919.
Cardinali, G. Art. *Frumentatio* in De Ruggiero, *Dizionario Epigrafico,* III, pp. 225 *sqq.*
Cavaignac, E. *Population et Capital.* Strasbourg-Paris, 1923.
De Sanctis, G. *Storia dei Romani,* III. Turin, 1916.
Drachmann, A. B. *Sagunt und die Ebro-Grenze in der Verhandlungen zwischen Rom und Karthago,* 220–218. Kgl. Danske Videnskab. Selskab. Hist. fil. Meddelelser, III. 3. 1920.
Duff, J. Wight. *A Literary History of Rome.* Ed. 7. London, 1927.
Frank, T. *Rome, Marseilles and Carthage.* In Military Historian, 1916, pp. 394–406.
Gelzer, M. *Die Nobilität der römischen Republik.* Leipzig, 1912.
Holleaux, M. *Rome, la Grèce et les monarchies hellénistiques.* Paris, 1921.
Jullian, C. *Histoire de la Gaule.* I. Paris, 1908.
Kahrstedt, U. *Geschichte der Karthager von* 218. Berlin, 1913. (= Meltzer's *Geschichte der Karthager* III.)
Klingmüller, F. *Die Idee des Staatseigentums am römischen Provinzialboden.* Phil. LXIX, 1910, p. 71.
Lauterbach, A. *Untersuchungen zur Geschichte der Unterwerfung von Oberitalien durch die Römer.* Breslau, 1905.
Meyer, E. *Untersuchungen zur Geschichte des zweiten punischen Krieges,* I, III. Kleine Schriften. II. Halle, 1924.
Münzer, F. Art. *Q. Fabius Maximus, C. Flaminius, M. Claudius Marcellus,* in P.W.

Niese, B. Art. *Galli* in P.W.

Pais, E. *Storia della Sardegna e della Corsica durante il dominio romano.* Rome, 1923.

Reid, J. S. *Problems of the Second Punic War.* J.R.S. 1913, pp. 171–190.

Rostowzew, M. *Studien zur Geschichte des römischen Kolonates.* Leipzig, 1910.

Schnabel, P. *Zur Vorgeschichte des zweiten punischen Krieges.* Klio, xx, 1925, p. 110.

Solari, A. *Delle Guerre dei Romani coi Liguri per la conquista del territorio lunese pisano.* In Pais, Studi storici, 1, 1908, p. 58.

—— *Topografia storica dell' Etruria.* Rome, 1915–20.

Täubler, E. *Die Vorgeschichte des zweiten punischen Kriegs.* Berlin, 1921.

CHAPTER XXVI
THE ROMANS IN ILLYRIA

(Section I. The early relations of Rome with the Greek World)

A. ANCIENT SOURCES

(*a*) *The "treaty" between Rome and Rhodes.*
Polybius, xxx, 5, 6 (omitting the words τοῖς πρὸς ἑκατόν).

(*b*) *Rome and Ptolemy II.*
Livy, *per.* xiv.
Eutropius, ii, 15.
Dionysius of Halicarnassus, *Antiq. Roman.* xx, 14, 1–2.
Dio Cassius, frag. 41 (Boissevain, i, p. 139).
Zonaras, viii, 6, 11.
Valerius Maximus, iv, 3, 9.
Justin, xviii, 2, 9.

(*c*) *Rome and Apollonia.*
Livy, *per.* xv.
Valerius Maximus, vi, 6, 5.
Dio Cassius, frag. 42 (Boissevain, i, p. 141).
Zonaras, viii, 7, 3.

(*d*) *The "treaty" between Rome and Seleucus II.*
Suetonius, *Claud.* 25.

(*e*) *The "offer of assistance" by Rome to Ptolemy III.*
Eutropius, iii, 1.

(*f*) *The Roman intervention in Acarnania.*
Justin, xxviii, 1, 5–2.

(*g*) *The first Roman embassy in Greece.*
Polybius, ii, 12, 7.

B. MODERN WORKS

Bandelin, E. *De rebus inter Aegyptios et Romanos intercedentibus....* Diss. Halle,
  1893. pp. 6 *sqq.*
Beloch, K. J. *Griechische Geschichte.* 2nd ed. iv, 1. Berlin-Leipzig, 1925, pp. 290,
  n. 2, 634, 663 *sq.* iv, 2. Berlin-Leipzig, 1927. p. 531.
Cary, M. *The early Roman treaties with Tarentum and Rhodes.* J.P. xxxv, 1920,
  p. 170.
Colin, G. *Rome et la Grèce de 200 à 146 avant J.-C.* Paris, 1905. pp. 30 *sqq.*
De Sanctis, G. *Storia dei Romani*, ii. Turin, 1907. pp. 426 *sqq.* iii, 1. Turin,
  1916. pp. 275 *sqq.*
Holleaux, M. *Rome, la Grèce et les monarchies hellénistiques au IIIᵉ siècle avant
  J.-C.* Paris, 1921. pp. 1–22, 29 *sqq.*
Lehmann-Haupt, C. F. *Vom pyrrhischen und ersten syrischen zum chremonideischen
  Kriege.* Ἐπιτύμβιον H. Swoboda dargebracht. Reichenberg, 1927. pp. 152 *sqq.*
Meyer, Ed. *Kleine Schriften*, ii. Halle, 1924. pp. 381 *sqq.*
Niese, B. *Geschichte der griechischen und makedonischen Staaten...*, ii. Gotha,
  1899. pp. 66, n. 2, 153, n. 4, 281.
Norden, E. *Ennius und Vergilius.* Leipzig, 1915. pp. 59 *sqq.* See Pasquali, G.,
  G.G.A. clxxvii, 1915, p. 598, n. 1.
Täubler, E. *Imperium Romanum*, i. Leipzig-Berlin, 1913. pp. 202 *sqq.*

Walek, Th. *La politique romaine en Grèce et dans l'Orient hellénistique au IIIe* *siècle.* Rev. Phil. XLIX, 1925, pp. 118 *sqq.*
Willrich, H. *Caligula.* Klio, III, 1903, p. 404.

(*Sections II–IX*)

A. ANCIENT SOURCES

1. *Inscription*

C.I.L. I², 1, pp. 47, 173 (ad ann. 526). See also: Pais, E. *Fasti triumphales populi* *Romani.* Rome, 1920. I, pp. 12, 112. II, pl. XII.

2. *Literary*

Appian, *Illyrica*, 7–8.
Dio Cassius, frag. 49 (Boissevain, I, pp. 180 *sqq.*), frag. 53 (*ib.* p. 187).
Eutropius, III, 4.
Florus, I, 21 (II, 5).
Livy, *per.* XX.
Orosius, IV, 13, 2.
Pliny, *N. H.* XXXIV, 24.
Polybius, II, 2–12; III, 16, 18–19; IV, 16, 6–9, 19, 7–9, 29, 66, 4–5; V, 3, 3, 4, 3, 95, 1–4, 108, 1–9; VII, 9, 13–14.
Trogus, *prol.* XXVIII.
Zonaras, VIII, 19, 3–7, 20, 11–13.

B. MODERN WORKS

1. Illyria: Topography, Ethnography, Archæology, etc.; History of Illyria before the Roman Wars

Bauer, A. *Die Anfänge österreichischer Geschichte.* Arch.-epigr. Mitt. aus Öster- reich-Ungarn, XVIII, 1895, p. 129.
Beloch, K. J. *op. cit.* IV, 1, pp. 635–7; IV, 2, pp. 531–3.
Casson, S. *Macedonia, Thrace and Illyria.* Oxford, 1926.
Grosse. Art. *Lembus* in P.W.
v. Hahn, J. G. *Albanesische Studien*, I. Vienna, 1853.
Ippen, Th. A. *Skutari und die nordalbanische Küstenebene:* Zur Kunde der Balkan- halbinsel. Reisen und Beobachtungen herausgegeben von C. Patsch. Heft 5. Sarajevo, 1907.
Kiepert, H. and R. *Formae Orbis antiqui*, tab. XVI, XVII, with explanatory text. Berlin, 1908; 1894.
Kiepert, H. *Lehrbuch der alten Geographie.* Berlin, 1878. pp. 352 *sqq.*; pp. 355–8, §§ 315–16.
Krahe, H. *Die alten balkanillyrischen geographischen Namen.* Heidelberg, 1925.
Kroll, W. Art. *Seeraub* in P.W.
Ormerod, H. A. *Piracy in the ancient world.* Liverpool-London, 1924.
Pace, B. *Frustuli Illirici.* Annuario della R. Scuola archeol. di Atene, III, 1916– 20, p. 286.
Patsch, C. *Das Sandschak Berat in Albanien.* Schriften der Balkankommission der Akad. der Wiss. in Wien; Antiq. Abteil. III. Vienna, 1904.
—— Art. *Dardani* in P.W.
—— *Aus dem Albanesischen Nationalmuseum.* Jahreshefte, XXIII, 1926, Beiblatt, cols. 209 *sqq.*
Philippson, A. Art. *Dassaretis* in P.W.
Praschniker, C. *Muzakhia und Malakastra.* Jahreshefte, XXI–XXII, 1922, Beiblatt, col. 5. (With plans of the ruins and environs of Apollonia.)

Praschniker, C. and Schober A. *Archäol. Forschungen in Albanien und Monte-negro.* Schriften der Balkankommission der Akad. der Wiss. in Wien; Antiq. Abteil. VIII. Vienna, 1919.

Rey, L. *Fouilles de la Mission française à Apollonie d'Illyrie et à Durazzo* (1923–1924). Albania, Revue d'archéologie, d'histoire, d'art et des sciences appliquées en Albanie et dans les Balkans; année 1925.

Schober, A. *Zur Topographie von Dyrrachium.* Jahreshefte, XXIII, 1926, Beiblatt, cols. 231 *sqq.*

Schütt, C. *Untersuchungen zur Geschichte der alten Illyrier.* Diss. Breslau, 1910.

v. Thallóczy, L. *Illyrisch-albanische Forschungen.* Munich and Leipzig, 1916.

Tomaschek, W. Art. *Ardiaioi* in P.W.

Torr, C. *Ancient ships.* Cambridge, 1894. p. 115.

Veith, G. *Der Feldzug von Dyrrhachium zwischen Caesar und Pompejus.* (With 9 maps and very full bibliography.) Vienna, 1920.

Vulič, N. Art. *Illyricum* in P.W.

Zippel, G. *Die römische Herrschaft in Illyrien.* Leipzig, 1877. pp. 5–43.

2. The two Roman wars in Illyria

(See also the General Bibliography)

Bauer, A. *op. cit.* pp. 136 *sqq.*

Beloch, K. J. *op. cit.* IV, 1, pp. 664–7, 731 *sq.*, IV, 2, p. 262.

Büttner-Wobst, Th. Art. *Demetrios von Pharos* in P.W. Supplementband 1.

Cichorius, C. *Römische Studien.* Leipzig-Berlin, 1922. p. 190.

De Sanctis, G. *op. cit.* III, 1, pp. 292–304, 322–7.

Ferrabino, A. *Il problema della unità nazionale nella Grecia.* 1. *Arato di Sicione.* Contributi alla Scienza dell' Antichità pubbl. da G. De Sanctis e L. Pareti. Florence, 1921. p. 232.

Frank, T. *Roman Imperialism.* New York, 1914. p. 116 *sq.*

Hill, G. F. *Historical Roman Coins.* 1909. pp. 36 *sq.*, 44 *sqq.*

Holleaux, M. *op. cit.* pp. 22–8, 97–129, 130–8.

—— *La politique romaine en Grèce et dans l'Orient hellénistique au IIIᵉ siècle; réponse à M. Th. Walek.* Rev. Phil. L, 1926, pp. 46 *sqq.*, 194 *sqq.*

Niese, B. *op. cit.* pp. 276–86, 436–8.

Pais, E. *Storia di Roma durante le guerre puniche,* 1. Rome, 1927. pp. 166 *sqq.*

Täubler, E. *op. cit.* p. 25 and note 2.

—— *Die Vorgeschichte des zweiten punischen Krieg* . Berlin, 1921. pp. 12 *sqq.*

Walek, Th. *op. cit.* Rev. Phil. XLIX, 1925, pp. 28 *qq.*

Zippel, G. *op. cit.* pp. 46 *sqq.*

GENERAL INDEX

Romans are entered under their gentile names, and for purposes of identification, the year of their first or most relevant tenure of office, usually the consulship (cos.), is inserted. The use of these dates does not assert their historical veracity.

Abaeocritus of Boeotia, 218, 732
Abantidas, tyrant of Sicyon, 219, 222
Abdera, in Spain, 770, 786
— in Thrace, 717, 719, 722
Abila (Seleuceia), 192
Abydos, 719
Academy, the New, 237, 298
Acarnania, 744; Pyrrhus and, 83, 96; Lysimachus and, 96; League, 217, 747; and Rome, 823; alliance with Aetolia, 217; Illyrians and, 831
Acerrae, 593, 813
Acestorides of Corinth, and Syracuse, 620; peace with Carthage, 620
Achaea, Achaean League: 8, 23, 34, 100, 210, 216, 222, 719; alliance with Aetolia, 744; Aratus and, 732 sqq.; and Arcadian League, 708; Aratus and Cleomenes and, 756; coinage, 736; constitution of, 735 sqq.; Demetrius and, 84; Ptolemy III and, 734; Pyrrhus and, 214; synodos, synkletos, 737; territory of, 750
Achaea Phthiotis, 217, 748, 752
Achaemenids, 93
Achaeus, cousin of Seleucus III, 723 sqq., 728
Acholla, 682
Acichorius, 103 sq.
Acilius, C., 316
Acrae, 675
Acragas, see Agrigentum
Acre, 728, see Ptolemaïs
Acrotatus, son of Areus, 214, 219, 708
— son of Cleomenes II of Sparta, 622
Adaeus, dynast of Cypsela, 719
Adherbal, 687
Administration, Celtic, 72; of Eastern monarchies, 28 sqq.; Etruscan, 439; of new Hellenistic monarchies in general, 24; Ptolemaic, 116 sqq.; Roman, 2, 441 sqq., 521 sqq., 550 sqq., 817 sqq.; Roman, in Sicily, 793 sqq.; Seleucid, 24, 161 sqq.
Adonis, cult of, in Egypt, 145; Seleucids and cult of, 195
Adriatic, piracy in the, 824 sqq.
adrogatio, adoption by, 412, 428

Adys (Uthina), 682
Aebutius, T. (cos. 499), 489
Aediles, curule, 526 sq.; plebeian, 451, 481; and food-control, 550 sq.; and imperium, 442
Aeful-um (-ae), 510
Aegae, royal tombs at, 213
Aegates Islands, battle of, 692
Aegean Islands, 76; League of, 126; piracy in, 85
Aegina, 750
Aegium, 759
Aegosthena, 736
Aelius, L., Stilo, grammarian, 327
— Q., Tubero, historian, 537
— Sextus, Paetus Catus (cos. 198), 327, 463, 534; Aelianum ius, 327
Aemilius, L., Barbula (cos. 281), at Tarentum, 643 sq.
— L., Mamercinus (cons. trib. 377), 527, 578; (mag. equit. 368), 525
— L., Papus (cos. 225), at Telamon, 812
— L., Paullus (cos. 219), 815, 848
— M. (dictator, 433), 522
— M., Lepidus (cos. 232), 806
— M., Paullus (cos. 255), at Hermaean promontory, 684
— Mamercus Mamercinus (cos. 339), 502, 507, 525
— Q., Barbula (cos. 317, 311), 604 sq., 642
— Q., Papus (cos. 278), 650
Aeneas and Rome, 347, 363 sqq., 697
Aeneas Tacticus, military manuals of, 83
Aenianes, 106, 218
Aenus, 719
Aeolis, 184; Gauls and, 105, 721
Aequi, 406, 491 sqq., 494, 500 sq., 583; wars with Rome, 497, 500 sq., 509 sq., 575 sq.; and Volsci, 503; and Samnium, 606
Aequimelium, 325
Aeschrion, 629 sq.
Aesernia, 596
Aesis, river, 657
Aetius, doxographer, 238
Aetna, Agathocles and, 619

Aetolia, Aetolian League, 23, 80, 84, 89, 95, 207; alliance with Acarnania, 217; and Achaean League, 744; Amphictyonic League and, 210, 733; Antigonus Gonatas and, 99, 211, 217; invaded by Areus, 99; army of, 208; art and letters, 209; rivalry of Boeotia with, 102, 218; treaty with Boeotia, 83; invades Boeotia, 732; constitution and policy of, 208 sqq.; and Elis, 733; Gauls and, 102 sq., 208; and Illyria, 828 sq.; and Laconia, 744; Lysimachus and, 89; and Ptolemy III, 758; Pyrrhus and, 82 sqq., 95, 213

Aezani, 183

Africa, central, and Egypt, 133 sq.; northern and Egypt, 134; Agathocles of Syracuse and, 622–630

Agathoclea, mistress of Ptolemy IV, 727 sq.

Agathocles, minister of Ptolemy IV, 727
— of Cyzicus, 365
— of Syracuse, Ch. XIX, 77, 258, 261; character of, 636 sq.; early rises and falls, 618 sqq.; African campaigns of, 622–630; and Carthage, 622 sqq.; coinage, 621, 634; and Croton, 619, 635, 641; and Etruria, 630, 635; and Italiote Greeks, 635; and S. Italy, 634 sqq.; Mamertine mercenaries with, 635, 667; attacks Messana, 622; and Rome, 635; tyrant of Syracuse, 621; and Tarentum, 641; results of rule, 636 sq.
— II, 636
— son of Lysimachus, 80, 83, 88, 97

Agathos Daimon, 115

Agathostratus, Rhodian admiral, 713; statue of, at Delos, 714

Agelaus of Naupactus, appeal for Hellenic unity, 768

Ager Albanus, 349, 401
— Gallicus, 657; distribution of, 806 sq.
— Pomptinus, and food-supply, 537; distribution of, 538
— privatus, 468, 470, 537 sqq.
— publicus, 468, 546, 657, 797; the Aventine and, 459, 473; allotments of, 546; extent of, in regal Rome, 471; plebs and, 471, 473, 537 sq.; senators and, 808; Spurius Cassius and, 471 sqq.
— Romanus, 403, 409, 420, 452; Servius Tullius and, 434; after Veii, 516 sq.; division of, into tribus rusticae, 434; expansion of, after battle of Algidus, 538
— Rutulus, 340 sq., 404
— Tiburtinus, 404, 488, 500
— Veiens, rustic tribes on, 516

Agesilaus, party leader at Sparta, 742 sq.

Agesipolis, king of Sparta, 765

Agiatis, wife of Agis IV, 750

Agis IV of Sparta, 259, 734; condition of Sparta, 739 sqq.; reforms of, 741 sqq.

Agriculture, Celtic, 45, 73; Egyptian, 137 sqq.; in N. Italy, 559; in Latium, 334, 342 sqq.; in Italy, 334, 469; Roman, 466 sq., 475 sq., 546; Seleucid, 182 sq.; in Sicily, 794 sq.

Agrigentum (Acragas), 799; Agathocles and, 620, 622 sq., 633; Pyrrhus and, 651; Rome and, 673, 793; capture of, by Rome, 676 sq., by Carthalo, 685

Agron of Illyria, 747 sq., 827 sqq.

Aguilar, necropolis of, 786

Agyrium, Timoleon and, 617; Hiero II and, 690

Ahala, see Servilius

Ahriman, 6 sq.

Ahura-mazda, 6, 12, 14, 15, 156

Aigosages, the, 726

Ake-Ptolemaïs, 190, 192

Akkad, 188

'Akra Leuke, 780

Alalia, battle of, 769, 779

Alba Fucens, colony at, 608
— Longa, 341, 349, 364, 377, 401, 404, 431; colonies, 346; League, 350, 405; ager Albanus, 349, 401; plebs of, admitted to citizenship, 419; war with Rome, 377; Albani Longani Bovillenses, 401

Alban Lake, 513 sq.

Albanus Mons, 339 sq., 349

Albion, 51, 53 n., 771

Alcaeus of Messene, 269, 274

Alcia, wife of Agathocles, 635

Alcinoe, Aetolian poetess, 209

Alcmaeon, 285

Alebos, river (Vinalapò), 787

Aleppo, Seleucids and, 184

Aleria, 679

Aletrium, 606

Alexander, general of Antiochus III, 723
— Aetolus, tragic poet, 203, 209, 253, 272
— Balas, 194
— son of Cassander, 77, 79, 83
— of Corinth, revolt of, 715
— son of Craterus, tyrant of Corinth, 221 sqq.; revolt of, 221, 222; honoured as Benefactor, 221
— son of Demetrius, 77
— I of Epirus, treaty with Rome, 594, 640; in Illyria, 708; and Italy, 824
— the Great, 1, 4, 12, 15, 20, 23, 36, 158, 166, 194, 212; and the succession to, Ch. III passim; and the Alexandrian Academy, 251; the Celts and, 64 sq.; official imperial cult of, 17, 113; Danubian peoples and, 64; deified, 14, 17; conquest of Egypt, 137; Illyrians, expedition against, 64 sq.; in India, 118; national monarchy of, 9; conquest of Persia, 10; policy of fusing races, 37; the Triballi, expedition against, 64 sq.;

results of his work, 108; effect of conquests, on thought, 230, and on geographical knowledge, 261; see vol. VI

Alexander Jannaeus, 192, 194;
— II, son of Pyrrhus, 82, 214, 826; and Achaean League, 217 sq.

Alexandreschate, on the Jaxartes, 174

Alexandria, 12, 24 sq., 27, 29, 30 sq., 130, 146, 193, 249; Academy and Lyceum at, 251 sq.; 'Alexandria next Egypt,' 121; Alexandria and Greek literature, 253; art at, 147, 154; constitution of, 121 sq.; culture at, 30 sq., 46 sq.; economic centre of Egypt, 111; native population of Egypt and, 115; Greeks in, 28, 30 sq., 148 sq.; Hellenism of, 148 sq.; immigrants from the East, 111; industry at, 135; lighthouse at, 29; Mausoleum and Library at, 143, 251; Memphis, rivalry with, 115, 148, 151; Museum at, 29, 251 sq.; Peripatetics at, 251; Phoenician cities and, 191; mixed population of, 111 sq.; religion at, 145 sq.; science and scholarship at, 147, 203; trade centre, 32; Greek traders in, 111; after First Syrian war, 704
— in Arachosia (Candahar), 174
— Ariana (Herat), 174
— on the Etymandrus (Helmund), 174

Alexandrian Literature, Ch. VIII; biography, 261; geography, 261 sqq.; Greek debt to, 250, 253 sq.; history, 256–261; mythography, 265; oratory and rhetoric, 250, 255 sq.; philosophy, 249; poetry and drama, 249, 266–283; popular prose works, 264 sq.; prose, 249, 255–266; first Ptolemies and, 297; Tragic Pleiad at, 267
— Science and Mathematics, Ch. IX; biology and botany, 288 sq.; mathematics, 290–311; medicine and surgery, 284–288

Aleximachus, 103

Algidus, Mt, 501; battle of, 503, 506 sq., 509

Alicante, 787

Allia, river, battle of, 564, 596

Alliances, see also Treaties; Athens and Sparta, 707; Boeotia and Aetolia, 82; Carthage and Etruria, 769; Demetrius and Seleucus, 77; Egypt and Sparta, 706; Lysimachus, Seleucus and Ptolemy, 78; Massiliotes and Iberians, 781; Pyrrhus and Lysimachus, 89; Rome and Arretium, 605, and Caere, 575, and Falerii, 587, 800, and Gabii, 402, and Hernici and Latins, 492, and Hiero, 674, and Mamertines, 672, and Saguntum, 789, and Samnites, 586

Allies, war of the (220–217), 763 sqq.

Allifae, 597, 605, 607

Alonis, 780

Alpine passes, Celts and, 61 sqq.

Alsium, colony at, 690

Althia (Althaia), 789

Amanic Gates, 88

Amantia, 836

Amanus, river, 88

Amastris, 77, 105

Ambarvalia, 399

Ambigatus legend, 58, 60, 66

Ambracia, and Aetolian League, 748; Pyrrhus and, 83, 211

Ambracus, 765

Ameinias, general of Antigonus II, and Cassandreia, 107, 214 sq.

Amestris, wife of Lysimachus, at Heraclea, 77; murdered, 90

Amiternum, 613 sq.

Amitrochates, 173

Ammonites, 183

Amometus, 265

Amon, Amon-Re, 12, 14, 18 sq.

Amphictyonic League, 104, 210, 217, 764

Amphilochia, Pyrrhus and, 83; and Aetolian League, 748

Amphipolis, coinage, 85, 198

Amphisseans, at defence of Delphi, 103

Amynander, 748

Amyzon, 180

Anacreon, 274

Anagnia, 425, 492; civitas sine suffragio conferred on, 606

Anaitis, 182

Anapus plain, 624; river, 632

Anatolia, 111, 156 sq.

Anaxagoras, 292

ancilia, the, 426

Ancus Marcius, 362, 371, 377 sq., 402, 418, 474

Ancyra, Gauls settled in, 106; battle at, in War of the Brothers, 720

Andalusia, 774

Andosini, 782

Andragoras, Seleucid general, 720

Andromachus of Aspendus, 729
— uncle of Seleucus III, 723

Andros, battle of, 718

Anicius, Q., 533, 548

Aniensis tribus, 510

Anio, river, 338, 340, 403 sq.; Gauls at, 572

Antagoras of Rhodes, poet, 94, 203, 273

Antalcidas, Peace of, 321

Antander, 619, 631 sq.

Antemnae, 400, 403

Anthedon, 192

Anthemusias, 174

Antias, Q. Valerius, historian, 317, 436, 461

Antigone, daughter of Berenice, 77, 84

Antigoneia, vase festival at Delos, 715, 862
— passes of, 830

Antigoneia, in Atintania, 201, 836; in Bithynia, refounded by Lysimachus and re-named Nicaea, 92; near Cassandreia, 201; on the Orontes, demolished by Seleucus, 76; in Paeonia, 201; in the Troad, re-named Troas Alexandria, 91 sq.

Antigonids, 26, 82, 94; and Rome, 218

Antigonus I, 36, 88; and Babylon, 93; and deification, 15, 91; see vol. VI

— II, Gonatas, 10, 87, 94–96, 162, 200; and Aetolia, 211, 217; treaty with Antiochus, 100, 102, and Aratus, 222; at Argos, 215; army of, 201; and Athens, 89, 96 sq., 203, 206, 217, 220 sq., 706, 708; institutes festival of Basileia, 107; and Boeotia, 82, 207; in Chremonidean War, 705 sqq.; coin-age of, 107, 200 sq., 714, 719; and Corinth, 205, 214, 215, 223, 711 sq., 733; victory at Cos, 713, 862 sq.; deified, 107, 221; and Egypt, 213; and Gauls, 107, 201; and Greece, 201, 205 sq.; defeat by Keraunos, 99; king of Macedonia, 106 sqq., 197 sqq.; kingship, basis of, 202; literary circle, 203 sq.; and Menedemus, 94 sq.; and Peloponnese, 207, 219 sq.; and Philochorus, 712; and Pyrrhus, 83, 89, 95, 197, 213; and Rhodes, 207; and Seleucus, 93; and Sparta, 216, 220; and Thessalian League, 200; and Thessaly, 107, 200; and Winged Victory, 714; and Zeno, 94 sq., 202, 220

— III, Doson, invades Arcadia, 760; in Caria, 722; constitutional position of, 751; and Corinth, 842; Dardanians and, 762 sq.; Hellenic League of, 8, 759; and Illyria, 839, 845; and Laconia, 760; Philip V, guardian of, 751; and Rome, 839 sqq.; and Thessalian League, 751

— of Carystus, 251, 261, 264, 273

antigrapheus, Egyptian, 121

Antimachus of Colophon, 268, 271

Antioch, in Caria, 181 n.

— on the Orontes, 12, 25, 27, 30 sq., 88, 121, 158, 169, 174, 185, 188, 193 sq., 195; founded by Seleucus, 76; non-Greek inhabitants of, 185; Antiochus III and library at, 250; in Laodicean War, 716

— in Persis, 189

— in Pisidia, 181 n.

— in Scythia, 174

Antioch-Nisibis, 725

Antiochia Margiana (Merv), 174

Antiochis, mother of Attalus I, 721

Antiochus Hierax, 720, 726

— I, Soter, 93, 98 sq., 104 sq., 157 sqq., 161 sq., 173, 175, 178, 180, 188; treaty with Antigonus, 100, 102; and Babylon, 187 sq.; deified as Saviour, 16, 106; de-feated by Eumenes, 710; defeat of Gauls,

702; and Hellenism in Asia, 710; and literature, 250; mercenaries of, with Gauls, 102; and Miletus, 77; policy in Syria and Mesopotamia, 184; and Northern League, 701; Soter, 702 sq.; peace with Ptolemy II, 704

— II, Theos, 19, 161, 172, 181, 184, 188, 709 sqq.; and Asia Minor, 159; and Gauls of Galatia, 720 sq.; and Ptolemy II, 715; and Seleucus II, 722

— III, the Great, 162 sq., 167; character of, 723; at Doura, 725; invades Egypt, 726; Greek writers at court of, 699 n.; and Jewish colonies in Asia Minor, 171; letters of, 194; and literature, 250; in Marsyas valley, 724; victory of, at Panion, 190; defeat of, at Raphia, 730 sq.; and Rome, 155, 159, 172 sqq.; in Fourth Syrian War, 728 sqq.

— IV, Epiphanes, 159 sq., 172; at Jeru-salem, 163; and religious persecution, 164; policy of founding cities, 184, 189; and Babylon, 188; policy at Uruk, 188; and Hellenism, 189

— VII, Sidetes, 159 sqq.

— VIII, Grypus, Seleuceia in Pieria and, 186

— IX, Cyzicenus, 165 n.

— of Ascalon, 237

— of Commagene, 256

Antipater, son of Cassander, and the succes-sion to Alexander, 79 sq., 89 sqq., 197

— nephew of Cassander, 80, 102; Etesias, 107, 143

— the Regent, 14, 94

Antipatreia, 836, 855

Antiphanes of Berga, 265

Antiphon, orator, 225 n.

— mathematician, 294 sq.

Antistius Labeo, jurist, 329 sq.

Antium, 405, 474, 498, 510, 541, 576, 578; in Latin War, 590 sq.; piracy at, 586; Roman colony, 592; and Roman fleet, 678

Antoninus and Faustina, temple of, 354

Antoninus Pius, 314

Antonius, Q., Merenda (cons. trib. 422), 520

— T., Merenda (Decemvir), 460, 520

Antony, Mark, 313; and the Pergamene Library, 253

Anubis, cult of, 5, 7, 93 n., 146

Anxur (Tarracina), 339, 498, 510; colonists of, 416; see also Tarracina

Aoüs pass, 101, 219, 830 n.

Apama, daughter of Antiochus I, 704, 712

— wife of Seleucus I, 77, 93

Apamea Cibotos, 158, 700

— on the Orontes, 158, 169, 185, 701

— by Sipylus, battle of, 171, 179

Apelles, guardian of Philip V, 763 sq., 766 sq.

Aphrodite, 13, 265
Aphroditopolis papyrus of Menander, 227
Apiolae, 390
apokletoi, Aetolian, 209
Apollo, temple of, at Didyma, 175; Didymean, statue of, 174, 198; temple of, at Thermum, 208; at Delphi, and Gauls, 103; cult of, at Rome, 514; eponymous magistrate at Miletus, 709, 712
— Helios-Hermes, 5
Apollodorus, an Athenian chronographer, 235 *n.*, 262
— comic poet, Plautus and, 226, 226 *n.*
— tyrant of Cassandreia, 102 *sq.*, 107, 220, 740
Apollonia, 826, 836; Pyrrhus and, 83, 185, 192; alleged alliance with Rome, 823; *deditio* to Rome, 834; and Macedon, 839 *n.*
Apolloniatis, 724
Apollonis, Attalid foundation, 180
— wife of Attalus I, 721
Apollonius, *dioiketes* of Ptolemy II, 29, 119 *sqq.*, 128, 132, 135, 141, 146; court of, 116
— cadet of Alexandria, 123
— of Perga, geometer, 290, 299 *sq.*, 307–310
— Rhodius, 146; librarian at Alexandria, 253, 262, 267–277
Apollophanes, 'archon of the S. Dorians in Marissa,' 191
— physician to Antiochus III, 725
Appian, 314; on Pyrrhus, 638 *n.*
Appian Way, 401, 593
Appius, *see* Claudii
— Herdonius, 494 *sq.*
Apulia, Greek culture in, 584; and Rome in Samnite Wars, 598; Pyrrhus and, 656
Apustius, L., Fullo (cos. 226), 806
Aqua Marcia, 377
Aquilii, 695
Aquilius, C. (cos. 487), 325
— C., Florus (cos. 259), in Sicily, 679
Aquilonia, 613
Arabia, Arabian trade, 134, 175
Aradus, 190, 704, 712
Aramaea, 160 *sq.*
Arantides, Macedonian goddesses, 198
Aratus of Sicyon, character of, 222; General of Achaean League, 733, 863; and Aetolia, 743; and Argos, 735, 745; and Aristomachus, 749; and Athens, 735, 745, 749; and Boeotia, 732; at Caphyae, 753; and Cleomenes, 753, 755 *sqq.*; attacks Corinth, 734; and Egypt, 718, 722; and Lydiades, 746, 749; and Peloponnese, 223; and Ptolemy III, 726; and Sparta, 743
— of Soli, poet, 94, 108, 203, 250, 268, 270

Arbitration, increase of, in Greece, 211
Arbocala, 789
Arcadia, Demetrius and, 84; Eastern, 219; League, 707, 736
Arcesilas of Pitane, 105, 217, 221 *sq.*, 224, 237, 298
Archagathus, son of Agathocles, 629 *sq.*, 635
— II, 636
Archidamia, 743
Archidamus of Sparta, and S. Italy, 589, 824; and Tarentum, 640
archidikastes, Egyptian, 119
Archimedes of Syracuse, 263, 290, 299, 301 *sqq.*, 303–306, 820; Cicero and, 303
archiphylakitai, Egyptian, 124
Architecture, Celtic, 73; Roman, 466, influenced by Etruscans, 384 *sqq.*, 399, 464, by Greeks and Sicilians, 698
Archytas, 293
Ardea, 339 *sqq.*, 364, 404, 436, 488, 503, 521, 565, 577, 591
Ardiaeans, and Celts, 826
Aretos, Macedonian god, 197
Areus of Sparta, 214 *sq.*, 219; invades Aetolia, 99; in Chremonidean War, 706 *sqq.*; coinage of, 99 *sq.*
Arganthonius, king of Tartessus, 770
Argei, ritual of, 359; Fifth Sanctuary of, 564
Argolid, the, 84, 99
Argos, Demetrius and, 76, 84, 207; Antigonus Gonatas and, 99, 215, 707; Pyrrhus and, 215; Aratus and, 745, 759; Cleomenes and, 757
Ariana (Herat), 159, 174
Ariarathes the Persian, 710, 718
Aribazus, 716
Aricia, 339, 344, 348, 351, 369, 401, 404, 439, 577; league, 350 *sq.*, 405; battle of, 396 *sq.*, 487 *sq.*; cult of Diana at, 344, 348, 374, 405, 439; and Latin League, 401; *rex nemorensis* at, 409; admitted to Roman citizenship, 591
Ariminum, 438, 537; colony at, 657, 807
Aristaeus, 307
— 'the elder,' 298
Aristarchus, grammarian, 253, 254, 271
— of Samos, mathematician, 297, 301 *sq.*, 309 *sq.*, 311
Aristeas, Ps.-, Epistle of, 116 *sq.*
Aristippus, of Argos, Antigonus Gonatas and, 215; Aratus and, 735, 745
Aristobulus, historian, 259
Aristodama of Smyrna, poetess, 209
Aristodemus of Cumae, 395 *sq.*
— 'the Good', tyrant of Megalopolis, 219, 222
Aristodicides, 181
Aristomachus, tyrant of Argos, 219, 221 *sq.*, 735, 745, 749, 753, 757, 759

Ariston, 224

Aristophanes, and the New Comedy, 228
— of Byzantium, 227, 254

Aristotimus, Elis and, 216

Aristotle, 29, 224, 238 *sqq.*; on deification, 13; followers of, 237; and Egyptian kings, 252; *Ethics* of, 230; ideal monarchy of, 36; and the new philosophies, 230; *Poetics* of, 271; *Politics* of, 33; and Stoicism, 239; influence of, on science at Alexandria, 284, 288 *sqq.*; and mathematics, 296, 299; on condition of Sparta, 739

Aristoxenus of Tarentum, 238, 261, 554

Armenia, 88, 196

Armies: of Agathocles in Africa, 630; of Antigonus at Sellasia, 760; of Carthage, against Agathocles, 625, and in Punic War, 677; of Cleomenes at Sellasia, 760; of Demetrius, 84 *sq.*; of Gauls, in N. Italy, 101 *sq.*, 561, at the Allia, 561 *sq.*, at Telamon, 811; Greek, against Gauls, 102; of Hasdrubal in Spain, 788; of Macedonia, 198, 200 *sqq.*; of Pyrrhus at Tarentum, 643, at Heraclea, 644 *sq.*; of Ptolemies, 110 *sq.*, 113, 117 *sq.*; at Raphia, 729; of early Rome, 431 *sqq.*, 435; of Rome and military pay, 512, 811 *sq.*; of Rome at the Allia, 562 *sq.*, at Asculum, 647, at Drepana, 687, in Samnite Wars, 600 *sq.*, at Telamon, 760 *sq.*, in Sicily, 672, 813 *sq.*; of Seleucids, 169 *sqq.*

Arnensis tribus, 574

Arno, river, 805

Arpinum, 440, 607, 659; admitted to Roman citizenship, 608

Arretium, 613; Roman treaty with, 605; besieged by Senones, 638

Arrhidaeus, 107

Arrian, 258 *sq.*

Arsaces, chief of the Parni, 719
— II, 720, 722

Arsacids, 26

Arsinoe, in Ceos (formerly Poiessa), 707
— in Cilicia, 704
— (Methana) in the Argolid, 708
— (Patara), 704
— (Teucheira), 713
— in valley of the Marsyas, 192
— I, wife of Ptolemy II, 97 *sq.*; deified, 17, 138; coin portrait of, 97
— II, daughter of Ptolemy I, wife of Ptolemy II, 77, 89, 92 *sq.*, 99; in Syrian Wars, 703 *sq.*; coinage, 703; statues of, at Athens and Olympia, 705; cult names, 705
— III (Cleopatra), sister and wife of Ptolemy IV, 730

Art, in Alexandria, 147; Carthaginian, in Spain, 779; Celtic, 42, 47 *sqq.*, Greek

influence on, 44; Greek art, in Egypt, 153, in Spain, 777; Hellenistic and Chinese, 174, 196; Phoenician, in Spain, 773 *n.*, 779; Roman, Etruscan influence on, 385 *sq.*; Tartessian, 773. *See further* vol. VIII

Artabazanes of Aderbaijan, 725

Artemidorus, 778

Artemis, temple of, at Ephesus, 91, 198

Arthashastra, 154

Arval rites, 399

Aryium, C. (Ortegal), 771

Ascalon, 192

Ascanius, 364

Asclepiades of Samos, 266 *sqq.*, 272 *sq.*, 282

Asclepius, 4, 13, 146

Asconius Pedianus, commentator on Cicero, 330, 413, 450, 453 *sq.*, 461

Asculum, battle of, 647 *sq.*; Rome and, 657

Asia, centre of world's commerce, 212; Demetrius and, 76, 80, 85; Egypt and, 108; Lysimachus and, 97; mixed population of, 10

Asia Minor, Cassander and, 76; Celts in, 65; general character of, 176 *sq.*; Egypt and, 131; Gauls in, 26, 105 *sq.*, 720 *sq.*; Graeco-Macedonian cities in, 158; Greek cities in, 173, 177 *sq.*; Greek settlers in, 178 *sq.*; Hellenism in, 194; land, 177, 181 *sqq.*; Lysimachus and, 90; new cities in, 180 *sq.*; satrapies of, 166 and *n.*; Seleucid administration of, 156 *sq.*, 159, 163, 177–184; Seleucus II and, 720; temple lands, 183; Zoroastrianism in, 6 *sq.*

Asianic style of oratory, 256

Asoka and Hellenistic kings, 204

Aspendus, 704

Aspis (Clupea), 626; Roman landing at, 682

Assemblies, Roman, *see* Comitia, Concilium

Assyria, 156

Astacus, in Bithynia, destroyed by Lysimachus, 91, 100

Astauene, 720

Astrology, 4

Astronomy, 290, 295, 298, 301 *sq.*, 310 *sq.*

asylia, 180; cities of Phoenicia and Palestine coast and, 190, 211

Asylum *inter duos lucos*, 368 *sq.*

Atargatis, 5, 7

Atarneus, 184, 710

Ateius Capito, 417

Atellan farces, 593

Aternius, A., 324, 458 and *n.*, 459, 519

Athamania, 748

Athelhard of Bath, and Euclid, 299

Athena, Pheidias' statue of, 79

Athenaeus, admiral of Antiochus I, 173, 181
— of Naucratis, on the Alexandrians, 250

Athenaeus, writer on engines of war, 307
Athene Alkis, 201
Athens, Antigonus Gonatas and, 203, 206, 217, 220, 224, 708; rites of Atargatis in, 5; in Chremonidean War, 706 sq.; as a city state, 10, 23; and Delphi, 206; Demetrius and, 76, 78, 84; Demochares and, 86; independent, 748 sq.; after Macedonian rule, 224; Nationalist party at, 81 sq., 89, 100, 206, 213, 217, 706; Phoenicians at, 190 sq.; political importance lost, 221; Ptolemy I and, 85; Ptolemy III and, 749; Pyrrhus at, 87; Rome and, 824 sq.
— New Age, spirit of, 224 sqq.; Classical age ended, 224; Comedy, the New, 225–230; and Epicurus and Epicureanism, 231–234, 243–248; philosophies, the new, 229 sq.; older schools, 237 sq.; and Stoicism, 238–242; Zeno and, 235 sq.
Atilii of Calatia, 695
Atilius, A., Calatinus (cos. 258), 680; at Panormus, 685
— C., Bulbus (censor, 234), 806
— C., Regulus (cos. 256, 250), 630, 687
— L., Luscus (cons. trib. 44), 520
— M., Regulus (cos. 294), 613
— M., Regulus (cos. 256), 630, 680; in Africa, 681 sqq.; and Carthaginian peace offers, 683; a prisoner, 689
Atina, 603 n., 606 sq., 613
Atintania, Pyrrhus and, 83; King's Land, 199, 201; Rome and, 219 n.; Demetrius II and, 744; Epirus and, 748; Illyria and, 831, 834
Attalids, worship of, 20, 26; patronage of arts and letters, 251; see further vol. VIII
Attalus I, 178, 721 sqq.; refuses tribute to Gauls, 721; statuary at Pergamum, 722; and Antiochus III, 726
Atticus, friend of Cicero, 322 sqq.
Attius Clausus, 373, 416, 420, 470
— Tullius, 499
Attus Navius, 431
auctoritas patrum, 393, 413, 450, 482 sq., 530, 535
Audoleon of Paeonia, 85, 89, 96
Aufidena, 596, 611
Auguratorium, the, 564
Augurs, Etruria and, 384, 429 sq.; Romulus and, 353, 429; functions of, 430 sq.; and comitia tributa, 483; and plebs, 535; 'borrowed' auspices, 551; extispicium, 384; auspicatio, 384
Augustus: 15, 313, 329, 340, 514; and dedication of Cornelius Cossus, 316, 507; Roma et Augustus, cult of, 11
Aulius, Q., 601
Aulon (Valona), 836
Aulus Gellius, 227, 316, 330, 457
Aulus Vibenna, 391

Aurelian, 363
Aurelii, 694
Aurelius, C. (cos. 248), 689
Aurunci, 587 n., 602
Ausonians (Ausones), 584, 662
auspicatio, 384
Autariatae, Gauls and, 747; and Macedonia, 197
Autolycus of Pitane, 298
auxilium, 448; plebs and, 456 sq.
Avienus, Ora Maritima, 51, 59, 770 n.
Avroman, in Media, 167 sqq., 187
Axius, pass, 219
— river, 747, 827
Aylesford culture, 70
Azotus, 192

Baalbek, Seleucids and, 184
Ba'alim, 156
Babylon, 12, 98, 163, 175; Antigonus I and, 93; Antiochus I and, 93, 187 sq.; Antiochus IV and, 188 sq.; cuneiform tablets from, 187; Hellenism and, 189; under early Seleucids, 188; Seleucus and, 93
Babylonia, 7, 10, 156, 163; Antiochus IV and, 189, 194; Graeco-Macedonian cities in, 158; Greek settlers in, 170; Jewish colonists from, 180; and science, 290; under the Seleucids, 184, 187
Bactria, 26, 93, 158, 174, 189, 717; coinage, 719; revolt of, 159
Baebelo, 778
Baetis, river and valley, 772, 779, 792
Baetocaece, 183; temple of Zeus at, 184
Baeton, 259
Bagradas valley, 682; defeat of Regulus at, 684
Balearic Isles, 770; slingers, 773
Bambyce, Hierapolis, 93 n., 184, 189
Barce (Ptolemaïs), 713
Bargusii, 782
Basileia, festival of, instituted by Antigonus Gonatas, 107
Bastarnae, 316, 747
Bastulo- (Basto-) Phoenicians, 778
Bathanattus, king of the Scordisci, 102
Bedu, deity of Edessa, 197 sq.
Beisan (Scythopolis), 729
Bel, 12, 156; temple of, at Elam, 163, 195
Belbinate, the, 753
Belgae, origin and language of, 56; invasion of N.E. Gaul, 59; of S.E. Britain, 70
Bellovesus, 60, 63
Beneventum (Malventum), 438, 660; battle of, 653
Berenice, queen of Ptolemy I, 16, 77, 96
— daughter of Ptolemy II, 715 sq.
— of Cyrene, wife of Ptolemy III, 712 sq., 716; Coma Berenices, 302, 717

Berenice (formerly Euhesperides), 713
Berenikis, founded by Pyrrhus, 83
Beroea, 85, 200
Berosus, 260
Berybraces, 772
Berytus, 190 sq.
Bias of Priene, 769
Bion, of Borysthenes, Cynic, 204, 255, 264
— of Smyrna, 281
Bithynia, 76, 90, 100, 105; Seleucids and, 159, 177
Bithys, general of Demetrius II, 746
Black Sea, coinage in the cities of, 90 sq.; mines on, 169
Bodostar, 689
Bodyguards, Macedonian, 9, 11, 201
Boeotia, Boeotians, 64, 79, 99 sq., 104, 207, 218; revolt in, 81; alliance with Aetolia, 82 sqq.; and Aetolia, 102, 732, 744; Demetrius and, 82, 87; in Egypt, 122; Gauls and, 102 sqq.
Boëtius, and Euclid, 299
Boii, 63; flat graves of, 44 sqq.; in Bohemia, 45; inhumation cemeteries, 70; invasion of Italy, 556, 809 sqq.; defeat of, at Lake Vadimo, 639; at Telamon, 812 sq.
Bola, 469, 510, 575, 606
Bolgius, 101 sq.
Bologna, funeral stelae of, 556
Bolsena, 658
Bomilcar and Agathocles, 626 sqq.; and revolution in Carthage, 628
Borsippa, 188
Bostar, Carthaginian general, at Aspis, 682
Bovianum Undecimanorum, 614
— Vetus, 596, 611, 614
Bovillae, 350, 401 sq.
Brennus, leader of the Gauls: invasion of Macedonia, 101–104, of Greece, 102; army of, 101; at Delphi, 103; compared with Xerxes, 102
— leader against Rome, in Gallic wars, 561
British Isles, Celts in, 47; Greeks and, 50; minting in, 47; Pytheas and, 53 n.; trade with Egypt, 134; S.E. and Belgae, 70
Brittany, and tin, 50, 771, 775; Pytheas and, 53
Brochi, 724, 728
Bronze Age, the Cornish tin trade in, 50 n., 69; Latium in, 332 sq.
— early, tumulus culture of, 55 and n.; climate of, 71; see also beginning of Ch. XI
Bronze work, Celtic, 43 sqq., 49; Greek, 49; Tartessian, 771 sqq.
Brothers, War of the, 720 sqq.
Brundisium, colony at, 656, 690
Bruttii, Agathocles and the, 619, 634, 640; League, coinage of, 655
Brutus, see under Junius

Buddhism, Northern India and, 204
Burial, Celtic, 43 sqq.; chariot-burials, 43, 72; 'Chieftains' Graves,' 43, 72; flat graves, 44 sqq., 55, 59, 63, 69, 72; Italian cemeteries, 45; in Latium, 333, 336 sq., 354 sq., 356, 367, 381, 385 sq., 417, 496 sq.
Byblus, 190
Bylazora, 751, 767
Byllis, Bylliones, 836
Byzantium, 85, 90; and Northern League, 98 sq.; Gauls and, 104, 107; war with Rhodes, 726; and Philip V, 767 sq.

Cabum, 349, 364
Cacus, 364; Caci Scalae, 353
Caecilii, 696
Caecilius, L., Metellus (cos. 284), at Arretium, 638
— L., Metellus (cos. 251), 686, 820
Caeles Vibenna, 383, 391
Caelus Vivenna, 391; see also Caeles Vibenna
Caeninenses, the, 313, 403
Caere, 388, 439, 465, 505, 575, 604, 657; and Veii, 515; and Rome, 517, 659; and Gauls, 565, 571; Regolini-Galassi tombs at, 382; Tarchnas tomb at, 396 sq.
'caerea,' Iberian, 785
Caesar, see under Julius
caetra, caetrati, Iberian, 784
Caïcus valley, 709 sq.
Calabria, 634
Calatia, 598, 603, 695
Cales, 552, 660; colony at, 541, 594
Callatis, coinage, 91
Callicrates of Samos, at Miletus, 702; in Cilicia, 704; statue of, 705
Callimachus, 143, 146, 262, 264 sq., 270–283, 727; and Library at Alexandria, 252 sq.; and Ptolemy II, 705, 717
Callinicus, cult name of Seleucus II, 718
Callippus of Cyzicus, 311
— son of Moerocles, 100, 102, 706
Callisthenes of Olynthus, 257
Callium, burnt by Gauls, 102; rebuilt, 213
Calpurnius, L., Piso (cos. 133), historian, 317, 325 sq., 453
— — (cos. 58), 455
Calynda in Caria, the Ptolemies and, 128, 130
Camarina, 632, 680, 685
Cambaules, and Thrace, 101
Camerinum, 605, 609, 612
Camillus, see under Furius
Campania, Campanians, 339 sq., 382 sq., 395 sq., 465 sq., 588; culture and manufactures in, 592 n.; mercenaries with Agathocles, 635; at Rhegium, 654, 656, 664; mutiny of Roman troops in, 529
Canuleius, C., 419, 519; see also under Lex
Canusium, 600

capanne in the Palatine, 356

Capena, 383; and Veii, 515, 561; Rome and, 516 *sq.*

— Porta, 383

Caphyae, 219, 707, 747, 750; battle of, 764

Capito, Ateius, jurist, 330

— Sinnius, 330

Capitoline Triad, the, 375, 383 *sq.*

Capitolium Vetus, 496

Cappadocia, Lysimachus and, 76; Great, 159

Capua, taken by Sabellians, 584; citizenship granted to, 592; after Latin War, 592 *sq.*; and Cumae, 594 *sq.*; Pyrrhus and, 646

caput, see Citizenship

Caranis, ruins of, 144

Carchemish, Seleucids and, 184

Cardia, 91

Caria, 76, 78, 92, 126, 128, 129 and *n.*, 719

Carinae, *mureus terreus* of the, 347, 356

Carpetani, 782, 789

Carsioli, colony at, 608 *sq.*

Cartagena (New Carthage), foundation of, 787 *sqq.*; silver mines of, 778, 792

Carthage: Agathocles and, 622 *sqq.*; commerce and industry, 665 *sq.*; constitution of, 666; Etruria and, 347; Hellenization of, 191; Pyrrhus and, 650 *sqq.*; revolution in, 628; and Sardinia, 803 *sq.*; sea power of, 670; Sicily, 622 *sqq.*, policy in, 649 *sqq.*; territory, limits of, 682; trade policy of, 665, 669; Rome, contrasted with, 465, 666, 669; *see* Punic War, First, Ch. XXI; and Rome, after war, 802 *sqq.*; treaties with, first, 402, 405, 436, 465, 491, 649, 774, *see* chron. note, 859 *sqq.*; later treaties, 580, 586, 607, 649, 672, 776, 781 *sqq.*, and Spain, Ch. XXIV; Etruscan allies, 769; and Massilia, 774; first empire in Spain, 774, lost, 781; conquest of Tartessus, 773 *sqq.*; voyage of Pytheas of Massilia, 50 *n.*, 53, 262, 780 *sq.*; defeat of, at Himera, 480; reconquest of Spain, 781; Roman embassy to Hamilcar, 787, to Hasdrubal, 788; Ebro treaty, 788; empire in Spain, 220 B.C., 791 *sq.*

Carthalo, Carthaginian general, 685, 688 *sq.*

Carvilius, Sp. (cos. 293), 547, 613

— (cos. 234), in Sardinia, 805

Casa Faustuli, 356, 564

Casiana, 185

Casinum, 339

Cassander, and Argos, 76; treaty with Athens, 78; and Atintania, 219; and Corcyra, 76; deified, 198; and Euhemerus, 265; and Four Years War, 81; and Greece, 78; after Ipsus, 75–78; and King's Land in Chalcidice, 199; policy of, 205

Cassandreia, 85, 90 *sq.*, 97 *sqq.*, 107, 198, 200, 202, 220; revolution in, 101 *sq.*, 740

Cassianum foedus, 405, 487–493, 504, 549, 564, 578, 862

Cassiodorus, Chronicle of, 325

Cassiterides, 50

Cassius, Dio Cocceianus, historian, History of Rome, 314; on Pyrrhus, 638 *n.*; on First Punic War, 665 *n.*

— L., Hemina, annalist, 317, 327, 554, 860

— Sp., Vecellinus (cos. 486), 312, 395, 461, 478, 480; and agrarian campaign, 471 *sq.*; *see Cassianum foedus*

castes, in Egypt, India, Judaea, 34

Castor of Rhodes, Chronicle of, 318

Castores, temple of, 456

Castrum Novum, maritime colony at, 638, 657, 838

Catana, Pyrrhus and, 651; Rome and, 675

Cato, the elder, 318, 320, 326

Catullus, Callimachus and, 276

Catulus, *see* Lutatius

Caudium, battle and peace of, 599

Caulonia, Dionysius I and, 640

Caunus, in Caria, 78, 92, 95, 130, 701

Celaenae (Apamea Cibotos), 105, 158

Celsus, 285 *sq.*

Celtiberi, 559, 782 *sq.*

Celtic-Iberian culture, 60, 782 *sq.*

Celto-Greeks in Asia Minor, 559

Celto-Ligurians in maritime Alps, 559

Celto-Scythians, 559

Celts, coming of the, Ch. II *passim*; La Tène period, 42–48 and Ch. II *passim*; chronology of, 42; area of culture, 43 *sqq.*; art of, 47 *sq.*; *see also unde* Gauls

— Alexander and, 64 *sq.*; in Asia Minor, 46, 64 *sq.*; in Bavaria, 46, 65; in Castile, 59; in Dacia, 65; Delphi attacked, 46, 65; in Cisalpine Gaul, 45, 70; in Greece, 64, 70; in Italy, 45, 60; in Macedonia, 65; in Thrace, 65; in Transylvania, 65

— agriculture, 45; architecture, 68, 73; art, Greek influence on, 44, 47 *sq.*

— Celtic populations, character of, 57; coinage, 46 *sq.*; currency, adoption of, 46; early home of, 54 *sqq.*; funeral rites, 42 *sqq.*, 55; Galatae and Celts, 56; government, 72; language, 57 *sq.*; life and character of, 71 *sqq.*; material culture, 43 *sqq.*; mountain-names, 53 *sqq.*; physique, 57; religion, 72; river-names, 54 *sq.*; trade-routes, 52 *sqq.*; early traders, Greek world and, 49 *sqq.*; warfare, 73; weapons, 43 *sqq.*, 73; zone-beaker people, 54 *sq.*

— Goidelic, 407

— migrations, 59–71; causes of, 66–71; pass finds, 61; S.W. France and Spain, 59 *sq.*; Italy, 60–64; Alpine passes, 60–64; south-eastward, 64 *sq.*

Celtic sites: Auriol, 46; Berru, 43; Boden-
bach, 70; Boii, 44 sq.; Borsód, 65;
Braubach, 44; Carniola, 46; Eifel, south-
ern, 69; Eygenbilsen, 68; Glastonbury,
44; Hagenau, 43; Haulzy, 60, 67; Huns-
rück, 69; Lisnacroghera, 48; Massilia
(Ligurian), 49; Montefortino, 45; La
Gorge-Meillet, 43; Montfercaut, 46;
Munkacz, 65; 'Nyrax,' 49; Plouhinec,
44; Rastatt, 43; St Pol-de-Léon, 44;
Silivaş, 65; Somme Bionne, 43; Stutt-
gart, 43; Túrócz, 65; Ulm, 43; Waldal-
gesheim, 45; Wallis, 62; see map 1
Cempsi, 771
Cempsicum, C. (Espichel), 771
Cenchreae, 848
Cenomani, 556, 559, 811 sq.
Censorinus, 311
Censors, 424, 443, 521 sqq.; functions of,
522 sqq.; and imperium, 442
Census, 433 sqq., 521, 811
Centuripa, 675, 794
Ceos, 745, 748, 763
Cephallenia, 748, 766
Cephaloedium, 633
Cercidas of Megalopolis, 274, 755 sq., 761
sq.
Ceres, Liber and Libera, temple of, 466
Ceretes, 772
Cerethrius, in Thrace, 101, 106 sq.
Cerfennia, 607
'Cermalus' (Palatine), 354, 357
'Cerro de los Santos,' statues of, 773
Cessetani, 782
Chaeremon, 230
Chaeronea, Aetolian victory at, 732
Chalcedon, 98, 100
Chalcidice, King's Land in, 199 sq.
Chalcis, 81, 85, 212, 216, 221, 715
Chaldaea, 5
Chamaeleon, 26
Chandragupta, 154, 173, 196
Chaones, League with Molossi and Thes-
protes, 83
Chares of Mitylene, 259
Charilaus, magistrate at Neapolis, 595
Charisius, 256
Chasles, Michael, and Euclid, 301; and
Archimedes, 305
Chersonese, under the Ptolemies, 126, 719
Chilonis, 742 sqq.
China (under Han dynasty), trade with
Egypt, 134; art, 174; influence of
Hellenistic art and civilization on, 174,
196
Chios, 719, 748, 767; Aetolia and, 733, 763
Choerilus, 270
chrematistai, Egyptian, 119
Chremonidean War, 206, 705 sqq.; Greece
after, 218 sqq.
Chremonides, 29, 220, 706 sq., 713

Christianity, and Hellenism, 2; deification
and, 22; Epicurus and, 233; Stoics and
pre-Christian thought, 236
Chronology, of La Tène period, 42; early
Roman, 321 sq., 371 sq.; of foedus
Cassianum, 491; of war with Fidenae,
401, 508; of Veientane Wars, 506 sq., 511
sqq.; of Gallic sack of Rome, 561 n.; of
Gallic incursions, 570, 572; of Illyrian
Wars, 834 n.; see also chron. notes
Chryseis, wife of Demetrius II, 751
Chrysippus, 238 sq.
Cibyra, in Pisidia, 184
Cicero, on aediles, 551; and sphere of Archimedes, 303; on Roman citizenship, 447;
on Epicurus, 244 sq.; on Decemvirs, 464;
on early historical writing, 319 sqq.; on
early Rome, 330, Ch. XIII passim; on
imperium, 408; on officia, 242; on powers
of magistrates, 442; on Rome and Sicily,
793 n.; on tribunes, 453 sqq.; on Tus-
culum and consular families, 548; on
Twelve Tables, 312
Cieros, 77
Cilbiceni, 771 sq., 778
Cilicia, Demetrius and Seleucus and, 78, 88,
93; policy of Antiochus Epiphanes in,
189; in Second Syrian War, 712
Cilnii of Arretium, 609
Cincinnatus, L., Quinctius, dictator, 326,
501 sq.
Cincius, L., lexicographer and jurist, 329,
405, 419
— L., Alimentus, annalist, 316, 326
Cineas, minister of Pyrrhus, 83; as envoy
to Rome, 642, 645, 648, 650
Circeii, 405 sq., 509 sq., 590, 862
Cisauna, 610
Cissa, 782
Citizenship, Roman: see also Isopolity,
Sympolity, 415 sq., 569; plebs and, 419;
granted to: Acerrae, 593; plebs of Alba,
418; Anagnia, 606; Aricia, 591; Arpinum, 608; Caere, 659; Campanians,
588; Capua, 592; gens Claudia, 416;
Cumae, 592; Etruria, part of, 639;
Formiae, 592; Fundi, 592; Lanuvium,
591; Latium, 659; Nomentum, 591;
Pedum, 591; Privernum, 594; Praetuttians, 659; Sabines, 494, 616, 658; slaves,
531 sq.; Suessula, 592; Trebula, 608; see
map 13
City-states, 2, 4, 8, 22 sqq., 31 sq., 230, 254;
Alexander's conquests and, 225; Aristotle on, 33; Athens, Rhodes, Sparta, 10,
23; cosmopolitanism and, 16; Cynics on,
33 sqq.; dependent polis and its protector,
24 sqq.; disintegration of, 33, and its
effect on Greeks, 110; frontiers of, 25, 27;
homogeneity of, gone, 25; individualism
and, 33 sqq.; leagues and, 23 sq.; Stoics

and, 37 *sqq.*; substitutes for, 33 *sqq.*;
decay of urban nationalism, 22 *sq.*;
weakness of, 22 *sqq.*
— new foundations, **24** *sqq.*, Chs. III–V;
administration of, **29**; as centres of
culture, 29 *sq.*
Cius, 98
Clastidium, battle of, 813
Claudia, gens, 417 *sqq.*, 470, 494 *sq.*
Claudian plebiscite, 808
Claudii, the, 641
— Marcelli, 418
Claudius, Emperor, 389 *sqq.*; and Mastarna,
520
— Appius (Decemvir), 459 *sqq.*, 494; *see*
Attus Clausus
— — (dictator, 362), 526, 576
— — Caecus (cos. 307), 611; censorship
of, 531, 818; speech on peace with
Pyrrhus, 647
— — Caudex (cos. 264), 672 *sqq.*
— — Pulcher (cos. 54), 412
— C. (mil. trib. 264), 672
— M., Marcellus (cos. 222), 529; at
Clastidium, 814, 820 *sq.*
— P., Pulcher (cos. 249), defeated at
Drepana, 687
— Q., Quadrigarius, historian, 317, 526, 554
Clazomenae, 719
Cleanthes, 238, 242, 268, 302
Clearchus of Soli, 261
Cleinias, tyrant of Sicyon, 222
Cleitarchus of Colophon, 258, 264
Clement of Alexandria, 143
Cleombrotus, 743
Cleomenes III of Sparta, 259, 726, 728;
invades Achaea, 756; and Achaean
League, 756 *sq.*; and Antigonus Doson,
758 *sqq.*; and Aratus, 755 *sqq.*; and
Argos, 757, 761, 863; death of, 762;
and Ptolemy IV, 752, 756 *sqq.*, 762;
Ptolemy III and, 756; revolution of,
753 *sqq.*
Cleonae, battle of, 745
Cleonymus the Spartan, 77, 214, 607, 609,
634, 824
Cleopatra, and the Pergamene Library, 253
clientes, 420 *sqq.*, 470
Cloaca Maxima, 354, 359, 386, 390
Clodius, 412; *see also* Claudius
— P., annalist, 554
Cloelius, Q., Siculus, 542
Cluilius, C., Alban king, 377, 401
Clusium, 397; Gauls at, 554, 561 *sq.*, 812
Clustumina tribus, 435 *n.*, 452
Cnidus, 98, 105, 704
Cnossos, 765
Coele-Syria, under the Ptolemies, 126;
coast towns of, under the Seleucids, 159
sq., 173; satrapies of, 129 *sq.*, 166 *n.*; in
Syrian Wars, 700, 702

coemptio, 423 *sq.*
Coinage, of Achaean League, 736; of
Agathocles, 621, 634; of Alexander, 90,
141; of Amphipolis, 85, 198; Antigonid tetradrachms, 714, 752 *n.*; of Antigonus Gonatas, 107, 200 *sq.*, 714, 719;
of Antioch, 165; of Areus of Sparta, 99
sq.; of Arsinoe, 97; of Athens, 141, 220;
of Bactria, 719; Black Sea cities, 90;
Britain, 47; of Bruttian League, 655;
of Callatis, 91; Campanian, 662; Celtic
copies of Greek, 46 *sq.* (Regenbogenschüsselchen); of Cleomenes III, 754; of
Cumae, 584 *n.*; of Cyrenaic League, 713;
of Delphi, 213; of Demetrius, 80, 85, 92;
of Diodotus, 719; of Emporiae, 46; of
Ephesus, 91; Etruscan, 662; of S. France,
pre-Celtic, 46; of Locri, 654; of Lysimachus, 90 *sq.*; of Macedonia, 213; of
Massilia, 46 *sq.*; of Miletus, 92; of Pella,
85; Persian, 141; of Philetaerus, 709; of
Philip II, 46 *sq.*; of Philip V, 751; of
the Ptolemies, 99, 141 *sq.*, 176, 713; of
Ptolemy II, and Arsinoe, 753; of Rhode,
46; Roman, early, 47, 324, 433, 489,
607 *sq.*, 649, 662 *sqq.*; Romano-Campanian, 367, 608 and *n.*; of Seleuceia
in Pieria, 188; of Seleuceia on Tigris, 165;
of Seleucids, 164 *sq.*, 176; of Seleucus II,
719; of Seleucus, son of Antiochus I, 710;
of Sicilian cities, 799; of Sinope, 90;
of Tyre, 165
Colaeus of Samos, at Tartessus, 51
Collatia, 404
collegium, 34 *sqq.*
Collina tribus, 434
Colonies, colonization: Carthaginian, 665;
Hellenic, 3, 179 *sq.*, 188; *see* maps 3
and 4; of Latin League, 659; Massiliote,
Emporiae and Rhode, 810; Phoenician,
191; early Roman, 473 *sq.*
— Roman, 473 *sq.*, 540 *sqq.*; methods and
object of, 659; status of, 541; *coloniae
civium Romanorum,* 541; colonies established at: Alba Fucens, 608, Alsium,
690, Antium, 474, 541, 552, 592, Anxur, 416, Ardea, 591, Ariminum, 438,
440, 657, Brundisium, 656, 690, Cales,
541, Carsioli, 608, Castrum Novum, 638,
657, Circeii, 406, 510, 591, Cosa, 660,
Firmum, 657, Fregellae, 594, Fregenae,
690, Hadria, 542, 638, Interamna, 603,
Luceria, 601, 641, Malventum (Beneventum), 654, Minturnae, 613, Nepete,
517, 575, 591, Nequinum (Narnia), 609,
Norba, 498, 591, Ostia, 378, 541, Paestum, 653, Pontia, 603, Saticula, 603,
Satricum, 576, 578, 592, 602, Sena Gallica, 542, Setia, 541, 591, Signia, 498,
591, Sinuessa, 613, Sora, 608, Spoletium,
800, Suessa, 602, Sutrium, 517, 575, 591,

Tarracina, 594, Tauromenium, 315, Urso, 430 n., Velitrae, 474, 576 sq., 592, Venusia, 639; see map 12

Colophon, 91, 719

Comedy, the New, 224–230, 250; influence of politics on, 224 sq.; Aristophanes and, 228; Euripides and, 228

Cominium, 613 sq.

Comitia, 410; contio and, 410; concilia and, 451
— calata, 412
— centuriata, 413, 432 sqq., 482 sq.; reform of, 801
— curiata, 410 sq., 412 sq., 433; plebs and, 423
— tributa, 453, 455 sq., 483

commercium, 422, 549, 591

Commontorius, founds kingdom of Tylis, 107

Companions, Macedonian, ἑταῖροι, 9, 11, 171, 201

Concilium plebis tributum, 455

Concolitanus, 813

confarreatio, 422

Conon of Samos, and Coma Berenices, 302 sqq., 717

Consentia, restored by Alexander of Epirus, 640

Consualia, the, 368 sq.

Consuls, 320 sq., 331, 396, 412, 437 sq., 443, 481, 484, 520, 818; and Senate, 449, 818; restored after Decemvirate, 460; and censors, 523; and plebs, 525 sqq., 583; imperium of, 459; earliest plebeian, 664

Contenebra, 574

Contestani, 782

conubium, 419, 422, 460, 483, 519, 525, 549, 591

Copernicus, 292

Cora, 341, 488, 518, 577, 591

Corcyra, Cassander and, 76, 634; Pyrrhus and, 83 sq., 95, 634, 826; Demetrius and, 84, 634; Agathocles and, 634; Cleonymus and, 634; and Illyria, 831, 833

Corcyra Nigra (Curzola), 825

Corduba, statues of, 773

Corinth, and Achaean League, 746; Antigonus Doson and, 757; Antigonus Gonatas and, 205 sq., 214, 216, 223, 707, 710, 715, 733; Cleomenes and, 758; commercial position of, 212; Demetrius Poliorcetes and, 76, 81, 84 sqq., 96; in Laodicean War, 715 sq.; Roman embassy to, 841 sq.; in Second Syrian War, 710 sq.

Coriolanus, see Marcius

Corne, Mte, 348

Cornelia, gens, 417

Cornelii Scipiones, 417

Cornelius, A., Cossus (cos. 428), 438,

575 sq., 578; and spolia opima, 316, 507 sqq.
— Cn., Asina (cos. 260), 679; at Panormus, 685
— Cn., Blasio (cos. 270), at Rhegium, 656; in Sicily, 680
— Cn., Scipio (cos. 222), at Clastidium, 814
— L., Lentulus (cos. 275), 653
— L., Scipio Barbatus (cos. 298), 438, 610 sq.
— P., Dolabella (cos. 283), defeats Boii, 639
— P., Lentulus (cos. 236), 806
— P., Rufinus (cos. 277), 654
— P., Scipio (cos. 259), 679; see also under Fronto

Cornwall, 50

Corragus, 178, 180

Corsica, 804; Corsi, 805; Etruscans and, 770; in First Punic War, 679; Roman protectorate, 804 sq.

Cortona, Roman treaty with, 605

Cortuosa, 574

Coruncanius, C., envoy to Illyria, 831
— L., envoy to Illyria, 831 sq.
— T. (cos. 280), jurist, 328, 548, 646

Corvus, the, 678, 682

Cos, battle of, 159, 712; its effect in Asia Minor, 159; Theocritus at, 278; see also chron. note 2, 862 sqq.

Cosa, 657, 660

Cosmopolitanism, in religion, 5; monarchy and, 11, 33 sqq.; and the New Comedy and philosophy, 224 sq.; Stoics and Epicureans and, 225

Crassus, see under Licinius

Craterus, general of Alexander, 12
— officer of Antigonus Gonatas, 95, 206 sq., 216, 707
— historian, 65 n., 203, 206, 216

Crates, philosopher, 203, 238; Demetrius and, 87
— of Mallus, Stoic grammarian, 251
— of Thebes, 274

Cratippus, 256

cremation, 55, 60, 69, 70; in La Tène period, 43 sqq.; in Latium, 334, 336 sq., 340, 354 sqq., 367, 496 sq.

Cremera, battle of, 420 n., 504 sqq.

Cremona, colony of, 814

Crete, Cretans, 126, 211, 214; and Egyptian army, 117; politeumata of, in Egypt, 122; in Social War, 765, 768

Crimisus, battle of, 617

Croton, Crotonians, Dionysius I and, 64, 640; Agathocles and, 619, 635, 641; Syracuse and, 634 sq.; under Roman control, 650; Pyrrhus and, 654; taken by Pyrrhus, 652; in Roman federation, 654; socii navales, 656

Crustumerium, 340, 403, 435 *n.*, 452, 488, 511; Clustumina tribus, 452

Ctesibius, 297, 307

Ctesiphon, 724

Cumae, 476; first settlers in, 347; Chalcidic colonists of, 380; culture of, 584; Sabellians and, 584; coinage, 584 *n.*; citizenship granted to, 592 *sq.*; parties at, 594 *sq.*; see also Cyme

Cures, Numa and, 376

Curia Hostilia, 377

— of the Salii, 564

Curiae, origin of, 410 *sqq.*

Curio maximus, earliest plebeian, 423

Curius, M'., Dentatus (cos. 290), 547 *sq.*, 615 *sq.*, 641, 653, 809; and Senones, 638

Cyclades, 76, 221, 704, 745

Cyme, in Aeolis, 726

— in Italy, battle of, 779

Cynaetha, 757, 764

Cynetes, 49, 771 *sq.*

Cynics, ideal wise man of, 16, 33; Epicurus and, 37 *sq.*; ideal king of, 202

Cyprus, 78, 133, 716; Demetrius and, 76; under the Ptolemies, 78, 126 *sq.*, 136, 167

Cypsela on the Hebrus, 719

Cyrene and Cyrenaica, 222; under Ptolemies, 126 *sq.*, 712 *sq.*; League, 127, 713; Ophellas, viceroy of, 626

Cyrrhestice, revolt in, 725

Cyzicus, 100; Gauls and, 105

Dacia, Celts in, 65

Daïmachus, 173

Dalmatians, 825

Damas, 619

Damascus, 175, 184, 702, 718

Damastes, 780

Damophilus, Greek artist at Rome, 467

Danube, 49, 82; upper and middle region of, Celts in, 54, 64 *sq.*

Daphne, review at, 171, 181

Dardanelles, 98, 100; Demetrius and, 77; Gauls and, 104 *sq.*, 726

Dardanians, 101, 747 *sq.*, 751, 827 *sq.*, 833

Darius I of Persia, 134, 166

— III of Persia, 15

Darron, god of healing, 197

Dassaretae, 836

Daunians, 585

'Dea Dia,' precinct of, 399

Debt, at Rome, 469, 475, 524 *sq.*, 553; law of, 476–480; money at interest, 529, 542 *sqq.*; legislation, 543 *sqq.*; *mutuum*, 543; see also *nexum*

Decapolis, the (in Transjordania), 192

Decemvirs, 437 *sq.*, 440, 447, 457 *sqq.*, 480 *sq.*; abdication of, 460; code of Ten Tables, 460; legislation of, 546; and *provocatio*, 447, 459

— *stlitibus iudicandis*, 481

Decius, P., Mus (cos. 340), 590

— — (cos. 312), 417, 547, 611 *sq.*

— — (cos. 279), 647

decuriae, 424, 431

Deidameia, daughter of Pyrrhus II, 747

— wife of Demetrius, 76 *sq.*

Deification, 13–22; of Alexander, 14, 91; of Antigonus I, 15, 91; of Antigonus Gonatas, 107, 221; of Antiochus I, 16, 106; of Attalids, 20; of Cassander, 13, 198; of Demetrius, 22; of Dion, 13; of Dionysius I, 13; of Lanassa, 84; of Lysander, 13; of Lysimachus, 91, 93, 198; of Pharaoh, 14 *sq.*, 17 *sq.*; of Philip II, 13 *sq.*; of Philip V, 198; of Philocles, 92; of Plato, 13; of Ptolemy I and Berenice, 16 *sq.*, 19, 92; of Ptolemy II, 101, and Arsinoe, 17, 705; of Ptolemy III, 749

— and absolutism, 16; Alexander, official imperial cult of, 14, 17, 115; Aristotle on, 13; change in form of, 22; city and provincial cults, 19 *sq.*; complex character of, 20 *sqq.*; in Egypt, 14, 17 *sq.*; Greek background of, 13, 15; Hellenistic king-worship, 17, unknown in Rome, 372; in Macedonia, 202; Pergamum and, 20; posthumous (heroization), 14, 16 *sq.*; Ptolemies, imperial cult of, 17 *sqq.*; rulers, urban cult of, 15 *sq.*; Seleucids, imperial cult of, 19 *sq.*; Successors to Alexander and, 15

— Cult-names: Amon, 14, 18 *sq.*; Apollo Soter, 16; Benefactor (Euergetes), 93; Brother-Sister Gods, 17; Chalkioikos (Arsinoe II), 706; Deliverer, 92; Horus, 18 *sq.*; Osiris, 18 *sq.*; Queen and Sister, 162 *sq.*; Saviour (Soter), 92; Theoi Soteres, Theos, 20; Theos Adelphos, 19; Theos Euergetes, 19, 21; Theos Philopator, 19; Zeus Nicator, 16

Deinocrates, 631 *sqq.*

Deldo, Bastarnian chief, 508

Delos, 28, 745, 763; commercial position of, 212; cult of Osiris at, 146 *n.*; *paroikoi* at, 24; Phoenician and Syrian traders at, 175; Ptolemy I and, 92; Seleucids and, 159; Stratonice and, 93; vase festival at, 101

Delphi, 89, 191, 206, 217, 316; Aetolians and, 83, 209; statue of Aetolia at, 104; offering of Camillus at, 513; attacked by Celts, 65, 103; coinage, 213

Demades, on Athens, 224

Demaratus, tyrant of Aeolis, 184

Demeter, and Kore, festival of, 96; temple of, at Argos, 215; cult-name of Lanassa, 84

Demetrias, 81, 89, 96, 100, 205, 211, 216, 750, 759; built by Demetrius, 80 *sq.*

Demetrius I, Poliorcetes, 76–96, 194, 205, 207, 223; army of, 84 *sq.*; in Asia, 87 *sq.*;

and Athens, 21 *sq.*, 76, 78 *sqq.*, 84; coinage, 80, 85, 92; at Corcyra, 84; at Corinth, 76; defeated by Seleucus, 88; deified, 21, 81; and Euboean League, 81; and Greece, 80 *sqq.*; and Ionia, 87 *sq.*; and Lysimachus, 77; king of Macedonia, 79 *sq.*; and Pyrrhus, 77, 82 *sqq.*; attacks Sparta, 79; and Thebes, 82; and Thessaly, 80; power and fall of, 84 *sqq.*
— II, 708, 733; war with Greek Leagues, 744 *sqq.*; in the Aegean, 745; and Argos, 745; and Peloponnese, 746 *sq.*; and Illyria, 828; and Dardanians, 833
— the Fair, son of Demetrius I, 217, 712 *sq.*
— of Phalerum, 21, 29, 31; and PtolemyI, 114; and Museum at Alexandria, 251; oratory of, 255 *sq.*
— of Pharos, 760, 765; and Corcyra, 834; rebels against Rome, 844 *sqq.*; and Macedonia, 848; and Philip V, 851 *sq.*
— of Scepsis, 251
Demochares, and Demetrius, 78, 81, 86, 89; decree for Demosthenes, 100, 206; decree in honour of, 217; character of, 86
Democritus, 232, 243 *n.*, 293
Demodamas of Miletus, 174
Demophanes, 222, 713
Demosthenes, 100, 206, 224
Diana, cult of, at Aricia, 344, 348, 374, 405, 429; temple of, on the Aventine, 350 *sq.*, 392, 466
Diaspora, Graeco-Macedonian, 3, 12, 27, 145
Dicaearchus the Peripatetic, 90, 238, 261, 264, 780 *sq.*
Dictator, 418, 437–445; and *provocatio*, 448
Didyma, temple statue of, 77; the oracle at, 162 *n.*
diffarreatio, 422
Dimale (Dimallum), 836, 847
Dinostratus, 293
Dio Chrysostom, 143
Diocles, mathematician, 309
Diodorus Siculus, 204, 259, 265, 322, 326 *n.*, 395, 459 *sq.*, 485 *n.*, 511; authority of, 314 *sqq.*; on Agathocles, 617 *n.*; on Celts, 73; on Gallic wars, 554; on Pyrrhus, 638 *n.*; on First Punic War, 665 *n.*, 689; on early Roman history, 318; on fifth-century Rome, 485 *n.*; on first treaty with Carthage, chron. note, 859 *sqq.*
Diodotus, Diodotids, 26, 159; coinage, 719
Diogeneia, festival, 749
Diogenes, Macedonian commander of the Piraeus, 748 *sq.*
— of Oenoanda, 225 *n.*, 232 and *n.*, 244
— governor of Susiana, 724 *sq.*
Diognetus, Alexander's officer, 259
— admiral of Antiochus III, 729

dioiketes, Egyptian, 120, 124, 127, 129, 130, 146
Dion, in Palestine, 192
— of Syracuse, deified, 13
Dionysiac rites, in Egypt and Jerusalem, 5; artists, 212; Great Dionysia, the, 30
Dionysius of Halicarnassus, 313 *sq.*, 458 *n.*; Alexandrian prose writers, 255 *sq.*; on *comitia* and *concilium plebis*, 483; on *curiae*, 411; on *foedus Cassianum*, 490; on Gallic wars, 554; on isopolity, 550; on Rome in fifth century, 485 *n.*; on Roman colonies, 474; on early Roman history, 313 *sq.*, 370 *n.*, 373 *n.*, 458 *n.*, 485 *n.*
— I of Syracuse, 476, 621; Celtic and Iberian mercenaries, 64, 571; cities founded by, 825; deified, 13; power in Adriatic, 825; Rhegium sacked by, 321 *sq.*; *see* vol. VI
— II, the Younger, 825; and Gallic mercenaries, 571
— *epistolographos* of Antiochus IV, 181
— of Heraclea, philosopher, 94
— the Thracian, and the first Greek Grammar, 254
Dionysus Zagreus, Eleusino-Orphic, mysteries of, 145 *sq.*
Dioscuri, at Lake Regillus, 489
Diphilus, Plautus and, 226 and *n.*
Dium, 765
Dodona, 83, 213, 766
Dolopes, the, 218
Domitius, Cn., Calvinus (cos. 283), 533
— Cn., Calvinus (cos. 53, 40), 313
Donatus, 450
Dora (Tantura), 190, 192, 728
Dorimachus, 763 *sq.*, 766
Doris, 218
Dositheus, 302
Doura on the Tigris, 724 *sq.*
Doura-Europus, 167 *sq.*, 186 *sq.*, 194, 724
Drama, Roman, Sicilian influence on, 697
Drepana, battle of, 686 *sqq.*; Rome and, 793
Drilo (Drin), river, 827
Drinus, river, 836
Dromichaetes, Lysimachus and, 82, 91
Dropion, 219
Druids, 58 *sq.*, 71
Drynemetos, sanctuary of Gauls, 106
Duillii, 696
Duillius, 697 *sq.*
— C., at Mylae, 679
— Kaeso, 552
— M. (trib. plebis 470), 325, 481
Duoviri aedi dedicandae, 552
— *navales*, 552, 603
— *perduellionis*, 331
Duris, historian, 75 *n.*, 238, 258 *sqq.*; tyrant of Samos, 98, 282; on Agathocles, 617 *n.*
Duronia, 613

Dyme, 766; revolt of, 99
Dyrrachium (Epidamnus) in Illyrian War, 826, 834

Ebro, the treaty of, 788 and *n.*, 810, 843
Ebusus (Ibiza), 773
Ecbatana, 189
Ecdemus, 222, 713
Ecetra, 498
Echedorides, Macedonian nymphs, 198
Echetla, 674
Ecnomus, Mt, 623
Edeco, 782
Edessa, 174, 188 *sq.*, 197 *sq.*
Edetani, 782
Edfu, 146
Egeria, cult of, 351, 374
Egypt, under Alexander, 110; Asia and, 108; castes in, 34; local cults in, 6; deification in, 17 *sqq.*; Demetrius and, 77; Dionysiac rites in, 5; Greek cities in, 118, 120 *sq.*; Greek mercenaries and traders in, 110; Greek population and, 110, 144; guilds, 34, 150; Hellenization of, 2, 115, 144, 149 *sqq.*, 152; Jews in, 111 *sq.*, 120; Lysimachus and, 96 *sq.*; monarchy in, 36; natives and immigrants, 110, 144 *sq.*; new Hellenistic kingdoms and, 101; Peripatetics in, 249
— against Syria and Macedonia, Ch. XXII; danger of a strong Macedonia, 699; issues between, and Syria, 700 *sq.*; policy of Ptolemies, 700; after First Syrian War, 704 *sq.*; Chremonidean War, 705; and Athenian Nationalists, 706; alliance with Sparta, 706; war of Eumenes, 709 *sq.*; Second Syrian War, 710 *sqq.*; battle of Cos, 713; Third Syrian War (Laodicean), 715 *sqq.*; battle of Andros, 718; sea-power lost, 718 *sq.*; War of the Brothers, 720 *sqq.*; Fourth Syrian War, 726; ceases to be a great military power, 727; native Egyptians with Ptolemy IV, 738
— Ptolemaic, Ch. IV; administration of, 116; agriculture, 131 *sq.*; army, 110, 113, 117; art, 147, 154; civil service, 119; coinage, 141 *sq.*; corvée, the, 140 *sq.*; 'country', administration of: nomes, toparchies, *komai*, 123 *sq.*, population of, 112; 'courts,' 116; culture, 149 *sq.*; economic conditions, 111, 130 *sq.*; finance, 28, 120 *sq.*; fleet, 110, 118; foreign policy, 136; Greeks and Egyptians, 144, 152 *sq.*; guilds, 150; Hellenism, 115, 144, 149, 152; immigrants, 111 *sq.*, 114; insurrections and their results, 151 *sq.*; justice, administration of, 120; *katoikoi*, 118 *sq.*; kings, cult of, 17, 113 *sq.*; *kleroi*, 117 *sq.*; land, 138; liturgies, 141; mercenaries in war and peace, 110, 117; monopolies, 129,

140; *politeumata* and *polis*, 122; population, native, 125, 153, non-Egyptian, 122; priesthoods, 149; provinces, administration of, 126 *sqq.*; religion, 112, 115, 145 *sq.*; slavery, 135; social life, 142 *sqq.*; *stathmoi*, 117; taxation of Egypt, 136 *sqq.*, of provinces, 129; trade and industry, 133 *sqq.*, 139; transport, 124, 140 *sq.*
ekades, 186
eklogistes, Egyptian, 121
Elaea, 709
Elam, temple of Bel at, 163
Elatea, 89
Elaus, 758
Elba, 381
Elche (Helice, Ilici), 787; 'Lady of Elche,' 785
Eleusis, 79, 89, 221; Eleusino-Orphic mysteries, 145
Eleutherna in Crete, 752
Eleutherus, river, 700 *n.*
Elis, Sparta and, 84; Antigonus I and, 99; Pyrrhus and, 214; Antigonus II and, 216; Aetolia and, 733, 744; and Illyrian pirates, 826; Philip V and, 852
Elymais, Greek settlers in, 170
Emathia, 197
Emesa, 184
Emporiae, coinage, 46; Hasdrubal and, 810
Enna, 651, 680
Ennius, 265, 318, 320, 369, 373; on Pyrrhus, 644, 647
Eperatus, Achaean general, 766
Epetium, 325
Ephesus, Antiochus I and, 712 *sq.*; temple of Artemis at, 91; coinage, 91; council of elders at, 91; Demetrius and, 76, 87; Gauls and, 105; Lysimachus and, 78, 91; Ptolemies and, 126; Seleucizers in, 93; in First Syrian War, 710
Ephorus of Cyme, 51, 257 *sq.*, 318, 554
Epictetus, 230, 236
Epicurus, 231–234, 243–248; cosmogony of, 37 *sqq.*; and individualism, 37; ideal life, 38; and cosmopolitanism, 225; swerve, doctrine of the, 244
Epidamnus (Dyrrachium), 826
Epidaurus, 734, 758
Epigenes, officer of Seleucus III, 723
epigonoi, epigone, Egyptian, 117
Epirus: and Acarnania, 217; and Alexander's Successors, 80 *sqq.*; civil war in, 747; decline of, 826, 828; Demetrius and, 84; end of Aeacid dynasty, 838; Epirote Alliance, 83; and Illyria, 219, alliance with, 748, invaded by, 830; literature of, 83; Lysimachus and, 213; in Social War, 764
epistatai, Macedonian, 200 *sq.*
epistolographos, Egyptian, 119

equites, 522; *equo privato*, 512, 522; *equitum centuriae*, 409, 431 *sqq.*, 433, 435
Era, of Parthia, 159, 720
— Seleucid, 20, 75, 161
eranoi, 212
Erasistratus, physiologist, 284 *sqq.*, 297
Eratosthenes of Cyrene, 174, 204, 224, 253, 255, 260 *sq.*, 262 *sqq.*, 299, 306 *sq.*, 321, 726 *sq.*, 781
Eretria, 94; Antigonus Gonatas and, 107 *sq.*, 216 *sq.*; Alexander, son of Craterus, and, 221
Eretum, 340
Erginus, 734 *sq.*
Erymnon, Aetolian officer in Syracuse, 631
Erythrae, the Gauls and, 105; Seleucids and, 178 *sq.*; in Laodicean War, 719
Eryx, Mt, Pyrrhus and, 651
E-sagila, temple, 188
Eshmunazar, dynasty of, 192
Esquilina tribus, 434
Etitovius, 556
Etruria, Etruscans, 402 *sq.*; origins, 378 *sqq.*; commerce, 381; culture, 379 *sqq.*; decadence of, 558; epigraphy, 382; *Etrusca disciplina*, 429; language, 379 *n.*; religion, 383 *sqq.*, 387; serfdom in, 658
— — Agathocles and, 630, 635; Campania and, 395 *sq.*; Carthage and, 347, 769, 779; Gauls and, 555 *sq.*; and N. Italy, 556, 558; Latium and, 396, 398; league, 439, 515, 562; Phoenicians and, 381; Rome, war with, 604 *sqq.*; southern, Roman conquest of, 511 *sqq.*; re-conquest after Gallic Wars, 574; settlers in Rome, 398; supremacy in Rome, 338; Roman supremacy in, 402 *sq.*; and Roman federation, 662, 805; influence on Rome, 337, 378 *sqq.*, 382 *sqq.*, 388 *sqq.*, 398; weakness of, 515 *sqq.*, 558
Euboea, league, 81; Demetrius and, 84, 95; Antigonus II and, 100, 205, 216, 221
Eucleidas, brother of Cleomenes III, 755, 761 *sq.*
Euclid, 290, 294 *sqq.*, 298 *sqq.*; translations and editions of, 299, 304, 307 *sq.*
Euctemon, 780
Eudemus of Rhodes, history of mathematics, 238, 296
Eudoxus of Cnidus, 290, 294 *sqq.*, 296, 298, 300, 302, 304; and Plato, 295
Euhemerus, 16, 265
Euhesperides, renamed Berenice, 713
Eumachus, 629 *sq.*
Eumenes, Alexander's secretary, 172
Eumenes I of Pergamum, War of, 709 *sq.*; alliance with Ptolemy II, 709; Antiochus I defeated by, 710; in the Laodicean War, 719
— kinsman of above, revolt of, 712
— II, Rome and, 178

Euphantus of Olynthus, tutor of Antigonus Gonatas, 94
Euphorion of Chalcis, 221, 249 *sq.*, 271, 281
Euphrates, river, 158, 189
Euripides, 267; and the New Comedy, 228
Euryalus, 532
Eurycleidas of Cephissia, 748
Eurydice, wife of Ptolemy I, 77, 87, 96, 99; mercenaries of, 102; deified, 102
— daughter of Lysimachus, 79, 92
Eutocius, commentator on Apollonius, 307
Eutropius, historian, 315
Evander, 364 *sq.*
extispicium, Etruscan origin of, 384, 429
E-zida, temple, 188

Fabii, the, 417; at the Cremera, 420 *n.*, 504 *sqq.*; and consulship, 527
Fabius, C. (*mag. equit.* 315), 601
— C., Ambustus (? cos. 360), 575 *sq.*
— C., Pictor, artist, 316
— M., Ambustus (? interrex, 355), 525, 528
— M., Vibulanus (cos. 480), 504 *sq.*
— Q., Ambustus (cons. trib. 391), 552 *n.*
— Q., Gurges (cos. 292), 615
— Q., Maximus Cunctator, 820
— Q., Maximus Rullianus (cos. 310, 304, 297), 532, 535, 537, 547, 551, 598, 601, 605, 611 *sq.*, 861
— Q., Maximus Servilianus (cos. 142), 317
— Q., M. f. Vibulanus (cos. 467), 473 *sq.*
— Q., Pictor, historian, 316, 321, 860
Fabrateria (Vetus), 594
Fabricius, C., Luscinus (cos. 282), and Thurii, 641; and Pyrrhus, 647 *sq.*; triumph of, 650
Face-urn culture, peoples of, 69
falarica, Iberian, 784
Falerii, Falisci, 326 *n.*, 338, 401, 515, 575, 614; treaty with Rome, 512, 516 *sq.*, 561; alliance with Rome, 587, 604; sacked by Rome, 800
Falerna tribus, 600
fasces, Etruscan origin of, 384
Fasti, the, Consular, 313, 319, 323 *sqq.*, 328 *sq.*, 375, 391, 397, 421, 437, 440, 459, 520, 527, 529
— Triumphal, 313, 323, 326, 329, 547, 555, 581, 588, 592, 598, 609 *n.*, 611, 650, 657
Fasti of Ovid, 276
Faunus, 365
Faustulus, 356
Fayûm, the, 109, 132, 138, 144, 148, 150
Federation, Roman, 639, 646, 654, 658–664; territory of full citizenship, 659; without franchise, 659; *see also* League
Felsina, 556
Ferentinum, 510, 576, 606, 611

Festivals:
— Hellenistic: Antigoneia, 715, 862; Basileia, 107; of Demeter and Kore, 96; Diogeneia, 749; Dionysia, the Great, 30; Nemea, at Cleonae, 745; Nikephoria, 723; Paneia, 718; Philadelpheia, 705; Philetaireia, 709; Ptolemaiea, 101, 703, 715, 716; Soteria, 98, 104, 718, quadriennial, 733; Stratoniceia, 715, 862
— Roman: Ambarvalia, 399; Consualia, 368 sq.; Fordicidia, 411; Fornacalia, 411; Lupercalia, 365; Poplifugia, 395, 408; Regifugium, 394, 407 sq.; Robigalia, 399; Septimontium, 355, 357 sq., 362, 372, 418; Vinalia, 343
Festus, Rufius, historian, 315, 440, 442, 449
— Sex. Pompeius, lexicographer, 329 sq., 331
fetiales, 331, 377, 429
Ficana, 378, 402
Ficorini cista, 548
Ficulea, 340, 403
ficus ruminalis, 356, 366 sq.
Fidenae, 340, 382, 403, 435, 465, 504, 511, 514; revolt of, 507, 574; under Roman control, 509
Fides, temple of, at Rome, 698
Finance: Ptolemaic, 28, 120 sq.; of Lysimachus, 90; Roman, in Sicily, 793 sqq.; Seleucid, 173
Firmum, colony at, 657, 660, 838
flamen Dialis, 344, 409, 422, 426; Numa and, 374
flamines, 412, 426
Flamininus, see under Quinctius
Flaminius, C. (cos. 223), 813; and distribution of Ager Gallicus, 806 sq.
Flavius, Cn., curule aedile, 327, 463, 532, 533 sq.
Flora, temple of, at Rome, 698
Florus, 315, 452 n.
Food-supply, control of, in Rome in fifth century, 474 sqq.; plebs and, 536 sq.; aediles and, 551
Fordicidia, 411
Forentum, 600
Formiae, 440 and n.; citizenship granted to, 592
Fornacalia, 411
Fortuna Muliebris, temple of, 499
Forum Romanum, 353
— Ulpium, 353, 359
France, E. and N.E., Celts and, 43; Greek influence on, 48
Freedmen, 522; and Senate, 531, 533; at Volsinii, 658; at Rome, enrolled in city tribes, 806
Fregellae, 594, 598, 602
Fregenae, colony at, 690
Frentani, 585, 604, 609, 661
Fronto, M. Cornelius, jurist, 314
Frusino, 606

Fufetius, Mettius, 401
Fulvii, 547 sq., 696
Fulvius, Cn., in Samnium, 611 sq.
— Cn., Centumalus (cos. 229), in Illyria, 834 sq.
— L., Curvus (cos. 322), 547, 591
— M., Curvus (cos. 305), 606
— Q., Flaccus (cos. I, 237), 813
— Q., Nobilior (cos. 153), 375
— Ser., Nobilior (cos. 255), at Hermaean promontory, 684
Fundi, 440 and n.; citizenship granted to, 592
Furius, C., Pacilus (censor, 435), 521
— L., Camillus, 587 n., 590
— M., pontifex maximus, 454
— M., Camillus, and Veii, 511 sq., 524; Hernici, 575; and offering at Delphi, 513; and Gauls, 554, 565; and reforms after Gallic Wars, 566 sqq.; speech after Gallic invasion, 514; victory over Latins, 578
— P., Philus (cos. 223), 813
— Sp. (cons. trib. 378), 577

Gabii, 350, 404 sq.; treaty with Rome, 393 sq., 405
Gabinius, A. (cos. 58 B.C.), 455
Gadara (Seleuceia), 192, 729
Gades, and trade with Carthage, 665; Tyrian colony, 770, 775, 778 sq.
Gaesati, Celtic mercenaries, 62, 811
Gaius, Institutes of, 327, 330
Galatae, and Celts, 56 sqq.
Galatia (Northern Phrygia), 173; Gauls settled in, 106
Galen, on Alexandrine anatomists, 285 sqq.
Gallic sites: Bologna, 555 sq., 560; Felsina, 555, 557; Filottrano, 560; Marzabotto, 555 sq.; Montefortino, 555, 560; Ornavasso, 555, 560; Soldo, 555, 560; see also under Celts
Gamala, 190; (?) Philoteria, 192
Gandhara, and Hellenism, 196
Gaul, Cisalpine, Celtic settlement in, 45, 70; Belgic invasion of, 59; trade with Egypt, 134
Gauls (Galatae), see also Celts; Aetolians and, 102; Antigonus and, 102; mercenaries with Antigonus, 201, 213; army of, 101 sq.; in Asia Minor, 26, 104 sqq., 701, 720 sq.; at Delphi, 103, 316; invade Greece, 102; Greek army and, 102; conquest of N. Italy by, 555 sqq., causes of, 537 sqq.; invade Macedonia, 101 sqq., 107; and Menedemus, 94 sq.; settled in N. Phrygia (Galatia), 106; Seleucids and, 106, 159; settlers in Serbia, 201; in Thrace, 101, 106, 201; wars with Rome, Ch. XVII passim, 808–815; battle of the Allia, 564 sq.; raids, 570 sqq.; sack of Rome by, 564 sq.; consequences to Rome of invasions, 570 sqq., 578 sqq.

Gavius Pontius, Samnite general at Cau-
dium, 599
Gaza, 190, 192; the Ptolemies and, 130,
161, 175
Gazoria, Macedonian goddess, 197
Geganius, L. (cons. trib. 378), 577
— M., Macerinus (censor 435), 521
Gela, Agathocles at, 620, 622 *sq.*, 632
Gellius, Cn., historian, 317
— Egnatius, Samnite general, 613
gens, in early Rome, 415 *sq.*; in early
Senate, 423 *sqq.*; and *familia*, 415 *sq.*;
religious ties of, 417; ownership of land,
416 *sq.*; plebeian *gentes*, 418 *sq.*; patrician,
transition to *plebs*, 421
Genucii, and consulship, 527
Genucius, L. (cos. 362), 576
— (trib. pl. 342), 529
— T. (? cos. 451), 459
Genusus, river, 836, 855
Gerasa (Antioch), 192
Gerizim, Mount, temple on, and Sidonians,
191
Geron, 775
Gerrha, 724, 728
Getae, Lysimachus and the, 82
Gherard of Cremona, 299
Gibraltar, the Straits of, 262; Carthage and,
52, 775 *sq.*, 780 *sq.*
Glaucias, king of the Taulantini, 826
— physician, 287
Glaucon, 29, 86, 220, 706
Gomphi, 752
Gongylus, tyrant of Aeolis, 184
Gonni, 200
Gorgasus, Greek artist at Rome, 467
Gortyn, 745
Gracchanus, Junius Congus, *De potestatibus*
of, 327
Gracchus, Gaius, 473
— Tiberius, 471, 807; and *ager publicus*,
538; and Iberians, 786
Graeco-Macedonian cities, in Syria, 158, 164
Greece, Greeks: and the succession to Alex-
ander, 78 *sq.*; Babylon, Greeks in, 188;
Celts and, 57, 64, 70; after the Chre-
monidean War, 218–222; Demetrius
and, 80; in Egypt, 110, 144, 152 *sq.*;
initiative in West lost, 1; invaded by
Gauls, 102 *sqq.*; Greece and Macedon,
2 *sq.*; Greek coastal towns of Macedonia,
200; Greek Leagues and Macedonia,
Ch. XXIII; and Macedonia, 2 *sq.*, Ch. VI
passim; Macedonia, Greek mercenaries
in, 201; Phoenicians in, 190; after
Pyrrhus, 216 *sqq.*; Seleucids and, 157,
168; social and economic changes 275–
217 B.C., 211 *sqq.*; in Western Mediterranean, 363
— — Rome, relations with, 514 *sq.*: first
official contact with, 840; and Rome,

influence of, contrasted, 2 *sq.*; Greeks of
Magna Graecia, Rome and, 26; Rome,
embassy of philosophers to, 316; influence
of, at Rome, 467; and early Roman
legends, 363 *sqq.*, 369
— — in Alexandria, 28; Alexandria,
literary debt to, 250; art in Hellenistic
period, 174; in Asia, 10; and early Celtic
traders, 49 *sqq.*; Greek cities in Egypt,
120 *sq.*; communities and deification of
rulers, 15; Leagues, 8; literature and Alexandrian scholars, 253 *sq.*; mathematics,
science, 7; monarchy in, 9 *sq.*; monarchy,
Greek thought and, 36 *sq.*; philosophy
and science separated, 7; political theory
and the *oecumene*, 37
Guadalquivir, river, 51, 772
Guilds, 34 *sq.*; in Egypt, 150 *sq.*; of Phoenician cities, 191; Roman, 464
Gyga, Macedonian goddess, 197 *sq.*
Gymnetes, Iberian, 772, 782
Gythium, 762

Hadad, Syrian cult of, 7
Hadranum under Aetna, 675
Hadria, 542, 557, 638, 660, 838
Hadrumetum, captured by Agathocles, 626
Halae, 218
Halaesa, Hiero II and, 668; Rome and,
675, 794; charter of, 799
Halcyoneus, son of Antigonus Gonatas,
202, 214 *sq.*, 221, 708
Halicarnassus, 98, 105, 156, 184; under the
Ptolemies, 128, 130
Halicyae, Pyrrhus and, 651; and Rome,
676, 794
Hallstatt period, Ch. II *passim*
Halycus, river, 630
Halys, river, 105
Hamilcar, Punic governor of Sicily (c. 320
B.C.), and Syracusan oligarchs, 622 *sq.*
— son of Gisco, 623, 625 *sq.*, 631 *sqq.*
— Carthaginian general in First Punic
War, 678, 680 *sqq.*
— Barca, in Sicily, 690 *sqq.*; conducts
peace negotiations, 692; and re-conquest
of Spain, 781, 786 *sqq.*; Roman embassy
to, 809; and Mercenary Revolt, 782
Hannibal, Carthaginian admiral in First
Punic War, 668; at Agrigentum, 676 *sq.*;
at Mylae, 679
— in Spain, 49, 789 *sqq.*; at Sagun-
tum, 790; strategy at Trasimene and
Gereonium, 784; and Spanish place-
names, 791; and Rome's war with
Antiochus, 791; Hannibalis Insula, 791;
Hannibalis Portus, 791; Hannibalis
scalae, 791; Hannibalis speculae, 791
Hanno, Carthaginian admiral in First
Punic War, 673, 677, 681
— 'the Great,' 666, 689, 803

Hanno, Carthaginian general (310 B.C.), 626
— Carthaginian navigator, 776
harmostai, Macedonian, 200
Harpasus in Caria, battle of, 721
Harpocrates, Egyptian cult of, 5, 7
Harpstedt culture, 67
Hasdrubal, Carthaginian general in First Punic War, 680, 685, 686
— governor of Spain, 787 *sq.*, 809 *sq.*
Hecataeus of Abdera, 265
— of Miletus, on Celts, 49
Hecatombaeum, battle of, 756
Hecatomnus, 184
Hedylus of Samos, 266, 282
Hegesias of Magnesia, 250, 256, 258 *sq.*
Heirkte, 651, 690
Helenus, son of Pyrrhus, 214, 653
Helice, 787
Helicranum, 830
Hellenic League, 759 *sqq.*, 846
Hellenism, Ch. I *passim*; age of experiment, 3; age, scientific and materialistic, 29; in Alexandria, 148; Antiochus I and, 710; Antiochus Epiphanes and, 189; in Carthage, 191; influence of art on Chinese art, 174, 196; Christianity and, 2; cosmopolitanism, 2, 5, 11, 33 *sqq.*; in East, failure of, 115, 189; in Egypt, 6, 115, 144, 149 *sq.*, 152; Gandhara and, 196; Greek philosophy and science separated, 7; individualism, 2, 4, 33 *sqq.*; Judaism and, 2, 6; kingship, basis of Macedonian, 11; leaders, Macedonian, 2; literature, effect on, 3; in Macedonia, 2; Oriental religions and, 7; in Palestine, 160, 189, 192; in Phoenicia, 190 *sq.*; poetry, 251, 272; religion and, 4 *sqq.*; at Rome, 824; Seleucids and, 160, 174, 189, 194 *sq.*; of native Sikels, 617; religious syncretism 5; in Thrace, 107; Zoroastrianism and, 6
Hellenistic kingdoms, the new, Chs. III, IV, XXII; administration of, 28 *sq.*, Chs. IV, V; new capitals and Athens, 4; as centres of culture, 30 *sq.*; natural frontiers, absence of, 27; native populations of, 28; strength and weakness of, 32
— Science and Mathematics, Ch. IX *passim*; medicine and surgery, 284–288; philosophy and medicine, 286 *sq.*; biology and botany, 288 *sq.*; mathematics, 290–311; early Ptolemies and, 297
Helleno-memphites, in Egypt, 122
Helorum, 675
Helvetii, in N. Switzerland, 44 *sq.*
Hemeroscopium, 769, 773, 780
Hera, cult of, in Egypt, 145
Heraclea, in Italy, restored by Alexander of Epirus, 640; battle of, 644 *sq.*; alliance with Rome, 650
— on Latmus, renamed Pleistarchea, 76 *sq.*

Heraclea, Pontica, 75 *n.*, 81, 92, 105; navy of, 85, 90; Ptolemy II and, 98 *sq.*
— in Sicily, 633, 651, 799
Heracleides of Pontus, 301, 554; and Plato, 295
— of Tarentum, 287
— son of Agathocles, 628, 635
— party leader at Syracuse, 618 *sqq.*
Heracleitus of Athmonon, 206, 221
— of Ephesus, 239
— of Halicarnassus, 283
Heraea, 745, 762
Herat (Alexandria Ariana), 174
Herbessus, Hiero II and, 690
Herculaneum, the *tetrapharmakos* from, 234
Hercules, Pillars of, 776, 780
— Musarum, temple of, 375
Hercynian forest, Celts in, 60
heredium of *bina iugera*, 342, 416 *sq.*, 469
Hermaean promontory (Cape Bon), Carthage and Agathocles at, 625
Hermagoras of Temnos, 256
Hermeias the Carian, minister of Seleucus III and Antiochus III, 181, 723 *sqq.*
Hermesianax of Colophon, 266, 273 *sq.*, 279
Hermias, nesiarch, and the Philadelpheia, 705
Hermione, 219, 750, 758
Hermippus, 261
Hermocrates, 258 *sq.*
Hermogenes, 100
Hermotimus of Colophon, 298
Hermupolis, 144
Hernici, 340, 349, 406, 471, 492, 500, 575 *sq.*, 592, 606 *sq.*
Herodas, 143, 252, 267, 269, 279 *sqq.*
Herodotus, 780; on Celts, 49, 51; on Etruscans, 379 *sq.*, 394
Heroïzation, 14, 16 *sq.*
Heron of Alexandria, 299, 303 *sq.*
Heroopolis, Ptolemy II at, 704
Herophilus, anatomist, 284 *sqq.*, 297
Hesiod, Callimachus and, 276
Hestiaeotis, 752
Hiberus (Rio Tinto), 771
Hicetas of Syracuse, 292
Hierapolis, 184
Hierapytna in Crete, 752
Hiero I of Syracuse, 396
— II, 278, 303; and Leges Hieronicae, 637; and Mamertines, 667 *sq.*; alliance with Rome, 674 *sq.*, 690; and Alexandria, 796
Hierocles the Carian, 89, 206, 216
Hieron, tyrant of Priene, 77
Hieronymus of Rhodes, the Peripatetic, 221
— of Cardia, 75 *n.*, 81, 90, 95, 203, 214 *sq.*, 259, 644; *harmost* of Boeotia, 81
Himera, battle of (480 B.C.), 778 *sq.*
Himeras, river, battle of (311 B.C.), 623 *sq.*

Himilco, Carthaginian explorer, 776
Hipparchus of Nicaea, 264, 302, 310 sq.
Hippias of Elis, 293
Hippo (Bizerta), 682, 691
Hippocrates of Chios, 293, 299
— of Cos, 285 sq.
Hippomedon, 743
Hipponax, 268, 274
Hipponium, Agathocles and, 635, 641;
Dionysius I and, 640
Hippou Akra (Bizerta), 629
Hirpini, 654, 661
Histiaea, 216
Historiae Augustae Scriptores, 143
Histria, pirates at, 815; Livy on, 825
Hittites, 156
Homer, editions of, by Alexandrians, 254,
274; Eratosthenes on Homeric question,
263
Honos, temple of, at Rome, 698
Horace, 514; debt to Alexandrian poets,
268
Horatii and Curiatii, 377, 401
Horatius, M. (cons. trib. 378), 577
— M., Barbatus (cos. 449), 460, 462, 481
— M., Pulvillus (cos. 509), 436, 859, 861
— Cocles, 397; statue of, in the Comitium,
319
Hortensius, Q. (dictator 287), 451, 482, 553
Horus, 18 sq.; (Harpocrates), 146
Hostilia gens, 377, 418
Hostilii, Catones, 377
Hostilius, C., Mancinus (cos. 137), 600
Hypaspistae, Macedonian, 170
hvpomnematographos, Egyptian, 119
Hyrcania, 720
Hyrcanus, son of Tobias, 183

Iambulus, 265, 741
Iapygians, Agathocles and, 641
Iberians, 64, 771; agriculture, 784; armour,
784; art and literature, 785; dwellings,
785; funeral rites, 785; institutions of,
783 sqq.; mercenaries with Carthaginians
and Romans, 783; place-names, 789;
religion, 786; situation of, 782; strategy
and tactics, 784
Ibiza (Ebusus), 779
Ichnae, 174
Icilian rogation, 361
Icilius, L. (trib. pl. 456), 472
Ictis, 52 sq.
Ida, Mt, 709
Idumea, 122
Ierne, 51, 53 n., 771
Iguvium, Tables of, 409, 411
Ileates, 771
Ilercavones, 782, 791
Ilium, Ilians, League of, 24, 91; Troas and,
92; and tyrants, 98, 105, 219; Antiochus
I and, 161

Illyria, Illyrians, piracy, 824 sqq.; origins
of, 826; limits of state, 827; menace to
Greece, 827; navy of, 827; under Agron
and Teuta, 827 sqq.; wars with Rome,
831 sqq., 848 sqq., causes of, 824, 832 sq.,
838; and Italian commerce, 829, 831 sq.;
and Epirus, 219, 820; Roman envoys to,
831; treaty with Rome, 835, 852; Illyrian
territory, 827, 836; under Roman protectorate, 857; Paxos, battle of, 833 sq.
— Alexander and, 64; Celts in, 65;
southern, 83, 95; Gauls and, 102
Imbros, Lysimachus and, 92
imperium, 327, 408, 412 sq., 437, 520;
plebs and, 447, 455 sq.; nature of, 441
sqq.; limitations of, 442 sq.; contrasted
with potestas, 441 sqq.; of kings, 408, 413,
444, 455; of consuls, 443, 459, 502; minor
magistrates and, 455; of praetors, decemvirs, military tribunes, 442 sq.; abrogatio
imperii, 444; precautions against abuse of,
443, 456; quaestors and, 523; and fines,
457; prorogatio imperii, 530
India, 159, 196; castes in, 34
Indigetes, 772, 782
Individualism, 33 sqq.; Greek, 2; in Hellenistic age, 4; and pure science, 4;
Epicurus and, 37; Zeno and, 37; and
the New Comedy and philosophy,
224
Indortes, Iberian officer, 787
Insubres, 556, 811, 813 sq.
Interamna Larinas, 603, 613 sq., 660
— Nahars, 614
intercessio, 444, 457, 520 n., 525, 550
interregnum, 407, 413, 424, 437 n., 442 sqq.,
450, 460, 528
Ionia, Demetrius and, 76 sq., 87; Ionian
League, 24, 77 sq., 91, 737; Lysimachus
and, 78, 87 sq., 91; Gauls and, 105;
under the Ptolemies, 128; Ionian Greeks
and science, 290; and Sardinia, 769
Ipsus, battle of, 75 sq.; see Vol. VI
Iran, Iranians, Greek manufactures in, 174;
Hellenism in, 5 sq.; settlers in Media,
187; the Seleucids and, 155 sq., 159 sqq.;
in army of Seleucids, 170; mercenaries in
Seleucid army, 170
Ireland, sacra insula, 51; Iwerio, 52
Iris, river, 105
Iron Age, Early, in Central Europe, 41;
Hallstatt period, 41 sqq., 46 sqq.; Urn-
field Culture, 55, 57, 59, 61; La Tène
period, 41 sqq.; art of, 42, 61; pass finds,
61, 62 sq., 65, 68, 70 sq.; second Iron
Age, 42; Hallstatt pottery, 59; Hallstatt
Tumulus Culture, 59 sq.; climate in, 61;
Latium in, 335 sq.
Iron Gate, the (Demir Kapu), 102
Isauria, Seleucids and, 183
Isis, 5, 7, 146

Island League, the, 24, 84, 92, 128, 714, 737; breaks up, 715

Isocrates, 9, 780; influence of, on Hellenistic prose, 255, 257

Isopolity, 550; Aetolian, 210, 733; Roman, 393 sq., 748

Issa, 825, 835

Isthmian Games, Romans admitted to, 841

Istolatius, Iberian officer, 787

Istria, Celts and, 64

Italy, 2, 49, 57; agriculture in, 469; art, 546 n.; Celtic invasion of, 60 sqq.; central, Roman conquest of, Ch. XVIII; early inhabitants of, 233 sqq.; northern, and Gauls, 555 sqq., 571, and Rome, 805 sqq., Phoenician traders in, 191; Roman policy in, 817; southern, and Agathocles, 624 sqq.; western, Roman hegemony of, 518; see also under Rome

Itanus, in Crete, 704

Ius, fas, 427 sq.
— Aelianum, 327
— civile, 327, 550; plebs and, 422
— Flavianum, 327, 463, 534
— migrandi, and Latin League, 550
— Papirianum, 312, 327
— suffragii, plebs and, 423

Janus, temple of, at Rome, 698; gates closed, 809

Jason (in Macc. II), 172

Jaxartes, river, 76, 174

Jews, Judaism, 192, 231; Jerusalem, Antiochus III and, 164, 192; Jews in Asia, 10, 24; in Alexandria, 111 sq., 120 sq.; in Egypt, 120; colonists in Lydia and Phrygia, 180; Dionysiac rites in, 5; Hellenism and, 2, 6, 160; Judaea as a temple state, 193; Ptolemy IV and, 727

Joppa, 192

Josephus, 180, 191 sq.

Julius Caesar, on Celts, 61; in Gaul, 66
— L., Caesar (cos. 64), 329

Junius, C., Brutus (cos. 291, 277), triumph of, 650
— C., Bubulcus (cos. 317), 547, 600, 605, 609
— D., Brutus (cos. 325), 598
— — — (cos. 292), 614
— L., Brutus, the First Consul, 397, 414, 432, 436, 444, 449, 453, 859, 861
— L., Pullus (cos. 249), at Drepana, 687

Juno Moneta, temple of, 320 sq.

Juppiter Feretrius, 316, 384, 507
— Latiaris, 344, 348 sq., 350, 364, 405
— Optimus Maximus, temple of, 464

Jurists, Roman, as authorities for history, 326 sqq.

Justin, on Agathocles, 617 n.; on new Hellenistic kingdoms, 75 n.; on Pyrrhus, 638 n.; on Brother-War, 699 n.

Justinian, 330

katoikoi, Egyptian, 118; Macedonian, 171; Seleucid, 169; katoikiai, 32

Kautilia, Arthashastra of, 154

Khabur, river, 158

Khnum (the 'Potter'), 115

'Kinsmen,' Macedonian, 201

kleroi, Egyptian, 117; Macedonian, 171, 182, 186; klerouchoi, Egyptian, 118, 126; Seleucid, 169, 186

koine, the, 36 sq.

Koloë, in Lydia, battle of, 721

Kom-Ombos, 146

komai, Egyptian, administration, 123

Kore and Demeter, festival of, 96

Korupedion, battle of, 98

Kurdistan, 160

Kuthah, 188

Labeo, Antistius, jurist, 329 sq.

Labici, 488, 500 sq., 510; via Labicana, 339

Lacetani, 782

Lachares, Athens and, 78 sq.

Lacinian headland, 640

Laconia, Pyrrhus in, 214; and Illyrian pirates, 826

Ladoceia, battle of, 753

Laelius Felix, jurist, 330, 411, 451, 482

Laeetani, 782

Laevius Egerius, 488

Lamia, 732

Lanassa, wife of Pyrrhus, deified, 84, 634, 636

Land, allotments of, in Egypt, 137 sqq.; in Macedonia, 199 sq.; Roman, 416 sq.; ager Gallicus, 806 sq.; of ager publicus, 470 sqq., 537 sqq., 808; of Aventine, 472 sq.; in Campania, 593; citizen settlements, 593; of conquered territory, 417, 471, 538 sqq.; debtors' land, 479; Spurius Cassius and, 471 sq.; in Sparta, 741; Seleucid, 171 sqq., 179 sqq.

Land, Roman, private ownership of, 468 sqq.; limit to holdings of, 538 sqq.

Lanuvium, 411, 439, 488, 577; granted Roman citizenship, 591

Laodice, wife of Antiochus II, 172, 181, 188, 712, 715 sq.
— wife of Antiochus III, 162, 724
— wife of Mithridates of Pontus, 718

Laodicea, in Palestine, 191
— in Phrygia, on the Lycus, 181 n., 725
— in Syria (foundation of Seleucus I), 158, 185

Laodicean War, 715 sqq.

laokritai, Egyptian, 119 sq.

Lapis Niger, 351, 564

Larcius (Largius), T., 441, 507

Larichus, 181

Larissa, 79, 185, 767

Lars Porsenna, 389, 397, 432, 504, 507
Larymna, 218
Lasion, 756, 766
La Tène period, 559, Ch. II *passim*; *see also* Celts, Early Iron Age
Latin language, Etruscan elements in, 382, 387, 391, 439; Sicilian, 697
Latium, Latins: Aeneas and, 363 *sqq.*; agriculture in, 342; ancestors of, 333; commerce, 466; Latin communities, 345 *sqq.*; and Etruria, 338, 396; federal movement in, 404 *sqq.*; frontiers of, 340; early geography of, 337–340; League, treaty with Romans, 312, 348 *sqq.*, 393, 404 *sqq.*, 517 *sq.*, 549 *sq.*; products of, 341 *sqq.*; Roman citizenship and, 547 *sqq.*; and Rome: Latin Leagues and, 487 *sqq.*, treaty with, 392 *sq.*, 586, war with, 577 *sq.*, 586 *sqq.*; social life in, 344 *sqq.*; Latin unity, beginnings of, 348 *sqq.*
Laurentes, Laurentum, 405, 488; 'Laurentes Lauinates', 345
Laus, 584, 640
Lautulae, 594; battle of, 601
Lavinium, 348, 351, 364, 404, 406, 488, 577; worship of Aphrodite at, 364
Law, private, in early Rome, 428 *sq.*
League, defined, 7 *n.*; substitute for provincial nationalism, 23; Acarnanian, 217, 747, 759; Achaean, 8, 23, 34, 100, 207, 210, 214, 220, 222, 718, 732–739, 746, 759, 842; Aegean Islands, 126; Aetolian, 23, 208 *sqq.*; Alban, 349, 405; Amphictyonic, 104, 210, 217; Arcadian, 219, 707, 736; Arician, 350 *sq.*, 405; Boeotian, 210, 759; Capuan, 589, 593; Cyrenaic, 127, 713; Demetrius, 740; Doson's new Hellenic, 759; Epirote, 83; Etruscan cities, 439, 515, 562; Euboean, 81, 759; Hellenic, 2, 8, 76, 759, 842; Hernican, 493; Ionian, 24, 77, 91, 105, 737; Islanders, 24, 84, 92, 128, 705, 714 *sq.*, 737; Italiote, 640; Latin, 312, 348 *sq.*, 393, 401 *sq.*, 404 *sqq.*, 487 *sqq.*, 517 *sq.*, 659 *sq.*; Lucanian, 585 *sq.*; of the Macedonians, 571, 759; Northern, 98 *sq.*, 701; Nucerian, 601; Paeonia, 219; Pan-hellenic, 737, 740, 759; Peloponnesian, 99; Phocis, 28, 759; Samnite, 585; Thessalian, 80, 200, 751, 759
Lebedus, 91; re-named Ptolemaïs, 719
lembi, 825
Lemnos, 92, 99
Lemonia tribus, 434
Lentulus, *see* Cornelius
Leonidas, son of Cleonymus, 742 *sq.*, 752
— of Tarentum, 282
Leonnatus, officer of Alexander, 12
Leonnorius, 'king' of the Tolistoagii, 104
Leontini, 642 *sqq.*, 674 *sq.*
Leontius, 766 *sq.*
Leosthenes, 760

Lepidus, the triumvir, 328; *see under* Aemilius
Lepontii, 556, 560
Leptines, Syracusan general, 632
Leptis, Magna, 682; Minor, 682
Lesbos, 719
Leucadia, 643
Lex, leges: Acilia Repetundarum, 420; Aemilia, 522, 533; Agraria of 111 B.C., 328; *arae Dianae in Aventino*, 392; Aternia Tarpeia, 324, 457; Canuleia, 483, 519; Coloniae Genetivae Juliae, 430 *n.*; *curiata*, 412 and *n.*; *fenebris*, 529, 544 *sq.*; Genuciae, 484; Hieronica, 636 *sqq.*, 795 *sq.*; Hortensia, 327, 482, 664, 671, 819; Icilia de Aventino publicando, 350, 361, 472 *sq.*; Julia Papiria, 457; Licinio-Sextian, 438 *sq.*, 483, 524 *sqq.*, 528, 538 *sqq.*; Maenia, 535; Marcia, 544; Menenia Sestia, 457; Ogulnia, and the Pontifical College, 320, 324, 427, 429, 459; Ovinia, 522, 818; Poetelia, 545 *sq.*; Publilia, 453; *regiae*, ascribed to Numa, 376; *sacrata militaris*, 529; Tarpeia, 324; Valeria, 395, 447, 455; Valerio-Horatian, 480 *sqq.*
Libici, Gallic tribe, 556
Liburni, Livy on, 825; *liburnae*, 825
Libyans, Agathocles and, 626 *sq.*, 630
Liby-phoenicians, 771
Licinio-Sextian laws of 367 B.C., 438 *sq.*, 483, 524 *sqq.*, 528, 538 *sqq.*
Licinii, and consulship, 527
Licinius, C. (*mag. equit.* 368), 525
— C., Macer, historian, 317, 320, 461, 503, 521, 533, 537
— C., Stolo (? cos. 361), 524 *sq.*; and ager publicus, 538 *sq.*; and debt, 542; and Hernici, 576
— M., Crassus (cos. 30); and *spolia opima*, 316, 508
— P., Calvus (cons. trib. 400), 449, 520
Lictors, 423
Ligurians, Celts and, 49 *sq.*, 52, 559, 771; Rome and, 805
Lilybaeum, besieged by Pyrrhus, 651 *sq.*; in First Punic War, 680, 687; Rome and, 793, 798
Limnaea, 752, 766 *sq.*
Limnaeus, 184
Lingones, 556, 811
Lipari islands, 561
Lissus, 835, 838
Liturgies, Egyptian, 141
Livius Andronicus, 655, 697, 824
— M., Salinator (cos. 219), 815, 848
Livy: on augurs, 429; on first treaty with Carthage, chron. note, 860 *sqq.*; on Celts, 60 *sq.*, 63; on censorship, 521; on chronology, early Roman, 322 *sq.*; on comitia centuriata, 423; on constitutional

struggle, 526; on *duoviri perduellionis*, 331; on Fasti, 321, 323; on Liburni and Histri, 825; on *plebiscita*, 481, 483; on First Punic War, 665 *n.*; on Pyrrhus, 638 *n.*; on early Rome, 312, 370 *n.*; on fifth-century Rome, 485 *n.*; on Samnite Wars, 613; on Ten Tables, 460; on tribes, 409; on tribunes, 450; on usury, 529; on Veii, 512 *sqq.*; on Volsci, 497, 499

Locri, Dionysius I and, 64, 640; Roman garrison at, 645; captured by Pyrrhus, 652; in Roman federation, 654; coinage, 654; attacked by Hamilcar Barca, 690

Locris, Eastern, 81, 83 *sq.*, 207, 218; Locrians and Gauls, 102; Western, 83; and Aetolian League, 210, 218; Opuntian, 218; Epicnemidian, 218

Longanus river, battle of, 668

Longarus, king of Dardania, **747**

Longula, battle of, 605

Lucanians, 661; and cities of Magna Graecia, 661; culture of, mainly Greek, 584; and Dionysius I, 639; league, 584; and Oenotria, 584; and Rome, 639 *sq.*; and Tarentum, 640

Lucentum (Alicante), 780

Luceres, 409, 429

Luceria, foundation of, 640; colony at, 601, 641, 646, 660; and the Social War, 319

Lucian, 234

Lucretia, Sextus Tarquinius and, 394

Lucretius, Sp., 436

— T., poet, 232 *sqq.*, 239, 243 *sqq.*

'Lupa Capitolina,' 366

Lupercal, the, Lupercalia, 356, 365

Lusitania, 783 *n.*

lustrum, 410, 521, 523

Lutarius, 'king' of the Trocmi, 104

Lutatii, 695

Lutatius, C., Catulus (cos. 242), wins victory at Aegates I., 691 *sq.*; negotiates peace with Carthage, 692 *sq.*

Lycaeum, battle of, 753

Lycaonia, Seleucids and, 183

Lychnidus, Lake, 855

Lycia, Lycians, 78; Egypt and, 105, 122, 126, 128, 712, 719; under the Seleucids, 183

Lycon, philosopher, 221

Lycophron of Chalcis, tragedian, 94, 107, 253, 267, 281, 653

Lycurgus, king of Sparta (219 B.C.), 765

Lycus of Rhegium, 554

Lydia, 167; Jewish colonists in, 180; Seleucus II and, 720

Lydiades of Megalopolis, 734, 746, 749, 753

Lynceus of Samos, 264

Lyons inscription, 391

Lysander of Sparta, deified, 13, 742 *sq.*

Lysandra, daughter of Ptolemy I, 77, 80, 97

Lysanias, 184

Lysias, in Phrygia, 184; family of, in Phrygia, 720

— son of Philomelus, 184

— tyrant of Lebanon, 190

Lysimacheia, 90 *sqq.*, 98, 106, 180, 202, 206, 719; restored by Antiochus III, 171

— in Mysia, 92

Lysimachus, the Successor, after Ipsus, 76 *sqq.*, 89–94; coalition with Seleucus and Ptolemy, 78, 85; and Asia Minor, 90; coinage, 90 *sq.*; deified, 91, 93, 198; Demetrius and, 77, 79, 93; and Egypt, 96 *sq.*; and Ephesus, 78, 91; and Epirus, 96; fall of, 97 *sq.*; attacks the Getae, 82; invades Macedonia, 85, 89; king of Macedonia, 90; and learning, 90; navy of, 85; realm of, 90 *sq.*; policy towards cities, 91; trade and finance of, 90

— brother of Ptolemy III, 727

Macedonia, Macedonians, 197–204; and Aetolia, 744; Antigonus invades, 106; army, 9, 12, 32, 198; Body-Guards, 9, 11; Celts in, 65; cities, government of, 200; city assemblies, 200; cities and army, 200 *sqq.*; Companions, 9, 11; Corinth and, 205 *sq.*; court of, 11; Crown Council, 11; Dardanians invade, 748; Demetrius, king of, 79 *sq.*, 84; export trade, 199; federalism and, 751 *sq.*; Gaulish mercenaries in, 107; Gauls invade, 101–106; Greece and, 2 *sq.*, 23, Ch. VI *passim*; Greek coastal towns of, 200; Greek leagues and, Ch. XXIII; hegemony of, in Hellas, 12; Hellenism in, 2, 205; imperialism, 2, 4; after Ipsus, Ch. III; kingship, 11; King's Land, 199 *sqq.*; land, 199; League of the Macedonians, 751, 759; and literature, 203 *sqq.*, 250; monarchy in, 8 *sqq.*; and her neighbours, 205 *sq.*; population of, 197; and Ptolemaic god-kingship, 18; Pyrrhus and, 85, 89, 213; religion, 197 *sq.*; revenue, 198; and Rome, 839 *sq.*, 844; Royal Pages, 9, 11; Seleucids and, 157; and Sparta, 30, 207; and Syria against Egypt, Ch. XXII; and Thessaly, 200

machimoi, Egyptian, 117 *sq.*

Macrobius, *Saturnalia* of, 330

Maeandrius, Chronicle of, 260

Maecia tribus, 591

Maelius, Sp., sedition of, 324 *sq.*; and food-supply, 536 *sq.*

Maenace, 769 *sq.*, 774 *sq.*, 778

Maenius, C. (cos. 338), 547, 590

Magas, governor of Cyrenaica, Antiochus I and, 704, 712

— brother of Ptolemy IV, 728

Magi, 6

Magna Graecia, Rome and Greeks of, 26, 583 *sq.*, 607, 640 *sqq.*
Magnesia, on the Maeander, 87, 103, 182, 189, 719
— by Sipylus, 171 and *n.*; battle of, 171 and *n.*, 178 *sq.*
— (Thessalian), 759
Mago, in Sicily, 649 *sq.*, 665; negotiates Carthaginian treaty with Rome, 665, 672; house of Mago, 769
Mago (Port Mahon), capital of Minorca, 773
Malaca, 411, 770, 775
Malchus, Carthaginian general in Sicily and Sardinia, 769
Malis, 102; and Aetolian League, 210
Mallus, 719
Malventum (Beneventum), battle of, 653; colony at, 654
Mamertines, Pyrrhus and, 652; and Hiero II, 667 *sq.*; and Carthage, 668, 673; mercenaries with Agathocles, 635, 667; alliance with Rome, 667 *sqq.*
Mamilii, 695
Mamilius, Octavius (Octavus) of Tusculum, 396, 489
— Q. (cos. 262), in Sicily, 676
mancipium, 417, 468, 477
Manetho, 146, 260
Manlii, and consulship, 527
Manlius, A. (Decemvir), 459
— C. (cos. 480), 577
— Cn. (cons. trib. 379), 504 *sq.*
— L., Capitolinus (dictator, 363), 552
— L., Vulso (cos. 250), 687
— M., Capitolinus (cos. 392), 395, 524, 542
— P., Capitolinus (cons. trib. 379), 525, 577
— T., Torquatus (cos. I. 347), 427, 526, 567, 570, 572, 590
— — — (cos. 235, 224), 813
Mantinea, 84, 219, 706, 708, 735, 746 *sq.*, 753, 756, 760; refounded by Aratus as Antigoneia, 762
Mantua, 557 *sq.*
Manumission, 455, 532
Marathus, 704
Marcellus, *see* Claudii
Marcia, gens, 418
Marcius, C., Rutilus (cos. 357), 326 *n.*, 378, 527, 544, 575; first plebeian dictator and censor, 418
— — (cos. 310), 605 *sq.*
— Cn., Coriolanus, 457, 476, 498 *sq.*, 501
— Q., Rex (praetor, 144), 377
Marduk, 156
Margus, river, 827
Marissa, 191
Marius, C., 619
Marmaridae, 704

Marne culture, 52; peoples of, 56 *sq.*, 67; chariot burials, 43, 67, 72; pottery, 44; tumuli and flat graves, 44
Maronea, 719
Marrucini, 585, 604 *sq.*, 609, 661
Marsi, 585, 604, 606, 609, 661
Marsyas valley, 700, 702, 704
Massilia, Massiliotes: foundation of, 769, 773; and Carthage, 774, 776 *sq.*, 780, 787; Celts and, 46 *sq.*, 49, 51; Delphic Treasury, 513 *sq.*; and Rome, 514, 640
Mastarna, Servius Tullus and, 389 *sqq.*
Mastia, Mastieni, 771 *sq.*, 777 *sq.*, 789 *n.*
Mathematics, 4; and science at Alexandria, Ch. IX *passim*
Mausolus, 184 (*see* vol. VI)
Medeon, 748, 828
Media, 88, 159 *sq.*, 167, 169, 174; Atropatene, 166 *n.*; Greek settlers in, 170; Iranian settlers in, 187
Mediolanum (Milan), 814
Medullia, 403
Megaleas, 766 *sq.*
Megalopolis, 707, 734, 760; Demetrius and, 207; Pyrrhus at, 214 *sq.*; Antigonus Gonatas and, 99, 216, 221; and Achaean League, 746; Cleomenes and, 755 *sqq.*, 760
Megara, Megarians: 102, 216, 707, 734; Demetrius and, 81, 84, 100; and Achaean League, 736
— Hyblaea, 675
— near Apamea, 185
Megasthenes, 173, 260
Meleager of Gadara, 195, 250, 272, 281
— brother of Ptolemy Keraunos, 102
Melita (Malta), Regulus at, 680
Melitaea, 767
Melkart, 776
Melpum, 556 *sq.*
Memnon, historian, 75
Memphis, 12, 122, 123; Greeks in, 112, 115; Alexandria, rivalry with, 115, 151; cloth works at, 135; under the Ptolemies, 144 *sqq.*
Menaechmus, 296, 298
Menander, 224, 226–230; Plautus and Terence and, 226 *n.*
Mendes, 134
Menedemus, tyrant of Croton, 635
— of Eretria, 94 *sq.*, 107, 204, 216
Menenius, M., Agrippa (cos. 503), 473
— T., Lanatus (cos. 452), 324
Menippus of Gadara, 264, 274
Menon, history of medicine, 238, 287
Mercenaries, of Agathocles, 635, 657; of Antigonus II, 95; of Arsinoe, 99; Campanian, 635, 651, 676, of Carthaginians, 620; Celtic and Iberian, of Dionysius I, 64; Celtic, of Tartessians, 787; of Demetrius, 77, 85; of Eurydice, 102; *Gaesati*, 811; Gallic, of Latin cities, 571, 578; in

Greek army, 102; Iberian, 783; in Macedonian army, 198; of Ptolemies—Greek, 110; in First Punic War, 693; Samnite, at Neapolis, 595; at Sellasia, 760 *sq.*; Spartan, at Carthage, 684

Meropis, 257

Merv (Antiochia Margiana), 174

Mesopotamia, Seleucid policy in, 76, 159 *sq.*, 163, 164, 167, 184, 194; under Seleucids, 184 *sqq.*; Graeco-Macedonian cities in, 158; Greek settlers in, 170; Arab sheikhs in, 175; Jewish colonists from, 180

Messana, Agathocles and, 622; Campanian mercenaries and, 635, 651; and Hiero II, 667 *sq.*; Rome and, 667 *sq.*

Messapia, Pyrrhus and, 656

Messene, 84, 214, 733, 764, 826

Metapontum, 584, 607, 640

Metellus, *see under* Caecilius

Methana (re-named Arsinoe), 708, 719

Metics, Spartan, 743, 753 *sq.*, 765

Metilius, plebiscite of, 817

Metrodorus, 90

Mettius Fufetius, 377, 401

Micion, 749

Miletus, 212; Apollo, eponymous magistrate at, 709, 712; coinage, 92; Demetrius at, 87; Egypt and, 105; Lysimachus and, 78, 92; the Ptolemies and, 128, 181, 701 *sqq.*; Seleucus I and, 77, 98, 162 *n.*, 178; in Syrian Wars, 710, 712, 719

Milo, officer of Pyrrhus, 653

Milyad, the, 704, 726

Mimnermus, 274

Minturnae, colony at, 613

Minucia gens, 418

Minucius, L. (cos. 458), 324, 454, 502, 536

— M., Faesus, augur, 324

— T. (?cos. 451), 459

Mithras, cult of, in Asia Minor, 146, 195

Mithres, finance minister of Lysimachus, 90

Mithridates I, of Parthia, Rome and, 160

— first king of Pontus, Northern League and, 98; Gauls and, 104 *sqq.*; kingdom of, 105; and Seleucus II, 720

Mitylene, 763

Mitylus of Illyria, 708

Mnesimachus, inscription, 171 *n.*, 172, 182

Moagetes, 184, 720

Moloch, 626

Molon, satrap of Media, insurrection of, 181; Seleucus III and, 723; revolt and death of, 723 *sqq.*

Molossi, 83

Monarchy, 7–12; Aegeadae, 9; Alexander, 9 *sqq.*; Aristotle on, 13; Aristotle's ideal king, 36; in Asia, 12; new royal capitals as centres of culture, 30 *sqq.*; cosmopolitanism and Hellenistic kingship, 11; in Greece, 8; Greek thought and, 36; kingship, Hellenistic and Macedonian, 11; in Macedonia, 12, 198; new monarchies, 25 *sqq.*, Ch. III *passim*; Persia, Alexander's conquest of, and, 10 *sq.*; in Persia, 12, 14, 36; Philip, national monarchy of, 9; Plato's ideal king, 36; Rome and, 8, 11; Rome, primitive monarchy of, 407 *sqq.*; in western world, 10

Mongolia, northern, woollen textiles from Syria in, 174 *sq.*

Monti Cimini, 337

Morgantia, 620

Moschus, 281

Mount Gerizim, temple on, 191

Mucius, P., Scaevola (cos. 133), 319 *sq.*, 327 *sq.*

— Q., Scaevola (cos. 95), 327, 330, 415, 451

Munychia, 79, 97, 206

Murgantia, 611

Mutina (Modena), 557

Mylae, battle of, 679

Mylasa, 184

Myndus, 704

Myrina, 726

Mysteries, Graeco-Oriental 'fake-,' 7; mystery-cults, 4; *see also* Eleusis

Nabis of Sparta, 757

Naevius, 689, 697, 824

Naia, festival of, 83

Nanaia, temple of, 163, 187

Narnia, Roman colony of, 609; *see also* Nequinum

Naucratis, Greeks in, 112, 121, 144

Naupactus, 208; peace of, 768, 854

Nazarene cult Hellenized, 7

Neanthes, annalist of Cyzicus, 260

Neapolis (Naples), 584, 594 *sq.*, 659, 678; Pyrrhus and, 646; and Rome, 530, 640; Sabellians and, 584

Nearchus, tyrant of Orchomenus, 746

— admiral of Alexander, 259, 262

Neetum, 675, 794

Nemea, 745

Nemi, inscription of, 497, 501

Neo-Pythagoreans, on kingship, 114, 233

Nepete, colony of, 517, 561, 569, 574 *sq.*, 604, 660

Nepos, Cornelius, 257, 665 *n.*

Nequinum, 609; *see also* Narnia

Nerulum, 600 *n.*

New Carthage, 787 *sq.*

nexum, 478 *sq.*, 545 *sq.*, 549; *see also* Debt

Nicaea, wife of Lysimachus, 80; and Antigoneia, 92

— wife of Alexander, tyrant of Corinth, 221, 223

Nicander, 270

Nicanor, founder of Doura, 168

Nicephorium, 174

Nicocles, tyrant of Sicyon, 222

Nicolaus the Aetolian, general of Ptolemy IV, 728 sq.
Nicomedes of Bithynia, 100, 104, 106, 701
— geometer, 293, 309
Nicomedia, 100
Nicophanes, 756
Nicoteles, epitaph on, 282
Nikephoria, festival instituted by Attalus I, 723
Ninus, Story of, 266
Nippur, 188
Nisaea, 216
Nisibis, 174, 189
Nisyrus, law against tyrants, 98, 219
Nobility, the new Roman, 546 sqq.
Nola, and Cumae, 595; in Samnite Wars, 598, 603
Nomentum, 340, 403, 439, 488, 578; Roman citizenship granted to, 591
Nomes, nomoi, in Egypt, administration of, 123 sq.
Nonius, grammarian, 330
Norba, 341, 350, 474, 487, 498, 518, 577, 589 n.
'Nordic' culture, 66, 68; area, 60; zone, 56, 59, 66, 69, 71; pressure on Gauls in central Germany, 69
Northern League, 98 sqq., 701
Noutria, 835
Nuceria, 601, 603, 606
Numa Pompilius, 331, 371, 374–376, 424, 427, 496; Calendar of, 343, 358, 374 sqq.; origin of name, 376; and religious institutions, 425 sqq.; commentarii of, 331
Numantia, siege of, 783
Numidia, Carthaginian trade with, 665; in First Punic War, 683, 685
nuraghi, 805
Nymphis, 81, 98
Nymphius, magistrate at Neapolis, 595
'Nyrax, a Celtic city,' 49
Nysa on the Maeander, 180
— Scythopolis, 192

Oaxus (Vaxus), 748
Ocriculum, 605, 609
Octavii, 419
Odessus, 91
Odilienberg, 68, 73
Odrysae, the, 107
Oea, 682
Oeniadae, 217, 765
Oenopides of Chios, 292, 299
Oenotria, 655; and Lucanians, 584
Oenus valley (Kelephina), 760
Oestrymnians, 50 sqq., 771
Oestrymnis (Brittany), 771
Ogulnii, aediles (296 B.C.), 367; see also Lex Ogulnia
Olba, in Cilicia, 184
Olbia, in Sardinia, 679

Olcades, 782, 789
Olenus, 207, 736
Olympia, 31
Olympias, 733, 747
Olympichus, in Caria, 184, 720
Olympiodorus, Athenian general, 81, 86, 89
Olynthus, 198
Onesicritus, at Lysimachus' court, 90
Onomarchus, and Delphi, 513
Ophellas, officer of Alexander, Agathocles and, 626 sqq.
Opheltas, 755
Ophiussa, C. (Roca), 771
Opis, 187, 201
Oppius, Mons, 358
Opus, 218
Ora Maritima, of Avienus, 51, 59, 770 n. 1
Oratory, Asianic style, 256
Orchomenus, 219, 707, 746 sq., 760, 762
Orestis, 198
Oretani (Orissi, Oretes), 789
Oricus, 836
Orissi (Oretani, Oretes), 782, 787
Orontes, river, 158
Oropus, 216
Orosius, historian, 315
Orpheus, 274
Ortygia, 651
Orvieto, triple temple at, 383
Oscans, 5; dialect, 336; Sabellians and, 584 sq.
Osiris, 14, 18 sq.; (Osorapis), 145; cult of, at Delos, 146 n.
Ostia, 378, 402, 474; as naval base, 678
Ostimii, 53
Otacilii, 695
Otacilius, M'., Crassus (cos. 263), 674
Otranto, Straits of, 824
Ovinius, 531; tribunician law of, 449; see also Lex Ovinia
Oxyrhynchus, 144, 314

Pachynus, Cape, 685
Paeligni, 585, 589, 604, 661; Samnium and, 606 sq.; Rome and, 609
Paeonia, Lysimachus and, 96; Gauls and, 101; King's Land, 199 sqq.; League, 219, 747 sq., 751
Paestum, 657; colony at, 654
Pagasae, 80 sq., 211
— Gulf of, 81
Palaeopolis, 595 n.
Palaephatus, 265
Palatina tribus, 434
Pale, 766
palefitte, 334
Palestine, coast towns of, 130; under the Ptolemies, 126, 729; under the Seleucids, 157 sqq., 166 n., 167, 173, 175, 190 sqq.; Hellenization of, 160, 192; trade with Egypt, 135; rising in, after Raphia, 729

Pallanteion (Pallantium), cult of Evander at, 365
Pallantium (Pallanteion), 753
Palumbinum, 614
Palos, C., 771, 774, 777, 780, 782, 787
Pamphylia, Seleucids and, 183; in Second Syrian War, 712
Panactum, 220 sq.
Panara, shrine of Zeus Triphylios at, 265
Panaro, river, 344
Panathenaea, the Great, 30, 206
Paneia, vase festival at Delos, 718
Pangaeus, Mt, silver mines of, 199
Panhellenic League, 737, 740; see also under Hellenic
Panion, battle of, 190
Pannonia, Celts in, 65
Panormus, in First Punic War, 680, 685 sq.; Rome and, 798
Pantauchus, 84
Paphlagonia, 105
Papiria gens, 312, 418 sq., 806
Papirianum, ius, 312, 327
Papirius, L., Cursor (cos. 326), 545, 598, 601, 605
—— —— (cos. 293), 613, 655
— L., Mugillanus (cos. 444), 521
— L., Paetus (friend of Cicero), 418
— M. (pont. max.), 454
— (cos. 231), 805 sq.
Pappus, 298 sqq., 303 sq., 307, 309
paradoxa, Hellenistic collections of, 264
Paraetonium, Greeks in, 112, 121
Parapotamia, 724
Parauaea, Pyrrhus and, 83, 96
Parma, 557
Parni, the, 719
paroikoi, 24
Parthenius, 270
Parthia, 26, 720; Era of, 159, 720; Seleucids and, 174 sq., 190
Parthinians, 827, 834
Passaron, 83
Patara (Arsinoe), 704
paterfamilias, 468, 549; patria potestas, 414 sq., 422 sq.; priestly functions of, 425
Patrae, revolt of, 99
patres, patrician members of the Senate, 413, 419, 423 sq., 449; and the army, 435; and clientes, 420 sqq., 470; and comitia centuriata, 482; and conubium, 422, 525; families, extinction of, 421; and gentes, 415, 417; and land, 470 sq., 473 sq.; minorum gentium, 419, 424, 449; patrum auctoritas, 413, 450, 482 sq., 530; plebs, struggle with, 450–484, Ch. XVI, see also plebs; transitio ad plebem, 418, 421, 527; plebiscita binding on, 481; privileges of, 450
Patrocles, general of Seleucus I, 88, 100, 173, 262

Patroclus, Macedonian admiral, in Chremonidean War, 707, 710
Patroclus' Camp (island of Sunium), 707
patroni, 420 sq., 470
Paullus, see under Aemilius
Paxos, 841; battle of, 833 sq.
Pedieis, the, and Priene, 88
Pedum, 488, 500 sq., 573, 578; in Latin War, 590; Roman citizenship conferred on, 591
Pegae, 736
Pelagonia, 855
Pella (Bounomos), 25, 197, 200, 203 sq.; coinage, 85; worship of Pan at, 107
— in Palestine, 192
Pellene, 735, 757
Peloponnese, Celts in, 70; Demetrius and, 76, 78; League revived by Areus, 99; Antigonus and, 207, 216; the Ptolemies and, 126; after the Chremonidean War, 219; invaded by Pyrrhus, 214 sq.; free from Macedonia, 750
Peltuinum, 605
Pelusium, 130, 133, 139, 728
Pentri, 654, 661
Peraea, 190
Perdiccas, 231 (see vol. VI)
perduellio, perduellis, 331, 446 sq., 458; duoviri perduellionis, 446, 524
Pergamum, 12, 20, 24, 26 sq., 30 sq., 97, 709 sq.; Antiochus III and, 159, 176, 184; the Gauls and, 105, 127; patronage of arts and letters, 251; Pergamene Library, 253; sculpture, 65 n.; see vol. VIII
Perigenes, admiral of Ptolemy IV, 729
Peripatetics, 37; on kingship, 114, 237 sq.; in Egypt, 114, 249, 251; Demetrius and, 251; at Athens, 251; prose writings of, 255, 261; influence of, on Hellenistic prose, 255
Periplus, Massiliote, 51 sq., 59, 774 sq.; voyage from Massilia to Tartessus, 770
Perrhaebia, 217
Persaeus, philosopher, Antigonus and, 202, 204, 217; epistates of Corinth, 223, 235 n.
Persephone, temple of, at Locri, 652
Persepolis, 12
Perseus, mathematician, 309
Perseus of Macedon, Rome's war with, 655
Persia, Persian: immigrants to, from Aegean Archipelago, 7; Alexander's conquest of, 10, 12; monarchy in, 11, 36; proskynesis, 15, 183; trade routes in Asia Minor, 175; Sasanian, 196
Persis, 156, 159, 160; Greek settlers in, 170
Perusia, Roman alliance with, 605, 613
Pesaro (Pisaurum), 557; bilingual inscription from, 385, 430
Pessinus, 106, 156
Petra (in Arabia), 175
— (in Sicily), revolt of, 686

πεζέταιροι, 9
Phaedrus, of Sphettus, Athens and, 78 sq.; Demetrius and, 81 sq., 86, 206; nationalist party at Athens and, 217
Phalaecus, 268
Phalanna, 200
Phanocles, 271
phantasiai, Stoic doctrine of, 237
Pharae, 99, 766
Pharaoh Necho, 134
Pharaohs: Pharaoh Ptolemy, deification of, 6, 14 sq., 17 sqq.; army of, 110, 114
Pharisees, 236
Pharos, 825 sq., 850
Pharsalus, 752
Phaselis, 704
Pheidias, mathematician, 302
Phigalea, 707; Aetolia and, 733, 764
Phila, near Tempe, foundation of, 745
Phila, wife of Demetrius, 77 sq.; suicide of, 85, 94
— wife of Antigonus Gonatas, 100, 108, 702; statue of, at Delos, 714
Philadelpheia, vase festival at, 705
Philadelphia, in Cilicia, 704
— in the Fayûm, 122, 144
— in Palestine (Rabbath-Ammon), 190, 192 sq., 729
Philemon, 226; dream of, 708
Philetaireia, under Ida, 709
Philetaireia, vase festival at Delos, 709
Philetaerus, of Pergamum, 97 sqq., 100, 105; coinage, 709
Philetas of Cos, 266, 271, 273, 277 sq.; Ptolemy I and, 297
Philinus of Agrigentum, 287, 859
Philip II, and Corinthian League, 8, 751; national monarchy of, 9; conquest of Greece, 10; deified, 13 sq.; coinage, 46 sq.
— IV of Macedon, 79
— V of Macedon, 94, 198, 205, 219 n., 269, 744, 751, 845; character of, 763; coinage, 751; Aratus and, 764, 766; and Thermum, 852; and Rome, 852; and Scerdilaidas, 848, 854 sq.; and Antigonus Doson, 851 sq.; letter to Larissa, 532, 853
Philippides of Cephale, 81, 86, 89, 96
— of Paeania, Athens and, 78, 81
Philippopolis (Thronium), 768
Philippus of Medma (or Opus), pupil of Plato, 299
Philistus of Syracuse, 256 sq.; on Gallic Wars, 554
Philo of Byzantium, 307
Philochorus, 260, 712
Philocles, admiral of Demetrius, 92, 191
Philolaus, 292
Philomelium, in Phrygia, 184, 720
Philopoemen, 760 sq.
Philosophy, *see* chap. VII *passim*; Greek, and

science, 7; the New, influence of politics on, 224, 230–248; older schools, 237 sq.; and medicine, 285 sq.
Philoteria, in Palestine, 192, 729
Phintias, 688
Phlius, 219, 750, 757
Phocaeans, found Massilia and Hemeroscopium, 769; end of thalassocracy of W. Mediterranean, 769; trade with Tartessus, 770, 773
Phocis, 51, 81, 83 sq., 89; Gauls and, 102 sqq., 207; Amphictyonic League and, 104; League, 218; Aetolia and, 733
Phoenice, 748, 830
Phoenicia, Phoenicians: cities, and Alexandria, 191; colonization, 191; in Cyprus, 238; Egyptian Greeks in, 190 sq.; and Etruscans, 381; in Greece, 190 sqq.; Hellenized, 190 sq.; traders in Italy, 191; in Laodicean War, 718; trade with Palestine, 135; and Ptolemies, 126, 130, 136, 190 sq.; and Seleucids, 156, 160, 166 n., 167, 173, 175, 190 sqq.
Phoenix of Colophon, 91, 268, 274 sqq.
Phraates II, Rome and, 160
Phrygia, Phrygians, northern Gauls in, 105 sq.; in Egypt, 122; Jewish colonists in, 180
Phrynichus, Attic tragedian, 267
Phthia, wife of Demetrius II, 733, 744
Phylacia, 746
phylakitai, Egyptian, 124 sq.
Phylarchus, 197 n., 211, 214, 258 sq.; on condition of Sparta, 739 sq.
Phyle, 221
Picentes, 604, 609; and Greeks of S. Italy, 583 sq.; in Ager Gallicus, 657; citizenship granted to, 801
Pillars of Hercules, 49
Pindar, 780
Pinnes, 827
Piracy, in the Aegean, 85, 107, 704; at Antium, 586; Illyrian, 824 sqq.
Piraeus (the), 79, 84, 85, 89, 90, 100, 220
Pisa, 805
Pisaurum (Pesaro), 557
Pisidia, 105; Seleucids and, 183
Pisis of Thespiae, 81
Piso, *see* Calpurnius
Pissaeum, 855
Pitane, 105, 710
Placentia (Piacenza), colony of, 816; the Piacenza liver, 384
Plane-tree Pass, 729
Plato, Atlantis of, 780; deified, 13; and Eudoxus, 294; ideal monarchy, 36; and mathematics, 295 sq.; and the new philosophy, 230
Plautii, and consulship, 528, 548
Plautius, C., Proculus (cos. 358), 527, 576
— C., Venox (Venno) (cos. 341), 528, 589 n.

Plautius, C. Venox (censor 312), 531

Plautus, and the New Comedy, adaptations from, 226 and *n*.

plebs, origin of, 420 *sq*.; institutions, origin of, 455; and *patres*, 414; *patres*, struggle with, 450–457, Ch. XVI, causes of, 419 *sq*., 452, 462, 470, position of *plebs* at close of, 552 *sqq*.; aristocracy, new plebeian, 546 *sqq*.; and augurate, 459, 535; and *auxilium*, 448, 456 *sqq*.; and censorship, 528; and citizenship, 528; civic rights of, 422 *sqq*.; and clientship, 421; and colonies, 541 *sq*.; and comitia centuriata, 423; and consulship, 421, 518, 527 *sqq*., 582; and *conubium*, 419, 422, 460, 483, 519; and debt and usury, 475 *sq*., 544 *sq*.; Decemvirs and, 459; and dictatorship, 482, 528; and food-supply, 474 *sqq*., 479, 536 *sq*.; plebeian *gentes*, 418; and *intercessio*, 457; and administration of justice, 457; and ownership of land, 470 *sqq*., 536 *sqq*.; and law code, 458 *sqq*.; marriage forms of, 422; and military service, 472; officers of, *see* aediles, tribunes; plebeian nobles, 546, 581; *plebis concilia*, 451 *sqq*., 456 *sq*.; *plebiscita*, 451, 481 *sqq*., 523, 531, 664, with force of *leges*, 481 *sqq*., valid for all Quirites, 530, 553; and *pontifices*, 545; *plebs* and *populus*, 451 *sq*.; and quaestorship, 523 *sq*.; and *secessio*, 452 *sq*., 460; and *suffragii ius*, 423; and Senate, 449, 553; *transitio ad plebem*, 418, 421, 483, 527; and Valerio-Horatian laws, 480 *sqq*.

Pleistarchea (Heraclea on Latmos), 76

Pleistarchus, brother of Cassander, 76, 78

Pliny, the Elder, 53, 311, 317, 468, 533 *sq*.

Plutarch, 172, 214, 231, 259, 370 *n*., 449, 457, 470; on Demetrius I, 75 *n*.; on kings of Rome, 370 *n*.; on Pyrrhus, 75 *n*., 638 *n*., 644, 648; on Aratus, Agis and Cleomenes, 732 *n*., 743

Pluto, 146

Poetelius, C., Libo Visolus (cos. 360, 346, 326), 527, 545 *sq*., 573

—— —— son of above, 533, 545

Poiessa in Ceos, re-named Arsinoe, 707

Polemon, 203, 235, 238, 251

politeumata, Egyptian, military character of, 122

Polyaenus, on Agathocles, 617 *n*.

Polybius, on Achaean League, 732 *n*.; on War of Allies, 732 *n*.; on Aratus, 756 *sq*.; on first treaty with Carthage, 486, *see* chron. note, 859; on *Gaesati*, 61 *sq*.; on Gallic Wars, 554, 793 *n*.; on Illyrian Wars, 822 *n*., 827; on Peace of Naupactus, 768; on Ptolemies and Palestine, 729; on Ptolemy IV, 727; on First Punic War, 665 *n*., 656; on early Roman chronology, 486; on Roman embassies to Greece, 823; on Saguntum, 790; on battle of Sellasia, 760 *sq*., see chron. note, 863; on Syrian Wars, 699 *n*.; on Truceless War, 803

Polycrates the Argive, 29

Polygnotus, painter, 235

Pomerium, 359 *sq*. and *n*., 362, 400, 448

Pometia, 341, 406, 476, 487 *sq*., 498

Pompeii, 603; decorative painting at, 147; prosperity of, 593

Pompeius, Cn., Magnus (cos. 70), 330

— Sex., Festus, 329

Pompilii, 418

Pomponii (coss. 233, 231), 806

Pomponius (cos. 233), in Sardinia, 805

— Q., 552

— Sextus, jurist, 326 *sq*., 330, 482

Pomptina tribus, 577

Pomptine marshes, 576 *sq*.; annexation of, 578, 580

Pomptinus ager, 537

pontifex, pontifex maximus, 312, 319, 407, 412; functions of, 422, 426 *sqq*.; in private law, 428 *sq*.; *plebs* and, 535

Pontus, 76, 90, 100; the new kingdom of, 104 *sq*.; Seleucus I and, 159, 177

Popillia gens, 418

Popillius, M., Laenas (cos. 359), 527 *sq*., 563, 573, 859

Poplicius, M., Malleolus (cos. 232), 806

Poplifugia, 395, 408

Poplilia tribus, 577, 586, 801

populus, 344 *sq*., 440, 519; comitia centuriata and, 435; sovereignty of, 444 *sq*.; and *plebs*, 451 *sq*.; and *caput*, 458; and *provocatio*, 446 *sq*.

Poseidippus of Pella, epigrammatist, 203, 266, 282, 705

— comic poet, 226

Poseidon, cult of, in Egypt, 145

Posidonia, 584, 594, 640

Posidonius, 58; and Hellenism, 194 *sq*., 299, 319, 594

Postumius, A., Albinus (censor, 234 B.C.). 806

— A., Albus (cos. 496), 489

— A., Tubertus (dictator 431), 502

— L. (cos. 294), 612 *sq*.

— L. (cos. 262), in Sicily, 676

— L., Albinus (cos. 229), 834 *sq*.

— L., Megellus (cos. 305), 552, 615

— M. (cons. trib. 426), 551

— Sp., Albinus (cos. 321), 598

— Sp., Albus, and Decemvirate, 459

Pottery, Celtic, 43 *sqq*.; Greek and Italian influence on, 44; in Central Europe, 44; in N.E. France, 44; in Brittany, 44; in Rhine area, 44; in Neckar, 45; Iberian, 785; Greek, 49; chip-carved, 55; Hallstatt, 59; Lower Rhenish, 67

praefectus annonae, 530
— *urbi*, 424, 436
Praeneste, 339, 350, 488, 501, 510, 518, 591; Bernardini and Barberini tombs at, 382; connection with Caere, 465; Calendar of, 329, 408; commercial revival at, 546; Etruscan, 347; and Volsci, 576 *sq.*
Praetors, 424, 437 *sqq.*, 481, 526 *sq.*; and *imperium*, 442 *sq.*; in Sardinia, 805; in Sicily, 798; *urbanus* and *peregrinus*, 818
Praetuttii, 604, 638
Praxagoras, physician, 285
Prepelaus, general of Lysimachus, 89
Priene, 77, 87 *sq.*, 91, 719; Soteria festival at, 98; Gauls and, 105; and Samos, 260; and Rhodes, 260
Priscian, 350
Privernum, 326 *n.*, 548 *n.*, 589 *n.*, 594, 600
Probus, 363
Proclus, 298 *sq.*
prorogatio imperii, 443, 530 *sq.*, 533
proskynesis, Persian, 15
Provinces, Roman: Corsica and Sardinia, 805; Sicily, 793
provocatio, 377, 445, 447 *sq.*, 455, 459 *sq.*, 535; *plebs* and, 481
Prusias of Bithynia, 726
Prytanis, lawgiver at Megalopolis, 762
Pseudo-Scylax, 537, 557, 584 *sq.*, 780; *periplus* of, 49
Psophis, 766
Ptolemaeus, king of Epirus, 214, 747
— son of Lysimachus, 91, 99, 101, 107, 127, 129, 213, 703, 705 *sq.*; revolt of, against Ptolemy II, 711
— son of Thraseas, 729
Ptolemaieia, vase festival at Delos, 101, 703 *n.*; second, 715; third, 716
Ptolemais, daughter of Ptolemy I, 77, 87
— Athenian tribe, 758
Ptolemaïs, 112, 121 *sq.*, 127, 144; (Acre), 728; (Barce), 713; (Lebedus), 719
Ptolemies (*see also* Egypt, Ptolemaic): 26 *sq.*; and Alexandria, Library and Museum at, 251; and city state, 27; coinage, 141 *sq.*, 176, 713; cult of, official imperial, 17, 114 *sq.*; Egypt, results of policy in, 153 *sq.*; and Hellenism, 115; letters and science, 250; Phoenicia and Palestine, coasts of, 190; power, foundation of, 113 *sq.*; Seleucids, rivalry with, 157; Syrian Wars, policy in, 700
Ptolemy I, Soter, 76 *sq.*, 87, 89, 92, 123, 136; and state cult of Alexander, 17; and the Academy at Alexandria, 251 *sq.*; army and fleet of, 110 *sq.*; and Cyrene, 127; deified, 16, 19, 92; Demetrius of Phalerum and, 114, 297; satrap of Egypt, 110; and Egyptian religion, 19; and Greek and Macedonian immigrants, 111; power of, its philosophic basis,

113 *sq.*; and provinces, 126; founds Ptolemaïs, 112; Seleucus and Lysimachus, coalition with, 85 *sq.*; writings of, 259, 297
— II, Philadelphus, 97, 105, 114, 123, 126, 134, 159, 181, 202, 213, 261; Callimachus' prophecy, 705; and Caria, 129 *n.*; coinage of, 142; court of, 116 *sq.*; and currency, 141; deification of, 17, 19, 101; and Ethiopia, 261; the Fayûm and, 144; festival in honour of Ptolemy I, 101; great festivals, 143; vase festival at Delos, 101; fleet of, 711; kingship, basis of, 202; and Library at Alexandria, 252; as patron of science, 297; sea power of, 101; and Syria, 105; Theocritus and, 278; embassy to Rome, 653, 823; in Asia Minor, 701 *sq.*; possessions at end of First Syrian War, 704; peace with Antigonus, 708, 713; mutiny of mercenaries, 712
— III, Euergetes I, 115, 117, 126, 129; adopted by Arsinoe II, 703; and Achaean League, 750; and Aratus, 222; and Asia Minor, 159; and Callimachus, 275; character of, 726; deified, 749; and Eratosthenes, 262; insurrection under, 151; and mathematics, 297; supports revolt of Alexander son of Craterus, 221
— IV, Philopator, 115, 117, 143; and deification, 17; and cult of Dionysus, 145, 727; insurrections under, 151
— VI, Philometor, 123
— Keraunos, 46, 96 *sqq.*; defeats Antigonus, 99; Gauls and, 101; Lysimachus and, 96 *sq.*; Ptolemy II and, 701; Seleucus and, 98 *sq.*; death of, 101
— the Geographer, 53; and Hipparchus, 310
Publilius, Q., Philo (cos. 339), first plebeian dictator, 482; legislation of, 482 *sq.*; first proconsul, 530, 595; in Campania, 593 *n.*; besieges Neapolis, 595; in Samnite Wars, 601 *sq.*; impeachment of, 547, 602
Punic War, the First, Ch. XXI; causes of, 635, 656, 670 *sqq.*; Sicily, conditions in, 667 *sq.*; Messana occupied, 667; crossing to Sicily, by Rome, 676 *sqq.*; Roman alliance with Hiero, 673 *sqq.*; capture of Agrigentum by Rome, 676 *sq.*, by Carthage, 685; Roman fleets, 678 *sq.*; battle of Mylae, 679; battle of Thermae, 680; battle of Tyndaris, 680; battle of Ecnomus, 681 *sq.*; Regulus in Africa, 681 *sqq.*; capture of Aspis, 682; Regulus offers peace, 683; defeat of Regulus, 684; Roman victory at Hermaean promontory, 684; Roman fleet wrecked, 685, off Palinurus, 686; capture of Panormus, 685; Romans attack Lilybaeum, 687; Roman naval defeat at Drepana, 687; peace negotiations fail,

689; Hamilcar captures Mt Eryx, 691; government loan at Rome, 691; Roman victory at Aegates Islands, 692; peace terms, 692; Roman and Carthaginian strategy compared, 693 *sqq.*; effects of war on Rome, 695 *sqq.*

Puteoli, 175

Pylos, in Messenia, in Illyrian War, 847

Pyrgion, archon at Athens, 321

Pyrrhon the Sceptic, 203, 230

Pyrrhus, king of Epirus, 77, 79, 82 *sqq.*; kingdom of, 83; in Egypt, 77, 83; and Demetrius, 79, 82 *sqq.*; and Lysimachus, 85, 89 *sq.*; and Antigonus Gonatas, 89, 95; treaty with Acarnania, 96; at Athens, 87; raids Macedonia, 85; raids Thessaly, 82, and Corcyra, 95; Ch. xx *passim*; character of, 82 *sq.*, 642 *sq.*; war in Italy, 644 *sqq.*; at Tarentum, 641 *sqq.*, 651; Hannibal on, 642, 644; Pyrrhic victory at Heraclea, 644 *sq.*; peace negotiations, 646 *sqq.*; victory at Asculum, 647; war in Sicily, 648 *sqq.*; Carthage and, 651 *sq.*; defeat at Beneventum, 653; war with Antigonus Gonatas, 213, 646, in Thessaly 213; assaults Sparta, 214, death at Argos, 215

Pythagoras, 377; and mathematics, 290 *sqq.*

Pythagoreans, and science and mathematics, 291 *sq.*, 299 *sq.*

Pytheas of Massilia, 45; his voyage, 50 *n.*, 53 *sq.* and *n.*, 262, 780 *sq.*

Pythian festival in Athens, 84

— Games, Pyrrhus and, 84

Pyxus, 584

Quaestors, 327, 446 *sq.*, 455; and *imperium*, 523; Julius Caesar and, 483; *quaestores—aerarii, parricidii*, 446

Quinctius, Kaeso (son of L. Cincinnatus), 457, 502

— L., Cincinnatus (cos. 460), 501 *sq.*

— T. (cos. 468), 420

— T., Cincinnatus (cons. trib. 388), 566

— T., Flamininus (cos. 198), 205

— T., Poenus (dict. 361), 526, 572

— T., Rocus, 331

— T., Trogus, 447 *n.*

Quintilian's appreciation of Menander, 227

Quirina tribus, 801

Quirinus, and Romulus, 365, 372

Rabbath-Ammon (Philadelphia), 192 *sq.*, 729

Rabuleius, M. (trib. pl. 488), 460

Ramnenses, 409, 429, 431

Raphia, 192; battle of, 171, 729 *sqq.*; effect of, on native Egyptians, 731

Ratumena Porta, 383

Ravenna, 557

Red Sea ports, 133, 173

Regia, the, 313, 320, 407; position of, 372; Numa and, 375 *sq.*

Regifugium, 34, 407 *sq.*

Regillus, Lake, battle of, 487 *sqq.*

Regulus, *see under* Atilius

Religion: Asclepius, 4; astrology, 4; Christianity and Hellenism, 2 *sqq.*; cosmopolitanism in, 5; in Egypt, 6 *sq.*, 19, 113 *sqq.*, 145 *sq.*; *gentes* and, 417; Iranian, 2, 6; Judaism, 2, 6; Macedonian, 4, 197 *sq.*; mystery-cults, 4; Numa and, 374; Oriental, Hellenized, 7; and philosophy, 231; religious syncretism, 5; in early Rome, 425–431; Rome and Etruscan, 383 *sq.*, 387; Zoroastrianism, 6

Remus and Romulus, legend of, 353, 366 *sq.*

rex, hatred of name, 395; primary functions of, 372, 408 *sq.*; and comitia curiata, 412 *sq.*

rex sacrorum, 407 *sq.* and *n.*, 418, 528

Rhamnus, 79

Rhegium, 640; besieged by Dionysius, 321 *sq.*; Agathocles and, 619, 635; Pyrrhus and, 645; Roman garrison at, 643, 650, 656; Campanians in, 664; ally of Rome, 794

Rhianus, 254, 269

Rhine, Middle, Celts and, 43; Lower, Celtic migration from, 60

Rhizon, 827, 835

Rhode, coinage, 46; Hasdrubal and, 810

Rhodes, 23, 31, 99; navy of, 85; Seleucids and, 159, 175; Antigonus Gonatas and, 207; the *Rhodian Sea-Law*, 208; trade centre, 32, 212; Colossus of, 207; and Samos and Priene, 260; government of, 207; supposed 'Treaty of Commerce and Friendship' with Rome, 822; in Second Syrian War, 713; war with Byzantium, 726, and Philip V, 767 *sq.*; in Illyrian War, 847

Rhōmos, 365 *sqq.*

Roads: trade routes in the East, 117; Roman: *see under* Via

Robigalia, 399 *sq.*

Roman federation, *see* Federation

Rome: early history of, sources for, Ch. x; earlier annalists, 312 *sq.*, 316–319, and sources used by, 319 *sq.*; antiquarians, 326; archaeological discovery, 332; chronology, systems of, 321 *sq.*; coinage, 325; Fasti, 313 *sqq.*; foundation, date of, 321; historians, 313 *sqq.*; jurists, 326 *sqq.*; *libri augurales*, 328 *sq.*; magistrates, lists of, 313, 323 *sqq.*; early monuments, 312 *sq.*; triumphs, lists of, 323, 326 *n.*

— institutions, officials, life (*see also separate headings*): aediles, plebeian, 440, 442, 451, 454 *sqq.*, 481, curule, 526 *sq.*; agriculture, 467, 468–473, 479; army, 431 *sq.*,

435, military pay, 512, 537 *sq.*; augurs, 328, 384, 429 *sqq.*, 482, and *plebs*, 459; *auxilium*, 448, 456 *sqq.*; *caput*, 7, 811; censors, 424, 442 *sq.*, 445, 520 *sqq.*, 802, 818 *sq.*; census, 433 *sqq.*, 521; *centuriae*, 409, 431; *clientes*, *patroni*, 420 *sq.*, and *plebs*, 451, 470; coinage, 433, 489, 542, 640, 662 *sq.*; colonies, early, 473 *sq.*; comitia, concilium, 444; comitia calata, 412; comitia centuriata, 412 *sq.*, 432 *sqq.*, 455, 664, reform of, 801 *sqq.*, 806, 817 *sq.*; comitia curiata, 410 *sqq.*; comitia populi tributa, 453, 455; *commercium*, 422, 591 and *n.*; consuls, 396, 437 *sq.*, 443, 520, and Senate, 449, and *plebs*, 525 *sqq.*, and *imperium*, 459, restored after Decemvirate, 460; *conubium*, 419 *sq.*, 422, 460, 483, 519, 525, 591 and *n.*; criminal jurisdiction, 445 *sq.*; culture, Greek influence on, 467; curiae, origin of, 410 *sqq.*, 424, 428, 431, 442, and land tenure, 468 *sqq.*; debt, law of, 476 *sqq.*, 524, and slavery, 479; Decemvirs, 437 *sq.*, 440, 447, 467, 480 *sq.*, and consular power, 438, abdication of, 460; Dictators, 418, 437–445; *equites*, 522; *equitum centuriae*, 409; *fetiales*, 331, 377, 429; fines, 457 *sqq.*, 521, 525; *flamines*, 409, 412, 422, 426; fleets, 678 *sq.*; food-supply, 474 *sqq.*, 479, 535 *sqq.*; *gens*, family and, 415 *sqq.*, religious ties of, 417, plebeian, 418; guilds, 464; *heredium*, 342, 415 *sqq.*, of *bina iugera*, 342, 416, 469; *imperium*, *see under separate heading*: industry and commerce, 464 *sqq.*; *intercessio*, 444, 457, 459, 481; land, land tenure, 468–473; *ager publicus*, 535 *sqq.*; *lustrum*, 410, 453, 521; magistrates, powers and limitations of, 441 *sqq.*; priestly functions of, 425 *sq.*; *mancipium*, 417, 468; *manumissio*, 455, 532; military institutions, 431 *sq.*; monarchy, primitive, 407 *sq.*; *mos maiorum*, 445, 448, 450; *municipium*, 569; *paterfamilias*, 414 *sq.*, 425 *sq.*; *pax deorum*, 425, 428; *populus*, 413, 454, appeal to, 447, sovereignty of, 444 *sq.*; *praefectus urbi*, 436; praetors, 437 *sqq.*, 818; *prorogatio*, 443; *provocatio*, 377, 447 *sq.*, 457, 460, 481; quaestors, 327, 446 *sq.*, 455, 485; *Regifugium*, 394, 407 *sq.*; *rex*, functions of, 408 *sq.*, 412; *rex sacrorum*, 407 *sq.*, 418, 528; religious institutions, 425–431; people, primitive divisions of, 409 *sqq.*; Salii, colleges of, 426; Senate, *see under separate heading*; trade and industry, 464; tribes, three primitive, 409, 411, 'Servian' tribes, number increased, 434 *sq.*, 574, 591, 594, 600; tribunes, military, 431 *sq.*, 437 *sq.*, 519, plebeian, 443 *sq.*, 451 *sq.*; *tributum* (war tax), 522 *sq.*; triumvirs, 442 *n.*, 533

— founding of, Ch. XI: date of, 321; *see also* Latium; site of, 351 *sqq.*; hills, 352, 357 *sq.*; settlements of, 355 *sq.*; Roma Quadrata, 356 *sqq.*; Septimontium, 357 *sqq.*; walls, 360 *sqq.*; *pomerium*, 359 *sq.*, 362, 448; foundation legends, 363–369; Greek legend of origin, 363 *sqq.*; Aeneas, coming of, 363 *sq.*, 697; Romulus and Remus, 365 *sqq.*; Sabine women, the, 368 *sq.*
— kings of, Ch. XII, *see also separate headings*: tradition, value of, 370 *sqq.*; chronology, 371 *sq.*; king-god theories, 372; Sabine settlements, 373 *sq.*; a Latin city, 378; Etruscans in Rome, 378–387; Etruscan influence on, 382 *sqq.*; Rome and Western Mediterranean, 387; monarchy, fall of, 395 *sqq.*; government under later kings, 397 *sqq.*; Etruscan settlements in, 398; spread of authority in regal period, 399 *sqq.*; territory, earliest limits of, 399 *sq.*; wars of kings, 400 *sqq.*; conquest, beginnings of, 402 *sq.*; territory at end of regal period, 399 *sqq.*; and the Latin Leagues, 312, 404 *sqq.*, 487–493
— early Republic: legends of, 324 *sqq.*; successors of kings, 436 *sqq.*; Senate, early Republican, 448 *sqq.*; plebeian institutions, 450–456; *plebs* and *patres*, 456–462; the Twelve Tables, 462 *sqq.*; land tenure, 468 *sqq.*; early colonization, 473 *sq.*; debt, law of, 476 *sqq.*; Valerio-Horatian laws, 480–484; federation, 616, 639, 654, 658 *sqq.*
— Aequi, wars with, 497 *sqq.*, 509, 575; Antigonid pretenders and, 218; Antiochus III and, 155, 172; and Capua, 595; and Carthage: first treaty with, 402, 465, chron. n. 859 *sqq.*, First Punic War, Ch. XXI, policy towards after war, 802 *sqq.*, naval supremacy after war, 829; *see also* Carthage, Punic War, First; and early colonization, 473 *sq.*; drama, Sicilian influence on, 697; and Epicureanism, 232 *sq.*; and Etruria, 378 *sqq.*, war with, 604 *sqq.*, Rome's debt to, 383 *sqq.*; and Falerii, 800; and federation, 639, 654, 658 *sqq.*; *ager Gallicus*, distribution of, 806 *sqq.*; and Gauls: wars with, Ch. XVII, consequences of, 565 *sq.*, 570 *sqq.*, 579, 821, continuous raids of, 570 *sqq.*, recovery after war, 566 *sqq.*; and Greece: 32, 514 *sq.*, first official contact with, 840, embassies to Athens and Corinth, 842 *sq.*, no Hellenic policy, 842, culture, Greek influence on, 467, and Greek letters, 369, and Greeks of Magna Graecia and Sicily, 26, 583 *sq.*, 607, 640 *sqq.*,; and Hellenism, 824; alliance with Hernici, 492 *sq.*, war with, 575 *sq.*, 606 *sq.*; and Illyria, Ch. XXVI, *see also* Illyria;

and Italy: conquest of, Ch. XVIII, 800 *sqq.*, policy in, 815 *sqq.*, N. Italy, 805 *sqq.*, Central, Ch. XVIII; and Latium: war with, 577 *sq.*, 586 *sqq.*, after war, 591 *sqq.*, 594 *sqq.*, Latin Leagues and, 404 *sqq.*, treaties with, 392 *sq.*, 586, *see also* Latium; and Macedonia, 839 *sq.*, 851 *sqq.*; and Neapolis, 595; and Pyrrhus, war with, 644 *sqq.*, *see also* Pyrrhus; and Samnites: treaty with, 580, 585, wars with, 597 *sqq.*; and Sardinia, 804 *sqq.*; and Seleucids and, 155, 190; and Sicily, 476, 793–800; Tarquinii, war with, 574 *sq.*; and Veii, 437, 504–516, *see also* Veii; and Volsci, 497 *sq.*, 576 *sqq.*, *see also* Volsci; and Western Mediterranean, 387

Romulea, 611

Romulus, 313, 364 *sqq.*, 371, 373 *sq.*, 409, 431; the tomb of, 312; Casa Romuli, 344, 356; and Remus, 353, 365, 367 *sq.*; Rhōmos, 365 *sqq.*; and early Senate, 419, 424; and Quirinus, 372; and land, 468

Royal Guards, Egyptian, 117

— Pages, Macedonian, 9, 11, 201

Rubicon, river, 647

Rufinus, *see under* Cornelius

Rufrium, 597

Russia, S., trade with Egypt, 134

Rutuli, 339 *sqq.*; Rutulus populus Ardeatis, 345

Sabatina tribus, 574

Sabazius, cult of, in Thrace, 146; Dionysius, 165, 727

Sabellians, 639, 660

Sabines, 340, 412, 638; origin of, 493 *sq.*; settlement at Rome, 336, 373, 376, 496; penetration gradual, 494 *sqq.*; rape of Sabine women, 368 *sq.*; Romulus and, 409; Tatius and, 424; burial forms of, 496; possible confusion with Samnites, 615; *cives sine suffragio*, 616; receive full franchise from Rome, 658, 801

'Sabines,' 357, 381

Sabratha, 682

sacra insula = Ireland, 51

Saefes, 771

Saepinum, 614

Saguntum, Carthage and, 783; Carthaginian capture of, 790; under Roman protection, 847

Saïte period, 110, 112 (*see* vols. IV and VI)

Salamis, 85, 221

Salii, college of, 426; Collini, 496; Curia of, 564

Sallentini, 533

Salluvii, 556

Salmantica (Salamanca), 789

Salt-pans, Romulus and, 338, 402; and *septem pagi*, 504

Salus, temple of, 316

Samaria, 192; Antiochus and, 729; Ptolemies and, 190

Samnium, Samnites: Pyrrhus and, 646; League, extent of, 585; Lucanians and, 641; *ver sacrum*, 583, 615; *meddix tuticus*, 596; political system of, 596 *sq.*; Latins and, 589; treaties with Rome, 580, 585 *sq.*, 589; warfare, system of, 595; wars with Rome, Ch. XVIII, tradition untrustworthy, 581 *sq.*, 600; alleged first war, 588; Alexander of Epirus and, 594; Rome's policy towards, 594 *sqq.*; Roman military problem and, 595 *sqq.*; Caudium, battle and peace of, 599; Sentinum, battle of, 612 *sq.*; final Roman victory, 613 *sqq.*; possible confusion of 'Samnite' and 'Sabine,' 615

Samos, Samians, 13, 15; Lysimachus and, 91; Ptolemy II and, 98; Antiochus II and, 182; and Rhodes, 260; and Priene, 260; in Second Syrian War, 712; in Laodicean War, 719

Samothrace, Lysimachus and, 92 *sq.*, 99; the Ptolemies and, 126, 128; Ptolemy II and, 712; temples at, 714 *n.*; Winged Victory of, 714

Sandrakottos, ambassador of Seleucus to India, 260

Saon, epitaph, 282 *sq.*

Sapinia tribus, 409

Sarapis, cult of, 5; and Greeks, 17, 145 *sq.*, 727

Sarcophagi, Sidonian, 191

Sardes, 87, 97, 106, 156, 158, 167, 182, 720; Mnesimachus inscription from, 171, 172

Sardinia, Carthage and, 665, 769; in First Punic War, 680; revolt of mercenaries in, 803; a Roman province, 804 *sq.*

Sarsina, Gallic settlement at, 657

Saticula, 542, 601, 607, 660

Satricum, 347; colony, 569, 576, 578, 592; rebellion at, 511, 602; and Gauls, 570

Saturn, island (Berlenga), 771

— temple of, at Rome, 466

Satyrus, 261

Sauadai, Macedonian water-spirits, 198

Scaevola, *see under* Mucius

'Scandza, island of' = Norway, 53

Scaptia tribus, 591

Scepsis, Scepsians, 92 *sq.*

Scerdilaidas, 765, 827, 830, 844; and Demetrius of Pharos, 847; and Philip V, 848, 851 *sq.*; attack on Philip, 854 *sq.*

Scidrus, 584

Science, Greek, 4, 7; and mathematics at Alexandria, Ch. IX *passim*

Scipio, *see under* Cornelius

Scodra (Scutari), 827

Scopas, 763 *sq.*, 766

Scordisci, 102, 536, 747

Sculpture, Delphic, 65 *n.*; Pergamene, 65 *n.*, 251; *see* vol. VIII
Scutari (Scodra), lake of, 827
Scylax of Caryanda, 780
Scylax, Pseudo-, *see* Pseudo-Scylax
Scythopolis (Beisan), 729
secessio, 452 *sq.*, 460, 553
Segéda, 784
Segesta, Agathocles and, 633; Pyrrhus and, 651; and Rome, 676, 679, 794; 'immune,' 799
Segovesus, 60, 63
Seleuceia, in Cilicia, 719
— on the Eulaeus, 167
— by Merom, 192
— in Pieria, 158, 174 *sq.*, 716, 718 *sq.*, 728; Athens and, 185 *sq.*; coinage of, 188; Seleucus II and, 185
— on the Tigris, 12, 25, 93, 121, 158, 717; coinage of, 164, 188; mixed population of, 174, 187 *sq.*
Seleucid Era, 75
Seleucids, and their Empire, Ch. V *passim*; army of, 169 *sqq.*; Asia Minor and, 159, 163, 176–184; Babylonia under, 184 *sqq.*; character of, 155 *sq.*; old Greek cities in, 178 *sq.*, 180 *sqq.*; new coinage, 164 *sq.*, 176; court and central administration, 164 *sq.*; economic policy, 173 *sq.*; Era, 20, 75, 161; fleet, 172; Gauls and, 106, 159; Graeco-Macedonian settlements, 158 *sqq.*, 176; guilds, 191; Hellenism, 115, 160 *sq.*, 189, 194 *sqq.*; imperial cult of, 19 *sq.*; and India, 260 *sq.*; *katoikoi*, 169, 171 *sq.*; kings, cult of, 162 *sqq.*; King's Land, 181; the king's power, 161 *sqq.*; *klerouchoi*, 169; law, 168; and literature, 250 *sq.*; Mesopotamia under, 184 *sqq.*; military colonies, 178 *sqq.*; non-Greek population, 164; Palestine under, 190 *sqq.*; Phoenicia under, 190 *sqq.*; policy of, 157 *sq.*; problem of, 155 *sqq.*; provinces and administration of, 165 *sqq.*; Ptolemies, rivalry with, 157; religion, 163 *sq.*; results of work, 194 *sqq.*; Rome and, 159 *sqq.*; satrapies, administration of, 166 *sq.*; *stathmoi*, 171; *symmachia*, 177 *sq.*; Syria under, 184 *sqq.*; taxation, 167 *sq.*, 192, 194; temple lands, 183; temple states, 193; trade and manufactures, 176; trade routes, 174 *sq.*
Seleucis, Antiochus I and revolt in, 701
Seleucus, son of Antiochus I, 105, 702, 709; coins of, 710
— I, Nicator, 111, 155 *sqq.*, 161, 168, 173 *sqq.*, 178, 184, 187 *sqq.*; deified, 16, 20; Syria and Mesopotamia and, 76, 184; alliance with Demetrius, 77, 93; navy of, 85; coalition with Lysimachus and Ptolemy, 85; capture of Demetrius, 88, 93, 96

— II, Callinicus, 185, 188, 712, 716 *sqq.*, 720, 722
— III, Soter, 723 *sqq.*
— of Seleuceia, astronomer, 195, 302
Selge in Pisidia, 726
Selinus, 633, 651
Sellasia, battle of, 760 *sqq.*; *see also* chron. note, 863 *sq.*
Semo Sancus Dius Fidius, temple of, 393
Sempronius, C., Atratinus (cos. 423), 510, 551 *sq.*
— C., Blaesus (cos. 253), 686
— C., Tuditanus (cos. 129), annalist, 317, 327, 689
— L., Atratinus (cos. 443), 521; *see also* under Gracchus
Sena Gallica, citizen colony at, 638
Senate, Senators, Roman: Council of Elders, 413 *sq.*; *patres*, 413 *sq.*, 419 *sq.*, 423 *sqq.*; Romulus and, 419, 424; formation of, in early Rome, 419; early Republican, 448 *sqq.*; earliest plebeian in, 449; and struggle of the orders, 449; powers of, 450, 807, 818; change in *personnel* of, 546 *sqq.*; and freedmen, 531, 533; *Senatus consultum ultimum*, 524
Senatusconsultum, de Bacchanalibus, 410
Seneca, the elder, 266
— the younger, 236, 239 *sq.*, 256
Senones, 60 *sq.*; in N. Italy, 556; treaty with Rome, 573; defeated by Rome, 638
Sentinum, 607; battle of, 612 *sq.*
Sepias, Cape, 81
Septuagint, the, 148
sepulcretum in Forum, 386
Serfs, and *tribus rusticae*, 435 *n.* 2; in Etruria, 658; Neumann's theory, 435 *n.*
Sergius, L., Fidenas (cos. 437), 508
— M'., 331
Sertorius, 784, 786
Servilius, C., Ahala, 325 *sq.*, 536
— Cn., Caepio (cos. 253), 686
— P., Geminus (cos. 248), 689
— P., Isauricus (cos. 48), 329
— Q., Ahala (cos. 365, 362 and ? 342), 527, 529, 573, 577 *sq.*
— Q., Priscus Structus (cos. 468), 420
— Q., Priscus Structus Fidenas (dict. 435), 508
— Sp., Priscus (censor 378), 542
Servius on the Aeneid, 319
— Tullius, 328, 331, 360, 387 *sqq.*, 391 *sq.*, 398, 419; and comitia centuriata, 423, 431 *sqq.*; and temple of Diana on Aventine, 348, 350, 392; and Latin League, 401; and Mastarna, 390 *sqq.*; reforms of, 434 *sqq.*; Servian Wall, 360, 398, 563, 567
Sestius, P., Capitolinus (cos. 452), 324, 459
Sestos, 719
Setia, colony, 541, 569, 577 *sq.*, 589 *n.*, 591

Seven Hills of Rome, names of the, 425
sex suffragia, 409
Sexi, 770
Sextius, L., Sextinus, first plebeian consul, 524 *sq.*, 526 *sq.*; and *ager publicus*, 538 *sq.*; and debt, 542 *sq.*
Shechem, 19
Siccius, Cn. L., Dentatus, 325
— T., 325
Sicily: under Agathocles, Ch. XIX; and Carthage, Chs. XIX, XXI; civil wars in, 619 *sqq.*, 632 *sqq.*; Greek cities in, alliance of, 617; Hellenization of native Sicels, 617; Pyrrhus in, 649 *sqq.*; Pyrrhus' withdrawal from, 652
— and Rome: after conquest, Ch. XXV; taxation, 793 *sqq.*; tithe, collection of, 794 *sq.*, exemption from, 793 *sq.*; allied and immune cities, 793 *sq.*; legal status of land, 797 *sq.*; Lex Hieronica, 795 *sq.*; Roman administration of, 798 *sqq.*; coinage, 799; Roman drama, influence on, 697
Sicinius, L., 453
— L., Dentatus, 325
— T., 325
Sicyon, 84, 216, 222, 734, 757
Sidicini, 589 *sq.*
Sidon, 76, 78, 92, 190 *sqq.*
Sierra Morena, 778, 789
Signia, 341, 350, 487, 498, 518, 578, 591
Silva Arsia, battle of, 396
— Maesia, 402
Simias of Rhodes, 266, 271, 273
Simonides of Magnesia, 250
Simplicius, commentaries on Aristotle, 238, 299
Sinope, coinage, 90 *sq.*
Sinuessa, 613
Slavery, slaves, 414, 658, 677, 745, 760, 806; Stoics and, 211 *sq.*, 455, 742; in early Rome, 414; Crete and, 211; Phylarchus on, 211; enfranchisement of, in Rome, 531 *sq.*; Philip V on Roman policy, 532; manumission of, tax on, 455; and debtors, 479; freeing of, at Volsinii, 658; importation into Egypt, 135
Smyrna, 92, 93 *n.*; Seleucids and, 171 *n.*, 178, 717, 719 *sq.*
Social War (Greek War of the Allies), 763 *sqq.*
socii navales, 655 *sq.*, 673, 678, 812
Socrates, 237
Sogdiana, 15, 26, 158 *sq.*
soldurii, Iberian, 783
Soli, 716, 719
Solinus, C. Julius, geographer, 322
solliferrea, Celtic, 59
Solon, 381, 433, 459, 461, 477 *sq.*
Solus, revolt from Carthage, 686

Sophists, φύσις, νόμοι, 33; and cosmopolitanism, 225 and *n.*
Sophocles, worship of, at Athens, 16
Sophron, 268; Theocritus and, 279
— Seleucid commander, 719
Sora, 587 *n.*, 602, 606 *sq.*, 659; colony at, 608
Soracte, 337
Soranus, 285
Sosibius of Alexandria, minister of Ptolemy IV, 724, 727 *sq.*; patron of Callimachus, 29, 271, 727
— the younger, 29
Sosiphanes of Syracuse, dramatist, 697
Sosistratus, politician at Syracuse, 618 *sq.*, 622, 635
— tyrant of Acragas, in Ortygia, 651 *sq.*
Sosthenes, general of Lysimachus, 88, 102, 106 *sq.*
Sosthenis, city of the Aenianes, 106
Sostratus of Cnidus, and Egypt, 29, 713 *sq.*
Sotas of Priene, 105
Soteria, festival of, at Delphi, 104, 733; at Priene, 98, 718
Spain, 49; and tin, 50; trade with Egypt, 134; Carthaginians in, Ch. XXIV; natural wealth of, 770; Carthaginian conquest of, 773 *sqq.*; re-conquest of, by Carthage, 781; challenge to Rome, 789 *sq.*; place-names and Hannibal, 794; Carthaginian archaeological finds in, 779, Greek, 779 *sq.*
Sparta, Demetrius and, 79 *sq.*, 84; attacked by Pyrrhus, 214 *sq.*; Antigonus Gonatas and, 216, 220; in Chremonidean War, 706 *sq.*; Aratus and, 734; Agis IV, reforms of, 739 *sqq.*; law and debts, 742 *sq.*; *perioeci*, 743; metics, 743, 753 *sq.*; federalism and, 751 *sq.*; Cleomenes' revolution in, 752 *sqq.*; reform of debts and land, 754 *sq.*; effect on Peloponnese, 755
Spartocus, dynast of the Crimea, 89; Spartocids, 91
Spercheus, river, 102, 104
Spes, temple of, at Rome, 698
Sphaerus, 742, 754
Spoletium, colony at, 801
spolia opima, 316, 507 *sqq.*
Stagirus, 201
stathmoi, in Egypt, 117; in Syria, 171
Stellatina tribus, 574
Stilo, L. Aelius, grammarian, 327
Stilpo, Ptolemy I, and, 297
Stoics, 235 *sqq.*, 238–242; and cosmopolitanism, 37, 225, 240; *ataraxia*, 37; *summum bonum*, 38; *autarkeia*, 38; natural law, 39; individualism, 37 *sqq.*; Rome and, 40; on kingship, 114, 202; science and, 203; and slavery, 211 *sq.*; and Homer, 263; physics, 239; psychology and ethics, 241 *sq.*
Stone Age, in Central Europe, 54

Stone-cist culture: burial rite, 69; peoples of, 69

Strabo, 260; on Alexandria, 143, 252; on Pytheas, 53; on Celts, 72, 74

strategos, in Ptolemaic Egypt, 122 *sqq.*; in Ptolemaic provinces, 126 *sq.*

Strato of Lampsacus, 301; Ptolemy II and, 297

Stratocles, Athens and, 78 *sq.*, 81 *sq.*

Stratonice, daughter of Antiochus II, 718 wife of Demetrius II of Macedon, 77, 715, 722

— wife of Seleucus I, 93 and *n.*, 223

— (Stratoni), 201

Stratoniceia, vase festival at Delos, 715, 862

Stratus, 217

Strombichus, 86

Strymon, river, 827

Stymphalus, 757

Subura, the, 358

Successors, the: and deification, 15; policy of, 36 *sq.*, 78, Ch. III *passim*; position of new kingdoms, 275 B.C., 108, 156; wars of, 117; Graeco-Macedonian armies of, 12, 110 *sq.*; Stoics and Cynics and, 202, 250; literature in transition period of, 250; and geographical discovery, 261

Succusana tribus, 434

Suessa Aurunca, 590, 660; colony at, 602

— Pometia, 390, 497

Suessula, citizenship granted to, 592 *sq.*

Suetonius, 329, 419

suffragii, ius, plebeians and, 423; *see also under* Citizenship

Suidas, 262, 275, 281

Sulpicius, C., Longus (cos. III, 314), victory at Tarracina, 602

— C., Paterculus (cos. 258), 679

— C., Peticus (cos. I, 364), 527, 566, 568, 573

— P., Camerinus, and Decemvirate, 459

— P., Saverrio (cos. 304), 607

— — — (cos. 279), 647

— Ser., Rufus, jurist, 327

Sunium, 221, 707

Suovetaurilia, 344

Susa, 174, 189

Susiana, 158 *sqq.*, 167, 187, 194

Sutrium, 517, 561, 569, 574 *sq.*, 590, 604, 605, 660

Switzerland, Celtic antiquities in, 41; Celts in, 45

Syene, 144

Sympolities, 7 *n.*, 171 *n.*, 210, 735; *see also under* Citizenship

Syncretism, religious, 5 *sqq.*

synedrion, of Hellenic Leagues, 2, 23

Synoecism (*synoikismos*), 81, 91 *sq.*, 180

Syracuse, chap. XIX *passim*; Six Hundred at, 618 *sq.*; revolution in, 619; blockaded by Agathocles, 620, and by Carthaginians, 624 *sqq.*; suzerainty of, over Sicels, 620;

Hiero II of Syracuse, 667 *sqq.*; and Rome, 673 *sqq.*

Syria, *see also* Seleucid Empire, chap. V *passim*; Syrians in Alexandria, 111; Egypt and, 133, 135; Graeco-Macedonian settlements in, 157, 170; Hellenism in, 2; Ptolemies and, 135 *sq.*; revolt against Antiochus, 100; Seleucid policy in, 158 *sqq.*, 164, 184; trade with China, 196; temple lands in, 183; *see also* Palestine

— and Macedonia against Egypt, Ch. XXII; First Syrian War, 699 *sqq.*; and Ptolemy I, 700; invaded by Ptolemy II, 700 *sqq.*; Second Syrian War, 710 *sqq.*; Third (Laodicean) War, 715 *sq.*; War of the Brothers, 720 *sqq.*; Fourth Syrian War, 726 *sqq.*

'Talassio' and Talasius, 369

'Tanist' in Ireland, 407

Tarentum, leader of Italiote cities, 584 *sq.*, 640; Archidamus of Sparta and, 640; Alexander of Epirus and, 640; Agathocles and, 619, 641; Cleonymus and, 634, 640; Pyrrhus and, 642 *sq.*; and Rome, 641 *sqq.*, 655 *sq.*; and Thurii, 642 *sq.*

Tarpeius, 324, 458 and *n.*, 519

Tarquinii, 347, 388 *sqq.*, 515, 604; war with Rome, 574 *sq.*; alliance with Rome, 604 *sq.*

Tarquinii, Etruscan origin of the, 382

Tarquinius, L., Collatinus, 406, 436, 444

— L., Priscus, 60, 387 *sq.*, 398, 409, 419, 424, 431

— L., Superbus, 378, 389 *sq.*, 393 *sqq.*, 403, 436, 497

— Sextus, and Lucretia, 394

Tarracina, colony, 405 *sq.*, 469, 594; (Anxur), 511, 861 *sq.*; battle of, 602

Tarsus, 156

Tartessus, Celts and, 50 *sq.*; Greeks and, 51; Carthage and, 771 *sqq.*; empire of, 770, 772; culture in, 772; trade and industry, 772 *sq.*; art, 772 *sq.*; architecture, 773; literature, 773; conquest of, by Spain, 773 *sqq.*

Taulantini, 826

Taurasia, 610

Taurini, 810

Taurion, general of Philip V, 767, 848

Tauromenium, colonization of, 315; Pyrrhus and, 651; Rome and, 675, 794

Taurus, the, 88, 97, 156

Taxation: of Demetrius, 84; of Gauls, 106; Macedonian, *see* Ch. VI; Ptolemaic, 129 *sqq.*, 136 *sqq.*; *see also* Ch. IV; Seleucid, 178 *sqq.*; *see also* Ch. V; Roman *tributum*, 522; Roman, of Sardinia, 805, of Sicily, 793 *sqq.*

Taxila, 196

Teanum, 600

Tectosages, 45, 104 *sq.*, 721

Tegea, 219, 706, 747, 762

Telamon, battle of, 579, 812 *sq.*

Telegonus, 363

Tellus, victims offered to, 411

Telmessus, in Lycia, 129, 719

Tempe, 81

Temples: of Aphrodite at Pergamum, 721; of Apollo at Delphi, 103; of Artemis at Ephesus, 91; of Atargatis, 93 *n.*; of Didyma, 77; in Egypt, 112, 124; of Juno at Falerii, 801; of Juppiter Latiaris, 348, 364, 405; of Nanaia, 187; triple temple at Orvieto (Juppiter, Juno, Minerva), 383; of Persephone, at Locri, 652; of Salus, 316; Seleucid policy towards, 183; of Zeus Amarios at Aegium, 736

Temples at Rome: of Antoninus and Faustina, 354; of Castor, 455; of the Castores, 466; of Ceres, Liber and Libera, 456, 466, 481; of Diana on the Aventine, 350 *sq.*, 392, 405, 466, 472; of Faunus, 365, 385; of Fides, 698; of Flora, 698 *n.*; of Fortuna Muliebris, 499; of Hercules Musarum, 375; of Honos, 698; of Janus, 698; of Juno Moneta, 320 *sq.*; of Juppiter Capitolinus, 383 *n.*, 385, 436, 464; of Juppiter Feretrius, 316, 507; of Saturn, 446, 466; of Semo Sanctus Dius Fidius, 393; of Spes, 698; of Tempests, 698

Temple-states, 193

Tempsa, 640

Tencteri, Gauls and, 66

Tenos, 763

Ten Tables, code of, 460; *see also* Twelve Tables

Teos, 91

Terence, and New Comedy, 226 and *n.*

Terentilius, C., Harsa, *rogatio* of, 459, 461, 502

Terentius, M., Varro, *see* Varro

Teretina tribus, 610

Terina, restored by Alexander of Epirus, 640

Termessus, 156

Terminus, 400

terramara, *terremaricoli*, 334 *sq.*, 336, 343, 427

Tertullian, 286

tetrapharmakos, the, from Herculaneum, 234

Teucer, house of, 184

Teucheira, re-named Arsinoe, 713

Teuta, 827 *sqq.*, 844; Roman envoys to, 831 *sq.*; treaty with Rome, 835; Antigonus Doson and, 839; and Epirus, 747, 748

Thales, 290

Thapsus, captured by Agathocles, **626**

Tharros, 779

Thasos, 92

Thaulos, god of war, 197 *sq.*

Theadelphia, ruins of, 144

Theaetetus, 294, 300

Thebes, in Boeotia, 10, 30, 82, 84, 87, 748

— in Egypt, 12, 112, 144, 146, 151

— Phthiotic, 81, 211, 767

Themisonium, 105

Theocritus, 114, 143 *sqq.*, 266 *sqq.*, 271 *sqq.*, 277, 668, 704

Theodorus of Cyrene, 293 *sq.*

Theodotus of Aetolia, general of Ptolemy III, 724, 728

Theon of Alexandria, 299, 303 *sq.*

— of Smyrna, 307

Theophrastus, 230, 238; and botany, 288; Ptolemy I and, 297

Theopompus of Chios, 257 *sq.*, 260

Theoxena, wife of Agathocles, 635

Thera, 92, 126, 704, 714

Thermae, 618, 633; battle of, 680

Thermopylae, Gauls at, 102 *sq.*

Thermum, 208, 766 *sq.*, 852; Thermica at, 208

Thesprotians, League with Chaones and Molossi, 83

Thessaliotis, 752, 762

Thessalonica, 198, 200, 213, 412

Thessalonice, wife of Cassander, 79

Thessaly, Demetrius and, 80, 84; Thessalian League, 80, 200; Pyrrhus and, 82, 89 *sq.*; Lysimachus and, 90; Gauls in, 102; Antigonus II and, 107, 200; Assemblies of, 200, and Amphictyonic League, 217; Aetolia and, 748

Theveste, Hanno's expedition to, 666

Thoenon, tyrant of Syracuse, blockaded in Ortygia, 651 *sq.*

Thrace, 82; Celts in, 70; Lysimachus and, 90; Gauls invade, 101; interior lost to Hellenism, 107; in part under the Ptolemies, 126

Thronium re-named Philippopolis, 768

Thule, 53, 262

Thurii, Dionysius I and, 640; and Rome, 641 *sqq.*

Thyateira, 106, 171 *n.*

Tiber, river, 338, 340, 347, 378, 382, 404, 464 *sq.*

Tibur, 338, 341, 355, 404, 488, 500 *sq.*, 577 *sq.*, 591

Tigris, river, 158, 189

Timaeus of Tauromenium, 49, 53, 258 *sq.*, 263, 321 *sq.*, 554, 617 *n.*, 676

Timagenes, 58

Timarchus the Aetolian, captures Samos, 712; tyrant of Miletus, 712

Timoleon, policy of, in Sicily, 617 *sq.*

Timon of Phlius, the 'sillographer,' 203, 230, 252

Timosthenes, admiral of Philadelphus, 261

Timotheus, and Sarapis, 146

Timoxenus, 758 *sq.*, 863

Tin, mines in Cornwall, Brittany, Spain, 50; trade in, by Celts, 50 *sq.*, by Tartessus, 771, by Carthage, 775 *sq.*

Tios, 77, 98, 105

Tiridates (Arsaces II), 720

Titienses, 409, 429

Titus Tatius, 367, 371, 373, 376, 409, 424

Tlepolemus, regent of Egypt, 29 *sq.*

Tobias, Zeno's correspondent, 160, 193

Tolistoagii (Tolistovagi *or* Tolistobogii), 104 *sqq.*, 721

Tolumnius, Lars of Veii, 316, 507 *sq.*

Toparchies, in Egypt, administration of, 123

Totoës, Macedonian god, 197

Tragic Pleiad at Alexandria, 267

Tragyrium, 825

Trajan, 353; Trajan column, 353

Transjordania, 160, 192 *sq.*

Treaties, Roman: Ardea, 503, 521; Capena, 517; Carthage, 402, 405, 436, 465, 491, 580, 586, 607, 669, 692 *sq.*, 788; *Cassianum foedus*, 405, 487, 493, 578; Falerii, 516 *sq.*, 800; Fidenae, 507; Hiero II, 690; Latin Leagues, 312; Latins, 392 *sq.*, 586; Lavinium, 405 *sq.*; Samnites, 580, 593 *n.*; Senones, 573

Trebia, (Trebbia) river, 364; battle of, 645

Trebonius, L., 519

Trerus, river, 339 *sq.*, 465, 492, 493

Triballi, and Alexander, 64

Tribes, Roman: three primitive, 409, 431; and *curia*, 411; *tribus rusticae*, 425, 434, 516; urban, 532; comitia tributa populi, 455; tribus—Aniensis, 610, Arnensis, 574, Clustumina, 435 *n.*, Collina, 434, Esquilina, 434, Falerna, 600, Lemonia, 434, Maecia, 591, Oufentina, 589 *n.*, 594, 600, Palatina, 434, Pomptina, 577, 586, Poplilia, 577, 586, Quirina, 801, Sabatina, 574, Sapinia, 409, Scaptia, 591, Stellatina, 574, Succusana, 434, Teretina, 610, Tromentina, 574, Velina, 801

Tribunes, military, with consular power, 437 *sq.*, 442, 449, 519 *sq.*, 525 *sqq.*; *tribuni celerum*, 432, 436

Tribunes: plebeian, 451, 460, 480; numbers and election of, 443 *sq.*, 453 *sq.*; sacrosanctity of, 454 *sq.*, 481; and *intercessio*, 550; and *auxilium*, 448

Tricca, 752

Trichonis, Lake, 767

Trifanum, battle of, 590

trimarkisia, 73

Triparadeisus, pact of, 161; *see* vol. VI

Triphylia, 766

Tripolis, in Phoenicia, 190

Tritaea, 766; revolt against Antigonus, 99

Triteuta, 827, 844

Triumphs, lists of, 323, 326, 329; right to grant, 519; *see under* Fasti

Triumvirs, 442 *n.*; *t. nocturnus*, 533; *coloniae deducendae*, 533

Troad, the, 159; Seleucids and, 177

Troas, and Ilium, 92

— Alexandria (Antigoneia), 91

Trocmi, 104 *sqq.*

Troezen, Antigonus Gonatas and, 207, 214; and Achaean League, 734, 758

Trogus, Pompeius, 554

Troilum, 614

Tromentina tribus, 574

'Truceless War,' the, 803

Tubero, L. Aelius, annalist, 318, 320; *see also under* Aelius

Tullius, M'., 391

— M., Cicero, *see* Cicero

— Servius, *see* Servius Tullius

Tullus Hostilius, 331, 341, 371; and Alba, 377, 401 *sq.*, 419, 431

Tumuli: in Burgundy, 57; in Lorraine, 57; of Hallstatt period, 59; Haulzy, 60; of La Tène period, 43 *sqq.*, 68; in Alaise-Württemberg, 57; in Bavaria, 57; cemeteries in S.W. France, 59

Tumulus culture, of Bronze Age, 55 *n.*; Lower Rhenish, 56, 59, 67 *sq.*; tumulus peoples, 69; of Bronze Age, 55 *n.*

Tunis, 626 *sq.*

Turdetani, 791 *sq.*

Turris Stratonis, 190

Tusculum, 339, 351, 363, 404, 425, 440, 488 *sq.*, 501, 504, 518, 548; Roman citizenship granted to, 569, 591

Twelve Tables, code of the, 312, 327, 415, 438, 456 *n.*, 534; and *mancipium*, 417; the Decemvirate and, 458 *sqq.*; and Solon's code, 461; and Rome in fifth century, 462–467; and acquisition of property in land by *usus*, 468; and debt, 476; and *provocatio*, 481

Tyche = Chance, 2, 40; the New Comedy and, 226, 229; Stoics and, 236

Tylis, kingdom of, founded by Gauls, 107

Tymphaea, Pyrrhus and, 83, 96

Tyndaris, Hiero II and, 668; battle of, 680; revolt of, 686

Tyre, 76, 78, 92, 190 *sq.*, 728; coinage, 165

Tyrol, Celtic finds in, 62 *sq.*

Tyrrhenian Sea, 837

Tzetzes, on Alexandrian Library, 252

Ulpian, 327, 446

Umbria, Umbrians, 336, 386, 811; in Samnite War, 603; Rome and, 609

Urnfield Culture, 55 *sq.*

Urso, charter of, 430 *n.*

Uruk, 167 *sq.*; cuneiform tablets from, 187 *sq.*; Antiochus Epiphanes and, 188

Usipetes, Gaul and, 66
Utica, 682, 803

Vaccaei, 789
Vadimo, Lake, battle of, 605, 639
Valerio-Horatian Laws, 480 sqq.
Valerius, L., Potitus (cos. 449), 460, 462, 481, 519
— M'., Messalla (cos. 263), 674, 676
— M., Corvus (cos. 348), 567, 587, 859
— M., Maximus (cos. 300), 535
— M., Messalla (cos. 53), 329, 410
— P., Laevinus (cos. 280), 643 sqq.
— P., Publicola (cos. 509), 397, 436, 446 sq., 449, 457, 470, 478
— — — (cons. trib. 377), 578
— Q., Antias, historian, 317, 436, 461
Vallis Murcia, 356, 362
Valona (Aulon), 836
Vardar (Upper Axius), 747
Varia (Vicovaro), 340
Varro, M., Terentius, 322, 329 sqq., 408 sqq., 431 n., 440, 450, 452, 468
Vaxus (Oaxus), 748
Veii, 312, 338, 360, 382, 388, 397, 402 sqq.; Grotta Oscura of, 359; struggle with Rome, 497, 504–509, chronology of, 506 sq., 511 sqq.; siege and fall of, 511–516, 561; ager Veiens, 516; and Gauls, 565
Velabrum, 353
Velia, 614, 640
— at Rome, 353
Velina tribus, 801
Velitrae, 341, 410, 474, 498, 510, 548 n., 570, 576 sq., 592
Velleius Paterculus, 541, 547
Veneti, 556, 589
Venetia, 811
Vennonius, 317, 434 sq.
Venus, worship of, at Lavinium, 348
Venus, C. (Higuer), 771
Venusia, Latin colony at, 639, 646, 660
Vergil, 340, 363, 464, 514, 676; Theocritus and, 281
Verginia, legend of, 460 sq., 481
Verginius, A., 459
Verres, 418, 796
Verrius Flaccus, grammarian, 329, 408, 432
Verrugo, revolt at, 510
ver sacrum, 583, 615
Verulae, 606
Vestal Virgins, 411, 426
Vestini, 585, 598, 604, 609, 661
Vetulonia, 343; and fasces, 384 sq.
Veturii, 600
Veturius, Sp., 460 n.
— T. (cos. 321), in Samnite Wars, 598
— T., Calvinus (cos. 334), 529
Via Aemilia 557, Appia, 401, Campana, 399, Claudia, 400, Labicana, 339, Latina,

339, Laurentina, 400, Salaria, 356, 400, 402, Valeria, 338
Villa Boscoreale fresco, 87, 107
Villanovan culture, 55; in Latium, 335 sqq., 341; in Etruria, 379 sqq.
Vinalia, 343
Virdumarus, 814
Viriathus, 784
Vitellia, Roman colony at, 510
Vitruvius, 307
Volnius, 409
Volsci, 341, 349, 406, 440, 491 sqq., 494, 586; wars with Rome, 497 sqq., 509 sq., 576 sq., 587; and Aequi, 503 sq.
Volsinii (Orvieto), 401, 561, 605, 613; Etruscans of, 397, and Roman federation, 638 sq., 646; slaves freed, 658
Volterra, 381
Voltumnae fanum, Etruscans at, 515
Volumnii, origin of, 604 n.
Volumnius, L. (cos. 308), 606, 611
Vulca of Veii, 385, 388, 394
Vulcan, cult of, at Ostia, 378
Vulci, 394, 397; Etruscans of, and Roman federation, 638 sq., 646

Walls, Roman, 360 sqq., 386, 398, 563, 567

Xandos, Macedonian god, 197
Xanthippus of Phocis, 89
— Spartan mercenary captain, Regulus defeated by, 684
Xenocrates, 235
Xenodicus, 632
Xenoetas, 724
Xenomedes, 271
Xenophanes, 184
Xenophon, 256, 631

Yahweh, 15, 156

Zagros, Mt, 725
Zeirene, Macedonian goddess, 197
Zelea, 184
Zeno, steward of Apollonius, correspondence of, 116, 119, 128, 130, 132, 139, 141, 143, 152 sq., 190, 193
— admiral of Ptolemy I, at Athens, 86
— of Citium, Stoic, 195, 231, 235 sq., 237 sqq.; his ideal wise man, 16; cosmogony of, 37; and individualism, 37; Demochares and, 86; Antigonus Gonatas and, 94 sq., 202; death of, 220 sq.; Republic of, 225; decree for, 221; and Egyptian embassy to Athens, 706; homonoia, 741
— of Elea, 294
Zenodorus, 309
Zenodotus of Ephesus, 253, 266, 274; and Homer, 254
Zephyrion, temple of Arsinoe II at, 705
Zervan-Aion, 7

Zeugma on the Euphrates, 174
Zeus, cult of, in Egypt, 145 *sq.*; Z.
    Amarios, temple of, at Aegium, 736;
    Zeus-Ammon-Yahweh-Ahura Mazda-
    Jupiter, 5; Z. Triphylios, shrine of, at
    Paneia, 265
Zeuxis, 180
Ziaelas of Bithynia, 720 *sq.*

Ziboetes, king of Bithynia, 90, 97, 100; son
    of, 100, 104
Zonaras, Joannes, historian, 314; on Pyr-
    rhus, 638 *n.*; on Rome and Sicily, 793 *n.*
Zone-beaker people, 54 *sqq.*
Zopyrion, 91
Zoroastrianism, in Asia Minor, 6 *sq.*; *see
    also* Ahura-Mazda

INDEX TO MAPS

Maps have their own indexes, and reference is made here only to the number of the map. The alphabetical arrangement ignores the usual prefixes (lake, etc.). Names followed by figures in parentheses are of sites marked on map 1.

	Facing page		Facing page
1. Map to illustrate the coming of the Celts	41	9. The struggle of Egypt against Macedonia and Syria	699
2. The Hellenistic Kingdoms c. 275	75	10. Greece, Macedonia and S. Illyria in 228 B.C.	768
3. Hellenistic Egypt	109	11. Carthaginian possessions in Spain c. 220 B.C.	769
4. Hellenistic Asia	155	12. Map to illustrate Roman colonization	820
5. Rome and her Neighbours in the Fifth Century	333	13. Map to illustrate the extension of Roman citizenship	820
6. Site of Rome	351	14. Illyria	825
7. The Roman conquest of central Italy	581		
8. S. Italy and Sicily	617		

Aachen (16), 1
Aar, R., 1
Abdera, 2, 9, 10, 11
Abila, 4
Abydos, 9
Acarnania, 10
Acerrae, 7
Achaean League, 10
Acrae, 8
Acroceraunium Pr., 10, 14
Acrolissus, 14
Adige, R., 1
Adriatic Sea, 1, 10, 14
Adys (Uthina), 8
Aefulum(ae)?, 5
Aegates I., 8
Aegean Sea, 10
Aegium, 10
Aelana, 3, 4
Aenus, 9
Aequi, 5, 7, 12
Aesernia, 7, 12
Aesis, 12
Aethiopia, 3
Aetna, Mt, 8
Aetolian League, 10
Aezani, 4
Agrigentum (Acragas), 8
Agyrium, 8
Ake, 3, 4
Akkad, 4
Akra Leuke (Alicante), 11
Alaise (32), 1
Alba Fucens, 7, 12
Alba Longa, 5
Aletrium, 7, 13

Alexandria, 2, 3, 4, 9
Alexandria-Antioch, 4
Alexandria (Arbela), 4
Alexandria Troas, 4
Alexandropolis, 4
Algidus, Mt, 5
Alicante, 11
Allifae, 7
Alonis, 11
Alsium, 12
Amanis, R., 2
Amanteia (Plojča), 14
Amastris, 4
Ambracia, 2, 10
Ambracian Gulf, 10, 14
Amiternum, 7
Ampelone (?), 3
Amphipolis, 2, 10
Amphipolis (Thapsacus), 4
Amu Daria, R., 2
Amyzon, 4
Anagnia, 5, 7
Anapus, R., 8
Anas, R. (Guadiana), 11
Ancona, 13
Ancyra, 4, 9
Andernach, 1
Andros, 9, 10
Aniensis tribus, 13
Anio, R., 5
Antemnae, 5
Anthedon, 4
Anthemus, 4
Antigoneia, 10, 14
Antigoneia, Pass of, 14
Antioch, 2, 4, 9

Antioch-Adana, 4
Antioch-Alabanda, 4
Antioch-Edessa (Orrhoë), 4
Antioch-Gerasa, 4
Antioch-Hippos, 4
Antioch-Mallus, 4
Antioch-Nisibis, 4
Antioch-Nysa, 4
Antioch-Tarsus, 4
Antipatreia, 10
Antipatreia (Berat), 14
Anti-Paxos, 14
Antium, 5, 7, 12
Anxur (Tarracina), 5, 7
Aoüs, R. (Voioussa), 10, 14
Apamea, 2, 4, 9
Apamea (Celaenae), 4
Apamea (Myrleia), 4
Apollinopolis, 3
Apollonia, 3, 4, 10, 14
Apollonia-Tripolis, 4
Apollonis, 4
Appia, Via, 7
Apsus, R. (Semeni), 10, 14
Apulia, 7, 12
Aquilonia (Lacedogna), 7
Aquinum, 13
Arabia, 2, 3, 4
Arachosia, 2
Aradus, 2, 4, 9
Aral Sea, 2
Arbela, 4
Arbocala, 11
Ardea, 5, 7, 12
Ardiaei, 14
Arethusa, 4

Argos, 10
Aria, 2, 4
Ariarathea, 4
Aricia, 5
Ariminum, 12
Arius, R., 2
Armenia, 2
Arnensis tribus, 13
Arpi, 7, 13
Arpinum, 7
Arretium, 7
Arsinoe (?), 3, 4
Arsinoe-Cleopatris, 3
Arsinoe (Crocodilopolis), 3
Arsinoe-Ephesus, 4
Arsinoe (Patara), 4
Arsinoe-Teucheira, 3
Artemita, 4
Aryium Pr. (C. Ortegal), 11
Ascalon, 4
Asculum, 13
Ashdod, 4
Aspendus, 9
Aspis (Clupea), 8
Atarneus, 9
Atella, 7
Aternus, R., 7
Athamania, 10
Athens, 2, 10
Atina, 7
Atintania, 10, 14
Atrek, R., 2
Atropatene (Aderbaïjan), 2
Attaleia, 4
Attica, 10
Aufidena, 7
Aulon (Valona), 14
Auriol (20), 1
Aurunci, 7
Avens, R., 5
Aventine, 6
Aventine, Little, 6
Axius, R., 10
Axius, R. (Vardar), 14
Azotus (Ashdod), 4

Baalbek, 4
Babylon, 2, 4
Babylonia, 2, 4
Bactra, 2
Bactria, 2
Baetis, R., 11
Baetocaece, 4
Bagradas, R., 8
Balaneia, 4
Baleares I., 11
Bambyce, 4
Barbanna, R. (Boïanna), 10, 14
Barce, 3
Baria, 11
Bastuli, 11

Beneventum, 12
Berenice, 3
Berenice Epidires, 3
Berenice-Euhesperides, 3
Berenice Hormos (?), 3
Berenice-Pella, 4
Berenice the Golden, 3
Berlenga I., 11
Bernardino, 1
Beroea, 10
Beroea (Haleb), 4
Berru (30), 1
Berytus, 9
Bethshan, 4
Bithynia, 2, 4, 9
Black Sea, 1, 2, 4, 9
Blaundus, 4
Bodenbach (34), 1
Boeotian League, 10
Bologna (40), 1
Borsippa, 4
Bostra, 4
Bovianum Undecimanorum, 7
Bovianum Vetus, 7
Bovillae, 5
Bracciano, L., 5
Bradanus, R., 7
Brattia, 14
Braubach (10), 1
Brenner, 1
Brundisium (Brindisi), 8, 10, 12, 14
Bruttium, 8
Bubastis, 3
Budapest (36), 1
Byblus, 4
Bylazora, 10
Bylliones, 14
Byllis, 14
Byzantium, 2, 4, 9

Cabul, 2
Cabul, R., 2
Cadi, 4
Caelian, 6
Caere, 5, 7
Caïcus, R., 9
Calatia, 7
Cales, 7, 12
Calliope, 4
Calycadnus, R., 9
Calynda, 4
Camarina, 8
Camerinum, 7, 13
Campania, 5, 7
Campus Martius, 6
Candahar, 2
Canopus, 3
Canusium, 13
Capena, 5

Caphyae, 10
Capitoline, 6
Cappadocia, 2, 4, 9
Capua, 7
Caranis, 3
Carchemish, 4
Cardia, 4
Caria, 2, 4, 9
Carmania, 2, 4
Carpetani, 11
Carsioli, 5, 7, 12
Carsulae, 7
Carthage, 8
Carthage, New (Mastia), 11
Carthaginian Empire (in Spain), 11
Carystus, 10
Casinum, 5
Caspian Sea, 2, 4
Cassandreia, 9, 10
Cassiope, 14
Castrum Novum, 12
Castulo, 11
Catana, 8
Cataract, first, 3
Cataract, second, 3
Caudium, 7
Caulonia, 8
Caunus, 2, 4, 9
Cavo, Mte, 5
Celaenae, 4
Celtiberi, 11
Celtici, 11
Cempsicum Pr. (Espichel, C.), 11
Cenchreae, 10
Centuripa, 8
Ceos, 9
Cephallenia, 10
Cephaloedium, 8
Cerasus, 4
Cerfennia, 7
Cermalus, 6
Cevennes, Mts, 1
Chaeronea, 10
Chala, 4
Chalcedon, 2
Chalcis, 4, 10
Chaldaea, 2, 4
Chaonia, 4, 10, 14
Charrae (Harran), 4
Chios, 9
Cibyra, 4, 9
Cilicia, 2, 4, 9
Cimini, Mti, 5, 7
Circeii, 5, 7, 12
Circello, C., 5
Circus Maximus, 6
Cisauna, 7
Cispius, 6
Cius, 2

Clazomenae, 9
Cleonae, 10
Cleopatra (?), 3
Clupea (Aspis), 8
Clusium, 7
Clustumina tribus, 13
Cnidus, 4, 9
Coele-Syria, 2, 3, 9
Col di Tenda, 1
Collatia, 5
Cologne (14), 1
Colophon, 9
Cominium (?), 7
Cominium Ocritum, 7
Commagene, 2, 4
Coptos, 3
Cora, 5, 13
Corbilo (23?), 1
Corcyra, 10, 14
Corcyra Nigra (Curzola), 14
Corduba, 11
Corfinium, 13
Corinth, 10
Corniculani, Mti, 5
Cortona, 7
Cos, 9
Cosa, 12
Cosentia, 8
Cremera, R., 5
Crete, 2, 9
Crimea, 2
Crocodilopolis, 3
Croton, 8
Crustumerium, 5
Ctesiphon, 4
Cumae, 7
Curia Hostilia, 6
Cutha, 4
Cyme, 9
Cynaetha, 10
Cynetes, 11
Cyprus, 2, 4, 9
Cypsela, 9
Cyrenaica, 3
Cyrene, 2, 3
Cyrrhestice, 2
Cyrrhus, 4
Cyrus, R., 4
Cyzicus, 2, 4, 9

Dalmatae, 14
Damascus, 2, 3, 4, 9
Danube, R., 1, 9
Dardania, 2, 10, 14
Dassaratae, 14
Dauni, 7
Dedan, 3
Delos, 9, 10
Delphi, 2, 10
Demetrias, 2, 10
Demetrias (?), 4

Dinaric Alps, 1
Diomedis Pr., 14
Dionysopolis, 4
Dium, 4, 10
Diz, R., 2
Docimeum, 4
Dodona, 10, 14
Dora, 4, 9
Dorylaeum, 4
Doubs, R., 1
Doura, 4
Doura-Europus, 2, 4
Douro, R., 11
Drangiana, 2, 4
Drave, R., 1
Drepana, 8
Drilo, R. (Drin), 10, 14
Drinus, R. (Drina), 14
Duisburg (15), 1
du Raz, Pt, 1
Dyme, 10
Dyrrhachium s. Epidamnus
    (Durazzo), 10, 14

Ebro, R., 11
Ebusus, 11
Ecbatana, 2, 4
Echetla, 8
Ecnomus, C., 8
Edessa, 2, 10
Egypt, 2, 4, 9
Egyptian Empire, 2
Eifel, 1
Elaea, 4, 9
Elbe, R., 1
Elephantine, 3
Eleutherus, R., 9
Elis, 10
Emesa, 4
Emporiae, 1, 11
Ems, R., 1
Enna, 8
Eordaicus, R. ?(Devol), 14
Epetium, 14
Ephesus, 9
Epidamnus (Dyrrhachium),
    10, 14
Epidaurus, 10
Epiphaneia (Ecbatana), 4
Epiphaneia (Hamath), 4
Epirus, 2, 10, 14
Eretria, 10
Eretum, 5, 7
Erythrae, 4, 9
Eryx, Mt, 8
Espichel, C. (Cempsicum
    Pr.), 11
Esquiline, 6
Este (39), 1
Etruria, 7, 12
Etrusci, 13

Euboea, 10
Eumeneia, 4
Eupatoria, 4
Euphrates, R., 2, 3, 4
Europus (Carchemish), 4
Europus (Rhagae), 4
Eurydiceia-Smyrna, 4
Eusebeia-Mazaca, 4
Eusebeia-Tyana, 4
Eygenbilsen (17), 1

Fabrateria Vetus, 7
Fagutal, 6
Falerii, 5, 7
Falerna tribus, 13
Fayûm, 3
Ferentinum, 5, 13
Ficana, 5
Ficulea, 5
Fidenae, 5
Firmum, 12
Forentum, 7
Formiae, 7
Forum Boarium, 6
Forum Romanum, 6
Frascati, 5
Fregellae, 7, 12
Fregenae, 12
Frentani, 7, 12
Frusino, 7
Fucine Lake, 5
Fundi, 7

Gabae (?), 4
Gabii, 5
Gadara, 3, 4, 9
Gades, 11
Galaesus, R., 8
Galatia, 2, 4, 9
Gamala (?), 4
Garganus, Pr., 7
Gata, C., 11
Gauls, 7, 12
Gauls of Tylis, 2, 9
Gaza, 2, 3, 4, 9
Gedrosia, 2
Gela, 8
Genèvre, Mt, 1
Genoa, 1
Genusus, R. (Scoumbi), 10,
    14
Gerrha, 4
Gerrhaeans, 4
Gibraltar, Straits of, 11
Glastonbury (26), 1
Gomphi, 10
Gonni, 10
Gorge-Meillet, La (29), 1
Grumentum, 8
Guadalquivir, R. (Baetis),
    11

Guadarrama, Sierra de, 11
Guadiana, R. (Anas), 11
Guadiaro, R., 11
Gythium, 10

Hadranum, 8
Hadria, 10, 12
Hadrumetum, 8
Hagenau (3), 1
Halaesa, 8
Haleb, 4
Halicarnassus, 4, 9
Halicyae, 8
Halle (35), 1
Hallstatt (2), 1
Halycus, R., 8
Halys, R., 2, 4, 9
Hamath, 4
Hannibalis, Portus, 11
Harran, 4
Harz, Mt, 1
Haulzy (27), 1
Hausrück, Mts, 1
Hecatompylos, 4
Helicranum (?), 14
Heliopolis, 3
Helmund, R., 2
Helorum, 8
Hemeroscopium, 11
Heraclea, 2, 4, 8, 9, 10
Heraclea-Achaia (?), 4
Heracleopolis, 3
Heraea, 10
Herat, 2
Herbessus, 8
Herculaneum, 7
Heri Rud, R. (Arius), 2
Hermaeum Pr., 8
Hermione, 10
Hermupolis, 3
Hernici, 5, 7, 12
Heroopolis, 9
Hiberus, R. (Rio Tinto), 11
Hierapolis, 4
Hierapolis (Bambyce), 4
Hieropolis-Castabala, 4
Higuer, C. (Venus Pr.), 11
Hingol, R. (Tomerus), 2
Hipponium, 8
Histiaea (Oreus), 10
Hyblaea, 8
Hydrus, 10
Hydrus (Otranto), 14
Hyrcania, 2
Hyrcanis, 4

Iathrippa, 3
Ichnae, 4
Ida, Mt, 9
Ilici, 11
Ilium, 4

Illyria, 10
Indian Ocean, 2, 4
Indus, R., 2
Inn, R., 1
Insula Tiberina, 6
Interamna (Larinas), 7, 12
Interamna Nahars, 7, 13
Ionian Sea, 10, 14
Issa (Lissa), 14
Italy, 10
Itanus, 9

Janiculum, 6
Jaxartes, R. (Syr Daria), 2
Jerusalem, 4, 9
Joppa, 4
Jordan, R., 9
Jucar, R., 11
Julier, 1
Jura, Mts, 1

Karna, 3
Katabani, 3
Kleiner Gleichberg (33), 1
Kodza, 1
Kom-Ombo, 3

Labeates, L. (Scutari), 10, 14
Labici, 5
Lacedogna, 7
Lacinium Pr., 8
Laconia, 10
Lamia, 10
Land's End, 1
Laodicea, 4, 9
Laodicea-Berytus, 4
Laodicea the Burnt, 4
Larissa, 4, 10
Larissa (Sizara), 4
La Tène (1), 1
Latium, 7
Latopolis, 3
Lautulae, 7
Lavinium, 5
Lebanon, Mt, 9
Lebedus, 9
Lemnos, 10
Leontini, 8
Lepini, Mti, 5
Leptis, 8
Lesbos, 9
Leucas, 10
Libba, 4
Libya, 3
Lihyanites, 3
Lilybaeum, 8
Limnaea, 10
Lipara, 8
Liparaean I., 8
Lippe, R., 1
Liris, R., 5, 7

Lissus (Alessio), 10, 14
Locri, 8
Loire, R., 1
Longanus, R., 8
Lucania, 7, 8, 12
Luceria, 7, 12
Lusitani, 11
Lychnidus, 14
Lychnidus, L. (Ochrida), 10, 14
Lycia, 2, 4, 9
Lycopolis, 3
Lydia, 2, 4, 9
Lysias, 4
Lysimacheia, 2, 4, 9

Maas, R., 1
Macedonia, 2, 9, 10, 14
Macedonopolis (?), 4
Maeander, R., 9
Maecia tribus, 13
Maenace, 11
Magnesia, 4, 9, 10
Mago, 11
Main, R., 1
Mainz (8), 1
Malaca, 11
Malakastra, 14
Mallus, 9
Mantinea, 10
Marathus, 9
Margus, R. (Morava), 14
Mariaba, 3
Marino, 5
Marisa, 4
Marne, R., 1
Maronea, 9
Maros, R., 1
Marrucini, 7, 12
Marsi, 7, 12
Marsyas Valley, 9
Massilia, 1, 11
Mastia (New Carthage), 11
Mastieni, 11
Mauryan Empire, 2
Medeon, 10
Media, 2, 4
Mediterranean Sea, 1, 2, 3, 4, 9
Megalopolis, 10
Megara, 8, 10
Mehren (12), 1
Melita I., 8
Melitaea, 10
Melite, 14
Memphis, 2, 3, 9
Mendes, 3
Meroe, 3
Mesopotamia, 2, 4
Messana, 8
Messene, 10

Messenia, 10
Metapontum, 7, 8, 13
Methana, 10
Methone (?), 4
Milan, 1
Miletus, 2, 4, 9
Minab, R. (Amanis), 2
Minæans, 3
Minturnae, 7, 12
Montefortino (41), 1
Monte Mario, 6
Monte Verde, 6
Montfercaut (31), 1
Morena, Sierra, 11
Morgantia, 8
Mosel, R., 1
Mulde, R., 1
Munkacz (37), 1
Murgantia, 7
Murghab, R., 2
Muzhakhia, 14
Mylae, 8
Myndus, 9
Myos Hormos, 3
Myrina, 9
Myrleia, 4
Mysia, 4
Mytistratus, 8

Nabatæans, 3, 4
Nacrasa, 4
Nao, C., 11
Nar, R., 7
Narenta, R., 1
Narnia, 7, 12
Naro, R. (Narenta), 14
Naucratis, 3
Naupactus, 10
Neapolis, 4, 7, 13
Neckar, R., 1
Neetum, 8
Nemi, L. di, 5
Nepete, 5, 7, 12
Nequinum (Narnia), 7
Nerulum, 8
Nestus, R., 10
Nicatoris (?), 4
Nicea, 4
Nicephorium, 4
Nicomedia, 4
Nicopolis, 4
Nile, R., 2, 3, 4
Nippur, 4
Nisibis, 2
Nola, 7, 13
Nomentum, 5
Norba, 5, 7, 12
North Sea, 1
Nuceria, 7
Numantia, 11
Numicus, R., 5

Nymphaeum Pr., 14

Ochrida, L. (Lychnidus), 14
Ocriculum, 7
Oder, R., 1
Odilienberg (18), 1
Oeniadae, 10
Olba, 4
Olcades, 11
Onchesmus (Santi Quaranta), 14
Ophiussa Pr. (Roca, C.), 11
Opis, 4
Oppius, 6
Opus, 10
Orchoi (Uruk), 4
Orchomenus, 10
Oretani, 11
Oretum, 11
Oricus, 14
Orontes, R., 4, 9
Oropus, 10
Orrhoë, 4
Orte, 5
Ortegal, C. (Aryium Pr.), 11
Orthosia, 4
Ostia, 5, 7, 12
Otranto, Straits of, 14
Ouessant I., 1
Oufentina tribus, 13
Oxus, R. (Amu Daria), 2, 4
Oxyrhynchus, 3

Pachynus, C., 8
Paeligni, 7, 12
Paeonia, 2, 10
Paestum, 7, 12
Palatine, 6
Pale, 10
Palestine, 2, 3, 9
Palinurus, C., 8
Palmyra, 4
Palos, C., 11
Pamphylia, 4, 9
Panormus, 8
Pantano secco, 5
Paphlagonia, 2, 4
Paraetonium, 3
Parapotamia, 2, 4
Parauaea, 14
Parthia, 2, 4
Parthini, 10, 14
Pasitigris, R., 2
Passaron, 10
Patara, 4, 9
Patrae, 10
Paxos, 10, 14
Pedum, 5, 7
Pella, 2, 10
Pellene, 10
Peltae, 4

Peltuinum, 7
Pelusium, 3, 4, 9
Pergamum, 2, 4, 9
Persepolis, 2, 4
Persian Gulf, 2, 4
Persis, 2, 4
Perusia, 7
Pessinus, 4
Petelia, 8
Petra, 2, 3, 4, 8, 9
Phalanna, 10
Pharae, 10
Pharnacia (Cerasus), 4
Pharos (Lesina), 14
Pharsalus, 10
Phaselis, 9
Phasis, 4
Phigalea, 10
Phila, 10
Philadelphia, 3, 4, 9
Philadelphia (Rabbath-Ammon), 3, 4
Philae, 3
Philetaireia, 4
Philomelium, 4, 9
Philometoris (?), 3
Philotera (?), 3
Philoteria, 4
Philoteris, 3
Phintias, 8
Phlius, 10
Phocaea, 9
Phocis, 10
Phoenice, 10, 14
Phoenicia, 9
Phra, 4
Phrygia, 2, 4, 9
Picenum, 7, 12
Pincian, 6
Pinna, 7
Pisidia, 2, 4, 9
Pitane, 9
Pithom-Heroopolis, 3
Pleistarcheia-Heraclea, 4
Plouhinec (24), 1
Po, R., 1
Poimanenum, 4
Polytimetus, R., 2
Pometia (?), 5
Pompeii, 7
Pomptina tribus, 13
Pomptine Marshes, 5
Pontia (313), 12
Pontiae I., 7
Pontus, 2, 4, 9
Poplilia tribus, 13
Portus Hannibalis, 11
Posidonia (Paestum), 7, 12
Praeneste, 5, 7, 13
Praetuttii, 7, 12
Presba, L. of, 14

Priene, 9
Privernum, 7
Prophthasia (?), 4
Prusa, 4
Prusias-Cierus, 4
Prusias-Cius, 4
Psophis, 10
Ptolemaïs, 3, 4, 9
Ptolemaïs (Ake), 3
Ptolemaïs (Akз), 4
Ptolemaïs Epitheras, 3
Ptolemaïs Hormos, 3
Ptolemaïs-Lebedus, 4
Pulcrum Pr., 8
Pydna, 10
Pylos, 10
Pyrenees, 11

Quirina tribus, 13
Quirinal, 6

Rabbath-Ammon, 3, 4
Raphia, 3, 4, 9
Rastatt (4), 1
Reate, 5, 7
Red Sea, 2, 3, 4
Regia, 6
Regillus, L., 5
Rhagae, 4
Rhegium, 8
Rhine, R., 1
Rhinocolura, 3
Rhizon (Risano), 10, 14
Rhizonic Gulf (Bocche di Cattaro), 10, 14
Rhode (21), 1, 11
Rhodes, 2, 4, 9
Rhône, R., 1
Roca, C. (Ophiussa Pr.), 11
Roman Protectorate in Illyria, 10
Rome, 5, 7, 12
Romulea, 7
Rosas, Gulf of, 11
Rufrium, 7

Saale, R., 1
Sabæans, 3
Sabatina tribus, 13
Sabini, 7, 12
Sacrum, Pr., 11
Saepinum, 7
Sagrus, R., 7
Saguntum, 11
St Bernard, Gt, 1
St Bernard, Lit., 1
St Gotthard, 1
St Mathieu, Pt, 1
Saint-Pol-de-Léon (25), 1
Sais, 3

Salamantica (Salamanca), 11
Salamis, 4
Samaria, 4, 9
Samnites, 13
Samnium, 7, 12
Samos, 2, 9
Samosata, 4
Samothrace, 9
Sangarius, R., 2
Saône, R., 1
Sardes, 2, 4, 9
Sason I., 14
Saticula, 7, 12
Satricum, 5, 7, 12
Save, R., 1
Scaptia tribus, 13
Scardus, Mons, 14
Scepsis, 4
Scodra (Scutari), 10, 14
Scythopolis (Bethshan), 4, 9
Segesta, 8
Seine, R., 1
Seleuceia-Abila, 4
Seleuceia in Cilicia, 4, 9
Seleuceia the Iron, 4
Seleuceia-Mopsuestia, 4
Seleuceia (Opis), 4
Seleuceia in Pieria, 4, 9
Seleuceia (Susa), 4
Seleuceia (on the Tigris), 2, 3, 4
Seleuceia-Tralles, 4
Seleuceia Zeugma, 4
Seleucid Empire, 2
Seleucid Syria, 2
Selge, 4, 9
Selinuntiae, 8
Selinus, 8
Sellasia, 10
Sena Gallica, 12
Senones, 7
Sentinum, 7
Sepulcretum at Rome, 6
Sestos, 9
Setia, 7, 12
Sexi, 11
Sicyon, 10
Sidicini, 7
Sidon, 4, 9
Siebengebirge, 1
Sieg, R., 1
Signia, 5, 7, 12
Silarus, R., 7
Silivas (38), 1
Silva Arsia (?), 5
Silva Maesia (?) 5
Singara, 4
Sinope, 2, 4
Sinuessa, 7, 12
Sippar, 4
Sizara, 4

Smyrna, 9
Sogdiana, 2
Soli, 9
Solus, 8
Somme-Bionne (28), 1
Sora, 7, 12
Soracte, Mt, 5
Soteira, 4
Sparta, 2, 10
Splügen, 1
Spoletium, 12
Stellatina tribus, 13
Stratonicea, 4
Stratonis Turris, 4
Stratus, 10
Strymon, R., 10
Stuttgart (5), 1
Stymphalus, 10
Subura, 6
Suessa, 7, 12
Suessula, 7
Suez, Gulf of, 9
Susa, 2, 4
Susiana, 2, 4
Sutrium, 5, 7, 12
Syene, 3
Synnada, 4
Syracuse, 8
Syrian Desert, 3, 4

Tagus, R., 11
Tarentum, 7, 8, 10, 13, 14
Tarentum, Gulf of, 8
Tarquinii, 5, 7
Tarracina (Anxur), 5, 7, 12
Tarraco, 11
Tarsus, 2, 9
Tartessus, 11
Taunus, Mt, 1
Taurasia, 7
Tauromenium, 8
Tavium, 4
Teanum, 7
Teanum Apulum, 13
Tegea, 10
Teima, 3
Telmessus, 4, 9
Tentyra, 3
Teos, 9
Teretina tribus, 13
Termessus, 4
Teutoburger Wald, 1
Thapsacus, 4
Thapsus, 8
Thasos, 10
Theadelphia, 3
Thebes, 3, 10
Themisonium, 4
Thera, 9
Thermae, 8
Thermae (Selinuntiae), 8

Thermopylae, 10
Thermum, 10
Thessalonica, 9, 10
Thessaly, 2
Thrace, 2, 9, 10
Thronium, 10
Thurii, 8
Thüringer Wald, 1
Thyateira, 4, 9
Tiber, R., 5, 6, 7
Tibur, 5, 7, 13
Ticino, R., 1
Tigris, R., 2, 4
Tinto, Rio (Hiberus), 11
Tios, 2, 4
Tisza, R., 1
Toletum (Toledo), 11
Tomarus, Mons, 14
Tomeros, R. (Hingol), 2
Torto, R. (Numicus), 5
Tragyrium (Trau), 14
Trapezus, 2
Trerus, R., 5, 7
Trèves (13), 1
Tricca, 10

Tripolis, 4
Tritaea, 10
Troezen, 10
Trogodyte Coast, 3
Tromentina tribus, 13
Tunis, 8
Turin, 1
Tusculum, 5, 7
Tyndaris, 8
Tyre, 2, 3, 4, 9

Ulm (6), 1
Umbria, 7, 12
Uruk, 4
Uthina (Adys), 8
Utica, 8
Uzboi Channel, 2

Vaccaei, 11
Vallis Murcia, 6
Valona (Aulon), 14
Van, L., 2
Vardar, R. (Axius), 14
Varia, 5
Vaticanus, Mons, 6

Veii, 5
Velabrum, 6
Velia, 6
Velia (Elea), 7
Velina tribus, 13
Velitrae, 5, 7, 12
Venus Pr. (C. Higuer), 11
Venusia, 7, 12
Verona, 1
Vestini, 7, 12
Vesuvius, Mt, 7
Vettones, 11
Viminal, 6
Volsci, 5, 7, 12
Volsinii, 7
Volturnus, R., 5, 7
Vulci, 5

Waldalgesheim (9), 1
Weser, R., 1
Worms (7), 1

Zacynthus, 10
Zeugma, 2

INDEX OF PASSAGES REFERRED TO

Aelius Gallus

ap. Fest. 424 L.   428

Aeneas Tacticus

XVI, 5–8   735 *n.*

Alexander of Aetolia

ap. Anth. Pal. VII, 709   743 *n.*

Ammianus Marcellinus

XV, 9, 4   58
XV, 9–12   71 *n.*

Appian

Bas. 1   340 *n.*
Bell. Civ. 1, 8   538
   1, 54   545 *n.*
Bell. Samn. 7   588 *n.*, 641
Celt. 1, 2   64
Ill. 7–8   822 *n.*
Ital. 8   513 *n.*
  9   542
Sic. 1–2   665 *n.*
Syr. 61   161
  62   166 *n.*

Aristotle

Ath. Pol. II, 2   469 *n.*
Eud. Eth. III, 1   58 *n.*
Nic. Eth. III, 9, 7   58 *n.*
Pol. II, 11   666
  III, 9, 1280 *a*   36, 777
  III, 13, 1284 *a*   13 *n.*

Arius

ap. Euseb. *Praep. Ev.* XV,
  xv, 3   240

Arrian

Anab. I, 4, 6   64 *n.*
Dissertation, II, xi, 1   230 *n.*
Ind. 30   262

Asconius

ed. Clark, p. 40, ll. 16 *sq.*
               401 *n.*
    p. 58   447
in Cornelianam, p. 76   453 *n.*
in Milonianam, p. 47   457 *n.*

Asconius, pseudo-

in Div. in Caecil.   522 *n.*

Athenaeus

I, 22 D   252
IV, 184 B   250
XIII, 597 B   274

Athenaeus (mech.)

ap. Vitruvium, X, 13   775

Aulus Gellius

II, 23, 5 *sqq.*   227
V, 19   428
X, 15, 3   344 *n.*
XIII, 16   410
XIV, 7, 8   330
XV, 27   451
XVII, 2, 10   463 *n.*
XX, 1, 45–52   479 *n.*

Avienus

Ora Maritima, ll. 96–8   51
l. 108   51
l. 109   51
l. 112   52
l. 113 *sq.*   51
ll. 114 *sqq.*   51
ll. 130 *sqq.*   51, 52
l. 360   778 *n.*
ll. 380 *sqq.*, 406 *sq.*   776

Caesar

B.G. I, i   56
  V, 12   50 *n.*

Callimachus

Ep. IX [W.-M.]   283
  XIX [W.-M.]   282
Hecale   272
Hymn to Apollo, 1 *sqq.*   269

Cassius Hemina

frag. 17 P.   470 *n.*

Cato

ap. Fest. p. 268 L.   430 *n.*
de agri cult., ad init.
       477 *n.*, 545 and *n.*
Orig. frag. 18 P.   335
  22 P.   439
  58 P. 345 *n.*, 346 *n.*,
        350, 487 *n.*
  62 P.   406 *n.*
  77 P.   319 *n.*, 475 *n.*
  84 P.   860 *n.*
  95 *e* P.   539 *n.*

Celsus

pref.   286 *n.*

Censorinus

de die nat. 20, 2   375 *n.*
  23, 8   463 *n.*

Chrysippus

ap. Plutarch. *Moral.*
  1044 C *sqq.*   240 *n.*
  1053 F   239

Cicero

Acad. I, 45   237
  II, 77   237
ad Att. IV, 18, 2   412 *n.*
  VI, 1, 8   534
  IX, 9   329
ad Brut. I, 5, 4   413
ad fam. IX, 21   418
Brutus, 16, 62   323 *sq.*
  19, 75   326
de domo sua 14, 38   414, 483
  49, 127   552
de fin. I, 19   245
  I, 30   246
  I, 42–53   248
  I, 60   232 *n.*
  III, 4   231 *n.*
  III, 10   238
  III, 16–22   235 *n.*
  III, 22   242
  III, 50   242
  III, 63 *sq.*   240
  IV, 56   242
de leg. agr. II, 7, 17   444
de leg. I, 2, 6   319
  II, 12, 31   430 *n.*, 451
  II, 22, 55   418
  II, 22, 56   328, 417
  II, 23, 59   327, 463 *n.*
  II, 25, 64   461
  III, 3, 6   448
  III, 3, 8   408 *n.*, 442
  III, 4, 11   447
  III, 20, 48   328
de nat. deor. I, 15, 38   16 *n.*
  I, 16   238
  I, 44, 122   431
  I, 69   245
  II, 13–22   240 *n.*
de off. 31, 112   552 *n.*
de Orat. I, 39, 176   417 *sq.*
  I, 57, 245   478 *n.*
  II, 12, 52   319
de Rep. I, 40, 63   440
  II, 8, 14   409

Cicero

de Rep. II, 9, 16	421, 468 n.
II, 13, 25	413 n.
II, 14, 26	417, 468 n.
II, 17, 31	413 n.
II, 18	321
II, 20, 36	431
II, 31, 54	447
II, 34, 59	478 n.
II, 35, 60	446, 521
II, 36, 61 sqq.	461
II, 52	321 n.
de senect. 16, 56	326
in Pison. 68 sqq.	232 n.
in Verr. I, 45, 115	418
V, 14, 36	551
Phil. IX, 2, 4	508 n.
pro Arch. 5, 9	328
pro Balbo, 23, 53	489
pro Caecin. 35, 102	549
pro Flacc. 7, 15	444
pro Planc. 8, 19	548
24, 58	548
pro Sull. 7, 23	548
pro Tull. 5, 47	455 n.
Topica, 4, 23	468 n.
6, 29	415
Tusc. I, 2, 5	4 n.
I, 77	248
II, 13	231 n.
III, 6	231 n.
V, 5	231 n.
V, 25	230 n.
V, 108	225 n.

Cincius Alimentus

ap. Fest. p. 276 L.	405
frag. 6 P.	536 n.

Claudius

Letter to Alexandrines, I, 66	
	25 n.

Claudius Quadrigarius

frag. 57 P.	615 n.

Cleanthes

ap. Epictetus, Manual, 52	
	240 n.

Demetrius

de eloc. 285	224 n.

de viris illust.

7, 7; Chron. anni, 354,	
p. 144	475 n.
20, 3	540 n.
26	547

Digest

I, 2, 2	326

Dio Cassius

frags. 22	480 n.
29	526 n.
49	822 n.
53	822 n.

Diodorus

I, 4	319
IV, 56	49
V, 9	755
V, 16	773 n.
V, 20	776 n.
V, 22	52
V, 32	58
VII, frag. 5	321
VII, 5, 9	341 n., 346 n.
XI, 40, 5	501
XI, 53	318
XI, 53, 6	505
XI, 68	453
XII, 24	319
XII, 25	319, 480
XII, 31	584 n.
XII, 76	584 n.
XII, 80, 6	508
XIII, 42	606 n.
XIII, 94, 95	758 n.
XIV, 16, 5	512
XIV, 98, 5	517
XIV, 102	318
XIV, 102, 4	510 n., 538 n.
XIV, 116	318, 565
XIV, 117	318, 576 n., 606 n.
XIV, 117, 4	517
XVI, 31	326 n.
XVI, 69, 1	859
XVI, 90, 2	590 n.
XVIII, 56, 2	14
XIX, 10	588 n.
XIX, 72	319
XIX, 76	602 n.
XX, 36	531 n.
XX, 90	606 n., 607 n.
XXII, 7, 5	859
XXIII, 18	684 n.

Diogenes Laertius

VII, 5	235 n.
VII, 25	238, 242
VII, 28	235 n.
VII, 108	242
VII, 110	241
X, 9	233 n.
X, 46–53	244
X, 75	232 n.
X, 79 sq.	243
X, 85 sqq.	243
X, 97	243
X, 104	243
X, 118	247
X, 125	246
X, 129	247
X, 131 sq.	247

Diogenes Laertius

X, 134	244
X, 139	247
X, 148 art. XXVII	248

Diogenes of Oenoanda

frag. 8	243 n.
10	232 n.
24 etc.	225 n.

Dionysius of Halicarnassus

I, 30, 2	379
I, 53, 2	406 n.
I, 55, 1	406 n.
I, 72, 2	363 n.
I, 74	321
I, 79	326
II, 7, 4	468 n.
II, 9	421 n.
II, 46, 3	495 n.
II, 70, 1	496 n.
III, 1, 4	468 n.
III, 34, 3	405
IV, 26, 5	351 n., 392
IV, 49, 1	406 n.
IV, 49, 2	349, 405
IV, 58, 4	393 n.
V, 26, 3	476 n.
V, 43, 2	474 n.
V, 60, 4	474 n., 507
V, 61, 3	346 n., 401, 488
VI, 18, 2	405 n.
VI, 83, 4	478 n.
VI, 89	458 n.
VI, 94, 3	466 n.
VI, 95, 2	489
VII, 1–2	476 n.
VII, 1, 4	476
VII, 12, 3	343 n.
VII, 12, 5	474 n.
VII, 50	457
VIII, 14 sqq.	499
VIII, 69, 2	492
VIII, 69, 3–4	471 n.
VIII, 72	550
VIII, 76	472
VIII, 81, 3	472 n.
IX, 15	420 n.
IX, 25	475 n.
IX, 41	483
IX, 59, 1	474 n.
X, 32, 4	350, 472
XI, 45	481
XI, 59 sq.	519
XI, 63	521 n.
XV, 3	588 n.
XV, 4	590 n.
XVII–XVIII, 5	552 n.
XVIII	609 n.
XIX, 10	588 n.

Ephorus

frag. 132 Jac.	58 n.

Epictetus

Manual, 7   236
   52   240

Epicurus

ap. Cic. *de fin.* I, 30   246
ap. Diog. Laert. X, 125   246
   X, 139   247
ep. to Herodotus, ap. Diog.
   Laert. X, 46–53   244
   X, 79 *sq.*   243
   X, 97, 104   243
ep. to Menoeceus, ap. Diog.
   Laert. X, 118, 131 *sq.* 247
   X, 134   244
ep. to Pythocles, ap. Diog.
   Laert. X, 85 *sqq.*   243
frag. 409, 67 (Usener)   246
   469   247

Eusebius

II, p. 118, Schoene   78 n.
Praep. Ev. XV, XV, 3   240

Eutropius

III, 1   823

Fabius Pictor

frags. 5 *a*, 5 *b* P.   367

Fenestella

frag. 7 P.   343

Festus

48 L.   393 n.
71 L.   344 n.
108 L.   523
128 L.   487 n.
166 L.   490
176 L.   478 n.
180 L.   324
216 L.   448
249 L.   430, 438
264 L.   530 n.
268 L.   324, 430 n., 457
274 L.   417
276 L.   405, 490
290 L.   449
310 L.   357 n.
328 L.   365 and n.
424 L.   428, 516
450 L.   505 n.
458 sq. L.   357 n.
464 L.   516
476 L.   469 n.
500 L.   328

Frontinus

de aquaeductibus, cap. 7
   443 n.

Gaius

Inst. I, 3   482
   II, 42, 54   468 n.
   IV, 23   544 n.

Hellanicus of Lesbos

ap. Dion. Hal. I, 72, 2 363 n.
(*F.G.H.* frag. 53
   = *F.H.G.* frag. 84)

Heracleides Criticus

ap. F.H.G. II, p. 263   80 n.

Hermesianax

ap. Athenaeum, XIII, 597 B
   274

Herodotus

I, 94   379
II, 33   49
IV, 49   49

Homer

Iliad XV, 201–3   714

Horace

Ep. I, iv, 16   232 n.

Josephus

Ant. XII, 148   180
   XII, 169 *sqq.*   129
   XII, 258–264   191
   XIV, 115 *sqq.*   127
Vita, 12   236

Justin

XX, 5   64
XX, 5, 7   66
XXIV, 4   66
XXVIII, 1, 5–2   823
XLIII, 5, 2   774 n., 777 n.
XLIV, 5, 1   774 n.
Lex Coloniae Genetivae
Juliae (cap. 66)   430 n.

Lindian Chronicle

C, ll. 97 *sqq.*   862
C, ll. 127 *sqq.*   747 n.

Livy

I, 9, 12   369
I, 14, 3   406 n.
I, 23, 3   400 n.
I, 26   331, 445
I, 30   419 n.
I, 31, 1   341
I, 32   413
I, 36   431 and n.
I, 49, 3   393 n.
I, 53, 2   497
I, 56, 3   406 n.
I, 60, 2   397
II, 9, 6   465 n., 476 n.
II, 13, 25   413 n.

Livy

II, 16   494
II, 16, 8   341 n.
II, 17, 31   413 n.
II, 18   437
II, 21   434
II, 27, 5   475 n.
II, 31, 4   474 n.
II, 33, 9   489
II, 34, 6   474 n.
II, 34, 7   476 n.
II, 38, 1   487
II, 39, 2 *sqq.*   499
II, 39, 5   400 n.
II, 41   446
II, 41, 1   471 n., 492 n.
II, 41, 8   476 n.
II, 42, 5   466 n.
II, 56, 3   423 n.
III, 1, 5   473 n., 474 n.
III, 6   551
III, 13, 6   457
III, 15–18   494
III, 30   454 n.
III, 31   459 n.
III, 55   437, 480
IV, 4   419 n.
IV, 6   520 n.
IV, 7, 2   520
IV, 7, 10 *sqq.*   503 n.
IV, 11, 3   473 n.
IV, 11, 5   503 n.
IV, 12   519 n.
IV, 12, 3 *sqq.*   537 n.
IV, 13, 7   536 n.
IV, 16   324
IV, 16, 2   537 n.
IV, 20, 5 *sqq.*   507
IV, 25, 3   514
IV, 25, 4   537 n.
IV, 26, 6, 7   502
IV, 29, 5, 6   502 n.
IV, 30   520 n.
IV, 36, 2   537 n.
IV, 37   584 n.
IV, 43, 6   537 n.
IV, 44   584 n.
IV, 44, 7   537 n.
IV, 47, 7   469 n.
IV, 49   606 n.
IV, 49, 11 *sq.*   537 n.
IV, 52, 2 *sq.*   537 n.
IV, 52, 4   537 n.
IV, 53, 3   510
IV, 53, 4 *sqq.*   537 n.
IV, 58, 1 *sq.*   512
IV, 60, 9   512
V, 2, 8   576 n.
V, 10 *sq.*   519 n.
V, 12   520
V, 12, 3 *sq.*   537 n.

Livy

V, 16, 5	515 n.
V, 24, 4	510 n.
V, 25, 8 sq.	514
V, 29, 3	510 n.
V, 30, 8	538 n.
V, 34	58, 60, 61 n.
V, 35	61 n.
V, 48	565 n.
V, 51–54	514 n.
V, 52	412 n.
VI, 1	552 n.
VI, 1, 10	463 n.
VI, 2	565 sq., 606 n.
VI, 2, 8	576 n.
VI, 5, 1–5	538 n.
VI, 6, 1	538 n.
VI, 11, 8 sq.	542 n.
VI, 21, 4	538 n.
VI, 31, 2	542 n.
VI, 32, 1	361
VI, 35, 4	543 n.
VI, 35, 5	539 n.
VI, 35, 14	543 n.
VI, 38, 9	525
VI, 39, 2	543 n.
VI, 41	414, 483
VI, 42	414
VII, 12, 7	491
VII, 16, 1	477 n., 544 n.
VII, 16, 9	540 n.
VII, 20, 9	361
VII, 24	563
VII, 27, 2	860
VII, 27, 3–4	544 n.
VII, 28, 9	544 n.
VII, 29–VIII, 2	588 n.
VII, 38, 1	589
VII, 42	544 n.
VIII, 4	590
VIII, 5	427
VIII, 8, 19	590 n.
VIII, 11	592
VIII, 11, 11	590 n.
VIII, 12	482
VIII, 14	549, 592
VIII, 21, 11	469 n.
VIII, 22	551 n.
VIII, 22–3	595 n.
VIII, 25–6	595 n.
VIII, 28	545 n.
VIII, 28, 9	546 n.
VIII, 37	548 n.
VIII, 40	323, 547
IX, 26	602
IX, 28, 6	603 n.
IX, 36, 3	387
IX, 43, 26	860
IX, 46	435, 443 n., 532, 533 n., 552
X, 8	417

Livy

X, 8, 8	525 n.
X, 9, 10–11	537 n.
X, 10, 5	609 n.
X, 11, 9	537 n.
X, 13	610
X, 13, 14	540 n.
X, 23, 11–12	367
X, 31	551
X, 38–46	613
XXIV, 44	615 n.
XXVII, 10, 7	474 n.
XXXI, 2	409
XXXIV, 17 sqq.	787
XXXIV, 62, 3	682 n.
XXXV, 9, 3	341
XXXV, 44	615 n.
XXXVII, 54, 22	194
XXXIX, 15	444

Lucian

Alexander, 47, 61	234

Lucretius

I, 1021–8	245
II, 14–19	247
II, 177–181	246
II, 217–214, 243–250, 251–260	245
II, 646–651	246
III, 978 sqq.	232 n.
V, 1–14, 43–54	233 sq.
V, 187–199	246
V, 526–533	243 n.
V, 772–1457	232 n.

Lycophron

Alexandria, ll. 1226–33	281

Macrobius

Sat. I, 8, 1	466 n.
I, 12, 16	375 n.

Marcus Aurelius

V, 20	236
VI, 44	240

Martial

VII, 73, 4	496 n.

Menander

Epitrepontes, 544–569	229
frag. 50	230
125	226 n.
166	226 n.
355	229
481	226 n.
531	229
602	225
604	230

Orosius

III, 7, 1	860

Ovid

Amores, I, xv, 17 sq.	228
Fast. II, 527 sqq.	411
II, 682	400 n.
VI, 721 sqq.	503 n.

Pausanias

VI, 19, 2–4	772 n.
X, 8, 6	774 n.
X, 19	73 n.

Pindar

Isth. III, 31	776 n.
Nem. III, 21	776 n.
IV, 69	776 n.
Ol. III, 44	776 n.

Piso

frag. 27 P.	533

Plato

Politicus, 294 A, 296 sqq.	13 n.
303 B	13 n.
Prot. 337 C	225 n.

Plautus

Mostellaria, 1149–51	226 n.

Pliny the Elder

N.H. II, 140	397 n.
II, 169	776 n.
III, 56 sqq.	346
III, 69	349
VI, 49	174
VII, 136	548
VII, 212	463
XIV, 88–91	343 n.
XVI, 37	482 n.
XVI, 242 sqq.	348 n.
XVIII, 7	469 n.
XVIII, 15	537 n.
XVIII, 18	538 n.
XVIII, 285	399
XIX, 50	416
XXVIII, 17	430 n.
XXVIII, 146	344 n.
XXXI, 41	377
XXXI, 89	465 n.
XXXIV, 21	537 n.
XXXIV, 23	373 n., 509 n.
XXXV, 154	467 n.
XXXV, 157	385

Plutarch

Aratus, 41	758 n., 863
53	864
Camillus, XXXIX	526 n.
XXXIX, 5	538 n.
Cleomenes, XXXII	864
XXXIX	526 n.
Demetrius, VIII	224 n.
T. Gracchus, 8, 2	538 n.

Plutarch

Mor. 7 D	231 n.
329 A	225 n.
360 C	202 n.
1044 C sqq.	240 n.
1053 F	239
1070 A, F	242 n.
Numa, XVII, 2	464
Pomp. XIII	532 n.
Publicola, I, 1	495 n.
XXI, 6	469 n., 470 n.
Quaest. Rom. I	422 n.
VI	343 n.
Romulus, 11	335
Solon, XXII	381

Polyaenus

V, 18	862

Polybius

ap. Strab. IV, 208	63
I, 6	321 n.
I, 10, 5	781
II, 1, 6	774
II, 6, 4	845 n.
II, 8, 5	845 n.
II, 9, 8	834 n.
II, 12, 1, 2	835 n.
II, 13, 7	788
II, 17	72
II, 18	526
II, 19	612
II, 21	72
II, 22 sq.	62
II, 24	811 n.
II, 37, 11	34 n.
II, 41, 10	220
II, 45, 1 sq.	834 n.
II, 46, 1–3	834 n.
II, 52, 3	863
II, 53, 2	863
II, 60, 2	863 sq.
II, 70	843, 845 n.
II, 70, 4	863
III, 18, 1	845 n.
III, 22	777
III, 22, 3	859
III, 22, 7	778 n.
III, 24	587, 781, 859
III, 24, 6	860
III, 25	649, 859
III, 26	672
III, 26, 1, 2	859
III, 30, 1	788 n.
III, 40 sqq.	49
III, 59	225
III, 86, 7	758 n.
III, 87, 6	532 n., 758 n.
III, 103, 4	758 n.
IV, 26, 7	737 sq.
IV, 29, 2	845 n.

Polybius

IV, 35, 8	863
V, 4, 3	845 n.
V, 42, 3	724 n.
V, 65	730 n.
V, 79	730 n.
V, 90	184
IX, 29, 6	220
XVI, 21	30
XVIII, 55	127
XXII, 7, 5	859
XXIX, 21	226 n.
XXX, 5, 6	823

Pomponius

Dig. 1, 2, 2, 7	534

Posidonius

ap. Strab. III, 147	792 n.

Priscian

VII, 69	860

Proclus

Comm. on Eucl. I, p. 84	291 n.

Propertius

IV, 1, 28	385

Quintilian

III, 6, 84	479 n.
X, 1, 69	227
X, 1, 95	329 n.

Sallust

Hist. I, frag. 11 M.	470 n.
III, frag. 48 M.	414

Seneca

de beneficiis, I, vi, 2; ep. XCV, 57	241
de clementia, I, 6	242
de otio, IV, 1	240
de vita beata, 13	247

Servius

ad Aen. I, 422	383 n.

Silius Italicus

VIII, 483 sqq.	385 n.

Solinus

I, 31	321 n.

Stobaeus

eclogae, II, 90	242

Strabo

ap. Joseph. Ant. XIV	115 sqq., 127
I, 15	224 n.
III, 147	792 n.

Strabo

III, 149	774 n.
IV	71
IV, 189	58
IV, 208	63
V, 230	338 n., 399
V, 231	390 n.
V, 232	364
VII, 301	64 n.
XVI, 752	185
XVII, 793 sqq.	251

Suetonius

Claud. 25	823

Suidas

s.v. Antipatros	14
s.v. βασιλεία, no. 2	202

Tacitus

Ann. III, 26	435
VI, 16, 3	476, 545 n.
XI, 22	446
XI, 24	391 n., 548 n.
XI, 25	449
XII, 24	359 n.

Terence

Heautontimorumenus, 110 sq.	225 n.
I, 1, 25	225

Tertullian

de anima, 10	286

Theophrastus

περί βασιλείας, II	114
Hist. Pl. V. 8, 1, 3	342

Thucydides

I, 13	774 n.
VI, 4, 2; 5, 2	372 n.

Timaeus

ap. Diod. Sic. IV, 56	49
V, 16	773 n.

Timon of Phlius

ap. Athen. I, 22 D	252

Twelve Tables

III, 1 sqq.	480 n.
III, 4	479 n.
III, 6	479 n.
VI, 1	478 n.
VI, 3	468 n.

Valerius Maximus

III, 2, 8	510
IV, 3, 5	538 n.
VI, 3, 2	480 n.
VI, 5, 2	510

Varro

ap. Non. s.v. *consulum*	438
ap. Solin, I, 17	357 n.
L.L. v, 41	358 n.
v, 43	351 n.
v, 45 sqq.	359
v, 48	356 n.
v, 54	357 n.
v, 55	373 n., 409
v, 143	359 n.
v, 155	377
v, 158	496 n.
VI, 33	375 n.
VI, 90 sqq.	446
VII, 105	545 n.
R.R. I, 2, 9	539 n.
I, 10	416
I, 10, 2	469 n.

Velleius Paterculus

I, 8	322 n.
I, 14, 2	517
II, 8, 3	536 n.

Vergil

Aen. VI, 609	420 n.
VI, 775	341 n.
VII, 761 sq.	344 n.
Georg. I, 269	427

Verrius Flaccus

C.I.L. I², p. 236	399

Veterum Stoicorum Fragmenta

von Arnim) III, 157, 175	39

Vitruvius

X, 13	775

Zeno

ap. Stobaeum, *eclogae*, II, 90	242

Zonaras

epitome VII, 9	449 n.
VII, 17, 6	527 n.

Ecclesiastes

ix, 1	226 n.

1 Maccabees

iii, 29	167

2 Maccabees

iv, 19 sqq.	172
vi	191

Inscriptions

B.C.H. XLV, 1921, p. 150, no. 3	212 n.
XLV, 1921, p. 153, no. 6	92 n.

Inscriptions

C.I.E. II, no. 5275, p. 161	
	388 n.
C.I.L. I², p. 177	536 n.
I², p. 236	399 n.
Dessau, 212	391 n., 520
1371	345 n.
2988	401 n.
4958	384 n., 430
5011	401 n.
5048	338 n., 399 n.
6188, 6189	401 n.
6190	401 n.
6245	355
Ditt.³ 241, ll. 37, 66, 81,	
119	708 n.
392	645
410	173
475	185
543	532
543, IV	853 n.
Durrbach, *Choix*, no. 127	
	116 n.
I.G. XI, ii, 114	862
XI, ii, 116	862
XI, iv, 114, 116	708 n.
XII, v, 898	708 n.
Ineditum Vaticanum, 3	385 n.
Inschr. v. Magn. 80, 81, 181 n.	
122, d. 4	182
v. Priene, 37, ll. 134,	
153	181
Mnesimachus inscription	
	171 n., 182
O.G.I.S. 4	14
211	171 n.
212	162
213	162 n.
214	162 n., 175
217	170
219	161 sq., 716 n.
219, 24	716 n.
219, 26	162
221, 54	173
223	179
224	162, 716 n.
225	166, 172, 182
227, 6	162
229	171 n.
229, 13	177
230	167 n.
233	163 n., 189
237, 5	162
238	166 n.
244	162
245	163 n.
246	163 n.

Inscriptions

O.G.I.S. 256	165 n.
257	186
262	183
265	550 n.
502	183
Rehm, *Milet*, I, iii, no. 139	
	862
I, vii, p. 295	21
I, no. 123,	
l. 37	98 n.
I, no. 123, ll.	
1, 38	708 n.
S.E.G. I, 74	207 n.
I, 335	455 n.
I, 342	116 n.
I, 366	182
II, 663	178
II, 864	122

Papyri

Herculaneum, no. 1418, col. XXXIIIª (XXIIIª)	107 n.
P. Cairo Zen. 59001	118 n.
59003	121 n.
59006	121 n.
59012	130, 139
59016	127
59019, l. 6	107 n.
59021	141
59034	146
59036	118 n., 863
59037	129 and n., 130
59045	129 n.
59046	129 n.
59077	130
59093	130
59132	118 n.
59136	118 n.
P. Cornell I	119
P. Freib. 2, ii, 4	21 n.
P. Heid. 47, 48	118 n.
P. Lond. I, p. 603	118 n.
P. Oxyrh. I, xii	588 n.
IV, 668	314 n.
X, 1241	253 n.
XIII, 1611, ll. 38 sqq.	114
P.S.I. IV, no. 332, l. 16	862
IV, 429, 505	127
V, no. 502, l. 24	862
V, 541	717 n.
P. Tebt. 8	129 sq.
Symbolae Osloenses, fasc. V, 1927	862 sq.

HELLENISTIC DYNASTIES

I. The Ptolemies

	B.C.
Ptol. I Soter	–283
Ptol. II Philadelphus	285–246
Ptol. III Euergetes I	246–221
Ptol. IV Philopator	221–203
Ptol. V Epiphanes	203–181/0
Ptol. VI Philometor	181/0–145
Ptol. VII Euergetes II (Physcon)	145–116
Ptol. VIII Soter II (Lathyrus)	116–108/7
	88–80
Ptol. IX Alexander I	108/7–88
Ptol. X Alexander II	80
Ptol. XI Auletes	80–51
⌠Ptol. XII	51–48
⌡Cleopatra VII	
⌠Ptol. XIII	
⌡Cleopatra VII	47–44
⌠Cleopatra VII	
⌡Ptol. XIV Caesar (Caesarion)	? 44–30

II. The Seleucids

	B.C.
Seleucus I Nicator	–280
Antiochus I Soter	280–262/1
Antiochus II Theos	261–247
Seleucus II Callinicus	247–226
Seleucus III Soter	226–223
Antiochus III (the Great)	223–187
Seleucus IV Philopator	187–175
Antiochus IV Epiphanes	175–163
Antiochus V Eupator	163–162
Demetrius I Soter	162–150
Alexander Balas	150–145
Demetrius II Nicator	145–139/8
Antiochus VI Epiphanes	145–142/1
Antiochus VII (Sidetes)	139/8–129
Demetrius II Nicator	129–125
⌠Cleopatra Thea	125–121
⌡Antiochus VIII (Grypus)	125–121
Antiochus VIII (Grypus)	121–96
Antiochus IX (Cyzicenus)	115–95

III. The Antigonids

	B.C.
Antigonus I	–301
Demetrius I (Poliorcetes)	307–283
Antigonus II (Gonatas)	283–239
Demetrius II	239–229
Antigonus III (Doson)	229–221
Philip V	221–179
Perseus	179–168

IV. The Attalids

	B.C.
Attalus I Soter	241–197
Eumenes II Soter	197–160/59
Attalus II	160/59–139/8
Attalus III	139/8–133

THE FAMILY OF LYSIMACHUS

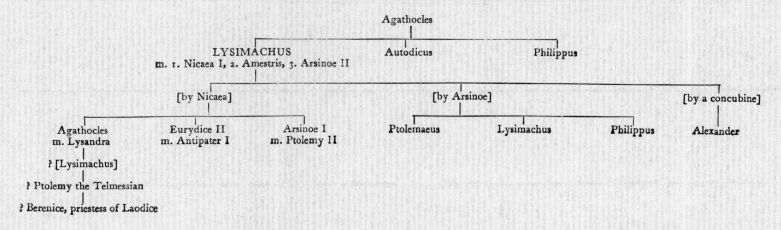

Agathocles

LYSIMACHUS — Autodicus — Philippus
m. 1. Nicaea I, 2. Amestris, 3. Arsinoe II

[by Nicaea] — [by Arsinoe] — [by a concubine]

Agathocles m. Lysandra — Eurydice II m. Antipater I — Arsinoe I m. Ptolemy II — Ptolemaeus — Lysimachus — Philippus — Alexander

? [Lysimachus]

? Ptolemy the Telmessian

? Berenice, priestess of Laodice

THE ATTALIDS

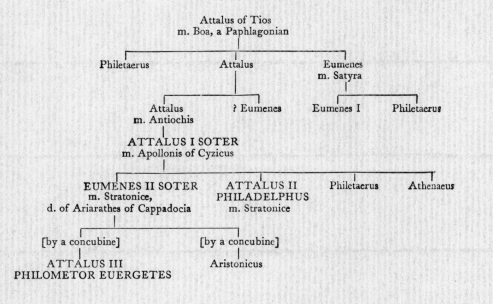

Attalus of Tios
m. Boa, a Paphlagonian

Philetaerus — Attalus — Eumenes m. Satyra

Attalus m. Antiochis — ? Eumenes — Eumenes I — Philetaerus

ATTALUS I SOTER
m. Apollonis of Cyzicus

EUMENES II SOTER
m. Stratonice,
d. of Ariarathes of Cappadocia — ATTALUS II PHILADELPHUS m. Stratonice — Philetaerus — Athenaeus

[by a concubine] — [by a concubine]

ATTALUS III
PHILOMETOR EUERGETES — Aristonicus

THE KINGS OF EPIRUS

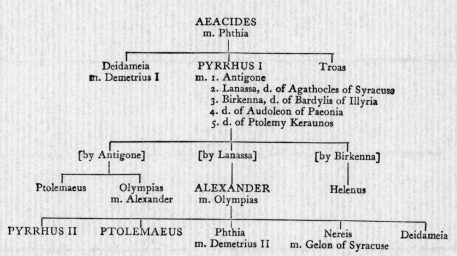

AEACIDES
m. Phthia

Deidameia m. Demetrius I — PYRRHUS I
m. 1. Antigone
2. Lanassa, d. of Agathocles of Syracuse
3. Birkenna, d. of Bardylis of Illyria
4. d. of Audoleon of Paeonia
5. d. of Ptolemy Keraunos — Troas

[by Antigone] — [by Lanassa] — [by Birkenna]

Ptolemaeus — Olympias m. Alexander — ALEXANDER m. Olympias — Helenus

PYRRHUS II — PTOLEMAEUS — Phthia m. Demetrius II — Nereis m. Gelon of Syracuse — Deidameia

THE FAMILY OF ANTIPATER

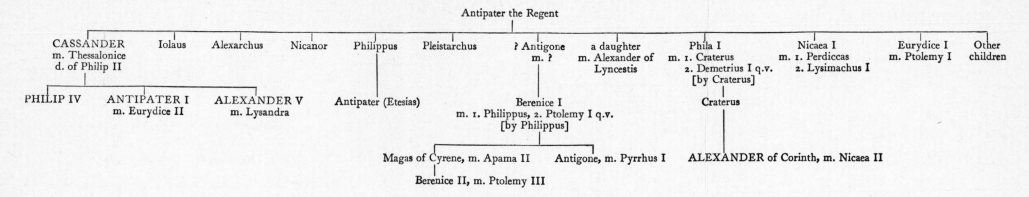

THE ANTIGONIDS

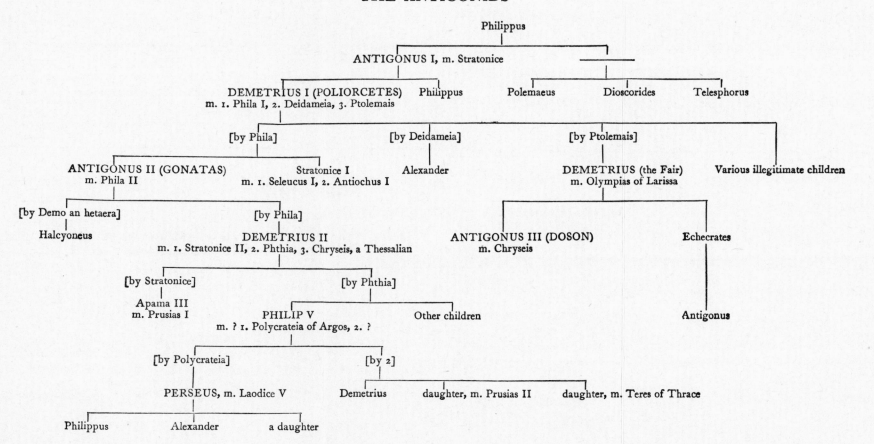

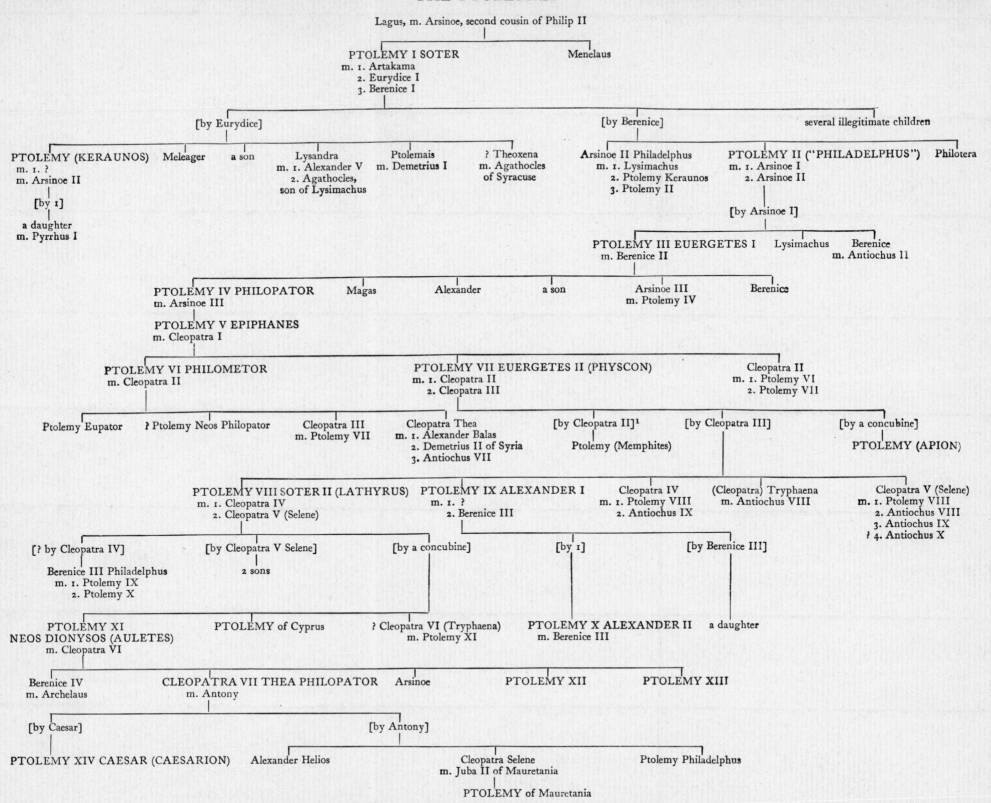

Lagus, m. Arsinoe, second cousin of Philip II

PTOLEMY I SOTER
m. 1. Artakama
2. Eurydice I
3. Berenice I

Menelaus

[by Eurydice]

[by Berenice]

several illegitimate children

PTOLEMY (KERAUNOS)
m. 1. ?
m. Arsinoe II

[by 1]

a daughter
m. Pyrrhus I

Meleager

a son

Lysandra
m. 1. Alexander V
2. Agathocles,
son of Lysimachus

Ptolemais
m. Demetrius I

? Theoxena
m. Agathocles
of Syracuse

Arsinoe II Philadelphus
m. 1. Lysimachus
2. Ptolemy Keraunos
3. Ptolemy II

PTOLEMY II ("PHILADELPHUS")
m. 1. Arsinoe I
2. Arsinoe II

Philotera

[by Arsinoe I]

PTOLEMY III EUERGETES I
m. Berenice II

Lysimachus

Berenice
m. Antiochus II

PTOLEMY IV PHILOPATOR
m. Arsinoe III

Magas

Alexander

a son

Arsinoe III
m. Ptolemy IV

Berenice

PTOLEMY V EPIPHANES
m. Cleopatra I

PTOLEMY VI PHILOMETOR
m. Cleopatra II

PTOLEMY VII EUERGETES II (PHYSCON)
m. 1. Cleopatra II
2. Cleopatra III

Cleopatra II
m. 1. Ptolemy VI
2. Ptolemy VII

Ptolemy Eupator

? Ptolemy Neos Philopator

Cleopatra III
m. Ptolemy VII

Cleopatra Thea
m. 1. Alexander Balas
2. Demetrius II of Syria
3. Antiochus VII

[by Cleopatra II][1]

Ptolemy (Memphites)

[by Cleopatra III]

[by a concubine]

PTOLEMY (APION)

PTOLEMY VIII SOTER II (LATHYRUS)
m. 1. Cleopatra IV
2. Cleopatra V (Selene)

PTOLEMY IX ALEXANDER I
m. 1. ?
2. Berenice III

Cleopatra IV
m. 1. Ptolemy VIII
2. Antiochus IX

(Cleopatra) Tryphaena
m. Antiochus VIII

Cleopatra V (Selene)
m. 1. Ptolemy VIII
2. Antiochus VIII
3. Antiochus IX
? 4. Antiochus X

[? by Cleopatra IV]

Berenice III Philadelphus
m. 1. Ptolemy IX
2. Ptolemy X

[by Cleopatra V Selene]

2 sons

[by a concubine]

[by 1]

[by Berenice III]

PTOLEMY XI
NEOS DIONYSOS (AULETES)
m. Cleopatra VI

PTOLEMY of Cyprus

? Cleopatra VI (Tryphaena)
m. Ptolemy XI

PTOLEMY X ALEXANDER II
m. Berenice III

a daughter

Berenice IV
m. Archelaus

CLEOPATRA VII THEA PHILOPATOR
m. Antony

Arsinoe

PTOLEMY XII

PTOLEMY XIII

[by Caesar]

[by Antony]

PTOLEMY XIV CAESAR (CAESARION)

Alexander Helios

Cleopatra Selene
m. Juba II of Mauretania

Ptolemy Philadelphus

PTOLEMY of Mauretania

[1] Some believe they had another son; see E. R. Bevan, *A history of Egypt under the Ptolemaic dynasty*, p. 309, n. 3.

Antiochus
m. Laodice

SELEUCUS I NICATOR
m. 1. Apama I, d. of Spitamenes
2. Stratonice I

[by Apama]

[by Stratonice]

Phila II
m. Antigonus II

ANTIOCHUS I SOTER
m. Stratonice I

Achaeus

Seleucus

ANTIOCHUS II THEOS
m. 1. Laodice I
2. Berenice, d. of Ptolemy II

Apama II
m. Magas

Stratonice II
m. Demetrius II

Alexander

Andromachus

Antiochis
m. Attalus

Laodice I
m. Antiochus II

[by Laodice]

[by Berenice]

a son

SELEUCUS II CALLINICUS
m. Laodice II

Antiochus (Hierax)
m. d. of Ziaelas
of Bithynia

Stratonice
m. Ariarathes III
of Cappadocia

Laodice
m. Mithridates II
of Pontus

Laodice II
m. Seleucus II

Achaeus
m. Laodice, ? a d. of Mithridates II
of Pontus or of Antiochus Hierax

SELEUCUS III SOTER

Antiochis

ANTIOCHUS III (the Great)
m. 1. Laodice III, d. of Mithridates II of Pontus
2. Euboea of Chalcis
[by Laodice]

Antiochus
m. Laodice IV

SELEUCUS IV PHILOPATOR
m. ?

ANTIOCHUS IV EPIPHANES
m. Laodice (? IV)

Cleopatra I
m. Ptolemy V

Laodice IV
m. Antiochus

Antiochis
m. Ariarathes IV of Cappadocia

Nysa
m. Pharnaces I
of Pontus

a SON

DEMETRIUS I SOTER
m. ?

Laodice V
m. Perseus

ANTIOCHUS V EUPATOR

Laodice
? m. Mithridates V
of Pontus

ALEXANDER (BALAS), pretended son of Antiochus IV
m. Cleopatra Thea

DEMETRIUS II NICATOR
m. 1. Cleopatra Thea
2. Rhodogune, d. of Mithridates I of Parthia

ANTIOCHUS VII EUERGETES (SIDETES)
m. Cleopatra Thea

Antigonus

ANTIOCHUS VI EPIPHANES DIONYSUS

[by Cleopatra]

[by Rhodogune]

Children

SELEUCUS V

**ANTIOCHUS VIII
PHILOMETOR (GRYPUS)**
m. 1. (Cleopatra) Tryphaena
2. Cleopatra V (Selene)
[by Tryphaena]

Laodice
m. Phraates II of Parthia

Laodice

? Laodice

Antiochus

? Seleucus

ANTIOCHUS IX PHILOPATOR (CYZICENUS)
m. 1. ?
2. Cleopatra IV
3. Cleopatra V (Selene)
[by 1]

**SELEUCUS VI
EPIPHANES
NICATOR**

**ANTIOCHUS XI
EPIPHANES
PHILADELPHUS**

**PHILIP I
EPIPHANES
PHILADELPHUS**

**DEMETRIUS III
PHILOPATOR SOTER
(EUKAIROS)**

**ANTIOCHUS XII
DIONYSUS**

Laodice Thea
Philadelphus
m. Mithridates I of
Commagene

ANTIOCHUS X EUSEBES PHILOPATOR
m. ? Cleopatra V (Selene)

PHILIP II

ANTIOCHUS I
of Commagene

ANTIOCHUS XIII (ASIATICUS)   A son

The Aegean, Egypt, and Asia	Literature, Philosophy, Science, and Art	B.C.
301 Partition of Antigonus' kingdom		301
300 Foundation of Antioch	*Floruit* of Duris of Samos and of Timaeus	300
299 Alliance of Seleucus and Demetrius	c. 300 *Floruit* of Eutychides, the sculptor Zeno and Epicurus at Athens Revival of Greek poetry (Philetas of Cos, Simias of Rhodes, Asclepiades of Samos)	
296 Coalition against Demetrius 295 Ptolemy acquires Cyprus, Seleucus Cilicia, and Lysimachus (ultimately) Ionia		295
292 Antiochus I joint king of the far East	Euclid at Alexandria 292 Death of Menander	
	c. 290 *Floruit* of Hermesianax and Phoenix of Colophon *Floruit* of Chares of Lindus, and rise of Rhodian School of sculpture	290
	288 Strato of Lampsacus succeeds Theophrastus as head of Peripatetic school	
Before 287 Ptolemy divorces Eurydice and marries Berenice 286 Ptolemy acquires Tyre, Sidon, the Island League and the command of the sea	c. 287 Birth of Archimedes	285
285 *Spring* Ptolemy II joint king. Demetrius surrenders to Seleucus	c. 285 *Floruit* of Leonidas of Tarentum *Floruit* of the anatomists Herophilus and Erasistratus Zenodotus first head of the Alexandrian Library	
283 *Late* Death of Ptolemy I. Ptolemy II becomes sole king	283 *onwards* Brilliant literary patronage of Ptolemy II; Callimachus, Apollonius Rhodius, Theocritus, Herodas, the Tragic Pleiad, etc.	
281 *Summer* Lysimachus defeated and killed by Seleucus at Korupedion 280 *Early* Death of Seleucus and accession of Antiochus I. War between Antigonus and Antiochus. The first Ptolemaieia founded at Delos 279 *Autumn* Treaty between Antigonus and Antiochus	280 *Floruit* of Aristarchus of Samos *Floruit* of Euhemerus	280
278 The Gauls cross to Asia. Miletus Egyptian 277 Gallic terror in Asia Minor		
276 First Syrian War. Antiochus I defeats Ptolemy II in Syria *Winter* 276–5 Ptolemy II marries Arsinoe II 275 Antiochus I defeats the Gauls End of Babylon's civil existence 274 Egyptian conquests in Asia Minor 273 *or* 272 End of the First Syrian War	276–5 Aratus of Soli at the court of Antigonus Gonatas	2?
	272 Livius Andronicus brought to Rome	
270 July 9 Death of Arsinoe II	270 Death of Epicurus	270
266 *Spring* Beginning of Chremonidean War		265
263 Eumenes I succeeds Philetaerus as dynast of Pergamum 262 Ephesus Egyptian 262–1 (*Between October and April*) Death of Antiochus I and accession of Antiochus II 261 Peace between Ptolemy II and Antigonus 260 Beginning of Second Syrian War 259 Death of Magas of Cyrene. Antiochus II recovers Ephesus 258 Demetrius the Fair king of Cyrene 258 *or* 256 Battle of Cos; end of Egypt's sea-command	262 End of the *Atthis* of Philochorus 261 Death of Zeno. He is succeeded by Cleanthes of Assus c. 260 Apollonius Rhodius head of Alexandrian Library	260
255 General peace. Antigonus secures the Island League		255

B.C.	THE WESTERN MEDITERRANEAN	ITALY AND SICILY	GREECE AND MACEDONIA
	c. 300 Celtic conquest of Southern Gaul		301 The League of Corinth breaks up: government of centre party at Athens under Phaedrus
300	300 Carthaginian Empire in South and Eastern Spain slowly weakening	*c.* 300 Agathocles captures Corcyra	
		299 Latin colony at Narnia	
		c. 298 Agathocles besieges Croton	297 Death of Cassander and his son Philip IV
			Division of Macedonia between his younger sons
295		*c.* 295 Agathocles seizes Hipponium	295 Lachares seizes power at Athens
		295 Roman victory at Sentinum	
			294 Demetrius Poliorcetes takes Athens and becomes king of Macedonia
			293 Foundation of Demetrias: end of centre party at Athens: Phaedrus joins Demetrius
290		291 Latin colony at Venusia	291 Demetrius takes Thebes
		Latin colonies at Hadria and Castrum Novum	Demetrius' wars with Aetolia and Pyrrhus
		290 End of Samnite War. Rome annexes Sabines as *cives sine suffragio*	
		289 Death of Agathocles. The Mamertines seize Messana	289 Demetrius prepares to invade Asia
		Warfare in Sicily	288 *Early* Coalition against Demetrius
			July Nationalist government at Athens
			About September Fall of Demetrius. Pyrrhus and Lysimachus partition Macedonia
		287 The Hortensian Laws	287 Demetrius crosses to Asia
285		*c.* 285 Thurii decrees honours to a Roman tribune	285 Demetrius surrenders to Seleucus
			Lysimachus king of all Macedonia
		284 M'. Curius defeats the Senones	284 Lysimachus conquers Paeonia
		Citizen colony at Sena	283 *Spring* Death of Demetrius. His son, Antigonus Gonatas, takes the royal title
		283 Defeat of Boii and Etruscans at Lake Vadimo	
		282 Rome helps Thurii against the Lucanians	281 Death of Lysimachus. Antigonus takes Athens
280	280 Sicilian cities threatened by Carthage	280 Pyrrhus lands in Italy: Roman defeat at Heraclea	280 Ptolemy Keraunos king of Macedonia. Beginning of the Achaean League
	279–8 Carthage encourages Rome against Pyrrhus	279 *Spring* Rome rejects Pyrrhus' peace-offer	279 *Early* Gauls invade Macedonia. Death of Keraunos
		Roman defeat at Asculum	*Autumn-winter* Gauls invade, and are driven out of, Greece
		279–8 Further Roman negotiations with Pyrrhus. Treaty with Carthage	
		278 *Autumn* Pyrrhus crosses into Sicily	278–246 Expansion of the Aetolian League
		277–6 Inconclusive campaigns of Pyrrhus in Sicily	277 Anarchy in Macedonia. Antigonus defeats the Gauls at Lysimacheia
			276 Antigonus king of Macedonia
			Winter He marries Phila, sister of Antiochus I
275		275 Pyrrhus returns to Italy: is defeated near Beneventum: leaves Italy	275 Return of Pyrrhus from Italy
		273 Latin colonies at Cosa and Paestum	274 Pyrrhus overruns Macedonia
		Egyptian envoys received at Rome	
		272 Capture of Tarentum by Papirius Cursor	272 Death of Pyrrhus
270		270 Capture of Rhegium	? 270 Antigonus annexes Euboea
		268 Latin colonies at Ariminum and Beneventum	
		Full citizenship granted to the Sabines	267 *Early* Coalition of Athens, Sparta, and Egypt against Antigonus
		Denarial currency founded	*Autumn* Chremonides moves the declaration of war.
265		*c.* 265 Hiero proclaimed king of Syracuse	265 Battle of Corinth. Death of Areus II of Sparta
		264 Latin colony at Firmum: Rome in alliance with the Mamertines. Appius Claudius dispatched to Sicily. First Punic War begins	
		263 Hiero becomes ally of Rome. Latin colony at Aesernia	? 263 *or* 262 Death of Acrotatus of Sparta
		262 Warfare in Sicily: capture of Agrigentum	262 *Late* Antigonus takes Athens
		Naval victory of Duillius off Mylae	
260			261 Peace between Ptolemy II and Antigonus
			? 258 Aristodemus becomes tyrant of Megalopolis
	256 Regulus lands in Africa, defeats the Carthaginians, and winters at Tunis	257 Naval victory of Regulus off Tyndaris	
		256 Naval victory off Ecnomus	
255	255 Regulus' army defeated	255 Roman fleet wrecked off Pachynus	255 Restoration of autonomy to Athens
	Roman naval victory off Cape Hermaeum		

THE AEGEAN, EGYPT, AND ASIA	LITERATURE, PHILOSOPHY, SCIENCE, AND ART	B.C.
253 Antigoneia founded at Delos		
252 Antiochus II joins Egypt and marries Berenice II		
Between 250 and 227 Bactria and Parthia become independent	*c.* 250 Arcesilas head of the New Academy	250
249 Second Ptolemaieia founded at Delos	Birth of Plautus	
	Floruit of Hegesias of Magnesia	
247 1 Nisan: the Parthian era	Death of Timaeus	
Winter Death of Antiochus II and accession **of Seleucus II**		
246 *January* Death of Ptolemy II and accession of Ptolemy III		
Early Third Ptolemaieia founded at Delos. **Third Syrian** War begins		
246 *or early* 245 Battle of Andros	*c.* 246 Eratosthenes head of the Alexandrian Library	
245 Paneia and Soteria founded at Delos		245
241 Peace between Seleucus II and Ptolemy III		
Death of Eumenes I and accession of Attalus I		
Between 241 and 236 War of the Brothers (Seleucus II and Antiochus Hierax). Ended before 236; Hierax rules Asia Minor		
	c. 240 First plays of Livius Andronicus	240
	Antigonus of Carystus, sculptor and author	
	c. 239 Birth of Ennius	
	c. 236 *Floruit* of Apollonius of Perga	233
	First play of Naevius	
	Dedications of Attalus I, by sculptors of the First Pergamene School	
Before 230 Attalus I defeats the Gauls and takes the royal title		
230–229 War of Attalus I with Antiochus Hierax	231 Chrysippus head of the Stoic school	230
228 Attalus I master of Seleucid Asia Minor		
227 Antigonus Doson's expedition to Caria		
226 Death of Seleucus II and accession of Seleucus III		
	c. 225 *Floruit* of Rhianus	225
223 Death of Seleucus III and accession of **Antiochus** III		
223 *to* 220 Achaeus recovers Seleucid Asia Minor		
221 Death of Ptolemy III (July at earliest, October at latest) and accession of Ptolemy IV	*c.* 220 *Floruit* of Euphorion	220
220 Antiochus III subdues Molon's revolt. Revolt of Achaeus	220 Starting-point of main theme of Polybius' history	
219 Fourth Syrian War begins. Rhodes declares war on Byzantium		
Death of Cleomenes in Egypt		
217 *June* 22 Battle of Raphia. Peace between Antiochus III and Ptolemy IV		217

B.C. See chronological note 3, p. 863 *sq.*

B.C.	THE WESTERN MEDITERRANEAN	ITALY AND SICILY	GREECE AND MACEDONIA
		253 Roman fleet wrecked off Palinurus	253 *or* 252 Revolt of Alexander of Corinth
		253–242 Stalemate on land and sea: Roman naval losses	
250			*c.* 252 Death of Aristodemus
			251 Aratus frees Sicyon
	Punic Army penetrates Numidia. Capture of Theveste	248 Roman alliance with Hiero renewed	
		247 Hamilcar Barca starts Carthaginian offensive in Sicily	*c.* 247 Death of Alexander of Corinth
		246 Latin colony at Brundisium	246 (*At latest*) Antigonus recovers Corinth
245			245 Aetolia defeats Boeotia at Chaeronea
			Aratus' first Generalship of the Achaean League
	260–237 Carthaginians lose power in Eastern Spain	243 Fleet built by Rome from voluntary loans	244 Agis IV becomes king of Sparta
		242 Institution of praetor peregrinus	243 Aratus takes Corinth
		241 Lutatius Catulus defeats Hanno in naval battle off Drepana (Aegates Insulae). Carthage asks for peace, entrusting Hamilcar with negotiations. Latin colony at Spoletium. Rome occupies Sicily	241 *or* 240 Death of Agis IV
240	240–237 War of the Mercenaries ('Truceless War')	*c.* 240 Reform of Centuriate Assembly	*c.* 240 Death of Alexander of Epirus
			c. 240–230 Growth of power of Illyria under King Agron
			239 *Early* Death of Antigonus Gonatas and accession of Demetrius II
	238 Occupation of Sardinia and (later) Corsica by Rome		? 238 War of Demetrius with the Leagues begins
	237 End of War of the Mercenaries: Hamilcar goes to Spain.		237 Cleomenes III becomes king at Sparta
235	235 Carthaginian conquests in Spain		235 Battle of Cleonae. Megalopolis joins the Achaean League
		232 Distribution of *ager Gallicus* in small lots carried by Flaminius	233 Battle of Phylacia
230	231 Roman envoys confer with Hamilcar		230 Teuta succeeds Agron. Illyrian expedition to Epirus
	? 230 Roman treaty with Saguntum. (See pp. 788, 809)		Romans demand reparation from Teuta
	Death of Hamilcar. Hasdrubal becomes general in Spain	229 First Illyrian War. Corcyra, Dyrrhachium, Apollonia, and Issa become Roman allies	229 *Spring* Death of Demetrius II. Antigonus Doson king of Macedonia
			Battle of Paxos.
			Argos joins the Achaean League: great expansion of
			229–8 Athens recovers independence
	c. 228 Foundation of New Carthage	228 Teuta of Illyria surrenders: Demetrius made ruler of Pharos	228 War begins between Sparta and Achaean League
		Roman protectorate on the Illyrian coast	(Cleomenic War). Roman envoys at Athens and Corinth
	227 Sardinia and Corsica made a Roman province	227 Four praetors elected annually.	227 Revolution at Sparta
		Sicily and Sardinia under praetors	
	226 Ebro Treaty between Rome and Hasdrubal	225 Invading Gauls routed at Telamon	226 Battle of Hecatombaeum
225			225 Argos and Corinth join Cleomenes. Aratus negotiates Antigonus
			224 *Spring* Aratus dictator: alliance with Antigonus
			224 Antigonus takes Argos, and (*winter*) forms the Hellenic League
		223 Flaminius defeats the Insubres	223 Antigonus and Aratus destroy Mantinea
			Cleomenes razes Megalopolis
		222 Battle of Clastidium. Insubres surrender to Rome	222 *July* Battle of Sellasia. Antigonus takes Sparta
	221 Death of Hasdrubal: Hannibal becomes general in Spain		221 *Autumn* Death of Antigonus Doson and accession of Philip
220	219 *Spring* Hannibal attacks Saguntum	220 Construction of Via Flaminia	220 The War of the Allies begins
	Roman envoys at Carthage	219 Second Illyrian War.	219 Demetrius of Pharos flees to Philip V
	Late autumn Fall of Saguntum		
	218 *Spring* War declared between Rome and Carthage. Hannibal sets out for Italy	218 Latin colonies at Placentia and Cremona	218 Victories of Philip V. Sack of Thermum
		Hannibal wins battles of Ticinus and Trebia	
217		217 *Spring* Hannibal wins victory at Trasimene	217 (*About August*) Peace of Naupactus

¹ These events, with the defection of Corinth, fall one year later if the Battle of Sellasia is placed in 221